HANDBOOK OF ECONOMIC FORECASTING
VOLUME 1

HANDBOOKS IN ECONOMICS

24

Series Editors

KENNETH J. ARROW
MICHAEL D. INTRILIGATOR

ELSEVIER

AMSTERDAM • BOSTON • HEIDELBERG • LONDON
NEW YORK • OXFORD • PARIS • SAN DIEGO
SAN FRANCISCO • SINGAPORE • SYDNEY • TOKYO

N·H

HANDBOOK OF ECONOMIC FORECASTING

VOLUME 1

Edited by

GRAHAM ELLIOTT
CLIVE W.J. GRANGER
ALLAN TIMMERMANN
University of California, San Diego

ELSEVIER

AMSTERDAM • BOSTON • HEIDELBERG • LONDON
NEW YORK • OXFORD • PARIS • SAN DIEGO
SAN FRANCISCO • SINGAPORE • SYDNEY • TOKYO

N·H

North-Holland is an imprint of Elsevier
Radarweg 29, PO Box 211, 1000 AE Amsterdam, The Netherlands
The Boulevard, Langford Lane, Kidlington, Oxford OX5 1GB, UK

First edition 2006

Library of Congress Cataloging-in-Publication Data
A catalog record for this book is available from the Library of Congress

British Library Cataloguing in Publication Data
A catalogue record for this book is available from the British Library

ISBN-13: 978-0-444-51395-3
ISBN-10: 0-444-51395-7

ISSN: 0169-7218 (Handbooks in Economics series)
ISSN: 1574-0706 (Handbook of Economic Forecasting series)

For information on all North-Holland publications
visit our website at books.elsevier.com

Printed and bound in the United Kingdom
Transferred to Digital Print 2011

INTRODUCTION TO THE SERIES

The aim of the *Handbooks in Economics* series is to produce Handbooks for various branches of economics, each of which is a definitive source, reference, and teaching supplement for use by professional researchers and advanced graduate students. Each Handbook provides self-contained surveys of the current state of a branch of economics in the form of chapters prepared by leading specialists on various aspects of this branch of economics. These surveys summarize not only received results but also newer developments, from recent journal articles and discussion papers. Some original material is also included, but the main goal is to provide comprehensive and accessible surveys. The Handbooks are intended to provide not only useful reference volumes for professional collections but also possible supplementary readings for advanced courses for graduate students in economics.

KENNETH J. ARROW and MICHAEL D. INTRILIGATOR

PUBLISHER'S NOTE

For a complete overview of the Handbooks in Economics Series, please refer to the listing at the end of this volume.

CONTENTS OF THE HANDBOOK

VOLUME 1

CONTENTS OF VOLUME 1

PART 1

FORECASTING METHODOLOGY

Chapter 1

BAYESIAN FORECASTING

JOHN GEWEKE and CHARLES WHITEMAN

Department of Economics, University of Iowa, Iowa City, IA 52242-1000

Contents

Handbook of Economic Forecasting, Volume 1
Edited by Graham Elliott, Clive W.J. Granger and Allan Timmermann

DOI: 10.1016/S1574-0706(05)01001-3

Abstract

Bayesian forecasting is a natural product of a Bayesian approach to inference. The Bayesian approach in general requires explicit formulation of a model, and conditioning on known quantities, in order to draw inferences about unknown ones. In Bayesian forecasting, one simply takes a subset of the unknown quantities to be future values of some variables of interest. This chapter presents the principles of Bayesian forecasting, and describes recent advances in computational capabilities for applying them that have dramatically expanded the scope of applicability of the Bayesian approach. It describes historical developments and the analytic compromises that were necessary prior to recent developments, the application of the new procedures in a variety of examples, and reports on two long-term Bayesian forecasting exercises.

Keywords

Markov chain Monte Carlo, predictive distribution, probability forecasting, simulation, vector autoregression

JEL classification: C530, C110, C150

> *... in terms of forecasting ability, ... a good Bayesian will beat a non-Bayesian, who will do better than a bad Bayesian.*
>
> [C.W.J. Granger (1986, p. 16)]

1. Introduction

Forecasting involves the use of information at hand – hunches, formal models, data, etc. – to make statements about the likely course of future events. In technical terms, conditional on what one knows, what can one say about the future? The Bayesian approach to inference, as well as decision-making and forecasting, involves conditioning on what is known to make statements about what is not known. Thus "Bayesian forecasting" is a mild redundancy, because forecasting is at the core of the Bayesian approach to just about anything. The parameters of a model, for example, are no more known than future values of the data thought to be generated by that model, and indeed the Bayesian approach treats the two types of unknowns in symmetric fashion. The future values of an economic time series simply constitute another function of interest for the Bayesian analysis.

Conditioning on what is known, of course, means using prior knowledge of structures, reasonable parameterizations, etc., and it is often thought that it is the use of prior information that is the salient feature of a Bayesian analysis. While the use of such information is certainly a distinguishing feature of a Bayesian approach, it is merely an implication of the principles that one should fully specify what is known and what is unknown, and then condition on what is known in making probabilistic statements about what is unknown.

Until recently, each of these two principles posed substantial technical obstacles for Bayesian analyses. Conditioning on known data and structures generally leads to integration problems whose intractability grows with the realism and complexity of the problem's formulation. Fortunately, advances in numerical integration that have occurred during the past fifteen years have steadily broadened the class of forecasting problems that can be addressed routinely in a careful yet practical fashion. This development has simultaneously enlarged the scope of models that can be brought to bear on forecasting problems using either Bayesian or non-Bayesian methods, and significantly increased the quality of economic forecasting. This chapter provides both the technical foundation for these advances, and the history of how they came about and improved economic decision-making.

The chapter begins in Section 2 with an exposition of Bayesian inference, emphasizing applications of these methods in forecasting. Section 3 describes how Bayesian inference has been implemented in posterior simulation methods developed since the late 1980's. The reader who is familiar with these topics at the level of Koop (2003) or Lancaster (2004) will find that much of this material is review, except to establish notation, which is quite similar to Geweke (2005). Section 4 details the evolution of Bayesian forecasting methods in macroeconomics, beginning from the seminal work of Zellner (1971). Section 5 provides selectively chosen examples illustrating other Bayesian forecasting models, with an emphasis on their implementation through posterior simulators. The chapter concludes with some practical applications of Bayesian vector autoregressions.

2. Bayesian inference and forecasting: A primer

Bayesian methods of inference and forecasting all derive from two simple principles.

1. *Principle of explicit formulation.* Express all assumptions using formal probability statements about the joint distribution of future events of interest and relevant events observed at the time decisions, including forecasts, must be made.
2. *Principle of relevant conditioning.* In forecasting, use the distribution of future events conditional on observed relevant events and an explicit loss function.

The fun (if not the devil) is in the details. Technical obstacles can limit the expression of assumptions and loss functions or impose compromises and approximations. These obstacles have largely fallen with the advent of posterior simulation methods described in Section 3, methods that have themselves motivated entirely new forecasting models. In practice those doing the technical work with distributions [investigators, in the dichotomy drawn by Hildreth (1963)] and those whose decision-making drives the list of future events and the choice of loss function (Hildreth's clients) may not be the same. This poses the question of what investigators should report, especially if their clients are anonymous, an issue to which we return in Section 3.3. In these and a host of other tactics, the two principles provide the strategy.

This analysis will provide some striking contrasts for the reader who is both new to Bayesian methods and steeped in non-Bayesian approaches. Non-Bayesian methods employ the first principle to varying degrees, some as fully as do Bayesian methods, where it is essential. All non-Bayesian methods violate the second principle. This leads to a series of technical difficulties that are symptomatic of the violation: no treatment of these difficulties, no matter how sophisticated, addresses the essential problem. We return to the details of these difficulties below in Sections 2.1 and 2.2. At the end of the day, the failure of non-Bayesian methods to condition on what is known rather than what is unknown precludes the integration of the many kinds of uncertainty that is essential both to decision making as modeled in mainstream economics and as it is understood by real decision-makers. Non-Bayesian approaches concentrate on uncertainty about the future conditional on a model, parameter values, and exogenous variables, leading to a host of practical problems that are once again symptomatic of the violation of the principle of relevant conditioning. Section 3.3 details these difficulties.

2.1. Models for observables

Bayesian inference takes place in the context of one or more models that describe the behavior of a $p \times 1$ vector of observable random variables $\mathbf{y}_t$ over a sequence of discrete time units $t = 1, 2, \ldots$. The history of the sequence at time t is given by $\mathbf{Y}_t = \{\mathbf{y}_s\}_{s=1}^t$. The sample space for $\mathbf{y}_t$ is ψ_t, that for $\mathbf{Y}_t$ is Ψ_t, and $\psi_0 = \Psi_0 = \{\emptyset\}$. A model, A, specifies a corresponding sequence of probability density functions

$$p(\mathbf{y}_t \mid \mathbf{Y}_{t-1}, \boldsymbol{\theta}_A, A) \tag{1}$$

in which $\boldsymbol{\theta}_A$ is a $k_A \times 1$ vector of unobservables, and $\boldsymbol{\theta}_A \in \Theta_A \subseteq \mathbb{R}^k$. The vector $\boldsymbol{\theta}_A$ includes not only parameters as usually conceived, but also latent variables convenient in model formulation. This extension immediately accommodates non-standard distributions, time varying parameters, and heterogeneity across observations; Albert and Chib (1993), Carter and Kohn (1994), Fruhwirth-Schnatter (1994) and DeJong and Shephard (1995) provide examples of this flexibility in the context of Bayesian time series modeling.

The notation $p(\cdot)$ indicates a generic probability density function (p.d.f.) with respect to Lebesgue measure, and $P(\cdot)$ the corresponding cumulative distribution function (c.d.f.). We use continuous distributions to simplify the notation; extension to discrete and mixed continuous–discrete distributions is straightforward using a generic measure ν. The probability density function (p.d.f.) for $\mathbf{Y}_T$, conditional on the model and unobservables vector $\boldsymbol{\theta}_A$, is

$$p(\mathbf{Y}_T \mid \boldsymbol{\theta}_A, A) = \prod_{t=1}^{T} p(\mathbf{y}_t \mid \mathbf{Y}_{t-1}, \boldsymbol{\theta}_A, A). \tag{2}$$

When used alone, expressions like $\mathbf{y}_t$ and $\mathbf{Y}_T$ denote random vectors. In Equations (1) and (2) $\mathbf{y}_t$ and $\mathbf{Y}_T$ are arguments of functions. These uses are distinct from the observed values themselves. To preserve this distinction explicitly, denote observed $\mathbf{y}_t$ by $\mathbf{y}_t^o$ and observed $\mathbf{Y}_T$ by $\mathbf{Y}_T^o$. In general, the superscript o will denote the observed value of a random vector. For example, the *likelihood function* is $L(\boldsymbol{\theta}_A; \mathbf{Y}_T^o, A) \propto p(\mathbf{Y}_T^o \mid \boldsymbol{\theta}_A, A)$.

2.1.1. An example: Vector autoregressions

Following Sims (1980) and Litterman (1979) (which are discussed below), vector autoregressive models have been utilized extensively in forecasting macroeconomic and other time series owing to the ease with which they can be used for this purpose and their apparent great success in implementation. Adapting the notation of Litterman (1979), the VAR specification for

$$p(\mathbf{y}_t \mid \mathbf{Y}_{t-1}, \boldsymbol{\theta}_A, A)$$

is given by

$$\mathbf{y}_t = \mathbf{B}_D D_t + \mathbf{B}_1 \mathbf{y}_{t-1} + \mathbf{B}_2 \mathbf{y}_{t-2} + \cdots + \mathbf{B}_m \mathbf{y}_{t-m} + \varepsilon_t \tag{3}$$

where A now signifies the autoregressive structure, D_t is a deterministic component of dimension d, and $\varepsilon_t \overset{\text{iid}}{\sim} N(0, \boldsymbol{\Psi})$. In this case,

$$\boldsymbol{\theta}_A = (\mathbf{B}_D, \mathbf{B}_1, \ldots, \mathbf{B}_m, \boldsymbol{\Psi}).$$

2.1.2. An example: Stochastic volatility

Models with time-varying volatility have long been standard tools in portfolio allocation problems. Jacquier, Polson and Rossi (1994) developed the first fully Bayesian approach to such a model. They utilized a time series of latent volatilities $\mathbf{h} = (h_1, \ldots, h_T)'$:

$$h_1 \mid (\sigma_\eta^2, \phi, A) \sim N\left[0, \sigma_\eta^2/(1 - \phi^2)\right], \tag{4}$$

$$h_t = \phi h_{t-1} + \sigma_\eta \eta_t \quad (t = 2, \ldots, T). \tag{5}$$

An observable sequence of asset returns $\mathbf{y} = (y_1, \ldots, y_T)'$ is then conditionally independent,

$$y_t = \beta \exp(h_t/2)\varepsilon_t; \tag{6}$$

$(\varepsilon_t, \eta_t)' \mid A \overset{\text{iid}}{\sim} N(\mathbf{0}, \mathbf{I}_2)$. The $(T + 3) \times 1$ vector of unobservables is

$$\boldsymbol{\theta}_A = \left(\beta, \sigma_\eta^2, \phi, h_1, \ldots, h_T\right)'. \tag{7}$$

It is conventional to speak of $(\beta, \sigma_\eta^2, \phi)$ as a parameter vector and $\mathbf{h}$ as a vector of latent variables, but in Bayesian inference this distinction is a matter only of language, not substance. The unobservables $\mathbf{h}$ can be any real numbers, whereas $\beta > 0$, $\sigma_\eta > 0$, and $\phi \in (-1, 1)$. If $\phi > 0$ then the observable sequence $\{y_t^2\}$ exhibits the positive serial correlation characteristic of many sequences of asset returns.

2.1.3. The forecasting vector of interest

Models are means, not ends. A useful link between models and the purposes for which they are formulated is a vector of interest, which we denote $\boldsymbol{\omega} \in \Omega \subseteq \mathbb{R}^q$. The vector of interest may be unobservable, for example the monetary equivalent of a change in welfare, or the change in an equilibrium price vector, following a hypothetical policy change. In order to be relevant, the model must not only specify (1), but also

$$p(\boldsymbol{\omega} \mid \mathbf{Y}_T, \boldsymbol{\theta}_A, A). \tag{8}$$

In a forecasting problem, by definition, $\{\mathbf{y}'_{T+1}, \ldots, \mathbf{y}'_{T+F}\} \in \boldsymbol{\omega}'$ for some $F > 0$. In some cases $\boldsymbol{\omega}' = (\mathbf{y}'_{T+1}, \ldots, \mathbf{y}'_{T+F})$ and it is possible to express $p(\boldsymbol{\omega} \mid \mathbf{Y}_T, \boldsymbol{\theta}_A) \propto p(\mathbf{Y}_{T+F} \mid \boldsymbol{\theta}_A, A)$ in closed form, but in general this is not so. Suppose, for example, that a stochastic volatility model of the form (5)–(6) is a means to the solution of a financial decision making problem with a 20-day horizon so that $\boldsymbol{\omega} = (y_{T+1}, \ldots, y_{T+20})'$. Then there is no analytical expression for $p(\boldsymbol{\omega} \mid \mathbf{Y}_T, \boldsymbol{\theta}_A, A)$ with $\boldsymbol{\theta}_A$ defined as it is in (7). If $\boldsymbol{\omega}$ is extended to include $(h_{T+1}, \ldots, h_{T+20})'$ as well as $(y_{T+1}, \ldots, y_{T+20})'$, then the expression is simple. Continuing with an analytical approach then confronts the original problem of integrating over $(h_{T+1}, \ldots, h_{T+20})'$ to obtain $p(\boldsymbol{\omega} \mid \mathbf{Y}_T, \boldsymbol{\theta}_A, A)$. But it also highlights the fact that it is easy to simulate from this extended definition of $\boldsymbol{\omega}$ in a way that is, today, obvious:

$$h_t \mid \left(h_{t-1}, \sigma_\eta^2, \phi, A\right) \sim N\left(\phi h_{t-1}, \sigma_\eta^2\right),$$

$$y_t \mid (h_t, \beta, A) \sim N\left[0, \beta^2 \exp(h_t)\right] \quad (t = T+1, \ldots, T+20).$$

Since this produces a simulation from the joint distribution of $(h_{T+1}, \ldots, h_{T+20})'$ and $(y_{T+1}, \ldots, y_{T+20})'$, the "marginalization" problem simply amounts to discarding the simulated $(h_{T+1}, \ldots, h_{T+20})'$.

A quarter-century ago, this idea was far from obvious. Wecker (1979), in a paper on predicting turning points in macroeconomic time series, appears to have been the first to have used simulation to access the distribution of a problematic vector of interest $\boldsymbol{\omega}$ or functions of $\boldsymbol{\omega}$. His contribution was the first illustration of several principles that have emerged since and will appear repeatedly in this survey. One is that while producing marginal from joint distributions analytically is demanding and often impossible, in simulation it simply amounts to discarding what is irrelevant. (In Wecker's case the future y_{T+s} were irrelevant in the vector that also included indicator variables for turning points.) A second is that formal decision problems of many kinds, from point forecasts to portfolio allocations to the assessment of event probabilities can be solved using simulations of $\boldsymbol{\omega}$. Yet another insight is that it may be much simpler to introduce intermediate conditional distributions, thereby enlarging $\boldsymbol{\theta}_A$, $\boldsymbol{\omega}$, or both, retaining from the simulation only that which is relevant to the problem at hand. The latter idea was fully developed in the contribution of Tanner and Wong (1987).

2.2. *Model completion with prior distributions*

The generic model for observables (2) is expressed conditional on a vector of unobservables, $\boldsymbol{\theta}_A$, that includes unknown parameters. The same is true of the model for the vector of interest $\boldsymbol{\omega}$ in (8), and this remains true whether one simulates from this distribution or provides a full analytical treatment. Any workable solution of a forecasting problem must, in one way or another, address the fact that $\boldsymbol{\theta}_A$ is unobserved. A similar issue arises if there are alternative models A – different functional forms in (2) and (8) – and we return to this matter in Section 2.3.

2.2.1. *The role of the prior*

The Bayesian strategy is dictated by the first principle, which demands that we work with $p(\boldsymbol{\omega} \mid \mathbf{Y}_T, A)$. Given that $p(\mathbf{Y}_T \mid \boldsymbol{\theta}_A, A)$ has been specified in (2) and $p(\boldsymbol{\omega} \mid \mathbf{Y}_T, \boldsymbol{\theta}_A)$ in (8), we meet the requirements of the first principle by specifying

$$p(\boldsymbol{\theta}_A \mid A), \tag{9}$$

because then

$$p(\boldsymbol{\omega} \mid \mathbf{Y}_T, A) \propto \int_{\Theta_A} p(\boldsymbol{\theta}_A \mid A) p(\mathbf{Y}_T \mid \boldsymbol{\theta}_A, A) p(\boldsymbol{\omega} \mid \mathbf{Y}_T, \boldsymbol{\theta}_A, A)\, \mathrm{d}\boldsymbol{\theta}_A.$$

The density $p(\boldsymbol{\theta}_A \mid A)$ defines the *prior distribution* of the unobservables. For many practical purposes it proves useful to work with an intermediate distribution, the *poste-*

rior distribution of the unobservables whose density is

$$p(\boldsymbol{\theta}_A \mid \mathbf{Y}_T^o, A) \propto p(\boldsymbol{\theta}_A \mid A) p(\mathbf{Y}_T^o \mid \boldsymbol{\theta}_A, A)$$

and then $p(\boldsymbol{\omega} \mid \mathbf{Y}_T^o, A) = \int_{\Theta_A} p(\boldsymbol{\theta}_A \mid \mathbf{Y}_T^o, A) p(\boldsymbol{\omega} \mid \mathbf{Y}_T^o, \boldsymbol{\theta}_A, A) \, \mathrm{d}\boldsymbol{\theta}_A$.

Much of the prior information in a complete model comes from the specification of (1): for example, Gaussian disturbances limit the scope for outliers regardless of the prior distribution of the unobservables; similarly in the stochastic volatility model outlined in Section 2.1.2 there can be no "leverage effects" in which outliers in period $T + 1$ are more likely following a negative return in period T than following a positive return of the same magnitude. The prior distribution further refines what is reasonable in the model.

There are a number of ways that the prior distribution can be articulated. The most important, in Bayesian economic forecasting, have been the closely related principles of shrinkage and hierarchical prior distributions, which we take up shortly. Substantive expert information can be incorporated, and can improve forecasts. For example DeJong, Ingram and Whiteman (2000) and Ingram and Whiteman (1994) utilize dynamic stochastic general equilibrium models to provide prior distributions in vector autoregressions to the same good effect that Litterman (1979) did with shrinkage priors (see Section 4.3 below). Chulani, Boehm and Steece (1999) construct a prior distribution, in part, from expert information and use it to improve forecasts of the cost, schedule and quality of software under development. Heckerman (1997) provides a closely related approach to expressing prior distributions using Bayesian belief networks.

2.2.2. *Prior predictive distributions*

Regardless of how the conditional distribution of observables and the prior distribution of unobservables are formulated, together they provide a distribution of observables with density

$$p(\mathbf{Y}_T \mid A) = \int_{\Theta_A} p(\boldsymbol{\theta}_A \mid A) p(\mathbf{Y}_T \mid \boldsymbol{\theta}_A) \, \mathrm{d}\boldsymbol{\theta}_A, \tag{10}$$

known as the *prior predictive density*. It summarizes the whole range of phenomena consistent with the complete model and it is generally very easy to access by means of simulation. Suppose that the values $\boldsymbol{\theta}_A^{(m)}$ are drawn i.i.d. from the prior distribution, an assumption that we denote $\boldsymbol{\theta}_A^{(m)} \overset{\text{iid}}{\sim} p(\boldsymbol{\theta}_A \mid A)$, and then successive values of $\mathbf{y}_t^{(m)}$ are drawn independently from the distributions whose densities are given in (1),

$$\mathbf{y}_t^{(m)} \overset{\text{id}}{\sim} p(\mathbf{y}_t \mid \mathbf{Y}_{t-1}^{(m)}, \boldsymbol{\theta}_A^{(m)}, A) \quad (t = 1, \ldots, T;\ m = 1, \ldots, M). \tag{11}$$

Then the simulated samples $\mathbf{Y}_T^{(m)} \overset{\text{iid}}{\sim} p(\mathbf{Y}_T \mid A)$. Notice that so long as prior distributions of the parameters are tractable, this exercise is entirely straightforward. The vector autoregression and stochastic volatility models introduced above are both easy cases.

The prior predictive distribution summarizes the substance of the model and emphasizes the fact that the prior distribution and the conditional distribution of observables are inseparable components, a point forcefully argued a quarter-century ago in a seminal paper by Box (1980). It can also be a very useful tool in understanding a model – one that can greatly enhance research productivity, as emphasized in recent papers by Geweke (1998), Geweke and McCausland (2001) and Gelman (2003) as well as in recent Bayesian econometrics texts by Lancaster (2004, Section 2.4) and Geweke (2005, Section 5.3.1). This is because simulation from the prior predictive distribution is generally much simpler than formal inference (Bayesian or otherwise) and can be carried out relatively quickly when a model is first formulated. One can readily address the question of whether an observed function of the data $g(\mathbf{Y}_T^o)$ is consistent with the model by checking to see whether it is within the support of $p[g(\mathbf{Y}_T) \mid A]$ which in turn is represented by $g(\mathbf{Y}_T^{(m)})$ $(m = 1, \ldots, M)$. The function g could, for example, be a unit root test statistic, a measure of leverage, or the point estimate of a long-memory parameter.

2.2.3. Hierarchical priors and shrinkage

A common technique in constructing a prior distribution is the use of intermediate parameters to facilitate expressing the distribution. For example suppose that the prior distribution of a parameter μ is Student-t with location parameter $\underline{\mu}$, scale parameter $\underline{h}^{-1}$ and ν degrees of freedom. The underscores, here, denote parameters of the prior distribution, constants that are part of the model definition and are assigned numerical values. Drawing on the familiar genesis of the t-distribution, the same prior distribution could be expressed $(\underline{\nu}/\underline{h})h \sim \chi^2(\underline{\nu})$, the first step in the hierarchical prior, and then $\mu \mid h \sim N(\underline{\mu}, h^{-1})$, the second step. The unobservable h is an intermediate device useful in expressing the prior distribution; such unobservables are sometimes termed *hyperparameters* in the literature. A prior distribution with such intermediate parameters is a *hierarchical prior*, a concept introduced by Lindley and Smith (1972) and Smith (1973). In the case of the Student-t distribution this is obviously unnecessary, but it still proves quite convenient in conjunction with the posterior simulators discussed in Section 3.

In the formal generalization of this idea the complete model provides the prior distribution by first specifying the distribution of a vector of hyperparameters $\boldsymbol{\theta}_A^*$, $p(\boldsymbol{\theta}_A^* \mid A)$, and then the prior distribution of a parameter vector $\boldsymbol{\theta}_A$ conditional on $\boldsymbol{\theta}_A^*$, $p(\boldsymbol{\theta}_A \mid \boldsymbol{\theta}_A^*, A)$. The distinction between a hyperparameter and a parameter is that the distribution of the observable is expressed, directly, conditional on the latter: $p(\mathbf{Y}_T \mid \boldsymbol{\theta}_A, A)$. Clearly one could have more than one layer of hyperparameters and there is no reason why $\boldsymbol{\theta}_A^*$ could not also appear in the observables distribution.

In other settings hierarchical prior distributions are not only convenient, but essential. In economic forecasting important instances of hierarchical prior arise when there are many parameters, say $\theta_1, \ldots, \theta_r$, that are thought to be similar but about whose common central tendency there is less information. To take the simplest case, that of a multivariate normal prior distribution, this idea could be expressed by means of a variance matrix with large on-diagonal elements $\underline{h}^{-1}$, and off-diagonal elements $\underline{\rho}\underline{h}^{-1}$, with $\underline{\rho}$ close to 1.

Equivalently, this idea could be expressed by introducing the hyperparameter θ^*, then taking

$$\theta^* \mid A \sim N(0, \rho \underline{h}^{-1}) \tag{12}$$

followed by

$$\theta_i \mid (\theta^*, A) \sim N[\theta^*, (1-\rho)\underline{h}^{-1}], \tag{13}$$

$$\mathbf{y}_t \mid (\theta_1, \ldots, \theta_r, A) \sim p(\mathbf{y}_t \mid \theta_1, \ldots, \theta_r) \quad (t = 1, \ldots, T). \tag{14}$$

This idea could then easily be merged with the strategy for handling the Student-*t* distribution, allowing some outliers among θ_i (a Student-*t* distribution conditional on θ^*), thicker tails in the distribution of θ^*, or both.

The application of hierarchical priors in (12)–(13) is an example of shrinkage. The concept is familiar in non-Bayesian treatments as well (for example, ridge regression) where its formal motivation originated with James and Stein (1961). In the Bayesian setting shrinkage is toward a common unknown mean θ^*, for which a posterior distribution will be determined by the data, given the prior.

This idea has proven to be vital in forecasting problems in which there are many parameters. Section 4 reviews its application in vector autoregressions and its critical role in turning mediocre into superior forecasts in that model. Zellner and Hong (1989) used this strategy in forecasting growth rates of output for 18 different countries, and it proved to minimize mean square forecast error among eight competing treatments of the same model. More recently Tobias (2001) applied the same strategy in developing predictive intervals in the same model. Zellner and Chen (2001) approached the problem of forecasting US real GDP growth by disaggregating across sectors and employing a prior that shrinks sector parameters toward a common but unknown mean, with a payoff similar to that in Zellner and Hong (1989). In forecasting long-run returns to over 1,000 initial public offerings Brav (2000) found a prior with shrinkage toward an unknown mean essential in producing superior results.

2.2.4. *Latent variables*

Latent variables, like the volatilities h_t in the stochastic volatility model of Section 2.1.2, are common in econometric modelling. Their treatment in Bayesian inference is no different from the treatment of other unobservables, like parameters. In fact latent variables are, formally, no different from hyperparameters. For the stochastic volatility model Equations (4)–(5) provide the distribution of the latent variables (hyperparameters) conditional on the parameters, just as (12) provides the hyperparameter distribution in the illustration of shrinkage. Conditional on the latent variables $\{h_t\}$, (6) indicates the observables distribution, just as (14) indicates the distribution of observables conditional on the parameters.

In the formal generalization of this idea the complete model provides a conventional prior distribution $p(\boldsymbol{\theta}_A \mid A)$, and then the distribution of a vector of latent variables $\mathbf{z}$

conditional on $\boldsymbol{\theta}_A$, $p(\mathbf{z} \mid \boldsymbol{\theta}_A, A)$. The observables distribution typically involves both $\mathbf{z}$ and $\boldsymbol{\theta}_A$: $p(\mathbf{Y}_T \mid \mathbf{z}, \boldsymbol{\theta}_A, A)$. Clearly one could also have a hierarchical prior distribution for $\boldsymbol{\theta}_A$ in this context as well.

Latent variables are convenient, but not essential, devices for describing the distribution of observables, just as hyperparameters are convenient but not essential in constructing prior distributions. The convenience stems from the fact that the likelihood function is otherwise awkward to express, as the reader can readily verify for the stochastic volatility model. In these situations Bayesian inference then has to confront the problem that it is impractical, if not impossible, to evaluate the likelihood function or even to provide an adequate numerical approximation. Tanner and Wong (1987) provided a systematic method for avoiding analytical integration in evaluating the likelihood function, through a simulation method they described as data augmentation. Section 5.2.2 provides an example.

This ability to use latent variables in a routine and practical way in conjunction with Bayesian inference has spawned a generation of Bayesian time series models useful in prediction. These include state space mixture models [see Carter and Kohn (1994, 1996) and Gerlach, Carter and Kohn (2000)], discrete state models [see Albert and Chib (1993) and Chib (1996)], component models [see West (1995) and Huerta and West (1999)] and factor models [see Geweke and Zhou (1996) and Aguilar and West (2000)]. The last paper provides a full application to the applied forecasting problem of foreign exchange portfolio allocation.

2.3. Model combination and evaluation

In applied forecasting and decision problems one typically has under consideration not a single model A, but several alternative models $A_1, \ldots, A_J$. Each model is comprised of a conditional observables density (1), a conditional density of a vector of interest $\boldsymbol{\omega}$ (8) and a prior density (9). For a finite number of models, each fully articulated in this way, treatment is dictated by the principle of explicit formulation: extend the formal probability treatment to include all J models. This extension requires only attaching prior probabilities $p(A_j)$ to the models, and then conducting inference and addressing decision problems conditional on the universal model specification

$$\left\{p(A_j),\, p(\boldsymbol{\theta}_{A_j} \mid A_j),\, p(\mathbf{Y}_T \mid \boldsymbol{\theta}_{A_j}, A_j),\, p(\boldsymbol{\omega} \mid \mathbf{Y}_T, \boldsymbol{\theta}_{A_j}, A_j)\right\} \quad (j = 1, \ldots, J). \tag{15}$$

The J models are related by their prior predictions for a common set of observables $\mathbf{Y}_T$ and a common vector of interest $\boldsymbol{\omega}$. The models may be quite similar: some, or all, of them might have the same vector of unobservables $\boldsymbol{\theta}_A$ and the same functional form for $p(\mathbf{Y}_T \mid \boldsymbol{\theta}_A, A)$, and differ only in their specification of the prior density $p(\boldsymbol{\theta}_A \mid A_j)$. At the other extreme some of the models in the universe might be simple or have a few unobservables, while others could be very complex with the number of unobservables, which include any latent variables, substantially exceeding the number of observables. There is no nesting requirement.

2.3.1. Models and probability

The penultimate objective in Bayesian forecasting is the distribution of the vector of interest $\boldsymbol{\omega}$, conditional on the data $\mathbf{Y}_T^o$ and the universal model specification $A = \{A_1, \ldots, A_J\}$. Given (15) the formal solution is

$$p(\boldsymbol{\omega} \mid \mathbf{Y}_T^o, A) = \sum_{j=1}^{J} p(\boldsymbol{\omega} \mid \mathbf{Y}_T^o, A_j) p(A_j \mid \mathbf{Y}_T^o), \tag{16}$$

known as *model averaging*. In expression (16),

$$p(A_j \mid \mathbf{Y}_T^o, A) = p(\mathbf{Y}_T^o \mid A_j) p(A_j \mid A) / p(\mathbf{Y}_T^o \mid A) \tag{17}$$

$$\propto p(\mathbf{Y}_T^o \mid A_j) p(A_j \mid A). \tag{18}$$

Expression (17) is the posterior probability of model A_j. Since these probabilities sum to 1, the values in (18) are sufficient. Of the two components in (18) the second is the prior probability of model A_j. The first is the *marginal likelihood*

$$p(\mathbf{Y}_T^o \mid A_j) = \int_{\Theta_{A_j}} p(\mathbf{Y}_T^o \mid \boldsymbol{\theta}_{A_j}, A_j) p(\boldsymbol{\theta}_{A_j} \mid A_j) \, \mathrm{d}\boldsymbol{\theta}_{A_j}. \tag{19}$$

Comparing (19) with (10), note that (19) is simply the prior predictive density, evaluated at the realized outcome $\mathbf{Y}_T^o$ – the data.

The ratio of posterior probabilities of the models A_j and A_k is

$$\frac{P(A_j \mid \mathbf{Y}_T^o)}{P(A_k \mid \mathbf{Y}_T^o)} = \frac{P(A_j)}{P(A_k)} \cdot \frac{p(\mathbf{Y}_T^o \mid A_j)}{p(\mathbf{Y}_T^o \mid A_k)}, \tag{20}$$

known as the *posterior odds ratio* in favor of model A_j versus model A_k. It is the product of the *prior odds ratio* $P(A_j \mid A)/P(A_k \mid A)$, and the ratio of marginal likelihoods $p(\mathbf{Y}_T^o \mid A_j)/p(\mathbf{Y}_T^o \mid A_k)$, known as the *Bayes factor*. The Bayes factor, which may be interpreted as updating the prior odds ratio to the posterior odds ratio, is independent of the other models in the universe $A = \{A_1, \ldots, A_J\}$. This quantity is central in summarizing the evidence in favor of one model, or theory, as opposed to another one, an idea due to Jeffreys (1939). The significance of this fact in the statistics literature was recognized by Roberts (1965), and in econometrics by Leamer (1978). The Bayes factor is now a practical tool in applied statistics; see the reviews of Draper (1995), Chatfield (1995), Kass and Raftery (1996) and Hoeting et al. (1999).

2.3.2. A model is as good as its predictions

It is through the marginal likelihoods $p(\mathbf{Y}_T^o \mid A_j)$ $(j = 1, \ldots, J)$ that the observed outcome (data) determines the relative contribution of competing models to the posterior distribution of the vector of interest $\boldsymbol{\omega}$. There is a close and formal link between a model's marginal likelihood and the adequacy of its out-of-sample predictions. To establish this link consider the specific case of a forecasting horizon of F periods, with

$\omega' = (\mathbf{y}'_{T+1}, \ldots, \mathbf{y}'_{T+F})$. The *predictive density* of $\mathbf{y}_{T+1}, \ldots, \mathbf{y}_{T+F}$, conditional on the data $\mathbf{Y}_T^o$ and a particular model A is

$$p(\mathbf{y}_{T+1}, \ldots, \mathbf{y}_{T+F} \mid \mathbf{Y}_T^o, A). \tag{21}$$

The predictive density is relevant after formulation of the model A and observing $\mathbf{Y}_T = \mathbf{Y}_T^o$, but before observing $\mathbf{y}_{T+1}, \ldots, \mathbf{y}_{T+F}$. Once $\mathbf{y}_{T+1}, \ldots, \mathbf{y}_{T+F}$ are known, we can evaluate (21) at the observed values. This yields the *predictive likelihood* of $\mathbf{y}_{T+1}^o, \ldots, \mathbf{y}_{T+F}^o$ conditional on $\mathbf{Y}_T^o$ and the model A, the real number $p(\mathbf{y}_{T+1}^o, \ldots, \mathbf{y}_{T+F}^o \mid \mathbf{Y}_T^o, A)$. Correspondingly, the *predictive Bayes factor* in favor of model A_j, versus the model A_k, is

$$p(\mathbf{y}_{T+1}^o, \ldots, \mathbf{y}_{T+F}^o \mid \mathbf{Y}_T^o, A_j) / p(\mathbf{y}_{T+1}^o, \ldots, \mathbf{y}_{T+F}^o \mid \mathbf{Y}_T^o, A_k).$$

There is an illuminating link between predictive likelihood and marginal likelihood that dates at least to Geisel (1975). Since

$$\begin{aligned} p(\mathbf{Y}_{T+F} \mid A) &= p(\mathbf{Y}_{T+F} \mid \mathbf{Y}_T, A) p(\mathbf{Y}_T \mid A) \\ &= p(\mathbf{y}_{T+1}, \ldots, \mathbf{y}_{T+F} \mid \mathbf{Y}_T, A) p(\mathbf{Y}_T \mid A), \end{aligned}$$

the predictive likelihood is the ratio of marginal likelihoods

$$p(\mathbf{y}_{T+1}^o, \ldots, \mathbf{y}_{T+F}^o \mid \mathbf{Y}_T^o, A) = p(\mathbf{Y}_{T+F}^o \mid A) / p(\mathbf{Y}_T^o \mid A).$$

Thus the predictive likelihood is the factor that updates the marginal likelihood, as more data become available.

This updating relationship is quite general. Let the strictly increasing sequence of integers $\{s_j \ (j = 0, \ldots, q)\}$ with $s_0 = 1$ and $s_q = T$ partition T periods of observations $\mathbf{Y}_T^o$. Then

$$p(\mathbf{Y}_T^o \mid A) = \prod_{\tau=1}^{q} p(\mathbf{y}_{s_{\tau-1}+1}^o, \ldots, \mathbf{y}_{s_\tau}^o \mid \mathbf{Y}_{s_{\tau-1}}^o, A). \tag{22}$$

This decomposition is central in the updating and prediction cycle that

1. Provides a probability density for the next $s_\tau - s_{\tau-1}$ periods

$$p(\mathbf{y}_{s_{\tau-1}+1}, \ldots, \mathbf{y}_{s_\tau} \mid \mathbf{Y}_{s_{\tau-1}}^o, A),$$

2. After these events are realized evaluates the fit of this probability density by means of the predictive likelihood

$$p(\mathbf{y}_{s_{\tau-1}+1}^o, \ldots, \mathbf{y}_{s_\tau}^o \mid \mathbf{Y}_{s_{\tau-1}}^o, A),$$

3. Updates the posterior density

$$p(\boldsymbol{\theta}_A \mid \mathbf{Y}_{s_\tau}^o, A) \propto p(\boldsymbol{\theta}_A \mid \mathbf{Y}_{s_{\tau-1}}^o, A) p(\mathbf{y}_{s_{\tau-1}+1}^o, \ldots, \mathbf{y}_{s_\tau}^o \mid \mathbf{Y}_{s_{\tau-1}}^o, \boldsymbol{\theta}_A, A),$$

4. Provides a probability density for the next $s_{\tau+1} - s_\tau$ periods

$$p(\mathbf{y}_{s_\tau+1}, \ldots, \mathbf{y}_{s_{\tau+1}} \mid \mathbf{Y}^o_{s_\tau}, A) = \int_{\Theta_A} p(\boldsymbol{\theta}_A \mid \mathbf{Y}^o_{s_\tau}, A) p(\mathbf{y}_{s_\tau+1}, \ldots, \mathbf{y}_{s_{\tau+1}} \mid \mathbf{Y}^o_{s_\tau}, \boldsymbol{\theta}_A, A) \, d\boldsymbol{\theta}_A.$$

This system of updating and probability forecasting in real time was termed *prequential* (a combination of probability forecasting and sequential prediction) by Dawid (1984). Dawid carefully distinguished this process from statistical forecasting systems that do not fully update: for example, using a "plug-in" estimate of $\boldsymbol{\theta}_A$, or using a posterior distribution for $\boldsymbol{\theta}_A$ that does not reflect all of the information available at the time the probability distribution over future events is formed.

Each component of the multiplicative decomposition in (22) is the realized value of the predictive density for the following $s_\tau - s_{\tau-1}$ observations, formed after $s_{\tau-1}$ observations are in hand. In this, well-defined, sense the marginal likelihood incorporates the out-of-sample prediction record of the model A. Equations (16), (18) and (22) make precise the idea that in model averaging, the weight assigned to a model is proportional to the product of its out-of-sample predictive likelihoods.

2.3.3. *Posterior predictive distributions*

Model combination completes the Bayesian structure of analysis, following the principles of explicit formulation and relevant conditioning set out at the start of this section (p. 7). There are many details in this structure important for forecasting, yet to be described. A principal attraction of the Bayesian structure is its internal logical consistency, a useful and sometimes distinguishing property in applied economic forecasting. But the external consistency of the structure is also critical to successful forecasting: a set of bad models, no matter how consistently applied, will produce bad forecasts. Evaluating external consistency requires that we compare the set of models with unarticulated alternative models. In so doing we step outside the logical structure of Bayesian analysis. This opens up an array of possible procedures, which cannot all be described here. One of the earliest, and still one of the most complete descriptions of these possible procedures is the seminal 1980 paper by Box (1980) that appears with comments by a score of discussants. For a similar more recent symposium, see Bayarri and Berger (1998) and their discussants.

One of the most useful tools in the evaluation of external consistency is the *posterior predictive distribution*. Its density is similar to the prior predictive density, except that the prior is replaced by the posterior:

$$p(\widetilde{\mathbf{Y}}_T \mid \mathbf{Y}^o_T, A) = \int_{\Theta_A} p(\boldsymbol{\theta}_A \mid \mathbf{Y}^o_T, A) p(\widetilde{\mathbf{Y}}_T \mid \mathbf{Y}^o_T, \boldsymbol{\theta}_A, A) \, d\boldsymbol{\theta}_A. \tag{23}$$

In this expression $\widetilde{\mathbf{Y}}_T$ is a random vector: the outcomes, given model A and the data $\mathbf{Y}^o_T$, that might have occurred but did not. Somewhat more precisely, if the time series "experiment" could be repeated, (23) would be the predictive density for the outcome of the repeated experiment. Contrasts between $\widetilde{\mathbf{Y}}_T$ and $\mathbf{Y}_T^o$ are the basis of assessing the external validity of the model, or set of models, upon which inference has been conditioned. If one is able to simulate unobservables $\boldsymbol{\theta}_A^{(m)}$ from the posterior distribution (more on this in Section 3) then the simulation $\widetilde{\mathbf{Y}}_T^{(m)}$ follows just as the simulation of $\mathbf{Y}_T^{(m)}$ in (11).

The process can be made formal by identifying one or more subsets S of the range Ψ_T of $\mathbf{Y}_T$. For any such subset $P(\widetilde{\mathbf{Y}}_T \in S \mid \mathbf{Y}_T^o, A)$ can be evaluated using the simulation approximation $M^{-1} \sum_{m=1}^{M} I_S(\widetilde{\mathbf{Y}}_T^{(m)})$. If $P(\widetilde{\mathbf{Y}}_T \in S \mid \mathbf{Y}_T^o, A) = 1 - \alpha$, α being a small positive number, and $\mathbf{Y}_T^o \notin S$, there is evidence of external inconsistency of the model with the data. This idea goes back to the notion of "surprise" discussed by Good (1956): we have observed an event that is very unlikely to occur again, were the time series "experiment" to be repeated, independently, many times. The essentials of this idea were set out by Rubin (1984) in what he termed "model monitoring by posterior predictive checks". As Rubin emphasized, there is no formal method for choosing the set S (see, however, Section 2.4.1 below). If S is defined with reference to a scalar function g as $\{\widetilde{\mathbf{Y}}_T\colon g_1 \leqslant g(\widetilde{\mathbf{Y}}_T) \leqslant g_2\}$ then it is a short step to reporting a "p-value" for $g(\mathbf{Y}_T^o)$. This idea builds on that of the probability integral transform introduced by Rosenblatt (1952), stressed by Dawid (1984) in prequential forecasting, and formalized by Meng (1994); see also the comprehensive survey of Gelman et al. (1995).

The purpose of posterior predictive exercises of this kind is not to conduct hypothesis tests that lead to rejection or non-rejection of models; rather, it is to provide a diagnostic that may spur creative thinking about new models that might be created and brought into the universe of models $A = \{A_1, \ldots, A_J\}$. This is the idea originally set forth by Box (1980). Not all practitioners agree: see the discussants in the symposia in Box (1980) and Bayarri and Berger (1998), as well as the articles by Edwards, Lindman and Savage (1963) and Berger and Delampady (1987). The creative process dictates the choice of S, or of $g(\widetilde{\mathbf{Y}}_T)$, which can be quite flexible, and can be selected with an eye to the ultimate application of the model, a subject to which we return in the next section. In general the function $g(\widetilde{\mathbf{Y}}_T)$ could be a pivotal test statistic (e.g., the difference between the first order statistic and the sample mean, divided by the sample standard deviation, in an i.i.d. Gaussian model) but in the most interesting and general cases it will not (e.g., the point estimate of a long-memory coefficient). In checking external validity, the method has proven useful and flexible; for example see the recent work by Koop (2001) and Geweke and McCausland (2001) and the texts by Lancaster (2004, Section 2.5) and Geweke (2005, Section 5.3.2). Brav (2000) utilizes posterior predictive analysis in examining alternative forecasting models for long-run returns on financial assets.

Posterior predictive analysis can also temper the forecasting exercise when it is clear that there are features $g(\widetilde{\mathbf{Y}}_T)$ that are poorly described by the combination of models considered. For example, if model averaging consistently under- or overestimates $P(\widetilde{\mathbf{Y}}_T \in S \mid \mathbf{Y}_T^o, A)$, then this fact can be duly noted if it is important to the client. Since there is no presumption that there exists a true model contained within the set of models considered, this sort of analysis can be important. For more details, see Draper (1995) who also provides applications to forecasting the price of oil.

2.4. Forecasting

To this point we have considered the generic situation of J competing models relating a common vector of interest $\boldsymbol{\omega}$ to a set of observables $\mathbf{Y}_T$. In forecasting problems $(\mathbf{y}'_{T+1}, \ldots, \mathbf{y}'_{T+F}) \in \boldsymbol{\omega}$. Sections 2.1 and 2.2 showed how the principle of explicit formulation leads to a recursive representation of the complete probability structure, which we collect here for ease of reference. For each model A_j, a prior model probability $p(A_j \mid A)$, a prior density $p(\boldsymbol{\theta}_{A_j} \mid A_j)$ for the unobservables $\boldsymbol{\theta}_{A_j}$ in that model, a conditional observables density $p(\mathbf{Y}_T \mid \boldsymbol{\theta}_{A_j}, A_j)$, and a vector of interest density $p(\boldsymbol{\omega} \mid \mathbf{Y}_T, \boldsymbol{\theta}_{A_j}, A_j)$ imply

$$p\{[A_j, \boldsymbol{\theta}_{A_j}\ (j = 1, \ldots, J)], \mathbf{Y}_T, \boldsymbol{\omega} \mid A\}$$
$$= \sum_{j=1}^{J} p(A_j \mid A) \cdot p(\boldsymbol{\theta}_{A_j} \mid A_j) \cdot p(\mathbf{Y}_T \mid \boldsymbol{\theta}_{A_j}, A_j) \cdot p(\boldsymbol{\omega} \mid \mathbf{Y}_T, \boldsymbol{\theta}_{A_j}, A_j).$$

The entire theory of Bayesian forecasting derives from the application of the principle of relevant conditioning to this probability structure. This leads, in order, to the posterior distribution of the unobservables in each model

$$p(\boldsymbol{\theta}_{A_j} \mid \mathbf{Y}_T^o, A_j) \propto p(\boldsymbol{\theta}_{A_j} \mid A_j) p(\mathbf{Y}_T^o \mid \boldsymbol{\theta}_{Aj}, A_j) \quad (j = 1, \ldots, J), \tag{24}$$

the predictive density for the vector of interest in each model

$$p(\boldsymbol{\omega} \mid \mathbf{Y}_T^o, A_j) = \int_{\Theta_{A_j}} p(\boldsymbol{\theta}_{A_j} \mid \mathbf{Y}_T^o, A_j) p(\boldsymbol{\omega} \mid \mathbf{Y}_T^o, \boldsymbol{\theta}_{A_j})\, \mathrm{d}\boldsymbol{\theta}_{A_j}, \tag{25}$$

posterior model probabilities

$$p(A_j \mid \mathbf{Y}_T^o, A) \propto p(A_j \mid A) \cdot \int_{\Theta_{A_j}} p(\mathbf{Y}_T^o \mid \boldsymbol{\theta}_{A_j}, A_j) p(\boldsymbol{\theta}_{A_j} \mid A_j)\, \mathrm{d}\boldsymbol{\theta}_{A_j}$$
$$(j = 1 \ldots, J), \tag{26}$$

and, finally, the predictive density for the vector of interest,

$$p(\boldsymbol{\omega} \mid \mathbf{Y}_T^o, A) = \sum_{j=1}^{J} p(\boldsymbol{\omega} \mid \mathbf{Y}_T^o, A_j) p(A_j \mid \mathbf{Y}_T^o, A). \tag{27}$$

The density (25) involves one of the elements of the recursive formulation of the model and consequently, as observed in Section 2.2.2, simulation from the corresponding distribution is generally straightforward. Expression (27) involves not much more than simple addition. Technical hurdles arise in (24) and (26), and we shall return to a general treatment of these problems using posterior simulators in Section 3. Here we emphasize the incorporation of the final product (27) in forecasting – the decision of what to report about the future. In Sections 2.4.1 and 2.4.2 we focus on (24) and (25), suppressing the model subscripting notation. Section 2.4.3 returns to issues associated with forecasting using combinations of models.

2.4.1. Loss functions and the subjective decision maker

The elements of Bayesian decision theory are isomorphic to those of the classical theory of expected utility in economics. Both Bayesian decision makers and economic agents associate a cardinal measure with all possible combinations of relevant random elements in their environment – both those that they cannot control, and those that they do. The latter are called *actions* in Bayesian decision theory and choices in economics. The mapping to a cardinal measure is a *loss function* in the Bayesian decision theory and a utility function in economics, but except for a change in sign they serve the same purpose. The decision maker takes the *Bayes action* that minimizes the expected value of his loss function; the economic agent makes the choice that maximizes the expected value of her utility function.

In the context of forecasting the relevant elements are those collected in the vector of interest $\boldsymbol{\omega}$, and for a single model the relevant density is (25). The Bayesian formulation is to find an action $\mathbf{a}$ (a vector of real numbers) that minimizes

$$E\big[L(\mathbf{a},\boldsymbol{\omega}) \mid \mathbf{Y}_T^o, A\big] = \int_\Omega \int_{\Theta_A} L(\mathbf{a},\boldsymbol{\omega}) p\big(\boldsymbol{\omega} \mid \mathbf{Y}_T^o, A\big)\,\mathrm{d}\boldsymbol{\omega}. \tag{28}$$

The solution of this problem may be denoted $\mathbf{a}(\mathbf{Y}_T^o, A)$. For some well-known special cases these solutions take simple forms; see Bernardo and Smith (1994, Section 5.1.5) or Geweke (2005, Section 2.5). If the loss function is quadratic, $L(\mathbf{a},\boldsymbol{\omega}) = (\mathbf{a}-\boldsymbol{\omega})'\mathbf{Q}(\mathbf{a}-\boldsymbol{\omega})$, where $\mathbf{Q}$ is a positive definite matrix, then $\mathbf{a}(\mathbf{Y}_T^o, A) = E(\mathbf{a} \mid \mathbf{Y}_T^o, A)$; point forecasts that are expected values assume a quadratic loss function. A zero-one loss function takes the form $L(\mathbf{a},\boldsymbol{\omega};\varepsilon) = 1 - \int_{N_\varepsilon(\mathbf{a})}(\boldsymbol{\omega})$, where $N_\varepsilon(\mathbf{a})$ is an open ε-neighborhood of $\mathbf{a}$. Under weak regularity conditions, as $\varepsilon \to 0$, $\mathbf{a} \to \arg\max_{\boldsymbol{\omega}} p(\boldsymbol{\omega} \mid \mathbf{Y}_T^o, A)$.

In practical applications asymmetric loss functions can be critical to effective forecasting; for one such application see Section 6.2 below. One example is the linear-linear loss function, defined for scalar ω as

$$L(a,\omega) = (1-q)\cdot(a-\omega)I_{(-\infty,a)}(\omega) + q\cdot(\omega-a)I_{(a,\infty)}(\omega), \tag{29}$$

where $q \in (0,1)$; the solution in this case is $a = P^{-1}(q \mid \mathbf{Y}_T^o, A)$, the qth quantile of the predictive distribution of ω. Another is the linear-exponential loss function studied by Zellner (1986):

$$L(a,\omega) = \exp\big[r(a-\omega)\big] - r(a-\omega) - 1,$$

where $r \neq 0$; then (28) is minimized by

$$a = -r^{-1}\log\big\{E\big[\exp(-r\omega)\big] \mid \mathbf{Y}_T^o, A\big\};$$

if the density (25) is Gaussian, this becomes

$$a = E\big(\omega \mid \mathbf{Y}_T^o, A\big) - (r/2)var\big(\omega \mid \mathbf{Y}_T^o, A\big).$$

The extension of both the quantile and linear-exponential loss functions to the case of a vector function of interest $\boldsymbol{\omega}$ is straightforward.

Forecasts of discrete future events also emerge from this paradigm. For example, a business cycle downturn might be defined as $\omega = y_{T+1} < y_T^o > y_{T-1}^o$ for some measure of real economic activity y_t. More generally, any future event may be denoted $\Omega_0 \subseteq \Omega$. Suppose there is no loss given a correct forecast, but loss L_1 in forecasting $\omega \in \Omega_0$ when in fact $\omega \notin \Omega_0$, and loss L_2 in forecasting $\omega \notin \Omega_0$ when in fact $\omega \in \Omega_0$. Then the forecast is $\omega \in \Omega_0$ if

$$\frac{L_1}{L_2} < \frac{P(\omega \in \Omega_0 \mid \mathbf{Y}_T^o, A)}{P(\omega \notin \Omega_0 \mid \mathbf{Y}_T^o, A)}$$

and $\omega \notin \Omega_0$ otherwise. For further details on event forecasts and combinations of event forecasts with point forecasts see Zellner, Hong and Gulati (1990).

In simulation-based approaches to Bayesian inference a random sample $\boldsymbol{\omega}^{(m)}$ ($m = 1, \ldots, M$) represents the density $p(\boldsymbol{\omega} \mid \mathbf{Y}_T^o, A)$. Shao (1989) showed that

$$\arg\max_{\mathbf{a}} M^{-1} \sum_{m=1}^{M} L\big(\mathbf{a}, \boldsymbol{\omega}^{(m)}\big) \overset{\text{a.s.}}{\rightarrow} \arg\max_{\mathbf{a}} E\big[L(\mathbf{a}, \boldsymbol{\omega}) \mid \mathbf{Y}_T^o, A\big]$$

under weak regularity conditions that serve mainly to assure the existence and uniqueness of $\arg\max_{\mathbf{a}} E[L(\mathbf{a}, \boldsymbol{\omega}) \mid \mathbf{Y}_T^o, A]$. See also Geweke (2005, Theorems 4.1.2, 4.2.3 and 4.5.3). These results open up the scope of tractable loss functions to those that can be minimized for fixed $\boldsymbol{\omega}$.

Once in place, loss functions often suggest candidates for the sets S or functions $g(\widetilde{\mathbf{Y}}_T)$ used in posterior predictive distributions as described in Section 2.3.3. A generic set of such candidates stems from the observation that a model provides not only the optimal action $\mathbf{a}$, but also the predictive density of $L(\mathbf{a}, \boldsymbol{\omega}) \mid (\mathbf{Y}_T^o, A)$ associated with that choice. This density may be compared with the realized outcomes $L(\mathbf{a}, \boldsymbol{\omega}^o) \mid (\mathbf{Y}_T^o, A)$. This can be done for one forecast, or for a whole series of forecasts. For example, $\mathbf{a}$ might be the realization of a trading rule designed to minimize expected financial loss, and L the financial loss from the application of the trading rule; see Geweke (1989b) for an early application of this idea to multiple models.

Non-Bayesian formulations of the forecasting decision problem are superficially similar but fundamentally different. In non-Bayesian approaches it is necessary to introduce the assumption that there is a data generating process $f(\mathbf{Y}_T \mid \boldsymbol{\theta})$ with a fixed but unknown vector of parameters $\boldsymbol{\theta}$, and a corresponding generating process for the vector of interest $\boldsymbol{\omega}$, $f(\boldsymbol{\omega} \mid \mathbf{Y}_T, \boldsymbol{\theta})$. In so doing these approaches condition on unknown quantities, sewing the seeds of internal logical contradiction that subsequently re-emerge, often in the guise of interesting and challenging problems. The formulation of the forecasting problem, or any other decision-making problem, is then to find a mapping from all possible outcomes $\mathbf{Y}_T$, to actions $\mathbf{a}$, that minimizes

$$E\big\{L\big[\mathbf{a}(\mathbf{Y}_T), \boldsymbol{\omega}\big]\big\} = \int_{\boldsymbol{\Omega}} \int_{\Psi_T} L\big[\mathbf{a}(\mathbf{Y}_T), \boldsymbol{\omega}\big] f(\mathbf{Y}_T \mid \boldsymbol{\theta}) f(\boldsymbol{\omega} \mid \mathbf{Y}_T, \boldsymbol{\theta})\, \mathrm{d}\mathbf{Y}_T\, \mathrm{d}\boldsymbol{\omega}. \tag{30}$$

Isolated pedantic examples aside, the solution of this problem invariably involves the unknown $\boldsymbol{\theta}$. The solution of the problem is infeasible because it is ill-posed, assuming that which is unobservable to be known and thereby violating the principle of relevant conditioning. One can replace $\boldsymbol{\theta}$ with an estimator $\widehat{\boldsymbol{\theta}}(\mathbf{Y}_T)$ in different ways and this, in turn, has led to a substantial literature on an array of procedures. The methods all build upon, rather than address, the logical contradictions inherent in this approach. Geisser (1993) provides an extensive discussion; see especially Section 2.2.2.

2.4.2. Probability forecasting and remote clients

The formulation (24)–(25) is a synopsis of the prequential approach articulated by Dawid (1984). It summarizes all of the uncertainty in the model (or collection of models, if extended to (27)) relevant for forecasting. From these densities remote clients with different loss functions can produce forecasts **a**. These clients must, of course, share the same collection of (1) prior model probabilities, (2) prior distributions of unobservables, and (3) conditional observables distributions, which is asking quite a lot. However, we shall see in Section 3.3.2 that modern simulation methods allow remote clients some scope in adjusting prior probabilities and distributions without repeating all the work that goes into posterior simulation. That leaves the collection of observables distributions $p(\mathbf{Y}_T \mid \boldsymbol{\theta}_{A_j}, A_j)$ as the important fixed element with which the remote client must work, a constraint common to all approaches to forecasting.

There is a substantial non-Bayesian literature on probability forecasting and the expression of uncertainty about probability forecasts; see Chapter 5 in this volume. It is necessary to emphasize the point that in Bayesian approaches to forecasting there is no uncertainty about the predictive density $p(\boldsymbol{\omega} \mid \mathbf{Y}_T^o)$ given the specified collection of models; this is a consequence of consistency with the principle of relevant conditioning. The probability integral transform of the predictive distribution $P(\boldsymbol{\omega} \mid \mathbf{Y}_T^o)$ provides candidates for posterior predictive analysis. Dawid (1984, Section 5.3) pointed out that not only is the marginal distribution of $P^{-1}(\boldsymbol{\omega} \mid \mathbf{Y}_T)$ uniform on (0, 1), but in a prequential updating setting of the kind described in Section 2.3.2 these outcomes are also i.i.d. This leads to a wide variety of functions $g(\widetilde{\mathbf{Y}}_T)$ that might be used in posterior predictive analysis. [Kling (1987) and Kling and Bessler (1989) applied this idea in their assessment of vector autoregression models.] Some further possibilities were discussed in recent work by Christoffersen (1998) that addressed interval forecasts; see also Chatfield (1993).

Non-Bayesian probability forecasting addresses a superficially similar but fundamentally different problem, that of estimating the predictive density inherent in the data generating process, $f(\boldsymbol{\omega} \mid \mathbf{Y}_T^o, \boldsymbol{\theta})$. The formulation of the problem in this approach is to find a mapping from all possible outcomes $\mathbf{Y}_T$ into functions $p(\boldsymbol{\omega} \mid \mathbf{Y}_T)$ that minimizes

$$E\{L[p(\boldsymbol{\omega} \mid \mathbf{Y}_T), f(\boldsymbol{\omega} \mid \mathbf{Y}_T, \boldsymbol{\theta})]\} = \int_\Omega \int_{\Psi_T} L[p(\boldsymbol{\omega} \mid \mathbf{Y}_T), f(\boldsymbol{\omega} \mid \mathbf{Y}_T, \boldsymbol{\theta})] \times f(\mathbf{Y}_T \mid \boldsymbol{\theta}) f(\boldsymbol{\omega} \mid \mathbf{Y}_T, \boldsymbol{\theta})\, \mathrm{d}\mathbf{Y}_T\, \mathrm{d}\boldsymbol{\omega}. \tag{31}$$

In contrast with the predictive density, the minimization problem (31) requires a loss function, and different loss functions will lead to different solutions, other things the same, as emphasized by Weiss (1996).

The problem (31) is a special case of the frequentist formulation of the forecasting problem described at the end of Section 2.4.1. As such, it inherits the internal inconsistencies of this approach, often appearing as challenging problems. In their recent survey of density forecasting using this approach Tay and Wallis (2000, p. 248) pinpointed the challenge, if not its source: "While a density forecast can be seen as an acknowledgement of the uncertainty in a point forecast, it is itself uncertain, and this second level of uncertainty is of more than casual interest if the density forecast is the direct object of attention .... How this might be described and reported is beginning to receive attention."

2.4.3. *Forecasts from a combination of models*

The question of how to forecast given alternative models available for the purpose is a long and well-established one. It dates at least to the 1963 work of Barnard (1963) in a paper that studied airline data. This was followed by a series of influential papers by Granger and coauthors [Bates and Granger (1969), Granger and Ramanathan (1984), Granger (1989)]; Clemen (1989) provides a review of work before 1990. The papers in this and the subsequent forecast combination literature all addressed the question of how to produce a superior forecast given competing alternatives. The answer turns in large part on what is available. Producing a superior forecast, given only competing point forecasts, is distinct from the problem of aggregating the information that produced the competing alternatives [see Granger and Ramanathan (1984, p. 198) and Granger (1989, pp. 168–169)]. A related, but distinct, problem is that of combining probability distributions from different and possibly dependent sources, taken up in a seminal paper by Winkler (1981).

In the context of Section 2.3, forecasting from a combination of models is straightforward. The vector of interest $\boldsymbol{\omega}$ includes the relevant future observables $(\mathbf{y}_{T+1}, \ldots, \mathbf{y}_{T+F})$, and the relevant forecasting density is (16). Since the minimand $E[L(\mathbf{a}, \boldsymbol{\omega}) \mid \mathbf{Y}_T^o, A]$ in (28) is defined with respect to this distribution, there is no substantive change. Thus the combination of models leads to a single predictive density, which is a weighted average of the predictive densities of the individual models, the weights being proportional to the posterior probabilities of those models. This predictive density conveys all uncertainty about $\boldsymbol{\omega}$, conditional on the collection of models and the data, and point forecasts and other actions derive from the use of a loss function in conjunction with it.

The literature acting on this paradigm has emerged rather slowly, for two reasons. One has to do with computational demands, now largely resolved and discussed in the next section; Draper (1995) provides an interesting summary and perspective on this aspect of prediction using combinations of models, along with some applications. The other is that the principle of explicit formulation demands not just point forecasts of competing models, but rather (1) their entire predictive densities $p(\boldsymbol{\omega} \mid \mathbf{Y}_T^o, A_j)$ and (2) their marginal likelihoods. Interestingly, given the results in Section 2.3.2, the latter requirement is equivalent to a record of the one-step-ahead predictive likelihoods $p(\mathbf{y}_t^o \mid \mathbf{Y}_{t-1}^o, A_j)$ $(t = 1, \ldots, T)$ for each model. It is therefore not surprising that most of the prediction work based on model combination has been undertaken using models also designed by the combiners. The feasibility of this approach was demonstrated by Zellner and coauthors [Palm and Zellner (1992), Min and Zellner (1993)] using purely analytical methods. Petridis et al. (2001) provide a successful forecasting application utilizing a combination of heterogeneous data and Bayesian model averaging.

2.4.4. *Conditional forecasting*

In some circumstances, selected elements of the vector of future values of $\mathbf{y}$ may be known, making the problem one of conditional forecasting. That is, restricting attention to the vector of interest $\boldsymbol{\omega} = (\mathbf{y}_{T+1}, \ldots, \mathbf{y}_{T+F})'$, one may wish to draw inferences regarding $\boldsymbol{\omega}$ treating $(S_1\mathbf{y}_{T+1}', \ldots, S_F\mathbf{y}_{T+F}') \equiv \mathbf{S}\boldsymbol{\omega}$ as known for $q \times p$ "selection" matrices $(S_1, \ldots, S_F)$, which could select elements or linear combinations of elements of future values. The simplest such situation arises when one or more of the elements of $\mathbf{y}$ become known before the others, perhaps because of staggered data releases. More generally, it may be desirable to make forecasts of some elements of $\mathbf{y}$ given views that others follow particular time paths as a way of summarizing features of the joint predictive distribution for $(\mathbf{y}_{T+1}, \ldots, \mathbf{y}_{T+F})$.

In this case, focusing on a single model, A, (25) becomes

$$p(\boldsymbol{\omega} \mid \mathbf{S}\boldsymbol{\omega}, \mathbf{Y}_T^o, A) = \int_{\Theta_A} p(\boldsymbol{\theta}_A \mid \mathbf{S}\boldsymbol{\omega}, \mathbf{Y}_T^o, A) p(\boldsymbol{\omega} \mid \mathbf{S}\boldsymbol{\omega}, \mathbf{Y}_T^o, \boldsymbol{\theta}_A) \, d\boldsymbol{\theta}_A. \tag{32}$$

As noted by Waggoner and Zha (1999), this expression makes clear that the conditional predictive density derives from the *joint* density of $\boldsymbol{\theta}_A$ and $\boldsymbol{\omega}$. Thus it is not sufficient, for example, merely to know the conditional predictive density $p(\boldsymbol{\omega} \mid \mathbf{Y}_T^o, \boldsymbol{\theta}_A)$, because the pattern of evolution of $(\mathbf{y}_{T+1}, \ldots, \mathbf{y}_{T+F})$ carries information about which $\boldsymbol{\theta}_A$ are likely, and vice versa.

Prior to the advent of fast posterior simulators, Doan, Litterman and Sims (1984) produced a type of conditional forecast from a Gaussian vector autoregression (see (3)) by working directly with the mean of $p(\boldsymbol{\omega} \mid \mathbf{S}\boldsymbol{\omega}, \mathbf{Y}_T^o, \bar{\boldsymbol{\theta}}_A)$, where $\bar{\boldsymbol{\theta}}_A$ is the posterior mean of $p(\boldsymbol{\theta}_A \mid \mathbf{Y}_T^o, A)$. The former can be obtained as the solution of a simple least squares problem. This procedure of course ignores the uncertainty in $\boldsymbol{\theta}_A$.

More recently, Waggoner and Zha (1999) developed two procedures for calculating conditional forecasts from VARs according to whether the conditions are regarded as "hard" or "soft". Under "hard" conditioning, $\mathbf{S}\boldsymbol{\omega}$ is treated as known, and (32) must be evaluated. Waggoner and Zha (1999) develop a Gibbs sampling procedure to do so. Under "soft" conditioning, $\mathbf{S}\boldsymbol{\omega}$ is regarded as lying in a pre-specified interval, which makes it possible to work directly with the unconditional predictive density (25), obtaining a sample of $\mathbf{S}\boldsymbol{\omega}$ in the appropriate interval by simply discarding those samples $\mathbf{S}\boldsymbol{\omega}$ which do not. The advantage to this procedure is that (25) is generally straightforward to obtain, whereas $p(\boldsymbol{\omega} \mid \mathbf{S}\boldsymbol{\omega}, \mathbf{Y}_T^o, \boldsymbol{\theta}_A)$ may not be.

Robertson, Tallman and Whiteman (2005) provide an alternative to these conditioning procedures by approximating the relevant conditional densities. They specify the conditioning information as a set of moment conditions (e.g., $E\mathbf{S}\boldsymbol{\omega} = \hat{\boldsymbol{\omega}}_{\mathbf{S}}$; $E(\mathbf{S}\boldsymbol{\omega} - \hat{\boldsymbol{\omega}}_{\mathbf{S}})(\mathbf{S}\boldsymbol{\omega} - \hat{\boldsymbol{\omega}}_{\mathbf{S}})' = \mathbf{V}_{\omega}$), and work with the density (i) that is closest to the unconditional in an information-theoretic sense and that also (ii) satisfies the specified moment conditions. Given a sample $\{\boldsymbol{\omega}^{(m)}\}$ from the unconditional predictive, the new, minimum-relative-entropy density is straightforward to calculate; the original density serves as an importance sampler for the conditional. Cogley, Morozov and Sargent (2005) have utilized this procedure in producing inflation forecast fan charts from a time-varying parameter VAR.

3. Posterior simulation methods

The principle of relevant conditioning in Bayesian inference requires that one be able to access the posterior distribution of the vector of interest $\boldsymbol{\omega}$ in one or more models. In all but simple illustrative cases this cannot be done analytically. A posterior simulator yields a pseudo-random sequence $\{\boldsymbol{\omega}^{(1)}, \ldots, \boldsymbol{\omega}^{(M)}\}$ that can be used to approximate posterior moments of the form $E[h(\boldsymbol{\omega}) \mid \mathbf{Y}_T^o, A]$ arbitrarily well: the larger is M, the better is the approximation. Taken together, these algorithms are known generically as posterior simulation methods. While the motivating task, here, is to provide a simulation representative of $p(\boldsymbol{\omega} \mid \mathbf{Y}_T^o, A)$, this section will both generalize and simplify the conditioning, in most cases, and work with the density $p(\boldsymbol{\theta} \mid I)$, $\boldsymbol{\theta} \in \Theta \subseteq \mathbb{R}^k$, and $p(\boldsymbol{\omega} \mid \boldsymbol{\theta}, I)$, $\boldsymbol{\omega} \in \boldsymbol{\Omega} \subseteq \mathbb{R}^q$, I denoting "information". Consistent with the motivating problem, we shall assume that there is no difficulty in drawing $\boldsymbol{\omega}^{(m)} \overset{\text{iid}}{\sim} p(\boldsymbol{\omega} \mid \boldsymbol{\theta}, I)$.

The methods described in this section all utilize as building blocks the set of distributions from which it is possible to produce pseudo-i.i.d. sequences of random variables or vectors. We shall refer to such distributions as conventional distributions. This set includes, of course, all of those found in standard mathematical applications software. There is a gray area beyond these distributions; examples include the Dirichlet (or multivariate beta) and Wishart distributions. What is most important, in this context, is that posterior distributions in all but the simplest models lead almost immediately to distributions from which it is effectively impossible to produce pseudo-i.i.d. sequences of random vectors. It is to these distributions that the methods discussed in this section are addressed. The treatment in this section closely follows portions of Geweke (2005, Chapter 4).

3.1. Simulation methods before 1990

The applications of simulation methods in statistics and econometrics before 1990, including Bayesian inference, were limited to sequences of independent and identically distributed random vectors. The state of the art by the mid-1960s is well summarized in Hammersly and Handscomb (1964) and the early impact of these methods in

Bayesian econometrics is evident in Zellner (1971). A survey of progress as of the end of this period is Geweke (1991) written at the dawn of the application of Markov chain Monte Carlo (MCMC) methods in Bayesian statistics.[1] Since 1990 MCMC methods have largely supplanted i.i.d. simulation methods. MCMC methods, in turn, typically combine several simulation methods, and those developed before 1990 are important constituents in MCMC.

3.1.1. *Direct sampling*

In direct sampling $\boldsymbol{\theta}^{(m)} \overset{\text{iid}}{\sim} p(\boldsymbol{\theta} \mid I)$. If $\boldsymbol{\omega}^{(m)} \sim p(\boldsymbol{\omega} \mid \boldsymbol{\theta}^{(m)}, I)$ is a conditionally independent sequence, then $\{\boldsymbol{\theta}^{(m)}, \boldsymbol{\omega}^{(m)}\} \overset{\text{iid}}{\sim} p(\boldsymbol{\theta} \mid I)p(\boldsymbol{\omega} \mid \boldsymbol{\theta}, I)$. Then for any existing moment $E[h(\boldsymbol{\theta}, \boldsymbol{\omega}) \mid I]$, $M^{-1}\sum_{m=1}^{M} h(\boldsymbol{\theta}^{(m)}, \boldsymbol{\omega}^{(m)}) \overset{\text{a.s.}}{\rightarrow} E[h(\boldsymbol{\theta}, \boldsymbol{\omega}) \mid I]$; this property, for any simulator, is widely termed *simulation-consistency*. An entirely conventional application of the Lindeberg–Levy central limit theorem provides a basis of assessing the accuracy of the approximation. The conventional densities $p(\boldsymbol{\theta} \mid I)$ from which direct sampling is possible coincide, more or less, with those for which a fully analytical treatment of Bayesian inference and forecasting is possible. An excellent example is the fully Bayesian and entirely analytical solution of the problem of forecasting turning points by Min and Zellner (1993).

The Min–Zellner treatment addresses only one-step-ahead forecasting. Forecasting successive steps ahead entails increasingly nonlinear functions that rapidly become intractable in a purely analytical approach. This problem was taken up in Geweke (1988) for multiple-step-ahead forecasts in a bivariate Gaussian autoregression with a conjugate prior distribution. The posterior distribution, like the prior, is normal-gamma. Forecasts F steps ahead based on a quadratic loss function entail linear combinations of posterior moments of order F from a multivariate Student-t distribution. This problem plays to the comparative advantage of direct sampling in the determination of posterior expectations of nonlinear functions of random variables with conventional distributions. It nicely illustrates two variants on direct sampling that can dramatically increase the speed and accuracy of posterior simulation approximations.

1. The first variant is motivated by the fact that the conditional mean of the F-step ahead realization of $\mathbf{y}_t$ is a deterministic function of the parameters. Thus, the function of interest $\boldsymbol{\omega}$ is taken to be this mean, rather than a simulated realization of $\mathbf{y}_t$.
2. The second variant exploits the fact that the posterior distribution of the variance matrix of the disturbances (denoted $\boldsymbol{\theta}_2$, say) in this model is inverted Wishart, and

[1] Ironically, MCMC methods were initially developed in the late 1940's in one of the first applications of simulation methods using electronic computers, to the design of thermonuclear weapons [see Metropolis et al. (1953)]. Perhaps not surprisingly, they spread first to disciplines with the greatest access to computing power: see the application to image restoration by Geman and Geman (1984).

the conditional distribution of the coefficients ($\boldsymbol{\theta}_1$, say) is Gaussian. Corresponding to the generated sequence $\boldsymbol{\theta}_1^{(m)}$, consider also $\widetilde{\boldsymbol{\theta}}_1^{(m)} = 2E(\boldsymbol{\theta}_1 \mid \boldsymbol{\theta}_2^{(m)}, I) - \boldsymbol{\theta}_1^{(m)}$. Both $\boldsymbol{\theta}^{(m)\prime} = (\boldsymbol{\theta}_1^{(m)\prime}, \boldsymbol{\theta}_2^{(m)\prime})$ and $\widetilde{\boldsymbol{\theta}}^{(m)\prime} = (\widetilde{\boldsymbol{\theta}}_1^{(m)\prime}, \boldsymbol{\theta}_2^{(m)\prime})$ are i.i.d. sequences drawn from $p(\boldsymbol{\theta} \mid I)$. Take $\boldsymbol{\omega}^{(m)} \sim p(\boldsymbol{\omega} \mid \boldsymbol{\theta}^{(m)}, I)$ and $\widetilde{\boldsymbol{\omega}}^{(m)} \sim p(\boldsymbol{\omega} \mid \widetilde{\boldsymbol{\theta}}^{(m)}, I)$. (In the forecasting application of Geweke (1988) these latter distributions are deterministic functions of $\boldsymbol{\theta}^{(m)}$ and $\widetilde{\boldsymbol{\theta}}^{(m)}$.) The sequences $h(\boldsymbol{\omega}^{(m)})$ and $h(\widetilde{\boldsymbol{\omega}}^{(m)})$ will also be i.i.d. and, depending on the nature of the function h, may be negatively correlated because $cov(\boldsymbol{\theta}_1^{(m)}, \widetilde{\boldsymbol{\theta}}_1^{(m)}, I) = -var(\boldsymbol{\theta}_1^{(m)} \mid I) = -var(\widetilde{\boldsymbol{\theta}}_1^{(m)} \mid I)$. In many cases the approximation error occurred using $(2M)^{-1} \sum_{m=1}^{M} [h(\boldsymbol{\omega}^{(m)}) + h(\widetilde{\boldsymbol{\omega}}^{(m)})]$ may be much smaller than that occurred using $M^{-1} \sum_{m=1}^{M} h(\boldsymbol{\omega}^{(m)})$.

The second variant is an application of antithetic sampling, an idea well established in the simulation literature [see Hammersly and Morton (1956) and Geweke (1996a, Section 5.1)]. In the posterior simulator application just described, given weak regularity conditions and for a given function h, the sequences $h(\boldsymbol{\omega}^{(m)})$ and $h(\widetilde{\boldsymbol{\omega}}^{(m)})$ become more negatively correlated as sample size increases [see Geweke (1988, Theorem 1)]; hence the term *antithetic acceleration*. The first variant has acquired the monicker *Rao–Blackwellization* in the posterior simulation literature, from the Rao–Blackwell Theorem, which establishes $var[E(\boldsymbol{\omega} \mid \boldsymbol{\theta}, I)] \leqslant var(\boldsymbol{\omega} \mid I)$. Of course the two methods can be used separately. For one-step ahead forecasts, the combination of the two methods drives the variance of the simulation approximation to zero; this is a close reflection of the symmetry and analytical tractability exploited in Min and Zellner (1993). For near-term forecasts the methods reduce variance by more than 99% in the illustration taken up in Geweke (1988); as the forecasting horizon increases the reduction dissipates, due to the increasing nonlinearity of h.

3.1.2. Acceptance sampling

Acceptance sampling relies on a conventional source density $p(\boldsymbol{\theta} \mid S)$ that approximates $p(\boldsymbol{\theta} \mid I)$, and then exploits an acceptance–rejection procedure to reconcile the approximation. The method yields a sequence $\boldsymbol{\theta}^{(m)} \overset{\text{iid}}{\sim} p(\boldsymbol{\theta} \mid I)$; as such, it renders the density $p(\boldsymbol{\theta} \mid I)$ conventional, and in fact acceptance sampling is the "black box" that produces pseudo-random variables in most mathematical applications software; for a review see Geweke (1996a).

Figure 1 provides the intuition of acceptance sampling. The heavy curve is the target density $p(\theta \mid I)$, and the lower bell-shaped curve is the source density $p(\boldsymbol{\theta} \mid S)$. The ratio $p(\theta \mid I)/p(\boldsymbol{\theta} \mid S)$ is bounded above by a constant a. In Figure 1, $p(1.16 \mid I)/p(1.16 \mid S) = a = 1.86$, and the lightest curve is $a \cdot p(\boldsymbol{\theta} \mid S)$. The idea is to draw θ^* from the source density, which has kernel $a \cdot p(\theta^* \mid S)$, but to accept the draw with probability $p(\theta^*)/a \cdot p(\theta^* \mid S)$. For example if $\theta^* = 0$, then the draw is accepted with probability 0.269, whereas if $\theta^* = 1.16$ then the draw is accepted with probability 1. The accepted values in fact simulate i.i.d. drawings from the target density $p(\theta \mid I)$.

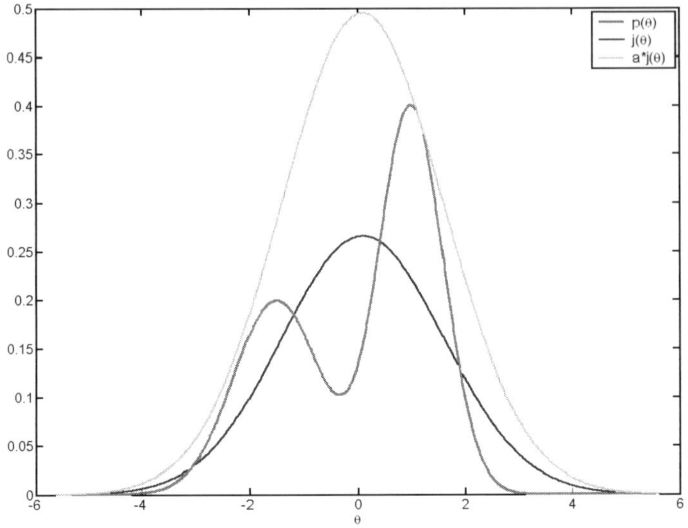

Figure 1. Acceptance sampling.

While Figure 1 is necessarily drawn for scalar θ it should be clear that the principle applies for vector $\boldsymbol{\theta}$ of any finite order. In fact this algorithm can be implemented using a kernel $k(\boldsymbol{\theta} \mid I)$ of the density $p(\boldsymbol{\theta} \mid I)$ i.e., $k(\boldsymbol{\theta} \mid I) \propto p(\boldsymbol{\theta} \mid I)$, and this can be important in applications where the constant of integration is not known. Similarly we require only a kernel $k(\boldsymbol{\theta} \mid S)$ of $p(\boldsymbol{\theta} \mid S)$, and let $a_k = \sup_{\boldsymbol{\theta} \in \boldsymbol{\Theta}} k(\boldsymbol{\theta} \mid I)/k(\boldsymbol{\theta} \mid S)$. Then for each draw m the algorithm works as follows.

1. Draw u uniform on $[0, 1]$.
2. Draw $\boldsymbol{\theta}^* \sim p(\boldsymbol{\theta} \mid S)$.
3. If $u > k(\boldsymbol{\theta}^* \mid I)/a_k k(\boldsymbol{\theta}^* \mid S)$ return to step 1.
4. Set $\boldsymbol{\theta}^{(m)} = \boldsymbol{\theta}^*$.

To see why the algorithm works, let Θ^* denote the support of $p(\boldsymbol{\theta} \mid S)$; $a < \infty$ implies $\Theta \subseteq \Theta^*$. Let $c_I = k(\boldsymbol{\theta} \mid I)/p(\boldsymbol{\theta} \mid I)$ and $c_S = k(\boldsymbol{\theta} \mid S)/p(\boldsymbol{\theta} \mid S)$. The unconditional probability of proceeding from step 3 to step 4 is

$$\int_{\boldsymbol{\Theta}^*} \left\{k(\boldsymbol{\theta} \mid I)/\left[a_k k(\boldsymbol{\theta} \mid S)\right]\right\} p(\boldsymbol{\theta} \mid S)\, \mathrm{d}\boldsymbol{\theta} = c_I/a_k c_S. \tag{33}$$

Let A be any subset of Θ. The unconditional probability of proceeding from step 3 to step 4 with $\boldsymbol{\theta} \in A$ is

$$\int_A \left\{k(\boldsymbol{\theta} \mid I)/\left[a_k k(\boldsymbol{\theta} \mid S)\right]\right\} p(\boldsymbol{\theta} \mid S)\, \mathrm{d}\boldsymbol{\theta} = \int_A k(\boldsymbol{\theta} \mid I)\, \mathrm{d}\boldsymbol{\theta}/a_k c_S. \tag{34}$$

The probability that $\boldsymbol{\theta} \in A$, conditional on proceeding from step 3 to step 4, is the ratio of (34) to (33), which is $\int_A k(\boldsymbol{\theta} \mid I)\, \mathrm{d}\boldsymbol{\theta}/c_I = \int_A p(\boldsymbol{\theta} \mid I)\, \mathrm{d}\boldsymbol{\theta}$.

Regardless of the choices of kernels the unconditional probability in (33) is $c_I/a_k c_S = \inf_{\boldsymbol{\theta}\in\boldsymbol{\Theta}} p(\boldsymbol{\theta} \mid S)/p(\boldsymbol{\theta} \mid I)$. If one wishes to generate M draws of $\boldsymbol{\theta}$ using acceptance sampling, the expected number of times one will have to draw u, draw $\boldsymbol{\theta}^*$, and compute $k(\boldsymbol{\theta}^* \mid I)/[a_k k(\boldsymbol{\theta}^* \mid S)]$ is $M \cdot \sup_{\boldsymbol{\theta}\in\Theta} p(\boldsymbol{\theta} \mid I)/p(\boldsymbol{\theta} \mid S)$. The computational efficiency of the algorithm is driven by those $\boldsymbol{\theta}$ for which $p(\boldsymbol{\theta} \mid S)$ has the greatest relative undersampling. In most applications the time consuming part of the algorithm is the evaluation of the kernels $k(\boldsymbol{\theta} \mid S)$ and $k(\boldsymbol{\theta} \mid I)$, especially the latter. (If $p(\boldsymbol{\theta} \mid I)$ is a posterior density, then evaluation of $k(\boldsymbol{\theta} \mid I)$ entails computing the likelihood function.) In such cases this is indeed the relevant measure of efficiency.

Since $\boldsymbol{\theta}^{(m)} \overset{\text{iid}}{\sim} p(\boldsymbol{\theta} \mid I)$, $\boldsymbol{\omega}^{(m)} \overset{\text{iid}}{\sim} p(\boldsymbol{\omega} \mid I) = \int_\Theta p(\boldsymbol{\theta} \mid I)p(\boldsymbol{\omega} \mid \boldsymbol{\theta}, I)\,\mathrm{d}\boldsymbol{\theta}$. Acceptance sampling is limited by the difficulty in finding an approximation $p(\boldsymbol{\theta} \mid S)$ that is efficient, in the sense just described, and by the need to find $a_k = \sup_{\boldsymbol{\theta}\in\boldsymbol{\Theta}} k(\boldsymbol{\theta} \mid I)/k(\boldsymbol{\theta} \mid S)$. While it is difficult to generalize, these tasks are typically more difficult the greater the number of elements of $\boldsymbol{\theta}$.

3.1.3. Importance sampling

Rather than accept only a fraction of the draws from the source density, it is possible to retain all of them, and consistently approximate the posterior moment by appropriately weighting the draws. The probability density function of the source distribution is then called the *importance sampling density*, a term due to Hammersly and Handscomb (1964), who were among the first to propose the method. It appears to have been introduced to the econometrics literature by Kloek and van Dijk (1978).

To describe the method, denote the source density by $p(\boldsymbol{\theta} \mid S)$ with support Θ^*, and an arbitrary kernel of the source density by $k(\boldsymbol{\theta} \mid S) = c_S \cdot p(\boldsymbol{\theta} \mid S)$ for any $c_S \neq 0$. Denote an arbitrary kernel of the target density by $k(\boldsymbol{\theta} \mid I) = c_I \cdot p(\boldsymbol{\theta} \mid I)$ for any $c_I \neq 0$, the i.i.d. sequence $\boldsymbol{\theta}^{(m)} \sim p(\boldsymbol{\theta} \mid S)$, and the sequence $\boldsymbol{\omega}^{(m)}$ drawn independently from $p(\boldsymbol{\omega} \mid \boldsymbol{\theta}^{(m)}, I)$. Define the weighting function $w(\boldsymbol{\theta}) = k(\boldsymbol{\theta} \mid I)/k(\boldsymbol{\theta} \mid S)$. Then the approximation of $\bar{h} = E[h(\boldsymbol{\omega}) \mid I]$ is

$$\bar{h}^{(M)} = \frac{\sum_{m=1}^{M} w(\boldsymbol{\theta}^{(m)})h(\boldsymbol{\omega}^{(m)})}{\sum_{m=1}^{M} w(\boldsymbol{\theta}^{(m)})}. \tag{35}$$

Geweke (1989a) showed that if $E[h(\boldsymbol{\omega}) \mid I]$ exists and is finite, and $\Theta^* \supseteq \Theta$, then $\bar{h}^{(M)} \overset{\text{a.s.}}{\rightarrow} \bar{h}$. Moreover, if $var[h(\boldsymbol{\omega}) \mid I]$ exists and is finite, and if $w(\boldsymbol{\theta})$ is bounded above on Θ, then the accuracy of the approximation can be assessed using the Lindeberg–Levy central limit theorem with an appropriately approximated variance [see Geweke (1989a, Theorem 2) or Geweke (2005, Theorem 4.2.2)]. In applications of importance sampling, this accuracy can be summarized in terms of the *numerical standard error* of $\bar{h}^{(M)}$, its sampling standard deviation in independent runs of length M of the importance sampling simulation, and in terms of the *relative numerical efficiency* of $\bar{h}^{(M)}$, the ratio of simulation size in a hypothetical direct simulator to that required using importance sampling to achieve the same numerical standard error. These summaries of accuracy can be used with other simulation methods as well, including the Markov chain Monte Carlo algorithms described in Section 3.2.

To see why importance sampling produces a simulation-consistent approximation of $E[h(\boldsymbol{\omega}) \mid I]$, notice that

$$E\big[w(\boldsymbol{\theta}) \mid S\big] = \int_{\Theta} \frac{k(\boldsymbol{\theta} \mid I)}{k(\boldsymbol{\theta} \mid S)} p(\boldsymbol{\theta} \mid S)\,\mathrm{d}\boldsymbol{\theta} = \frac{c_I}{c_S} \equiv \overline{w}.$$

Since $\{\boldsymbol{\omega}^{(m)}\}$ is i.i.d. the strong law of large numbers implies

$$M^{-1} \sum_{m=1}^{M} w\big(\boldsymbol{\theta}^{(m)}\big) \overset{\text{a.s.}}{\to} \overline{w}. \tag{36}$$

The sequence $\{w(\boldsymbol{\theta}^{(m)}),\ h(\boldsymbol{\omega}^{(m)})\}$ is also i.i.d., and

$$\begin{aligned}
E\big[w(\boldsymbol{\theta})h(\boldsymbol{\omega}) \mid I\big] &= \int_{\Theta} w(\boldsymbol{\theta})\left[\int_{\Omega} h(\boldsymbol{\omega})p(\boldsymbol{\omega} \mid \boldsymbol{\theta}, I)\,\mathrm{d}\boldsymbol{\omega}\right]p(\boldsymbol{\theta} \mid S)\,\mathrm{d}\boldsymbol{\theta} \\
&= (c_I/c_S)\int_{\Theta}\int_{\Omega} h(\boldsymbol{\omega})p(\boldsymbol{\omega} \mid \boldsymbol{\theta}, I)p(\boldsymbol{\theta} \mid I)\,\mathrm{d}\boldsymbol{\omega}\,\mathrm{d}\boldsymbol{\theta} \\
&= (c_I/c_S)E\big[h(\boldsymbol{\omega}) \mid I\big] = \overline{w} \cdot \bar{h}.
\end{aligned}$$

By the strong law of large numbers,

$$M^{-1} \sum_{m=1}^{M} w\big(\boldsymbol{\theta}^{(m)}\big)h\big(\boldsymbol{\omega}^{(m)}\big) \overset{\text{a.s.}}{\to} \overline{w} \cdot \bar{h}. \tag{37}$$

The fraction in (35) is the ratio of the left-hand side of (37) to the left-hand side of (36).

One of the attractive features of importance sampling is that it requires only that $p(\boldsymbol{\theta} \mid I)/p(\boldsymbol{\theta} \mid S)$ be bounded, whereas acceptance sampling requires that the supremum of this ratio (or that for kernels of the densities) be known. Moreover, the known supremum is required in order to implement acceptance sampling, whereas the boundedness of $p(\boldsymbol{\theta} \mid I)/p(\boldsymbol{\theta} \mid S)$ is utilized in importance sampling only to exploit a central limit theorem to assess numerical accuracy. An important application of importance sampling is in providing remote clients with a simple way to revise prior distributions, as discussed below in Section 3.3.2.

3.2. Markov chain Monte Carlo

Markov chain Monte Carlo (MCMC) methods are generalizations of direct sampling. The idea is to construct a Markov chain $\{\boldsymbol{\theta}^{(m)}\}$ with continuous state space Θ and unique invariant probability density $p(\boldsymbol{\theta} \mid I)$. Following an initial transient or *burn-in* phase, the distribution of $\boldsymbol{\theta}^{(m)}$ is approximately that of the density $p(\boldsymbol{\theta} \mid I)$. The exact sense in which this approximation holds is important. We shall touch on this only briefly; for full detail and references see Geweke (2005, Section 3.5). We continue to assume that

$\boldsymbol{\omega}$ can be simulated directly from $p(\boldsymbol{\omega} \mid \boldsymbol{\theta}, I)$, so that given $\{\boldsymbol{\theta}^{(m)}\}$ the corresponding $\boldsymbol{\omega}^{(m)} \sim p(\boldsymbol{\omega} \mid \boldsymbol{\theta}^{(m)}, I)$ can be drawn.

Markov chain methods have a history in mathematical physics dating back to the algorithm of Metropolis et al. (1953). This method, which was described subsequently in Hammersly and Handscomb (1964, Section 9.3) and Ripley (1987, Section 4.7), was generalized by Hastings (1970), who focused on statistical problems, and was further explored by Peskun (1973). A version particularly suited to image reconstruction and problems in spatial statistics was introduced by Geman and Geman (1984). This was subsequently shown to have great potential for Bayesian computation by Gelfand and Smith (1990). Their work, combined with data augmentation methods [see Tanner and Wong (1987)] has proven very successful in the treatment of latent variables in econometrics. Since 1990 application of MCMC methods has grown rapidly: new refinements, extensions, and applications appear constantly. Accessible introductions are Gelman et al. (1995), Chib and Greenberg (1995) and Geweke (2005); a good collection of applications is Gilks, Richardson and Spiegelhaldter (1996). Section 5 provides several applications of MCMC methods in Bayesian forecasting models.

3.2.1. The Gibbs sampler

Most posterior densities $p(\boldsymbol{\theta}_A \mid \mathbf{Y}_T^o, A)$ do not correspond to any conventional family of distributions. On the other hand, the conditional distributions of subvectors of $\boldsymbol{\theta}_A$ often do, which is to say that the conditional posterior distributions of these subvectors are conventional. This is partially the case in the stochastic volatility model described in Section 2.1.2. If, for example, the prior distribution of ϕ is truncated Gaussian and those of β^2 and σ_η^2 are inverted gamma, then the conditional posterior distribution of ϕ is truncated normal and those of β^2 and σ_η^2 are inverted gamma. (The conditional posterior distributions of the latent volatilities h_t are unconventional, and we return to this matter in Section 5.5.)

This motivates the simplest setting for the Gibbs sampler. Suppose $\boldsymbol{\theta}' = (\boldsymbol{\theta}_1', \boldsymbol{\theta}_2')$ has density $p(\boldsymbol{\theta}_1, \boldsymbol{\theta}_2 \mid I)$ of unconventional form, but that the conditional densities $p(\boldsymbol{\theta}_1 \mid \boldsymbol{\theta}_2, I)$ and $p(\boldsymbol{\theta}_2 \mid \boldsymbol{\theta}_1, I)$ are conventional. Suppose (hypothetically) that one had access to an initial drawing $\boldsymbol{\theta}_2^{(0)}$ taken from $p(\boldsymbol{\theta}_2 \mid I)$, the marginal density of $\boldsymbol{\theta}_2$. Then after iterations $\boldsymbol{\theta}_1^{(m)} \sim p(\boldsymbol{\theta}_1 \mid \boldsymbol{\theta}_2^{(m-1)}, I)$, $\boldsymbol{\theta}_2^{(m)} \sim p(\boldsymbol{\theta}_2 \mid \boldsymbol{\theta}_1^{(m)}, I)$ $(m = 1, \ldots, M)$ one would have a collection $\boldsymbol{\theta}^{(m)} = (\boldsymbol{\theta}_1'^{(m)}, \boldsymbol{\theta}_2'^{(m)})' \sim p(\boldsymbol{\theta} \mid I)$. The extension of this idea to more than two components of $\boldsymbol{\theta}$, given a *blocking* $\boldsymbol{\theta}' = (\boldsymbol{\theta}_1', \ldots, \boldsymbol{\theta}_B')$ and an initial $\boldsymbol{\theta}^{(0)} \sim p(\boldsymbol{\theta} \mid I)$, is immediate, cycling through

$$\boldsymbol{\theta}_b^{(m)} \sim p\big[\boldsymbol{\theta}^{(b)} \,\big|\, \boldsymbol{\theta}_a^{(m)}(a < b), \boldsymbol{\theta}_a^{(m-1)}(a > b), I\big]$$
$$(b = 1, \ldots, B;\ m = 1, 2, \ldots). \tag{38}$$

Of course, if it were possible to make an initial draw from this distribution, then independent draws directly from $p(\boldsymbol{\theta} \mid I)$ would also be possible. The purpose of that assumption here is to marshal an informal argument that the density $p(\boldsymbol{\theta} \mid I)$ is an invariant density of this Markov chain: that is, if $\boldsymbol{\theta}^{(m)} \sim p(\boldsymbol{\theta} \mid I)$, then $\boldsymbol{\theta}^{(m+s)} \sim p(\boldsymbol{\theta} \mid I)$ for all $s > 0$.

It is important to elucidate conditions for $\boldsymbol{\theta}^{(m)}$ to converge in distribution to $p(\boldsymbol{\theta} \mid I)$ given any $\boldsymbol{\theta}^{(0)} \in \Theta$. Note that even if $\boldsymbol{\theta}^{(0)}$ were drawn from $p(\boldsymbol{\theta} \mid I)$, the argument just given demonstrates only that any single $\boldsymbol{\theta}^{(m)}$ is also drawn from $p(\boldsymbol{\theta} \mid I)$. It does not establish that a single sequence $\{\boldsymbol{\theta}^{(m)}\}$ is representative of $p(\boldsymbol{\theta} \mid I)$. Consider the example shown in Figure 2(a), in which $\Theta = \Theta_1 \cup \Theta_2$, and the Gibbs sampling algorithm has blocks θ_1 and θ_2. If $\boldsymbol{\theta}^{(0)} \in \Theta_1$, then $\boldsymbol{\theta}^{(m)} \in \Theta_1$ for $m = 1, 2, \ldots$. Any single $\boldsymbol{\theta}^{(m)}$ is just as representative of $p(\boldsymbol{\theta} \mid I)$ as is the single drawing $\boldsymbol{\theta}^{(0)}$, but the same cannot be said of the collection $\{\boldsymbol{\theta}^{(m)}\}$. Indeed, $\{\boldsymbol{\theta}^{(m)}\}$ could be highly misleading. In the example shown in Figure 2(b), if $\boldsymbol{\theta}^{(0)}$ is the indicated point at the lower left vertex of the triangular closed support of $p(\boldsymbol{\theta} \mid I)$, then $\boldsymbol{\theta}^{(m)} = \boldsymbol{\theta}^{(0)}\ \forall m$. What is required is that the Gibbs sampling Markov chain $\{\boldsymbol{\theta}^{(m)}\}$ with transition density $p(\boldsymbol{\theta}^{(m)} \mid \boldsymbol{\theta}^{(m-1)}, G)$ defined in (38) be ergodic. That is, if $\boldsymbol{\omega}^{(m)} \sim p(\boldsymbol{\omega} \mid \boldsymbol{\theta}, I)$ and $E[h(\boldsymbol{\theta}, \boldsymbol{\omega}) \mid I]$ exists, then we require $M^{-1} \sum_{m=1}^{M} h(\boldsymbol{\theta}^{(m)}, \boldsymbol{\omega}^{(m)}) \xrightarrow{\text{a.s.}} E[h(\boldsymbol{\theta}, \boldsymbol{\omega}) \mid I]$. Careful statement of the weakest sufficient conditions demands considerably more theoretical apparatus than can be developed here; for this, see Tierney (1994). Somewhat

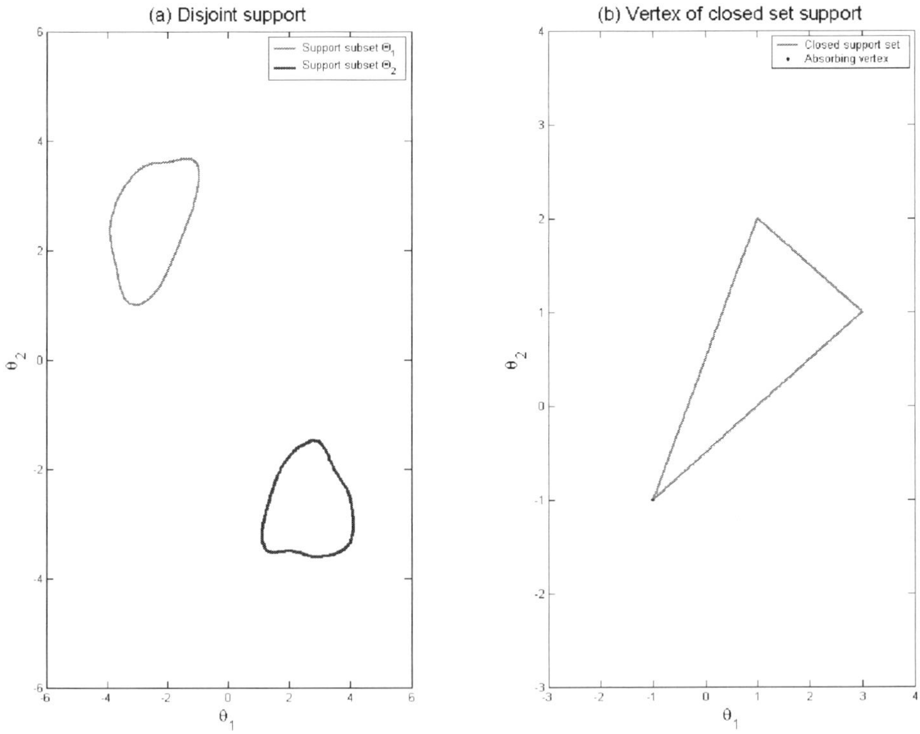

Figure 2. Two examples in which a Gibbs sampling Markov chain will be reducible.

stronger, but still widely applicable, conditions are easier to state. For example, if for any Lebesgue measurable A with $\int_A p(\boldsymbol{\theta} \mid I)\,\mathrm{d}\boldsymbol{\theta} > 0$ it is the case that in the Markov chain (38) $P(\boldsymbol{\theta}^{(m+1)} \in A \mid \boldsymbol{\theta}^{(m)}, G) > 0$ for any $\boldsymbol{\theta}^{(m)} \in \Theta$, then the Markov chain is ergodic. (Clearly neither example in Figure 2 satisfies this condition.) For this and other simple conditions see Geweke (2005, Section 4.5).

3.2.2. The Metropolis–Hastings algorithm

The Metropolis–Hastings algorithm is defined by a probability density function $p(\boldsymbol{\theta}^* \mid \boldsymbol{\theta}, H)$ indexed by $\boldsymbol{\theta} \in \Theta$ and with density argument $\boldsymbol{\theta}^*$. The random vector $\boldsymbol{\theta}^*$ generated from $p(\boldsymbol{\theta}^* \mid \boldsymbol{\theta}^{(m-1)}, H)$ is a candidate value for $\boldsymbol{\theta}^{(m)}$. The algorithm sets $\boldsymbol{\theta}^{(m)} = \boldsymbol{\theta}^*$ with probability

$$\alpha\big(\boldsymbol{\theta}^* \mid \boldsymbol{\theta}^{(m-1)}, H\big) = \min\left\{\frac{p(\boldsymbol{\theta}^* \mid I)/p(\boldsymbol{\theta}^* \mid \boldsymbol{\theta}^{(m-1)}, H)}{p(\boldsymbol{\theta}^{(m-1)} \mid I)/p(\boldsymbol{\theta}^{(m-1)} \mid \boldsymbol{\theta}^*, H)}, 1\right\}; \tag{39}$$

otherwise, $\boldsymbol{\theta}^{(m)} = \boldsymbol{\theta}^{(m-1)}$. Conditional on $\boldsymbol{\theta} = \boldsymbol{\theta}^{(m-1)}$ the distribution of $\boldsymbol{\theta}^*$ is a mixture of a continuous distribution with density given by $u(\boldsymbol{\theta}^* \mid \boldsymbol{\theta}, H) = p(\boldsymbol{\theta}^* \mid \boldsymbol{\theta}, H)\alpha(\boldsymbol{\theta}^* \mid \boldsymbol{\theta}, H)$, corresponding to the accepted candidates, and a discrete distribution with probability mass $r(\boldsymbol{\theta} \mid H) = 1 - \int_\Theta u(\boldsymbol{\theta}^* \mid \boldsymbol{\theta}, H)\,\mathrm{d}\boldsymbol{\theta}^*$ at the point $\boldsymbol{\theta}$, which is the probability of drawing a $\boldsymbol{\theta}^*$ that will be rejected. The entire transition density can be expressed using the Dirac delta function as

$$p\big(\boldsymbol{\theta}^{(m)} \mid \boldsymbol{\theta}^{(m-1)}, H\big) = u\big(\boldsymbol{\theta}^{(m)} \mid \boldsymbol{\theta}^{(m-1)}, H\big) + r\big(\boldsymbol{\theta}^{(m-1)} \mid H\big)\delta_{\boldsymbol{\theta}^{(m-1)}}\big(\boldsymbol{\theta}^{(m)}\big). \tag{40}$$

The intuition behind this procedure is evident on the right-hand side of (39), and is in many respects similar to that in acceptance and importance sampling. If the transition density $p(\boldsymbol{\theta}^* \mid \boldsymbol{\theta}, H)$ makes a move from $\boldsymbol{\theta}^{(m-1)}$ to $\boldsymbol{\theta}^*$ quite likely, relative to the target density $p(\boldsymbol{\theta} \mid I)$ at $\boldsymbol{\theta}^*$, and a move back from $\boldsymbol{\theta}^*$ to $\boldsymbol{\theta}^{(m-1)}$ quite unlikely, relative to the target density at $\boldsymbol{\theta}^{(m-1)}$, then the algorithm will place a low probability on actually making the transition and a high probability on staying at $\boldsymbol{\theta}^{(m-1)}$. In the same situation, a prospective move from $\boldsymbol{\theta}^*$ to $\boldsymbol{\theta}^{(m-1)}$ will always be made because draws of $\boldsymbol{\theta}^{(m-1)}$ are made infrequently relative to the target density $p(\boldsymbol{\theta} \mid I)$.

This is the most general form of the Metropolis–Hastings algorithm, due to Hastings (1970). The Metropolis et al. (1953) form takes $p(\boldsymbol{\theta}^* \mid \boldsymbol{\theta}, H) = p(\boldsymbol{\theta} \mid \boldsymbol{\theta}^*, H)$, which in turn leads to a simplification of the acceptance probability: $\alpha(\boldsymbol{\theta}^* \mid \boldsymbol{\theta}^{(m-1)}, H) = \min[p(\boldsymbol{\theta}^* \mid I)/p(\boldsymbol{\theta}^{(m-1)} \mid I), 1]$. A leading example of this form is the *Metropolis random walk*, in which $p(\boldsymbol{\theta}^* \mid \boldsymbol{\theta}, H) = p(\boldsymbol{\theta}^* - \boldsymbol{\theta} \mid H)$ and the latter density is symmetric about $\mathbf{0}$, for example that of the multivariate normal distribution with mean $\mathbf{0}$. Another special case is the *Metropolis independence chain* [see Tierney (1994)] in which $p(\boldsymbol{\theta}^* \mid \boldsymbol{\theta}, H) = p(\boldsymbol{\theta}^* \mid H)$. This leads to $\alpha(\boldsymbol{\theta}^* \mid \boldsymbol{\theta}^{(m-1)}, H) = \min[w(\boldsymbol{\theta}^*)/w(\boldsymbol{\theta}^{(m-1)}), 1]$, where $w(\boldsymbol{\theta}) = p(\boldsymbol{\theta} \mid I)/p(\boldsymbol{\theta} \mid H)$. The independence chain is closely related to acceptance sampling and importance sampling. But rather than place a low probability of acceptance or a low weight on a draw that is too likely relative to the target distribution, the independence chain assigns a low probability of transition to that candidate.

There is a simple two-step argument that motivates the convergence of the sequence $\{\boldsymbol{\theta}^{(m)}\}$, generated by the Metropolis–Hastings algorithm, to the distribution of interest. [This approach is due to Chib and Greenberg (1995).] First, note that if a transition probability density function $p(\boldsymbol{\theta}^{(m)} \mid \boldsymbol{\theta}^{(m-1)}, T)$ satisfies the *reversibility condition*

$$p\big(\boldsymbol{\theta}^{(m-1)} \mid I\big)p\big(\boldsymbol{\theta}^{(m)} \mid \boldsymbol{\theta}^{(m-1)}, T\big) = p\big(\boldsymbol{\theta}^{(m)} \mid I\big)p\big(\boldsymbol{\theta}^{(m-1)} \mid \boldsymbol{\theta}^{(m)}, T\big)$$

with respect to $p(\boldsymbol{\theta} \mid I)$, then

$$\begin{aligned}
&\int_{\Theta} p\big(\boldsymbol{\theta}^{(m-1)} \mid I\big)p\big(\boldsymbol{\theta}^{(m)} \mid \boldsymbol{\theta}^{(m-1)}, T\big)\,\mathrm{d}\boldsymbol{\theta}^{(m-1)} \\
&\quad = \int_{\Theta} p\big(\boldsymbol{\theta}^{(m)} \mid I\big)p\big(\boldsymbol{\theta}^{(m-1)} \mid \boldsymbol{\theta}^{(m)}, T\big)\,\mathrm{d}\boldsymbol{\theta}^{(m-1)} \\
&\quad = p\big(\boldsymbol{\theta}^{(m)} \mid I\big)\int_{\Theta} p\big(\boldsymbol{\theta}^{(m-1)} \mid \boldsymbol{\theta}^{(m)}, T\big)\,\mathrm{d}\boldsymbol{\theta}^{(m-1)} = p\big(\boldsymbol{\theta}^{(m)} \mid I\big).
\end{aligned} \tag{41}$$

Expression (41) indicates that if $\boldsymbol{\theta}^{(m-1)} \sim p(\boldsymbol{\theta} \mid I)$, then the same is true of $\boldsymbol{\theta}^{(m)}$. The density $p(\boldsymbol{\theta} \mid I)$ is an invariant density of the Markov chain with transition density $p(\boldsymbol{\theta}^{(m)} \mid \boldsymbol{\theta}^{(m-1)}, T)$.

The second step in this argument is to consider the implications of the requirement that the Metropolis–Hastings transition density $p(\boldsymbol{\theta}^{(m)} \mid \boldsymbol{\theta}^{(m-1)}, H)$ be reversible with respect to $p(\boldsymbol{\theta} \mid I)$,

$$p\big(\boldsymbol{\theta}^{(m-1)} \mid I\big)p\big(\boldsymbol{\theta}^{(m)} \mid \boldsymbol{\theta}^{(m-1)}, H\big) = p\big(\boldsymbol{\theta}^{(m)} \mid I\big)p\big(\boldsymbol{\theta}^{(m-1)} \mid \boldsymbol{\theta}^{(m)}, H\big).$$

For $\boldsymbol{\theta}^{(m-1)} = \boldsymbol{\theta}^{(m)}$ the requirement holds trivially. For $\boldsymbol{\theta}^{(m-1)} \neq \boldsymbol{\theta}^{(m)}$ it implies that

$$\begin{aligned}
&p\big(\boldsymbol{\theta}^{(m-1)} \mid I\big)p\big(\boldsymbol{\theta}^{*} \mid \boldsymbol{\theta}^{(m-1)}, H\big)\alpha\big(\boldsymbol{\theta}^{*} \mid \boldsymbol{\theta}^{(m-1)}, H\big) \\
&\quad = p\big(\boldsymbol{\theta}^{*} \mid I\big)p\big(\boldsymbol{\theta}^{(m-1)} \mid \boldsymbol{\theta}^{*}, H\big)\alpha\big(\boldsymbol{\theta}^{(m-1)} \mid \boldsymbol{\theta}^{*}, H\big).
\end{aligned} \tag{42}$$

Suppose without loss of generality that

$$p\big(\boldsymbol{\theta}^{(m-1)} \mid I\big)p\big(\boldsymbol{\theta}^{*} \mid \boldsymbol{\theta}^{(m-1)}, H\big) > p\big(\boldsymbol{\theta}^{*} \mid I\big)p\big(\boldsymbol{\theta}^{(m-1)} \mid \boldsymbol{\theta}^{*}, H\big).$$

If $\alpha(\boldsymbol{\theta}^{(m-1)} \mid \boldsymbol{\theta}^{*}, H) = 1$ and

$$\alpha\big(\boldsymbol{\theta}^{*} \mid \boldsymbol{\theta}^{(m-1)}, H\big) = \frac{p(\boldsymbol{\theta}^{*} \mid I)p(\boldsymbol{\theta}^{(m-1)} \mid \boldsymbol{\theta}^{*}, H)}{p(\boldsymbol{\theta}^{(m-1)} \mid I)p(\boldsymbol{\theta}^{*} \mid \boldsymbol{\theta}^{(m-1)}, H)},$$

then (42) is satisfied.

3.2.3. Metropolis within Gibbs

Different MCMC methods can be combined in a variety of rich and interesting ways that have been important in solving many practical problems in Bayesian inference. One of the most important in econometric modelling has been the Metropolis within Gibbs algorithm. Suppose that in attempting to implement a Gibbs sampling algorithm, a conditional density $p[\boldsymbol{\theta}_{(b)} \mid \boldsymbol{\theta}_{(a)}\ (a \neq b)]$ is intractable. The density is not of any known form, and efficient acceptance sampling algorithms are not at hand. This occurs in the stochastic volatility example, for the volatilities $h_1, \ldots, h_T$.

This problem can be addressed by applying the Metropolis–Hastings algorithm in block b of the Gibbs sampler while treating the other blocks in the usual way. Specifically, let $p(\boldsymbol{\theta}^*_{(b)} \mid \boldsymbol{\theta}, H_b)$ be the density (indexed by $\boldsymbol{\theta}$) from which candidate $\boldsymbol{\theta}^*_{(b)}$ is drawn. At iteration m, block b, of the Gibbs sampler draw $\boldsymbol{\theta}^*_{(b)} \sim p(\boldsymbol{\theta}^*_{(b)} \mid \boldsymbol{\theta}^{(m)}_a (a < b), \boldsymbol{\theta}^{(m-1)}_a (a \geqslant b), H_b)$, and set $\boldsymbol{\theta}^{(m)}_{(b)} = \boldsymbol{\theta}^*_{(b)}$ with probability

$$\begin{aligned}
&\alpha\big[\boldsymbol{\theta}^*_{(b)} \mid \boldsymbol{\theta}^{(m)}_a (a < b), \boldsymbol{\theta}^{(m-1)}_a (a \geqslant b), H_b\big] \\
&\quad = \min\left\{ \frac{p[\boldsymbol{\theta}^{(m)}_a (a < b), \boldsymbol{\theta}^*_b, \boldsymbol{\theta}^{(m-1)}_a (a > b) \mid I]}{p[\boldsymbol{\theta}^*_{(b)} \mid \boldsymbol{\theta}^{(m)}_a (a < b), \boldsymbol{\theta}^{(m-1)}_a (a \geqslant b), H_b]} \right/ \\
&\qquad \left. \frac{p[\boldsymbol{\theta}^{(m)}_a (a < b), \boldsymbol{\theta}^{(m-1)}_a (a \geqslant b) \mid I]}{p[\boldsymbol{\theta}^{(m-1)}_b \mid \boldsymbol{\theta}^{(m)}_a (a < b), \boldsymbol{\theta}^*_b, \boldsymbol{\theta}^{(m-1)}_a (a > b), H_b]}, 1 \right\}.
\end{aligned}$$

If $\boldsymbol{\theta}^{(m)}_{(b)}$ is not set to $\boldsymbol{\theta}^*_{(b)}$, then $\boldsymbol{\theta}^{(m)}_{(b)} = \boldsymbol{\theta}^{(m-1)}_{(b)}$. The procedure for $\boldsymbol{\theta}_{(b)}$ is exactly the same as for a standard Metropolis step, except that $\boldsymbol{\theta}_a$ $(a \neq b)$ also enters the density $p(\boldsymbol{\theta} \mid I)$ and transition density $p(\boldsymbol{\theta} \mid H)$. It is usually called a *Metropolis within Gibbs step*.

To see that $p(\boldsymbol{\theta} \mid I)$ is an invariant density of this Markov chain, consider the simple case of two blocks with a Metropolis within Gibbs step in the second block. Adapting the notation of (40), describe the Metropolis step for the second block by

$$p\big(\boldsymbol{\theta}^*_{(2)} \mid \boldsymbol{\theta}_{(1)}, \boldsymbol{\theta}_{(2)}, H_2\big) = u\big(\boldsymbol{\theta}^*_{(2)} \mid \boldsymbol{\theta}_{(1)}, \boldsymbol{\theta}_{(2)}, H_2\big) + r(\boldsymbol{\theta}_{(2)} \mid \boldsymbol{\theta}_{(1)}, H_2)\delta_{\boldsymbol{\theta}_{(2)}}\big(\boldsymbol{\theta}^*_{(2)}\big)$$

where

$$u\big(\boldsymbol{\theta}^*_{(2)} \mid \boldsymbol{\theta}_{(1)}, \boldsymbol{\theta}_{(2)}, H_2\big) = \alpha\big(\boldsymbol{\theta}^*_{(2)} \mid \boldsymbol{\theta}_{(1)}, \boldsymbol{\theta}_{(2)}, H_2\big) p\big(\boldsymbol{\theta}^*_{(2)} \mid \boldsymbol{\theta}_{(1)}, \boldsymbol{\theta}_{(2)}, H_2\big)$$

and

$$r(\boldsymbol{\theta}_{(2)} \mid \boldsymbol{\theta}_{(1)}, H_2) = 1 - \int_{\Theta_2} u\big(\boldsymbol{\theta}^*_{(2)} \mid \boldsymbol{\theta}_{(1)}, \boldsymbol{\theta}_{(2)}, H_2\big)\, d\boldsymbol{\theta}^*_{(2)}. \tag{43}$$

The one-step transition density for the entire chain is

$$p\big(\boldsymbol{\theta}^* \mid \boldsymbol{\theta}, G\big) = p\big(\boldsymbol{\theta}^*_{(1)} \mid \boldsymbol{\theta}_{(2)}, I\big) p\big(\boldsymbol{\theta}^*_{(2)} \mid \boldsymbol{\theta}_{(1)}, \boldsymbol{\theta}_{(2)}, H_2\big).$$

Then $p(\boldsymbol{\theta} \mid I)$ is an invariant density of $p(\boldsymbol{\theta}^* \mid \boldsymbol{\theta}, G)$ if

$$\int_{\Theta} p(\boldsymbol{\theta} \mid I) p\big(\boldsymbol{\theta}^* \mid \boldsymbol{\theta}, G\big)\, d\boldsymbol{\theta} = p\big(\boldsymbol{\theta}^* \mid I\big). \tag{44}$$

To establish (44), begin by expanding the left-hand side,

$$\int_{\Theta} p(\boldsymbol{\theta} \mid I) p\big(\boldsymbol{\theta}^* \mid \boldsymbol{\theta}, G\big)\, d\boldsymbol{\theta} = \int_{\Theta_2} \int_{\Theta_1} p(\boldsymbol{\theta}_{(1)}, \boldsymbol{\theta}_{(2)} \mid I)\, d\boldsymbol{\theta}_{(1)} p\big(\boldsymbol{\theta}^*_{(1)} \mid \boldsymbol{\theta}_{(2)}, I\big)$$

$$\times \left[u\left(\boldsymbol{\theta}^*_{(2)} \mid \boldsymbol{\theta}^*_{(1)}, \boldsymbol{\theta}_{(2)}, H_2\right) + r\left(\boldsymbol{\theta}_{(2)} \mid \boldsymbol{\theta}^*_{(1)}, H_2\right)\delta_{\boldsymbol{\theta}_{(2)}}\left(\boldsymbol{\theta}^*_{(2)}\right)\right] \mathrm{d}\boldsymbol{\theta}_{(2)}$$

$$= \int_{\Theta_2} p(\boldsymbol{\theta}_{(2)} \mid I) p\left(\boldsymbol{\theta}^*_{(1)} \mid \boldsymbol{\theta}_{(2)}, I\right) u\left(\boldsymbol{\theta}^*_{(2)} \mid \boldsymbol{\theta}^*_{(1)}, \boldsymbol{\theta}_{(2)}, H_2\right) \mathrm{d}\boldsymbol{\theta}_{(2)} \tag{45}$$

$$+ \int_{\Theta_2} p(\boldsymbol{\theta}_{(2)} \mid I) p\left(\boldsymbol{\theta}^*_{(1)} \mid \boldsymbol{\theta}_{(2)}, I\right) r\left(\boldsymbol{\theta}_{(2)} \mid \boldsymbol{\theta}^*_{(1)}, H_2\right)\delta_{\boldsymbol{\theta}_{(2)}}\left(\boldsymbol{\theta}^*_{(2)}\right) \mathrm{d}\boldsymbol{\theta}_{(2)}. \tag{46}$$

In (45) and (46) we have used the fact that

$$p(\boldsymbol{\theta}_{(2)} \mid I) = \int_{\Theta_1} p(\boldsymbol{\theta}_{(1)}, \boldsymbol{\theta}_{(2)} \mid I) \, \mathrm{d}\boldsymbol{\theta}_{(1)}.$$

Using Bayes rule (45) is the same as

$$p\left(\boldsymbol{\theta}^*_{(1)} \mid I\right) \int_{\Theta_2} p\left(\boldsymbol{\theta}_{(2)} \mid \boldsymbol{\theta}^*_{(1)}, I\right) u\left(\boldsymbol{\theta}^*_{(2)} \mid \boldsymbol{\theta}^*_{(1)}, \boldsymbol{\theta}_{(2)}, H_2\right) \mathrm{d}\boldsymbol{\theta}_{(2)}. \tag{47}$$

Carrying out the integration in (46) yields

$$p\left(\boldsymbol{\theta}^*_{(2)} \mid I\right) p\left(\boldsymbol{\theta}^*_{(1)} \mid \boldsymbol{\theta}^*_{(2)}, I\right) r\left(\boldsymbol{\theta}^*_{(2)} \mid \boldsymbol{\theta}^*_{(1)}, H_2\right). \tag{48}$$

Recalling the reversibility of the Metropolis step,

$$p\left(\boldsymbol{\theta}_{(2)} \mid \boldsymbol{\theta}^*_{(1)}, I\right) u\left(\boldsymbol{\theta}^*_{(2)} \mid \boldsymbol{\theta}^*_{(1)}, \boldsymbol{\theta}_{(2)}, H_2\right) = p\left(\boldsymbol{\theta}^*_{(2)} \mid \boldsymbol{\theta}^*_{(1)}, I\right) u\left(\boldsymbol{\theta}_{(2)} \mid \boldsymbol{\theta}^*_{(1)}, \boldsymbol{\theta}^*_{(2)}, H_2\right)$$

and so (47) becomes

$$p\left(\boldsymbol{\theta}^*_{(1)} \mid I\right) p\left(\boldsymbol{\theta}^*_{(2)} \mid \boldsymbol{\theta}^*_{(1)}, I\right) \int_{\Theta_2} u\left(\boldsymbol{\theta}_{(2)} \mid \boldsymbol{\theta}^*_{(1)}, \boldsymbol{\theta}^*_{(2)}, H_2\right) \mathrm{d}\boldsymbol{\theta}_{(2)}. \tag{49}$$

We can express (48) as

$$p\left(\boldsymbol{\theta}^*_{(1)}, \boldsymbol{\theta}^*_{(2)} \mid I\right) r\left(\boldsymbol{\theta}^*_{(2)} \mid \boldsymbol{\theta}^*_{(1)}, H_2\right). \tag{50}$$

Finally, recalling (43), the sum of (49) and (50) is $p(\boldsymbol{\theta}^*_{(1)}, \boldsymbol{\theta}^*_{(2)} \mid I)$, thus establishing (44).

This demonstration of invariance applies to the Gibbs sampler with b blocks, with a Metropolis within Gibbs step for one block, simply through the convention that Metropolis within Gibbs is used in the last block of each iteration. Metropolis within Gibbs steps can be used for several blocks, as well. The argument for invariance proceeds by mathematical induction, and the details are the same.

Sections 5.2.1 and 5.5 provide applications of Metropolis within Gibbs in Bayesian forecasting models.

3.3. *The full Monte*

We are now in a position to complete the practical Bayesian agenda for forecasting by means of simulation. This process integrates several sources of uncertainty about the future. These are summarized from a non-Bayesian perspective in the most widely used graduate econometrics textbook [Greene (2003, p. 576)] as

(1) uncertainty about parameters ("which will have been estimated");
(2) uncertainty about forecasts of exogenous variables; and
(3) uncertainty about unobservables realized in the future.

To these most forecasters would add, along with Diebold (1998, pp. 291–292) who includes (1) and (3) but not (2) in his list,

(4) uncertainty about the model itself.

Greene (2003) points out that for the non-Bayesian forecaster, "In practice handling the second of these errors is largely intractable while the first is merely extremely difficult." The problem with parameters in non-Bayesian approaches originates in the violation of the principle of relevant conditioning, as discussed in the conclusions of Sections 2.4.2 and 2.4.3. The difficulty with exogenous variables is grounded in violation of the principle of explicit formulation: a so-called exogenous variable in this situation is one whose joint distribution with the forecasting vector of interest $\boldsymbol{\omega}$ should have been expressed explicitly, but was not.[2] This problem is resolved every day in decision-making, either formally or informally, in any event. If there is great uncertainty about the joint distribution of some relevant variables and the forecasting vector of interest, that uncertainty should be incorporated in the prior distribution, or in uncertainty about the appropriate model.

We turn first to the full integration of the first three sources of uncertainty using posterior simulators (Section 3.3.1) and then to the last source (Section 3.3.2).

3.3.1. *Predictive distributions and point forecasts*

Section 2.4 summarized the probability structure of the recursive formulation of a single model A: the prior density $p(\boldsymbol{\theta}_A \mid A)$, the density of the observables $p(\mathbf{Y}_T \mid \boldsymbol{\theta}_A, A)$, and the density of future observables $\boldsymbol{\omega}$, $p(\boldsymbol{\omega} \mid \mathbf{Y}_T, \boldsymbol{\theta}_A, A)$. It is straightforward to simulate from the corresponding distributions, and this is useful in the process of model formulation as discussed in Section 2.2. The principle of relevant conditioning, however, demands that we work instead with the distribution of the unobservables ($\boldsymbol{\theta}_A$ and $\boldsymbol{\omega}$) conditional on the observables, $\mathbf{Y}_T$, and the assumptions of the model, A:

$$p(\boldsymbol{\theta}_A, \boldsymbol{\omega} \mid \mathbf{Y}_T, A) = p(\boldsymbol{\theta}_A \mid \mathbf{Y}_T, A) p(\boldsymbol{\omega} \mid \boldsymbol{\theta}_A, \mathbf{Y}_T, A).$$

Substituting the observed values (data) $\mathbf{Y}_T^o$ for $\mathbf{Y}_T$, we can access this distribution by means of a posterior simulator for the first component on the right, followed by simulation from the predictive density for the second component:

$$\boldsymbol{\theta}_A^{(m)} \sim p(\boldsymbol{\theta}_A \mid \mathbf{Y}_T^o, A), \quad \boldsymbol{\omega}^{(m)} \sim p(\boldsymbol{\omega} \mid \boldsymbol{\theta}_A^{(m)}, \mathbf{Y}_T^o, A). \tag{51}$$

[2] The formal problem is that "exogenous variables" are not ancillary statistics when the vector of interest includes future outcomes. In other applications of the same model, they may be. This distinction is clear in the Bayesian statistics literature; see, e.g., Bernardo and Smith (1994, Section 5.1.4) or Geweke (2005, Section 2.2.2).

The first step, posterior simulation, has become practicable for most models by virtue of the innovations in MCMC methods summarized in Section 3.2. The second simulation is relatively simple, because it is part of the recursive formulation. The simulations $\boldsymbol{\theta}_A^{(m)}$ from the posterior simulator will not necessarily be i.i.d. (in the case of MCMC) and they may require weighting (in the case of importance sampling) but the simulations are *ergodic*: i.e., so long as $E[h(\boldsymbol{\theta}_A, \boldsymbol{\omega}) \mid \mathbf{Y}_T^o, A]$ exists and is finite,

$$\frac{\sum_{m=1}^{M} w^{(m)} h(\boldsymbol{\theta}_A^{(m)}, \boldsymbol{\omega}^{(m)})}{\sum_{m=1}^{M} w^{(m)}} \overset{\text{a.s.}}{\rightarrow} E\big[h(\boldsymbol{\theta}_A, \boldsymbol{\omega}) \mid \mathbf{Y}_T^o, A\big]. \tag{52}$$

The weights $w^{(m)}$ in (52) come into play for importance sampling. There is another important use for weighted posterior simulation, to which we return in Section 3.3.2.

This full integration of sources of uncertainty by means of simulation appears to have been applied for the first time in the unpublished thesis of Litterman (1979) as discussed in Section 4. The first published full applications of simulation methods in this way in published papers appear to have been Monahan (1983) and Thompson and Miller (1986), which built on Thompson (1984). This study applied an autoregressive model of order 2 with a conventional improper diffuse prior [see Zellner (1971, p. 195)] to quarterly US unemployment rate data from 1968 through 1979, forecasting for the period 1980 through 1982. Section 4 of their paper outlines the specifics of (51) in this case. They computed posterior means of each of the 12 predictive densities, corresponding to a joint quadratic loss function; predictive variances; and centered 90% predictive intervals. They compared these results with conventional non-Bayesian procedures [see Box and Jenkins (1976)] that equate unknown parameters with their estimates, thus ignoring uncertainty about these parameters. There were several interesting findings and comparisons.

1. The posterior means of the parameters and the non-Bayesian point estimates are similar: $y_t = 0.441 + 1.596 y_{t-1} - 0.669 y_{t-2}$ for the former and $y_t = 0.342 + 1.658 y_{t-1} - 0.719 y_{t-2}$ for the latter.
2. The point forecasts from the predictive density and the conventional non-Bayesian procedure depart substantially over the 12 periods, from unemployment rates of 5.925% and 5.904%, respectively, one-step-ahead, to 6.143% and 5.693%, respectively, 12 steps ahead. This is due to the fact that an F-step-ahead mean, conditional on parameter values, is a polynomial of order F in the parameter values: predicting farther into the future involves an increasingly non-linear function of parameters, and so the discrepancy between the mean of the nonlinear function and the non-linear function of the mean also increases.
3. The Bayesian 90% predictive intervals are generally wider than the corresponding non-Bayesian intervals; the difference is greatest 12 steps ahead, where the width is 5.53% in the former and 5.09% in the latter. At 12 steps ahead the 90% intervals are (3.40%, 8.93%) and (3.15%, 8.24%).
4. The predictive density is platykurtic; thus a normal approximation of the predictive density (today a curiosity, in view of the accessible representation (51))

produces a 90% predictive density that is too wide, and the discrepancy increases for predictive densities farther into the future: 5.82% rather than 5.53%, 12 steps ahead.

Thompson and Miller did not repeat their exercise for other forecasting periods, and therefore had no evidence on forecasting reliability. Nor did they employ the shrinkage priors that were, contemporaneously, proving so important in the successful application of Bayesian vector autoregressions at the Federal Reserve Bank of Minneapolis. We return to that project in Section 6.1.

3.3.2. Model combination and the revision of assumptions

Incorporation of uncertainty about the model itself is rarely discussed, and less frequently acted upon; Greene (2003) does not even mention it. This lacuna is rational in non-Bayesian approaches: since uncertainty cannot be integrated in the context of one model, it is premature, from this perspective, even to contemplate this task. Since model-specific uncertainty has been resolved, both as a theoretical and as a practical matter, in Bayesian forecasting, the problem of model uncertainty is front and center. Two variants on this problem are integrating uncertainty over a well-defined set of models, and bringing additional, but similar, models into such a group in an efficient manner.

Extending the expression of uncertainty to a set of J specified models is straightforward in principle, as detailed in Section 2.3. From (24)–(27) it is clear that the additional technical task is the evaluation of the marginal likelihoods

$$p(\mathbf{Y}_T^o \mid A_j) = \int_{\Theta_{A_j}} p(\mathbf{Y}_T^o \mid \boldsymbol{\theta}_{A_j}, A_j) p(\boldsymbol{\theta}_{A_j} \mid A_j) \, \mathrm{d}\boldsymbol{\theta}_{A_j} \quad (j = 1, \ldots, J).$$

With few exceptions simulation approximation of the marginal likelihood is not a special case of approximating a posterior moment in the model A_j. One such exception of practical importance involves models A_j and A_k with a common vector of unobservables $\boldsymbol{\theta}_A$ and likelihood $p(\mathbf{Y}_T^o \mid \boldsymbol{\theta}_A, A_j) = p(\mathbf{Y}_T^o \mid \boldsymbol{\theta}_A, A_k)$ but different prior densities $p(\boldsymbol{\theta}_A \mid A_j)$ and $p(\boldsymbol{\theta}_A \mid A_k)$. (For example, one model might incorporate a set of inequality restrictions while the other does not.) If $p(\boldsymbol{\theta}_A \mid A_k)/p(\boldsymbol{\theta}_A \mid A_j)$ is bounded above on the support of $p(\boldsymbol{\theta}_A \mid A_j)$, and if $\boldsymbol{\theta}_A^{(m)} \sim p(\boldsymbol{\theta}_A \mid \mathbf{Y}_T^o, A_j)$ is ergodic then

$$M^{-1} \sum_{m=1}^{M} p(\boldsymbol{\theta}_A^{(m)} \mid A_k) / p(\boldsymbol{\theta}_A^{(m)} \mid A_j) \xrightarrow{\text{a.s.}} p(\mathbf{Y}_T^o \mid A_k) / p(\mathbf{Y}_T^o \mid A_j); \tag{53}$$

see Geweke (2005, Section 5.2.1).

For certain types of posterior simulators, simulation-consistent approximation of the marginal likelihood is also straightforward: see Geweke (1989b, Section 5) or Geweke (2005, Section 5.2.2) for importance sampling, Chib (1995) for Gibbs sampling, Chib and Jeliazkov (2001) for the Metropolis–Hastings algorithm, and Meng and Wong (1996) for a general theoretical perspective. An approach that is more general, but often computationally less efficient in these specific cases, is the density ratio method of

Gelfand and Dey (1994), also described in Geweke (2005, Section 5.2.4). These approaches, and virtually any conceivable approach, require that it be possible to evaluate or approximate with substantial accuracy the likelihood function. This condition is not necessary in MCMC posterior simulators, and this fact has been central to the success of these simulations in many applications, especially those with latent variables. This, more or less, defines the rapidly advancing front of attack on this important technical issue at the time of this writing.

Some important and practical modifications can be made to the set of models over which uncertainty is integrated, without repeating the exercise of posterior simulation. These modifications all exploit reweighting of the posterior simulator output. One important application is updating posterior distributions with new data. In a real-time forecasting situation, for example, one might wish to update predictive distributions minute-by-minute, whereas as a full posterior simulation adequate for the purposes at hand might take more than a minute (but less than a night). Suppose the posterior simulation utilizes data through time T, but the predictive distribution is being formed at time $T^* > T$. Then

$$\begin{aligned}
p(\boldsymbol{\omega} \mid \mathbf{Y}_{T^*}^o, A) &= \int_{\Theta_A} p(\boldsymbol{\theta}_A \mid \mathbf{Y}_{T^*}^o, A) p(\boldsymbol{\omega} \mid \boldsymbol{\theta}_A, \mathbf{Y}_{T^*}^o, A)\, \mathrm{d}\boldsymbol{\theta}_A \\
&= \int_{\Theta_A} p(\boldsymbol{\theta}_A \mid \mathbf{Y}_T^o, A) \frac{p(\boldsymbol{\theta}_A \mid \mathbf{Y}_{T^*}^o, A)}{p(\boldsymbol{\theta}_A \mid \mathbf{Y}_T^o, A)} p(\boldsymbol{\omega} \mid \boldsymbol{\theta}_A, \mathbf{Y}_{T^*}^o, A)\, \mathrm{d}\boldsymbol{\theta}_A \\
&\propto \int_{\Theta_A} p(\boldsymbol{\theta}_A \mid \mathbf{Y}_T^o, A) p(\mathbf{y}_{T+1}^o, \ldots, \mathbf{y}_{T^*}^o \mid \boldsymbol{\theta}_A, A) \\
&\quad \times p(\boldsymbol{\omega} \mid \boldsymbol{\theta}_A, \mathbf{Y}_{T^*}^o, A)\, \mathrm{d}\boldsymbol{\theta}_A.
\end{aligned}$$

This suggests that one might use the simulator output $\boldsymbol{\theta}^{(m)} \sim p(\boldsymbol{\theta}_A \mid \mathbf{Y}_T^o, A)$, taking $\boldsymbol{\omega}^{(m)} \sim p(\boldsymbol{\omega} \mid \boldsymbol{\theta}_A^{(m)}, \mathbf{Y}_{T^*}^o, A)$ but reweighting the simulator output to approximate $E[h(\boldsymbol{\omega}) \mid \mathbf{Y}_{T^*}^o, A]$ by

$$\sum_{m=1}^{M} p(\mathbf{y}_{T+1}^o, \ldots, \mathbf{y}_{T^*}^o \mid \boldsymbol{\theta}_A^{(m)}, A) h(\boldsymbol{\omega}^{(m)}) \Big/ \sum_{m=1}^{M} p(\mathbf{y}_{T+1}^o, \ldots, \mathbf{y}_{T^*}^o \mid \boldsymbol{\theta}_A^{(m)}, A). \quad (54)$$

This turns out to be correct; for details see Geweke (2000). One can show that (54) is a simulation-consistent approximation of $E[h(\boldsymbol{\omega}) \mid \mathbf{Y}_{T^*}^o, A]$ and in many cases the updating requires only spreadsheet arithmetic. There are central limit theorems on which to base assessments of the accuracy of the approximations; these require more advanced, but publicly available, software; see Geweke (1999) and Geweke (2005, Sections 4.1 and 5.4).

The method of reweighting can also be used to bring into the fold models with the same likelihood function but different priors, or to explore the effect of modifying the prior, as (53) suggests. In that context A_k denotes the new model, with a prior distribution that is more informative in the sense that $p(\boldsymbol{\theta}_A \mid A_k)/p(\boldsymbol{\theta}_A \mid A_j)$ is bounded above on the support of Θ_{A_j}. Reweighting the posterior simulator output

$\boldsymbol{\theta}_{A_j}^{(m)} \sim p(\boldsymbol{\theta}_{A_j} \mid \mathbf{Y}_T^o, A_j)$ by $p(\boldsymbol{\theta}_{A_j}^{(m)} \mid A_k)/p(\boldsymbol{\theta}_{A_j}^{(m)} \mid A_j)$ provides the new simulation-consistent set of approximations. Moreover, the exercise yields the marginal likelihood of the new model almost as a by-product, because

$$M^{-1} \sum_{m=1}^{M} p(\boldsymbol{\theta}_{A_j}^{(m)} \mid A_k) / p(\boldsymbol{\theta}_{A_j}^{(m)} \mid A_j) \xrightarrow{\text{a.s.}} p(\mathbf{Y}_T^o \mid A_k) / p(\mathbf{Y}_T^o \mid A_j). \tag{55}$$

This suggests a pragmatic reason for investigators to use prior distributions $p(\boldsymbol{\theta}_A \mid A_j)$ that are uninformative, in this sense: clients can tailor the simulator output to their more informative priors $p(\boldsymbol{\theta}_A \mid A_k)$ by reweighting.

4. 'Twas not always so easy: A historical perspective

The procedures outlined in the previous section accommodate, at least in principle (and much practice), very general likelihood functions and prior distributions, primarily because numerical substitutes are available for analytic evaluation of expectations of functions of interest. But prior to the advent of inexpensive desktop computing in the mid-1980's, Bayesian prediction was an analytic art. The standard econometric reference for Bayesian work of any such kind was Zellner (1971), which treats predictive densities at a level of generality similar to that in Section 2.3.2 above, and in detail for Gaussian location, regression, and multiple regression problems.

4.1. In the beginning, there was diffuseness, conjugacy, and analytic work

In these specific examples, Zellner's focus was on the diffuse prior case, which leads to the usual normal-gamma posterior. To illustrate his approach to prediction in the normal regression model, let $p = 1$ and write the model (a version of Equation (1)) as

$$\mathbf{Y}_T = \mathbf{X}_T \boldsymbol{\beta} + \mathbf{u}_T \tag{56}$$

where:

- $\mathbf{X}_T$ – a $T \times k$ matrix, with rank k, of observations on the independent variables,
- $\boldsymbol{\beta}$ – a $k \times 1$ vector of regression coefficients,
- $\mathbf{u}_T$ – a $T \times 1$ vector of error terms, assumed Gaussian with mean zero and variance matrix $\sigma^2 \mathbf{I}_T$.

Zellner (1971, Section 3.2) employs the "diffuse" prior specification $p(\boldsymbol{\beta}, \sigma) \propto \frac{1}{\sigma}$. With this prior, the joint density for the parameters and the q-step prediction vector $\widetilde{\mathbf{Y}} = \{y_s\}_{s=T+1}^{T+q}$, assumed to be generated by

$$\widetilde{\mathbf{Y}} = \widetilde{\mathbf{X}} \boldsymbol{\beta} + \tilde{\mathbf{u}},$$

(a version of (8)) is given by

$$p(\widetilde{\mathbf{Y}}, \boldsymbol{\beta}, \sigma \mid \mathbf{Y}_T, \mathbf{X}_T, \widetilde{\mathbf{X}}) = p(\widetilde{\mathbf{Y}} \mid \boldsymbol{\beta}, \sigma, \widetilde{\mathbf{X}}) p(\boldsymbol{\beta}, \sigma \mid \mathbf{Y}_T, \mathbf{X}_T)$$

which is the product of the conditional Gaussian predictive for $\widetilde{\mathbf{Y}}$ given the parameters, and independent variables and the posterior density for $\boldsymbol{\beta}$ and σ, which is given by

$$p(\boldsymbol{\beta}, \sigma \mid \mathbf{Y}_T, \mathbf{X}_T) \propto \sigma^{-(T+1)} \exp\{-(\mathbf{Y}_T - \mathbf{X}_T\beta)'(\mathbf{Y}_T - \mathbf{X}_T\beta)/2\sigma^2\} \tag{57}$$

and which in turn can be seen to be the product of a conditional Gaussian density for $\boldsymbol{\beta}$ given σ and the data and an inverted gamma density for σ given the data. In fact, the joint density is

$$\begin{aligned} &p(\widetilde{\mathbf{Y}}, \boldsymbol{\beta}, \sigma \mid \mathbf{Y}_T, \mathbf{X}_T, \widetilde{\mathbf{X}}) \\ &\quad \propto \sigma^{-(T+q+1)} \exp\left\{-\frac{(\mathbf{Y}_T - \mathbf{X}_T\beta)'(\mathbf{Y}_T - \mathbf{X}_T\beta) + (\widetilde{\mathbf{Y}} - \widetilde{\mathbf{X}}\beta)'(\widetilde{\mathbf{Y}} - \widetilde{\mathbf{X}}\beta)}{2\sigma^2}\right\}. \end{aligned}$$

To obtain the predictive density (21), $p(\widetilde{\mathbf{Y}} \mid \mathbf{Y}_T, \mathbf{X}_T, \widetilde{\mathbf{X}})$, Zellner marginalizes analytically rather than numerically. He does so in two steps: first, he integrates with respect to σ to obtain

$$\begin{aligned} &p(\widetilde{\mathbf{Y}}, \boldsymbol{\beta} \mid \mathbf{Y}_T, \mathbf{X}_T, \widetilde{\mathbf{X}}) \\ &\quad \propto \left[(\mathbf{Y}_T - \mathbf{X}_T\boldsymbol{\beta})'(\mathbf{Y}_T - \mathbf{X}_T\boldsymbol{\beta}) + (\widetilde{\mathbf{Y}} - \widetilde{\mathbf{X}}\boldsymbol{\beta})'(\widetilde{\mathbf{Y}} - \widetilde{\mathbf{X}}\boldsymbol{\beta})\right]^{-(T+q)/2} \end{aligned}$$

and then completes the square in $\boldsymbol{\beta}$, rearranges, integrates and obtains

$$\begin{aligned} &p(\widetilde{\mathbf{Y}} \mid \mathbf{Y}_T, \mathbf{X}_T, \widetilde{\mathbf{X}}) \\ &\quad \propto \left[\mathbf{Y}_T'\mathbf{Y}_T + \widetilde{\mathbf{Y}}'\widetilde{\mathbf{Y}} - (\mathbf{X}_T'\mathbf{Y}_T + \widetilde{\mathbf{X}}'\widetilde{\mathbf{Y}})' M^{-1} (\mathbf{X}_T'\mathbf{Y}_T + \widetilde{\mathbf{X}}'\widetilde{\mathbf{Y}})\right]^{-(T-k+q)/2} \end{aligned}$$

where $\mathbf{M} = \mathbf{X}_T'\mathbf{X}_T + \widetilde{\mathbf{X}}'\widetilde{\mathbf{X}}$. After considerable additional algebra to put this into "a more intelligible form", Zellner obtains

$$p(\widetilde{\mathbf{Y}} \mid \mathbf{Y}_T, \mathbf{X}_T, \widetilde{\mathbf{X}}) \propto \left[T - k + (\widetilde{\mathbf{Y}} - \widetilde{\mathbf{X}}\hat{\boldsymbol{\beta}})'\mathbf{H}(\widetilde{\mathbf{Y}} - \widetilde{\mathbf{X}}\hat{\boldsymbol{\beta}})\right]^{-(T-k+q)}$$

where $\hat{\boldsymbol{\beta}} = (\mathbf{X}_T'\mathbf{X}_T)^{-1}\mathbf{X}_T'\mathbf{Y}_T$ is the in-sample ordinary least squares estimator, $\mathbf{H} = (1/s^2)(I - \widetilde{\mathbf{X}}\mathbf{M}^{-1}\widetilde{\mathbf{X}}')$, and $s^2 = \frac{1}{T-k}(\mathbf{Y}_T - \mathbf{X}_T\hat{\boldsymbol{\beta}})'\mathbf{H}(\mathbf{Y}_T - \mathbf{X}_T\hat{\boldsymbol{\beta}})$. This formula is then recognized as the multivariate Student-t density, meaning that $\widetilde{\mathbf{Y}}$ is distributed as such with mean $\widetilde{\mathbf{X}}\hat{\boldsymbol{\beta}}$ (provided $T - k > 1$) and covariance matrix $\frac{T-k}{T-k-2}\mathbf{H}^{-1}$ (provided $T - k > 2$). Zellner notes that a linear combination of the elements of $\widetilde{\mathbf{Y}}$ (his example of such a function of interest is a discounted sum) will be distributed as univariate Student-t, so that expectations of such linear combinations can be calculated as a matter of routine, but he does not elaborate further. In the multivariate regression model [Zellner (1971, Section 8.2)], similar calculations to those above lead to a generalized or matrix Student-t predictive distribution.

Zellner's treatment of the Bayesian prediction problem constituted the state of the art at the beginning of the 1970's. In essence, linear models with Gaussian errors and flat priors could be utilized, but not much more generality than this was possible. Slightly greater generality was available if the priors were *conjugate*. Such priors leave the posterior in the same form as the likelihood. In the Gaussian regression case, this means a normal-gamma prior (conditional normal for the regression coefficients, inverted gamma for the residual standard deviation) and a normal likelihood. As Section 2 makes clear, there is no longer need for conjugacy and simple likelihoods, as developments of the past 15 years have made it possible to replace "integration by Arnold Zellner" with "integration by Monte Carlo", in some cases using MC methods developed by Zellner himself [e.g., Zellner and Min (1995); Zellner and Chen (2001)].

4.2. The dynamic linear model

In 1976, P.J. Harrison and C.F. Stevens [Harrison and Stevens (1976)] read a paper with a title that anticipates ours before the Royal Statistical Society in which they remarked that "[c]ompared with current forecasting fashions our views may well appear radical". Their approach involved the dynamic linear model (see also Chapter 7 in this volume), which is a version of a state-space observer system:

$$\mathbf{y}_t = \mathbf{x}_t'\boldsymbol{\beta}_t + \mathbf{u}_t,$$
$$\boldsymbol{\beta}_t = G\boldsymbol{\beta}_{t-1} + \mathbf{w}_t$$

with $\mathbf{u}_t \overset{\text{iid}}{\sim} N(0, \mathbf{U}_t)$ and $\mathbf{w}_t \overset{\text{iid}}{\sim} N(0, \mathbf{W}_t)$. Thus the slope parameters are treated as latent variables, as in Section 2.2.4. As Harrison and Stevens note, this generalizes the standard linear Gaussian model (one of Zellner's examples) by permitting time variation in $\boldsymbol{\beta}$ and the residual covariance matrix. Starting from a prior distribution for $\boldsymbol{\beta}_0$ Harrison and Stevens calculate posterior distributions for $\boldsymbol{\beta}_t$ for $t = 1, 2, \ldots$ via the (now) well-known Kalman filter recursions. They also discuss prediction formulae for $\mathbf{y}_{T+k}$ at time T under the assumption (i) that $\mathbf{x}_{T+k}$ is known at T, and (ii) $\mathbf{x}_{T+k}$ is unknown at T. They note that their predictions are "distributional in nature, and derived from the current parameter uncertainty" and that "[w]hile it is natural to think of the expectations of the future variate values as "forecasts" there is no need to single out the expectation for this purpose ... if the consequences of an error in one direction are more serious that an error of the same magnitude in the opposite direction, then the forecast can be biased to take this into account" (cf. Section 2.4.1).

Harrison and Stevens take up several examples, beginning with the standard regression model, the "static case". They note that in this context, their Bayesian–Kalman filter approach amounts to a

> computationally neat and economical method of revising regression coefficient estimates as fresh data become available, without effectively re-doing the whole calculation all over again and without any matrix inversion. This has been previously pointed out by Plackett (1950) and others but its practical importance seems to have been almost completely missed. (p. 215)

Other examples they treat include the linear growth model, additive seasonal model, periodic function model, autoregressive models, and moving average models. They also consider treatment of multiple possible models, and integrating across them to obtain predictions, as in Section 2.3.

Note that the Harrison–Stevens approach generalized what was possible using Zellner's (1971) book, but priors were still conjugate, and the underlying structure was still Gaussian. The structures that could be handled were more general, but the statistical assumptions and nature of prior beliefs accommodated were quite conventional. Indeed, in his discussion of Harrison–Stevens, Chatfield (1976) remarks that

> ... you do not need to be Bayesian to adopt the method. If, as the authors suggest, the general purpose default priors work pretty well for most time series, then one does not need to supply prior information. So, despite the use of Bayes' theorem inherent in Kalman filtering, I wonder if *Adaptive Forecasting* would be a better description of the method. (p. 231)

The fact remains, though, that latent-variable structure of the forecasting model does put uncertainty about the parameterization on a par with the uncertainty associated with the stochastic structure of the observables themselves.

4.3. The Minnesota revolution

During the mid- to late-1970's, Christopher Sims was writing what would become "Macroeconomics and reality", the lead article in the January 1980 issue of *Econometrica*. In that paper, Sims argued that identification conditions in conventional large-scale econometric models that were routinely used in (non Bayesian) forecasting and policy exercises, were "incredible" – either they were normalizations with no basis in theory, or "based" in theory that was empirically falsified or internally inconsistent. He proposed, as an alternative, an approach to macroeconomic time series analysis with little theoretical foundation other than statistical stationarity. Building on the Wold decomposition theorem, Sims argued that, exceptional circumstances aside, vectors of time series could be represented by an autoregression, and further, that such representations could be useful for assessing features of the data even though they reproduce only the first and second moments of the time series and not the entire probabilistic structure or "data generation process".

With this as motivation, Robert Litterman (1979) took up the challenge of devising procedures for forecasting with such models that were intended to compete directly with large-scale macroeconomic models then in use in forecasting. Betraying a frequentist background, much of Litterman's effort was devoted to dealing with "multicollinearity problems and large sampling errors in estimation". These "problems" arise because in (3), each of the equations for the p variables involves m lags of each of p variables, resulting in mp^2 coefficients in $\mathbf{B}_1, \ldots, \mathbf{B}_m$. To these are added the parameters $\mathbf{B}_D$ associated with the deterministic components, as well as the $p(p+1)$ distinct parameters in $\boldsymbol{\Psi}$.

Litterman (1979) treats these problems in a distinctly classical way, introducing "restrictions in the form of priors" in a subsection on "Biased estimation". While he notes that "each of these methods may be given a Bayesian interpretation", he discusses reduction of sampling error in classical estimation of the parameters of the normal linear model (56) via the standard ridge regression estimator [Hoerl and Kennard (1970)]

$$\boldsymbol{\beta}_R^k = \left(\mathbf{X}_T'\mathbf{X}_T + \varrho\mathbf{I}_k\right)^{-1}\mathbf{X}_T'\mathbf{Y}_T,$$

the Stein (1974) class

$$\boldsymbol{\beta}_S^k = \left(\mathbf{X}_T'\mathbf{X}_T + \varrho\mathbf{X}_T'\mathbf{X}_T\right)^{-1}\mathbf{X}_T'\mathbf{Y}_T,$$

and, following Maddala (1977), the "generalized ridge"

$$\boldsymbol{\beta}_S^k = \left(\mathbf{X}_T'\mathbf{X}_T + \varrho\boldsymbol{\Delta}^{-1}\right)^{-1}\left(\mathbf{X}_T'\mathbf{Y}_T + \varrho\boldsymbol{\Delta}^{-1}\theta\right). \tag{58}$$

Litterman notes that the latter "corresponds to a prior distribution on β of $N(\theta, \lambda^2\Delta)$ with $\varrho = \sigma^2/\lambda^2$". (Both parameters σ^2 and λ^2 are treated as known.) Yet Litterman's next statement is frequentist: "The variance of this estimator is given by $\sigma^2(\mathbf{X}_T'\mathbf{X}_T + \varrho\boldsymbol{\Delta}^{-1})^{-1}$". It is clear from his development that he has the "Bayesian" shrinkage in mind as a way of reducing the sampling variability of otherwise frequentist estimators.

Anticipating a formulation to come, Litterman considers two shrinkage priors (which he refers to as "generalized ridge estimators") designed specifically with lag distributions in mind. The canonical distributed lag model for scalar y and x is given by

$$y_t = \alpha + \beta_0 x_t + \beta_1 x_{t-1} + \cdots + \beta_l x_{t-m} + u_t. \tag{59}$$

The first prior, due to Leamer (1972), shrinks the mean and variance of the lag coefficients at the same geometric rate with the lag, and covariances between the lag coefficients at a different geometric rate according to the distance between them:

$$E\beta_i = \upsilon\rho^i,$$
$$cov(\beta_i, \beta_j) = \lambda^2\omega^{|i-j|}\rho^{i+j-2}$$

with $0 < \rho, \omega < 1$. The hyperparameters ρ, and ω control the decay rates, while υ and λ control the scale of the mean and variance. The spirit of this prior lives on in the "Minnesota" prior to be discussed presently.

The second prior is Shiller's (1973) "smoothness" prior, embodied by

$$\mathbf{R}[\beta_1, \ldots, \beta_m]' = \mathbf{w}, \quad \mathbf{w} \sim N\left(0, \sigma_w^2 I_{m-2}\right) \tag{60}$$

where the matrix R incorporates smoothness restrictions by "differencing" adjacent lag coefficients; for example, to embody the notion that second differences between lag coefficients are small (that the lag distribution is quadratic), R is given by

$$R = \begin{bmatrix} 1 & -2 & 1 & 0 & 0 & & \ldots & & 0 \\ 0 & 1 & -2 & 1 & 0 & 0 & \ldots & & 0 \\ & & \ddots & \ddots & \ddots & \ddots & & & \\ 0 & 0 & \ldots & & & & 1 & -2 & 1 \end{bmatrix}.$$

Having introduced these priors, Litterman dismisses the latter, quoting Sims: "... the whole notion that lag distributions in econometrics ought to be smooth is ... at best weakly supported by theory or evidence" [Sims (1974, p. 317)]. In place of a smooth lag distribution, Litterman (1979, p. 20) assumed that "a reasonable approximation of the behavior of an economic variable is a random walk around an unknown, deterministic component". Further, Litterman operated equation by equation, and therefore assumed that the parameters for equation i of the autoregression (3) were centered around

$$y_{it} = y_{i,t-1} + d_{it} + \varepsilon_{it}.$$

Litterman goes on to describe the prior:

> The parameters are all assumed to have means of zero except the coefficient on the first lag of the dependent variable, which is given a prior mean of one. The parameters are assumed to be uncorrelated with each other and to have standard deviations which decrease the further back they are in the lag distributions. In general, the prior distribution on lag coefficients of the dependent variable is much looser, that is, has larger standard deviations, than it is on other variables in the system. (p. 20)

A footnote explains that while the prior represents Litterman's opinion, "it was developed with the aid of many helpful suggestions from Christopher Sims" [Litterman (1979, p. 96)]. Inasmuch as these discussions and the prior development took place during the course of Litterman's dissertation work at the University of Minnesota under Sims's direction, the prior has come to be known as the "Minnesota" or "Litterman" prior. Prior information on deterministic components is taken to be diffuse, though he does use the simple first order stationary model

$$y_{1t} = \alpha + \beta y_{1,t-1} + \varepsilon_{1t}$$

to illustrate the point that the mean $M_1 = E(y_{1t})$ and persistence (β) are related by $M_1 = \alpha/(1-\beta)$, indicating that priors on the deterministic components independent of the lag coefficients are problematic. This notion was taken up by Schotman and van Dijk (1991) in the unit root literature.

The remainder of the prior involves the specification of the standard deviation of the coefficient on lag l of variable j in equation i: δ^l_{ij}. This is specified by

$$\delta^l_{ij} = \begin{cases} \dfrac{\lambda}{l^{\gamma_1}} & \text{if } i = j, \\ \dfrac{\lambda\gamma_2\hat{\sigma}_i}{l^{\gamma_1}\hat{\sigma}_j} & \text{if } i \neq j \end{cases} \tag{61}$$

where γ_1 is a hyperparameter greater than 1.0, γ_2 and λ are scale factors, and $\hat{\sigma}_i$ and $\hat{\sigma}_j$ are the estimated residual standard deviations in unrestricted ordinary least squares estimates of equations i and j of the system. [In subsequent work, e.g., Litterman (1986), the residual standard deviation estimates were from univariate autoregressions.] Alternatively, the prior can be expressed as

$$\mathbf{R}_i\boldsymbol{\beta}_i = \mathbf{r}_i + \mathbf{v}_i, \quad \mathbf{v}_i \sim N(0, \lambda^2\mathbf{I}_{mp}) \tag{62}$$

where $\boldsymbol{\beta}_i$ represents the lag coefficients in equation i (the ith row of $B_1, B_2, \ldots, B_l$ in Equation (3)), R_i is a diagonal matrix with zeros corresponding to deterministic components and elements λ/δ_{ij}^l corresponding to the lth lag of variable j, and r_i is a vector of zeros except for a one corresponding to the first lag of variable i. Note that specification of the prior involves choosing the prior hyperparameters for "overall tightness" λ, the "decay" γ_1, and the "other's weight" γ_2. Subsequent modifications and embellishments (encoded in the principal software developed for this purpose, RATS) involved alternative specifications for the decay rate (harmonic in place of geometric), and generalizations of the meaning of "other" (some "others" are more equal than others).

Litterman is careful to note that the prior is being applied equation by equation, and that he will "indeed estimate each equation separately". Thus the prior was to be implemented one equation at a time, with known parameter values in the mean and variance; this meant that the "estimator" corresponded to Theil's (1963) mixed estimator, which could be implemented using the generalized ridge formula (58). With such an estimator, $\tilde{\mathbf{B}} = (\tilde{B}_D, \tilde{B}_1, \ldots, \tilde{B}_m)$, forecasts were produced recursively via (3). Thus the one-step-ahead forecast so produced will correspond to the mean of the predictive density, but ensuing steps will not owing to the nonlinear interactions between forecasts and the B_js. (For an example of the practical effect of this phenomenon, see Section 3.3.1.)

Litterman noted a possible loss of "efficiency" associated with his equation-by-equation treatment, but argued that the loss was justified because of the "computational burden" of a full system treatment, due to the necessity of inverting the large cross-product matrix of right-hand-side variables. This refers to the well-known result that equation-by-equation ordinary least squares estimation is sampling-theoretic efficient in the multiple linear regression model when the right-hand-side variables are the same in all equations. Unless $\boldsymbol{\Psi}$ is diagonal, this does not hold when the right-hand-side variables differ across equations. This, coupled with the way the prior was implemented led Litterman to reason that a system method would be more "efficient". To see this, suppose that $p > 1$ in (3), stack observations on variable i in the $T \times 1$ vector $\mathbf{Y}_{iT}$, the $T \times pm + d$ matrix with row t equal to $(D_t', y_{t-1}', \ldots, y_{t-m}')$ as $\mathbf{X}_T$ and write the equation i analogue of (56) as

$$\mathbf{Y}_{iT} = \mathbf{X}_T \boldsymbol{\beta}_i + \mathbf{u}_{iT}. \tag{63}$$

Obtaining the posterior mean associated with the prior (62) is straightforward using a "trick" of mixed estimation: simply append "dummy variables" r_i to the bottom of $\mathbf{Y}_{iT}$ and R_i to the bottom of $\mathbf{X}_T$, and apply OLS to the resulting system. This produces the appropriate analogue of (58). But now the right-hand-side variables for equation i are of the form

$$\begin{bmatrix} \mathbf{X}_T \\ R_i \end{bmatrix}$$

which are of course not the same across equations. In a sampling-theory context with multiple equations with explanatory variables of this form, the "efficient" estimator is the seemingly-unrelated-regression [see Zellner (1971)] estimator, which is not the same as OLS applied equation-by-equation. In the special case of diagonal $\mathbf{\Psi}$, however, equation-by-equation calculations are sufficient to compute the posterior mean of the VAR parameters. Thus Litterman's (1979) "loss of efficiency" argument suggests that a perceived computational burden in effect forced him to make unpalatable assumptions regarding the off-diagonal elements of $\mathbf{\Psi}$.

Litterman also sidestepped another computational burden (at the time) of treating the elements of the prior as unknown. Indeed, the use of estimated residual standard deviations in the specification of the prior is an example of the "empirical" Bayesian approach. He briefly discussed the difficulties associated with treating the parameters of the prior as unknown, but argued that the required numerical integration of the resulting distribution (the diffuse prior version of which is Zellner's (57) above) was "not feasible". As is clear from Section 2 above (and 5 below), ten years later, feasibility was not a problem.

Litterman implemented his scheme on a three-variable VAR involving real GNP, M1, and the GNP price deflator using a quarterly sample from 1954:1 to 1969:4, and a forecast period 1970:1 to 1978:1. In undertaking this effort, he introduced a recursive evaluation procedure. First, he estimated the model (obtained $\tilde{\mathbf{B}}$) using data through 1969:4 and made predictions for 1 through K steps ahead. These were recorded, the sample updated to 1970:1, the model re-estimated, and the process was repeated for each quarter through 1977:4. Various measures of forecast accuracy (mean absolute error, root mean squared error, and Theil's U – the ratio of the root mean squared error to that of a no-change forecast) were then calculated for each of the forecast horizons 1 through K. Estimation was accomplished by the Kalman filter, though it was used only as a computational device, and none of its inherent Bayesian features were utilized. Litterman's comparison to McNees's (1975) forecast performance statistics for several large-scale macroeconometric models suggested that the forecasting method worked well, particularly at horizons of about two to four quarters.

In addition to traditional measures of forecast accuracy, Litterman also devoted substantial effort to producing Fair's (1980) "estimates of uncertainty". These are measures of forecast accuracy that embody adjustments for changes in the variances of the forecasts over time. In producing these measures for his Bayesian VARs, Litterman anticipated much of the essence of posterior simulation that would be developed over the next fifteen years. The reason is that Fair's method decomposes forecast uncertainty into several sources, of which one is the uncertainty due to the need to estimate the coefficients of the model. Fair's version of the procedure involved simulation from the frequentist *sampling* distribution of the coefficient estimates, but Litterman explicitly indicated the need to stochastically simulate from the posterior distribution of the VAR parameters as well as the distribution of the error terms. Indeed, he generated 50 (!) random samples from the (equation-by-equation, empirical Bayes' counterpart to the) predictive density for a six variable, four-lag VAR. Computations required 1024 seconds on the CDC Cyber 172 computer at the University of Minnesota, a computer that was fast by the standards of the time.

Doan, Litterman and Sims (1984, DLS) built on Litterman, though they retained the equation-by-equation mode of analysis he had adopted. Key innovations included accommodation of time variation via a Kalman filter procedure like that used by Harrison and Stevens (1976) for the dynamic linear model discussed above, and the introduction of new features of the prior to reflect views that sums of own lag coefficients in each equation equal unity, further reflecting the random walk prior. [Sims (1992) subsequently introduced a related additional feature of the prior reflecting the view that variables in the VAR may be cointegrated.]

After searching over prior hyperparameters (overall tightness, degree of time variation, etc.) DLS produced a "prior" involving small time variation and some "bite" from the sum-of-lag coefficients restriction that improved pseudo-real time forecast accuracy modestly over univariate predictions for a large (10 variable) model of macroeconomic time series. They conclude the improvement is "... substantial relative to differences in forecast accuracy ordinarily turned up in comparisons across methods, even though it is not large relative to total forecast error." (pp. 26–27)

4.4. After Minnesota: Subsequent developments

Like DLS, Kadiyala and Karlsson (1993) studied a variety of prior distributions for macroeconomic forecasting, and extended the treatment to full system-wide analysis. They began by noting that Litterman's (1979) equation-by-equation formulation has an interpretation as a multivariate analysis, albeit with a Gaussian prior distribution for the VAR coefficients characterized by a diagonal, known, variance-covariance matrix. (In fact, this "known" covariance matrix is data determined owing to the presence of estimated residual standard deviations in Equation (61).) They argue that diagonality is a more troublesome assumption (being "rarely supported by data") than the one that the covariance matrix is known, and in any case introduce four alternatives that relax them both.

Horizontal concatenation of equations of the form (63) and then vertically stacking (vectorizing) yields the Kadiyala and Karlsson (1993) formulation

$$\mathbf{y}_T = (\mathbf{I}_p \otimes \mathbf{X}_T)\mathbf{b} + \mathbf{U}_T \tag{64}$$

where now $\mathbf{y}_T = vec(\mathbf{Y}_{1T}, \mathbf{Y}_{2T}, \ldots, \mathbf{Y}_{pT})$, $\mathbf{b} = vec(\boldsymbol{\beta}_1, \boldsymbol{\beta}_2, \ldots, \boldsymbol{\beta}_p)$, and $\mathbf{U}_T = vec(\mathbf{u}_{1T}, \mathbf{u}_{2T}, \ldots, \mathbf{u}_{pT})$. Here $\mathbf{U}_T \sim N(0, \boldsymbol{\Psi} \otimes \mathbf{I}_T)$. The Minnesota prior treats $var(\mathbf{u}_{iT})$ as fixed (at the unrestricted OLS estimate $\hat{\sigma}_i$) and $\boldsymbol{\Psi}$ as diagonal, and takes, for autoregression model A,

$$\boldsymbol{\beta}_i \mid A \sim N(\underline{\boldsymbol{\beta}}_i, \underline{\boldsymbol{\Sigma}}_i)$$

where $\underline{\boldsymbol{\beta}}_i$ and $\underline{\boldsymbol{\Sigma}}_i$ are the prior mean and covariance hyperparameters. This formulation results in the Gaussian posteriors

$$\boldsymbol{\beta}_i \mid \mathbf{y}_T, A \sim N(\bar{\boldsymbol{\beta}}_i, \bar{\boldsymbol{\Sigma}}_i)$$

where (recall (58))

$$\bar{\boldsymbol{\beta}}_i = \bar{\boldsymbol{\Sigma}}_i\left(\underline{\boldsymbol{\Sigma}}_i^{-1}\underline{\boldsymbol{\beta}}_i + \hat{\sigma}_i^{-1}\mathbf{X}_T'\mathbf{Y}_{iT}\right),$$
$$\bar{\boldsymbol{\Sigma}}_i = \left(\underline{\boldsymbol{\Sigma}}_i^{-1} + \hat{\sigma}_i^{-1}\mathbf{X}_T'\mathbf{X}_T\right)^{-1}.$$

Kadiyala and Karlsson's first alternative is the "normal-Wishart" prior, which takes the VAR parameters to be Gaussian conditional on the innovation covariance matrix, and the covariance matrix not to be known but rather given by an inverted Wishart random matrix:

$$\begin{aligned} &\mathbf{b} \mid \boldsymbol{\Psi} \sim N(\underline{\mathbf{b}}, \boldsymbol{\Psi} \otimes \underline{\boldsymbol{\Omega}}), \\ &\boldsymbol{\Psi} \sim IW(\underline{\boldsymbol{\Psi}}, \alpha) \end{aligned} \tag{65}$$

where the inverse Wishart density for $\boldsymbol{\Psi}$ given degrees of freedom parameter α and "shape" $\underline{\boldsymbol{\Psi}}$ is proportional to $|\boldsymbol{\Psi}|^{-(\alpha+p+1)/2}\exp\{-0.5\mathrm{tr}\boldsymbol{\Psi}^{-1}\underline{\boldsymbol{\Psi}}\}$ [see, e.g., Zellner (1971, p. 395)]. This prior is the natural conjugate prior for $\mathbf{b}$, $\boldsymbol{\Psi}$. The posterior is given by

$$\mathbf{b} \mid \boldsymbol{\Psi}, \mathbf{y_T}, A \sim N\left(\bar{\mathbf{b}}, \boldsymbol{\Psi} \otimes \bar{\boldsymbol{\Omega}}\right),$$
$$\boldsymbol{\Psi} \mid \mathbf{y_T}, A \sim IW\left(\bar{\boldsymbol{\Psi}}, T + \alpha\right)$$

where the posterior parameters $\bar{\mathbf{b}}$, $\bar{\boldsymbol{\Omega}}$, and $\bar{\boldsymbol{\Psi}}$ are simple (though notationally cumbersome) functions of the data and the prior parameters $\underline{\mathbf{b}}$, $\underline{\boldsymbol{\Omega}}$, and $\underline{\boldsymbol{\Psi}}$. Simple functions of interest can be evaluated analytically under this posterior, and for more complicated functions, evaluation by posterior simulation is trivial given the ease of sampling from the inverted Wishart [see, e.g., Geweke (1988)].

But this formulation has a drawback, noted long ago by Rothenberg (1963), that the Kronecker structure of the prior covariance matrix enforces an unfortunate symmetry on ratios of posterior variances of parameters. To take an example, suppress deterministic components ($d = 0$) and consider a 2-variable, 1-lag system ($p = 2$, $m = 1$):

$$y_{1t} = B_{1,11}y_{1t-1} + B_{1,12}y_{2t-1} + \varepsilon_{1t},$$
$$y_{2t} = B_{1,21}y_{1t-1} + B_{1,22}y_{2t-1} + \varepsilon_{2t}.$$

Let $\boldsymbol{\Psi} = [\psi_{ij}]$ and $\bar{\boldsymbol{\Omega}} = [\bar{\sigma}_{ij}]$. Then the posterior covariance matrix for $\mathbf{b} = (B_{1,11}\ B_{1,12}\ B_{1,21}\ B_{1,22})'$ is given by

$$\boldsymbol{\Psi} \otimes \bar{\boldsymbol{\Omega}} = \begin{bmatrix} \psi_{11}\bar{\sigma}_{11} & \psi_{11}\bar{\sigma}_{12} & \psi_{12}\bar{\sigma}_{11} & \psi_{12}\bar{\sigma}_{12} \\ \psi_{11}\bar{\sigma}_{21} & \psi_{11}\bar{\sigma}_{22} & \psi_{12}\bar{\sigma}_{21} & \psi_{12}\bar{\sigma}_{22} \\ \psi_{21}\bar{\sigma}_{11} & \psi_{21}\bar{\sigma}_{12} & \psi_{22}\bar{\sigma}_{11} & \psi_{22}\bar{\sigma}_{12} \\ \psi_{21}\bar{\sigma}_{21} & \psi_{21}\bar{\sigma}_{22} & \psi_{22}\bar{\sigma}_{21} & \psi_{22}\bar{\sigma}_{22} \end{bmatrix},$$

so that

$$\begin{aligned} var(B_{1,11})/var(B_{1,21}) &= \psi_{11}\bar{\sigma}_{11}/\psi_{22}\bar{\sigma}_{11} \\ &= var(B_{1,12})/var(B_{1,22}) = \psi_{11}\bar{\sigma}_{22}/\psi_{22}\bar{\sigma}_{22}. \end{aligned}$$

That is, under the normal-Wishart prior, the ratio of the posterior variance of the "own" lag coefficient in first equation to that of the "other" lag coefficient in second equation is identical to the ratio of the posterior variance of the "other" lag coefficient in first equation to the "own" lag coefficient in second equation: ψ_{11}/ψ_{22}. This is a very unattractive feature in general, and runs counter to the spirit of the Minnesota prior view that there is greater certainty about each equation's "own" lag coefficients than the "others". As Kadiyala and Karlsson (1993) put it, this "force(s) us to treat all equations symmetrically".

Like the normal-Wishart prior, the "diffuse" prior

$$p(\mathbf{b}, \boldsymbol{\Psi}) \propto |\boldsymbol{\Psi}|^{-(p+1)/2} \tag{66}$$

results in a posterior with the same form as the likelihood, with

$$\mathbf{b} \mid \boldsymbol{\Psi} \sim N\left(\hat{\mathbf{b}}, \boldsymbol{\Psi} \otimes \left(\mathbf{X}_{\mathbf{T}}'\mathbf{X}_{\mathbf{T}}\right)^{-1}\right)$$

where now $\hat{\mathbf{b}}$ is the ordinary least squares (equation-by-equation, of course) estimator of $\mathbf{b}$, and the marginal density for $\boldsymbol{\Psi}$ is again of the inverted Wishart form. Symmetric treatment of all equations is also feature of this formulation owing to the product form of the covariance matrix. Yet this formulation has found application (see, e.g., Section 5.2) because its use is very straightforward.

With the "normal-diffuse" prior

$$\mathbf{b} \sim N(\underline{\mathbf{b}}, \underline{\boldsymbol{\Sigma}}),$$
$$p(\boldsymbol{\Psi}) \propto |\boldsymbol{\Psi}|^{-(p+1)/2}$$

of Zellner (1971, p. 239), Kadiyala and Karlsson (1993) relaxed the implicit symmetry assumption at the cost of an analytically intractable posterior. Indeed, Zellner had advocated the prior two decades earlier, arguing that "the price is well worth paying". Zellner's approach to the analytic problem was to integrate $\boldsymbol{\Psi}$ out of the joint posterior for $\mathbf{b}$, $\boldsymbol{\Psi}$ and to approximate the result (a product of generalized multivariate Student t and multivariate Gaussian densities) using the leading (Gaussian) term in a Taylor series expansion. This approximation has a form not unlike (65), with mean given by a matrix-weighted average of the OLS estimator and the prior mean. Indeed, the similarity of Litterman's initial attempts to treat residual variances in his prior as unknown, which he regarded as computationally expensive at the time, to Zellner's straightforward approximation apparently led Litterman to abandon pursuit of a fully Bayesian analysis in favor of the mixed estimation strategy. But by the time Kadiyala and Karlsson (1993) appeared, initial development of fast posterior simulators [e.g., Drèze (1977), Kloek and van Dijk (1978), Drèze and Richard (1983), and Geweke (1989a)] had occurred, and they proceeded to utilize importance-sampling-based Monte Carlo methods for this normal-diffuse prior and a fourth, extended natural conjugate prior [Drèze and Morales (1976)], with only a small apology: "Following Kloek and van Dijk (1978), we have chosen to evaluate Equation (5) using Monte Carlo integration instead of standard numerical integration techniques. Standard numerical integration is relatively inefficient when the integral has a high dimensionality ..."

A natural byproduct of the adoption of posterior simulation is the ability to work with the correct predictive density without resort to the approximations used by Litterman (1979), Doan, Litterman and Sims (1984), and other successors. Indeed, Kadiyala and Karlsson's (1993) Equation (5) is precisely the posterior mean of the predictive density (our (23)) with which they were working. (This is not the *first* such treatment, as production forecasts from full predictive densities have been issued for Iowa tax revenues (see Section 6.2) since 1990, and the shell code for carrying out such calculations in the diffuse prior case appeared in the RATS manual in the late 1980's.)

Kadiyala and Karlsson (1993) conducted three small forecasting "horse race" competitions amongst the four priors, using hyperparameters similar to those recommended by Doan, Litterman and Sims (1984). Two experiments involved quarterly Canadian M2 and real GNP from 1955 to 1977; the other involved monthly data on the U.S. price of wheat, along with wheat export shipments and sales, and an exchange rate index for the U.S. dollar. In a small sample of the Canadian data, the normal-diffuse prior won, followed closely by the extended-natural-conjugate and Minnesota priors; in a larger data set, the normal-diffuse prior was the clear winner. For the monthly wheat data, no one procedure dominated, though priors that allowed for dependencies across equation parameters were generally superior.

Four years later, Kadiyala and Karlsson (1997) analyzed the same four priors, but by then the focus had shifted from the pure forecasting performance of the various priors to the numerical performance of posterior samplers and associated predictives. Indeed, Kadiyala and Karlsson (1997) provide both importance sampling and Gibbs sampling schemes for simulating from each of the posteriors they considered, and provide information regarding numerical efficiencies of the simulation procedures.

Sims and Zha (1999), which was submitted for publication in 1994, and Sims and Zha (1998), completed the Bayesian treatment of the VAR by generalizing procedures for implementing prior views regarding the structure of cross-equation errors. In particular, they wrote (3) in the form

$$\mathbf{C}_0\mathbf{y}_t = \mathbf{C}_D D_t + \mathbf{C}_1\mathbf{y}_{t-1} + \mathbf{C}_2\mathbf{y}_{t-2} + \cdots + \mathbf{C}_m\mathbf{y}_{t-m} + \mathbf{u}_t \tag{67}$$

with

$$E\mathbf{u}_t\mathbf{u}_t' = \mathbf{I}$$

which accommodates various identification schemes for $\mathbf{C}_0$. For example, one route for passing from (3) to (67) is via "Choleski factorization" of $\boldsymbol{\Sigma}$ as $\boldsymbol{\Sigma} = \boldsymbol{\Sigma}^{1/2}\boldsymbol{\Sigma}^{1/2'}$ so that $\mathbf{C}_0 = \boldsymbol{\Sigma}^{-1/2}$ and $\mathbf{u}_t = \Sigma^{-1/2}\varepsilon_t$. This results in exact identification of parameters in $\mathbf{C}_0$, but other "overidentification" schemes are possible as well. Sims and Zha (1999) worked directly with the likelihood, thus implicitly adopting a diffuse prior for $\mathbf{C}_0, \mathbf{C}_D, \mathbf{C}_1, \ldots, \mathbf{C}_m$. They showed that conditional on $\mathbf{C}_0$, the posterior ("likelihood") for the other parameters is Gaussian, but the marginal for $\mathbf{C}_0$ is not of any standard form. They indicated how to sample from it using importance sampling, but in application used a random walk Metropolis-chain procedure utilizing a multivariate-t candidate generator. Subsequently, Sims and Zha (1998) showed how to adopt an informative Gaussian prior for $\mathbf{C}_D, \mathbf{C}_1, \ldots, \mathbf{C}_m | \mathbf{C}_0$ together with a general (diffuse or informative) prior for $\mathbf{C}_0$ and concluded with the "hope that this will allow the transparency and reproducibility of Bayesian methods to be more widely available for tasks of forecasting and policy analysis" (p. 967).

5. Some Bayesian forecasting models

The vector autoregression (VAR) is the best known and most widely applied Bayesian economic forecasting model. It has been used in many contexts, and its ability to improve forecasts and provide a vehicle for communicating uncertainty is by now well established. We return to a specific application of the VAR illustrating these qualities in Section 6. In fact Bayesian inference is now widely undertaken with many models, for a variety of applications including economic forecasting. This section surveys a few of the models most commonly used in economics. Some of these, for example ARMA and fractionally integrated models, have been used in conjunction with methods that are not only non-Bayesian but are also not likelihood-based because of the intractability of the likelihood function. The technical issues that arise in numerical maximization of the likelihood function, on the one hand, and the use of simulation methods in computing posterior moments, on the other, are distinct. It turns out, in these cases as well as in many other econometric models, that the Bayesian integration problem is easier to solve than is the non-Bayesian optimization problem. We provide some of the details in Sections 5.2 and 5.3 below.

The state of the art in inference and computation is an important determinant of which models have practical application and which do not. The rapid progress in posterior simulators since 1990 is an increasingly important influence in the conception and creation of new models. Some of these models would most likely never have been substantially developed, or even emerged, without these computational tools, reviewed in Section 3. An example is the stochastic volatility model, introduced in Section 2.1.2 and discussed in greater detail in Section 5.5 below. Another example is the state space model, often called the dynamic linear model in the statistics literature, which is described briefly in Section 4.2 and in more detail in Chapter 7 of this volume. The monograph by West and Harrison (1997) provides detailed development of the Bayesian formulation of this model, and that by Pole, West and Harrison (1994) is devoted to the practical aspects of Bayesian forecasting.

These models all carry forward the theme so important in vector autoregressions: priors matter, and in particular priors that cope sensibly with an otherwise profligate parameterization are demonstrably effective in improving forecasts. That was true in the earliest applications when computational tools were very limited, as illustrated in Section 4 for VARs, and here for autoregressive leading indicator models (Section 5.1). This fact has become even more striking as computational tools have become more sophisticated. The review of cointegration and error correction models (Section 5.4) constitutes a case study in point. More generally models that are preferred, as indicated by Bayes factors, should lead to better decisions, as measured by ex post loss, for the reasons developed in Sections 2.3.2 and 2.4.1. This section closes with such a comparison for time-varying volatility models.

5.1. Autoregressive leading indicator models

In a series of papers [Garcia-Ferer et al. (1987), Zellner and Hong (1989), Zellner, Hong and Gulati (1990), Zellner, Hong and Min (1991), Min and Zellner (1993)] Zellner and coauthors investigated the use of leading indicators, pooling, shrinkage, and time-varying parameters in forecasting real output for the major industrialized countries. In every case the variable modeled was the growth rate of real output; there was no presumption that real output is cointegrated across countries. The work was carried out entirely analytically, using little beyond what was available in conventional software at the time, which limited attention almost exclusively to one-step-ahead forecasts. A principal goal of these investigations was to improve forecasts significantly using relatively simple models and pooling techniques.

The observables model in all of these studies is of the form

$$y_{it} = \alpha_0 + \sum_{s=1}^{3} \alpha_s y_{i,t-s} + \boldsymbol{\beta}' \mathbf{z}_{i,t-1} + \varepsilon_{it}, \quad \varepsilon_{it} \overset{\text{iid}}{\sim} N\big(0, \sigma^2\big), \tag{68}$$

with y_{it} denoting the growth rate in real GNP or real GDP between year $t-1$ and year t in country i. The vector $\mathbf{z}_{i,t-1}$ comprises the leading indicators. In Garcia-Ferer et al. (1987) and Zellner and Hong (1989) $\mathbf{z}_{it}$ consisted of real stock returns in country i in years $t-1$ and t, the growth rate in the real money supply between years $t-1$ and t, and world stock return defined as the median real stock return in year t over all countries in the sample. Attention was confined to nine OECD countries in Garcia-Ferer et al. (1987). In Zellner and Hong (1989) the list expanded to 18 countries but the original group was reported separately, as well, for purposes of comparison.

The earliest study, Garcia-Ferer et al. (1987), considered five different forecasting procedures and several variants on the right-hand-side variables in (68). The period 1954–1973 was used exclusively for estimation, and one-step-ahead forecast errors were recorded for each of the years 1974 through 1981, with estimates being updated before each forecast was made. Results for root mean square forecast error, expressed in units of growth rate percentage, are given in Table 1. The model LI1 includes only the two stock returns in $\mathbf{z}_{it}$; LI2 adds the world stock return and LI3 adds also the growth rate in the real money supply. The time varying parameter (TVP) model utilizes a conventional state-space representation in which the variance in the coefficient drift is $\sigma^2/2$. The pooled models constrain the coefficients in (68) to be the same for all countries. In the variant "Shrink 1" each country forecast is an equally-weighted average of the own country forecast and the average forecast for all nine countries; unequally-weighted

Table 1
Summary of forecast RMSE for 9 countries in Garcia-Ferer et al. (1987)

	Estimation method				
	(None)	OLS	TVP	Pool	Shrink 1
Growth rate = 0	3.09				
Random walk growth rate	3.73				
AR(3)		3.46			
AR(3)-LI1		2.70	2.52	3.08	
AR(3)-LI2		2.39		2.62	
AR(3)-LI3		2.23	1.82	2.22	1.78

Table 2
Summary of forecast RMSE for 18 countries in Zellner and Hong (1989)

	Estimation method				
	(None)	OLS	Pool	Shrink 1	Shrink 2
Growth rate = 0	3.07				
Random walk growth rate	3.02				
Growth rate = Past average	3.09				
AR(3)		3.00			
AR(3)-LI3		2.62	2.14	2.32	2.13

averages (unreported here) produce somewhat higher root mean square error of forecast.

The subsequent study by Zellner and Hong (1989) extended this work by adding nine countries, extending the forecasting exercise by three years, and considering an alternative shrinkage procedure. In the alternative, the coefficient estimates are taken to be a weighted average of the least squares estimates for the country under consideration, and the pooled estimates using all the data. The study compared several weighting schemes, and found that a weight of one-sixth on the country estimates and five-sixths on the pooled estimates minimized the out-of-sample forecast root mean square error. These results are reported in the column "Shrink 2" in Table 2.

Garcia-Ferer et al. (1987) and Zellner and Hong (1989) demonstrated the returns both to the incorporation of leading indicators and to various forms of pooling and shrinkage. Combined, these two methods produce root mean square errors of forecast somewhat smaller than those of considerably more complicated OECD official forecasts [see Smyth (1983)], as described in Garcia-Ferer et al. (1987) and Zellner and Hong (1989). A subsequent investigation by Min and Zellner (1993) computed formal posterior odds ratios between the most competitive models. Consistent with the results described here, they found that odds rarely exceeded 2 : 1 and that there was no systematic gain from combining forecasts.

5.2. Stationary linear models

Many routine forecasting situations involve linear models of the form $y_t = \boldsymbol{\beta}'\mathbf{x}_t + \boldsymbol{\varepsilon}_t$, in which $\boldsymbol{\varepsilon}_t$ is a stationary process, and the covariates $\mathbf{x}_t$ are ancillary – for example they may be deterministic (e.g., calendar effects in asset return models), they may be controlled (e.g., traditional reduced form policy models), or they may be exogenous and modelled separately from the relationship between $\mathbf{x}_t$ and y_t.

5.2.1. The stationary AR(p) model

One of the simplest models of serial correlation in $\boldsymbol{\varepsilon}_t$ is an autoregression of order p. The contemporary Bayesian treatment of this problem [see Chib and Greenberg (1994) or Geweke (2005, Section 7.1)] exploits the structure of MCMC posterior simulation algorithms, and the Gibbs sampler in particular, by decomposing the posterior distribution into manageable conditional distributions for each of several groups of parameters.

Suppose

$$\varepsilon_t = \sum_{s=1}^{p} \phi_s \varepsilon_{t-s} + u_t,\ u_t \mid (\varepsilon_{t-1}, \varepsilon_{t-2}, \ldots) \overset{\text{iid}}{\sim} N\big(0, h^{-1}\big),$$

and

$$\boldsymbol{\phi} = (\phi_1, \ldots, \phi_p)' \in S_p = \left\{\boldsymbol{\phi}\colon \left|1 - \sum_{s=1}^{p} \phi_s z^s\right| \neq 0\ \forall z\colon |z| \leqslant 1\right\} \subseteq \mathbb{R}^p.$$

There are three groups of parameters: $\boldsymbol{\beta}$, $\boldsymbol{\phi}$, and h. Conditional on $\boldsymbol{\phi}$, the likelihood function is of the classical generalized least squares form and reduces to that of ordinary least squares by means of appropriate linear transformations. For $t = p+1, \ldots, T$ these transformations amount to $y_t^* = y_t - \sum_{s=1}^{p} \phi_s y_{t-s}$ and $\mathbf{x}_t^* = \mathbf{x}_t - \sum_{s=1}^{p} \mathbf{x}_{t-s}\phi_s$. For $t = 1, \ldots, p$ the p Yule–Walker equations

$$\begin{bmatrix} 1 & \rho_1 & \cdots & \rho_{p-1} \\ \rho_1 & 1 & \cdots & \rho_{p-2} \\ \vdots & \vdots & \ddots & \vdots \\ \rho_{p-1} & \rho_{p-2} & \cdots & 1 \end{bmatrix} \begin{pmatrix} \phi_1 \\ \phi_2 \\ \vdots \\ \phi_p \end{pmatrix} = \begin{pmatrix} \rho_1 \\ \rho_2 \\ \vdots \\ \rho_p \end{pmatrix}$$

can be inverted to solve for the autocorrelation coefficients $\boldsymbol{\rho} = (\rho_1, \ldots, \rho_p)'$ as a linear function of $\boldsymbol{\phi}$. Then construct the $p \times p$ matrix $\mathbf{R}_p(\boldsymbol{\phi}) = [\rho_{|i-j|}]$, let $\mathbf{A}_p(\boldsymbol{\rho})$ be a Choleski factor of $[\mathbf{R}_p(\boldsymbol{\phi})]^{-1}$, and then take $(y_1^*, \ldots, y_p^*)' = \mathbf{A}_p(\boldsymbol{\rho})(y_1, \ldots, y_p)'$. Creating $\mathbf{x}_1^*, \ldots, \mathbf{x}_p^*$ by means of the same transformation, the linear model $y_t^* = \boldsymbol{\beta}'\mathbf{x}_t^* + \varepsilon_t^*$ satisfies the assumptions of the textbook normal linear model. Given a normal prior for $\boldsymbol{\beta}$ and a gamma prior for h, the conditional posterior distributions come from these same families; variants on these prior distributions are straightforward; see Geweke (2005, Sections 2.1 and 5.3).

On the other hand, conditional on $\boldsymbol{\beta}$, h, $\mathbf{X}$ and $\mathbf{y}^o$,

$$\mathbf{e} = \begin{pmatrix} \varepsilon_{p+1} \\ \varepsilon_{p+2} \\ \vdots \\ \varepsilon_T \end{pmatrix} \quad \text{and} \quad \mathbf{E} = \begin{bmatrix} \varepsilon_p & \cdots & \varepsilon_1 \\ \varepsilon_{p+1} & \cdots & \varepsilon_2 \\ \vdots & & \vdots \\ \varepsilon_{T-1} & \cdots & \varepsilon_{T-p} \end{bmatrix}$$

are known. Further denoting $\mathbf{X}_p = [\mathbf{x}_1, \ldots, \mathbf{x}_p]'$ and $\mathbf{y}_p = (y_1, \ldots, y_p)'$, the likelihood function is

$$p(\mathbf{y}^o \mid \mathbf{X}, \boldsymbol{\beta}, \boldsymbol{\phi}, h)$$
$$= (2\pi)^{-T/2} h^{T/2} \exp\bigl[-h(\mathbf{e} - \mathbf{E}\boldsymbol{\phi})'(\mathbf{e} - \mathbf{E}\boldsymbol{\phi})/2\bigr] \tag{69}$$
$$\times \bigl|\mathbf{R}_p(\boldsymbol{\phi})\bigr|^{-1/2} \exp\bigl[-h\bigl(\mathbf{y}_p^o - \mathbf{X}_p\boldsymbol{\beta}\bigr)'\mathbf{R}_p(\boldsymbol{\phi})^{-1}\bigl(\mathbf{y}_p^o - \mathbf{X}_p\boldsymbol{\beta}\bigr)/2\bigr]. \tag{70}$$

The expression (69), treated as a function of $\boldsymbol{\phi}$, is the kernel of a p-variate normal distribution. If the prior distribution of $\boldsymbol{\phi}$ is Gaussian, truncated to S_p, then the same is true of the product of this prior and (69). (Variants on this prior can be accommodated through reweighting as discussed in Section 3.3.2.) Denote expression (70) as $r(\boldsymbol{\beta}, h, \boldsymbol{\phi})$, and note that, interpreted as a function of $\boldsymbol{\phi}$, $r(\boldsymbol{\beta}, h, \boldsymbol{\phi})$ does not correspond to the kernel of any tractable multivariate distribution. This apparent impediment to an MCMC algorithm can be addressed by means of a Metropolis within Gibbs step, as discussed in Section 3.2.3. At iteration m a Metropolis within Gibbs step for $\boldsymbol{\phi}$ draws a candidate $\boldsymbol{\phi}^*$ from the Gaussian distribution whose kernel is the product of the untruncated Gaussian prior distribution of $\boldsymbol{\phi}$ and (69), using the current values $\boldsymbol{\beta}^{(m)}$ of $\boldsymbol{\beta}$ and $h^{(m)}$ of h. From (70) the acceptance probability for the candidate is

$$\min\left[\frac{r(\boldsymbol{\beta}^{(m)}, h^{(m)}, \boldsymbol{\phi}^*) I_{S_p}(\boldsymbol{\phi}^*)}{r(\boldsymbol{\beta}^{(m)}, h^{(m)}, \boldsymbol{\phi}^{(m-1)})}, 1\right].$$

5.2.2. The stationary ARMA(p, q) model

The incorporation of a moving average component

$$\varepsilon_t = \sum_{s=1}^{p} \phi_s \varepsilon_{t-s} + \sum_{s=1}^{q} \theta_s u_{t-s} + u_t$$

adds the parameter vector $\boldsymbol{\theta} = (\theta_1, \ldots, \theta_q)'$ and complicates the recursive structure. The first broad-scale attack on the problem was Monahan (1983) who worked without the benefit of modern posterior simulation methods and was able to treat only $p + q \leqslant 2$. Nevertheless he produced exact Bayes factors for five alternative models, and obtained up to four-step ahead predictive means and standard deviations for each model. He applied his methods in several examples developed originally in Box and Jenkins (1976). Chib and Greenberg (1994) and Marriott et al. (1996) approached the problem by means of data augmentation, adding unobserved pre-sample values to the vector of unobservables. In Marriott et al. (1996) the augmented data are $\boldsymbol{\varepsilon}_0 = (\varepsilon_0, \ldots, \varepsilon_{1-p})'$ and $\mathbf{u}_0 = (u_0, \ldots, u_{1-q})'$. Then [see Marriott et al. (1996, pp. 245–246)]

$$p(\varepsilon_1, \ldots, \varepsilon_T \mid \boldsymbol{\phi}, \boldsymbol{\theta}, h, \boldsymbol{\varepsilon}_0, \mathbf{u}_0) = (2\pi)^{-T/2} h^{T/2} \exp\left[-h \sum_{t=1}^{T} (\varepsilon_t - \mu_t)^2/2\right] \tag{71}$$

with

$$\mu_t = \sum_{s=1}^{p} \phi_s \varepsilon_{t-s} - \sum_{s=1}^{t-1} \theta_s (\varepsilon_{t-s} - \mu_{t-s}) - \sum_{s=t}^{q} \theta_s \varepsilon_{t-s}. \tag{72}$$

(The second summation is omitted if $t = 1$, and the third is omitted if $t > q$.)

The data augmentation scheme is feasible because the conditional posterior density of $\mathbf{u}_0$ and $\boldsymbol{\varepsilon}_0$,

$$p(\boldsymbol{\varepsilon}_0, \mathbf{u}_0 \mid \boldsymbol{\phi}, \boldsymbol{\theta}, h, \mathbf{X}_T, \mathbf{y}_T) \tag{73}$$

is that of a Gaussian distribution and is easily computed [see Newbold (1974)]. The product of (73) with the density corresponding to (71)–(72) yields a Gaussian kernel for the presample $\boldsymbol{\varepsilon}_0$ and $\mathbf{u}_0$. A draw from this distribution becomes one step in a Gibbs sampling posterior simulation algorithm. The presence of (73) prevents the posterior conditional distribution of $\boldsymbol{\phi}$ and $\boldsymbol{\theta}$ from being Gaussian. This complication may be handled just as it was in the case of the AR(p) model, using a Metropolis within Gibbs step.

There are a number of variants on these approaches. Chib and Greenberg (1994) show that the data augmentation vector can be reduced to $\max(p, q + 1)$ elements, with some increase in complexity. As an alternative to enforcing stationarity in the Metropolis within Gibbs step, the transformation of $\boldsymbol{\phi}$ to the corresponding vector of partial autocorrelations [see Barndorff-Nielsen and Schou (1973)] may be inverted and the Jacobian computed [see Monahan (1984)], thus transforming S_p to a unit hypercube. A similar treatment can restrict the roots of $1 - \sum_{s=1}^{q} \theta_s z^s$ to the exterior of the unit circle [see Marriott et al. (1996)].

There are no new essential complications introduced in extending any of these models or posterior simulators from univariate (ARMA) to multivariate (VARMA) models. On the other hand, VARMA models lead to large numbers of parameters as the number of variables increases, just as in the case of VAR models. The BVAR (Bayesian Vector Autoregression) strategy of using shrinkage prior distributions appears not to have been applied in VARMA models. The approach has been, instead, to utilize exclusion restrictions for many parameters, the same strategy used in non-Bayesian approaches. In a Bayesian set-up, however, uncertainty about exclusion restrictions can be incorporated in posterior and predictive distributions. Ravishanker and Ray (1997a) do exactly this, in extending the model and methodology of Marriott et al. (1996) to VARMA models. Corresponding to each autoregressive coefficient ϕ_{ijs} there is a multiplicative Bernoulli random variable γ_{ijs}, indicating whether that coefficient is excluded, and similarly for each moving average coefficient θ_{ijs} there is a Bernoulli random variable δ_{ijs}:

$$y_{it} = \sum_{j=1}^{n}\sum_{s=1}^{p} \gamma_{ijs}\phi_{ijs}y_{j,t-s} + \sum_{j=1}^{n}\sum_{s=1}^{q} \theta_{ijs}\delta_{ijs}\varepsilon_{j,t-s} + \varepsilon_{it} \quad (i = 1, \ldots, n).$$

Prior probabilities on these random variables may be used to impose parsimony, both globally and also differentially at different lags and for different variables; independent Bernoulli prior distributions for the parameters γ_{ijs} and δ_{ijs}, embedded in a hierarchical prior with beta prior distributions for the probabilities, are the obvious alternatives to *ad hoc* non-Bayesian exclusion decisions, and are quite tractable. The conditional posterior distributions of the γ_{ijs} and δ_{ijs} are individually conditionally Bernoulli. This strategy is one of a family of similar approaches to exclusion restrictions in regression models [see George and McCulloch (1993) or Geweke (1996b)] and has also been employed in univariate ARMA models [see Barnett, Kohn and Sheather (1996)]. The posterior MCMC sampling algorithm for the parameters ϕ_{ijs} and δ_{ijs} also proceeds one parameter at a time; Ravishanker and Ray (1997a) report that this algorithm is computationally efficient in a three-variable VARMA model with $p = 3$, $q = 1$, applied to a data set with 75 quarterly observations.

5.3. Fractional integration

Fractional integration, also known as long memory, first drew the attention of economists because of the improved multi-step-ahead forecasts provided by even the simplest variants of these models as reported in Granger and Joyeux (1980) and Porter-Hudak (1982). In a fractionally integrated model $(1 - L)^d y_t = u_t$, where

$$(1 - L)^d = \sum_{j=0}^{\infty} \binom{d}{j} (-L)^j = \sum_{j=1}^{\infty} \frac{(-1)^j \Gamma(d-1)}{\Gamma(j-1)\Gamma(d-j-1)} L^j$$

and u_t is a stationary process whose autocovariance function decays geometrically. The fully parametric version of this model typically specifies

$$\phi(L)(1 - L)^d (y_t - \mu) = \theta(L)\varepsilon_t, \tag{74}$$

with $\phi(L)$ and $\theta(L)$ being polynomials of specified finite order and ε_t being serially uncorrelated; most of the literature takes $\varepsilon_t \overset{\text{iid}}{\sim} N(0, \sigma^2)$. Sowell (1992a, 1992b) first derived the likelihood function and implemented a maximum likelihood estimator. Koop et al. (1997) provided the first Bayesian treatment, employing a flat prior distribution for the parameters in $\phi(L)$ and $\theta(L)$, subject to invertibility restrictions. This study used importance sampling of the posterior distribution, with the prior distribution as the source distribution. The weighting function $w(\boldsymbol{\theta})$ is then just the likelihood function, evaluated using Sowell's computer code. The application in Koop et al. (1997) used quarterly US real GNP, 1947–1989, a standard data set for fractionally integrated models, and polynomials in $\phi(L)$ and $\theta(L)$ up to order 3. This study did not provide any evaluation of the efficiency of the prior density as the source distribution in the importance sampling algorithm; in typical situations this will be poor if there are a half-dozen or more dimensions of integration. In any event, the computing times reported[3] indicate that subsequent more sophisticated algorithms are also much faster.

Much of the Bayesian treatment of fractionally integrated models originated with Ravishanker and coauthors, who applied these methods to forecasting. Pai and Ravishanker (1996) provided a thorough treatment of the univariate case based on a Metropolis random-walk algorithm. Their evaluation of the likelihood function differs from Sowell's. From the autocovariance function $r(s)$ corresponding to (74) given in Hosking (1981) the Levinson–Durbin algorithm provides the partial regression coefficients ϕ_j^k in

$$\mu_t = E(y_t \mid \mathbf{Y}_{t-1}) = \sum_{j=1}^{t-1} \phi_j^{t-1} y_{t-j}. \tag{75}$$

The likelihood function then follows from

$$y_t \mid \mathbf{Y}_{t-1} \sim N\left(\mu_t, \nu_t^2\right), \nu_t^2 = \left[r(0)/\sigma^2\right] \prod_{j=1}^{t-1} \left[1 - \left(\phi_j^j\right)^2\right]. \tag{76}$$

Pai and Ravishanker (1996) computed the maximum likelihood estimate as discussed in Haslett and Raftery (1989). The observed Fisher information matrix is the variance matrix used in the Metropolis random-walk algorithm, after integrating μ and σ^2 analytically from the posterior distribution. The study focused primarily on inference for the parameters; note that (75)–(76) provide the basis for sampling from the predictive distribution given the output of the posterior simulator.

A multivariate extension of (74), without cointegration, may be expressed

$$\Phi(L)\mathbf{D}(L)(\mathbf{y}_t - \boldsymbol{\mu}) = \Theta(L)\boldsymbol{\varepsilon}_t$$

in which $\mathbf{y}_t$ is $n \times 1$, $\mathbf{D}(L) = diag[(1-L)^{d_1}, \ldots, (1-L)^{d_n}]$, $\Phi(L)$ and $\Theta(L)$ are $n \times n$ matrix polynomials in L of specified order, and $\boldsymbol{\varepsilon}_t \overset{\text{iid}}{\sim} N(\mathbf{0}, \boldsymbol{\Sigma})$. Ravishanker and Ray (1997b, 2002) provided an exact Bayesian treatment and a forecasting application of this model. Their approach blends elements of Marriott et al. (1996) and Pai and Ravishanker (1996). It incorporates presample values of $\mathbf{z}_t = \mathbf{y}_t - \boldsymbol{\mu}$ and the pure fractionally integrated process $\mathbf{a}_t = \mathbf{D}(L)^{-1}\boldsymbol{\varepsilon}_t$ as latent variables. The autocovariance function $\mathbf{R}^a(s)$ of $\mathbf{a}_t$ is obtained recursively from

$$r^a(0)_{ij} = \sigma_{ij} \frac{\Gamma(1-d_i-d_j)}{\Gamma(1-d_i)\Gamma(1-d_j)}, \quad r^a(s)_{ij} = -\frac{1-d_i-s}{s-d_j} r^a(s-1)_{ij}.$$

[3] Contrast Koop et al. (1997, footnote 12) with Pai and Ravishanker (1996, p. 74).

The autocovariance function of $\mathbf{z}_t$ is then

$$\mathbf{R}^z(s) = \sum_{i=1}^{\infty}\sum_{j=0}^{\infty} \mathbf{\Psi}_i \mathbf{R}^a(s+i-j)\mathbf{\Psi}'_j$$

where the coefficients $\mathbf{\Psi}_j$ are those in the moving average representation of the ARMA part of the process. Since these decay geometrically, truncation is not a serious issue. This provides the basis for a random walk Metropolis-within-Gibbs step constructed as in Pai and Ravishanker (1996). The other blocks in the Gibbs sampler are the presample values of $\mathbf{z}_t$ and $\mathbf{a}_t$, plus $\boldsymbol{\mu}$ and $\mathbf{\Sigma}$. The procedure requires on the order of n^3T^2 operations and storage of order n^2T^2; $T = 200$ and $n = 3$ requires a gigabyte of storage. If likelihood is computed conditional on all presample values being zero the problem is computationally much less demanding, but results differ substantially.

Ravishanker and Ray (2002) provide details of drawing from the predictive density, given the output of the posterior simulator. Since the presample values are a by-product of each iteration, the latent vectors $\mathbf{a}_t$ can be computed by means of $\mathbf{a}_t = -\sum_{i=1}^{p} \mathbf{\Phi}_i \mathbf{z}_{t-i} + \sum_{i=1}^{q} \mathbf{\Theta}_r \mathbf{a}_{t-r}$. Then sample $\mathbf{a}_t$ forward using the autocovariance function of the pure long-memory process, and finally apply the ARMA recursions to these values. The paper applies a simple version of the model ($n = 3$; $q = 0$; $p = 0$ or 1) to sea temperatures off the California coast. The coefficients of fractional integration are all about 0.4 when $p = 0$; $p = 1$ introduces the usual difficulties in distinguishing between long memory and slow geometric decay of the autocovariance function. There are substantial interactions in the off-diagonal elements of $\mathbf{\Phi}(L)$, but the study does not take up fractional cointegration.

5.4. Cointegration and error correction

Cointegration restricts the long-run behavior of multivariate time series that are otherwise nonstationary. Error correction models (ECMs) provide a convenient representation of cointegration, and there is by now an enormous literature on inference in these models. By restricting the behavior of otherwise nonstationary time series, cointegration also has the promise of improving forecasts, especially at longer horizons. Coming hard on the heels of Bayesian vector autoregressions, ECMs were at first thought to be competitors of VARs:

> One could also compare these results with estimates which are obviously misspecified such as least squares on differences or Litterman's Bayesian Vector Autoregression which shrinks the parameter vector toward the first difference model which is itself misspecified for this system. The finding that such methods provided inferior forecasts would hardly be surprising. [Engle and Yoo (1987, pp. 151–152)]

Shoesmith (1995) carefully compared and combined the error correction specification and the prior distributions pioneered by Litterman, with illuminating results. He used the quarterly, six-lag VAR in Litterman (1980) for real GNP, the implicit GNP price deflator, real gross private domestic investment, the three-month treasury bill rate and the money supply (M1). Throughout the exercise, Shoesmith repeatedly tested for lag length and the outcome consistently indicated six lags. The period 1959:1 through 1981:4 was the base estimation period, followed by 20 successive five-year experimental forecasts: the first was for 1982:1 through 1986:4; and the last was for 1986:4 through 1991:3 based on estimates using data from 1959:1 through 1986:3. Error correction specification tests were conducted using standard procedures [see Johansen (1988)]. For all the samples used, these procedures identified the price deflator as I(2), all other variables as I(1), and two cointegrating vectors.

Shoesmith compared forecasts from Litterman's model with six other models. One, VAR/I1, was a VAR in I(1) series (i.e., first differences for the deflator and levels for all other variables) estimated by least squares, not incorporating any shrinkage or other prior. The second, ECM, was a conventional ECM, again with no shrinkage. The other four models all included the Minnesota prior. One of these models, BVAR/I1, differs from Litterman's model only in replacing the deflator with its first difference. Another, BECM, applies the Minnesota prior to the conventional ECM, with no shrinkage or other restrictions applied to the coefficients on the error correction terms. Yet another variant, BVAR/I0, applies the Minnesota prior to a VAR in I(0) variables (i.e., second differences for the deflator and first differences for all other variables). The final model, BECM/5Z, is identical to BECM except that five cointegrating relationships are specified, an intentional misreading of the outcome of the conventional procedure for determining the rank of the error correction matrix.

The paper offers an extensive comparison of root mean square forecasting errors for all of the variables. These are summarized in Table 3, by first forming the ratio of mean square error in each model to its counterpart in Litterman's model, and then averaging the ratios across the six variables.

The most notable feature of the results is the superiority of the BECM forecasts, which is realized at all forecasting horizons but becomes greater at more distant horizons. The ECM forecasts, by contrast, do not dominate those of either the original Litterman VAR or the BVAR/I1, contrary to the conjecture in Engle and Yoo (1987). The results show that most of the improvement comes from applying the Minnesota prior to a model that incorporates stationary time series: BVAR/I0 ranks second at all horizons, and the ECM without shrinkage performs poorly relative to BVAR/I0 at all horizons. In fact the VAR with the Minnesota prior and the error correction models are not competitors, but complementary methods of dealing with the profligate parameterization in multivariate time series by shrinking toward reasonable models with fewer parameters. In the case of the ECM the shrinkage is a hard, but data driven, restriction, whereas in the Minnesota prior it is soft, allowing the data to override in cases where the more parsimoniously parameterized model is less applicable. The possibilities for employing both have hardly been exhausted. Shoesmith (1995) suggested that this may be a promising avenue for future research.

Table 3
Comparison of forecast RMSE in Shoesmith (1995)

	Horizon		
	1 quarter	8 quarters	20 quarters
VAR/I1	1.33	1.00	1.14
ECM	1.28	0.89	0.91
BVAR/I1	0.97	0.96	0.85
BECM	0.89	0.72	0.45
BVAR/I0	0.95	0.87	0.59
BECM/5Z	0.99	1.02	0.88

This experiment incorporated the Minnesota prior utilizing the mixed estimation methods described in Section 4.3, appropriate at the time to the investigation of the relative contributions of error correction and shrinkage in improving forecasts. More recent work has employed modern posterior simulators. A leading example is Villani (2001), which examined the inflation forecasting model of the central bank of Sweden. This model is expressed in error correction form

$$\Delta \mathbf{y}_t = \boldsymbol{\mu} + \boldsymbol{\alpha}\boldsymbol{\beta}'\mathbf{y}_{t-1} + \sum_{s=1}^{p} \boldsymbol{\Gamma}_s \Delta \mathbf{y}_{t-s} + \boldsymbol{\varepsilon}_t, \quad \boldsymbol{\varepsilon}_t \overset{\text{iid}}{\sim} N(\mathbf{0}, \boldsymbol{\Sigma}). \tag{77}$$

It incorporates GDP, consumer prices and the three-month treasury rate, both Swedish and weighted averages of corresponding foreign series, as well as the trade-weighted exchange rate. Villani limits consideration to models in which $\boldsymbol{\beta}$ is 7×3, based on the bank's experience. He specifies four candidate coefficient vectors: for example, one based on purchasing power parity and another based on a Fisherian interpretation of the nominal interest rate given a stationary real rate. This forms the basis for competing models that utilize various combinations of these vectors in $\boldsymbol{\beta}$, as well as unknown cointegrating vectors. In the most restrictive formulations three vectors are specified and in the least restrictive all three are unknown. Villani specifies conventional uninformative priors for $\boldsymbol{\alpha}$, $\boldsymbol{\beta}$ and $\boldsymbol{\Sigma}$, and conventional Minnesota priors for the parameters $\boldsymbol{\Gamma}_s$ of the short-run dynamics. The posterior distribution is sampled using a Gibbs sampler blocked in $\boldsymbol{\mu}$, $\boldsymbol{\alpha}$, $\boldsymbol{\beta}$, $\{\boldsymbol{\Gamma}_s\}$ and $\boldsymbol{\Sigma}$.

The paper utilizes data from 1972:2 through 1993:3 for inference. Of all of the combinations of cointegrating vectors, Villani finds that the one in which all three are unrestricted is most favored. This is true using both likelihood ratio tests and an informal version (necessitated by the improper priors) of posterior odds ratios. This unrestricted specification ("$\boldsymbol{\beta}$ empirical" in the table below), as well as the most restricted one ("$\boldsymbol{\beta}$ specified"), are carried forward for the subsequent forecasting exercise. This exercise compares forecasts over the period 1994–1998, reporting forecast root mean square errors for the means of the predictive densities for price inflation ("Bayes ECM"). It also computes forecasts from the maximum likelihood estimates, treating these estimates as

Table 4
Comparison of forecast RMSE in Villani (2001)

	β	
	specified	empirical
Bayes ECM	0.485	0.488
ML unrestricted ECM	0.773	0.694
ML restricted ECM	0.675	0.532

known coefficients ("ML unrestricted ECM"), and finds the forecast root mean square error. Finally, it constrains many of the coefficients to zero, using conventional stepwise deletion procedures in conjunction with maximum likelihood estimation, and again finds the forecast root mean square error. Taking averages of these root mean square errors over forecasting horizons of one to eight quarters ahead yields comparison given in Table 4. The Bayesian ECM produces by far the lowest root mean square error of forecast, and results are about the same whether the restricted or unrestricted version of the cointegrating vectors are used. The forecasts based on restricted maximum likelihood estimates benefit from the additional restrictions imposed by stepwise deletion of coefficients, which is a crude from of shrinkage. In comparison with Shoesmith (1995), Villani (2001) has the further advantage of having used a full Monte Carlo simulation of the predictive density, whose mean is the Bayes estimate given a squared-error loss function.

These findings are supported by other studies that have made similar comparisons. An earlier literature on regional forecasting, of which the seminal paper is Lesage (1990), contains results that are broadly consistent but not directly comparable because of the differences in variables and data. Amisano and Serati (1999) utilized a three-variable VAR for Italian GDP, consumption and investment. Their approach was closer to mixed estimation than to full Bayesian inference. They employed not only a conventional Minnesota prior for the short-run dynamics, but also applied a shrinkage prior to the factor loading vector $\boldsymbol{\alpha}$ in (77). This combination produced a smaller root mean square error, for forecasts from one to twenty quarters ahead, than either a traditional VAR with a Minnesota prior, or an ECM that shrinks the short-run dynamics but not $\boldsymbol{\alpha}$.

5.5. *Stochastic volatility*

In classical linear processes, for example the vector autoregression (3), conditional means are time varying but conditional variances are not. By now it is well established that for many time series, including returns on financial assets, conditional variances in fact often vary greatly. Moreover, in the case of financial assets, conditional variances are fundamental to portfolio allocation. The ARCH family of models provides conditional variances that are functions of past realizations, likelihood functions that are relatively easy to evaluate, and a systematic basis for forecasting and solving the allocation problem. Stochastic volatility models provide an alternative approach, first motivated by autocorrelated information flows [see Tauchen and Pitts (1983)] and as discrete approximations to diffusion processes utilized in the continuous time asset pricing literature [see Hull and White (1987)]. The canonical univariate model, introduced in Section 2.1.2, is

$$\begin{aligned} y_t &= \beta \exp(h_t/2)\varepsilon_t, \quad h_t = \phi h_{t-1} + \sigma_\eta \eta_t, \\ & h_1 \sim N\left[0, \sigma_\eta^2/\left(1-\phi^2\right)\right], \quad (\varepsilon_t, \eta_t)' \overset{\text{iid}}{\sim} N(\mathbf{0}, \mathbf{I}_2). \end{aligned} \tag{78}$$

Only the return y_t is observable. In the stochastic volatility model there are two shocks per time period, whereas in the ARCH family there is only one. As a consequence the stochastic volatility model can more readily generate extreme realizations of y_t. Such a realization will have an impact on the variance of future realizations if it arises because of an unusually large value of η_t, but not if it is due to large ε_t. Because h_t is a latent process not driven by past realizations of y_t, the likelihood function cannot be evaluated directly. Early applications like Taylor (1986) and Melino and Turnbull (1990) used method of moments rather than likelihood-based approaches.

Jacquier, Polson and Rossi (1994) were among the first to point out that the formulation of (78) in terms of latent variables is, by contrast, very natural in a Bayesian formulation that exploits a MCMC posterior simulator. The key insight is that conditional on the sequence of latent volatilities $\{h_t\}$, the likelihood function for (78) factors into a component for β and one for σ_η^2 and ϕ. Given an inverted gamma prior distribution for β^2 the posterior distribution of β^2 is also inverted gamma, and given an independent inverted gamma prior distribution for σ_η^2 and a truncated normal prior distribution for ϕ, the posterior distribution of (σ_η^2, ϕ) is the one discussed at the start of Section 5.2. Thus, the key step is sampling from the posterior distribution of $\{h_t\}$ conditional on $\{y_t^o\}$ and the parameters $(\beta, \sigma_\eta^2, \phi)$. Because $\{h_t\}$ is a first order Markov process, the conditional distribution of a single h_t given $\{h_s, s \neq t\}$, $\{y_t\}$ and $(\beta, \sigma_\eta^2, \phi)$ depends only on h_{t-1}, h_{t+1}, y_t and $(\beta, \sigma_\eta^2, \phi)$. The log-kernel of this distribution is

$$-\frac{(h_t - \mu_t)^2}{2\sigma_\eta^2/(1+\phi^2)} - \frac{h_t}{2} - \frac{y_t^2 \exp(-h_t)}{2\beta^2} \tag{79}$$

with

$$\mu_t = \frac{\phi(h_{t+1} + h_{t-1})}{1+\phi^2} - \frac{\sigma_\eta^2}{2(1+\phi^2)}.$$

Since the kernel is non-standard, a Metropolis-within-Gibbs step can be used for the draw of each h_t. The candidate distribution in Jacquier, Polson and Rossi (1994) is inverted gamma, with parameters chosen to match the first two moments of the candidate density and the kernel.

There are many variants on this Metropolis-within-Gibbs step. Shephard and Pitt (1997) took a second-order Taylor series expansion of (79) about $h_t = \mu_t$, and then used a Gaussian proposal distribution with the corresponding mean and variance. Alternatively, one could find the mode of (79) and the second derivative at the mode to create a Gaussian proposal distribution. The practical limitation in all of these approaches is that sampling the latent variables h_t one at a time generates serial correlation in the MCMC algorithm: loosely speaking, the greater is $|\phi|$, the greater is the serial correlation in the Markov chain. An example in Shephard and Pitt (1997), using almost 1,000 daily exchange rate returns, showed a relative numerical efficiency (as defined in Section 3.1.3) for ϕ of about 0.001; the posterior mean of ϕ is 0.982. The Gaussian proposal distribution is very effective, with a high acceptance rate. The difficulty is in the serial correlation in the draws of h_t from one iteration to the next.

Shephard and Pitt (1997) pointed out that there is no reason, in principle, why the latent variables h_t need to be drawn one at a time. The conditional posterior distribution of a subset $\{h_t, \ldots, h_{t+k}\}$ of $\{h_t\}$, conditional on $\{h_s, s < t, s > t + k\}$, $\{y_t\}$, and $(\beta, \sigma_\eta^2, \phi)$ depends only on h_{t-1}, h_{t+k+1}, $(y_t, \ldots, y_{t+k})$ and $(\beta, \sigma_\eta^2, \phi)$. Shephard and Pitt derived a multivariate Gaussian proposal distribution for $\{h_t, \ldots, h_{t+k}\}$ in the same way as the univariate proposal distribution for h_t. As all of the $\{h_t\}$ are blocked into subsets $\{h_t, \ldots, h_{t+k}\}$ that are fewer in number but larger in size the conditional correlation between the blocks diminishes, and this decreases the serial correlation in the MCMC algorithm. On the other hand, the increasing dimension of each block means that the Gaussian proposal distribution is less efficient, and the proportion of draws rejected in each Metropolis–Hastings step increases. Shephard and Pitt discussed methods for choosing the number of subsets that achieves an overall performance near the best attainable. In their exchange rate example 10 or 20 subsets of $\{h_t\}$, with 50 to 100 latent variables in each subset, provided the most efficient algorithm. The relative numerical efficiency of ϕ was about 0.020 for this choice.

Kim, Shephard and Chib (1998) provided yet another method for sampling from the posterior distribution. They began by noting that nothing is lost by working with $\log(y_t^2) = \log(\beta) + h_t + \log \varepsilon_t^2$. The disturbance term has a log-$\chi^2(1)$ distribution. This is intractable, but can be well-approximated by a mixture of seven normal distributions. Conditional on the corresponding seven latent states, most of the posterior distribution, including the latent variables $\{h_t\}$, is jointly Gaussian, and the $\{h_t\}$ can therefore be marginalized analytically. Each iteration of the resulting MCMC algorithm provides values of the parameter vector $(\beta, \sigma_\eta^2, \phi)$; given these values and the data, it is straightforward to draw $\{h_t\}$ from the Gaussian conditional posterior distribution. The algorithm is very efficient, there now being seven rather than T latent variables. The unique invariant distribution of the Markov chain is that of the posterior distribution based on the mixture approximation rather than the actual model. Conditional on the drawn values of the $\{h_t\}$ it is easy to evaluate the ratio of the true to the approximate posterior distribution. The approximate posterior distribution may thus be regarded as the source distribution in an importance sampling algorithm, and posterior moments can be computed by means of reweighting as discussed in Section 3.1.3.

Bos, Mahieu and van Dijk (2000) provided an interesting application of stochastic volatility and competing models in a decision-theoretic prediction setting. The decision problem is hedging holdings of a foreign currency against fluctuations in the relevant exchange rate. The dollar value of a unit of foreign currency holdings in period t is the exchange rate S_t. If held to period $t+1$ the dollar value of these holdings will be S_{t+1}. Alternatively, at time t the unit of foreign currency may be exchanged for a contract for forward delivery of F_t dollars in period $t+1$. By covered interest parity, $F_t = S_t \exp(r^h_{t,t+1} - r^f_{t,t+1})$, where $r^h_{t,\tau}$ and $r^f_{t,\tau}$ are the risk-free home and foreign currency interest rates, respectively, each at time t with a maturity of τ periods. Bos et al. considered optimal hedging strategy in this context, corresponding to a CRRA utility function $U(W_t) = (W_t^\gamma - 1)/\gamma$. Initial wealth is $W_t = S_t$, and the fraction H_t is hedged by purchasing contracts for forward delivery of dollars. Taking advantage of the scale-invariance of $U(W_t)$, the decision problem is

$$\max_{H_t} \gamma^{-1} \bigl\langle E\bigl\{\bigl[(1-H_t)S_{t+1} + H_t F_t\bigr]/S_t \mid \Phi_t\bigr\}^\gamma - 1\bigr\rangle.$$

Bos et al. took $\Phi_t = \{S_{t-j}\ (j \geqslant 0)\}$ and constrained $H_t \in [0,1]$. It is sufficient to model the continuously compounded exchange rate return $s_t = \log(S_t/S_{t-1})$, because

$$\bigl[(1-H_t)S_{t+1} + H_t F_t\bigr]/S_t = (1-H_t)\exp(s_{t+1}) + H_t \exp\bigl(r_t^h - r_t^f\bigr).$$

The study considered eight alternative models, all special cases of the state space model

$$s_t = \mu_t + \varepsilon_t, \qquad \varepsilon_t \sim \bigl(0, \sigma^2_{\varepsilon,t}\bigr),$$
$$\mu_t = \rho\mu_{t-1} + \eta_t, \qquad \eta_t \overset{\text{iid}}{\sim} N\bigl(0, \sigma^2_\eta\bigr).$$

The two most competitive models are GARCH(1, 1)-t,

$$\sigma^2_{\varepsilon,t} = \omega + \delta\sigma^2_{\varepsilon,t-1} + \alpha\varepsilon^2_{t-1}, \qquad \varepsilon_t \sim t\bigl[0, (\nu-2)\sigma^2_{\varepsilon,t}, \nu\bigr],$$

and the stochastic volatility model

$$\sigma^2_{\varepsilon,t} = \mu_h + \phi\bigl(\sigma^2_{\varepsilon,t-1} - \mu_h\bigr) + \zeta_t, \qquad \zeta_t \sim N\bigl(0, \sigma^2_\zeta\bigr).$$

After assigning similar proper priors to the models, the study used MCMC to simulate from the posterior distribution of each model. The algorithm for GARCH(1, 1)-t copes with the Student-t distribution by data augmentation as proposed in Geweke (1993). Conditional on these latent variables the likelihood function has the same form as in the GARCH(1, 1) model. It can be evaluated directly, and Metropolis-within-Gibbs steps are used for ν and the block of parameters $(\sigma^2_\varepsilon, \delta, \alpha)$. The Kim, Shephard and Chib (1998) algorithm is used for the stochastic volatility model.

Bos et al. applied these models to the overnight hedging problem for the dollar and Deutschmark. They used daily data from January 1, 1982 through December 31, 1997 for inference, and the period from January 1, 1998 through December 31, 1999 to evaluate optimal hedging performance using each model. The log-Bayes factor in favor of the stochastic volatility model is about 15. (The log-Bayes factors in favor of the

Table 5
Realized utility for alternative hedging strategies

	White noise	GARCH-t	Stoch. vol.	RW hedge
Marginal likelihood	−4305.9	−4043.4	−4028.5	
$\sum U_t$ ($\gamma = -10$)	−2.24	−0.01	3.10	3.35
$\sum U_t$ ($\gamma = -2$)	0.23	7.42	7.69	6.73
$\sum U_t$ ($\gamma = 0$)	5.66	7.40	9.60	7.56

stochastic volatility model, against the six models other than GARCH(1, 1)-t considered, are all over 100.) Given the output of the posterior simulators, solving the optimal hedging problem is a simple and straightforward calculus problem, as described in Section 3.3.1. The performance of any sequence of hedging decisions $\{H_t\}$ over the period $T+1, \ldots, T+F$ can be evaluated by the ex post realized utility

$$\sum_{t=T+1}^{T+F} U_t = \gamma^{-1} \sum_{t=T+1}^{T+F} \bigl[(1-H_t)S_{t+1} + H_t F_t\bigr]/S_t.$$

The article undertook this exercise for all of the models considered as well as some benchmark *ad hoc* decision rules. In addition to the GARCH(1, 1)-t and stochastic volatility models, the exercise included a benchmark model in which the exchange return s_t is Gaussian white noise. The best-performing *ad hoc* decision rule is the random walk strategy, which sets the hedge ratio to one (zero) if the foreign currency depreciated (appreciated) in the previous period. The comparisons are given in Table 5.

The stochastic volatility model leads to higher realized utility than does the GARCH-t model in all cases, and it outperforms the random walk hedge model except for the most risk-averse utility function. Hedging strategies based on the white noise model are always inferior. Model combination would place almost all weight on the stochastic volatility model, given the Bayes factors, and so the decision based on model combination, discussed in Sections 2.4.3 and 3.3.2, leads to the best outcome.

6. Practical experience with Bayesian forecasts

This section describes two long-term experiences with Bayesian forecasting: The Federal Reserve Bank of Minneapolis national forecasting project, and The Iowa Economic Forecast produced by The University of Iowa Institute for Economic Research. This is certainly not an exhaustive treatment of the production usage of Bayesian forecasting methods; we describe these experiences because they are well documented [Litterman (1986), McNees (1986), Whiteman (1996)] and because we have personal knowledge of each.

6.1. National BVAR forecasts: The Federal Reserve Bank of Minneapolis

Litterman's thesis work at the University of Minnesota ("the U") was coincident with his employment as a research assistant in the Research Department at the Federal Reserve Bank of Minneapolis (the "Bank"). In 1978 and 1979, he wrote a computer program, "Predict" to carry out the calculations described in Section 4. At the same time, Thomas Doan, also a graduate student at the U and likewise a research assistant at the Bank, was writing code to carry out regression, ARIMA, and other calculations for staff economists. Thomas Turner, a staff economist at the Bank, had modified a program written by Christopher Sims, "Spectre", to incorporate regression calculations using complex arithmetic to facilitate frequency-domain treatment of serial correlation. By the summer of 1979, Doan had collected his own routines in a flexible shell and incorporated the features of Spectre and Predict (in most cases completely recoding their routines) to produce the program RATS (for "Regression Analysis of Time Series"). Indeed, Litterman (1979) indicates that some of the calculations for his paper were carried out in RATS. The program subsequently became a successful Doan-Litterman commercial venture, and did much to facilitate the adoption of BVAR methods throughout academics and business.

It was in fact Litterman himself who was responsible for the Bank's focus on BVAR forecasts. He had left Minnesota in 1979 to take a position as Assistant Professor of Economics at M.I.T., but was hired back to the Bank two years later. Based on work carried out while a graduate student and subsequently at M.I.T., in 1980 Litterman began issuing monthly forecasts using a six-variable BVAR of the type described in Section 4. The six variables were: real GNP, the GNP price deflator, real business fixed investment, the 3-month Treasury bill rate, the unemployment rate, and the money supply (M1). Upon his return to the Bank, the BVAR for these variables [described in Litterman (1986)] became known as the "Minneapolis Fed model".

In his description of five years of monthly experience forecasting with the BVAR model, Litterman (1986) notes that unlike his competition at the time – large, expensive commercial forecasts produced by the likes of Data Resources Inc. (DRI), Wharton Econometric Forecasting Associates (WEFA), and Chase – his forecasts were produced mechanically, without judgemental adjustment. The BVAR often produced forecasts very different from the commercial predictions, and Litterman notes that they were sometimes regarded by recipients (Litterman's mailing list of academics, which included both of us) as too "volatile" or "wild". Still, his procedure produced real time forecasts that were "at least competitive with the best forecasts commercially available" [Litterman (1986, p. 35)]. McNees's (1986) independent assessment, which also involved comparisons with an even broader collection of competitors was that Litterman's BVAR was "generally the most accurate or among the most accurate" for real GNP, the unemployment rate, and investment. The BVAR price forecasts, on the other hand, were among the least accurate.

Subsequent study by Litterman resulted in the addition of an exchange rate measure and stock prices that improved, at least experimentally, the performance of the model's price predictions. Other models were developed as well; Litterman (1984) describes a 46-variable monthly national forecasting model, while Amirizadeh and Todd (1984) describe a five-state model of the 9th Federal Reserve District (that of the Minneapolis Fed) involving 3 or 4 equations per state. Moreover, the models were used regularly in Bank discussions, and reports based on them appeared regularly in the Minneapolis Fed *Quarterly Review* [e.g., Litterman (1984), Litterman (1985)].

In 1986, Litterman left the Bank to go to Goldman–Sachs. This required dissolution of the Doan–Litterman joint venture, and Doan subsequently formed Estima, Inc. to further develop and market RATS. It also meant that forecast production fell to staff economists whose research interests were not necessarily focused on the further development of BVARs [e.g., Roberds and Todd (1987), Runkle (1988), Miller and Runkle (1989), Runkle (1989, 1990, 1991)]. This, together with the pain associated with explaining the inevitable forecast errors, caused enthusiasm for the BVAR effort at the Bank to wane over the ensuing half dozen years, and the last *Quarterly Review* "outlook" article based on a BVAR forecast appeared in 1992 [Runkle (1992)]. By the spring of 1993, the Bank's BVAR efforts were being overseen by a research assistant (albeit a quite capable one), and the authors of this paper were consulted by the leadership of the Bank's Research Department regarding what steps were required to ensure academic currency and reliability of the forecasting effort. The cost – our advice was to employ a staff economist whose research would be complementary to the production of forecasts – was regarded as too high given the configuration of economists in the department, and development of the forecasting model and procedures at the Bank effectively ceased.

Cutting-edge development of Bayesian forecasting models reappeared relatively soon within the Federal Reserve System. In 1995, Tao Zha, who had written a Minnesota thesis under the direction of Chris Sims, moved from the University of Saskatchewan to the Federal Reserve Bank of Atlanta, and began implementing the developments described in Sims and Zha (1998, 1999) to produce regular forecasts for internal briefing purposes. These efforts, which utilize the over-identified procedures described in Section 4.4, are described in Robertson and Tallman (1999a, 1999b) and Zha (1998), but there is no continuous public record of forecasts comparable to Litterman's "Five Years of Experience".

6.2. Regional BVAR forecasts: economic conditions in Iowa

In 1990, Whiteman became Director of the Institute for Economic Research at the University of Iowa. Previously, the Institute had published forecasts of general economic conditions and had produced tax revenue forecasts for internal use of the state's Department of Management by judgmentally adjusting the product of a large commercial forecaster. These forecasts had not been especially accurate and were costing the state tens of thousands of dollars each year. As a consequence, an "Iowa Economic Forecast" model was constructed based on BVAR technology, and forecasts using it have been issued continuously each quarter since March 1990.

The Iowa model consists of four linked VARs. Three of these involve income, real income, and employment, and are treated using mixed estimation and the priors outlined in Litterman (1979) and Doan, Litterman and Sims (1984). The fourth VAR, for predicting aggregate state tax revenue, is much smaller, and fully Bayesian predictive densities are produced from it under a diffuse prior.

The income and employment VARs involve variables that were of interest to the Iowa Forecasting Council, a group of academic and business economists that met quarterly to advise the Governor on economic conditions. The nominal income VAR includes total nonfarm income and four of its components: wage and salary disbursements, property income, transfers, and farm income. These five variables together with their national analogues, four lags of each, and a constant and seasonal dummy variables complete the specification of the model for the observables. The prior is Litterman's (1979) (recall specifications (61) and (62), with a generalization of the "other's weight" that embodies the notion that national variables are much more likely to be helpful in predicting Iowa variables than the converse. Details can be found in Whiteman (1996) and Otrok and Whiteman (1998). The real income VAR is constructed in parallel fashion after deflating each income variable by the GDP deflator.

The employment VAR is constructed similarly, using aggregate Iowa employment (nonfarm employment) together with the state's population and five components of employment: durable and nondurable goods manufacturing employment, and employment in services and wholesale and retail trade. National analogues of each are used for a total of 14 equations. Monthly data available from the U.S. Bureau of Labor Statistics and Iowa's Department of Workforce Development are aggregated to a quarterly basis. As in the income VAR, four lags, a constant, and seasonal dummies are included. The prior is very similar to the one employed in the income VARs.

The revenue VAR incorporates two variables: total personal income and total tax receipts (on a cash basis.) The small size was dictated by data availability at the time of the initial model construction: only seven years' of revenue data were available on a consistent accounting standard as of the beginning of 1990. Monthly data are aggregated to a quarterly basis; other variables include a constant and seasonal dummies. Until 1997, two lags were used; thereafter, four were employed. The prior is diffuse, as in (66).

Each quarter, the income and employment VARs are "estimated" (via mixed estimation), and [as in Litterman (1979) and Doan, Litterman and Sims (1984)] parameter estimates so obtained are used to produce forecasts using the chain rule of forecasting for horizons of 12 quarters. Measures of uncertainty at each horizon are calculated each quarter from a pseudo-real time forecasting experiment [recall the description of Litterman's (1979) experiment] over the 40 quarters immediately prior to the end of the sample. Forecasts and uncertainty measures are published in the "Iowa Economic Forecast".

Production of the revenue forecasts involves normal-Wishart sampling. In particular, each quarter, the Wishart distribution is sampled repeatedly for innovation covariance matrices; using each such sampled covariance matrix, a conditionally Gaussian parameter vector and a sequence of Gaussian errors is drawn and used to seed a dynamic

Table 6
Iowa revenue growth forecasts

Loss factor	FY05	FY06	FY07	FY08
1	1.9	4.4	3.3	3.6
2	1.0	3.5	2.5	2.9
3	0.6	3.0	2.0	2.4
4	0.3	2.7	1.7	2.1
5	0.0	2.5	1.5	1.9

simulation of the VAR. These quarterly results are aggregated to annual figures and used to produce graphs of predictive densities and distribution functions. Additionally, asymmetric linear loss forecasts [see Equation (29)] are produced. As noted above, this amounts to reporting quantiles of the predictive distribution. In the notation of (29), reports are for integer "loss factors" (ratios $(1-q)/q$); an example from July 2004 is given in Table 6.

The forecasts produced by the income, employment, and revenue VARs are discussed by the Iowa Council of Economic Advisors (which replaced the Iowa Economic Forecast Council in 2004) and also the Revenue Estimating Conference (REC). The latter body consists of three individuals, of whom two are appointed by the Governor and the third is agreed to by the other two. It makes the official state revenue forecast using whatever information it chooses to consider. Regarding the use and interpretation of a predictive density forecast by state policymakers, one of the members of the REC during the 1990s, Director of the Department of Management, Gretchen Tegler remarked, "It lets the decision-maker choose how certain they want to be" [Cedar Rapids Gazette (2004)]. By law, the official estimate is binding in the sense that the governor cannot propose, and the legislature may not pass, expenditure bills that exceed 99% of revenue predicted to be available in the relevant fiscal year. The estimate is made by December 15 of each year, and conditions the Governor's "State of the State" address in early January, and the legislative session that runs from January to May.

Whiteman (1996) reports on five years of experience with the procedures. Although there are not competitive forecasts available, he compares forecasting results to historical data revisions and expectations of policy makers. During the period 1990–1994, personal income in the state ranged from about \$50 billion to \$60 billion. Root mean squared one-step ahead forecast errors relative to first releases of the data averaged \$1 billion. The data themselves were only marginally more accurate: root mean squared revisions from first release to second release averaged \$864 million. The revenue predictions made for the on-the-run fiscal year prior to the December REC meeting had root mean squared errors of 2%. Tegler's assessment: "If you are within 2 percent, you are phenomenal" [Cedar Rapids Gazette (2004)]. Subsequent difficulties in forecasting during fiscal years 2000 and 2001 (in the aftermath of a steep stock market decline and during an unusual national recession), which were widespread across the country in fact led to a reexamination of forecasting methods in the state in 2003–2004. The outcome of this was a reaffirmation of official faith in the approach, perhaps reflecting former State Comptroller Marvin Seldon's comment at the inception of BVAR use in Iowa revenue forecasting: "If you can find a revenue forecaster who can get you within 3 percent, keep him" [Seldon (1990)].

References

Aguilar, O., West, M. (2000). "Bayesian dynamic factor models and portfolio allocation". Journal of Business and Economic Statistics 18, 338–357.

Albert, J.H., Chib, S. (1993). "Bayes inference via Gibbs sampling of autoregressive time-series subject to Markov mean and variance shifts". Journal of Business and Economic Statistics 11, 1–15.

Amirizadeh, H., Todd, R. (1984). "More growth ahead for ninth district states". Federal Reserve Bank of Minneapolis Quarterly Review 4, 8–17.

Amisano, G., Serati, M. (1999). "Forecasting cointegrated series with BVAR models". Journal of Forecasting 18, 463–476.

Barnard, G.A. (1963). "New methods of quality control". Journal of the Royal Statistical Society Series A 126, 255–259.

Barndorff-Nielsen, O.E., Schou, G. (1973). "On the reparameterization of autoregressive models by partial autocorrelations". Journal of Multivariate Analysis 3, 408–419.

Barnett, G., Kohn, R., Sheather, S. (1996). "Bayesian estimation of an autoregressive model using Markov chain Monte Carlo". Journal of Econometrics 74, 237–254.

Bates, J.M., Granger, C.W.J. (1969). "The combination of forecasts". Operations Research 20, 451–468.

Bayarri, M.J., Berger, J.O. (1998). "Quantifying surprise in the data and model verification". In: Berger, J.O., Bernardo, J.M., Dawid, A.P., Lindley, D.V., Smith, A.F.M. (Eds.), Bayesian Statistics, vol. 6. Oxford University Press, Oxford, pp. 53–82.

Berger, J.O., Delampady, M. (1987). "Testing precise hypotheses". Statistical Science 2, 317–352.

Bernardo, J.M., Smith, A.F.M. (1994). Bayesian Theory. Wiley, New York.

Bos, C.S., Mahieu, R.J., van Dijk, H.K. (2000). "Daily exchange rate behaviour and hedging of currency risk". Journal of Applied Econometrics 15, 671–696.

Box, G.E.P. (1980). "Sampling and Bayes inference in scientific modeling and robustness". Journal of the Royal Statistical Society Series A 143, 383–430.

Box, G.E.P., Jenkins, G.M. (1976). Time Series Analysis, Forecasting and Control. Holden-Day, San Francisco.

Brav, A. (2000). "Inference in long-horizon event studies: A Bayesian approach with application to initial public offerings". The Journal of Finance 55, 1979–2016.

Carter, C.K., Kohn, R. (1994). "On Gibbs sampling for state-space models". Biometrika 81, 541–553.

Carter, C.K., Kohn, R. (1996). "Markov chain Monte Carlo in conditionally Gaussian state space models". Biometrika 83, 589–601.

Cedar Rapids Gazette. (2004). "Rain or shine? Professor forecasts funding," Sunday, February 1.

Chatfield, C. (1976). "Discussion on the paper by Professor Harrison and Mr. Stevens". Journal of the Royal Statistical Society. Series B (Methodological) 38 (3), 231–232.

Chatfield, C. (1993). "Calculating interval forecasts". Journal of Business and Economic Statistics 11, 121–135.

Chatfield, C. (1995). "Model uncertainty, data mining, and statistical inference". Journal of the Royal Statistical Society Series A 158, 419–468.

Chib, S. (1995). "Marginal likelihood from the Gibbs output". Journal of the American Statistical Association 90, 1313–1321.

Chib, S. (1996). "Calculating posterior distributions and modal estimates in Markov mixture models". Journal of Econometrics 75, 79–97.

Chib, S., Greenberg, E. (1994). "Bayes inference in regression models with ARMA(p, q) errors". Journal of Econometrics 64, 183–206.
Chib, S., Greenberg, E. (1995). "Understanding the Metropolis–Hastings algorithm". The American Statistician 49, 327–335.
Chib, S., Jeliazkov, J. (2001). "Marginal likelihood from the Metropolis–Hastings output". Journal of the American Statistical Association 96, 270–281.
Christoffersen, P.F. (1998). "Evaluating interval forecasts". International Economic Review 39, 841–862.
Chulani, S., Boehm, B., Steece, B. (1999). "Bayesian analysis of empirical software engineering cost models". IEEE Transactions on Software Engineering 25, 573–583.
Clemen, R.T. (1989). "Combining forecasts – a review and annotated bibliography". International Journal of Forecasting 5, 559–583.
Cogley, T., Morozov, S., Sargent, T. (2005). "Bayesian fan charts for U.K. inflation: Forecasting and sources of uncertainty in an evolving monetary system," Journal of Economic Dynamics and Control, in press.
Dawid, A.P. (1984). "Statistical theory: The prequential approach". Journal of the Royal Statistical Society Series A 147, 278–292.
DeJong, D.N., Ingram, B.F., Whiteman, C.H. (2000). "A Bayesian approach to dynamic macroeconomics". Journal of Econometrics 98, 203–223.
DeJong, P., Shephard, N. (1995). "The simulation smoother for time series models". Biometrika 82, 339–350.
Diebold, F.X. (1998). Elements of Forecasting. South-Western College Publishing, Cincinnati.
Doan, T., Litterman, R.B., Sims, C.A. (1984). "Forecasting and conditional projection using realistic prior distributions". Econometric Reviews 3, 1–100.
Draper, D. (1995). "Assessment and propagation of model uncertainty". Journal of the Royal Statistical Society Series B 57, 45–97.
Drèze, J.H. (1977). "Bayesian regression analysis using poly-t densities". Journal of Econometrics 6, 329–354.
Drèze, J.H., Morales, J.A. (1976). "Bayesian full information analysis of simultaneous equations". Journal of the American Statistical Association 71, 919–923.
Drèze, J.H., Richard, J.F. (1983). "Bayesian analysis of simultaneous equation systems". In: Griliches, Z., Intrilligator, M.D. (Eds.), Handbook of Econometrics, vol. I. North-Holland, Amsterdam, pp. 517–598.
Edwards, W., Lindman, H., Savage, L.J. (1963). "Bayesian statistical inference for psychological research". Psychological Review 70, 193–242.
Engle, R.F., Yoo, B.S. (1987). "Forecasting and testing in cointegrated systems". Journal of Econometrics 35, 143–159.
Fair, R.C. (1980). "Estimating the expected predictive accuracy of econometric models". International Economic Review 21, 355–378.
Fruhwirth-Schnatter, S. (1994). "Data augmentation and dynamic linear models". Journal of Time Series Analysis 15, 183–202.
Garcia-Ferer, A., Highfield, R.A., Palm, F., Zellner, A. (1987). "Macroeconomic forecasting using pooled international data". Journal of Business and Economic Statistics 5, 53–67.
Geisel, M.S. (1975). "Bayesian comparison of simple macroeconomic models". In: Fienberg, S.E., Zellner, A. (Eds.), Studies in Bayesian Econometrics and Statistics: In Honor of Leonard J. Savage. North-Holland, Amsterdam, pp. 227–256.
Geisser, S. (1993). Predictive Inference: An Introduction. Chapman and Hall, London.
Gelfand, A.E., Dey, D.K. (1994). "Bayesian model choice: Asymptotics and exact calculations". Journal of the Royal Statistical Society Series B 56, 501–514.
Gelfand, A.E., Smith, A.F.M. (1990). "Sampling based approaches to calculating marginal densities". Journal of the American Statistical Association 85, 398–409.
Gelman, A. (2003). "A Bayesian formulation of exploratory data analysis and goodness-of-fit testing". International Statistical Review 71, 369–382.
Gelman, A., Carlin, J.B., Stern, H.S., Rubin, D.B. (1995). Bayesian Data Analysis. Chapman and Hall, London.

Geman, S., Geman, D. (1984). "Stochastic relaxation, Gibbs distributions and the Bayesian restoration of images". IEEE Transactions on Pattern Analysis and Machine Intelligence 6, 721–741.
George, E., McCulloch, R.E. (1993). "Variable selection via Gibbs sampling". Journal of the American Statistical Association 99, 881–889.
Gerlach, R., Carter, C., Kohn, R. (2000). "Efficient Bayesian inference for dynamic mixture models". Journal of the American Statistical Association 95, 819–828.
Geweke, J. (1988). "Antithetic acceleration of Monte Carlo integration in Bayesian inference". Journal of Econometrics 38, 73–90.
Geweke, J. (1989a). "Bayesian inference in econometric models using Monte Carlo integration". Econometrica 57, 1317–1340.
Geweke, J. (1989b). "Exact predictive densities in linear models with ARCH disturbances". Journal of Econometrics 40, 63–86.
Geweke, J. (1991). "Generic, algorithmic approaches to Monte Carlo integration in Bayesian inference". Contemporary Mathematics 115, 117–135.
Geweke, J. (1993). "Bayesian treatment of the independent Student-*t* linear model". Journal of Applied Econometrics 8, S19–S40.
Geweke, J. (1996a). "Monte Carlo simulation and numerical integration". In: Amman, H., Kendrick, D., Rust, J. (Eds.), Handbook of Computational Economics. North-Holland, Amsterdam, pp. 731–800.
Geweke, J. (1996b). "Variable selection and model comparison in regression". In: Berger, J.O., Bernardo, J.M., Dawid, A.P., Smith, A.F.M. (Eds.), Bayesian Statistics, vol. 5. Oxford University Press, Oxford, pp. 609–620.
Geweke, J. (1998). "Simulation methods for model criticism and robustness analysis". In: Berger, J.O., Bernardo, J.M., Dawid, A.P., Smith, A.F.M. (Eds.), Bayesian Statistics, vol. 6. Oxford University Press, Oxford, pp. 275–299.
Geweke, J. (1999). "Using simulation methods for Bayesian econometric models: Inference, development and communication". Econometric Reviews 18, 1–126.
Geweke, J. (2000). "Bayesian communication: The BACC system". In: 2000 Proceedings of the Section on Bayesian Statistical Sciences of the American Statistical Association, pp. 40–49.
Geweke, J. (2005). Contemporary Bayesian Econometrics and Statistics. Wiley, New York.
Geweke, J., McCausland, W. (2001). "Bayesian specification analysis in econometrics". American Journal of Agricultural Economics 83, 1181–1186.
Geweke, J., Zhou, G. (1996). "Measuring the pricing error of the arbitrage pricing theory". The Review of Financial Studies 9, 557–587.
Gilks, W.R., Richardson, S., Spiegelhaldter, D.J. (1996). Markov Chain Monte Carlo in Practice. Chapman and Hall, London.
Good, I.J. (1956). "The surprise index for the multivariate normal distribution". Annals of Mathematical Statistics 27, 1130–1135.
Granger, C.W.J. (1986). "Comment" (on McNees, 1986). Journal of Business and Economic Statistics 4, 16–17.
Granger, C.W.J. (1989). "Invited review: Combining forecasts – twenty years later". Journal of Forecasting 8, 167–173.
Granger, C.W.J., Joyeux, R. (1980). "An introduction to long memory time series models and fractional differencing". Journal of Time Series Analysis 1, 15–29.
Granger, C.W.J., Ramanathan, R. (1984). "Improved methods of combining forecasts". Journal of Forecasting 3, 197–204.
Greene, W.H. (2003). Econometric Analysis, fifth ed. Prentice-Hall, Upper Saddle River, NJ.
Hammersly, J.M., Handscomb, D.C. (1964). Monte Carlo Methods. Methuen and Company, London.
Hammersly, J.M., Morton, K.H. (1956). "A new Monte Carlo technique: Antithetic variates". Proceedings of the Cambridge Philosophical Society 52, 449–474.
Harrison, P.J., Stevens, C.F. (1976). "Bayesian forecasting". Journal of the Royal Statistical Society Series B (Methodological) 38 (3), 205–247.

Haslett, J., Raftery, A.E. (1989). "Space-time modeling with long-memory dependence: Assessing Ireland's wind power resource". Applied Statistics 38, 1–50.

Hastings, W.K. (1970). "Monte Carlo sampling methods using Markov chains and their applications". Biometrika 57, 97–109.

Heckerman, D. (1997). "Bayesian networks for data mining". Data Mining and Knowledge Discovery 1, 79–119.

Hildreth, C. (1963). "Bayesian statisticians and remote clients". Econometrica 31, 422–438.

Hoerl, A.E., Kennard, R.W. (1970). "Ridge regression: Biased estimation for nonorthogonal problems". Technometrics 12, 55–67.

Hoeting, J.A., Madigan, D., Raftery, A.E., Volinsky, C.T. (1999). "Bayesian model averaging: A tutorial". Statistical Science 14, 382–401.

Hosking, J.R.M. (1981). "Fractional differencing". Biometrika 68, 165–176.

Huerta, G., West, M. (1999). "Priors and component structures in autoregressive time series models". Journal of the Royal Statistical Society Series B 61, 881–899.

Hull, J., White, A. (1987). "The pricing of options on assets with stochastic volatilities". Journal of Finance 42, 281–300.

Ingram, B.F., Whiteman, C.H. (1994). "Supplanting the Minnesota prior – forecasting macroeconomic time series using real business-cycle model priors". Journal of Monetary Economics 34, 497–510.

Iowa Economic Forecast, produced quarterly by the Institute for Economic Research in the Tippie College of Business at The University of Iowa. Available at www.biz.uiowa.edu/econ/econinst.

Jacquier, C., Polson, N.G., Rossi, P.E. (1994). "Bayesian analysis of stochastic volatility models". Journal of Business and Economic Statistics 12, 371–389.

James, W., Stein, C. (1961). "Estimation with quadratic loss". In: Proceedings of the Fourth Berkeley Symposium on Mathematical Statistics and Probability. University of California Press, Berkeley, pp. 361–379.

Jeffreys, H. (1939). Theory of Probability. Clarendon Press, Oxford.

Johansen, S. (1988). "Statistical analysis of cointegration vectors". Journal of Economic Dynamics and Control 12, 231–254.

Kadiyala, K.R., Karlsson, S. (1993). "Forecasting with generalized Bayesian vector autoregressions". Journal of Forecasting 12, 365–378.

Kadiyala, K.R., Karlsson, S. (1997). "Numerical methods for estimation and inference in Bayesian VAR-models". Journal of Applied Econometrics 12, 99–132.

Kass, R.E., Raftery, A.E. (1996). "Bayes factors". Journal of the American Statistical Association 90, 773–795.

Kim, S., Shephard, N., Chib, S. (1998). "Stochastic volatility: Likelihood inference and comparison with ARCH models". Review of Economic Studies 64, 361–393.

Kling, J.L. (1987). "Predicting the turning points of business and economic time series". Journal of Business 60, 201–238.

Kling, J.L., Bessler, D.A. (1989). "Calibration-based predictive distributions: An application of prequential analysis to interest rates, money, prices and output". Journal of Business 62, 477–499.

Kloek, T., van Dijk, H.K. (1978). "Bayesian estimates of equation system parameters: An application of integration by Monte Carlo". Econometrica 46, 1–20.

Koop, G. (2001). "Bayesian inference in models based on equilibrium search theory". Journal of Econometrics 102, 311–338.

Koop, G. (2003). Bayesian Econometrics. Wiley, Chichester.

Koop, G., Ley, E., Osiewalski, J., Steel, M.F.J. (1997). "Bayesian analysis of long memory and persistence using ARFIMA models". Journal of Econometrics 76, 149–169.

Lancaster, T. (2004). An Introduction to Modern Bayesian Econometrics. Blackwell, Malden, MA.

Leamer, E.E. (1972). "A class of informative priors and distributed lag analysis". Econometrica 40, 1059–1081.

Leamer, E.E. (1978). Specification Searches. Wiley, New York.

Lesage, J.P. (1990). "A comparison of the forecasting ability of ECM and VAR models". The Review of Economics and Statistics 72, 664–671.

Lindley, D., Smith, A.F.M. (1972). "Bayes estimates for the linear model". Journal of the Royal Statistical Society Series B 34, 1–41.
Litterman, R.B. (1979). "Techniques of forecasting using vector autoregressions". Working Paper 115, Federal Reserve Bank of Minneapolis.
Litterman, R.B. (1980). "A Bayesian procedure for forecasting with vector autoregressions". Working Paper, Massachusetts Institute of Technology.
Litterman, R.B. (1984). "Above average national growth in 1985 and 1986". Federal Reserve Bank of Minneapolis Quarterly Review.
Litterman, R.B. (1985). "How monetary policy in 1985 affects the outlook". Federal Reserve Bank of Minneapolis Quarterly Review.
Litterman, R.B. (1986). "Forecasting with Bayesian vector autoregressions – 5 years of experience". Journal of Business and Economic Statistics 4, 25–38.
Maddala, G.S. (1977). Econometrics. McGraw-Hill, New York.
Marriott, J., Ravishanker, N., Gelfand, A., Pai, J. (1996). "Bayesian analysis of ARMA processes: Complete sampling-based inference under exact likelihoods". In: Barry, D.A., Chaloner, K.M., Geweke, J. (Eds.), Bayesian Analysis in Econometrics and Statistics: Essays in Honor of Arnold Zellner. Wiley, New York, pp. 243–256.
McNees, S.K. (1975). "An evaluation of economic forecasts". New England Economic Review, 3–39.
McNees, S.K. (1986). "Forecasting accuracy of alternative techniques: A comparison of U.S. macroeconomic forecasts". Journal of Business and Economic Statistics 4, 5–15.
Melino, A., Turnbull, S. (1990). "Pricing foreign currency options with stochastic volatility". Journal of Econometrics 45, 7–39.
Meng, X.L. (1994). "Posterior predictive p-values". Annals of Statistics 22, 1142–1160.
Meng, X.L., Wong, W.H. (1996). "Simulating ratios of normalizing constants via a simple identity: A theoretical exploration". Statistica Sinica 6, 831–860.
Metropolis, N., Rosenbluth, A.W., Rosenbluth, M.N., Teller, A.H., Teller, E. (1953). "Equation of state calculations by fast computing machines". The Journal of Chemical Physics 21, 1087–1092.
Miller, P.J., Runkle, D.E. (1989). "The U.S. economy in 1989 and 1990: Walking a fine line". Federal Reserve Bank of Minneapolis Quarterly Review.
Min, C.K., Zellner, A. (1993). "Bayesian and non-Bayesian methods for combining models and forecasts with applications to forecasting international growth rates". Journal of Econometrics 56, 89–118.
Monahan, J.F. (1983). "Fully Bayesian analysis of ARMA time series models". Journal of Econometrics 21, 307–331.
Monahan, J.F. (1984). "A note on enforcing stationarity in autoregressive moving average models". Biometrika 71, 403–404.
Newbold, P. (1974). "The exact likelihood for a mixed autoregressive moving average process". Biometrika 61, 423–426.
Otrok, C., Whiteman, C.H. (1998). "What to do when the crystal ball is cloudy: Conditional and unconditional forecasting in Iowa". Proceedings of the National Tax Association, 326–334.
Pai, J.S., Ravishanker, N. (1996). "Bayesian modelling of ARFIMA processes by Markov chain Monte Carlo methods". Journal of Forecasting 15, 63–82.
Palm, F.C., Zellner, A. (1992). "To combine or not to combine – Issues of combining forecasts". Journal of Forecasting 11, 687–701.
Peskun, P.H. (1973). "Optimum Monte-Carlo sampling using Markov chains". Biometrika 60, 607–612.
Petridis, V., Kehagias, A., Petrou, L., Bakirtzis, A., Kiartzis, S., Panagiotou, H., Maslaris, N. (2001). "A Bayesian multiple models combination method for time series prediction". Journal of Intelligent and Robotic Systems 31, 69–89.
Plackett, R.L. (1950). "Some theorems in least squares". Biometrica 37, 149–157.
Pole, A., West, M., Harrison, J. (1994). Applied Bayesian Forecasting and Time Series Analysis. Chapman and Hall, London.
Porter-Hudak, S. (1982). "Long-term memory modelling – a simplified spectral approach". Ph.D. thesis, University of Wisconsin, Unpublished.

RATS, computer program available from Estima, 1800 Sherman Ave., Suite 612, Evanston, IL 60201.
Ravishanker, N., Ray, B.K. (1997a). "Bayesian analysis of vector ARMA models using Gibbs sampling". Journal of Forecasting 16, 177–194.
Ravishanker, N., Ray, B.K. (1997b). "Bayesian analysis of vector ARFIMA process". Australian Journal of Statistics 39, 295–311.
Ravishanker, N., Ray, B.K. (2002). "Bayesian prediction for vector ARFIMA processes". International Journal of Forecasting 18, 207–214.
Ripley, R.D. (1987). Stochastic Simulation. Wiley, New York.
Roberds W., Todd R. (1987). "Forecasting and modelling the U.S. economy in 1986–1988". Federal Reserve Bank of Minneapolis Quarterly Review.
Roberts, H.V. (1965). "Probabilistic prediction". Journal of the American Statistical Association 60, 50–62.
Robertson, J.C., Tallman, E.W. (1999a). "Vector autoregressions: Forecasting and reality". Federal Reserve Bank of Atlanta Economic Review 84 (First Quarter), 4–18.
Robertson, J.C., Tallman, E.W. (1999b). "Improving forecasts of the Federal funds rate in a policy model". Journal of Business and Economic Statistics 19, 324–930.
Robertson, J.C., Tallman, E.W., Whiteman, C.H. (2005). "Forecasting using relative entropy". Journal of Money, Credit, and Banking 37, 383–401.
Rosenblatt, M. (1952). "Remarks on a multivariate transformation". Annals of Mathematical Statistics 23, 470–472.
Rothenberg, T.J. (1963). "A Bayesian analysis of simultaneous equation systems". Report 6315, Econometric Institute, Netherlands School of Economics, Rotterdam.
Rubin, D.B. (1984). "Bayesianly justifiable and relevant frequency calculations for the applied statistician". Annals of Statistics 12, 1151–1172.
Runkle, D.E. (1988). "Why no crunch from the crash?". Federal Reserve Bank of Minneapolis Quarterly Review.
Runkle, D.E. (1989). "The U.S. economy in 1990 and 1991: Continued expansion likely". Federal Reserve Bank of Minneapolis Quarterly Review.
Runkle, D.E. (1990). "Bad news from a forecasting model of the U.S. economy". Federal Reserve Bank of Minneapolis Quarterly Review.
Runkle, D.E. (1991). "A bleak outlook for the U.S. economy". Federal Reserve Bank of Minneapolis Quarterly Review.
Runkle, D.E. (1992). "No relief in sight for the U.S. economy". Federal Reserve Bank of Minneapolis Quarterly Review.
Schotman, P., van Dijk, H.K. (1991). "A Bayesian analysis of the unit root in real exchange rates". Journal of Econometrics 49, 195–238.
Seldon, M. (1990). Personal communication to Whiteman.
Shao, J. (1989). "Monte Carlo approximations in Bayesian decision theory". Journal of the American Statistical Association 84, 727–732.
Shephard, N., Pitt, M.K. (1997). "Likelihood analysis of non-Gaussian measurement time series". Biometrika 84, 653–667.
Shiller, R.J. (1973). "A distributed lag estimator derived from smoothness priors". Econometrica 41, 775–788.
Shoesmith, G.L. (1995). "Multiple cointegrating vectors, error correction, and forecasting with Litterman's model". International Journal of Forecasting 11, 557–567.
Sims, C.A. (1974). "Distributed lags". In: Intrilligator, M.D., Kendrick, P.A. (Eds.), Frontiers of Quantitative Economics, vol. II. North-Holland, Amsterdam, pp. 239–332.
Sims, C.A. (1980). "Macroeconomics and reality". Econometrica 48, 1–48.
Sims, C.A. (1992). "A nine-variable probabilistic macroeconomic forecasting model". In: Stock, J.H., Watson, M.W. (Eds.), Business Cycles, Indicators, and Forecasting. University of Chicago Press, Chicago.
Sims, C.A., Zha, T.A. (1998). "Bayesian methods for dynamic multivariate models". International Economic Review 39, 949–968.
Sims, C.A., Zha, T.A. (1999). "Error bands for impulse responses". Econometrica 67, 1113–1155.

Smith, A.F.M. (1973). "A general Bayesian linear model". Journal of the Royal Statistical Society Series B 35, 67–75.

Smyth, D.J. (1983). "Short-run macroeconomic forecasting: The OECD performance". Journal of Forecasting 2, 37–49.

Sowell, F. (1992a). "Maximum likelihood estimation of stationary univariate fractionally integrated models". Journal of Econometrics 53, 165–188.

Sowell, F. (1992b). "Modeling long-run behavior with the fractional ARIMA model". Journal of Monetary Economics 29, 277–302.

Stein, C.M. (1974). "Multiple regression". In: Olkin, I. (Ed.), Contributions to Probability and Statistics: Essays in Honor of Harold Hotelling. Stanford University Press, Stanford.

Tanner, M.A., Wong, H.W. (1987). "The calculation of posterior distributions by data augmentation". Journal of the American Statistical Association 82, 528–540.

Tauchen, G., Pitts, M. (1983). "The price–variability–volume relationship on speculative markets". Econometrica 51, 485–505.

Tay, A.S., Wallis, K.F. (2000). "Density forecasting: A survey". Journal of Forecasting 19, 235–254.

Taylor, S. (1986). Modelling Financial Time Series. Wiley, New York.

Theil, H. (1963). "On the use of incomplete prior information in regression analysis". Journal of the American Statistical Association 58, 401–414.

Thompson, P.A. (1984). "Bayesian multiperiod prediction: Forecasting with graphics". Ph.D. thesis, University of Wisconsin, Unpublished.

Thompson, P.A., Miller, R.B. (1986). "Sampling the future: A Bayesian approach to forecasting from univariate time series models". Journal of Business and Economic Statistics 4, 427–436.

Tierney, L. (1994). "Markov chains for exploring posterior distributions". Annals of Statistics 22, 1701–1762.

Tobias, J.L. (2001). "Forecasting output growth rates and median output growth rates: A hierarchical Bayesian approach". Journal of Forecasting 20, 297–314.

Villani, M. (2001). "Bayesian prediction with cointegrated vector autoregressions". International Journal of Forecasting 17, 585–605.

Waggoner, D.F., Zha, T. (1999). "Conditional forecasts in dynamic multivariate models". Review of Economics and Statistics 81, 639–651.

Wecker, W. (1979). "Predicting the turning points of a time series". Journal of Business 52, 35–50.

Weiss, A.A. (1996). "Estimating time series models using the relevant cost function". Journal of Applied Econometrics 11, 539–560.

West, M. (1995). "Bayesian inference in cyclical component dynamic linear models". Journal of the American Statistical Association 90, 1301–1312.

West, M., Harrison, J. (1997). Bayesian Forecasting and Dynamic Models, second ed. Springer, New York.

Whiteman, C.H. (1996). "Bayesian prediction under asymmetric linear loss: Forecasting state tax revenues in Iowa". In: Johnson, W.O., Lee, J.C., Zellner, A. (Eds.), Forecasting, Prediction and Modeling in Statistics and Econometrics, Bayesian and non-Bayesian Approaches. Springer, New York.

Winkler, R.L. (1981). "Combining probability distributions from dependent information sources". Management Science 27, 479–488.

Zellner, A. (1971). An Introduction to Bayesian Inference in Econometrics. Wiley, New York.

Zellner, A. (1986). "Bayesian estimation and prediction using asymmetric loss functions". Journal of the American Statistical Association 81, 446–451.

Zellner, A., Chen, B. (2001). "Bayesian modeling of economies and data requirements". Macroeconomic Dynamics 5, 673–700.

Zellner, A., Hong, C. (1989). "Forecasting international growth rates using Bayesian shrinkage and other procedures". Journal of Econometrics 40, 183–202.

Zellner, A., Hong, C., Gulati, G.M. (1990). "Turning points in economic time series, loss structures and Bayesian forecasting". In: Geisser, S., Hodges, J.S., Press, S.J., Zellner, A. (Eds.), Bayesian and Likelihood Methods in Statistics and Econometrics: Essays in Honor of George A. Barnard. North-Holland, Amsterdam, pp. 371–393.

Zellner, A., Hong, C., Min, C.K. (1991). "Bayesian exponentially weighted autoregression, time-varying parameter, and pooling techniques". Journal of Econometrics 49, 275–304.

Zellner, A., Min, C.K. (1995). "Gibbs sampler convergence criteria". Journal of the American Statistical Association 90, 921–927.

Zha, T.A. (1998). "A dynamic multivariate model for use in formulating policy". Federal Reserve Bank of Atlanta Economic Review 83 (First Quarter), 16–29.

Chapter 2

FORECASTING AND DECISION THEORY

CLIVE W.J. GRANGER and MARK J. MACHINA

Department of Economics, University of California, San Diego, La Jolla, CA 92093-0508

Contents

Handbook of Economic Forecasting, Volume 1
Edited by Graham Elliott, Clive W.J. Granger and Allan Timmermann

DOI: 10.1016/S1574-0706(05)01002-5

Abstract

When forecasts of the future value of some variable, or the probability of some event, are used for purposes of ex ante planning or decision making, then the preferences, opportunities and constraints of the decision maker will all enter into the ex post evaluation of a forecast, and the ex post comparison of alternative forecasts. After a presenting a brief review of early work in the area of forecasting and decision theory, this chapter formally examines the manner in which the features of an agent's decision problem combine to generate an appropriate *decision-based loss function* for that agent's use in forecast evaluation. Decision-based loss functions are shown to exhibit certain necessary properties, and the relationship between the functional form of a decision-based loss function and the functional form of the agent's underlying utility function is characterized. In particular, the standard squared-error loss function is shown to imply highly restrictive and not particularly realistic properties on underlying preferences, which are *not* justified by the use of a standard local quadratic approximation. A class of more realistic loss functions ("location-dependent loss functions") is proposed.

Keywords

forecasting, loss functions, decision theory, decision-based loss functions

JEL classification: C440, C530

Preface

This chapter has two sections. Section 1 presents a fairly brief history of the interaction of forecasting and decision theory, and Section 2 presents some more recent results.

1. History of the field

1.1. Introduction

A decision maker (either a private agent or a public policy maker) must inevitably consider the future, and this requires forecasts of certain important variables. There also exist forecasters – such as scientists or statisticians – who may or may not be operating independently of a decision maker. In the classical situation, forecasts are produced by a single forecaster, and there are several potential users, namely the various decision makers. In other situations, each decision maker may have several different forecasts to choose between.

A decision maker will typically have a payoff or utility function $U(x, \alpha)$, which depends upon some uncertain variable or vector x which will be realized and observed at a future time T, as well as some decision variable or vector α which must be chosen out of a set $\mathcal{A}$ at some earlier time $t < T$. The decision maker can base their choice of α upon a current scalar forecast (a "point forecast") x_F of the variable x, and make the choice $\alpha(x_F) \equiv \arg\max_{\alpha \in \mathcal{A}} U(x_F, \alpha)$. Given the realized value x_R, the decision maker's *ex post* utility $U(x_R, \alpha(x_F))$ can be compared with the maximum possible utility they could have attained, namely $U(x_R, \alpha(x_R))$. This shortfall can be averaged over a number of such situations, to obtain the decision maker's average loss in terms of foregone payoff or utility. If one is forecasting in a stochastic environment, perfect forecasting will not be possible and this average long-term loss will be strictly positive. In a deterministic world, it could be zero.

Given some measure of the loss arising from an imperfect forecast, different forecasting methods can be compared, or different combinations selected.

In his 1961 book *Economic Forecasts and Policy*, Henri Theil outlined many versions of the above type of situation, but paid more attention to the control activities of the policy maker. He returned to these topics in his 1971 volume *Applied Economic Forecasting*, particularly in the general discussion of Chapter 1 and the mention of loss functions in Chapter 2. These two books cover a wide variety of topics in both theory and applications, including discussions of certainty equivalence, interval and distributional forecasts, and non-quadratic loss functions. This emphasis on the links between decision makers and forecasters was not emphasized by other writers for at least another quarter of a century, which shows how farsighted Theil could be. An exception is an early contribution by White (1966).

Another major development was Bayesian decision analysis, with important contributions by DeGroot (1970) and Berger (1985), and later by West and Harrison (1989,

1997). Early in their book, on page 14, West and Harrison state "A statistician, economist or management scientist usually looks at a decision as comprising a forecast or belief, and a utility, or reward, function". Denote Y as the outcome of a future random quantity which is "conditional on your decision α expressed through a forward or probability function $P(Y|\alpha)$. A reward function $u(Y, \alpha)$ expresses your gain or loss if Y happens when you take decision α". In such a case, the expected reward is

$$r(\alpha) = \int u(Y, \alpha)\,\mathrm{d}P(Y|\alpha) \tag{1}$$

and the optimal decision is taken to be the one that maximizes this expected reward. The parallel with the "expected utility" literature is clear.

The book continues by discussing a dynamic linear model (denoted DLM) using a state-space formulation. There are clear similarities with the Kalman filtering approach, but the development is quite different. Although West and Harrison continue to develop the "Bayesian maximum reward" approach, according to their index the words "decision" and "utility" are only used on page 14, as mentioned above. Although certainly important in Bayesian circles, it was less influential elsewhere. This also holds for the large body of work known as "statistical decision theory", which is largely Bayesian.

The later years of the Twentieth Century produced a flurry of work, published around the year 2000. Chamberlain (2000) was concerned with the general topic of econometrics and decision theory – in particular, with the question of how econometrics can influence decisions under uncertainty – which leads to considerations of distributional forecasts or "predictive distributions". Naturally, one needs a criterion to evaluate procedures for constructing predictive distributions, and Chamberlain chose to use risk robustness and to minimize regret risk. To construct predictive distributions, Bayes methods were used based on parametric models. One application considered an individual trying to forecast their future earnings using their personal earnings history and data on the earnings trajectories of others.

1.2. The Cambridge papers

Three papers from the Department of Economics at the University of Cambridge moved the discussion forward. The first, by Granger and Pesaran (2000a), first appeared as a working paper in 1996. The second, also by Granger and Pesaran (2000b), appeared as a working paper in 1999. The third, by Pesaran and Skouras (2002), appeared as a working paper in 2000.

Granger and Pesaran (2000a) review the classic case in which there are two states of the world, which we here call "good" and "bad" for convenience. A forecaster provides a probability forecast $\hat{\pi}$ (resp. $1-\hat{\pi}$) that the good (resp. bad) state will occur. A decision maker can decide whether or not to take some action on the basis of this forecast, and a completely general payoff or profit function is allowed. The notation is illustrated in Table 1. The Y_{ij}'s are the utility or profit payoffs under each state and action, net of any costs of the action. A simple example of states is that a road becoming icy and dangerous

Table 1

Action	State	
	Good	Bad
Yes	Y_{11}	Y_{12}
No	Y_{21}	Y_{22}

is the bad state, whereas the road staying clear is the good state. The potential action could be to add sand to the road. If $\hat{\pi}$ is the forecast probability of the good state, then the action should be undertaken if

$$\frac{\hat{\pi}}{1-\hat{\pi}} > \frac{Y_{22} - Y_{12}}{Y_{11} - Y_{21}}. \tag{2}$$

This case of two states with predicted probabilities of $\hat{\pi}$ and $1 - \hat{\pi}$ is the simplest possible example of a predictive distribution. An alternative type of forecast, which might be called an "event forecast", consists of the forecaster simply announcing the event that is judged to have the highest probability. Granger and Pesaran (2000a) show that using an event forecast will be suboptimal compared to using a predictive distribution. Although the above example is a very simple case, the advantages of using an economic cost function along with a decision-theoretic approach, rather than some statistical measure such as least squares, are clearly illustrated.

Granger and Pesaran (2000b) continue their consideration of this type of model, but turn to loss functions suggested for the evaluation of the meteorological forecasts. A well-known example is the Kuipers Score (*KS*) defined by

$$KS = H - F \tag{3}$$

where H is the fraction (over time) of bad events that were *correctly* forecast to occur, and F is the fraction of good events that had been incorrectly forecast to have come out bad (sometimes termed the "false alarm rate"). Random forecasts would produce an average KS value of zero. Although this score would seem to be both useful and interpretable, it turns out to have some undesirable properties. The first is that it cannot be defined for a one-shot case, since regardless of the prediction and regardless of the realized event, one of the fractions H or F must take the undefined form $0/0$. A generalization of this undesirable property is that the Kuipers Score cannot be guaranteed to be well-defined for *any* prespecified sample size (either time series or cross-sectional), since for any sample size n, the score is similarly undefined whenever all the realized events are good, or all the realized events are bad.

Although the above properties would appear serious from a theoretical point of view, one might argue that any practical application would involve a prediction history where incorrect forecasts of both types had occurred, so that both H and F would be well-defined. But even in that case, another undesirable property of the Kuipers Score can manifest itself, namely that the neither the score itself, nor its ranking of alternative

Table 2

Year	Realized event	A's forecast	B's forecast	A's 5-year score	B's 5-year score	A's 10-year score	B's 5-year score
1	good	good	good	$H^A_{1-5} = 1$	$H^B_{1-5} = 0$		
2	good	bad	good				
3	good	bad	good	$F^A_{1-5} = \frac{3}{4}$	$F^B_{1-5} = \frac{1}{4}$		
4	good	bad	bad				
5	bad	bad	good	$KS^A_{1-5} = \frac{1}{4}$	$KS^B_{1-5} = -\frac{1}{4}$	$H^A_{1-10} = \frac{2}{5}$	$H^B_{1-10} = \frac{3}{5}$
						$F^A_{1-10} = \frac{3}{5}$	$F^B_{1-10} = \frac{2}{5}$
6	bad	bad	bad	$H^A_{5-10} = \frac{1}{4}$	$H^B_{5-10} = \frac{3}{4}$	$KS^A_{1-10} = -\frac{1}{5}$	$KS^B_{1-10} = \frac{1}{5}$
7	bad	good	bad				
8	bad	good	bad	$F^A_{5-10} = 0$	$F^B_{5-10} = 1$		
9	bad	good	good				
10	good	good	bad	$KS^A_{5-10} = \frac{1}{4}$	$KS^B_{5-10} = -\frac{1}{4}$		

forecasters, will exhibit the natural uniform dominance property with respect to combining or partitioning sample populations. We illustrate this with the following example, where a 10-element sample is partitioned into two 5-element subsamples, and where the history of two forecasters, A and B, are as given in Table 2. For this data, forecaster A is seen to have a higher Kuipers score than forecaster B for the first five-year period, and also for the second five-year period, but A has a lower Kuipers score than B for the whole decade – a property which is clearly undesirable, whether or not our evaluation is based on an underlying utility function. The intuition behind this occurrence is that the two components H and F of the Kuipers score are given equal weight in the formula $KS = H - F$ even though the number of data points they refer to (the number of periods with realized bad events versus the number of periods with realized good events) needn't be equal, and the fraction of bad versus good events in each of two subperiods can be vastly different from the fraction over the combined period. Researchers interested in applying this type of evaluation measure to situations involving the aggregation/disaggregation of time periods, or time periods of different lengths, would be better off with the simpler measure defined by the overall fraction of events (be they good *or* bad) that were correctly forecast.

Granger and Pesaran (2000b) also examine the relationship between other statistical measures of forecast accuracy and tests of stock market timing, and with a detailed application to stock market data. Models for stock market returns have emphasized expected risk-adjusted returns rather than least-squares fits – that is, an economic rather than a statistical measure of quality of the model.

Pesaran and Skouras (2002) is a survey paper, starting with the above types of results and then extending them to predictive distributions, with a particular emphasis on the role of decision-based forecast evaluation. The paper obtains closed-form results for a variety of random specifications and cost or utility functions, such as Gaussian distributions combined with negative exponential utility. Attention is given to a general survey of the use of cost functions with predictive distributions, with mention of the possible use of scoring rules, as well as various measures taken from meteorology. See also Elliott and Lieli (2005).

Although many of the above results are well known in the Bayesian decision theory literature, they were less known in the forecasting area, where the use of the whole distribution rather than just the mean, and an economic cost function linked with a decision maker, were not usually emphasized.

1.3. Forecasting versus statistical hypothesis testing and estimation

Although the discussion of this chapter is in terms of forecasting some yet-to-be-realized random variable, it will be clear to readers of the literature that most of our analysis and results also apply to the statistical problem of testing a hypothesis whose truth value is already determined (though not yet known), or to the statistical problem of estimating some parameter whose numerical value is also already determined (though not yet observed, or not directly observable). The case of hypothesis testing will correspond to the forecasting of binary events as illustrated in the above table, and that of numerical parameter estimation will correspond to that of predicting a real-valued variable, as examined in Section 2 below.

2. Forecasting with decision-based loss functions

2.1. Background

In practice, statistical forecasts are typically *produced* by one group of agents ("forecasters") and *consumed* by a different group ("clients"), and the procedures and desires of the two groups typically do not interact. After the fact, alternative forecasts or forecast methods are typically *evaluated* by means of statistical loss functions, which are often chosen primarily on grounds of statistical convenience, with little or no reference to the particular goals or preferences of the client.

But whereas *statistical science* is like any other science in seeking to conduct a "search for truth" that is uninfluenced by the particular interests of the end user, *statistical decisions* are like any other decision in that they should be driven by the goals and preferences of the particular decision maker. Thus, if one forecasting method has a lower bias but higher average squared error than a second one, clients with different goals or preferences may disagree on which of the two techniques is "best" – or at least, which one is best for them. Here we examine the process of forecast evaluation from the point of view of serving clients who have a need or a use for such information in making some upcoming decision. Each such situation will generate its own loss function, which is called a *decision-based loss function*.

Although it serves as a sufficient construct for forecast evaluation, a decision-based loss function is *not* simply a direct representation of the decision maker's underlying preferences. A decision maker's ultimate goal is not to achieve "zero loss", but rather, to achieve maximum utility or payoff (or expected utility or expected payoff). Furthermore, decision-based loss functions are not derived from preferences alone: Any decision problem that involves maximizing utility or payoff (or its expectation) is subject to certain opportunities or constraints, and the nature and extent of these opportunities or constraints will also be reflected in its implied decision-based loss function.

The goal here is to provide a systematic examination of the relationship between decision problems and their associated loss functions. We ask general questions, such as "Can every statistical loss function be derived from some well-specified decision problem?" or "How big is the family of decision problems that generate a given loss function?" We can also ask more specific questions, such as "What does the use of *squared-error loss* reveal or imply about a decision maker's underlying decision problem (i.e. their preferences and/or constraints)?" In addressing such questions, we hope to develop a better understanding of the use of loss functions as tools in forecast evaluation and parameter estimation.

The following analysis is based Pesaran and Skouras (2002) and Machina and Granger (2005). Section 2.2 lays out a framework and derives some of the basic categories and properties of decision-based loss functions. Section 2.3 treats the reverse question of deriving the family of underlying decision problems that generate a given loss function, as well as the restrictions on preferences that are implicitly imposed by the selection of specific functional forms, such as squared-error loss or error-based loss. Given that these restrictions turn out to be stronger than we would typically choose to impose, Section 2.4 describes a more general, "location-dependent" approach to the analysis of general loss functions, which preserves most of the intuition of the standard cases. Section 2.5 examines the above types of questions when we replace point forecasts of an uncertain variable with distribution forecasts. Potentially one can extend the approach to partial distribution forecasts such as moment or quantile forecasts, but these topics are not considered here.

2.2. *Framework and basic analysis*

2.2.1. *Decision problems, forecasts and decision-based loss functions*

A decision maker would only have a material interest in forecasts of some uncertain variable x if such information led to "planning benefits" – that is, if their optimal choice in some intermediate decision might depend upon this information. To represent this, we assume the decision maker has an *objective function* (either a utility or a profit function) $U(x, \alpha)$ that depends upon the realized value of x (assumed to lie in some closed interval $\mathcal{X} \subset \mathbf{R}^1$), as well as upon some *choice variable* α to be selected out of some closed interval $\mathcal{A} \subset \mathbf{R}^1$ after the forecast is learned, but before x is realized. We thus define a *decision problem* to consist of the following components:

$$\begin{aligned}&\text{uncertain variable} \quad x \in \mathcal{X},\\&\text{choice variable and choice set} \quad \alpha \in \mathcal{A},\\&\text{objective function} \quad U(\cdot,\cdot): \mathcal{X} \times \mathcal{A} \to \mathbf{R}^1.\end{aligned} \tag{4}$$

Forecasts of x can take several forms. A forecast consisting of a single value $x_F \in \mathcal{X}$ is termed a *point forecast*. For such forecasts, the decision maker's *optimal action function* $\alpha(\cdot)$ is given by

$$\alpha(x_F) \equiv \arg\max_{\alpha \in \mathcal{A}} U(x_F, \alpha) \quad \text{all } x_F \in \mathcal{X}. \tag{5}$$

The objective function $U(\cdot,\cdot)$ can be measured in either utils or dollars. When $U(\cdot,\cdot)$ is posited exogenously (as opposed from being derived from a loss function as in Theorem 1), we assume it is such that (5) has interior solutions $\alpha(x_F)$, and also that it satisfies the following conditions on its second and cross-partial derivatives, which ensure that $\alpha(x_F)$ is unique and is increasing in x_F:

$$U_{\alpha\alpha}(x, \alpha) < 0, \quad U_{x\alpha}(x, \alpha) > 0 \quad \text{all } x \in \mathcal{X}, \text{ all } \alpha \in \mathcal{A}. \tag{6}$$

Forecasts are invariably subject to error. Intuitively, the "loss" arising from a forecast value of x_F, when x turns out to have a realized value of x_R, is simply the loss in utility or profit due to the imperfect prediction, or in other words, the amount by which utility or profit falls short of what it would have been if the decision maker had instead possessed "perfect information" and been able to exactly foresee the realized value x_R. Accordingly, we define the *point-forecast/point-realization loss function* induced by the decision problem (4) by

$$L(x_R, x_F) \equiv U\big(x_R, \alpha(x_R)\big) - U\big(x_R, \alpha(x_F)\big) \quad \text{all } x_R, x_F \in \mathcal{X}. \tag{7}$$

Note that in defining the loss arising from the imperfection of forecasts, the realized utility or profit level $U(x_R, \alpha(x_F))$ is compared with what it would have been *if the forecast had instead been equal to the realized value* (that is, compared with $U(x_R, \alpha(x_R))$), and *not* with what utility or profit would have been *if the realization had instead been equal to the forecast* (that is, compared with $U(x_F, \alpha(x_F))$). For example, given that a firm faces a realized output price of x_R, it would have been best if it had had this same value as its forecast, and we measure loss relative to this counterfactual. But given that it received and planned on the basis of a price forecast of x_F, it is *not* best that the realized price also come in at x_F, since any *higher* realized output price would lead to *still higher* profits. Thus, there is no reason why $L(x_R, x_F)$ should necessarily be symmetric (or skew-symmetric) in x_R and x_F. Under our assumptions, the loss function $L(x_R, x_F)$ from (7) satisfies the following properties:

$$\begin{aligned}&L(x_R, x_F) \geqslant 0, \quad L(x_R, x_F)|_{x_R = x_F} = 0,\\&L(x_R, x_F) \text{ is increasing in } x_F \text{ for all } x_F > x_R,\\&L(x_R, x_F) \text{ is decreasing in } x_F \text{ for all } x_F < x_R.\end{aligned} \tag{8}$$

As noted, forecasts of x can take several forms. Whereas a point forecast x_F conveys information on the general "location" of x, it conveys no information as to x's potential variability. On the other hand, forecasters who seek to formally communicate their own extent of uncertainty, or alternatively, who seek to communicate their knowledge of the stochastic mechanism that generates x, would report a *distribution forecast* $F_F(\cdot)$ consisting of a cumulative distribution function over the interval $\mathcal{X}$. A decision maker receiving a distribution forecast, and who seeks to maximize expected utility or expected profits, would have an optimal action function $\alpha(\cdot)$ defined by

$$\alpha(F_F) \equiv \arg\max_{\alpha \in \mathcal{A}} \int U(x, \alpha)\, \mathrm{d}F_F(x) \quad \text{all } F_F(\cdot) \text{ over } \mathcal{X} \tag{9}$$

and a *distribution-forecast/point-realization loss* function defined by

$$L(x_R, F_F) \equiv U\big(x_R, \alpha(x_R)\big) - U\big(x_R, \alpha(F_F)\big) \quad \text{all } x \in \mathcal{X}, \text{ all } F_F(\cdot) \text{ over } \mathcal{X}. \tag{10}$$

Under our previous assumptions on $U(\cdot, \cdot)$, each distribution forecast $F_F(\cdot)$ has a unique *point-forecast equivalent* $x_F(F_F)$ that satisfies $\alpha(x_F(F_F)) = \alpha(F_F)$ [e.g., Pratt, Raiffa and Schaifer (1995, 24.4.2)]. Since the point-forecast equivalent $x_F(F_F)$ generates the same optimal action as the distribution forecast $F_F(\cdot)$, it will lead to the same loss, so that we have $L(x_R, x_F(F_F)) \equiv L(x_R, F_F)$ for all $x_R \in \mathcal{X}$ and all distributions $F_F(\cdot)$ over $\mathcal{X}$.

Under our assumptions, the loss function $L(x_R, F_F)$ from (10) satisfies the following properties, where "increasing or decreasing in $F_F(\cdot)$" is with respect to first order stochastically dominating changes in $F_F(\cdot)$:

$$\begin{aligned} &L(x_R, F_F) \geqslant 0, \quad L(x_R, F_F)|_{x_R = x_F(F_F)} = 0, \\ &L(x_R, F_F) \text{ is increasing in } F_F(\cdot) \text{ for all } F_F(\cdot) \text{ such that } x_F(F_F) > x_R, \\ &L(x_R, F_F) \text{ is decreasing in } F_F(\cdot) \text{ for all } F_F(\cdot) \text{ such that } x_F(F_F) < x_R. \end{aligned} \tag{11}$$

It should be noted that throughout, these loss functions are quite general in form, and are not being constrained to any specific class.

2.2.2. *Derivatives of decision-based loss functions*

For point forecasts, the optimal action function $\alpha(\cdot)$ from (5) satisfies the first-order conditions

$$U_\alpha\big(x, \alpha(x)\big) \underset{x}{\equiv} 0. \tag{12}$$

Differentiating this identity with respect to x yields

$$\alpha'(x) \equiv -\frac{U_{x\alpha}(x, \alpha(x))}{U_{\alpha\alpha}(x, \alpha(x))} \tag{13}$$

and hence

$$\alpha''(x) \equiv -\frac{U_{xx\alpha}(x,\alpha(x)) \cdot U_{\alpha\alpha}(x,\alpha(x)) - U_{x\alpha}(x,\alpha(x)) \cdot U_{x\alpha\alpha}(x,\alpha(x))}{U_{\alpha\alpha}(x,\alpha(x))^2}$$

$$- \frac{U_{x\alpha\alpha}(x,\alpha(x)) \cdot U_{\alpha\alpha}(x,\alpha(x)) - U_{x\alpha}(x,\alpha(x)) \cdot U_{\alpha\alpha\alpha}(x,\alpha(x))}{U_{\alpha\alpha}(x,\alpha(x))^2} \cdot \alpha'(x)$$

$$\equiv -\frac{U_{xx\alpha}(x,\alpha(x))}{U_{\alpha\alpha}(x,\alpha(x))} + 2 \cdot \frac{U_{x\alpha}(x,\alpha(x)) \cdot U_{x\alpha\alpha}(x,\alpha(x))}{U_{\alpha\alpha}(x,\alpha(x))^2}$$

$$- \frac{U_{x\alpha}(x,\alpha(x))^2 \cdot U_{\alpha\alpha\alpha}(x,\alpha(x))}{U_{\alpha\alpha}(x,\alpha(x))^3}. \tag{14}$$

By (7) and (12), the derivative of $L(x_R, x_F)$ with respect to small departures from a perfect forecast is

$$\left.\frac{\partial L(x_R, x_F)}{\partial x_F}\right|_{x_F = x_R} \equiv -U_\alpha\big(x_R, \alpha(x_F)\big)\big|_{x_F = x_R} \cdot \alpha'(x_F)\big|_{x_F = x_R} \equiv 0. \tag{15}$$

Calculating $L(x_R, x_F)$'s derivatives at general values of x_R and x_F yields

$$\begin{aligned}
\frac{\partial L(x_R, x_F)}{\partial x_R} &\equiv U_x\big(x_R, \alpha(x_R)\big) + U_\alpha\big(x_R, \alpha(x_R)\big) \cdot \alpha'(x_R) - U_x\big(x_R, \alpha(x_F)\big), \\
\frac{\partial L(x_R, x_F)}{\partial x_F} &\equiv -U_\alpha\big(x_R, \alpha(x_F)\big) \cdot \alpha'(x_F), \\
\frac{\partial^2 L(x_R, x_F)}{\partial x_R^2} &\equiv U_{xx}\big(x_R, \alpha(x_R)\big) + U_{x\alpha}\big(x_R, \alpha(x_R)\big) \cdot \alpha'(x_R) \\
&\quad + U_{x\alpha}\big(x_R, \alpha(x_R)\big) \cdot \alpha'(x_R) + U_{\alpha\alpha}\big(x_R, \alpha(x_R)\big) \cdot \alpha'(x_R)^2 \\
&\quad + U_\alpha\big(x_R, \alpha(x_R)\big) \cdot \alpha''(x_R) - U_{xx}\big(x_R, \alpha(x_F)\big), \\
\frac{\partial^2 L(x_R, x_F)}{\partial x_R \partial x_F} &\equiv -U_{x\alpha}\big(x_R, \alpha(x_F)\big) \cdot \alpha'(x_F), \\
\frac{\partial^2 L(x_R, x_F)}{\partial x_F^2} &\equiv -U_{\alpha\alpha}\big(x_R, \alpha(x_F)\big) \cdot \alpha'(x_F)^2 - U_\alpha\big(x_R, \alpha(x_F)\big) \cdot \alpha''(x_F).
\end{aligned} \tag{16}$$

2.2.3. *Inessential transformations of a decision problem*

One can potentially learn a lot about decision problems or families of decision problems by asking what changes can be made to them without altering certain features of their solution. This section presents a relevant application of this approach.

A transformation of any decision problem (4) is said to be *inessential* if it does not change its implied loss function, even though it may change other attributes, such as the formula for its optimal action function or the formula for its ex post payoff or utility. For point-forecast loss functions $L(\cdot,\cdot)$, there exist two types of inessential transformations:

Inessential relabelings of the choice variable: Given a decision problem with objective function $U(\cdot,\cdot):\mathcal{X}\times\mathcal{A}\to\mathbf{R}^1$, any one-to-one mapping $\varphi(\cdot)$ from $\mathcal{A}$ into an arbitrary space $\mathcal{B}$ will generate what we term an *inessential relabeling* $\beta=\varphi(\alpha)$ of the choice variable, with objective function $U^*(\cdot,\cdot):\mathcal{X}\times\mathcal{B}^*\to\mathbf{R}^1$ and choice set $\mathcal{B}^*\subseteq\mathcal{B}$ defined by

$$U^*(x,\beta)\equiv U\big(x,\varphi^{-1}(\beta)\big),\qquad \mathcal{B}^*=\varphi(\mathcal{A})=\big\{\varphi(\alpha)\mid\alpha\in\mathcal{A}\big\}.\tag{17}$$

The optimal action function $\beta(\cdot):\mathcal{X}\to\mathcal{B}^*$ for this transformed decision problem is related to that of the original problem by

$$\begin{aligned}\beta(x_F)&\equiv\arg\max_{\beta\in\mathcal{B}^*}U^*(x_F,\beta)\equiv\arg\max_{\beta\in\mathcal{B}^*}U\big(x,\varphi^{-1}(\beta)\big)\\&\equiv\varphi\big(\arg\max_{\alpha\in\mathcal{A}}U(x_F,\alpha)\big)\equiv\varphi\big(\alpha(x_F)\big).\end{aligned}\tag{18}$$

The loss function for the transformed problem is the same as for the original problem, since

$$\begin{aligned}L^*(x_R,x_F)&\equiv U^*\big(x_R,\beta(x_R)\big)-U^*\big(x_R,\beta(x_F)\big)\\&\equiv U\big(x_R,\varphi^{-1}\big(\beta(x_R)\big)\big)-U\big(x_R,\varphi^{-1}\big(\beta(x_F)\big)\big)\\&\equiv U\big(x_R,\alpha(x_R)\big)-U\big(x_R,\alpha(x_F)\big)\equiv L(x_R,x_F).\end{aligned}\tag{19}$$

While any one-to-one mapping $\varphi(\cdot)$ will generate an inessential transformation of the original decision problem, there is a unique "most natural" such transformation, namely the one generated by the mapping $\varphi(\cdot)=\alpha^{-1}(\cdot)$, which relabels each choice α with the forecast value x_F that would have led to that choice – we refer to this labeling as the *forecast-equivalent labeling* of the choice variable. Technically, the map $\alpha^{-1}(\cdot)$ is not defined over the entire space $\mathcal{A}$, but just over the subset $\{\alpha(x)\mid x\in\mathcal{X}\}\subseteq\mathcal{A}$ of actions that are optimal for some x. However, that suffices for the following decision problem to be considered an inessential transformation of the original decision problem:

$$\hat{U}(x,x_F)\underset{x,x_F}{\equiv}U\big(x,\alpha(x_F)\big),\qquad \hat{\mathcal{B}}=\varphi(\mathcal{A})=\big\{\varphi(\alpha)\mid\alpha\in\mathcal{A}\big\}.\tag{20}$$

We refer to (20) as the *canonical form* of the original decision problem, note that its optimal action function is given by $\hat{\alpha}(x_F)\equiv x_F$, and observe that $\hat{U}(x,x_F)$ can be interpreted as the formula for the amount of *ex post* utility (or profit) resulting from a realized value of x when the decision maker had optimally responded to a point forecast of x_F.

Inessential transformations of the objective function: A second type of inessential transformation consists of adding an arbitrary function $\xi(\cdot):\mathcal{X}\to\mathbf{R}^1$ to the original objective function, to obtain a new function $U^{**}(x,\alpha)\equiv U(x,\alpha)+\xi(x)$. Since $U_\alpha(x_F,\alpha)\equiv U^{**}_\alpha(x_F,\alpha)$, the first order condition (12) is unchanged, so the optimal action functions $\alpha^{**}(\cdot)$ and $\alpha(\cdot)$ for the two problems are identical. But since the ex post utility levels for the two problems are related by $U^{**}(x,\alpha^{**}(x_F))\equiv$

$U(x, \alpha(x_F)) + \xi(x)$, their canonical forms are related by $\hat{U}^{**}(x, x_F) \equiv \hat{U}(x, x_F) + \xi(x)$ and $\hat{\mathcal{B}} = \mathcal{A}$, which would, for example, allow $\hat{U}^{**}(x, x_F)$ to be increasing in x when $\hat{U}(x, x_F)$ was decreasing in x, or vice versa. However, the loss functions for the two problems will be identical, since:

$$\begin{aligned} L^{**}(x_R, x_F) &\equiv U^{**}\big(x_R, \alpha^{**}(x_R)\big) - U^{**}\big(x_R, \alpha^{**}(x_F)\big) \\ &\equiv U\big(x_R, \alpha(x_R)\big) - U\big(x_R, \alpha(x_F)\big) \equiv L(x_R, x_F). \end{aligned} \tag{21}$$

Theorem 1 below will imply that these two forms, namely inessential relabelings of the choice variable and inessential additive transformations of the objective function, exhaust the class of loss-function-preserving transformations of a decision problem.

2.3. Recovery of decision problems from loss functions

In practice, loss functions are typically *not* derived from an underlying decision problem as in the previous section, but rather, are postulated exogenously. But since we have seen that decision-based loss functions inherit certain necessary properties, it is worth asking precisely when a given loss function (or functional form) can or cannot be viewed as being derived from an underlying decision problem. In cases when they can, it is then worth asking about the restrictions this loss function or functional form implies about the underlying utility or profit function or constraints.

2.3.1. Recovery from point-forecast loss functions

Machina and Granger (2005) demonstrate that for an arbitrary point-forecast/point-realization loss function $L(\cdot, \cdot)$ satisfying (8), the class of objective functions that generate $L(\cdot, \cdot)$ has the following specification:

THEOREM 1. *For arbitrary function $L(\cdot, \cdot)$ that satisfies the properties* (8)*, an objective function $U(\cdot, \cdot) : \mathcal{X} \times \mathcal{A} \to \mathbf{R}^1$ with strictly monotonic optimal action function $\alpha(\cdot)$ will generate $L(\cdot, \cdot)$ as its loss function if and only if it takes the form*

$$U(x, \alpha) \equiv f(x) - L\big(x, g(\alpha)\big) \tag{22}$$

for some function $f(\cdot) : \mathcal{X} \to \mathbf{R}^1$ and monotonic function $g(\cdot) : \mathcal{A} \to \mathcal{X}$.

This theorem states that an objective function $U(x, \alpha)$ and choice space $\mathcal{A}$ are consistent with the loss function $L(x_R, x_F)$ if and only if they can be obtained from the function $-L(x_R, x_F)$ by one or both of the two types of inessential transformations described in the previous section. This result serves to highlight the close, though not unique, relationship between decision makers' loss functions and their underlying decision problems.

To derive the canonical form of the objective function (22) for given choice of $f(\cdot)$ and $g(\cdot)$, recall that each loss function $L(x_R, x_F)$ is minimized with respect to x_F when

x_F is set equal to x_R, so that the optimal action function for the objective function (22) takes the form $\alpha(x) \equiv g^{-1}(x)$. This in turn implies that its canonical form $\hat{U}(x, x_F)$ is given by

$$\hat{U}(x, x_F) \equiv U\big(x, \alpha(x_F)\big) \equiv f(x) - L\big(x, g\big(\alpha(x_F)\big)\big) \equiv f(x) - L(x, x_F). \quad (23)$$

2.3.2. *Implications of squared-error loss*

The most frequently used loss function in statistics is unquestionably the *squared-error form*

$$L_{\text{Sq}}(x_R, x_F) \equiv k \cdot (x_R - x_F)^2, \quad k > 0, \quad (24)$$

which is seen to satisfy the properties (8). Theorem 1 thus implies the following result:

COROLLARY 1. *For arbitrary squared-error function $L_{Sq}(x_R, x_F) \equiv k \cdot (x_R - x_F)^2$ with $k > 0$, an objective function $U(\cdot, \cdot) : \mathcal{X} \times \mathcal{A} \to \mathbf{R}^1$ with strictly monotonic optimal action function $\alpha(\cdot)$ will generate $L_{\text{Sq}}(\cdot, \cdot)$ as its loss function if and only if it takes the form*

$$U(x, \alpha) \equiv f(x) - k \cdot \big(x - g(\alpha)\big)^2 \quad (25)$$

for some function $f(\cdot) : \mathcal{X} \to \mathbf{R}^1$ and monotonic function $g(\cdot) : \mathcal{A} \to \mathcal{X}$.

Since utility or profit functions of the form (25) are not particularly standard, it is worth describing some of their properties. One property, which may or may not be realistic for a decision setting, is that changes in the level of the choice variable α do not affect the *curvature* (i.e. the second and higher order derivatives) of $U(x, \alpha)$ with respect to x, but only lead to uniform changes in the *level* and *slope* with respect to x – that is to say, for any pair of values $\alpha_1, \alpha_2 \in \mathcal{A}$, the difference $U(x, \alpha_1) - U(x, \alpha_2)$ is an affine function of x.[1]

A more direct property of the form (25) is revealed by adopting the forecast-equivalent labeling of the choice variable to obtain its canonical form $\hat{U}(x, x_F)$ from (20), which as we have seen, specifies the level of utility or profit resulting from an actual realized value of x and the action that would have been optimal for a realized value of x_F. Under this labeling, the objective function implied by the squared-error loss function $L_{\text{Sq}}(x_R, x_F)$ is seen (by (23)) to take the form

$$\hat{U}(x, x_F) \equiv f(x) - L_{\text{Sq}}(x, x_F) \equiv f(x) - k \cdot (x - x_F)^2. \quad (26)$$

In terms of our earlier example, this states that when a firm faces a realized output price of x, its shortfall from optimal profits due to *having planned* for an output price of x_F only depends upon the difference between x and x_F (and in particular, upon the

[1] Specifically, (25) implies $U(x, \alpha_1) - U(x, \alpha_2) \equiv -k \cdot [g(\alpha_1)^2 - g(\alpha_2)^2] + 2 \cdot k \cdot [g(\alpha_1) - g(\alpha_2)] \cdot x$.

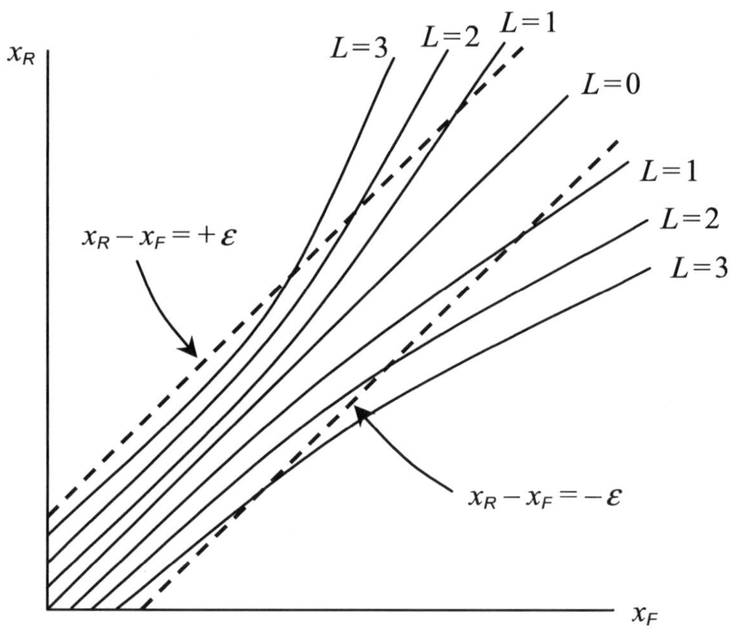

Figure 1. Level curves of a general loss function $L(x_R, x_F)$ and the band $|x_R - x_F| \leqslant \varepsilon$.

square of this difference), and not upon how high or how low the two values might both be. Thus, the profit shortfall from having underpredicted a realized output price of \$10 by one dollar is the same as the profit shortfall from having underpredicted a realized output price of \$2 by one dollar. This is clearly unrealistic in any decision problem which exhibits "wealth effects" or "location effects" in the uncertain variable, such as a firm which could make money if the realized output price was \$7 (so there would be a definite loss in profits from having underpredicted the price by \$1), but would want to shut down if the realized output price was only \$4 (in which case there would be no profit loss at all from having underpredicted the price by \$1).

2.3.3. *Are squared-error loss functions appropriate as "local approximations"?*

One argument for the squared-error form $L_{\text{Sq}}(x_R, x_F) \equiv k \cdot (x_R - x_F)^2$ is that if the forecast errors $x_R - x_F$ are not too big – that is, if the forecaster is good enough at prediction – then this functional form is the natural second-order approximation to any smooth loss function that exhibits the necessary properties of being zero when $x_R = x_F$ (from (8)) and having zero first-order effect for small departures from a perfect forecast (from (15)).

However, the fact that $x_R - x_F$ may always be close to zero *does not* legitimize the use of the functional form $k \cdot (x_R - x_F)^2$ as a second-order approximation to a general smooth bivariate loss function $L(x_R, x_F)$, even one that satisfies $L(0,0) = 0$ and $\partial L(x_R, x_F)/\partial x_F|_{x_R=x_F} = 0$. Consider Figure 1, which illustrates the level curves of some smooth loss function $L(x_R, x_F)$, along with the region where $|x_R - x_F|$ is less than or equal to some small value ε, which is seen to constitute a constant-width band about the 45° line. This region does *not* constitute a small neighborhood in $\mathbf{R}^2$, even as $\varepsilon \to 0$. In particular, the second order approximation to $L(x_R, x_F)$ when x_R and x_F are both small and approximately equal to each other is *not* the same as the second-order approximation to $L(x_R, x_F)$ when x_R and x_F are both large and approximately equal to each other. Legitimate second-order approximations to $L(x_R, x_F)$ can only be taken in over *small neighborhoods of points* in $\mathbf{R}^2$, and not over *bands* (even narrow bands) about the 45° line. The "quadratic approximation" $L_{\mathrm{Sq}}(x_R, x_F) \equiv k \cdot (x_R - x_F)^2$ over such bands is not justified by Taylor's theorem.

2.3.4. *Implications of error-based loss*

By the year 2000, virtually all stated loss functions were of the form (27) – that is, a single-argument function of the forecast error $x_R - x_F$ which satisfies the properties (8):

$$L_{\mathrm{err}}(x_R, x_F) \equiv H(x_R - x_F), \qquad H(\cdot) \geqslant 0,\ H(0) = 0,\ H(\cdot) \text{ quasiconcave}. \tag{27}$$

Consider what Theorem 1 implies about this general *error-based form*:

COROLLARY 2. *For arbitrary error-based function $L_{\mathrm{err}}(x_R, x_F) \equiv H(x_R - x_F)$ satisfying* (27), *an objective function $U(\cdot,\cdot) : \mathcal{X} \times \mathcal{A} \to \mathbf{R}^1$ with strictly monotonic optimal action function $\alpha(\cdot)$ will generate $L_{\mathrm{err}}(\cdot,\cdot)$ as its loss function if and only if it takes the form*

$$U(x, \alpha) \equiv f(x) - H\big(x - g(\alpha)\big) \tag{28}$$

for some function $f(\cdot) : \mathcal{X} \to \mathbf{R}^1$ and monotonic function $g(\cdot) : \mathcal{A} \to \mathcal{X}$.

Formula (28) highlights the fact that the use of an error-based loss function of the form (27) implicitly assumes that the decision maker's underlying problem is again "location-independent", in the sense that the utility loss from having made an ex post nonoptimal choice $\alpha \neq g^{-1}(x_R)$ only depends upon the *difference* between the values x_R and $g(\alpha)$, and not their general levels, so that it is again subject to the remarks following Equation (26). This location-independence is even more starkly illustrated in formula (28)'s canonical form, namely $\hat{U}(x, x_F) \equiv f(x) - H(x - x_F)$.

2.4. *Location-dependent loss functions*

Given a loss function $L(x_R, x_F)$ which is location-dependent and hence does *not* take the form (27), we can nevertheless retain most of our error-based intuition by defining $e = x_R - x_F$ and defining $L(x_R, x_F)$'s associated *location-dependent error-based form* by

$$H(x_R, e) \equiv L(x_R, x_R - e) \tag{29}$$

which implies

$$L(x_R, x_F) \equiv H(x_R, x_R - x_F). \tag{30}$$

In this case Theorem 1 implies that the utility function (22) takes the form

$$U(x, \alpha) \equiv f(x) - H\big(x, x - g(\alpha)\big) \tag{31}$$

for some $f(\cdot)$ and monotonic $g(\cdot)$. This is seen to be a generalization of Corollary 2, where the error-based function $H(x - g(\alpha))$ is replaced by a location-dependent form $H(x, x - g(\alpha))$. Such a function, with canonical form $\hat{U}(x, x_F) \equiv f(x) - H(x, x - x_F)$, would be appropriate when the decision maker's sensitivity to a unit error was different for prediction errors about high values of the variable x than for prediction errors about low values of this variable.

2.5. *Distribution-forecast and distribution-realization loss functions*

Although the traditional form of forecast used was the point forecast, there has recently been considerable interest in the use of distribution forecasts. As motivation, consider "forecasting" the number that will come up on a biased (i.e. "loaded") die. There is little point to giving a scalar point forecast – rather, since there will be irreducible uncertainty, the forecaster is better off studying the die (e.g., rolling it many times) and reporting the six face probabilities. We refer to such a forecast as a *distribution forecast*. The decision maker bases their optimal action upon the distribution forecast $F_F(\cdot)$ by solving the first order condition

$$\int U_\alpha(x, \alpha)\, \mathrm{d}F_F(x) = 0 \tag{32}$$

to obtain the optimal action function

$$\alpha(F_F) \equiv \arg\max_{\alpha \in \mathcal{A}} \int U(x, \alpha)\, \mathrm{d}F_F(x). \tag{33}$$

For the case of a distribution forecast $F_F(\cdot)$, the reduced-form payoff function takes the form

$$R(x_R, F_F) \equiv U\Big(x_R, \arg\max_{\alpha \in \mathcal{A}} \int U(x, \alpha)\, \mathrm{d}F_F(x)\Big) \equiv U\big(x_R, \alpha(F_F)\big). \tag{34}$$

Recall that the *point-forecast equivalent* is defined as the value $x_F(F_F)$ that satisfies

$$\alpha\big(x_F(F_F)\big) = \alpha(F_F) \tag{35}$$

and in the case of a single realization x_R, the *distribution-forecast/point-realization loss function* is given by

$$L(x_R, F_F) \equiv U\big(x_R, \alpha(x_R)\big) - U\big(x_R, \alpha(F_F)\big). \tag{36}$$

In the case of T successive throws of the same loaded die, there is a sense in which the "best case scenario" is when the forecaster has correctly predicted each of the successive realized values $x_{R1}, \ldots, x_{RT}$. However, when it is taken as given that the successive throws are independent, and when the forecaster is restricted to offering a single distribution forecast $F_F(\cdot)$ which must be provided prior to any of the throws, then the "best case" distribution forecast is the one that turns out to match the empirical distribution $F_R(\cdot)$ of the sequence of realizations, which we can call its "histogram". We thus define the *distribution-forecast/distribution-realization loss function* by

$$L(F_R, F_F) \equiv \int U\big(x, \alpha(F_R)\big)\, \mathrm{d}F_R(x) - \int U\big(x, \alpha(F_F)\big)\, \mathrm{d}F_R(x) \tag{37}$$

and observe that much of the above point-realization based analysis can be extended to such functions.

References

Berger, J.O. (1985). Statistical Decision Theory and Bayesian Analysis, second ed. Springer-Verlag, New York.

Chamberlain, G. (2000). "Econometrics and decision theory". Journal of Econometrics 95, 255–283.

DeGroot, M.H. (1970). Optimal Statistical Decisions. McGraw Hill, New York.

Elliott, G., Lieli, R., (2005). "Predicting binary outcomes". Working Paper, Department of Economics, University of California, San Diego.

Granger, C.W.J., Pesaran, M.H. (2000a). "A decision-theoretic approach to forecast evaluation". In: Chan, W.S., Li, W.K., Tong, H. (Eds.), Statistics and Finance: An Interface. Imperial College Press, London.

Granger, C.W.J., Pesaran, M.H. (2000b). "Economic and statistical measures of forecast accuracy". Journal of Forecasting 19, 537–560.

Machina, M.J., Granger, C.W.J., (2005). "Decision-based forecast evaluation". Manuscript, Department of Economics, University of California, San Diego.

Pesaran, M.H., Skouras, S. (2002). "Decision-based methods for forecast evaluation". In: Clements, M.P., Hendry, D.F. (Eds.), A Companion to Economic Forecasting. Blackwell, Oxford.

Pratt, J.W., Raiffa, H., Schlaifer, R. (1995). Introduction to Statistical Decision Theory, second ed. MIT Press, Cambridge, MA.

Theil, H. (1961). Economic Forecasts and Policy, second ed. North-Holland, Amsterdam.

Theil, H. (1971). Applied Economic Forecasting. North-Holland, Amsterdam.

West, M., Harrison, J. (1989). Bayesian Forecasting and Dynamic Models. Springer-Verlag, New York.

West, M., Harrison, J. (1997). Bayesian Forecasting and Dynamic Models, second ed. Springer-Verlag, New York.

White, D.J. (1966). "Forecasts and decision making". Journal of Mathematical Analysis and Applications 14, 163–173.

Chapter 3

FORECAST EVALUATION

KENNETH D. WEST

University of Wisconsin

Contents

Handbook of Economic Forecasting, Volume 1
Edited by Graham Elliott, Clive W.J. Granger and Allan Timmermann

DOI: 10.1016/S1574-0706(05)01003-7

Abstract

This chapter summarizes recent literature on asymptotic inference about forecasts. Both analytical and simulation based methods are discussed. The emphasis is on techniques applicable when the number of competing models is small. Techniques applicable when a large number of models is compared to a benchmark are also briefly discussed.

Keywords

forecast, prediction, out of sample, prediction error, forecast error, parameter estimation error, asymptotic irrelevance, hypothesis test, inference

JEL classification: C220, C320, C520, C530

1. Introduction

This chapter reviews asymptotic methods for inference about moments of functions of predictions and prediction errors. The methods may rely on conventional asymptotics or they may be bootstrap based. The relevant class of applications are ones in which the investigator uses a long time series of predictions and prediction errors as a model evaluation tool. Typically the evaluation is done retrospectively rather than in real time. A classic example is Meese and Rogoff's (1983) evaluation of exchange rate models.

In most applications, the investigator aims to compare two or more models. Measures of relative model quality might include ratios or differences of mean, mean-squared or mean-absolute prediction errors; correlation between one model's prediction and another model's realization (also known as forecast encompassing); or comparisons of utility or profit-based measures of predictive ability. In other applications, the investigator focuses on a single model, in which case measures of model quality might include correlation between prediction and realization, lack of serial correlation in one step ahead prediction errors, ability to predict direction of change, or bias in predictions.

Predictive ability has long played a role in evaluation of econometric models. An early example of a study that retrospectively set aside a large number of observations for predictive evaluation is Wilson (1934, pp. 307–308). Wilson, who studied monthly price data spanning more than a century, used estimates from the first half of his data to forecast the next twenty years. He then evaluated his model by computing the correlation between prediction and realization.[1] Growth in data and computing power has led to widespread use of similar predictive evaluation techniques, as is indicated by the applications cited below.

To prevent misunderstanding, it may help to stress that the techniques discussed here are probably of little relevance to studies that set aside one or two or a handful of observations for out of sample evaluation. The reader is referred to textbook expositions about confidence intervals around a prediction, or to proposals for simulation methods such as Fair (1980). As well, the paper does not cover density forecasts. Inference about such forecasts is covered in the Handbook Chapter 5 by Corradi and Swanson (2006). Finally, the paper takes for granted that one wishes to perform out of sample analysis. My purpose is to describe techniques that can be used by researchers who have decided, for reasons not discussed in this chapter, to use a non-trivial portion of their samples for prediction. See recent work by Chen (2004), Clark and McCracken (2005b) and Inoue and Kilian (2004a, 2004b) for different takes on the possible power advantages of using out of sample tests.

Much of the paper uses tests for equal mean squared prediction error (MSPE) for illustration. MSPE is not only simple, but it is also arguably the most commonly used measure of predictive ability. The focus on MSPE, however, is done purely for expositional reasons. This paper is intended to be useful for practitioners interested in a

[1] Which, incidentally and regrettably, turned out to be negative.

wide range of functions of predictions and prediction errors that have appeared in the literature. Consequently, results that are quite general are presented. Because the target audience is practitioners, I do not give technical details. Instead, I give examples, summarize findings and present guidelines.

Section 2 illustrates the evolution of the relevant methodology. Sections 3–8 discuss inference when the number of models under evaluation is small. "Small" is not precisely defined, but in sample sizes typically available in economics suggests a number in the single digits. Section 3 discusses inference in the unusual, but conceptually simple, case in which none of the models under consideration rely on estimated regression parameters to make predictions. Sections 4 and 5 relax this assumption, but for reasons described in those sections assume that the models under consideration are nonnested. Section 4 describes when reliance on estimated regression parameters is irrelevant asymptotically, so that Section 3 procedures may still be applied. Section 5 describes how to account for reliance on estimated regression parameters. Sections 6 and 7 consider nested models. Section 6 focuses on MSPE, Section 7 other loss functions. Section 8 summarizes the results of previous sections. Section 9 briefly discusses inference when the number of models being evaluated is large, possibly larger than the sample size. Section 10 concludes.

2. A brief history

I begin the discussion with a brief history of methodology for inference, focusing on mean squared prediction errors (MSPE).

Let e_{1t} and e_{2t} denote one step ahead prediction errors from two competing models. Let their corresponding second moments be

$$\sigma_1^2 \equiv \mathrm{E}e_{1t}^2 \quad \text{and} \quad \sigma_2^2 \equiv \mathrm{E}e_{2t}^2.$$

(For reasons explained below, the assumption of stationarity – the absence of a t subscript on σ_1^2 and σ_2^2 – is not always innocuous. For the moment, I maintain it for consistency with the literature about to be reviewed.) One wishes to test the null

$$\mathrm{H}_0\colon \quad \sigma_1^2 - \sigma_2^2 = 0,$$

or perhaps construct a confidence interval around the point estimate of $\sigma_1^2 - \sigma_2^2$.

Observe that $\mathrm{E}(e_{1t} - e_{2t})(e_{1t} + e_{2t}) = \sigma_1^2 - \sigma_2^2$. Thus $\sigma_1^2 - \sigma_2^2 = 0$ if and only if the covariance or correlation between $e_{1t} - e_{2t}$ and $e_{1t} + e_{2t}$ is zero. Let us suppose initially that (e_{1t}, e_{2t}) is i.i.d. Granger and Newbold (1977) used this observation to suggest testing $\mathrm{H}_0\colon \sigma_1^2 - \sigma_2^2 = 0$ by testing for zero correlation between $e_{1t} - e_{2t}$ and $e_{1t}+e_{2t}$. This procedure was earlier proposed by Morgan (1939) in the context of testing for equality between variances of two normal random variables. Granger and Newbold (1977) assumed that the forecast errors had zero mean, but Morgan (1939) indicates that this assumption is not essential. The Granger and Newbold test was extended to multistep, serially correlated and possibly non-normal prediction errors by Meese and Rogoff (1988) and Mizrach (1995).

Ashley, Granger and Schmalensee (1980) proposed a test of equal MSPE in the context of nested models. For nested models, equal MSPE is theoretically equivalent to a test of Granger non-causality. Ashley, Granger and Schmalensee (1980) proposed executing a standard F-test, but with out of sample prediction errors used to compute restricted and unrestricted error variances. Ashley, Granger and Schmalensee (1980) recommended that tests be one-sided, testing whether the unrestricted model has smaller MSPE than the restricted (nested) model: it is not clear what it means if the restricted model has a significantly smaller MSPE than the unrestricted model.

The literature on predictive inference that is a focus of this chapter draws on now standard central limit theory introduced into econometrics research by Hansen (1982) – what I will call "standard results" in the rest of the discussion. Perhaps the first explicit use of standard results in predictive inference is Christiano (1989). Let $f_t = e_{1t}^2 - e_{2t}^2$. Christiano observed that we are interested in the mean of f_t, call it $\mathrm{E} f_t \equiv \sigma_1^2 - \sigma_2^2$.[2] And there are standard results on inference about means – indeed, if f_t is i.i.d. with finite variance, introductory econometrics texts describe how to conduct inference about $\mathrm{E} f_t$ given a sample of $\{f_t\}$. A random variable like $e_{1t}^2 - e_{2t}^2$ may be non-normal and serially correlated. But results in Hansen (1982) apply to non-i.i.d. time series data. (Details below.)

One of Hansen's (1982) conditions is stationarity. Christiano acknowledged that standard results might not apply to his empirical application because of a possible failure of stationarity. Specifically, Christiano compared predictions of models estimated over samples of increasing size: the first of his 96 predictions relied on models estimated on quarterly data running from 1960 to 1969, the last from 1960 to 1988. Because of increasing precision of estimates of the models, forecast error variances might decline over time. (This is one sense in which the assumption of stationarity was described as "not obviously innocuous" above.)

West, Edison and Cho (1993) and West and Cho (1995) independently used standard results to compute test statistics. The objects of interest were MSPEs and a certain utility based measure of predictive ability. Diebold and Mariano (1995) proposed using the same standard results, also independently, but in a general context that allows one to be interested in the mean of a general loss or utility function. As detailed below, these papers explained either in context or as a general principle how to allow for multistep, non-normal, and conditionally heteroskedastic prediction errors.

The papers cited in the preceding two paragraphs all proceed without proof. None directly address the possible complications from parameter estimation noted by Christiano (1989). A possible approach to allowing for these complications in special cases is in Hoffman and Pagan (1989) and Ghysels and Hall (1990). These papers showed how

[2] Actually, Christiano looked at root mean squared prediction errors, testing whether $\sigma_1 - \sigma_2 = 0$. For clarity and consistency with the rest of my discussion, I cast his analysis in terms of MSPE.

standard results from Hansen (1982) can be extended to account for parameter estimation in out of sample tests of instrument residual orthogonality when a fixed parameter estimate is used to construct the test. [Christiano (1989), and most of the forecasting literature, by contrast updates parameter estimate as forecasts progress through the sample.] A general analysis was first presented in West (1996), who showed how standard results can be extended when a sequence of parameter estimates is used, and for the mean of a general loss or utility function.

Further explication of developments in inference about predictive ability requires me to start writing out some results. I therefore call a halt to the historical summary. The next section begins the discussion of analytical results related to the papers cited here.

3. A small number of nonnested models, Part I

Analytical results are clearest in the unusual (in economics) case in which predictions do not rely on estimated regression parameters, an assumption maintained in this section but relaxed in future sections.

Notation is as follows. The object of interest is $\mathrm{E}f_t$, an $(m \times 1)$ vector of moments of predictions or prediction errors. Examples include MSPE, mean prediction error, mean absolute prediction error, covariance between one model's prediction and another model's prediction error, mean utility or profit, and means of loss functions that weight positive and negative errors asymmetrically as in Elliott and Timmermann (2003). If one is comparing models, then the elements of $\mathrm{E}f_t$ are expected differences in performance. For MSPE comparisons, and using the notation of the previous section, for example, $\mathrm{E}f_t = \mathrm{E}e_{1t}^2 - \mathrm{E}e_{2t}^2$. As stressed by Diebold and Mariano (1995), this framework also accommodates general loss functions or measures of performance. Let $\mathrm{E}g_{it}$ be the measure of performance of model i – perhaps MSPE, perhaps mean absolute error, perhaps expected utility. Then when there are two models, $m = 1$ and $\mathrm{E}f_t = \mathrm{E}g_{1t} - \mathrm{E}g_{2t}$.

We have a sample of predictions of size P. Let $\bar{f}^* \equiv P^{-1}\sum_t f_t$ denote the $m \times 1$ sample mean of f_t. (The reason for the "*" superscript will become apparent below.) If we are comparing two models with performance of model i measured by $\mathrm{E}g_{it}$, then of course $\bar{f}^* \equiv P^{-1}\sum_t(g_{1t} - g_{2t}) \equiv \bar{g}_1 - \bar{g}_2 =$ the difference in performance of the two models, over the sample. For simplicity and clarity, assume covariance stationarity – neither the first nor second moments of f_t depend on t. At present (predictions do not depend on estimated regression parameters), this assumption is innocuous. It allows simplification of formulas. The results below can be extended to allow moment drift as long as time series averages converge to suitable constants. See Giacomini and White (2003). Then under well-understood and seemingly weak conditions, a central limit theorem holds:

$$\sqrt{P}\big(\bar{f}^* - \mathrm{E}f_t\big) \sim_A \mathrm{N}\big(0, V^*\big), \quad V^* \equiv \sum_{j=-\infty}^{\infty} \mathrm{E}(f_t - \mathrm{E}f_t)(f_{t-j} - \mathrm{E}f_t)'. \tag{3.1}$$

See, for example, White (1984) for the "well-understood" phrase of the sentence prior to (3.1); see below for the "seemingly weak" phrase. Equation (3.1) is the "standard result" referenced above. The $m \times m$ positive semidefinite matrix V^* is sometimes called the long run variance of f_t. If f_t is serially uncorrelated (perhaps i.i.d.), then $V^* = \mathrm{E}(f_t - \mathrm{E}f_t)(f_t - \mathrm{E}f_t)'$. If, further, $m = 1$ so that f_t is a scalar, $V^* = \mathrm{E}(f_t - \mathrm{E}f_t)^2$.

Suppose that V^* is positive definite. Let $\hat{V}^*$ be a consistent estimator of V^*. Typically $\hat{V}^*$ will be constructed with a heteroskedasticity and autocorrelation consistent covariance matrix estimator. Then one can test the null

$$\mathrm{H}_0\colon\quad \mathrm{E}f_t = 0 \tag{3.2}$$

with a Wald test:

$$\bar{f}^{*\prime}\hat{V}^{*-1}\bar{f}^* \sim_A \chi^2(m). \tag{3.3}$$

If $m = 1$ so that f_t is a scalar, one can test the null with a t-test:

$$\begin{aligned} &\bar{f}^*/\big[\hat{V}^*/P\big]^{1/2} \sim_A \mathrm{N}(0, 1), \\ &\hat{V}^* \to_p V^* \equiv \sum_{j=-\infty}^{\infty} \mathrm{E}(f_t - \mathrm{E}f_t)(f_{t-j} - \mathrm{E}f_t). \end{aligned} \tag{3.4}$$

Confidence intervals can be constructed in obvious fashion from $[\hat{V}^*/P]^{1/2}$.

As noted above, the example of the previous section maps into this notation with $m = 1$, $f_t = e_{1t}^2 - e_{2t}^2$, $\mathrm{E}f_t = \sigma_1^2 - \sigma_2^2$, and the null of equal predictive ability is that $\mathrm{E}f_t = 0$, i.e., $\sigma_1^2 = \sigma_2^2$. Testing for equality of MSPE in a set of $m + 1$ models for $m > 1$ is straightforward, as described in the next section. To give an illustration or two of other possible definitions of f_t, sticking for simplicity with $m = 1$: If one is interested in whether a forecast is unbiased, then $f_t = e_{1t}$ and $\mathrm{E}f_t = 0$ is the hypothesis that the model 1 forecast error is unbiased. If one is interested in mean absolute error, $f_t = |e_{1t}| - |e_{2t}|$, and $\mathrm{E}f_t = 0$ is the hypothesis of equal mean absolute prediction error. Additional examples are presented in a subsequent section below.

For concreteness, let me return to MSPE, with $m = 1$, $f_t = e_{1t}^2 - e_{2t}^2$, $\bar{f}^* \equiv P^{-1}\sum_t(e_{1t}^2 - e_{2t}^2)$. Suppose first that (e_{1t}, e_{2t}) is i.i.d. Then so, too, is $e_{1t}^2 - e_{2t}^2$, and $V^* = \mathrm{E}(f_t - \mathrm{E}f_t)^2 = \mathrm{variance}(e_{1t}^2 - e_{2t}^2)$. In such a case, as the number of forecast errors $P \to \infty$ one can estimate V^* consistently with $\hat{V}^* = P^{-1}\sum_t(f_t - \bar{f}^*)^2$. Suppose next that (e_{1t}, e_{2t}) is a vector of τ step ahead forecast errors whose (2×1) vector of Wold innovations is i.i.d. Then (e_{1t}, e_{2t}) and $e_{1t}^2 - e_{2t}^2$ follow MA$(\tau - 1)$ processes, and $V^* = \sum_{j=-\tau+1}^{\tau-1}\mathrm{E}(f_t - \mathrm{E}f_t)(f_{t-j} - \mathrm{E}f_t)$. One possible estimator of V^* is the sample analogue. Let $\hat{\Gamma}_j = P^{-1}\sum_{t>|j|}(f_t - \bar{f}^*)(f_{t-|j|} - \bar{f}^*)$ be an estimate of $\mathrm{E}(f_t - \mathrm{E}f_t)(f_{t-j} - \mathrm{E}f_t)$, and set $\hat{V}^* = \sum_{j=-\tau+1}^{\tau-1}\hat{\Gamma}_j$. It is well known, however, that this estimator may not be positive definite if $\tau > 0$. Hence one may wish to use an estimator that is both consistent and positive semidefinite by construction [Newey and West (1987, 1994), Andrews (1991), Andrews and Monahan (1994), den Haan and

Levin (2000)]. Finally, under some circumstances, one will wish to use a heteroskedasticity and autocorrelation consistent estimator of V^* even when (e_{1t}, e_{2t}) is a one step forecast error. This will be the case if the second moments follow a GARCH or related process, in which case there will be serial correlation in $f_t = e_{1t}^2 - e_{2t}^2$ even if there is no serial correlation in (e_{1t}, e_{2t}).

But such results are well known, for f_t a scalar or vector, and for f_t relevant for MSPE or other moments of predictions and prediction errors. The "seemingly weak" conditions referenced above Equation (3.1) allow for quite general forms of dependence and heterogeneity in forecasts and forecast errors. I use the word "seemingly" because of some ancillary assumptions that are not satisfied in some relevant applications. First, the number of models m must be "small" relative to the number of predictions P. In an extreme case in which $m > P$, conventional estimators will yield $\hat{V}^*$ that is not of full rank. As well, and more informally, one suspects that conventional asymptotics will yield a poor approximation if m is large relative to P. Section 9 briefly discusses alternative approaches likely to be useful in such contexts.

Second, and more generally, V^* must be full rank. When the number of models $m = 2$, and MSPE is the object of interest, this rules out $e_{1t}^2 = e_{2t}^2$ with probability 1 (obviously). It also rules out pairs of models in which $\sqrt{P}(\hat{\sigma}_1^2 - \hat{\sigma}_2^2) \to_p 0$. This latter condition is violated in applications in which one or both models make predictions based on estimated regression parameters, and the models are nested. This is discussed in Sections 6 and 7 below.

4. A small number of nonnested models, Part II

In the vast majority of economic applications, one or more of the models under consideration rely on estimated regression parameters when making predictions. To spell out the implications for inference, it is necessary to define some additional notation. For simplicity, assume that one step ahead prediction errors are the object of interest. Let the total sample size be $T + 1$. The last P observations of this sample are used for forecast evaluation. The first R observations are used to construct an initial set of regression estimates that are then used for the first prediction. We have $R + P = T + 1$. Schematically:

$$\begin{array}{ccc} & R \text{ observations} & & P \text{ observations} & \\ | & \text{———————————} & | & \text{———————————} & | \\ 1 & & R & & T+1=R+P \end{array} \tag{4.1}$$

Division of the available data into R and P is taken as given.

In the forecasting literature, three distinct schemes figure prominently in how one generates the sequence of regression estimates necessary to make predictions. Asymptotic results differ slightly for the three, so it is necessary to distinguish between them. Let β denote the vector of regression parameters whose estimates are used to make predictions. In the *recursive* scheme, the size of the sample used to estimate β grows as one makes predictions for successive observations. One first estimates β with data from 1 to R and uses the estimate to predict observation $R + 1$ (recall that I am assuming one step ahead predictions, for simplicity); one then estimates β with data from 1 to $R + 1$, with the new estimate used to predict observation $R + 2; \ldots$; finally, one estimates β with data from 1 to T, with the final estimate used to predict observation $T + 1$. In the *rolling* scheme, the sequence of β's is always generated from a sample of size R. The first estimate of β is obtained with a sample running from 1 to R, the next with a sample running from 2 to $R + 1, \ldots$, the final with a sample running from $T - R + 1$ to T. In the *fixed* scheme, one estimates β just once, using data from 1 to R. In all three schemes, the number of predictions is P and the size of the smallest regression sample is R. Examples of applications using each of these schemes include Faust, Rogers and Wright (2004) (recursive), Cheung, Chinn and Pascual (2003) (rolling) and Ashley, Granger and Schmalensee (1980) (fixed). The fixed scheme is relatively attractive when it is computationally difficult to update parameter estimates. The rolling scheme is relatively attractive when one wishes to guard against moment or parameter drift that is difficult to model explicitly.

It may help to illustrate with a simple example. Suppose one model under consideration is a univariate zero mean AR(1): $y_t = \beta^* y_{t-1} + e_{1t}$. Suppose further that the estimator is ordinary least squares. Then the sequence of P estimates of β^* are generated as follows for $t = R, \ldots, T$:

$$\begin{aligned}
&\text{recursive:} && \hat{\beta}_t = \left[\sum_{s=1}^{t}(y_{s-1}^2)\right]^{-1}\left[\sum_{s=1}^{t} y_{s-1}y_s\right]; \\
&\text{rolling:} && \hat{\beta}_t = \left[\sum_{s=t-R+1}^{t}(y_{s-1}^2)\right]^{-1}\left[\sum_{s=t-R+1}^{t} y_{s-1}y_s\right]; \\
&\text{fixed:} && \hat{\beta}_t = \left[\sum_{s=1}^{R}(y_{s-1}^2)\right]^{-1}\left[\sum_{s=1}^{R} y_{s-1}y_s\right].
\end{aligned} \tag{4.2}$$

In each case, the one step ahead prediction error is $\hat{e}_{t+1} \equiv y_{t+1} - y_t\hat{\beta}_t$. Observe that for the fixed scheme $\hat{\beta}_t = \hat{\beta}_R$ for all t, while $\hat{\beta}_t$ changes with t for the rolling and recursive schemes.

I will illustrate with a simple MSPE example comparing two linear models. I then introduce notation necessary to define other moments of interest, sticking with linear models for expositional convenience. An important asymptotic result is then stated. The next section outlines a general framework that covers all the simple examples in this section, and allows for nonlinear models and estimators.

So suppose there are two least squares models, say $y_t = X_{1t}'\beta_1^* + e_{1t}$ and $y_t = X_{2t}'\beta_2^* + e_{2t}$. (Note the dating convention: X_{1t} and X_{2t} can be used to predict y_t, for example $X_{1t} = y_{t-1}$ if model 1 is an AR(1).) The population MSPEs are $\sigma_1^2 \equiv \mathrm{E}e_{1t}^2$ and $\sigma_2^2 \equiv \mathrm{E}e_{2t}^2$. (Absence of a subscript t on the MSPEs is for simplicity and without substance.) Define the sample one step ahead forecast errors and sample MSPEs as

$$\hat{e}_{1t+1} \equiv y_{t+1} - X'_{1t+1}\hat{\beta}_{1t}, \quad \hat{e}_{2t+1} \equiv y_{t+1} - X'_{2t+1}\hat{\beta}_{2t},$$
$$\hat{\sigma}_1^2 = P^{-1}\sum_{t=R}^{T}\hat{e}_{1t+1}^2, \quad \hat{\sigma}_2^2 = P^{-1}\sum_{t=R}^{T}\hat{e}_{2t+1}^2. \tag{4.3}$$

With MSPE the object of interest, one examines the difference between the sample MSPEs $\hat{\sigma}_1^2$ and $\hat{\sigma}_2^2$. Let

$$\hat{f}_t \equiv \hat{e}_{1t}^2 - \hat{e}_{2t}^2, \quad \bar{f} \equiv P^{-1}\sum_{t=R}^{T}\hat{f}_{t+1} \equiv \hat{\sigma}_1^2 - \hat{\sigma}_2^2. \tag{4.4}$$

Observe that $\bar{f}$ defined in (4.4) differs from $\bar{f}^*$ defined above (3.1) in that $\bar{f}$ relies on $\hat{e}$'s, whereas $\bar{f}^*$ relies on e's.

The null hypothesis is $\sigma_1^2 - \sigma_2^2 = 0$. One way to test the null would be to substitute $\hat{e}_{1t}$ and $\hat{e}_{2t}$ for e_{1t} and e_{2t} in the formulas presented in the previous section. If $(e_{1t}, e_{2t})'$ is i.i.d., for example, one would set $\hat{V}^* = P^{-1}\sum_{t=R}^{T}(\hat{f}_{t+1} - \bar{f})^2$, compute the t-statistic

$$\bar{f}/[\hat{V}^*/P]^{1/2} \tag{4.5}$$

and use standard normal critical values. [I use the "*" in $\hat{V}^*$ for both $P^{-1}\sum_{t=R}^{T}(\hat{f}_{t+1} - \bar{f})^2$ (this section) and for $P^{-1}\sum_{t=R}^{T}(f_{t+1} - \bar{f}^*)^2$ (previous section) because under the asymptotic approximations described below, both are consistent for the long run variance of f_{t+1}.]

Use of (4.5) is not obviously an advisable approach. Clearly, $\hat{e}_{1t}^2 - \hat{e}_{2t}^2$ is polluted by error in estimation of β_1 and β_2. It is not obvious that sample averages of $\hat{e}_{1t}^2 - \hat{e}_{2t}^2$ (i.e., $\bar{f}$) have the same asymptotic distribution as those of $e_{1t}^2 - e_{2t}^2$ (i.e., $\bar{f}^*$). Under suitable conditions (see below), a key factor determining whether the asymptotic distributions are equivalent is whether or not the two models are nested. If they are nested, the distributions are not equivalent. Use of (4.5) with normal critical values is not advised. This is discussed in a subsequent section.

If the models are not nested, West (1996) showed that when conducting inference about MSPE, parameter estimation error is *asymptotically irrelevant*. I put the phrase in italics because I will have frequent recourse to it in the sequel: "asymptotic irrelevance" means that one conduct inference by applying standard results to the mean of the loss function of interest, treating parameter estimation error as irrelevant.

To explain this result, as well as to illustrate when asymptotic irrelevance does not apply, requires some – actually, considerable – notation. I will phase in some of this notation in this section, with most of the algebra deferred to the next section. Let β^* denote the $k \times 1$ population value of the parameter vector used to make predictions. Suppose for expositional simplicity that the model(s) used to make predictions are linear,

$$y_t = X_t'\beta^* + e_t \tag{4.6a}$$

if there is a single model,

$$y_t = X_{1t}'\beta_1^* + e_{1t}, \quad y_t = X_{2t}'\beta_2^* + e_{2t}, \quad \beta^* \equiv (\beta_1^{*\prime}, \beta_2^{*\prime})', \tag{4.6b}$$

if there are two competing models. Let $f_t(\beta^*)$ be the random variable whose expectation is of interest. Then leading scalar ($m = 1$) examples of $f_t(\beta^*)$ include:

$$f_t(\beta^*) = e_{1t}^2 - e_{2t}^2 = (y_t - X_{1t}'\beta_1^*)^2 - (y_t - X_{2t}'\beta_2^*)^2 \tag{4.7a}$$

($\mathrm{E}f_t = 0$ means equal MSPE);

$$f_t(\beta^*) = e_t = y_t - X_t'\beta^* \tag{4.7b}$$

($\mathrm{E}f_t = 0$ means zero mean prediction error);

$$f_t(\beta^*) = e_{1t}X_{2t}'\beta_2^* = (y_t - X_{1t}'\beta_1^*)X_{2t}'\beta_2^* \tag{4.7c}$$

[$\mathrm{E}f_t = 0$ means zero correlation between one model's prediction error and another model's prediction, an implication of forecast encompassing proposed by Chong and Hendry (1986)];

$$f_t(\beta^*) = e_{1t}(e_{1t} - e_{2t}) = (y_t - X_{1t}'\beta_1^*)[(y_t - X_{1t}'\beta_1^*) - (y_t - X_{2t}'\beta_2^*)] \tag{4.7d}$$

[$\mathrm{E}f_t = 0$ is an implication of forecast encompassing proposed by Harvey, Leybourne and Newbold (1998)];

$$f_t(\beta^*) = e_{t+1}e_t = (y_{t+1} - X_{t+1}'\beta^*)(y_t - X_t'\beta^*) \tag{4.7e}$$

($\mathrm{E}f_t = 0$ means zero first order serial correlation);

$$f_t(\beta^*) = e_tX_t'\beta^* = (y_t - X_t'\beta^*)X_t'\beta^* \tag{4.7f}$$

($\mathrm{E}f_t = 0$ means the prediction and prediction error are uncorrelated);

$$f_t(\beta^*) = |e_{1t}| - |e_{2t}| = |y_t - X_{1t}'\beta_1^*| - |y_t - X_{2t}'\beta_2^*| \tag{4.7g}$$

($\mathrm{E}f_t = 0$ means equal mean absolute error).

More generally, $f_t(\beta^*)$ can be per period utility or profit, or differences across models of per period utility or profit, as in Leitch and Tanner (1991) or West, Edison and Cho (1993).

Let $\hat{f}_{t+1} \equiv f_{t+1}(\hat{\beta}_t)$ denote the sample counterpart of $f_{t+1}(\beta^*)$, with $\bar{f} \equiv P^{-1}\sum_{t=R}^{T}\hat{f}_{t+1}$ the sample mean evaluated at the series of estimates of β^*. Let $\bar{f}^* = P^{-1}\sum_{t=R}^{T} f_{t+1}(\beta^*)$ denote the sample mean evaluated at β^*. Let F denote the $(1 \times k)$ derivative of the expectation of f_t, evaluated at β^*:

$$F = \frac{\partial \mathrm{E}f_t(\beta^*)}{\partial \beta}. \tag{4.8}$$

For example, $F = -\mathrm{E}X_t'$ for mean prediction error (4.7b).

Then under mild conditions,

$$\sqrt{P}(\bar{f} - \mathrm{E}f_t) = \sqrt{P}(\bar{f}^* - \mathrm{E}f_t) + F \times (P/R)^{1/2} \times [\mathrm{O}_p(1) \text{ terms from the sequence of estimates of } \beta^*] + \mathrm{o}_p(1). \tag{4.9}$$

Some specific formulas are in the next section. Result (4.9) holds not only when f_t is a scalar, as I have been assuming, but as well when f_t is a vector. (When f_t is a vector of dimension (say) m, F has dimension $m \times k$.)

Thus, uncertainty about the estimate of $\mathrm{E}f_t$ can be decomposed into uncertainty that would be present even if β^* were known and, possibly, additional uncertainty due to estimation of β^*. The qualifier "possibly" results from at least three sets of circumstances in which error in estimation of β^* is asymptotically irrelevant: (1) $F = 0$; (2) $P/R \to 0$; (3) the variance of the terms due to estimation of β^* is exactly offset by the covariance between these terms and $\sqrt{P}(\bar{f}^* - \mathrm{E}f_t)$. For cases (1) and (2), the middle term in (4.9) is identically zero ($F = 0$) or vanishes asymptotically ($P/R \to 0$), implying that $\sqrt{P}(\bar{f} - \mathrm{E}f_t) - \sqrt{P}(\bar{f}^* - \mathrm{E}f_t) \to_p 0$; for case (3) the asymptotic variances of $\sqrt{P}(\bar{f} - \mathrm{E}f_t)$ and $\sqrt{P}(\bar{f}^* - \mathrm{E}f_t)$ happen to be the same. In any of the three sets of circumstances, *inference can proceed as described in the previous section.* This is important because it simplifies matters if one can abstract from uncertainty about β^* when conducting inference.

To illustrate each of the three circumstances:

1. For MSPE in our linear example $F = (-2\mathrm{E}X'_{1t}e_{1t}, 2\mathrm{E}X'_{2t}e_{2t})'$. So $F = 0_{1\times k}$ if the predictors are uncorrelated with the prediction error.[3] Similarly, $F = 0$ for mean absolute prediction error (4.7g) ($\mathrm{E}[|e_{1t}| - |e_{2t}|]$) when the prediction errors have a median of zero, conditional on the predictors. (To prevent confusion, it is to be emphasized that MSPE and mean absolute error are unusual in that asymptotic irrelevance applies even when P/R is not small. In this sense, my focus on MSPE is a bit misleading.)

Let me illustrate the implications with an example in which f_t is a vector rather than a scalar. Suppose that we wish to test equality of MSPEs from $m + 1$ competing models, under the assumption that the forecast error vector $(e_{1t}, \ldots, e_{m+1,t})'$ is i.i.d. Define the $m \times 1$ vectors

$$f_t \equiv \left(e_{1t}^2 - e_{2t}^2, \ldots, e_{1t}^2 - e_{m+1,t}^2\right)', \quad \hat{f}_t = \left(\hat{e}_{1t}^2 - \hat{e}_{2t}^2, \ldots, \hat{e}_{1t}^2 - \hat{e}_{m+1,t}^2\right)',$$
$$\bar{f} = P^{-1} \sum_{t=R}^{T} \hat{f}_{t+1}. \tag{4.10}$$

The null is that $\mathrm{E}f_t = 0_{m\times 1}$. (Of course, it is arbitrary that the null is defined as discrepancies from model 1's squared prediction errors; test statistics are identical regardless of the model used to define f_t.) Then under the null

$$\bar{f}'\hat{V}^{*-1}\bar{f} \sim_A \chi^2(m), \quad \hat{V}^* \to_p V^* \equiv \sum_{j=-\infty}^{\infty} \mathrm{E}(f_t - \mathrm{E}f_t)(f_{t-j} - \mathrm{E}f_t)', \tag{4.11}$$

[3] Of course, one would be unlikely to forecast with a model that *a priori* is expected to violate this condition, though prediction is sometimes done with realized right hand side endogenous variables [e.g., Meese and Rogoff (1983)]. But prediction exercise do sometimes find that this condition does not hold. That is, out of sample prediction errors display correlation with the predictors (even though in sample residuals often display zero correlation by construction). So even for MSPE, one might want to account for parameter estimation error when conducting inference.

where, as indicated, $\hat{V}^*$ is a consistent estimate of the $m \times m$ long run variance of f_t. If $f_t \equiv (e_{1t}^2 - e_{2t}^2, \ldots, e_{1t}^2 - e_{m+1,t}^2)'$ is serially uncorrelated (sufficient for which is that $(e_{1t}, \ldots, e_{m+1,t})'$ is i.i.d.), then a possible estimator of V is simply

$$\hat{V}^* = P^{-1} \sum_{t=R}^{T} (\hat{f}_{t+1} - \bar{f})(\hat{f}_{t+1} - \bar{f})'.$$

If the squared forecast errors display persistence (GARCH and all that), a robust estimator of the variance-covariance matrix should be used [Hueng (1999), West and Cho (1995)].

2. One can see in (4.9) that asymptotic irrelevance holds quite generally when $P/R \to 0$. The intuition is that the relatively large sample (big R) used to estimate β produces small uncertainty relative to uncertainty that would be present in the relatively small sample (small P) even if one knew β. The result was noted informally by Chong and Hendry (1986). Simulation evidence in West (1996, 2001), McCracken (2004) and Clark and McCracken (2001) suggests that $P/R < 0.1$ more or less justifies using the asymptotic approximation that assumes asymptotic irrelevance.

3. This fortunate cancellation of variance and covariance terms occurs for certain moments and loss functions, when estimates of parameters needed to make predictions are generated by the recursive scheme (but not by the rolling or fixed schemes), and when forecast errors are conditionally homoskedastic. These loss functions are: mean prediction error; serial correlation of one step ahead prediction errors; zero correlation between one model's forecast error and another model's forecast. This is illustrated in the discussion of Equation (7.2) below.

To repeat: When asymptotic irrelevance applies, one can proceed as described in Section 3. One need not account for dependence of forecasts on estimated parameter vectors. When asymptotic irrelevance does not apply, matters are more complicated. This is discussed in the next sections.

5. A small number of nonnested models, Part III

Asymptotic irrelevance fails in a number of important cases, at least according to the asymptotics of West (1996). Under the rolling and fixed schemes, it fails quite generally. For example, it fails for mean prediction error, correlation between realization and prediction, encompassing, and zero correlation in one step ahead prediction errors [West and McCracken (1998)]. Under the recursive scheme, it similarly fails for such moments when prediction errors are not conditionally homoskedastic. In such cases, asymptotic inference requires accounting for uncertainty about parameters used to make predictions.

The general result is as follows. One is interested in an $(m \times 1)$ vector of moments $\mathrm{E} f_t$, where f_t now depends on observable data through a $(k \times 1)$ unknown parameter vector β^*. If moments of predictions or prediction errors of competing sets of regressions are to be compared, the parameter vectors from the various regressions are stacked to form β^*. It is assumed that $\mathrm{E}f_t$ is differentiable in a neighborhood around β^*. Let $\hat{\beta}_t$ denote an estimate of β^* that relies on data from period t and earlier. Let $\tau \geqslant 1$ be the forecast horizon of interest; $\tau = 1$ has been assumed in the discussion so far. Let the total sample available be of size $T + \tau$. The estimate of $\mathrm{E}f_t$ is constructed as

$$\bar{f} = P^{-1} \sum_{t=R}^{T} f_{t+\tau}(\hat{\beta}_t) \equiv P^{-1} \sum_{t=R}^{T} \hat{f}_{t+\tau}. \tag{5.1}$$

The models are assumed to be parametric. The estimator of the regression parameters satisfies

$$\hat{\beta}_t - \beta^* = B(t)H(t), \tag{5.2}$$

where $B(t)$ is $k \times q$, $H(t)$ is $q \times 1$ with

(a) $B(t) \overset{\text{a.s.}}{\rightarrow} B$, B a matrix of rank k;

(b) $H(t) = t^{-1} \sum_{s=1}^{t} h_s(\beta^*)$ (recursive), $H(t) = R^{-1} \sum_{s=t-R+1}^{t} h_s(\beta^*)$ (rolling), $H(t) = R^{-1} \sum_{s=1}^{R} h_s(\beta^*)$ (fixed), for a $(q \times 1)$ orthogonality condition $h_s(\beta^*)$ orthogonality condition that satisfies

(c) $\mathrm{E}h_s(\beta^*) = 0$.

Here, h_t is the score if the estimation method is maximum likelihood, or the GMM orthogonality condition if GMM is the estimator. The matrix $B(t)$ is the inverse of the Hessian (ML) or linear combination of orthogonality conditions (GMM), with large sample counterpart B. In exactly identified models, $q = k$. Allowance for overidentified GMM models is necessary to permit prediction from the reduced form of simultaneous equations models, for example. For the results below, various moment and mixing conditions are required. See West (1996) and Giacomini and White (2003) for details.

It may help to pause to illustrate with linear least squares examples. For the least squares model (4.6a), in which $y_t = X_t'\beta^* + e_t$,

$$h_t = X_t e_t. \tag{5.3a}$$

In (4.6b), in which there are two models $y_t = X_{1t}'\beta_1^* + e_{1t}$, $y_t = X_{2t}'\beta_2^* + e_{2t}$, $\beta^* \equiv (\beta_1^{*\prime}, \beta_2^{*\prime})'$,

$$h_t = \left(X_{1t}'e_{1t}, X_{2t}'e_{2t}\right)', \tag{5.3b}$$

where $h_t = h_t(\beta^*)$ is suppressed for simplicity. The matrix B is $k \times k$:

$$\begin{aligned} &B = \left(\mathrm{E}X_{1t}X_{1t}'\right)^{-1} \quad \text{(model (4.6a))}, \\ &B = \operatorname{diag}\left[\left(\mathrm{E}X_{1t}X_{1t}'\right)^{-1}, \left(\mathrm{E}X_{2t}X_{2t}'\right)^{-1}\right] \quad \text{(model (4.6b))}. \end{aligned} \tag{5.4}$$

If one is comparing two models with $\mathrm{E}g_{it}$ and $\bar{g}_i$ the expected and sample mean performance measure for model i, $i = 1, 2$, then $\mathrm{E}f_t = \mathrm{E}g_{1t} - \mathrm{E}g_{2t}$ and $\bar{f} = \bar{g}_1 - \bar{g}_2$.

To return to the statement of results, which require conditions such as those in West (1996), and which are noted in the bullet points at the end of this section. Assume a large sample of both predictions and prediction errors,

$$P \to \infty, \quad R \to \infty, \quad \lim_{T\to\infty} \frac{P}{R} = \pi, \quad 0 \leqslant \pi < \infty. \tag{5.5}$$

An expansion of $\bar{f}$ around $\bar{f}^*$ yields

$$\sqrt{P}(\bar{f} - \mathrm{E}f_t) = \sqrt{P}(\bar{f}^* - \mathrm{E}f_t) + F(P/R)^{1/2}\bigl[BR^{1/2}\bar{H}\bigr] + \mathrm{o}_p(1) \tag{5.6}$$

which may also be written

$$P^{-1/2}\sum_{t=R}^{T}\bigl[f(\hat{\beta}_{t+1}) - \mathrm{E}f_t\bigr]$$
$$= P^{-1/2}\sum_{t=R}^{T}\bigl[f_{t+1}(\beta^*) - \mathrm{E}f_t\bigr] + F(P/R)^{1/2}\bigl[BR^{1/2}\bar{H}\bigr] + \mathrm{o}_p(1). \tag{5.6$'$}$$

The first term on the right-hand side of (5.6) and (5.6)′ – henceforth (5.6), for short – represents uncertainty that would be present even if predictions relied on the population value of the parameter vector β^*. The limiting distribution of this term was given in (3.1). The second term on the right-hand side of (5.6) results from reliance of predictions on estimates of β^*. To account for the effects of this second term requires yet more notation. Write the long run variance of $(f'_{t+1}, h'_t)'$ as

$$S = \begin{bmatrix} V^* & S_{fh} \\ S'_{fh} & S_{hh} \end{bmatrix}. \tag{5.7}$$

Here, $V^* \equiv \sum_{j=-\infty}^{\infty} \mathrm{E}(f_t - \mathrm{E}f_t)(f_{t-j} - \mathrm{E}f_t)'$ is $m \times m$, $S_{fh} = \sum_{j=-\infty}^{\infty} \mathrm{E}(f_t - \mathrm{E}f_t)h'_{t-j}$ is $m \times k$, and $S_{hh} \equiv \sum_{j=-\infty}^{\infty} \mathrm{E}h_t h'_{t-j}$ is $k \times k$, and f_t and h_t are understood to be evaluated at β^*. The asymptotic ($R \to \infty$) variance–covariance matrix of the estimator of β^* is

$$V_\beta \equiv BS_{hh}B'. \tag{5.8}$$

With π defined in (5.5), define the scalars λ_{fh}, λ_{hh} and $\lambda \equiv (1 + \lambda_{hh} - 2\lambda_{fh})$, as in the following table:

Sampling scheme	λ_{fh}	λ_{hh}	λ
Recursive	$1 - \pi^{-1}\ln(1+\pi)$	$2[1 - \pi^{-1}\ln(1+\pi)]$	1
Rolling, $\pi \leqslant 1$	$\frac{\pi}{2}$	$\pi - \frac{\pi^2}{3}$	$1 - \frac{\pi^2}{3}$
Rolling, $\pi > 1$	$1 - \frac{1}{2\pi}$	$1 - \frac{1}{3\pi}$	$\frac{2}{3\pi}$
Fixed	0	π	$1 + \pi$

(5.9)

Finally, define the $m \times k$ matrix F as in (4.8), $F \equiv \partial \mathrm{E}f_t(\beta^*)/\partial\beta$.

Then $P^{-1/2}\sum_{t=R}^{T}[f(\hat{\beta}_{t+1})-\mathrm{E}f_t]$ is asymptotically normal with variance-covariance matrix

$$V = V^* + \lambda_{fh}\big(FBS'_{fh} + S_{fh}B'F'\big) + \lambda_{hh}FV_\beta F'. \tag{5.10}$$

V^* is the long run variance of $P^{-1/2}\big[\sum_{t=R}^{T} f_{t+1}(\beta^*) - \mathrm{E}f_t\big]$ and is the same object as V^* defined in (3.1), $\lambda_{hh}FV_\beta F'$ is the long run variance of $F(P/R)^{1/2}[BR^{1/2}\bar{H}]$, and $\lambda_{fh}(FBS'_{fh} + S_{fh}B'F')$ is the covariance between the two.

This completes the statement of the general result. To illustrate the expansion (5.6) and the asymptotic variance (5.10), I will temporarily switch from my example of comparison of MSPEs to one in which one is looking at mean prediction error. The variable f_t is thus redefined to equal the prediction error, $f_t = e_t$, and $\mathrm{E}f_t$ is the moment of interest. I will further use a trivial example, in which the only predictor is the constant term, $y_t = \beta^* + e_t$. Let us assume as well, as in the Hoffman and Pagan (1989) and Ghysels and Hall (1990) analyses of predictive tests of instrument-residual orthogonality, that the fixed scheme is used and predictions are made using a single estimate of β^*. This single estimate is the least squares estimate on the sample running from 1 to R, $\hat{\beta}_R \equiv R^{-1}\sum_{s=1}^{R} y_s$. Now, $\hat{e}_{t+1} = e_{t+1} - (\hat{\beta}_R - \beta^*) = e_{t+1} - R^{-1}\sum_{s=1}^{R} e_s$. So

$$P^{-1/2}\sum_{t=R}^{T}\hat{e}_{t+1} = P^{-1/2}\sum_{t=R}^{T}e_{t+1} - (P/R)^{1/2}\left(R^{-1/2}\sum_{s=1}^{R}e_s\right). \tag{5.11}$$

This is in the form (4.9) or (5.6)′, with: $F = -1$, $R^{-1/2}\sum_{s=1}^{R} e_s = [\mathrm{O}_p(1)$ terms due to the sequence of estimates of $\beta^*]$, $B \equiv 1$, $\bar{H} = (R^{-1}\sum_{s=1}^{R} e_s)$ and the $\mathrm{o}_p(1)$ term identically zero.

If e_t is well behaved, say i.i.d. with finite variance σ^2, the bivariate vector $(P^{-1/2}\sum_{t=R}^{T} e_{t+1}, R^{-1/2}\sum_{s=1}^{R} e_s)'$ is asymptotically normal with variance covariance matrix $\sigma^2 I_2$. It follows that

$$P^{-1/2}\sum_{t=R}^{T}e_{t+1} - (P/R)^{1/2}\left(R^{-1/2}\sum_{s=1}^{R}e_s\right) \sim_A \mathrm{N}\big(0, (1+\pi)\sigma^2\big). \tag{5.12}$$

The variance in the normal distribution is in the form (5.10), with $\lambda_{fh} = 0$, $\lambda_{hh} = \pi$, $V^* = FV_\beta F' = \sigma^2$. Thus, use of $\hat{\beta}_R$ rather than β^* in predictions inflates the asymptotic variance of the estimator of mean prediction error by a factor of $1+\pi$.

In general, when uncertainty about β^* matters asymptotically, the adjustment to the standard error that would be appropriate if predictions were based on population rather than estimated parameters is increasing in:

- The ratio of number of predictions P to number of observations in smallest regression sample R. Note that in (5.10) as $\pi \to 0$, $\lambda_{fh} \to 0$ and $\lambda_{hh} \to 0$; in the specific example (5.12) we see that if P/R is small, the implied value of π is small and the adjustment to the usual asymptotic variance of σ^2 is small; otherwise the adjustment can be big.

- The variance–covariance matrix of the estimator of the parameters used to make predictions.

Both conditions are intuitive. Simulations in West (1996, 2001), West and McCracken (1998), McCracken (2000), Chao, Corradi and Swanson (2001) and Clark and McCracken (2001, 2003) indicate that with plausible parameterizations for P/R and uncertainty about β^*, failure to adjust the standard error can result in very substantial size distortions. It is possible that $V < V^*$ – that is, accounting for uncertainty about regression parameters may *lower* the asymptotic variance of the estimator.[4] This happens in some leading cases of practical interest when the rolling scheme is used. See the discussion of Equation (7.2) below for an illustration.

A consistent estimator of V results from using the obvious sample analogues. A possibility is to compute λ_{fh} and λ_{hh} from (5.10) setting $\pi = P/R$. (See Table 1 for the implied formulas for λ_{fh}, λ_{hh} and λ.) As well, one can estimate F from the sample average of $\partial f(\hat{\beta}_t)/\partial\beta$, $\hat{F} = P^{-1}\sum_{t=R}^{T} \partial f(\hat{\beta}_t)/\partial\beta$;[5] estimate V_β and B from one of the sequence of estimates of β^*. For example, for mean prediction error, for the fixed scheme, one might set

$$\hat{F} = -P^{-1}\sum_{t=R}^{T} X'_{t+1}, \quad \hat{B} = \left(R^{-1}\sum_{s=1}^{R} X_s X'_s\right)^{-1},$$

Table 1
Sample analogues for λ_{fh}, λ_{hh} and λ

	Recursive	Rolling, $P \leqslant R$	Rolling, $P > R$	Fixed
λ_{fh}	$1 - \frac{R}{P}\ln(1 + \frac{P}{R})$	$\frac{1}{2}\frac{P}{R}$	$1 - \frac{1}{2}\frac{R}{P}$	0
λ_{hh}	$2[1 - \frac{R}{P}\ln(1 + \frac{P}{R})]$	$\frac{P}{R} - \frac{1}{3}\frac{P^2}{R^2}$	$1 - \frac{1}{3}\frac{R}{P}$	$\frac{P}{R}$
λ	1	$1 - \frac{1}{3}\frac{P^2}{R^2}$	$\frac{2R}{3P}$	$1 + \frac{P}{R}$

Notes:
1. The recursive, rolling and fixed schemes are defined in Section 4 and illustrated for an AR(1) in Equation (4.2).
2. P is the number of predictions, R the size of the smallest regression sample. See Section 4 and Equation (4.1).
3. The parameters λ_{fh}, λ_{hh} and λ are used to adjust the asymptotic variance covariance matrix for uncertainty about regression parameters used to make predictions. See Section 5 and Tables 2 and 3.

[4] Mechanically, such a fall in asymptotic variance indicates that the variance of terms resulting from estimation of β^* is more than offset by a negative covariance between such terms and terms that would be present even if β^* were known.

[5] See McCracken (2000) for an illustration of estimation of F for a non-differentiable function.

$$\hat{V}_\beta \equiv \left(R^{-1}\sum_{s=1}^{R} X_s X_s'\right)^{-1}\left(R^{-1}\sum_{s=1}^{R} X_s X_s' \hat{e}_s^2\right)\left(R^{-1}\sum_{s=1}^{R} X_s X_s'\right)^{-1}.$$

Here, $\hat{e}_s$, $1 \leqslant s \leqslant R$, is the in-sample least squares residual associated with the parameter vector $\hat{\beta}_R$ that is used to make predictions and the formula for $\hat{V}_\beta$ is the usual heteroskedasticity consistent covariance matrix for $\hat{\beta}_R$. (Other estimators are also consistent, for example sample averages running from 1 to T.) Finally, one can combine these with an estimate of the long run variance S constructed using a heteroskedasticity and autocorrelation consistent covariance matrix estimator [Newey and West (1987, 1994), Andrews (1991), Andrews and Monahan (1994), den Haan and Levin (2000)].

Alternatively, one can compute a smaller dimension long run variance as follows. Let us assume for the moment that f_t and hence V are scalar. Define the (2×1) vector $\hat{g}_t$ as

$$\hat{g}_t = \begin{bmatrix} \hat{f}_t \\ \hat{F}\hat{B}\hat{h}_t \end{bmatrix}. \tag{5.13}$$

Let g_t be the population counterpart of $\hat{g}_t$, $g_t \equiv (f_t, FBh_t)'$. Let Ω be the (2×2) long run variance of g_t, $\Omega \equiv \sum_{j=-\infty}^{\infty} \mathrm{E} g_t g_{t-j}'$. Let $\hat{\Omega}$ be an estimate of Ω. Let $\hat{\Omega}_{ij}$ be the (i, j) element of $\hat{\Omega}$. Then one can consistently estimate V with

$$\hat{V} = \hat{\Omega}_{11} + 2\lambda_{fh}\hat{\Omega}_{12} + \lambda_{hh}\hat{\Omega}_{22}. \tag{5.14}$$

The generalization to vector f_t is straightforward. Suppose f_t is say $m \times 1$ for $m \geqslant 1$. Then

$$\hat{g}_t = \begin{bmatrix} f_t \\ FBh_t \end{bmatrix}.$$

is $2m \times 1$, as is $\hat{g}_t$; Ω and $\hat{\Omega}$ are $2m \times 2m$. One divides $\hat{\Omega}$ into four $(m \times m)$ blocks, and computes

$$\hat{V} = \hat{\Omega}(1,1) + \lambda_{fh}\big[\hat{\Omega}(1,2) + \hat{\Omega}(2,1)\big] + \lambda_{hh}\hat{\Omega}(2,2). \tag{5.15}$$

In (5.15), $\hat{\Omega}(1,1)$ is the $m \times m$ block in the upper left hand corner of $\hat{\Omega}$, $\hat{\Omega}(1,2)$ is the $m \times m$ block in the upper right hand corner of $\hat{\Omega}$, and so on.

Alternatively, in some common problems, and if the models are linear, regression based tests can be used. By judicious choice of additional regressors [as suggested for in-sample tests by Pagan and Hall (1983), Davidson and MacKinnon (1984) and Wooldridge (1990)], one can "trick" standard regression packages into computing standard errors that properly reflect uncertainty about β^*. See West and McCracken (1998) and Table 3 below for details, Hueng and Wong (2000), Avramov (2002) and Ferreira (2004) for applications.

Conditions for the expansion (5.6) and the central limit result (5.10) include the following.

- Parametric models and estimators of β are required. Similar results may hold with nonparametric estimators, but, if so, these have yet to be established. Linearity is not required. One might be basing predictions on nonlinear time series models, for example, or restricted reduced forms of simultaneous equations models estimated by GMM.
- At present, results with I(1) data are restricted to linear models [Corradi, Swanson and Olivetti (2001), Rossi (2003)]. Asymptotic irrelevance continues to apply when $F = 0$ or $\pi = 0$. When those conditions fail, however, the normalized estimator of $\mathrm{E}f_t$ typically is no longer asymptotically normal. (By I(1) data, I mean I(1) data entered in levels in the regression model. Of course, if one induces stationarity by taking differences or imposing cointegrating relationships prior to estimating β^*, the theory in the present section is applicable quite generally.)
- Condition (5.5) holds. Section 7 discusses implications of an alternative asymptotic approximation due to Giacomini and White (2003) that holds R fixed.
- For the recursive scheme, condition (5.5) can be generalized to allow $\pi = \infty$, with the same asymptotic approximation. (Recall that π is the limiting value of P/R.) Since $\pi < \infty$ has been assumed in existing theoretical results for rolling and fixed, researchers using those schemes should treat the asymptotic approximation with extra caution if $P \gg R$.
- The expectation of the loss function f must be differentiable in a neighborhood of β^*. This rules out direction of change as a loss function.
- A full rank condition on the long run variance of $(f'_{t+1}, (Bh_t)')'$. A necessary condition is that the long run variance of f_{t+1} is full rank. For MSPE, and i.i.d. forecast errors, this means that the variance of $e^2_{1t} - e^2_{2t}$ is positive (note the absence of a "^" over e^2_{1t} and e^2_{2t}). This condition will fail in applications in which the models are nested, for in that case $e_{1t} \equiv e_{2t}$. Of course, for the sample forecast errors, $\hat{e}_{1t} \neq \hat{e}_{2t}$ (note the "^") because of sampling error in estimation of β^*_1 and β^*_2. So the failure of the rank condition may not be apparent in practice. McCracken's (2004) analysis of nested models shows that under the conditions of the present section apart from the rank condition, $\sqrt{P}(\hat{\sigma}^2_1 - \hat{\sigma}^2_2) \rightarrow_p 0$. The next two sections discuss inference for predictions from such nested models.

6. A small number of models, nested: MSPE

Analysis of nested models per se does not invalidate the results of the previous sections. A rule of thumb is: if the rank of the data becomes degenerate when regression parameters are set at their population values, then a rank condition assumed in the previous sections likely is violated. When only two models are being compared, "degenerate" means identically zero.

Consider, as an example, out of sample tests of Granger causality [e.g., Stock and Watson (1999, 2002)]. In this case, model 2 might be a bivariate VAR, model 1 a univariate AR that is nested in model 2 by imposing suitable zeroes in the model 2 regression vector. If the lag length is 1, for example:

$$\text{Model 1:}\quad y_t = \beta_{10} + \beta_{11}y_{t-1} + e_{1t} \equiv X_{1t}'\beta_1^* + e_{1t},\quad X_{1t} \equiv (1, y_{t-1})',$$
$$\beta_1^* \equiv (\beta_{10}, \beta_{11})'; \tag{6.1a}$$
$$\text{Model 2:}\quad y_t = \beta_{20} + \beta_{21}y_{t-1} + \beta_{22}x_{t-1} + e_{2t} \equiv X_{2t}'\beta_2^* + e_{2t},$$
$$X_{2t} \equiv (1, y_{t-1}, x_{t-1})',\quad \beta_2^* \equiv (\beta_{20}, \beta_{21}, \beta_{22})'. \tag{6.1b}$$

Under the null of no Granger causality from x to y, $\beta_{22} = 0$ in model 2. Model 1 is then nested in model 2. Under the null, then,

$$\beta_2^{*\prime} = (\beta_1^{*\prime}, 0),\quad X_{1t}'\beta_1^* = X_{2t}'\beta_2^*,$$

and the disturbances of model 2 and model 1 are identical: $e_{2t}^2 - e_{1t}^2 \equiv 0$, $e_{1t}(e_{1t} - e_{2t}) = 0$ and $|e_{1t}| - |e_{2t}| = 0$ for all t. So the theory of the previous sections does not apply if MSPE, $\text{cov}(e_{1t}, e_{1t} - e_{2t})$ or mean absolute error is the moment of interest. On the other hand, the random variable $e_{1t+1}x_t$ is nondegenerate under the null, so one can use the theory of the previous sections to examine whether $\text{E}e_{1t+1}x_t = 0$. Indeed, Chao, Corradi and Swanson (2001) show that (5.6) and (5.10) apply when testing $\text{E}e_{1t+1}x_t = 0$ with out of sample prediction errors.

The remainder of this section considers the implications of a test that does fail the rank condition of the theory of the previous section – specifically, MSPE in nested models. This is a common occurrence in papers on forecasting asset prices, which often use MSPE to test a random walk null against models that use past data to try to predict changes in asset prices. It is also a common occurrence in macro applications, which, as in example (6.1), compare univariate to multivariate forecasts. In such applications, the asymptotic results described in the previous section will no longer apply. In particular, and under essentially the technical conditions of that section (apart from the rank condition), when $\hat{\sigma}_1^2 - \hat{\sigma}_2^2$ is normalized so that its limiting distribution is non-degenerate, that distribution is non-normal.

Formal characterization of limiting distributions has been accomplished in McCracken (2004) and Clark and McCracken (2001, 2003, 2005a, 2005b). This characterization relies on restrictions not required by the theory discussed in the previous section. These restrictions include:

(6.2a) The objective function used to estimate regression parameters must be the same quadratic as that used to evaluate prediction. That is:
- The estimator must be nonlinear least squares (ordinary least squares of course a special case).
- For multistep predictions, the "direct" rather than "iterated" method must be used.[6]

[6] To illustrate these terms, consider the univariate example of forecasting $y_{t+\tau}$ using y_t, assuming that mathematical expectations and linear projections coincide. The objective function used to evaluate predictions is $\text{E}[y_{t+\tau} - \text{E}(y_{t+\tau} \mid y_t)]^2$. The "direct" method estimates $y_{t+\tau} = y_t\gamma + u_{t+\tau}$ by least squares, uses $y_t\hat{\gamma}_t$

(6.2b) A pair of models is being compared. That is, results have not been extended to multi-model comparisons along the lines of (3.3).

McCracken (2004) shows that under such conditions, $\sqrt{P}(\hat{\sigma}_1^2 - \hat{\sigma}_2^2) \to_p 0$, and derives the asymptotic distribution of $P(\hat{\sigma}_1^2 - \hat{\sigma}_2^2)$ and certain related quantities. (Note that the normalizing factor is the prediction sample size P rather than the usual $\sqrt{P}$.) He writes test statistics as functionals of Brownian motion. He establishes limiting distributions that are asymptotically free of nuisance parameters under certain additional conditions:

(6.2c) one step ahead predictions and conditionally homoskedastic prediction errors, or

(6.2d) the number of additional regressors in the larger model is exactly 1 [Clark and McCracken (2005a)].

Condition (6.2d) allows use of the results about to be cited, in conditionally heteroskedastic as well as conditionally homoskedastic environments, and for multiple as well as one step ahead forecasts. Under the additional restrictions (6.2c) or (6.2d), McCracken (2004) tabulates the quantiles of $P(\hat{\sigma}_1^2 - \hat{\sigma}_2^2)/\hat{\sigma}_2^2$. These quantiles depend on the number of additional parameters in the larger model and on the limiting ratio of P/R. For conciseness, I will use "(6.2)" to mean

Conditions (6.2a) and (6.2b) hold, as does either or both of conditions (6.2c) and (6.2d). (6.2)

Simulation evidence in Clark and McCracken (2001, 2003, 2005b), McCracken (2004), Clark and West (2005a, 2005b) and Corradi and Swanson (2005) indicates that in MSPE comparisons in nested models the usual statistic (4.5) is non-normal not only in a technical but in an essential practical sense: use of standard critical values usually results in very poorly sized tests, with *far* too few rejections. As well, the usual statistic has very poor power. For both size and power, the usual statistic performs worse the larger the number of irrelevant regressors included in model 2. The evidence relies on one-sided tests, in which the alternative to $\mathrm{H_0}$: $\mathrm{E}e_{1t}^2 - \mathrm{E}e_{2t}^2 = 0$ is

$$\mathrm{H_A}: \quad \mathrm{E}e_{1t}^2 - \mathrm{E}e_{2t}^2 > 0. \tag{6.3}$$

Ashley, Granger and Schmalensee (1980) argued that in nested models, the alternative to equal MSPE is that the larger model outpredicts the smaller model: it does not make sense for the population MSPE of the parsimonious model to be smaller than that of the larger model.

to forecast, and computes a sample average of $(y_{t+\tau} - y_t\hat{\gamma}_t)^2$. The "iterated" method estimates $y_{t+1} = y_t\beta + e_{t+1}$, uses $y_t(\hat{\beta}_t)^\tau$ to forecast, and computes a sample average of $[y_{t+\tau} - y_t(\hat{\beta}_t)^\tau]^2$. Of course, if the AR(1) model for y_t is correct, then $\gamma = \beta^\tau$ and $u_{t+\tau} = e_{t+\tau} + \beta e_{t+\tau-1} + \cdots + \beta^{\tau-1}e_{t+1}$. But if the AR(1) model is incorrect, the two forecasts may differ, even in a large sample. See Ing (2003) and Marcellino, Stock and Watson (2004) for theoretical and empirical comparison of direct and iterated methods.

To illustrate the sources of these results, consider the following simple example. The two models are:

$$\text{Model 1: } y_t = e_t; \quad \text{Model 2: } y_t = \beta^* x_t + e_t; \quad \beta^* = 0;$$
$$e_t \text{ a martingale difference sequence with respect to past } y\text{'s and } x\text{'s.} \tag{6.4}$$

In (6.4), all variables are scalars. I use x_t instead of X_{2t} to keep notation relatively uncluttered. For concreteness, one can assume $x_t = y_{t-1}$, but that is not required. I write the disturbance to model 2 as e_t rather than e_{2t} because the null (equal MSPE) implies $\beta^* = 0$ and hence that the disturbance to model 2 is identically equal to e_t. Nonetheless, for clarity and emphasis I use the "2" subscript for the sample forecast error from model 2, $\hat{e}_{2t+1} \equiv y_{t+1} - x_{t+1}\hat{\beta}_t$. In a finite sample, the model 2 sample forecast error differs from the model 1 forecast error, which is simply y_{t+1}. The model 1 and model 2 MSPEs are

$$\hat{\sigma}_1^2 \equiv P^{-1}\sum_{t=R}^{T} y_{t+1}^2, \quad \hat{\sigma}_2^2 \equiv P^{-1}\sum_{t=R}^{T} \hat{e}_{2t+1}^2 \equiv P^{-1}\sum_{t=R}^{T}\left(y_{t+1} - x_{t+1}\hat{\beta}_t\right)^2. \tag{6.5}$$

Since

$$\hat{f}_{t+1} \equiv y_{t+1}^2 - \left(y_{t+1} - x_{t+1}\hat{\beta}_t\right)^2 = 2y_{t+1}x_{t+1}\hat{\beta}_t - \left(x_{t+1}\hat{\beta}_t\right)^2$$

we have

$$\bar{f} \equiv \hat{\sigma}_1^2 - \hat{\sigma}_2^2 = 2\left(P^{-1}\sum_{t=R}^{T} y_{t+1}x_{t+1}\hat{\beta}_t\right) - \left[P^{-1}\sum_{t=R}^{T}\left(x_{t+1}\hat{\beta}_t\right)^2\right]. \tag{6.6}$$

Now,

$$-\left[P^{-1}\sum_{t=R}^{T}\left(x_{t+1}\hat{\beta}_t\right)^2\right] \leqslant 0$$

and under the null ($y_{t+1} = e_{t+1} \sim$ i.i.d.)

$$2\left(P^{-1}\sum_{t=R}^{T} y_{t+1}x_{t+1}\hat{\beta}_t\right) \approx 0.$$

So under the null it will generally be the case that

$$\bar{f} \equiv \hat{\sigma}_1^2 - \hat{\sigma}_2^2 < 0 \tag{6.7}$$

or: the *sample* MSPE from the null model will tend to be *less* than that from the alternative model.

The intuition will be unsurprising to those familiar with forecasting. If the null is true, the alternative model introduces noise into the forecasting process: the alternative model attempts to estimate parameters that are zero in population. In finite samples, use of the noisy estimate of the parameter will *raise* the estimated MSPE of the alternative model relative to the null model. So if the null is true, the model 1 MSPE should be smaller by the amount of estimation noise.

To illustrate concretely, let me use the simulation results in Clark and West (2005b). As stated in (6.3), one tailed tests were used. That is, the null of equal MSPE is rejected at (say) the 10 percent level only if the alternative model predicts better than model 1:

$$\begin{aligned}
&\bar{f}/\big[\hat{V}^*/P\big]^{1/2} = \big(\hat{\sigma}_1^2 - \hat{\sigma}_2^2\big)/\big[\hat{V}^*/P\big]^{1/2} > 1.282,\\
&\hat{V}^* = \text{estimate of long run variance of } \hat{\sigma}_1^2 - \hat{\sigma}_2^2, \text{ say,}\\
&\hat{V}^* = P^{-1}\sum_{t=R}^{T}\big(\hat{f}_{t+1} - \bar{f}\big)^2 = P^{-1}\sum_{t=R}^{T}\big[\hat{f}_{t+1} - \big(\hat{\sigma}_1^2 - \hat{\sigma}_2^2\big)\big]^2 \quad \text{if } e_t \text{ is i.i.d.}
\end{aligned} \tag{6.8}$$

Since (6.8) is motivated by an asymptotic approximation in which $\hat{\sigma}_1^2 - \hat{\sigma}_2^2$ is centered around zero, we see from (6.7) that the test will tend to be undersized (reject too infrequently). Across 48 sets of simulations, with DGPs calibrated to match key characteristics of asset price data, Clark and West (2005b) found that the median size of a nominal 10% test using the standard result (6.8) was less than 1%. The size was better with bigger R and worse with bigger P. (Some alternative procedures (described below) had median sizes of 8–13%.) The power of tests using "standard results" was poor: rejection of about 9%, versus 50–80% for alternatives.[7] Non-normality also applies if one normalizes differences in MSPEs by the unrestricted MSPE to produce an out of sample F-test. See Clark and McCracken (2001, 2003), and McCracken (2004) for analytical and simulation evidence of marked departures from normality.

Clark and West (2005a, 2005b) suggest adjusting the difference in MSPEs to account for the noise introduced by the inclusion of irrelevant regressors in the alternative model. If the null model has a forecast $\hat{y}_{1t+1}$, then (6.6), which assumes $\hat{y}_{1t+1} = 0$, generalizes to

$$\hat{\sigma}_1^2 - \hat{\sigma}_2^2 = -2P^{-1}\sum_{t=R}^{T}\hat{e}_{1t+1}\big(\hat{y}_{1t+1} - \hat{y}_{2t+1}\big) - P^{-1}\sum_{t=R}^{T}\big(\hat{y}_{1t+1} - \hat{y}_{2t+1}\big)^2. \tag{6.9}$$

To yield a statistic better centered around zero, Clark and West (2005a, 2005b) propose adjusting for the negative term $-P^{-1}\sum_{t=R}^{T}(\hat{y}_{1t+1} - \hat{y}_{2t+1})^2$. They call the result *MSPE-adjusted*:

$$\begin{aligned}
&P^{-1}\sum_{t=R}^{T}\hat{e}_{1t+1}^2 - \left[P^{-1}\sum_{t=R}^{T}\hat{e}_{2t+1}^2 - P^{-1}\sum_{t=R}^{T}\big(\hat{y}_{1t+1} - \hat{y}_{2t+1}\big)^2\right]\\
&\quad \equiv \hat{\sigma}_1^2 - \big(\hat{\sigma}_2^2\text{-adj}\big).
\end{aligned} \tag{6.10}$$

[7] Note that (4.5) and the left-hand side of (6.8) are identical, but that Section 4 recommends the use of (4.5) while the present section recommends against use of (6.8). At the risk of beating a dead horse, the reason is that Section 4 assumed that models are non-nested, while the present section assumes that they are nested.

$\hat{\sigma}_2^2$-adj, which is smaller than $\hat{\sigma}_2^2$ by construction, can be thought of as the MSPE from the larger model, adjusted downwards for estimation noise attributable to inclusion of irrelevant parameters.

Viable approaches to testing equal MSPE in nested models include the following (with the first two summarizing the previous paragraphs):

1. Under condition (6.2), use critical values from Clark and McCracken (2001) and McCracken (2004), [e.g., Lettau and Ludvigson (2001)].
2. Under condition (6.2), or when the null model is a martingale difference, adjust the differences in MSPEs as in (6.10), and compute a standard error in the usual way. The implied t-statistic can be obtained by regressing $\hat{e}_{1t+1}^2 - [\hat{e}_{2t+1}^2 - (\hat{y}_{1t+1} - \hat{y}_{2t+1})^2]$ on a constant and computing the t-statistic for a coefficient of zero. Clark and West (2005a, 2005b) argue that standard normal critical values are approximately correct, even though the statistic is non-normal according to asymptotics of Clark and McCracken (2001).

   It remains to be seen whether the approaches just listed in points 1 and 2 perform reasonably well in more general circumstances – for example, when the larger model contains several extra parameters, and there is conditional heteroskedasticity. But even if so other procedures are possible.
3. If $P/R \to 0$, Clark and McCracken (2001) and McCracken (2004) show that asymptotic irrelevance applies. So for small P/R, use standard critical values [e.g., Clements and Galvao (2004)]. Simulations in various papers suggest that it generally does little harm to ignore effects from estimation of regression parameters if $P/R \leqslant 0.1$. Of course, this cutoff is arbitrary. For some data, a larger value is appropriate, for others a smaller value.
4. For MSPE and one step ahead forecasts, use the standard test if it rejects: if the standard test rejects, a properly sized test most likely will as well [e.g., Shintani (2004)].[8]
5. Simulate/bootstrap your own standard errors [e.g., Mark (1995), Sarno, Thornton and Valente (2005)]. Conditions for the validity of the bootstrap are established in Corradi and Swanson (2005).

Alternatively, one can swear off MSPE. This is discussed in the next section.

7. A small number of models, nested, Part II

Leading competitors of MSPE for the most part are encompassing tests of various forms. Theoretical results for the first two statistics listed below require condition (6.2),

[8] The restriction to one step ahead forecasts is for the following reason. For multiple step forecasts, the difference between model 1 and model 2 MSPEs presumably has a negative expectation. And simulations in Clark and McCracken (2003) generally find that use of standard critical values results in too few rejections. But sometimes there are too many rejections. This apparently results because of problems with HAC estimation of the standard error of the MSPE difference (private communication from Todd Clark).

and are asymptotically non-normal under those conditions. The remaining statistics are asymptotically normal, and under conditions that do not require (6.2).

1. Of various variants of encompassing tests, Clark and McCracken (2001) find that power is best using the Harvey, Leybourne and Newbold (1998) version of an encompassing test, normalized by unrestricted variance. So for those who use a non-normal test, Clark and McCracken (2001) recommend the statistic that they call "Enc-new":

$$\text{Enc-new} = \bar{f} = \frac{P^{-1}\sum_{t=R}^{T}\hat{e}_{1t+1}(\hat{e}_{1t+1}-\hat{e}_{2t+1})}{\hat{\sigma}_2^2},$$

$$\hat{\sigma}_2^2 \equiv P^{-1}\sum_{t=R}^{T}\hat{e}_{2t+1}^2. \tag{7.1}$$

2. It is easily seen that MSPE-adjusted (6.10) is algebraically identical to $2P^{-1} \times \sum_{t=R}^{T}\hat{e}_{1t+1}(\hat{e}_{1t+1}-\hat{e}_{2t+1})$. This is the sample moment for the Harvey, Leybourne and Newbold (1998) encompassing test (4.7d). So the conditions described in point (2) at the end of the previous section are applicable.
3. Test whether model 1's prediction error is uncorrelated with model 2's predictors or the subset of model 2's predictors not included in model 1 [Chao, Corradi and Swanson (2001)], $f_t = e_{1t}X_{2t}'$ in our linear example or $f_t = e_{1t}x_{t-1}$ in example (6.1). When both models use estimated parameters for prediction (in contrast to (6.4), in which model 1 does not rely on estimated parameters), the Chao, Corradi and Swanson (2001) procedure requires adjusting the variance–covariance matrix for parameter estimation error, as described in Section 5. Chao, Corradi and Swanson (2001) relies on the less restricted environment described in the section on nonnested models; for example, it can be applied in straightforward fashion to joint testing of multiple models.
4. If $\beta_2^* \neq 0$, apply an encompassing test in the form (4.7c), $0 = \mathrm{E}e_{1t}X_{2t}'\beta_2^*$. Simulation evidence to date indicates that in samples of size typically available, this statistic performs poorly with respect to both size and power [Clark and McCracken (2001), Clark and West (2005a)]. But this statistic also neatly illustrates some results stated in general terms for nonnested models. So to illustrate those results: With computation and technical conditions similar to those in West and McCracken (1998), it may be shown that when $\bar{f} = P^{-1}\sum_{t=R}^{T}\hat{e}_{1t+1}X_{2t+1}'\hat{\beta}_{2t}$, $\beta_2^* \neq 0$, and the models are nested, then

$$\sqrt{P}\bar{f} \sim_A \mathrm{N}(0, V), \quad V \equiv \lambda V^*, \quad \lambda \text{ defined in (5.9)},$$

$$V^* \equiv \sum_{j=-\infty}^{\infty} \mathrm{E}e_t e_{t-j}\left(X_{2t}'\beta_2^*\right)\left(X_{2t-j}'\beta_2^*\right). \tag{7.2}$$

Given an estimate of V^*, one multiplies the estimate by λ to obtain an estimate of the asymptotic variance of $\sqrt{P}\bar{f}$. Alternatively, one divides the t-statistic by $\sqrt{\lambda}$.

Observe that $\lambda = 1$ for the recursive scheme: this is an example in which there is the cancellation of variance and covariance terms noted in point 3 at the end of Section 4. For the fixed scheme, $\lambda > 1$, with λ increasing in P/R. So uncertainty about parameter estimates inflates the variance, with the inflation factor increasing in the ratio of the size of the prediction to regression sample. Finally, for the rolling scheme $\lambda < 1$. So use of (6.8) will result in *smaller* standard errors and larger t-statistics than would use of a statistic that ignores the effect of uncertainty about β^*. The magnitude of the adjustment to standard errors and t-statistics is increasing in the ratio of the size of the prediction to regression sample.

5. If $\beta_2^* = 0$, and if the rolling or fixed (but *not* the recursive) scheme is used, apply the encompassing test just discussed, setting $\bar{f} = P^{-1}\sum_{t=R}^{T} e_{1t+1}X'_{2t+1}\hat{\beta}_{2t}$. Note that in contrast to the discussion just completed, there is no "^" over e_{1t+1}: because model 1 is nested in model 2, $\beta_2^* = 0$ means $\beta_1^* = 0$, so $e_{1t+1} = y_{t+1}$ and e_{1t+1} is observable. One can use standard results – asymptotic irrelevance applies. The factor of λ that appears in (7.2) resulted from estimation of β_1^*, and is now absent. So $V = V^*$; if, for example, e_{1t} is i.i.d., one can consistently estimate V with $\hat{V} = P^{-1}\sum_{t=R}^{T}(e_{1t+1}X'_{2t+1}\hat{\beta}_{2t})^2$.[9]
6. If the rolling or fixed regression scheme is used, construct a conditional rather than unconditional test [Giacomini and White (2003)]. This paper makes both methodological and substantive contributions. The methodological contributions are twofold. First, the paper explicitly allows data heterogeneity (e.g., slow drift in moments). This seems to be a characteristic of much economic data. Second, while the paper's conditions are broadly similar to those of the work cited above, its asymptotic approximation holds R fixed while letting $P \to \infty$.

   The substantive contribution is also twofold. First, the objects of interest are moments of $\hat{e}_{1t}$ and $\hat{e}_{2t}$ rather than e_t. (Even in nested models, $\hat{e}_{1t}$ and $\hat{e}_{2t}$ are distinct because of sampling error in estimation of regression parameters used to make forecasts.) Second, and related, the moments of interest are conditional ones, say $\mathrm{E}(\hat{\sigma}_1^2 - \hat{\sigma}_2^2 \mid \text{lagged } y\text{'s and } x\text{'s})$. The Giacomini and White (2003) framework allows general conditional loss functions, and may be used in nonnested as well as nested frameworks.

[9] The reader may wonder whether asymptotic normality violates the rule of thumb enunciated at the beginning of this section, because $f_t = e_{1t}X'_{2t}\beta_2^*$ is identically zero when evaluated at population $\beta_2^* = 0$. At the risk of confusing rather than clarifying, let me briefly note that the rule of thumb still applies, but only with a twist on the conditions given in the previous section. This twist, which is due to Giacomini and White (2003), holds R fixed as the sample size grows. Thus in population the random variable of interest is $f_t = e_{1t}X'_{2t}\hat{\beta}_{2t}$, which for the fixed or rolling schemes is nondegenerate for all t. (Under the recursive scheme, $\hat{\beta}_{2t} \to_p 0$ as $t \to \infty$, which implies that f_t is degenerate for large t.) It is to be emphasized that technical conditions (R fixed vs. $R \to \infty$) are not arbitrary. Reasonable technical conditions should reasonably rationalize finite sample behavior. For tests of equal MSPE discussed in the previous section, a vast range of simulation evidence suggests that the $R \to \infty$ condition generates a reasonably accurate asymptotic approximation (i.e., non-normality is implied by the theory and is found in the simulations). The more modest array of simulation evidence for the R fixed approximation suggests that this approximation might work tolerably for the moment $\mathrm{E}e_{1t}X'_{2t}\beta_{2t}^*$, provided the rolling scheme is used.

8. Summary on small number of models

Let me close with a summary. An expansion and application of the asymptotic analysis of the preceding four sections is given in Tables 2 and 3A–3C. The rows of Table 2 are organized by sources of critical values. The first row is for tests that rely on standard results. As described in Sections 3 and 4, this means that asymptotic normal critical values are used without explicitly taking into account uncertainty about regression parameters used to make forecasts. The second row is for tests that rely on asymptotic normality, but only after adjusting for such uncertainty as described in Section 5 and in some of the final points of this section. The third row is for tests for which it would be ill-advised to use asymptotic normal critical values, as described in preceding sections.

Tables 3A–3C present recommended procedures in settings with a small number of models. They are organized by class of application: Table 3A for a single model, Table 3B for a pair of nonnested models, and Table 3C for a pair of nested models. Within each table, rows are organized by the moment being studied.

Tables 2 and 3A–3C aim to make specific recommendations. While the tables are self-explanatory, some qualifications should be noted. First, the rule of thumb that asymptotic irrelevance applies when $P/R < 0.1$ (point A1 in Table 2, note to Table 3A) is just a rule of thumb. Second, as noted in Section 4, asymptotic irrelevance for MSPE or mean absolute error (point A2 in Table 2, rows 1 and 2 in Table 3B) requires that the prediction error is uncorrelated with the predictors (MSPE) or that the disturbance is symmetric conditional on the predictors (mean absolute error). Otherwise, one will need to account for uncertainty about parameters used to make predictions. Third, some of the results in A3 and A4 (Table 2) and the regression results in Table 3A, rows 1–3, and Table 3B, row 3, have yet to be noted. They are established in West and McCracken (1998). Fourth, the suggestion to run a regression on a constant and compute a HAC t-stat (e.g., Table 3B, row 1) is just one way to operationalize a recommendation to use standard results. This recommendation is given in non-regression form in Equation (4.5). Finally, the tables are driven mainly by asymptotic results. The reader should be advised that simulation evidence to date seems to suggest that in seemingly reasonable sample sizes the asymptotic approximations sometimes work poorly. The approximations generally work poorly for long horizon forecasts [e.g., Clark and McCracken (2003), Clark and West (2005a)], and also sometimes work poorly even for one step ahead forecasts [e.g., rolling scheme, forecast encompassing (Table 3B, line 3, and Table 3C, line 3), West and McCracken (1998), Clark and West (2005a)].

9. Large number of models

Sometimes an investigator will wish to compare a large number of models. There is no precise definition of large. But for samples of size typical in economics research, procedures in this section probably have limited appeal when the number of models is say in the single digits, and have a great deal of appeal when the number of models is

Table 2
Recommended sources of critical values, small number of models

Source of critical values	Conditions for use
A. Use critical values associated with asymptotic normality, abstracting from any dependence of predictions on estimated regression parameters, as illustrated for scalar hypothesis test in (4.5) and a vector test in (4.11).	1. Prediction sample size P is small relative to regression sample size R, say $P/R < 0.1$ (any sampling scheme or moment, nested or nonnested models). 2. MSPE or mean absolute error in nonnested models. 3. Sampling scheme is recursive, moment of interest is mean prediction error or correlation between a given model's prediction error and prediction. 4. Sampling scheme is recursive, one step ahead conditionally homoskedastic prediction errors, moment of interest is either: (a) first order autocorrelation or (b) encompassing in the form (4.7c). 5. MSPE, nested models, equality of MSPE rejects (implying that it will also reject with an even smaller p-value if an asymptotically valid test is used).
B. Use critical values associated with asymptotic normality, but adjust test statistics to account for the effects of uncertainty about regression parameters.	1. Mean prediction error, first order autocorrelation of one step ahead prediction errors, zero correlation between a prediction error and prediction, encompassing in the form (4.7c) (with the exception of point C3), encompassing in the form (4.7d) for nonnested models. 2. Zero correlation between a prediction error and another model's vector of predictors (nested or nonnested) [Chao, Corradi and Swanson (2001)]. 3. A general vector of moments or a loss or utility function that satisfies a suitable rank condition. 4. MSPE, nested models, under condition (6.2), after adjustment as in (6.10).
C. Use non-standard critical values.	1. MSPE or encompassing in the form (4.7d), nested models, under condition (6.2): use critical values from McCracken (2004) or Clark and McCracken (2001). 2. MSPE, encompassing in the form (4.7d) or mean absolute error, nested models, and in contexts not covered by A5, B4 or C1: simulate/bootstrap your own critical values. 3. Recursive scheme, $\beta_1^* = 0$, encompassing in the form (4.7c): simulate/bootstrap your own critical values.

Note: Rows B and C assume that P/R is sufficiently large, say $P/R \geqslant 0.1$, that there may be nonnegligible effects of estimation uncertainty about parameters used to make forecasts. The results in row A, points 2–5, apply whether or not P/R is large.

Table 3A
Recommended procedures, small number of models.
Tests of adequacy of a single model, $y_t = X_t'\beta^* + e_t$

Description	Null hypothesis	Recommended procedure	Asymptotic normal critical values?
1. Mean prediction error (bias)	$\mathrm{E}(y_t - X_t'\beta^*) = 0$, or $\mathrm{E}e_t = 0$	Regress prediction error on a constant, divide HAC t-stat by $\sqrt{\lambda}$.	Y
2. Correlation between prediction error and prediction (efficiency)	$\mathrm{E}(y_t - X_t'\beta^*)X_t'\beta^* = 0$, or $\mathrm{E}e_t X_t'\beta^* = 0$	Regress $\hat{e}_{t+1}$ on $X_{t+1}'\hat{\beta}_t$, divide HAC t-stat by $\sqrt{\lambda}$, or regress y_{t+1} on prediction $X_{t+1}'\hat{\beta}_t$, divide HAC t-stat (for testing coefficient value of 1) by $\sqrt{\lambda}$.	Y
3. First order correlation of one step ahead prediction errors	$\mathrm{E}(y_{t+1} - X_{t+1}'\beta^*)(y_t - X_t'\beta^*) = 0$, or $\mathrm{E}e_{t+1}e_t = 0$.	a. Prediction error conditionally homoskedastic: 1. Recursive scheme: regress $\hat{e}_{t+1}$ on $\hat{e}_t$, use OLS t-stat. 2. Rolling or fixed schemes: regress $\hat{e}_{t+1}$ on $\hat{e}_t$ and X_t, use OLS t-tstat on coefficient on $\hat{e}_t$. b. Prediction error conditionally heteroskedastic: adjust standard errors as described in Section 5 above.	Y

Notes:
1. The quantity λ is computed as described in Table 1. "HAC" refers to a heteroskedasticity and autocorrelation consistent covariance matrix. Throughout, it is assumed that predictions rely on estimated regression parameters and that P/R is large enough, say $P/R \geqslant 0.1$, that there may be nonnegligible effects of such estimation. If P/R is small, say $P/R < 0.1$, any such effects may well be negligible, and one can use standard results as described in Sections 3 and 4.
2. Throughout, the alternative hypothesis is the two-sided one that the indicated expectation is nonzero (e.g., for row 1, $\mathrm{H_A}$: $\mathrm{E}e_t \neq 0$).

Table 3B
Recommended procedures, small number of models.
Tests comparing a pair of nonnested models, $y_t = X'_{1t}\beta_1^* + e_{1t}$ vs. $y_t = X'_{2t}\beta_2^* + e_{2t}$, $X'_{1t}\beta_1^* \neq X'_{2t}\beta_2^*$, $\beta_2^* \neq 0$

Description	Null hypothesis	Recommended procedure	Asymptotic normal critical values?
1. Mean squared prediction error (MSPE)	$\mathrm{E}(y_t - X'_{1t}\beta_1^*)^2 - \mathrm{E}(y_t - X'_{2t}\beta_2^*)^2 = 0$, or $\mathrm{E}e_{1t}^2 - \mathrm{E}e_{2t}^2 = 0$	Regress $\hat{e}_{1t+1}^2 - \hat{e}_{2t+1}^2$ on a constant, use HAC t-stat.	Y
2. Mean absolute prediction error (MAPE)	$\mathrm{E}\lvert y_t - X'_{1t}\beta_1^*\rvert - \mathrm{E}\lvert y_t - X'_{2t}\beta_2^*\rvert = 0$, or $\mathrm{E}\lvert e_{1t}\rvert - \mathrm{E}\lvert e_{2t}\rvert = 0$	Regress $\lvert\hat{e}_{1t}\rvert - \lvert\hat{e}_{2t}\rvert$ on a constant, use HAC t-stat.	Y
3. Zero correlation between model 1's prediction error and the prediction from model 2 (forecast encompassing)	$\mathrm{E}(y_t - X'_{1t}\beta_1^*)X'_{2t}\beta_2^* = 0$, or $\mathrm{E}e_{1t}X'_{2t}\beta_2^* = 0$	a. Recursive scheme, prediction error e_{1t} homoskedastic conditional on both X_{1t} and X_{2t}: regress $\hat{e}_{1t+1}$ on $X'_{2t+1}\hat{\beta}_{2t}$, use OLS t-stat. b. Recursive scheme, prediction error e_{1t} conditionally heteroskedastic, or rolling or fixed scheme: regress $\hat{e}_{1t+1}$ on $X'_{2t+1}\hat{\beta}_{2t}$ and X_{1t}, use HAC t-stat on coefficient on $X'_{2t+1}\hat{\beta}_{2t}$.	Y
4. Zero correlation between model 1's prediction error and the difference between the prediction errors of the two models (another form of forecast encompassing)	$\mathrm{E}(y_t - X'_{1t}\beta_1^*) \times [(y_t - X'_{1t}\beta_1^*) - (y_t - X'_{2t}\beta_2^*)] = 0$, or $\mathrm{E}e_{1t}(e_{1t} - e_{2t}) = 0$	Adjust standard errors as described in Section 5 above and illustrated in West (2001).	Y
5. Zero correlation between model 1's prediction error and the model 2 predictors	$\mathrm{E}(y_t - X'_{1t}\beta_1^*)X_{2t} = 0$, or $\mathrm{E}e_{1t}X_{2t} = 0$	Adjust standard errors as described in Section 5 above and illustrated in Chao, Corradi and Swanson (2001).	Y

See notes to Table 3A.

Table 3C

Recommended procedures, small number of models.

Tests of comparing a pair of nested models, $y_t = X'_{1t}\beta_1^* + e_{1t}$ vs. $y_t = X'_{2t}\beta_2^* + e_{2t}$, $X_{1t} \subset X_{2t}$, $X'_{2t} = (X'_{1t}, X'_{22t})'$

Description	Null hypothesis	Recommended procedure	Asympt. normal critical values?
1. Mean squared prediction error (MSPE)	$\mathrm{E}(y_t - X'_{1t}\beta_1^*)^2 - \mathrm{E}(y_t - X'_{2t}\beta_2^*)^2 = 0$, or $\mathrm{E}e_{1t}^2 - \mathrm{E}e_{2t}^2 = 0$	a. If condition (6.2) applies: either (1) use critical values from McCracken (2004), or	N
		(2) compute MSPE-adjusted (6.10).	Y
		b. Equality of MSPE rejects (implying that it will also reject with an even smaller p-value if an asymptotically valid test is used).	Y
		c. Simulate/bootstrap your own critical values.	N
2. Mean absolute prediction error (MAPE)	$\mathrm{E}\lvert y_t - X'_{1t}\beta_1^*\rvert - \mathrm{E}\lvert y_t - X'_{2t}\beta_2^*\rvert = 0$, or $\mathrm{E}\lvert e_{1t}\rvert - \mathrm{E}\lvert e_{2t}\rvert = 0$	Simulate/bootstrap your own critical values.	N
3. Zero correlation between model 1's prediction error and the prediction from model 2 (forecast encompassing)	$\mathrm{E}(y_t - X'_{1t}\beta_1^*)X'_{2t}\beta_2^* = 0$, or $\mathrm{E}e_{1t}X'_{2t}\beta_2^* = 0$	a. $\beta_1^* \neq 0$: regress $\hat{e}_{1t+1}$ on $X'_{2t+1}\hat{\beta}_{2t}$, divide HAC t-stat by $\sqrt{\lambda}$.	Y
		b. $\beta_1^* = 0$ ($\Rightarrow \beta_2^* = 0$): (1) Rolling or fixed scheme: regress $\hat{e}_{1t+1}$ on $X'_{2t+1}\hat{\beta}_{2t}$, use HAC t-stat.	Y
		(2) $\beta_1^* = 0$, recursive scheme: simulate/bootstrap your own critical values.	N
4. Zero correlation between model 1's prediction error and the difference between the prediction errors of the two models (another form of forecast encompassing)	$\mathrm{E}(y_t - X'_{1t}\beta_1^*) \times [(y_t - X'_{1t}\beta_1^*) - (y_t - X'_{2t}\beta_2^*)] = 0$ or $\mathrm{E}e_{1t}(e_{1t} - e_{2t}) = 0$	a. If condition (6.2) applies: either (1) use critical values from Clark and McCracken (2001), or	N
		(2) use standard normal critical values.	Y
		b. Simulate/bootstrap your own critical values.	N
5. Zero correlation between model 1's prediction error and the model 2 predictors	$\mathrm{E}(y_t - X'_{1t}\beta_1^*)X_{22t} = 0$, or $\mathrm{E}e_{1t}X_{22t} = 0$	Adjust standard errors as described in Section 5 above and illustrated in Chao et al. (2001).	Y

1. See note 1 to Table 3A. 2. Under the null, the coefficients on X_{22t} (the regressors included in model 2 but not model 1) are zero. Thus, $X'_{1t}\beta_1^* = X'_{2t}\beta_2^*$ and $e_{1t} = e_{2t}$. 3. Under the alternative, one or more of the coefficients on X_{22t} are nonzero. In rows 1–4, the implied alternative is one sided: $\mathrm{E}e_{1t}^2 - \mathrm{E}e_{2t}^2 > 0$, $\mathrm{E}\lvert e_{1t}\rvert - \mathrm{E}\lvert e_{2t}\rvert > 0$, $\mathrm{E}e_{1t}X'_{2t}\beta_2^* > 0$, $\mathrm{E}e_{1t}(e_{1t} - e_{2t}) > 0$. In row 5, the alternative is two sided, $\mathrm{E}e_{1t}X_{22t} \neq 0$.

into double digits or above. White's (2000) empirical example examined 3654 models using a sample of size 1560. An obvious problem is controlling size, and, independently, computational feasibility.

I divide the discussion into (A) applications in which there is a natural null model, and (B) applications in which there is no natural null.

(A) Sometimes one has a natural null, or benchmark, model, which is to be compared to an array of competitors. The leading example is a martingale difference model for an asset price, to be compared to a long list of methods claimed in the past to help predict returns. Let model 1 be the benchmark model. Other notation is familiar: For model i, $i = 1, \ldots, m+1$, let $\hat{g}_{it}$ be an observation on a prediction or prediction error whose sample mean will measure performance. For example, for MSPE, one step ahead predictions and linear models, $\hat{g}_{it} = \hat{e}_{it}^2 = (y_t - X_{it}'\hat{\beta}_{i,t-1})^2$. Measure performance so that smaller values are preferred to larger values – a natural normalization for MSPE, and one that can be accomplished for other measures simply by multiplying by -1 if necessary. Let $\hat{f}_{it} = \hat{g}_{1t} - \hat{g}_{i+1,t}$ be the difference in period t between the benchmark model and model $i+1$.

One wishes to test the null that the benchmark model is expected to perform at least as well as any other model. One aims to test

$$\mathrm{H}_0\colon \quad \max_{i=1,\ldots,m} \mathrm{E}g_{it} \leqslant 0 \tag{9.1}$$

against

$$\mathrm{H}_A\colon \quad \max_{i=1,\ldots,m} \mathrm{E}g_{it} > 0. \tag{9.2}$$

The approach of previous sections would be as follows. Define an $m \times 1$ vector

$$\hat{f}_t = \left(\hat{f}_{1t}, \hat{f}_{2t}, \ldots, \hat{f}_{mt}\right)'; \tag{9.3}$$

compute

$$\begin{aligned}\bar{f} &\equiv P^{-1}\sum \hat{f}_t \equiv \left(\bar{f}_1, \bar{f}_2, \ldots, \bar{f}_m\right)' \\ &\equiv (\bar{g}_1 - \bar{g}_2, \bar{g}_1 - \bar{g}_3, \ldots, \bar{g}_1 - \bar{g}_{m+1})';\end{aligned} \tag{9.4}$$

construct the asymptotic variance covariance matrix of $\bar{f}$. With small m, one could evaluate

$$\bar{\nu} \equiv \max_{i=1,\ldots,m} \sqrt{P}\bar{f}_i \tag{9.5}$$

via the distribution of the maximum of a correlated set of normals. If $P \ll R$, one could likely even do so for nested models and with MSPE as the measure of performance (per note 1 in Table 2A). But that is computationally difficult. And in any event, when m is large, the asymptotic theory relied upon in previous sections is doubtful.

White's (2000) "reality check" is a computationally convenient bootstrap method for construction of p-values for (9.1). It assumes asymptotic irrelevance $P \ll R$ though the actual asymptotic condition requires $P/R \to 0$ at a sufficiently rapid rate [White (2000, p. 1105)]. The basic mechanics are as follows:

(1) Generate prediction errors, using the scheme of choice (recursive, rolling, fixed).
(2) Generate a series of bootstrap samples as follows. For bootstrap repetitions $j = 1, \ldots, N$:
   (a) Generate a new sample by sampling with replacement from the prediction errors. There is no need to generate bootstrap samples of parameters used for prediction because asymptotic irrelevance is assumed to hold. The bootstrap generally needs to account for possible dependency of the data. White (2000) recommends the stationary bootstrap of Politis and Romano (1994).
   (b) Compute the difference in performance between the benchmark model and model $i + 1$, for $i = 1, \ldots, m$. For bootstrap repetition j and model $i + 1$, call the difference $\bar{f}_{ij}^{*}$.
   (c) For $\bar{f}_i$ defined in (9.4), compute and save $\bar{\nu}_j^{*} \equiv \max_{i=1,\ldots,m} \sqrt{P}(\bar{f}_{ij}^{*} - \bar{f}_i)$.
(3) To test whether the benchmark can be beaten, compare $\bar{\nu}$ defined in (9.5) to the quantiles of the $\bar{\nu}_j^{*}$.

While White (2000) motivates the method for its ability to tractably handle situations where the number of models is large relative to sample size, the method can be used in applications with a small number of models as well [e.g., Hong and Lee (2003)].

White's (2000) results have stimulated the development of similar procedures. Corradi and Swanson (2005) indicate how to account for parameter estimation error, when asymptotic irrelevance does not apply. Corradi, Swanson and Olivetti (2001) present extensions to cointegrated environments. Hansen (2003) proposes studentization, and suggests an alternative formulation that has better power when testing for superior, rather than equal, predictive ability. Romano and Wolf (2003) also argue that test statistics be studentized, to better exploit the benefits of bootstrapping.

(B) Sometimes there is no natural null. McCracken and Sapp (2003) propose that one gauge the "false discovery rate" of Storey (2002). That is, one should control the fraction of rejections that are due to type I error. Hansen, Lunde and Nason (2004) propose constructing a set of models that contain the best forecasting model with prespecified asymptotic probability.

10. Conclusions

This paper has summarized some recent work about inference about forecasts. The emphasis has been on the effects of uncertainty about regression parameters used to make forecasts, when one is comparing a small number of models. Results applicable for a comparison of a large number of models were also discussed. One of the highest priorities for future work is development of asymptotically normal or otherwise nuisance parameter free tests for equal MSPE or mean absolute error in a pair of nested models. At present only special case results are available.

Acknowledgements

I thank participants in the January 2004 preconference, two anonymous referees, Pablo M. Pincheira-Brown, Todd E. Clark, Peter Hansen and Michael W. McCracken for helpful comments. I also thank Pablo M. Pincheira-Brown for research assistance and the National Science Foundation for financial support.

References

Andrews, D.W.K. (1991). "Heteroskedasticity and autocorrelation consistent covariance matrix estimation". Econometrica 59, 1465–1471.

Andrews, D.W.K., Monahan, J.C. (1994). "An improved heteroskedasticity and autocorrelation consistent covariance matrix estimator". Econometrica 60, 953–966.

Ashley, R., Granger, C.W.J., Schmalensee, R. (1980). "Advertising and aggregate consumption: An analysis of causality". Econometrica 48, 1149–1168.

Avramov, D. (2002). "Stock return predictability and model uncertainty". Journal of Financial Economics 64, 423–458.

Chao, J., Corradi, V., Swanson, N.R. (2001). "Out-of-sample tests for Granger causality". Macroeconomic Dynamics 5, 598–620.

Chen, S.-S. (2004). "A note on in-sample and out-of-sample tests for Granger causality". Journal of Forecasting. In press.

Cheung, Y.-W., Chinn, M.D., Pascual, A.G. (2003). "Empirical exchange rate models of the nineties: Are any fit to survive?". Journal of International Money and Finance. In press.

Chong, Y.Y., Hendry, D.F. (1986). "Econometric evaluation of linear macro-economic models". Review of Economic Studies 53, 671–690.

Christiano, L.J. (1989). "P^*: Not the inflation forecaster's Holy Grail". Federal Reserve Bank of Minneapolis Quarterly Review 13, 3–18.

Clark, T.E., McCracken, M.W. (2001). "Tests of equal forecast accuracy and encompassing for nested models". Journal of Econometrics 105, 85–110.

Clark, T.E., McCracken, M.W. (2003). "Evaluating long horizon forecasts". Manuscript, University of Missouri.

Clark, T.E., McCracken, M.W. (2005a). "Evaluating direct multistep forecasts". Manuscript, Federal Reserve Bank of Kansas City.

Clark, T.E., McCracken, M.W. (2005b). "The power of tests of predictive ability in the presence of structural breaks". Journal of Econometrics 124, 1–31.

Clark, T.E., West, K.D. (2005a). "Approximately normal tests for equal predictive accuracy in nested models". Manuscript, University of Wisconsin.

Clark, T.E., West, K.D. (2005b). "Using out-of-sample mean squared prediction errors to test the martingale difference hypothesis". Journal of Econometrics. In press.

Clements, M.P., Galvao, A.B. (2004). "A comparison of tests of nonlinear cointegration with application to the predictability of US interest rates using the term structure". International Journal of Forecasting 20, 219–236.

Corradi, V., Swanson, N.R., Olivetti, C. (2001). "Predictive ability with cointegrated variables". Journal of Econometrics 104, 315–358.

Corradi V., Swanson N.R. (2005). "Nonparametric bootstrap procedures for predictive inference based on recursive estimation schemes". Manuscript, Rutgers University.

Corradi, V., Swanson, N.R. (2006). "Predictive density evaluation". In: Elliott, G., Granger, C.W.J., Timmermann, A. (Eds.), Handbook of Economic Forecasting. Elsevier, Amsterdam. Chapter 5 in this volume.

Davidson, R., MacKinnon, J.G. (1984). "Model specification tests based on artificial linear regressions". International Economic Review 25, 485–502.

den Haan, W.J, Levin, A.T. (2000). "Robust covariance matrix estimation with data-dependent VAR prewhitening order". NBER Technical Working Paper No. 255.

Diebold, F.X., Mariano, R.S. (1995). "Comparing predictive accuracy". Journal of Business and Economic Statistics 13, 253–263.

Elliott, G., Timmermann, A. (2003). "Optimal forecast combinations under general loss functions and forecast error distributions". Journal of Econometrics. In press.

Fair, R.C. (1980). "Estimating the predictive accuracy of econometric models". International Economic Review 21, 355–378.

Faust, J., Rogers, J.H., Wright, J.H. (2004). "News and noise in G-7 GDP announcements". Journal of Money, Credit and Banking. In press.

Ferreira, M.A. (2004). "Forecasting the comovements of spot interest rates". Journal of International Money and Finance. In press.

Ghysels, E., Hall, A. (1990). "A test for structural stability of Euler conditions parameters estimated via the generalized method of moments estimator". International Economic Review 31, 355–364.

Giacomini, R. White, H. (2003). "Tests of conditional predictive ability". Manuscript, University of California at San Diego.

Granger, C.W.J., Newbold, P. (1977). Forecasting Economic Time Series. Academic Press, New York.

Hansen, L.P. (1982). "Large sample properties of generalized method of moments estimators". Econometrica 50, 1029–1054.

Hansen, P.R. (2003). "A test for superior predictive ability". Manuscript, Stanford University.

Hansen, P.R., Lunde, A., Nason, J. (2004). "Model confidence sets for forecasting models". Manuscript, Stanford University.

Harvey, D.I., Leybourne, S.J., Newbold, P. (1998). "Tests for forecast encompassing". Journal of Business and Economic Statistics 16, 254–259.

Hoffman, D.L., Pagan, A.R. (1989). "Practitioners corner: Post sample prediction tests for generalized method of moments estimators". Oxford Bulletin of Economics and Statistics 51, 333–343.

Hong, Y., Lee, T.-H. (2003). "Inference on predictability of foreign exchange rates via generalized spectrum and nonlinear time series models". Review of Economics and Statistics 85, 1048–1062.

Hueng, C.J. (1999). "Money demand in an open-economy shopping-time model: An out-of-sample-prediction application to Canada". Journal of Economics and Business 51, 489–503.

Hueng, C.J., Wong, K.F. (2000). "Predictive abilities of inflation-forecasting models using real time data". Working Paper No 00-10-02, The University of Alabama.

Ing, C.-K. (2003). "Multistep prediction in autoregressive processes". Econometric Theory 19, 254–279.

Inoue, A., Kilian, L. (2004a). "In-sample or out-of-sample tests of predictability: Which one should we use?". Econometric Reviews. In press.

Inoue, A., Kilian, L. (2004b). "On the selection of forecasting models". Manuscript, University of Michigan.

Leitch, G., Tanner, J.E. (1991). "Economic forecast evaluation: Profits versus the conventional error measures". American Economic Review 81, 580–590.

Lettau, M., Ludvigson, S. (2001). "Consumption, aggregate wealth, and expected stock returns". Journal and Finance 56, 815–849.

Marcellino, M., Stock, J.H., Watson, M.W. (2004). "A comparison of direct and iterated multistep AR methods for forecasting macroeconomic time". Manuscript, Princeton University.

Mark, N. (1995). "Exchange rates and fundamentals: Evidence on long-horizon predictability". American Economic Review 85, 201–218.

McCracken, M.W. (2000). "Robust out of sample inference". Journal of Econometrics 99, 195–223.

McCracken, M.W. (2004). "Asymptotics for out of sample tests of causality". Manuscript, University of Missouri.

McCracken, M.W., Sapp, S. (2003). "Evaluating the predictability of exchange rates using long horizon regressions". Journal of Money, Credit and Banking. In press.

Meese, R.A., Rogoff, K. (1983). "Empirical exchange rate models of the seventies: Do they fit out of sample?". Journal of International Economics 14, 3–24.
Meese, R.A., Rogoff, K. (1988). "Was it real? The exchange rate – interest differential over the modern floating rate period". Journal of Finance 43, 933–948.
Mizrach, B. (1995). "Forecast comparison in L_2". Manuscript, Rutgers University.
Morgan, W.A. (1939). "A test for significance of the difference between two variances in a sample from a normal bivariate population". Biometrika 31, 13–19.
Newey, W.K., West, K.D. (1987). "A simple, positive semidefinite, heteroskedasticity and autocorrelation consistent covariance matrix". Econometrica 55, 703–708.
Newey, W.K., West, K.D. (1994). "Automatic lag selection in covariance matrix estimation". Review of Economic Studies 61, 631–654.
Pagan, A.R., Hall, A.D. (1983). "Diagnostic tests as residual analysis". Econometric Reviews 2, 159–218.
Politis, D.N., Romano, J.P. (1994). "The stationary bootstrap". Journal of the American Statistical Association 89, 1301–1313.
Romano, J.P., Wolf, M. (2003). "Stepwise multiple testing as formalize data snooping". Manuscript, Stanford University.
Rossi, B. (2003). "Testing long-horizon predictive ability with high persistence the Meese–Rogoff puzzle". International Economic Review. In press.
Sarno, L., Thornton, D.L., Valente, G. (2005). "Federal funds rate prediction". Journal of Money, Credit and Banking. In press.
Shintani, M. (2004). "Nonlinear analysis of business cycles using diffusion indexes: Applications to Japan and the US". Journal of Money, Credit and Banking. In press.
Stock, J.H., Watson, M.W. (1999). "Forecasting inflation". Journal of Monetary Economics 44, 293–335.
Stock, J.H., Watson, M.W. (2002). "Macroeconomic forecasting using diffusion indexes". Journal of Business and Economic Statistics 20, 147–162.
Storey, J.D. (2002). "A direct approach to false discovery rates". Journal of the Royal Statistical Society, Series B 64, 479–498.
West, K.D. (1996). "Asymptotic inference about predictive ability". Econometrica 64, 1067–1084.
West, K.D. (2001). "Tests of forecast encompassing when forecasts depend on estimated regression parameters". Journal of Business and Economic Statistics 19, 29–33.
West, K.D., Cho, D. (1995). "The predictive ability of several models of exchange rate volatility". Journal of Econometrics 69, 367–391.
West, K.D., Edison, H.J., Cho, D. (1993). "A utility based comparison of some models of exchange rate volatility". Journal of International Economics 35, 23–46.
West, K.D., McCracken, M.W. (1998). "Regression based tests of predictive ability". International Economic Review 39, 817–840.
White, H. (1984). Asymptotic Theory for Econometricians. Academic Press, New York.
White, H. (2000). "A reality check for data snooping". Econometrica 68, 1097–1126.
Wilson, E.B. (1934). "The periodogram of American business activity". The Quarterly Journal of Economics 48, 375–417.
Wooldridge, J.M. (1990). "A unified approach to robust, regression-based specification tests". Econometric Theory 6, 17–43.

Chapter 4

FORECAST COMBINATIONS

ALLAN TIMMERMANN
UCSD

Contents

Handbook of Economic Forecasting, Volume 1
Edited by Graham Elliott, Clive W.J. Granger and Allan Timmermann

DOI: 10.1016/S1574-0706(05)01004-9

Abstract

Forecast combinations have frequently been found in empirical studies to produce better forecasts on average than methods based on the ex ante best individual forecasting model. Moreover, simple combinations that ignore correlations between forecast errors often dominate more refined combination schemes aimed at estimating the theoretically optimal combination weights. In this chapter we analyze theoretically the factors that determine the advantages from combining forecasts (for example, the degree of correlation between forecast errors and the relative size of the individual models' forecast error variances). Although the reasons for the success of simple combination schemes are poorly understood, we discuss several possibilities related to model misspecification, instability (non-stationarities) and estimation error in situations where the number of models is large relative to the available sample size. We discuss the role of combinations under asymmetric loss and consider combinations of point, interval and probability forecasts.

Keywords

forecast combinations, pooling and trimming, shrinkage methods, model misspecification, diversification gains

JEL classification: C53, C22

1. Introduction

Multiple forecasts of the same variable are often available to decision makers. This could reflect differences in forecasters' subjective judgements due to heterogeneity in their information sets in the presence of private information or due to differences in modelling approaches. In the latter case, two forecasters may well arrive at very different views depending on the maintained assumptions underlying their forecasting models, e.g., constant versus time-varying parameters, linear versus nonlinear forecasting models, etc.

Faced with multiple forecasts of the same variable, an issue that immediately arises is how best to exploit information in the individual forecasts. In particular, should a single dominant forecast be identified or should a combination of the underlying forecasts be used to produce a pooled summary measure? From a theoretical perspective, unless one can identify ex ante a particular forecasting model that generates smaller forecast errors than its competitors (and whose forecast errors cannot be hedged by other models' forecast errors), forecast combinations offer diversification gains that make it attractive to combine individual forecasts rather than relying on forecasts from a single model. Even if the best model could be identified at each point in time, combination may still be an attractive strategy due to diversification gains, although its success will depend on how well the combination weights can be determined.

Forecast combinations have been used successfully in empirical work in such diverse areas as forecasting Gross National Product, currency market volatility, inflation, money supply, stock prices, meteorological data, city populations, outcomes of football games, wilderness area use, check volume and political risks, cf. Clemen (1989). Summarizing the simulation and empirical evidence in the literature on forecast combinations, Clemen (1989, p. 559) writes "The results have been virtually unanimous: combining multiple forecasts leads to increased forecast accuracy ... in many cases one can make dramatic performance improvements by simply averaging the forecasts." More recently, Makridakis and Hibon (2000) conducted the so-called M3-competition which involved forecasting 3003 time series and concluded (p. 458) "The accuracy of the combination of various methods outperforms, on average, the specific methods being combined and does well in comparison with other methods." Similarly, Stock and Watson (2001, 2004) undertook an extensive study across numerous economic and financial variables using linear and nonlinear forecasting models and found that, on average, pooled forecasts outperform predictions from the single best model, thus confirming Clemen's conclusion. Their analysis has been extended to a large European data set by Marcellino (2004) with essentially the same conclusions.

A simple portfolio diversification argument motivates the idea of combining forecasts, cf. Bates and Granger (1969). Its premise is that, perhaps due to presence of private information, the information set underlying the individual forecasts is often unobserved to the forecast user. In this situation it is not feasible to pool the underlying information sets and construct a 'super' model that nests each of the underlying forecasting models. For example, suppose that we are interested in forecasting some variable, y, and that two predictions, $\hat{y}_1$ and $\hat{y}_2$ of its conditional mean are available. Let the first forecast be based on the variables x_1, x_2, i.e., $\hat{y}_1 = g_1(x_1, x_2)$, while the second forecast is based on the variables x_3, x_4, i.e., $\hat{y}_2 = g_2(x_3, x_4)$. Further, suppose that all variables enter with non-zero weights in the forecasts and that the x-variables are imperfectly correlated. If $\{x_1, x_2, x_3, x_4\}$ were observable, it would be natural to construct a forecasting model based on all four variables, $\hat{y}_3 = g_3(x_1, x_2, x_3, x_4)$. On the other hand, if only the forecasts, $\hat{y}_1$ and $\hat{y}_2$ are observed by the forecast user (while the underlying variables are unobserved) then the only option is to combine these forecasts, i.e. to elicit a model of the type $\hat{y} = g_c(\hat{y}_1, \hat{y}_2)$. More generally, the forecast user's information set, $\mathcal{F}$, may comprise n individual forecasts, $\mathcal{F} = \{\hat{y}_1, \ldots, \hat{y}_n\}$, where $\mathcal{F}$ is often not the union of the information sets underlying the individual forecasts, $\bigcup_{i=1}^{n} \mathcal{F}_i$, but a much smaller subset. Of course, the higher the degree of overlap in the information sets used to produce the underlying forecasts, the less useful a combination of forecasts is likely to be, cf. Clemen (1987).

It is difficult to fully appreciate the strength of the diversification or hedging argument underlying forecast combination. Suppose the aim is to minimize some loss function belonging to a family of convex loss functions, $\mathcal{L}$, and that some forecast, $\hat{y}_1$, stochastically dominates another forecast, $\hat{y}_2$, in the sense that expected losses for all loss functions in $\mathcal{L}$ are lower under $\hat{y}_1$ than under $\hat{y}_2$. While this means that it is not rational for a decision maker to choose $\hat{y}_2$ over $\hat{y}_1$ in isolation, it is easy to construct examples where some combination of $\hat{y}_1$ and $\hat{y}_2$ generates a smaller expected loss than that produced using $\hat{y}_1$ alone.

A second reason for using forecast combinations referred to by, inter alia, Figlewski and Urich (1983), Kang (1986), Diebold and Pauly (1987), Makridakis (1989), Sessions and Chattererjee (1989), Winkler (1989), Hendry and Clements (2002) and Aiolfi and Timmermann (2006) and also thought of by Bates and Granger (1969), is that individual forecasts may be very differently affected by structural breaks caused, for example, by institutional change or technological developments. Some models may adapt quickly and will only temporarily be affected by structural breaks, while others have parameters that only adjust very slowly to new post-break data. The more data that is available after the most recent break, the better one might expect stable, slowly adapting models to perform relative to fast adapting ones as the parameters of the former are more precisely estimated. Conversely, if the data window since the most recent break is short, the faster adapting models can be expected to produce the best forecasting performance. Since it is typically difficult to detect structural breaks in 'real time', it is plausible that on average, i.e., across periods with varying degrees of stability, combinations of forecasts from models with different degrees of adaptability will outperform forecasts from individual models. This intuition is confirmed in Pesaran and Timmermann (2005).

A third and related reason for forecast combination is that individual forecasting models may be subject to misspecification bias of unknown form, a point stressed particularly by Clemen (1989), Makridakis (1989), Diebold and Lopez (1996) and Stock and Watson (2001, 2004). Even in a stationary world, the true data generating process is likely to be more complex and of a much higher dimension than assumed by the most flexible and general model entertained by a forecaster. Viewing forecasting models as local approximations, it is implausible that the same model dominates all others at all points in time. Rather, the best model may change over time in ways that can be difficult to track on the basis of past forecasting performance. Combining forecasts across different models can be viewed as a way to make the forecast more robust against such misspecification biases and measurement errors in the data sets underlying the individual forecasts. Notice again the similarity to the classical portfolio diversification argument for risk reduction: Here the portfolio is the combination of forecasts and the source of risk reflects incomplete information about the target variable and model misspecification possibly due to non-stationarities in the underlying data generating process.

A fourth argument for combination of forecasts is that the underlying forecasts may be based on different loss functions. This argument holds even if the forecasters observe the same information set. Suppose, for example, that forecaster A strongly dislikes large negative forecast errors while forecaster B strongly dislikes large positive forecast errors. In this case, forecaster A is likely to under-predict the variable of interest (so the forecast error distribution is centered on a positive value), while forecaster B will over-predict it. If the bias is constant over time, there is no need to average across different forecasts since including a constant in the combination equation will pick up any unwanted bias. Suppose, however, that the optimal amount of bias is proportional to the conditional variance of the variable, as in Christoffersen and Diebold (1997) and Zellner (1986). Provided that the two forecasters adopt a similar volatility model (which is not implausible since they are assumed to share the same information set), a forecast user with a more symmetric loss function than was used to construct the underlying forecasts could find a combination of the two forecasts better than the individual ones.

Numerous arguments against using forecast combinations can also be advanced. Estimation errors that contaminate the combination weights are known to be a serious problem for many combination techniques especially when the sample size is small relative to the number of forecasts, cf. Diebold and Pauly (1990), Elliott (2004) and Yang (2004). Although non-stationarities in the underlying data generating process can be an argument for using combinations, it can also lead to instabilities in the combination weights and lead to difficulties in deriving a set of combination weights that performs well, cf. Clemen and Winkler (1986), Diebold and Pauly (1987), Figlewski and Urich (1983), Kang (1986) and Palm and Zellner (1992). In situations where the information sets underlying the individual forecasts are unobserved, most would agree that forecast combinations can add value. However, when the full set of predictor variables used to construct different forecasts is observed by the forecast user, the use of a combination strategy instead of attempting to identify a single best "super" model can be challenged, cf. Chong and Hendry (1986) and Diebold (1989).

It is no coincidence that these arguments against forecast combinations seem familiar. In fact, there are many similarities between the forecast combination problem and the standard problem of constructing a single econometric specification. In both cases a subset of predictors (or individual forecasts) has to be selected from a larger set of potential forecasting variables and the choice of functional form mapping this information into the forecast as well as the choice of estimation method have to be determined. There are clearly important differences as well. First, it may be reasonable to assume that the individual forecasts are unbiased in which case the combined forecast will also be unbiased provided that the combination weights are constrained to sum to unity and an intercept is omitted. Provided that the unbiasedness assumption holds for each forecast, imposing such parameter constraints can lead to efficiency gains. One would almost never want to impose this type of constraint on the coefficients of a standard regression model since predictor variables can differ significantly in their units, interpretation and scaling. Secondly, if the individual forecasts are generated by quantitative models whose parameters are estimated recursively there is a potential generated regressor problem which could bias estimates of the combination weights. In part this explains why using simple averages based on equal weights provides a natural benchmark. Finally, the forecasts that are being combined need not be point forecasts but could take the form of interval or density forecasts.

As a testimony to its important role in the forecasting literature, many high-quality surveys of forecast combinations have already appeared, cf. Clemen (1989), Diebold and Lopez (1996) and Newbold and Harvey (2001). This survey differs from earlier ones in many important ways, however. First, we put more emphasis on the theory underlying forecast combinations, particularly in regard to the diversification argument which is common also in portfolio analysis. Second, we deal in more depth with recent topics – some of which were emphasized as important areas of future research by Diebold and Lopez (1996) – such as combination of probability forecasts, time-varying combination weights, combination under asymmetric loss and shrinkage.

The chapter is organized as follows. We first develop the theory underlying the general forecast combination problem in Section 2. The following section discusses estimation methods for the linear forecast combination problem. Section 4 considers nonlinear combination schemes and combinations with time-varying weights. Section 5 discusses shrinkage combinations while Section 6 covers combinations of interval or density forecasts. Section 7 extracts main conclusions from the empirical literature and Section 8 concludes.

2. The forecast combination problem

Consider the problem of forecasting at time t the future value of some target variable, y, after h periods, whose realization is denoted y_{t+h}. Since no major new insights arise from the case where y is multivariate, to simplify the exposition we shall assume that $y_{t+h} \in \mathbb{R}$. We shall refer to t as the time of the forecast and h as the forecast horizon. The information set at time t will be denoted by $\mathcal{F}_t$ and we assume that $\mathcal{F}_t$ comprises an N – vector of forecasts $\hat{\mathbf{y}}_{t+h,t} = (\hat{y}_{t+h,t,1}, \hat{y}_{t+h,t,2}, \ldots, \hat{y}_{t+h,t,N})'$ in addition to the histories of these forecasts up to time t and the history of the realizations of the target variable, i.e. $\mathcal{F}_t = \{\hat{\mathbf{y}}_{h+1,1}, \hat{\mathbf{y}}_{t+h,t}, y_1, \ldots, y_t\}$. A set of additional information variables, $\mathbf{x}_t$, can easily be included in the problem.

The general forecast combination problem seeks an aggregator that reduces the information in a potentially high-dimensional vector of forecasts, $\hat{\mathbf{y}}_{t+h,t} \in \mathbb{R}^N$, to a lower dimensional summary measure, $C(\hat{\mathbf{y}}_{t+h,t}; \boldsymbol{\omega}_c) \in \mathbb{R}^c \subset \mathbb{R}^N$, where $\boldsymbol{\omega}_c$ are the parameters associated with the combination. If only a point forecast is of interest, then a one-dimensional aggregator will suffice. For example, a decision maker interested in using forecasts to determine how much to invest in a risky asset may want to use not only information on either the mode, median or mean forecast, but also to consider the degree of dispersion across individual forecasts as a way to measure the uncertainty or 'disagreement' surrounding the forecasts. How low-dimensional the combined forecast should be is not always obvious. Outside the MSE framework, it is not trivially true that a scalar aggregator that summarizes all relevant information can always be found.

Forecasts do not intrinsically have direct value to decision makers. Rather, they become valuable only to the extent that they can be used to improve decision makers' actions, which in turn affect their loss or utility. Point forecasts generally provide insufficient information for a decision maker or forecast user who, for example, may be interested in the degree of uncertainty surrounding the forecast. Nevertheless, the vast majority of studies on forecast combinations has dealt with point forecasts so we initially focus on this case. We let $\hat{y}^c_{t+h,t} = C(\hat{\mathbf{y}}_{t+h,t}; \boldsymbol{\omega}_{t+h,t})$ be the combined point forecast as a function of the underlying forecasts $\hat{\mathbf{y}}_{t+h,t}$ and the parameters of the combination, $\boldsymbol{\omega}_{t+h,t} \in \mathcal{W}_t$, where $\mathcal{W}_t$ is often assumed to be a compact subset of $\mathbb{R}^N$ and $\boldsymbol{\omega}_{t+h,t}$ can be time-varying but is adapted to $\mathcal{F}_t$. For example, equal weights would give $g(\hat{\mathbf{y}}_{t+h,t}; \boldsymbol{\omega}_{t+h,t}) = (1/N)\sum_{j=1}^N \hat{y}_{t+h,t,j}$. Our choice of notation reflects that we will mostly be thinking of $\boldsymbol{\omega}_{t+h,t}$ as combination weights, although the parameters need not always have this interpretation.

2.1. Specification of loss function

To simplify matters we follow standard practice and assume that the loss function only depends on the forecast error from the combination, $e^c_{t+h,t} = y_{t+h} - g(\hat{\mathbf{y}}_{t+h,t}; \boldsymbol{\omega}_{t+h,t})$, i.e. $L = L(e_{t+h,t})$. The vast majority of work on forecast combinations assumes this type of loss, in part because point forecasts are far more common than distribution forecasts and in part because the decision problem underlying the forecast situation is not worked out in detail. However, it should also be acknowledged that this loss function embodies a set of restrictive assumptions on the decision problem, cf. Granger and Machina (2006) and Elliott and Timmermann (2004). In Section 6 we cover the more general case that combines interval or distribution forecasts.

The parameters of the optimal combination, $\boldsymbol{\omega}^*_{t+h,t} \in \mathcal{W}_t$, solve the problem

$$\boldsymbol{\omega}^*_{t+h,t} = \underset{\boldsymbol{\omega}_{t+h,t} \in \mathcal{W}_t}{\arg\min}\ \mathrm{E}\big[L\big(e^c_{t+h,t}(\boldsymbol{\omega}_{t+h,t})\big)|\mathcal{F}_t\big]. \tag{1}$$

Here the expectation is taken over the conditional distribution of $e_{t+h,t}$ given $\mathcal{F}_t$. Clearly optimality is established within the assumed family $\hat{y}^c_{t+h,t} = C(\hat{\mathbf{y}}_{t+h,t}; \boldsymbol{\omega}_{t+h,t})$. Elliott and Timmermann (2004) show that, subject to a set of weak technical assumptions on the loss and distribution functions, the combination weights can be found as the solution to the following Taylor series expansion around $\mu_{e_{t+h,t}} = \mathrm{E}[e_{t+h,t}|\mathcal{F}_t]$:

$$\boldsymbol{\omega}^*_{t+h,t} = \underset{\boldsymbol{\omega}_{t+h,t}\in\mathcal{W}_t}{\arg\min} \left\{ L(\mu_{e_{t+h,t}}) + \frac{1}{2}L''_{\mu_e}\mathrm{E}\big[(e_{t+h,t} - \mu_{e_{t+h,t}})^2|\mathcal{F}_t\big] \right. \\ \left. + \sum_{m=3}^{\infty} L^m_{\mu_e} \sum_{i=0}^{m} \frac{1}{i!(m-i)!}\mathrm{E}\big[e^{m-i}_{t+h,t}\mu^i_{e_{t+h,t}}|\mathcal{F}_t\big] \right\} \tag{2}$$

where $L^k_{\mu_e} \equiv \partial^k L(e_{t+h,t})/\partial^k e|_{e_{t+h,t}=\mu_{e_{t+h,t}}}$. In general, the entire moment generating function of the forecast error distribution and all higher-order derivatives of the loss function will influence the optimal combination weights which therefore reflect both the shape of the loss function and the forecast error distribution.

The expansion in (2) suggests that the collection of individual forecasts $\hat{\mathbf{y}}_{t+h,t}$ is useful in as far as it can predict any of the conditional moments of the forecast error distribution of which a decision maker cares. Hence, $\hat{y}_{t+h,t,i}$ gets a non-zero weight in the combination if for any moment, $e^m_{t+h,t}$, for which $L^m_{\mu_e} \neq 0$, $\partial\mathrm{E}[e^m_{t+h,t}|\mathcal{F}_t]/\partial\hat{y}_{t+h,t,i} \neq 0$. For example, if the vector of point forecasts can be used to predict the mean, variance, skew and kurtosis, but no other moments of the forecast error distribution, then the combined summary measure could be based on those summary measures of $\hat{\mathbf{y}}_{t+h,t}$ that predict the first through fourth moments.

Oftentimes it is simply assumed that the objective function underlying the combination problem is mean squared error (MSE) loss

$$L(y_{t+h}, \hat{y}_{t+h,t}) = \theta(y_{t+h} - \hat{y}_{t+h,t})^2, \quad \theta > 0. \tag{3}$$

For this case, the combined or consensus forecast seeks to choose a (possibly time-varying) mapping $C(\hat{\mathbf{y}}_{t+h,t}; \boldsymbol{\omega}_{t+h,t})$ from the N-vector of individual forecasts $\hat{\mathbf{y}}_{t+h,t}$ to the real line, $\mathcal{Y}_{t+h,t} \to \mathcal{R}$ that best approximates the conditional expectation, $\mathrm{E}[y_{t+h}|\hat{\mathbf{y}}_{t+h,t}]$.[1]

Two levels of aggregation are thus involved in the combination problem. The first step summarizes individual forecasters' private information to produce point forecasts $\hat{y}_{t+h,t,i}$. The only difference to the standard forecasting problem is that the 'input' variables are forecasts from other models or subjective forecasts. This may create a generated regressor problem that can bias the estimated combination weights, although this aspect is often ignored. It could in part explain why combinations based on estimated weights often do not perform well. The second step aggregates the vector of point forecasts $\hat{\mathbf{y}}_{t+h,t}$ to the consensus measure $C(\hat{\mathbf{y}}_{t+h,t}; \boldsymbol{\omega}_{t+h,t})$. Information is lost in both steps. Conversely, the second step is likely to lead to far simpler and more parsimonious forecasting models when compared to a forecast based on the full set of individual

[1] To see this, take expectations of (3) and differentiate with respect to $C(\hat{\mathbf{y}}_{t+h,t}; \boldsymbol{\omega}_{t+h,t})$ to get $C^*(\hat{\mathbf{y}}_{t+h,t}; \boldsymbol{\omega}_{t+h,t}) = \mathrm{E}[Y_{t+h}|\mathcal{F}_t]$.

forecasts or a "super model" based on individual forecasters' information variables. In general, we would expect information aggregation to increase the bias in the forecast but also to reduce the variance of the forecast error. To the extent possible, the combination should optimally trade off these two components. This is particularly clear under MSE loss, where the objective function equals the squared bias plus the forecast error variance, $\mathrm{E}[e^2_{t+h,t}] = \mathrm{E}[e_{t+h,t}]^2 + \mathrm{Var}(e_{t+h,t})$.[2]

2.2. Construction of a super model – pooling information

Let $\mathcal{F}^c_t = \bigcup_{i=1}^N \mathcal{F}_{it}$ be the union of the forecasters' individual information sets, or the 'super' information set. If $\mathcal{F}^c_t$ were observed, one possibility would be to model the conditional mean of y_{t+h} as a function of all these variables, i.e.

$$\hat{y}_{t+h,t} = C_s\big(\mathcal{F}^c_t; \boldsymbol{\theta}_{t+h,t,s}\big). \tag{4}$$

Individual forecasts, i, instead take the form $\hat{y}_{t+h,t,i} = C_i(\mathcal{F}_{it}; \boldsymbol{\theta}_{t+h,t,i})$.[3] If only the individual forecasts $\hat{y}_{t+h,t,i}$ $(i = 1, \ldots, N)$ are observed, whereas the underlying information sets $\{\mathcal{F}_{it}\}$ are unobserved by the forecast user, the combined forecast would be restricted as follows:

$$\hat{y}_{t+h,t,i} = C_c\big(\hat{y}_{t+h,t,1}, \ldots, \hat{y}_{t+h,t,N}; \boldsymbol{\theta}_{t+h,t,c}\big). \tag{5}$$

Normally it would be better to pool all information rather than first filter the information sets through the individual forecasting models. This introduces the usual efficiency loss through the two-stage estimation and also ignores correlations between the underlying information sources. There are several potential problems with pooling the information sets, however. One problem is – as already mentioned – that individual information sets may not be observable or too costly to combine. Diebold and Pauly (1990, p. 503) remark that "While pooling of forecasts is suboptimal relative to pooling of information sets, it must be recognized that in many forecasting situations, particularly in real time, pooling of information sets is either impossible or prohibitively costly." Furthermore, in cases with many relevant input variables and complicated dynamic and nonlinear effects, constructing a "super model" using the pooled information set, $\mathcal{F}^c_t$, is not likely to provide good forecasts given the well-known problems associated with high-dimensional kernel regressions, nearest neighbor regressions, or other

[2] Clemen (1987) demonstrates that an important part of the aggregation of individual forecasts towards an aggregate forecast is an assessment of the dependence among the underlying models' ('experts') forecasts and that a group forecast will generally be less informative than the set of individual forecasts. In fact, group forecasts only provide a sufficient statistic for collections of individual forecasts provided that both the experts and the decision maker agree in their assessments of the dependence among experts. This precludes differences in opinion about the correlation structure among decision makers. Taken to its extreme, this argument suggests that experts should not attempt to aggregate their observed information into a single forecast but should simply report their raw data to the decision maker.

[3] Notice that we use $\boldsymbol{\omega}_{t+h,t}$ for the parameters involved in the combination of the forecasts, $\hat{y}_{t+h,t}$, while we use $\boldsymbol{\theta}_{t+h,t}$ for the parameters relating the underlying information variables in $\mathcal{F}_t$ to y_{t+h}.

nonparametric methods. Although individual forecasting models will be biased and may omit important variables, this bias can more than be compensated for by reductions in parameter estimation error in cases where the number of relevant predictor variables is much greater than N, the number of forecasts.[4]

2.3. Linear forecast combinations under MSE loss

While in general there is no closed-form solution to (1), one can get analytical results by imposing distributional restrictions or restrictions on the loss function. Unless the mapping, C, from $\hat{\mathbf{y}}_{t+h,t}$ to y_{t+h} is modeled nonparametrically, optimality results for forecast combination must be established within families of parametric combination schemes of the form $\hat{y}^c_{t+h,t} = C(\hat{\mathbf{y}}_{t+h,t}; \boldsymbol{\omega}_{t+h,t})$. The general class of combination schemes in (1) comprises nonlinear as well as time-varying combination methods. We shall return to these but for now concentrate on the family of linear combinations, $\mathcal{W}^l_t \subset \mathcal{W}_t$, which are more commonly used.[5] To this end we choose weights, $\boldsymbol{\omega}_{t+h,t} = (\omega_{t+h,t,1}, \ldots, \omega_{t+h,t,N})'$ to produce a combined forecast of the form

$$\hat{y}^c_{t+h,t} = \boldsymbol{\omega}'_{t+h,t}\hat{\mathbf{y}}_{t+h,t}. \tag{6}$$

Under MSE loss, the combination weights are easy to characterize in population and only depend on the first two moments of the joint distribution of y_{t+h} and $\hat{\mathbf{y}}_{t+h,t}$,

$$\begin{pmatrix} y_{t+h} \\ \hat{\mathbf{y}}_{t+h,t} \end{pmatrix} \sim \left(\begin{pmatrix} \mu_{yt+h,t} \\ \boldsymbol{\mu}_{\hat{\mathbf{y}}t+h,t} \end{pmatrix} \begin{pmatrix} \sigma^2_{yt+h,t} & \boldsymbol{\sigma}'_{y\hat{\mathbf{y}}t+h,t} \\ \boldsymbol{\sigma}_{y\hat{\mathbf{y}}t+h,t} & \boldsymbol{\Sigma}_{\hat{\mathbf{y}}\hat{\mathbf{y}}t+h,t} \end{pmatrix} \right). \tag{7}$$

Minimizing $\mathrm{E}[e^2_{t+h,t}] = \mathrm{E}[(y_{t+h} - \boldsymbol{\omega}'_{t+h,t}\hat{\mathbf{y}}_{t+h,t})^2]$, we have

$$\begin{aligned} \boldsymbol{\omega}^*_{t+h,t} = \underset{\boldsymbol{\omega}_{t+h,t} \in \mathcal{W}^l_t}{\arg\min} \Big(& \big(\mu_{yt+h,t} - \boldsymbol{\omega}'_{t+h,t}\boldsymbol{\mu}_{\hat{\mathbf{y}}t+h,t}\big)^2 + \sigma^2_{yt+h,t} \\ & + \boldsymbol{\omega}'_{t+h,t}\boldsymbol{\Sigma}_{\hat{\mathbf{y}}\hat{\mathbf{y}}t+h,t}\boldsymbol{\omega}_{t+h,t} - 2\boldsymbol{\omega}'_{t+h,t}\boldsymbol{\sigma}_{y\hat{\mathbf{y}}t+h,t} \Big). \end{aligned}$$

This yields the first order condition

$$\begin{aligned} \frac{\partial \mathrm{E}[e^2_{t+h,t}]}{\partial \boldsymbol{\omega}_{t+h,t}} &= -\big(\mu_{yt+h,t} - \boldsymbol{\omega}'_{t+h,t}\boldsymbol{\mu}_{\hat{\mathbf{y}}t+h,t}\big)\boldsymbol{\mu}_{\hat{\mathbf{y}}t+h,t} + \boldsymbol{\Sigma}_{\hat{\mathbf{y}}\hat{\mathbf{y}}t+h,t}\boldsymbol{\omega}_{t+h,t} - \boldsymbol{\sigma}_{y\hat{\mathbf{y}}t+h,t} \\ &= \mathbf{0}. \end{aligned}$$

Assuming that $\boldsymbol{\Sigma}_{\hat{\mathbf{y}}\hat{\mathbf{y}}t+h,t}$ is invertible, this has the solution

$$\boldsymbol{\omega}^*_{t+h,t} = \big(\boldsymbol{\mu}_{\hat{\mathbf{y}}t+h,t}\boldsymbol{\mu}'_{\hat{\mathbf{y}}t+h,t} + \boldsymbol{\Sigma}_{\hat{\mathbf{y}}\hat{\mathbf{y}}t+h,t}\big)^{-1}\big(\boldsymbol{\mu}_{\hat{\mathbf{y}}t+h,t}\mu_{yt+h,t} + \boldsymbol{\sigma}_{y\hat{\mathbf{y}}t+h,t}\big). \tag{8}$$

[4] When the true forecasting model mapping $\mathcal{F}^c_t$ to y_{t+h} is infinite-dimensional, the model that optimally balances bias and variance may depend on the sample size with a dimension that grows as the sample size increases.

[5] This, of course, does not rule out that the *estimated* weights vary over time as will be the case when the weights are updated recursively as more data becomes available.

This solution is optimal in population whenever y_{t+h} and $\hat{\mathbf{y}}_{t+h,t}$ are joint Gaussian since in this case the conditional expectation $\mathrm{E}[y_{t+h}|\hat{\mathbf{y}}_{t+h,t}]$ will be linear in $\hat{\mathbf{y}}_{t+h,t}$. For the moment we ignore time-variations in the conditional moments in (8), but as we shall see later on, the weights can facilitate such effects by allowing them to vary over time. A constant can trivially be included as one of the forecasts so that the combination scheme allows for an intercept term, a strategy recommended (under MSE loss) by Granger and Ramanathan (1984) and – for a more general class of loss functions – by Elliott and Timmermann (2004). Assuming that a constant is included, the optimal (population) values of the constant and the combination weights, $\omega^*_{0t+h,t}$ and $\boldsymbol{\omega}^*_{t+h,t}$, simplify as follows:

$$\begin{aligned} \omega^*_{0t+h,t} &= \mu_{yt+h,t} - \boldsymbol{\omega}^{*\prime}_{t+h,t}\boldsymbol{\mu}_{\hat{\mathbf{y}}t+h,t}, \\ \boldsymbol{\omega}^*_{t+h,t} &= \boldsymbol{\Sigma}^{-1}_{\hat{\mathbf{y}}\hat{\mathbf{y}}t+h,t}\boldsymbol{\sigma}_{y\hat{\mathbf{y}}t+h,t}. \end{aligned} \tag{9}$$

These weights depend on the full conditional covariance matrix of the forecasts, $\boldsymbol{\Sigma}_{\hat{\mathbf{y}}\hat{\mathbf{y}}t+h,t}$. In general the weights have an intuitive interpretation and tend to be larger for more accurate forecasts that are less strongly correlated with other forecasts. Notice that the constant, $\omega^*_{0t+h,t}$, corrects for any biases in the weighted forecast $\boldsymbol{\omega}^{*\prime}_{t+h,t}\hat{\mathbf{y}}_{t+h,t}$.

In the following we explore some interesting special cases to demonstrate the determinants of gains from forecast combination.

2.3.1. Diversification gains

Under quadratic loss it is easy to illustrate the population gains from different forecast combination schemes. This is an important task since, as argued by Winkler (1989, p. 607) "The better we understand which sets of underlying assumptions are associated with which combining rules, the more effective we will be at matching combining rules to forecasting situations." To this end we consider the simple combination of two forecasts that give rise to errors $e_1 = y - \hat{y}_1$ and $e_2 = y - \hat{y}_2$. Without risk of confusion we have dropped the time and horizon subscripts. Assuming that the individual forecast errors are unbiased, we have $e_1 \sim (0, \sigma_1^2)$, $e_2 \sim (0, \sigma_2^2)$ where $\sigma_1^2 = \mathrm{var}(e_1)$, $\sigma_2^2 = \mathrm{var}(e_2)$, $\sigma_{12} = \rho_{12}\sigma_1\sigma_2$ is the covariance between e_1 and e_2 and ρ_{12} is their correlation. Suppose that the combination weights are restricted to sum to one, with weights $(\omega, 1-\omega)$ on the first and second forecast, respectively. The forecast error from the combination $e^c = y - \omega\hat{y}_1 - (1-\omega)\hat{y}_2$ takes the form

$$e^c = \omega e_1 + (1-\omega)e_2. \tag{10}$$

By construction this has zero mean and variance

$$\sigma_c^2(\omega) = \omega^2\sigma_1^2 + (1-\omega)^2\sigma_2^2 + 2\omega(1-\omega)\sigma_{12}. \tag{11}$$

Differentiating with respect to ω and solving the first order condition, we have

$$\omega^* = \frac{\sigma_2^2 - \sigma_{12}}{\sigma_1^2 + \sigma_2^2 - 2\sigma_{12}},$$
$$1 - \omega^* = \frac{\sigma_1^2 - \sigma_{12}}{\sigma_1^2 + \sigma_2^2 - 2\sigma_{12}}. \tag{12}$$

A greater weight is assigned to models producing more precise forecasts (lower forecast error variances). A negative weight on a forecast clearly does not mean that it has no value to a forecaster. In fact when $\rho_{12} > \sigma_2/\sigma_1$ the combination weights are not convex and one weight will exceed unity, the other being negative, cf. Bunn (1985).

Inserting ω^* into the objective function (11), we get the expected squared loss associated with the optimal weights:

$$\sigma_c^2(\omega^*) = \frac{\sigma_1^2\sigma_2^2(1-\rho_{12}^2)}{\sigma_1^2 + \sigma_2^2 - 2\rho_{12}\sigma_1\sigma_2}. \tag{13}$$

It can easily be verified that $\sigma_c^2(\omega^*) \leqslant \min(\sigma_1^2, \sigma_2^2)$. In fact, the diversification gain will only be zero in the following special cases (i) σ_1 or σ_2 equal to zero; (ii) $\sigma_1 = \sigma_2$ and $\rho_{12} = 1$; or (iii) $\rho_{12} = \sigma_1/\sigma_2$.

It is interesting to compare the variance of the forecast error from the optimal combination (12) to the variance of the combination scheme that weights the forecasts inversely to their relative mean squared error (MSE) values and hence ignores any correlation between the forecast errors:

$$\omega_{\text{inv}} = \frac{\sigma_2^2}{\sigma_1^2 + \sigma_2^2}, \qquad 1 - \omega_{\text{inv}} = \frac{\sigma_1^2}{\sigma_1^2 + \sigma_2^2}. \tag{14}$$

These weights result in a forecast error variance

$$\sigma_{\text{inv}}^2 = \frac{\sigma_1^2\sigma_2^2(\sigma_1^2 + \sigma_2^2 + 2\rho_{12}\sigma_1\sigma_2)}{(\sigma_1^2 + \sigma_2^2)^2}. \tag{15}$$

After some algebra we can derive the ratio of the forecast error variance under this scheme relative to its value under the optimal weights, $\sigma_c^2(\omega^*)$ in (13):

$$\frac{\sigma_{\text{inv}}^2}{\sigma_c^2(\omega^*)} = \left(\frac{1}{1-\rho_{12}^2}\right)\left(1 - \left(\frac{2\sigma_{12}}{\sigma_1^2 + \sigma_2^2}\right)^2\right). \tag{16}$$

If $\sigma_1 \neq \sigma_2$, this exceeds unity unless $\rho_{12} = 0$. When $\sigma_1 = \sigma_2$, this ratio is always unity irrespective of the value of ρ_{12} and in this case $\omega_{\text{inv}} = \omega^* = 1/2$. Equal weights are optimal when combining two forecasts provided that the two forecast error variances are identical, irrespective of the correlation between the two forecast errors.

Another interesting benchmark is the equal-weighted combination $\hat{y}^{\text{ew}} = (1/2)(\hat{y}_1 + \hat{y}_2)$. Under these weights the variance of the forecast error is

$$\sigma_{\text{ew}}^2 = \frac{1}{4}\sigma_1^2 + \frac{1}{4}\sigma_2^2 + \frac{1}{2}\sigma_1\sigma_2\rho_{12} \tag{17}$$

so the ratio $\sigma_{\text{ew}}^2/\sigma_c^2(\omega^*)$ becomes:

$$\frac{\sigma_{\text{ew}}^2}{\sigma_c^2(\omega^*)} = \frac{(\sigma_1^2 + \sigma_2^2)^2 - 4\sigma_{12}^2}{4\sigma_1^2\sigma_2^2(1 - \rho_{12}^2)}, \tag{18}$$

which in general exceeds unity unless $\sigma_1 = \sigma_2$.

Finally, as a measure of the diversification gain obtained from combining the two forecasts it is natural to compare $\sigma_c^2(\omega^*)$ to $\min(\sigma_1^2, \sigma_2^2)$. Suppose that $\sigma_1 > \sigma_2$ and define $\kappa = \sigma_2/\sigma_1$ so that $\kappa < 1$. We then have

$$\frac{\sigma_c^2(\omega^*)}{\sigma_2^2} = \frac{1 - \rho_{12}^2}{1 + \kappa^2 - 2\rho_{12}\kappa}. \tag{19}$$

Figure 1 shows this expression graphically as a function of ρ_{12} and κ. The diversification gain is a complicated function of the correlation between the two forecast errors, ρ_{12},

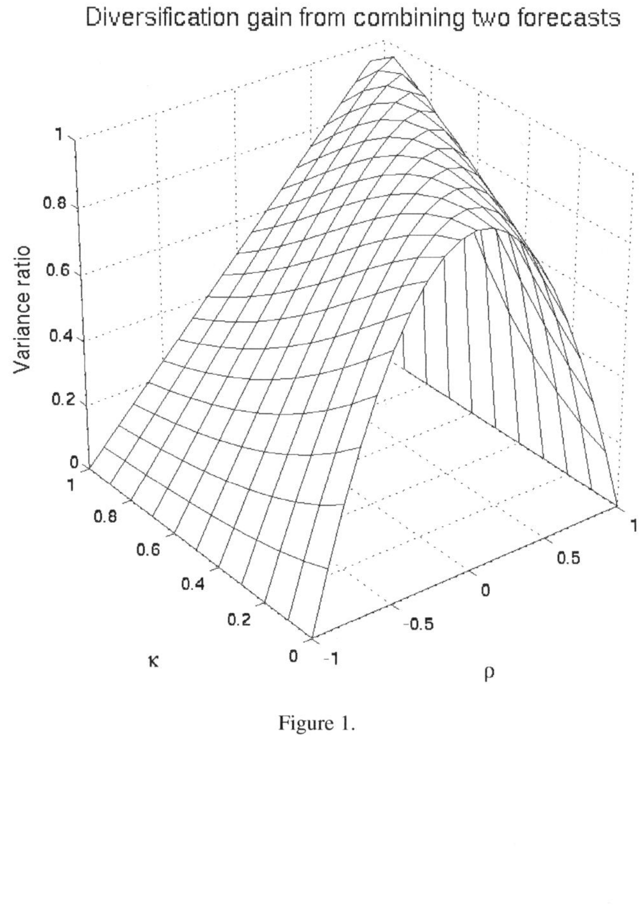

Figure 1.

and the variance ratio of the forecast errors, κ. In fact, the derivative of the efficiency gain with respect to either κ or ρ_{12} changes sign even for reasonable parameter values. Differentiating (19) with respect to ρ_{12}, we have

$$\frac{\partial(\sigma_c^2(\omega^*)/\sigma_2^2)}{\partial\rho_{12}} \propto \kappa\rho_{12}^2 - (1+\kappa^2)\rho_{12} + \kappa.$$

This is a second order polynomial in ρ_{12} with roots (assuming $\kappa < 1$)

$$\frac{1+\kappa^2 \pm (1-\kappa^2)}{2\kappa} = (\kappa;\, 1/\kappa).$$

Only when $\kappa = 1$ (so $\sigma_1^2 = \sigma_2^2$) does it follow that the efficiency gain will be an increasing function of ρ_{12} – otherwise it will change sign, being positive on the interval $[-1; \kappa]$ and negative on $[\kappa; 1]$ as can be seen from Figure 1. The figure shows that diversification through combination is more effective (in the sense that it results in the largest reduction in the forecast error variance for a given change in ρ_{12}) when $\kappa = 1$.

2.3.2. *Effect of bias in individual forecasts*

Problems can arise for forecast combinations when one or more of the individual forecasts is biased, the combination weights are constrained to sum to unity and an intercept is omitted from the combination scheme. Min and Zellner (1993) illustrate how bias in one or more of the forecasts along with a constraint that the weights add up to unity can lead to suboptimality of combinations. Let $y - \hat{y}_1 = e_1 \sim (0, \sigma^2)$ and $y - \hat{y}_2 = e_2 \sim (\mu_2, \sigma^2)$, $\text{cov}(e_1, e_2) = \sigma_{12} = \rho_{12}\sigma^2$, so $\hat{y}_1$ is unbiased while $\hat{y}_2$ has a bias equal of μ_2. Then the MSE of $\hat{y}_1$ is σ^2, while the MSE of $\hat{y}_2$ is $\sigma^2 + \mu_2^2$. The MSE of the combined forecast $\hat{y}_c = \omega\hat{y}_1 + (1-\omega)\hat{y}_2$ relative to that of the best forecast $(\hat{y}_1)$ is

$$\text{MSE}(\hat{y}_c) - \text{MSE}(\hat{y}_1) = (1-\omega)\sigma^2\left((1-\omega)\left(\frac{\mu_2}{\sigma}\right)^2 - 2\omega(1-\rho_{12})\right),$$

so $\text{MSE}(\hat{y}_c) > \text{MSE}(\hat{y}_1)$ if

$$\left(\frac{\mu_2}{\sigma}\right)^2 > \frac{2\omega(1-\rho_{12})}{1-\omega}.$$

This condition always holds if $\rho_{12} = 1$. Furthermore, the larger the bias, the more likely it is that the combination will not dominate the first forecast. Of course the problem here is that the combination is based on variances and not the mean squared forecast errors which would account for the bias.

2.4. *Optimality of equal weights – general case*

Equally weighted combinations occupy a special place in the forecast combination literature. They are frequently either imposed on the combination scheme or used as a point towards which the unconstrained combination weights are shrunk. Given their special role, it is worth establishing more general conditions under which they are optimal in a population sense. This sets a benchmark that proves helpful in understanding their good finite-sample performance in simulations and in empirical studies with actual data.

Let $\boldsymbol{\Sigma}_e = \mathrm{E}[\mathbf{ee}']$ be the covariance matrix of the individual forecast errors where $\mathbf{e} = \boldsymbol{\iota} y - \hat{\mathbf{y}}$ and $\boldsymbol{\iota}$ is an $N \times 1$ column vector of ones. Again we drop time and horizon subscripts without any risk of confusion. From (7) and assuming that the individual forecasts are unbiased, so $\boldsymbol{\iota}\hat{\boldsymbol{\mu}}'_{\mathbf{y}} = \boldsymbol{\mu}'_{\hat{\mathbf{y}}} \cdot \boldsymbol{\iota}'$, the vector of forecast errors has second moment

$$\begin{aligned}\boldsymbol{\Sigma}_e &= \mathrm{E}\big[y^2\boldsymbol{\iota}\boldsymbol{\iota}' + \hat{\mathbf{y}}\hat{\mathbf{y}}' - 2y\boldsymbol{\iota}\hat{\mathbf{y}}'\big] \\ &= \big(\sigma_y^2 + \mu_y^2\big)\boldsymbol{\iota}\boldsymbol{\iota}' + \boldsymbol{\mu}_{\hat{\mathbf{y}}}\boldsymbol{\mu}'_{\hat{\mathbf{y}}} + \boldsymbol{\Sigma}_{\hat{\mathbf{y}}\hat{\mathbf{y}}} - 2\boldsymbol{\iota}\boldsymbol{\sigma}'_{y\hat{\mathbf{y}}} - 2\mu_y\boldsymbol{\iota}\boldsymbol{\mu}'_{\hat{\mathbf{y}}}.\end{aligned} \tag{20}$$

Consider minimizing the expected forecast error variance subject to the constraint that the weights add up to one:

$$\begin{aligned}&\min\ \boldsymbol{\omega}'\boldsymbol{\Sigma}_e\boldsymbol{\omega} \\ &\text{s.t.}\quad \boldsymbol{\omega}'\boldsymbol{\iota} = 1.\end{aligned} \tag{21}$$

The constraint ensures unbiasedness of the combined forecast provided that $\boldsymbol{\mu}_{\hat{\mathbf{y}}} = \mu_y\boldsymbol{\iota}$ so that

$$\mu_y^2\boldsymbol{\iota}\boldsymbol{\iota}' + \boldsymbol{\mu}_{\hat{\mathbf{y}}}\boldsymbol{\mu}'_{\hat{\mathbf{y}}} - 2\mu_y\boldsymbol{\iota}\boldsymbol{\mu}'_{\hat{\mathbf{y}}} = 0.$$

The Lagrangian associated with (21) is

$$\mathcal{L} = \boldsymbol{\omega}'\boldsymbol{\Sigma}_e\boldsymbol{\omega} - \lambda(\boldsymbol{\omega}'\boldsymbol{\iota} - 1)$$

which yields the first order condition

$$\boldsymbol{\Sigma}_e\boldsymbol{\omega} = \frac{\lambda}{2}\boldsymbol{\iota}. \tag{22}$$

Assuming that $\boldsymbol{\Sigma}_e$ is invertible, after pre-multiplying by $\boldsymbol{\Sigma}_e^{-1}\boldsymbol{\iota}'$ and recalling that $\boldsymbol{\iota}'\boldsymbol{\omega} = 1$ we get $\lambda/2 = (\boldsymbol{\iota}'\boldsymbol{\Sigma}_e^{-1}\boldsymbol{\iota})^{-1}$. Inserting this in (22) we have the frequently cited formula for the optimal weights:

$$\boldsymbol{\omega}^* = \big(\boldsymbol{\iota}'\boldsymbol{\Sigma}_e^{-1}\boldsymbol{\iota}\big)^{-1}\boldsymbol{\Sigma}_e^{-1}\boldsymbol{\iota}. \tag{23}$$

Now suppose that the forecast errors have the same variance, σ^2, and correlation, ρ. Then we have

$$\begin{aligned}\boldsymbol{\Sigma}_e^{-1} &= \frac{1}{\sigma^2(1-\rho)}\left(\mathbf{I} - \frac{\rho}{1+(N-1)\rho}\boldsymbol{\iota}\boldsymbol{\iota}'\right) \\ &= \frac{1}{\sigma^2(1-\rho)(1+(N-1)\rho)}\big((1+(N-1)\rho)\mathbf{I} - \rho\boldsymbol{\iota}\boldsymbol{\iota}'\big),\end{aligned}$$

where $\mathbf{I}$ is the $N \times N$ identity matrix. Inserting this in (23) we have

$$\boldsymbol{\Sigma}_e^{-1}\boldsymbol{\iota} = \frac{\boldsymbol{\iota}}{\sigma^2(1+(N-1)\rho)},$$

$$\left(\boldsymbol{\iota}'\boldsymbol{\Sigma}_e^{-1}\boldsymbol{\iota}\right)^{-1} = \frac{\sigma^2(1+(N-1)\rho)}{N},$$

so

$$\boldsymbol{\omega}^* = \left(\frac{1}{N}\right)\boldsymbol{\iota}. \tag{24}$$

Hence equal-weights are optimal in situations with an arbitrary number of forecasts when the individual forecast errors have the same variance and identical pair-wise correlations. Notice that the property that the weights add up to unity only follows as a result of imposing the constraint $\boldsymbol{\iota}'\boldsymbol{\omega} = 1$ and need not otherwise hold more generally.

2.5. Optimal combinations under asymmetric loss

Recent work has seen considerable interest in analyzing the effect of asymmetric loss on optimal predictions, cf., inter alia, Christoffersen and Diebold (1997), Granger and Pesaran (2000) and Patton and Timmermann (2004). These papers show that the standard properties of an optimal forecast under MSE loss case to hold under asymmetric loss. These properties include lack of bias, absence of serial correlation in the forecast error at the single-period forecast horizon and increasing forecast error variance as the horizon grows. It is therefore not surprising that asymmetric loss also affects combination weights. To illustrate the significance of the shape of the loss function for the optimal combination weights, consider linex loss. The linex loss function is convenient to use since it allows us to characterize the optimal forecast analytically. It takes the form, cf. Zellner (1986),

$$L(e_{t+h,t}) = \exp(ae_{t+h,t}) - ae_{t+h,t} + 1, \tag{25}$$

where a is a scalar that controls the aversion towards either positive ($a > 0$) or negative ($a < 0$) forecast errors and $e_{t+h,t} = (y_{t+h} - \omega_{0t+h,t} - \boldsymbol{\omega}'_{t+h,t}\hat{\mathbf{y}}_{t+h,t})$. First, suppose that the target variable and forecast are joint Gaussian with moments given in (7). Using the well-known result that if $X \sim N(\mu, \sigma^2)$, then $\mathrm{E}[\mathrm{e}^x] = \exp(\mu + \sigma^2/2)$, the optimal combination weights $(\omega^*_{0t+h,t}, \boldsymbol{\omega}^*_{t+h,t})$ which minimize the expected loss $E[L(e_{t+h,t})|\mathcal{F}_t]$, solve

$$\begin{aligned}\min_{\omega_{0t+h,t},\boldsymbol{\omega}_{t+h,t}} \exp\Bigg(& a\left(\mu_{yt+h,t} - \omega_{0t+h,t} - \boldsymbol{\omega}'_{t+h,t}\boldsymbol{\mu}_{\hat{\mathbf{y}}t+h,t}\right)\\ &+ \frac{a^2}{2}\left(\sigma^2_{yt+h,t} + \boldsymbol{\omega}'_{t+h,t}\boldsymbol{\Sigma}_{\hat{\mathbf{y}}\hat{\mathbf{y}}t+h,t}\boldsymbol{\omega}_{t+h,t} - 2\boldsymbol{\omega}'_{t+h,t}\boldsymbol{\sigma}_{y\hat{\mathbf{y}}t+h,t}\right)\Bigg)\\ &- a\left(\mu_{yt+h,t} - \omega_{0t+h,t} - \boldsymbol{\omega}'_{t+h,t}\boldsymbol{\mu}_{\hat{\mathbf{y}}t+h,t}\right).\end{aligned}$$

Taking derivatives, we get the first order conditions

$$\exp\Big(a\big(\mu_{yt+h,t} - \omega_{0t+h,t} - \boldsymbol{\omega}'_{t+h,t}\boldsymbol{\mu}_{\hat{\mathbf{y}}t+h,t}\big) + \frac{a^2}{2}\big(\sigma^2_{yt+h,t} + \boldsymbol{\omega}'_{t+h,t}\boldsymbol{\Sigma}_{\hat{\mathbf{y}}\hat{\mathbf{y}}t+h,t}\boldsymbol{\omega}_{t+h,t} - 2\boldsymbol{\omega}'_{t+h,t}\boldsymbol{\sigma}_{y\hat{\mathbf{y}}t+h,t}\big)\Big) = 1, \tag{26}$$

$$\Big(-a\boldsymbol{\mu}_{\hat{\mathbf{y}}t+h,t} + \frac{a^2}{2}(2\boldsymbol{\Sigma}_{\hat{\mathbf{y}}\hat{\mathbf{y}}t+h,t}\boldsymbol{\omega}_{t+h,t} - 2\boldsymbol{\sigma}_{y\hat{\mathbf{y}}t+h,t})\Big) + a\boldsymbol{\mu}_{\hat{\mathbf{y}}t+h,t} = 0.$$

It follows that $\boldsymbol{\omega}^*_{t+h,t} = \boldsymbol{\Sigma}^{-1}_{\hat{\mathbf{y}}\hat{\mathbf{y}}t+h,t}\boldsymbol{\sigma}_{y\hat{\mathbf{y}}t+h,t}$ which when inserted in the first equation gives the optimal solution

$$\begin{aligned}\omega^*_{0t+h,t} &= \mu_{yt+h,t} - \boldsymbol{\omega}^{*\prime}_{t+h,t}\boldsymbol{\mu}_{\hat{\mathbf{y}}t+h,t} + \frac{a}{2}\big(\sigma^2_{yt+h,t} - \boldsymbol{\omega}^{*\prime}_{t+h,t}\boldsymbol{\sigma}_{y\hat{\mathbf{y}}t+h,t}\big),\\ \boldsymbol{\omega}^*_{t+h,t} &= \boldsymbol{\Sigma}^{-1}_{\hat{\mathbf{y}}\hat{\mathbf{y}}t+h,t}\boldsymbol{\sigma}_{y\hat{\mathbf{y}}t+h,t}.\end{aligned} \tag{27}$$

Notice that the optimal combination weights, $\boldsymbol{\omega}^*_{t+h,t}$, are unchanged from the case with MSE loss, (9), while the intercept accounts for the shape of the loss function and depends on the parameter a. In fact, the optimal combination will have a bias, $\frac{a}{2}(\sigma^2_{yt+h,t} - \boldsymbol{\omega}^{*\prime}_{t+h,t}\boldsymbol{\sigma}_{y\hat{\mathbf{y}}t+h,t})$, that reflects the dispersion of the forecast error evaluated at the optimal combination weights.

Next, suppose that we allow for a non-Gaussian forecast error distribution by assuming that the joint distribution of $(y_{t+h}\ \hat{\mathbf{y}}'_{t+h,t})'$ is a mixture of two Gaussian distributions driven by a state variable, S_{t+h}, which can take two values, i.e. $s_{t+h} = 1$ or $s_{t+h} = 2$ so that

$$\begin{pmatrix} y_{t+h} \\ \hat{\mathbf{y}}_{t+h,t} \end{pmatrix} \sim N\left(\begin{pmatrix} \mu_{ys_{t+h}} \\ \boldsymbol{\mu}_{\hat{\mathbf{y}}s_{t+h}} \end{pmatrix}, \begin{pmatrix} \sigma^2_{ys_{t+h}} & \boldsymbol{\sigma}'_{y\hat{\mathbf{y}}s_{t+h}} \\ \boldsymbol{\sigma}_{y\hat{\mathbf{y}}s_{t+h}} & \boldsymbol{\Sigma}_{\hat{\mathbf{y}}\hat{\mathbf{y}}s_{t+h}} \end{pmatrix}\right). \tag{28}$$

Furthermore, suppose that $P(S_{t+h} = 1) = p$, while $P(S_{t+h} = 2) = 1 - p$. The two regimes could correspond to recession and expansion states for the economy [Hamilton (1989)] or bull and bear states for financial markets, cf. Guidolin and Timmermann (2005).

Under this model,

$$\begin{aligned} e_{t+h,t} &= y_{t+h} - \omega_{0t+h,t} - \boldsymbol{\omega}'_{t+h,t}\hat{\mathbf{y}}_{t+h,t} \\ &\sim N\big(\mu_{ys_{t+h}} - \omega_{0t+h,t} - \boldsymbol{\omega}'_{t+h,t}\boldsymbol{\mu}_{\hat{\mathbf{y}}s_{t+h}}, \sigma^2_{ys_{t+h}} + \boldsymbol{\omega}'_{t+h,t}\boldsymbol{\Sigma}_{\hat{\mathbf{y}}s_{t+h}}\boldsymbol{\omega}_{t+h,t} \\ &\qquad - 2\boldsymbol{\omega}'_{t+h,t}\boldsymbol{\sigma}_{y\hat{\mathbf{y}}s_{t+h}}\big). \end{aligned}$$

Dropping time and horizon subscripts, the expected loss under this distribution, $\mathrm{E}[L(e_{t+h,t})|\hat{\mathbf{y}}_{t+h,t}]$, is proportional to

$$p\left\{\exp\left(a\left(\mu_{y1} - \omega_0 - \boldsymbol{\omega}'\boldsymbol{\mu}_{\hat{\mathbf{y}}1}\right) + \frac{a^2}{2}\left(\sigma_{y1}^2 + \boldsymbol{\omega}'\boldsymbol{\Sigma}_{\hat{\mathbf{y}}\hat{\mathbf{y}}1}\boldsymbol{\omega} - 2\boldsymbol{\omega}'\boldsymbol{\sigma}_{y\hat{\mathbf{y}}1}\right)\right) - a(\mu_{y1} - \omega_0 - \boldsymbol{\omega}'\boldsymbol{\mu}_{\hat{\mathbf{y}}1})\right\}$$
$$+ (1-p)\left\{\exp\left(a\left(\mu_{y2} - \omega_0 - \boldsymbol{\omega}'\boldsymbol{\mu}_{\hat{\mathbf{y}}2}\right) + \frac{a^2}{2}\left(\sigma_{y2}^2 + \boldsymbol{\omega}'\boldsymbol{\Sigma}_{\hat{\mathbf{y}}\hat{\mathbf{y}}2}\boldsymbol{\omega} - 2\boldsymbol{\omega}'\boldsymbol{\sigma}_{y\hat{\mathbf{y}}2}\right)\right) - a\left(\mu_{y2} - \omega_0 - \boldsymbol{\omega}'\boldsymbol{\mu}_{\hat{\mathbf{y}}2}\right)\right\}.$$

Taking derivatives, we get the following first order conditions for ω_0 and $\boldsymbol{\omega}$:

$$p\left(\exp(\xi_1) - 1\right) + (1-p)\left(\exp(\xi_2) - 1\right) = 0,$$

$$p\left(\exp(\xi_1)\left(-\boldsymbol{\mu}_{\hat{\mathbf{y}}1} + a(\boldsymbol{\Sigma}_{\hat{\mathbf{y}}\hat{\mathbf{y}}1}\boldsymbol{\omega} - \boldsymbol{\sigma}_{y\hat{\mathbf{y}}1})\right) + \boldsymbol{\mu}_{\hat{\mathbf{y}}1}\right)$$
$$+ (1-p)\left(\exp(\xi_2)\left(-\boldsymbol{\mu}_{\hat{\mathbf{y}}2} + a(\boldsymbol{\Sigma}_{\hat{\mathbf{y}}\hat{\mathbf{y}}2}\boldsymbol{\omega} - \boldsymbol{\sigma}_{y\hat{\mathbf{y}}2})\right) + \boldsymbol{\mu}_{\hat{\mathbf{y}}2}\right) = 0,$$

where

$$\xi_{s_{t+1}} = a\left(\mu_{ys_{t+1}} - \omega_0 - \boldsymbol{\omega}'\boldsymbol{\mu}_{\hat{\mathbf{y}}s_{t+1}}\right) + \frac{a^2}{2}\left(\sigma_{ys_{t+1}}^2 + \boldsymbol{\omega}'\boldsymbol{\Sigma}_{\hat{\mathbf{y}}\hat{\mathbf{y}}s_{t+1}}\boldsymbol{\omega} - 2\boldsymbol{\omega}'\boldsymbol{\sigma}_{y\hat{\mathbf{y}}s_{t+1}}\right).$$

In general this gives a set of $N+1$ highly nonlinear equations in ω_0 and $\boldsymbol{\omega}$. The exception is when $\boldsymbol{\mu}_{\hat{\mathbf{y}}1} = \boldsymbol{\mu}_{\hat{\mathbf{y}}2}$, in which case (using the first order condition for ω_0) the first order condition for $\boldsymbol{\omega}$ simplifies to

$$p\exp(\xi_1)(\boldsymbol{\Sigma}_{\hat{\mathbf{y}}\hat{\mathbf{y}}1}\boldsymbol{\omega} - \boldsymbol{\sigma}_{y\hat{\mathbf{y}}1}) + (1-p)\exp(\xi_2)(\boldsymbol{\Sigma}_{\hat{\mathbf{y}}\hat{\mathbf{y}}2}\boldsymbol{\omega} - \boldsymbol{\sigma}_{y\hat{\mathbf{y}}2}) = \mathbf{0}.$$

When $\boldsymbol{\Sigma}_{\hat{\mathbf{y}}\hat{\mathbf{y}}2} = \varphi\boldsymbol{\Sigma}_{\hat{\mathbf{y}}\hat{\mathbf{y}}1}$ and $\boldsymbol{\sigma}_{y\hat{\mathbf{y}}2} = \varphi\boldsymbol{\sigma}_{y\hat{\mathbf{y}}1}$, for any $\varphi > 0$, the solution to this equation again corresponds to the optimal weights for the MSE loss function, (9):

$$\boldsymbol{\omega}^* = \boldsymbol{\Sigma}_{\hat{\mathbf{y}}\hat{\mathbf{y}}1}^{-1}\sigma_{y\hat{\mathbf{y}}1}. \tag{29}$$

This restriction represents a very special case and ensures that the joint distribution of $(y_{t+h}, \hat{\mathbf{y}}_{t+h,t})$ is elliptically symmetric – a class of distributions that encompasses the multivariate Gaussian. This is a special case of the more general result by Elliott and Timmermann (2004): If the joint distribution of $(y_{t+h}\,\hat{\mathbf{y}}'_{t+h,t})'$ is elliptically symmetric and the expected loss can be written as a function of the mean and variance of the forecast error, μ_e and σ_e^2, i.e., $\mathrm{E}[L(e_t)] = g(\mu_e, \sigma_e^2)$, then the optimal forecast combination weights, $\boldsymbol{\omega}^*$, take the form (29) and hence do not depend on the shape of the loss function (other than for certain technical conditions). Conversely, the constant (ω_0) reflects this shape. Thus, under fairly general conditions on the loss functions, a forecast enters into the optimal combination with a non-zero weight if and only if its optimal weight under MSE loss is non-zero. Conversely, if elliptical symmetry fails to hold, then it is quite possible that a forecast may have a non-zero weight under loss functions other than MSE loss but not under MSE loss and vice versa. The latter case is likely to be most relevant empirically since studies using regime switching models often find that, although the mean parameters may be constrained to be identical across regimes, the variance-covariance parameters tend to be very different across regimes, cf., e.g., Guidolin and Timmermann (2005).

This example can be used to demonstrate that a forecast that adds value (in the sense that it is uncorrelated with the outcome variable) only a small part of the time when other forecasts break down, will be included in the optimal combination. We set all mean parameters equal to one, $\mu_{y1} = \mu_{y2} = 1$, $\boldsymbol{\mu}_{\hat{\mathbf{y}}1} = \boldsymbol{\mu}_{\hat{\mathbf{y}}2} = \boldsymbol{\iota}$, so bias can be ignored, while the variance-covariance parameters are chosen as follows:

$$\sigma_{y1} = 3; \quad \sigma_{y2} = 1,$$
$$\boldsymbol{\Sigma}_{\hat{\mathbf{y}}\hat{\mathbf{y}}1} = 0.8 \times \sigma_{y1}^2 \times \mathbf{I}; \quad \boldsymbol{\Sigma}_{\hat{\mathbf{y}}\hat{\mathbf{y}}2} = 0.5 \times \sigma_{y2}^2 \times \mathbf{I},$$
$$\boldsymbol{\sigma}_{y\hat{\mathbf{y}}1} = \sigma_{y1} \times \sqrt{\operatorname{diag}(\boldsymbol{\Sigma}_{\hat{\mathbf{y}}\hat{\mathbf{y}}1})} \odot \begin{pmatrix} 0.9 \\ 0.2 \end{pmatrix},$$
$$\boldsymbol{\sigma}_{y\hat{\mathbf{y}}2} = \sigma_{y2} \times \sqrt{\operatorname{diag}(\boldsymbol{\Sigma}_{\hat{\mathbf{y}}\hat{\mathbf{y}}2})} \odot \begin{pmatrix} 0.0 \\ 0.8 \end{pmatrix},$$

where $\odot$ is the Hadamard or element by element multiplication operator.

In Table 1 we show the optimal weight on the two forecasts as a function of p for two different values of a, namely $a = 1$, corresponding to strongly asymmetric loss, and $a = 0.1$, representing less asymmetric loss. When $p = 0.05$ and $a = 1$, so there is only a five percent chance that the process is in state 1, the optimal weight on model 1 is 35%. This is lowered to only 8% when the asymmetry parameter is reduced to $a = 0.1$. Hence the low probability event has a greater effect on the optimal combination weights the higher the degree of asymmetry in the loss function and the higher the variability of such events.

This example can also be used to demonstrate why forecast combinations may work when the underlying predictors are generated under different loss functions. Suppose that two forecasters have linex loss with parameters $a_1 > 0$ and $a_2 < 0$ and suppose

Table 1
Optimal combination weights under asymmetric loss.

$a = 1$			$a = 0.1$		
p	ω_1^*	ω_2^*	p	ω_1^*	ω_2^*
0.05	0.346	0.324	0.05	0.081	0.365
0.10	0.416	0.314	0.10	0.156	0.353
0.25	0.525	0.297	0.25	0.354	0.323
0.50	0.636	0.280	0.50	0.620	0.283
0.75	0.744	0.264	0.75	0.831	0.250
0.90	0.842	0.249	0.90	0.940	0.234

that both have access to the same information set and use the same model to forecast the mean and variance of Y, $\hat{\mu}_{yt+h,t}$, $\hat{\sigma}^2_{yt+h,1}$. Their forecasts are then computed as [assuming normality, cf. Christoffersen and Diebold (1997)]

$$\hat{y}_{t+h,t,1} = \hat{\mu}_{yt+h,t} + \frac{a_1}{2}\hat{\sigma}^2_{yt+h,t},$$
$$\hat{y}_{t+h,t,2} = \hat{\mu}_{yt+h,t} + \frac{a_2}{2}\hat{\sigma}^2_{yt+h,t}.$$

Each forecast includes an optimal bias whose magnitude is time-varying. For a forecast user with symmetric loss, neither of these forecasts is particularly useful as each is biased. Furthermore, the bias cannot simply be taken out by including a constant in the forecast combination regression since the bias is time-varying. However, in this simple case, there exists an exact linear combination of the two forecasts that is unbiased:

$$\hat{y}^c_{t+1,t} = \omega\hat{y}_{t+h,t,1} + (1-\omega)\hat{y}_{t+h,t,2}, \qquad \omega = \frac{-a_2}{a_1 - a_2}.$$

Of course this is a special case, but it nevertheless does show how biases in individual forecasts can either be eliminated or reduced in a forecast combination.

2.6. *Combining as a hedge against non-stationarities*

Hendry and Clements (2002) argue that forecast combinations may work well empirically because they provide insurance against what they refer to as extraneous (deterministic) structural breaks. They consider a wide array of simulation designs for the break and find that combinations work well under a shift in the intercept of a single variable in the data generating process. In addition when two or more positively correlated predictor variables are subject to shifts in opposite directions, forecast combinations can be expected to lead to even larger reductions in the MSE. Their analysis considers the case where a break occurs after the estimation period and does not affect the parameter estimates of the individual forecasting models. They establish conditions on the size of the post-sample break ensuring that an equal-weighted combination out-performs the individual forecasts.[6]

In support of the interpretation that structural breaks or model instability may explain the good average performance of forecast combination methods, Stock and Watson (2004) report that the performance of combined forecasts tends to be far more stable than that of the individual constituent forecasts entering in the combinations. Interestingly, however, many of the combination methods that attempt to build in time-variations in the combination weights (either in the form of discounting of past performance or time-varying parameters) have generally not proved to be successful, although there have been exceptions.

[6] See also Winkler (1989) who argues (p. 606) that "... in many situations there is no such thing as a 'true' model for forecasting purposes. The world around us is continually changing, with new uncertainties replacing old ones."

It is easy to construct examples of specific forms of non-stationarities in the underlying data generating process for which simple combinations work better than the forecast from the best single model. Aiolfi and Timmermann (2006) study the following simple model for changes or shifts in the data generating process:

$$\begin{aligned} y_t &= S_t f_{1t} + (1 - S_t) f_{2t} + \varepsilon_{yt}, \\ \hat{y}_{1t} &= f_{1t} + \varepsilon_{1t}, \\ \hat{y}_{2t} &= f_{2t} + \varepsilon_{2t}. \end{aligned} \tag{30}$$

All variables are assumed to be Gaussian with factors $f_{1t} \sim N(\mu_1, \sigma_{f_1}^2)$, $f_{2t} \sim N(\mu_2, \sigma_{f_2}^2)$ and innovations $\varepsilon_{yt} \sim N(0, \sigma_{\varepsilon_y}^2)$, $\varepsilon_{1t} \sim N(0, \sigma_{\varepsilon_1}^2)$, $\varepsilon_{2t} \sim N(0, \sigma_{\varepsilon_2}^2)$. Innovations are mutually uncorrelated and uncorrelated with the factors, while $\mathrm{Cov}(f_{1t}, f_{2t}) = \sigma_{f_1 f_2}$. In addition, the state transition probabilities are constant: $P(S_t = 1) = p$, $P(S_t = 0) = 1 - p$. Let β_1 be the population projection coefficient of y_t on $\hat{y}_{1t}$ while β_2 is the population projection coefficient of y_t on $\hat{y}_{2t}$, so that

$$\begin{aligned} \beta_1 &= \frac{p\sigma_{f_1}^2 + (1-p)\sigma_{f_1 f_2}}{\sigma_{f_1}^2 + \sigma_{\varepsilon_1}^2}, \\ \beta_2 &= \frac{(1-p)\sigma_{f_2}^2 + p\sigma_{f_1 f_2}^2}{\sigma_{f_2}^2 + \sigma_{\varepsilon_2}^2}. \end{aligned}$$

The first and second moments of the forecast errors $e_{it} = y_t - \hat{y}_{it}$, can then be characterized as follows:

- Conditional on $S_t = 1$:

$$\begin{pmatrix} e_{1t} \\ e_{2t} \end{pmatrix} \sim N\left(\begin{pmatrix} (1-\beta_1)\mu_1 \\ \mu_1 - \beta_2\mu_2 \end{pmatrix}, \right.$$
$$\left. \begin{pmatrix} (1-\beta_1)^2\sigma_{f_1}^2 + \beta_1^2\sigma_{\varepsilon_1}^2 + \sigma_{\varepsilon_y}^2 & (1-\beta_1)\sigma_{f_1}^2 + \sigma_{\varepsilon_y}^2 \\ (1-\beta_1)\sigma_{f_1}^2 + \sigma_{\varepsilon_y}^2 & \sigma_{f_1}^2 + \beta_2^2\sigma_{f_2}^2 + \beta_2^2\sigma_{\varepsilon_2}^2 + \sigma_{\varepsilon_y}^2 \end{pmatrix} \right).$$

- Conditional on $S_t = 0$:

$$\begin{pmatrix} e_{1t} \\ e_{2t} \end{pmatrix} \sim N\left(\begin{pmatrix} \mu_2 - \beta_1\mu_1 \\ (1-\beta_2)\mu_2 \end{pmatrix}, \right.$$
$$\left. \begin{pmatrix} \beta_1^2\sigma_{f_1}^2 + \sigma_{f_2}^2 + \beta_1^2\sigma_{\varepsilon_1}^2 + \sigma_{\varepsilon_y}^2 & (1-\beta_2)\sigma_{f_2}^2 + \sigma_{\varepsilon_y}^2 \\ (1-\beta_2)\sigma_{f_2}^2 + \sigma_{\varepsilon_y}^2 & (1-\beta_2)^2\sigma_{f_2}^2 + \beta_2^2\sigma_{\varepsilon_2}^2 + \sigma_{\varepsilon_y}^2 \end{pmatrix} \right).$$

Under the joint model for $(y_t, \hat{y}_{1t}, \hat{y}_{2t})$ in (30), Aiolfi and Timmermann (2006) show that the population MSE of the equal-weighted combined forecast will be lower than the population MSE of the best model provided that the following condition holds:

$$\frac{1}{3}\left(\frac{p}{1-p}\right)^2 \frac{1+\psi_2}{1+\psi_1} < \frac{\sigma_{f_2}^2}{\sigma_{f_1}^2} < 3\left(\frac{p}{1-p}\right)^2 \frac{1+\psi_2}{1+\psi_1}. \tag{31}$$

Here $\psi_1 = \sigma^2_{\varepsilon_1}/\sigma^2_{f_1}$, $\psi_2 = \sigma^2_{\varepsilon_2}/\sigma^2_{f_2}$ are the noise-to-signal ratios for forecasts one and two, respectively. Hence if $p = 1-p = 1/2$ and $\psi_1 = \psi_2$, the condition in (31) reduces to

$$\frac{1}{3} < \frac{\sigma^2_{f_2}}{\sigma^2_{f_1}} < 3,$$

suggesting that equal-weighted combinations will provide a hedge against 'breaks' for a wide range of values of the relative factor variance. How good an approximation this model provides for actual data can be debated, but regime shifts have been widely documented for first and second moments of, *inter alia*, output growth, stock and bond returns, interest rates and exchange rates.

Conversely, when combination weights have to be estimated, instability in the data generating process may cause under-performance relative to that of the best individual forecasting model. Hence we can construct examples where combination is the dominant strategy in the absence of breaks or other forms of non-stationarities, but becomes inferior in the presence of breaks. This is likely to happen if the conditional distribution of the target variable given a particular forecast is stationary, whereas the correlations between the forecasts changes. In this case the combination weights will change but the individual models' performance remain the same.

3. Estimation

Forecast combinations, while appealing in theory, are at a disadvantage over a single forecast model because they introduce parameter estimation error in cases where the combination weights need to be estimated. This is an important point – so much so, that seemingly suboptimal combination schemes such as equal-weighting have widely been found to dominate combination methods that would be optimal in the absence of parameter estimation errors. Finite-sample errors in the estimates of the combination weights can lead to poor performance of combination schemes that dominate in large samples.[7]

3.1. To combine or not to combine

The first question to answer in the presence of multiple forecasts of the same variable is whether or not to combine the forecasts or rather simply attempt to identify the single

[7] Yang (2004) demonstrates theoretically that linear forecast combinations can lead to far worse performance than those from the best single forecasting model due to large variability in estimates of the combination weights and proposes a range of recursive methods for updating the combination weights that ensure that combinations achieve a performance similar to that of the best individual forecasting method up to a constant penalty term and a proportionality factor.

best forecasting model. Here it is important to distinguish between the situation where the information sets underlying the individual forecasts is observed from that where they are unobserved to the forecast user. When the information sets are unobserved it is often justified to combine forecasts provided that the private (non-overlapping) parts of the information sets are sufficiently important. Whether this is satisfied can be difficult to assess, but diagnostics such as the correlation between forecasts or forecast errors can be considered.

When forecast users do have access to the full information set used to construct the individual forecasts, Chong and Hendry (1986) and Diebold (1989) argue that combinations may be less justified. Successful combination indicates misspecification of the individual models and so a better individual model should be sought. Finding a 'best' model may of course be rather difficult if the space of models included in the search is high dimensional and the time-series short. As Clemen (1989) nicely puts it: "Using a combination of forecasts amounts to an admission that the forecaster is unable to build a properly specified model. Trying ever more elaborate combining models seems to add insult to injury as the more complicated combinations do not generally perform that well."

Simple tests of whether one forecast dominates another forecast are neither sufficient nor necessary for settling the question of whether or not to combine. This follows since we can construct examples where (in population) forecast $\hat{y}_1$ dominates forecast $\hat{y}_2$ (in the sense that it leads to lower expected loss), yet it remains optimal to combine the two forecasts.[8] Similarly, we can construct examples where forecast $\hat{y}_1$ and $\hat{y}_2$ generate identical expected loss, yet it is not optimal to combine them – most obviously if they are perfectly correlated, but also due to estimation errors in the combination weights.

What is called for more generally is a test of whether one forecast – or a set of forecasts – encompasses all information contained in another forecast (or sets of forecasts). In the context of MSE loss functions, forecast encompassing tests have been developed by Chong and Hendry (1986). Point forecasts are sufficient statistics under MSE loss and a test of pair-wise encompassing can be based on the regression

$$y_{t+h} = \beta_0 + \beta_1 \hat{y}_{t+h,t,1} + \beta_2 \hat{y}_{t+h,t,2} + e_{t+h,t}, \quad t = 1, 2, \ldots, T - h. \tag{32}$$

Forecast 1 encompasses forecast 2 when the parameter restriction $(\beta_0\ \beta_1\ \beta_2) = (0\ 1\ 0)$ holds, while conversely if forecast 2 encompasses forecast 1 we have $(\beta_0\ \beta_1\ \beta_2) = (0\ 0\ 1)$. All other outcomes mean that there is some information in both forecasts which can then be usefully exploited. Notice that this is an argument that only holds in population. It is still possible in small samples that ignoring one forecast can lead to better out-of-sample forecasts even though, asymptotically, the coefficient on the omitted forecast in (32) differs from zero.

[8] Most obviously, under MSE loss, when $\sigma(y - \hat{y}_1) > \sigma(y - \hat{y}_2)$, and $cor(y - \hat{y}_1, y - \hat{y}_2) \neq \sigma(y - \hat{y}_2)/\sigma(y - \hat{y}_1)$, it will generally be optimal to combine the two forecasts, cf. Section 2.

More generally, a test that the forecast of some model, e.g., model 1, encompasses all other models can be based on a test of $\beta_2 = \cdots = \beta_N = 0$ in the regression

$$y_{t+h} - \hat{y}_{t+h,t,1} = \beta_0 + \sum_{i=2}^{N} \beta_i \hat{y}_{t+h,t,i} + e_{t+h,t}.$$

Inference is complicated by whether forecasting models are nested or non-nested, cf. West (2006), Chapter 3 in this Handbook, and the references therein.

In situations where the data is not very informative and it is not possible to identify a single dominant model, it makes sense to combine forecasts. Makridakis and Winkler (1983) explain this well (p. 990): "When a single method is used, the risk of not choosing the best method can be very serious. The risk diminishes rapidly when more methods are considered and their forecasts are averaged. In other words, the choice of the best method or methods becomes less important when averaging." They demonstrate this point by showing that the forecasting performance of a combination strategy improves as a function of the number of models involved in the combination, albeit at a decreasing rate.

Swanson and Zeng (2001) propose to use model selection criteria such as the SIC to choose which subset of forecasts to combine. This approach does not require formal hypothesis testing so that size distortions due to the use of sequential pre-tests, can be avoided. Of course, consistency of the selection approach must be established in the context of the particular sampling experiment appropriate for a given forecasting situation. In empirical work reported by these authors the combination chosen by SIC appears to provide the best overall performance and rarely gets dominated by other methods in out-of-sample forecasting experiments.

Once it has been established whether to combine or not, there are various ways in which the combination weights, $\hat{\boldsymbol{\omega}}_{t+h,t}$, can be estimated. We will discuss some of these methods in what follows. A theme that is common across estimators is that estimation errors in forecast combinations are generally important especially in cases where the number of forecasts, N, is large relative to the length of the time-series, T.

3.2. Least squares estimators of the weights

It is common to assume a linear-in-weights model and estimate combination weights by ordinary least squares, regressing realizations of the target variable, y_τ on the N-vector of forecasts, $\hat{\mathbf{y}}_\tau$ using data over the period $\tau = h, \ldots, t$:

$$\hat{\boldsymbol{\omega}}_{t+h,t} = \left(\sum_{\tau=1}^{t-h} \hat{\mathbf{y}}_{\tau+h,\tau} \hat{\mathbf{y}}'_{\tau+h,\tau} \right)^{-1} \sum_{\tau=1}^{t-h} \hat{\mathbf{y}}_{\tau+h,\tau} y_{\tau+h}. \tag{33}$$

Different versions of this basic least squares projection have been proposed. Granger and Ramanathan (1984) consider three regressions

$$\begin{aligned}
&\text{(i)} \quad y_{t+h} = \omega_{0h} + \boldsymbol{\omega}_h' \hat{\mathbf{y}}_{t+h,t} + \varepsilon_{t+h}, \\
&\text{(ii)} \quad y_{t+h} = \boldsymbol{\omega}_h' \hat{\mathbf{y}}_{t+h,t} + \varepsilon_{t+h}, \\
&\text{(iii)} \quad y_{t+h} = \boldsymbol{\omega}_h' \hat{\mathbf{y}}_{t+h,t} + \varepsilon_{t+h}, \quad \text{s.t.} \quad \boldsymbol{\omega}_h' \boldsymbol{\iota} = 1.
\end{aligned} \tag{34}$$

The first and second of these regressions can be estimated by standard least squares, the only difference being that the second equation omits an intercept term. The third regression omits an intercept and can be estimated through constrained least squares. The first, and most general, regression does not require that the individual forecasts are unbiased since any bias can be adjusted through the intercept term, ω_{0h}. In contrast, the third regression is motivated by an assumption of unbiasedness of the individual forecasts. Imposing that the weights sum to one then guarantees that the combined forecast is also unbiased. This specification may not be efficient, however, as the latter constraint can lead to efficiency losses as $\mathrm{E}[\hat{\mathbf{y}}_{t+h,t}\varepsilon_{t+h}] \neq \mathbf{0}$. One could further impose convexity constraints $0 \leqslant \omega_{h,i} \leqslant 1$, $i = 1, \ldots, N$, to rule out that the combined forecast lies outside the range of the individual forecasts.

Another reason for imposing the constraint $\boldsymbol{\omega}_h' \boldsymbol{\iota} = 1$ has been discussed by Diebold (1988). He proposes the following decomposition of the forecast error from the combination regression:

$$\begin{aligned}
e^c_{t+h,t} &= y_{t+h} - \omega_{0h} - \boldsymbol{\omega}_h' \hat{\mathbf{y}}_{t+h,t} \\
&= -\omega_{0h} + \left(1 - \boldsymbol{\omega}_h' \boldsymbol{\iota}\right) y_{t+h} + \boldsymbol{\omega}_h' \left(y_{t+h} \boldsymbol{\iota} - \hat{\mathbf{y}}_{t+h,t}\right) \\
&= -\omega_{0h} + \left(1 - \boldsymbol{\omega}_h' \boldsymbol{\iota}\right) y_{t+h} + \boldsymbol{\omega}_h' \mathbf{e}_{t+h,t},
\end{aligned} \tag{35}$$

where $\mathbf{e}_{t+h,t}$ is the $N \times 1$ vector of h-period forecast errors from the individual models. Oftentimes the target variable, y_{t+h}, is quite persistent whereas the forecast errors from the individual models are not serially correlated even when $h = 1$. It follows that unless it is imposed that $1 - \boldsymbol{\omega}_h' \boldsymbol{\iota} = 0$, then the forecast error from the combination regression typically will be serially correlated and hence be predictable itself.

3.3. Relative performance weights

Estimation errors in the combination weights tend to be particularly large due to difficulties in precisely estimating the covariance matrix, $\boldsymbol{\Sigma}_e$. One answer to this problem is to simply ignore correlations across forecast errors. Combination weights that reflect the performance of each individual model relative to the performance of the average model, but ignore correlations across forecasts have been proposed by Bates and Granger (1969) and Newbold and Granger (1974). Both papers argue that correlations can be poorly estimated and should be ignored in situations with many forecasts and short time-series. This effectively amounts to treating $\boldsymbol{\Sigma}_e$ as a diagonal matrix, cf. Winkler and Makridakis (1983).

Stock and Watson (2001) propose a broader set of combination weights that also ignore correlations between forecast errors but base the combination weights on the models' relative MSE performance raised to various powers. Let $\mathrm{MSE}_{t+h,t,i} =$

$(1/v)\sum_{\tau=t-v}^{t} e^2_{\tau,\tau-h,i}$ be the ith forecasting model's MSE at time t, computed over a window of the previous v periods. Then

$$\hat{y}^c_{t+h,t} = \sum_{i=1}^{N} \hat{\omega}_{t+h,t,i}\hat{y}_{t+h,t,i}, \quad \hat{\omega}_{t+h,t,i} = \frac{(1/\mathrm{MSE}^{\kappa}_{t+h,t,i})}{\sum_{j=1}^{N}(1/\mathrm{MSE}^{\kappa}_{t+h,t,j})}. \tag{36}$$

Setting $\kappa = 0$ assigns equal weights to all forecasts, while forecasts are weighted by the inverse of their MSE when $\kappa = 1$. The latter strategy has been found to work well in practice as it does not require estimating the off-diagonal parameters of the covariance matrix of the forecast errors. Such weights therefore disregard any correlations between forecast errors and so are only optimal in large samples provided that the forecast errors are truly uncorrelated.

3.4. Moment estimators

Outside the quadratic loss framework one can base estimation of the combination weights directly on the loss function, cf. Elliott and Timmermann (2004). Let the realized loss in period $t + h$ be

$$L(e_{t+h,t}; \boldsymbol{\omega}) = L\big(\boldsymbol{\omega}|y_{t+h}, \hat{\mathbf{y}}_{t+h,t}, \boldsymbol{\psi}_L\big),$$

where $\boldsymbol{\psi}_L$ are the (given) parameters of the loss function. Then $\tilde{\boldsymbol{\omega}}_h = (\omega_{0h}\ \boldsymbol{\omega}'_h)'$ can be obtained as an M-estimator based on the sample analog of $\mathrm{E}[L(e_{t+h,t})]$ using a sample of $T - h$ observations $\{y_\tau, \hat{\mathbf{y}}_{\tau,\tau-h}\}_{\tau=h+1}^{T}$:

$$\bar{L}(\boldsymbol{\omega}) = (T-h)^{-1} \sum_{\tau=h+1}^{T} L\big(e_{\tau,\tau-h}\big(\tilde{\boldsymbol{\omega}}_h\big); \boldsymbol{\theta}_L\big).$$

Taking derivatives, one can use the generalized method of moments (GMM) to estimate $\boldsymbol{\omega}_{T+h,T}$ from the quadratic form

$$\min_{\tilde{\boldsymbol{\omega}}_h} \left(\sum_{\tau=h+1}^{T} \mathbf{L}'\big(e_{\tau,\tau-h}\big(\tilde{\boldsymbol{\omega}}_h\big); \boldsymbol{\psi}_L\big)\right)' \boldsymbol{\Lambda}^{-1} \left(\sum_{\tau=h+1}^{T} \mathbf{L}'\big(e_{\tau,\tau-h}\big(\tilde{\boldsymbol{\omega}}_h\big); \boldsymbol{\psi}_L\big)\right), \tag{37}$$

where $\boldsymbol{\Lambda}$ is a (positive definite) weighting matrix and $\mathbf{L}'$ is a vector of derivatives of the moment conditions with respect to $\tilde{\boldsymbol{\omega}}_h$. Consistency and asymptotic normality of the estimated weights is easily established under standard regularity conditions.

3.5. Nonparametric combination schemes

The estimators considered so far require stationarity at least for the moments involved in the estimation. To be empirically successful, they also require a reasonably large data sample (relative to the number of models, N) as they otherwise tend not to be robust to outliers, cf. Gupta and Wilton (1987, p. 358): "… combination weights derived using minimum variance or regression are not robust given short data samples, instability or nonstationarity. This leads to poor performance in the prediction sample." In many applications the number of forecasts, N, is large relatively to the length of the time-series, T. In this case, it is not feasible to estimate the combination weights by OLS. Simple combination schemes such as an equal-weighted average of forecasts $y^{\text{ew}}_{t+h,t} = \boldsymbol{\iota}'\hat{\mathbf{y}}_{t+h,t}/N$ or weights based on the inverse MSE-values offer are an attractive option in this situation.

Simple, rank-based weighting schemes can also be constructed and have been used with some success in mean-variance analysis in finance, cf. Wright and Satchell (2003). These take the form $\boldsymbol{\omega}_{t+h,t} = f(\mathcal{R}_{t,t-h,1}, \ldots, \mathcal{R}_{t,t-h,N})$, where $\mathcal{R}_{t,t-h,i}$ is the rank of the ith model based on its h-period performance up to time t. The most common scheme in this class is to simply use the median forecast as proposed by authors such as Armstrong (1989), Hendry and Clements (2002) and Stock and Watson (2001, 2004). Alternatively one can consider a triangular weighting scheme that lets the combination weights be inversely proportional to the models' rank, cf. Aiolfi and Timmermann (2006):

$$\hat{\omega}_{t+h,t,i} = \mathcal{R}^{-1}_{t,t-h,i} \Bigg/ \left(\sum_{i=1}^{N} \mathcal{R}^{-1}_{t,t-h,i} \right). \tag{38}$$

Again this combination ignores correlations across forecast errors. However, since ranks are likely to be less sensitive to outliers, this weighting scheme can be expected to be more robust than the weights in (33) or (36).

Another example in this class is spread combinations. These have been proposed by Aiolfi and Timmermann (2006) and consider weights of the form

$$\hat{\omega}_{t+h,t,i} = \begin{cases} \dfrac{1+\bar{\omega}}{\alpha N} & \text{if } \mathcal{R}_{t,t-h,i} \leqslant \alpha N, \\ 0 & \text{if } \alpha N < \mathcal{R}_{t,t-h,i} < (1-\alpha)N, \\ \dfrac{-\bar{\omega}}{\alpha N} & \text{if } \mathcal{R}_{t,t-h,i} \leqslant (1-\alpha)N, \end{cases} \tag{39}$$

where α is the proportion of top models that – based on performance up to time t – gets a weight of $(1+\bar{\omega})/\alpha N$. Similarly, a proportion α of models gets a weight of $-\bar{\omega}/\alpha N$. The larger the value of α, the wider the set of top and bottom models that are used in the combination. Similarly, the larger is $\bar{\omega}$, the bigger the difference in weights on top and bottom models. The intuition for such spread combinations can be seen from (12) when $N = 2$ so $\alpha = 1/2$. Solving for ρ_{12} we see that $\omega^* = 1 + \bar{\omega}$ provided that

$$\rho_{12} = \frac{1}{2\bar{\omega}+1}\left(\frac{\sigma_2}{\sigma_1}\bar{\omega} + \frac{\sigma_1}{\sigma_2}(1+\bar{\omega}) \right).$$

Hence if $\sigma_1 \approx \sigma_2$, spread combinations are close to optimal provided that $\rho_{12} \approx 1$. The second forecast provides a hedge for the performance of the first forecast in this situation. In general, spread portfolios are likely to work well when the forecasts are strongly collinear.

Gupta and Wilton (1987) propose an odds ratio combination approach based on a matrix of pair-wise odds ratios. Let π_{ij} be the probability that the ith forecasting model outperforms the jth model out-of-sample. The ratio $o_{ij} = \pi_{ij}/\pi_{ji}$ is then the odds that model i will outperform model j and $o_{ij} = 1/o_{ji}$. Filling out the $N \times N$ odds ratio matrix O with i, j element o_{ij} requires specifying $N(N-1)/2$ pairs of probabilities of outperformance, π_{ij}. An estimate of the combination weight ω is obtained from the solution to the system of equations $(\mathbf{O} - N\mathbf{I})\boldsymbol{\omega} = \mathbf{0}$. Since $\mathbf{O}$ has unit rank with a trace equal to N, $\boldsymbol{\omega}$ can be found as the normalized eigenvector associated with the largest (and only non-zero) eigenvalue of $\mathbf{O}$. This approach gives weights that are insensitive to small changes in the odds ratio and so does not require large amounts of data. Also, as it does not account for dependencies between the models it is likely to be less sensitive to changes in the covariance matrix than the regression approach. Conversely, it can be expected to perform worse if such correlations are important and can be estimated with sufficient precision.[9]

3.6. Pooling, clustering and trimming

Rather than combining the full set of forecasts, it is often advantageous to discard the models with the worst performance (trimming). Combining only the best models goes under the header 'use sensible models' in Armstrong (1989). This is particularly important when forecasting with nonlinear models whose predictions are often implausible and can lie outside the empirical range of the target variable. One can base whether or not to trim – and by how much to trim – on formal tests or on more loose decision rules.

To see why trimming can be important, suppose a fraction α of the forecasting models contain valuable information about the target variable while a fraction $1-\alpha$ is pure noise. It is easy to see in this extreme case that the optimal forecast combination puts zero weight on the pure noise forecasts. However, once combination weights have to be estimated, forecasts that only add marginal information should be dropped from the combination since the cost of their inclusion – increased parameter estimation error – is not matched by similar benefits.

[9] Bunn (1975) proposes a combination scheme with weights reflecting the probability that a model produces the lowest loss, i.e.

$$p_{t+h,t,i} = \Pr\big(L(e_{t+h,t,i}) < L(e_{t+h,t,j})\big) \quad \text{for all } j \neq i,$$

$$\hat{y}^c_{t+h,t} = \sum_{i=1}^{N} p_{t+h,t,i}\,\hat{y}_{t+h,t,i}.$$

Bunn discusses how $p_{t+h,t,i}$ can be updated based on a model's track historical record using the proportion of times up to the current period where a model outperformed its competitors.

The 'thick modeling' approach – thus named because it seeks to exploit information in a cross-section (thick set) of models – proposed by Granger and Jeon (2004) is an example of a trimming scheme that removes poorly performing models in a step that precedes calculation of combination weights. Granger and Jeon argue that "an advantage of thick modeling is that one no longer needs to worry about difficult decisions between close alternatives or between deciding the outcome of a test that is not decisive".

Grouping or clustering of forecasts can be motivated by the assumption of a common factor structure underlying the forecasting models. Consider the factor model

$$\begin{aligned} Y_{t+h} &= \mu_y + \boldsymbol{\beta}_y' \mathbf{f}_{t+h} + \varepsilon_{yt+h}, \\ \hat{\mathbf{y}}_{t+h,t} &= \boldsymbol{\mu}_{\hat{\mathbf{y}}} + \mathbf{B}\mathbf{f}_{t+h} + \boldsymbol{\varepsilon}_{t+h}, \end{aligned} \tag{40}$$

where $\mathbf{f}_{t+h}$ is an $n_f \times 1$ vector of factor realizations satisfying $\mathrm{E}[\mathbf{f}_{t+h}\varepsilon_{yt+h}] = \mathbf{0}$, $\mathrm{E}[\mathbf{f}_{t+h}\boldsymbol{\varepsilon}_{t+h}'] = \mathbf{0}$ and $\mathrm{E}[\mathbf{f}_{t+h}\mathbf{f}_{t+h}'] = \boldsymbol{\Sigma}_f$. $\boldsymbol{\beta}_y$ is an $n_f \times 1$ vector while $\mathbf{B}$ is an $N \times n_f$ matrix of factor loadings. For simplicity we assume that the factors have been orthogonalized. This will obviously hold if they are constructed as the principal components from a large data set and can otherwise be achieved through rotation. Furthermore, all innovations ε are serially uncorrelated with zero mean, $\mathrm{E}[\varepsilon_{yt+h}^2] = \sigma_{\varepsilon_y}^2$, $\mathrm{E}[\varepsilon_{yt+h}\boldsymbol{\varepsilon}_{t+h}] = \mathbf{0}$ and the noise in the individual forecasts is assumed to be idiosyncratic (model specific), i.e.,

$$\mathrm{E}[\varepsilon_{it+h}\varepsilon_{jt+h}] = \begin{cases} \sigma_{\varepsilon_i}^2 & \text{if } i = j, \\ 0 & \text{if } i \neq j. \end{cases}$$

We arrange these values on a diagonal matrix $\mathrm{E}[\boldsymbol{\varepsilon}_{t+h}\boldsymbol{\varepsilon}_{t+h}'] = \mathbf{D}_\varepsilon$. This gives the following moments:

$$\begin{pmatrix} y_{t+h} \\ \hat{\mathbf{y}}_{t+h,t} \end{pmatrix} \sim \left(\begin{pmatrix} \mu_y \\ \boldsymbol{\mu}_{\hat{\mathbf{y}}} \end{pmatrix}, \begin{pmatrix} \boldsymbol{\beta}_y'\boldsymbol{\Sigma}_f\boldsymbol{\beta}_y + \sigma_{\varepsilon_y}^2 & \boldsymbol{\beta}_y'\boldsymbol{\Sigma}_f\mathbf{B}' \\ \mathbf{B}\boldsymbol{\Sigma}_f\boldsymbol{\beta}_y & \mathbf{B}\boldsymbol{\Sigma}_f\mathbf{B}' + \mathbf{D}_\varepsilon \end{pmatrix} \right).$$

Also suppose either that $\boldsymbol{\mu}_{\hat{\mathbf{y}}} = \mathbf{0}$, $\mu_y = 0$ or a constant is included in the combination scheme. Then the first order condition for the optimal weights is, from (8),

$$\boldsymbol{\omega}^* = \left(\mathbf{B}\boldsymbol{\Sigma}_f\mathbf{B}' + \mathbf{D}_\varepsilon\right)^{-1}\mathbf{B}\boldsymbol{\Sigma}_f\boldsymbol{\beta}_y. \tag{41}$$

Further suppose that the N forecasts of the n_f factors can be divided into appropriate groups according to their factor loading vectors $\mathbf{b}_i$ such that $\sum_{i=1}^{n_f} \dim(\mathbf{b}_i) = N$:

$$\mathbf{B} = \begin{pmatrix} \mathbf{b}_1 & \mathbf{0} & \dots & \mathbf{0} \\ \mathbf{0} & \mathbf{b}_2 & \mathbf{0} & \dots \\ \vdots & \mathbf{0} & \ddots & \mathbf{0} \\ \mathbf{0} & \dots & \mathbf{0} & \mathbf{b}_{n_f} \end{pmatrix}.$$

Then the first term on the right-hand side of (41) is given by

$$\mathbf{B}\boldsymbol{\Sigma}_f\mathbf{B}' + \mathbf{D}_{\boldsymbol{\varepsilon}} = \begin{pmatrix} \mathbf{b}_1\mathbf{b}_1' & \mathbf{0} & \cdots & \mathbf{0} \\ \mathbf{0} & \mathbf{b}_2\mathbf{b}_2' & \mathbf{0} & \cdots \\ \vdots & \mathbf{0} & \ddots & \mathbf{0} \\ \mathbf{0} & \cdots & \mathbf{0} & \mathbf{b}_{n_f}\mathbf{b}_{n_f}' \end{pmatrix} \mathbf{D}_{\sigma_F^2} + \mathbf{D}_{\boldsymbol{\varepsilon}}, \tag{42}$$

where $\mathbf{D}_{\sigma_F}$ is a diagonal matrix with $\sigma_{f_1}^2$ in its first n_1 diagonal places followed by $\sigma_{f_2}^2$ in the next n_2 diagonal places and so on and $\mathbf{D}_\varepsilon$ is a diagonal matrix with $\mathrm{Var}(\varepsilon_{it})$ as the ith diagonal element. Thus the matrix in (42) and its inverse will be block diagonal. Provided that the forecasts tracking the individual factors can be grouped and have similar factor exposure ($\mathbf{b}_i$) within each group, this suggests that little is lost by pooling forecasts within each cluster and ignoring correlations across clusters. In a subsequent step, sample counterparts of the optimal combination weights for the grouped forecasts can be obtained by least-squares estimation. In this way, far fewer combination weights (n_f rather than N) have to be estimated. This can be expected to decrease forecast errors and thus improve forecasting performance.

Building on these ideas Aiolfi and Timmermann (2006) propose to sort forecasting models into clusters using a K-mean clustering algorithm based on their past MSE performance. As the previous argument suggests, one could alternatively base clustering on correlation patterns among the forecast errors.[10] Their method identifies K clusters. Let $\hat{\mathbf{y}}_{t+h,t}^k$ be the $p_k \times 1$ vector containing the subset of forecasts belonging to cluster k, $k = 1, 2, \ldots, K$. By ordering the clusters such that the first cluster contains models with the lowest historical MSE values, Aiolfi and Timmermann consider three separate strategies. The first simply computes the average forecast across models in the cluster of previous best models:

$$\hat{y}_{t+h,t}^{\mathrm{CPB}} = (\boldsymbol{\iota}_{p_1}'/p_1)\hat{\mathbf{y}}_{t+h,t}^1. \tag{43}$$

A second combination strategy identifies a small number of clusters, pools forecasts within each cluster and then estimates optimal weights on these pooled predictions by least squares:

$$\hat{y}_{t+h,t}^{\mathrm{CLS}} = \sum_{k=1}^{K} \hat{\omega}_{t+h,t,k}\big[(\boldsymbol{\iota}_{p_k}'/p_k)\hat{\mathbf{y}}_{t+h,t}^k\big], \tag{44}$$

where $\hat{\omega}_{t+h,t,k}$ are least-squares estimates of the optimal combination weights for the K clusters. This strategy is likely to work well if the variation in forecasting performance within each cluster is small relative to the variation in forecasting performance across clusters.

[10] The two clustering methods will be similar if σ_{F_i} varies significantly across factors and the factor exposure vectors, $\mathbf{b}_i$, and error variances $\sigma_{\varepsilon_i}^2$ are not too dissimilar across models. In this case forecast error variances will tend to cluster around the factors that the various forecasting models are most exposed to.

Finally, the third strategy pools forecasts within each cluster, estimates least squares combination weights and then shrinks these towards equal weights in order to reduce the effect of parameter estimation error

$$\hat{y}^{\mathrm{CSW}}_{t+h,t} = \sum_{k=1}^{K} \hat{s}_{t+h,t,k}\big[\big(\iota'_{p_k}/p_k\big)\hat{\mathbf{y}}^k_{t+h,t}\big],$$

where $\hat{s}_{t+h,t,k}$ are the shrinkage weights for the K clusters computed as $\hat{s}_{t+h,t,k} = \lambda\hat{\omega}_{t+h,t,k} + (1-\lambda)\frac{1}{K}$, $\lambda = \max\{0, 1 - \kappa(\frac{K}{t-h-K})\}$. The higher is κ, the higher the shrinkage towards equal weights.

4. Time-varying and nonlinear combination methods

So far our analysis has concentrated on forecast combination schemes that assumed constant and linear combination weights. While this follows naturally in the case with MSE loss and a time-invariant Gaussian distribution for the forecasts and realization, outside this framework it is natural to consider more general combination schemes. Two such families of special interest that generalize (6) are linear combinations with time-varying weights:

$$\hat{y}^c_{t+h,t} = \omega_{0t+h,t} + \boldsymbol{\omega}'_{t+h,t}\hat{\mathbf{y}}_{t+h,t}, \tag{45}$$

where $\omega_{0t+h,t}$, $\boldsymbol{\omega}'_{t+h,t}$ are adapted to $\mathcal{F}_t$, and nonlinear combinations with constant weights:

$$\hat{y}^c_{t+h,t} = C\big(\hat{\mathbf{y}}_{t+h,t}, \boldsymbol{\omega}\big), \tag{46}$$

where $C(.)$ is some function that is nonlinear in the parameters, $\boldsymbol{\omega}$, in the vector of forecasts, $\hat{\mathbf{y}}_{t+h,t}$, or in both. There is a close relationship between time-varying and nonlinear combinations. For example, nonlinearities in the true data generating process can lead to time-varying covariances for the forecast errors and hence time-varying weights in the combination of (misspecified) forecasts.

We next describe some of the approaches within these classes that have been proposed in the literature.

4.1. Time-varying weights

When the joint distribution of $(y_{t+h}\ \hat{\mathbf{y}}'_{t+h,t})'$ – or at least its first and second moments – vary over time, it can be beneficial to let the combination weights change over time. Indeed, Bates and Granger (1969) and Newbold and Granger (1974) suggested either assigning a disproportionately large weight to the model that has performed best most recently or using an adaptive updating scheme that puts more emphasis on recent performance in assigning the combination weights. Rather than explicitly modeling the structure of the time-variation in the combination weights, Bates and Granger proposed five adaptive estimation schemes based on exponential discounting or the use of rolling estimation windows.

The first combination scheme uses a rolling window of the most recent v observations based on the forecasting models' relative performance[11]

$$\hat{\boldsymbol{\omega}}_{t,t-h,i}^{\mathrm{BG1}} = \frac{(\sum_{\tau=t-v+1}^{t} e_{\tau,\tau-h,i}^2)^{-1}}{\sum_{j=1}^{N}(\sum_{\tau=t-v+1}^{t} e_{\tau,\tau-h,j}^2)^{-1}}. \tag{47}$$

The shorter is v, the more weight is put on the models' recent track record and the larger the part of the historical data that is discarded. If $v = t$, an expanding window is used and this becomes a special case of (36). Correlations between forecast errors are ignored by this scheme.

The second rolling window scheme accounts for such correlations across forecast errors but, again, only uses the most recent v observations for estimation:

$$\begin{aligned} \hat{\boldsymbol{\omega}}_{t,t-h}^{\mathrm{BG2}} &= \frac{\hat{\boldsymbol{\Sigma}}_{et,t-h}^{-1}\boldsymbol{\iota}}{\boldsymbol{\iota}'\hat{\boldsymbol{\Sigma}}_{et,t-h}^{-1}\boldsymbol{\iota}}, \\ \hat{\boldsymbol{\Sigma}}_{et,t-h}[i,j] &= v^{-1}\sum_{\tau=t-v+1}^{t} e_{\tau,\tau-h,i}e_{\tau,\tau-h,j}. \end{aligned} \tag{48}$$

The third combination scheme uses adaptive updating captured by the parameter $\alpha \in (0, 1)$, which tends to smooth the time-series evolution in the combination weights:

$$\hat{\omega}_{t,t-h,i}^{\mathrm{BG3}} = \alpha\hat{\omega}_{t-1,t-h-1,i} + (1-\alpha)\frac{(\sum_{\tau=t-v+1}^{t} e_{\tau,\tau-h,i}^2)^{-1}}{\sum_{j=1}^{N}(\sum_{\tau=t-v+1}^{t} e_{\tau,\tau-h,j}^2)^{-1}}. \tag{49}$$

The closer to unity is α, the smoother the weights will generally be.

The fourth and fifth combination methods are based on exponential discounting versions of the first two methods and take the form

$$\hat{\omega}_{t,t-h,i}^{\mathrm{BG4}} = \frac{(\sum_{\tau=1}^{t} \lambda^{\tau} e_{\tau,\tau-h,i}^2)^{-1}}{\sum_{j=1}^{N}(\sum_{\tau=1}^{t} \lambda^{\tau} e_{\tau,\tau-h,j}^2)^{-1}}, \tag{50}$$

where $\lambda \geqslant 1$ and higher values of λ correspond to putting more weight on recent data. This scheme does not put a zero weight on any of the past forecast errors whereas the rolling window methods entirely ignore observations more than v periods old. If $\lambda = 1$, there is no discounting of past performance and the formula becomes a special case of (36). However, it is common to use a discount factor such as $\lambda = 1.05$ or $\lambda = 1.10$, although the chosen value will depend on factors such as data frequency, evidence of instability, forecast horizon, etc.

[11] While we write the equations for the weights for general h, adjustments can be made when $h \geqslant 2$ which induces serial correlation in the forecast errors.

Finally, the fifth scheme estimates the variance and covariance of the forecast errors using exponential discounting:

$$\hat{\omega}_{t,t-h}^{\mathrm{BG5}} = \frac{\hat{\boldsymbol{\Sigma}}_{et,t-h}^{-1}\boldsymbol{\iota}}{\boldsymbol{\iota}'\hat{\boldsymbol{\Sigma}}_{et,t-h}^{-1}\boldsymbol{\iota}},$$
$$\hat{\boldsymbol{\Sigma}}_{et,t-h}[i,j] = \sum_{\tau=h+1}^{t} \lambda^{\tau} e_{\tau,\tau-h,i} e_{\tau,\tau-h,j}. \tag{51}$$

Putting more weight on recent data means reducing the weight on past data and tends to increase the variance of the parameter estimates. Hence it will typically lead to poorer performance if the underlying data generating process is truly covariance stationary. Conversely, the underlying time-variations have to be quite strong to justify not using an expanding window. See Pesaran and Timmermann (2005) for further analysis of this point.

Diebold and Pauly (1987) embed these schemes in a general weighted least squares setup that chooses combination weights to minimize the weighted average of forecast errors from the combination. Let $e_{t,t-h}^{c} = y_t - \boldsymbol{\omega}'\hat{\mathbf{y}}_{t,t-h}$ be the forecast error from the combination. Then one can minimize

$$\sum_{t=h+1}^{T} \sum_{\tau=h+1}^{T} \gamma_{t,\tau} e_{t,t-h}^{c} e_{\tau,\tau-h}^{c}, \tag{52}$$

or equivalently, $\mathbf{e}^{c\prime}\boldsymbol{\Gamma}\boldsymbol{e}^{c}$, where $\boldsymbol{\Gamma}$ is a $(T-h)\times(T-h)$ matrix with $[t,\tau]$ element $\gamma_{t,\tau}$ and $\mathbf{e}^{c}$ is a $(T-h)\times 1$ vector of errors from the forecast combination. Assuming that $\boldsymbol{\Gamma}$ is diagonal, equal-weights on all past observations correspond to $\gamma_{tt} = 1$ for all t, linearly declining weights can be represented as $\gamma_{tt} = t$, and geometrically declining weights take the form $\gamma_{tt} = \lambda^{T-t}$, $0 < \lambda \leqslant 1$. Finally, Diebold and Pauly introduce two new weighting schemes, namely nonlinearly declining weights, $\gamma_{tt} = t^{\lambda}$, $\lambda \geqslant 0$, and the Box–Cox transform weights

$$\gamma_{tt} = \begin{cases} (t^{\lambda}-1)/\lambda & \text{if } 0 < \lambda \leqslant 1, \\ \ln(t) & \text{if } \lambda = 0. \end{cases}$$

These weights can be either declining at an increasing rate or at a decreasing rate, depending on the sign of $\lambda - 1$. This is clearly an attractive feature and one that, e.g., the geometrically declining weights do not have.

Diebold and Pauly also consider regression-based combinations with time-varying parameters. For example, if both the intercept and slope of the combination regression are allowed to vary over time,

$$\hat{y}_{t+h} = \sum_{i=1}^{N} \left(g_t^i + \mu_t^i\right) \hat{y}_{t+h,t,i},$$

where $g^i(t) + \mu_t^i$ represent random variation in the combination weights. This approach explicitly models the evolution in the combination weights as opposed to doing this indirectly through the weighting of past and current forecast errors.

Instead of using adaptive schemes for updating the parameter estimates, an alternative is to explicitly model time-variations in the combination weights. A class of combination schemes considered by, e.g., Sessions and Chattererjee (1989), Zellner, Hong and Min (1991) and LeSage and Magura (1992) lets the combination weights evolve smoothly according to a time-varying parameter model:

$$\begin{aligned} y_{t+h} &= \tilde{\boldsymbol{\omega}}'_{t+h,t}\mathbf{z}_{t+h} + \varepsilon_{t+h}, \\ \tilde{\boldsymbol{\omega}}_{t+h,t} &= \tilde{\boldsymbol{\omega}}_{t,t-h} + \boldsymbol{\eta}_{t+h}, \end{aligned} \tag{53}$$

where $\mathbf{z}_{t+h} = (1\, \hat{\mathbf{y}}'_{t+h,t})'$ and $\tilde{\boldsymbol{\omega}}_{t+h,t} = (\omega_{0t+h,t}\, \boldsymbol{\omega}'_{t+h,t})'$. It is typically assumed that (for $h = 1$) $\varepsilon_{t+h} \sim \text{iid}(0, \sigma_\varepsilon^2)$, $\boldsymbol{\eta}_{t+h} \sim \text{iid}(0, \boldsymbol{\Sigma}_\eta^2)$ and $\text{Cov}(\varepsilon_{t+h}, \boldsymbol{\eta}_{t+h}) = \mathbf{0}$.

Changes in the combination weights may instead occur more discretely, driven by some switching indicator, $I_{\mathbf{e}}$, cf. Deutsch, Granger and Terasvirta (1994):

$$y_{t+h} = I_{\mathbf{e}_t \in A}\left(\omega_{01} + \boldsymbol{\omega}'_1 \hat{\mathbf{y}}_{t+h,t}\right) + (1 - I_{\mathbf{e}_t \in A})\left(\omega_{02} + \boldsymbol{\omega}'_2 \hat{\mathbf{y}}_{t+h,t}\right) + \varepsilon_{t+h}. \tag{54}$$

Here $\mathbf{e}_t = \boldsymbol{\iota} y_t - \hat{\mathbf{y}}_{t,t-h}$ is the vector of period-t forecast errors; $I_{\mathbf{e}_t \in A}$ is an indicator function taking the value unity when $\mathbf{e}_t \in A$ and zero otherwise, for A some pre-defined set defining the switching condition. This provides a broad class of time-varying combination schemes as $I_{\mathbf{e}_t \in A}$ can depend on past forecast errors or other variables in a number of ways. For example, $I_{\mathbf{e}_t \in A}$ could be unity if the forecast error is positive, zero otherwise.

Engle, Granger and Kraft (1984) propose time-varying combining weights that follow a bivariate ARCH scheme and are constrained to sum to unity. They assume that the distribution of the two forecast errors $\mathbf{e}_{t+h,t} = (e_{t+h,t,1}\, e_{t+h,t,2})'$ is bivariate Gaussian $N(\mathbf{0}, \boldsymbol{\Sigma}_{t+h,t})$ where $\boldsymbol{\Sigma}_{t+h,t}$ is the conditional covariance matrix.

A flexible mixture model for time-variation in the combination weights has been proposed by Elliott and Timmermann (2005). This approach is able to track both sudden and discrete as well as more gradual shifts in the joint distribution of $(y_{t+h}\, \hat{\mathbf{y}}'_{t+h,t})$. Suppose that the joint distribution of $(y_{t+h}\, \hat{\mathbf{y}}'_{t+h,t})$ is driven by an unobserved state variable, S_{t+h}, which assumes one of n_s possible values, i.e. $S_{t+h} \in (1, \dots, n_s)$. Conditional on a given realization of the underlying state, $S_{t+h} = s_{t+h}$, the joint distribution of y_{t+h} and $\hat{\mathbf{y}}_{t+h,t}$ is assumed to be Gaussian

$$\left.\begin{pmatrix} y_{t+h} \\ \hat{\mathbf{y}}_{t+h,t} \end{pmatrix}\right|_{s_{t+h}} \sim N\left(\begin{pmatrix} \mu_{ys_{t+h}} \\ \boldsymbol{\mu}_{\hat{\mathbf{y}}s_{t+h}} \end{pmatrix}, \begin{pmatrix} \sigma^2_{ys_{t+h}} & \boldsymbol{\sigma}'_{y\hat{\mathbf{y}}s_{t+h}} \\ \boldsymbol{\sigma}_{y\hat{\mathbf{y}}s_{t+h}} & \boldsymbol{\Sigma}_{\hat{\mathbf{y}}\hat{\mathbf{y}}s_{t+h}} \end{pmatrix}\right). \tag{55}$$

This is similar to (7) but now conditional on S_{t+h}, which is important. This model generalizes (28) to allow for an arbitrary number of states. State transitions are assumed to be driven by a first-order Markov chain $\mathbf{P} = \Pr(S_{t+h} = s_{t+h}|S_t = s_t)$

$$\mathbf{P} = \begin{pmatrix} p_{11} & p_{12} & \cdots & p_{1n_s} \\ p_{21} & p_{22} & \cdots & \vdots \\ \vdots & \vdots & \cdots & p_{n_s-1n_s} \\ p_{n_s1} & \cdots & p_{n_sn_s-1} & p_{n_sn_s} \end{pmatrix}. \tag{56}$$

Conditional on $S_{t+h} = s_{t+h}$, the expectation of y_{t+h} is linear in the prediction signals, $\hat{\mathbf{y}}_{t+h,t}$, and thus takes the form of state-dependent intercept and combination weights:

$$\mathrm{E}[y_{t+h}|\hat{\mathbf{y}}_{t+h,t}, s_{t+h}] = \mu_{ys_{t+h}} + \boldsymbol{\sigma}'_{y\hat{\mathbf{y}}s_{t+h}}\boldsymbol{\Sigma}^{-1}_{\hat{\mathbf{y}}\hat{\mathbf{y}}s_{t+h}}(\hat{\mathbf{y}}_{t+h,t} - \boldsymbol{\mu}_{\hat{\mathbf{y}}s_{t+h}}). \tag{57}$$

Accounting for the fact that the underlying state is unobservable, the conditionally expected loss given current information, $\mathcal{F}_t$, and state probabilities, $\pi_{s_{t+h},t}$, becomes:

$$\mathrm{E}[e^2_{t+h}|\pi_{s_{t+h},t}, \mathcal{F}_t] = \sum_{s_{t+h}=1}^{n_s} \pi_{s_{t+h},t}\{\mu^2_{es_{t+h}} + \sigma^2_{es_{t+h}}\}, \tag{58}$$

where $\pi_{s_{t+h},t} = \Pr(S_{t+h} = s_{t+h}|\mathcal{F}_t)$ is the probability of being in state s_{t+h} in period $t+h$ conditional on current information, $\mathcal{F}_t$. Assuming a linear combination conditional on $\mathcal{F}_t$, $\pi_{s_{t+h},t}$ the optimal combination weights, $\omega^*_{0t+h,t}$, $\boldsymbol{\omega}^*_{t+h,t}$ become [cf. Elliott and Timmermann (2005)]

$$\begin{aligned} \omega^*_{0t+h,t} &= \sum_{s_{t+h}=1}^{n_s} \pi_{s_{t+h},t}\mu_{ys_{t+h}} - \left(\sum_{s_{t+h}=1}^{n_s} \pi_{s_{t+h},t}\boldsymbol{\mu}'_{\hat{\mathbf{y}}s_{t+h}}\right)\boldsymbol{\omega}_{th} \equiv \bar{\mu}_{yt} - \bar{\boldsymbol{\mu}}'_{\hat{\mathbf{y}}t}\boldsymbol{\omega}_{th}, \\ \boldsymbol{\omega}^*_{t+h,t} &= \left(\sum_{s_{t+h}=1}^{n_s} \pi_{s_{t+h},t}(\boldsymbol{\mu}_{\hat{\mathbf{y}}s_{t+h}}\boldsymbol{\mu}'_{\hat{\mathbf{y}}s_{t+h}} + \boldsymbol{\Sigma}_{\hat{\mathbf{y}}s_{t+h}}) - \bar{\boldsymbol{\mu}}_{\hat{\mathbf{y}}t}\bar{\boldsymbol{\mu}}'_{\hat{\mathbf{y}}t}\right)^{-1} \\ &\quad \times \left(\sum_{s_{t+h}=1}^{n_s} \pi_{s_{t+h},t}(\mu_{ys_{t+h}}\boldsymbol{\mu}_{\hat{\mathbf{y}}s_{t+h}} + \boldsymbol{\sigma}_{y\hat{\mathbf{y}}s_{t+h}}) - \bar{\mu}_{yt+h,t}\bar{\boldsymbol{\mu}}_{\hat{\mathbf{y}}t+h,t}\right), \end{aligned} \tag{59}$$

where $\bar{\mu}_{yt+h,t} = \sum_{s_{t+h}=1}^{n_s} \pi_{s_{t+h},t}\mu_{ys_{t+h}}$ and $\bar{\boldsymbol{\mu}}_{\hat{\mathbf{y}}t+h,t} = \sum_{s_{t+h}=1}^{n_s} \pi_{s_{t+h},t}\boldsymbol{\mu}_{\hat{\mathbf{y}}s_{t+h}}$. The standard weights in (8) can readily be obtained by setting $n_s = 1$.

It follows from (59) that the (conditionally) optimal combination weights will vary as the state probabilities vary over time as a function of the arrival of new information provided that $\mathbf{P}$ is of rank greater than one.

4.2. Nonlinear combination schemes

Two types of nonlinearities can be considered in forecast combinations. First, nonlinear functions of the forecasts can be used in the combination which is nevertheless linear in the unknown parameters:

$$\hat{y}^c_{t+h,t} = \omega_0 + \boldsymbol{\omega}'C(\hat{\mathbf{y}}_{t+h,t}). \tag{60}$$

Here $C(\hat{\mathbf{y}}_{t+h,t})$ is a function of the underlying forecasts that typically includes a lead term that is linear in $\hat{\mathbf{y}}_{t+h,t}$ in addition to higher order terms similar to a Volterra or Taylor series expansion. The nonlinearity in (60) only enters through the shape of the transformation $C(.)$ so the unknown parameters can readily be estimated by OLS although the small-sample properties of such estimates could be an issue due to possible outliers. A second and more general combination method considers nonlinearities in the combination parameters, i.e.

$$\hat{y}^c_{t+h,t} = C(\hat{\mathbf{y}}_{t+h,t}, \boldsymbol{\omega}). \tag{61}$$

There does not appear to be much work in this area, possibly because estimation errors already appear to be large in linear combination schemes. They can be expected to be even larger for nonlinear combinations whose parameters are generally less robust and more sensitive to outliers than those of the linear schemes. Techniques from the Handbook Chapter 9 by White (2006) could be readily used in this context, however.

One paper that does estimate nonlinear combination weights is the study by Donaldson and Kamstra (1996). This uses artificial neural networks to combine volatility forecasts from a range of alternative models. Their combination scheme takes the form

$$\begin{aligned}
\hat{y}^c_{t+h,t} &= \beta_0 + \sum_{j=1}^{N} \beta_j \hat{y}_{t+h,t,j} + \sum_{i=1}^{p} \delta_i g(\mathbf{z}_{t+h,t}\boldsymbol{\gamma}_i),\\
g(\mathbf{z}_{t+h,t}\boldsymbol{\gamma}_i) &= \left(1 + \exp\left(-\left(\gamma_{0,i} + \sum_{j=1}^{N} \gamma_{1,j} z_{t+h,t,j}\right)\right)\right)^{-1},\\
z_{t+h,t,j} &= (\hat{y}_{t+h,t,j} - \bar{y}_{t+h,t})/\hat{\sigma}_{yt+h,t},\\
p &\in \{0, 1, 2, 3\}.
\end{aligned} \tag{62}$$

Here $\bar{y}_{t+h,t}$ is the sample estimate of the mean of y across the forecasting models while $\hat{\sigma}_{yt+h,t}$ is the sample estimate of the standard deviation using data up to time t. This network uses logistic nodes. The linear model is nested as a special case when $p = 0$ so no nonlinear terms are included. In an out-of-sample forecasting experiment for volatility in daily stock returns, Donaldson and Kamstra find evidence that the neural net combination applied to two underlying forecasts (a moving average variance model and a GARCH(1,1) model) outperforms traditional combination methods.

5. Shrinkage methods

In cases where the number of forecasts, N, is large relative to the sample size, T, the sample covariance matrix underlying standard combinations is subject to considerable estimation uncertainty. Shrinkage methods aim to trade off bias in the combination weights against reduced parameter estimation error in estimates of the combination weights. Intuition for how shrinkage works is well summarized by Ledoit and Wolf (2004, p. 2): "The crux of the method is that those estimated coefficients in the sample covariance matrix that are extremely high tend to contain a lot of positive error and therefore need to be pulled downwards to compensate for that. Similarly, we compensate for the negative error that tends to be embedded inside extremely low estimated coefficients by pulling them upwards." This problem can partially be resolved by imposing more structure on the estimator in a way that reduces estimation error although the key question remains how much and which structure to impose. Shrinkage methods let the forecast combination weights depend on the sample size relative to the number of cross-sectional models to be combined.

Diebold and Pauly (1990) propose to shrink towards equal-weights. Consider the standard linear regression model underlying most forecast combinations and for simplicity drop the time and horizon subscripts:

$$\mathbf{y} = \hat{\mathbf{y}}\boldsymbol{\omega} + \boldsymbol{\varepsilon}, \quad \boldsymbol{\varepsilon} \sim N(\mathbf{0}, \sigma^2\mathbf{I}), \tag{63}$$

where $\mathbf{y}$ and $\boldsymbol{\varepsilon}$ are $T \times 1$ vectors, $\hat{\mathbf{y}}$ is the $T \times N$ matrix of forecasts and $\boldsymbol{\omega}$ is the $N \times 1$ vector of combination weights. The standard normal-gamma conjugate prior $\sigma^2 \sim IG(s_0^2, v_0)$, $\boldsymbol{\omega}|\sigma \sim N(\boldsymbol{\omega}_0, \mathbf{M})$ implies that

$$P(\boldsymbol{\omega}, \sigma) \propto \sigma^{-N-v_0-1} \exp\left(\frac{-(v_0 s_0^2 + (\boldsymbol{\omega} - \boldsymbol{\omega}_0)'\mathbf{M}(\boldsymbol{\omega} - \boldsymbol{\omega}_0))}{2\sigma^2}\right). \tag{64}$$

Under normality of $\boldsymbol{\varepsilon}$ the likelihood function for the data is

$$L(\boldsymbol{\omega}, \sigma|\mathbf{y}, \hat{\mathbf{y}}) \propto \sigma^{-T} \exp\left(\frac{-(\mathbf{y} - \hat{\mathbf{y}}\boldsymbol{\omega})'(\mathbf{y} - \hat{\mathbf{y}}\boldsymbol{\omega})}{2\sigma^2}\right) \tag{65}$$

These results can be combined to give the marginal posterior for $\boldsymbol{\omega}$ with mean

$$\bar{\boldsymbol{\omega}} = (\mathbf{M} + \hat{\mathbf{y}}'\hat{\mathbf{y}})^{-1}(\mathbf{M}\boldsymbol{\omega}_0 + \hat{\mathbf{y}}'\hat{\mathbf{y}}\hat{\boldsymbol{\omega}}), \tag{66}$$

where $\hat{\boldsymbol{\omega}} = (\hat{\mathbf{y}}'\hat{\mathbf{y}})^{-1}\hat{\mathbf{y}}'\mathbf{y}$ is the least squares estimate of $\boldsymbol{\omega}$. Using a prior for $\mathbf{M}$ that is proportional to $\hat{\mathbf{y}}'\hat{\mathbf{y}}$, $\mathbf{M} = g\hat{\mathbf{y}}'\hat{\mathbf{y}}$, we get

$$\bar{\boldsymbol{\omega}} = (g\hat{\mathbf{y}}'\hat{\mathbf{y}} + \hat{\mathbf{y}}'\hat{\mathbf{y}})^{-1}(g\hat{\mathbf{y}}'\hat{\mathbf{y}}\boldsymbol{\omega}_0 + \hat{\mathbf{y}}'\hat{\mathbf{y}}\hat{\boldsymbol{\omega}}),$$

which can be used to obtain

$$\bar{\boldsymbol{\omega}} = \boldsymbol{\omega}_0 + \frac{\hat{\boldsymbol{\omega}} - \boldsymbol{\omega}_0}{1+g}. \tag{67}$$

Clearly, the larger the value of g, the stronger the shrinkage towards the mean of the prior, $\boldsymbol{\omega}_0$, whereas small values of g suggest putting more weight on the data.

Alternatively, empirical Bayes methods can be used to estimate g. Suppose the prior for $\boldsymbol{\omega}$ conditional on σ is Gaussian $N(\boldsymbol{\omega}_0, \tau^2\mathbf{A}^{-1})$. Then the posterior for $\boldsymbol{\omega}$ is also Gaussian, $N(\bar{\boldsymbol{\omega}}, \boldsymbol{\tau}^{-2}\mathbf{A} + \sigma^{-2}\hat{\mathbf{y}}'\hat{\mathbf{y}})$ and σ^2 and τ^2 can be replaced by the estimates [cf.

Diebold and Pauly (1990)]

$$\hat{\sigma}^2 = \frac{(\mathbf{y} - \hat{\mathbf{y}}\hat{\boldsymbol{\omega}})'(\mathbf{y} - \hat{\mathbf{y}}\hat{\boldsymbol{\omega}})}{T},$$

$$\hat{\tau}^2 = \frac{(\hat{\boldsymbol{\omega}} - \boldsymbol{\omega}_0)'(\hat{\boldsymbol{\omega}} - \boldsymbol{\omega}_0)}{\operatorname{tr}(\hat{\mathbf{y}}'\hat{\mathbf{y}})^{-1}} - \hat{\sigma}^2.$$

This gives rise to an empirical Bayes estimator of $\boldsymbol{\omega}$ whose posterior mean is

$$\bar{\boldsymbol{\omega}} = \boldsymbol{\omega}_0 + \left(\frac{\hat{\tau}^2}{\hat{\sigma}^2 + \hat{\tau}^2}\right)(\hat{\boldsymbol{\omega}} - \boldsymbol{\omega}_0). \tag{68}$$

The empirical Bayes combination shrinks $\hat{\boldsymbol{\omega}}$ towards $\boldsymbol{\omega}_0$ and amounts to setting $g = \hat{\sigma}^2/\hat{\tau}^2$ in (67). Notice that if $\hat{\sigma}^2/\hat{\tau}^2 \to 0$, the OLS estimator is obtained while if $\hat{\sigma}^2/\hat{\tau}^2 \to \infty$, the prior estimate $\boldsymbol{\omega}_0$ is obtained as a special case. Diebold and Pauly argue that the combination weights should be shrunk towards the equal-weighted (simple) average so the combination procedure gives a convex combination of the least-squares and equal weights.

Stock and Watson (2004) also propose shrinkage towards the arithmetic average of forecasts. Let $\hat{\omega}_{T,T-h,i}$ be the least-squares estimator of the weight on the ith model in the forecast combination based on data up to period T. The combination weights considered by Stock and Watson take the form (assuming $T > h + N + 1$)

$$\omega_{T,T-h,i} = \psi\hat{\omega}_{T,T-h,i} + (1 - \psi)(1/N),$$

$$\psi = \max\bigl(0, 1 - \kappa N/(T - h - N - 1)\bigr),$$

where κ regulates the strength of the shrinkage. Stock and Watson consider values $\kappa = 1/4$, $1/2$ or 1. As the sample size, T, rises relative to N, the least squares estimate gets a larger weight. Indeed, if T grows at a faster rate than N, the least squares weight will, in the limit, get a weight of unity.

5.1. Shrinkage and factor structure

In a portfolio application Ledoit and Wolf (2003) propose to shrink the weights towards a point implied by a single factor structure common from finance.[12] Suppose that the

[12] The problem of forming mean–variance efficient portfolios in finance is mathematically equivalent to that of combining forecasts, cf. Dunis, Timmermann and Moody (2001). In finance, the standard optimization problem minimizes the portfolio variance $\boldsymbol{\omega}'\boldsymbol{\Sigma}\boldsymbol{\omega}$ subject to a given portfolio return, $\boldsymbol{\omega}'\boldsymbol{\mu} = \mu_0$, where $\boldsymbol{\mu}$ is a vector of mean returns while $\boldsymbol{\Sigma}$ is the covariance matrix of asset returns. Imposing also the constraint that the portfolio weights sum to unity, we have

$$\min_{\boldsymbol{\omega}} \boldsymbol{\omega}'\boldsymbol{\Sigma}\boldsymbol{\omega}$$

$$\text{s.t.} \quad \boldsymbol{\omega}'\boldsymbol{\iota} = 1,$$

$$\boldsymbol{\omega}'\boldsymbol{\mu} = \mu_0.$$

individual forecast errors are affected by a single common factor, f_{et}:

$$e_{it} = \alpha_i + \beta_i f_{et} + \varepsilon_{it} \tag{69}$$

where the idiosyncratic residuals, ε_{it}, are assumed to be orthogonal across forecasting models and uncorrelated with f_{et}. This single factor model has a long tradition in finance but is also a natural starting point for forecasting purposes since forecast errors are generally strongly positively correlated. Letting $\sigma^2_{f_e}$ be the variance of f_{et}, the covariance matrix of the forecast errors becomes

$$\boldsymbol{\Sigma}_{ef} = \sigma^2_{f_e}\boldsymbol{\beta}\boldsymbol{\beta}' + \mathbf{D}_\varepsilon, \tag{70}$$

where $\boldsymbol{\beta} = (\beta_1 \ldots \beta_N)'$ is the vector of factor sensitivities, while $\mathbf{D}_\varepsilon$ is a diagonal matrix with the individual values of $\text{Var}(\varepsilon_{it})$ on the diagonal. Estimation of $\boldsymbol{\Sigma}_{ef}$ requires determining only $2N+1$ parameters. Consistent estimates of these parameters are easily obtained by estimating (69) by OLS, equation by equation, to get

$$\hat{\boldsymbol{\Sigma}}_{ef} = \hat{\sigma}^2_{f_e}\hat{\boldsymbol{\beta}}\hat{\boldsymbol{\beta}}' + \hat{\mathbf{D}}_\varepsilon.$$

Typically this covariance matrix is biased due to the assumption that $\mathbf{D}_\varepsilon$ is diagonal. For example, there may be more than a single common factor in the forecast errors and some forecasts may omit the same relevant variable in which case blocks of forecast errors will be correlated. Though biased, the single factor covariance matrix is typically surrounded by considerably smaller estimation errors than the unconstrained matrix, $\text{E}[\mathbf{ee}']$, which can be estimated by

$$\hat{\boldsymbol{\Sigma}}_e = \frac{1}{T-h}\sum_{\tau=h}^{T} \mathbf{e}_{\tau,\tau-h}\mathbf{e}'_{\tau,\tau-h},$$

where $\mathbf{e}_{\tau,\tau-h}$ is an $N \times 1$ vector of forecast errors. This estimator requires estimating $N(N+1)/2$ parameters. Using $\hat{\boldsymbol{\Sigma}}_{ef}$ as the shrinkage point, Ledoit and Wolf (2003) propose minimizing the following quadratic loss as a function of the shrinkage parameter, α,

$$L(\alpha) = \left\|\alpha\hat{\boldsymbol{\Sigma}}_{ef} + (1-\alpha)\hat{\boldsymbol{\Sigma}}_e - \boldsymbol{\Sigma}_e\right\|^2,$$

where $\|.\|^2$ is the Frobenius norm, i.e. $\|\mathbf{Z}\|^2 = \text{trace}(\mathbf{Z}^2)$, $\hat{\boldsymbol{\Sigma}}_e = (1/T)\mathbf{e}(\mathbf{I} - \boldsymbol{\iota}\boldsymbol{\iota}'/T)\mathbf{e}'$ is the sample covariance matrix and $\boldsymbol{\Sigma}_e$ is the true matrix of squared forecast errors, $\text{E}[\mathbf{ee}']$,

This problem has the solution

$$\boldsymbol{\omega}^* = \boldsymbol{\Sigma}^{-1}(\boldsymbol{\mu}\boldsymbol{\iota})\left[(\boldsymbol{\mu}\boldsymbol{\iota})'\boldsymbol{\Sigma}^{-1}(\boldsymbol{\mu}\boldsymbol{\iota})\right]^{-1}\begin{pmatrix}\mu_0\\1\end{pmatrix}.$$

In the forecast combination problem the constraint $\boldsymbol{\omega}'\boldsymbol{\iota} = 1$ is generally interpreted as guaranteeing an unbiased combined forecast – assuming of course that the individual forecasts are also unbiased. The only difference to the optimal solution from the forecast combination problem is that a minimum variance portfolio is derived for each separate value of the mean portfolio return, μ_0.

where $\mathbf{e}$ is an $N \times T$ matrix of forecast errors. Letting $\hat{f}_{ij}$ be the (i, j) entry of $\hat{\mathbf{\Sigma}}_{ef}$, $\hat{\sigma}_{ij}$ the (i, j) element of $\hat{\mathbf{\Sigma}}_e$ and ϕ_{ij} the (i, j) element of the single factor covariance matrix, $\mathbf{\Sigma}_{ef}$, while σ_{ij} is the (i, j) element of $\mathbf{\Sigma}_e$, they demonstrate that the optimal shrinkage takes the form

$$\alpha^* = \frac{1}{T}\frac{\pi - \rho}{\gamma} + \mathrm{O}\left(\frac{1}{T^2}\right),$$

where

$$\pi = \sum_{i=1}^{N}\sum_{j=1}^{N} \mathrm{AsyVar}\left(\sqrt{T}\hat{\sigma}_{ij}\right),$$

$$\rho = \sum_{i=1}^{N}\sum_{j=1}^{N} \mathrm{AsyCov}\left(\sqrt{T}\hat{f}_{ij}, \sqrt{T}\hat{\sigma}_{ij}\right),$$

$$\gamma = \sum_{i=1}^{N}\sum_{j=1}^{N} (\phi_{ij} - \sigma_{ij})^2.$$

Hence, π measures the (scaled) sum of asymptotic variances of the sample covariance matrix ($\hat{\mathbf{\Sigma}}_e$), ρ measures the (scaled) sum of asymptotic covariances of the sample covariance matrix ($\hat{\mathbf{\Sigma}}_e$) and the single-factor covariance matrix ($\hat{\mathbf{\Sigma}}_{ef}$), while γ measures the degree of misspecification (bias) in the single factor model. Ledoit and Wolf propose consistent estimators $\hat{\pi}$, $\hat{\rho}$ and $\hat{\gamma}$ under the assumption of IID forecast errors.[13]

5.2. Constraints on combination weights

Shrinkage bears an interesting relationship to portfolio weight constraints in finance. It is commonplace to consider minimization of portfolio variance subject to a set of equality and inequality constraints on the portfolio weights. Portfolio weights are often constrained to be non-negative (due to no short selling) and not to exceed certain upper bounds (due to limits on ownership in individual stocks). Reflecting this, let $\hat{\Sigma}$ be an estimate of the covariance matrix for some cross-section of asset returns with row i, column j element $\hat{\Sigma}[i, j]$ and consider the optimization program

$$\begin{aligned} \boldsymbol{\omega}^* &= \arg\min_{\omega} \frac{1}{2}\boldsymbol{\omega}'\hat{\Sigma}\boldsymbol{\omega} \\ \text{s.t.} \quad & \boldsymbol{\omega}'\boldsymbol{\iota} = 1, \\ & \omega_i \geqslant 0, \quad i = 1, \ldots, N, \\ & \omega_i \leqslant \bar{\omega}, \quad i = 1, \ldots, N. \end{aligned} \tag{71}$$

[13] It is worth pointing out that the assumption that $\mathbf{e}$ is IID is unlikely to hold for forecast errors which could share common dynamics in first, second or higher order moments or even be serially correlated, cf. Diebold (1988).

This gives a set of Kuhn–Tucker conditions:

$$\sum_j \hat{\Sigma}[i,j]\omega_j - \lambda_i + \delta_i = \lambda_0 \geqslant 0, \quad i = 1, \ldots, N,$$

$$\lambda_i \geqslant 0 \quad \text{and} \quad \lambda_i = 0 \quad \text{if } \omega_i > 0,$$

$$\delta_i \geqslant 0 \quad \text{and} \quad \delta_i = 0 \quad \text{if } \omega_i < \bar{\omega}.$$

Lagrange multipliers for the lower and upper bounds are collected in the vectors $\boldsymbol{\lambda} = (\lambda_1, \ldots, \lambda_N)'$ and $\boldsymbol{\delta} = (\delta_1, \ldots, \delta_N)'$; λ_0 is the Lagrange multiplier for the constraint that the weights sum to one.

Constraints on combination weights effectively have two effects. First, they shrink the largest elements of the covariance matrix towards zero. This reduces the effects of estimation error that can be expected to be strongest for assets with extreme weights. The second effect is that it may introduce specification errors to the extent that the true population values of the optimal weights actually lie outside the assumed interval.

Jaganathan and Ma (2003) show the following result. Let

$$\tilde{\boldsymbol{\Sigma}} = \hat{\boldsymbol{\Sigma}} + (\boldsymbol{\delta}\boldsymbol{\iota}' + \boldsymbol{\iota}\boldsymbol{\delta}') - (\boldsymbol{\lambda}\boldsymbol{\iota}' + \boldsymbol{\iota}\boldsymbol{\lambda}'). \tag{72}$$

Then $\tilde{\boldsymbol{\Sigma}}$ is symmetric and positive semi-definite. Constructing a solution to the inequality constrained problem (71) is shown to be equivalent to finding the optimal weights for the unconstrained quadratic form based on the modified covariance matrix in (72) $\tilde{\boldsymbol{\Sigma}} = \hat{\boldsymbol{\Sigma}} + (\boldsymbol{\delta}\boldsymbol{\iota}' + \boldsymbol{\iota}\boldsymbol{\delta}') - (\boldsymbol{\lambda}\boldsymbol{\iota}' + \boldsymbol{\iota}\boldsymbol{\lambda}')$.

Furthermore, it turns out that $\tilde{\boldsymbol{\Sigma}}$ can be interpreted as a shrinkage version of $\hat{\boldsymbol{\Sigma}}$. To see this, consider the weights that are affected by the lower bound so $\tilde{\boldsymbol{\Sigma}} = \hat{\boldsymbol{\Sigma}} - (\boldsymbol{\lambda}\boldsymbol{\iota}' + \boldsymbol{\iota}\boldsymbol{\lambda}')$. When the constraint for the lower bound is binding (so a combination weight would have been negative), the covariances of a particular forecast error with all other errors are reduced by the strictly positive Lagrange multipliers and its variance is shrunk. Imposing the non-negativity constraints shrinks the largest covariance estimates that would have resulted in negative weights. Since the largest estimates of the covariance are more likely to be the result of estimation error, such shrinkage can have the effect of reducing estimation error and have the potential to improve out-of-sample performance of the combination.

In the case of the upper bounds, those forecasts whose unconstrained weights would have exceeded $\bar{\omega}$ are also the ones for which the variance and covariance estimates tend to be smallest. These forecasts have strictly positive Lagrange multipliers on the upper bound constraint, meaning that their forecast error variance will be increased by $2\delta_i$ while the covariances in the modified covariance matrix $\tilde{\boldsymbol{\Sigma}}$ will be increased by $\delta_i + \delta_j$. Again this corresponds to shrinkage towards the cross-sectional average of the variances and covariances.

6. Combination of interval and probability distribution forecasts

So far we have focused on combining point forecasts. This, of course, reflects the fact that the vast majority of academic studies on forecasting only report point forecasts. However, there has been a growing interest in studying interval and probability distribution forecasts and an emerging literature in economics is considering the scope for using combination methods for such forecasts. This is preceded by the use of combined probability forecasting in areas such as meteorology, cf. Sanders (1963). Genest and Zidek (1986) present a broad survey of various techniques in this area.

6.1. The combination decision

As in the case of combinations of point forecasts it is natural to ask whether the best strategy is to use only a single probability forecast or a combination of these. This is related to the concept of forecast encompassing which generalizes from point to density forecasts as follows. Suppose we are considering combining N distribution forecasts $f_1, \dots, f_N$ whose joint distribution with y is $P(y, f_1, f_2, \dots, f_N)$. Factoring this into the product of the conditional distribution of y given $f_1, \dots, f_N$, $P(y|f_1, \dots, f_N)$, and the marginal distribution of the forecasts, $P(f_1, \dots, f_N)$, we have

$$P(y, f_1, f_2, \dots, f_N) = P(y|f_1, \dots, f_N)P(f_1, \dots, f_N). \tag{73}$$

A probability forecast that does not provide information about y given all the other probability density forecasts is referred to as extraneous by Clemen, Murphy and Winkler (1995). If the ith forecast is extraneous we must have

$$P(y|f_1, f_2, \dots, f_N) = P(y|f_1, f_2, \dots, f_{i-1}, f_{i+1}, \dots, f_N). \tag{74}$$

If (74) holds, probability forecast f_i does not contain any information that is useful for forecasting y given the other $N-1$ probability forecasts. Only if forecast i does not satisfy (74) does it follow that this model is not encompassed by the other models. Interestingly, adding more forecasting models (i.e. increasing N) can lead a previously extraneous model to become non-extraneous if it contains information about the relationship between the existing $N-1$ methods and the new forecasts.

For pairwise comparison of probability forecasts, Clemen, Murphy and Winkler (1995) define the concept of sufficiency. This concept is important because if forecast 1 is sufficient for forecast 2, then 1's forecasts will be of greater value to *all* users than forecast 2. Conversely, if neither model is sufficient for the other we would expect some forecast users to prefer model 1 while others prefer model 2. To illustrate this concept, consider two probability forecasts, $f_1 = P_1(x = 1)$ and $f_2 = P_2(x = 1)$ of some event, X, where $x = 1$ if the event occurs while it is zero otherwise. Also let $v_1(f) = P(f_1 = f)$ and $v_2(g) = P(f_2 = g)$, where $f, g \in \mathcal{G}$, and $\mathcal{G}$ is the set of permissible probabilities. Forecast 1 is then said to be sufficient for forecast 2 if there exists a stochastic transformation $\zeta(g|f)$ such that for all $g \in \mathcal{G}$,

$$\sum_f \zeta(g|f)v_1(f) = v_2(g),$$

$$\sum_f \zeta(g|f) f v_1(f) = g v_2(g).$$

The function $\zeta(g|f)$ is said to be a stochastic transformation provided that it lies between zero and one and integrates to unity. It represents an additional randomization that has the effect of introducing noise into the first forecast.

6.2. Combinations of probability density forecasts

Combinations of probability density or distribution forecasts impose new requirements beyond those we saw for combinations of point forecasts, namely that the combination must be convex with weights confined to the zero-one interval so that the probability forecast never becomes negative and always sums to one.

This still leaves open a wide set of possible combination schemes. An obvious way to combine a collection of probability forecasts $\{F_{t+h,t,1}, \ldots, F_{t+h,t,N}\}$ is through the convex combination ("linear opinion pool"):

$$\bar{F}^c = \sum_{i=1}^{N} \omega_{t+h,t,i} F_{t+h,t,i}, \tag{75}$$

with $0 \leqslant \omega_{t+h,t,i} \leqslant 1$ $(i = 1, \ldots, N)$ and $\sum_{i=1}^{N} \omega_{t+h,t,i} = 1$ to ensure that the combined probability forecast is everywhere non-negative and integrates to one. The generalized linear opinion pool adds an extra probability forecast, $F_{t+h,t,0}$, and takes the form

$$\bar{F}^c = \sum_{i=0}^{N} \omega_{t+h,t,i} F_{t+h,t,i}. \tag{76}$$

Under this scheme the weights are allowed to be negative $\omega_0, \omega_1, \ldots, \omega_n \in [-1, 1]$ although they still are restricted to sum to unity: $\sum_{i=0}^{N} \omega_{t+h,t,i} = 1. F_{t+h,t,0}$ can be shown to exist under conditions discussed by Genest and Zidek (1986).

Alternatively, one can adopt a logarithmic combination of densities

$$\bar{f}^l = \prod_{i=1}^{N} f_{t+h,t,i}^{\omega_{t+h,t,i}} \Big/ \int \prod_{i=1}^{N} f_{t+h,t,i}^{\omega_{t+h,t,i}} \, \mathrm{d}\mu, \tag{77}$$

where $\{\omega_{t+h,t,1}, \ldots, \omega_{t+h,t,N}\}$ are weights chosen such that the integral in the denominator is finite and μ is the underlying probability measure. This combination is less dispersed than the linear combination and is also unimodal, cf. Genest and Zidek (1986).

6.3. Bayesian methods

Bayesian approaches have been widely used to construct combinations of probability forecasts. For example, Min and Zellner (1993) propose combinations based on posterior odds ratios. Let p_1 and p_2 be the posterior probabilities of two models (a fixed parameter and a time-varying parameter model in their application) while $k = p_1/p_2$ is the posterior odds ratio of the two models. Assuming that the two models, M_1 and M_2, are exhaustive the proposed combination scheme has a conditional mean of

$$\begin{aligned}\mathrm{E}[y] &= p_1\mathrm{E}[y|M_1] + (1-p_1)\mathrm{E}[y|M_2] \\ &= \frac{k}{1+k}\mathrm{E}[y|M_1] + \frac{1}{1+k}\mathrm{E}[y|M_2].\end{aligned} \tag{78}$$

Palm and Zellner (1992) propose a combination method that accounts for the full correlation structure between the forecast errors. They model the one-step forecast errors from the individual models as follows:

$$y_{t+1} - \hat{y}_{it+1,t} = \theta_i + \varepsilon_{it+1} + \eta_{t+1}, \tag{79}$$

where θ_i is the bias in the ith model's forecast – reflecting perhaps the forecaster's asymmetric loss, cf. Zellner (1986) – ε_{it+1} is an idiosyncratic forecast error and η_{t+1} is a common component in the forecast errors reflecting an unpredictable component of the outcome variable. It is assumed that both $\varepsilon_{it+1} \sim N(0, \sigma_i^2)$ and $\eta_{t+1} \sim N(0, \sigma_\eta^2)$ are serially uncorrelated (as well as mutually uncorrelated) Gaussian variables with zero mean.

For the case with zero bias ($\theta_i = 0$), Winkler (1981) shows that when $\varepsilon_{it+1} + \eta_{t+1}$ ($i = 1, \ldots, N$) has known covariance matrix, $\mathbf{\Sigma}_0$, the predictive density function of y_{t+1} given an N-vector of forecasts $\hat{\mathbf{y}}_{t+1,t} = (\hat{y}_{t+1,t,1}, \ldots, \hat{y}_{t+1,t,N})'$ is Gaussian with mean $\boldsymbol{\iota}'\mathbf{\Sigma}_0^{-1}\hat{\mathbf{y}}_{t+1,t}/\boldsymbol{\iota}'\mathbf{\Sigma}_0\boldsymbol{\iota}$ and variance $\boldsymbol{\iota}'\mathbf{\Sigma}_0^{-1}\boldsymbol{\iota}$. When the covariance matrix of the N time-varying parts of the forecast errors $\varepsilon_{it+1} + \eta_{t+1}$, $\mathbf{\Sigma}$, is unknown but has an inverted Wishart prior $IW(\mathbf{\Sigma}|\mathbf{\Sigma}_0, \delta_0, N)$ with $\delta_0 \geqslant N$, the predictive distribution of y_{T+1} given $\mathcal{F}_T = \{y_1, \ldots, y_T, \hat{\mathbf{y}}_{2,1}, \ldots, \hat{\mathbf{y}}_{T,T-1}, \hat{\mathbf{y}}_{T+1,T})$ is a univariate student-t with degrees of freedom parameter $\delta_0 + N - 1$, mean $m^* = \boldsymbol{\iota}'\mathbf{\Sigma}_0^{-1}\hat{\mathbf{y}}_{T+1,T}/\boldsymbol{\iota}'\mathbf{\Sigma}_0^{-1}\boldsymbol{\iota}$ and variance $(\delta_0 + N - 1)s^{*2}/(\delta_0 + N - 3)$, where $s^{*2} = (\delta_0 + (m^*\boldsymbol{\iota} - \hat{\mathbf{y}}_{T+1,T})'\mathbf{\Sigma}_0^{-1}(m^*\boldsymbol{\iota} - \hat{\mathbf{y}}_{T+1,T}))/(\delta_0 + N - 1)\boldsymbol{\iota}'\mathbf{\Sigma}_0^{-1}\boldsymbol{\iota}$.

Palm and Zellner (1992) extend these results to allow for a non-zero bias. Given a set of N forecasts $\hat{\mathbf{y}}_{t+1,t}$ over T periods they express the forecast errors $y_t - \hat{y}_{t,t-1,i} = \theta_i + \varepsilon_{it} + \eta_t$ as a $T \times N$ multivariate regression model:

$$\mathbf{Y} = \boldsymbol{\iota\theta} + \mathbf{U}.$$

Suppose that the structure of the forecast errors (79) is reflected in a Wishart prior for $\mathbf{\Sigma}^{-1}$ with v degrees of freedom and covariance matrix $\mathbf{\Sigma}_0 = \mathbf{\Sigma}_{\varepsilon 0} + \sigma_{\eta 0}^2\boldsymbol{\iota\iota}'$ (with known parameters v, $\boldsymbol{\Sigma}_{\varepsilon 0}$, $\sigma_{\eta 0}^2$):

$$P(\boldsymbol{\Sigma}^{-1}) \propto |\boldsymbol{\Sigma}^{-1}|^{(v-N-1)/2}|\boldsymbol{\Sigma}_0^{-1}|^{-v/2}\exp\left(-\frac{1}{2}\mathrm{tr}(\boldsymbol{\Sigma}_0\boldsymbol{\Sigma}^{-1})\right).$$

Assuming a sample of T observations and a likelihood function

$$L(\boldsymbol{\theta}, \boldsymbol{\Sigma}^{-1}|\mathcal{F}_T) \propto |\boldsymbol{\Sigma}^{-1}|^{-T/2}\exp\left(-\frac{1}{2}\mathrm{tr}(\mathbf{S}\boldsymbol{\Sigma}^{-1}) - \frac{1}{2}\mathrm{tr}((\boldsymbol{\theta}-\hat{\boldsymbol{\theta}})\boldsymbol{\iota}'\boldsymbol{\iota}(\boldsymbol{\theta}-\hat{\boldsymbol{\theta}})'\boldsymbol{\Sigma}^{-1})\right),$$

where $\hat{\boldsymbol{\theta}} = (\boldsymbol{\iota}'\boldsymbol{\iota})^{-1}\boldsymbol{\iota}'\mathbf{Y}$ and $\mathbf{S} = (\mathbf{Y}-\boldsymbol{\iota}\hat{\boldsymbol{\theta}}')'(\mathbf{Y}-\boldsymbol{\iota}\hat{\boldsymbol{\theta}}')$, Palm and Zellner derive the predictive distribution function of y_{T+1} given $\mathcal{F}_T$:

$$P(y_{T+1}|\mathcal{F}_T) \propto \left[1 + (y_{T+1} - \bar{\mu})^2/(T-1)s^{**2}\right]^{-(T+v)/2},$$

where $\bar{\mu} = \boldsymbol{\iota}'\bar{\mathbf{S}}^{-1}\hat{\boldsymbol{\mu}}/\boldsymbol{\iota}'\bar{\mathbf{S}}^{-1}\boldsymbol{\iota}$, $s^{**2} = [T+1+T(\bar{\mu}\boldsymbol{\iota}-\hat{\boldsymbol{\mu}})'\bar{\mathbf{S}}^{-1}(\bar{\mu}\boldsymbol{\iota}-\hat{\boldsymbol{\mu}})]/(T(T-1)\boldsymbol{\iota}'\bar{\mathbf{S}}^{-1}\boldsymbol{\iota})$, $\hat{\boldsymbol{\mu}} = \hat{y}_{T+1} - \hat{\boldsymbol{\theta}}$ and $\bar{\mathbf{S}} = \mathbf{S} + \boldsymbol{\Sigma}_0$. This approach provides a complete solution to the forecast combination problem that accounts for the joint distribution of forecast errors from the individual models.

6.3.1. Bayesian model averaging

Bayesian Model Averaging methods have been proposed by, inter alia, Leamer (1978), Raftery, Madigan and Hoeting (1997) and Hoeting et al. (1999) and are increasingly used in empirical studies, see, e.g., Jackson and Karlsson (2004). Under this approach, the predictive density can be computed by averaging over a set of models, $i = 1, \ldots, N$, each characterized by parameters $\boldsymbol{\theta}_i$:

$$f(y_{t+h}|\mathcal{F}_t) = \sum_{i=1}^{N} \Pr(M_i|\mathcal{F}_t) f_i(y_{t+h}, \boldsymbol{\theta}_i|\mathcal{F}_t), \tag{80}$$

where $\Pr(M_i|\mathcal{F}_t)$ is the posterior probability of model M_i obtained from the model priors $\Pr(M_i)$, the priors for the unknown parameters, $\Pr(\boldsymbol{\theta}_i|M_i)$, and the likelihood functions of the models under consideration. $f_i(y_{t+h}, \boldsymbol{\theta}_i|\mathcal{F}_t)$ is the density of y_{t+h} and $\boldsymbol{\theta}_i$ under the ith model, given information at time t, $\mathcal{F}_t$. Note that unlike the combination weights used for point forecasts such as (12), these weights do not account for correlations between forecasts. However, the approach is quite general and does not require the use of conjugate families of distributions. More details are provided in the Handbook Chapter 1 by Geweke and Whitemann (2006).

6.4. Combinations of quantile forecasts

Combinations of quantile forecasts do not pose any new issues except for the fact that the associated loss function used to combine quantiles is typically no longer continuous and differentiable. Instead predictions of the αth quantile can be related to the 'tick' loss function

$$L_\alpha(e_{t+h,t}) = (\alpha - 1_{e_{t+h,t}<0})e_{t+h,t},$$

where $1_{e_{t+h,t}<0}$ is an indicator function taking a value of unity if $e_{t+h,t} < 0$, and is otherwise zero, cf. Giacomini and Komunjer (2005). Given a set of quantile forecasts $q_{t+h,t,1}, \ldots, q_{t+h,t,N}$, quantile forecast combinations can then be based on formulas such as

$$q^c_{t+h,t} = \sum_{i=1}^{N} \omega_i q_{t+h,t,i},$$

possibly subject to constraints such as $\sum_{i=1}^{N} \omega_i = 1$.

More caution should be exercised when forming combinations of interval forecasts. Suppose that we have N interval forecasts each taking the form of a lower and an upper limit $\{l_{t+h,t,i}; u_{t+h,t,i}\}$. While weighted averages $\{\bar{l}^c_{t+h,t,i}; \bar{u}^c_{t+h,t,i}\}$

$$\begin{aligned} \bar{l}^c_{t+h,t,i} &= \sum_{i=1}^{N} \omega^l_{t+h,t,i} l_{t+h,t,i}, \\ \bar{u}^c_{t+h,t,i} &= \sum_{i=1}^{N} \omega^u_{t+h,t,i} u_{t+h,t,i} \end{aligned} \tag{81}$$

may seem natural, they are not guaranteed to provide correct coverage rates. To see this, consider the following two 97% confidence intervals for a normal mean:

$$\left[\bar{y} - 2.58\frac{\sigma}{T}, \bar{y} + 1.96\frac{\sigma}{T}\right],$$
$$\left[\bar{y} - 1.96\frac{\sigma}{T}, \bar{y} + 2.58\frac{\sigma}{T}\right].$$

The average of these confidence intervals, $[\bar{y} - 2.27\frac{\sigma}{T}, \bar{y} + 2.27\frac{\sigma}{T}]$ has a coverage of 97.7%. Combining confidence intervals may thus change the coverage rate.[14] The problem here is that the underlying end-points for the two forecasts (i.e. $\bar{y} - 2.58\frac{\sigma}{T}$ and $\bar{y} - 1.96\frac{\sigma}{T}$) are not estimates of the same quantiles. While it is natural to combine estimates of the same α-quantile, it is less obvious that combination of forecast intervals makes much sense unless one can be assured that the end-points are lined up and are estimates of the same quantiles.

[14] I am grateful to Mark Watson for suggesting this example.

7. Empirical evidence

The empirical literature on forecast combinations is voluminous and includes work in several areas such as management science, economics, operations research, meteorology, psychology and finance. The work in economics dates back to Reid (1968) and Bates and Granger (1969). Although details and results vary across studies, it is possible to extract some broad conclusions from much of this work. Such conclusions come with a stronger than usual caveat emptor since for each point it is possible to construct counter examples. This is necessarily the case since findings depend on the number of models, N (as well as their type), the sample size, T, the extent of instability in the underlying data set and the structure of the covariance matrix of the forecast errors (e.g., diagonal or with similar correlations).

Nevertheless, empirical findings in the literature on forecast combinations broadly suggest that (i) simple combination schemes are difficult to beat. This is often explained by the importance of parameter estimation error in the combination weights. Consequently, methods aimed at reducing such errors (such as shrinkage or combination methods that ignore correlations between forecasts) tend to perform well; (ii) forecasts based exclusively on the model with the best in-sample performance often leads to poor out-of-sample forecasting performance; (iii) trimming of the worst models and clustering of models with similar forecasting performance prior to combination can yield considerable improvements in forecasting performance, especially in situations involving large numbers of forecasts; (iv) shrinkage to simple forecast combination weights often improves performance; and (v) some time-variation or adaptive adjustment in the combination weights (or perhaps in the underlying models being combined) can often improve forecasting performance. In the following we discuss each of these points in more detail. The section finishes with a brief empirical application to a large macroeconomic data set from the G7 economies.

7.1. Simple combination schemes are hard to beat

It has often been found that simple combinations – that is, combinations that do not require estimating many parameters such as arithmetic averages or weights based on the inverse mean squared forecast error – do better than more sophisticated rules relying on estimating optimal weights that depend on the full variance-covariance matrix of forecast errors, cf. Bunn (1985), Clemen and Winkler (1986), Dunis, Laws and Chauvin (2001), Figlewski and Urich (1983) and Makridakis and Winkler (1983).

Palm and Zellner (1992, p. 699) concisely summarize the advantages of adopting a simple average forecast:

"1. Its weights are known and do not have to be estimated, an important advantage if there is little evidence on the performance of individual forecasts or if the parameters of the model generating the forecasts are time-varying;

2. In many situations a simple average of forecasts will achieve a substantial reduction in variance and bias through averaging out individual bias;

3. It will often dominate, in terms of MSE, forecasts based on optimal weighting if proper account is taken of the effect of sampling errors and model uncertainty on the estimates of the weights."

Despite the impressive empirical track record of equal-weighted forecast combinations we stress that the theoretical justification for this method critically depends on the ratio of forecast error variances not being too far away from unity. They also depend on the correlation between forecast errors not varying too much across pairs of models. Consistent with this, Gupta and Wilton (1987) find that the performance of equal weighted combinations depends strongly on the relative size of the variance of the forecast errors associated with different forecasting methods. When these are similar, equal weights perform well, while when larger differences are observed, differential weighting of forecasts is generally required.

Another reason for the good average performance of equal-weighted forecast combinations is related to model instability. If model instability is sufficiently important to render precise estimation of combination weights nearly impossible, equal-weighting of forecasts may become an attractive alternative as pointed out by Figlewski and Urich (1983), Clemen and Winkler (1986), Kang (1986), Diebold and Pauly (1987) and Palm and Zellner (1992).

Results regarding the performance of equal-weighted forecast combinations may be sensitive to the loss function underlying the problem. Elliott and Timmermann (2005) find in an empirical application that the optimal weights in a combination of inflation survey forecasts and forecasts from a simple autoregressive model strongly depend on the degree of asymmetry in the loss function. In the absence of loss asymmetry, the autoregressive forecast does not add much information. However, under asymmetric loss (in either direction), both sets of forecasts appear to contain information and have non-zero weights in the combined forecast. Their application confirms the frequent finding that equal-weights outperform estimated optimal weights under MSE loss. However, it also shows very clearly that this result can be overturned under asymmetric loss where use of estimated optimal weights may lead to smaller average losses out-of-sample.

7.2. Choosing the single forecast with the best track record is often a bad idea

Many studies have found that combination dominates the best individual forecast in out-of-sample forecasting experiments. For example, Makridakis et al. (1982) report that a simple average of six forecasting methods performed better than the underlying individual forecasts. In simulation experiments Gupta and Wilton (1987) also find combination superior to the single best forecast. Makridakis and Winkler (1983) report large gains from simply averaging forecasts from individual models over the performance of the best model. Hendry and Clements (2002) explain the better performance of combination methods over the best individual model by misspecification of the models caused by deterministic shifts in the underlying data generating process. Naturally, the models cannot be misspecified in the same way with regard to this source of change, or else diversification gains would be zero.

In one of the most comprehensive studies to date, Stock and Watson (2001) consider combinations of a range of linear and nonlinear models fitted to a very large set of US macroeconomic variables. They find strong evidence in support of using forecast combination methods, particularly the average or median forecast and the forecasts weighted by their inverse MSE. The overall dominance of the combination forecasts holds at the one, six and twelve month horizons. Furthermore, the best combination methods combine forecasts across many different time-series models.

Similarly, in a time-series simulation experiment, Winkler and Makridakis (1983) find that a weighted average with weights inversely proportional to the sum of squared errors or a weighted average with weights that depend on the exponentially discounted sum of squared errors perform better than the best individual forecasting model, equal-weighting or methods that require estimation of the full covariance matrix for the forecast errors.

Aiolfi and Timmermann (2006) find evidence of persistence in the out-of-sample performance of linear and nonlinear forecasting models fitted to a large set of macroeconomic time-series in the G7 countries. Models that were in the top and bottom quartiles when ranked by their historical forecasting performance have a higher than average chance of remaining in the top and bottom quartiles, respectively, in the out-of-sample period. They also find systematic evidence of 'crossings', where the previous best models become the worst models in the future or vice versa, particularly among the linear forecasting models. They find that many forecast combinations produce lower out-of-sample MSE than a strategy of selecting the previous best forecasting model irrespective of the length of the backward-looking window used to measure past forecasting performance.

7.3. Trimming of the worst models often improves performance

Trimming of forecasts can occur at two levels. First, it can be adopted as a form of outlier reduction rule [cf. Chan, Stock and Watson (1999)] at the initial stage that produces forecasts from the individual models. Second it can be used in the combination stage where models deemed to be too poor may be discarded. Since the first form of trimming has more to do with specification of the individual models underlying the forecast combination, we concentrate on the latter form of trimming which has been used successfully in many studies. Most obviously, when many forecasts get a weight close to zero, improvements due to reduced parameter estimation errors can be gained by dropping such models.

Winkler and Makridakis (1983) find that including very poor models in an equal-weighted combination can substantially worsen forecasting performance. Stock and Watson (2004) also find that the simplest forecast combination methods such as trimmed equal weights and slowly moving weights tend to perform well and that such combinations do better than forecasts from a dynamic factor model.

In their thick modeling approach, Granger and Jeon (2004) recommend trimming five or ten percent of the worst models, although the extent of the trimming will depend on the application at hand.

More aggressive trimming has also been proposed. In a forecasting experiment involving the prediction of stock returns by means of a large set of forecasting models, Aiolfi and Favero (2005) investigate the performance of a large set of trimming schemes. Their findings indicate that the best performance is obtained when the top 20% of the forecasting models is combined in the forecast so that 80% of the models (ranked by their R^2-value) are trimmed.

7.4. Shrinkage often improves performance

By and large shrinkage methods have performed quite well in empirical studies. In an empirical exercise containing four real-time forecasts of nominal and real GNP, Diebold and Pauly (1990) report that shrinkage weights systematically improve upon the forecasting performance over methods that select a single forecast or use least squares estimates of the combination weights. They direct the shrinkage towards a prior reflecting equal weights and find that the optimal degree of shrinkage tends to be large. Similarly, Stock and Watson (2004) find that shrinkage methods perform best when the degree of shrinkage (towards equal weights) is quite strong.

Aiolfi and Timmermann (2006) explore persistence in the performance of forecasting models by proposing a set of combination strategies that first pre-select models into either quartiles or clusters on the basis of the distribution of past forecasting performance across models. Then they pool forecasts within each cluster and estimate optimal combination weights that are shrunk towards equal weights. These conditional combination strategies lead to better average forecasting performance than simpler strategies in common use such as using the single best model or averaging across all forecasting models or a small subset of these.

Elliott (2004) undertakes a simulation experiment where he finds that although shrinkage methods always dominate least squares estimates of the combination weights, the performance of the shrinkage method can be quite sensitive to the shrinkage parameter and that none of the standard methods for determining this parameter work particularly well.

Given the similarity of the mean-variance optimization problem in finance to the forecast combination problem, it is not surprising that empirical findings in finance mirror those in the forecast combination literature. For example, it has generally been found in applications to asset returns that sample estimates of portfolio weights that solve a standard mean-variance optimization problem are extremely sensitive to small changes in sample means. In addition they are highly sensitive to variations in the inverse of the covariance matrix estimate, $\hat{\boldsymbol{\Sigma}}^{-1}$.

Jobson and Korkie (1980) show that the sample estimate of the optimal portfolio weights can be characterized as the ratio of two estimators, each of whose first and second moments can be derived in closed form. They use Taylor series expansions to derive an approximate solution for the first two moments of the optimal weights, noting that higher order moments can be characterized under additional normality assumptions. They also derive the asymptotic distribution of the portfolio weights for the case where N is fixed and T goes to infinity. In simulation experiments they demonstrate that the sample estimates of the portfolio weights are highly volatile and can take extreme values that lead to poor out-of-sample performance.

It is widely recognized in finance that imposing portfolio weight constraints generally leads to improved out-of-sample performance of mean-variance efficient portfolios. For example, Jaganathan and Ma (2003) find empirically that once such constraints are imposed on portfolio weights, other refinements of covariance matrix estimation have little additional effect on the variance of the optimal portfolio. Since they also demonstrate that portfolio weight constraints can be interpreted as a form of shrinkage, these findings lend support to using shrinkage methods as well.

Similarly, Ledoit and Wolf (2003) report that the out-of-sample standard deviation of portfolio returns based on a shrunk covariance matrix is significantly lower than the standard deviation of portfolio returns based on more conventional estimates of the covariance matrix.

Notice that shrinkage and trimming tend to work in opposite directions – at least if the shrinkage is towards equal weights. Shrinkage tends to give more similar weights to all models whereas trimming completely discards a subset of models. If some models produce extremely poor out-of-sample forecasts, shrinkage can be expected to perform poorly if the combined forecast is shrunk too aggressively towards an equal-weighted average. For this reason, shrinkage preceded by a trimming step may work well in many situations.

7.5. Limited time-variation in the combination weights may be helpful

Empirical evidence on the value of allowing for time-varying combinations in the combination weights is somewhat mixed. Time-variations in forecasts can be introduced either in the individual models underlying the combination or in the combination weights themselves and both approaches have been considered. The idea of time-varying forecast combinations goes back to the advent of the combination literature in economics. Bates and Granger (1969) used combination weights that were adaptively updated as did many subsequent studies such as Winkler and Makridakis (1983). Newbold and Granger (1974) considered values of the window length, v, in (47) and (48) between one and twelve periods and values of the discounting factor, λ, in (50) and (51) between 1 and 2.5. Their results suggested that there is an interior optimum around $v = 6, \alpha = 0.5$ for which the adaptive updating method (49) performs best whereas the rolling window combinations generally do best for the longest windows, i.e., $v = 9$ or $v = 12$, and the best exponential discounting was found for λ around 2 or 2.5. This is consistent with the finding by Bates and Granger (1969) that high values of the discounting factor tend to work best. A method that combines a Holt–Winters and stepwise autoregressive forecast was found to perform particularly well. Winkler and Makridakis (1983) report similar results and also find that the longer windows, v, in equations such as (47) and (48) tend to produce the most accurate forecasts, although in their study the best results among the discounting methods were found for relatively low values of the discount factor.

In a combination of forecasts from the Survey of Professional Forecasters and forecasts from simple autoregressive models applied to six macroeconomic variables, Elliott and Timmermann (2005) investigate the out-of-sample forecasting performance produced by different constant and time-varying forecasting schemes such as (57). Compared to a range of other time-varying forecast combination methods, a two-state regime switching method produces a lower MSE-value for four or five out of six cases. They argue that the evidence suggests that the best forecast combination method allows the combination weights to vary over time but in a mean-reverting manner. Unsurprisingly, allowing for three states leads to worse forecasting performance for four of the six variables under consideration.

Stock and Watson (2004) report that the combined forecasts that perform best in their study are the time-varying parameter (TVP) forecast with very little time variation, the simple mean and a trimmed mean. They conclude that "the results for the methods designed to handle time variation are mixed. The TVP forecasts sometimes work well but sometimes work quite poorly and in this sense are not robust; the larger the amount of time variation, the less robust are the forecasts. Similarly, the discounted MSE forecasts with the most discounting ... are typically no better than, and sometimes worse than, their counterparts with less or no discounting."

This leads them to conclude that "This "forecast combination puzzle" – the repeated finding that simple combination forecasts outperform sophisticated adaptive combination methods in empirical applications – is, we think, more likely to be understood in the context of a model in which there is widespread instability in the performance of individual forecast, but the instability is sufficiently idiosyncratic that the combination of these individually unstably performing forecasts can itself be stable."

7.6. Empirical application

To demonstrate the practical use of forecast combination techniques, we consider an empirical application to the seven-country data set introduced in Stock and Watson (2004). This data comprises up to 43 quarterly time series for each of the G7 economies (Canada, France, Germany, Italy, Japan, UK, and the US) over the period 1959Q1–1999Q4. Observations on some variables are only available for a shorter sample. The 43 series comprise the following categories: Asset returns, interest rates and spreads; measures of real economic activity; prices and wages; and various monetary aggregates. The data has been transformed as described in Stock and Watson (2004) and Aiolfi and Timmermann (2006) to deal with seasonality, outliers and stochastic trends, yielding between 46 and 71 series per country.

Forecasts are generated from bivariate autoregressive models of the type

$$y_{t+h} = c + A(L)y_t + B(L)x_t + \epsilon_{t+h}, \tag{82}$$

where x_t is a regressor other than y_t. Lag lengths are selected recursively using the BIC with between 1 and 4 lags of x_t and between 0 and 4 lags of y_t. All parameters are estimated recursively using an expanding data window. For more details, see Aiolfi and Timmermann (2006). The average number of forecasting models entertained ranges from 36 for France, through 67 for the US.

We consider three trimmed forecast combination schemes that take simple averages over the top 25%, top 50% and top 75% of forecast models ranked recursively by means of their forecasting performance up to the point in time where a new out-of-sample forecast gets computed. In addition we report the performance of the simple average (mean) forecast, the median forecast, the triangular forecast combination scheme (38) and the discounted mean squared forecast combination (50) with $\lambda = 1$ so the forecasting models get weighted by the inverse of their MSE-values. Out-of-sample forecasting performance is reported relative to the forecasting performance of the previous best (PB) model selected according to the forecasting performance up to the point where a new out-of-sample forecast is generated. Numbers below one indicate better MSE performance while numbers above one indicate worse performance relative to this benchmark. The out-of-sample period is 1970Q1–1999Q4.

Table 2 reports results averaged across variables within each country.[15] We show results for four forecast horizons, namely $h = 1, 2, 4$ and 8. For each country it is clear that simple trimmed forecast combinations perform very well and generally are better, the fewer models that get included, i.e. the more aggressive the trimming. Furthermore, gains can be quite large – on the order of 10–15% relative to the forecast from the previous best model. The median forecast also performs better on average than the previous best model, but is generally worse compared to some of the other combination schemes as is the discounted mean squared forecast error weighting scheme. Results are quite consistent across the seven countries.

Table 3 shows results averaged across countries but for the separate categories of variables. Gains from forecast combination tend to be greater for the economic activity variables and somewhat smaller for the monetary aggregates. There is also a systematic tendency for the forecasting performance of the combinations relative to the best single model to improve as the forecast horizon is extended from one-quarter to two or more quarters.

How consistent are these results across countries and variables? To investigate this question, Tables 4, 5 and 6 show disaggregate results for the US, Japan and France. Considerable variations in gains from forecast combinations emerge across countries, variables and horizons. Table 4 shows that gains in the US are very large for the economic activity variables but somewhat smaller for asset returns, interest rates and monetary aggregates. Compared to the US results, in Japan the best combinations perform relatively worse for economic activity variables and prices and wages but relatively better for the monetary aggregates, asset returns and interest rates. Finally in the case of

[15] I am grateful to Marco Aiolfi for carrying out these calculations.

Table 2

Linear Models. Out-of-sample forecasting performance of combination schemes applied to linear models. Each panel reports the out-of-sample MSFE – relative to that of the previous best (PB) model using an expanding window – averaged across variables, for different combination strategies, countries and forecast horizons (h).

	$h = 1$							
	TMB25%	TMB50%	TMB75%	Mean	Median	TK	DMSFE	PB
US	0.88	0.89	0.90	0.90	0.93	0.90	0.91	1.00
UK	0.91	0.91	0.92	0.92	0.93	0.91	0.92	1.00
Germany	0.92	0.93	0.93	0.92	0.95	0.92	0.92	1.00
Japan	0.93	0.94	0.94	0.94	0.97	0.94	0.94	1.00
Italy	0.90	0.90	0.91	0.91	0.93	0.90	0.91	1.00
France	0.93	0.93	0.94	0.94	0.96	0.93	0.94	1.00
Canada	0.91	0.91	0.92	0.92	0.94	0.91	0.92	1.00
	$h = 2$							
	TMB25%	TMB50%	TMB75%	Mean	Median	TK	DMSFE	PB
US	0.85	0.86	0.86	0.86	0.88	0.86	0.86	1.00
UK	0.90	0.90	0.90	0.91	0.92	0.90	0.91	1.00
Germany	0.90	0.90	0.91	0.91	0.93	0.90	0.91	1.00
Japan	0.90	0.91	0.92	0.92	0.94	0.91	0.92	1.00
Italy	0.89	0.89	0.89	0.89	0.90	0.89	0.89	1.00
France	0.88	0.88	0.88	0.88	0.89	0.88	0.88	1.00
Canada	0.90	0.90	0.91	0.90	0.94	0.90	0.90	1.00
	$h = 4$							
	TMB25%	TMB50%	TMB75%	Mean	Median	TK	DMSFE	PB
US	0.87	0.87	0.87	0.87	0.90	0.87	0.87	1.00
UK	0.86	0.86	0.86	0.86	0.87	0.86	0.86	1.00
Germany	0.90	0.90	0.91	0.91	0.92	0.90	0.91	1.00
Japan	0.91	0.93	0.95	0.96	0.98	0.94	0.97	1.00
Italy	0.86	0.85	0.85	0.85	0.86	0.85	0.85	1.00
France	0.88	0.88	0.88	0.88	0.89	0.88	0.88	1.00
Canada	0.85	0.85	0.86	0.86	0.88	0.85	0.86	1.00
	$h = 8$							
	TMB25%	TMB50%	TMB75%	Mean	Median	TK	DMSFE	PB
US	0.85	0.85	0.86	0.86	0.88	0.85	0.86	1.00
UK	0.88	0.88	0.89	0.89	0.91	0.88	0.89	1.00
Germany	0.90	0.91	0.91	0.91	0.92	0.90	0.91	1.00
Japan	0.85	0.85	0.85	0.85	0.86	0.85	0.85	1.00
Italy	0.89	0.89	0.90	0.90	0.91	0.89	0.90	1.00
France	0.90	0.90	0.90	0.90	0.92	0.90	0.90	1.00
Canada	0.86	0.87	0.87	0.87	0.88	0.86	0.86	1.00

Note: TMB25%, TMB50% and TMB75% use the mean forecast computed across the top 25%, 50% and 75% of models ranked by historical forecasting performance. Mean and median use the mean or median forecast across all models. TK is the forecast from a triangular weighting scheme (38), while DMSFE is the forecast produced by the discounted mean squared forecast error scheme in (50).

Table 3

Linear Models. Out-of-sample forecasting performance of combination schemes applied to linear models. Each panel reports the out-of-sample MSFE – relative to that of the previous best model using an expanding window – averaged across countries, for different combination strategies, categories of economic variables and forecast horizons (h).

	All							
	TMB25%	TMB50%	TMB75%	Mean	Median	TK	DMSFE	PB
$h=1$	0.91	0.92	0.92	0.92	0.94	0.92	0.92	1.00
$h=2$	0.89	0.89	0.89	0.89	0.91	0.89	0.90	1.00
$h=4$	0.88	0.88	0.88	0.88	0.90	0.88	0.89	1.00
$h=8$	0.87	0.88	0.88	0.88	0.90	0.88	0.88	1.00
	Returns and interest rates							
	TMB25%	TMB50%	TMB75%	Mean	Median	TK	DMSFE	PB
$h=1$	0.92	0.92	0.92	0.92	0.94	0.92	0.92	1.00
$h=2$	0.89	0.90	0.90	0.90	0.91	0.90	0.90	1.00
$h=4$	0.88	0.89	0.89	0.89	0.91	0.88	0.89	1.00
$h=8$	0.87	0.87	0.87	0.87	0.89	0.87	0.87	1.00
	Economic activity							
	TMB25%	TMB50%	TMB75%	Mean	Median	TK	DMSFE	PB
$h=1$	0.89	0.91	0.92	0.93	0.95	0.91	0.93	1.00
$h=2$	0.86	0.88	0.89	0.89	0.93	0.88	0.90	1.00
$h=4$	0.85	0.88	0.89	0.89	0.93	0.88	0.90	1.00
$h=8$	0.87	0.89	0.90	0.91	0.95	0.89	0.90	1.00
	Prices and wages							
	TMB25%	TMB50%	TMB75%	Mean	Median	TK	DMSFE	PB
$h=1$	0.90	0.91	0.91	0.91	0.93	0.91	0.91	1.00
$h=2$	0.89	0.89	0.89	0.89	0.91	0.89	0.89	1.00
$h=4$	0.86	0.86	0.87	0.87	0.88	0.86	0.87	1.00
$h=8$	0.87	0.86	0.86	0.86	0.88	0.86	0.86	1.00
	Monetary aggregates							
	TMB25%	TMB50%	TMB75%	Mean	Median	TK	DMSFE	PB
$h=1$	0.91	0.92	0.93	0.93	0.96	0.92	0.93	1.00
$h=2$	0.89	0.89	0.89	0.89	0.90	0.89	0.89	1.00
$h=4$	0.90	0.90	0.90	0.89	0.90	0.89	0.89	1.00
$h=8$	0.90	0.90	0.90	0.90	0.91	0.90	0.90	1.00

Note: see note of Table 2.

Table 4

Linear models US. Out-of-sample forecasting performance of combination schemes applied to linear models. Each panel reports the out-of-sample MSFE – relative to that of the previous best model using an expanding window – averaged across variables, for different combination strategies, categories of economic variables and forecast horizons (h).

	TMB25%	TMB50%	TMB75%	Mean	Median	TK	DMSFE	PB
				All				
$h = 1$	0.88	0.89	0.90	0.90	0.93	0.90	0.91	1.00
$h = 2$	0.85	0.86	0.86	0.86	0.88	0.86	0.86	1.00
$h = 4$	0.87	0.87	0.87	0.87	0.90	0.87	0.87	1.00
$h = 8$	0.85	0.85	0.86	0.86	0.88	0.85	0.86	1.00
				Returns and interest rates				
	TMB25%	TMB50%	TMB75%	Mean	Median	TK	DMSFE	PB
$h = 1$	0.89	0.89	0.89	0.89	0.91	0.89	0.89	1.00
$h = 2$	0.87	0.87	0.88	0.88	0.90	0.87	0.88	1.00
$h = 4$	0.90	0.90	0.90	0.90	0.92	0.90	0.90	1.00
$h = 8$	0.86	0.86	0.86	0.86	0.87	0.86	0.86	1.00
				Economic activity				
	TMB25%	TMB50%	TMB75%	Mean	Median	TK	DMSFE	PB
$h = 1$	0.86	0.90	0.91	0.92	0.94	0.90	0.92	1.00
$h = 2$	0.77	0.80	0.81	0.82	0.87	0.80	0.82	1.00
$h = 4$	0.80	0.83	0.84	0.84	0.90	0.83	0.84	1.00
$h = 8$	0.82	0.86	0.88	0.90	0.98	0.86	0.88	1.00
				Prices and wages				
	TMB25%	TMB50%	TMB75%	Mean	Median	TK	DMSFE	PB
$h = 1$	0.86	0.86	0.87	0.87	0.90	0.86	0.87	1.00
$h = 2$	0.84	0.85	0.84	0.85	0.86	0.84	0.85	1.00
$h = 4$	0.83	0.83	0.83	0.82	0.83	0.83	0.82	1.00
$h = 8$	0.80	0.79	0.79	0.79	0.81	0.79	0.79	1.00
				Monetary aggregates				
	TMB25%	TMB50%	TMB75%	Mean	Median	TK	DMSFE	PB
$h = 1$	0.92	0.95	0.97	0.98	1.03	0.96	0.98	1.00
$h = 2$	0.88	0.88	0.87	0.87	0.88	0.87	0.88	1.00
$h = 4$	0.87	0.88	0.88	0.88	0.90	0.88	0.88	1.00
$h = 8$	0.93	0.92	0.93	0.93	0.94	0.92	0.93	1.00

Note: see note of Table 2.

Table 5

Linear models: Japan. Out-of-sample forecasting performance of combination schemes applied to linear models. Each panel reports the out-of-sample MSFE – relative to that of the previous best model using an expanding window – averaged across variables, for different combination strategies, categories of economic variables and forecast horizons (h).

	All							
	TMB25%	TMB50%	TMB75%	Mean	Median	TK	DMSFE	PB
$h=1$	0.93	0.94	0.94	0.94	0.97	0.94	0.94	1.00
$h=2$	0.90	0.91	0.92	0.92	0.94	0.91	0.92	1.00
$h=4$	0.91	0.93	0.95	0.96	0.98	0.94	0.97	1.00
$h=8$	0.85	0.85	0.85	0.85	0.86	0.85	0.85	1.00
	Returns and interest rates							
	TMB25%	TMB50%	TMB75%	Mean	Median	TK	DMSFE	PB
$h=1$	0.94	0.95	0.96	0.96	1.00	0.95	0.96	1.00
$h=2$	0.92	0.93	0.93	0.93	0.95	0.93	0.94	1.00
$h=4$	0.91	0.93	0.94	0.95	0.98	0.93	0.96	1.00
$h=8$	0.81	0.81	0.82	0.82	0.83	0.81	0.82	1.00
	Economic activity							
	TMB25%	TMB50%	TMB75%	Mean	Median	TK	DMSFE	PB
$h=1$	0.97	0.99	1.00	1.00	1.02	0.99	1.00	1.00
$h=2$	0.91	0.93	0.94	0.95	0.96	0.93	0.95	1.00
$h=4$	0.99	1.00	1.03	1.05	1.06	1.01	1.06	1.00
$h=8$	0.89	0.88	0.88	0.89	0.89	0.88	0.88	1.00
	Prices and wages							
	TMB25%	TMB50%	TMB75%	Mean	Median	TK	DMSFE	PB
$h=1$	0.90	0.92	0.93	0.92	0.94	0.92	0.92	1.00
$h=2$	0.91	0.93	0.93	0.93	0.97	0.92	0.93	1.00
$h=4$	0.90	0.95	0.98	0.99	1.03	0.96	1.00	1.00
$h=8$	0.90	0.90	0.89	0.89	0.91	0.89	0.90	1.00
	Monetary aggregates							
	TMB25%	TMB50%	TMB75%	Mean	Median	TK	DMSFE	PB
$h=1$	0.89	0.90	0.89	0.89	0.91	0.89	0.89	1.00
$h=2$	0.85	0.85	0.85	0.85	0.86	0.85	0.85	1.00
$h=4$	0.87	0.87	0.87	0.87	0.88	0.87	0.86	1.00
$h=8$	0.84	0.83	0.83	0.83	0.83	0.83	0.83	1.00

Note: see note of Table 2.

Table 6

Linear models: France. Out-of-sample forecasting performance of combination schemes applied to linear models. Each panel reports the out-of-sample MSFE – relative to that of the previous best model using an expanding window – averaged across variables, for different combination strategies, categories of economic variables and forecast horizons (h).

	All							
	TMB25%	TMB50%	TMB75%	Mean	Median	TK	DMSFE	PB
$h=1$	0.93	0.93	0.94	0.94	0.96	0.93	0.94	1.00
$h=2$	0.88	0.88	0.88	0.88	0.89	0.88	0.88	1.00
$h=4$	0.88	0.88	0.88	0.88	0.89	0.88	0.88	1.00
$h=8$	0.90	0.90	0.90	0.90	0.92	0.90	0.90	1.00
	Returns and interest rates							
	TMB25%	TMB50%	TMB75%	Mean	Median	TK	DMSFE	PB
$h=1$	0.94	0.94	0.95	0.94	0.97	0.94	0.95	1.00
$h=2$	0.89	0.89	0.89	0.89	0.89	0.89	0.89	1.00
$h=4$	0.89	0.89	0.89	0.89	0.90	0.89	0.89	1.00
$h=8$	0.89	0.89	0.90	0.89	0.91	0.89	0.90	1.00
	Economic activity							
	TMB25%	TMB50%	TMB75%	Mean	Median	TK	DMSFE	PB
$h=1$	0.80	0.80	0.81	0.82	0.85	0.80	0.83	1.00
$h=2$	0.75	0.76	0.77	0.77	0.79	0.76	0.77	1.00
$h=4$	0.78	0.77	0.77	0.78	0.78	0.77	0.77	1.00
$h=8$	0.84	0.84	0.84	0.84	0.86	0.83	0.84	1.00
	Prices and wages							
	TMB25%	TMB50%	TMB75%	Mean	Median	TK	DMSFE	PB
$h=1$	0.96	0.96	0.96	0.97	0.98	0.96	0.97	1.00
$h=2$	0.90	0.90	0.91	0.90	0.92	0.90	0.90	1.00
$h=4$	0.86	0.85	0.85	0.85	0.86	0.85	0.85	1.00
$h=8$	0.91	0.90	0.90	0.91	0.93	0.90	0.91	1.00
	Monetary aggregates							
	TMB25%	TMB50%	TMB75%	Mean	Median	TK	DMSFE	PB
$h=1$	0.88	0.89	0.91	0.91	0.94	0.90	0.91	1.00
$h=2$	0.85	0.86	0.86	0.87	0.90	0.86	0.87	1.00
$h=4$	1.06	1.07	1.08	1.09	1.11	1.07	1.09	1.00
$h=8$	0.99	1.01	1.01	1.01	1.05	1.00	1.01	1.00

Note: see note of Table 2.

France, we uncover a number of cases where, for the forecasts of monetary aggregates, in fact none of the combinations beat the previous best model.

8. Conclusion

In his classical survey of forecast combinations, Clemen (1989, p. 567) concluded that "Combining forecasts has been shown to be practical, economical and useful. Underlying theory has been developed, and many empirical tests have demonstrated the value of composite forecasting. We no longer need to justify this methodology."

In the early days of the combination literature the set of forecasts was often taken as given, but recent experiments undertaken by Stock and Watson (2001, 2004) and Marcellino (2004) let the forecast user control both the number of forecasting models as well as the types of forecasts that are being combined. This opens a whole new set of issues: is it best to combine forecasts from linear models with different regressors or is it better to combine forecasts produced by different families of models, e.g., linear and nonlinear, or maybe the same model using estimators with varying degrees of robustness? The answer to this depends of course on the type of misspecification or instability the model combination can hedge against. Unfortunately this is typically unknown so general answers are hard to come by.

Since then, combination methods have gained even more ground in the forecasting literature, largely because of the strength of the empirical evidence suggesting that these methods systematically perform better than alternatives based on forecasts from a single model. Stable, equal weights have so far been the workhorse of the combination literature and have set a benchmark that has proved surprisingly difficult to beat. This is surprising since – on theoretical grounds – one would not expect any particular combination scheme to be dominant, since the various methods incorporate restrictions on the covariance matrix that are designed to trade off bias against reduced parameter estimation error. The optimal bias can be expected to vary across applications, and the scheme that provides the best trade-off is expected to depend on the sample size, the number of forecasting models involved, the ratio of the variance of individual models' forecast errors as well as their correlations and the degree of instability in the underlying data generating process.

Current research also provides encouraging pointers towards modifications of this simple strategy that can improve forecasting. Modest time-variations in the combination weights and trimming of the worst models have generally been found to work well, as has shrinkage towards equal weights or some other target requiring the estimation of a relatively modest number of parameters, particularly in applications with combinations of a large set of forecasts.

Acknowledgements

This research was sponsored by NSF grant SES0111238. I am grateful to Marco Aiolfi, Graham Elliott and Clive Granger for many discussions on the topic. Barbara Rossi and Mark Watson provided detailed comments and suggestions that greatly improved the paper. Comments from seminar participants at the UCSD Rady School forecasting conference were also helpful.

References

Aiolfi, M., Favero, C.A. (2005). "Model uncertainty, thick modeling and the predictability of stock returns". Journal of Forecasting 24, 233–254.

Aiolfi, M., Timmermann, A. (2006). "Persistence of forecasting performance and combination strategies". Journal of Econometrics. In press.

Armstrong, J.S. (1989). "Combining forecasts: The end of the beginning or the beginning of the end". International Journal of Forecasting 5, 585–588.

Bates, J.M., Granger, C.W.J. (1969). "The combination of forecasts". Operations Research Quarterly 20, 451–468.

Bunn, D.W. (1975). "A Bayesian approach to the linear combination of forecasts". Operations Research Quarterly 26, 325–329.

Bunn, D.W. (1985). "Statistical efficiency in the linear combination of forecasts". International Journal of Forecasting 1, 151–163.

Chan, Y.L., Stock, J.H., Watson, M.W. (1999). "A dynamic factor model framework for forecast combination". Spanish Economic Review 1, 91–122.

Chong, Y.Y., Hendry, D.F. (1986). "Econometric evaluation of linear macro-economic models". Review of Economic Studies 53, 671–690.

Christoffersen, P., Diebold, F.X. (1997). "Optimal prediction under asymmetrical loss". Econometric Theory 13, 806–817.

Clemen, R.T. (1987). "Combining overlapping information". Management Science 33, 373–380.

Clemen, R.T. (1989). "Combining forecasts: A review and annotated bibliography". International Journal of Forecasting 5, 559–581.

Clemen, R.T., Murphy, A.H., Winkler, R.L. (1995). "Screening probability forecasts: Contrasts between choosing and combining". International Journal of Forecasting 11, 133–145.

Clemen, R.T., Winkler, R.L. (1986). "Combining economic forecasts". Journal of Business and Economic Statistics 4, 39–46.

Deutsch, M., Granger, C.W.J., Terasvirta, T. (1994). "The combination of forecasts using changing weights". International Journal of Forecasting 10, 47–57.

Diebold, F.X. (1988). "Serial correlation and the combination of forecasts". Journal of Business and Economic Statistics 6, 105–111.

Diebold, F.X. (1989). "Forecast combination and encompassing: Reconciling two divergent literatures". International Journal of Forecasting 5, 589–592.

Diebold, F.X., Lopez, J.A. (1996). "Forecast evaluation and combination". In: Maddala, G.S., Rao, C.R. (Eds.), Statistical Methods in Finance, Handbook of Statistics, vol. 14. Elsevier, Amsterdam, pp. 241–268.

Diebold, F.X., Pauly, P. (1987). "Structural change and the combination of forecasts". Journal of Forecasting 6, 21–40.

Diebold, F.X., Pauly, P. (1990). "The use of prior information in forecast combination". International Journal of Forecasting 6, 503–508.

Donaldson, R.G., Kamstra, M. (1996). "Forecast combining with neural networks". Journal of Forecasting 15, 49–61.

Dunis, C., Laws, J., Chauvin, S. (2001). "The use of market data and model combinations to improve forecast accuracy". In: Dunis, C., Timmermann, A., Moody, J.E. (Eds.), Development in Forecasts Combination and Portfolio Choice. Wiley, Oxford.

Dunis, C.L., Timmermann, A., Moody, J.E. (Eds.) (2001). Developments in Forecasts Combination and Portfolio Choice. Wiley, Oxford.

Elliott, G. (2004). "Forecast combination with many forecasts". Mimeo, Department of Economics, University of California, San Diego.

Elliott, G., Timmermann, A. (2004). "Optimal forecast combinations under general loss functions and forecast error distributions". Journal of Econometrics 122, 47–79.

Elliott, G., Timmermann, A. (2005). "Optimal forecast combination weights under regime switching". International Economic Review 46, 1081–1102.

Engle, R.F., Granger, C.W.J., Kraft, D. (1984). "Combining competing forecasts of inflation using a bivariate ARCH model". Journal of Economic Dynamics and Control 8, 151–165.

Figlewski, S., Urich, T. (1983). "Optimal aggregation of money supply forecasts: Accuracy, profitability and market efficiency". Journal of Finance 28, 695–710.

Genest, S., Zidek, J. (1986). "Combining probability distributions: A critique and an annotated bibliography". Statistical Science 1, 114–148.

Geweke, J., Whitemann, C. (2006). "Bayesian forecasting". In: Elliott, G., Granger, C.W.J., Timmermann, A. (Eds.), Handbook of Economic Forecasting. Elsevier, Amsterdam, pp. 3–79. Chapter 1 in this volume.

Giacomini, R., Komunjer, I. (2005). "Evaluation and combination of conditional quantile forecasts". Journal of Business and Economic Statistics 23, 416–431.

Granger, C.W.J., Jeon, Y. (2004). "Thick modeling". Economic Modelling 21, 323–343.

Granger, C.W.J., Machina, M.J. (2006). "Forecasting and decision theory". In: Elliott, G., Granger, C.W.J., Timmermann, A. (Eds.), Handbook of Economic Forecasting. Elsevier, Amsterdam, pp. 81–98. Chapter 2 in this volume.

Granger, C.W.J., Pesaran, M.H. (2000). "Economic and statistical measures of forecast accuracy". Journal of Forecasting 19, 537–560.

Granger, C.W.J., Ramanathan, R. (1984). "Improved methods of combining forecasts". Journal of Forecasting 3, 197–204.

Guidolin, M., Timmermann, A. (2005). "Optimal forecast combination weights under regime shifts with an application to US interest rates". Mimeo, Federal Reserve Bank of St. Louis and the Department of Economics, University of California, San Diego.

Gupta, S., Wilton, P.C. (1987). "Combination of forecasts: An extension". Management Science 33, 356–372.

Hamilton, J.H. (1989). "A new approach to the economic analysis of nonstationary time series and the business cycle". Econometrica 57, 357–384.

Hendry, D.F., Clements, M.P. (2002). "Pooling of forecasts". Econometrics Journal 5, 1–26.

Hoeting, J.A., Madigan, D., Raftery, A.E., Volinsky, C.T. (1999). "Bayesian model averaging: A tutorial". Statistical Science 14, 382–417.

Jackson, T., Karlsson, S. (2004). "Finding good predictors for inflation: A Bayesian model averaging approach". Journal of Forecasting 23, 479–498.

Jaganathan, R., Ma, T. (2003). "Risk reduction in large portfolios: Why imposing the wrong constraints helps". Journal of Finance 58, 1651–1684.

Jobson, J.D., Korkie, B. (1980). "Estimation for Markowitz efficient portfolios". Journal of the American Statistical Association 75, 544–554.

Kang, H. (1986). "Unstable weights in the combination of forecasts". Management Science 32, 683–695.

Leamer, E. (1978). Specification Searches. Wiley, Oxford.

Ledoit, O., Wolf, M. (2003). "Improved estimation of the covariance matrix of stock returns with an application to portfolio election". Journal of Empirical Finance 10, 603–621.

Ledoit, O., Wolf, M. (2004). "Honey, I shrunk the sample covariance matrix". Journal of Portfolio Management.

LeSage, J.P., Magura, M. (1992). "A mixture-model approach to combining forecasts". Journal of Business and Economic Statistics 10, 445–453.

Makridakis, S. (1989). "Why combining works?". International Journal of Forecasting 5, 601–603.

Makridakis, S., Hibon, M. (2000). "The M3-competition: Results, conclusions and implications". International Journal of Forecasting 16, 451–476.

Makridakis, S., Winkler, R.L. (1983). "Averages of forecasts: Some empirical results". Management Science 29, 987–996.
Makridakis, S., Andersen, A., Carbone, R., Fildes, R., Hibon, M., Lewandowski, R., Newton, J., Parzen, E., Winkler, R. (1982). "The accuracy of extrapolation (time series) methods: Results of a forecasting competition". Journal of Forecasting 1, 111–153.
Marcellino, M. (2004). "Forecast pooling for short time series of macroeconomic variables". Oxford Bulletin of Economic and Statistics 66, 91–112.
Min, C.-K., Zellner, A. (1993). "Bayesian and non-Bayesian methods for combining models and forecasts with applications to forecasting international growth rates". Journal of Econometrics 56, 89–118.
Newbold, P., Granger, C.W.J. (1974). "Experience with forecasting univariate time series and the combination of forecasts". Journal of the Royal Statistical Society Series A 137, 131–146.
Newbold, P., Harvey, D.I. (2001). "Forecast combination and encompassing". In: Clements, M.P., Hendry, D.F. (Eds.), A Companion to Economic Forecasting. Blackwell, Oxford.
Palm, F.C., Zellner, A. (1992). "To combine or not to combine? Issues of combining forecasts". Journal of Forecasting 11, 687–701.
Patton, A., Timmermann, A. (2004). "Properties of optimal forecasts under asymmetric loss and nonlinearity". Mimeo, London School of Economics and Department of Economics, University of California, San Diego.
Pesaran, M.H., Timmermann, A. (2005). "Selection of estimation window in the presence of breaks". Mimeo, Cambridge University and Department of Economics, University of California, San Diego.
Raftery, A.E., Madigan, D., Hoeting, J.A. (1997). "Bayesian model averaging for linear regression models". Journal of the American Statistical Association 92, 179–191.
Reid, D.J. (1968). "Combining three estimates of gross domestic product". Economica 35, 431–444.
Sanders, F. (1963). "On subjective probability forecasting". Journal of Applied Meteorology 2, 196–201.
Sessions, D.N., Chatterjee, S. (1989). "The combining of forecasts using recursive techniques with nonstationary weights". Journal of Forecasting 8, 239–251.
Stock, J.H., Watson, M. (2001). "A comparison of linear and nonlinear univariate models for forecasting macroeconomic time series". In: Engle, R.F., White, H. (Eds.), Festschrift in Honour of Clive Granger. Cambridge University Press, Cambridge, pp. 1–44.
Stock, J.H., Watson, M. (2004). "Combination forecasts of output growth in a seven-country data set". Journal of Forecasting 23, 405–430.
Swanson, N.R., Zeng, T. (2001). "Choosing among competing econometric forecasts: Regression-based forecast combination using model selection". Journal of Forecasting 6, 425–440.
West, K.D. (2006). "Forecast evaluation". In: Elliott, G., Granger, C.W.J., Timmermann, A. (Eds.), Handbook of Economic Forecasting. Elsevier, Amsterdam, pp. 99–134. Chapter 3 in this volume.
White, H. (2006). "Approximate nonlinear forecasting methods". In: Elliott, G., Granger, C.W.J., Timmermann, A. (Eds.), Handbook of Economic Forecasting. Elsevier, Amsterdam, pp. 459–512. Chapter 9 in this volume.
Winkler, R.L. (1981). "Combining probability distributions from dependent information sources". Management Science 27, 479–488.
Winkler, R.L. (1989). "Combining forecasts: A philosophical basis and some current issues". International Journal of Forecasting 5, 605–609.
Winkler, R.L., Makridakis, S. (1983). "The combination of forecasts". Journal of the Royal Statistical Society Series A 146, 150–157.
Wright, S.M., Satchell, S.E. (2003). "Generalized mean-variance analysis and robust portfolio diversification". In: Satchell, S.E., Scowcroft, A. (Eds.), Advances in Portfolio Construction and Implementation. Butterworth Heinemann, London, pp. 40–54.
Yang, Y. (2004). "Combining forecasts procedures: Some theoretical results". Econometric Theory 20, 176–190.
Zellner, A. (1986). "Bayesian estimation and prediction using asymmetric loss functions". Journal of the American Statistical Association 81, 446–451.
Zellner, A., Hong, C., Min, C.-k. (1991). "Forecasting turning points in international output growth rates using Bayesian exponentially weighted autoregression, time-varying parameter, and pooling techniques". Journal of Econometrics 49, 275–304.

Chapter 5

PREDICTIVE DENSITY EVALUATION

VALENTINA CORRADI

Queen Mary, University of London

NORMAN R. SWANSON

Rutgers University

Contents

Handbook of Economic Forecasting, Volume 1
Edited by Graham Elliott, Clive W.J. Granger and Allan Timmermann

DOI: 10.1016/S1574-0706(05)01005-0

Abstract

This chapter discusses estimation, specification testing, and model selection of predictive density models. In particular, predictive density estimation is briefly discussed, and a variety of different specification and model evaluation tests due to various authors including Christoffersen and Diebold [Christoffersen, P., Diebold, F.X. (2000). "How relevant is volatility forecasting for financial risk management?". Review of Economics and Statistics 82, 12–22], Diebold, Gunther and Tay [Diebold, F.X., Gunther, T., Tay, A.S. (1998). "Evaluating density forecasts with applications to finance and management". International Economic Review 39, 863–883], Diebold, Hahn and Tay [Diebold, F.X., Hahn, J., Tay, A.S. (1999). "Multivariate density forecast evaluation and calibration in financial risk management: High frequency returns on foreign exchange". Review of Economics and Statistics 81, 661–673], White [White, H. (2000). "A reality check for data snooping". Econometrica 68, 1097–1126], Bai [Bai, J. (2003). "Testing parametric conditional distributions of dynamic models". Review of Economics and Statistics 85, 531–549], Corradi and Swanson [Corradi, V., Swanson, N.R. (2005a). "A test for comparing multiple misspecified conditional distributions". Econometric Theory 21, 991–1016; Corradi, V., Swanson, N.R. (2005b). "Nonparametric bootstrap procedures for predictive inference based on recursive estimation schemes". Working Paper, Rutgers University; Corradi, V., Swanson, N.R. (2006a). "Bootstrap conditional distribution tests in the presence of dynamic misspecification". Journal of Econometrics, in press; Corradi, V., Swanson, N.R. (2006b). "Predictive density and conditional confidence interval accuracy tests". Journal of Econometrics, in press], Hong and Li [Hong, Y.M., Li, H.F. (2003). "Nonparametric specification testing for continuous time models with applications to term structure of interest rates". Review of Financial Studies, 18, 37–84], and others are reviewed. Extensions of some existing techniques to the case of out-of-sample evaluation are also provided, and asymptotic results associated with these extensions are outlined.

Keywords

block bootstrap, density and conditional distribution, forecast accuracy testing, mean square error, parameter estimation error, parametric and nonparametric methods, prediction, rolling and recursive estimation scheme

JEL classification: C22, C51

Part I: Introduction

1. Estimation, specification testing, and model evaluation

The topic of predictive density evaluation has received considerable attention in economics and finance over the last few years, a fact which is not at all surprising when one notes the importance of predictive densities to virtually all public and private institutions involved with the construction and dissemination of forecasts. As a case in point, consider the plethora of conditional mean forecasts reported by the news media. These sorts of predictions are not very useful for economic decision making unless confidence intervals are also provided. Indeed, there is a clear need when forming macroeconomic policies and when managing financial risk in the insurance and banking industries to use predictive confidence intervals or entire predictive conditional distributions. One such case is when value at risk measures are constructed in order to assess the amount of capital at risk from small probability events, such as catastrophes (in insurance markets) or monetary shocks that have large impact on interest rates [see Duffie and Pan (1997) for further discussion]. Another case is when maximizing expected utility of an investor who is choosing an optimal asset allocation of stocks and bonds, in which case there is a need to model the joint distribution of the assets [see Guidolin and Timmermann (2005, 2006) for a discussion of this and related applications]. Finally, it is worth noting that density forecasts may be useful in multi-step ahead prediction contexts using nonlinear models, even if interest focuses only on point forecasts of the conditional mean [see Chapter 8 in this Handbook by Teräsvirta (2006)]. In this chapter we shall discuss some of the tools that are useful in such situations, with particular focus on estimation, specification testing, and model evaluation. Additionally, we shall review various tests for the evaluation of point predictions.[1]

There are many important historical precedents for predictive density estimation, testing, and model selection. From the perspective of estimation, the parameters characterizing distributions, conditional distributions and predictive densities can be constructed using innumerable well established techniques, including maximum likelihood, (simulated generalized) methods of moments, and a plethora of other estimation techniques. Additionally, one can specify parametric models, nonparametric models, and semiparametric models. For example, a random variable of interest, say y_t, may be assumed to have a particular distribution, say $F(u|\theta_0) = P(y \leqslant u|\theta_0) = \Phi(u) = \int_{-\infty}^{u} f(y)\,\mathrm{d}y$, where $f(y) = \frac{1}{\sigma\sqrt{2\pi}}\mathrm{e}^{-(y-\mu)^2/(2\sigma^2)}$. Here, the consistent maximum likelihood estimator of θ_0 is $\widehat{\mu} = n^{-1}\sum_{t=1}^{T} y_t$, and $\widehat{\sigma}^2 = n^{-1}\sum_{t=1}^{T}(y_t - \widehat{\mu})^2$, where T is the

[1] In this chapter, the distinction that is made between specification testing and model evaluation (or predictive accuracy testing) is predicated on the fact that specification tests often consider only one model. Such tests usually attempt to ascertain whether the model is misspecified, and they usually assume correct specification under the null hypothesis. On the other hand, predictive accuracy tests compare multiple models and should (in our view) allow for various forms of misspecification, under both hypotheses.

sample size. This example corresponds to the case where the variable of interest is a martingale difference sequence and so there is no potentially useful (conditioning) information which may help in prediction. Then, the predictive density for y_t is simply $\widehat{f}(y) = \frac{1}{\hat{\sigma}\sqrt{2\pi}} e^{-(y-\hat{\mu})^2/(2\hat{\sigma}^2)}$. Alternatively, one may wish to use a nonparametric estimator. For example, if the functional form of the distribution is unknown, one might choose to construct a kernel density estimator. In this case, one would construct $\widehat{f}(y) = \frac{1}{T\lambda}\sum_{t=1}^{T}\kappa(\frac{y_t-y}{\lambda})$, where κ is a kernel function and λ is the bandwidth parameter that satisfies a particular rate condition in order to ensure consistent estimation, such as $\lambda = O(T^{-1/5})$. Nonparametric density estimators converge to the true underlying density at a nonparametric (slow) rate. For this reason, a valid alternative is the use of empirical distributions, which instead converge to the cumulative distribution (CDF) at a parametric rate [see, e.g., Andrews (1993) for a thorough overview of empirical distributions, and empirical processes in general]. In particular, the empirical distribution is crucial in our discussion of predictive density because it is useful in estimation, testing, and model evaluation; and has the property that $\frac{1}{\sqrt{T}}\sum_{i=1}^{T}(1\{y_t \leqslant u\} - F(u|\theta_0))$ satisfies a central limit theorem.

Of course, in economics it is natural to suppose that better predictions can be constructed by conditioning on other important economic variables. Indeed, discussions of predictive density are usually linked to discussions of conditional distribution, where we define conditioning information as $Z^t = (y_{t-1}, \ldots, y_{t-v}, X_t, \ldots, X_{t-w})$ with v, w finite, and where X_t may be vector valued. In this context, we could define a parametric model, say $F(u|Z^t, \theta)$ to characterize the conditional distribution $F_0(u|Z^t, \theta_0) = \Pr(Y_t \leqslant u|Z^t)$. Needless to say, our model would be misspecified, unless $F = F_0$.

Alternatively, one may wish to estimate and evaluate a group of alternative models, say $F_1(u|Z^t, \theta_1^\dagger), \ldots, F_m(u|Z^t, \theta_m^\dagger)$, where the parameters in these distributions correspond to the probability limits of the estimated parameters, and m is the number of models to be estimated and evaluated. Estimation in this context can be carried out in much the same way as when unconditional models are estimated. For example, one can construct a conditional distribution model by postulating that $y_t|Z^t \sim N(\theta' Z^t, \sigma^2)$, estimate θ by least square, σ^2 using least square residuals and then forming predictive confidence intervals or the entire predictive density. The foregoing discussion underscores the fact that there are numerous well established estimation techniques which one can use to estimate predictive density models, and hence which one can use to make associated probabilistic statements such as: "There is 0.9 probability, based on the use of my particular model, that inflation next period will lie between 4 and 5 percent." Indeed, for a discussion of estimation, one need merely pick up any basic or advanced statistics and/or econometrics text. Naturally, and as one might expect, the appropriateness of a particular estimation technique hinges on two factors. The first is the nature of the data. Marketing survey data are quite different from aggregate measures of economic activity, and there are well established literatures describing appropriate models and estimation techniques for these and other varieties of data, from spatial to panel, and from time series to cross sectional. Given that there is already a huge literature on the topic of estimation, we shall hereafter assume that the reader has at her/his disposal software and know-how concerning model estimation [for some discussion of estimation in cross sectional, panel, and time series models, for example, the reader might refer to Baltagi (1995), Bickel and Doksum (1977), Davidson and MacKinnon (1993), Hamilton (1994), White (1994), and Wooldridge (2002), to name but a very few]. The second factor upon which the appropriateness of a particular estimation strategy hinges concerns model specification. In the context of model specification and evaluation, it is crucial to make it clear in empirical settings whether one is assuming that a model is correctly specified (prior to estimation), or whether the model is simply an approximation, possibly from amongst a group of many "approximate models", from whence some "best" predictive density model is to be selected. The reason this assumption is important is because it impacts on the assumed properties of the residuals from the first stage conditional mean regression in the above example, which in turn impacts on the validity and appropriateness of specification testing and model evaluation techniques that are usually applied after a model has been estimated.

The focus in this chapter is on the last two issues, namely specification testing and model evaluation. One reason why we are able to discuss both of these topics in a (relatively) short handbook chapter is that the literature on the subjects is not near so large as that for estimation; although it is currently growing at an impressive rate! The fact that the literature in these areas is still relatively underdeveloped is perhaps surprising, given that the "tools" used in specification testing and model evaluation have been around for so long, and include such important classical contributions as the Kolmogorov–Smirnov test [see, e.g., Kolmogorov (1933) and Smirnov (1939)], various results on empirical processes [see, e.g., Andrews (1993) and the discussion in Chapter 19 of van der Vaart (1998) on the contributions of Glivenko, Cantelli, Doob, Donsker and others], the probability integral transform [see, e.g., Rosenblatt (1952)], and the Kullback–Leibler Information Criterion [see, e.g., White (1982) and Vuong (1989)]. However, the immaturity of the literature is perhaps not so surprising when one considers that many of the contributions in the area depend upon recent advances including results validating the use of the bootstrap [see, e.g., Horowitz (2001)] and the invention of crucial tools for dealing with parameter estimation error [see, e.g., Ghysels and Hall (1990), Khmaladze (1981, 1988) and West (1996)], for example.

We start by outlining various contributions which are from the literature on (consistent) specification testing [see, e.g., Bierens (1982, 1990) and Bierens and Ploberger (1997)]. An important feature of such tests is that if one subsequently carries out a series of these tests, such as when one performs a series of specification tests using alternative conditional distributions [e.g., the conditional Kolmogorov–Smirnov test of Andrews (1997)], then sequential test bias arises (i.e. critical values may be incorrectly sized, and so inference based on such sequential tests may be incorrect). Additionally, it may be difficult in some contexts to justify the assumption under the null that a model is correctly specified, as we may want to allow for possible dynamic misspecification under the null, for example. After all, if two tests for the correct specification of two different models are carried out sequentially, then surely one of the models is misspecified under the null, implying that the critical values of one of the two tests may be incorrect, as we shall shortly illustrate. It is in this sense that the idea of model evaluation in which a group of models are jointly compared, and in which case all models are allowed to be misspecified, is important, particularly from the perspective of prediction. Also, there are many settings for which the objective is not to find the correct model, but rather to select the "best" model (based on a given metric or loss function to be used for predictive evaluation) from amongst a group of models, all of which are approximations to some underlying unknown model. Nevertheless, given that advances in multiple model comparison under misspecification derive to a large extent from earlier advances in (correct) specification testing, and given that specification testing and model evaluation are likely most powerful when used together, we shall discuss tools and techniques in both areas.

Although a more mature literature, there is still a great amount of activity in the area of tests for the correct specification of conditional distributions. One reason for this is that testing for the correct conditional distribution is equivalent to jointly evaluating many conditional features of a process, including the conditional mean, variance, and symmetry. Along these lines, Inoue (2001) constructs tests for generic conditional aspects of a distribution, and Bai and Ng (2001) construct tests for conditional asymmetry. These sorts of tests can be generalized to the evaluation of predictive intervals and predictive densities, too.

One group of tests that we discuss along these lines is that due to Corradi and Swanson (2006a). In their paper, they construct Kolmogorov type conditional distribution tests in the presence of both dynamic misspecification and parameter estimation error. As shall be discussed shortly, the approach taken by these authors differs somewhat from much of the related literature because they construct a statistics that allow for dynamic misspecification under both hypotheses, rather than assuming correct dynamic specification under the null hypothesis. This difference can be most easily motivated within the framework used by Diebold, Gunther and Tay (1998, DGT), Hong (2001), and Bai (2003). In their paper, DGT use the probability integral transform to show that $F_t(y_t|\Im_{t-1}, \theta_0)$ is identically and independently distributed as a uniform random variable on $[0, 1]$, where $F_t(\cdot|\Im_{t-1}, \theta_0)$ is a parametric distribution with underlying parameter θ_0, y_t is again our random variable of interest, and $\Im_{t-1}$ is the information set containing all "relevant" past information (see below for further discussion). They thus suggest using the difference between the empirical distribution of $F_t(y_t|\Im_{t-1}, \widehat{\theta}_T)$ and the $45°$-degree line as a measure of "goodness of fit", where $\widehat{\theta}_T$ is some estimator of θ_0. This approach has been shown to be very useful for financial risk management [see, e.g., Diebold, Hahn and Tay (1999)], as well as for macroeconomic forecasting [see, e.g., Diebold, Tay and Wallis (1998) and Clements and Smith (2000, 2002)]. Likewise, Bai (2003) proposes a Kolmogorov type test of $F_t(u|\Im_{t-1}, \theta_0)$ based on the comparison of $F_t(y_t|\Im_{t-1}, \widehat{\theta}_T)$ with the CDF of a uniform on $[0, 1]$. As a consequence of using estimated parameters, the limiting distribution of his test reflects the contribution of parameter estimation error and is not nuisance parameter free. To overcome this problem, Bai (2003) uses a novel approach based on a martingalization argument to construct a modified Kolmogorov test which has a nuisance parameter free limiting distribution. This test has power against violations of uniformity but not against violations of independence (see below for further discussion). Hong (2001) proposes another related interesting test, based on the generalized spectrum, which has power against both uniformity and independence violations, for the case in which the contribution of parameter estimation error vanishes asymptotically. If the null is rejected, Hong (2001) also proposes a test for uniformity robust to non independence, which is based on the comparison between a kernel density estimator and the uniform density. All of these tests are discussed in detail below. In summary, two features differentiate the tests of Corradi and Swanson (2006a, CS) from the tests outlined in the other papers mentioned above. First, CS assume strict stationarity. Second, CS allow for dynamic misspecification under the null hypothesis. The second feature allows CS to obtain asymptotically valid critical values even when the conditioning information set does not contain all of the relevant past history. More precisely, assume that we are interested in testing for correct specification, given a particular information set which may or may not contain all of the relevant past information. This is important when a Kolmogorov test is constructed, as one is generally faced with the problem of defining $\Im_{t-1}$. If enough history is not included, then there may be dynamic misspecification. Additionally, finding out how much information (e.g., how many lags) to include may involve pre-testing, hence leading to a form of sequential test bias. By allowing for dynamic misspecification, such pre-testing is not required.

To be more precise, critical values derived under correct specification given $\Im_{t-1}$ are not in general valid in the case of correct specification given a subset of $\Im_{t-1}$. Consider the following example. Assume that we are interested in testing whether the conditional distribution of $y_t|y_{t-1}$ is $N(\alpha_1^\dagger y_{t-1}, \sigma_1)$. Suppose also that in actual fact the "relevant" information set has $\Im_{t-1}$ including both y_{t-1} and y_{t-2}, so that the true conditional model is $y_t|\Im_{t-1} = y_t|y_{t-1}, y_{t-2} = N(\alpha_1 y_{t-1} + \alpha_2 y_{t-2}, \sigma_2)$, where $\alpha_1^\dagger$ differs from α_1. In this case, correct specification holds with respect to the information contained in y_{t-1}; but there is dynamic misspecification with respect to y_{t-1}, y_{t-2}. Even without taking account of parameter estimation error, the critical values obtained assuming correct dynamic specification are invalid, thus leading to invalid inference. Stated differently, tests that are designed to have power against both uniformity and independence violations (i.e. tests that assume correct dynamic specification under H_0) will reject; an inference which is incorrect, at least in the sense that the "normality" assumption is *not* false. In summary, if one is interested in the particular problem of testing for correct specification for a given information set, then the CS approach is appropriate, while if one is instead interested in testing for correct specification assuming that $\Im_{t-1}$ is known, then the other tests discussed above are useful – these are some of the tests discussed in the second part of this chapter, and all are based on probability integral transforms and Kolmogorov–Smirnov distance measures.

In the third part of this chapter, attention is turned to the case of density model evaluation. Much of the development in this area stems from earlier work in the area of point evaluation, and hence various tests of conditional mean models for nested and nonnested models, both under assumption of correct specification, and under the assumption that all models should be viewed as "approximations", are first discussed. These tests include important ones by Diebold and Mariano (1995), West (1996), White (2000), and many others. Attention is then turned to a discussion of predictive density selection. To illustrate the sort of model evaluation tools that are discussed, consider the following. Assume that we are given a group of (possibly) misspecified conditional distributions, $F_1(u|Z^t, \theta_1^\dagger), \ldots, F_m(u|Z^t, \theta_m^\dagger)$, and assume that the objective is to compare these models in terms of their "closeness" to the true conditional distribution, $F_0(u|Z^t, \theta_0) = \Pr(Y_{t+1} \leqslant u|Z^t)$. Corradi and Swanson (2005a, 2006b) consider such a problem. If $m > 2$, they follow White (2000), in the sense that a particular conditional distribution model is chosen as the "benchmark" and one tests the null hypothesis that no competing model can provide a more accurate approximation of the "true" conditional distribution against the alternative that at least one competitor outperforms the benchmark model. However, unlike White, they evaluate predictive densities rather than point forecasts. Pairwise comparison of alternative models, in which no benchmark needs to be specified, follows from their results as a special case. In their context, accuracy is measured using a distributional analog of mean square error. More precisely, the squared (approximation) error associated with model i, $i = 1, \ldots, m$, is measured in terms of $E((F_i(u|Z^{t+1}, \theta_i^\dagger) - F_0(u|Z^{t+1}, \theta_0))^2)$, where $u \in U$, and U is a possibly unbounded set on the real line. The case of evaluation of multiple conditional confidence interval models is analyzed too.

Another well known measure of distributional accuracy which is also discussed in Part III is the Kullback–Leibler Information Criterion (KLIC). The KLIC is useful because the "most accurate" model can be shown to be that which minimizes the KLIC (see below for more details). Using the KLIC approach, Giacomini (2002) suggests a weighted version of the Vuong (1989) likelihood ratio test for the case of dependent observations, while Kitamura (2002) employs a KLIC based approach to select among misspecified conditional models that satisfy given moment conditions. Furthermore, the KLIC approach has been recently employed for the evaluation of dynamic stochastic general equilibrium models [see, e.g., Schörfheide (2000), Fernandez-Villaverde and Rubio-Ramirez (2004), and Chang, Gomes and Schorfheide (2002)]. For example, Fernandez-Villaverde and Rubio-Ramirez (2004) show that the KLIC-best model is also the model with the highest posterior probability. In general, there is no reason why either of the above two measures of accuracy is more "natural". These tests are discussed in detail in the chapter.

As a further preamble to this chapter, we now present Table 1 which summarizes selected testing and model evaluation papers. The list of papers in the table is undoubtedly incomplete, but nevertheless serves as a rough benchmark to the sorts of papers and results that are discussed in this chapter. The primary reason for including the table is to summarize in a directly comparable manner the assumptions made in the various papers. Later on, assumptions are given as they appear in the original papers, and are gathered in Appendix A.

Table 1
Summary of selected specification testing and model evaluation papers

Paper	Eval	Test	Misspec	Loss	PEE	Horizon	Nesting	CV
Bai (2003)[1]	S	CD	C	NA	Yes	$h = 1$	NA	Standard
Corradi and Swanson (2006a)[2]	S	CD	D	NA	Yes	$h = 1$	NA	Boot
Diebold, Gunther and Tay (1998)[2]	S	CD	C	NA	No	$h = 1$	NA	NA
Hong (2001)	S	CD	C, D, G	NA	No	$h = 1$	NA	Standard
Hong and Li (2003)[1]	S	CD	C, D, G	NA	Yes	$h = 1$	NA	Standard
Chao, Corradi and Swanson (2001)	S	CM	D	D	Yes	$h \geqslant 1$	NA	Boot
Clark and McCracken (2001, 2003)	S, P	CM	C	D	Yes	$h \geqslant 1$	N,A	Boot,Standard
Corradi and Swanson (2002)[3]	S	CM	D	D	Yes	$h \geqslant 1$	NA	Boot
Corradi and Swanson (2006b)	M	CD	G	D	Yes	$h \geqslant 1$	O	Boot
Corradi, Swanson and Olivetti (2001)	P	CM	C	D	Yes	$h \geqslant 1$	O	Standard
Diebold, Hahn and Tay (1999)	M	CD	C	NA	No	$h \geqslant 1$	NA	NA
Diebold and Mariano (1995)	P	CM	G	N	No	$h \geqslant 1$	O	Standard
Giacomini (2002)	P	CD	G	NA	Yes	$h \geqslant 1$	A	Standard
Giacomini and White (2003)[5]	P	CM	G	D	Yes	$h \geqslant 1$	A	Standard
Li and Tkacz (2006)	S	CD	C	NA	Yes	$h \geqslant 1$	NA	Standard
Rossi (2005)	P	CM	C	D	Yes	$h \geqslant 1$	O	Standard
Thompson (2002)	S	CD	C	NA	Yes	$h \geqslant 1$	NA	Standard
West (1996)	P	CM	C	D	Yes	$h \geqslant 1$	O	Standard
White (2000)[4]	M	CM	G	N	Yes	$h \geqslant 1$	O	Boot

[1]See extension in this paper to the out-of-sample case.

[2]Extension to multiple horizon follows straightforwardly if the marginal distribution of the errors is normal, for example; otherwise extension is not always straightforward.

[3]This is the only predictive accuracy test from the listed papers that is consistent against generic (nonlinear) alternatives.

[4]See extension in this paper to predictive density evaluation, allowing for parameter estimation error.

[5]Parameters are estimated using a fixed window of observations, so that parameters do not approach their probability limits, but are instead treated as mixing variables under the null hypothesis.

Notes: The table provides a summary of various tests currently available. For completeness, some tests of conditional mean are also included, particularly when they have been, or could be, extended to the case of conditional distribution evaluation. Many tests are considered ancillary, or have been omitted due to ignorance. Many other tests are discussed in the papers cited in this table. "NA" entries denote "Not Applicable". Columns and mnemonics used are defined as follows:

- Eval = Evaluation is of: Single model (S); Pair of models (P); Multiple models (M).
- Test = Test is of: Conditional Distribution (CD); Conditional Mean (CM).
- Misspec = Misspecification assumption under H_0: Correct specification (C); Dynamic misspecification allowed (D); General misspecification allowed (G).
- Loss = Loss function assumption: Differentiable (D); may be non-differentiable (N).
- PEE = Parameter estimation error: accounted for (yes); not accounted for (no).
- Horizon = Prediction horizon: 1-step ($h = 1$); multi-step ($h \geqslant 1$).
- Nesting = Assumption vis nestedness of models: (at least One) nonnested model required (O); Nested models (N); Any combination (A).
- CV = Critical values constructed via: Standard limiting distribution or nuisance parameter free nonstandard distribution (Standard); Bootstrap or other procedure (Boot).

Part II: Testing for Correct Specification of Conditional Distributions

2. Specification testing and model evaluation in-sample

There are several instances in which a "good" model for the conditional mean and/or variance is not adequate for the task at hand. For example, financial risk management involves tracking the entire distribution of a portfolio; or measuring certain distributional aspects, such as value at risk [see, e.g., Duffie and Pan (1997)]. In these cases, the choice of the best loss function specific model for the conditional mean may not be of too much help. The reader is also referred to the papers by Guidolin and Timmermann (2006, 2005) for other interesting financial applications illustrating cases where models of conditional mean and/or variance are not adequate for the task at hand.

Important contributions that go beyond the examination of models of conditional mean include assessing the correctness of (out-of-sample) conditional interval prediction [Christoffersen (1998)] and assessing volatility predictability by comparing unconditional and conditional interval forecasts [Christoffersen and Diebold (2000)].[2] Needless to say, correct specification of the conditional distribution implies correct specification of all conditional aspects of the model. Perhaps in part for this reason, there has been growing interest in recent years in providing tests for the correct specification of conditional distributions. In this section, we analyze the issue of testing for the correct specification of the conditional distribution, distinguishing between the case in which we condition on the entire history and that in which we condition on a given information set, thus allowing for dynamic misspecification. In particular, we illustrate with some detail recent important work by Diebold, Gunther and Tay (1998), based on the probability integral transformation [see also Diebold, Hahn and Tay (1999) and Christoffersen and Diebold (2000)]; by Bai (2003), based on Kolmogorov tests and martingalization techniques; by Hong (2001), based on the notion of generalized cross-spectrum; and by Corradi and Swanson (2006a), based on Kolmogorov type tests. We begin by considering the in-sample version of the tests, in which the same set of observations is used for both estimation and testing. Further, we provide an out-of-sample version of these tests, in which the first subset of observations is used for estimation and the last subset is used for testing. In the out-of-sample case, parameters are generally estimated using either a recursive or a rolling estimation scheme. Thus, we first review important results by West (1996) and West and McCracken (1998) about the limiting distribution of m-estimators and GMM estimators in a variety of contexts, such as recursive and rolling estimation schemes.[3] As pointed in Section 3.3 below, asymptotic critical values for both the in-sample and out-of-sample versions of the statistic by Corradi and Swanson can be obtained via an application of the bootstrap. While

[2] Prediction confidence intervals are also discussed in Granger, White and Kamstra (1989), Diebold, Tay and Wallis (1998), Clements and Taylor (2001), and the references cited therein. See also Zheng (2000).

[3] See also Dufour, Ghysels and Hall (1994) and Ghysels and Hall (1990) for related discussion and results.

the asymptotic behavior of (full sample) bootstrap m-estimators is already well known, see the literature cited below, this is no longer true for the case of bootstrap estimators based on either a recursive or a rolling scheme. This issue is addressed by Corradi and Swanson (2005b, 2006b) and summarized in Sections 3.4.1 and 3.4.2 below.

2.1. *Diebold, Gunther and Tay approach – probability integral transform*

In a key paper in the field, Diebold, Gunther and Tay (1998, DGT) use the probability integral transform [see, e.g., Rosenblatt (1952)] to show that $F_t(y_t|\Im_{t-1},\theta_0) = \int_{-\infty}^{y_t} f_t(y|\Im_{t-1},\theta_0)$, is identically and independently distributed as a uniform random variable on [0, 1], whenever $F_t(y_t|\Im_{t-1},\theta_0)$ is dynamically correctly specified for the CDF of $y_t|\Im_{t-1}$. Thus, they suggest to use the difference between the empirical distribution of $F_t(y_t|\Im_{t-1},\widehat{\theta}_T)$ and the 45°-degree line as a measure of "goodness of fit", where $\widehat{\theta}_T$ is some estimator of θ_0. Visual inspection of the plot of this difference gives also some information about the deficiency of the candidate conditional density, and so may suggest some way of improving it. The univariate framework of DGT is extended to a multivariate framework in Diebold, Hahn and Tay (1999, DHT), in order to allow to evaluate the adequacy of density forecasts involving cross-variable interactions. This approach has been shown to be very useful for financial risk management [see, e.g., DGT (1998) and DHT (1999)], as well as for macroeconomic forecasting [see Diebold, Tay and Wallis (1998), where inflation predictions based on professional forecasts are evaluated, and see Clements and Smith (2000), where predictive densities based on nonlinear models of output and unemployment are evaluated]. Important closely related work in the area of the evaluation of volatility forecasting and risk management is discussed in Christoffersen and Diebold (2000). Additional tests based on the DGT idea of comparing the empirical distribution of $F_t(y_t|\Im_{t-1},\widehat{\theta}_T)$ with the 45°-degree line have been suggested by Bai (2003), Hong (2001), Hong and Li (2003), and Corradi and Swanson (2006a).

2.2. *Bai approach – martingalization*

Bai (2003) considers the following hypotheses:

$$H_0\colon\quad \Pr(y_t \leqslant y|\Im_{t-1},\theta_0) = F_t(y|\Im_{t-1},\theta_0), \quad \text{a.s. for some } \theta_0 \in \Theta, \tag{1}$$

$$H_A\colon\quad \text{the negation of } H_0, \tag{2}$$

where $\Im_{t-1}$ contains all the relevant history up to time $t-1$. In this sense, the null hypotheses corresponds with dynamic correct specification of the conditional distribution.

Bai (2003) proposes a Kolmogorov type test based on the comparison of $F_t(y|\Im_{t-1},\theta_0)$ with the CDF of a uniform random variable on [0, 1]. In practice, we need to replace the unknown parameters, θ_0, with an estimator, say $\widehat{\theta}_T$. Additionally, we often do not observe the full information set $\Im_{t-1}$, but only a subset of it, say $Z^t \subseteq \Im_{t-1}$. Therefore, we need to approximate $F_t(y|\Im_{t-1},\theta_0)$ with $F_t(y|Z^{t-1},\widehat{\theta}_T)$. Hereafter, for notational simplicity, define

$$\widehat{U}_t = F_t\big(y_t|Z^{t-1},\widehat{\theta}_T\big), \tag{3}$$

$$\widetilde{U}_t = F_t\big(y_t|Z^{t-1}, \theta^\dagger\big), \tag{4}$$

$$U_t = F_t(y_t|\Im_{t-1}, \theta_0), \tag{5}$$

where $\theta^\dagger = \theta_0$ whenever Z^{t-1} contains all useful information in $\Im_{t-1}$, so that in this case $\widetilde{U}_t = U_t$. As a consequence of using estimated parameters, the limiting distribution of his test reflects the contribution of parameter estimation error and is not nuisance parameter free. In fact, as shown in his Equations (1)–(4),

$$\begin{aligned}\widehat{V}_T(r) &= \frac{1}{\sqrt{T}} \sum_{t=1}^{T} \big(1\{\widehat{U}_t \leqslant r\} - r\big) \\ &= \frac{1}{\sqrt{T}} \sum_{t=1}^{T} \big(1\{\widetilde{U}_t \leqslant r\} - r\big) + \bar{g}(r)'\sqrt{T}\big(\widehat{\theta}_T - \theta^\dagger\big) + o_P(1) \\ &= \frac{1}{\sqrt{T}} \sum_{t=1}^{T} \big(1\{U_t \leqslant r\} - r\big) + \bar{g}(r)'\sqrt{T}\big(\widehat{\theta}_T - \theta_0\big) + o_P(1),\end{aligned} \tag{6}$$

where the last equality holds only if Z^{t-1} contains all useful information in $\Im_{t-1}$.[4] Here,

$$\bar{g}(r) = \operatorname*{plim}_{T\to\infty} \frac{1}{T} \sum_{t=1}^{T} \frac{\partial F_t}{\partial \theta}\big(x|Z^{t-1}, \theta^\dagger\big)\bigg|_{x = F_t^{-1}(r|Z^{t-1}, \theta^\dagger)}.$$

Also, let

$$g(r) = \big(1, \bar{g}(r)'\big).$$

To overcome the nuisance parameter problem, Bai uses a novel approach based on a martingalization argument to construct a modified Kolmogorov test which has a nuisance parameter free limiting distribution. In particular, let $\dot{g}$ be the derivative of g, and let $C(r) = \int_r^1 \dot{g}(\tau)\dot{g}(\tau)'\,d\tau$. Bai's test statistic (Equation (5), p. 533) is defined as:

$$\widehat{W}_T(r) = \widehat{V}_T(r) - \int_0^r \left(\dot{g}(s)C^{-1}(s)\dot{g}(s)' \int_s^1 \dot{g}(\tau)\,d\widehat{V}_T(\tau)\right) ds, \tag{7}$$

where the second term may be difficult to compute, depending on the specific application. Several examples, including GARCH models and (self-exciting) threshold autoregressive models are provided in Section IIIB of Bai (2003). The limiting distribution of the statistic in (7) is obtained under assumptions BAI–BAI4, which are listed in Appendix A. It is of note that stationarity is not required. (Note also that BAI4 below rules out non-negligible differences between the information in Z^{t-1} and $\Im_{t-1}$, with respect to the model of interest.).

The following result can be proven.

[4] Note that $\widehat{U}_t$ should be defined for $t > s$, where s is the largest lags contained in the information set Z^{t-1}, however for notational simplicity we start all summation from $t = 1$, as if $s = 0$.

THEOREM 2.1 (From Corollary 1 in Bai (2003)). *Let* BAI1–BAI4 *hold, then under* H_0,

$$\sup_{r\in[0,1]} \left|\widehat{W}_T(r)\right| \xrightarrow{d} \sup_{r\in[0,1]} \left|W(r)\right|,$$

where $W(r)$ *is a standard Brownian motion. Therefore, the limiting distribution is nuisance parameter free and critical values can be tabulated.*

Now, suppose there is dynamic misspecification, so that $\Pr(y_t \leqslant y|\Im_{t-1}, \theta_0) \neq \Pr(y_t \leqslant y|Z^{t-1}, \theta^{\dagger})$. In this case, critical values relying on the limiting distribution in Theorem 2.1 are no longer valid. However, if $F(y_t|Z^{t-1}, \theta^{\dagger})$ is correctly specified for $\Pr(y_t \leqslant y|Z^{t-1}, \theta^{\dagger})$, uniformity still holds, and there is no guarantee that the statistic diverges. Thus, while Bai's test has unit asymptotic power against violations of uniformity, is does not have unit asymptotic power against violations of independence. Note that in the case of dynamic misspecification, assumption BAI4 is violated. Also, the assumption cannot be checked from the data, in general. In summary, the limiting distribution of Kolmogorov type tests is affected by dynamic misspecification. Critical values derived under correct dynamic specification are not in general valid in the case of correct specification given a subset of the full information set. Consider the following example. Assume that we are interested in testing whether the conditional distribution of $y_t|y_{t-1}$ is $N(\alpha_1^{\dagger} y_{t-1}, \sigma_1)$. Suppose also that in actual fact the "relevant" information set has Z^{t-1} including both y_{t-1} and y_{t-2}, so that the true conditional model is $y_t|Z^{t-1} = y_t|y_{t-1}, y_{t-2} = N(\alpha_1 y_{t-1} + \alpha_2 y_{t-2}, \sigma_2)$, where $\alpha_1^{\dagger}$ differs from α_1. In this case, we have correct specification with respect to the information contained in y_{t-1}; but we have dynamic misspecification with respect to y_{t-1}, y_{t-2}. Even without taking account of parameter estimation error, the critical values obtained assuming correct dynamic specification are invalid, thus leading to invalid inference.

2.3. *Hong and Li approach – a nonparametric test*

As mentioned above, the Kolmogorov test of Bai does not necessarily have power against violations of independence. A test with power against violations of both independence and uniformity has been recently suggested by Hong and Li (2003), who also draw on results by Hong (2001). Their test is based on the comparison of the joint nonparametric density of $\widehat{U}_t$ and $\widehat{U}_{t-j}$, as defined in (3), with the product of two $UN[0,1]$ random variables. In particular, they introduce a boundary modified kernel which ensures a "good" nonparametric estimator, even around 0 and 1. This forms the basis for a test which has power against both non-uniformity and non-independence. For any $j > 0$, define

$$\widehat{\phi}(u_1, u_2) = (n-j)^{-1} \sum_{\tau=j+1}^{n} K_h\left(u_1, \widehat{U}_\tau\right) K_h\left(u_2, \widehat{U}_{\tau-j}\right), \tag{8}$$

where

$$K_h(x,y) = \begin{cases} \dfrac{h^{-1}(\frac{x-y}{h})}{\int_{-(x/h)}^{1} k(u)\,\mathrm{d}u} & \text{if } x \in [0,h), \\[2ex] h^{-1}\left(\dfrac{x-y}{h}\right) & \text{if } x \in [h, 1-h), \\[2ex] \dfrac{h^{-1}(\frac{x-y}{h})}{\int_{-1}^{(1-x)/h} k(u)\,\mathrm{d}u} & \text{if } x \in [1-h, 1]. \end{cases} \tag{9}$$

In the above expression, h defines the bandwidth parameter, although in later sections (where confusion cannot easily arise), h is used to denote forecast horizon. As an example, one might use,

$$k(u) = \frac{15}{16}\left(1-u^2\right)^2 1\left\{|u| \leqslant 1\right\}.$$

Also, define

$$\widehat{M}(j) = \int_0^1 \int_0^1 \left(\widehat{\phi}(u_1,u_2) - 1\right)^2 \mathrm{d}u_1\,\mathrm{d}u_2 \tag{10}$$

and

$$\widehat{Q}(j) = \frac{(n-j)\widehat{M}(j) - A_h^0}{V_0^{1/2}}, \tag{11}$$

with

$$A_h^0 = \left(\left(h^{-1}-2\right)\int_{-1}^{1} k^2(u)\,\mathrm{d}u + 2\int_0^1 \int_{-1}^{b} k_b(u)\,\mathrm{d}u\,\mathrm{d}b\right)^2 - 1,$$

$$k_b(\cdot) = \frac{k(\cdot)}{\int_{-1}^{b} k(v)\,\mathrm{d}v},$$

and

$$V_0 = 2\left(\int_{-1}^{1}\left(\int_{-1}^{1} k(u+v)k(v)\,\mathrm{d}v\right)^2 \mathrm{d}u\right)^2.$$

The limiting distribution of $\widehat{Q}(j)$ is obtained by Hong and Li (2003) under assumptions HL1–HL4, which are listed in Appendix A.[5]

Given this setup, the following result can be proven.

[5] Hong et al. specialize their test to the case of testing continuous time models. However, as they point out, it is equally valid for discrete time models.

THEOREM 2.2 (From Theorem 1 in Hong and Li (2003)). *Let* HL1–HL4 *hold. If* $h = cT^{-\delta}$, $\delta \in (0, 1/5)$, *then under* H_0 (*i.e. see* (1)), *for any* $j > 0$, $j = o(T^{1-\delta(5-2/v)})$, $\widehat{Q}(j) \xrightarrow{d} N(0, 1)$.

Once the null is rejected, it remains of interest to know whether the rejection is due to violation of uniformity or to violation of independence (or both). Broadly speaking, violations of independence arises in the case of dynamic misspecification (Z^t does not contain enough information), while violations of uniformity arise when we misspecify the functional form of f_t when constructing $\widehat{U}_t$. Along these lines, Hong (2001) proposes a test for uniformity, which is robust to dynamic misspecification. Define, the hypotheses of interest as:

$$H_0: \quad \Pr\left(y_t \leqslant y|Z^{t-1}, \theta^\dagger\right) = F_t\left(y|Z^{t-1}, \theta^\dagger\right), \quad \text{a.s. for some } \theta_0 \in \Theta, \tag{12}$$

$$H_A: \quad \text{the negation of } H_0, \tag{13}$$

where $F_t(y|Z^{t-1}, \theta^\dagger)$ may differ from $F_t(y|\Im_{t-1}, \theta_0)$. The relevant test is based on the comparison of a kernel estimator of the marginal density of $\widehat{U}_t$ with the uniform density, and has a standard normal limiting distribution under the null in (12). Hong (2001) also provides a test for the null of independence, which is robust to violations of uniformity.

Note that the limiting distribution in Theorem 2.2, as well as the limiting distribution of the uniformity (independence) test which is robust to non-uniformity (non-independence) in Hong (2001) are all asymptotically standard normal, regardless of the fact that we construct the statistic using $\widehat{U}_t$ instead on U_t. This is due to the feature that parameter estimators converge at rate $T^{1/2}$, while the statistics converge at nonparametric rates. The choice of the bandwidth parameter and the slower rate of convergence are thus the prices to be paid for not having to directly account for parameter estimation error.

2.4. Corradi and Swanson approach

Corradi and Swanson (2006a) suggest a test for the null hypothesis of correct specification of the conditional distribution, for a given information set which is, as usual, called Z^t, and which, as above, does not necessarily contain all relevant historical information. The test is again a Kolmogorov type test, and is based on the fact that under the null of correct (but not necessarily dynamically correct) specification of the conditional distribution, U_t is distributed as [0, 1]. As with Hong's (2001) test, this test is thus robust to violations of independence. As will become clear below, the advantages of the test relative to that of Hong (2001) is that it converges at a parametric rate and there is no need to choose the bandwidth parameter. The disadvantage is that the limiting distribution is not nuisance parameters free and hence one needs to rely on bootstrap techniques in order to obtain valid critical values. Define:

$$V_{1T} = \sup_{r \in [0,1]} \left|V_{1T}(r)\right|, \tag{14}$$

where

$$V_{1T}(r) = \frac{1}{\sqrt{T}} \sum_{t=1}^{T} \left(1\{\widehat{U}_t \leqslant r\} - r\right),$$

and

$$\widehat{\theta}_T = \arg\max_{\theta \in \Theta} \frac{1}{T} \sum_{t=1}^{T} \ln f(y_t | X_t, \theta).$$

Note that the above statistic is similar to that of Bai (2003). However, there is no "extra" term to cancel out the effect of parameter estimation error. The reason is that Bai's martingale transformation argument does not apply to the case in which the score is not a martingale difference process (so that (dynamic) misspecification is not allowed for when using his test).

The standard rationale underlying the above test, which is known to hold when $Z^{t-1} = \Im_{t-1}$, is that under H_0 (given above as (12)), $F(y_t|Z^{t-1}, \theta_0)$ is distributed independently and uniformly on [0, 1]. The uniformity result also holds under dynamic misspecification. To see this, let $c_f^r(Z^{t-1})$ be the rth critical value of $f(\cdot|Z^{t-1}, \theta_0)$, where f is the density associated with $F(\cdot|Z^{t-1}, \theta_0)$ (i.e. the conditional distribution under the null).[6] It then follows that,

$$\begin{aligned}
&\Pr\left(F\left(y_t|Z^{t-1}, \theta_0\right) \leqslant r\right) \\
&\quad = \Pr\left(\int_{-\infty}^{y_t} f\left(y|Z^{t-1}, \theta_0\right) \mathrm{d}y \leqslant r\right) \\
&\quad = \Pr\left(1\left\{y_t \leqslant c_f^r\left(Z^{t-1}\right)\right\} = 1\middle|Z^{t-1}\right) = r, \quad \text{for all } r \in [0, 1],
\end{aligned}$$

if $y_t|Z^{t-1}$ has density $f(\cdot|Z^{t-1}, \theta_0)$. Now, if the density of $y_t|Z^{t-1}$ is different from $f(\cdot|Z^{t-1}, \theta_0)$, then,

$$\Pr\left(1\left\{y_t \leqslant c_f^r\left(Z^{t-1}\right)\right\} = 1\middle|Z^{t-1}\right) \neq r,$$

for some r with nonzero Lebesgue measure on [0, 1]. However, under dynamic misspecification, $F(y_t|Z^{t-1}, \theta_0)$ is no longer independent (or even martingale difference), in general, and this will clearly affect the covariance structure of the limiting distribution of the statistic. Theorem 2.3 below relies on Assumptions CS1–CS3, which are listed in Appendix A.

Of note is that CS2 imposes mild smoothness and moment restrictions on the cumulative distribution function under the null, and is thus easily verifiable. Also, we use CS2(i)–(ii) in the study of the limiting behavior of V_{1T} and CS2(iii)–(iv) in the study of V_{2T}.

[6] For example, if $f(Y|X_t, \theta_0) \sim N(\alpha X_t, \sigma^2)$, then $c_f^{0.95}(X_t) = 1.645 + \sigma\alpha X_t$.

THEOREM 2.3 (From Theorem 1 in Corradi and Swanson (2006a)). *Let* CS1, CS2(i)–(ii) *and* CS3 *hold. Then*:

(i) *Under* H_0, $V_{1T} \Rightarrow \sup_{r\in[0,1]} |V_1(r)|$, *where* V *is a zero mean Gaussian process with covariance kernel* $K_1(r, r')$ *given by*:

$$\begin{aligned}
E\big(V_1(r)V_1(r')\big) &= K_1(r, r') \\
&= E\left(\sum_{s=-\infty}^{\infty}\left(1\big\{F\big(y_1|Z^0,\theta_0\big) \leqslant r\big\} - r\right)\right. \\
&\qquad \left.\times \left(1\big\{F\big(y_s|Z^{s-1},\theta_0\big) \leqslant r'\big\} - r'\right)\right) \\
&\quad + E\big(\nabla_\theta F\big(x(r)|Z^{t-1},\theta_0\big)\big)' A(\theta_0) \\
&\qquad \times \sum_{s=-\infty}^{\infty} E\big(q_1(\theta_0)q_s(\theta_0)'\big)A(\theta_0)E\big(\nabla_\theta F\big(x(r')|Z^{t-1},\theta_0\big)\big) \\
&\quad - 2E\big(\nabla_\theta F\big(x(r)|Z^{t-1},\theta_0\big)\big)' A(\theta_0) \\
&\qquad \times \sum_{s=-\infty}^{\infty} E\big(\big(1\big\{F\big(y_1|Z^0,\theta_0\big) \leqslant r\big\} - r\big)q_s(\theta_0)'\big),
\end{aligned}$$

with $q_s(\theta_0) = \nabla_\theta \ln f_s(y_s|Z^{s-1},\theta_0)$, $x(r) = F^{-1}(r|Z^{t-1},\theta_0)$, *and* $A(\theta_0) = (E(\nabla_\theta q_s(\theta_0)\nabla_\theta q_s(\theta_0)'))^{-1}$.

(ii) *Under* H_A, *there exists an* $\varepsilon > 0$ *such that*

$$\lim_{T\to\infty} \Pr\left(\frac{1}{T^{1/2}} V_{1T} > \varepsilon\right) = 1.$$

Notice that the limiting distribution is a zero mean Gaussian process, with a covariance kernel that reflects both dynamic misspecification as well as the contribution of parameter estimation error. Thus, the limiting distribution is not nuisance parameter free and so critical values cannot be tabulated.

Corradi and Swanson (2006a) also suggest another Kolmogorov test, which is no longer based on the probability integral transformation, but can be seen as an extension of the conditional Kolmogorov (CK) test of Andrews (1997) to the case of time series data and possible dynamic misspecification.

In a related important paper, Li and Tkacz (2006) discuss an interesting approach to testing for correct specification of the conditional density which involves comparing a nonparametric kernel estimate of the conditional density with the density implied under the null hypothesis. As in Hong and Li (2003) and Hong (2001), the Tkacz and Li test is characterized by a nonparametric rate. Of further note is that Whang (2000, 2001) also proposes a version of Andrews' CK test for the correct specification, although his focus is on conditional mean, and not conditional distribution.

A conditional distribution version of the CK test is constructed by comparing the empirical joint distribution of y_t and Z^{t-1} with the product of the distribution of $y_t|Z^t$ and the empirical CDF of Z^{t-1}. In practice, the empirical joint distribution, say $\widehat{H}_T(u, v) = \frac{1}{T}\sum_{t=1}^{T} 1\{y_t \leqslant u\}1\{Z^{t-1} < v\}$, and the semi-empirical/semi-parametric analog of $F(u, v, \theta_0)$, say $\widehat{F}_T(u, v, \widehat{\theta}_T) = \frac{1}{T}\sum_{t=1}^{T} F(u|Z^{t-1}, \widehat{\theta}_T)1\{Z^{t-1} < v\}$ are used, and the test statistic is:

$$V_{2T} = \sup_{u \times v \in U \times V} \left|V_{2T}(u, v)\right|, \tag{15}$$

where U and V are compact subsets of $\Re$ and $\Re^d$, respectively, and

$$V_{2T}(u, v) = \frac{1}{\sqrt{T}}\sum_{t=1}^{T}\Big(\big(1\{y_t \leqslant u\} - F\big(u|Z^{t-1}, \widehat{\theta}_T\big)\big)1\big\{Z^{t-1} \leqslant v\big\}\Big).$$

Note that V_{2T} is given in Equation (3.9) of Andrews (1997).[7] Note also that when computing this statistic, a grid search over $U \times V$ may be computationally demanding when V is high-dimensional. To avoid this problem, Andrews shows that when all (u, v) combinations are replaced with (y_t, Z^{t-1}) combinations, the resulting test is asymptotically equivalent to $V_{2T}(u, v)$.

THEOREM 2.4 (From Theorem 2 in Corradi and Swanson (2006a)). *Let* CS1, CS2(iii)–(iv) *and* CS3 *hold. Then*:

(i) *Under* H_0, $V_{2T} \Rightarrow \sup_{u \times v \in U \times V} |Z(u, v)|$, *where* V_{2T} *is defined in* (15) *and* Z *is a zero mean Gaussian process with covariance kernel* $K_2(u, v, u', v')$ *given by*:

$$\begin{aligned}
&E\Bigg(\sum_{s=-\infty}^{\infty}\big(\big(1\{y_1 \leqslant u\} - F\big(u|Z^0, \theta_0\big)\big)1\{X_0 \leqslant v\}\big)\\
&\quad \times \big(\big(1\{y_s \leqslant u'\} - F\big(u|Z^{s-1}, \theta_0\big)\big)1\{X_s \leqslant v'\}\big)\Bigg)\\
&\quad + E\big(\nabla_\theta F\big(u|Z^0, \theta_0\big)'1\big\{Z^0 \leqslant v\big\}\big)A(\theta_0)\\
&\quad \times \sum_{s=-\infty}^{\infty} q_0(\theta_0)q_s(\theta_0)'A(\theta_0)E\big(\nabla_\theta F\big(u'|Z^0, \theta_0\big)1\big\{Z^0 \leqslant v'\big\}\big)\\
&\quad - 2\sum_{s=-\infty}^{\infty}\big(\big(1\{y_0 \leqslant u\} - F\big(u|Z^0, \theta_0\big)\big)1\big\{Z^0 \leqslant v\big\}\big)\\
&\quad \times E\big(\nabla_\theta F\big(u'|Z^0, \theta_0\big)'1\big\{Z^0 \leqslant v'\big\}\big)A(\theta_0)q_s(\theta_0).
\end{aligned}$$

[7] Andrews (1997), for the case of iid observations, actually addresses the more complex situation where U and V are unbounded sets in $\Re$ and $\Re^d$, respectively. We believe that an analogous result for the case of dependent observations holds, but showing this involves proofs for stochastic equicontinuity which are quite demanding.

(ii) *Under H_A, there exists an $\varepsilon > 0$ such that*

$$\lim_{T\to\infty} \Pr\left(\frac{1}{T^{1/2}} V_{2T} > \varepsilon\right) = 1.$$

As in Theorem 2.3, the limiting distribution is a zero mean Gaussian process with a covariance kernel that reflects both dynamic misspecification as well as the contribution of parameter estimation error. Thus, the limiting distribution is not nuisance parameter free and so critical values cannot be tabulated. Below, we outline a bootstrap procedure that takes into account the joint presence of parameter estimation error and possible dynamic misspecification.

2.5. Bootstrap critical values for the V_{1T} and V_{2T} tests

Given that the limiting distributions of V_{1T} and V_{2T} are not nuisance parameter free, one approach is to construct bootstrap critical values for the tests. In order to show the first order validity of the bootstrap, it thus remains to obtain the limiting distribution of the bootstrapped statistic and show that it coincides with the limiting distribution of the actual statistic under H_0. Then, a test with correct asymptotic size and unit asymptotic power can be obtained by comparing the value of the original statistic with bootstrapped critical values.

If the data consists of iid observations, we should consider proceeding along the lines of Andrews (1997), by drawing B samples of T iid observations from the distribution under H_0, conditional on the observed values for the covariates, Z^{t-1}. The same approach could also be used in the case of dependence, if H_0 were correct dynamic specification (i.e. if $Z^{t-1} = \Im_{t-1}$); in fact, in that case we could use a parametric bootstrap and draw observations from $F(y_t|Z^t, \widehat{\theta}_T)$. However, if instead $Z^{t-1} \subset \Im_{t-1}$, using the parametric bootstrap procedure based on drawing observations from $F(y_t|Z^{t-1}, \widehat{\theta}_T)$ does not ensure that the long run variance of the resampled statistic properly mimics the long run variance of the original statistic; thus leading in general to the construction of invalid asymptotic critical values.

The approach used by Corradi and Swanson (2006a) involves comparing the empirical CDF of the resampled series, evaluated at the bootstrap estimator, with the empirical CDF of the actual series, evaluated at the estimator based on the actual data. For this, they use the overlapping block resampling scheme of Künsch (1989), as follows:[8] At each replication, draw b blocks (with replacement) of length l from the sample $W_t = (y_t, Z^{t-1})$, where $T = lb$. Thus, the first block is equal to

[8] Alternatively, one could use the stationary bootstrap of Politis and Romano (1994a, 1994b). The main difference between the block bootstrap and the stationary bootstrap of Politis and Romano (1994a, PR) is that the former uses a deterministic block length, which may be either overlapping as in Künsch (1989) or non-overlapping as in Carlstein (1986), while the latter resamples using blocks of random length. One important feature of the PR bootstrap is that the resampled series, conditional on the sample, is stationary, while a series resampled from the (overlapping or non-overlapping) block bootstrap is nonstationary, even if the original

$W_{i+1}, \ldots, W_{i+l}$, for some i, with probability $1/(T-l+1)$, the second block is equal to $W_{i+1}, \ldots, W_{i+l}$, for some i, with probability $1/(T-l+1)$, and so on for all blocks. More formally, let I_k, $k = 1, \ldots, b$, be iid discrete uniform random variables on $[0, 1, \ldots, T-l]$, and let $T = bl$. Then, the resampled series, $W_t^* = (y_t^*, X_t^*)$, is such that $W_1^*, W_2^*, \ldots, W_l^*, W_{l+1}^*, \ldots, W_T^* = W_{I_1+1}, W_{I_1+2}, \ldots, W_{I_1+l}, W_{I_2}, \ldots, W_{I_b+l}$, and so a resampled series consists of b blocks that are discrete iid uniform random variables, conditional on the sample. Also, let $\widehat{\theta}_T^*$ be the estimator constructed using the resampled series. For V_{1T}, the bootstrap statistic is:

$$V_{1T}^* = \sup_{r\in[0,1]} \left|V_{1T}^*(r)\right|,$$

where

$$V_{1T}^*(r) = \frac{1}{\sqrt{T}} \sum_{t=1}^{T} \left(1\left\{F\left(y_t^* | Z^{*,t-1}, \widehat{\theta}_T^*\right) \leqslant r\right\} - 1\left\{F\left(y_t | Z^{t-1}, \widehat{\theta}_T\right) \leqslant r\right\}\right), \tag{16}$$

and

$$\widehat{\theta}_T^* = \arg\max_{\theta\in\Theta} \frac{1}{T} \sum_{t=1}^{T} \ln f\left(y_t^* | Z^{*,t-1}, \theta\right).$$

The rationale behind the choice of (16) is the following. By a mean value expansion it can be shown that

$$\begin{aligned} V_{1T}^*(r) = {} & \frac{1}{\sqrt{T}} \sum_{t=1}^{T} \left(1\left\{F\left(y_t^* | Z^{*,t-1}, \theta^\dagger\right) \leqslant r\right\} - 1\left\{F\left(y_t | Z^{t-1}, \theta^\dagger\right) \leqslant r\right\}\right) \\ & - \frac{1}{T} \sum_{t=1}^{T} \nabla_\theta F\left(y_t | Z^{t-1}, \theta^\dagger\right) \sqrt{T}\left(\widehat{\theta}_T^* - \widehat{\theta}_T\right) + o_{P^*}(1) \ \Pr\text{-}P, \end{aligned} \tag{17}$$

where P^* denotes the probability law of the resampled series, conditional on the sample; P denotes the probability law of the sample; and where "$o_{P^*}(1)$ Pr-P", means a term approaching zero according to P^*, conditional on the sample and for all samples except a set of measure approaching zero. Now, the first term on the right-hand side of (17) can be treated via the empirical process version of the block bootstrap, suggesting that the term has the same limiting distribution as $\frac{1}{\sqrt{T}}\sum_{t=1}^{T}(1\{F(y_t|Z^{t-1}, \theta^\dagger) \leqslant r\} - E(1\{F(y_t|Z^{t-1}, \theta^\dagger) \leqslant r\}))$, where $E(1\{F(y_t|X_t, \theta^\dagger) \leqslant r\}) = r$ under H_0, and is different from r under H_A, conditional of the sample. If $\sqrt{T}(\widehat{\theta}_T^* - \widehat{\theta}_T)$ has the same

sample is strictly stationary. However, Lahiri (1999) shows that all block bootstrap methods, regardless of whether the block length is deterministic or random, have a first order bias of the same magnitude, but the bootstrap with deterministic block length has a smaller first order variance. In addition, the overlapping block bootstrap is more efficient than the non-overlapping block bootstrap.

limiting distribution as $\sqrt{T}(\widehat{\theta}_T - \theta^\dagger)$, conditionally on the sample and for all samples except a set of measure approaching zero, then the second term on the right-hand side of (17) will properly capture the contribution of parameter estimation error to the covariance kernel. For the case of dependent observations, the limiting distribution of $\sqrt{T}(\widehat{\theta}^*_T - \widehat{\theta}_T)$ for a variety of quasi maximum likelihood (QMLE) and GMM estimators has been examined in numerous papers in recent years.

For example, Hall and Horowitz (1996) and Andrews (2002) show that the block bootstrap provides improved critical values, in the sense of asymptotic refinement, for "studentized" GMM estimators and for tests of over-identifying restrictions, in the case where the covariance across moment conditions is zero after a given number of lags.[9] In addition, Inoue and Shintani (2006) show that the block bootstrap provides asymptotic refinements for linear over-identified GMM estimators for general mixing processes. In the present context, however, one cannot "studentize" the statistic, and we are thus unable to show second order refinement, as mentioned above. Instead, and again as mentioned above, the approach of Corradi and Swanson (2006a) is to show first order validity of $\sqrt{T}(\widehat{\theta}^*_T - \widehat{\theta}_T)$. An important recent contribution which is useful in the current context is that of Goncalves and White (2002, 2004) who show that for QMLE estimators, the limiting distribution of $\sqrt{T}(\widehat{\theta}^*_T - \widehat{\theta}_T)$ provides a valid first order approximation to that of $\sqrt{T}(\widehat{\theta}_T - \theta^\dagger)$ for heterogeneous and near epoch dependent series.

THEOREM 2.5 (From Theorem 3 of Corradi and Swanson (2006a)). *Let* CS1, CS2(i)–(ii) *and* CS3 *hold, and let* $T = bl$, *with* $l = l_T$, *such that as* $T \to \infty$, $l_T^2/T \to 0$. *Then,*

$$P\left(\omega\colon \sup_{x\in\Re}\left|P^*\left[V^*_{1T}(\omega) \leqslant u\right] - P\left[\sup_{r\in[0,1]} \frac{1}{\sqrt{T}}\sum_{t=1}^{T}\left(1\left\{F\left(y_t|Z^{t-1},\widehat{\theta}_T\right) \leqslant r\right\} - E\left(1\left\{F\left(y_t|Z^{t-1},\theta^\dagger\right) \leqslant r\right\}\right)\right) \leqslant x\right]\right| > \varepsilon\right) \to 0.$$

Thus, V^*_{1T} has a well defined limiting distribution under both hypotheses, which under the null coincides with the same limiting distribution of V_{1T}, Pr-P, as $E(1\{F(y_t|Z^{t-1}, \theta^\dagger) \leqslant r\}) = r$. Now, define $V^*_{2T} = \sup_{u\times v\in U\times V} |V^*_{2T}(u, v)|$, where

$$V^*_{2T}(u, v) = \frac{1}{\sqrt{T}}\sum_{t=1}^{T}\Big(\big(1\{y^*_t \leqslant u\} - F\big(u|Z^{*,t-1}, \widehat{\theta}^*_T\big)\big)1\{Z^{*,t-1} \leqslant v\} - \big(1\{y_t \leqslant u\} - F\big(u|Z^{t-1}, \widehat{\theta}_T\big)\big)1\{Z^{t-1} \leqslant v\}\Big).$$

[9] Andrews (2002) shows first order validity and asymptotic refinements of the equivalent k-step estimator of Davidson and MacKinnon (1999), which only requires the construction of a closed form expression at each bootstrap replication, thus avoiding nonlinear optimization at each replication.

THEOREM 2.6 (From Theorem 4 of Corradi and Swanson (2006a)). *Let* CS1, CS2(iii)–(iv) *and* CS3 *hold, and let* $T = bl$, *with* $l = l_T$, *such that as* $T \to \infty$, $l_T^2/T \to 0$. *Then,*

$$P\Bigg(\omega\colon \sup_{x\in\Re}\Bigg|P^*\big[V_{2T}^*(\omega) \leqslant x\big]$$

$$\times P\Bigg[\sup_{u\times v\in U\times V} \frac{1}{\sqrt{T}}\sum_{t=1}^{T}\Big(\big(1\{y_t \leqslant u\} - F\big(u|Z^{t-1}, \widehat{\theta}_T\big)\big)1\big\{Z^{t-1} \leqslant v\big\}$$

$$- E\big(\big(1\{y_t \leqslant u\} - F\big(u|Z^{t-1}, \theta^\dagger\big)\big)1\big\{Z^{t-1} \leqslant v\big\}\big)\Big) \leqslant x\Bigg] > \varepsilon\Bigg|\Bigg) \to 0.$$

In summary, from Theorems 2.5 and 2.6, we know that V_{1T}^* (resp. V_{2T}^*) has a well defined limiting distribution, conditional on the sample and for all samples except a set of probability measure approaching zero. Furthermore, the limiting distribution coincides with that of V_{1T} (resp. V_{2T}), under H_0. The above results suggest proceeding in the following manner. For any bootstrap replication, compute the bootstrapped statistic, V_{1T}^* (resp. V_{2T}^*). Perform B bootstrap replications (B large) and compute the percentiles of the empirical distribution of the B bootstrapped statistics. Reject H_0 if V_{1T} (V_{2T}) is greater than the $(1-\alpha)$th-percentile. Otherwise, do not reject H_0. Now, for all samples except a set with probability measure approaching zero, V_{1T} (V_{2T}) has the same limiting distribution as the corresponding bootstrapped statistic, under H_0. Thus, the above approach ensures that the test has asymptotic size equal to α. Under the alternative, V_{1T} (V_{2T}) diverges to infinity, while the corresponding bootstrap statistic has a well defined limiting distribution. This ensures unit asymptotic power. Note that the validity of the bootstrap critical values is based on an infinite number of bootstrap replications, although in practice we need to choose B. Andrews and Buchinsky (2000) suggest an adaptive rule for choosing B, Davidson and MacKinnon (2000) suggest a pretesting procedure ensuring that there is a "small probability" of drawing different conclusions from the ideal bootstrap and from the bootstrap with B replications, for a test with a given level. However, in the current context, the limiting distribution is a functional of a Gaussian process, so that the explicit density function is not known; and thus one cannot directly apply the approaches suggested in the papers above. In Monte Carlo experiments, Corradi and Swanson (2006a) show that finite sample results are quite robust to the choice of B. For example, they find that even for values of B as small as 100, the bootstrap has good finite sample properties.

Needless to say, if the parameters are estimated using T observations, and the statistic is constructed using only R observations, with $R = o(T)$, then the contribution of parameter estimation error to the covariance kernel is asymptotically negligible. In this case, it is not necessary to compute $\widehat{\theta}_T^*$. For example, when bootstrapping critical values for a statistic analogous to V_{1T}, but constructed using R observations, say V_{1R}, one can instead construct V_{1R}^* as follows:

$$V_{1R}^* = \sup_{r\in[0,1]} \frac{1}{\sqrt{R}} \sum_{t=1}^{R} \left(1\left\{F\left(y_t^*|Z^{*,t-1}, \widehat{\theta}_T\right) \leqslant r\right\} - 1\left\{F\left(y_t|Z^{t-1}, \widehat{\theta}_T\right) \leqslant r\right\}\right). \tag{18}$$

The intuition for this statistic is that $\sqrt{R}(\widehat{\theta}_T - \theta^\dagger) = o_p(1)$, and so the bootstrap estimator of θ is not needed in order to mimic the distribution of $\sqrt{T}(\widehat{\theta}_T - \theta^\dagger)$. Analogs of V_{1R} and V_{1R}^* can similarly be constructed for V_{2T}. However, Corradi and Swanson (2006a) do not suggest using this approach because of the cost to finite sample power, and also because of the lack of an adaptive, data-driven rule for choosing R.

2.6. *Other related work*

Most of the test statistics described above are based on testing for the uniformity on [0, 1] and/or independence of $F_t(y_t|Z^{t-1}, \theta_0) = \int_{-\infty}^{y_t} f_t(y|Z^{t-1}, \theta_0)$. Needless to say, if $F_t(y_t|Z^{t-1}, \theta_0)$ is iid $UN[0, 1]$, then $\Phi^{-1}(F_t(y_t|Z^{t-1}, \theta_0))$, where Φ denotes the CDF of a standard normal, is iid $N(0, 1)$.

Berkowitz (2001) proposes a likelihood ratio test for the null of (standard) normality against autoregressive alternatives. The advantage of his test is that is easy to implement and has standard limiting distribution, while the disadvantage is that it only has unit asymptotic power against fixed alternatives.

Recently, Bontemps and Meddahi (2003, 2005, BM) introduce a novel approach to testing distributional assumptions. More precisely, they derive set of moment conditions which are satisfied under the null of a particular distribution. This leads to a GMM type test. Of interest is the fact that, the tests suggested by BM do not suffer of the parameter estimation error issue, as the suggested moment condition ensure that the contribution of estimation uncertainty vanishes asymptotically. Furthermore, if the null is rejected, by looking at which moment condition is violated one can get some guidance on how to "improve" the model. Interestingly, BM (2003) point out that, a test for the normality of $\Phi^{-1}(F_t(y_t|Z^{t-1}, \theta_0))$ is instead affected by the contribution of estimation uncertainty, because of the double transformation. Finally, other tests for normality have been recently suggested by Bai and Ng (2005) and by Duan (2003).

3. Specification testing and model selection out-of-sample

In the previous section we discussed in-sample implementation of tests for the correct specification of the conditional distribution for the entire or for a given information set. Thus, the same set of observations were to be used for both estimation and model evaluation. In this section, we outline out-of-sample versions of the same tests, where the sample is split into two parts, and the latter portion is used for validation. Indeed, going back at least as far as Granger (1980) and Ashley, Granger and Schmalensee (1980), it has been noted that if interest focuses on assessing the predictive accuracy of different models, it should be of interest to evaluate them in an out of sample manner – namely by looking at predictions and associated prediction errors. This is particularly true if all models are assumed to be approximations of some "true" underlying unknown model (i.e. if all models may be misspecified). Of note is that Inoue and Kilian (2004) claim that in-sample tests are more powerful than simulated out-of-sample variants thereof. Their findings are based on the examination of standard tests that assume correct specification under the null hypothesis. As mentioned elsewhere in this chapter, in a recent series of papers, Corradi and Swanson (2002, 2005a, 2005b, 2006a, 2006b) relax the correct specification assumption, hence addressing the fact that standard tests are invalid in the sense of having asymptotic size distortions when the model is misspecified under the null.

Of further note is that the probability integral transform approach has frequently been used in an out-of-sample fashion [see, e.g., the empirical applications in DGT (1998) and Hong (2001)], and hence the tests discussed above (which are based on the probability integral transform approach of DGT) should be of interest from the perspective of out-of-sample evaluation. For this reason, and for sake of completeness, in this section we provide out-of-sample versions of all of the test statistics in Sections 2.2–2.4. This requires some preliminary results on the asymptotic behavior of recursive and rolling estimators, as these results have not yet been published elsewhere [see Corradi and Swanson (2005b, 2006b)].

3.1. Estimation and parameter estimation error in recursive and rolling estimation schemes – West as well as West and McCracken results

In out-of-sample model evaluation, the sample of T observations is split into R observations to be used for estimation, and P observations to be used for forecast construction, predictive density evaluation, and generally for model validation and selection. In this context, it is assumed that $T = R + P$. In out-of-sample contexts, parameters are usually estimated using either recursive or rolling estimation schemes. In both cases, one constructs a sequence of P estimators, which are in turn used in the construction of P h-step ahead predictions and prediction errors, where h is the forecast horizon.

In the recursive estimation scheme, one constructs the first estimator using the first R observations, say $\widehat{\theta}_R$, the second using observations up to $R+1$, say $\widehat{\theta}_{R+1}$, and so on until one has a sequence of P estimators, $(\widehat{\theta}_R, \widehat{\theta}_{R+1}, \ldots, \widehat{\theta}_{R+P-1})$. In the sequel, we consider the generic case of extremum estimators, or m-estimators, which include ordinary least squares, nonlinear least squares, and (quasi) maximum-likelihood estimators. Define the recursive estimator as:[10]

$$\widehat{\theta}_{t,\mathrm{rec}} = \arg\min_{\theta\in\Theta} \frac{1}{t}\sum_{j=1}^{t} q\left(y_j, Z^{j-1}, \theta\right), \quad t = R, R+1, \ldots, R+P-1, \tag{19}$$

[10] For notational simplicity, we begin all summations at $t = 1$. Note, however, that in general if Z^{t-1} contains information up to the sth lag, say, then summation should be initiated at $t = s + 1$.

where $q(y_j, Z^{j-1}, \theta_i)$ denotes the objective function (i.e. in (quasi) MLE, $q(y_j, Z^{j-1}, \theta_i) = -\ln f(y_j, Z^{j-1}, \theta_i)$, with f denoting the (pseudo) density of y^t given Z^{t-1}).[11]

In the rolling estimation scheme, one constructs a sequence of P estimators using a rolling window of R observations. That is, the first estimator is constructed using the first R observations, the second using observations from 2 to $R+1$, and so on, with the last estimator being constructed using observations from $T-R$ to $T-1$, so that we have a sequence of P estimators, $(\widehat{\theta}_{R,R}, \widehat{\theta}_{R+1,R}, \ldots, \widehat{\theta}_{R+P-1,R})$.[12]

In general, it is common to assume that P and R grow as T grows. This assumption is maintained in the sequel. Notable exceptions to this approach are Giacomini and White (2003),[13] who propose using a rolling scheme with a fixed window that does not increase with the sample size, so that estimated parameters are treated as mixing variables, and Pesaran and Timmermann (2004a, 2004b) who suggest rules for choosing the window of observations, in order to take into account possible structure breaks.

Turning now to the rolling estimation scheme, define the relevant estimator as:

$$\widehat{\theta}_{t,\mathrm{rol}} = \arg\min_{\theta \in \Theta} \frac{1}{R} \sum_{j=t-R+1}^{t} q\big(y_j, Z^{j-1}, \theta\big), \quad R \leqslant t \leqslant T-1. \tag{20}$$

In the case of in-sample model evaluation, the contribution of parameter estimation error is summarized by the limiting distribution of $\sqrt{T}(\widehat{\theta}_T - \theta^\dagger)$, where $\theta^\dagger$ is the probability limit of $\widehat{\theta}_T$. This is clear, for example, from the proofs of Theorems 2.3 and 2.4 above, which are given in Corradi and Swanson (2006a). On the other hand, in the case of recursive and rolling estimation schemes, the contribution of parameter estimation error is summarized by the limiting distribution of $\frac{1}{\sqrt{P}} \sum_{t=R}^{T-1} (\widehat{\theta}_{t,\mathrm{rec}} - \theta^\dagger)$ and $\frac{1}{\sqrt{P}} \sum_{t=R}^{T-1} (\widehat{\theta}_{t,\mathrm{rol}} - \theta^\dagger)$ respectively. Under mild conditions, because of the central limit theorem, $(\widehat{\theta}_{t,\mathrm{rec}} - \theta^\dagger)$ and $(\widehat{\theta}_{t,\mathrm{rol}} - \theta^\dagger)$ are $O_P(R^{-1/2})$. Thus, if P grows at a slower rate than R (i.e. if $P/R \to 0$, as $T \to \infty$), then $\frac{1}{\sqrt{P}} \sum_{t=R}^{T-1} (\widehat{\theta}_{t,\mathrm{rec}} - \theta^\dagger)$ and $\frac{1}{\sqrt{P}} \sum_{t=R}^{T-1} (\widehat{\theta}_{t,\mathrm{rol}} - \theta^\dagger)$ are asymptotically negligible. In other words, if the in-sample portion of the data used for estimation is "much larger" than the out-of-sample portion of the data to be used for predictive accuracy testing and generally for model evaluation, then the contribution of parameter estimation error is asymptotically negligible.

[11] Generalized method of moments (GMM) estimators can be treated in an analogous manner. As one is often interested in comparing misspecified models, we avoid using over-identified GMM estimators in our discussion. This is because, as pointed out by Hall and Inoue (2003), one cannot obtain asymptotic normality for over-identified GMM in the misspecified case.

[12] Here, for simplicity, we have assumed that in-sample estimation ends with period $T-R$ to $T-1$. Thus, we are implicitly assuming that $h=1$, so that P out-of-sample predictions *and* prediction errors can be constructed.

[13] The Giacomini and White (2003) test is designed for conditional mean evaluation, although it can likely be easily extended to the case of conditional density evaluation. One important advantage of this test is that it is valid for both nested and nonnested models (see below for further discussion).

A key result which is used in all of the subsequent limiting distribution results discussed in this chapter is the derivation of the limiting distribution of $\frac{1}{\sqrt{P}}\sum_{t=R}^{T-1}(\widehat{\theta}_{t,\mathrm{rec}} - \theta^{\dagger})$ [see West (1996)] and of $\frac{1}{\sqrt{P}}\sum_{t=R}^{T-1}(\widehat{\theta}_{t,\mathrm{rol}} - \theta^{\dagger})$ [see West and McCracken (1998)]. Their results follow, given Assumptions W1 and W2, which are listed in Appendix A.

THEOREM 3.1 (From Lemma 4.1 and Theorem 4.1 in West (1996)). *Let* W1 *and* W2 *hold. Also, as $T \to \infty$, $P/R \to \pi$, $0 < \pi < \infty$. Then,*

$$\frac{1}{\sqrt{P}}\sum_{t=R}^{T-1}\left(\widehat{\theta}_{t,\mathrm{rec}} - \theta^{\dagger}\right) \xrightarrow{d} N\left(0, 2\Pi A^{\dagger} C_{00} A^{\dagger}\right),$$

where $\Pi = (1 - \pi^{-1}\ln(1+\pi))$, $C_{00} = \sum_{j=-\infty}^{\infty} E((\nabla_{\theta} q(y_{1+s}, Z^{s}, \theta^{\dagger}))(\nabla_{\theta} q(y_{1+s+j}, Z^{s+j}, \theta^{\dagger}))')$, *and* $A^{\dagger} = E(-\nabla_{\theta_i}^2 q(y_t, Z^{t-1}, \theta^{\dagger}))$.

THEOREM 3.2 (From Lemmas 4.1 and 4.2 in West (1996) and McCracken (2004a)). *Let* W1 *and* W2 *hold. Also, as $T \to \infty$, $P/R \to \pi$, $0 < \pi < \infty$. Then,*

$$\frac{1}{\sqrt{P}}\sum_{t=R}^{T-1}\left(\widehat{\theta}_{t,\mathrm{rol}} - \theta^{\dagger}\right) \xrightarrow{d} N(0, 2\Pi C_{00}),$$

where for $\pi \leqslant 1$, $\Pi = \pi - \frac{\pi^2}{3}$ and for $\pi > 1$, $\Pi = 1 - \frac{1}{3\pi}$. Also, C_{00} and $A^{\dagger}$ defined as in Theorem 3.1.

Of note is that a closely related set of results to those discussed above, in the context of GMM estimators, structural break tests, and predictive tests is given in Dufour, Ghysels and Hall (1994) and Ghysels and Hall (1990). Note also that in the proceeding discussion, little mention is made of π. However, it should be stressed that although our asymptotics do not say anything about the choice of π, some of the tests discussed below have nonstandard limit distributions that have been tabulated for various values of π, and choice thereof can have a discernible impact on finite sample test performance.

3.2. Out-of-sample implementation of Bai as well as Hong and Li tests

We begin by analyzing the out-of-sample versions of Bai's (2003) test. Define the out-of-sample version of the statistic in (6) for the recursive case, as

$$\widehat{V}_{P,\mathrm{rec}} = \frac{1}{\sqrt{P}}\sum_{t=R}^{T-1}\left(1\left\{F_{t+1}\left(y_{t+1}|Z^{t}, \widehat{\theta}_{t,\mathrm{rec}}\right) \leqslant r\right\} - r\right), \tag{21}$$

and for the rolling case as

$$\widehat{V}_{P,\mathrm{rol}} = \frac{1}{\sqrt{P}}\sum_{t=R}^{T-1}\left(1\left\{F_{t+1}\left(y_{t+1}|Z^{t}, \widehat{\theta}_{t,\mathrm{rol}}\right) \leqslant r\right\} - r\right), \tag{22}$$

where $\widehat{\theta}_{t,\text{rec}}$ and $\widehat{\theta}_{t,\text{rol}}$ are defined as in (19) and (20), respectively. Also, define

$$\widehat{W}_{P,\text{rec}}(r) = \widehat{V}_{P,\text{rec}}(r) - \int_0^r \left(\dot{g}(s) C^{-1}(s) \dot{g}(s)' \int_s^1 \dot{g}(\tau) \, \mathrm{d}\widehat{V}_{P,\text{rec}}(\tau) \right) \mathrm{d}s$$

and

$$\widehat{W}_{P,\text{rol}}(r) = \widehat{V}_{P,\text{rol}}(r) - \int_0^r \left(\dot{g}(s) C^{-1}(s) \dot{g}(s)' \int_s^1 \dot{g}(\tau) \, \mathrm{d}\widehat{V}_{P,\text{rol}}(\tau) \right) \mathrm{d}s.$$

Let BAI1, BAI2 and BAI4 be as given in Appendix A, and modify BAI3 as follows:

BAI3′: $(\widehat{\theta}_{t,\text{rec}} - \theta_0) = \mathrm{O}_P(P^{-1/2})$, uniformly in t.[14]
BAI3″: $(\widehat{\theta}_{t,\text{rol}} - \theta_0) = \mathrm{O}_P(P^{-1/2})$, uniformly in t.[15]

Given this setup, the following proposition holds.

PROPOSITION 3.2. *Let* BAI1, BAI2, BAI4 *hold and assume that as* $T \to \infty$, $P/R \to \pi$, *with* $\pi < \infty$. *Then,*

(i) *If* BAI3′ *hold, under the null hypothesis in* (1), $\sup_{r\in[0,1]} \widehat{W}_{P,\text{rec}}(r) \xrightarrow{d} \sup_{r\in[0,1]} W(r)$.

(ii) *If* BAI3″ *hold, under the null hypothesis in* (1), $\sup_{r\in[0,1]} \widehat{W}_{P,\text{rol}}(r) \xrightarrow{d} \sup_{r\in[0,1]} W(r)$.

PROOF. See Appendix B. □

Turning now to an out-of-sample version of the Hong and Li test, note that these tests can be defined as in Equations (8)–(11) above, by replacing $\widehat{U}_t$ in (8) with $\widehat{U}_{t,\text{rec}}$

[14] Note that BAI3′ is satisfied under mild conditions, provided $P/R \to \pi$ with $\pi < \infty$. In particular,

$$P^{1/2}(\widehat{\theta}_t - \theta_0) = \left(\frac{1}{t} \sum_{j=1}^{t} \nabla_\theta^2 q_j(\bar{\theta}_t) \right)^{-1} \left(\frac{P^{1/2}}{t} \sum_{j=1}^{t} \nabla_\theta q_j(\theta_0) \right).$$

Now, by uniform law of large numbers, $(\frac{1}{t}\sum_{j=1}^{t} \nabla_\theta^2 q_j(\bar{\theta}_t))^{-1} - (\frac{1}{t}\sum_{j=1}^{t} E(\nabla_\theta^2 q_j(\theta_0)))^{-1} \xrightarrow{\text{pr}} 0$. Let $t = [Tr]$, with $(1+\pi)^{-1} \leqslant r \leqslant 1$. Then,

$$\frac{P^{1/2}}{[Tr]} \sum_{j=1}^{[Tr]} \nabla_\theta q_j(\theta_0) = \sqrt{\frac{P}{T}} \frac{1}{r} \frac{1}{\sqrt{T}} \sum_{j=1}^{[Tr]} \nabla_\theta q_j(\theta_0).$$

For any r, $\frac{1}{r}\frac{1}{\sqrt{T}} \sum_{j=1}^{[Tr]} \nabla_\theta q_j(\theta_0)$ satisfies a CLT and so is $\mathrm{O}_P(T^{-1/2})$ and so $\mathrm{O}(P^{-1/2})$. As r is bounded away from zero, and because of stochastic equicontinuity in r,

$$\sup_{r\in[(1+\pi)^{-1},1]} \sqrt{\frac{P}{T}} \frac{1}{r} \frac{1}{\sqrt{T}} \sum_{j=1}^{[Tr]} \nabla_\theta q_j(\theta_0) = \mathrm{O}_P(P^{-1/2}).$$

[15] BAI3″ is also satisfied under mild assumptions, by the same arguments used in the footnote above.

and $\widehat{U}_{t,\mathrm{rol}}$, respectively, where

$$\widehat{U}_{t+1,\mathrm{rec}} = F_{t+1}\big(y_{t+1}|Z^t, \widehat{\theta}_{t,\mathrm{rec}}\big) \quad \text{and} \quad \widehat{U}_{t+1,\mathrm{rol}} = F_{t+1}\big(y_{t+1}|Z^t, \widehat{\theta}_{t,\mathrm{rol}}\big), \tag{23}$$

with $\widehat{\theta}_{t,\mathrm{rec}}$ and $\widehat{\theta}_{t,\mathrm{rol}}$ defined as in (19) and (20). Thus, for the recursive estimation case, it follows that

$$\widehat{\phi}_{\mathrm{rec}}(u_1, u_2) = (P - j)^{-1} \sum_{\tau=R+j+1}^{T-1} K_h\big(u_1, \widehat{U}_{\tau,\mathrm{rec}}\big) K_h\big(u_2, \widehat{U}_{\tau-j,\mathrm{rec}}\big),$$

where $n = T = R + P$. For the rolling estimation case, it follows that

$$\widehat{\phi}_{\mathrm{rol}}(u_1, u_2) = (P - j)^{-1} \sum_{\tau=R+j+1}^{T-1} K_h\big(u_1, \widehat{U}_{\tau,\mathrm{rol}}\big) K_h\big(u_2, \widehat{U}_{\tau-j,\mathrm{rol}}\big).$$

Also, define

$$\widehat{M}_{\mathrm{rec}}(j) = \int_0^1 \int_0^1 \big(\widehat{\phi}_{\mathrm{rec}}(u_1, u_2) - 1\big)^2 \, \mathrm{d}u_1 \, \mathrm{d}u_2,$$

$$\widehat{M}_{\mathrm{rol}}(j) = \int_0^1 \int_0^1 \big(\widehat{\phi}_{\mathrm{rol}}(u_1, u_2) - 1\big)^2 \, \mathrm{d}u_1 \, \mathrm{d}u_2$$

and

$$\widehat{Q}_{\mathrm{rec}}(j) = \frac{(n - j)\widehat{M}_{\mathrm{rec}}(j) - A_h^0}{V_0^{1/2}}, \qquad \widehat{Q}_{\mathrm{rol}}(j) = \frac{(n - j)\widehat{M}_{\mathrm{rol}}(j) - A_h^0}{V_0^{1/2}}.$$

The following proposition then holds.

PROPOSITION 3.3. *Let* HL1–HL4 *hold. If* $h = cP^{-\delta}$, $\delta \in (0, 1/5)$, *then under the null in* (1), *and for any* $j > 0$, $j = \mathrm{o}(P^{1-\delta(5-2/v)})$, *if as* $P, R \to \infty$, $P/R \to \pi$, $\pi < \infty$, $\widehat{Q}_{\mathrm{rec}}(j) \xrightarrow{d} N(0, 1)$ *and* $\widehat{Q}_{\mathrm{rol}}(j) \xrightarrow{d} N(0, 1)$.

The statement in the proposition above follows straightforwardly by the same arguments used in the proof of Theorem 1 in Hong and Li (2003). Additionally, and as noted above, the contribution of parameter estimation error is of order $\mathrm{O}_P(P^{1/2})$, while the statistic converges at a nonparametric rate, depending on the bandwidth parameter. Therefore, regardless of the estimation scheme used, the contribution of parameter estimation error is asymptotically negligible.

3.3. Out-of-sample implementation of Corradi and Swanson tests

We now outline out-of-sample versions of the Corradi and Swanson (2006a) tests. First, redefine the statistics using the above out-of-sample notation as

$$V_{1P,\mathrm{rec}} = \sup_{r \in [0,1]} \big|V_{1P,\mathrm{rec}}(r)\big|, \qquad V_{1P,\mathrm{rol}} = \sup_{r \in [0,1]} \big|V_{1P,\mathrm{rol}}(r)\big|$$

where

$$V_{1P,\mathrm{rec}}(r) = \frac{1}{\sqrt{P}} \sum_{t=R}^{T-1} \left(1\left\{\widehat{U}_{t+1,\mathrm{rec}} \leqslant r\right\} - r\right)$$

and

$$V_{1P,\mathrm{rol}}(r) = \frac{1}{\sqrt{P}} \sum_{t=R}^{T-1} \left(1\left\{\widehat{U}_{t+1,\mathrm{rol}} \leqslant r\right\} - r\right),$$

with $\widehat{U}_{t,\mathrm{rec}}$ and $\widehat{U}_{t,\mathrm{rol}}$ defined as in (23). Further, define

$$V_{2P,\mathrm{rec}} = \sup_{u\times v\in U\times V} \left|V_{2P,\mathrm{rec}}(u,v)\right|, \qquad V_{2P,\mathrm{rol}} = \sup_{u\times v\in U\times V} \left|V_{2P,\mathrm{rol}}(u,v)\right|,$$

where

$$V_{2P,\mathrm{rec}}(u,v) = \frac{1}{\sqrt{P}} \sum_{t=R}^{T-1} \left(\left(1\{y_{t+1} \leqslant u\} - F\left(u|Z^t, \widehat{\theta}_{t,\mathrm{rec}}\right)\right) 1\left\{Z^t \leqslant v\right\}\right)$$

and

$$V_{2P,\mathrm{rol}}(u,v) = \frac{1}{\sqrt{P}} \sum_{t=R}^{T-1} \left(\left(1\{y_{t+1} \leqslant u\} - F\left(u|Z^t, \widehat{\theta}_{t,\mathrm{rol}}\right)\right) 1\left\{Z^t \leqslant v\right\}\right).$$

Hereafter, let $V_{1P,J} = V_{1P,\mathrm{rec}}$ when $J = 1$ and $V_{1P,J} = V_{1P,\mathrm{rol}}$ when $J = 2$ and similarly, $V_{2P,J} = V_{2P,\mathrm{rec}}$ when $J = 1$ and $V_{2P,J} = V_{2P,\mathrm{rol}}$ when $J = 2$. The following propositions then hold.

PROPOSITION 3.4. *Let* CS1, CS2(i)–(ii) *and* CS3 *hold. Also, as* $P, R \to \infty$, $P/R \to \pi$, $0 < \pi < \infty$.[16] *Then for* $J = 1, 2$:

(i) *Under* H_0, $V_{1P,J} \Rightarrow \sup_{r\in[0,1]} |V_{1,J}(r)|$, *where* $V_{1,J}$ *is a zero mean Gaussian process with covariance kernel* $K_{1,J}(r, r')$ *given by*:

$$\begin{aligned} K_{1,J}(r,r') = {} & E\Bigg(\sum_{s=-\infty}^{\infty} \left(1\left\{F\left(y_1|Z^0,\theta_0\right) \leqslant r\right\} - r\right) \\ & \times \left(1\left\{F\left(y_s|Z^{s-1},\theta_0\right) \leqslant r'\right\} - r'\right)\Bigg) \\ & + \Pi_J E\left(\nabla_\theta F\left(x(r)|Z^{t-1},\theta_0\right)\right)' A(\theta_0) \\ & \times \sum_{s=-\infty}^{\infty} E\left(q_1(\theta_0) q_s(\theta_0)'\right) A(\theta_0) E\left(\nabla_\theta F\left(x(r')|Z^{t-1},\theta_0\right)\right) \end{aligned}$$

[16] Note that for $\pi = 0$, the contribution of parameter estimation error is asymptotically negligible, and so the covariance kernel is the same as that given in Theorem 2.3.

$$- 2C\Pi_J E\big(\nabla_\theta F\big(x(r)|Z^{t-1}, \theta_0\big)\big)' A(\theta_0) \times \sum_{s=-\infty}^{\infty} E\big(\big(1\big\{F\big(y_1|Z^0, \theta_0\big) \leqslant r\big\} - r\big) q_s(\theta_0)'\big)$$

with $q_s(\theta_0) = \nabla_\theta \ln f_s(y_s|Z^{s-1}, \theta_0)$, $x(r) = F^{-1}(r|Z^{t-1}, \theta_0)$, $A(\theta_0) = (E(\nabla_\theta q_s(\theta_0)\nabla_\theta q_s(\theta_0)'))^{-1}$, $\Pi_1 = 2(1 - \pi^{-1}\ln(1+\pi))$, *and* $C\Pi_1 = (1 - \pi^{-1}\ln(1+\pi))$. *For* $J = 2$, $j = 1$ *and* $P \leqslant R$, $\Pi_2 = (\pi - \frac{\pi^2}{3})$, $C\Pi_2 = \frac{\pi}{2}$, *and for* $P > R$, $\Pi_2 = (1 - \frac{1}{3\pi})$ *and* $C\Pi_2 = (1 - \frac{1}{2\pi})$.

(ii) *Under* H_A, *there exists an* $\varepsilon > 0$ *such that*

$$\lim_{T\to\infty} \Pr\left(\frac{1}{P^{1/2}} V_{1T,J} > \varepsilon\right) = 1, \quad J = 1, 2.$$

PROOF. See Appendix B. □

PROPOSITION 3.5. *Let* CS1, CS2(iii)–(iv) *and* CS3 *hold. Also, as* $P, R \to \infty$, $P/R \to \pi$, $0 < \pi < \infty$. *Then for* $J = 1, 2$:

(i) *Under* H_0, $V_{2P,J} \Rightarrow \sup_{u\times v\in U\times V} |Z_J(u, v)|$, *where* $V_{2P,J}$ *is defined as in* (15) *and* Z *is a zero mean Gaussian process with covariance kernel* $K_{2,J}(u, v, u', v')$ *given by*:

$$E\left(\sum_{s=-\infty}^{\infty} \big(\big(1\{y_1 \leqslant u\} - F\big(u|Z^0, \theta_0\big)\big)1\{X_0 \leqslant v\}\big) \times \big(\big(1\{y_s \leqslant u'\} - F\big(u|Z^{s-1}, \theta_0\big)\big)1\{X_s \leqslant v'\}\big)\right)$$
$$+ \Pi_J E\big(\nabla_\theta F\big(u|Z^0, \theta_0\big)' 1\big\{Z^0 \leqslant v\big\}\big) A(\theta_0) \times \sum_{s=-\infty}^{\infty} q_0(\theta_0) q_s(\theta_0)' A(\theta_0) E\big(\nabla_\theta F\big(u'|Z^0, \theta_0\big) 1\big\{Z^0 \leqslant v'\big\}\big)$$
$$- 2C\Pi_J \sum_{s=-\infty}^{\infty} \big(\big(1\{y_0 \leqslant u\} - F\big(u|Z^0, \theta_0\big)\big)1\big\{Z^0 \leqslant v\big\}\big) \times E\big(\nabla_\theta F\big(u'|Z^0, \theta_0\big)' 1\big\{Z^0 \leqslant v'\big\}\big) A(\theta_0) q_s(\theta_0)\big),$$

where Π_J *and* $C\Pi_J$ *are defined as in the statement of Proposition* 3.4.

(ii) *Under* H_A, *there exists an* $\varepsilon > 0$ *such that*

$$\lim_{T\to\infty} \Pr\left(\frac{1}{T^{1/2}} V_{2T} > \varepsilon\right) = 1.$$

PROOF. See Appendix B. □

It is immediate to see that the limiting distributions in Propositions 3.4 and 3.5 differ from the ones in Theorems 2.3 and 2.4 only up to terms Π_j and $C\Pi_j$, $j = 1, 2$. On the other hand, we shall see that valid asymptotic critical values cannot be obtained by directly following the bootstrap procedure described in Section 2.5. Below, we outline how to obtain valid bootstrap critical values in the recursive and in the rolling estimation cases, respectively.

3.4. Bootstrap critical for the $V_{1P,J}$ and $V_{2P,J}$ tests under recursive estimation

When forming the block bootstrap for recursive m-estimators, it is important to note that earlier observations are used more frequently than temporally subsequent observations when forming test statistics. On the other hand, in the standard block bootstrap, all blocks from the original sample have the same probability of being selected, regardless of the dates of the observations in the blocks. Thus, the bootstrap estimator, say $\widehat{\theta}^*_{t,\mathrm{rec}}$, which is constructed as a direct analog of $\widehat{\theta}_{t,\mathrm{rec}}$, is characterized by a location bias that can be either positive or negative, depending on the sample that we observe. In order to circumvent this problem, we suggest a re-centering of the bootstrap score which ensures that the new bootstrap estimator, which is no longer the direct analog of $\widehat{\theta}_{t,\mathrm{rec}}$, is asymptotically unbiased. It should be noted that the idea of re-centering is not new in the bootstrap literature for the case of full sample estimation. In fact, re-centering is necessary, even for first order validity, in the case of over-identified generalized method of moments (GMM) estimators [see, e.g., Hall and Horowitz (1996), Andrews (2002, 2004), and Inoue and Shintani (2006)]. This is due to the fact that, in the over-identified case, the bootstrap moment conditions are not equal to zero, even if the population moment conditions are. However, in the context of m-estimators using the full sample, re-centering is needed only for higher order asymptotics, but not for first order validity, in the sense that the bias term is of smaller order than $T^{-1/2}$ [see, e.g., Andrews (2002)]. However, in the case of recursive m-estimators the bias term is instead of order $T^{-1/2}$, and so it does contribute to the limiting distribution. This points to a need for re-centering when using recursive estimation schemes, and such re-centering is discussed in the next subsection.

3.4.1. The recursive PEE bootstrap

We now show how the Künsch (1989) block bootstrap can be used in the context of a recursive estimation scheme. At each replication, draw b blocks (with replacement) of length l from the sample $W_t = (y_t, Z^{t-1})$, where $bl = T - 1$. Thus, the first block is equal to $W_{i+1}, \ldots, W_{i+l}$, for some $i = 0, \ldots, T - l - 1$, with probability $1/(T - l)$, the second block is equal to $W_{i+1}, \ldots, W_{i+l}$, again for some $i = 0, \ldots, T - l - 1$, with probability $1/(T - l)$, and so on, for all blocks. More formally, let I_k, $k = 1, \ldots, b$, be iid discrete uniform random variables on $[0, 1, \ldots, T - l + 1]$. Then, the resampled series, $W_t^* = (y_t^*, Z^{*,t-1})$, is such that $W_1^*, W_2^*, \ldots, W_l^*, W_{l+1}^*, \ldots, W_T^* =$

$W_{I_1+1}, W_{I_1+2}, \ldots, W_{I_1+l}, W_{I_2}, \ldots, W_{I_b+l}$, and so a resampled series consists of b blocks that are discrete iid uniform random variables, conditional on the sample.

Suppose we define the bootstrap estimator, $\widehat{\theta}^*_{t,\mathrm{rec}}$, to be the direct analog of $\widehat{\theta}_{t,\mathrm{rec}}$. Namely,

$$\widehat{\theta}^*_{t,\mathrm{rec}} = \arg\min_{\theta\in\Theta} \frac{1}{t}\sum_{j=1}^{t} q\big(y^*_j, Z^{*,j-1}, \theta\big), \quad R \leqslant t \leqslant T-1. \tag{24}$$

By first order conditions, $\frac{1}{t}\sum_{j=1}^{t} \nabla_\theta q(y^*_j, Z^{*,j-1}, \widehat{\theta}^*_{t,\mathrm{rec}}) = 0$, and via a mean value expansion of $\frac{1}{t}\sum_{j=1}^{t} \nabla_\theta q(y^*_j, Z^{*,j-1}, \widehat{\theta}^*_{t,\mathrm{rec}})$ around $\widehat{\theta}_{t,\mathrm{rec}}$, after a few simple manipulations, we have that

$$\begin{aligned}
&\frac{1}{\sqrt{P}}\sum_{t=R}^{T-1}\big(\widehat{\theta}^*_{t,\mathrm{rec}} - \widehat{\theta}_{t,\mathrm{rec}}\big)\\
&\quad = \frac{1}{\sqrt{P}}\sum_{t=R}^{T-1}\left(\left(\frac{1}{t}\sum_{j=1}^{t}\nabla^2_\theta q\big(y^*_j, Z^{*,j-1}, \bar{\theta}_{t,\mathrm{rec}}\big)\right)^{-1}\right.\\
&\qquad \left.\times \frac{1}{t}\sum_{j=1}^{t}\nabla_\theta q\big(y^*_j, Z^{*,j-1}, \widehat{\theta}_{t,\mathrm{rec}}\big)\right)\\
&\quad = A_i^\dagger \frac{1}{\sqrt{P}}\sum_{t=R}^{T-1}\left(\frac{1}{t}\sum_{j=1}^{t}\nabla_\theta q\big(y^*_j, Z^{*,j-1}, \widehat{\theta}_{t,\mathrm{rec}}\big)\right) + o_{P^*}(1) \ \mathrm{Pr}\text{-}P\\
&\quad = A_i^\dagger \frac{a_{R,0}}{\sqrt{P}}\sum_{t=1}^{R}\nabla_\theta q\big(y^*_j, Z^{*,j-1}, \widehat{\theta}_{t,\mathrm{rec}}\big)\\
&\qquad + A_i^\dagger \frac{1}{\sqrt{P}}\sum_{j=1}^{P-1} a_{R,j}\nabla_\theta q\big(y^*_{R+j}, Z^{*,R+j-1}, \widehat{\theta}_{t,\mathrm{rec}}\big)\\
&\qquad + o_{P^*}(1) \ \mathrm{Pr}\text{-}P,
\end{aligned} \tag{25}$$

where $\bar{\theta}^*_{t,\mathrm{rec}} \in (\widehat{\theta}^*_{t,\mathrm{rec}}, \widehat{\theta}_{t,\mathrm{rec}})$, $A^\dagger = E(\nabla^2_\theta q(y_j, Z^{j-1}, \theta^\dagger))^{-1}$, $a_{R,j} = \frac{1}{R+j} + \frac{1}{R+j+1} + \cdots + \frac{1}{R+P-1}$, $j = 0, 1, \ldots, P-1$, and where the last equality on the right-hand side of (25) follows immediately, using the same arguments as those used in Lemma A5 of West (1996). Analogously,

$$\begin{aligned}
&\frac{1}{\sqrt{P}}\sum_{t=R}^{T-1}\big(\widehat{\theta}_{t,\mathrm{rec}} - \theta^\dagger\big)\\
&\quad = A^\dagger \frac{a_{R,0}}{\sqrt{P}}\sum_{t=s}^{R}\nabla_\theta q\big(y_j, Z^{j-1}, \theta^\dagger\big)
\end{aligned}$$

$$+ A^{\dagger} \frac{1}{\sqrt{P}} \sum_{j=1}^{P-1} a_{R,j} \nabla_{\theta} q\left(y_{R+j}, Z^{R+j-1}, \theta^{\dagger}\right) + o_P(1). \tag{26}$$

Now, given the definition of $\theta^{\dagger}$, $E(\nabla_{\theta} q(y_j, Z^{j-1}, \theta^{\dagger})) = 0$ for all j, and $\frac{1}{\sqrt{P}} \times \sum_{t=R}^{T-1} (\widehat{\theta}_{t,\text{rec}} - \theta^{\dagger})$ has a zero mean normal limiting distribution [see Theorem 4.1 in West (1996)]. On the other hand, as any block of observations has the same chance of being drawn,

$$E^*\left(\nabla_{\theta} q\left(y_j^*, Z^{*,j-1}, \widehat{\theta}_{t,\text{rec}}\right)\right) = \frac{1}{T-1} \sum_{k=1}^{T-1} \nabla_{\theta} q\left(y_k, Z^{k-1}, \widehat{\theta}_{t,\text{rec}}\right) + \mathrm{O}\left(\frac{l}{T}\right) \ \mathrm{Pr}\text{-}P, \tag{27}$$

where the $\mathrm{O}(\frac{l}{T})$ term arises because the first and last l observations have a lesser chance of being drawn [see, e.g., Fitzenberger (1997)].[17] Now, $\frac{1}{T-1} \sum_{k=1}^{T-1} \nabla_{\theta} q(y_k, Z^{k-1}, \widehat{\theta}_{t,\text{rec}}) \neq 0$, and is instead of order $\mathrm{O}_P(T^{-1/2})$. Thus, $\frac{1}{\sqrt{P}} \sum_{t=R}^{T-1} \frac{1}{T-1} \sum_{k=1}^{T-1} \nabla_{\theta} q(y_k, Z^{k-1}, \widehat{\theta}_{t,\text{rec}}) = \mathrm{O}_P(1)$, and does not vanish in probability. This clearly contrasts with the full sample case, in which $\frac{1}{T-1} \sum_{k=1}^{T-1} \nabla_{\theta} q(y_k, Z^{k-1}, \widehat{\theta}_T) = 0$, because of the first order conditions. Thus, $\frac{1}{\sqrt{P}} \sum_{t=R}^{T-1} (\widehat{\theta}^*_{t,\text{rec}} - \widehat{\theta}_{t,\text{rec}})$ cannot have a zero mean normal limiting distribution, but is instead characterized by a location bias that can be either positive or negative depending on the sample.

Given (27), our objective is thus to have the bootstrap score centered around $\frac{1}{T-1} \sum_{k=1}^{T-1} \nabla_{\theta} q(y_k, Z^{k-1}, \widehat{\theta}_{t,\text{rec}})$. Hence, define a new bootstrap estimator, $\widetilde{\theta}^*_{t,\text{rec}}$, as:

$$\widetilde{\theta}^*_{t,\text{rec}} = \arg\min_{\theta \in \Theta} \frac{1}{t} \sum_{j=1}^{t} \left(q\left(y_j^*, Z^{*,j-1}, \theta\right) - \theta' \left(\frac{1}{T} \sum_{k=1}^{T-1} \nabla_{\theta} q\left(y_k, Z^{k-1}, \widehat{\theta}_{t,\text{rec}}\right) \right) \right), \tag{28}$$

$R \leqslant t \leqslant T-1$.[18]

Given first order conditions,

$$\frac{1}{t} \sum_{j=1}^{t} \left(\nabla_{\theta} q\left(y_j^*, Z^{*,j-1}, \widetilde{\theta}^*_{t,\text{rec}}\right) - \left(\frac{1}{T} \sum_{k=1}^{T-1} \nabla_{\theta} q\left(y_k, Z^{k-1}, \widehat{\theta}_{t,\text{rec}}\right) \right) \right) = 0,$$

[17] In fact, the first and last observation in the sample can appear only at the beginning and end of the block, for example.

[18] More precisely, we should define

$$\widetilde{\theta}^*_{i,t} = \arg\min_{\theta_i \in \Theta_i} \frac{1}{t-s} \sum_{j=s}^{t} \left(q_i\left(y_j^*, Z^{*,j-1}, \theta_i\right) - \theta_i' \left(\frac{1}{T-s} \sum_{k=s}^{T-1} \nabla_{\theta_i} q_i\left(y_k, Z^{k-1}, \widehat{\theta}_{i,t}\right) \right) \right).$$

However, for notational simplicity we approximate $\frac{1}{t-s}$ and $\frac{1}{T-s}$ with $\frac{1}{t}$ and $\frac{1}{T}$.

and via a mean value expansion of $\frac{1}{t}\sum_{j=1}^{t}\nabla_\theta q(y_j^*, Z^{*,j-1}, \widetilde{\theta}_{t,\text{rec}}^*)$ around $\widehat{\theta}_{t,\text{rec}}$, after a few simple manipulations, we have that

$$\frac{1}{\sqrt{P}}\sum_{t=R}^{T-1}\left(\widetilde{\theta}_{t,\text{rec}}^* - \widehat{\theta}_{t,\text{rec}}\right)$$
$$= A^\dagger \frac{1}{\sqrt{P}}\sum_{t=R}^{T}\left(\frac{1}{t}\sum_{j=s}^{t}\left(\nabla_\theta q\left(y_j^*, Z^{*,j-1}, \widehat{\theta}_{t,\text{rec}}\right)\right.\right.$$
$$\left.\left.- \left(\frac{1}{T}\sum_{k=s}^{T-1}\nabla_\theta q\left(y_k, Z^{k-1}, \widehat{\theta}_{t,\text{rec}}\right)\right)\right)\right) + o_{P^*}(1)\ \text{Pr-}P.$$

Given (27), it is immediate to see that the bias associated with $\frac{1}{\sqrt{P}}\sum_{t=R}^{T-1}(\widetilde{\theta}_{t,\text{rec}}^* - \widehat{\theta}_{t,\text{rec}})$ is of order $\mathrm{O}(lT^{-1/2})$, conditional on the sample, and so it is negligible for first order asymptotics, as $l = \mathrm{o}(T^{1/2})$.

The following result pertains given the above setup.

THEOREM 3.6 (From Theorem 1 in Corradi and Swanson (2005b)). *Let* CS1 *and* CS3 *hold. Also, assume that as* $T \to \infty$, $l \to \infty$, *and that* $\frac{l}{T^{1/4}} \to 0$. *Then, as* T, P *and* $R \to \infty$,

$$P\left(\omega\colon \sup_{v\in\Re^{\varrho(i)}}\left|P_T^*\left(\frac{1}{\sqrt{P}}\sum_{t=R}^{T}\left(\widetilde{\theta}_{t,\text{rec}}^* - \theta^\dagger\right) \leqslant v\right)\right.\right.$$
$$\left.\left.- P\left(\frac{1}{\sqrt{P}}\sum_{t=R}^{T}\left(\widehat{\theta}_{t,\text{rec}} - \theta^\dagger\right) \leqslant v\right)\right| > \varepsilon\right) \to 0,$$

where P_T^* *denotes the probability law of the resampled series, conditional on the* (*entire*) *sample.*

Broadly speaking, Theorem 3.6 states that $\frac{1}{\sqrt{P}}\sum_{t=R}^{T-1}(\widetilde{\theta}_{t,\text{rec}}^* - \theta^\dagger)$ has the same limiting distribution as $\frac{1}{\sqrt{P}}\sum_{t=R}^{T-1}(\widehat{\theta}_{t,\text{rec}} - \theta^\dagger)$, conditional on the sample, and for all samples except a set with probability measure approaching zero. As outlined in the following sections, application of Theorem 3.6 allows us to capture the contribution of (recursive) parameter estimation error to the covariance kernel of the limiting distribution of various statistics.

3.4.2. $V_{1P,J}$ and $V_{2P,J}$ bootstrap statistics under recursive estimation

One can apply the results above to provide a bootstrap statistic for the case of the recursive estimation scheme. Define

$$V_{1P,\text{rec}}^* = \sup_{r\in[0,1]}\left|V_{1P,\text{rec}}^*(r)\right|,$$

where

$$V^*_{1P,\text{rec}}(r) = \frac{1}{\sqrt{P}} \sum_{t=R}^{T-1} \left(1\left\{ F\left(y^*_{t+1} | Z^{*,t}, \widetilde{\theta}^*_{t,\text{rec}}\right) \leqslant r \right\} - \frac{1}{T} \sum_{j=1}^{T-1} 1\left\{ F\left(y_{j+1} | Z^j, \widehat{\theta}_{t,\text{rec}}\right) \leqslant r \right\} \right). \tag{29}$$

Also define,

$$V^*_{2P,\text{rec}} = \sup_{u \times v \in U \times V} V^*_{2P,\text{rec}}(u, v)$$

where

$$V^*_{2P,\text{rec}}(u, v) = \frac{1}{\sqrt{P}} \sum_{t=R}^{T-1} \left(\left(1\left\{ y^*_{t+1} \leqslant u \right\} - F\left(u | Z^{*,t}, \widetilde{\theta}^*_{t,\text{rec}}\right)\right) 1\left\{ Z^{*,t} \leqslant v \right\} - \frac{1}{T} \sum_{j=1}^{T-1} \left(1\{ y_{j+1} \leqslant u \} - F\left(u | Z^j, \widehat{\theta}_{t,\text{rec}}\right)\right) 1\left\{ Z^j \leqslant v \right\} \right). \tag{30}$$

Note that bootstrap statistics in (29) and (30) are different from the "usual" bootstrap statistics, which are defined as the difference between the statistic computed over the sample observations and over the bootstrap observations. For brevity, just consider $V^*_{1P,\text{rec}}$. Note that each bootstrap term, say $1\{F(y^*_{t+1}|Z^{*,t}, \widetilde{\theta}^*_{t,\text{rec}}) \leqslant r\}$, $t \geqslant R$, is recentered around the (full) sample mean $\frac{1}{T} \sum_{j=1}^{T-1} 1\{F(y_{j+1}|Z^j, \widehat{\theta}_{t,\text{rec}}) \leqslant r\}$. This is necessary as the bootstrap statistic is constructed using the last P resampled observations, which in turn have been resampled from the full sample. In particular, this is necessary regardless of the ratio P/R. If $P/R \to 0$, then we do not need to mimic parameter estimation error, and so could simply use $\widehat{\theta}_{1,t,\tau}$ instead of $\widetilde{\theta}^*_{1,t,\tau}$, but we still need to recenter any bootstrap term around the (full) sample mean. This leads to the following proposition.

PROPOSITION 3.7. *Let* CS1, CS2(i)–(ii) *and* CS3 *hold. Also, assume that as* $T \to \infty$, $l \to \infty$, *and that* $\frac{l}{T^{1/4}} \to 0$. *Then, as* T, P *and* $R \to \infty$,

$$P\left(\omega\colon \sup_{x \in \Re} \left| P^*\left[V^*_{1P,\text{rec}}(\omega) \leqslant u \right] - P\left[\sup_{r \in [0,1]} \frac{1}{\sqrt{P}} \sum_{t=R}^{T-1} \left(1\left\{ F\left(y_{t+1} | Z^t, \theta^\dagger\right) \leqslant r \right\} - E\left(1\left\{ F\left(y_{t+1} | Z^t, \theta^\dagger\right) \leqslant r \right\}\right)\right) \leqslant x \right] \right| > \varepsilon \right) \to 0.$$

PROOF. See Appendix B. □

PROPOSITION 3.8. *Let* CS1, CS2(iii)–(iv) *and* CS3 *hold. Also, assume that as* $T \to \infty$, $l \to \infty$, *and that* $\frac{l}{T^{1/4}} \to 0$. *Then, as* T, P *and* $R \to \infty$,

$$P\left(\omega: \sup_{x\in\Re}\left|P^*\left[V^*_{2P,\mathrm{rec}}(\omega) \leqslant x\right]\right.\right.$$
$$\times P\left[\sup_{u\times v\in U\times V}\frac{1}{\sqrt{P}}\sum_{t=R}^{T-1}\left(\left(1\{y_{t+1}\leqslant u\} - F\left(u|Z^t,\theta^\dagger\right)\right)1\left\{Z^t \leqslant v\right\}\right.\right.$$
$$\left.\left.\left.\left. - E\left(\left(1\{y_{t+1}\leqslant u\} - F\left(u|Z^t,\theta^\dagger\right)\right)1\left\{Z^t\leqslant v\right\}\right)\right) \leqslant x\right]\right| > \varepsilon\right) \to 0.$$

PROOF. See Appendix B. □

The same remarks given below Theorems 2.5 and 2.6 apply here.

3.5. Bootstrap critical for the $V_{1P,J}$ and $V_{2P,J}$ tests under rolling estimation

In the rolling estimation scheme, observations in the middle of the sample are used more frequently than observations at either the beginning or the end of the sample. As in the recursive case, this introduces a location bias to the usual block bootstrap, as under standard resampling with replacement, any block from the original sample has the same probability of being selected. Also, the bias term varies across samples and can be either positive or negative, depending on the specific sample. In the sequel, we shall show how to properly recenter the objective function in order to obtain a bootstrap rolling estimator, say $\widetilde{\theta}^*_{t,\mathrm{rol}}$ such that $\frac{1}{\sqrt{P}}\sum_{t=R}^{T-1}(\widetilde{\theta}^*_{t,\mathrm{rol}} - \widehat{\theta}_{t,\mathrm{rol}})$ has the same limiting distribution as $\frac{1}{\sqrt{P}}\sum_{t=R}^{T-1}(\widehat{\theta}_{t,\mathrm{rol}} - \theta^\dagger)$, conditionally on the sample.

Resample b overlapping blocks of length l from $W_t = (y_t, Z^{t-1})$, as in the recursive case and define the rolling bootstrap estimator as,

$$\widetilde{\theta}^*_{t,\mathrm{rol}} = \arg\max_{\theta_i\in\Theta_i}\frac{1}{R}\sum_{j=t-R+1}^{t}\left(q\left(y^*_j, Z^{*,j-1},\theta\right)\right.$$
$$\left. - \theta'\left(\frac{1}{T}\sum_{k=s}^{T-1}\nabla_\theta q\left(y_k, Z^{k-1},\widehat{\theta}_{t,\mathrm{rol}}\right)\right)\right).$$

THEOREM 3.9 (From Proposition 2 in Corradi and Swanson (2005b)). *Let* CS1 *and* CS3 *hold. Also, assume that as* $T \to \infty$, $l \to \infty$, *and that* $\frac{l}{T^{1/4}} \to 0$. *Then, as* T, P *and* $R \to \infty$,

$$P\left(\omega\colon \sup_{v \in \Re^{\varrho(i)}} \left| P_T^*\left(\frac{1}{\sqrt{P}} \sum_{t=R}^{T} \left(\widetilde{\theta}_{t,\mathrm{rol}}^* - \widehat{\theta}_{t,\mathrm{rol}}\right) \leqslant v\right) - P\left(\frac{1}{\sqrt{P}} \sum_{t=R}^{T} \left(\widehat{\theta}_{t,\mathrm{rol}} - \theta^{\dagger}\right) \leqslant v\right)\right| > \varepsilon\right) \to 0.$$

Finally note that in the rolling case, $V_{1P,\mathrm{rol}}^*$, $V_{2P,\mathrm{rol}}^*$ can be constructed as in (29) and (30), $\widetilde{\theta}_{t,\mathrm{rec}}^*$ and $\widehat{\theta}_{t,\mathrm{rec}}$ with $\widetilde{\theta}_{t,\mathrm{rol}}^*$ and $\widehat{\theta}_{t,\mathrm{rol}}$, and the same statement as in Propositions 3.7 and 3.8 hold.

Part III: Evaluation of (Multiple) Misspecified Predictive Models

4. Pointwise comparison of (multiple) misspecified predictive models

In the previous two sections we discussed several in-sample and out of sample tests for the null of either correct dynamic specification of the conditional distribution or for the null of correct conditional distribution for given information set. Needless to say, the correct (either dynamically, or for a given information set) conditional distribution is the best predictive density. However, it is often sensible to account for the fact that all models may be approximations, and so may be misspecified. The literature on point forecast evaluation does indeed acknowledge that the objective of interest is often to choose a model which provides the best (loss function specific) out-of-sample predictions, from amongst a set of potentially misspecified models, and not just from amongst models that may only be dynamically misspecified, as is the case with some of the tests discussed above. In this section we outline several popular tests for comparing the relative out-of-sample accuracy of misspecified models in the case of point forecasts. We shall distinguish among three main groups of tests: (i) tests for comparing two nonnested models, (ii) tests for comparing two (or more) nested models, and (iii) tests for comparing multiple models, where at least one model is non-nested. In the next section, we broaden the scope by considering tests for comparing misspecified predictive density models.[19]

[19] It should be noted that the contents of this section of the chapter have broad overlap with a number of topics discussed in the Chapter 3 in this Handbook by Ken West (2006). For further details, the reader is referred to that chapter.

4.1. Comparison of two nonnested models: Diebold and Mariano test

Diebold and Mariano (1995, DM) propose a test for the null hypothesis of equal predictive ability that is based in part on the pairwise model comparison test discussed in Granger and Newbold (1986). The Diebold and Mariano test allows for nondifferentiable loss functions, but does not explicitly account for parameter estimation error, instead relying on the assumption that the in-sample estimation period is growing more quickly than the out-of-sample prediction period, so that parameter estimation error vanishes asymptotically. West (1996) takes the more general approach of explicitly allowing for parameter estimation error, although at the cost of assuming that the loss function used is differentiable. Let $u_{0,t+h}$ and $u_{1,t+h}$ be the h-step ahead prediction error associated with predictions of y_{t+h}, using information available up to time t. For example, for $h = 1$, $u_{0,t+1} = y_{t+1} - \kappa_0(Z_0^{t-1}, \theta_0^\dagger)$, and $u_{1,t+1} = y_{t+1} - \kappa_1(Z_1^{t-1}, \theta_1^\dagger)$, where Z_0^{t-1} and Z_1^{t-1} contain past values of y_t and possibly other conditioning variables. Assume that the two models be nonnested (i.e. Z_0^{t-1} not a subset of Z_1^{t-1} – and vice-versa – and/or $\kappa_1 \neq \kappa_0$). As lucidly pointed out by Granger and Pesaran (1993), when comparing misspecified models, the ranking of models based on their predictive accuracy depends on the loss function used. Hereafter, denote the loss function as g, and as usual let $T = R + P$, where only the last P observations are used for model evaluation. Under the assumption that $u_{0,t}$ and $u_{1,t}$ are strictly stationary, the null hypothesis of equal predictive accuracy is specified as:

$$H_0\colon \quad E\big(g(u_{0,t}) - g(u_{1t})\big) = 0$$

and

$$H_A\colon \quad E\big(g(u_{0,t}) - g(u_{1t})\big) \neq 0.$$

In practice, we do not observe $u_{0,t+1}$ and $u_{1,t+1}$, but only $\widehat{u}_{0,t+1}$ and $\widehat{u}_{1,t+1}$, where $\widehat{u}_{0,t+1} = y_{t+1} - \kappa_0(Z_0^t, \widehat{\theta}_{0,t})$, and where $\widehat{\theta}_{0,t}$ is an estimator constructed using observations from 1 up to t, $t \geqslant R$, in the recursive estimation case, and between $t - R + 1$ and t in the rolling case. For brevity, in this subsection we just consider the recursive scheme. Therefore, for notational simplicity, we simply denote the recursive estimator for model i, $\widehat{\theta}_{0,t}$, $\widehat{\theta}_{0,t,\text{rec}}$. Note that the rolling scheme can be treated in an analogous manner. Of crucial importance is the loss function used for estimation. In fact, as we shall show below if we use the same loss function for estimation and model evaluation, the contribution of parameter estimation error is asymptotically negligible, regardless of the limit of the ratio P/R as $T \to \infty$. Here, for $i = 0, 1$

$$\widehat{\theta}_{i,t} = \arg\min_{\theta_i \in \Theta_i} \frac{1}{t} \sum_{j=1}^{t} q\big(y_j - \kappa_i\big(Z_i^{j-1}, \theta_i\big)\big), \quad t \geqslant R.$$

In the sequel, we rely on the assumption that g is continuously differentiable. The case of non-differentiable loss functions is treated by McCracken (2000, 2004b). Now,

$$\begin{aligned}\frac{1}{\sqrt{P}}\sum_{t=R}^{T-h} g(\widehat{u}_{i,t+1}) &= \frac{1}{\sqrt{P}}\sum_{t=R}^{T-1} g(u_{i,t+1}) + \frac{1}{\sqrt{P}}\sum_{t=R}^{T-1} \nabla g(\bar{u}_{i,t+1})(\widehat{\theta}_{i,t} - \theta_i^{\dagger}) \\ &= \frac{1}{\sqrt{P}}\sum_{t=R}^{T-1} g(u_{i,t+1}) + E(\nabla g(u_{i,t+1}))\frac{1}{\sqrt{P}}\sum_{t=R}^{T-1}(\widehat{\theta}_{i,t} - \theta_i^{\dagger}) \\ &\quad + o_P(1). \end{aligned} \tag{31}$$

It is immediate to see that if $g = q$ (i.e. the same loss is used for estimation and model evaluation), then $E(\nabla g(u_{i,t+1})) = 0$ because of the first order conditions. Of course, another case in which the second term on the right-hand side of (31) vanishes is when $P/R \to 0$ (these are the cases DM consider). The limiting distribution of the right-hand side in (31) is given in Section 3.1. The Diebold and Mariano test is

$$DM_P = \frac{1}{\sqrt{P}}\frac{1}{\widehat{\sigma}_P}\sum_{t=R}^{T-1}\bigl(g(\widehat{u}_{0,t+1}) - g(\widehat{u}_{1,t+1})\bigr),$$

where

$$\begin{aligned}&\frac{1}{\sqrt{P}}\sum_{t=R}^{T-1}\bigl(g(\widehat{u}_{0,t+1}) - g(\widehat{u}_{1,t+1})\bigr) \\ &\quad \xrightarrow{d} N\bigl(0, S_{gg} + 2\Pi F_0' A_0 S_{h_0 h_0} A_0 F_0 \\ &\qquad + 2\Pi F_1' A_1 S_{h_1 h_1} A_1 F_1 - \Pi\bigl(S_{gh_0}' A_0 F_0 + F_0' A_0 S_{gh_0}\bigr) \\ &\qquad - 2\Pi\bigl(F_1' A_1 S_{h_1 h_0} A_0 F_0 + F_0' A_0 S_{h_0 h_1} A_1 F_1\bigr) \\ &\qquad + \Pi\bigl(S_{gh_1}' A_1 F_1 + F_1' A_1 S_{gh_1}\bigr)\bigr),\end{aligned}$$

with

$$\begin{aligned}\widehat{\sigma}_P^2 = {}& \widehat{S}_{gg} + 2\Pi \widehat{F}_0' \widehat{A}_0 \widehat{S}_{h_0 h_0} + 2\Pi \widehat{F}_1' \widehat{A}_1 S_{h_1 h_1} \widehat{A}_1 \widehat{F}_1 \\ & - 2\Pi\bigl(\widehat{F}_1' \widehat{A}_1 \widehat{S}_{h_1 h_0} \widehat{A}_0 \widehat{F}_0 + \widehat{F}_0' \widehat{A}_0 \widehat{S}_{h_0 h_1} \widehat{A}_1 \widehat{F}_1\bigr) \\ & + \Pi\bigl(\widehat{S}_{gh_1}' \widehat{A}_1 \widehat{F}_1 + \widehat{F}_1' \widehat{A}_1 \widehat{S}_{gh_1}\bigr),\end{aligned}$$

where for $i, l = 0, 1$, $\Pi = \Pi = 1 - \pi^{-1}\ln(1+\pi)$, and $q_t(\widehat{\theta}_{i,t}) = q(y_t - \kappa_i(Z_i^{t-1}, \widehat{\theta}_{i,t})$,

$$\widehat{S}_{h_i h_l} = \frac{1}{P}\sum_{\tau=-l_P}^{l_P} w_\tau \sum_{t=R+l_P}^{T-l_P} \nabla_\theta q_t(\widehat{\theta}_{i,t}) \nabla_\theta q_{t+\tau}(\widehat{\theta}_{l,t})',$$

$$\widehat{S}_{fh_i} = \frac{1}{P}\sum_{\tau=-l_P}^{l_P} w_\tau \times \sum_{t=R+l_P}^{T-l_P}\left(\left(g(\widehat{u}_{0,t}) - g(\widehat{u}_{1,t})\right) - \frac{1}{P}\sum_{t=R}^{T-1}\left(g(\widehat{u}_{0,t+1}) - g(\widehat{u}_{1,t+1})\right)\right) \times \nabla_\beta q_{t+\tau}(\widehat{\theta}_{i,t})',$$

$$\widehat{S}_{gg} = \frac{1}{P}\sum_{\tau=-l_P}^{l_P} w_\tau \sum_{t=R+l_P}^{T-l_P}\left(g(\widehat{u}_{0,t}) - g(\widehat{u}_{1,t}) - \frac{1}{P}\sum_{t=R}^{T-1}\left(g(\widehat{u}_{0,t+1}) - g(\widehat{u}_{1,t+1})\right)\right) \times \left(g(\widehat{u}_{0,t+\tau}) - g(\widehat{u}_{1,t+\tau}) - \frac{1}{P}\sum_{t=R}^{T-1}\left(g(\widehat{u}_{0,t+1}) - g(\widehat{u}_{1,t+1})\right)\right)$$

with $w = 1 - (\frac{\tau}{l_P+1})$, and where

$$\widehat{F}_i = \frac{1}{P}\sum_{t=R}^{T-1}\nabla_{\theta_i} g(\widehat{u}_{i,t+1}), \qquad \widehat{A}_i = \left(-\frac{1}{P}\sum_{t=R}^{T-1}\nabla^2_{\theta_i} q(\widehat{\theta}_{i,t})\right)^{-1}.$$

PROPOSITION 4.1 (From Theorem 4.1 in West (1996)). *Let* W1–W2 *hold. Also, assume that g is continuously differentiable, then, if as $P \to \infty$, $l_p \to \infty$ and $l_P/P^{1/4} \to 0$, then as $P, R \to \infty$, under H_0, $DM_P \xrightarrow{d} N(0,1)$ and under H_A,* $\Pr(P^{-1/2}|DM_P| > \varepsilon) \to 1$, *for any $\varepsilon > 0$.*

Recall that it is immediate to see that if either $g = q$ or $P/R \to 0$, then the estimator of the long-run variance collapses to $\widehat{\sigma}_P^2 = \widehat{S}_{gg}$. The proposition is valid for the case of short-memory series. Corradi, Swanson and Olivetti (2001) consider DM tests in the context of cointegrated series, and Rossi (2005) in the context of processes with roots local to unity.

The proposition above has been stated in terms of one-step ahead prediction errors. All results carry over to the case of $h > 1$. However, in the multistep ahead case, one needs to decide whether to compute "direct" h-step ahead forecast errors (i.e. $\widehat{u}_{i,t+h} = y_{t+h} - \kappa_i(Z_i^{t-h}, \widehat{\theta}_{i,t})$) or to compute iterated h-ahead forecast errors (i.e. first predict y_{t+1} using observations up to time t, and then use this predicted value in order to predict y_{t+2}, and so on). Within the context of VAR models, Marcellino, Stock and Watson (2006) conduct an extensive and careful empirical study in order to examine the properties of these direct and indirect approaches to prediction.

Finally, note that when the two models are nested, so that $u_{0,t} = u_{1,t}$ under H_0, both the numerator of the DM_P statistic and $\widehat{\sigma}_P$ approach zero in probability at the same rate, if $P/R \to 0$, so that the DM_P statistic no longer has a normal limiting distribution under the null. The asymptotic distribution of the Diebold–Mariano statistic in the nested case has been recently provided by McCracken (2004a), who shows that the limiting distribution is a functional over Brownian motions. Comparison of nested models is the subject of the next subsection.

4.2. Comparison of two nested models

In several instances we may be interested in comparing nested models, such as when forming out-of-sample Granger causality tests. Also, in the empirical international finance literature, an extensively studied issue concerns comparing the relative accuracy of models driven by fundamentals against random walk models. Since the seminal paper by Meese and Rogoff (1983), who find that no economic models can beat a random walk in terms of their ability to predict exchange rates, several papers have further examined the issue of exchange rate predictability, a partial list of which includes Berkowitz and Giorgianni (2001), Mark (1995), Kilian (1999a), Clarida, Sarno and Taylor (2003), Kilian and Taylor (2003), Rossi (2005), Clark and West (2006), and McCracken and Sapp (2005). Indeed, the debate about predictability of exchange rates was one of the driving force behind the literature on out-of-sample comparison of nested models.

4.2.1. Clark and McCracken tests

Within the context of nested linear models, Clark and McCracken (2001, CMa) propose some easy to implement tests, under the assumption of martingale difference prediction errors (these tests thus rule out the possibility of dynamic misspecification under the null model). Such tests are thus tailored for the case of one-step ahead prediction. This is because h-step ahead prediction errors follow an MA$(h-1)$ process. For the case where $h > 1$, Clark and McCracken (2003, CMb) propose a different set tests. We begin by outlining the CMa tests.

Consider the following two nested models. The restricted model is

$$y_t = \sum_{j=1}^{q} \beta_j y_{t-j} + \epsilon_t \tag{32}$$

and the unrestricted model is

$$y_t = \sum_{j=1}^{q} \beta_j y_{t-j} + \sum_{j=1}^{k} \alpha_j x_{t-j} + u_t. \tag{33}$$

The null and the alternative hypotheses are formulated as:

$$H_0\colon\quad E\left(\epsilon_t^2\right) - E\left(u_t^2\right) = 0,$$
$$H_A\colon\quad E\left(\epsilon_t^2\right) - E\left(u_t^2\right) > 0,$$

so that it is implicitly assumed that the smaller model cannot outperform the larger. This is actually the case when the loss function is quadratic and when parameters are estimated by LS, which is the case considered by CMa. Note that under the null hypothesis, $u_t = \epsilon_t$, and so DM tests are not applicable in the current context. We use assumptions CM1 and CM2, listed in Appendix A, in the sequel of this section. Note that CM2 requires that the larger model is dynamically correctly specified, and requires u_t to be conditionally homoskedastic. The three different tests proposed by CMa are

$$ENC\text{-}T = (P-1)^{1/2} \frac{\bar{c}}{\left(P^{-1}\sum_{t=R}^{T-1}(c_{t+1}-\bar{c})\right)^{1/2}},$$

where $c_{t+1} = \widehat{\epsilon}_{t+1}(\widehat{\epsilon}_{t+1} - \widehat{u}_{t+1})$, $\bar{c} = P^{-1}\sum_{t=R}^{T-1} c_{t+1}$, and where $\widehat{\epsilon}_{t+1}$ and $\widehat{u}_{t+1}$ are residuals from the LS estimation. Additionally,

$$ENC\text{-}REG = (P-1)^{1/2} \frac{P^{-1}\sum_{t=R}^{T-1}(\widehat{\epsilon}_{t+1}(\widehat{\epsilon}_{t+1} - \widehat{u}_{t+1}))}{\left(P^{-1}\sum_{t=R}^{T-1}(\widehat{\epsilon}_{t+1} - \widehat{u}_{t+1})^2 P^{-1}\sum_{t=R}^{T-1}\widehat{\epsilon}_{t+1}^2 - \bar{c}^2\right)^{1/2}},$$

and

$$ENC\text{-}NEW = P\frac{\bar{c}}{P^{-1}\sum_{t=1}\widehat{u}_{t+1}^2}.$$

Of note is that the encompassing t-test given above is proposed by Harvey, Leybourne and Newbold (1997).

PROPOSITION 4.2 (From Theorems 3.1, 3.2, 3.3 in CMa). *Let* CM1–CM2 *hold. Then under the null,*

(i) *If as* $T \to \infty$, $P/R \to \pi > 0$, *then ENC-T and ENC-REG converge in distribution to* Γ_1/Γ_2 *where* $\Gamma_1 = \int_{(1+\pi)^{-1}}^{1} s^{-1} W'(s)\,\mathrm{d}W(s)$ *and* $\Gamma_2 = \int_{(1+\pi)^{-1}}^{1} s^{-2} W'(s) W(s)\,\mathrm{d}s$. *Here,* $W(s)$ *is a standard k-dimensional Brownian motion (note that k is the number of restrictions or the number of extra regressors in the larger model). Also, ENC-NEW converges in distribution to* Γ_1, *and*

(ii) *If as* $T \to \infty$, $P/R \to \pi = 0$, *then ENC-T and ENC-REG converge in distribution to* $N(0,1)$, *and ENC-NEW converges to* 0 *in probability.*

Thus, for $\pi > 0$ all three tests have non-standard limiting distributions, although the distributions are nuisance parameter free. Critical values for these statistics under $\pi > 0$ have been tabulated by CMa for different values of k and π.

It is immediate to see that CM2 is violated in the case of multiple step ahead prediction errors. For the case of $h > 1$, CMb provide modified versions of the above tests in order to allow for MA$(h-1)$ errors. Their modification essentially consists of using a robust covariance matrix estimator in the context of the above tests.[20] Their new version of the *ENC-T* test is

$$ENC\text{-}T' = (P-h+1)^{1/2} \times \frac{\frac{1}{P-h+1}\sum_{t=R}^{T-h}\widehat{c}_{t+h}}{\left(\frac{1}{P-h+1}\sum_{j=-\bar{j}}^{\bar{j}}\sum_{t=R+j}^{T-h} K(\frac{j}{M})(\widehat{c}_{t+h}-\bar{c})(\widehat{c}_{t+h-j}-\bar{c})\right)^{1/2}}, \quad (34)$$

[20] The tests are applied to the problem of comparing linear economic models of exchange rates in McCracken and Sapp (2005), using critical values constructed along the lines of the discussion in Kilian (1999b).

where $\widehat{c}_{t+h} = \widehat{\epsilon}_{t+h}(\widehat{\epsilon}_{t+h} - \widehat{u}_{t+h})$, $\bar{c} = \frac{1}{P-h+1}\sum_{t=R}^{T-\tau}\widehat{c}_{t+h}$, $K(\cdot)$ is a kernel (such as the Bartlett kernel), and $0 \leqslant K(\frac{j}{M}) \leqslant 1$, with $K(0) = 1$, and $M = o(P^{1/2})$. Note that $\bar{j}$ does not grow with the sample size. Therefore, the denominator in *ENC-T'* is a consistent estimator of the long run variance only when $E(c_t c_{t+|k|}) = 0$ for all $|k| > h$ (see Assumption A3 in CMb). Thus, the statistic takes into account the moving average structure of the prediction errors, but still does not allow for dynamic misspecification under the null. Another statistic suggested by CMb is the Diebold Mariano statistic with nonstandard critical values. Namely,

$$\mathit{MSE}\text{-}T' = (P-h+1)^{1/2} \times \frac{\frac{1}{P-h+1}\sum_{t=R}^{T-h}\widehat{d}_{t+h}}{\left(\frac{1}{P-h+1}\sum_{j=-\bar{j}}^{\bar{j}}\sum_{t=R+j}^{T-h}K(\frac{j}{M})(\widehat{d}_{t+h}-\bar{d})(\widehat{d}_{t+h-j}-\bar{d})\right)^{1/2}},$$

where $\widehat{d}_{t+h} = \widehat{u}_{t+h}^2 - \widehat{\epsilon}_{t+h}^2$, and $\bar{d} = \frac{1}{P-h+1}\sum_{t=R}^{T-\tau}\widehat{d}_{t+h}$.

The limiting distributions of the *ENC-T'* and *MSE-T* statistics are given in Theorems 3.1 and 3.2 in CMb, and for $h > 1$ contain nuisance parameters so their critical values cannot be directly tabulated. CMb suggest using a modified version of the bootstrap in Kilian (1999a) to obtain critical values.[21]

4.2.2. Chao, Corradi and Swanson tests

A limitation of the tests above is that they rule out possible dynamic misspecification under the null. A test which does not require correct dynamic specification and/or conditional homoskedasticity is proposed by Chao, Corradi and Swanson (2001). Of note, however, is that the Clark and McCracken tests are one-sided while the Chao, Corradi and Swanson test are two-sided, and so may be less powerful in small samples. The test statistic is

$$m_P = P^{-1/2}\sum_{t=R}^{T-1}\widehat{\epsilon}_{t+1}X_t, \tag{35}$$

where $\widehat{\epsilon}_{t+1} = y_{t+1} - \sum_{j=1}^{p-1}\widehat{\beta}_{t,j}y_{t-j}$, $X_t = (x_t, x_{t-1}, \ldots x_{t-k-1})'$. We shall formulate the null and the alternative as

$$\widetilde{H}_0\colon\quad E(\epsilon_{t+1}x_{t-j}) = 0, \quad j = 0, 1, \ldots k-1,$$

$$\widetilde{H}_A\colon\quad E(\epsilon_{t+1}x_{t-j}) \neq 0 \quad \text{for some } j,\ j = 0, 1, \ldots, k-1.$$

The idea underlying the test is very simple, if $\alpha_1 = \alpha_2 = \cdots = \alpha_k = 0$ in Equation (32), then ϵ_t is uncorrelated with the past of X. Thus, models including lags of X_t do not "outperform" the smaller model. In the sequel we shall require assumption CSS, which is listed in Appendix A.

[21] For the case of $h = 1$, the limit distribution of *ENC-T'* corresponds with that of *ENC-T*, given in Proposition 4.2, and the limiting distribution is derived by McCracken (2000).

PROPOSITION 4.3 (From Theorem 1 in Chao, Corradi and Swanson (2001)). *Let* CCS *hold. As $T \to \infty$, $P, R \to \infty$, $P/R \to \pi, 0 \leqslant \pi < \infty$,*

(i) *Under $\widetilde{H}_0$, for $0 < \pi < \infty$,*

$$m_P \xrightarrow{d} N\big(0, S_{11} + 2\big(1 - \pi^{-1}\ln(1+\pi)\big)F'MS_{22}MF \\ - \big(1 - \pi^{-1}\ln(1+\pi)\big)\big(F'MS_{12} + S_{12}'MF\big)\big).$$

In addition, for $\pi = 0, m_P \xrightarrow{d} N(0, S_{11})$, where $F = E(Y_t X_t')$, $M = \operatorname{plim}\big(\frac{1}{t}\sum_{j=q}^{t} Y_j Y_j'\big)^{-1}$, and $Y_j = (y_{j-1}, \ldots, y_{j-q})'$, so that M is a $q \times q$ matrix, F is a $q \times k$ matrix, Y_j is a $k \times 1$ vector, S_{11} is a $k \times k$ matrix, S_{12} is a $q \times k$ matrix, and S_{22} is a $q \times q$ matrix, with

$$S_{11} = \sum_{j=-\infty}^{\infty} E\big((X_t\varepsilon_{t+1} - \mu)(X_{t-j}\varepsilon_{t+1-j} - \mu)'\big),$$

where $\mu = E(X_t\epsilon_{t+1})$, $S_{22} = \sum_{j=-\infty}^{\infty} E((Y_{t-1}\varepsilon_t)(Y_{t-1-j}\varepsilon_{t-j})')$ and

$$S_{12}' = \sum_{j=-\infty}^{\infty} E\big((\epsilon_{t+1}X_t - \mu)(Y_{t-1-j}\epsilon_{t-j})'\big).$$

(ii) *Under $\widetilde{H}_A$, $\lim_{P\to\infty} \Pr(|\frac{m_P}{P^{1/2}}| > 0) = 1$.*

COROLLARY 4.4 (From Corollary 2 in Chao, Corradi and Swanson (2001)). *Let Assumption* CCS *hold. As $T \to \infty$, $P, R \to \infty$, $P/R \to \pi, 0 \leqslant \pi < \infty$, $l_T \to \infty$, $l_T/T^{1/4} \to 0$,*

(i) *Under $\widetilde{H}_0$, for $0 < \pi < \infty$,*

$$m_P'\Big(\widehat{S}_{11} + 2\big(1 - \pi^{-1}\ln(1+\pi)\big)\widehat{F}'\widehat{M}\widehat{S}_{22}\widehat{M}\widehat{F} \\ - \big(1 - \pi^{-1}\ln(1+\pi)\big)\big(\widehat{F}'\widehat{M}\widehat{S}_{12} + \widehat{S}_{12}'\widehat{M}\widehat{F}\big)^{-1}\Big)^{-1} m_P \xrightarrow{d} \chi_k^2, \tag{36}$$

where $\widehat{F} = \frac{1}{P}\sum_{t=R}^{T} Y_t X_t'$, $\widehat{M} = \big(\frac{1}{P}\sum_{t=R}^{T-1} Y_t Y_t'\big)r^{-1}$, and

$$\widehat{S}_{11} = \frac{1}{P}\sum_{t=R}^{T-1}(\widehat{\epsilon}_{t+1}X_t - \widehat{\mu}_1)(\widehat{\epsilon}_{t+1}X_t - \widehat{\mu}_1)' \\ + \frac{1}{P}\sum_{t=\tau}^{l_T} w_\tau \sum_{t=R+\tau}^{T-1}(\widehat{\epsilon}_{t+1}X_t - \widehat{\mu}_1)(\widehat{\epsilon}_{t+1-\tau}X_{t-\tau} - \widehat{\mu}_1)' \\ + \frac{1}{P}\sum_{t=\tau}^{l_T} w_\tau \sum_{t=R+\tau}^{T-1}(\widehat{\epsilon}_{t+1-\tau}X_{t-\tau} - \widehat{\mu}_1)(\widehat{\epsilon}_{t+1}X_t - \widehat{\mu}_1)',$$

where $\widehat{\mu}_1 = \frac{1}{P}\sum_{t=R}^{T-1}\widehat{\epsilon}_{t+1}X_t$,

$$\widehat{S}'_{12} = \frac{1}{P}\sum_{\tau=0}^{l_T} w_\tau \sum_{t=R+\tau}^{T-1} \left(\widehat{\epsilon}_{t+1-\tau}X_{t-\tau} - \widehat{\mu}_1\right)\left(Y_{t-1}\widehat{\epsilon}_t\right)' + \frac{1}{P}\sum_{\tau=1}^{l_T} w_\tau \sum_{t=R+\tau}^{T-1} \left(\widehat{\epsilon}_{t+1}X_t - \widehat{\mu}_1\right)\left(Y_{t-1-\tau}\widehat{\epsilon}_{t-\tau}\right)',$$

and

$$\widehat{S}_{22} = \frac{1}{P}\sum_{t=R}^{T-1}\left(Y_{t-1}\widehat{\epsilon}_t\right)\left(Y_{t-1}\widehat{\epsilon}_t\right)' + \frac{1}{P}\sum_{\tau=1}^{l_T} w_\tau \sum_{t=R+\tau}^{T-1} \left(Y_{t-1}\widehat{\epsilon}_t\right)\left(Y_{t-1-\tau}\widehat{\epsilon}_{t-\tau}\right)' + \frac{1}{P}\sum_{\tau=1}^{l_T} w_\tau \sum_{t=R+\tau}^{T-1} \left(Y_{t-1-\tau}\widehat{\epsilon}_{t-\tau}\right)\left(Y_{t-1}\widehat{\epsilon}_t\right)',$$

with $w_\tau = 1 - \frac{\tau}{l_T+1}$.

In addition, for $\pi = 0$, $m'_p\widehat{S}_{11}m_p \xrightarrow{d} \chi^2_k$.

(ii) *Under* $\widetilde{H}_A$, $m'_p\widehat{S}_{11}^{-1}m_p$ *diverges at rate* P.

Two final remarks: (i) note that the test can be easily applied to the case of multistep-ahead prediction, it suffices to replace "1" with "h" above; (ii) linearity of neither the null nor the larger model is required. In fact the test, can be equally applied using residuals from a nonlinear model and using a nonlinear function of X_t, rather than simply using X_t.

4.3. Comparison of multiple models: The reality check

In the previous subsection, we considered the issue of choosing between two competing models. However, in a lot of situations many different competing models are available and we want to be able to choose the best model from amongst them. When we estimate and compare a very large number of models using the same data set, the problem of data mining or data snooping is prevalent. Broadly speaking, the problem of data snooping is that a model may appear to be superior by chance and not because of its intrinsic merit (recall also the problem of sequential test bias). For example, if we keep testing the null hypothesis of efficient markets, using the same data set, eventually we shall find a model that results in rejection. The data snooping problem is particularly serious when there is no economic theory supporting an alternative hypothesis. For example, the data snooping problem in the context of evaluating trading rules has been pointed out by Brock, Lakonishok and LeBaron (1992), as well as Sullivan, Timmermann and White (1999, 2001).

4.3.1. White's reality check and extensions

White (2000) proposes a novel approach for dealing with the issue of choosing amongst many different models. Suppose there are m models, and we select model 1 as our benchmark (or reference) model. Models $i = 2, \dots, m$ are called the competitor (alternative) models. Typically, the benchmark model is either a simple model, our favorite model, or the most commonly used model. Given the benchmark model, the objective is to answer the following question: "Is there any model, amongst the set of $m-1$ competitor models, that yields more accurate predictions (for the variable of interest) than the benchmark?".

In this section, let the generic forecast error be $u_{i,t+1} = y_{t+1} - \kappa_i(Z^t, \theta_i^\dagger)$, and let $\widehat{u}_{i,t+1} = y_{t+1} - \kappa_i(Z^t, \widehat{\theta}_{i,t})$, where $\kappa_i(Z^t, \widehat{\theta}_{i,t})$ is the conditional mean function under model i, and $\widehat{\theta}_{i,t}$ is defined as in Section 3.1. Assume that the set of regressors may vary across different models, so that Z^t is meant to denote the collection of all potential regressors. Following White (2000), define the statistic

$$S_P = \max_{k=2,\dots,m} S_P(1,k),$$

where

$$S_P(1,k) = \frac{1}{\sqrt{P}} \sum_{t=R}^{T-1} \bigl(g(\widehat{u}_{1,t+1}) - g(\widehat{u}_{k,t+1})\bigr), \quad k = 2, \dots, m.$$

The hypotheses are formulated as

$$H_0\colon \quad \max_{k=2,\dots,m} E\bigl(g(u_{1,t+1}) - g(g_{k,t+1})\bigr) \leqslant 0,$$

$$H_A\colon \quad \max_{k=2,\dots,m} E\bigl(g(u_{1,t+1}) - g(u_{k,t+1})\bigr) > 0,$$

where $u_{k,t+1} = y_{t+1} - \kappa_k(Z^t, \theta_{k,t}^\dagger)$, and $\theta_{k,t}^\dagger$ denotes the probability limit of $\theta_{i,t}$.

Thus, under the null hypothesis, no competitor model, amongst the set of the $m-1$ alternatives, can provide a more (loss function specific) accurate prediction than the benchmark model. On the other hand, under the alternative, at least one competitor (and in particular, the best competitor) provides more accurate predictions than the benchmark. Now, let W1 and W2 be as stated in Appendix A, and assume WH, also stated in Appendix A. Note that WH requires that at least one of the competitor models has to be nonnested with the benchmark model.[22] We have:

[22] This is for the same reasons as discussed in the context of the Diebold and Mariano test.

PROPOSITION 4.5 (Parts (i) and (iii) are from Proposition 2.2 in White (2000)). *Let* W1–W2 *and* WH *hold. Then, under* H_0,

$$\max_{k=2,\dots,m}\big(S_P(1,k)-\sqrt{P}E\big(g(u_{1,t+1})-g(u_{k,t+1})\big)\big)\xrightarrow{d}\max_{k=2,\dots,m}S(1,k), \tag{37}$$

where $S=(S(1,2),\dots,S(1,n))$ *is a zero mean Gaussian process with covariance kernel given by* V, *with* V *a* $m\times m$ *matrix, and*:

(i) *If parameter estimation error vanishes (i.e. if either* P/R *goes to zero and/or the same loss function is used for estimation and model evaluation,* $g=q$, *where* q *is again the objective function), then for* $i=1,\dots,m-1$, $V=[v_{i,i}]=S_{g_ig_i}$; *and*

(ii) *If parameter estimation error does not vanish (i.e. if* $P/R\to 0$ *and* $g\neq q$), *then for* $i,j=1,\dots,m-1$

$$V=[v_{i,i}]=S_{g_ig_i}+2\Pi\mu_1'A_1^{\dagger}C_{11}A_1^{\dagger}\mu_1+2\Pi\mu_i'A_i^{\dagger}C_{ii}A_i^{\dagger}\mu_i$$
$$-4\Pi\mu_1'A_1^{\dagger}C_{1i}A_i^{\dagger}\mu_i+2\Pi S_{g_iq_1}A_1^{\dagger}\mu_1-2\Pi S_{g_iq_i}A_i^{\dagger}\mu_i,$$

where

$$S_{g_ig_i}=\sum_{\tau=-\infty}^{\infty}E\big(\big(g(u_{1,1})-g(u_{i,1})\big)\big(g(u_{1,1+\tau})-g(u_{i,1+\tau})\big)\big),$$

$$C_{ii}=\sum_{\tau=-\infty}^{\infty}E\Big(\big(\nabla_{\theta_i}q_i\big(y_{1+s},Z^s,\theta_i^{\dagger}\big)\big)\big(\nabla_{\theta i}q_i\big(y_{1+s+\tau},Z^{s+\tau},\theta_i^{\dagger}\big)\big)'\Big),$$

$$S_{g_iq_i}=\sum_{\tau=-\infty}^{\infty}E\Big(\big(g(u_{1,1})-g(u_{i,1})\big)\big(\nabla_{\theta i}q_i\big(y_{1+s+\tau},Z^{s+\tau},\theta_i^{\dagger}\big)\big)'\Big),$$

$B_i^{\dagger}=(E(-\nabla_{\theta_i}^2q_i(y_t,Z^{t-1},\theta_i^{\dagger})))^{-1}$, $\mu_i=E(\nabla_{\theta_i}g(u_{i,t+1}))$, *and* $\Pi=1-\pi^{-1}\ln(1+\pi)$.

(iii) *Under* H_A, $\Pr(\frac{1}{\sqrt{P}}|S_P|>\varepsilon)\to 1$, *as* $P\to\infty$.

PROOF. For the proof of part (ii), see Appendix B. □

Note that under the null, the least favorable case arises when $E(g(u_{1,t+1})-g(u_{k,t+1}))=0$, $\forall k$. In this case, the distribution of S_P coincides with that of $\max_{k=2,\dots,m}(S_P(1,k)-\sqrt{P}E(g(u_{1,t+1})-g(u_{k,t+1})))$, so that S_P has the above limiting distribution, which is a functional of a Gaussian process with a covariance kernel that reflects uncertainty due to dynamic misspecification and possibly to parameter estimation error. Additionally, when all competitor models are worse than the benchmark, the statistic diverges to minus infinity at rate $\sqrt{P}$. Finally, when only some competitor models are worse than the benchmark, the limiting distribution provides a conservative test, as S_P will always be smaller than

$$\max_{k=2,\ldots,m} \left(S_P(1,k) - \sqrt{P}E\left(g(u_{1,t+1}) - g(u_{k,t+1})\right)\right),$$

asymptotically. Of course, when H_A holds, the statistic diverges to plus infinity at rate $\sqrt{P}$.

We now outline how to obtain valid asymptotic critical values for the limiting distribution on the right-hand side of (37), regardless whether the contribution of parameter estimation error vanishes or not. As noted above, such critical values are conservative, except for the least favorable case under the null. We later outline two ways of alleviating this problem, one suggested by Hansen (2005) and another, based on subsampling, suggested by Linton, Maasoumi and Whang (2004).

Recall that the maximum of a Gaussian process is not Gaussian in general, so that standard critical values cannot be used to conduct inference on S_P. As pointed out by White (2000), one possibility in this case is to first estimate the covariance structure and then draw 1 realization from an $(m-1)$-dimensional normal with covariance equal to the estimated covariance structure. From this realization, pick the maximum value over $k = 2, \ldots, m$. Repeat this a large number of times, form an empirical distribution using the maximum values over $k = 2, \ldots, m$, and obtain critical values in the usual way. A drawback to this approach is that we need to rely on an estimator of the covariance structure based on the available sample of observations, which in many cases may be small relative to the number of models being compared. Furthermore, whenever the forecasting errors are not martingale difference sequences (as in our context), heteroskedasticity and autocorrelation consistent covariance matrices should be estimated, and thus a lag truncation parameter must be chosen. Another approach which avoids these problems involves using the stationary bootstrap of Politis and Romano (1994a). This is the approach used by White (2000). In general, bootstrap procedures have been shown to perform well in a variety of finite sample contexts [see, e.g., Diebold and Chen (1996)]. White's suggested bootstrap procedure is valid for the case in which parameter estimation error vanishes asymptotically. His bootstrap statistic is given by:

$$S_P^{**} = \max_{k=2,\ldots m} \left|S_P^{**}(1,k)\right|, \tag{38}$$

where

$$S_P^{**}(1,k) = \frac{1}{\sqrt{P}} \sum_{t=R}^{T-1} \left(\left(g\left(\widehat{u}_{1,t+1}^{**}\right) - g\left(\widehat{u}_{1,t+1}\right)\right) - \left(g\left(\widehat{u}_{k,t+1}^{**}\right) - g\left(\widehat{u}_{k,t+1}\right)\right)\right),$$

and $\widehat{u}_{k,t+1}^{**} = y_{t+1}^{**} - \kappa_k(Z^{**,t}, \widehat{\theta}_{k,t})$, where y_{t+1}^{**} $Z^{**,t}$ denoted the resampled series. White uses the stationary bootstrap by Politis and Romano (1994a), but both the block bootstrap and stationary bootstrap deliver the same asymptotic critical values. Note that the bootstrap statistics "contains" only estimators based on the original sample: this is because in White's context PEE vanishes. Our approach to handling PEE is to apply the recursive PEE bootstrap outlined in Section 3.3 in order to obtain critical values which are asymptotically valid in the presence of nonvanishing PEE.

Define the bootstrap statistic as:

$$S_P^* = \max_{k=2,\dots,m} S_P^*(1,k),$$

where

$$\begin{aligned} S_P^*(1,k) = \frac{1}{\sqrt{P}} \sum_{t=R}^{T-1} \Bigg[& \left(g\left(y_{t+1}^* - \kappa_1\left(Z^{*,t}, \widetilde{\theta}_{1,t}^*\right)\right) - g\left(y_{t+1}^* - \kappa_k\left(Z^{*,t}, \widetilde{\theta}_{k,t}^*\right)\right)\right) \\ & - \frac{1}{T} \sum_{j=s}^{T-1} \left(g\left(y_{j+1} - \kappa_1\left(Z^j, \widehat{\theta}_{1,t}\right)\right)\right. \\ & \left. - g\left(y_{j+1} - \kappa_k\left(Z^j, \widehat{\theta}_{k,t}\right)\right)\right) \Bigg]. \end{aligned} \tag{39}$$

PROPOSITION 4.6 ((i) from Corollary 2.6 in White (2000), (ii) from Proposition 3 in Corradi and Swanson (2005b)). *Let* W1–W2 *and* WH *hold.*

(i) *If* $P/R \to 0$ *and/or* $g = q$, *then as* $P, R \to \infty$

$$P\left(\omega\colon \sup_{v \in \Re} \left| P_{R,P}^*\left(\max_{k=2,\dots,n} S_P^{**}(1,k) \leqslant v\right) - P\left(\max_{k=2,\dots,n} S_P^{\mu}(1,k) \leqslant v\right)\right| > \varepsilon\right) \\ \to 0,$$

(ii) *Let Assumptions* A1–A4 *hold. Also, assume that as* $T \to \infty$, $l \to \infty$, *and that* $\frac{l}{T^{1/4}} \to 0$. *Then, as* T, P *and* $R \to \infty$,

$$P\left(\omega\colon \sup_{v \in \Re} \left| P_T^*\left(\max_{k=2,\dots,n} S_P^*(1,k) \leqslant v\right) - P\left(\max_{k=2,\dots,n} S_P^{\mu}(1,k) \leqslant v\right)\right| > \varepsilon\right) \\ \to 0,$$

and

$$S_P^{\mu}(1,k) = S_P(1,k) - \sqrt{P} E\left(g(u_{1,t+1}) - g(u_{k,t+1})\right).$$

The above result suggests proceeding in the following manner. For any bootstrap replication, compute the bootstrap statistic, S_P^*. Perform B bootstrap replications (B large) and compute the quantiles of the empirical distribution of the B bootstrap statistics. Reject H_0, if S_P is greater than the $(1-\alpha)$th-percentile. Otherwise, do not reject. Now, for all samples except a set with probability measure approaching zero, S_P has the same limiting distribution as the corresponding bootstrapped statistic when $E(g(u_{1,t+1}) - g(u_{k,t+1})) = 0\ \forall k$, ensuring asymptotic size equal to α. On the other hand, when one or more competitor models are strictly dominated by the benchmark, the rule provides a test with asymptotic size between 0 and α (see above discussion).

Under the alternative, S_P diverges to (plus) infinity, while the corresponding bootstrap statistic has a well defined limiting distribution, ensuring unit asymptotic power.

In summary, this application shows that the block bootstrap for recursive m-estimators can be readily adapted in order to provide asymptotically valid critical values that are robust to parameter estimation error as well as model misspecification. In addition, the bootstrap statistics are very easy to construct, as no complicated adjustment terms involving possibly higher order derivatives need be included.

4.3.2. Hansen's approach applied to the reality check

As mentioned above, the critical values obtained via the empirical distribution of S_P^{**} or S_P^* are upper bounds whenever some competing models are strictly dominated by the benchmark. The issue of conservativeness is particularly relevant when a large number of dominated (bad) models are included in the analysis. In fact, such models do not contribute to the limiting distribution, but drive up the reality check p-values, which are obtained for the least favorable case under the null hypothesis. The idea of Hansen (2005)[23] is to eliminate the models which are dominated, while paying careful attention to not eliminate relevant models. In summary, Hansen defines the statistic

$$\widetilde{S}_P = \max\left\{\max_{k=2,\dots,m} \frac{S_P(1,k)}{\left(\widehat{\operatorname{var}}\frac{1}{P}\sum_{t=R}^{T-1}(g(\widehat{u}_{1,t+1}) - g(\widehat{u}_{k,t+1}))\right)^{1/2}}, 0\right\},$$

where $\widehat{\operatorname{var}}\frac{1}{P}\sum_{t=R}^{T-1}(g(\widehat{u}_{1,t+1}) - g(\widehat{u}_{k,t+1}))$ is defined in (40) below. In this way, the modified reality check statistic does not take into account strictly dominated models.

The idea of Hansen is also to impose the "entire" null (not only the least favorable component of the null) when constructing the bootstrap statistic. For this reason, he adds a recentering term. Define,

$$\widehat{\mu}_k = \frac{1}{P}\sum_{t=R}^{T-1}\left(g(\widehat{u}_{1,t+1}) - g(\widehat{u}_{k,t+1})\right)1\left\{g(\widehat{u}_{1,t+1}) - g(\widehat{u}_{k,t+1}) \geqslant A_{T,k}\right\},$$

where $A_{T,k} = \frac{1}{4}T^{-1/4}\sqrt{\widehat{\operatorname{var}}\frac{1}{P}\sum_{t=R}^{T-1}(g(\widehat{u}_{1,t+1}) - g(\widehat{u}_{k,t+1}))}$, with

$$\begin{aligned}
&\widehat{\operatorname{var}}\frac{1}{P}\sum_{t=R}^{T-1}\left(g(\widehat{u}_{1,t+1}) - g(\widehat{u}_{k,t+1})\right) \\
&\quad = B^{-1}\sum_{b=1}^{B}\left(\frac{1}{P}\sum_{t=R}^{T-1}\left(\left(g(\widehat{u}_{1,t+1}) - g(\widehat{u}_{k,t+1})\right) - \left(g(\widehat{u}^*_{1,t+1}) - g(\widehat{u}^*_{k,t+1})\right)\right)^2\right),
\end{aligned} \tag{40}$$

[23] A careful analysis of testing in the presence of composite null hypotheses is given in Hansen (2004).

and where B denotes the number of bootstrap replications. Hansen's bootstrap statistic is then defined as

$$\widetilde{S}_P^* = \max_{k=2,\ldots,m} \frac{\frac{1}{\sqrt{P}} \sum_{t=R}^{T-1} [(g(\widehat{u}_{1,t+1}^*) - g(\widehat{u}_{k,t+1}^*)) - \widehat{\mu}_k]}{\left(\widehat{\text{var}} \frac{1}{P} \sum_{t=R}^{T-1} (g(\widehat{u}_{1,t+1}) - g(\widehat{u}_{k,t+1}))\right)^{1/2}}.$$

P-values are then computed in terms of the number of times the statistic is smaller than the bootstrap statistic, and H_0 is rejected if, say, $\frac{1}{B} \sum_{b=1}^{B} 1\{\widetilde{S}_P \leqslant \widetilde{S}_P^*\}$ is below α. This procedure is valid, provided that the effect of parameter estimation error vanishes.

4.3.3. *The subsampling approach applied to the reality check*

The idea of subsampling is based on constructing a sequence of statistics using a (sub)sample of size b, where b grows with the sample size, but at a slower rate. Critical values are constructed using the empirical distribution of the sequence of statistics [see, e.g., the book by Politis, Romano and Wolf (1999)]. In the current context, let the subsampling size to be equal to b, where as $P \to \infty$, $b \to \infty$ and $b/P \to 0$. Define

$$S_{P,a,b} = \max_{k=2,\ldots,m} S_{P,a,b}(1,k), \quad a = R, \ldots, T-b-1,$$

where

$$S_{P,a,b}(1,k) = \frac{1}{\sqrt{b}} \sum_{t=a}^{a+b-1} \left(g(\widehat{u}_{1,t+1}) - g(\widehat{u}_{k,t+1})\right), \quad k = 2, \ldots, m.$$

Compute the empirical distribution of $S_{P,a,b}$ using $T-b-1$ statistics constructed using b observations. The rule is to reject if we get a value for S_P larger than the $(1-\alpha)$-critical value of the (subsample) empirical distribution, and do not reject otherwise. If $\max_{k=2,\ldots,m} E(g(u_{1,t+1}) - g(u_{k,t+1})) = 0$, then this rule gives a test with asymptotic size equal to α, while if $\max_{k=2,\ldots,m} E(g(u_{1,t+1}) - g(u_{k,t+1})) < 0$ (i.e. if all models are dominated by the benchmark), then the rule gives a test with asymptotic size equal to zero. Finally, under the alternative, $S_{P,a,b}$ diverges at rate $\sqrt{b}$, ensuring unit asymptotic power, provided that $b/P \to 0$. The advantage of subsampling over the block bootstrap, is that the test then has correct size when $\max_{k=2,\ldots,m} E(g(u_{1,t+1}) - g(u_{k,t+1})) = 0$, while the bootstrap approach gives conservative critical values, whenever $E(g(u_{1,t+1}) - g(u_{k,t+1})) < 0$ for some k. Note that the subsampling approach is valid also in the case of nonvanishing parameter estimation error. This is because each subsample statistic properly mimics the distribution of the actual statistic. On the other hand the subsampling approach has two drawbacks. First, subsampling critical values are based on a sample of size b instead of P. Second, the finite sample power may be rather low, as the subsampling quantiles under the alternative diverge at rate $\sqrt{b}$, while bootstrap quantiles are bounded under both hypotheses.[24]

[24] In a recent paper, Linton, Maasoumi and Whang (2004) apply the subsampling approach to the problem of testing for stochastic dominance; a problem characterized by a composite null, as in the reality check case.

4.3.4. The false discovery rate approach applied to the reality check

Another way to avoid sequential testing bias is to rely on bounds, such as (modified) Bonferroni bounds. However, a well known drawback of such an approach is that it is conservative, particularly when we compare a large number of models. Recently, a new approach, based on the false discovery rate (FDR) has been suggested by Benjamini and Hochberg (1995), for the case of independent statistics. Their approach has been extended to the case of dependent statistics by Benjamini and Yekutieli (2001).[25] The FDR approach allows one to select among alternative groups of models, in the sense that one can assess which group(s) contribute to the rejection of the null. The FDR approach has the objective of controlling the expected number of false rejections, and in practice one computes p-values associated with m hypotheses, and orders these p-values in increasing fashion, say $P_1 \leqslant \cdots \leqslant P_i \leqslant \cdots \leqslant P_m$. Then, all hypotheses characterized by $P_i \leqslant (1 - (i - 1)/m)\alpha$ are rejected, where α is a given significance level. Such an approach, though less conservative than Hochberg's (1988) approach, is still conservative as it provides bounds on p-values. More recently, Storey (2003) introduces the q-value of a test statistic, which is defined as the minimum possible false discovery rate for the null is rejected. McCracken and Sapp (2005) implement the q-value approach for the comparison of multiple exchange rate models. Overall, we think that a sound practical strategy could be to first implement the above reality check type tests. These tests can then be complemented by using a multiple comparison approach, yielding a better overall understanding concerning which model(s) contribute to the rejection of the null, if it is indeed rejected. If the null is not rejected, then one simply chooses the benchmark model. Nevertheless, even in this case, it may not hurt to see whether some of the individual hypotheses in their joint null hypothesis are rejected via a multiple test comparison approach.

4.4. A predictive accuracy test that is consistent against generic alternatives

So far we have considered tests for comparing one model against a fixed number of alternative models. Needless to say, such tests have power only against a given alternative. However, there may clearly be some other model with greater predictive accuracy. This is a feature of predictive ability tests which has already been addressed in the consistent specification testing literature [see, e.g., Bierens (1982, 1990), Bierens and Ploberger (1997), DeJong (1996), Hansen (1996), Lee, White and Granger (1993), Stinchcombe and White (1998)].

Corradi and Swanson (2002) draw on both the consistent specification and predictive accuracy testing literatures, and propose a test for predictive accuracy which is consistent against generic nonlinear alternatives, and which is designed for comparing nested

[25] Benjamini and Yekutieli (2001) show that the Benjamini and Hochberg (1995) FDR is valid when the statistics have positive regression dependency. This condition allows for multivariate test statistics with a nondiagonal correlation matrix.

models. The test is based on an out-of-sample version of the integrated conditional moment (ICM) test of Bierens (1982, 1990) and Bierens and Ploberger (1997).

Summarizing, assume that the objective is to test whether there exists any unknown alternative model that has better predictive accuracy than a given benchmark model, for a given loss function. A typical example is the case in which the benchmark model is a simple autoregressive model and we want to check whether a more accurate forecasting model can be constructed by including possibly unknown (non)linear functions of the past of the process or of the past of some other process(es).[26] Although this is the case that we focus on, the benchmark model can in general be any (non)linear model. One important feature of this test is that the same loss function is used for in-sample estimation and out-of-sample prediction [see Granger (1993) and Weiss (1996)].

Let the benchmark model be

$$y_t = \theta^{\dagger}_{1,1} + \theta^{\dagger}_{1,2} y_{t-1} + u_{1,t}, \tag{41}$$

where $\theta^{\dagger}_1 = (\theta^{\dagger}_{1,1}, \theta^{\dagger}_{1,2})' = \arg\min_{\theta_1 \in \Theta_1} E(q(y_t - \theta_{1,1} - \theta_{1,2} y_{t-1}))$, $\theta_1 = (\theta_{1,1}, \theta_{1,2})'$, y_t is a scalar, $q = g$, as the same loss function is used both for in-sample estimation and out-of-sample predictive evaluation, and everything else is defined above. The generic alternative model is:

$$y_t = \theta^{\dagger}_{2,1}(\gamma) + \theta^{\dagger}_{2,2}(\gamma) y_{t-1} + \theta^{\dagger}_{2,3}(\gamma) w\left(Z^{t-1}, \gamma\right) + u_{2,t}(\gamma), \tag{42}$$

where $\theta^{\dagger}_2(\gamma) = (\theta^{\dagger}_{2,1}(\gamma), \theta^{\dagger}_{2,2}(\gamma), \theta^{\dagger}_{2,3}(\gamma))' = \arg\min_{\theta_2 \in \Theta_2} E(q(y_t - \theta_{2,1} - \theta_{2,2} y_{t-1} - \theta_{2,3} w(Z^{t-1}, \gamma)))$, $\theta_2(\gamma) = (\theta_{2,1}(\gamma), \theta_{2,2}(\gamma), \theta_{2,3}(\gamma))'$, and $\theta_2 \in \Theta_2$, where Γ is a compact subset of $\Re^d$, for some finite d. The alternative model is called "generic" because of the presence of $w(Z^{t-1}, \gamma)$, which is a generically comprehensive function, such as Bierens' exponential, a logistic, or a cumulative distribution function [see, e.g., Stinchcombe and White (1998) for a detailed explanation of generic comprehensiveness]. One example has $w(Z^{t-1}, \gamma) = \exp(\sum_{i=1}^{s} \gamma_i \Phi(X_{t-i}))$, where Φ is a measurable one to one mapping from $\Re$ to a bounded subset of $\Re$, so that here $Z^t = (X_t, \ldots, X_{t-s+1})$, and we are thus testing for nonlinear Granger causality. The hypotheses of interest are:

$$H_0\colon \quad E\left(g(u_{1,t+1}) - g\left(u_{2,t+1}(\gamma)\right)\right) = 0, \tag{43}$$

$$H_A\colon \quad E\left(g(u_{1,t+1}) - g\left(u_{2,t+1}(\gamma)\right)\right) > 0. \tag{44}$$

Clearly, the reference model is nested within the alternative model, and given the definitions of $\theta^{\dagger}_1$ and $\theta^{\dagger}_2(\gamma)$, the null model can never outperform the alternative. For this reason, H_0 corresponds to equal predictive accuracy, while H_A corresponds to the case

[26] For example, Swanson and White (1997) compare the predictive accuracy of various linear models against neural network models using both in-sample and out-of-sample model selection criteria.

where the alternative model outperforms the reference model, as long as the errors above are loss function specific forecast errors. It follows that H_0 and H_A can be restated as:

$$H_0\colon\ \theta^{\dagger}_{2,3}(\gamma)=0 \quad \text{versus} \quad H_A\colon\ \theta^{\dagger}_{2,3}(\gamma)\neq 0,$$

for $\forall\gamma\in\Gamma$, except for a subset with zero Lebesgue measure. Now, given the definition of $\theta^{\dagger}_{2}(\gamma)$, note that

$$E\left(g'\big(y_{t+1}-\theta^{\dagger}_{2,1}(\gamma)-\theta^{\dagger}_{2,2}(\gamma)y_t-\theta^{\dagger}_{2,3}(\gamma)w(Z^t,\gamma)\big)\times\begin{pmatrix}-1\\ -y_t\\ -w(Z^t,\gamma)\end{pmatrix}\right)=0,$$

where g' is defined as above. Hence, under H_0 we have that $\theta^{\dagger}_{2,3}(\gamma)=0$, $\theta^{\dagger}_{2,1}(\gamma)=\theta^{\dagger}_{1,1}$, $\theta^{\dagger}_{2,2}(\gamma)=\theta^{\dagger}_{1,2}$, and $E(g'(u_{1,t+1})w(Z^t,\gamma))=0$. Thus, we can once again restate H_0 and H_A as:

$$\begin{aligned}&H_0\colon\ E\big(g'(u_{1,t+1})w\big(Z^t,\gamma\big)\big)=0 \quad \text{versus}\\ &H_A\colon\ E\big(g'(u_{1,t+1})w\big(Z^t,\gamma\big)\big)\neq 0,\end{aligned} \tag{45}$$

for $\forall\gamma\in\Gamma$, except for a subset with zero Lebesgue measure. Finally, define $\widehat{u}_{1,t+1}=y_{t+1}-(1\quad y_t)\widehat{\theta}_{1,t}$. The test statistic is:

$$M_P=\int_\Gamma m_P(\gamma)^2\phi(\gamma)\,\mathrm{d}\gamma, \tag{46}$$

and

$$m_P(\gamma)=\frac{1}{P^{1/2}}\sum_{t=R}^{T-1}g'\big(\widehat{u}_{1,t+1}\big)w\big(Z^t,\gamma\big), \tag{47}$$

where $\int_\Gamma\phi(\gamma)\,\mathrm{d}\gamma=1$, $\phi(\gamma)\geqslant 0$, and $\phi(\gamma)$ is absolutely continuous with respect to Lebesgue measure. In the sequel, we need Assumptions NV1–NV4, which are listed in Appendix A.

THEOREM 4.7 (From Theorem 1 in Corradi and Swanson (2002)). *Let* NV1–NV3 *hold. Then, the following results hold*:

(i) *Under* H_0,

$$M_P=\int_\Gamma m_P(\gamma)^2\phi(\gamma)\,\mathrm{d}\gamma\xrightarrow{d}\int_\Gamma Z(\gamma)^2\phi(\gamma)\,\mathrm{d}\gamma,$$

where $m_P(\gamma)$ *is defined in Equation* (47) *and* Z *is a Gaussian process with covariance kernel given by*:

$$K(\gamma_1,\gamma_2)=S_{gg}(\gamma_1,\gamma_2)+2\Pi\mu_{\gamma_1}A^{\dagger}S_{hh}A^{\dagger}\mu_{\gamma_2}+\Pi\mu'_{\gamma_1}A^{\dagger}S_{gh}(\gamma_2)+\Pi\mu'_{\gamma_2}A^{\dagger}S_{gh}(\gamma_1),$$

with $\mu_{\gamma_1} = E(\nabla_{\theta_1}(g'_{t+1}(u_{1,t+1})w(Z^t,\gamma_1)))$, $A^\dagger = (-E(\nabla^2_{\theta_1} q_1(u_{1,t})))^{-1}$,

$$S_{gg}(\gamma_1,\gamma_2) = \sum_{j=-\infty}^{\infty} E\big(g'(u_{1,s+1})w\big(Z^s,\gamma_1\big)g'(u_{1,s+j+1})w\big(Z^{s+j},\gamma_2\big)\big),$$

$$S_{hh} = \sum_{j=-\infty}^{\infty} E\big(\nabla_{\theta_1} q_1(u_{1,s})\nabla_{\theta_1} q_1(u_{1,s+j})'\big),$$

$$S_{gh}(\gamma_1) = \sum_{j=-\infty}^{\infty} E\big(g'(u_{1,s+1})w\big(Z^s,\gamma_1\big)\nabla_{\theta_1} q_1(u_{1,s+j})'\big),$$

and γ, γ_1, *and* γ_2 *are generic elements of* Γ. $\Pi = 1-\pi^{-1}\ln(1+\pi)$, *for* $\pi > 0$ *and* $\Pi = 0$ *for* $\pi = 0$, $z^q = (z_1,\ldots,z_q)'$, *and* γ, γ_1, γ_2 *are generic elements of* Γ.

(ii) *Under* H_A, *for* $\varepsilon > 0$ *and* $\delta < 1$,

$$\lim_{P\to\infty} \Pr\left(\frac{1}{P^\delta}\int_\Gamma m_P(\gamma)^2\phi(\gamma)\,\mathrm{d}\gamma > \varepsilon\right) = 1.$$

Thus, the limiting distribution under H_0 is a Gaussian process with a covariance kernel that reflects both the dependence structure of the data and, for $\pi > 0$, the effect of parameter estimation error. Hence, critical values are data dependent and cannot be tabulated.

Valid asymptotic critical values have been obtained via a conditional P-value approach by Corradi and Swanson (2002, Theorem 2). Basically, they have extended Inoue's (2001) to the case of non vanishing parameter estimation error. In turn, Inoue (2001) has extended this approach to allow for non-martingale difference score functions. A drawback of the conditional P-values approach is that the simulated statistic is of order $O_P(l)$, where l plays the same role of the block length in the block bootstrap, under the alternative. This may lead to a loss in power, specially with small and medium size samples. A valid alternative is provided by the block bootstrap for recursive estimation scheme.

Define,

$$\widetilde{\theta}^*_{1,t} = \big(\widetilde{\theta}^*_{1,1,t},\widetilde{\theta}^*_{1,2,t}\big)' = \arg\min_{\theta_1\in\Theta_1}\frac{1}{t}\sum_{j=2}^{t}\Bigg[g\big(y^*_j-\theta_{1,1}-\theta_{1,2}y^*_{j-1}\big) - \theta_1'\frac{1}{T}\sum_{i=2}^{T-1}\nabla_\theta g\big(y_i-\widehat{\theta}_{1,1,t}-\widehat{\theta}_{1,2,t}y_{i-1}\big)\Bigg]. \tag{48}$$

Also, define $\widetilde{u}^*_{1,t+1} = y^*_{t+1} - (1\quad y^*_t)\widetilde{\theta}^*_{1,t}$. The bootstrap test statistic is:

$$M^*_P = \int_\Gamma m^*_P(\gamma)^2\phi(\gamma)\,\mathrm{d}\gamma,$$

where

$$m_P^*(\gamma) = \frac{1}{P^{1/2}} \sum_{t=R}^{T-1} \Bigg(g'\big(y_{t+1}^* - (1 \quad y_t^*)\widetilde{\theta}_{1,t}^*\big) w\big(Z^{*,t}, \gamma\big) - \frac{1}{T} \sum_{i=1}^{T-1} g'\big(y_{i+1} - (1 \quad y_i)\widehat{\theta}_{1,t}\big) w\big(Z^i, \gamma\big) \Bigg). \tag{49}$$

THEOREM 4.8 (From Proposition 5 in Corradi and Swanson (2005b)). *Let Assumptions* NV1–NV4 *hold. Also, assume that as* $T \to \infty$, $l \to \infty$, *and that* $\frac{l}{T^{1/4}} \to 0$. *Then, as* T, P *and* $R \to \infty$,

$$P\left(\omega\colon \sup_{v \in \Re} \left| P_T^*\left(\int_\Gamma m_P^*(\gamma)^2 \phi(\gamma)\, d\gamma \leqslant v \right) - P\left(\int_\Gamma m_P^\mu(\gamma)^2 \phi(\gamma)\, d\gamma \leqslant v \right) \right| > \varepsilon \right) \to 0,$$

where $m_P^\mu(\gamma) = m_P(\gamma) - \sqrt{P} E(g'(u_{1,t+1}) w(Z^t, \gamma))$.

The above result suggests proceeding the same way as in the first application. For any bootstrap replication, compute the bootstrap statistic, M_P^*. Perform B bootstrap replications (B large) and compute the percentiles of the empirical distribution of the B bootstrap statistics. Reject H_0 if M_P is greater than the $(1-\alpha)$th-percentile. Otherwise, do not reject. Now, for all samples except a set with probability measure approaching zero, M_P has the same limiting distribution as the corresponding bootstrap statistic under H_0, thus ensuring asymptotic size equal to α. Under the alternative, M_P diverges to (plus) infinity, while the corresponding bootstrap statistic has a well defined limiting distribution, ensuring unit asymptotic power.

5. Comparison of (multiple) misspecified predictive density models

In Section 2 we outlined several tests for the null hypothesis of correct specification of the conditional distribution (some of which allowed for dynamic misspecification). Nevertheless, and as discussed above, most models are approximations of reality and therefore they are typically misspecified, and not just dynamically. In Section 4, we have seen that much of the recent literature on evaluation of point forecast models has already acknowledged the fact that models are typically misspecified. The purpose of this section is to merge these two strands of the literature and discuss recent tests for comparing misspecified conditional distribution models.

5.1. The Kullback–Leibler information criterion approach

A well-known measure of distributional accuracy is the Kullback–Leibler Information Criterion (KLIC), according to which we choose the model which minimizes the KLIC [see, e.g., White (1982), Vuong (1989), Giacomini (2002), and Kitamura (2002)]. In particular, choose model 1 over model 2, if

$$E\left(\log f_1\left(Y_t|Z^t, \theta_1^\dagger\right) - \log f_2\left(Y_t|Z^t, \theta_2^\dagger\right)\right) > 0.$$

For the iid case, Vuong (1989) suggests a likelihood ratio test for choosing the conditional density model that is closer to the "true" conditional density in terms of the KLIC. Giacomini (2002) suggests a weighted version of the Vuong likelihood ratio test for the case of dependent observations, while Kitamura (2002) employs a KLIC based approach to select among misspecified conditional models that satisfy given moment conditions.[27] Furthermore, the KLIC approach has recently been employed for the evaluation of dynamic stochastic general equilibrium models [see, e.g., Schörfheide (2000), Fernandez-Villaverde and Rubio-Ramirez (2004), and Chang, Gomes and Schorfheide (2002)]. For example, Fernandez-Villaverde and Rubio-Ramirez (2004) show that the KLIC-best model is also the model with the highest posterior probability.

The KLIC is a sensible measure of accuracy, as it chooses the model which on average gives higher probability to events which have actually occurred. Also, it leads to simple likelihood ratio type tests which have a standard limiting distribution and are not affected by problems associated with accounting for PEE.

However, it should be noted that if one is interested in measuring accuracy over a specific region, or in measuring accuracy for a given conditional confidence interval, say, this cannot be done in as straightforward manner using the KLIC. For example, if we want to evaluate the accuracy of different models for approximating the probability that the rate of inflation tomorrow, given the rate of inflation today, will be between 0.5% and 1.5%, say, we can do so quite easily using the square error criterion, but not using the KLIC.

5.2. *A predictive density accuracy test for comparing multiple misspecified models*

Corradi and Swanson (2005a, 2006b) introduce a measure of distributional accuracy, which can be interpreted as a distributional generalization of mean square error. In addition, Corradi and Swanson (2005a) apply this measure to the problem of selecting amongst multiple misspecified predictive density models. In this section we discuss these contributions to the literature.

5.2.1. *A mean square error measure of distributional accuracy*

As usual, consider forming parametric conditional distributions for a scalar random variable, y_t, given Z^t, where $Z^t = (y_{t-1}, \ldots, y_{t-s_1}, X_t, \ldots, X_{t-s_2+1})$ with s_1, s_2 finite. Define the group of conditional distribution models from which one is to select a "best"

[27] Of note is that White (1982) shows that quasi maximum likelihood estimators minimize the KLIC, under mild conditions.

model as $F_1(u|Z^t, \theta_1^\dagger), \ldots, F_m(u|Z^t, \theta_m^\dagger)$, and define the true conditional distribution as

$$F_0(u|Z^t, \theta_0) = \Pr(y_{t+1} \leqslant u|Z^t).$$

Hereafter, assume that $\theta_i^\dagger \in \Theta_i$, where Θ_i is a compact set in a finite dimensional Euclidean space, and let $\theta_i^\dagger$ be the probability limit of a quasi maximum likelihood estimator (QMLE) of the parameters of the conditional distribution under model i. If model i is correctly specified, then $\theta_i^\dagger = \theta_0$. If $m > 2$, follow White (2000). Namely, choose a particular conditional distribution model as the "benchmark" and test the null hypothesis that no competing model can provide a more accurate approximation of the "true" conditional distribution, against the alternative that at least one competitor outperforms the benchmark model. Needless to say, pairwise comparison of alternative models, in which no benchmark need be specified, follows as a special case. In this context, measure accuracy using the above distributional analog of mean square error. More precisely, define the mean square (approximation) error associated with model i, $i = 1, \ldots, m$, in terms of the average over U of $E((F_i(u|Z^t, \theta_i^\dagger) - F_0(u|Z^t, \theta_0))^2)$, where $u \in U$, and U is a possibly unbounded set on the real line, and the expectation is taken with respect to the conditioning variables. In particular, model 1 is more accurate than model 2, if

$$\int_U E\Big(\big(F_1(u|Z^t, \theta_1^\dagger) - F_0(u|Z^t, \theta_0)\big)^2 - \big(F_2(u|Z^t, \theta_2^\dagger) - F_0(u|Z^t, \theta_0)\big)^2\Big)\phi(u)\,\mathrm{d}u < 0,$$

where $\int_U \phi(u)\,\mathrm{d}u = 1$ and $\phi(u) \geqslant 0$, for all $u \in U \subset \Re$. This measure essentially integrates over different quantiles of the conditional distribution. For any given evaluation point, this measure defines a norm and it implies a standard goodness of fit measure. Note, that this measure of accuracy leads to straightforward evaluation of distributional accuracy over a given region of interest, as well as to straightforward evaluation of specific quantiles.

A conditional confidence interval version of the above condition which is more natural to use in applications involving predictive interval comparison follows immediately, and can be written as

$$E\Big(\big(\big(F_1(\bar{u}|Z^t, \theta_1^\dagger) - F_1(\underline{u}|Z^t, \theta_1^\dagger)\big) - \big(F_0(\bar{u}|Z^t, \theta_0) - F_0(\underline{u}|Z^t, \theta_0)\big)\big)^2 - \big(\big(F_2(\bar{u}|Z^t, \theta_2^\dagger) - F_2(\underline{u}|Z^t, \theta_2^\dagger)\big) - \big(F_0(\bar{u}|Z^t, \theta_0) - F_0(\underline{u}|Z^t, \theta_0)\big)\big)^2\Big) \leqslant 0.$$

5.2.2. *The tests statistic and its asymptotic behavior*

In this section, $F_1(\cdot|\cdot, \theta_1^\dagger)$ is taken as the benchmark model, and the objective is to test whether some competitor model can provide a more accurate approximation of

$F_0(\cdot|\cdot, \theta_0)$ than the benchmark. The null and the alternative hypotheses are:

$$H_0\colon \quad \max_{k=2,\dots,m} \int_U E\Big(\big(F_1\big(u|Z^t, \theta_1^\dagger\big) - F_0\big(u|Z^t, \theta_0\big)\big)^2 - \big(F_k\big(u|Z^t, \theta_k^\dagger\big) - F_0\big(u|Z^t, \theta_0\big)\big)^2\Big)\phi(u)\,\mathrm{d}u \leqslant 0 \tag{50}$$

versus

$$H_A\colon \quad \max_{k=2,\dots,m} \int_U E\Big(\big(F_1\big(u|Z^t, \theta_1^\dagger\big) - F_0\big(u|Z^t, \theta_0\big)\big)^2 - \big(F_k\big(u|Z^t, \theta_k^\dagger\big) - F_0\big(u|Z^t, \theta_0\big)\big)^2\Big)\phi(u)\,\mathrm{d}u > 0, \tag{51}$$

where $\phi(u) \geqslant 0$ and $\int_U \phi(u) = 1$, $u \in U \subset \Re$, U possibly unbounded. Note that for a given u, we compare conditional distributions in terms of their (mean square) distance from the true distribution. We then average over U. As discussed above, a possibly more natural version of the above hypotheses is in terms of conditional confidence intervals evaluation, so that the objective is to "approximate" $\Pr(\underline{u} \leqslant Y_{t+1} \leqslant \bar{u}|Z^t)$, and hence to evaluate a region of the predictive density. In that case, the null and alternative hypotheses can be stated as:

$$\begin{aligned} H_0'\colon \quad \max_{k=2,\dots,m} E\Big(&\big(\big(F_1\big(\bar{u}|Z^t, \theta_1^\dagger\big) - F_1\big(\underline{u}|Z^t, \theta_1^\dagger\big)\big) \\ &- \big(F_0\big(\bar{u}|Z^t, \theta_0\big) - F_0\big(\underline{u}|Z^t, \theta_0\big)\big)\big)^2 \\ &- \big(\big(F_k\big(\bar{u}|Z^t, \theta_k^\dagger\big) - F_k\big(\underline{u}|Z^t, \theta_k^\dagger\big)\big) \\ &- \big(F_0\big(\bar{u}|Z^t, \theta_0\big) - F_0\big(\underline{u}|Z^t, \theta_0\big)\big)\big)^2\Big) \leqslant 0 \end{aligned}$$

versus

$$\begin{aligned} H_A'\colon \quad \max_{k=2,\dots,m} E\Big(&\big(\big(F_1\big(\bar{u}|Z^t, \theta_1^\dagger\big) - F_1\big(\underline{u}|Z^t, \theta_1^\dagger\big)\big) \\ &- \big(F_0\big(\bar{u}|Z^t, \theta_0\big) - F_0\big(\underline{u}|Z^t, \theta_0\big)\big)\big)^2 \\ &- \big(\big(F_k\big(\bar{u}|Z^t, \theta_k^\dagger\big) - F_k\big(\underline{u}|Z^t, \theta_k^\dagger\big)\big) \\ &- \big(F_0\big(\bar{u}|Z^t, \theta_0\big) - F_0\big(\underline{u}|Z^t, \theta_0\big)\big)\big)^2\Big) > 0. \end{aligned}$$

Alternatively, if interest focuses on testing the null of equal accuracy of two conditional distribution models, say F_1 and F_k, we can simply state the hypotheses as:

$$H_0''\colon \quad \int_U E\Big(\big(F_1\big(u|Z^t, \theta_1^\dagger\big) - F_0\big(u|Z^t, \theta_0\big)\big)^2 - \big(F_k\big(u|Z^t, \theta_k^\dagger\big) - F_0\big(u|Z^t, \theta_0\big)\big)^2\Big)\phi(u)\,\mathrm{d}u = 0$$

versus

$$H_A''\colon \quad \int_U E\Big(\big(F_1\big(u|Z^t, \theta_1^\dagger\big) - F_0\big(u|Z^t, \theta_0\big)\big)^2$$

$$-\left(F_k\left(u|Z^t,\theta_k^\dagger\right)-F_0\left(u|Z^t,\theta_0\right)\right)^2\Big)\phi(u)\,\mathrm{d}u \neq 0,$$

or we can write the predictive density (interval) version of these hypotheses.

Needless to say, we do not know $F_0(u|Z^t)$. However, it is easy to see that

$$\begin{aligned} & E\Big(\left(F_1\left(u|Z^t,\theta_1^\dagger\right)-F_0\left(u|Z^t,\theta_0\right)\right)^2-\left(F_k\left(u|Z^t,\theta_k^\dagger\right)-F_0\left(u|Z^t,\theta_0\right)\right)^2\Big) \\ &\quad = E\left(\left(1\{y_{t+1}\leqslant u\}-F_1\left(u|Z^t,\theta_1^\dagger\right)\right)^2\right) \\ &\qquad - E\left(\left(1\{y_{t+1}\leqslant u\}-F_k\left(u|Z^t,\theta_k^\dagger\right)\right)^2\right), \end{aligned} \tag{52}$$

where the right-hand side of (52) does not require the knowledge of the true conditional distribution.

The intuition behind Equation (52) is very simple. First, note that for any given u, $E(1\{y_{t+1} \leqslant u\}|Z^t) = \Pr(y_{t+1} \leqslant u|Z^t) = F_0(u|Z^t,\theta_0)$. Thus, $1\{y_{t+1} \leqslant u\} - F_k(u|Z^t,\theta_k^\dagger)$ can be interpreted as an "error" term associated with computation of the conditional expectation under F_i. Now, $j = 1,\ldots,m$:

$$\begin{aligned} \mu_k^2(u) &= E\left(\left(1\{y_{t+1}\leqslant u\}-F_k\left(u|Z^t,\theta_k^\dagger\right)\right)^2\right) \\ &= E\Big(\left(\left(1\{y_{t+1}\leqslant u\}-F_0\left(u|Z^t,\theta_0\right)\right)-\left(F_k\left(u|Z^t,\theta_k^\dagger\right)-F_0\left(u|Z^t,\theta_0\right)\right)\right)^2\Big) \\ &= E\left(\left(1\{y_{t+1}\leqslant u\}-F_0\left(u|Z^t,\theta_0\right)\right)^2\right) \\ &\quad + E\left(\left(F_k\left(u|Z^t,\theta_k^\dagger\right)-F_0\left(u|Z^t,\theta_0\right)\right)^2\right), \end{aligned}$$

given that the expectation of the cross product is zero (which follows because $1\{y_{t+1} \leqslant u\} - F_0(u|Z^t,\theta_0)$ is uncorrelated with any measurable function of Z^t). Therefore,

$$\begin{aligned} \mu_1^2(u)-\mu_k^2(u) &= E\left(\left(F_1\left(u|Z^t,\theta_1^\dagger\right)-F_0\left(u|Z^t,\theta_0\right)\right)^2\right) \\ &\quad - E\left(\left(F_k\left(u|Z^t,\theta_k^\dagger\right)-F_0\left(u|Z^t,\theta_0\right)\right)^2\right). \end{aligned} \tag{53}$$

The statistic of interest is

$$Z_{P,j} = \max_{k=2,\ldots,m} \int_U Z_{P,u,j}(1,k)\phi(u)\,\mathrm{d}u, \qquad j=1,2, \tag{54}$$

where for $j = 1$ (rolling estimation scheme),

$$\begin{aligned} Z_{P,u,1}(1,k) &= \frac{1}{\sqrt{P}}\sum_{t=R}^{T-1}\Big(\left(1\{y_{t+1}\leqslant u\}-F_1\left(u|Z^t,\widehat{\theta}_{1,t,\mathrm{rol}}\right)\right)^2 \\ &\quad - \left(1\{y_{t+1}\leqslant u\}-F_k\left(u|Z^t,\widehat{\theta}_{k,t,\mathrm{rol}}\right)\right)^2\Big) \end{aligned}$$

and for $j = 2$ (recursive estimation scheme),

$$Z_{P,u,2}(1,k) = \frac{1}{\sqrt{P}}\sum_{t=R}^{T-1}\Big(\left(1\{y_{t+1}\leqslant u\}-F_1\left(u|Z^t,\widehat{\theta}_{1,\mathrm{rec}}\right)\right)^2$$

$$- \left(1\{y_{t+1} \leqslant u\} - F_k\left(u|Z^t, \widehat{\theta}_{k,t,\mathrm{rec}}\right)\right)^2\Big), \tag{55}$$

where $\widehat{\theta}_{i,t,\mathrm{rol}}$ and $\widehat{\theta}_{i,t,\mathrm{rec}}$ are defined as in (20) and in (19) in Section 3.1.

As shown above and in Corradi and Swanson (2005a), the hypotheses of interest can be restated as:

$$H_0\colon \quad \max_{k=2,\ldots,m} \int_U \left(\mu_1^2(u) - \mu_k^2(u)\right)\phi(u)\,\mathrm{d}u \leqslant 0$$

versus

$$H_A\colon \quad \max_{k=2,\ldots,m} \int_U \left(\mu_1^2(u) - \mu_k^2(u)\right)\phi(u)\,\mathrm{d}u > 0,$$

where $\mu_i^2(u) = E((1\{y_{t+1} \leqslant u\} - F_i(u|Z^t, \theta_i^\dagger))^2)$. In the sequel, we require Assumptions MD1–MD4, which are listed in Appendix A.

PROPOSITION 5.1 (From Proposition 1 in Corradi and Swanson (2006b)). *Let* MD1–MD4 *hold. Then,*

$$\max_{k=2,\ldots,m} \int_U \left(Z_{P,u,j}(1,k) - \sqrt{P}\left(\mu_1^2(u) - \mu_k^2(u)\right)\right)\phi_U(u)\,\mathrm{d}u$$
$$\xrightarrow{d} \max_{k=2,\ldots,m} \int_U Z_{1,k,j}(u)\phi_U(u)\,\mathrm{d}u,$$

where $Z_{1,k,j}(u)$ is a zero mean Gaussian process with covariance $C_{k,j}(u,u')$ ($j=1$ corresponds to rolling and $j=2$ to recursive estimation schemes), equal to:

$$E\Bigg(\sum_{j=-\infty}^{\infty} \left(\left(1\{y_{s+1} \leqslant u\} - F_1\left(u|Z^s, \theta_1^\dagger\right)\right)^2 - \mu_1^2(u)\right)$$
$$\times \left(\left(1\{y_{s+j+1} \leqslant u'\} - F_1\left(u'|Z^{s+j}, \theta_1^\dagger\right)\right)^2 - \mu_1^2(u')\right)\Bigg)$$
$$+ E\Bigg(\sum_{j=-\infty}^{\infty} \left(\left(1\{y_{s+1} \leqslant u\} - F_k\left(u|Z^s, \theta_k^\dagger\right)\right)^2 - \mu_k^2(u)\right)$$
$$\times \left(\left(1\{y_{s+j+1} \leqslant u'\} - F_k\left(u'|Z^{s+j}, \theta_k^\dagger\right)\right)^2 - \mu_k^2(u')\right)\Bigg)$$
$$- 2E\Bigg(\sum_{j=-\infty}^{\infty} \left(\left(1\{y_{s+1} \leqslant u\} - F_1\left(u|Z^s, \theta_1^\dagger\right)\right)^2 - \mu_1^2(u)\right)$$
$$\times \left(\left(1\{y_{s+j+1} \leqslant u'\} - F_k\left(u'|Z^{s+j}, \theta_k^\dagger\right)\right)^2 - \mu_k^2(u')\right)\Bigg)$$
$$+ 4\Pi_j m_{\theta_1^\dagger}(u)' A\left(\theta_1^\dagger\right)$$

$$
\begin{aligned}
&\times E\left(\sum_{j=-\infty}^{\infty} \nabla_{\theta_1} \ln f_1\left(y_{s+1}|Z^s, \theta_1^\dagger\right) \nabla_{\theta_1} \ln f_1\left(y_{s+j+1}|Z^{s+j}, \theta_1^\dagger\right)' \right) \\
&\times A\left(\theta_1^\dagger\right) m_{\theta_1^\dagger}(u') \\
&+ 4\Pi_j m_{\theta_k^\dagger}(u)' A\left(\theta_k^\dagger\right) \\
&\times E\left(\sum_{j=-\infty}^{\infty} \nabla_{\theta_k} \ln f_k\left(y_{s+1}|Z^s, \theta_k^\dagger\right) \nabla_{\theta_k} \ln f_k\left(y_{s+j+1}|Z^{s+j}, \theta_k^\dagger\right)' \right) \\
&\times A\left(\theta_k^\dagger\right) m_{\theta_k^\dagger}(u') \\
&- 4\Pi_j m_{\theta_1^\dagger}(u,)' A\left(\theta_1^\dagger\right) \\
&\times E\left(\sum_{j=-\infty}^{\infty} \nabla_{\theta_1} \ln f_1\left(y_{s+1}|Z^s, \theta_1^\dagger\right) \nabla_{\theta_k} \ln f_k\left(y_{s+j+1}|Z^{s+j}, \theta_k^\dagger\right)' \right) \\
&\times A\left(\theta_k^\dagger\right) m_{\theta_k^\dagger}(u') \\
&- 4C\Pi_j m_{\theta_1^\dagger}(u)' A\left(\theta_1^\dagger\right) \\
&\times E\left(\sum_{j=-\infty}^{\infty} \nabla_{\theta_1} \ln f_1\left(y_{s+1}|Z^s, \theta_1^\dagger\right) \right. \\
&\left. \times \left(\left(1\{y_{s+j+1} \leqslant u\} - F_1\left(u|Z^{s+j}, \theta_1^\dagger\right)\right)^2 - \mu_1^2(u)\right) \right) \\
&+ 4C\Pi_j m_{\theta_1^\dagger}(u)' A\left(\theta_1^\dagger\right) \\
&\times E\left(\sum_{j=-\infty}^{\infty} \nabla_{\theta_1} \ln f_1\left(y_{s+1}|Z^s, \theta_1^\dagger\right) \right. \\
&\left. \times \left(\left(1\{y_{s+j+1} \leqslant u\} - F_k\left(u|Z^{s+j}, \theta_k^\dagger\right)\right)^2 - \mu_k^2(u)\right) \right) \\
&- 4C\Pi_j m_{\theta_k^\dagger}(u)' A\left(\theta_k^\dagger\right) \\
&\times E\left(\sum_{j=-\infty}^{\infty} \nabla_{\theta_k} \ln f_k\left(y_{s+1}|Z^s, \theta_k^\dagger\right)' \right. \\
&\left. \times \left(\left(1\{y_{s+j+1} \leqslant u\} - F_k\left(u|Z^{s+j}, \theta_k^\dagger\right)\right)^2 - \mu_k^2(u)\right) \right) \\
&+ 4C\Pi_j m_{\theta_k^\dagger}(u)' A\left(\theta_k^\dagger\right)
\end{aligned}
$$

$$\times E\Bigg(\sum_{j=-\infty}^{\infty} \nabla_{\theta_k} \ln f_k\big(y_{s+1}|Z^s, \theta_k^\dagger\big)'$$

$$\times \big(\big(1\{y_{s+j+1} \leqslant u\} - F_1\big(u|Z^{s+j}, \theta_1^\dagger\big)\big)^2 - \mu_1^2(u)\big)\Bigg), \tag{56}$$

with

$$m_{\theta_i^\dagger}(u)' = E\big(\nabla_{\theta_i} F_i\big(u|Z^t, \theta_i^\dagger\big)'\big(1\{y_{t+1} \leqslant u\} - F_i\big(u|Z^t, \theta_i^\dagger\big)\big)\big)$$

and

$$A\big(\theta_i^\dagger\big) = A_i^\dagger = \big(E\big(-\nabla_{\theta_i}^2 \ln f_i\big(y_{t+1}|Z^t, \theta_i^\dagger\big)\big)\big)^{-1},$$

and for $j = 1$ *and* $P \leqslant R$, $\Pi_1 = (\pi - \frac{\pi^2}{3})$, $C\Pi_1 = \frac{\pi}{2}$, *and for* $P > R$, $\Pi_1 = (1 - \frac{1}{3\pi})$ *and* $C\Pi_1 = (1 - \frac{1}{2\pi})$. *Finally, for* $j = 2$, $\Pi_2 = 2(1 - \pi^{-1}\ln(1+\pi))$ *and* $C\Pi_2 = 0.5\Pi_2$.

From this proposition, note that when all competing models provide an approximation to the true conditional distribution that is as (mean square) accurate as that provided by the benchmark (i.e. when $\int_U (\mu_1^2(u) - \mu_k^2(u))\phi(u)\,du = 0, \forall k$), then the limiting distribution is a zero mean Gaussian process with a covariance kernel which is not nuisance parameter free. Additionally, when all competitor models are worse than the benchmark, the statistic diverges to minus infinity at rate $\sqrt{P}$. Finally, when only some competitor models are worse than the benchmark, the limiting distribution provides a conservative test, as Z_P will always be smaller than $\max_{k=2,\dots,m} \int_U (Z_{P,u}(1,k) - \sqrt{P}(\mu_1^2(u) - \mu_k^2(u)))\phi(u)\,du$, asymptotically. Of course, when H_A holds, the statistic diverges to plus infinity at rate $\sqrt{P}$.

For the case of evaluation of multiple conditional confidence intervals, consider the statistic:

$$V_{P,\tau} = \max_{k=2,\dots,m} V_{P,\underline{u},\bar{u},\tau}(1,k) \tag{57}$$

where

$$\begin{aligned} V_{P,\underline{u},\bar{u},\tau}(1,k) = \frac{1}{\sqrt{P}} \sum_{t=R}^{T-1} \Big(&\big(1\{\underline{u} \leqslant y_{t+1} \leqslant \bar{u}\} - \big(F_1\big(\bar{u}|Z^t, \widehat{\theta}_{1,t,\tau}\big) \\ &- F_1\big(\underline{u}|Z^t, \widehat{\theta}_{1,t,\tau}\big)\big)\big)^2 \\ &- \big(1\{\underline{u} \leqslant y_{t+1} \leqslant \bar{u}\} - \big(F_k\big(\bar{u}|Z^t, \widehat{\theta}_{k,t,\tau}\big) \\ &- F_k\big(\underline{u}|Z^t, \widehat{\theta}_{k,t,\tau}\big)\big)\big)^2\Big) \end{aligned} \tag{58}$$

where $s = \max\{s_1, s_2\}$, $\tau = 1, 2$, $\widehat{\theta}_{k,t,\tau} = \widehat{\theta}_{k,t,\mathrm{rol}}$ for $\tau = 1$, and $\widehat{\theta}_{k,t,\tau} = \widehat{\theta}_{k,t,\mathrm{rec}}$ for $\tau = 2$.

We then have the following result.

PROPOSITION 5.2 (From Proposition 1b in Corradi and Swanson (2006b)). *Let Assumptions* MD1–MD4 *hold. Then for* $\tau = 1$,

$$\max_{k=2,\ldots,m} \left(V_{P,\underline{u},\bar{u},\tau}(1,k) - \sqrt{P}\left(\mu_1^2 - \mu_k^2\right)\right) \xrightarrow{d} \max_{k=2,\ldots,m} V_{P,k,\tau}(\underline{u},\bar{u}),$$

where $V_{P,k,\tau}(\underline{u},\bar{u})$ *is a zero mean normal random variable with covariance* $c_{kk} = v_{kk} + p_{kk} + cp_{kk}$, *where* v_{kk} *denotes the component of the long-run variance matrix we would have in absence of parameter estimation error,* p_{kk} *denotes the contribution of parameter estimation error and* cp_{kk} *denotes the covariance across the two components. In particular*:

$$\begin{aligned}
v_{kk} = {} & E \sum_{j=-\infty}^{\infty} \Big(\Big(\big(1\{\underline{u} \leqslant y_{s+1} \leqslant \bar{u}\} - \big(F_1(\bar{u}|Z^s,\theta_1^\dagger) - F_1(\underline{u}|Z^s,\theta_1^\dagger)\big)\big)^2 - \mu_1^2\Big) \\
& \times \Big(\big(1\{\underline{u} \leqslant y_{s+1+j} \leqslant \bar{u}\} - \big(F_1(\bar{u}|Z^{s+j},\theta_1^\dagger) - F_1(\underline{u}|Z^{s+j},\theta_1^\dagger)\big)\big)^2 - \mu_1^2\Big)\Big) \\
& + E \sum_{j=-\infty}^{\infty} \Big(\Big(\big(1\{\underline{u} \leqslant y_{s+1} \leqslant \bar{u}\} - \big(F_k(\bar{u}|Z^s,\theta_k^\dagger) - F_k(\underline{u}|Z^s,\theta_k^\dagger)\big)\big)^2 - \mu_k^2\Big) \\
& \times \Big(\big(1\{\underline{u} \leqslant y_{s+1+j} \leqslant \bar{u}\} - \big(F_k(\bar{u}|Z^{s+j},\theta_k^\dagger) - F_k(\underline{u}|Z^{s+j},\theta_k^\dagger)\big)\big)^2 - \mu_k^2\Big)\Big) \\
& - 2E \sum_{j=-\infty}^{\infty} \Big(\Big(\big(1\{\underline{u} \leqslant y_{s+1} \leqslant \bar{u}\} - \big(F_1(\bar{u}|Z^s,\theta_1^\dagger) - F_1(\underline{u}|Z^s,\theta_1^\dagger)\big)\big)^2 - \mu_1^2\Big) \\
& \times \Big(\big(1\{\underline{u} \leqslant y_{s+1+j} \leqslant \bar{u}\} - \big(F_k(\bar{u}|Z^{s+j},\theta_k^\dagger) - F_k(\underline{u}|Z^{s+j},\theta_k^\dagger)\big)\big)^2 - \mu_k^2\Big)\Big),
\end{aligned} \tag{59}$$

$$\begin{aligned}
p_{kk} = {} & 4m'_{\theta_1^\dagger} A(\theta_1^\dagger) E\left(\sum_{j=-\infty}^{\infty} \nabla_{\theta_1} \ln f_1(y_{s+1}|Z^s,\theta_1^\dagger) \nabla_{\theta_1} \ln f_1(y_{s+1+j}|Z^{s+j},\theta_1^\dagger)'\right) \\
& \times A(\theta_1^\dagger) m_{\theta_1^\dagger} \\
& + 4m'_{\theta_k^\dagger} A(\theta_k^\dagger) E\left(\sum_{j=-\infty}^{\infty} \nabla_{\theta_k} \ln f_k(y_{s+1}|Z^s,\theta_k^\dagger) \nabla_{\theta_k} \ln f_k(y_{s+1+j}|Z^{s+j},\theta_k^\dagger)'\right) \\
& \times A(\theta_k^\dagger) m_{\theta_k^\dagger} \\
& - 8m'_{\theta_1^\dagger} A(\theta_1^\dagger) E\left(\sum_{j=-\infty}^{\infty} \nabla_{\theta_1} \ln f_1(y_{s+1}|Z^s,\theta_1^\dagger) \nabla_{\theta_k} \ln f_k(y_{s+1+j}|Z^{s+j},\theta_k^\dagger)'\right) \\
& \times A(\theta_k^\dagger) m_{\theta_k^\dagger},
\end{aligned} \tag{60}$$

$$\begin{aligned}
cp_{kk} = {} & -4m'_{\theta_1^\dagger} A(\theta_1^\dagger) E\Bigg(\sum_{j=-\infty}^{\infty} \nabla_{\theta_1} \ln f_1(y_{s+1}|Z^s, \theta_1^\dagger) \\
& \times \big((1\{\underline{u} \leqslant y_{s+j} \leqslant \bar{u}\} - (F_1(\bar{u}|Z^{s+j}, \theta_1^\dagger) - F_1(\underline{u}|Z^{s+j}, \theta_1^\dagger)))^2 - \mu_1^2 \big) \\
& + 8m'_{\theta_1^\dagger} A(\theta_1^\dagger) E\Bigg(\sum_{j=-\infty}^{\infty} \nabla_{\theta_1} \ln f_1(y_s|Z^s, \theta_1^\dagger) \\
& \times \big((1\{\underline{u} \leqslant y_{s+1+j} \leqslant \bar{u}\} - (F_k(\bar{u}|Z^{s+j}, \theta_k^\dagger) - F_k(\underline{u}|Z^{s+j}, \theta_k^\dagger)))^2 - \mu_k^2 \big) \Bigg) \\
& - 4m'_{\theta_k^\dagger} A(\theta_k^\dagger) E\Bigg(\sum_{j=-\infty}^{\infty} \nabla_{\theta_k} \ln f_k(y_{s+1}|Z^s, \theta_k^\dagger) \\
& \times \big((1\{\underline{u} \leqslant y_{s+j} \leqslant \bar{u}\} - (F_k(\bar{u}|Z^{s+j}, \theta_k^\dagger) - F_k(\underline{u}|Z^{s+j}, \theta_k^\dagger)))^2 - \mu_k^2 \big) \Bigg)
\end{aligned} \tag{61}$$

with

$$\begin{aligned}
m'_{\theta_i^\dagger} = {} & E\Big(\nabla_{\theta_i} \big(F_i(\bar{u}|Z^t, \theta_i^\dagger) - F_i(\bar{u}|Z^t, \theta_i^\dagger)\big) \\
& \times \big(1\{\underline{u} \leqslant y_t \leqslant \bar{u}\} - (F_i(\bar{u}|Z^t, \theta_i^\dagger) - F_i(\bar{u}|Z^t, \theta_i^\dagger)) \big) \Big)
\end{aligned}$$

and

$$A(\theta_i^\dagger) = \big(E(-\ln \nabla^2_{\theta_i} f_i(y_t|Z^t, \theta_i^\dagger)) \big)^{-1}.$$

An analogous result holds for the case where $\tau = 2$, and is omitted for the sake of brevity.

5.2.3. Bootstrap critical values for the density accuracy test

Turning now to the construction of critical values for the above test, note that using the bootstrap sampling procedures defined in Sections 3.4 or 3.5, one first constructs appropriate bootstrap samples. Thereafter, form bootstrap statistics as follows:

$$Z^*_{P,\tau} = \max_{k=2,\dots,m} \int_U Z^*_{P,u,\tau}(1,k)\phi(u)\,du,$$

where for $\tau = 1$ (rolling estimation scheme), and for $\tau = 2$ (recursive estimation scheme):

$$Z^*_{P,u,\tau}(1,k) = \frac{1}{\sqrt{P}} \sum_{t=R}^{T-1} \Bigg(\big((1\{y^*_{t+1} \leqslant u\} - F_1(u|Z^{*,t}, \widetilde{\theta}^*_{1,t,\tau}) \big)^2$$

$$- \left(1\left\{y^*_{t+1} \leqslant u\right\} - F_k\left(u|Z^{*,t}, \widetilde{\theta}^*_{k,t,\tau}\right)\right)^2\Big)$$
$$- \frac{1}{T}\sum_{j=s+1}^{T-1}\left(\left(1\{y_{j+1} \leqslant u\} - F_1\left(u|Z^i, \widehat{\theta}_{1,t,\tau}\right)\right)^2\right.$$
$$\left.- \left(1\{y_{j+1} \leqslant u\} - F_k\left(u|Z^j, \widehat{\theta}_{k,t,\tau}\right)\right)^2\right)\Bigg).$$

Note that each bootstrap term, say $1\{y^*_{t+1} \leqslant u\} - F_i(u|Z^{*,t}, \widetilde{\theta}^*_{i,t,\tau})$, $t \geqslant R$, is re-centered around the (full) sample mean $\frac{1}{T}\sum_{j=s+1}^{T-1}(1\{y_{j+1} \leqslant u\} - F_i(u|Z^i, \widehat{\theta}_{i,t,\tau}))^2$. This is necessary as the bootstrap statistic is constructed using the last P resampled observations, which in turn have been resampled from the full sample. In particular, this is necessary regardless of the ratio P/R. If $P/R \to 0$, then we do not need to mimic parameter estimation error, and so could simply use $\widehat{\theta}_{1,t,\tau}$ instead of $\widetilde{\theta}^*_{1,t,\tau}$, but we still need to recenter any bootstrap term around the (full) sample mean.

For the confidence interval case, define:

$$V^*_{P,\tau} = \max_{k=2,\dots,m} V^*_{P,\underline{u},\bar{u},\tau}(1,k),$$

$$V^*_{P,\underline{u},\bar{u},\tau}(1,k) = \frac{1}{\sqrt{P}}\sum_{t=R}^{T-1}\Big(\Big(1\left\{\underline{u} \leqslant y^*_{t+1} \leqslant \bar{u}\right\}$$
$$- \left(F_1\left(\bar{u}|Z^{*t}, \widetilde{\theta}^*_{1,t,\tau}\right) - F_1\left(\underline{u}|Z^{*t}, \widetilde{\theta}^*_{1,t,\tau}\right)\right)\Big)^2$$
$$- \left(1\left\{\underline{u} \leqslant y^*_{t+1} \leqslant \bar{u}\right\} - \left(F_k\left(\bar{u}|Z^{*t}, \widetilde{\theta}^*_{k,t,\tau}\right) - F_1\left(\underline{u}|Z^{*t}, \widetilde{\theta}^*_{k,t,\tau}\right)\right)\right)^2\Big)$$
$$- \frac{1}{T}\sum_{j=s+1}^{T-1}\Big(\Big(1\{\underline{u} \leqslant y_{i+1} \leqslant \bar{u}\}$$
$$- \left(F_1\left(\bar{u}|Z^j, \widehat{\theta}_{1,t,\tau}\right) - F_1\left(\underline{u}|Z^j, \widehat{\theta}_{1,t,\tau}\right)\right)\Big)^2$$
$$- \left(1\{\underline{u} \leqslant y_{j+1} \leqslant \bar{u}\} - \left(F_k\left(\bar{u}|Z^j, \widehat{\theta}_{k,t,\tau}\right) - F_1\left(\underline{u}|Z^j, \widehat{\theta}_{k,t,\tau}\right)\right)\right)^2\Big),$$

where, as usual, $\tau = 1, 2$. The following results then hold.

PROPOSITION 5.3 (From Proposition 6 in Corradi and Swanson (2006b)). *Let Assumptions* MD1–MD4 *hold. Also, assume that as $T \to \infty$, $l \to \infty$, and that $\frac{l}{T^{1/4}} \to 0$. Then, as T, P and $R \to \infty$, for $\tau = 1, 2$:*

$$P\left(\omega\colon \sup_{v\in\Re}\left|P^*_T\left(\max_{k=2,\dots,m}\int_U Z^*_{P,u,\tau}(1,k)\phi(u)\,du \leqslant v\right)\right.\right.$$
$$\left.\left.- P\left(\max_{k=2,\dots,m}\int_U Z^{\mu}_{P,u,\tau}(1,k)\phi(u)\,du \leqslant v\right)\right| > \varepsilon\right) \to 0,$$

where $Z^{\mu}_{P,u,\tau}(1,k) = Z_{P,u,\tau}(1,k) - \sqrt{P}(\mu_1^2(u) - \mu_k^2(u))$, *and where* $\mu_1^2(u) - \mu_k^2(u)$ *is defined as in Equation* (53).

PROPOSITION 5.4 (From Proposition 7 in Corradi and Swanson (2006b)). *Let Assumptions* MD1–MD4 *hold. Also, assume that as* $T \to \infty$, $l \to \infty$, *and that* $\frac{l}{T^{1/4}} \to 0$. *Then, as* T, P *and* $R \to \infty$, *for* $\tau = 1, 2$:

$$P\Big(\omega\colon \sup_{v\in\Re}\Big|P_T^*\Big(\max_{k=2,\ldots,m} V^*_{P,\underline{u},\bar{u},\tau}(1,k) \leqslant v\Big) - P\Big(\max_{k=2,\ldots,m} V^{\mu}_{P,\underline{u},\bar{u},\tau}(1,k) \leqslant v\Big)\Big| > \varepsilon\Big) \to 0,$$

where $V^{\mu}_{P,j}(1,k) = V_{P,j}(1,k) - \sqrt{P}(\mu_1^2 - \mu_k^2)$, *and where* $\mu_1^2 - \mu_k^2$ *is defined as in Equation* (53).

The above results suggest proceeding in the following manner. For brevity, just consider the case of $Z^*_{P,\tau}$. For any bootstrap replication, compute the bootstrap statistic, $Z^*_{P,\tau}$. Perform B bootstrap replications (B large) and compute the quantiles of the empirical distribution of the B bootstrap statistics. Reject H_0, if $Z_{P,\tau}$ is greater than the $(1-\alpha)$th-percentile. Otherwise, do not reject. Now, for all samples except a set with probability measure approaching zero, $Z_{P,\tau}$ has the same limiting distribution as the corresponding bootstrapped statistic when $E(\mu_1^2(u) - \mu_k^2(u)) = 0$, $\forall k$, ensuring asymptotic size equal to α. On the other hand, when one or more competitor models are strictly dominated by the benchmark, the rule provides a test with asymptotic size between 0 and α. Under the alternative, $Z_{P,\tau}$ diverges to (plus) infinity, while the corresponding bootstrap statistic has a well defined limiting distribution, ensuring unit asymptotic power. From the above discussion, we see that the bootstrap distribution provides correct asymptotic critical values only for the least favorable case under the null hypothesis; that is, when all competitor models are as good as the benchmark model. When $\max_{k=2,\ldots,m} \int_U (\mu_1^2(u) - \mu_k^2(u))\phi(u)\,du = 0$, but $\int_U (\mu_1^2(u) - \mu_k^2(u))\phi(u)\,du < 0$ for some k, then the bootstrap critical values lead to conservative inference. An alternative to our bootstrap critical values in this case is the construction of critical values based on subsampling [see, e.g., Politis, Romano and Wolf (1999, Chapter 3)]. Heuristically, construct $T - 2b_T$ statistics using subsamples of length b_T, where $b_T/T \to 0$. The empirical distribution of these statistics computed over the various subsamples properly mimics the distribution of the statistic. Thus, subsampling provides valid critical values even for the case where $\max_{k=2,\ldots,m} \int_U (\mu_1^2(u) - \mu_k^2(u))\phi(u)\,du = 0$, but $\int_U (\mu_1^2(u) - \mu_k^2(u))\phi(u)\,du < 0$ for some k. This is the approach used by Linton, Maasoumi and Whang (2004), for example, in the context of testing for stochastic dominance. Needless to say, one problem with subsampling is that unless the sample is very large, the empirical distribution of the subsampled statistics may yield a poor approximation of the limiting distribution of the statistic. An alternative approach for addressing the conservative nature of our bootstrap critical values is suggested in Hansen (2005). Hansen's idea is to recenter the bootstrap statistics using the sample mean, whenever the latter is larger than (minus) a bound of order $\sqrt{2T \log\log T}$. Otherwise, do not recenter the bootstrap statistics. In the current context, his approach leads to correctly sized inference when $\max_{k=2,\dots,m} \int_U (\mu_1^2(u) - \mu_k^2(u))\phi(u)\,\mathrm{d}u = 0$, but $\int_U (\mu_1^2(u) - \mu_k^2(u))\phi(u)\,\mathrm{d}u < 0$ for some k. Additionally, his approach has the feature that if all models are characterized by a sample mean below the bound, the null is "accepted" and no bootstrap statistic is constructed.

5.2.4. Empirical illustration – forecasting inflation

In this section we summarize the results of a simple stylized macroeconomic example from Corradi and Swanson (2006b) to illustrate how to apply the predictive density accuracy test discussed in Section 5.2.2. In particular, assume that the objective is to select amongst 4 different predictive density models for inflation, including a linear *AR* model and an *ARX* model, where the *ARX* model differs from the *AR* model only through the inclusion of unemployment as an additional explanatory variable. Assume also that 2 versions of each of these models are used, one assuming normality, and one assuming that the conditional distribution being evaluated follows a Student's t distribution with 5 degrees of freedom. Further, assume that the number of lags used in these models is selected via use of either the SIC or the AIC. This example can thus be thought of as an out-of-sample evaluation of simplified Phillips curve type models of inflation.

The data used were obtained from the St. Louis Federal Reserve website. For unemployment, we use the seasonally adjusted civilian unemployment rate. For inflation, we use the 12th difference of the log of the seasonally adjusted CPI for all urban consumers, all items. Both data series were found to be I(0), based on application of standard augmented Dickey–Fuller unit root tests. All data are monthly, and the sample period is 1954:1–2003:12. This 600 observation sample was broken into two equal parts for test construction, so that $R = P = 300$. Additionally, all predictions were 1-step ahead, and were constructed using the recursive estimation scheme discussed above.[28] Bootstrap percentiles were calculated based on 100 bootstrap replications, and we set $u \in U \subset [\mathit{Inf}_{\min}, \mathit{Inf}_{\max}]$, where Inf_t is the inflation variable being examined, and 100 equally spaced values for u across this range were used (i.e. $\phi(u)$ is the uniform density). Lags were selected as follows. First, and using only the initial R sample observations, autoregressive lags were selected according to both the SIC and the AIC. Thereafter, fixing the number of autoregressive lags, the number of lags of unemployment (Unem_t) was chosen, again using each of the SIC and the AIC. This framework enabled us to compare various permutations of 4 different models using the $Z_{P,2}$ statistic, where

$$Z_{P,2} = \max_{k=2,\dots,4} \int_U Z_{P,u,2}(1,k)\phi(u)\,\mathrm{d}u$$

[28] Results based on the rolling estimation scheme have been tabulated, and are available upon request from the authors.

and

$$Z_{P,u,2}(1,k) = \frac{1}{\sqrt{P}} \sum_{t=R}^{T-1} \Big(\big(1\{Inf_{t+1} \leqslant u\} - F_1\big(u|Z^t, \widehat{\theta}_{1,t,\mathrm{rec}}\big)\big)^2 - \big(1\{Inf_{t+1} \leqslant u\} - F_k\big(u|Z^t, \widehat{\theta}_{k,t,\mathrm{rec}}\big)\big)^2 \Big),$$

as discussed above. In particular, we consider (i) a comparison of *AR* and *ARX* models, with lags selected using the SIC; (ii) a comparison of *AR* and *ARX* models, with lags selected using the AIC; (iii) a comparison of *AR* models, with lags selected using either the SIC or the AIC; and (iv) a comparison of *ARX* models, with lags selected using either the SIC or the AIC. Recalling that each model is specified with either a Gaussian or Student's t error density, we thus have 4 applications, each of which involves the comparison of 4 different predictive density models. Results are gathered in Tables 2–5. The tables contain: mean square forecast errors – MSFE (so that our density accuracy results can be compared with model rankings based on conditional mean evaluation); lags used; $\int_U \frac{1}{\sqrt{P}} \sum_{t=R}^{T-1} (1\{Inf_{t+1} \leqslant u\} - F_1(u|Z^t, \widehat{\theta}_{1,t}))^2 \phi(u)\,\mathrm{d}u$ = DMSFE (for "ranking" based on our density type mean square error measures), and {50, 60, 70, 80, 90} split and full sample bootstrap percentiles for block lengths of {3, 5, 10, 15, 20} observations (for conducting inference using $Z_{P,2}$).

A number of results emerge, upon inspection of the tables. For example, notice that lower MSFEs are uniformly associated with models that have lags selected via the AIC. This rather surprising result suggests that parsimony is not always the best "rule of thumb" for selecting models for predicting conditional mean, and is a finding in agreement with one of the main conclusions of Marcellino, Stock and Watson (2006). Interestingly, though, the density based mean square forecast error measure that we consider (i.e. DMSFE) is not generally lower when the AIC is used. This suggests that the choice of lag selection criterion is sensitive to whether individual moments or entire distributions are being evaluated. Of further note is that $\max_{k=2,\ldots,4} \int_U Z_{P,u,2}(1,k)\phi(u)\,\mathrm{d}u$ in Table 2 is -0.046, which fails to reject the null hypothesis that the benchmark AR(1)-normal density model is at least as "good" as any other SIC selected model. Furthermore, when only AR models are evaluated (see Table 4), there is nothing gained by using the AIC instead of the SIC, and the normality assumption is again not "bested" by assuming fatter predictive density tails (notice that in this case, failure to reject occurs even when 50th percentiles of either the split or full sample recursive block bootstrap distributions are used to form critical values). In contrast to the above results, when either the AIC is used for all competitor models (Table 3), or when only ARX models are considered with lags selected by either SIC or AIC (Table 5), the null hypothesis of normality is rejected using 90th percentile critical values. Further, in both of these cases, the "preferred model", based on ranking according to DMSFE, is (i) an ARX model with Student's t errors (when only the AIC is used to select lags) or (ii) an ARX model with Gaussian errors and lags selected via the SIC (when only ARX models are compared). This result indicates the importance of comparing a wide variety of models.

Table 2
Comparison of autoregressive inflation models with and without unemployment using SIC

	Model 1 – Normal	Model 2 – Normal	Model 3 – Student's t	Model 4 – Student's t
Specification	AR	ARX	AR	ARX
Lag selection	SIC(1)	SIC(1,1)	SIC(1)	SIC(1,1)
MSFE	0.00083352	0.00004763	0.00083352	0.00004763
DMSFE	1.80129635	2.01137942	1.84758927	1.93272971
$Z_{P,u,2}(1,k)$	Benchmark	−0.21008307	−0.04629293	−0.13143336

Critical values

	Bootstrap with adjustment					Bootstrap without adjustment				
Percentile	3	5	10	15	20	3	5	10	15	20
50	0.094576	0.095575	0.097357	0.104290	0.105869	0.059537	0.062459	0.067246	0.073737	0.079522
60	0.114777	0.117225	0.128311	0.134509	0.140876	0.081460	0.084932	0.097435	0.105071	0.113710
70	0.142498	0.146211	0.169168	0.179724	0.200145	0.110945	0.110945	0.130786	0.145153	0.156861
80	0.178584	0.193576	0.221591	0.244199	0.260359	0.141543	0.146881	0.185892	0.192494	0.218076
90	0.216998	0.251787	0.307671	0.328763	0.383923	0.186430	0.196849	0.254943	0.271913	0.312400

Notes: Entires in the table are given in two parts (i) summary statistics, and (ii) bootstrap percentiles. In (i): "specification" lists the model used. For each specification, lags may be chosen either with the SIC or the AIC, and the predictive density may be either Gaussian or Student's t, as denoted in the various columns of the table. The bracketed entires beside SIC and AIC denote the number of lags chosen for the autoregressive part of the model and the number of lags of unemployment used, respectively. MSFE is the out-of-sample mean square forecast error based on evaluation of $P = 300$ 1-step ahead predictions using recursively estimated models, and DMSFE $= \int_U \frac{1}{\sqrt{P}} \sum_{t=R}^{T-1} (1\{Inf_{t+1} \leqslant u\} - F_1(u|Z^t, \widehat{\theta}_{1,t}))^2 \phi(u)\, du$, where $R = 300$, corresponding to the sample period from 1954:1–1978:12, is our analogous density based square error loss measure. Finally, $Z_{P,u,2}(1,k)$ is the accuracy test statistic, for each benchmark/alternative model comparison. The density accuracy test is the maximum across the $Z_{P,u,2}(1,k)$ values. In (ii) percentiles of the bootstrap empirical distributions under different block length sampling regimes are given. The "Bootstrap with adjustment" allows for parameter estimation error, while the "Bootstrap without adjustment" assumes that parameter estimation error vanishes asymptotically. Testing is carried out using 90th percentiles (see above for further details).

Table 3
Comparison of autoregressive inflation models with and without unemployment using AIC

	Model 1 – Normal	Model 2 – Normal	Model 3 – Student's t	Model 4 – Student's t
Specification	AR	ARX	AR	ARX
Lag selection	AIC(3)	AIC(3,1)	AIC(3)	AIC(3,1)
MSFE	0.00000841	0.00000865	0.00000841	0.00000865
DMSFE	2.17718449	2.17189485	2.11242940	2.10813786
$Z_{P,u,2}(1,k)$	Benchmark	0.00528965	0.06475509	0.06904664

Critical values

Percentile	Bootstrap with adjustment					Bootstrap without adjustment				
	3	5	10	15	20	3	5	10	15	20
50	−0.004056	−0.003820	−0.003739	−0.003757	−0.003722	-0.004542	−0.004448	−0.004316	−0.004318	−0.004274
60	−0.003608	−0.003358	−0.003264	−0.003343	−0.003269	-0.004318	−0.003999	−0.003911	−0.003974	−0.003943
70	−0.003220	−0.002737	−0.002467	−0.002586	−0.002342	-0.003830	−0.003384	−0.003287	−0.003393	−0.003339
80	−0.002662	−0.001339	−0.001015	−0.001044	−0.000321	-0.003148	−0.001585	−0.001226	−0.001340	−0.000783
90	−0.000780	0.001526	0.002828	0.002794	0.003600	−0.000925	0.001371	0.002737	0.002631	0.003422

Notes: See notes to Table 2.

Table 4
Comparison of autoregressive inflation models using SIC and AIC

	Model 1 – Normal	Model 2 – Normal	Model 3 – Student's t	Model 4 – Student's t
Specification	AR	AR	AR	AR
Lag selection	SIC(1)	AIC(3)	SIC(1)	AIC(3)
MSFE	0.00083352	0.00000841	0.00083352	0.00000841
DMSFE	1.80129635	2.17718449	1.84758927	2.11242940
$Z_{P,u,2}(1,k)$	Benchmark	−0.37588815	−0.04629293	−0.31113305

Critical values

	Bootstrap with adjustment					Bootstrap without adjustment				
Percentile	3	5	10	15	20	3	5	10	15	20
50	0.099733	0.104210	0.111312	0.114336	0.112498	0.063302	0.069143	0.078329	0.092758	0.096471
60	0.132297	0.147051	0.163309	0.169943	0.172510	0.099277	0.109922	0.121311	0.132211	0.135370
70	0.177991	0.193313	0.202000	0.217180	0.219814	0.133178	0.150112	0.162696	0.177431	0.185820
80	0.209509	0.228377	0.245762	0.279570	0.286277	0.177059	0.189317	0.210808	0.237286	0.244186
90	0.256017	0.294037	0.345221	0.380378	0.387672	0.213491	0.244186	0.280326	0.324281	0.330913

Notes: See notes to Table 2.

Table 5
Comparison of autoregressive inflation models with unemployment using SIC and AIC

	Model 1 – Normal	Model 2 – Normal	Model 3 – Student's t	Model 4 – Student's t
Specification	ARX	ARX	ARX	ARX
Lag selection	SIC(1,1)	AIC(3,1)	SIC(1,1)	AIC(3,1)
MSFE	0.00004763	0.00000865	0.00004763	0.00000865
DMSFE	2.01137942	2.17189485	1.93272971	2.10813786
$Z_{P,u,2}(1,k)$	Benchmark	−0.16051543	0.07864972	−0.09675844

Critical values

	Bootstrap with adjustment					Bootstrap without adjustment				
Percentile	3	5	10	15	20	3	5	10	15	20
50	0.013914	0.015925	0.016737	0.018229	0.020586	0.007462	0.012167	0.012627	0.014746	0.016022
60	0.019018	0.022448	0.023213	0.024824	0.027218	0.013634	0.016693	0.018245	0.019184	0.022048
70	0.026111	0.028058	0.029292	0.030620	0.033757	0.019749	0.022771	0.023878	0.025605	0.029439
80	0.031457	0.033909	0.038523	0.041290	0.043486	0.025395	0.027832	0.033134	0.034677	0.039756
90	0.039930	0.047533	0.052668	0.054634	0.060586	0.035334	0.042551	0.046784	0.049698	0.056309

Notes: See notes to Table 2.

If we were only to compare AR and ARX models using the AIC, as in Table 3, then we would conclude that ARX models beat AR models, and that fatter tails should replace Gaussian tails in error density specification. However, inspection of the density based MSFE measures across all models considered in the tables makes clear that the lowest DMSFE values are always associated with more parsimonious models (with lags selected using the SIC) that assume Gaussianity.

Acknowledgements

The authors owe great thanks to Clive W.J. Granger, whose discussions provided much of the impetus for the authors' own research that is reported in this paper. Thanks are also owed to Frank Diebold, Eric Ghysels, Lutz Kilian, and Allan Timmermann, and three anonymous referees for many useful comments on an earlier draft of this paper. Corradi gratefully acknowledges ESRC grant RES-000-23-0006, and Swanson acknowledges financial support from a Rutgers University Research Council grant.

Part IV: Appendices and References

Appendix A: Assumptions

Assumptions BAI1–BAI4 are used in Section 2.2.

BAI1: $F_t(y_t|Z^{t-1},\theta)$ and its density $f_t(y_t|Z^{t-1},\theta)$ are continuously differentiable in θ. $F_t(y|Z^{t-1},\theta)$ is strictly increasing in y, so that F_t^{-1} is well defined. Also,

$$E\sup_x\sup_\theta f_t\left(y_t|Z^{t-1},\theta\right)\leqslant M_1<\infty$$

and

$$E\sup_x\sup_\theta\left\|\frac{\partial F_t}{\partial\theta}\left(x|Z^{t-1},\theta\right)\right\|\leqslant M_1<\infty,$$

where the supremum is taken over all θ, such that $|\theta-\theta^\dagger|\leqslant MT^{-1/2}$, $M<\infty$.

BAI2: There exists a continuously differentiable function $\overline{g}(r)$, such that for every $M>0$,

$$\sup_{\substack{u,v\\|u-\theta^\dagger|\leqslant MT^{-1/2},|v-\theta^\dagger|\leqslant MT^{-1/2}}}\left\|\frac{1}{T}\sum_{t=1}^T\frac{\partial F_t}{\partial\theta}\left(F_t^{-1}(r|u)|v\right)-\overline{g}(r)\right\|=o_P(1),$$

where the $o_P(1)$ is uniform in $r\in[0,1]$. In addition, $\int_0^1\|\dot{g}(r)\|\,\mathrm{d}r<\infty$, $C(r)=\int_r^1\dot{g}(\tau)\dot{g}(\tau)'\,\mathrm{d}\tau$ is invertible for all r.

BAI3: $\sqrt{T}(\widehat{\theta}_T-\theta^\dagger)=O_P(1)$.

BAI4: The effect of using Z^{t-1} instead of $\Im_{t-1}$ is negligible. That is,

$$\sup_{u,|u-\theta_0|\leqslant MT^{-1/2}} T^{-1/2}\sum_{t=1}^{T}\big|F_t\big(F_t^{-1}(r|Z^{t-1},u)\Im_{t-1},\theta_0\big) - F_t\big(F_t^{-1}(r|\Im_{t-1},u)|\Im_{t-1},\theta_0\big)\big| = o_P(1)$$

Assumptions HL1–HL4 are used in Section 2.3.

HL1: (y_t, Z^{t-1}) are strong mixing with mixing coefficients $\alpha(\tau)$ satisfying $\sum_{\tau=0}^{\infty}\alpha(\tau)^{(\upsilon-1).\upsilon} \leqslant C < \infty$, with $\upsilon > 1$.
HL2: $f_t(y|Z^t,\theta)$ is twice continuously differentiable in θ, in a neighborhood of θ_0, and $\lim_{T\to\infty}\sum_{\tau=1}^{n} E\big|\frac{\partial U_t}{\partial\theta}\big|^4 \leqslant C$, $\lim_{T\to\infty}\sum_{\tau=1}^{n} E\sup_{\theta\in\Theta}\big|\frac{\partial^2 U_t}{\partial\theta\partial\theta'}\big|^2 \leqslant C$, for some constant C.
HL3: $\sqrt{T}(\widehat{\theta}_T - \theta^\dagger) = O_P(1)$, where $\theta^\dagger$ is the probability limit of $\widehat{\theta}_T$, and is equal to θ_0, under the null in (1).
HL4: The kernel function $k:[-1,1] \to \Re^+$ is a symmetric, bounded, twice continuously differentiable probability density, such that $\int_{-1}^{1} k(u)\,du = 0$ and $\int_{-1}^{1} k^2(u)\,du < \infty$.

Assumptions CS1–CS3 are used in Sections 2.4–2.5 and 3.3–3.5.

CS1: (y_t, Z^{t-1}), are jointly strictly stationary and strong mixing with size $-4(4+\psi)/\psi$, $0 < \psi < 1/2$.
CS2: (i) $F(y_t|Z^{t-1},\theta)$ is twice continuously differentiable on the interior of $\Theta \subset \Re^p$, Θ compact; (ii) $E(\sup_{\theta\in\Theta}|\nabla_\theta F(y_t|Z^t,\theta)_i|^{5+\psi}) \leqslant C < \infty$, $i = 1,\ldots,p$, where ψ is the same positive constant defined in CS1, and $\nabla_\theta F(y_t|Z^{t-1},\theta)_i$ is the ith element of $\nabla_\theta F(y_t|Z^{t-1},\theta)$; (iii) $F(u|Z^{t-1},\theta)$ is twice differentiable on the interior of $U\times\Theta$, where U and Θ are compact subsets of $\Re$ and $\Re^p$ respectively; and (iv) $\nabla_\theta F(u|Z^{t-1},\theta)$ and $\nabla_{u,\theta} F(u|Z^{t-1},\theta)$ are jointly continuous on $U\times\Theta$ and $4s$-dominated on $U\times\Theta$ for $s > 3/2$.
CS3: (i) $\theta^\dagger = \arg\max_{\theta\in\Theta} E(\ln f(y_1|Z^0,\theta))$ is uniquely identified, (ii) $f(y_t|Z^{t-1},\theta)$ is twice continuously differentiable in θ in the interior of Θ, (iii) the elements of $\nabla_\theta \ln f(y_t|Z^{t-1},\theta)$ and of $\nabla_\theta^2 \ln f(y_t|Z^{t-1},\theta)$ are $4s$-dominated on Θ, with $s > 3/2$, $E(-\nabla_\theta^2 \ln f(y_t|Z^{t-1},\theta))$ is positive definite uniformly in Θ.[29]

Assumptions W1–W2 are used in Sections 3.1, 4.1 and 4.3.

W1: (y_t, Z^{t-1}), with y_t scalar and Z^{t-1} an R^ζ-valued $(0 < \zeta < \infty)$ vector, is a strictly stationary and absolutely regular β-mixing process with size $-4(4+\psi)/\psi$, $\psi > 0$.

[29] Let $\nabla_\theta \ln f(y_t|X_t,\theta)_i$ be the ith element of $\nabla_\theta \ln f(y_t|X_t,\theta)$. For $4s$-domination on Θ, we require $|\nabla_\theta \ln f(y_t|X_t,\theta)_i| \leqslant m(X_t)$, for all i, with $E((m(X_t))^{4s}) < \infty$, for some function m.

W2: (i) $\theta^{\dagger}$ is uniquely identified (i.e. $E(q(y_t, Z^{t-1}, \theta)) > E(q(y_t, Z^{t-1}, \theta_i^{\dagger}))$ for any $\theta \neq \theta^{\dagger}$); (ii) q is twice continuously differentiable on the interior of Θ, and for Θ a compact subset of R^{ϱ}; (iii) the elements of $\nabla_{\theta} q$ and $\nabla_{\theta}^2 q$ are p-dominated on Θ, with $p > 2(2 + \psi)$, where ψ is the same positive constant as defined in W1; and (iv) $E(-\nabla_{\theta}^2 q(\theta))$ is negative definite uniformly on Θ.

Assumptions W1–W2 are used in Section 4.2.

CM1: (y_t, x_t) are strictly stationary, strong mixing processes, with size $\frac{-4(4+\delta)}{\delta}$, for some $\delta > 0$, and $E(y_t)^8 < \infty$, $E(x_t)^8$.

CM2: Let $z_t = (y_{t-1}, \ldots, y_{t-q}, x_{t-1}, \ldots, x_{t-q})$ and $E(z_t u_t | \Im_{t-1}) = 0$, where $\Im_{t-1}$ contains all the information at time $t-1$ generated by all the past of x_t and y_t. Also, $E(u_t^2 | \Im_{t-1}) = \sigma_u^2$.

Assumption CSS is used in Section 4.2.

CCS: (y_t, x_t) are strictly stationary, strong mixing processes, with size $\frac{-4(4+\delta)}{\delta}$, for some $\delta > 0$, and $E(y_t)^8 < \infty$, $E(x_t)^8 < \infty$, $E(\epsilon_t y_{t-j}) = 0$, $j = 1, 2, \ldots, q$.[30]

Assumption WH is used in Section 4.3.

WH: (i) κ_i is twice continuously differentiable on the interior of Θ_i and the elements of $\nabla_{\theta_i} \kappa_i(Z^t, \theta_i)$ and $\nabla_{\theta_i}^2 \kappa_i(Z^t, \theta_i)$ are p-dominated on Θ_i, for $i = 2, \ldots, m$, with $p > 2(2+\psi)$, where ψ is the same positive constant defined in W1; (ii) g is positive valued, twice continuously differentiable on Θ_i, and g, g' and g'' are p-dominated on Θ_i with p defined as in (i); and (iii) let

$$c_{kk} = \lim_{T \to \infty} \operatorname{Var}\left(\frac{1}{\sqrt{T}} \sum_{t=s}^{T} \left(g(u_{1,t+1}) - g(u_{k,t+1}) \right) \right), \quad k = 2, \ldots, m,$$

define analogous covariance terms, $c_{j,k}$, $j, k = 2, \ldots, m$, and assume that $[c_{j,k}]$ is positive semi-definite.

Assumptions NV1–NV4 are used in Section 4.4.

NV1: (i) (y_t, Z^t) is a strictly stationary and absolutely regular strong mixing sequence with size $-4(4 + \psi)/\psi$, $\psi > 0$, (ii) g is three times continuously differentiable in θ, over the interior of B, and $\nabla_{\theta} g$, $\nabla_{\theta}^2 g$, $\nabla_{\theta} g'$, $\nabla_{\theta}^2 g'$ are $2r$-dominated uniformly in Θ, with $r \geqslant 2(2 + \psi)$, (iii) $E(-\nabla_{\theta}^2 g_t(\theta))$ is negative definite, uniformly in Θ, (iv) w is a bounded, twice continuously differentiable function on the interior of Γ and $\nabla_{\gamma} w(z^t, \gamma)$ is bounded uniformly in Γ and (v) $\nabla_{\gamma} \nabla_{\theta} g_t'(\theta) w(Z^{t-1}, \gamma)$ is continuous on $\Theta \times \Gamma$, Γ a compact subset of $\Re^d$ and is $2r$-dominated uniformly in $\Theta \times \Gamma$, with $r \geqslant 2(2 + \psi)$.

[30] Note that the requirement $E(\epsilon_t y_{t-j}) = 0$, $j = 1, 2, \ldots, p$, is equivalent to the requirement that $E(y_t | y_{t-1}, \ldots, y_{t-p}) = \sum_{j=1}^{p-1} \beta_j y_{t-j}$. However, we allow dynamic misspecification under the null.

NV2: (i) $E(g'(y_t - \theta_{1,1} - \theta_{1,2}y_{t-1})) > E(g'(x_t - \theta_{1,1}^\dagger - \theta_{1,2}^\dagger x_{t-1}))$, $\forall \theta \neq \theta^\dagger$, and

$$\text{(ii)}\quad E\big(g'\big(y_t - \theta_{2,1} - \theta_{2,2}x_{t-1} - \theta_{2,3}w\big(Z^{t-1}, \gamma\big)\big)\big) > \inf_{\gamma} E\big(g'\big(y_t - \theta_{2,1}^\dagger(\gamma) - \theta_{2,2}^\dagger(\gamma)y_{t-1} - \theta_{2,3}^\dagger(\gamma)w\big(Z^{t-1}, \gamma\big)\big)\big)$$

for $\theta \neq \theta^\dagger(\gamma)$.

NV3: $T = R + P$, and as $T \to \infty$, $\frac{P}{R} \to \pi$, with $0 \leqslant \pi < \infty$.

NV4: For any t, s; $\forall\, i, j, k = 1, 2$; and for $\Delta < \infty$:

$$\text{(i)}\quad E\Big(\sup_{\theta \times \gamma \times \gamma^+ \in \Theta \times \Gamma \times \Gamma} \big|g_t'(\theta)w\big(Z^{t-1}, \gamma\big)\nabla_\theta^k g_s'(\theta)w\big(Z^{s-1}, \gamma^+\big)\big|^4\Big) < \Delta,$$

where $\nabla_\theta^k(\cdot)$ denotes the kth element of the derivative of its argument with respect to θ,

$$\text{(ii)}\quad E\Big(\sup_{\theta \in \Theta}\big|\big(\nabla_\theta^k\big(\nabla_\theta^i g_t(\theta)\big)\nabla_\theta^j g_s(\theta)\big)\big|^4\Big) < \Delta,$$

and

$$\text{(iii)}\quad E\Big(\sup_{\theta \times \gamma \in \Theta \times \Gamma}\big|\big(g_t'(\theta)w\big(Z^{t-1}, \gamma\big)\nabla_\theta^k\big(\nabla_\theta^j g_s(\theta)\big)\big)\big|^4\Big) < \Delta.$$

Assumptions MD1–MD4 are used in Section 5.2.

MD1: (y_t, X_t), with y_t scalar and X_t an R^ζ-valued $(0 < \zeta < \infty)$ vector, is a strictly stationary and absolutely regular β-mixing process with size $-4(4 + \psi)/\psi$, $\psi > 0$.

MD2: (i) $\theta_i^\dagger$ is uniquely identified (i.e. $E(\ln f_i(y_t, Z^{t-1}, \theta_i)) < E(\ln f_i(y_t, Z^{t-1}, \theta_i^\dagger))$ for any $\theta_i \neq \theta_i^\dagger$); (ii) $\ln f_i$ is twice continuously differentiable on the interior of Θ_i, for $i = 1, \ldots, m$, and for Θ_i a compact subset of $R^{\varrho(i)}$; (iii) the elements of $\nabla_{\theta_i} \ln f_i$ and $\nabla_{\theta_i}^2 \ln f_i$ are p-dominated on Θ_i, with $p > 2(2 + \psi)$, where ψ is the same positive constant as defined in Assumption A1; and (iv) $E(-\nabla_{\theta_i}^2 \ln f_i(\theta_i))$ is positive definite uniformly on Θ_i.

MD3: $T = R + P$, and as $T \to \infty$, $P/R \to \pi$, with $0 < \pi < \infty$.

MD4: (i) $F_i(u|Z^t, \theta_i)$ is continuously differentiable on the interior of Θ_i and $\nabla_{\theta_i} F_i(u|Z^t, \theta_i^\dagger)$ is $2r$-dominated on Θ_i, uniformly in u, $r > 2$, $i = 1, \ldots, m$;[31] and (ii) let

$$v_{kk}(u) = \operatorname*{plim}_{T\to\infty} \operatorname{Var}\Bigg(\frac{1}{\sqrt{T}}\sum_{t=s}^{T}\Big(\Big(\big(1\{y_{t+1} \leqslant u\} - F_1\big(u|Z^t, \theta_1^\dagger\big)\big)^2 - \mu_1^2(u)\Big) - \Big(\big(1\{y_{t+1} \leqslant u\} - F_k\big(u|Z^t, \theta_k^\dagger\big)\big)^2 - \mu_k^2(u)\Big)\Big)\Bigg),$$

$$k = 2, \ldots, m,$$

[31] We require that for $j = 1, \ldots, p_i$, $E(\nabla_\theta F_i(u|Z^t, \theta_i^\dagger))_j \leqslant D_t(u)$, with $\sup_t \sup_{u\in\Re} E(D_t(u)^{2r}) < \infty$.

define analogous covariance terms, $v_{j,k}(u)$, $j,k = 2,\ldots,m$, and assume that $[v_{j,k}(u)]$ is positive semi-definite, uniformly in u.

Appendix B: Proofs

PROOF OF PROPOSITION 3.2. For brevity, we just consider the case of recursive estimation. The case of rolling estimation schemes can be treated in an analogous way.

$$\begin{aligned}
\widehat{W}_{P,\mathrm{rec}} &= \frac{1}{\sqrt{P}} \sum_{t=R+1}^{T} \left(1\left\{F_t\left(y_t|Z^{t-1}, \widehat{\theta}_{t,\mathrm{rec}}\right) \leqslant r\right\} - r\right) \\
&= \frac{1}{\sqrt{P}} \sum_{t=R+1}^{T} \left(1\left\{F_t\left(y_t|Z^{t-1}, \theta_0\right) \leqslant F\left(F^{-1}\left(r|Z^{t-1}, \widehat{\theta}_{t,\mathrm{rec}}\right)\big|Z^{t-1}, \theta_0\right)\right\}\right. \\
&\quad \left. - r\right) \\
&= \frac{1}{\sqrt{P}} \sum_{t=R+1}^{T} \Big(1\left\{F_t\left(y_t|Z^{t-1}, \theta_0\right) \leqslant F\left(F^{-1}\left(r|Z^{t-1}, \widehat{\theta}_{t,\mathrm{rec}}\right)\big|Z^{t-1}, \theta_0\right)\right\} \\
&\quad - F\left(F^{-1}\left(r|Z^{t-1}, \widehat{\theta}_{t,\mathrm{rec}}\right)\big|Z^{t-1}, \theta_0\right)\Big) \\
&\quad + \frac{1}{\sqrt{P}} \sum_{t=R+1}^{T} \left(F\left(F^{-1}\left(r|Z^{t-1}, \widehat{\theta}_t\right)\big|Z^{t-1}, \theta_0\right) - r\right) \\
&= I_P + II_P.
\end{aligned}$$

We first want to show that:

(i) $I_P = \frac{1}{\sqrt{P}} \sum_{t=R+1}^{T} (1\{F_t(y_t|Z^{t-1}, \theta_0) \leqslant r\} - r) + o_P(1)$, uniformly in r, and

(ii) $II_P = \bar{g}(r) \frac{1}{\sqrt{P}} \sum_{t=R+1}^{T} (\widehat{\theta}_{t,\mathrm{rec}} - \theta_0) + o_P(1)$, uniformly in r.

Given BAI2, (ii) follows immediately. For (i), we need to show that

$$\begin{aligned}
&\frac{1}{\sqrt{P}} \sum_{t=R+1}^{T} \left(1\left\{F_t\left(y_t|Z^{t-1}, \theta_0\right) \leqslant r + \frac{\partial F_t}{\partial \theta}\left(F_t^{-1}\left(r|\bar{\theta}_{t,\mathrm{rec}}\right), \theta_0\right)\left(\widehat{\theta}_{t,\mathrm{rec}} - \theta_0\right)\right\}\right. \\
&\quad \left. - \left(r + \frac{\partial F_t}{\partial \theta}\left(F_t^{-1}\left(r|\bar{\theta}_{t,\mathrm{rec}}\right), \theta_0\right)\left(\widehat{\theta}_t - \theta_0\right)\right)\right) \\
&= \frac{1}{\sqrt{P}} \sum_{t=R+1}^{T} \left(1\left\{F_t(y_t|\Omega_{t-1}, \theta_0) \leqslant r\right\} - r\right) + o_P(1), \quad \text{uniformly in } r.
\end{aligned}$$

Given BAI3′, the equality above follows by the same argument as that used in the proof of Theorem 1 in Bai (2003). Given (i) and (ii), it follows that

$$\widehat{V}_{P,\text{rec}} = \frac{1}{\sqrt{P}} \sum_{t=R+1}^{T} \left(1\left\{F_t(y_t|\Omega_{t-1},\theta_0) \leqslant r\right\} - r\right)$$

$$+ \bar{g}(r)\frac{1}{\sqrt{P}} \sum_{t=R+1}^{T} \left(\widehat{\theta}_{t,\text{rec}} - \theta_0\right) + o_P(1), \tag{B.1}$$

uniformly in r, where $\bar{g}(r) = \operatorname{plim} \frac{1}{P} \sum_{t=R+1}^{T} \frac{\partial F_t}{\partial \theta}(F_t^{-1}(r|\bar{\theta}_{t,\text{rec}}), \theta_0)$, $\bar{\theta}_{t,\text{rec}} \in (\widehat{\theta}_{t,\text{rec}}, \theta_0)$.

The desired outcome follows if the martingalization argument applies also in the recursive estimation case and the parameter estimation error component cancel out in the statistic. Now, Equation A4 in Bai (2003) holds in the form of Equation (B.1) above. Also,

$$\widehat{W}_{P,\text{rol}}(r) = \widehat{V}_{P,\text{rol}}(r) - \int_0^r \left(\dot{g}(s)C^{-1}(s)\dot{g}(s)' \int_s^1 \dot{g}(\tau)\,\mathrm{d}\widehat{V}_{P,\text{rol}}(\tau)\right) \mathrm{d}s. \tag{B.2}$$

It remain to show that the parameter estimation error term, which enters into both $\widehat{V}_{P,\text{rol}}(r)$ and $\mathrm{d}\widehat{V}_{P,\text{rol}}(\tau)$, cancels out, as in the fixed estimation scheme. Notice that $g(r)$ is defined as in the fixed scheme. Now, it suffices to define the term c, which appears at the bottom of p. 543 (below Equation A6) in Bai (2003) as:

$$c = \frac{1}{\sqrt{P}} \sum_{t=R+1}^{T} \left(\widehat{\theta}_{t,\text{rec}} - \theta_0\right).$$

Then, the same argument used by Bai (2003) on p. 544 applies here, and the term $\frac{1}{\sqrt{P}} \sum_{t=R+1}^{T} (\widehat{\theta}_{t,\text{rec}} - \theta_0)$ on the right-hand side in (B.2) cancels out. □

PROOF OF PROPOSITION 3.4. (i) We begin by considering the case of recursive estimation. Given CS1 and CS3, $\widehat{\theta}_{t,\text{rec}} \overset{\text{a.s.}}{\to} \theta^\dagger$, with $\theta^\dagger = \theta_0$, under H_0. Given CS2(i), and following Bai (2003, pp. 545–546), we have that:

$$\frac{1}{\sqrt{P}} \sum_{t=R}^{T-1} \left(1\left\{F\left(y_{t+1}|Z^t, \widehat{\theta}_{t,\text{rec}}\right) \leqslant r\right\} - r\right)$$

$$= \frac{1}{\sqrt{P}} \sum_{t=R}^{T-1} \left(1\left\{F\left(y_{t+1}|Z^t, \theta_0\right) \leqslant F\left(F^{-1}\left(r|Z^t, \widehat{\theta}_{t,\text{rec}}\right)\big|Z^t, \theta_0\right)\right\} - r\right)$$

$$= \frac{1}{\sqrt{P}} \sum_{t=R}^{T-1} \left(1\left\{F\left(y_{t+1}|Z^t, \theta_0\right) \leqslant F\left(F^{-1}\left(r|Z^t, \widehat{\theta}_{t,\text{rec}}\right)\big|Z^t, \theta_0\right)\right\}\right.$$

$$\left. - F\left(F^{-1}\left(r|Z^t, \theta_0\right)\big|Z^t, \theta_0\right)\right)$$

$$- \frac{1}{\sqrt{P}} \sum_{t=R}^{T-1} \nabla_\theta F\left(F^{-1}\left(r|Z^t, \bar{\theta}_{t,\mathrm{rec}}\right)\big|Z^t, \theta_0\right)\left(\widehat{\theta}_{t,\mathrm{rec}} - \theta_0\right), \tag{B.3}$$

with $\bar{\theta}_{t,\mathrm{rec}} \in (\widehat{\theta}_{t,\mathrm{rec}}, \theta_0)$. Given CS1 and CS3, $(\widehat{\theta}_{t,\mathrm{rec}} - \theta_0) = \mathrm{O}_P(1)$, uniformly in t. Thus, the first term on the right-hand side of (B.3) can be treated by the same argument as that used in the proof of Theorem 1 in Corradi and Swanson (2006a). With regard to the last term on the right-hand side of (B.3), note that by the uniform law of large numbers for mixing processes,

$$\begin{aligned} &\frac{1}{\sqrt{P}} \sum_{t=R}^{T-1} \nabla_\theta F\left(F^{-1}\left(r|Z^t, \bar{\theta}_{t,\mathrm{rec}}\right)\big|Z^t, \theta_0\right)\left(\widehat{\theta}_{t,\mathrm{rec}} - \theta_0\right) \\ &\quad = E\left(\nabla_\theta F\left(x(r)|Z^{t-1}, \theta_0\right)\right)' \frac{1}{\sqrt{P}} \sum_{t=R}^{T-1} \left(\widehat{\theta}_{t,\mathrm{rec}} - \theta_0\right) + \mathrm{o}_P(1), \end{aligned} \tag{B.4}$$

where the $\mathrm{o}_P(1)$ term is uniform in r. The limiting distribution of $\frac{1}{\sqrt{P}} \sum_{t=R}^{T-1} (\widehat{\theta}_{t,\mathrm{rec}} - \theta_0)$, and so the key contribution of parameter estimation error, comes from Theorem 4.1 and Lemma 4.1 in West (1996). With regard to the rolling case, the same argument as above applies, with $\widehat{\theta}_{t,\mathrm{rec}}$ replaced by $\widehat{\theta}_{t,\mathrm{rol}}$. The limiting distribution of $\frac{1}{\sqrt{P}} \sum_{t=R}^{T-1} (\widehat{\theta}_{t,\mathrm{rec}} - \theta_0)$ is given by Lemma 4.1 and 4.2 in West and McCracken (1998). □

PROOF OF PROPOSITION 3.5. The proof is straightforward upon combining the proof of Theorem 2 in Corradi and Swanson (2006a) and the proof of Proposition 3.4. □

PROOF OF PROPOSITION 3.7. Note that:

$$\begin{aligned} &\frac{1}{\sqrt{P}} \sum_{t=R}^{T-1} \left(1\left\{F\left(y_{t+1}^* | Z^{*,t}, \widetilde{\theta}_{t,\mathrm{rec}}^*\right) \leqslant r\right\} - \frac{1}{T} \sum_{j=1}^{T-1} 1\left\{F\left(y_{j+1} | Z^j, \widehat{\theta}_{t,\mathrm{rec}}\right) \leqslant r\right\} \right) \\ &\quad = \frac{1}{\sqrt{P}} \sum_{t=R}^{T-1} \left(1\left\{F\left(y_{t+1}^* | Z^{*,t}, \widehat{\theta}_{t,\mathrm{rec}}\right) \leqslant r\right\} - \frac{1}{T} \sum_{j=1}^{T-1} 1\left\{F\left(y_{j+1} | Z^j, \widehat{\theta}_{t,\mathrm{rec}}\right) \leqslant r\right\} \right) \\ &\qquad - \frac{1}{\sqrt{P}} \sum_{t=R}^{T-1} \nabla_\theta F\left(F^{-1}\left(r|Z^t, \bar{\theta}_{t,\mathrm{rec}}^*\right)\big|Z^t, \theta_0\right)\left(\widetilde{\theta}_{t,\mathrm{rec}}^* - \widehat{\theta}_{t,\mathrm{rec}}\right), \end{aligned} \tag{B.5}$$

where $\bar{\theta}_{t,\mathrm{rec}}^* \in (\widetilde{\theta}_{t,\mathrm{rec}}^*, \widehat{\theta}_{t,\mathrm{rec}})$. Now, the first term on the right-hand side of (B.5) has the same limiting distribution as $\frac{1}{\sqrt{P}} \sum_{t=R}^{T-1} (1\{F(y_{t+1}|Z^t, \theta^\dagger) \leqslant r\} - E(1\{F(y_{j+1}|Z^j, \theta^\dagger) \leqslant r\}))$, conditional on the sample. Furthermore, given Theorem 3.6, the last term on the right-hand side of (B.5) has the same limiting distribution as

$$E\left(\nabla_\theta F\left(x(r)|Z^{t-1}, \theta_0\right)\right)' \frac{1}{\sqrt{P}} \sum_{t=R}^{T-1} \left(\widehat{\theta}_{t,\mathrm{rec}} - \theta^\dagger\right),$$

conditional on the sample. The rolling case follows directly, by replacing $\widetilde{\theta}^*_{t,\mathrm{rec}}$ and $\widehat{\theta}_{t,\mathrm{rec}}$ with $\widetilde{\theta}^*_{t,\mathrm{rol}}$ and $\widehat{\theta}_{t,\mathrm{rol}}$, respectively. □

PROOF OF PROPOSITION 3.8. The proof is similar to the proof of Proposition 3.7. □

PROOF OF PROPOSITION 4.5(ii). Note that, via a mean value expansion, and given A1, A2,

$$\begin{aligned} S_P(1,k) &= \frac{1}{P^{1/2}}\sum_{t=R}^{T-1}\big(g(\widehat{u}_{1,t+1}) - g(\widehat{u}_{k,t+1})\big) \\ &= \frac{1}{P^{1/2}}\sum_{t=R}^{T-1}\big(g(u_{1,t+1}) - g(u_{k,t+1})\big) \\ &\quad + \frac{1}{P}\sum_{t=R}^{T-1} g'(\bar{u}_{1,t+1})\nabla_{\theta_1}\kappa_1\big(Z^t,\bar{\theta}_{1,t}\big)P^{1/2}\big(\widehat{\theta}_{1,t} - \theta_1^\dagger\big) \\ &\quad - \frac{1}{P}\sum_{t=R}^{T-1} g'(\bar{u}_{k,t+1})\nabla_{\theta_k}\kappa_k\big(Z^t,\bar{\theta}_{k,t}\big)P^{1/2}\big(\widehat{\theta}_{k,t} - \theta_k^\dagger\big) \\ &= \frac{1}{P^{1/2}}\sum_{t=R}^{T-1}\big(g(u_{1,t+1}) - g(u_{k,t+1})\big) \\ &\quad + \mu_1\frac{1}{P^{1/2}}\sum_{t=R}^{T-1}\big(\widehat{\theta}_{1,t} - \theta_1^\dagger\big) - \mu_k\frac{1}{P^{1/2}}\sum_{t=R}^{T-1}\big(\widehat{\theta}_{k,t} - \theta_k^\dagger\big) + o_P(1), \end{aligned}$$

where $\mu_1 = E(g'(u_{1,t+1})\nabla_{\theta_1}\kappa_1(Z^t,\theta_1^\dagger))$, and μ_k is defined analogously. Now, when all competitors have the same predictive accuracy as the benchmark model, by the same argument as that used in Theorem 4.1 in West (1996),

$$\big(S_P(1,2),\dots,S_P(1,n)\big) \xrightarrow{d} N(0,V),$$

where V is the $n \times n$ matrix defined in the statement of the proposition. □

PROOF OF PROPOSITION 4.6(ii). For brevity, we just analyze model 1. In particular, note that:

$$\begin{aligned} &\frac{1}{P^{1/2}}\sum_{t=R}^{T-1}\big(g(\widehat{u}^*_{1,t+1}) - g(\widehat{u}_{1,t+1})\big) = \frac{1}{P^{1/2}}\sum_{t=R}^{T-1}\big(g(u^*_{1,t+1}) - g(u_{1,t+1})\big) \\ &\quad + \frac{1}{P^{1/2}}\sum_{t=R}^{T-1}\big(\nabla_{\theta_1} g(\bar{u}^*_{1,t+1})\big(\widehat{\theta}^*_{1,t} - \theta_1^\dagger\big) - \nabla_{\theta_1} g(\bar{u}_{1,t+1})\big(\widehat{\theta}_{1,t} - \theta_1^\dagger\big)\big), \end{aligned} \tag{B.6}$$

where $\bar{u}^*_{1,t+1} = y_{t+1} - \kappa_1(Z^{*,t}, \bar{\theta}^*_{1,t})$, $\bar{u}_{1,t+1} = y_{t+1} - \kappa_1(Z^t, \bar{\theta}_{1,t})$, $\bar{\theta}^*_{1,t} \in (\widehat{\theta}^*_{1,t}, \theta_1^\dagger)$ and $\bar{\theta}_{1,t} \in (\widehat{\theta}_{1,t}, \theta_1^\dagger)$. As an almost straightforward consequence of Theorem 3.5 in Künsch (1989), the first term on the right-hand side of (B.6) has the same limiting distribution as $P^{-1/2}\sum_{t=R}^{T-1}(g(u_{1,t+1}) - E(g(u_{1,t+1})))$. Additionally, the second line in (B.6) can be written as:

$$\begin{aligned}
&\frac{1}{P^{1/2}}\sum_{t=R}^{T-1}\nabla_{\theta_1} g\big(\bar{u}^*_{1,t+1}\big)\big(\widehat{\theta}^*_{1,t} - \widehat{\theta}_{1,t}\big) - \frac{1}{P^{1/2}}\sum_{t=R}^{T-1}\big(\nabla_{\theta_1} g\big(\bar{u}^*_{1,t+1}\big) \\
&\qquad - \nabla_{\theta_1} g(\bar{u}_{1,t+1})\big)\big(\widehat{\theta}_{1,t} - \theta_1^\dagger\big) \\
&\quad = \frac{1}{P^{1/2}}\sum_{t=R}^{T-1}\nabla_{\theta_1} g\big(\bar{u}^*_{1,t+1}\big)\big(\widehat{\theta}^*_{1,t} - \widehat{\theta}_{1,t}\big) + o^*_P(1)\ \text{Pr-}P \\
&\quad = \mu_1 B_1^\dagger \frac{1}{P^{1/2}}\sum_{t=R}^{T-1}\big(h^*_{1,t} - h_{1,t}\big) + o^*_P(1)\ \text{Pr-}P,
\end{aligned} \tag{B.7}$$

where $h^*_{1,t+1} = \nabla_{\theta_1} q_1(y^*_{t+1}, Z^{*,t}, \theta_1^\dagger)$ and $h_{1,t+1} = \nabla_{\theta_1} q_1(y_{t+1}, Z^t, \theta_1^\dagger)$. Also, the last line in (B.7) can be written as:

$$\begin{aligned}
&\mu_1 B_1^\dagger\left(a^2_{R,0}\frac{1}{P^{1/2}}\sum_{t=1}^{R}\big(h^*_{1,t} - h_{1,t}\big) + \frac{1}{P^{1/2}}\sum_{i=1}^{P-1} a_{R,i}\big(h^*_{1,R+i} - \bar{h}_{1,P}\big)\right) \\
&\quad - \mu_1 B_1^\dagger \frac{1}{P^{1/2}}\sum_{i=1}^{P-1} a_{R,i}\big(h_{1,R+i} - \bar{h}_{1,P}\big) + o^*_P(1)\ \text{Pr-}P,
\end{aligned} \tag{B.8}$$

where $\bar{h}_{1,P}$ is the sample average of $h_{1,t}$ computed over the last P observations. By the same argument used in the proof of Theorem 1 in Corradi and Swanson (2005b), the first line in (B.8) has the same limiting distribution as $\frac{1}{P^{1/2}}\sum_{t=R}^{T-1}(\widehat{\theta}_{1,t} - \theta_1^\dagger)$, conditional on sample. Therefore we need to show that the correction term for model 1 offsets the second line in (B.8), up to an o(1) Pr-P term. Let $h_{1,t+1}(\widehat{\theta}_{1,T}) = \nabla_{\theta_1} q_1(y_{t+1}, Z^t, \widehat{\theta}_{1,T})$ and let $\bar{h}_{1,P}(\widehat{\theta}_{1,T})$ be the sample average of $h_{1,t+1}(\widehat{\theta}_{1,T})$, over the last P observations. Now, by the uniform law of large numbers

$$\begin{aligned}
&\frac{1}{T}\sum_{t=s}^{T-1}\nabla_{\theta_1} g\big(\bar{u}^*_{1,t+1}\big)\left(\frac{1}{T}\sum_{t=s}^{T-1}\nabla^2_{\theta_1} q_1\big(y^*_t, Z^{*,t-1}, \widehat{\theta}_{1,T}\big)\right)^{-1} - \mu_1 B_1^\dagger \\
&\quad = o^*_P(1)\ \text{Pr-}P.
\end{aligned}$$

Also, by the same argument used in the proof of Theorem 1, it follows that,

$$\begin{aligned}
&\frac{1}{P^{1/2}}\sum_{i=1}^{P-1} a_{R,i}\big(h_{1,R+i} - \bar{h}_{1,P}\big) - \frac{1}{P^{1/2}}\sum_{i=1}^{P-1} a_{R,i}\big(h_{1,R+i}\big(\widehat{\theta}_{1,T}\big) - \bar{h}_{1,P}\big(\widehat{\theta}_{1,T}\big)\big) \\
&\quad = o(1)\ \text{Pr-}P.
\end{aligned}$$

□

References

Andrews, D.W.K. (1993). "An introduction to econometric applications of empirical process theory for dependent random variables". Econometric Reviews 12, 183–216.

Andrews, D.W.K. (1997). "A conditional Kolmogorov test". Econometrica 65, 1097–1128.

Andrews, D.W.K. (2002). "Higher-order improvements of a computationally attractive k-step bootstrap for extremum estimators". Econometrica 70, 119–162.

Andrews, D.W.K. (2004). "The block–block bootstrap: improved asymptotic refinements". Econometrica 72, 673–700.

Andrews, D.W.K., Buchinsky, M. (2000). "A three step method for choosing the number of bootstrap replications". Econometrica 68, 23–52.

Ashley, R., Granger, C.W.J., Schmalensee, R. (1980). "Advertising and aggregate consumption: An analysis of causality". Econometrica 48, 1149–1167.

Bai, J. (2003). "Testing parametric conditional distributions of dynamic models". Review of Economics and Statistics 85, 531–549.

Bai, J., Ng, S. (2001). "A consistent test for conditional symmetry in time series models". Journal of Econometrics 103, 225–258.

Bai, J., Ng, S. (2005). "Testing skewness, kurtosis and normality in time series data". Journal of Business and Economic Statistics 23, 49–61.

Baltagi, B.H. (1995). Econometric Analysis of Panel Data. Wiley, New York.

Benjamini, Y., Hochberg, Y. (1995). "Controlling the false discovery rate: A practical and powerful approach to multiple testing". Journal of the Royal Statistical Society Series B 57, 289–300.

Benjamini, Y., Yekutieli, Y. (2001). "The control of the false discovery rate in multiple testing under dependency". Annals of Statistics 29, 1165–1188.

Berkowitz, J. (2001). "Testing density forecasts with applications to risk management". Journal of Business and Economic Statistics 19, 465–474.

Berkowitz, J., Giorgianni, L. (2001). "Long-horizon exchange rate predictability?". Review of Economics and Statistics 83, 81–91.

Bickel, P.J., Doksum, K.A. (1977). Mathematical Statistics. Prentice-Hall, Englewood Cliffs, NJ.

Bierens, H.J. (1982). "Consistent model-specification tests". Journal of Econometrics 20, 105–134.

Bierens, H.J. (1990). "A consistent conditional moment test of functional form". Econometrica 58, 1443–1458.

Bierens, H.J., Ploberger, W. (1997). "Asymptotic theory of integrated conditional moments tests". Econometrica 65, 1129–1151.

Bontemps, C., Meddahi, N. (2003). "Testing distributional assumptions: A GMM approach". Working Paper, University of Montreal.

Bontemps, C., Meddahi, N. (2005). "Testing normality: A GMM approach". Journal of Econometrics 124, 149–186.

Brock, W., Lakonishok, J., LeBaron, B. (1992). "Simple technical trading rules and the stochastic properties of stock returns". Journal of Finance 47, 1731–1764.

Carlstein, E. (1986). "The use of subseries methods for estimating the variance of a general statistic from a stationary time series". Annals of Statistics 14, 1171–1179.

Chang, Y.S., Gomes, J.F., Schorfheide, F. (2002). "Learning-by-doing as a propagation mechanism". American Economic Review 92, 1498–1520.

Chao, J.C., Corradi, V., Swanson, N.R. (2001). "Out-of-sample tests for Granger causality". Macroeconomic Dynamics 5, 598–620.

Christoffersen, P.F. (1998). "Evaluating interval forecasts". International Economic Review 39, 841–862.

Christoffersen, P., Diebold, F.X. (2000). "How relevant is volatility forecasting for financial risk management?". Review of Economics and Statistics 82, 12–22.

Clarida, R.H., Sarno, L., Taylor, M.P. (2003). "The out-of-sample success of term structure models as exchange-rate predictors: A step beyond". Journal of International Economics 60, 61–83.

Clark, T.E., McCracken, M.W. (2001). "Tests of equal forecast accuracy and encompassing for nested models". Journal of Econometrics 105, 85–110.
Clark, T.E., McCracken, M.W. (2003). "Evaluating long horizon forecasts". Working Paper, University of Missouri–Columbia.
Clark, T.E., West, K.D. (2006). "Using out-of-sample mean squared prediction errors to test the martingale difference hypothesis". Journal of Econometrics. In press.
Clements, M.P., Smith, J. (2000). "Evaluating the forecast densities of linear and nonlinear models: Applications to output growth and unemployment". Journal of Forecasting 19, 255–276.
Clements, M.P., Smith, J. (2002). "Evaluating multivariate forecast densities: A comparison of two approaches". International Journal of Forecasting 18, 397–407.
Clements, M.P., Taylor, N. (2001). "Bootstrapping prediction intervals for autoregressive models". International Journal of Forecasting 17, 247–276.
Corradi, V., Swanson, N.R., Olivetti, C. (2001). "Predictive ability with cointegrated variables". Journal of Econometrics 104, 315–358.
Corradi, V., Swanson, N.R. (2002). "A consistent test for out of sample nonlinear predictive ability". Journal of Econometrics 110, 353–381.
Corradi, V., Swanson, N.R. (2005a). "A test for comparing multiple misspecified conditional distributions". Econometric Theory 21, 991–1016.
Corradi, V., Swanson, N.R. (2005b). "Nonparametric bootstrap procedures for predictive inference based on recursive estimation schemes". Working Paper, Rutgers University.
Corradi, V., Swanson, N.R. (2006a). "Bootstrap conditional distribution tests in the presence of dynamic misspecification". Journal of Econometrics. In press.
Corradi, V., Swanson, N.R. (2006b). "Predictive density and conditional confidence interval accuracy tests". Journal of Econometrics. In press.
Davidson, R., MacKinnon, J.G. (1993). Estimation and Inference in Econometrics. Oxford University Press, New York.
Davidson, R., MacKinnon, J.G. (1999). "Bootstrap testing in nonlinear models". International Economic Review 40, 487–508.
Davidson, R., MacKinnon, J.G. (2000). "Bootstrap tests: How many bootstraps". Econometric Reviews 19, 55–68.
DeJong, R.M. (1996). "The Bierens test under data dependence". Journal of Econometrics 72, 1–32.
Diebold, F.X., Chen, C. (1996). "Testing structural stability with endogenous breakpoint: A size comparison of analytical and bootstrap procedures". Journal of Econometrics 70, 221–241.
Diebold, F.X., Gunther, T., Tay, A.S. (1998). "Evaluating density forecasts with applications to finance and management". International Economic Review 39, 863–883.
Diebold, F.X., Hahn, J., Tay, A.S. (1999). "Multivariate density forecast evaluation and calibration in financial risk management: High frequency returns on foreign exchange". Review of Economics and Statistics 81, 661–673.
Diebold, F.X., Mariano, R.S. (1995). "Comparing predictive accuracy". Journal of Business and Economic Statistics 13, 253–263.
Diebold, F.X., Tay, A.S., Wallis, K.D. (1998). "Evaluating density forecasts of inflation: The survey of professional forecasters". In: Engle, R.F., White, H. (Eds.), Festschrift in Honor of C.W.J. Granger. Oxford University Press, Oxford.
Duan, J.C. (2003). "A specification test for time series models by a normality transformation". Working Paper, University of Toronto.
Duffie, D., Pan, J. (1997). "An overview of value at risk". Journal of Derivatives 4, 7–49.
Dufour, J.-M., Ghysels, E., Hall, A. (1994). "Generalized predictive tests and structural change analysis in econometrics". International Economic Review 35, 199–229.
Fernandez-Villaverde, J., Rubio-Ramirez, J.F. (2004). "Comparing dynamic equilibrium models to data". Journal of Econometrics 123, 153–187.
Fitzenberger, B. (1997). "The moving block bootstrap and robust inference for linear least square and quantile regressions". Journal of Econometrics 82, 235–287.

Ghysels, E., Hall, A. (1990). "A test for structural stability of Euler conditions parameters estimated via the generalized method of moments estimator". International Economic Review 31, 355–364.

Giacomini, R. (2002). "Comparing density forecasts via weighted likelihood ratio tests: Asymptotic and bootstrap methods". Working Paper, University of California, San Diego.

Giacomini, R., White, H. (2003). "Tests of conditional predictive ability". Working Paper, University of California, San Diego.

Goncalves, S., White, H. (2002). "The bootstrap of the mean for dependent heterogeneous arrays". Econometric Theory 18, 1367–1384.

Goncalves, S., White, H. (2004). "Maximum likelihood and the bootstrap for nonlinear dynamic models". Journal of Econometrics 119, 199–219.

Granger, C.W.J. (1980). "Testing for causality: A personal viewpoint". Journal of Economics and Dynamic Control 2, 329–352.

Granger, C.W.J. (1993). "On the limitations on comparing mean squared errors: A comment". Journal of Forecasting 12, 651–652.

Granger, C.W.J., Newbold, P. (1986). Forecasting Economic Time Series. Academic Press, San Diego.

Granger, C.W.J., Pesaran, M.H. (1993). "Economic and statistical measures of forecast accuracy". Journal of Forecasting 19, 537–560.

Granger, C.W.J., White, H., Kamstra, M. (1989). "Interval forecasing – an analysis based upon ARCH-quantile estimators". Journal of Econometrics 40, 87–96.

Guidolin, M., Timmermann, A. (2005). "Strategic asset allocation". Working Paper, University of California, San Diego.

Guidolin, M., Timmermann, A. (2006). "Term structure of risk under alternative econometric specifications". Journal of Econometrics. In press.

Hall, P., Horowitz, J.L. (1996). "Bootstrap critical values for tests based on generalized method of moments estimators". Econometrica 64, 891–916.

Hall, A.R., Inoue, A. (2003). "The large sample behavior of the generalized method of moments estimator in misspecified models". Journal of Econometrics, 361–394.

Hamilton, J.D. (1994). Time Series Analysis. Princeton University Press, Princeton.

Hansen, B.E. (1996). "Inference when a nuisance parameter is not identified under the null hypothesis". Econometrica 64, 413–430.

Hansen, P.R. (2004). "Asymptotic tests of composite hypotheses". Working Paper, Brown University.

Hansen, P.R. (2005). "A test for superior predictive ability". Journal of Business and Economic Statistics 23, 365–380.

Harvey, D.I., Leybourne, S.J., Newbold, P. (1997). "Tests for forecast encompassing". Journal of Business and Economic Statistics 16, 254–259.

Hochberg, Y. (1988). "A sharper Bonferroni procedure for multiple significance tests". Biometrika 75, 800–803.

Hong, Y. (2001). "Evaluation of out-of-sample probability density forecasts with applications to S&P 500 stock prices". Working Paper, Cornell University.

Hong, Y.M., Li, H.F. (2003). "Nonparametric specification testing for continuous time models with applications to term structure of interest rates". Review of Financial Studies 18, 37–84.

Horowitz, J. (2001). "The bootstrap". In: Heckman, J.J., Leamer, E. (Eds.), Handbook of Econometrics, vol. 5. Elsevier, Amsterdam.

Inoue, A. (2001). "Testing for distributional change in time series". Econometric Theory 17, 156–187.

Inoue, A., Kilian, L. (2004). "In-sample or out-of-sample tests of predictability: Which one should we use?". Econometric Reviews 23, 371–402.

Inoue, A., Shintani, M. (2006). "Bootstrapping GMM estimators for time series". Journal of Econometrics. In press.

Khmaladze, E. (1981). "Martingale approach in the theory of goodness of fit tests". Theory of Probability and Its Applications 20, 240–257.

Khmaladze, E. (1988). "An innovation approach to goodness of fit tests in R^m". Annals of Statistics 100, 789–829.

Kilian, L. (1999a). "Exchange rate and monetary fundamentals: What do we learn from long-horizon regressions?". Journal of Applied Econometrics 14, 491–510.

Kilian, L. (1999b). "Finite sample properties of percentile and percentile t-bootstrap confidence intervals for impulse responses". Review of Economics and Statistics 81, 652–660.

Kilian, L., Taylor, M.P. (2003). "Why is it so difficult to beat the random walk forecast of exchange rates?". Journal of International Economics 60, 85–107.

Kitamura, Y. (2002). "Econometric comparisons of conditional models". Working Paper, University of Pennsylvania.

Kolmogorov, A.N. (1933). "Sulla determinazione empirica di una legge di distribuzione". Giornale dell'Istituto degli Attuari 4, 83–91.

Künsch, H.R. (1989). "The jackknife and the bootstrap for general stationary observations". Annals of Statistics 17, 1217–1241.

Lahiri, S.N. (1999). "Theoretical comparisons of block bootstrap methods". Annals of Statistics 27, 386–404.

Lee, T.H., White, H., Granger, C.W.J. (1993). "Testing for neglected nonlinearity in time series models: A comparison of neural network methods and alternative tests". Journal of Econometrics 56, 269–290.

Li, F., Tkacz, G. (2006). "Consistent test for conditional density functions with time dependent data". Journal of Econometrics. In press.

Linton, O., Maasoumi, E., Whang, Y.J. (2004). "Testing for stochastic dominance: A subsampling approach". Working Paper, London School of Economics.

Marcellino, M., Stock, J., Watson, M. (2006). "A comparison of direct and iterated AR methods for forecasting macroeconomic series h-steps ahead". Journal of Econometrics. In press.

Mark, N.C. (1995). "Exchange rates and fundamentals: Evidence on long-horizon predictability". American Economic Review 85, 201–218.

McCracken, M.W. (2000). "Robust out-of-sample inference". Journal of Econometrics 99, 195–223.

McCracken, M.W. (2004a). "Asymptotics for out-of-sample tests of Granger causality". Working Paper, University of Missouri–Columbia.

McCracken, M.W. (2004b). "Parameter estimation error and tests of equal forecast accuracy between nonnested models". International Journal of Forecasting 20, 503–514.

McCracken, M.W., Sapp, S. (2005). "Evaluating the predictability of exchange rates using long horizon regressions: Mind your p's and q's". Journal of Money, Credit and Banking 37, 473–494.

Meese, R.A., Rogoff, K. (1983). "Empirical exchange rate models of the seventies: Do they fit out-of-sample?". Journal of International Economics 14, 3–24.

Pesaran, M.H., Timmermann, A. (2004a). "How costly is to ignore breaks when forecasting the direction of a time series?". International Journal of Forecasting 20, 411–425.

Pesaran, M.H., Timmermann, A. (2004b). "Selection of estimation window for strictly exogenous regressors". Working Paper, Cambridge University and University of California, San Diego.

Politis, D.N., Romano, J.P. (1994a). "The stationary bootstrap". Journal of the American Statistical Association 89, 1303–1313.

Politis, D.N., Romano, J.P. (1994b). "Limit theorems for weakly dependent Hilbert space valued random variables with application to the stationary bootstrap". Statistica Sinica 4, 461–476.

Politis, D.N., Romano, J.P., Wolf, M. (1999). Subsampling. Springer, New York.

Rosenblatt, M. (1952). "Remarks on a multivariate transformation". Annals of Mathematical Statistics 23, 470–472.

Rossi, B. (2005). "Testing long-horizon predictive ability with high persistence and the Meese–Rogoff puzzle". International Economic Review 46, 61–92.

Schörfheide, F. (2000). "Loss function based evaluation of DSGE models". Journal of Applied Econometrics 15, 645–670.

Smirnov, N. (1939). "On the estimation of the discrepancy between empirical curves of distribution for two independent samples". Bulletin Mathematique de l'Universite' de Moscou 2, 3–14.

Stinchcombe, M.B., White, H. (1998). "Consistent specification testing with nuisance parameters present only under the alternative". Econometric Theory 14, 295–325.

Storey, J.D. (2003). "The positive false discovery rate: A Bayesian interpretation and the q-value". Annals of Statistics 31, 2013–2035.

Sullivan, R., Timmermann, A., White, H. (1999). "Data-snooping, technical trading rule performance, and the bootstrap". Journal of Finance 54, 1647–1691.

Sullivan, R., Timmermann, A., White, H. (2001). "Dangers of data-mining: The case of calendar effects in stock returns". Journal of Econometrics 105, 249–286.

Swanson, N.R., White, H. (1997). "A model selection approach to real-time macroeconomic forecasting using linear models and artificial neural networks". Review of Economic Statistics 59, 540–550.

Teräsvirta, T. (2006). "Forecasting economic variables with nonlinear models". In: Elliott, G., Granger, C.W.J., Timmermann, A. (Eds.), Handbook of Economic Forecasting. Elsevier, Amsterdam, pp. 413–457. Chapter 8 in this volume.

Thompson, S.B. (2002). "Evaluating the goodness of fit of conditional distributions, with an application to affine term structure models". Working Paper, Harvard University.

van der Vaart, A.W. (1998). Asymptotic Statistics. Cambridge, New York.

Vuong, Q. (1989). "Likelihood ratio tests for model selection and non-nested hypotheses". Econometrica 57, 307–333.

Weiss, A. (1996). "Estimating time series models using the relevant cost function". Journal of Applied Econometrics 11, 539–560.

West, K.D. (1996). "Asymptotic inference about predictive ability". Econometrica 64, 1067–1084.

West, K.D. (2006). "Forecast evaluation". In: Elliott, G., Granger, C.W.J., Timmermann, A. (Eds.), Handbook of Economic Forecasting. Elsevier, Amsterdam, pp. 99–134. Chapter 3 in this volume.

West, K.D., McCracken, M.W. (1998). "Regression-based tests for predictive ability". International Economic Review 39, 817–840.

Whang, Y.J. (2000). "Consistent bootstrap tests of parametric regression functions". Journal of Econometrics, 27–46.

Whang, Y.J. (2001). "Consistent specification testing for conditional moment restrictions". Economics Letters 71, 299–306.

White, H. (1982). "Maximum likelihood estimation of misspecified models". Econometrica 50, 1–25.

White, H. (1994). Estimation, Inference and Specification Analysis. Cambridge University Press, Cambridge.

White, H. (2000). "A reality check for data snooping". Econometrica 68, 1097–1126.

Wooldridge, J.M. (2002). Econometric Analysis of Cross Section and Panel Data. MIT Press, Cambridge.

Zheng, J.X. (2000). "A consistent test of conditional parametric distribution". Econometric Theory 16, 667–691.

PART 2

FORECASTING MODELS

Chapter 6

FORECASTING WITH VARMA MODELS

HELMUT LÜTKEPOHL

Department of Economics, European University Institute, Via della Piazzuola 43, I-50133 Firenze, Italy
e-mail: helmut.luetkepohl@iue.it

Contents

Handbook of Economic Forecasting, Volume 1
Edited by Graham Elliott, Clive W.J. Granger and Allan Timmermann

DOI: 10.1016/S1574-0706(05)01006-2

Abstract

Vector autoregressive moving-average (VARMA) processes are suitable models for producing linear forecasts of sets of time series variables. They provide parsimonious representations of linear data generation processes. The setup for these processes in the presence of stationary and cointegrated variables is considered. Moreover, unique or identified parameterizations based on the echelon form are presented. Model specification, estimation, model checking and forecasting are discussed. Special attention is paid to forecasting issues related to contemporaneously and temporally aggregated VARMA processes. Predictors for aggregated variables based alternatively on past information in the aggregated variables or on disaggregated information are compared.

Keywords

echelon form, Kronecker indices, model selection, vector autoregressive process, vector error correction model, cointegration

JEL classification: C32

1. Introduction and overview

In this chapter linear models for the conditional mean of a stochastic process are considered. These models are useful for producing linear forecasts of time series variables. Even if nonlinear features may be present in a given series and, hence, nonlinear forecasts are considered, linear forecasts can serve as a useful benchmark against which other forecasts may be evaluated. As pointed out by Teräsvirta (2006) in this Handbook, Chapter 8, they may be more robust than nonlinear forecasts. Therefore, in this chapter linear forecasting models and methods will be discussed.

Suppose that K related time series variables are considered, $y_{1t}, \dots, y_{Kt}$, say. Defining $y_t = (y_{1t}, \dots, y_{Kt})'$, a linear model for the conditional mean of the data generation process (DGP) of the observed series may be of the vector autoregressive (VAR) form,

$$y_t = A_1 y_{t-1} + \cdots + A_p y_{t-p} + u_t, \tag{1.1}$$

where the A_i's $(i = 1, \dots, p)$ are $(K \times K)$ coefficient matrices and u_t is a K-dimensional error term. If u_t is independent over time (i.e., u_t and u_s are independent for $t \neq s$), the conditional mean of y_t, given past observations, is

$$y_{t|t-1} \equiv E(y_t | y_{t-1}, y_{t-2}, \dots) = A_1 y_{t-1} + \cdots + A_p y_{t-p}.$$

Thus, the model can be used directly for forecasting one period ahead and forecasts with larger horizons can be computed recursively. Therefore, variants of this model will be the basic forecasting models in this chapter.

For practical purposes the simple VAR model of order p may have some disadvantages, however. The A_i parameter matrices will be unknown and have to be replaced by estimators. For an adequate representation of the DGP of a set of time series of interest a rather large VAR order p may be required. Hence, a large number of parameters may be necessary for an adequate description of the data. Given limited sample information this will usually result in low estimation precision and also forecasts based on VAR processes with estimated coefficients may suffer from the uncertainty in the parameter estimators. Therefore it is useful to consider the larger model class of vector autoregressive moving-average (VARMA) models which may be able to represent the DGP of interest in a more parsimonious way because they represent a wider model class to choose from. In this chapter the analysis of models from that class will be discussed although special case results for VAR processes will occasionally be noted explicitly. Of course, this framework includes univariate autoregressive (AR) and autoregressive moving-average (ARMA) processes. In particular, for univariate series the advantages of mixed ARMA models over pure finite order AR models for forecasting was found in early studies [e.g., Newbold and Granger (1974)]. The VARMA framework also includes the class of unobserved component models discussed by Harvey (2006) in this Handbook who argues that these models forecast well in many situations.

The VARMA class has the further advantage of being closed with respect to linear transformations, that is, a linearly transformed finite order VARMA process has again a finite order VARMA representation. Therefore linear aggregation issues can be studied within this class. In this chapter special attention will be given to results related to forecasting contemporaneously and temporally aggregated processes.

VARMA models can be parameterized in different ways. In other words, different parameterizations describe the same stochastic process. Although this is no problem for forecasting purposes because we just need to have one adequate representation of the DGP, nonunique parameters are a problem at the estimation stage. Therefore the *echelon form* of a VARMA process is presented as a unique representation. Estimation and specification of this model form will be considered.

These models have first been developed for stationary variables. In economics and also other fields of applications many variables are generated by nonstationary processes, however. Often they can be made stationary by considering differences or changes rather than the levels. A variable is called integrated of order d ($I(d)$) if it is still nonstationary after taking differences $d - 1$ times but it can be made stationary or asymptotically stationary by differencing d times. In most of the following discussion the variables will be assumed to be stationary ($I(0)$) or integrated of order 1 ($I(1)$) and they may be cointegrated. In other words, there may be linear combinations of $I(1)$ variables which are $I(0)$. If cointegration is present, it is often advantageous to separate the cointegration relations from the short-run dynamics of the DGP. This can be done conveniently by allowing for an error correction or equilibrium correction (EC) term in the models and *EC echelon forms* will also be considered.

The model setup for stationary and integrated or cointegrated variables will be presented in the next section where also forecasting with VARMA models will be considered under the assumption that the DGP is known. In practice it is, of course, necessary to specify and estimate a model for the DGP on the basis of a given set of time series. Model specification, estimation and model checking are discussed in Section 3 and forecasting with estimated models is considered in Section 4. Conclusions follow in Section 5.

1.1. Historical notes

The successful use of univariate ARMA models for forecasting has motivated researchers to extend the model class to the multivariate case. It is plausible to expect that using more information by including more interrelated variables in the model improves the forecast precision. This is actually the idea underlying Granger's influential definition of causality [Granger (1969a)]. It turned out, however, that generalizing univariate models to multivariate ones is far from trivial in the ARMA case. Early on Quenouille (1957) considered multivariate VARMA models. It became quickly apparent, however, that the specification and estimation of such models was much more difficult than for univariate ARMA models. The success of the Box–Jenkins modelling strategy for univariate ARMA models in the 1970s [Box and Jenkins (1976), Newbold and Granger (1974), Granger and Newbold (1977, Section 5.6)] triggered further attempts of using the corresponding multivariate models and developing estimation and specification strategies. In particular, the possibility of using autocorrelations, partial autocorrelations and cross-correlations between the variables for model specification was explored. Because modelling strategies based on such quantities had been to some extent successful in the univariate Box–Jenkins approach, it was plausible to try multivariate extensions. Examples of such attempts are Tiao and Box (1981), Tiao and Tsay (1983, 1989), Tsay (1989a, 1989b), Wallis (1977), Zellner and Palm (1974), Granger and Newbold (1977, Chapter 7), Jenkins and Alavi (1981). It became soon clear, however, that these strategies were at best promising for very small systems of two or perhaps three variables. Moreover, the most useful setup of multiple time series models was under discussion because VARMA representations are not unique or, to use econometric terminology, they are not identified. Important early discussions of the related problems are due to Hannan (1970, 1976, 1979, 1981), Dunsmuir and Hannan (1976) and Akaike (1974). A rather general solution to the structure theory for VARMA models was later presented by Hannan and Deistler (1988). Understanding the structural problems contributed to the development of complete specification strategies. By now textbook treatments of modelling, analyzing and forecasting VARMA processes are available [Lütkepohl (2005), Reinsel (1993)].

The problems related to VARMA models were perhaps also relevant for a parallel development of pure VAR models as important tools for economic analysis and forecasting. Sims (1980) launched a general critique of classical econometric modelling and proposed VAR models as alternatives. A short while later the concept of cointegration was developed by Granger (1981) and Engle and Granger (1987). It is conveniently placed into the VAR framework as shown by the latter authors and Johansen (1995a). Therefore it is perhaps not surprising that VAR models dominate time series econometrics although the methodology and software for working with more general VARMA models is nowadays available. A recent previous overview of forecasting with VARMA processes is given by Lütkepohl (2002). The present review draws partly on that article and on a monograph by Lütkepohl (1987).

1.2. Notation, terminology, abbreviations

The following notation and terminology is used in this chapter. The *lag operator* also sometimes called *backshift operator* is denoted by L and it is defined as usual by $Ly_t \equiv y_{t-1}$. The *differencing operator* is denoted by Δ, that is, $\Delta y_t \equiv y_t - y_{t-1}$. For a random variable or random vector x, $x \sim (\mu, \Sigma)$ signifies that its mean (vector) is μ and its variance (covariance matrix) is Σ. The $(K \times K)$ identity matrix is denoted by I_K and the determinant and trace of a matrix A are denoted by $\det A$ and $\operatorname{tr} A$, respectively. For quantities $A_1, \dots, A_p$, $\operatorname{diag}[A_1, \dots, A_p]$ denotes the diagonal or block-diagonal matrix with $A_1, \dots, A_p$ on the diagonal. The natural logarithm of a real number is signified by log. The symbols $\mathbb{Z}$, $\mathbb{N}$ and $\mathbb{C}$ are used for the integers, the positive integers and the complex numbers, respectively.

DGP stands for data generation process. VAR, AR, MA, ARMA and VARMA are used as abbreviations for vector autoregressive, autoregressive, moving-average, autoregressive moving-average and vector autoregressive moving-average (process). Error correction is abbreviated as EC and VECM is short for vector error correction model. The echelon forms of VARMA and EC-VARMA processes are denoted by ARMA$_E$ and EC-ARMA$_E$, respectively. OLS, GLS, ML and RR abbreviate ordinary least squares, generalized least squares, maximum likelihood and reduced rank, respectively. LR and MSE are used to abbreviate likelihood ratio and mean squared error.

2. VARMA processes

2.1. Stationary processes

Suppose the DGP of the K-dimensional multiple time series, $y_1, \dots, y_T$, is stationary, that is, its first and second moments are time invariant. It is a (finite order) VARMA process if it can be represented in the general form

$$A_0 y_t = A_1 y_{t-1} + \cdots + A_p y_{t-p} + M_0 u_t + M_1 u_{t-1} + \cdots + M_q u_{t-q},$$
$$t = 0, \pm 1, \pm 2, \dots, \tag{2.1}$$

where $A_0, A_1, \dots, A_p$ are $(K \times K)$ autoregressive parameter matrices while $M_0, M_1, \dots, M_q$ are moving-average parameter matrices also of dimension $(K \times K)$. Defining the VAR and MA operators, respectively, as $A(L) = A_0 - A_1 L - \cdots - A_p L^p$ and $M(L) = M_0 + M_1 L + \cdots + M_q L^q$, the model can be written in more compact notation as

$$A(L) y_t = M(L) u_t, \quad t \in \mathbb{Z}. \tag{2.2}$$

Here u_t is a white-noise process with zero mean, nonsingular, time-invariant covariance matrix $E(u_t u_t') = \Sigma_u$ and zero covariances, $E(u_t u_{t-h}') = 0$ for $h = \pm 1, \pm 2, \dots$. The zero-order matrices A_0 and M_0 are assumed to be nonsingular. They will often be identical, $A_0 = M_0$, and in many cases they will be equal to the identity matrix, $A_0 = M_0 = I_K$. To indicate the orders of the VAR and MA operators, the process (2.1) is sometimes called a VARMA(p, q) process. Notice, however, that so far we have not made further assumptions regarding the parameter matrices so that some or all of the elements of the A_i's and M_j's may be zero. In other words, there may be a VARMA representation with VAR or MA orders less than p and q, respectively. Obviously, the VAR model (1.1) is a VARMA$(p, 0)$ special case with $A_0 = I_K$ and $M(L) = I_K$. It may also be worth pointing out that there are no deterministic terms such as nonzero mean terms in our basic VARMA model (2.1). These terms are ignored here for convenience although they are important in practice. The necessary modifications for deterministic terms will be discussed in Section 2.5.

The matrix polynomials in (2.2) are assumed to satisfy

$$\det A(z) \neq 0, \ |z| \leqslant 1, \quad \text{and} \quad \det M(z) \neq 0, \ |z| \leqslant 1 \quad \text{for } z \in \mathbb{C}. \tag{2.3}$$

The first of these conditions ensures that the VAR operator is *stable* and the process is stationary. Then it has a pure MA representation

$$y_t = \sum_{j=0}^{\infty} \Phi_i u_{t-i} \tag{2.4}$$

with MA operator $\Phi(L) = \Phi_0 + \sum_{i=1}^{\infty} \Phi_i L^i = A(L)^{-1}M(L)$. Notice that $\Phi_0 = I_K$ if $A_0 = M_0$ and in particular if both zero order matrices are identity matrices. In that case (2.4) is just the *Wold MA representation* of the process and, as we will see later, the u_t are just the one-step ahead forecast errors. Some of the forthcoming results are valid for more general stationary processes with Wold representation (2.4) which may not come from a finite order VARMA representation. In that case, it is assumed that the Φ_i's are absolutely summable so that the infinite sum in (2.4) is well-defined.

The second part of condition (2.3) is the usual *invertibility condition* for the MA operator which implies the existence of a pure VAR representation of the process,

$$y_t = \sum_{i=1}^{\infty} \Xi_i y_{t-i} + u_t, \tag{2.5}$$

where $A_0 = M_0$ is assumed and $\Xi(L) = I_K - \sum_{i=1}^{\infty} \Xi_i L^i = M(L)^{-1}A(L)$. Occasionally invertibility of the MA operator will not be a necessary condition. In that case, it is assumed without loss of generality that $\det M(z) \neq 0$, for $|z| < 1$. In other words, the roots of the MA operator are outside or on the unit circle. There are still no roots inside the unit circle, however. This assumption can be made without loss of generality because it can be shown that for an MA process with roots inside the complex unit circle an equivalent one exists which has all its roots outside and on the unit circle.

It may be worth noting at this stage already that every pair of operators $A(L)$, $M(L)$ which leads to the same transfer functions $\Phi(L)$ and $\Xi(L)$ defines an equivalent VARMA representation for y_t. This nonuniqueness problem of the VARMA representation will become important when parameter estimation is discussed in Section 3.

As specified in (2.1), we are assuming that the process is defined for all $t \in \mathbb{Z}$. For stable, stationary processes this assumption is convenient because it avoids considering issues related to initial conditions. Alternatively, one could define y_t to be generated by a VARMA process such as (2.1) for $t \in \mathbb{N}$, and specify the initial values $y_0, \ldots, y_{-p+1}, u_0, \ldots, u_{-q+1}$ separately. Under our assumptions they can be defined such that y_t is stationary. Another possibility would be to define fixed initial values or perhaps even $y_0 = \cdots = y_{-p+1} = u_0 = \cdots = u_{-q+1} = 0$. In general, such an assumption implies that the process is not stationary but just *asymptotically stationary*, that is, the first and second order moments converge to the corresponding quantities of the stationary process obtained by specifying the initial conditions accordingly or defining y_t for $t \in \mathbb{Z}$. The issue of defining initial values properly becomes more important for the nonstationary processes discussed in Section 2.2.

Both the MA and the VAR representations of the process will be convenient to work with in particular situations. Another useful representation of a stationary VARMA process is the state space representation which will not be used in this review, however. The relation between state space models and VARMA processes is considered, for example, by Aoki (1987), Hannan and Deistler (1988), Wei (1990) and Harvey (2006) in this Handbook, Chapter 7.

2.2. *Cointegrated $I(1)$ processes*

If the DGP is not stationary but contains some $I(1)$ variables, the levels VARMA form (2.1) is not the most convenient one for inference purposes. In that case, $\det A(z) = 0$ for $z = 1$. Therefore we write the model in EC form by subtracting $A_0 y_{t-1}$ on both sides and re-arranging terms as follows:

$$\begin{aligned} A_0 \Delta y_t = {} & \Pi y_{t-1} + \Gamma_1 \Delta y_{t-1} + \cdots + \Gamma_{p-1} \Delta y_{t-p+1} \\ & + M_0 u_t + M_1 u_{t-1} + \cdots + M_q u_{t-q}, \quad t \in \mathbb{N}, \end{aligned} \tag{2.6}$$

where $\Pi = -(A_0 - A_1 - \cdots - A_p) = -A(1)$ and $\Gamma_i = -(A_{i+1} + \cdots + A_p)$ $(i = 1, \ldots, p-1)$ [Lütkepohl and Claessen (1997)]. Here Πy_{t-1} is the EC term and $r = \operatorname{rk}(\Pi)$ is the cointegrating rank of the system which specifies the number of linearly independent cointegration relations. The process is assumed to be started at time $t = 1$ from some initial values $y_0, \ldots, y_{-p+1}, u_0, \ldots, u_{-q+1}$ to avoid infinite moments. Thus, the initial values are now of some importance. Assuming that they are zero is convenient because in that case the process is easily seen to have a pure EC-VAR or VECM representation of the form

$$\Delta y_t = \Pi^* y_{t-1} + \sum_{j=1}^{t-1} \Theta_j \Delta y_{t-j} + A_0^{-1} M_0 u_t, \quad t \in \mathbb{N}, \tag{2.7}$$

where Π^* and Θ_j $(j = 1, 2, \ldots)$ are such that

$$\begin{aligned} & I_K \Delta - \Pi^* L - \sum_{j=1}^{\infty} \Theta_j \Delta L^j \\ & \quad = A_0^{-1} M_0 M(L)^{-1} \left(A_0 \Delta - \Pi L - \Gamma_1 \Delta L - \cdots - \Gamma_{p-1} \Delta L^{p-1} \right). \end{aligned}$$

A similar representation can also be obtained if nonzero initial values are permitted [see Saikkonen and Lütkepohl (1996)]. Bauer and Wagner (2003) present a state space representation which is especially suitable for cointegrated processes.

2.3. *Linear transformations of VARMA processes*

As mentioned in the introduction, a major advantage of the class of VARMA processes is that it is closed with respect to linear transformations. In other words, linear transformations of VARMA processes have again a finite order VARMA representation. These transformations are very common and are useful to study problems of aggregation, marginal processes or averages of variables generated by VARMA processes etc.. In particular, the following result from Lütkepohl (1984) is useful in this context. Let

$$y_t = u_t + M_1 u_{t-1} + \cdots + M_q u_{t-q}$$

be a K-dimensional invertible MA(q) process and let F be an $(M \times K)$ matrix of rank M. Then the M-dimensional process $z_t = F y_t$ has an invertible MA($\breve{q}$) representation with $\breve{q} \leqslant q$. An interesting consequence of this result is that if y_t is a stable and invertible VARMA(p, q) process as in (2.1), then the linearly transformed process $z_t = F y_t$ has a stable and invertible VARMA$(\breve{p}, \breve{q})$ representation with $\breve{p} \leqslant (K - M + 1)p$ and $\breve{q} \leqslant (K - M)p + q$ [Lütkepohl (1987, Chapter 4) or Lütkepohl (2005, Corollary 11.1.2)].

These results are directly relevant for contemporaneous aggregation of VARMA processes and they can also be used to study temporal aggregation problems. To see this suppose we wish to aggregate the variables y_t generated by (2.1) over m subsequent periods. For instance, $m = 3$ if we wish to aggregate monthly data to quarterly figures. To express the temporal aggregation as a linear transformation we define

$$\mathbf{y}_\vartheta = \begin{bmatrix} y_{m(\vartheta-1)+1} \\ y_{m(\vartheta-1)+2} \\ \vdots \\ y_{m\vartheta} \end{bmatrix} \quad \text{and} \quad \mathbf{u}_\vartheta = \begin{bmatrix} u_{m(\vartheta-1)+1} \\ u_{m(\vartheta-1)+2} \\ \vdots \\ u_{m\vartheta} \end{bmatrix} \tag{2.8}$$

and specify the process

$$\mathcal{A}_0 \mathbf{y}_\vartheta = \mathcal{A}_1 \mathbf{y}_{\vartheta-1} + \cdots + \mathcal{A}_P \mathbf{y}_{\vartheta-P} + \mathcal{M}_0 \mathbf{u}_\vartheta + \mathcal{M}_1 \mathbf{u}_{\vartheta-1} + \cdots + \mathcal{M}_Q \mathbf{u}_{\vartheta-Q}, \tag{2.9}$$

where

$$\mathcal{A}_0 = \begin{bmatrix} A_0 & 0 & 0 & \ldots & 0 \\ -A_1 & A_0 & 0 & \ldots & 0 \\ -A_2 & -A_1 & A_0 & & \vdots \\ \vdots & \vdots & \vdots & \ddots & \\ -A_{m-1} & -A_{m-2} & -A_{m-3} & \ldots & A_0 \end{bmatrix},$$

$$\mathcal{A}_i = \begin{bmatrix} A_{im} & A_{im-1} & \ldots & A_{im-m+1} \\ A_{im+1} & A_{im} & \ldots & A_{im-m+2} \\ \vdots & \vdots & \ddots & \vdots \\ A_{im+m-1} & A_{im+m-2} & \ldots & A_{im} \end{bmatrix}, \quad i = 1, \ldots, P,$$

with $A_j = 0$ for $j > p$ and $\mathcal{M}_0, \ldots, \mathcal{M}_Q$ defined in an analogous manner. The order $P = \min\{n \in \mathbb{N} \mid nm \geqslant p\}$ and $Q = \min\{n \in \mathbb{N} \mid nm \geqslant q\}$. Notice that the time subscript of $\mathbf{y}_\vartheta$ is different from that of y_t. The new time index ϑ refers to another observation frequency than t. For example, if t refers to months and $m = 3$, ϑ refers to quarters.

Using the process (2.9), temporal aggregation over m periods can be represented as a linear transformation. In fact, different types of temporal aggregation can be handled. For instance, the aggregate may be the sum of subsequent values or it may be their average. Furthermore, temporal and contemporaneous aggregation can be dealt with simultaneously. In all of these cases the aggregate has a finite order VARMA representation if the original variables are generated by a finite order VARMA process and its structure can be analyzed using linear transformations. For another approach to study temporal aggregates see Marcellino (1999).

2.4. *Forecasting*

In this section forecasting with given VARMA processes is discussed to present theoretical results that are valid under ideal conditions. The effects of and necessary modifications due to estimation and possibly specification uncertainty will be treated in Section 4.

2.4.1. *General results*

When forecasting a set of variables is the objective, it is useful to think about a loss function or an evaluation criterion for the forecast performance. Given such a criterion, optimal forecasts may be constructed. VARMA processes are particularly useful for producing forecasts that minimize the forecast MSE. Therefore this criterion will be used here and the reader is referred to Granger (1969b) and Granger and Newbold (1977, Section 4.2) for a discussion of other forecast evaluation criteria.

Forecasts of the variables of the VARMA process (2.1) are obtained easily from the pure VAR form (2.5). Assuming an independent white noise process u_t, an optimal, minimum MSE h-step forecast at time τ is the conditional expectation given the y_t, $t \leqslant \tau$,

$$y_{\tau+h|\tau} \equiv E(y_{\tau+h}|y_\tau, y_{\tau-1}, \ldots).$$

It may be determined recursively for $h = 1, 2, \ldots$, as

$$y_{\tau+h|\tau} = \sum_{i=1}^{\infty} \Xi_i y_{\tau+h-i|\tau}, \tag{2.10}$$

where $y_{\tau+j|\tau} = y_{\tau+j}$ for $j \leqslant 0$. If the u_t do not form an independent but only uncorrelated white noise sequence, the forecast obtained in this way is still the best linear forecast although it may not be the best in a larger class of possibly nonlinear functions of past observations.

For given initial values, the u_t can also be determined under the present assumption of a known process. Hence, the h-step forecasts may be determined alternatively as

$$y_{\tau+h|\tau} = A_0^{-1}(A_1 y_{\tau+h-1|\tau} + \cdots + A_p y_{\tau+h-p|\tau}) + A_0^{-1} \sum_{i=h}^{q} M_i u_{\tau+h-i}, \tag{2.11}$$

where, as usual, the sum vanishes if $h > q$.

Both ways of computing h-step forecasts from VARMA models rely on the availability of initial values. In the pure VAR formula (2.10) all infinitely many past y_t are in principle necessary if the VAR representation is indeed of infinite order. In contrast, in order to use (2.11), the u_t's need to be known which are unobserved and can only be obtained if all past y_t or initial conditions are available. If only $y_1, \dots, y_\tau$ are given, the infinite sum in (2.10) may be truncated accordingly. For large τ, the approximation error will be negligible because the Ξ_i's go to zero quickly as $i \to \infty$. Alternatively, precise forecasting formulas based on $y_1, \dots, y_\tau$ may be obtained via the so-called *Multivariate Innovations Algorithm* of Brockwell and Davis (1987, Section 11.4).

Under our assumptions, the properties of the forecast errors for stable, stationary processes are easily derived by expressing the process (2.1) in Wold MA form,

$$y_t = u_t + \sum_{i=1}^{\infty} \Phi_i u_{t-i}, \tag{2.12}$$

where $A_0 = M_0$ is assumed (see (2.4)). In terms of this representation the optimal h-step forecast may be expressed as

$$y_{\tau+h|\tau} = \sum_{i=h}^{\infty} \Phi_i u_{\tau+h-i}. \tag{2.13}$$

Hence, the forecast errors are seen to be

$$y_{\tau+h} - y_{\tau+h|\tau} = u_{\tau+h} + \Phi_1 u_{\tau+h-1} + \cdots + \Phi_{h-1} u_{\tau+1}. \tag{2.14}$$

Thus, the forecast is unbiased (i.e., the forecast errors have mean zero) and the MSE or forecast error covariance matrix is

$$\Sigma_y(h) \equiv E\big[(y_{\tau+h} - y_{\tau+h|\tau})(y_{\tau+h} - y_{\tau+h|\tau})'\big] = \sum_{j=0}^{h-1} \Phi_j \Sigma_u \Phi_j'.$$

If u_t is normally distributed (Gaussian), the forecast errors are also normally distributed,

$$y_{\tau+h} - y_{\tau+h|\tau} \sim N\big(0, \Sigma_y(h)\big). \tag{2.15}$$

Hence, forecast intervals, etc. may be derived from these results in the familiar way under Gaussian assumptions.

It is also interesting to note that the forecast error variance is bounded by the covariance matrix of y_t,

$$\Sigma_y(h) \to_{h\to\infty} \Sigma_y \equiv E\big(y_t y_t'\big) = \sum_{j=0}^{\infty} \Phi_j \Sigma_u \Phi_j'. \tag{2.16}$$

Hence, forecast intervals will also have bounded length as the forecast horizon increases.

The situation is different if there are integrated variables. The formula (2.11) can again be used for computing the forecasts. Their properties will be different from those for stationary processes, however. Although the Wold MA representation does not exist for integrated processes, the Φ_j coefficient matrices can be computed in the same way as for stationary processes from the power series $A(z)^{-1}M(z)$ which still exists for $z \in \mathbb{C}$ with $|z| < 1$. Hence, the forecast errors can still be represented as in (2.14) [see Lütkepohl (2005, Chapters 6 and 14)]. Thus, formally the forecast errors look quite similar to those for the stationary case. Now the forecast error MSE matrix is unbounded, however, because the Φ_j's in general do not converge to zero as $j \to \infty$. Despite this general result, there may be linear combinations of the variables which can be forecast with bounded precision if the forecast horizon gets large. This situation arises if there is cointegration. For cointegrated processes it is of course also possible to base the forecasts directly on the EC form. For instance, using (2.6),

$$\Delta y_{\tau+h|\tau} = A_0^{-1}(\Pi y_{\tau+h-1|\tau} + \Gamma_1 \Delta y_{\tau+h-1|\tau} + \cdots + \Gamma_{p-1}\Delta y_{\tau+h-p+1|\tau}) + A_0^{-1}\sum_{i=h}^{q} M_i u_{\tau+h-i}, \tag{2.17}$$

and $y_{\tau+h|\tau} = y_{\tau+h-1|\tau} + \Delta y_{\tau+h|\tau}$ can be used to get a forecast of the levels variables.

As an illustration of forecasting cointegrated processes consider the following bivariate VAR model which has cointegrating rank 1:

$$\begin{bmatrix} y_{1t} \\ y_{2t} \end{bmatrix} = \begin{bmatrix} 0 & 1 \\ 0 & 1 \end{bmatrix}\begin{bmatrix} y_{1,t-1} \\ y_{2,t-1} \end{bmatrix} + \begin{bmatrix} u_{1t} \\ u_{2t} \end{bmatrix}. \tag{2.18}$$

For this process

$$A(z)^{-1} = (I_2 - A_1 z)^{-1} = \sum_{j=0}^{\infty} A_1^j z^j = \sum_{j=0}^{\infty} \Phi_j z^j$$

exists only for $|z| < 1$ because $\Phi_0 = I_2$ and

$$\Phi_j = A_1^j = \begin{bmatrix} 0 & 1 \\ 0 & 1 \end{bmatrix}, \quad j = 1, 2, \ldots,$$

does not converge to zero for $j \to \infty$. The forecast MSE matrices are

$$\Sigma_y(h) = \sum_{j=0}^{h-1} \Phi_j \Sigma_u \Phi_j' = \Sigma_u + (h-1)\begin{bmatrix} \sigma_2^2 & \sigma_2^2 \\ \sigma_2^2 & \sigma_2^2 \end{bmatrix}, \quad h = 1, 2, \ldots,$$

where σ_2^2 is the variance of u_{2t}. The conditional expectations are $y_{k,\tau+h|\tau} = y_{2,\tau}$ $(k = 1, 2)$. Assuming normality of the white noise process, $(1-\gamma)100\%$ forecast intervals are easily seen to be

$$y_{2,\tau} \pm c_{1-\gamma/2}\sqrt{\sigma_k^2 + (h-1)\sigma_2^2}, \quad k = 1, 2,$$

where $c_{1-\gamma/2}$ is the $(1-\gamma/2)100$ percentage point of the standard normal distribution. The lengths of these intervals increase without bounds for $h \to \infty$.

The EC representation of (2.18) is easily seen to be

$$\Delta y_t = \begin{bmatrix} -1 & 1 \\ 0 & 0 \end{bmatrix} y_{t-1} + u_t.$$

Thus, $\text{rk}(\Pi) = 1$ so that the two variables are cointegrated and some linear combinations can be forecasted with bounded forecast intervals. For the present example, multiplying (2.18) by

$$\begin{bmatrix} 1 & -1 \\ 0 & 1 \end{bmatrix}$$

gives

$$\begin{bmatrix} 1 & -1 \\ 0 & 1 \end{bmatrix} y_t = \begin{bmatrix} 0 & 0 \\ 0 & 1 \end{bmatrix} y_{t-1} + \begin{bmatrix} 1 & -1 \\ 0 & 1 \end{bmatrix} u_t.$$

Obviously, the cointegration relation $z_t = y_{1t} - y_{2t} = u_{1t} - u_{2t}$ is zero mean white noise and the forecast intervals for z_t, for any forecast horizon $h \geqslant 1$, are of constant length, $z_{\tau+h|\tau} \pm c_{1-\gamma/2}\sigma_z(h)$ or $[-c_{1-\gamma/2}\sigma_z, \ c_{1-\gamma/2}\sigma_z]$. Note that $z_{\tau+h|\tau} = 0$ for $h \geqslant 1$ and $\sigma_z^2 = \text{Var}(u_{1t}) + \text{Var}(u_{2t}) - 2\,\text{Cov}(u_{1t}, u_{2t})$ is the variance of z_t.

As long as theoretical results are discussed one could consider the first differences of the process, Δy_t, which also have a VARMA representation. If there is genuine cointegration, then Δy_t is overdifferenced in the sense that its VARMA representation has MA unit roots even if the MA part of the levels y_t is invertible.

2.4.2. Forecasting aggregated processes

We have argued in Section 2.3 that linear transformations of VARMA processes are often of interest, for example, if aggregation is studied. Therefore forecasts of transformed processes are also of interest. Here we present some forecasting results for transformed and aggregated processes from Lütkepohl (1987) where also proofs and further references can be found. We begin with general results which have immediate implications for contemporaneous aggregation. Then we will also present some results for temporally aggregated processes which can be obtained via the process representation (2.9).

Linear transformations and contemporaneous aggregation. Suppose y_t is a stationary VARMA process with pure, invertible Wold MA representation (2.4), that is, $y_t = \Phi(L)u_t$ with $\Phi_0 = I_K$, F is an $(M \times K)$ matrix with rank M and we are interested in forecasting the transformed process $z_t = Fy_t$. It was discussed in Section 2.3 that z_t also has a VARMA representation so that the previously considered techniques can be used for forecasting. Suppose that the corresponding Wold MA representation is

$$z_t = v_t + \sum_{i=1}^{\infty} \Psi_i v_{t-i} = \Psi(L)v_t. \tag{2.19}$$

From (2.13) the optimal h-step predictor for z_t at origin τ, based on its own past, is then

$$z_{\tau+h|\tau} = \sum_{i=h}^{\infty} \Psi_i v_{\tau+h-i}, \quad h = 1, 2, \ldots . \tag{2.20}$$

Another predictor may be based on forecasting y_t and then transforming the forecast,

$$z^o_{\tau+h|\tau} \equiv F y_{\tau+h|\tau}, \quad h = 1, 2, \ldots . \tag{2.21}$$

Before we compare the two forecasts $z^o_{\tau+h|\tau}$ and $z_{\tau+h|\tau}$ it may be of interest to draw attention to yet another possible forecast. If the dimension K of the vector y_t is large, it may be difficult to construct a suitable VARMA model for the underlying process and one may consider forecasting the individual components of y_t by univariate methods and then transforming the univariate forecasts. Because the component series of y_t can be obtained by linear transformations, they also have ARMA representations. Denoting the corresponding Wold MA representations by

$$y_{kt} = w_{kt} + \sum_{i=1}^{\infty} \theta_{ki} w_{k,t-i} = \theta_k(L) w_{kt}, \quad k = 1, \ldots, K, \tag{2.22}$$

the optimal univariate h-step forecasts are

$$y^u_{k,\tau+h|\tau} = \sum_{i=h}^{\infty} \theta_{ki} w_{k,\tau+h-i}, \quad k = 1, \ldots, K, \ h = 1, 2, \ldots . \tag{2.23}$$

Defining $y^u_{\tau+h|\tau} = (y^u_{1,\tau+h|\tau}, \ldots, y^u_{K,\tau+h|\tau})'$, these forecasts can be used to obtain an h-step forecast

$$z^u_{\tau+h|\tau} \equiv F y^u_{\tau+h|\tau} \tag{2.24}$$

of the variables of interest.

We will now compare the three forecasts (2.20), (2.21) and (2.24) of the transformed process z_t. In this comparison we denote the MSE matrices corresponding to the three forecasts by $\Sigma_z(h)$, $\Sigma^o_z(h)$ and $\Sigma^u_z(h)$, respectively. Because $z^o_{\tau+h|\tau}$ uses the largest information set, it is not surprising that it has the smallest MSE matrix and is hence the best one out of the three forecasts,

$$\Sigma_z(h) \geqslant \Sigma^o_z(h) \quad \text{and} \quad \Sigma^u_z(h) \geqslant \Sigma^o_z(h), \quad h \in \mathbb{N}, \tag{2.25}$$

where "$\geqslant$" means that the difference between the left-hand and right-hand matrices is positive semidefinite. Thus, forecasting the original process y_t and then transforming the forecasts is generally more efficient than forecasting the transformed process directly or transforming univariate forecasts. It is possible, however, that some or all of the forecasts are identical. Actually, for $I(0)$ processes, all three predictors always approach the same long-term forecast of zero. Consequently,

$$\Sigma_z(h), \Sigma^o_z(h), \Sigma^u_z(h) \to \Sigma_z \equiv E(z_t z_t') \quad \text{as } h \to \infty. \tag{2.26}$$

Moreover, it can be shown that if the one-step forecasts are identical, then they will also be identical for larger forecast horizons. More precisely we have,

$$z^o_{\tau+1|\tau} = z_{\tau+1|\tau} \Rightarrow z^o_{\tau+h|\tau} = z_{\tau+h|\tau}, \quad h = 1, 2, \ldots, \tag{2.27}$$

$$z^u_{\tau+1|\tau} = z_{\tau+1|\tau} \Rightarrow z^u_{\tau+h|\tau} = z_{\tau+h|\tau}, \quad h = 1, 2, \ldots, \tag{2.28}$$

and, if $\Phi(L)$ and $\Theta(L)$ are invertible,

$$z^o_{\tau+1|\tau} = z^u_{\tau+1|\tau} \Rightarrow z^o_{\tau+h|\tau} = z^u_{\tau+h|\tau}, \quad h = 1, 2, \ldots. \tag{2.29}$$

Thus, one may ask whether the one-step forecasts can be identical and it turns out that this is indeed possible. The following proposition which summarizes results of Tiao and Guttman (1980), Kohn (1982) and Lütkepohl (1984), gives conditions for this to happen.

PROPOSITION 1. *Let y_t be a K-dimensional stochastic process with MA representation as in* (2.12) *with $\Phi_0 = I_K$ and F an $(M \times K)$ matrix with rank M. Then, defining $\Phi(L) = I_K + \sum_{i=1}^{\infty} \Phi_i L^i$, $\Psi(L) = I_K + \sum_{i=1}^{\infty} \Psi_i L^i$ as in* (2.19) *and $\Theta(L) = \text{diag}[\theta_1(L), \ldots, \theta_K(L)]$ with $\theta_k(L) = 1 + \sum_{i=1}^{\infty} \theta_{ki} L^i$ $(k = 1, \ldots, K)$, the following relations hold*:

$$z^o_{\tau+1|\tau} = z_{\tau+1|\tau} \iff F\Phi(L) = \Psi(L)F, \tag{2.30}$$

$$z^u_{\tau+1|\tau} = z_{\tau+1|\tau} \iff F\Theta(L) = \Psi(L)F \tag{2.31}$$

and, if $\Phi(L)$ and $\Theta(L)$ are invertible,

$$z^o_{\tau+1|\tau} = z^u_{\tau+1|\tau} \iff F\Phi(L)^{-1} = F\Theta(L)^{-1}. \tag{2.32}$$

There are several interesting implications of this proposition. First, if y_t consists of independent components ($\Phi(L) = \Theta(L)$) and z_t is just their sum, i.e., $F = (1, \ldots, 1)$, then

$$z^o_{\tau+1|\tau} = z_{\tau+1|\tau} \iff \theta_1(L) = \cdots = \theta_K(L). \tag{2.33}$$

In other words, forecasting the individual components and summing up the forecasts is strictly more efficient than forecasting the sum directly whenever the components are not generated by stochastic processes with identical temporal correlation structures. Second, forecasting the univariate components of y_t individually can be as efficient a forecast for y_t as forecasting on the basis of the multivariate process if and only if $\Phi(L)$ is a diagonal matrix operator. Related to this result is a well-known condition for Granger-noncausality. For a bivariate process $y_t = (y_{1t}, y_{2t})'$, y_{2t} is said to be Granger-causal for y_{1t} if the former variable is helpful for improving the forecasts of the latter variable. In terms of the previous notation this may be stated by specifying $F = (1, 0)$ and defining y_{2t} as being Granger-causal for y_{1t} if $z^o_{\tau+1|\tau} = Fy_{\tau+1|\tau} = y^o_{1,\tau+1|\tau}$ is a better forecast than $z_{\tau+1|\tau}$. From (2.30) it then follows that y_{2t} is not Granger-causal for y_{1t} if and only if $\phi_{12}(L) = 0$, where $\phi_{12}(L)$ denotes the upper right hand element of $\Phi(L)$. This characterization of Granger-noncausality is well known in the related literature [e.g., Lütkepohl (2005, Section 2.3.1)].

It may also be worth noting that in general there is no unique ranking of the forecasts $z_{\tau+1|\tau}$ and $z^u_{\tau+1|\tau}$. Depending on the structure of the underlying process y_t and the transformation matrix F, either $\Sigma_z(h) \geqslant \Sigma^u_z(h)$ or $\Sigma_z(h) \leqslant \Sigma^u_z(h)$ will hold and the relevant inequality may be strict in the sense that the left-hand and right-hand matrices are not identical.

Some but not all the results in this section carry over to nonstationary $I(1)$ processes. For example, the result (2.26) will not hold in general if some components of y_t are $I(1)$ because in this case the three forecasts do not necessarily converge to zero as the forecast horizon gets large. On the other hand, the conditions in (2.30) and (2.31) can be used for the differenced processes. For these results to hold, the MA operator may have roots on the unit circle and hence overdifferencing is not a problem.

The previous results on linearly transformed processes can also be used to compare different predictors for temporally aggregated processes by setting up the corresponding process (2.9). Some related results will be summarized next.

Temporal aggregation. Different forms of temporal aggregation are of interest, depending on the types of variables involved. If y_t consists of stock variables, then temporal aggregation is usually associated with *systematic sampling*, sometimes called *skip-sampling* or *point-in-time sampling*. In other words, the process

$$\mathbf{s}_\vartheta = y_{m\vartheta} \tag{2.34}$$

is used as an aggregate over m periods. Here the aggregated process $\mathbf{s}_\vartheta$ has a new time index which refers to another observation frequency than the original subscript t. For example, if t refers to months and $m = 3$, then ϑ refers to quarters. In that case the process $\mathbf{s}_\vartheta$ consists of every third member of the y_t process. This type of aggregation contrasts with temporal aggregation of flow variables where a temporal aggregate is typically obtained by summing up consecutive values. Thus, aggregation over m periods gives the aggregate

$$\mathbf{z}_\vartheta = y_{m\vartheta} + y_{m\vartheta-1} + \cdots + y_{m\vartheta-m+1}. \tag{2.35}$$

Now if, for example, t refers to months and $m = 3$, then three consecutive observations are added to obtain the quarterly value. In the following we again assume that the disaggregated process y_t is stationary and invertible and has a Wold MA representation as in (2.12), $y_t = \Phi(L)u_t$ with $\Phi_0 = I_K$. As we have seen in Section 2.3, this implies that $\mathbf{s}_\vartheta$ and $\mathbf{z}_\vartheta$ are also stationary and have Wold MA representations. We will now discuss forecasting stock and flow variables in turn. In other words, we consider forecasts for $\mathbf{s}_\vartheta$ and $\mathbf{z}_\vartheta$.

Suppose first that we wish to forecast $\mathbf{s}_\vartheta$. Then the past aggregated values $\{\mathbf{s}_\vartheta, \mathbf{s}_{\vartheta-1}, \ldots\}$ may be used to obtain an h-step forecast $\mathbf{s}_{\vartheta+h|\vartheta}$ as in (2.13) on the basis of the MA representation of $\mathbf{s}_\vartheta$. If the disaggregate process y_t is available, another possible forecast results by systematically sampling forecasts of y_t which gives $\mathbf{s}^o_{\vartheta+h|\vartheta} = y_{m\vartheta+mh|m\vartheta}$. Using the results for linear transformations, the latter forecast generally has a lower MSE than $\mathbf{s}_{\vartheta+h|\vartheta}$ and the difference vanishes if the forecast horizon $h \to \infty$. For special processes the two predictors are identical, however. It follows from relation (2.30) of Proposition 1 that the two predictors are identical for $h = 1, 2, \ldots$, if and only if

$$\Phi(L) = \left(\sum_{i=0}^{\infty} \Phi_{im} L^{im}\right)\left(\sum_{i=0}^{m-1} \Phi_i L^i\right) \tag{2.36}$$

[Lütkepohl (1987, Proposition 7.1)]. Thus, there is no loss in forecast efficiency if the MA operator of the disaggregate process has the multiplicative structure in (2.36). This condition is, for instance, satisfied if y_t is a purely seasonal process with seasonal period m such that

$$y_t = \sum_{i=0}^{\infty} \Phi_{im} u_{t-im}. \tag{2.37}$$

It also holds if y_t has a finite order MA structure with MA order less than m. Interestingly, it also follows that there is no loss in forecast efficiency if the disaggregate process y_t is a VAR(1) process, $y_t = A_1 y_{t-1} + u_t$. In that case, the MA operator can be written as

$$\Phi(L) = \left(\sum_{i=0}^{\infty} A_1^{im} L^{im}\right)\left(\sum_{i=0}^{m-1} A_1^i L^i\right)$$

and, hence, it has the required structure.

Now consider the case of a vector of flow variables y_t for which the temporal aggregate is given in (2.35). For forecasting the aggregate $\mathbf{z}_\vartheta$ one may use the past aggregated values and compute an h-step forecast $\mathbf{z}_{\vartheta+h|\vartheta}$ as in (2.13) on the basis of the MA representation of $\mathbf{z}_\vartheta$. Alternatively, we may again forecast the disaggregate process y_t and aggregate the forecasts. This forecast is denoted by $\mathbf{z}^o_{\vartheta+h|\vartheta}$, that is,

$$\mathbf{z}^o_{\vartheta+h|\vartheta} = y_{m\vartheta+mh|m\vartheta} + y_{m\vartheta+mh-1|m\vartheta} + \cdots + y_{m\vartheta+mh-m+1|m\vartheta}. \tag{2.38}$$

Again the results for linear transformations imply that the latter forecast generally has a lower MSE than $\mathbf{z}_{\vartheta+h|\vartheta}$ and the difference vanishes if the forecast horizon $h \to \infty$. In this case equality of the two forecasts holds for small forecast horizons $h = 1, 2, \ldots$, if and only if

$$\left(1+L+\cdots+L^{m-1}\right)\left(\sum_{i=0}^{\infty}\Phi_i L^i\right)$$
$$=\left(\sum_{j=0}^{\infty}(\Phi_{jm}+\cdots+\Phi_{jm-m+1})L^{jm}\right)\left(\sum_{i=0}^{m-1}(\Phi_0+\Phi_1+\cdots+\Phi_i)L^i\right), \tag{2.39}$$

where $\Phi_j = 0$ for $j < 0$ [Lütkepohl (1987, Proposition 8.1)]. In other words, the two forecasts are identical and there is no loss in forecast efficiency from using the aggregate directly if the MA operator of y_t has the specified multiplicative structure upon multiplication by $(1 + L + \cdots + L^{m-1})$. This condition is also satisfied if y_t has the purely seasonal structure (2.37). However, in contrast to what was observed for stock variables, the two predictors are generally not identical if the disaggregate process y_t is generated by an MA process of order less than m.

It is perhaps also interesting to note that if there are both stock and flow variables in one system, then even if the underlying disaggregate process y_t is the periodic process (2.37), a forecast based on the disaggregate data may be better than directly forecasting the aggregate [Lütkepohl (1987, pp. 177–178)]. This result is interesting because for the purely seasonal process (2.37) using the disaggregate process will not result in superior forecasts if a system consisting either of stock variables only or of flow variables only is considered.

So far we have considered temporal aggregation of stationary processes. Most of the results can be generalized to $I(1)$ processes by considering the stationary process Δy_t instead of the original process y_t. Recall that forecasts for y_t can then be obtained from those of Δy_t. Moreover, in this context it may be worth taking into account that in deriving some of the conditions for forecast equality, the MA operator of the considered disaggregate process may have unit roots resulting from overdifferencing. A result which does not carry over to the $I(1)$ case, however, is the equality of long horizon forecasts based on aggregate or disaggregate variables. The reason is again that optimal forecasts of $I(1)$ variables do not settle down at zero eventually when $h \to \infty$.

Clearly, so far we have just discussed forecasting of known processes. In practice, the DGPs have to be specified and estimated on the basis of limited sample information. In that case quite different results may be obtained and, in particular, forecasts based on disaggregate processes may be inferior to those based on the aggregate directly. This issue is taken up again in Section 4.2 when forecasting estimated processes is considered.

Forecasting temporally aggregated processes has been discussed extensively in the literature. Early examples of treatments of temporal aggregation of time series are Abraham (1982), Amemiya and Wu (1972), Brewer (1973), Lütkepohl (1986a, 1986b), Stram and Wei (1986), Telser (1967), Tiao (1972), Wei (1978) and Weiss (1984) among many others. More recently, Breitung and Swanson (2002) have studied the implications of temporal aggregation when the number of aggregated time units goes to infinity. As mentioned previously, issues related to aggregating estimated processes and applications will be discussed in Section 4.2.

2.5. Extensions

So far we have considered processes which are too simple in some respects to qualify as DGPs of most economic time series. This was mainly done to simplify the exposition. Some important extensions will now be considered. In particular, we will discuss deterministic terms, higher order integration and seasonal unit roots as well as non-Gaussian processes.

2.5.1. Deterministic terms

An easy way to integrate deterministic terms in our framework is to simply add them to the stochastic part. In other words, we consider processes

$$y_t = \mu_t + x_t,$$

where μ_t is a deterministic term and x_t is the purely stochastic part which is assumed to have a VARMA representation of the type considered earlier. The deterministic part can, for example, be a constant, $\mu_t = \mu_0$, a linear trend, $\mu_t = \mu_0 + \mu_1 t$, or a higher order polynomial trend. Furthermore, seasonal dummy variables or other dummies may be included.

From a forecasting point of view, deterministic terms are easy to handle because by their very nature their future values are precisely known. Thus, in order to forecast y_t, we may forecast the purely stochastic process x_t as discussed earlier and then simply add the deterministic part corresponding to the forecast period. In this case, the forecast errors and MSE matrices are the same as for the purely stochastic process. Of course, in practice the deterministic part may contain unknown parameters which have to be estimated from data. For the moment this issue is ignored because we are considering known processes. It will become important, however, in Section 4, where forecasting estimated processes is discussed.

2.5.2. More unit roots

In practice the order of integration of some of the variables can be greater than one and $\det A(z)$ may have roots on the unit circle other than $z = 1$. For example, there may be seasonal unit roots. Considerable research has been done on these extensions of our basic models. See, for instance, Johansen (1995b, 1997), Gregoir and Laroque (1994) and Haldrup (1998) for discussions of the $I(2)$ and higher order integration frameworks, and Johansen and Schaumburg (1999) and Gregoir (1999a, 1999b) for research on processes with roots elsewhere on the unit circle. Bauer and Wagner (2003) consider state space representations for VARMA models with roots at arbitrary points on the unit circle.

As long as the processes are assumed to be known these issues do not create additional problems for forecasting because we can still use the general forecasting formulas for VARMA processes. Extensions are important, however, when it comes to model specification and estimation. In these steps of the forecasting procedure taking into account extensions in the methodology may be useful.

2.5.3. Non-Gaussian processes

If the DGP of a multiple time series is not normally distributed, point forecasts can be computed as before. They will generally still be best *linear* forecasts and may in fact be minimum MSE forecasts if u_t is independent white noise, as discussed in Section 2.4. In setting up forecast intervals the distribution has to be taken into account, however. If the distribution is unknown, bootstrap methods can be used to compute interval forecasts [e.g., Findley (1986), Masarotto (1990), Grigoletto (1998), Kabaila (1993), Kim (1999), Clements and Taylor (2001), Pascual, Romo and Ruiz (2004)].

3. Specifying and estimating VARMA models

As we have seen in the previous section, for forecasting purposes the pure VAR or MA representations of a stochastic process are quite useful. These representations are in general of infinite order. In practice, they have to be replaced by finite dimensional parameterizations which can be specified and estimated from data. VARMA processes are such finite dimensional parameterizations. Therefore, in practice, a VARMA model such as (2.1) or even a pure finite order VAR as in (1.1) will be specified and estimated as a forecasting tool.

As mentioned earlier, the operators $A(L)$ and $M(L)$ of the VARMA model (2.2) are not unique or not identified, as econometricians sometimes say. This nonuniqueness is problematic if the process parameters have to be estimated because a unique representation is needed for consistent estimation. Before we discuss estimation and specification issues related to VARMA processes we will therefore present identifying restrictions. More precisely, the echelon form of VARMA and EC-VARMA models will be presented. Then estimation procedures, model specification and diagnostic checking will be discussed.

3.1. The echelon form

Any pair of operators $A(L)$ and $M(L)$ that gives rise to the same VAR operator $\Xi(L) = I_K - \sum_{i=1}^{\infty} \Xi_i L^i = M(L)^{-1}A(L)$ or MA operator $\Phi(L) = A(L)^{-1}M(L)$ defines an equivalent VARMA process for y_t. Here $A_0 = M_0$ is assumed. Clearly, if we premultiply $A(L)$ and $M(L)$ by some invertible operator $D(L) = D_0 + D_1 L + \cdots + D_q L^q$ satisfying $\det(D_0) \neq 0$ and $\det D(z) \neq 0$ for $|z| \leqslant 1$, an equivalent VARMA representation is obtained. Thus, a first step towards finding a unique representation is to cancel common factors in $A(L)$ and $M(L)$. We therefore assume that the operator $[A(L) : M(L)]$ is *left-coprime*. To define this property, note that a matrix polynomial $D(z)$ and the corresponding operator $D(L)$ are *unimodular* if $\det D(z)$ is a constant which does not depend on z. Examples of unimodular operators are

$$D(L) = D_0 \quad \text{or} \quad D(L) = \begin{bmatrix} 1 & \delta L \\ 0 & 1 \end{bmatrix} \tag{3.1}$$

[see Lütkepohl (1996) for definitions and properties of matrix polynomials]. A matrix operator $[A(L) : M(L)]$ is called left-coprime if only unimodular operators $D(L)$ can be factored. In other words, if $[A(L) : M(L)]$ is left-coprime and operators $\bar{A}(L)$, $\bar{M}(L)$ and $D(L)$ exist such that $[A(L) : M(L)] = D(L)[\bar{A}(L) : \bar{M}(L)]$ holds, then $D(L)$ must be unimodular.

Although considering only left-coprime operators $[A(L) : M(L)]$ does not fully solve the nonuniqueness problem of VARMA representations it is a first step in the right direction because it excludes many possible redundancies. It does not rule out premultiplication by some nonsingular matrix, for example, and thus, there is still room for improvement. Even if $A_0 = M_0 = I_K$ is assumed, uniqueness of the operators is not achieved because there are unimodular operators $D(L)$ with zero-order matrix I_K, as seen in (3.1). Premultiplying $[A(L) : M(L)]$ by such an operator maintains left-coprimeness. Therefore more restrictions are needed for uniqueness. The echelon form discussed in the next subsections provides sufficiently many restrictions in order to ensure uniqueness of the operators. We will first consider stationary processes and then turn to EC-VARMA models.

3.1.1. Stationary processes

We assume that $[A(L) : M(L)]$ is left-coprime and we denote the klth elements of $A(L)$ and $M(L)$ by $\alpha_{kl}(L)$ and $m_{kl}(L)$, respectively. Let p_k be the maximum polynomial degree in the kth row of $[A(L) : M(L)]$, $k = 1, \dots, K$, and define

$$p_{kl} = \begin{cases} \min(p_k + 1, p_l) & \text{for } k > l, \\ \min(p_k, p_l) & \text{for } k < l, \end{cases} \qquad k, l = 1, \dots, K.$$

These quantities determine the number of free parameters in the operators $m_{kl}(L)$ in the echelon form. More precisely, the VARMA process is said to be in *echelon form* or, briefly, ARMA$_E$ form if the operators $A(L)$ and $M(L)$ satisfy the following restrictions [Lütkepohl and Claessen (1997), Lütkepohl (2002)]:

$$m_{kk}(L) = 1 + \sum_{i=1}^{p_k} m_{kk,i} L^i, \qquad \text{for } k = 1, \dots, K, \tag{3.2}$$

$$m_{kl}(L) = \sum_{i=p_k-p_{kl}+1}^{p_k} m_{kl,i} L^i, \quad \text{for } k \neq l, \tag{3.3}$$

and

$$\alpha_{kl}(L) = \alpha_{kl,0} - \sum_{i=1}^{p_k} \alpha_{kl,i} L^i, \quad \text{with } \alpha_{kl,0} = m_{kl,0} \quad \text{for } k, l = 1, \ldots, K. \tag{3.4}$$

Here the row degrees p_k $(k = 1, \ldots, K)$ are called the *Kronecker indices* [see Hannan and Deistler (1988), Lütkepohl (2005)].

To illustrate the echelon form we consider the following three-dimensional process from Lütkepohl (2002) with Kronecker indices $(p_1, p_2, p_3) = (1, 2, 1)$. It is easy to derive the p_{kl},

$$[p_{kl}] = \begin{bmatrix} \bullet & 1 & 1 \\ 1 & \bullet & 1 \\ 1 & 2 & \bullet \end{bmatrix}.$$

Using the implied operators from (3.3) and (3.4) gives the echelon form

$$\begin{bmatrix} 1 - \alpha_{11,1}L & -\alpha_{12,1}L & -\alpha_{13,1}L \\ -\alpha_{21,1}L - \alpha_{21,2}L^2 & 1 - \alpha_{22,1}L - \alpha_{22,2}L^2 & -\alpha_{23,1}L - \alpha_{23,2}L^2 \\ -\alpha_{31,1}L & \alpha_{32,0} - \alpha_{32,1}L & 1 - \alpha_{33,1}L \end{bmatrix} y_t$$

$$= \begin{bmatrix} 1 + m_{11,1}L & m_{12,1}L & m_{13,1}L \\ m_{21,2}L^2 & 1 + m_{22,1}L + m_{22,2}L^2 & m_{23,2}L^2 \\ m_{31,1}L & \alpha_{32,0} + m_{32,1}L & 1 + m_{33,1}L \end{bmatrix} u_t$$

which illustrates the kinds of restrictions imposed in the echelon form. Notice that, for example, $m_{12}(L) = m_{12,2}L^2$ has only one free parameter because $p_{12} = 1$, although $m_{12}(L)$ is a polynomial of order 2. In contrast, $p_{32} = 2$ and hence $m_{32}(L) = \alpha_{32,0} + m_{32,1}L$ has 2 free parameters although it is a polynomial of order 1. Consequently, the zero order term $(\alpha_{32,0})$ is left unrestricted. The model can be written alternatively as

$$\begin{aligned} \begin{bmatrix} 1 & 0 & 0 \\ 0 & 1 & 0 \\ 0 & \alpha_{32,0} & 1 \end{bmatrix} y_t = {} & \begin{bmatrix} \alpha_{11,1} & \alpha_{12,1} & \alpha_{13,1} \\ \alpha_{21,1} & \alpha_{22,1} & \alpha_{23,1} \\ \alpha_{31,1} & \alpha_{32,1} & \alpha_{33,1} \end{bmatrix} y_{t-1} \\ & + \begin{bmatrix} 0 & 0 & 0 \\ \alpha_{21,2} & \alpha_{22,2} & \alpha_{23,2} \\ 0 & 0 & 0 \end{bmatrix} y_{t-2} \\ & + \begin{bmatrix} 1 & 0 & 0 \\ 0 & 1 & 0 \\ 0 & \alpha_{32,0} & 1 \end{bmatrix} u_t + \begin{bmatrix} m_{11,1} & m_{12,1} & m_{13,1} \\ 0 & m_{22,1} & 0 \\ m_{31,1} & m_{32,1} & m_{33,1} \end{bmatrix} u_{t-1} \\ & + \begin{bmatrix} 0 & 0 & 0 \\ m_{21,2} & m_{22,2} & m_{23,2} \\ 0 & 0 & 0 \end{bmatrix} u_{t-2}. \end{aligned} \tag{3.5}$$

The zero order matrix $A_0 = M_0$ of an echelon form is always lower triangular and, in fact, it will often be an identity matrix. It will always be an identity matrix if the

Kronecker indices are ordered from smallest to largest. The restrictions on the zero order matrix are determined by the p_{kl}. Otherwise the VAR operator is just restricted by the Kronecker indices which specify maximum row degrees. For instance, in our example the first Kronecker index $p_1 = 1$ and hence, the $\alpha_{1l}(L)$ have degree 1 for $l = 1, 2, 3$ so that the first row of A_2 is zero. On the other hand, there are further zero restrictions imposed on the MA coefficient matrices which are implied by the p_{kl} which in turn are determined by the Kronecker indices p_1, p_2, p_3.

In the following we denote an echelon form with Kronecker indices $p_1, \dots, p_K$ by $\text{ARMA}_E(p_1, \dots, p_K)$. Thus, (3.5) is an $\text{ARMA}_E(1, 2, 1)$. Notice that it corresponds to a VARMA(p, p) representation in (2.1) with $p = \max(p_1, \dots, p_K)$. An ARMA_E form may have more zero coefficients than those specified by the restrictions from (3.2)–(3.4). In particular, there may be models where the AR and MA orders are not identical due to further zero restrictions. For example, if in (3.5) $m_{21,2} = m_{22,2} = m_{23,2} = 0$, we still have an $\text{ARMA}_E(1, 2, 1)$ form because the largest degree in the second row is still 2. Yet this representation would be categorized as a VARMA(2, 1) model in the standard terminology. Such over-identifying constraints are not ruled out by the echelon form. It does not need them to ensure uniqueness of the operator $[A(L) : M(L)]$ for a given VAR operator $\Xi(L)$ or MA operator $\Phi(L)$, however. Note also that every VARMA process can be written in echelon form. Thus, the echelon form does not exclude any VARMA processes.

The present specification of the echelon form does not restrict the autoregressive operator except for the maximum row degrees imposed by the Kronecker indices and the zero order matrix ($A_0 = M_0$). Additional identifying zero restrictions are placed on the moving average coefficient matrices attached to low lags of the error process u_t. This form of the echelon form was proposed by Lütkepohl and Claessen (1997) because it can be combined conveniently with the EC representation of a VARMA process, as we will see shortly. Thus, it is particularly useful for processes with cointegrated variables. It was called reverse echelon form by Lütkepohl (2005, Chapter 14) to distinguish it from the standard echelon form which is usually used for stationary processes. In that form the restrictions on low order lags are imposed on the VAR coefficient matrices [e.g., Hannan and Deistler (1988), Lütkepohl (2005, Chapter 12)].

3.1.2. $I(1)$ processes

If the EC form of the ARMA_E model is set up as in (2.6), the autoregressive short-run coefficient matrices $\Gamma_i = -(A_{i+1} + \cdots + A_p)$ $(i = 1, \dots, p-1)$ satisfy similar identifying constraints as the A_i's $(i = 1, \dots, p)$. More precisely, Γ_i obeys the same zero restrictions as A_{i+1} for $i = 1, \dots, p-1$. This structure follows from the specific form of the zero restrictions on the A_i's. If $\alpha_{kl,i}$ is restricted to zero by the echelon form this implies that the corresponding element $\alpha_{kl,j}$ of A_j is also zero for $j > i$. Similarly, the echelon form zero restrictions on Π are the same as those on $A_0 - A_1$. As an example we rewrite (3.5) in EC form as

$$\begin{bmatrix} 1 & 0 & 0 \\ 0 & 1 & 0 \\ 0 & \alpha_{32,0} & 1 \end{bmatrix} \Delta y_t = \begin{bmatrix} \pi_{11} & \pi_{12} & \pi_{13} \\ \pi_{21} & \pi_{22} & \pi_{23} \\ \pi_{31} & \pi_{32} & \pi_{33} \end{bmatrix} y_{t-1} + \begin{bmatrix} 0 & 0 & 0 \\ \gamma_{21,1} & \gamma_{22,1} & \gamma_{23,1} \\ 0 & 0 & 0 \end{bmatrix} \Delta y_{t-1}$$
$$+ \begin{bmatrix} 1 & 0 & 0 \\ 0 & 1 & 0 \\ 0 & \alpha_{32,0} & 1 \end{bmatrix} u_t + \begin{bmatrix} m_{11,1} & m_{12,1} & m_{13,1} \\ 0 & m_{22,1} & 0 \\ m_{31,1} & m_{32,1} & m_{33,1} \end{bmatrix} u_{t-1}$$
$$+ \begin{bmatrix} 0 & 0 & 0 \\ m_{21,2} & m_{22,2} & m_{23,2} \\ 0 & 0 & 0 \end{bmatrix} u_{t-2}.$$

Because the echelon form does not impose zero restrictions on A_1 if all Kronecker indices $p_k \geqslant 1$ $(k = 1, \dots, K)$, there are no echelon form zero restrictions on Π if all Kronecker indices are greater than zero as in the previous example. On the other hand, if there are zero Kronecker indices, this has consequences for the rank of Π and, hence, for the integration and cointegration structure of the variables. In fact, denoting by ϱ the number of zero Kronecker indices, it is easy to see that

$$\operatorname{rk}(\Pi) \geqslant \varrho. \tag{3.6}$$

This result is useful to remember when procedures for specifying the cointegrating rank of a VARMA system are considered.

The following three-dimensional $\text{ARMA}_E(0, 0, 1)$ model from Lütkepohl (2002) illustrates this issue:

$$y_t = \begin{bmatrix} 0 & 0 & 0 \\ 0 & 0 & 0 \\ \alpha_{31,1} & \alpha_{32,1} & \alpha_{33,1} \end{bmatrix} y_{t-1} + u_t + \begin{bmatrix} 0 & 0 & 0 \\ 0 & 0 & 0 \\ m_{31,1} & m_{32,1} & m_{33,1} \end{bmatrix} u_{t-1}. \tag{3.7}$$

Note that in this case $A_0 = M_0 = I_3$ because the Kronecker indices are ordered from smallest to largest. Two of the Kronecker indices are zero and, hence, according to (3.6), the cointegrating rank of this system must be at least 2. Using $\Pi = -(A_0 - A_1) = -I_K + A_1$, the EC form is seen to be

$$\Delta y_t = \begin{bmatrix} -1 & 0 & 0 \\ 0 & -1 & 0 \\ \pi_{31} & \pi_{32} & \pi_{33} \end{bmatrix} y_{t-1} + u_t + \begin{bmatrix} 0 & 0 & 0 \\ 0 & 0 & 0 \\ m_{31,1} & m_{32,1} & m_{33,1} \end{bmatrix} u_{t-1},$$

where $\pi_{31} = \alpha_{31,1}$, $\pi_{32} = \alpha_{32,1}$ and $\pi_{33} = -1 + \alpha_{33,1}$. The rank of

$$\Pi = \begin{bmatrix} -1 & 0 & 0 \\ 0 & -1 & 0 \\ \pi_{31} & \pi_{32} & \pi_{33} \end{bmatrix}$$

is clearly at least two.

In the following we use the acronym EC-ARMA_E for an EC-VARMA model which satisfies the echelon form restrictions. Because we now have unique representations of VARMA models we can discuss estimation of such models. Of course, to estimate an ARMA$_E$ or EC-ARMA$_E$ form we need to specify the Kronecker indices and possibly the cointegrating rank. We will discuss parameter estimation first and then consider model specification issues.

Before we go on with these topics, we mention that there are other ways to achieve uniqueness or identification of a VARMA representation. For example, Zellner and Palm (1974) and Wallis (1977) considered a *final equations form* representation which also solves the identification problem. It often results in rather heavily parameterized models [see Lütkepohl (2005, Chapter 12)] and has therefore not gained much popularity. Tiao and Tsay (1989) propose so-called *scalar component models* to overcome the identification problem. The idea is to consider linear combinations of the variables which can reveal simplifications of the general VARMA structure. The interested reader is referred to the aforementioned article. We have presented the echelon form here in some detail because it often results in parsimonious representations.

3.2. Estimation of VARMA models for given lag orders and cointegrating rank

For given Kronecker indices the ARMA$_E$ form of a VARMA DGP can be set up and estimated. We will consider this case first and then study estimation of EC-ARMA$_E$ models for which the cointegrating rank is given in addition to the Kronecker indices. Specification of the Kronecker indices and the cointegrating rank will be discussed in Sections 3.4 and 3.3, respectively.

3.2.1. ARMA$_E$ models

Suppose the white noise process u_t is normally distributed (Gaussian), $u_t \sim N(0, \Sigma_u)$. Given a sample $y_1, \dots, y_T$ and presample values $y_0, \dots, y_{p-1}, u_0, \dots, u_{q-1}$, the log-likelihood function of the VARMA model (2.1) is

$$l(\theta) = \sum_{t=1}^{T} l_t(\theta). \tag{3.8}$$

Here θ represents the vector of all parameters to be estimated and

$$l_t(\theta) = -\frac{K}{2}\log 2\pi - \frac{1}{2}\log\det\Sigma_u - \frac{1}{2}u_t'\Sigma_u^{-1}u_t,$$

where

$$u_t = M_0^{-1}(A_0 y_t - A_1 y_{t-1} - \cdots - A_p y_{t-p} - M_1 u_{t-1} - \cdots - M_q u_{t-q}).$$

It is assumed that the uniqueness restrictions of the ARMA$_E$ form are imposed and θ contains the freely varying parameters only. The initial values are assumed to be fixed and if the u_t ($t \leqslant 0$) are not available, they may be replaced by zero without affecting the asymptotic properties of the estimators.

Maximization of $l(\theta)$ is a nonlinear optimization problem which is complicated by the inequality constraints that ensure invertibility of the MA operator. Iterative optimization algorithms may be used here. Start-up values for such algorithms may be obtained as follows: An unrestricted long VAR model of order h_T, say, is fitted by OLS in a first step. Denoting the estimated residuals by $\hat{u}_t$, the ARMA$_E$ form can be estimated when all lagged u_t's are replaced by $\hat{u}_t$'s. If $A_0 \neq I_K$, then unlagged u_{jt} in equation k ($k \neq j$) may also be replaced by estimated residuals from the long VAR. The resulting parameter estimates can be used as starting values for an iterative algorithm.

If the DGP is stable and invertible and the parameters are identified, the ML estimator $\hat{\theta}$ has standard limiting properties, that is, $\hat{\theta}$ is consistent and

$$\sqrt{T}\big(\hat{\theta} - \theta\big) \xrightarrow{d} N(0, \Sigma_{\hat{\theta}}),$$

where $\xrightarrow{d}$ signifies convergence in distribution and $\Sigma_{\hat{\theta}}$ is the Gaussian inverse asymptotic information matrix. Asymptotic normality of the estimator holds even if the true distribution of the u_t's is not normal but satisfies suitable moment conditions. In that case the estimators are just quasi ML estimators, of course.

There has been some discussion of the likelihood function of VARMA models and its maximization [Tunnicliffe Wilson (1973), Nicholls and Hall (1979), Hillmer and Tiao (1979)]. Unfortunately, optimization of the Gaussian log-likelihood is not a trivial exercise. Therefore other estimation methods have been proposed in the literature [e.g., Koreisha and Pukkila (1987), Kapetanios (2003), Poskitt (2003), Bauer and Wagner (2002), van Overschee and DeMoor (1994)]. Of course, it is also straightforward to add deterministic terms to the model and estimate the associated parameters along with the VARMA coefficients.

3.2.2. EC-ARMA$_E$ models

If the cointegrating rank r is given and the DGP is a pure, finite order VAR(p) process, the corresponding VECM,

$$\Delta y_t = \alpha\beta' y_{t-1} + \Gamma_1 \Delta y_{t-1} + \cdots + \Gamma_{p-1} \Delta y_{t-p+1} + u_t, \tag{3.9}$$

can be estimated conveniently by RR regression, as shown in Johansen (1995a). Concentrating out the short-run dynamics by regressing Δy_t and y_{t-1} on $\Delta Y'_{t-1} = [\Delta y'_{t-1}, \ldots, \Delta y'_{t-p+1}]$ and denoting the residuals by R_{0t} and R_{1t}, respectively, the EC term can be estimated by RR regression from

$$R_{0t} = \alpha\beta' R_{1t} + u_t^c. \tag{3.10}$$

Because the decomposition $\Pi = \alpha\beta'$ is not unique, the estimators for α and β are not consistent whereas the resulting ML estimator for Π is consistent. However, because the matrices α and β have rank r, one way to make them unique is to choose

$$\beta' = \big[I_r : \beta'_{(K-r)}\big], \tag{3.11}$$

where $\beta_{(K-r)}$ is a $((K - r) \times r)$ matrix. This normalization is always possible upon a suitable ordering of the variables. The ML estimator of $\beta_{(K-r)}$ can be obtained by post-multiplying the RR estimator $\tilde{\beta}$ of β by the inverse of its first r rows and using the resulting last $K - r$ rows as the estimator $\breve{\beta}_{(K-r)}$ of $\beta_{(K-r)}$. This estimator is not only consistent but even superconsistent meaning that it converges at a faster rate than the usual $\sqrt{T}$ to the true parameter matrix $\beta_{(K-r)}$. In fact, it turns out that $T(\breve{\beta}_{(K-r)} - \beta_{(K-r)})$ converges weakly. As a result inference for the other parameters can be done as if the cointegration matrix β were known.

Other estimation procedures that can be used here as well were proposed by Ahn and Reinsel (1990) and Saikkonen (1992). In fact, in the latter article it was shown that the procedure can even be justified if the true DGP is an infinite order VAR process and only a finite order model is fitted, as long as the order goes to infinity with growing sample size. This result is convenient in the present situation where we are interested in VARMA processes, because we can estimate the cointegration relations in a first step on the basis of a finite order VECM without MA part. Then the estimated cointegration matrix can be used in estimating the remaining VARMA parameters. That is, the short-run parameters including the loading coefficients α and MA parameters of the EC-ARMA$_E$ form can then be estimated by ML conditional on the estimator for β. Because of the superconsistency of the estimator for the cointegration parameters this procedure maintains the asymptotic efficiency of the Gaussian ML estimator. Except for the cointegration parameters, the parameter estimators have standard asymptotic properties which are equivalent to those of the full ML estimators [Yap and Reinsel (1995)]. If the Kronecker indices are given, the echelon VARMA structure can also be taken into account in estimating the cointegration matrix.

As mentioned earlier, before a model can be estimated, the Kronecker indices and possibly the cointegrating rank have to be specified. These issues are discussed next.

3.3. Testing for the cointegrating rank

A wide range of proposals exists for determining the cointegrating ranks of pure VAR processes [see Hubrich, Lütkepohl and Saikkonen (2001) for a recent survey]. The most popular approach is due to Johansen (1995a) who derives likelihood ratio (LR) tests for the cointegrating rank of a pure VAR process. Because ML estimation of unrestricted VECMs with a specific cointegrating rank r is straightforward for Gaussian processes, the LR statistic for testing the pair of hypotheses H_0: $r = r_0$ versus H_1: $r > r_0$ is readily available by comparing the likelihood maxima for $r = r_0$ and $r = K$. The asymptotic distributions of the LR statistics are nonstandard and depend on the deterministic terms included in the model. Tables with critical values for various different cases are available in Johansen (1995a, Chapter 15). The cointegrating rank can be determined by checking sequentially the null hypotheses

$$H_0\colon r = 0, \quad H_0\colon r = 1, \quad \ldots, \quad H_0\colon r = K - 1$$

and choosing the cointegrating rank for which the first null hypothesis cannot be rejected in this sequence.

For our present purposes it is of interest that Johansen's LR tests can be justified even if a finite-order VAR process is fitted to an infinite order DGP, as shown by Lütkepohl and Saikkonen (1999). It is assumed in this case that the order of the fitted VAR process goes to infinity with the sample size and Lütkepohl and Saikkonen (1999) discuss the choice of the VAR order in this approach. Because the Kronecker indices are usually also unknown, choosing the cointegrating rank of a VARMA process by fitting a long VAR process is an attractive approach which avoids knowledge of the VARMA structure at the stage where the cointegrating rank is determined. So far the theory for this procedure seems to be available for processes with nonzero mean term only and not for other deterministic terms such as linear trends. It seems likely, however, that extensions to more general processes are possible.

An alternative way to proceed in determining the cointegrating rank of a VARMA process was proposed by Yap and Reinsel (1995). They extended the likelihood ratio tests to VARMA processes under the assumption that an identified structure of $A(L)$ and $M(L)$ is known. For these tests the Kronecker indices or some other identifying structure has to be specified first. If the Kronecker indices are known already, a lower bound for the cointegrating rank is also known (see (3.6)). Hence, in testing for the cointegrating rank, only the sequence of null hypotheses H_0: $r = \varrho$, H_0: $r = \varrho + 1, \ldots, H_0$: $r = K - 1$, is of interest. Again, the rank may be chosen as the smallest value for which H_0 cannot be rejected.

3.4. *Specifying the lag orders and Kronecker indices*

A number of proposals for choosing the Kronecker indices of ARMA_E models were made, see, for example, Hannan and Kavalieris (1984), Poskitt (1992), Nsiri and Roy (1992) and Lütkepohl and Poskitt (1996) for stationary processes and Lütkepohl and Claessen (1997), Claessen (1995), Poskitt and Lütkepohl (1995) and Poskitt (2003) for cointegrated processes. The strategies for specifying the Kronecker indices of cointegrated ARMA_E processes presented in this section are proposed in the latter two papers. Poskitt (2003, Proposition 3.3) presents a result regarding the consistency of the estimators of the Kronecker indices. A simulation study of the small sample properties of the procedures was performed by Bartel and Lütkepohl (1998). They found that the methods work reasonably well in small samples for the processes considered in their study. This section draws partly on Lütkepohl (2002, Section 8.4.1).

The specification method proceeds in two stages. In the first stage a long reduced-form VAR process of order h_T, say, is fitted by OLS giving estimates of the unobservable innovations u_t as in the previously described estimation procedure. In a second stage the estimated residuals are substituted for the unknown lagged u_t's in the ARMA_E form. A range of different models is estimated and the Kronecker indices are chosen by model selection criteria.

There are different possibilities for doing so within this general procedure. For example, one may search over all models associated with Kronecker indices which are smaller than some prespecified upper bound $p_{\max}$, $\{(p_1, \ldots, p_K) \mid 0 \leqslant p_k \leqslant p_{\max}, k = 1, \ldots, K\}$. The set of Kronecker indices is then chosen which minimizes the preferred model selection criterion. For systems of moderate or large dimensions this procedure is rather computer intensive and computationally more efficient search procedures have been suggested. One idea is to estimate the individual equations separately by OLS for different lag lengths. The lag length is then chosen so as to minimize a criterion of the general form

$$\Lambda_{k,T}(n) = \log \hat{\sigma}^2_{k,T}(n) + C_T n/T, \quad n = 0, 1, \ldots, P_T,$$

where C_T is a suitable function of the sample size T and $T\hat{\sigma}^2_{k,T}(n)$ is the residual sum of squares from a regression of y_{kt} on $(\hat{u}_{jt} - y_{jt})$ $(j = 1, \ldots, K,\ j \neq k)$ and y_{t-s} and $\hat{u}_{t-s}$ $(s = 1, \ldots, n)$. The maximum lag length P_T is also allowed to depend on the sample size.

In this procedure the echelon structure is not explicitly taken into account because the equations are treated separately. The kth equation will still be misspecified if the lag order is less than the true Kronecker index. Moreover, the kth equation will be correctly specified but may include redundant parameters and variables if the lag order is greater than the true Kronecker index. This explains why the criterion function $\Lambda_{k,T}(n)$ will possess a global minimum asymptotically when n is equal to the true Kronecker index, provided C_T is chosen appropriately. In practice, possible choices of C_T are $C_T = h_T \log T$ or $C_T = h_T^2$ [see Poskitt (2003) for more details on the procedure]. Poskitt and Lütkepohl (1995) and Poskitt (2003) also consider a modification of this procedure where coefficient restrictions derived from those equations in the system which have smaller Kronecker indices are taken into account. The important point to make here is that procedures exist which can be applied in a fully computerized model choice. Thus, model selection is feasible from a practical point of view although the small sample properties of these procedures are not clear in general, despite some encouraging but limited small sample evidence by Bartel and Lütkepohl (1998). Other procedures for specifying the Kronecker indices for stationary processes were proposed by Akaike (1976), Cooper and Wood (1982), Tsay (1989b) and Nsiri and Roy (1992), for example.

The Kronecker indices found in a computer automated procedure for a given time series should only be viewed as a starting point for a further analysis of the system under consideration. Based on the specified Kronecker indices a more efficient procedure for estimating the parameters may be applied (see Section 3.2) and the model may be subjected to a range of diagnostic tests. If such tests produce unsatisfactory results, modifications are called for. Tools for checking the model adequacy will be briefly summarized in the following section.

3.5. Diagnostic checking

As noted in Section 3.2, the estimators of an identified version of a stationary VARMA model have standard asymptotic properties. Therefore the usual t- and F-tests can be used to decide on possible overidentifying restrictions. When a parsimonious model without redundant parameters has been found, the residuals can be checked. According to our assumptions they should be white noise and a number of model-checking tools are tailored to check this assumption. For this purpose one may consider individual residual series or one may check the full residual vector at once. The tools range from visual inspection of the plots of the residuals and their autocorrelations to formal tests for residual autocorrelation and autocorrelation of the squared residuals to tests for non-normality and nonlinearity [see, e.g., Lütkepohl (2005), Doornik and Hendry (1997)]. It is also advisable to check for structural shifts during the sample period. Possible tests based on prediction errors are considered in Lütkepohl (2005). Moreover, when new data becomes available, out-of-sample forecasts may be checked. Model defects detected at the checking stage should lead to modifications of the original specification.

4. Forecasting with estimated processes

4.1. General results

To simplify matters suppose that the generation process of a multiple time series of interest admits a VARMA representation with zero order matrices equal to I_K,

$$y_t = A_1 y_{t-1} + \cdots + A_p y_{t-p} + u_t + M_1 u_{t-1} + \cdots + M_q u_{t-q}, \tag{4.1}$$

that is, $A_0 = M_0 = I_K$. Recall that in the echelon form framework this representation can always be obtained by premultiplying by A_0^{-1} if $A_0 \neq I_K$. We denote by $\hat{y}_{\tau+h|\tau}$ the h-step forecast at origin τ given in Section 2.4, based on estimated rather than known coefficients. For instance, using the pure VAR representation of the process,

$$\hat{y}_{\tau+h|\tau} = \sum_{i=1}^{h-1} \hat{\Xi}_i \hat{y}_{\tau+h-i|\tau} + \sum_{i=h}^{\infty} \hat{\Xi}_i y_{\tau+h-i}. \tag{4.2}$$

Of course, for practical purposes one may truncate the infinite sum at $i = \tau$ in (4.2). For the moment we will, however, consider the infinite sum and assume that the model represents the DGP. Thus, there is no specification error. For this predictor the forecast error is

$$y_{\tau+h} - \hat{y}_{\tau+h|\tau} = (y_{\tau+h} - y_{\tau+h|\tau}) + (y_{\tau+h|\tau} - \hat{y}_{\tau+h|\tau}),$$

where $y_{\tau+h|\tau}$ is the optimal forecast based on known coefficients and the two terms on the right-hand side are uncorrelated if only data up to period τ are used for estimation. In that case the first term can be written in terms of u_t's with $t > \tau$ and the second one contains only y_t's with $t \leqslant \tau$. Thus, the forecast MSE becomes

$$\begin{aligned}\Sigma_{\hat{y}}(h) &= \text{MSE}(y_{\tau+h|\tau}) + \text{MSE}(y_{\tau+h|\tau} - \hat{y}_{\tau+h|\tau}) \\ &= \Sigma_y(h) + E\big[(y_{\tau+h|\tau} - \hat{y}_{\tau+h|\tau})(y_{\tau+h|\tau} - \hat{y}_{\tau+h|\tau})'\big].\end{aligned} \tag{4.3}$$

The $\text{MSE}(y_{\tau+h|\tau} - \hat{y}_{\tau+h|\tau})$ can be approximated by $\Omega(h)/T$, where

$$\Omega(h) = E\left[\frac{\partial y_{\tau+h|\tau}}{\partial \theta'} \Sigma_{\tilde{\theta}} \frac{\partial y'_{\tau+h|\tau}}{\partial \theta}\right], \tag{4.4}$$

θ is the vector of estimated coefficients, and $\Sigma_{\tilde{\theta}}$ is its asymptotic covariance matrix [see Yamamoto (1980), Baillie (1981) and Lütkepohl (2005) for more detailed expressions for $\Omega(h)$ and Hogue, Magnus and Pesaran (1988) for an exact treatment of the AR(1) special case). If ML estimation is used, the covariance matrix $\Sigma_{\tilde{\theta}}$ is just the inverse asymptotic information matrix. Clearly, $\Omega(h)$ is positive semidefinite and the forecast MSE,

$$\Sigma_{\hat{y}}(h) = \Sigma_y(h) + \frac{1}{T}\Omega(h), \tag{4.5}$$

for estimated processes is larger (or at least not smaller) than the corresponding quantity for known processes, as one would expect. The additional term depends on the estimation efficiency because it includes the asymptotic covariance matrix of the parameter estimators. Therefore, estimating the parameters of a given process well is also important for forecasting. On the other hand, for large sample sizes T, the additional term will be small or even negligible.

Another interesting property of the predictor based on an estimated finite order VAR process is that under general conditions it is unbiased or has a symmetric distribution around zero [see Dufour (1985)]. This result even holds in finite samples and if a finite order VAR process is fitted to a series generated by a more general process, for instance, to a series generated by a VARMA process. A related result for univariate processes was also given by Pesaran and Timmermann (2005) and Ullah (2004, Section 6.3.1) summarizes further work related to prediction of estimated dynamic models. Schorfheide (2005) considers VAR forecasting under misspecification and possible improvements under quadratic loss.

It may be worth noting that deterministic terms can be accommodated easily, as discussed in Section 2.5. In the present situation the uncertainty in the estimators related to such terms can also be taken into account like that of the other parameters. If the deterministic terms are specified such that the corresponding parameter estimators are asymptotically independent of the other estimators, an additional term for the estimation uncertainty stemming from the deterministic terms has to be added to the forecast MSE matrix (4.5). For deterministic linear trends in univariate models more details are presented in Kim, Leybourne and Newbold (2004).

Various extensions of the previous results have been discussed in the literature. For example, Lewis and Reinsel (1985) and Lütkepohl (1985b) consider the forecast MSE for the case where the true process is approximated by a finite order VAR, thereby extending earlier univariate results by Bhansali (1978). Reinsel and Lewis (1987), Basu and Sen Roy (1987), Engle and Yoo (1987), Sampson (1991) and Reinsel and Ahn (1992) present results for processes with unit roots. Stock (1996) and Kemp (1999) assume that the forecast horizon h and the sample size T both go to infinity simultaneously. Clements and Hendry (1998, 1999) consider various other sources of possible forecast errors. Taking into account the specification and estimation uncertainty in multi-step forecasts, it makes also sense to construct a separate model for each specific forecast horizon h. This approach is discussed in detail by Bhansali (2002).

In practice, a model specification step precedes estimation and adds further uncertainty to the forecasts. Often model selection criteria are used in specifying the model orders, as discussed in Section 3.4. In a small sample comparison of various such criteria for choosing the order of a pure VAR process, Lütkepohl (1985a) found that more parsimonious criteria tend to select better forecasting models in terms of mean squared error than more profligate criteria. More precisely, the parsimonious Schwarz (1978) criterion often selected better forecasting models than the Akaike information criterion (AIC) [Akaike (1973)] even when the true model order was underestimated. Also Stock and Watson (1999), in a larger comparison of a range of univariate forecasting methods based on 215 monthly U.S. macroeconomic series, found that the Schwarz criterion performed slightly better than AIC. In contrast, based on 150 macro time series from different countries, Meese and Geweke (1984) obtained the opposite result. See, however, the analysis of the role of parsimony provided by Clements and Hendry (1998, Chapter 12). At this stage it is difficult to give well founded recommendations as to which procedure to use. Moreover, a large scale systematic investigation of the actual forecasting performance of VARMA processes relative to VAR models or univariate methods is not known to this author.

4.2. *Aggregated processes*

In Section 2.4 we have compared different forecasts for aggregated time series. It was found that generally forecasting the disaggregate process and aggregating the forecasts ($z^o_{\tau+h|\tau}$) is more efficient than forecasting the aggregate directly ($z_{\tau+h|\tau}$). In this case, if the sample size is large enough, the part of the forecast MSE due to estimation uncertainty will eventually be so small that the estimated $\hat{z}^o_{\tau+h|\tau}$ is again superior to the corresponding $\hat{z}_{\tau+h|\tau}$. There are cases, however, where the two forecasts are identical for known processes. Now the question arises whether in these cases the MSE term due to estimation errors will make one forecast preferable to its competitors. Indeed if estimated instead of known processes are used, it is possible that $\hat{z}^o_{\tau+h|\tau}$ looses its optimality relative to $\hat{z}_{\tau+h|\tau}$ because the MSE part due to estimation may be larger for the former than for the latter. Consider the case, where a number of series are simply added to obtain a univariate aggregate. Then it is possible that a simple parsimonious univariate ARMA model describes the aggregate well, whereas a large multivariate model is required for an adequate description of the multivariate disaggregate process. Clearly, it is conceivable that the estimation uncertainty in the multivariate case becomes considerably more important than for the univariate model for the aggregate. Lütkepohl (1987) shows that this may indeed happen in small samples. In fact, similar situations can not only arise for contemporaneous aggregation but also for temporal aggregation. Generally, if two predictors based on known processes are nearly identical, the estimation part of the MSE becomes important and generally the predictor based on the smaller model is then to be preferred.

There is also another aspect which is important for comparing forecasts. So far we have only taken into account the effect of estimation uncertainty on the forecast MSE. This analysis still assumes a known model structure and only allows for estimated parameters. In practice, model specification usually precedes estimation and usually there is additional uncertainty attached to this step in the forecasting procedure. It is also possible to explicitly take into account the fact that in practice models are only approximations to the true DGP by considering finite order VAR and AR approximations to infinite order processes. This has also been done by Lütkepohl (1987). Under these assumptions it is again found that the forecast $\hat{z}^o_{\tau+h|\tau}$ looses its optimality and forecasting the aggregate directly or forecasting the disaggregate series with univariate methods and aggregating univariate forecasts may become preferable.

Recent empirical studies do not reach a unanimous conclusion regarding the value of using disaggregate information in forecasting aggregates. For example, Marcellino, Stock and Watson (2003) found disaggregate information to be helpful while Hubrich (2005) and Hendry and Hubrich (2005) concluded that disaggregation resulted in forecast deterioration in a comparison based on euro area inflation data. Of course, there can be many reasons for the empirical results to differ from the theoretical ones. For example, the specification procedure is taken into account partially at best in theoretical comparisons or the data may have features that cannot be captured adequately by the models used in the forecast competition. Thus there is still considerable room to learn more about how to select a good forecasting model.

5. Conclusions

VARMA models are a powerful tool for producing linear forecasts for a set of time series variables. They utilize the information not only in the past values of a particular variable of interest but also allow for information in other, related variables. We have mentioned conditions under which the forecasts from these models are optimal under a MSE criterion for forecast performance. Even if the conditions for minimizing the forecast MSE in the class of all functions are not satisfied the forecasts will be best linear forecasts under general assumptions. These appealing theoretical features of VARMA models make them attractive tools for forecasting.

Special attention has been paid to forecasting linearly transformed and aggregated processes. Both contemporaneous as well as temporal aggregation have been studied. It was found that generally forecasting the disaggregated process and aggregating the forecasts is more efficient than forecasting the aggregate directly and thereby ignoring the disaggregate information. Moreover, for contemporaneous aggregation, forecasting the individual components with univariate methods and aggregating these forecasts was compared to the other two possible forecasts. Forecasting univariate components separately may lead to better forecasts than forecasting the aggregate directly. It will be inferior to aggregating forecasts of the fully disaggregated process, however. These results hold if the DGPs are known.

In practice the relevant model for forecasting a particular set of time series will not be known, however, and it is necessary to use sample information to specify and estimate a suitable candidate model from the VARMA class. We have discussed estimation methods and specification algorithms which are suitable at this stage of the forecasting process for stationary as well as integrated processes. The nonuniqueness or lack of identification of general VARMA representations turned out to be a major problem at this stage. We have focused on the echelon form as one possible parameterization that allows to overcome the identification problem. The echelon form has the advantage of providing a relatively parsimonious VARMA representation in many cases. Moreover, it can be extended conveniently to cointegrated processes by including an EC term. It is described by a set of integers called Kronecker indices. Statistical procedures were presented for specifying these quantities. We have also presented methods for determining the cointegrating rank of a process if some or all of the variables are integrated. This can be done by applying standard cointegrating rank tests for pure VAR processes because these tests maintain their usual asymptotic properties even if they are performed on the basis of an approximating VAR process rather than the true DGP. We have also briefly discussed issues related to checking the adequacy of a particular model. Overall a coherent strategy for specifying, estimating and checking VARMA models has been presented. Finally, the implications of using estimated rather than known processes for forecasting have been discussed.

If estimation and specification uncertainty are taken into account it turns out that forecasts based on a disaggregated multiple time series may not be better and may in fact be inferior to forecasting an aggregate directly. This situation is in particular likely to occur if the DGPs are such that efficiency gains from disaggregation do not exist or are small and the aggregated process has a simple structure which can be captured with a parsimonious model.

Clearly, VARMA models also have some drawbacks as forecasting tools. First of all, linear forecasts may not always be the best choice [see Teräsvirta (2006) in this Handbook, Chapter 8, for a discussion of forecasting with nonlinear models]. Second, adding more variables in a system does not necessarily increase the forecast precision. Higher dimensional systems are typically more difficult to specify than smaller ones. Thus, considering as many series as possible in one system is clearly not a good strategy unless some form of aggregation of the information in the series is used. The increase in estimation and specification uncertainty may offset the advantages of using additional information. VARMA models appear to be most useful for analyzing small sets of time series. Choosing the best set of variables for a particular forecasting exercise may not be an easy task. In conclusion, although VARMA models are an important forecasting tool and automatic procedures exist for most steps in the modelling, estimation and forecasting task, the actual success may still depend on the skills of the user of these tools in identifying a suitable set of time series to be analyzed in one system. Also, of course, the forecaster has to decide whether VARMA models are suitable in a given situation or some other model class should be considered.

Acknowledgements

I thank Kirstin Hubrich and two anonymous readers for helpful comments on an earlier draft of this chapter.

References

Abraham, B. (1982). "Temporal aggregation and time series". International Statistical Review 50, 285–291.

Ahn, S.K., Reinsel, G.C. (1990). "Estimation of partially nonstationary multivariate autoregressive models". Journal of the American Statistical Association 85, 813–823.

Akaike, H. (1973). "Information theory and an extension of the maximum likelihood principle". In: Petrov, B., Csáki, F. (Eds.), 2nd International Symposium on Information Theory. Académiai Kiadó, Budapest, pp. 267–281.

Akaike, H. (1974). "Stochastic theory of minimal realization". IEEE Transactions on Automatic Control AC-19, 667–674.

Akaike, H. (1976). "Canonical correlation analysis of time series and the use of an information criterion". In: Mehra, R.K., Lainiotis, D.G. (Eds.), Systems Identification: Advances and Case Studies. Academic Press, New York, pp. 27–96.

Amemiya, T., Wu, R.Y. (1972). "The effect of aggregation on prediction in the autoregressive model". Journal of the American Statistical Association 67, 628–632.

Aoki, M. (1987). State Space Modeling of Time Series. Springer-Verlag, Berlin.

Baillie, R.T. (1981). "Prediction from the dynamic simultaneous equation model with vector autoregressive errors". Econometrica 49, 1331–1337.

Bartel, H., Lütkepohl, H. (1998). "Estimating the Kronecker indices of cointegrated echelon form VARMA models". Econometrics Journal 1, C76–C99.

Basu, A.K., Sen Roy, S. (1987). "On asymptotic prediction problems for multivariate autoregressive models in the unstable nonexplosive case". Calcutta Statistical Association Bulletin 36, 29–37.

Bauer, D., Wagner, M. (2002). "Estimating cointegrated systems using subspace algorithms". Journal of Econometrics 111, 47–84.

Bauer, D., Wagner, M. (2003). "A canonical form for unit root processes in the state space framework". Diskussionsschriften 03-12, Universität Bern.

Bhansali, R.J. (1978). "Linear prediction by autoregressive model fitting in the time domain". Annals of Statistics 6, 224–231.

Bhansali, R.J. (2002). "Multi-step forecasting". In: Clements, M.P., Hendry, D.F. (Eds.), A Companion to Economic Forecasting. Blackwell, Oxford, pp. 206–221.

Box, G.E.P., Jenkins, G.M. (1976). Time Series Analysis: Forecasting and Control. Holden-Day, San Francisco.

Breitung, J., Swanson, N.R. (2002). "Temporal aggregation and spurious instantaneous causality in multiple time series models". Journal of Time Series Analysis 23, 651–665.

Brewer, K.R.W. (1973). "Some consequences of temporal aggregation and systematic sampling for ARMA and ARMAX models". Journal of Econometrics 1, 133–154.

Brockwell, P.J., Davis, R.A. (1987). Time Series: Theory and Methods. Springer-Verlag, New York.

Claessen, H. (1995). Spezifikation und Schätzung von VARMA-Prozessen unter besonderer Berücksichtigung der Echelon Form. Verlag Joseph Eul, Bergisch-Gladbach.

Clements, M.P., Hendry, D.F. (1998). Forecasting Economic Time Series. Cambridge University Press, Cambridge.

Clements, M.P., Hendry, D.F. (1999). Forecasting Non-stationary Economic Time Series. MIT Press, Cambridge, MA.

Clements, M.P., Taylor, N. (2001). "Bootstrap prediction intervals for autoregressive models". International Journal of Forecasting 17, 247–267.

Cooper, D.M., Wood, E.F. (1982). "Identifying multivariate time series models". Journal of Time Series Analysis 3, 153–164.

Doornik, J.A., Hendry, D.F. (1997). Modelling Dynamic Systems Using PcFiml 9.0 for Windows. International Thomson Business Press, London.

Dufour, J.-M. (1985). "Unbiasedness of predictions from estimated vector autoregressions". Econometric Theory 1, 387–402.

Dunsmuir, W.T.M., Hannan, E.J. (1976). "Vector linear time series models". Advances in Applied Probability 8, 339–364.

Engle, R.F., Granger, C.W.J. (1987). "Cointegration and error correction: Representation, estimation and testing". Econometrica 55, 251–276.

Engle, R.F., Yoo, B.S. (1987). "Forecasting and testing in cointegrated systems". Journal of Econometrics 35, 143–159.

Findley, D.F. (1986). "On bootstrap estimates of forecast mean square errors for autoregressive processes". In: Allen, D.M. (Ed.), Computer Science and Statistics: The Interface. North-Holland, Amsterdam, pp. 11–17.

Granger, C.W.J. (1969a). "Investigating causal relations by econometric models and cross-spectral methods". Econometrica 37, 424–438.

Granger, C.W.J. (1969b). "Prediction with a generalized cost of error function". Operations Research Quarterly 20, 199–207.

Granger, C.W.J. (1981). "Some properties of time series data and their use in econometric model specification". Journal of Econometrics 16, 121–130.

Granger, C.W.J., Newbold, P. (1977). Forecasting Economic Time Series. Academic Press, New York.

Gregoir, S. (1999a). "Multivariate time series with various hidden unit roots, part I: Integral operator algebra and representation theorem". Econometric Theory 15, 435–468.

Gregoir, S. (1999b). "Multivariate time series with various hidden unit roots, part II: Estimation and test". Econometric Theory 15, 469–518.

Gregoir, S., Laroque, G. (1994). "Polynomial cointegration: Estimation and test". Journal of Econometrics 63, 183–214.

Grigoletto, M. (1998). "Bootstrap prediction intervals for autoregressions: Some alternatives". International Journal of Forecasting 14, 447–456.

Haldrup, N. (1998). "An econometric analysis of I(2) variables". Journal of Economic Surveys 12, 595–650.

Hannan, E.J. (1970). Multiple Time Series. Wiley, New York.

Hannan, E.J. (1976). "The identification and parameterization of ARMAX and state space forms". Econometrica 44, 713–723.

Hannan, E.J. (1979). "The statistical theory of linear systems". In: Krishnaiah, P.R. (Ed.), Developments in Statistics. Academic Press, New York, pp. 83–121.

Hannan, E.J. (1981). "Estimating the dimension of a linear system". Journal of Multivariate Analysis 11, 459–473.

Hannan, E.J., Deistler, M. (1988). The Statistical Theory of Linear Systems. Wiley, New York.

Hannan, E.J., Kavalieris, L. (1984). "Multivariate linear time series models". Advances in Applied Probability 16, 492–561.

Harvey, A. (2006). "Forecasting with unobserved components time series models". In: Elliott, G., Granger, C.W.J., Timmermann, A. (Eds.), Handbook of Economic Forecasting. Elsevier, Amsterdam, pp. 327–412. Chapter 7 in this volume.

Hendry, D.F., Hubrich, K. (2005). "Forecasting aggregates by disaggregates". Discussion paper, European Central Bank.

Hillmer, S.C., Tiao, G.C. (1979). "Likelihood function of stationary multiple autoregressive moving average models". Journal of the American Statistical Association 74, 652–660.

Hogue, A., Magnus, J., Pesaran, B. (1988). "The exact multi-period mean-square forecast error for the first-order autoregressive model". Journal of Econometrics 39, 327–346.

Hubrich, K. (2005). "Forecasting euro area inflation: Does aggregating forecasts by HICP component improve forecast accuracy?". International Journal of Forecasting 21, 119–136.

Hubrich, K., Lütkepohl, H., Saikkonen, P. (2001). "A review of systems cointegration tests". Econometric Reviews 20, 247–318.

Jenkins, G.M., Alavi, A.S. (1981). "Some aspects of modelling and forecasting multivariate time series". Journal of Time Series Analysis 2, 1–47.

Johansen, S. (1995a). Likelihood-Based Inference in Cointegrated Vector Autoregressive Models. Oxford University Press, Oxford.

Johansen, S. (1995b). "A statistical analysis of cointegration for I(2) variables". Econometric Theory 11, 25–59.

Johansen, S. (1997). "Likelihood analysis of the I(2) model". Scandinavian Journal of Statistics 24, 433–462.

Johansen, S., Schaumburg, E. (1999). "Likelihood analysis of seasonal cointegration". Journal of Econometrics 88, 301–339.

Kabaila, P. (1993). "On bootstrap predictive inference for autoregressive processes". Journal of Time Series Analysis 14, 473–484.

Kapetanios, G. (2003). "A note on an iterative least-squares estimation method for ARMA and VARMA models". Economics Letters 79, 305–312.

Kemp, G.C.R. (1999). "The behavior of forecast errors from a nearly integrated AR(1) model as both sample size and forecast horizon become large". Econometric Theory 15, 238–256.

Kim, J.H. (1999). "Asymptotic and bootstrap prediction regions for vector autoregression". International Journal of Forecasting 15, 393–403.

Kim, T.H., Leybourne, S.J., Newbold, P. (2004). "Asymptotic mean-squared forecast error when an autoregression with linear trend is fitted to data generated by an I(0) or I(1) process". Journal of Time Series Analysis 25, 583–602.

Kohn, R. (1982). "When is an aggregate of a time series efficiently forecast by its past?". Journal of Econometrics 18, 337–349.

Koreisha, S.G., Pukkila, T.M. (1987). "Identification of nonzero elements in the polynomial matrices of mixed VARMA processes". Journal of the Royal Statistical Society, Series B 49, 112–126.

Lewis, R., Reinsel, G.C. (1985). "Prediction of multivariate time series by autoregressive model fitting". Journal of Multivariate Analysis 16, 393–411.

Lütkepohl, H. (1984). "Linear transformations of vector ARMA processes". Journal of Econometrics 26, 283–293.

Lütkepohl, H. (1985a). "Comparison of criteria for estimating the order of a vector autoregressive process". Journal of Time Series Analysis 6, 35–52;
"Correction". Journal of Time Series Analysis 8 (1987) 373.

Lütkepohl, H. (1985b). "The joint asymptotic distribution of multistep prediction errors of estimated vector autoregressions". Economics Letters 17, 103–106.

Lütkepohl, H. (1986a). "Forecasting temporally aggregated vector ARMA processes". Journal of Forecasting 5, 85–95.

Lütkepohl, H. (1986b). "Forecasting vector ARMA processes with systematically missing observations". Journal of Business & Economic Statistics 4, 375–390.

Lütkepohl, H. (1987). Forecasting Aggregated Vector ARMA Processes. Springer-Verlag, Berlin.

Lütkepohl, H. (1996). Handbook of Matrices. Wiley, Chichester.
Lütkepohl, H. (2002). "Forecasting cointegrated VARMA processes". In: Clements, M.P., Hendry, D.F. (Eds.), A Companion to Economic Forecasting. Blackwell, Oxford, pp. 179–205.
Lütkepohl, H. (2005). New Introduction to Multiple Time Series Analysis. Springer-Verlag, Berlin.
Lütkepohl, H., Claessen, H. (1997). "Analysis of cointegrated VARMA processes". Journal of Econometrics 80, 223–239.
Lütkepohl, H., Poskitt, D.S. (1996). "Specification of echelon form VARMA models". Journal of Business & Economic Statistics 14, 69–79.
Lütkepohl, H., Saikkonen, P. (1999). "Order selection in testing for the cointegrating rank of a VAR process". In: Engle, R.F., White, H. (Eds.), Cointegration, Causality, and Forecasting. A Festschrift in Honour of Clive W.J. Granger. Oxford University Press, Oxford, pp. 168–199.
Marcellino, M. (1999). "Some consequences of temporal aggregation in empirical analysis". Journal of Business & Economic Statistics 17, 129–136.
Marcellino, M., Stock, J.H., Watson, M.W. (2003). "Macroeconomic forecasting in the Euro area: Country specific versus area-wide information". European Economic Review 47, 1–18.
Masarotto, G. (1990). "Bootstrap prediction intervals for autoregressions". International Journal of Forecasting 6, 229–239.
Meese, R., Geweke, J. (1984). "A comparison of autoregressive univariate forecasting procedures for macroeconomic time series". Journal of Business & Economic Statistics 2, 191–200.
Newbold, P., Granger, C.W.J. (1974). "Experience with forecasting univariate time series and combination of forecasts". Journal of the Royal Statistical Society, Series A 137, 131–146.
Nicholls, D.F., Hall, A.D. (1979). "The exact likelihood of multivariate autoregressive moving average models". Biometrika 66, 259–264.
Nsiri, S., Roy, R. (1992). "On the identification of ARMA echelon-form models". Canadian Journal of Statistics 20, 369–386.
Pascual, L., Romo, J., Ruiz, E. (2004). "Bootstrap predictive inference for ARIMA processes". Journal of Time Series Analysis 25, 449–465.
Pesaran, M.H., Timmermann, A. (2005). "Small sample properties of forecasts from autoregressive models under structural breaks". Journal of Econometrics 129, 183–217.
Poskitt, D.S. (1992). "Identification of echelon canonical forms for vector linear processes using least squares". Annals of Statistics 20, 196–215.
Poskitt, D.S. (2003). "On the specification of cointegrated autoregressive moving-average forecasting systems". International Journal of Forecasting 19, 503–519.
Poskitt, D.S., Lütkepohl, H. (1995). "Consistent specification of cointegrated autoregressive moving average systems". Discussion paper 54, SFB 373, Humboldt-Universität zu Berlin.
Quenouille, M.H. (1957). The Analysis of Multiple Time-Series. Griffin, London.
Reinsel, G.C. (1993). Elements of Multivariate Time Series Analysis. Springer-Verlag, New York.
Reinsel, G.C., Ahn, S.K. (1992). "Vector autoregressive models with unit roots and reduced rank structure: Estimation, likelihood ratio test, and forecasting". Journal of Time Series Analysis 13, 353–375.
Reinsel, G.C., Lewis, A.L. (1987). "Prediction mean square error for non-stationary multivariate time series using estimated parameters". Economics Letters 24, 57–61.
Saikkonen, P. (1992). "Estimation and testing of cointegrated systems by an autoregressive approximation". Econometric Theory 8, 1–27.
Saikkonen, P., Lütkepohl, H. (1996). "Infinite order cointegrated vector autoregressive processes: Estimation and inference". Econometric Theory 12, 814–844.
Sampson, M. (1991). "The effect of parameter uncertainty on forecast variances and confidence intervals for unit root and trend stationary time-series models". Journal of Applied Econometrics 6, 67–76.
Schorfheide, F. (2005). "VAR forecasting under misspecification". Journal of Econometrics 128, 99–136.
Schwarz, G. (1978). "Estimating the dimension of a model". Annals of Statistics 6, 461–464.
Sims, C.A. (1980). "Macroeconomics and reality". Econometrica 48, 1–48.
Stock, J.H. (1996). "VAR, error correction and pretest forecasts at long horizons". Oxford Bulletin of Economics and Statistics 58, 685–701.

Stock, J.H., Watson, M.W. (1999). "A comparison of linear and nonlinear univariate models for forecasting macroeconomic time series". In: Engle, R.F., White, H. (Eds.), Cointegration, Causality, and Forecasting. A Festschrift in Honour of Clive W.J. Granger. Oxford University Press, Oxford, pp. 1–44.

Stram, D.O., Wei, W.W.S. (1986). "Temporal aggregation in the ARIMA process". Journal of Time Series Analysis 7, 279–292.

Telser, L.G. (1967). "Discrete samples and moving sums in stationary stochastic processes". Journal of the American Statistical Association 62, 484–499.

Teräsvirta, T. (2006). "Forecasting economic variables with nonlinear models". In: Elliott, G., Granger, C.W.J., Timmermann, A. (Eds.), Handbook of Economic Forecasting. Elsevier, Amsterdam, pp. 413–457. Chapter 8 in this volume.

Tiao, G.C. (1972). "Asymptotic behaviour of temporal aggregates of time series". Biometrika 59, 525–531.

Tiao, G.C., Box, G.E.P. (1981). "Modeling multiple time series with applications". Journal of the American Statistical Association 76, 802–816.

Tiao, G.C., Guttman, I. (1980). "Forecasting contemporal aggregates of multiple time series". Journal of Econometrics 12, 219–230.

Tiao, G.C., Tsay, R.S. (1983). "Multiple time series modeling and extended sample cross-correlations". Journal of Business & Economic Statistics 1, 43–56.

Tiao, G.C., Tsay, R.S. (1989). "Model specification in multivariate time series (with discussion)". Journal of the Royal Statistical Society, Series B 51, 157–213.

Tsay, R.S. (1989a). "Identifying multivariate time series models". Journal of Time Series Analysis 10, 357–372.

Tsay, R.S. (1989b). "Parsimonious parameterization of vector autoregressive moving average models". Journal of Business & Economic Statistics 7, 327–341.

Tunnicliffe Wilson, G. (1973). "Estimation of parameters in multivariate time series models". Journal of the Royal Statistical Society, Series B 35, 76–85.

Ullah, A. (2004). Finite Sample Econometrics. Oxford University Press, Oxford.

van Overschee, P., DeMoor, B. (1994). "N4sid: Subspace algorithms for the identification of combined deterministic-stochastic systems". Automatica 30, 75–93.

Wallis, K.F. (1977). "Multiple time series analysis and the final form of econometric models". Econometrica 45, 1481–1497.

Wei, W.W.S. (1978). "Some consequences of temporal aggregation in seasonal time series models". In: Zellner, A. (Ed.), Seasonal Analysis of Economic Time Series. U.S. Department of Commerce, Bureau of the Census, pp. 433–444.

Wei, W.W.S. (1990). Time Series Analysis: Univariate and Multivariate Methods. Addison-Wesley, Redwood City, CA.

Weiss, A.A. (1984). "Systematic sampling and temporal aggregation in time series models". Journal of Econometrics 26, 271–281.

Yamamoto, T. (1980). "On the treatment of autocorrelated errors in the multiperiod prediction of dynamic simultaneous equation models". International Economic Review 21, 735–748.

Yap, S.F., Reinsel, G.C. (1995). "Estimation and testing for unit roots in a partially nonstationary vector autoregressive moving average model". Journal of the American Statistical Association 90, 253–267.

Zellner, A., Palm, F. (1974). "Time series analysis and simultaneous equation econometric models". Journal of Econometrics 2, 17–54.

Chapter 7

FORECASTING WITH UNOBSERVED COMPONENTS TIME SERIES MODELS

ANDREW HARVEY

Faculty of Economics, University of Cambridge

Contents

Handbook of Economic Forecasting, Volume 1
Edited by Graham Elliott, Clive W.J. Granger and Allan Timmermann

DOI: 10.1016/S1574-0706(05)01007-4

Abstract

Structural time series models are formulated in terms of components, such as trends, seasonals and cycles, that have a direct interpretation. As well as providing a framework for time series decomposition by signal extraction, they can be used for forecasting and for 'nowcasting'. The structural interpretation allows extensions to classes of models that are able to deal with various issues in multivariate series and to cope with non-Gaussian observations and nonlinear models. The statistical treatment is by the state space form and hence data irregularities such as missing observations are easily handled. Continuous time models offer further flexibility in that they can handle irregular spacing. The paper compares the forecasting performance of structural time series models with ARIMA and autoregressive models. Results are presented showing how observations in linear state space models are implicitly weighted in making forecasts and hence how autoregressive and vector error correction representations can be obtained. The use of an auxiliary series in forecasting and nowcasting is discussed. A final section compares stochastic volatility models with GARCH.

Keywords

cycles, continuous time, Kalman filter, non-Gaussian models, state space, stochastic trend, stochastic volatility

JEL classification: C22, C32

1. Introduction

The fundamental reason for building a time series model for forecasting is that it provides a way of weighting the data that is determined by the properties of the time series. Structural time series models (STMs) are formulated in terms of unobserved components, such as trends and cycles, that have a direct interpretation. Thus they are designed to focus on the salient features of the series and to project these into the future. They also provide a way of weighting the observations for signal extraction, so providing a description of the series. This chapter concentrates on prediction, though signal extraction at the end of the period – that is filtering – comes within our remit under the heading of 'nowcasting'.

In an autoregression the past observations, up to a given lag, receive a weight obtained by minimizing the sum of squares of one step ahead prediction errors. As such they form a good baseline for comparing models in terms of one step ahead forecasting performance. They can be applied directly to nonstationary time series, though imposing unit roots by differencing may be desirable to force the eventual forecast function to be a polynomial; see Chapter 11 by Elliott in this Handbook. The motivation for extending the class of models to allow moving average terms is one of parsimony. Long, indeed infinite, lags can be captured by a small number of parameters. The book by Box and Jenkins (1976) describes a model selection strategy for this class of autoregressive-integrated-moving average (ARIMA) processes. Linear STMs have reduced forms belonging to the ARIMA class. The issue for forecasting is whether the implicit restrictions they place on the ARIMA models help forecasting performance by ruling out models that have unattractive properties.

1.1. Historical background

Structural time series models developed from *ad hoc* forecasting procedures,[1] the most basic of which is the exponentially weighted moving average (EWMA). The EWMA was generalized by Holt (1957) and Winters (1960). They introduced a slope component into the forecast function and allowed for seasonal effects. A somewhat different approach to generalizing the EWMA was taken by Brown (1963), who set up forecasting procedures in a regression framework and adopted the method of discounted least squares. These methods became very popular with practitioners and are still widely used as they are simple and transparent.

Muth (1960) was the first to provide a rationale for the EWMA in terms of a properly specified statistical model, namely a random walk plus noise. Nerlove and Wage (1964) extended the model to include a slope term. These are the simplest examples of structural time series models. However, the technology of the sixties was such that further development along these lines was not pursued at the time. It was some time before statisticians became acquainted with the paper in the engineering literature by Schweppe

[1] The procedures are ad hoc in that they are not based on a statistical model.

(1965) which showed how a likelihood function could be evaluated from the Kalman filter *via* the prediction error decomposition. More significantly, even if this result had been known, it could not have been properly exploited because of the lack of computing power.

The most influential work on time series forecasting in the sixties was carried out by Box and Jenkins (1976). Rather than rationalizing the EWMA by a structural model as Muth had done, Box and Jenkins observed that it could also be justified by a model in which the first differences of the variable followed a first-order moving average process. Similarly they noted that a rationale for the local linear trend extension proposed by Holt was given by a model in which second differences followed a second-order moving average process. A synthesis with the theory of stationary stochastic processes then led to the formulation of the class of ARIMA models, and the development of a model selection strategy. The estimation of ARIMA models proved to be a viable proposition at this time provided it was based on an approximate, rather than the exact, likelihood function.

Harrison and Stevens (1976) continued the work within the framework of structural time series models and were able to make considerable progress by exploiting the Kalman filter. Their response to the problems posed by parameter estimation was to adopt a Bayesian approach in which knowledge of certain key parameters was assumed. This led them to consider a further class of models in which the process generating the data switches between a finite number of regimes. This line of research has proved to be somewhat tangential to the main developments in the subject, although it is an important precursor to the econometric literature on regime switching.

Although the ARIMA approach to time series forecasting dominated the statistical literature in the 1970's and early 1980's, the structural approach was prevalent in control engineering. This was partly because of the engineers' familiarity with the Kalman filter which has been a fundamental algorithm in control engineering since its appearance in Kalman (1960). However, in a typical engineering situation there are fewer parameters to estimate and there may be a very large number of observations. The work carried out in engineering therefore tended to place less emphasis on maximum likelihood estimation and the development of a model selection methodology.

The potential of the Kalman filter for dealing with econometric and statistical problems began to be exploited in the 1970's, an early example being the work by Rosenberg (1973) on time-varying parameters. The subsequent development of a structural time series methodology began in the 1980's; see the books by Young (1984), Harvey (1989), West and Harrison (1989), Jones (1993) and Kitagawa and Gersch (1996). The book by Nerlove, Grether and Carvalho (1979) was an important precursor, although the authors did not use the Kalman filter to handle the unobserved components models that they fitted to various data sets.

The work carried out in the 1980s, and implemented in the STAMP package of Koopman et al. (2000), concentrated primarily on linear models. In the 1990's, the rapid developments in computing power led to significant advances in non-Gaussian and nonlinear modelling. Furthermore, as Durbin and Koopman (2000) together because both draw on computer intensive techniques such as Markov chain Monte Carlo and importance sampling. The availability of these methods tends to favour the use of unobserved component models because of their flexibility in being able to capture the features highlighted by the theory associated with the subject matter.

1.2. Forecasting performance

Few studies deal explicitly with the matter of comparing the forecasting performance of STMs with other time series methods over a wide range of data sets. A notable exception is Andrews (1994). In his abstract, he concludes: "The structural approach appears to perform quite well on annual, quarterly, and monthly data, especially for long forecasting horizons and seasonal data. Of the more complex forecasting methods, structural models appear to be the most accurate." There are also a number of illustrations in Harvey (1989) and Harvey and Todd (1983). However, the most compelling evidence is indirect and comes from the results of the M3 forecasting competitions; the most recent of these is reported in Makridakis and Hibon (2000). They conclude (on p. 460) as follows: "This competition has confirmed the original conclusions of M-competition using a new and much enlarged data set. In addition, it has demonstrated, once more, that simple methods developed by practicing forecasters (e.g., Brown's Simple and Gardner's Dampen (sic) Trend Exponential Smoothing) do as well, or in many cases better, than statistically sophisticated ones like ARIMA and ARARMA models." Although Andrews seems to class structural models as complex, the fact is that they include most of the simple methods as special cases. The apparent complexity comes about because estimation is (explicitly) done by maximum likelihood and diagnostic checks are performed.

Although the links between exponential smoothing methods and STMs have been known for a long time, and were stressed in Harvey (1984, 1989), this point has not always been appreciated in the forecasting literature. Section 2 of this chapter sets out the STMs that provide the theoretical underpinning for EWMA, double exponential smoothing and damped trend exponential smoothing. The importance of understanding the statistical basis of forecasting procedures is reinforced by a careful look at the so-called 'theta method', a new technique, introduced recently by Assimakopoulos and Nikolopoulos (2000). The theta method did rather well in the last M3 competition, with Makridakis and Hibon (2000, p. 460) concluding that: "Although this method seems simple to use ... and is not based on strong statistical theory, it performs remarkably well across different types of series, forecasting horizons and accuracy measures". However, Hyndman and Billah (2003) show that the underlying model is just a random walk with drift plus noise. Hence it is easily handled by a program such as STAMP and there is no need to delve into the details of a method the description of which is, in the opinion of Hyndman and Billah (2003, p. 287), "complicated, potentially confusing and involves several pages of algebra".

1.3. State space and beyond

The state space form (SSF) allows a general treatment of virtually any linear time series models through the general algorithms of the Kalman filter and the associated smoother. Furthermore, it permits the likelihood function to be computed. Section 6 reviews the SSF and presents some results that may not be well known but are relevant for forecasting. In particular, it gives the ARIMA and autoregressive (AR) representations of models in SSF. For multivariate series this leads to a method of computing the vector error correction model (VECM) representation of an unobserved component model with common trends. VECMs were developed by Johansen (1995) and are described in the chapter by Lutkepohl.

The most striking benefits of the structural approach to time series modelling only become apparent when we start to consider more complex problems. The direct interpretation of the components allows parsimonious multivariate models to be set up and considerable insight can be obtained into the value of, for example, using auxiliary series to improve the efficiency of forecasting a target series. Furthermore, the SSF offers enormous flexibility with regard to dealing with data irregularities, such as missing observations and observations at mixed frequencies. The study by Harvey and Chung (2000) on the measurement of British unemployment provides a nice illustration of how STMs are able to deal with forecasting and nowcasting when the series are subject to data irregularities. The challenge is how to obtain timely estimates of the underlying change in unemployment. Estimates of the numbers of unemployed according to the ILO definition have been published on a quarterly basis since the spring of 1992. From 1984 to 1991 estimates were published for the spring quarter only. The estimates are obtained from the Labour Force Survey (LFS), which consists of a rotating sample of approximately 60,000 households. Another measure of unemployment, based on administrative sources, is the number of people claiming unemployment benefit. This measure, known as the claimant count (CC), is available monthly, with very little delay and is an exact figure. It does not provide a measure corresponding to the ILO definition, but as Figure 1 shows it moves roughly in the same way as the LFS figure. There are thus two issues to be addressed. The first is how to extract the best estimate of the underlying monthly change in a series which is subject to sampling error and which may not have been recorded every month. The second is how to use a related series to improve this estimate. These two issues are of general importance, for example in the measurement of the underlying rate of inflation or the way in which monthly figures on industrial production might be used to produce more timely estimates of national income. The STMs constructed by Harvey and Chung (2000) follow Pfeffermann (1991) in making use of the SSF to handle the rather complicated error structure coming from the rotating sample. Using CC as an auxiliary series halves the RMSE of the estimator of the underlying change in unemployment.

STMs can also be formulated in continuous time. This has a number of advantages, one of which is to allow irregularly spaced observations to be handled. The SSF is easily adapted to cope with this situation. Continuous time modelling of flow variables

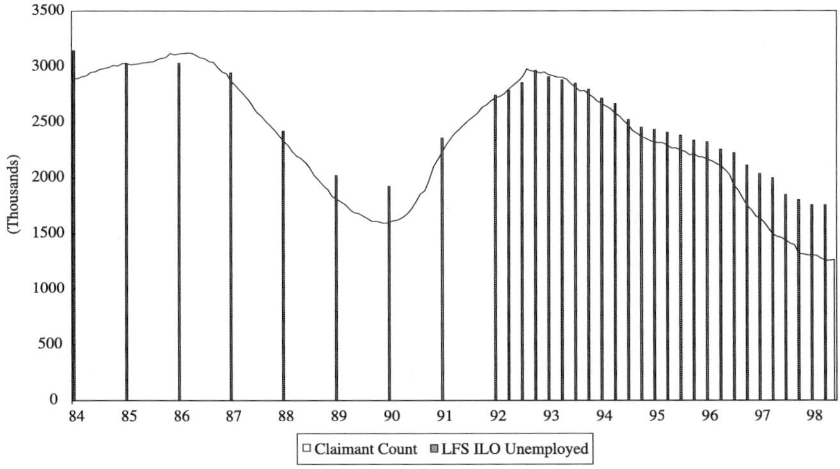

Figure 1. Annual and quarterly observations from the British labour force survey and the monthly claimant count.

offers the possibility of certain extensions such as making cumulative predictions over a variable lead time.

Some of the most exciting recent developments in time series have been in nonlinear and non-Gaussian models. The final part of this survey provides an introduction to some of the models that can now be handled. Most of the emphasis is on what can be achieved by computer intensive methods. For example, it is possible to fit STMs with heavy-tailed distributions on the disturbances, thereby making them robust with respect to outliers and structural breaks. Similarly, non-Gaussian models with stochastic components can be set up. However, for modelling an evolving mean of a distribution for count data or qualitative observations, it is interesting that the use of conjugate filters leads to simple forecasting procedures based around the EWMA.

2. Structural time series models

The simplest structural time series models are made up of a *stochastic trend* component, μ_t, and a random irregular term. The stochastic trend evolves over time and the practical implication of this is that past observations are discounted when forecasts are made. Other components may be added. In particular a cycle is often appropriate for economic data. Again this is stochastic, thereby giving the flexibility needed to capture the type of movements that occur in practice. The statistical formulations of trends and cycles are described in the subsections below. A convergence component is also considered and it is shown how the model may be extended to include explanatory variables and interventions. Seasonality is discussed in a later section. The general statistical treatment is by the state space form described in Section 6.

2.1. Exponential smoothing

Suppose that we wish to estimate the current level of a series of observations. The simplest way to do this is to use the sample mean. However, if the purpose of estimating the level is to use this as the basis for forecasting future observations, it is more appealing to put more weight on the most recent observations. Thus the estimate of the *current* level of the series is taken to be

$$m_T = \sum_{j=0}^{T-1} w_j y_{T-j} \tag{1}$$

where the w_j's are a set of weights that sum to unity. This estimate is then taken to be the forecast of future observations, that is

$$\widehat{y}_{T+l|T} = m_T, \quad l = 1, 2, \ldots \tag{2}$$

so the *forecast function* is a horizontal straight line. One way of putting more weight on the most recent observations is to let the weights decline exponentially. Thus,

$$m_T = \lambda \sum_{j=0}^{T-1} (1-\lambda)^j y_{T-j} \tag{3}$$

where λ is a *smoothing constant* in the range $0 < \lambda \leqslant 1$. (The weights sum to unity in the limit as $T \to \infty$.) The attraction of exponential weighting is that estimates can be updated by a simple recursion. If expression (3) is defined for any value of t from $t = 1$ to T, it can be split into two parts to give

$$m_t = (1-\lambda)m_{t-1} + \lambda y_t, \quad t = 1, \ldots, T \tag{4}$$

with $m_0 = 0$. Since m_t is the forecast of y_{t+1}, the recursion is often written with $\widehat{y}_{t+1|t}$ replacing m_t so that next period's forecast is a weighted average of the current observation and the forecast of the current observation made in the previous time period. This may be re-arranged to give

$$\widehat{y}_{t+1|t} = \widehat{y}_{t|t-1} + \lambda \widehat{v}_t, \quad t = 1, \ldots, T$$

where $\widehat{v}_t = y_t - \widehat{y}_{t|t-1}$ is the one-step-ahead prediction error and $\widehat{y}_{1|0} = 0$.

This method of constructing and updating forecasts of a level is known as an *exponentially weighted moving average* (EWMA) or *simple exponential smoothing*. The *smoothing constant*, λ, can be chosen so as to minimize the sum of squares of the prediction errors, that is, $S(\lambda) = \sum \widehat{v}_t^2$.

The EWMA is also obtained if we take as our starting point the idea that we want to form an estimate of the mean by minimizing a discounted sum of squares. Thus m_T is chosen by minimizing $S(\omega) = \sum \omega^j (y_{T-j} - m_T)^2$ where $0 < \omega \leqslant 1$. It is easily established that $\omega = 1 - \lambda$.

The forecast function for the EWMA procedure is a horizontal straight line. Bringing a slope, b_T, into the forecast function gives

$$\widehat{y}_{T+l|T} = m_T + b_T l, \quad l = 1, 2, \ldots. \tag{5}$$

Holt (1957) and Winters (1960) introduced an updating scheme for calculating m_T and b_T in which past observations are discounted by means of two smoothing constants, λ_0 and λ_1, in the range $0 < \lambda_0, \lambda_1 < 1$. Let m_{t-1} and b_{t-1} denote the estimates of the level and slope at time $t-1$. The one-step-ahead forecast is then

$$\widehat{y}_{t|t-1} = m_{t-1} + b_{t-1}. \tag{6}$$

As in the EWMA, the updated estimate of the level, m_t, is a linear combination of $\widehat{y}_{t|t-1}$ and y_t. Thus,

$$m_t = \lambda_0 y_t + (1 - \lambda_0)(m_{t-1} + b_{t-1}). \tag{7}$$

From this new estimate of m_t, an estimate of the slope can be constructed as $m_t - m_{t-1}$ and this is combined with the estimate in the previous period to give

$$b_t = \lambda_1(m_t - m_{t-1}) + (1 - \lambda_1)b_{t-1}. \tag{8}$$

Together these equations form Holt's recursions. Following the argument given for the EWMA, starting values may be constructed from the initial observations as $m_2 = y_2$ and $b_2 = y_2 - y_1$. Hence the recursions run from $t = 3$ to $t = T$. The closer λ_0 is to zero, the less past observations are discounted in forming a current estimate of the level. Similarly, the closer λ_1 is to zero, the less they are discounted in estimating the slope. As with the EWMA, these smoothing constants can be fixed *a priori* or estimated by minimizing the sum of squares of forecast errors.

2.2. Local level model

The *local level* model consists of a random walk plus noise,

$$y_t = \mu_t + \varepsilon_t, \quad \varepsilon_t \sim NID(0, \sigma_\varepsilon^2) \tag{9}$$

$$\mu_t = \mu_{t-1} + \eta_t, \quad \eta_t \sim NID(0, \sigma_\eta^2), \quad t = 1, \ldots, T, \tag{10}$$

where the irregular and level disturbances, ε_t and η_t respectively, are mutually independent and the notation $NID(0, \sigma^2)$ denotes normally and independently distributed with mean zero and variance σ^2. When σ_η^2 is zero, the level is constant. The signal–noise ratio, $q = \sigma_\eta^2/\sigma_\varepsilon^2$, plays the key role in determining how observations should be weighted for prediction and signal extraction. The higher is q, the more past observations are discounted in forecasting.

Suppose that we know the mean and variance of μ_{t-1} conditional on observations up to and including time $t-1$, that is $\mu_{t-1} \mid Y_{t-1} \sim N(m_{t-1}, p_{t-1})$. Then, from (10), $\mu_t \mid Y_{t-1} \sim N(m_{t-1}, p_{t-1} + \sigma_\eta^2)$. Furthermore, $y_t \mid Y_{t-1} \sim N(m_{t-1}, p_{t-1} + \sigma_\eta^2 + \sigma_\varepsilon^2)$ while the covariance between μ_t and y_t is $p_{t-1} + \sigma_\eta^2$. The information in y_t can be taken on board by invoking a standard result on the bivariate normal distribution[2] to give the conditional distribution at time t as $\mu_t \mid Y_t \sim N(m_t, p_t)$, where

$$m_t = m_{t-1} + \left[\left(p_{t-1} + \sigma_\eta^2\right)/\left(p_{t-1} + \sigma_\eta^2 + \sigma_\varepsilon^2\right)\right](y_t - m_{t-1}) \tag{11}$$

and

$$p_t = p_{t-1} + \sigma_\eta^2 - \left[\left(p_{t-1} + \sigma_\eta^2\right)^2/\left(p_{t-1} + \sigma_\eta^2 + \sigma_\varepsilon^2\right)\right]. \tag{12}$$

This process can be repeated as new observations become available. As we will see later this is a special case of the Kalman filter. But how should the filter be started? One possibility is to let $m_1 = y_1$, in which case $p_1 = \sigma_\varepsilon^2$. Another possibility is a diffuse prior in which the lack of information at the beginning of the series is reflected in an infinite value of p_0. However, if we set $\mu_0 \sim N(0, \kappa)$, update to get the mean and variance of μ_1 given y_1 and let $\kappa \to \infty$, the result is exactly the same as the first suggestion.

When updating is applied repeatedly, p_t becomes time invariant, that is $p_t \to p$. If we define $p_t^* = \sigma_\varepsilon^{-2} p_t$, divide both sides of (12) by σ_ε^2 and set $p_t^* = p_{t-1}^* = p^*$ we obtain

$$p^* = \left(-q + \sqrt{q^2 + 4q}\right)/2, \quad q \geqslant 0, \tag{13}$$

and it is clear that (11) leads to the EWMA, (4), with[3]

$$\lambda = (p^* + q)/(p^* + q + 1) = \left(-q + \sqrt{q^2 + 4q}\right)/2. \tag{14}$$

The conditional mean, m_t, is the minimum mean square error estimator (MMSE) of μ_t. The conditional variance, p_t, does not depend on the observations and so it is the unconditional MSE of the estimator. Because the updating recursions produce an estimator of μ_t which is a linear combination of the observations, we have adopted the convention of writing it as m_t. If the normality assumption is dropped, m_t is still the minimum mean square error linear estimator (MMSLE).

The conditional distribution of y_{T+l}, $l = 1, 2, \ldots,$ is obtained by writing

$$y_{T+l} = \mu_T + \sum_{j=1}^{l} \eta_{T+j} + \varepsilon_{T+l} = m_T + (\mu_T - m_T) + \sum_{j=1}^{l} \eta_{T+j} + \varepsilon_{T+l}.$$

[2] If y_1 and y_2 are jointly normal with means μ_1 and μ_2 and covariance matrix

$$\begin{bmatrix} \sigma_1^2 & \sigma_{12} \\ \sigma_{12} & \sigma_2^2 \end{bmatrix}$$

the distribution of y_2 conditional on y_1 is normal with mean $\mu_2 + (\sigma_{12}/\sigma_1^2)(y_1 - \mu_1)$ and variance $\sigma_2^2 - \sigma_{12}^2/\sigma_1^2$.

[3] If $q = 0$, then $\lambda = 0$ so there is no updating if we switch to the steady-state filter or use the EWMA.

Thus the *l-step* ahead predictor is the conditional mean, $\widetilde{y}_{T+l|T} = m_T$, and the forecast function is a horizontal straight line which passes through the final estimator of the level. The prediction MSE, the conditional variance of y_{T+l}, is

$$\mathrm{MSE}(\widetilde{y}_{T+l|T}) = p_T + l\sigma_\eta^2 + \sigma_\varepsilon^2 = \sigma_\varepsilon^2(p_T^* + lq + 1), \quad l = 1, 2. \tag{15}$$

This increases linearly with the forecast horizon, with p_T being the price paid for not knowing the starting point, μ_T. If T is reasonably large, then $p_T \simeq p$. Assuming σ_η^2 and σ_ε^2 to be known, a 95% prediction interval for y_{T+l} is given by $\widetilde{y}_{T+l|T} \pm 1.96\sigma_{T+l|T}$ where $\sigma_{T+l|T}^2 = \mathrm{MSE}(\widetilde{y}_{T+l|T}) = \sigma_\varepsilon^2 p_{T+l|T}$. Note that because the conditional distribution of y_{T+l} is available, it is straightforward to compute a point estimate that minimizes the expected loss; see Section 6.7.

When a series has been transformed, the conditional distribution of a future value of the original series, $y_{T+l}^\dagger$, will no longer be normal. If logarithms have been taken, the MMSE is given by the mean of the conditional distribution of $y_{T+l}^\dagger$ which, being lognormal, yields

$$E(y_{T+l}^\dagger \mid Y_T) = \exp(\widetilde{y}_{T+l|T} + 0.5\widetilde{\sigma}_{T+l|T}^2), \quad l = 1, 2, \ldots \tag{16}$$

where $\widetilde{\sigma}_{T+l|T}^2 = \sigma_\varepsilon^2 p_{T+l|T}$ is the conditional variance. A 95% prediction interval for $y_{T+l}^\dagger$, on the other hand, is straightforwardly computed as

$$\exp(\widetilde{y}_{T+l|T} - 1.96\widetilde{\sigma}_{T+l|T}^2) \leqslant y_{T+l}^\dagger \leqslant \exp(\widetilde{y}_{T+l|T} + 1.96\widetilde{\sigma}_{T+l|T}^2).$$

The model also provides the basis for using all the observations in the sample to calculate a MMSE of μ_t at all points in time. If μ_t is near the middle of a large sample then it turns out that

$$m_{t|T} \backsimeq \frac{\lambda}{2-\lambda} \sum_j (1-\lambda)^{|j|} y_{t+j}.$$

Thus there is exponential weighting on either side with a higher q meaning that the closest observations receive a higher weight. This is signal extraction; see Harvey and de Rossi (2005). A full discussion would go beyond the remit of this survey.

As regards estimation of q, the recursions deliver the mean and variance of the one-step ahead predictive distribution of each observation. Hence it is possible to construct a likelihood function in terms of the prediction errors, or *innovations*, $\nu_t = y_t - \widetilde{y}_{t|t-1}$. Once q has been estimated by numerically maximizing the likelihood function, the innovations can be used for diagnostic checking.

2.3. Trends

The *local linear trend* model generalizes the local level by introducing into (9) a stochastic slope, β_t, which itself follows a random walk. Thus,

$$\begin{aligned} \mu_t &= \mu_{t-1} + \beta_{t-1} + \eta_t, & \eta_t &\sim NID(0, \sigma_\eta^2), \\ \beta_t &= \beta_{t-1} + \zeta_t, & \zeta_t &\sim NID(0, \sigma_\zeta^2), \end{aligned} \tag{17}$$

where the irregular, level and slope disturbances, ε_t, η_t and ζ_t, respectively, are mutually independent. If both variances σ_η^2 and σ_ζ^2 are zero, the trend is deterministic. When only σ_ζ^2 is zero, the slope is fixed and the trend reduces to a random walk with drift. Allowing σ_ζ^2 to be positive, but setting σ_η^2 to zero gives an *integrated random walk* trend, which when estimated tends to be relatively smooth. This model is often referred to as the '*smooth trend*' model.

Provided σ_ζ^2 is strictly positive, we can generalize the argument used to obtain the local level filter and show that the recursion is as in (7) and (8) with the smoothing constants defined by

$$q_\eta = \left(\lambda_0^2 + \lambda_0^2\lambda_1 - 2\lambda_0\lambda_1\right)/(1-\lambda_0) \quad \text{and} \quad q_\zeta = \lambda_0^2\lambda_1^2/(1-\lambda_0)$$

where q_η and q_ζ are the relative variances $\sigma_\eta^2/\sigma_\varepsilon^2$ and $\sigma_\zeta^2/\sigma_\varepsilon^2$ respectively; see Harvey (1989, Chapter 4). If q_η is to be non-negative it must be the case that $\lambda_1 \leqslant \lambda_0/(2+\lambda_0)$; equality corresponds to the smooth trend. Double exponential smoothing, suggested by the principle of discounted least squares, is obtained by setting $q_\zeta = (q_\eta/2)^2$.

Given the conditional means of the level and slope, that is m_T and b_T, it is not difficult to see from (17) that the forecast function for MMSE prediction is

$$\widetilde{y}_{T+l|T} = m_T + b_T l, \quad l = 1, 2, \ldots. \tag{18}$$

The *damped trend* model is a modification of (17) in which

$$\beta_t = \rho\beta_{t-1} + \zeta_t, \quad \zeta_t \sim NID\left(0, \sigma_\zeta^2\right), \tag{19}$$

with $0 < \rho \leqslant 1$. As regards forecasting

$$\widetilde{y}_{T+l|T} = m_T + b_T + \rho b_T + \cdots + \rho^{l-1} b_T = m_T + \left[\left(1-\rho^l\right)/(1-\rho)\right]b_T$$

so the final forecast function is a horizontal line at a height of $m_T + b_T/(1-\rho)$. The model could be extended by adding a constant, $\bar{\beta}$, so that

$$\beta_t = (1-\rho)\bar{\beta} + \rho\beta_{t-1} + \zeta_t.$$

2.4. Nowcasting

The forecast function for local linear trend starts from the current, or '*real time*', estimate of the level and increases according to the current estimate of the slope. Reporting these estimates is an example of what is sometimes called '*nowcasting*'. As with forecasting, a UC model provides a way of weighting the observations that is consistent with the properties of the series and enables MSEs to be computed.

The underlying change at the end of a series – the *growth rate* for data in logarithms – is usually the focus of attention since it is the direction in which the series is heading. It is instructive to compare model-based estimators with simple, more direct, measures. The latter have the advantage of transparency, but may entail a loss of information. For example, the first difference at the end of a series, $\Delta y_T = y_T - y_{T-1}$, may be a very poor estimator of underlying change. This is certainly the case if y_t is the logarithm of the monthly price level: its difference is the rate of inflation and this 'headline' figure is known to be very volatile. A more stable measure of change is the rth difference divided by r, that is,

$$b_T^{(r)} = \frac{1}{r}\Delta_r y_T = \frac{y_T - y_{T-r}}{r}. \tag{20}$$

It is not unusual to measure the underlying monthly rate of inflation by subtracting the price level a year ago from the current price level and dividing by twelve. Note that since $\Delta_r y_t = \sum_{j=0}^{r-1} \Delta y_{t-j}$, $b_T^{(r)}$ is the average of the last r first differences.

Figure 2 shows the quarterly rate of inflation in the US together with the filtered estimator obtained from a local level model with q estimated to be 0.22. At the end of the series, in the first quarter of 1983, the underlying level was 0.011, corresponding to an annual rate of 4.4%. The RMSE was one fifth of the level. The headline figure is 3.1%, but at the end of the year it was back up to 4.6%.

The effectiveness of these simple measures of change depends on the properties of the series. If the observations are assumed to come from a local linear trend model with the current slope in the level equation,[4] then

$$\Delta y_t = \beta_t + \eta_t + \Delta\varepsilon_t, \quad t = 2, \ldots, T$$

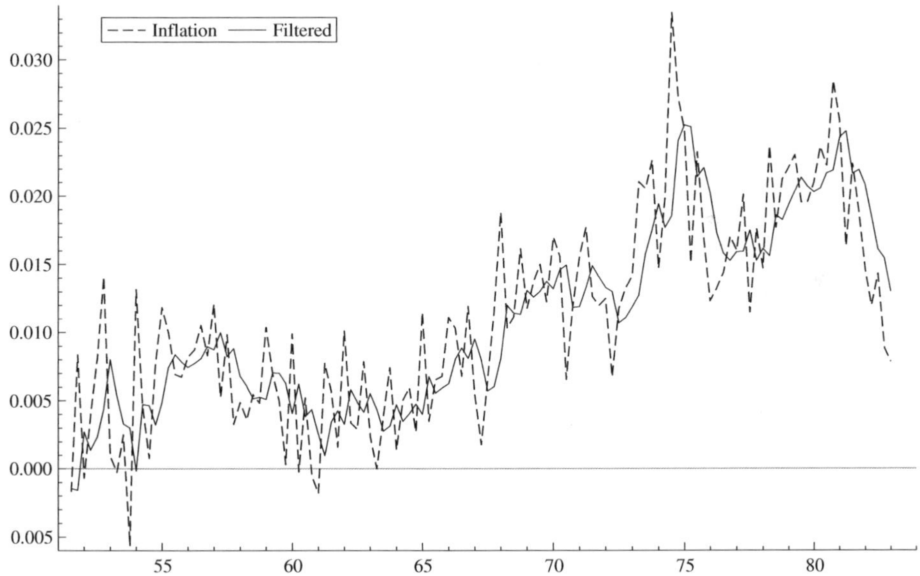

Figure 2. Quarterly rate of inflation in the U.S. with filtered estimates.

[4] Using the current slope, rather than the lagged slope, is for algebraic convenience.

Table 1
RMSEs of rth differences, $b_T^{(r)}$, as estimators of underlying change, relative to RMSE of corresponding estimator from the local linear trend model

r	$q=\sigma_\zeta^2/\sigma_\eta^2$			
	0.1	0.5	1	10
1	1.92	1.41	1.27	1.04
3	1.20	1.10	1.20	2.54
12	1.27	1.92	2.41	6.20
Mean lag	2.70	1	0.62	0.09

and it can be seen that taking Δy_T as an estimator of current underlying change, β_T, implies a MSE of $\sigma_\eta^2 + 2\sigma_\varepsilon^2$. Further manipulation shows that the MSE of $b_T^{(r)}$ as an estimator of β_T is

$$\mathrm{MSE}\big(b_T^{(r)}\big) = \mathrm{Var}\big\{b_T^{(r)} - \beta_T\big\} = \frac{(r-1)(2r-1)}{6r}\sigma_\zeta^2 + \frac{\sigma_\eta^2}{r} + \frac{2\sigma_\varepsilon^2}{r^2}. \tag{21}$$

When $\sigma_\varepsilon^2 = 0$, the irregular component is not present and so the trend is observed directly. In this case the first differences follow a local level model and the filtered estimate $\widetilde{\beta}_T$ is an EWMA of the Δy_t's. In the steady-state, $\mathrm{MSE}(\widetilde{\beta}_T)$ is as in (15) with σ_ε^2 replaced by σ_η^2 and $q = \sigma_\zeta^2/\sigma_\eta^2$. Table 1 shows some comparisons.

Measures of change are sometimes based on differences of rolling (moving) averages. The rolling average, Y_t, over the previous δ time periods is

$$Y_t = \frac{1}{\delta}\sum_{j=0}^{\delta-1} y_{t-j} \tag{22}$$

and the estimator of underlying change from rth differences is

$$B_T^{(r)} = \frac{1}{r}\Delta_r Y_T, \quad r = 1, 2, \ldots. \tag{23}$$

This estimator can also be expressed as a weighted average of current and past first differences. For example, if $r = 3$, then

$$B_T^{(3)} = \frac{1}{9}\Delta y_T + \frac{2}{9}\Delta y_{T-1} + \frac{1}{3}\Delta y_{T-2} + \frac{2}{9}\Delta y_{T-3} + \frac{1}{9}\Delta y_{T-4}.$$

The series of $B_T^{(3)\prime}s$ is quite smooth but it can be slow to respond to changes. An expression for the MSE of $B_T^{(r)}$ can be obtained using the same approach as for $b_T^{(r)}$. Some comparisons of MSEs can be found in Harvey and Chung (2000). As an example, in Table 1 the figures for $r = 3$ for the four different values of q are 1.17, 1.35, 1.61 and 3.88.

A change in the sign of the slope may indicate a *turning point*. The RMSE attached to a model-based estimate at a particular point in time gives some idea of significance. As new observations become available, the estimate and its (decreasing) RMSE may be monitored by a smoothing algorithm; see, for example, Planas and Rossi (2004).

2.5. Surveys and measurement error

Structural time series models can be extended to take account of sample survey error from a rotational design. The statistical treatment using the state space form is not difficult; see Pfeffermann (1991). Furthermore it permits changes over time that might arise, for example, from an increase in sample size or a change in survey design.

UK Labour force survey. Harvey and Chung (2000) model quarterly LFS as a stochastic trend but with a complex error coming from the rotational survey design. The implied weighting pattern of first differences for the estimator of the underlying change, computed from the SSF by the algorithm of Koopman and Harvey (2003), is shown in Figure 3 together with the weights for the level itself. It is interesting to contrast the weights for the slope with those of $B_T^{(3)}$ above.

2.6. Cycles

The stochastic cycle is

$$\begin{bmatrix} \psi_t \\ \psi_t^* \end{bmatrix} = \rho \begin{bmatrix} \cos\lambda_c & \sin\lambda_c \\ -\sin\lambda_c & \cos\lambda_c \end{bmatrix} \begin{bmatrix} \psi_{t-1} \\ \psi_{t-1}^* \end{bmatrix} + \begin{bmatrix} \kappa_t \\ \kappa_t^* \end{bmatrix}, \quad t = 1, \ldots, T, \tag{24}$$

where λ_c is frequency in radians, ρ is a damping factor and κ_t and κ_t^* are two mutually independent Gaussian white noise disturbances with zero means and common variance σ_κ^2. Given the initial conditions that the vector $(\psi_0, \psi_0^*)'$ has zero mean and covariance matrix $\sigma_\psi^2 \mathbf{I}$, it can be shown that for $0 \leqslant \rho < 1$, the process ψ_t is stationary

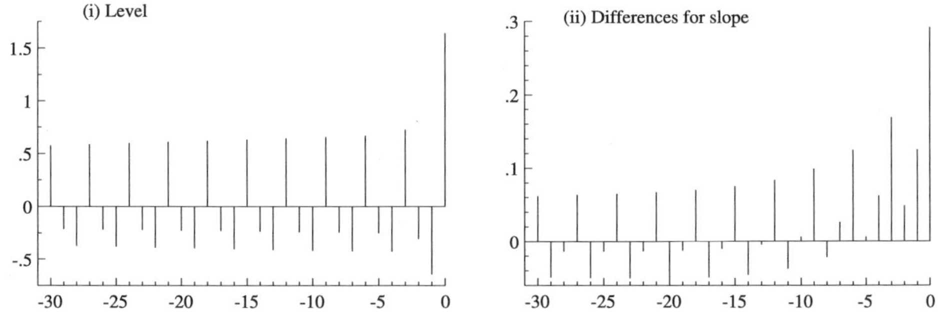

Figure 3. Weights used to construct estimates of the current level and slope of the LFS series.

and indeterministic with zero mean, variance $\sigma_\psi^2 = \sigma_\kappa^2/(1-\rho^2)$ and autocorrelation function (ACF)

$$\rho(\tau) = \rho^\tau \cos\lambda_c\tau, \quad \tau = 0, 1, 2, \ldots. \tag{25}$$

For $0 < \lambda_c < \pi$, the spectrum of ψ_t displays a peak, centered around λ_c, which becomes sharper as ρ moves closer to one; see Harvey (1989, p. 60). The period corresponding to λ_c is $2\pi/\lambda_c$.

Higher order cycles have been suggested by Harvey and Trimbur (2003). The *nth order stochastic cycle*, $\psi_{n,t}$, for positive integer n, is

$$\begin{aligned}
\begin{bmatrix}\psi_{1,t}\\ \psi_{1,t}^*\end{bmatrix} &= \rho\begin{bmatrix}\cos\lambda_c & \sin\lambda_c\\ -\sin\lambda_c & \cos\lambda_c\end{bmatrix}\begin{bmatrix}\psi_{1,t-1}\\ \psi_{1,t-1}^*\end{bmatrix} + \begin{bmatrix}\kappa_t\\ \kappa_t^*\end{bmatrix},\\
\begin{bmatrix}\psi_{i,t}\\ \psi_{i,t}^*\end{bmatrix} &= \rho\begin{bmatrix}\cos\lambda_c & \sin\lambda_c\\ -\sin\lambda_c & \cos\lambda_c\end{bmatrix}\begin{bmatrix}\psi_{i,t-1}\\ \psi_{i,t-1}^*\end{bmatrix} + \begin{bmatrix}\psi_{i-1,t-1}\\ \psi_{i-1,t-1}^*\end{bmatrix}, \qquad i = 2, \ldots, n.
\end{aligned} \tag{26}$$

The variance of the cycle for $n = 2$ is $\sigma_\psi^2 = \{(1+\rho^2)/(1-\rho^2)^3\}\sigma_\kappa^2$, while the ACF is

$$\rho(\tau) = \rho^\tau \cos(\lambda_c\tau)\left[1 + \frac{1-\rho^2}{1+\rho^2}\tau\right], \quad \tau = 0, 1, 2, \ldots. \tag{27}$$

The derivation and expressions for higher values of n are in Trimbur (2006).

For very short term forecasting, transitory fluctuations may be captured by a local linear trend. However, it is usually better to separate out such movements by including a stochastic cycle. Combining the components in an additive way, that is

$$y_t = \mu_t + \psi_t + \varepsilon_t, \quad t = 1, \ldots, T, \tag{28}$$

provides the usual basis for trend-cycle decompositions. The cycle may be regarded as measuring the output gap. Extracted higher order cycles tend to be smoother with more noise consigned to the irregular.

The *cyclical trend* model incorporates the cycle into the slope by moving it from (28) to the equation for the level:

$$\mu_t = \mu_{t-1} + \psi_{t-1} + \beta_{t-1} + \eta_t. \tag{29}$$

The damped trend is a special case corresponding to $\lambda_c = 0$.

2.7. Forecasting components

A UC model not only yields forecasts of the series itself, it also provides forecasts for the components and their MSEs.

US GDP. A trend plus cycle model, (28), was fitted to the logarithm of quarterly seasonally adjusted real per capita US GDP using STAMP. Figure 4 shows the forecasts for the series itself with one *RMSE* on either side, while Figures 5 and 6 show the forecasts for the logarithms of the cycle and the trend together with their smoothed

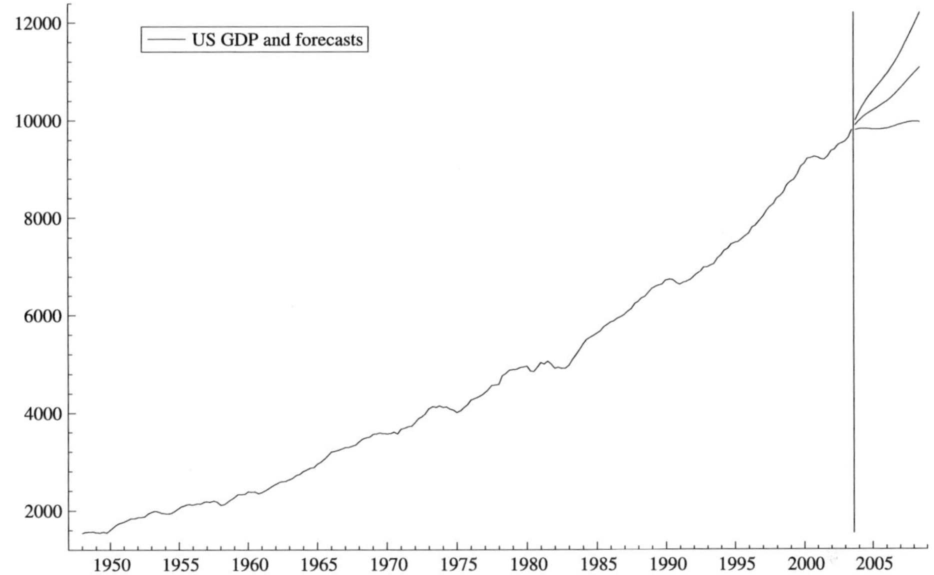

Figure 4. US GDP per capita and forecasts with 68% prediction interval.

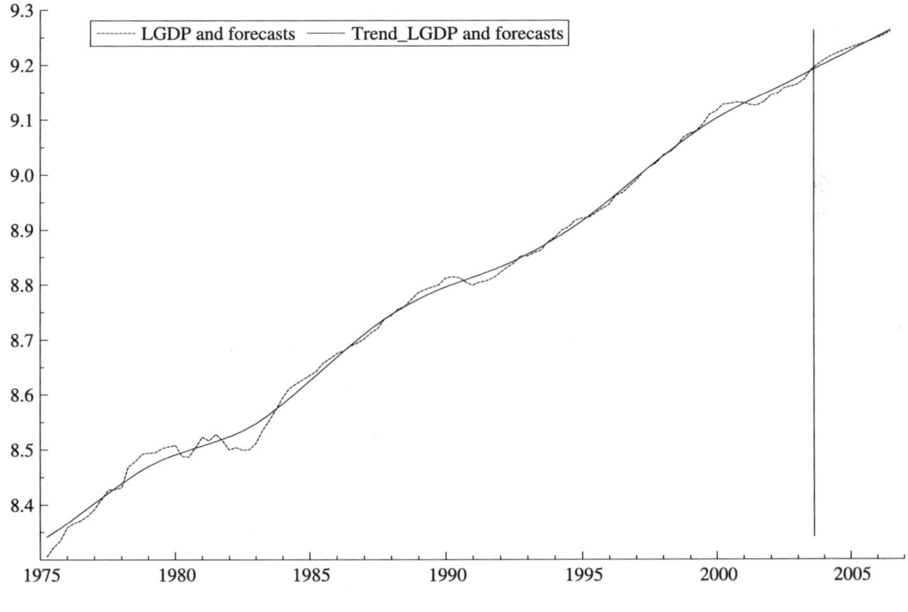

Figure 5. Trend in US GDP.

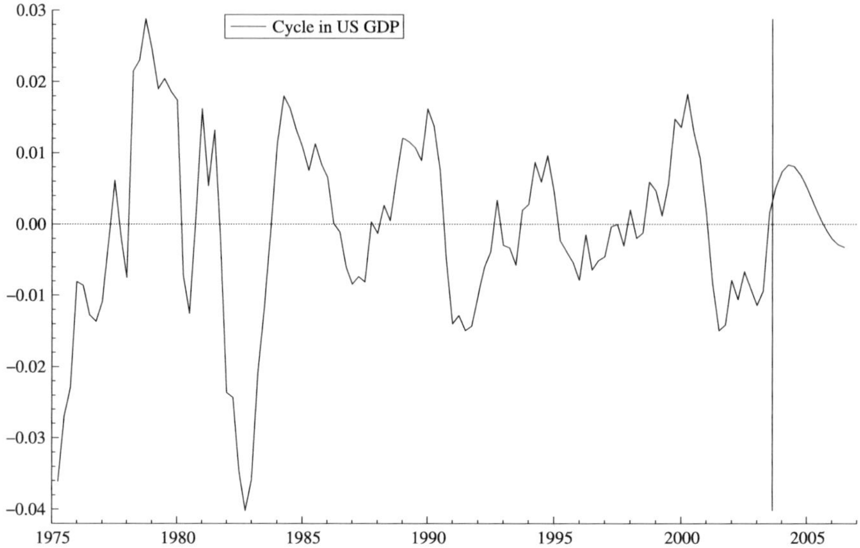

Figure 6. Cycle in US GDP.

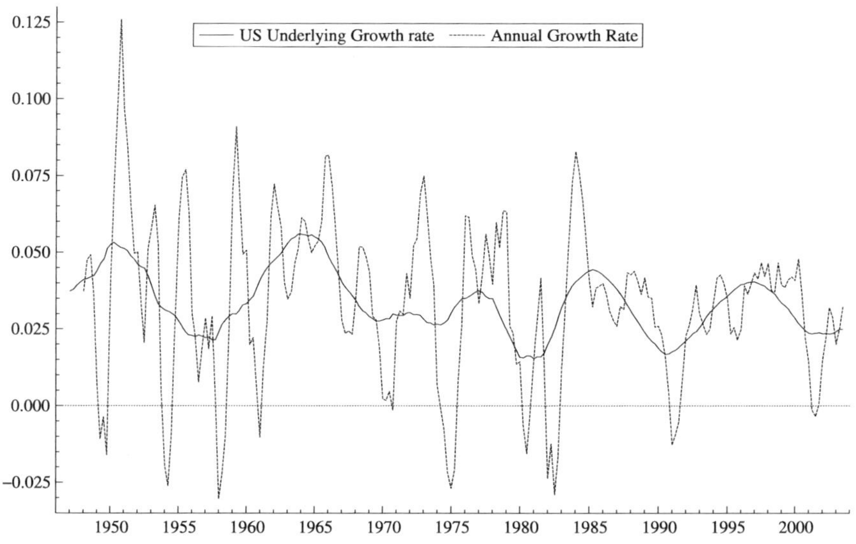

Figure 7. Smoothed estimates of slope of US per capita GDP and annual differences.

values since 1975. Figure 7 shows the annualized underlying growth rate (the estimate of the slope times four) and the fourth differences of the (logarithms of the) series. The latter is fairly noisy, though much smoother than first differences, and it includes the effect of temporary growth emanating from the cycle. The growth rate from the model, on the other hand, shows the long term growth rate and indicates how the prolonged upswings of the 1960's and 1990's are assigned to the trend rather than to the cycle. (Indeed it might be interesting to consider fitting a cyclical trend model with an additive cycle.) The estimate of the growth rate at the end of the series is 2.5%, with a RMSE of 1.2%, and this is the growth rate that is projected into the future.

Fitting a trend plus cycle model provides more scope for identifying turning points and assessing their significance. Different definitions of turning points might be considered, for example a change in sign of the cycle, a change in sign of its slope or a change in sign of the slope of the cycle and the trend together.

2.8. Convergence models

Long-run movements often have a tendency to converge to an equilibrium level. In an autoregressive framework this is captured by an error correction model (ECM). The UC approach is to add cycle and irregular components to an ECM so as to avoid confounding the transitional dynamics of convergence with short-term steady-state dynamics. Thus,

$$y_t = \alpha + \mu_t + \psi_t + \varepsilon_t, \quad t = 1, \ldots, T, \tag{30}$$

with

$$\mu_t = \phi\mu_{t-1} + \eta_t \quad \text{or} \quad \Delta\mu_t = (\phi - 1)\mu_{t-1} + \eta_t.$$

Smoother transitional dynamics, and hence a better separation into convergence and short-term components, can be achieved by specifying μ_t in (30) as

$$\begin{aligned} \mu_t &= \phi\mu_{t-1} + \beta_{t-1}, \\ \beta_t &= \phi\beta_{t-1} + \zeta_t, \end{aligned} \qquad t = 1, \ldots, T, \tag{31}$$

where $0 \leqslant \phi \leqslant 1$; the smooth trend model is obtained when $\phi = 1$. This second-order ECM can be expressed as

$$\Delta\mu_t = -(1-\phi)^2\mu_{t-1} + \phi^2\Delta\mu_{t-1} + \zeta_t$$

showing that the underlying change depends not only on the gap but also on the change in the previous time period. The variance and ACF can be obtained from the properties of an AR(2) process or by noting that the model is a special case of the second order cycle with $\lambda_c = 0$.

For the smooth convergence model the ℓ-step ahead forecast function, standardized by dividing by the current value of the gap, is $(1 + c\ell)\phi^\ell$, $\ell = 0, 1, 2, \ldots,$ where c is a constant that depends on the ratio, ω, of the gap in the current time period to the previous one, that is $\omega = \widetilde{\mu}_T/\widetilde{\mu}_{T-1|T}$. Since the one-step ahead forecast is $2\phi - \phi^2/\omega$, it follows that $c = 1 - \phi/\omega$, so

$$\widetilde{\mu}_{T+\ell|T} = \bigl(1 + (1-\phi/\omega)\ell\bigr)\phi^\ell\widetilde{\mu}_T, \quad \ell = 0, 1, 2, \ldots.$$

If $\omega = \phi$, the expected convergence path is the same as in the first order model. If ω is set to $(1+\phi^2)/2$, the convergence path evolves in the same way as the ACF. In this case, the slower convergence can be illustrated by noting, for example, that with $\phi = 0.96$, 39% of the gap can be expected to remain after 50 time periods as compared with only 13% in the first-order case. The most interesting aspect of the second-order model is that if the convergence process stalls sufficiently, the gap can be expected to widen in the short run as shown later in Figure 10.

3. ARIMA and autoregressive models

The reduced forms of the principal structural time series models[5] are ARIMA processes. The relationship between the structural and reduced forms gives considerable insight into the potential effectiveness of different ARIMA models for forecasting and the possible shortcomings of the approach.

From the theoretical point of view, the autoregressive representation of STMs is useful in that it shows how the observations are weighted when forecasts are made. From the practical point of view it indicates the kind of series for which autoregressions are unlikely to be satisfactory.

After discussing the ways in which ARIMA and autoregressive model selection methodologies contrast with the way in which structural time series models are chosen, we examine the rationale underlying single source of error STMs.

3.1. ARIMA models and the reduced form

An *autoregressive-integrated-moving average* model of order (p, d, q) is one in which the observations follow a stationary and invertible ARMA(p, q) process after they have been differenced d times. It is often denoted by writing, $y_t \sim$ ARIMA(p, d, q). If a constant term, θ_0, is included we may write

$$\Delta^d y_t = \theta_0 + \phi_1 \Delta^d y_{t-1} + \cdots + \phi_p \Delta^d y_{t-p} + \xi_t + \theta_1 \xi_{t-1} + \cdots + \theta_q \xi_{t-q} \qquad (32)$$

where $\phi_1, \ldots, \phi_p$ are the autoregressive parameters, $\theta_1, \ldots, \theta_q$ are the moving average parameters and $\xi_t \sim NID(0, \sigma^2)$. By defining polynomials in the lag operator, L,

$$\phi(L) = 1 - \phi_1 L - \cdots - \phi_p L^p \qquad (33)$$

and

$$\theta(L) = 1 + \theta_1 L + \cdots + \theta_q L^q \qquad (34)$$

[5] Some econometricians are unhappy with the use of the term 'structural' in this context. It was introduced by Engle (1978) to make the point that the reduced form, like the reduced form in a simultaneous equations model, is for forecasting only whereas the structural form attempts to model phenomena that are of direct interest to the economist. Once this is understood, the terminology seems quite reasonable. It is certainly better than the epithet 'dynamic linear models' favoured by West and Harrison (1989).

the model can be written more compactly as

$$\phi(L)\Delta^d y_t = \theta_0 + \theta(L)\xi_t. \tag{35}$$

A structural time series model normally contains several disturbance terms. Provided the model is linear, the components driven by these disturbances can be combined to give a model with a single disturbance. This is known as the *reduced form*. The reduced form is an ARIMA model, and the fact that it is derived from a structural form will typically imply restrictions on the parameter space. If these restrictions are not imposed when an ARIMA model of the implied order is fitted, we are dealing with the *unrestricted* reduced form.

The reduced forms of the principal structural models are set out below, and the restrictions on the ARIMA parameter space explored. Expressions for the reduced form parameters may, in principle, be determined by equating the autocovariances in the structural and reduced forms. In practice this is rather complicated except in the simplest cases. An algorithm is given in Nerlove, Grether and Carvalho (1979, pp. 70–78). General results for finding the reduced form for any model that can be put in state space form are given in Section 6.

Local level/random walk plus noise models: The reduced form is ARIMA(0, 1, 1). Equating the autocorrelations of first differences at lag one gives

$$\theta = \left[\left(q^2 + 4q\right)^{1/2} - 2 - q\right]/2 \tag{36}$$

where $q = \sigma_\eta^2/\sigma_\varepsilon^2$. Since $0 \leqslant q \leqslant \infty$ corresponds to $-1 \leqslant \theta \leqslant 0$, the MA parameter in the reduced form covers only half the usual parameter space. Is this a disadvantage or an advantage? The forecast function is an EWMA with $\lambda = 1 + \theta$ and if θ is positive the weights alternate between positive and negative values. This may be unappealing.

Local linear trend: The reduced form of the local linear trend is an ARIMA(0, 2, 2) process. The restrictions on the parameter space are more severe than in the case of the random walk plus noise model; see Harvey (1989, p. 69).

Cycles: The cycle has an ARMA(2, 1) reduced form. The MA part is subject to restrictions but the more interesting constraints are on the AR parameters. The roots of the AR polynomial are $\rho^{-1}\exp(\pm i\lambda_c)$. Thus, for $0 < \lambda_c < \pi$, they are a pair of complex conjugates with modulus ρ^{-1} and phase λ_c, and when $0 \leqslant \rho < 1$ they lie outside the unit circle. Since the roots of an AR(2) polynomial can be either real or complex, the formulation of the cyclical model effectively restricts the admissible region of the autoregressive coefficients to that part which is capable of giving rise to pseudo-cyclical behaviour. When a cycle is added to noise the reduced form is ARMA(2, 2).

Models constructed from several components may have quite complex reduced forms but with strong restrictions on the parameter space. For example the reduced form of the model made up of trend plus cycle and irregular is ARIMA(2, 2, 4). Unrestricted estimation of high order ARIMA models may not be possible. Indeed such models are unlikely to be selected by the ARIMA methodology. In the case of US GDP, for example, ARIMA(1, 1, 0) with drift gives a similar fit to the trend plus cycle model and hence will yield a similar one-step ahead forecasting performance; see Harvey and Jaeger (1993). The structural model may, however, forecast better several steps ahead.

3.2. *Autoregressive models*

The autoregressive representation may be obtained from the ARIMA reduced form or computed directly from the SSF as described in the next section. For more complex models computation from the SSF may be the only feasible option.

For the local level model, it follows from the ARIMA(0, 1, 1) reduced form that the first differences have a stationary autoregressive representation

$$\Delta y_t = -\sum_{j=1}^{\infty}(-\theta)^j \Delta y_{t-j} + \xi_t. \tag{37}$$

Expanding the difference operator and re-arranging gives

$$y_t = (1+\theta)\sum_{j=1}^{\infty}(-\theta)^{j-1} y_{t-j} + \xi_t \tag{38}$$

from which it is immediately apparent that the MMSE forecast of y_t at time $t-1$ is an EWMA. If changes in the level are dominated by the irregular, the signal–noise ratio is small and θ is close to minus one. As a result the weights decline very slowly and a low order autoregression may not give a satisfactory approximation. This issue becomes more acute in a local linear trend model as the slope will typically change rather slowly. One consequence of this is that unit root tests rarely point to autoregressive models in second differences as being appropriate; see Harvey and Jaeger (1993).

3.3. *Model selection in ARIMA, autoregressive and structural time series models*

An STM sets out to capture the salient features of a time series. These are often apparent from the nature of the series – an obvious example is seasonal data – though with many macroeconomic series there are strong reasons for wanting to fit a cycle. While the STM should be consistent with the correlogram, this typically plays a minor role. Indeed many models are selected without consulting it. Once a model has been chosen, diagnostic checking is carried out in the same way as for an ARIMA model.

ARIMA models are typically more parsimonious model than autoregressions. The MA terms are particularly important when differencing has taken place. Thus an ARIMA(0, 1, 1) is much more satisfactory than an autoregression if the true model is a random walk plus noise with a small signal–noise ratio. However, one of the drawbacks of ARIMA models as compared with STMs is that a parsimonious model may not pick up some of the more subtle features of a time series. As noted earlier, ARIMA model selection methodology will usually lead to an ARIMA(1, 1, 0) specification, with constant, for US GDP. For the data in Section 2.7, the constant term indicates a growth rate of 3.4%. This is bigger than the estimate for the structural model at the end of the series, one reason being that, as Figure 7 makes clear, the long-run growth rate has been slowly declining over the last fifty years.

ARIMA model selection is based on the premise that the ACF and related statistics can be accurately estimated and are stable over time. Even if this is the case, it can be difficult to identify moderately complex models with the result that important features of the series may be missed. In practice, the sampling error associated with the correlogram may mean that even simple ARIMA models are difficult to identify, particularly in small samples. STMs are more robust as the choice of model is not dependent on correlograms. ARIMA model selection becomes even more problematic with missing observations and other data irregularities. See Durbin and Koopman (2001, pp. 51–53) and Harvey (1989, pp. 80–81) for further discussion.

Autoregressive models can always be fitted to time series and will usually provide a decent baseline for one-step ahead prediction. Model selection is relatively straightforward. Unit root tests are usually used to determine the degree of differencing and lags are included in the final model according to statistical significance or a goodness of fit criterion.[6] The problems with this strategy are that unit root tests often have poor size and power properties and may give a result that depends on how serial correlation is handled. Once decisions about differencing have been made, there are different views about how best to select the lags to be included. Should gaps be allowed for example? It is rarely the case that 't-statistics' fall monotonically as the lag increases, but on the other hand creating gaps is often arbitrary and is potentially distorting. Perhaps the best thing is to do is to fix the lag length according to a goodness of fit criterion, in which case autoregressive modelling is effectively nonparametric.

Tests that are implicitly concerned with the order of differencing can also be carried out in a UC framework. They are stationarity rather than unit root tests, testing the null hypothesis that a component is deterministic. The statistical theory is actually more unified with the distributions under the null hypothesis coming from the family of Cramér–von Mises distributions; see Harvey (2001).

Finally, the forecasts from an ARIMA model that satisfies the reduced form restrictions of the STM will be identical to those from the STM and will have the same MSE. For nowcasting, Box, Pierce and Newbold (1987) show how the estimators of the level and slope can be extracted from the ARIMA model. These will be the same as those obtained from the STM. However, an MSE can only be obtained for a specified decomposition.

3.4. Correlated components

Single source of error (SSOE) models are a compromise between ARIMA and STMs in that they retain the structure associated with trends, seasonals and other components

[6] With US GDP, for example, this methodology again leads to ARIMA(1, 1, 0).

while easing the restrictions on the reduced form. For example for a local level we may follow Ord, Koehler and Snyder (1997) in writing

$$y_t = \mu_{t-1} + \xi_t, \quad t = 1, \ldots, T, \tag{39}$$

$$\mu_t = \mu_{t-1} + k\xi_t, \quad \xi_t \sim NID(0, \sigma^2). \tag{40}$$

Substituting for μ_t leads straight to an ARIMA(0, 1, 1) model, but one in which θ is no longer constrained to take only negative values, as in (36). However, invertibility requires that k lie between zero and two, corresponding to $|\theta| < 1$. For more complex models imposing the invertibility restriction[7] may not be quite so straightforward.

As already noted, using the full invertible parameter space of the ARIMA(0, 1, 1) model means that the weights in the EWMA can oscillate between positive and negative values. Chatfield et al. (2001) prefer this greater flexibility, while I would argue that it can often be unappealing. The debate raises the more general issue of why UC models are usually specified to have uncorrelated components. Harvey and Koopman (2000) point out that one reason is that this produces symmetric filters for signal extraction, while in SSOE models smoothing and filtering are the same. This argument may carry less weight for forecasting. However, the MSE attached to a filtered estimate in an STM is of some value for nowcasting; in the local level model, for example, the MSE in (15) can be interpreted as the contribution to the forecast MSE that arises from not knowing the starting value for the forecast function.

In the local level model, an assumption about the correlation between the disturbances – zero or one in the local level specifications just contrasted – is needed for identifiability. However, fixing correlations between disturbances is not always necessary. For example, Morley, Nelson and Zivot (2003) estimate the correlation in a model with trend and cycle components.

4. Explanatory variables and interventions

Explanatory variables can be added to unobserved components, thereby providing a bridge between regression and time series models. Thus

$$y_t = \mu_t + \mathbf{x}_t'\boldsymbol{\delta} + \varepsilon_t, \quad t = 1, \ldots, T \tag{41}$$

where $\mathbf{x}_t$ is a $k \times 1$ vector of observable exogenous[8] variables, some of which may be lagged values, and $\boldsymbol{\delta}$ is a $k \times 1$ vector of parameters. In a model of this kind the trend is allowing for effects that cannot be measured. If the stochastic trend is a random walk with drift, then first differencing yields a regression model with a stationary disturbance;

[7] In the STM invertibility of the reduced form is automatically ensured by the requirement that variances are not allowed to be negative.

[8] When x_t is stochastic, efficient estimation of $\boldsymbol{\delta}$ requires that we assume that it is independent of all disturbances, including those in the stochastic trend, in all time periods; this is strict exogeneity.

with a stochastic drift, second differences are needed. However, using the state space form allows the variables to remain in levels and this is a great advantage as regards interpretation; compare the transfer function models of Box and Jenkins (1976).

Spirits. The data set of annual observations on the per capita consumption of spirits in the UK, together with the explanatory variables of per capita income and relative price, is a famous one, having been used as a testbed for the Durbin–Watson statistic in 1951. The observations run from 1870 to 1938 and are in logarithms. A standard econometric approach would be to include a linear or quadratic time trend in the model with an AR(1) disturbance; see Fuller (1996, p. 522). The structural time series approach is simply to use a stochastic trend with the explanatory variables. The role of the stochastic trend is to pick up changes in tastes and habits that cannot be explicitly measured. Such a model gives a better fit than one with a deterministic trend and produces better forecasts. Figure 8 shows the multi-step forecasts produced from 1930 onwards, using the observed values of the explanatory variables. The lower graph shows a 68% prediction interval ($\pm$ one RMSE). Further details on this example can be found in the STAMP manual, Koopman et al. (2000, pp. 64–70).

US teenage unemployment. In a study of the relationship between teenage employment and minimum wages in the US, Bazen and Marimoutou (2002, p. 699) show that a structural time series model estimated up to 1979 "...accurately predicts what happens to teenage unemployment subsequently, when the minimum wage was frozen after

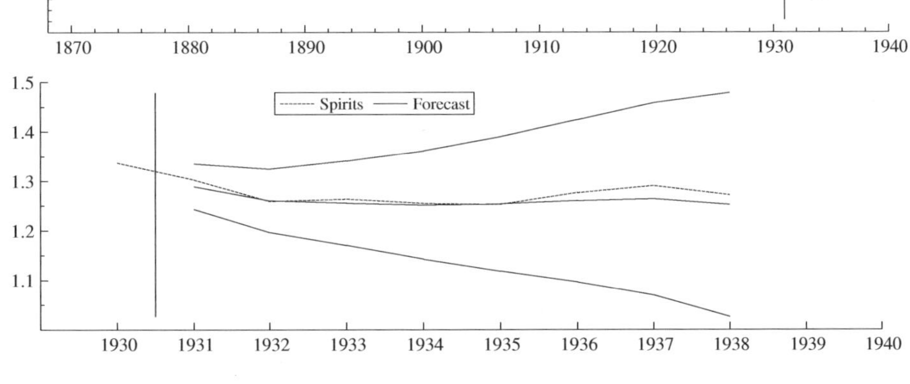

Figure 8. Multi-step forecasts for UK spirits from 1930.

1981 and then increased quite substantially in the 1990s." They note that "...previous models break down due to their inability to capture changes in the trend, cyclical and seasonal components of teenage employment".

Global warming. Visser and Molenaar (1995) use stationary explanatory variables to reduce the short term variability when modelling the trend in northern hemisphere temperatures.

4.1. Interventions

Intervention variables may be introduced into a model. Thus in a simple stochastic trend plus error model

$$y_t = \mu_t + \lambda w_t + \varepsilon_t, \quad t = 1, \ldots, T. \tag{42}$$

If an unusual event is to be treated as an outlier, it may be captured by a *pulse* dummy variable, that is,

$$w_t = \begin{cases} 0 & \text{for } t \neq \tau, \\ 1 & \text{for } t = \tau. \end{cases} \tag{43}$$

A structural break in the level at time τ may be modelled by a level shift dummy,

$$w_t = \begin{cases} 0 & \text{for } t < \tau, \\ 1 & \text{for } t \geqslant \tau \end{cases}$$

or by a pulse in the level equation, that is,

$$\mu_t = \mu_{t-1} + \lambda w_t + \beta_{t-1} + \eta_t$$

where w_t is given by (43). Similarly a change in the slope can be modelled in (42) by defining

$$w_t = \begin{cases} 0 & \text{for } t \leqslant \tau, \\ t - \tau & \text{for } t > \tau \end{cases}$$

or by putting a pulse in the equation for the slope. A piecewise linear trend emerges as a special case when there are no disturbances in the level and slope equations.

Modelling structural breaks by dummy variables is appropriate when they are associated with a change in policy or a specific event. The interpretation of structural breaks as large stochastic shocks to the level or slope will prove to be a useful way of constructing a robust model when their timing is unknown; see Section 9.4.

4.2. Time-varying parameters

A time-varying parameter model may be set up by letting the coefficients in (41) follow random walks, that is,

$$\boldsymbol{\delta}_t = \boldsymbol{\delta}_{t-1} + \boldsymbol{\upsilon}_t, \qquad \boldsymbol{\upsilon}_t \sim NID(\mathbf{0}, \mathbf{Q}).$$

The effect of $\mathbf{Q}$ being p.d. is to discount the past observations in estimating the latest value of the regression coefficient. Models in which the parameters evolve as stationary autoregressive processes have also been considered; see, for example, Rosenberg (1973). Chow (1984) and Nicholls and Pagan (1985) give surveys, while Wells (1996) investigates applications in finance.

5. Seasonality

A seasonal component, γ_t, may be added to a model consisting of a trend and irregular to give

$$y_t = \mu_t + \gamma_t + \varepsilon_t, \qquad t = 1, \ldots, T. \tag{44}$$

A fixed seasonal pattern may be modelled as

$$\gamma_t = \sum_{j=1}^{s} \gamma_j z_{jt}$$

where s is the number of seasons and the dummy variable z_{jt} is one in season j and zero otherwise. In order not to confound trend with seasonality, the coefficients, γ_j, $j = 1, \ldots, s$, are constrained to sum to zero. The seasonal pattern may be allowed to change over time by letting the coefficients evolve as random walks as in Harrison and Stevens (1976, pp. 217–218). If γ_{jt} denotes the effect of season j at time t, then

$$\gamma_{jt} = \gamma_{j,t-1} + \omega_{jt}, \qquad \omega_t \sim NID\big(0, \sigma_\omega^2\big), \ j = 1, \ldots, s. \tag{45}$$

Although all s seasonal components are continually evolving, only one affects the observations at any particular point in time, that is $\gamma_t = \gamma_{jt}$ when season j is prevailing at time t. The requirement that the seasonal components evolve in such a way that they always sum to zero is enforced by the restriction that the disturbances sum to zero at each point in time. This restriction is implemented by the correlation structure in

$$\operatorname{Var}(\boldsymbol{\omega}_t) = \sigma_\omega^2\big(\mathbf{I} - s^{-1}\mathbf{i}\mathbf{i}'\big) \tag{46}$$

where $\boldsymbol{\omega}_t = (\omega_{1t}, \ldots, \omega_{st})'$, coupled with initial conditions requiring that the seasonals sum to zero at $t = 0$. It can be seen from (46) that $\operatorname{Var}(\mathbf{i}'\boldsymbol{\omega}_t) = 0$.

In the *basic structural model* (BSM), μ_t in (44) is the local linear trend of (17), the irregular component, ε_t, is assumed to be random, and the disturbances in all three components are taken to be mutually uncorrelated. The signal–noise ratio associated

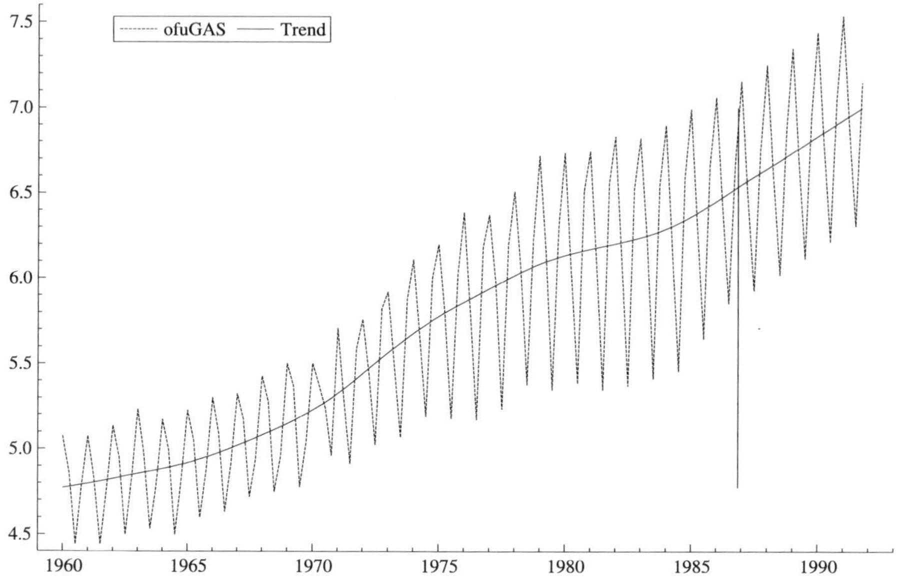

Figure 9. Trend and forecasts for 'Other final users' of gas in the UK.

with the seasonal, that is $q_\omega = \sigma_\omega^2/\sigma_\varepsilon^2$, determines how rapidly the seasonal changes relative to the irregular. Figure 9 shows the forecasts, made using the STAMP package of Koopman et al. (2000), for a quarterly series on the consumption of gas in the UK by 'Other final users'. The forecasts for the seasonal component are made by projecting the estimates of the γ_{jT}'s into the future. As can be seen, the seasonal pattern repeats itself over a period of one year and sums to zero. Another example of how the BSM successfully captures changing seasonality can be found in the study of alcoholic beverages by Lenten and Moosa (1999).

5.1. Trigonometric seasonal

Instead of using dummy variables, a fixed seasonal pattern may by modelled by a set of trigonometric terms at the seasonal frequencies, $\lambda_j = 2\pi j/s$, $j = 1, \ldots, [s/2]$, where [.] denotes rounding down to the nearest integer. The seasonal effect at time t is then

$$\gamma_t = \sum_{j=1}^{[s/2]} (\alpha_j \cos \lambda_j t + \beta_j \sin \lambda_j t). \tag{47}$$

When s is even, the sine term disappears for $j = s/2$ and so the number of trigonometric parameters, the α_j's and β_j's, is always $s - 1$. Provided that the full set of trigonometric terms is included, it is straightforward to show that the estimated seasonal pattern is the same as the one obtained with dummy variables.

The trigonometric components may be allowed to evolve over time in the same way as the stochastic cycle, (24). Thus,

$$\gamma_t = \sum_{j=1}^{[s/2]} \gamma_{jt} \tag{48}$$

with

$$\begin{aligned} \gamma_{jt} &= \gamma_{j,t-1}\cos\lambda_j + \gamma^*_{j,t-1}\sin\lambda_j + \omega_{jt}, \\ \gamma^*_{jt} &= -\gamma_{j,t-1}\sin\lambda_j + \gamma^*_{j,t-1}\cos\lambda_j + \omega^*_{jt}, \end{aligned} \qquad j = 1,\ldots,\big[(s-1)/2\big] \tag{49}$$

where ω_{jt} and ω^*_{jt} are zero mean white-noise processes which are uncorrelated with each other with a common variance σ_j^2 for $j = 1,\ldots,[(s-1)/2]$. The larger these variances, the more past observations are discounted in estimating the seasonal pattern. When s is even, the component at $j = s/2$ reduces to

$$\gamma_t = \gamma_{j,t-1}\cos\lambda_j + \omega_{jt}, \quad j = s/2. \tag{50}$$

The seasonal model proposed by Hannan, Terrell and Tuckwell (1970), in which α_j and β_j in (47) evolve as random walks, is effectively the same as the model above.

Assigning different variances to each harmonic allows them to evolve at varying rates. However, from a practical point of view it is usually desirable[9] to let these variances be the same except at $j = s/2$. Thus, for s even, $\mathrm{Var}(\omega_{jt}) = \mathrm{Var}(\omega^*_{jt}) = \sigma_j^2 = \overline{\sigma}^2_\omega$, $j = 1,\ldots,[(s-1)/2]$ and $\mathrm{Var}(\omega_{s/2,t}) = \overline{\sigma}^2_\omega/2$. As shown in Proietti (2000), this is equivalent to the dummy variable seasonal model, with $\sigma^2_\omega = 2\overline{\sigma}^2_\omega/s$ for s even and $\sigma^2_\omega = 2\overline{\sigma}^2_\omega/(s-1)$ for s odd.

A damping factor could very easily be introduced into the trigonometric seasonal model, just as in (24). However, since the forecasts would gradually die down to zero, such a seasonal component is not capturing the persistent effects of seasonality. In any case the empirical evidence, for example in Canova and Hansen (1995), clearly points to nonstationary seasonality.

5.2. *Reduced form*

The reduced form of the stochastic seasonal model is

$$\gamma_t = -\sum_{j=1}^{s-1} \gamma_{t-j} + \omega_t \tag{51}$$

with ω_t following an MA$(s-2)$ process. Thus the expected value of the seasonal effects over the previous year is zero. The simplicity of a *single shock* model, in which ω_t is

[9] As a rule, very little is lost in terms of goodness of fit by imposing this restriction. Although the model with different seasonal variances is more flexible, Bruce and Jurke (1996) show that it can lead to a significant increase in the roughness of the seasonal factors.

white noise, can be useful for pedagogic purposes. The relationship between this model and the *balanced dummy variable* model based on (45) is explored in Proietti (2000). In practice, it is usually preferable to work with the latter.

Given (51), it is easy to show that the reduced form of the BSM is such that $\Delta\Delta_s y_t \sim$ MA$(s + 1)$.

5.3. Nowcasting

When data are seasonally adjusted, revisions are needed as new observations become available and the estimates of the seasonal effects near the end of the series change. Often the revised figures are published only once a year and the changes to the adjusted figures can be quite substantial. For example, in the LFS, Harvey and Chung (2000) note that the figures for the slope estimate $b_T^{(3)}$, defined in (20), for February, March and April of 1998 were originally -6.4, 1.3 and -1.0 but using the revised data made available in early 1999 they became 7.9, 22.3 and -16.1, respectively. It appears that even moderate revisions in levels can translate into quite dramatic changes in differences, thereby rendering measures like $b_T^{(3)}$ virtually useless as a current indicator of change. Overall, the extent and timing of revisions casts doubt on the wisdom of estimating change from adjusted data, whatever the method used. Fitting models to unadjusted data has the attraction that the resulting estimates of change not only take account of seasonal movements but also reflect these movements in their RMSEs.

5.4. Holt–Winters

In the BSM the state vector is of length $s + 1$, and it is not easy to obtain analytic expressions for the steady-state form of the filtering equations. On the other hand, the extension of the Holt–Winters local linear trend recursions to cope with seasonality involves only a single extra equation. However, the component for each season is only updated every s periods and an adjustment has to be made to make the seasonal factors sum to zero. Thus there is a price to be paid for having only three equations because when the Kalman filter is applied to the BSM, the seasonal components are updated in every period and they automatically sum to zero. The Holt–Winters procedure is best regarded as an approximation to the Kalman filter applied to the BSM; why anyone would continue to use it is something of a mystery. Further discussion on different forms of additive and multiplicative Holt–Winters recursions can be found in Ord, Koehler and Snyder (1997).

5.5. Seasonal ARIMA models

For modelling seasonal data, Box and Jenkins (1976, Chapter 9) proposed a class of multiplicative seasonal ARIMA models; see also Chapter 13 by Ghysels, Osborn and Rodrigues in this Handbook. The most important model within this class has subsequently become known as the 'airline model' since it was originally fitted to a monthly series on UK airline passenger totals. The model is written as

$$\Delta\Delta_s y_t = (1+\theta L)\big(1+\Theta L^s\big)\xi_t \tag{52}$$

where $\Delta_s = 1 - L^s$ is the seasonal difference operator and θ and Θ are MA parameters which, if the model is to be invertible, must have modulus less than one. Box and Jenkins (1976, pp. 305–306) gave a rationale for the airline model in terms of EWMAs at monthly and yearly intervals.

Maravall (1985), compares the autocorrelation functions of $\Delta\Delta_s y_t$ for the BSM and airline model for some typical values of the parameters and finds them to be quite similar, particularly when the seasonal MA parameter, Θ, is close to minus one. In fact in the limiting case when Θ is equal to minus one, the airline model is equivalent to a BSM in which σ_ζ^2 and σ_ω^2 are both zero. The airline model provides a good approximation to the reduced form when the slope and seasonal are close to being deterministic. If this is not the case the implicit link between the variability of the slope and that of the seasonal component may be limiting.

The plausibility of other multiplicative seasonal ARIMA models can, to a certain extent, be judged according to whether they allow a canonical decomposition into trend and seasonal components; see Hillmer and Tiao (1982). Although a number of models fall into this category the case for using them is unconvincing. It is hardly surprising that most procedures for ARIMA model-based seasonal adjustment are based on the airline model. However, although the airline model may often be perfectly adequate as a vehicle for seasonal adjustment, it is of limited value for forecasting many economic time series. For example, it cannot deal with business cycle effects.

Pure AR models can be very poor at dealing with seasonality since seasonal patterns typically change rather slowly and this may necessitate the use of long seasonal lags. However, it is possible to combine an autoregression with a stochastic seasonal component as in Harvey and Scott (1994).

Consumption. A model for aggregate consumption provides a nice illustration of the way in which a simple parsimonious STM that satisfies economic considerations can be constructed. Using UK data from 1957q3 to 1992q2, Harvey and Scott (1994) show that a special case of the BSM consisting of a random walk plus drift, β, and a stochastic seasonal not only fits the data but yields a seasonal martingale difference that does little violence to the forward-looking theory of consumption. The unsatisfactory nature of an autoregression is illustrated in the paper by Osborn and Smith (1989) where sixteen lags are required to model seasonal differences. As regards ARIMA models, Osborn and Smith (1989) select a special case of the airline model in which $\theta = 0$. This contrasts with the reduced form for the structural model which has $\Delta_s c_t$ following an MA$(s-1)$ process (with non-zero mean). The seasonal ARIMA model matches the ACF but does not yield forecasts satisfying a seasonal martingale, that is $E[\Delta_s c_{t+s}] = s\beta$.

5.6. Extensions

It is not unusual for the level of a monthly time series to be influenced by *calendar effects*. Such effects arise because of changes in the level of activity resulting from variations in the composition of the calendar between years. The two main sources of calendar effects are trading day variation and moving festivals. They may both be introduced into a structural time series model and estimated along with the other components in the model. The state space framework allows them to change over time as in Dagum, Quenneville and Sutradhar (1992). Methods of detecting calendar effects are discussed in Busetti and Harvey (2003). As illustrated by Hillmer (1982, p. 388), failure to realise that calendar effects are present can distort the correlogram of the series and lead to inappropriate ARIMA models being chosen.

The treatment of *weekly, daily or hourly* observations raises a host of new problems. The structural approach offers a means of tackling them. Harvey, Koopman and Riani (1997) show how to deal with a weekly seasonal pattern by constructing a parsimonious but flexible model for the UK money supply based on time-varying splines and incorporating a mechanism to deal with moving festivals such as Easter. Harvey and Koopman (1993) also use time-varying splines to model and forecast hourly electricity data.

Periodic or *seasonal specific* models were originally introduced to deal with certain problems in environmental science, such as modelling river flows; see Hipel and McLeod (1994, Chapter 14). The key feature of such models is that separate stationary AR or ARMA model are constructed for each season. Econometricians have developed periodic models further to allow for nonstationarity within each season and constraints across the parameters in different seasons; see Franses and Papp (2004) and Chapter 13 by Ghysels, Osborn and Rodrigues in this Handbook. These approaches are very much within the autoregressive/unit root paradigm. The structural framework offers a more general way of capturing periodic features by allowing periodic components to be combined with components common to all seasons. These common components may exhibit seasonal heteroscedasticity, that is they may have different values for the parameters in different seasons. Such models have a clear interpretation and make explicit the distinction between an evolving seasonal pattern of the kind typically used in a structural time series model and genuine periodic effects. Proietti (1998) discusses these issues and gives the example of Italian industrial production where August behaves so differently from the other months that it is worth letting it have its own trend. There is further scope for work along these lines.

Krane and Wascher (1999) use state space methods to explore the interaction between *seasonality and business cycles*. They apply their methods to US employment and conclude that seasonal movements can be affected by business cycle developments.

Stochastic seasonal components can be combined with *explanatory variables* by introducing them into regression models in the same way as stochastic trends. The way in which this can give insight into the specification of dynamic regression models is illustrated in the paper by Harvey and Scott (1994) where it is suggested that seasonality in an error correction model be captured by a stochastic seasonal component. The model provides a good fit to UK consumption and casts doubt on the specification adopted in the influential paper of Davidson et al. (1978). Moosa and Kennedy (1998) reach the same conclusion using Australian data.

6. State space form

The statistical treatment of unobserved components models can be carried out efficiently and in great generality by using the state space form (SSF) and the associated algorithms of the Kalman filter and smoother.

The general linear state space form applies to a multivariate time series, $\mathbf{y}_t$, containing N elements. These observable variables are related to an $m \times 1$ vector, $\boldsymbol{\alpha}_t$, known as the *state vector*, through a *measurement equation*

$$\mathbf{y}_t = \mathbf{Z}_t\boldsymbol{\alpha}_t + \mathbf{d}_t + \boldsymbol{\varepsilon}_t, \quad t = 1, \ldots, T \tag{53}$$

where $\mathbf{Z}_t$ is an $N \times m$ matrix, $\mathbf{d}_t$ is an $N \times 1$ vector and $\boldsymbol{\varepsilon}_t$ is an $N \times 1$ vector of serially uncorrelated disturbances with mean zero and covariance matrix $\mathbf{H}_t$, that is $E(\boldsymbol{\varepsilon}_t) = \mathbf{0}$ and $\text{Var}(\boldsymbol{\varepsilon}_t) = \mathbf{H}_t$.

In general the elements of $\boldsymbol{\alpha}_t$ are not observable. However, they are known to be generated by a first-order Markov process,

$$\boldsymbol{\alpha}_t = \mathbf{T}_t\boldsymbol{\alpha}_{t-1} + \mathbf{c}_t + \mathbf{R}_t\boldsymbol{\eta}_t, \quad t = 1, \ldots, T \tag{54}$$

where $\mathbf{T}_t$ is an $m \times m$ matrix, $\mathbf{c}_t$ is an $m \times 1$ vector, $\mathbf{R}_t$ is an $m \times g$ matrix and $\boldsymbol{\eta}_t$ is a $g \times 1$ vector of serially uncorrelated disturbances with mean zero and covariance matrix, $\mathbf{Q}_t$, that is $E(\boldsymbol{\eta}_t) = \mathbf{0}$ and $\text{Var}(\boldsymbol{\eta}_t t) = \mathbf{Q}_t$. Equation (54) is the *transition equation.*

The specification of the state space system is completed by assuming that the initial state vector, $\boldsymbol{\alpha}_0$, has a mean of $\mathbf{a}_0$ and a covariance matrix $\mathbf{P}_0$, that is $E(\boldsymbol{\alpha}_0) = \mathbf{a}_0$ and $\text{Var}(\boldsymbol{\alpha}_0) = \mathbf{P}_0$, where $\mathbf{P}_0$ is positive semi-definite, and that the disturbances $\boldsymbol{\varepsilon}_t$ and $\boldsymbol{\eta}_t$ are uncorrelated with the initial state, that is $E(\boldsymbol{\varepsilon}_t\boldsymbol{\alpha}_0') = \mathbf{0}$ and $E(\boldsymbol{\eta}_t\boldsymbol{\alpha}_0') = \mathbf{0}$ for $t = 1, \ldots, T$. In what follows it will be assumed that the disturbances are uncorrelated with each other in all time periods, that is $E(\boldsymbol{\varepsilon}_t\boldsymbol{\eta}_s') = \mathbf{0}$ for all $s, t = 1, \ldots, T$, though this assumption may be relaxed, the consequence being a slight complication in some of the filtering formulae.

It is sometimes convenient to use the future form of the transition equation,

$$\boldsymbol{\alpha}_{t+1} = \mathbf{T}_t\boldsymbol{\alpha}_t + \mathbf{c}_t + \mathbf{R}_t\boldsymbol{\eta}_t, \quad t = 1, \ldots, T, \tag{55}$$

as opposed to the contemporaneous form of (54). The corresponding filters are the same unless $\boldsymbol{\varepsilon}_t$ and $\boldsymbol{\eta}_t$ are correlated.

6.1. Kalman filter

The Kalman filter is a recursive procedure for computing the optimal estimator of the state vector at time t, based on the information available at time t. This information consists of the observations up to and including $\mathbf{y}_t$. The system matrices,

$\mathbf{Z}_t, \mathbf{d}_t, \mathbf{H}_t, \mathbf{T}_t, \mathbf{c}_t, \mathbf{R}_t$ and $\mathbf{Q}_t$, together with $\mathbf{a}_0$ and $\mathbf{P}_0$ are assumed to be known in all time periods and so do not need to be explicitly included in the information set.

In a Gaussian model, the disturbances $\boldsymbol{\varepsilon}_t$ and $\boldsymbol{\eta}_t$, and the initial state, are all normally distributed. Because a normal distribution is characterized by its first two moments, the Kalman filter can be interpreted as updating the mean and covariance matrix of the conditional distribution of the state vector as new observations become available. The conditional mean minimizes the mean square error and when viewed as a rule for all realizations it is the minimum mean square error estimator (MMSE). Since the conditional covariance matrix does not depend on the observations, it is the unconditional MSE matrix of the MMSE. When the normality assumption is dropped, the Kalman filter is still optimal in the sense that it minimizes the mean square error within the class of all linear estimators; see Anderson and Moore (1979, pp. 29–32).

Consider the Gaussian state space model with observations available up to and including time $t-1$. Given this information set, let $\boldsymbol{\alpha}_{t-1}$ be normally distributed with known mean, $\mathbf{a}_{t-1}$, and $m \times m$ covariance matrix, $\mathbf{P}_{t-1}$. Then it follows from (54) that $\boldsymbol{\alpha}_t$ is normal with mean

$$\mathbf{a}_{t|t-1} = \mathbf{T}_t \mathbf{a}_{t-1} + \mathbf{c}_t \tag{56}$$

and covariance matrix

$$\mathbf{P}_{t|t-1} = \mathbf{T}_t \mathbf{P}_{t-1} \mathbf{T}_t' + \mathbf{R}_t \mathbf{Q}_t \mathbf{R}_t', \quad t = 1, \ldots, T.$$

These two equations are known as the *prediction equations*. The predictive distribution of the next observation, $\mathbf{y}_t$, is normal with mean

$$\tilde{\mathbf{y}}_{t|t-1} = \mathbf{Z}_t \mathbf{a}_{t|t-1} + \mathbf{d}_t \tag{57}$$

and covariance matrix

$$\mathbf{F}_t = \mathbf{Z}_t \mathbf{P}_{t|t-1} \mathbf{Z}_t' + \mathbf{H}_t, \quad t = 1, \ldots, T. \tag{58}$$

Once the new observation becomes available, a standard result on the multivariate normal distribution yields the *updating equations*,

$$\mathbf{a}_t = \mathbf{a}_{t|t-1} + \mathbf{P}_{t|t-1} \mathbf{Z}_t' \mathbf{F}_t^{-1} (\mathbf{y}_t - \mathbf{Z}_t \mathbf{a}_{t|t-1} - \mathbf{d}_t) \tag{59}$$

and

$$\mathbf{P}_t = \mathbf{P}_{t|t-1} - \mathbf{P}_{t|t-1} \mathbf{Z}_t' \mathbf{F}_t^{-1} \mathbf{Z}_t \mathbf{P}_{t|t-1},$$

as the mean and variance of the distribution of $\boldsymbol{\alpha}_t$ conditional on $\mathbf{y}_t$ as well as the information up to time $t-1$; see Harvey (1989, p. 109).

Taken together (56) and (59) make up the Kalman filter. If desired they can be written as a single set of recursions going directly from $\mathbf{a}_{t-1}$ to $\mathbf{a}_t$ or, alternatively, from $\mathbf{a}_{t|t-1}$ to $\mathbf{a}_{t+1|t}$. We might refer to these as, respectively, the *contemporaneous* and *predictive filter*. In the latter case

$$\mathbf{a}_{t+1|t} = \mathbf{T}_{t+1} \mathbf{a}_{t|t-1} + \mathbf{c}_{t+1} + \mathbf{K}_t \boldsymbol{\nu}_t \tag{60}$$

or

$$\mathbf{a}_{t+1|t} = (\mathbf{T}_{t+1} - \mathbf{K}_t\mathbf{Z}_t)\mathbf{a}_{t|t-1} + \mathbf{K}_t\mathbf{y}_t + (\mathbf{c}_{t+1} - \mathbf{K}_t\mathbf{d}_t) \tag{61}$$

where the gain matrix, $\mathbf{K}_t$, is given by

$$\mathbf{K}_t = \mathbf{T}_{t+1}\mathbf{P}_{t|t-1}\mathbf{Z}_t'\mathbf{F}_t^{-1}, \quad t = 1, \ldots, T. \tag{62}$$

The recursion for the covariance matrix,

$$\mathbf{P}_{t+1|t} = \mathbf{T}_{t+1}\big(\mathbf{P}_{t|t-1} - \mathbf{P}_{t|t-1}\mathbf{Z}_t'\mathbf{F}_t^{-1}\mathbf{Z}_t\mathbf{P}_{t|t-1}\big)\mathbf{T}_{t+1}' + \mathbf{R}_{t+1}\mathbf{Q}_{t+1}\mathbf{R}_{t+1}', \tag{63}$$

is a *Riccati equation.*

The starting values for the Kalman filter may be specified in terms of $\mathbf{a}_0$ and $\mathbf{P}_0$ or $\mathbf{a}_{1|0}$ and $\mathbf{P}_{1|0}$. Given these initial conditions, the Kalman filter delivers the optimal estimator of the state vector as each new observation becomes available. When all T observations have been processed, the filter yields the optimal estimator of the current state vector, and/or the state vector in the next time period, based on the full information set. A diffuse prior corresponds to setting $\mathbf{P}_0 = \kappa\mathbf{I}$, and letting the scalar κ go to infinity.

6.2. Prediction

In the Gaussian model, (53) and (54), the Kalman filter yields $\mathbf{a}_T$, the MMSE of $\boldsymbol{\alpha}_T$ based on all the observations. In addition it gives $\mathbf{a}_{T+1|T}$ and the one-step-ahead predictor, $\tilde{\mathbf{y}}_{T+1|T}$. As regards *multi-step prediction*, taking expectations, conditional on the information at time T, of the transition equation at time $T + \ell$ yields the recursion

$$\mathbf{a}_{T+l|T} = \mathbf{T}_{T+l}\mathbf{a}_{T+l-1|T} + \mathbf{c}_{T+l}, \quad l = 1, 2, 3, \ldots \tag{64}$$

with initial value $\mathbf{a}_{T|T} = \mathbf{a}_T$. Similarly,

$$\mathbf{P}_{T+l|T} = \mathbf{T}_{T+l}\mathbf{P}_{T+l-1|T}\mathbf{T}_{T+l}' + \mathbf{R}_{T+l}\mathbf{Q}_{T+l}\mathbf{R}_{T+l}', \quad l = 1, 2, 3, \ldots \tag{65}$$

with $\mathbf{P}_{T|T} = \mathbf{P}_T$. Thus $\mathbf{a}_{T+l|T}$ and $\mathbf{P}_{T+l|T}$ are evaluated by repeatedly applying the Kalman filter prediction equations. The MMSE of $\mathbf{y}_{T+l}$ can be obtained directly from $\mathbf{a}_{T+l|T}$. Taking conditional expectations in the measurement equation for $\mathbf{y}_{T+l}$ gives

$$E(\mathbf{y}_{T+l} \mid \mathbf{Y}_T) = \tilde{\mathbf{y}}_{T+l|T} = \mathbf{Z}_{T+l}\mathbf{a}_{T+l|T} + \mathbf{d}_{T+l}, \quad l = 1, 2, \ldots \tag{66}$$

with MSE matrix

$$\text{MSE}(\tilde{\mathbf{y}}_{T+l|T}) = \mathbf{Z}_{T+l}\mathbf{P}_{T+l|T}\mathbf{Z}_{T+l}' + \mathbf{H}_{T+l}, \quad l = 1, 2, \ldots. \tag{67}$$

When the normality assumption is relaxed, $\mathbf{a}_{T+l|T}$ and $\tilde{\mathbf{y}}_{T+l|T}$ are still minimum mean square *linear* estimators.

It is often of interest to see how past observations are weighted when forecasts are constructed: Koopman and Harvey (2003) give an algorithm for computing weights for $\mathbf{a}_T$ and weights for $\tilde{\mathbf{y}}_{T+l|T}$ are then obtained straightforwardly.

6.3. Innovations

The joint density function for the T sets of observations, $\mathbf{y}_1, \ldots, \mathbf{y}_T$, is

$$p(\mathbf{Y}; \boldsymbol{\psi}) = \prod_{t=1}^{T} p(\mathbf{y}_t \mid \mathbf{Y}_{t-1}) \tag{68}$$

where $p(\mathbf{y}_t \mid \mathbf{Y}_{t-1})$ denotes the distribution of $\mathbf{y}_t$ conditional on the information set at time $t-1$, that is $\mathbf{Y}_{t-1} = \{\mathbf{y}_{t-1}, \mathbf{y}_{t-2}, \ldots, \mathbf{y}_1\}$. In the Gaussian state space model, the conditional distribution of $\mathbf{y}_t$ is normal with mean $\widetilde{\mathbf{y}}_{t|t-1}$ and covariance matrix $\mathbf{F}_t$. Hence the $N \times 1$ vector of prediction errors or *innovations*,

$$\boldsymbol{\nu}_t = \mathbf{y}_t - \widetilde{\mathbf{y}}_{t|t-1}, \quad t = 1, \ldots, T, \tag{69}$$

is serially independent with mean zero and covariance matrix $\mathbf{F}_t$, that is, $\boldsymbol{\nu}_t \sim NID(\mathbf{0}, \mathbf{F}_t)$.

Re-arranging (69), (57) and (60) gives the *innovations form* representation

$$\begin{aligned} \mathbf{y}_t &= \mathbf{Z}_t \mathbf{a}_{t|t-1} + \mathbf{d}_t + \boldsymbol{\nu}_t, \\ \mathbf{a}_{t+1|t} &= \mathbf{T}_t \mathbf{a}_{t|t-1} + \mathbf{c}_t + \mathbf{K}_t \boldsymbol{\nu}_t. \end{aligned} \tag{70}$$

This mirrors the original SSF, with the transition equation as in (55), except that $\mathbf{a}_{t|t-1}$ appears in the place of the state and the disturbances in the measurement and transition equations are perfectly correlated. Since the model contains only one disturbance vector, it may be regarded as a reduced form with $\mathbf{K}_t$ subject to restrictions coming from the original structural form. The SSOE models discussed in Section 3.4 are effectively in innovations form but if this is the starting point of model formulation some way of putting constraints on $\mathbf{K}_t$ has to be found.

6.4. Time-invariant models

In many applications the state space model is time-invariant. In other words the system matrices $\mathbf{Z}_t$, $\mathbf{d}_t$, $\mathbf{H}_t$, $\mathbf{T}_t$, $\mathbf{c}_t$, $\mathbf{R}_t$ and $\mathbf{Q}_t$ are all independent of time and so can be written without a subscript. However, most of the properties in which we are interested apply to a system in which $\mathbf{c}_t$ and $\mathbf{d}_t$ are allowed to change over time and so the class of models under discussion is effectively

$$\mathbf{y}_t = \mathbf{Z}\boldsymbol{\alpha}_t + \mathbf{d}_t + \boldsymbol{\varepsilon}_t, \quad \mathrm{Var}(\boldsymbol{\varepsilon}_t) = \mathbf{H} \tag{71}$$

and

$$\boldsymbol{\alpha}_t = \mathbf{T}\boldsymbol{\alpha}_{t-1} + \mathbf{c}_t + \mathbf{R}\boldsymbol{\eta}_t, \quad \mathrm{Var}(\boldsymbol{\eta}_t) = \mathbf{Q} \tag{72}$$

with $E(\boldsymbol{\varepsilon}_t \boldsymbol{\eta}_s' t) = \mathbf{0}$ for all s, t and $\mathbf{P}_{1|0}$, $\mathbf{H}$ and $\mathbf{Q}$ p.s.d.

The principal STMS are time invariant and easily put in SSF with a measurement equation that, for univariate models, will be written

$$y_t = \mathbf{z}'\boldsymbol{\alpha}_t + \varepsilon_t, \quad t = 1, \ldots, T \tag{73}$$

with $\mathrm{Var}(\varepsilon_t) = H = \sigma_\varepsilon^2$. Thus state space form of the damped trend model, (19) is:

$$y_t = [1 \quad 0]\boldsymbol{\alpha}_t + \varepsilon_t, \tag{74}$$

$$\boldsymbol{\alpha}_t = \begin{bmatrix} \mu_t \\ \beta_t \end{bmatrix} = \begin{bmatrix} 1 & 1 \\ 0 & \rho \end{bmatrix} \begin{bmatrix} \mu_{t-1} \\ \beta_{t-1} \end{bmatrix} \begin{bmatrix} \eta_t \\ \zeta_t \end{bmatrix}. \tag{75}$$

The local linear trend is the same but with $\rho = 1$.

The Kalman filter applied to the model in (71) is in a steady state if the error covariance matrix is time-invariant, that is $\mathbf{P}_{t+1|t} = \mathbf{P}$. This implies that the covariance matrix of the innovations is also time-invariant, that is $\mathbf{F}_t = \mathbf{F} = \mathbf{ZPZ}' + \mathbf{H}$. The recursion for the error covariance matrix is therefore redundant in the steady state, while the recursion for the state becomes

$$\mathbf{a}_{t+1|t} = \mathbf{L}\mathbf{a}_{t|t-1} + \mathbf{K}\mathbf{y}_t + (\mathbf{c}_{t+1} - \mathbf{K}\mathbf{d}_t) \tag{76}$$

where the transition matrix is defined by

$$\mathbf{L} = \mathbf{T} - \mathbf{KZ} \tag{77}$$

and $\mathbf{K} = \mathbf{TPZ}'\mathbf{F}^{-1}$.

Letting $\mathbf{P}_{t+1|t} = \mathbf{P}_{t|t-1} = \mathbf{P}$ in (63) yields the algebraic Riccati equation

$$\mathbf{P} - \mathbf{TPT}' + \mathbf{TPZ}'\mathbf{F}^{-1}\mathbf{ZPT}' - \mathbf{RQR}' = \mathbf{0} \tag{78}$$

and the Kalman filter has a steady-state solution if there exists a time-invariant error covariance matrix, $\mathbf{P}$, that satisfies this equation. Although the solution to the Riccati equation was obtained for the local level model in (13), it is usually difficult to obtain an explicit solution. A discussion of various algorithms can be found in Ionescu, Oara and Weiss (1997).

The model is stable if the roots of $\mathbf{T}$ are less than one in absolute value, that is $|\lambda_i(\mathbf{T})| < 1, i = 1, \ldots, m$, and it can be shown that

$$\lim_{t\to\infty} \mathbf{P}_{t+1|t} = \mathbf{P} \tag{79}$$

with $\mathbf{P}$ independent of $\mathbf{P}_{1|0}$. Convergence to $\mathbf{P}$ is exponentially fast provided that $\mathbf{P}$ is the only p.s.d. matrix satisfying the algebraic Riccati equation. Note that with $\mathbf{d}_t$ time invariant and $\mathbf{c}_t$ zero the model is stationary. The stability condition can be readily checked but it is stronger than is necessary. It is apparent from (76) that what is needed is $|\lambda_i(\mathbf{L})| < 1, i = 1, \ldots, m$, but, of course, $\mathbf{L}$ depends on $\mathbf{P}$. However, it is shown in the engineering literature that the result in (79) holds if the system is detectable and stabilizable. Further discussion can be found in Anderson and Moore (1979, Section 4.4) and Burridge and Wallis (1988).

6.4.1. Filtering weights

If the filter is in a steady-state, the recursion for the predictive filter in (76) can be solved to give

$$\mathbf{a}_{t+1|t} = \sum_{j=0}^{\infty} \mathbf{L}^j \mathbf{K} \mathbf{y}_{t-j} + \sum_{j=0}^{\infty} \mathbf{L}^j \mathbf{c}_{t+1-j} + \sum_{j=0}^{\infty} \mathbf{L}^j \mathbf{K} \mathbf{d}_{t-j}. \tag{80}$$

Thus it can be seen explicitly how the filtered estimator is a weighted average of past observations. The one-step ahead predictor, $\widetilde{\mathbf{y}}_{t+1|t}$, can similarly be expressed in terms of current and past observations by shifting (57) forward one time period and substituting from (80). Note that when $\mathbf{c}_t$ and $\mathbf{d}_t$ are time-invariant, we can write

$$\mathbf{a}_{t+1|t} = (\mathbf{I} - \mathbf{L}L)^{-1}\mathbf{K}\mathbf{y}_t + (\mathbf{I} - \mathbf{L})^{-1}(\mathbf{c} - \mathbf{K}\mathbf{d}). \tag{81}$$

If we are interested in the weighting pattern for the current filtered estimator, as opposed to one-step ahead, the Kalman filtering equations need to be combined as

$$\mathbf{a}_t = \mathbf{L}^{\dagger}\mathbf{a}_{t-1} + \mathbf{K}^{\dagger}\mathbf{y}_t + \left(\mathbf{c}_t - \mathbf{K}^{\dagger}\mathbf{d}_t\right) \tag{82}$$

where $\mathbf{L}^{\dagger} = (\mathbf{I} - \mathbf{K}^{\dagger}\mathbf{Z})\mathbf{T}$ and $\mathbf{K}^{\dagger} = \mathbf{P}\mathbf{Z}'\mathbf{F}^{-1}$. An expression analogous to (81) is then obtained.

6.4.2. ARIMA representation

The ARIMA representation for any model in SSF can be obtained as follows. Suppose first that the model is stationary. The two equations in the steady-state innovations form may be combined to give

$$\mathbf{y}_t = \boldsymbol{\mu} + \mathbf{Z}(\mathbf{I} - \mathbf{T}L)^{-1}\mathbf{K}\boldsymbol{\nu}_{t-1} + \boldsymbol{\nu}_t. \tag{83}$$

The (*vector*) *moving-average representation* is therefore

$$\mathbf{y}_t = \boldsymbol{\mu} + \boldsymbol{\Psi}(L)\boldsymbol{\nu}_t \tag{84}$$

where $\boldsymbol{\Psi}(L)$ is a matrix polynomial in the lag operator

$$\boldsymbol{\Psi}(L) = \mathbf{I} + \mathbf{Z}(\mathbf{I} - \mathbf{T}L)^{-1}\mathbf{K}L. \tag{85}$$

Thus, given the steady-state solution, we can compute that MA coefficients.

If the stationarity assumption is relaxed, we can write

$$|\mathbf{I} - \mathbf{T}L|\mathbf{y}_t = \left[|\mathbf{I} - \mathbf{T}L|\mathbf{I} + \mathbf{Z}(\mathbf{I} - \mathbf{T}L)^{\dagger}\mathbf{K}L\right]\boldsymbol{\nu}_t \tag{86}$$

where $|\mathbf{I} - \mathbf{T}L|$ may contain unit roots. If, in a univariate model, there are d such unit roots, then the reduced form is an ARIMA(p, d, q) model with $p + d \leqslant m$. Thus in the local level model, we find, after some manipulation of (86), that

$$\Delta y_t = \nu_t - \nu_{t-1} + k\nu_{t-1} = \nu_t - (1 + p)^{-1}\nu_{t-1} = \nu_t + \theta\nu_{t-1} \tag{87}$$

confirming that the reduced form is ARIMA(0, 1, 1).

6.4.3. Autoregressive representation

Recalling the definition of an innovation vector in (69) we may write

$$\mathbf{y}_t = \mathbf{Z}\mathbf{a}_{t|t-1} + \mathbf{d} + \boldsymbol{\nu}_t.$$

Substituting for $\mathbf{a}_{t|t-1}$ from (81), lagged one time period, gives

$$\mathbf{y}_t = \boldsymbol{\delta} + \mathbf{Z}\sum_{j=1}^{\infty} \mathbf{L}^{j-1}\mathbf{K}\mathbf{y}_{t-j} + \boldsymbol{\nu}_t, \qquad \mathrm{Var}(\boldsymbol{\nu}_t) = \mathbf{F} \tag{88}$$

where

$$\boldsymbol{\delta} = \left(\mathbf{I} - \mathbf{Z}(\mathbf{I} - \mathbf{L})^{-1}\mathbf{K}\right)\mathbf{d} + \mathbf{Z}(\mathbf{I} - \mathbf{L})^{-1}\mathbf{c}. \tag{89}$$

The (*vector*) *autoregressive representation* is, therefore,

$$\boldsymbol{\Phi}(L)\mathbf{y}_t = \boldsymbol{\delta} + \boldsymbol{\nu}_t \tag{90}$$

where $\boldsymbol{\Phi}(L)$ is the matrix polynomial in the lag operator

$$\boldsymbol{\Phi}(L) = \mathbf{I} - \mathbf{Z}(\mathbf{I} - \mathbf{L}L)^{-1}\mathbf{K}L$$

and $\boldsymbol{\delta} = \boldsymbol{\Phi}(1)\mathbf{d} + \mathbf{Z}(\mathbf{I} - \mathbf{L})^{-1}\mathbf{c}$.

If the model is stationary, it may be written as

$$\mathbf{y}_t = \boldsymbol{\mu} + \boldsymbol{\Phi}^{-1}(L)\boldsymbol{\nu}_t \tag{91}$$

where $\boldsymbol{\mu}$ is as in the moving-average representation of (84). This implies that $\boldsymbol{\Phi}^{-1}(L) = \boldsymbol{\Psi}(L)$: hence the identity

$$\left(\mathbf{I} - \mathbf{Z}(\mathbf{I} - \mathbf{L}L)^{-1}\mathbf{K}L\right)^{-1} = \mathbf{I} + \mathbf{Z}(\mathbf{I} - \mathbf{T}L)^{-1}\mathbf{K}L.$$

6.4.4. Forecast functions

The forecast function for a time invariant model can be written as

$$\tilde{\mathbf{y}}_{T+l|T} = \mathbf{Z}\mathbf{a}_{T+l|T} = \mathbf{Z}\mathbf{T}^l\mathbf{a}_T, \qquad l = 1, 2, \ldots. \tag{92}$$

This is the MMSE of $\mathbf{y}_{T+\ell}$ in a Gaussian model. The weights assigned to current and past observations may be determined by substituting from (82). Substituting repeatedly from the recursion for the MSE of $\mathbf{a}_{T+l|T}$ gives

$$\mathrm{MSE}\left(\tilde{\mathbf{y}}_{T+l|T}\right) = \mathbf{Z}\mathbf{T}^l\mathbf{P}_T\mathbf{T}'^l\mathbf{Z}' + \mathbf{Z}\left(\sum_{j=0}^{l-1}\mathbf{T}^j\mathbf{R}\mathbf{Q}\mathbf{R}'\mathbf{T}'^j\right)\mathbf{Z}' + \mathbf{H}. \tag{93}$$

It is sometimes more convenient to use (80) to express $\tilde{\mathbf{y}}_{T+l|T}$ in terms of the predictive filter, that is as $\mathbf{Z}\mathbf{T}^{l-1}\mathbf{a}_{T+1|T}$. A corresponding expression for the MSE can be written down in terms of $\mathbf{P}_{T+1|T}$.

Local linear trend. The forecast function is as in (18), while from (93), the MSE is

$$\left(p_T^{(1,1)} + 2lp_T^{(1,2)} + l^2 p_T^{(2,2)}\right) + l\sigma_\eta^2 + \frac{1}{6}l(l-1)(2l-1)\sigma_\zeta^2 + \sigma_\varepsilon^2,$$
$$l = 1, 2, \ldots \tag{94}$$

where $p_T^{(i,j)}$ is the (ij)th element of the matrix $\mathbf{P}_T$. The third term, which is the contribution arising from changes in the slope, leads to the most dramatic increases as l increases. If the trend model were completely deterministic both the second and third terms would disappear. In a model where some components are deterministic, including them in the state vector ensures that their contribution to the MSE of predictions is accounted for by the elements of $\mathbf{P}_T$ appearing in the first term.

6.5. *Maximum likelihood estimation and the prediction error decomposition*

A state space model will normally contain unknown parameters, or hyperparameters, that enter into the system matrices. The vector of such parameters will be denoted by $\boldsymbol{\psi}$. Once the observations are available, the joint density in (68) can be reinterpreted as a likelihood function and written $L(\boldsymbol{\psi})$. The ML estimator of $\boldsymbol{\psi}$ is then found by maximizing $L(\boldsymbol{\psi})$. It follows from the discussion below (68) that the Gaussian likelihood function can be written in terms of the innovations, that is,

$$\log L(\boldsymbol{\psi}) = -\frac{NT}{2}\log 2\pi - \frac{1}{2}\sum_{t=1}^{T}\log|\mathbf{F}_t| - \frac{1}{2}\sum_{t=1}^{T}\boldsymbol{\nu}_t'\mathbf{F}_t^{-1}\boldsymbol{\nu}_t. \tag{95}$$

This is sometimes known as the *prediction error decomposition* form of the likelihood.

The maximization of $L\,(\boldsymbol{\psi})$ with respect to $\boldsymbol{\psi}$ will normally be carried out by some kind of numerical optimization procedure. A univariate model can usually be reparameterized so that $\boldsymbol{\psi} = [\boldsymbol{\psi}_*'\ \sigma_*^2]'$ where $\boldsymbol{\psi}_*$ is a vector containing $n-1$ parameters and σ_*^2 is one of the disturbance variances in the model. The Kalman filter can then be run independently of σ_*^2 and this allows it to be concentrated out of the likelihood function.

If prior information is available on all the elements of $\boldsymbol{\alpha}_0$, then $\boldsymbol{\alpha}_0$ has a proper prior distribution with known mean, $\mathbf{a}_0$, and bounded covariance matrix, $\mathbf{P}_0$. The Kalman filter then yields the exact likelihood function. Unfortunately, genuine prior information is rarely available. The solution is to start the Kalman filter at $t = 0$ with a diffuse prior. Suitable algorithms are discussed in Durbin and Koopman (2001, Chapter 5).

When parameters are estimated, the formula for $\text{MSE}(\widetilde{\mathbf{y}}_{T+l|T})$ in (67) will underestimate the true MSE because it does not take into account the extra variation, of $0(T^{-1})$, due to estimating $\boldsymbol{\psi}$. Methods of approximating this additional variation are discussed in Quenneville and Singh (2000). Using the bootstrap is also a possibility; see Stoffer and Wall (2004).

Diagnostic tests can be based on the standardized innovations, $\mathbf{F}_t^{-1/2}\boldsymbol{\nu}_t$. These residuals are serially independent if $\boldsymbol{\psi}$ is known, but when parameters are estimated the distribution of statistics designed to test for serially correlation are affected just as they are when an ARIMA model is estimated. Auxiliary residuals based on smoothed estimates of the disturbances $\boldsymbol{\varepsilon}_t$ and $\boldsymbol{\eta}_t$ are also useful; Harvey and Koopman (1992) show how they can give an indication of outliers or structural breaks.

6.6. Missing observations, temporal aggregation and mixed frequency

Missing observations are easily handled in the SSF simply by omitting the updating equations while retaining the prediction equations. Filtering and smoothing then go through automatically and the likelihood function is constructed using prediction errors corresponding to actual observations. When dealing with flow variables, such as income, the issue is one of temporal aggregation. This may be dealt with by the introduction of a cumulator variable into the state as described in Harvey (1989, Section 6.3). The ability to handle missing and temporally aggregated observations offers enormous flexibility, for example in dealing with observations at mixed frequencies. The unemployment series in Figure 1 provide an illustration.

It is sometimes necessary to make predictions of the cumulative effect of a flow variable up to a particular lead time. This is especially important in stock or production control problems in operations research. Calculating the correct MSE may be ensured by augmenting the state vector by a cumulator variable and making predictions from the Kalman filter in the usual way; see Johnston and Harrison (1986) and Harvey (1989, pp. 225–226). The continuous time solution described later in Section 8.3 is more elegant.

6.7. Bayesian methods

Since the state vector is a vector of random variables, a Bayesian interpretation of the Kalman filter as a way of updating a Gaussian prior distribution on the state to give a posterior is quite natural. The mechanics of filtering, smoothing and prediction are the same irrespective of whether the overall framework is Bayesian or classical. As regards initialization of the Kalman filter for a non-stationary state vector, the use of a proper prior is certainly not necessary from the technical point of view and a diffuse prior provides the solution in a classical framework.

The Kalman filter gives the mean and variance of the distribution of future observations, conditional on currently available observations. For the classical statistician, the conditional mean is the MMSE of the future observations while for the Bayesian it minimizes the expected loss for a symmetric loss function. With a quadratic loss function, the expected loss is given by the conditional variance. Further discussion can be found in Chapter 1 by Geweke and Whiteman in this Handbook.

The real differences in classical and Bayesian treatments arise when the parameters are unknown. In the classical framework these are estimated by maximum likelihood. Inferences about the state and predictions of future observations are then usually made conditional on the estimated values of the hyperparameters, though some approximation to the effect of parameter uncertainty can be made as noted at the end of Section 6.5. In a Bayesian set-up, on the other hand, the hyperparameters, as they are often called, are random variables. The development of simulation techniques based on Markov chain Monte Carlo (MCMC) has now made a full Bayesian treatment a feasible proposition. This means that it is possible to simulate a predictive distribution for future observations that takes account of hyperparameter uncertainty; see, for example, Carter and Kohn (1994) and Frühwirth-Schnatter (2004). The computations may be speeded up considerably by using the *simulation smoother* introduced by de Jong and Shephard (1995) and further developed by Durbin and Koopman (2002).

Prior distributions of variance parameters are often specified as inverted gamma distributions. This distribution allows a non-informative prior to be adopted as in Frühwirth-Schnatter (1994, p. 196). It is difficult to construct sensible informative priors for the variances themselves. Any knowledge we might have is most likely to be based on signal–noise ratios. Koop and van Dijk (2000) adopt an approach in which the signal–noise ratio in a random walk plus noise is transformed so as to be between zero and one. Harvey, Trimbur and van Dijk (2006) use non-informative priors on variances together with informative priors on the parameters λ_c and ρ in the stochastic cycle.

7. Multivariate models

The principal STMs can be extended to handle more than one series. Simply allowing for cross-correlations leads to the class of seemingly unrelated times series equation (SUTSE) models. Models with common factors emerge as a special case. As well as having a direct interpretation, multivariate structural time series models may provide more efficient inferences and forecasts. They are particularly useful when a target series is measured with a large error or is subject to a delay, while a related series does not suffer from these problems.

7.1. Seemingly unrelated times series equation models

Suppose we have N time series. Define the vector $\mathbf{y}_t = (y_{1t}, \ldots, y_{Nt})'$ and similarly for $\boldsymbol{\mu}_t$, $\boldsymbol{\psi}_t$ and $\boldsymbol{\varepsilon}_t$. Then a multivariate UC model may be set up as

$$\mathbf{y}_t = \boldsymbol{\mu}_t + \boldsymbol{\psi}_t + \boldsymbol{\varepsilon}_t, \quad \boldsymbol{\varepsilon}_t \sim NID(\mathbf{0}, \boldsymbol{\Sigma}_\varepsilon), \quad t = 1, \ldots, T \tag{96}$$

where $\boldsymbol{\Sigma}_\varepsilon$ is an $N \times N$ positive semi-definite matrix. The trend is

$$\begin{aligned} \boldsymbol{\mu}_t &= \boldsymbol{\mu}_{t-1} + \boldsymbol{\beta}_{t-1} + \boldsymbol{\eta}_t, \quad \boldsymbol{\eta}_t \sim NID(\mathbf{0}, \boldsymbol{\Sigma}_\eta), \\ \boldsymbol{\beta}_t &= \boldsymbol{\beta}_{t-1} + \boldsymbol{\zeta}_t, \quad \boldsymbol{\zeta}_t \sim NID(\mathbf{0}, \boldsymbol{\Sigma}_\zeta). \end{aligned} \tag{97}$$

The *similar cycle* model is

$$\begin{bmatrix} \boldsymbol{\psi}_t \\ \boldsymbol{\psi}_t^* \end{bmatrix} = \left[\rho \begin{bmatrix} \cos\lambda_c & \sin\lambda_c \\ -\sin\lambda_c & \cos\lambda_c \end{bmatrix} \otimes \mathbf{I}_N \right] \begin{bmatrix} \boldsymbol{\psi}_{t-1} \\ \boldsymbol{\psi}_{t-1}^* \end{bmatrix} + \begin{bmatrix} \boldsymbol{\kappa}_t \\ \boldsymbol{\kappa}_t^* \end{bmatrix}, \quad t = 1, \ldots, T \tag{98}$$

where $\boldsymbol{\psi}_t$ and $\boldsymbol{\psi}_t^*$ are $N \times 1$ vectors and $\boldsymbol{\kappa}_t$ and $\boldsymbol{\kappa}_t^*$ are $N \times 1$ vectors of the disturbances such that

$$E\left(\boldsymbol{\kappa}_t\boldsymbol{\kappa}_t'\right) = E\left(\boldsymbol{\kappa}_t^*\boldsymbol{\kappa}_t^{*'}\right) = \boldsymbol{\Sigma}_\kappa, \quad E\left(\boldsymbol{\kappa}_t\boldsymbol{\kappa}_t^{*'}\right) = \mathbf{0} \tag{99}$$

where $\boldsymbol{\Sigma}_\kappa$ is an $N \times N$ covariance matrix. The model allows the disturbances to be correlated across the series. Because the damping factor and the frequency, ρ and λ_c, are the same in all series, the cycles in the different series have similar properties; in particular, their movements are centered around the same period. This seems eminently reasonable if the cyclical movements all arise from a similar source such as an underlying business cycle. Furthermore, the restriction means that it is often easier to separate out trend and cycle movements when several series are jointly estimated.

Homogeneous models are a special case when all the covariance matrices, $\boldsymbol{\Sigma}_\eta$, $\boldsymbol{\Sigma}_\zeta$, $\boldsymbol{\Sigma}_\varepsilon$, and $\boldsymbol{\Sigma}_\kappa$, are proportional; see Harvey (1989, Chapter 8, Section 3). In this case, the same filter and smoother is applied to each series. Multivariate calculations are not required unless MSEs are needed.

7.2. Reduced form and multivariate ARIMA models

The reduced form of a SUTSE model is a multivariate ARIMA(p, d, q) model with p, d and q taking the same values as in the corresponding univariate case. General expressions may be obtained from the state space form using (86). Similarly the VAR representation may be obtained from (88).

The disadvantage of a VAR is that long lags may be needed to give a good approximation and the loss in degrees of freedom is compounded as the number of series increases. For ARIMA models the restrictions implied by a structural form are very strong – and this leads one to question the usefulness of the whole class. The fact that vector ARIMA models are far more difficult to estimate than VARs means that they have not been widely used in econometrics – unlike the univariate case, there are few, if any compensating advantages.

The issues can be illustrated with the multivariate random walk plus noise. The reduced form is the multivariate ARIMA(0, 1, 1) model

$$\Delta \mathbf{y}_t = \boldsymbol{\xi}_t + \boldsymbol{\Theta}\boldsymbol{\xi}_{t-1}, \quad \boldsymbol{\xi}_t \sim NID(\mathbf{0}, \boldsymbol{\Sigma}). \tag{100}$$

In the univariate case, the structural form implies that θ must lie between zero and minus one in the reduced form ARIMA(0, 1, 1) model. Hence only half the parameter space is admissible. In the multivariate model, the structural form not only implies restrictions on the parameter space in the reduced form, but also reduces its dimension. The total number of parameters in the structural form is $N(N+1)$ while in the unrestricted reduced form, the covariance matrix of $\boldsymbol{\xi}_t$ consists of $N(N+1)/2$ different elements but the MA parameter matrix contains N^2. Thus if N is five, the structural form contains thirty parameters while the unrestricted reduced form has forty. The restrictions are even tighter when the structural model contains several components.[10]

The reduced form of a SUTSE model is always invertible although it may not always be strictly invertible. In other words some of the roots of the MA polynomial for the reduced form may lie on, rather than outside, the unit circle. In the case of the multivariate random walk plus noise, the condition for strict invertibility of the stationary form is that $\mathbf{\Sigma}_\eta$ should be p.d. However, the Kalman filter remains valid even if $\mathbf{\Sigma}_\eta$ is only p.s.d. On the other hand, ensuring that $\mathbf{\Theta}$ satisfies the conditions of invertibility is technically more complex.

In summary, while the multivariate random walk plus noise has a clear interpretation and rationale, the meaning of the elements of $\mathbf{\Theta}$ is unclear, certain values may be undesirable and invertibility is difficult to impose.

7.3. *Dynamic common factors*

Reduced rank disturbance covariance matrices in a SUTSE model imply common factors. The most important cases arise in connection with the trend and this is our main focus. However, it is possible to have common seasonal components and common cycles. The common cycle model is a special case of the similar cycle model and is an example of what Engle and Kozicki (1993) call a common feature.

7.3.1. *Common trends and co-integration*

With $\mathbf{\Sigma}_\zeta = 0$ the trend in (97) is a random walk plus deterministic drift, $\boldsymbol{\beta}$. If the rank of $\mathbf{\Sigma}_\eta$ is $K < N$, the model can be written in terms of K common trends, $\boldsymbol{\mu}_t^\dagger$, that is,

$$\begin{aligned} \mathbf{y}_{1t} &= \boldsymbol{\mu}_t^\dagger + \boldsymbol{\varepsilon}_{1t}, \\ \mathbf{y}_{2t} &= \mathbf{\Pi}\boldsymbol{\mu}_t^\dagger + \bar{\boldsymbol{\mu}} + \boldsymbol{\varepsilon}_{2t} \end{aligned} \tag{101}$$

where $\mathbf{y}_t$ is partitioned into a $K \times 1$, vector $\mathbf{y}_{1t}$ and an $R \times 1$ vector $\mathbf{y}_{2t}$, $\boldsymbol{\varepsilon}_t$ is similarly partitioned, $\mathbf{\Pi}$ is an $R \times K$ matrix of coefficients and the $K \times 1$, vector $\boldsymbol{\mu}_t^\dagger$ follows a multivariate random walk with drift

$$\boldsymbol{\mu}_t^\dagger = \boldsymbol{\mu}_{t-1}^\dagger + \boldsymbol{\beta}^\dagger + \boldsymbol{\eta}_t^\dagger, \quad \boldsymbol{\eta}_t^\dagger \sim NID(\mathbf{0}, \mathbf{\Sigma}_\eta^\dagger) \tag{102}$$

with $\boldsymbol{\eta}_t^\dagger$ and $\boldsymbol{\beta}^\dagger$ being $K \times 1$ vectors and $\mathbf{\Sigma}_\eta^\dagger$ a $K \times K$ positive definite matrix.

The presence of common trends implies co-integration. In the local level model, (119), there exist $R = N - K$ co-integrating vectors. Let $\mathbf{A}$ be an $R \times N$ matrix partitioned as $\mathbf{A} = (\mathbf{A}_1, \mathbf{A}_2)$. The common trend system in (119) can be transformed to an

[10] No simple expressions are available for $\mathbf{\Theta}$ in terms of structural parameters in the multivariate case. However, its value may be computed from the steady-state by observing that $\mathbf{I} - \mathbf{T}L = (1 - L)\mathbf{I}$ and so, proceeding as in (86), one obtains the symmetric $N \times N$ moving average matrix, $\mathbf{\Theta}$, as $\mathbf{K} - \mathbf{I} = -\mathbf{L} = -(\mathbf{P} + \mathbf{I})^{-1}$.

equivalent co-integrating system by pre-multiplying by an $N \times N$ matrix

$$\begin{bmatrix} \mathbf{I}_K & \mathbf{0} \\ \mathbf{A}_1 & \mathbf{A}_2 \end{bmatrix}. \tag{103}$$

If $\mathbf{A} = (-\boldsymbol{\Pi}, \mathbf{I}_R)$ this is just

$$\begin{aligned} \mathbf{y}_{1t} &= \boldsymbol{\mu}_t^{\dagger} + \boldsymbol{\varepsilon}_{1t}, \\ \mathbf{y}_{2t} &= \boldsymbol{\Pi}\mathbf{y}_{1t} + \bar{\boldsymbol{\mu}} + \boldsymbol{\varepsilon}_t \end{aligned} \tag{104}$$

where $\boldsymbol{\varepsilon}_t = \boldsymbol{\varepsilon}_{2t} - \boldsymbol{\Pi}\boldsymbol{\varepsilon}_{1t}$. Thus the second set of equations consists of co-integrating relationships, $\mathbf{Ay}_t$, while the first set contains the common trends. This is a special case of the *triangular representation* of a co-integrating system.

The notion of co-breaking, as expounded in Clements and Hendry (1998), can be incorporated quite naturally into a common trends model by the introduction of a dummy variable, w_t, into the equation for the trend, that is,

$$\boldsymbol{\mu}_t^{\dagger} = \boldsymbol{\mu}_{t-1}^{\dagger} + \boldsymbol{\beta}^{\dagger} + \boldsymbol{\lambda} w_t + \boldsymbol{\eta}_t^{\dagger}, \quad \boldsymbol{\eta}_t^{\dagger} \sim NID\big(\mathbf{0}, \boldsymbol{\Sigma}_{\eta}^{\dagger}\big) \tag{105}$$

where $\boldsymbol{\lambda}$ is a $K \times 1$ vector of coefficients. Clearly the breaks do not appear in the R stationary series in $\mathbf{Ay}_t$.

7.3.2. Representation of a common trends model by a vector error correction model (VECM)

The VECM representation of a VAR

$$\mathbf{y}_t = \boldsymbol{\delta} + \sum_{j=1}^{\infty} \boldsymbol{\Phi}_j \mathbf{y}_{t-j} + \boldsymbol{\xi}_t \tag{106}$$

is

$$\Delta\mathbf{y}_t = \boldsymbol{\delta} + \boldsymbol{\Phi}^* \mathbf{y}_{t-1} + \sum_{r=1}^{\infty} \boldsymbol{\Phi}_r^* \Delta\mathbf{y}_{t-r} + \boldsymbol{\xi}_t, \quad \operatorname{Var}(\boldsymbol{\xi}_t) = \boldsymbol{\Sigma} \tag{107}$$

where the relationship between the $N \times N$ parameter matrices, $\boldsymbol{\Phi}_r^*$, and those in the VAR model is

$$\boldsymbol{\Phi}^* = -\boldsymbol{\Phi}(1) = \sum_{k=1}^{\infty} \boldsymbol{\Phi}_k - \mathbf{I}, \qquad \boldsymbol{\Phi}_j^* = -\sum_{k=j+1}^{\infty} \boldsymbol{\Phi}_k, \quad j = 1, 2, \ldots. \tag{108}$$

If there are R co-integrating vectors, contained in the $R \times N$ matrix $\mathbf{A}$, then $\boldsymbol{\Phi}^*$ contains K unit roots and $\boldsymbol{\Phi}^* = \boldsymbol{\Gamma}\mathbf{A}$, where $\boldsymbol{\Gamma}$ is $N \times R$; see Johansen (1995) and Chapter 6 by Lütkepohl in this Handbook.

If there are no restrictions on the elements of $\boldsymbol{\delta}$ they contain information on the $K \times 1$ vector of common slopes, $\boldsymbol{\beta}^*$, and on the $R \times 1$ vector of intercepts, $\boldsymbol{\mu}^*$, that constitutes the mean of $\mathbf{A}\mathbf{y}_t$. This is best seen by writing (107) as

$$\Delta \mathbf{y}_t = \mathbf{A}_{\perp}\boldsymbol{\beta}^* + \boldsymbol{\Gamma}(\mathbf{A}\mathbf{y}_{t-1} - \boldsymbol{\mu}^*) + \sum_{r=1}^{\infty} \boldsymbol{\Phi}_r^*\left(\Delta \mathbf{y}_{t-r} - \mathbf{A}_{\perp}\boldsymbol{\beta}^*\right) + \boldsymbol{\xi}_t \tag{109}$$

where $\mathbf{A}_{\perp}$ is an $N \times K$ matrix such that $\mathbf{A}\mathbf{A}_{\perp} = \mathbf{0}$, so that there are no slopes in the co-integrating vectors. The elements of $\mathbf{A}_{\perp}\boldsymbol{\beta}^*$ are the growth rates of the series. Thus,[11]

$$\boldsymbol{\delta} = \left(\mathbf{I} - \sum_{j=1}^{\infty} \boldsymbol{\Phi}_j^*\right)\mathbf{A}_{\perp}\boldsymbol{\beta}^* - \boldsymbol{\Gamma}\boldsymbol{\mu}^*. \tag{110}$$

Structural time series models have an implied triangular representation as we saw in (104). The connection with VECMs is not so straightforward. The coefficients of the VECM representation for any UC model with common (random walk plus drift) trends can be computed numerically by using the algorithm of Koopman and Harvey (2003). Here we derive analytic expressions for the VECM representation of a local level model, (101), noting that, in terms of the general state space model, $\mathbf{Z} = (\mathbf{I}, \boldsymbol{\Pi}')'$. The coefficient matrices in the VECM depend on the $K \times N$ steady-state Kalman gain matrix, $\mathbf{K}$, as given from the algebraic Riccati equations. Proceeding in this way can give interesting insights into the structure of the VECM.

From the vector autoregressive form of the Kalman filter, (88), noting that $\mathbf{T} = \mathbf{I}_K$, so $\mathbf{L} = \mathbf{I}_K - \mathbf{KZ}$, we have

$$\mathbf{y}_t = \boldsymbol{\delta} + \mathbf{Z}\left(\mathbf{I}_K - (\mathbf{I}_K - \mathbf{KZ})L\right)^{-1}\mathbf{K}\mathbf{y}_{t-1} + \boldsymbol{\nu}_t, \quad \mathrm{Var}(\boldsymbol{\nu}_t) = \mathbf{F}. \tag{111}$$

(Note that $\mathbf{F}$ and $\mathbf{K}$ depend on $\mathbf{Z}$, $\boldsymbol{\Sigma}_\eta$ and $\boldsymbol{\Sigma}_\varepsilon$ via the steady-state covariance matrix $\mathbf{P}$.) This representation corresponds to a VAR with $\boldsymbol{\nu}_t = \boldsymbol{\xi}_t$ and $\mathbf{F} = \boldsymbol{\Sigma}$. The polynomial in the infinite vector autoregression, (106), is, therefore,

$$\boldsymbol{\Phi}(L) = \mathbf{I}_N - \mathbf{Z}\left[\mathbf{I}_K - (\mathbf{I}_K - \mathbf{KZ})L\right]^{-1}\mathbf{K}L.$$

The matrix

$$\boldsymbol{\Phi}(1) = \mathbf{I}_N - \mathbf{Z}(\mathbf{KZ})^{-1}\mathbf{K} \tag{112}$$

has the property that $\boldsymbol{\Phi}(1)\mathbf{Z} = \mathbf{0}$ and $\mathbf{K}\boldsymbol{\Phi}(1) = \mathbf{0}$. Its rank is easily seen to be R, as required by the Granger representation theorem; this follows because it is idempotent and so the rank is equal to the trace.

The expression linking $\boldsymbol{\delta}$ to $\bar{\boldsymbol{\mu}}$ and $\boldsymbol{\beta}^{\dagger}$ is obtained from (89) as

$$\boldsymbol{\delta} = \left[\mathbf{I}_N - \mathbf{Z}(\mathbf{KZ})^{-1}\mathbf{K}\right]\begin{bmatrix}\mathbf{0}\\ \bar{\boldsymbol{\mu}}\end{bmatrix} + \mathbf{Z}(\mathbf{KZ})^{-1}\boldsymbol{\beta}^{\dagger} \tag{113}$$

[11] If we don't want time trends in the series, the growth rates must be set to zero so we must constrain $\boldsymbol{\delta}$ to depend only on the R parameters in $\boldsymbol{\mu}^*$ by setting $\boldsymbol{\delta} = -\boldsymbol{\Gamma}\boldsymbol{\mu}^*$. In the special case when $R = N$, there are no time trends and $\boldsymbol{\delta} = -\boldsymbol{\Gamma}\boldsymbol{\mu}^*$ is the unconditional mean.

since $\mathbf{d} = (\mathbf{0}', \overline{\boldsymbol{\mu}})'$. The vectors $\overline{\boldsymbol{\mu}}$ and $\boldsymbol{\beta}^{\dagger}$ contain N non-zero elements between them; thus the components of both level and growth are included in $\boldsymbol{\delta}$.

The coefficient matrices in the infinite VECM, (107), are $\boldsymbol{\Phi}^* = -\boldsymbol{\Phi}(1)$ and

$$\boldsymbol{\Phi}_j^* = -\mathbf{Z}[\mathbf{I}_K - \mathbf{KZ}]^j(\mathbf{KZ})^{-1}\mathbf{K}, \quad j = 1, 2, \ldots. \tag{114}$$

The VECM of (109) is given by setting $\mathbf{A}_{\perp} = \mathbf{Z} = (\mathbf{I}, \boldsymbol{\Pi}')'$ and $\boldsymbol{\beta}^* = \boldsymbol{\beta}^{\dagger}$. The $\mathbf{A}$ matrix is not unique for $N - K = R > 1$, but it can be set to $[-\boldsymbol{\Pi}, \mathbf{I}_R]$ and the $\boldsymbol{\Gamma}$ matrix must then satisfy $\boldsymbol{\Gamma}\mathbf{A} = \boldsymbol{\Phi}^*$. However, since $\mathbf{A}(\mathbf{0}', \overline{\boldsymbol{\mu}}')' = \boldsymbol{\mu}^*$, this choice of $\mathbf{A}$ implies $\overline{\boldsymbol{\mu}} = \boldsymbol{\mu}^*$. Hence it follows from (110) and (113) that $\boldsymbol{\Gamma}$ is given by the last R columns of $\boldsymbol{\Phi}^*$.

7.3.3. Single common trend

For a single common trend we may write

$$\mathbf{y}_t = \mathbf{z}\mu_t^{\dagger} + \boldsymbol{\varepsilon}_t, \quad t = 1, \ldots, T, \tag{115}$$

where $\mathbf{z}$ is a vector and $\mu_t^{\dagger}$ is a univariate random walk. It turns out that optimal filtering and smoothing can be carried out exactly as for a univariate local level model for $\overline{\overline{y}}_t = \overline{\sigma}_{\varepsilon}^2\mathbf{z}'\boldsymbol{\Sigma}_{\varepsilon}^{-1}\mathbf{y}_t$ with $\overline{q} = \sigma_{\eta}^2/\overline{\sigma}_{\varepsilon}^2$, where $\overline{\sigma}_{\varepsilon}^{-2} = \mathbf{z}'\boldsymbol{\Sigma}_{\varepsilon}^{-1}\mathbf{z}$. This result, which is similar to one in Kozicki (1999), is not entirely obvious since, unless the diagonal elements of $\boldsymbol{\Sigma}_{\varepsilon}$ are the same, univariate estimators would have different $q's$ and hence different smoothing constants. It has implications for estimating an underlying trend from a number of series. The result follows by applying a standard matrix inversion lemma, as in Harvey (1989, p. 108), to $\mathbf{F}_t^{-1}$ in the vector $\mathbf{k}_t = p_{t|t-1}\mathbf{z}'\mathbf{F}_t^{-1}$ to give

$$\mathbf{k}_t = \left[p_{t|t-1}^*/\left(p_{t|t-1}^* + 1\right)\right]\overline{\sigma}_{\varepsilon}^2\mathbf{z}'\boldsymbol{\Sigma}_{\varepsilon}^{-1} \tag{116}$$

where $p_{t|t-1}^* = \overline{\sigma}_{\varepsilon}^{-2}p_{t|t-1}$. Thus the Kalman filter can be run as a univariate filter for $\overline{\overline{y}}_t$. In the steady state, $\overline{p}^*$ is as in (13) but using $\overline{q}$ rather than q. Then from (116) we get $\mathbf{k} = [(\overline{p}^* + \overline{q})/(\overline{p}^* + \overline{q} + 1)]\overline{\sigma}_{\varepsilon}^2\mathbf{z}'\boldsymbol{\Sigma}_{\varepsilon}^{-1}$.

As regards the VECM representation, $\mathbf{I}_K - \mathbf{KZ} = 1 - \mathbf{k}'\mathbf{z}$ is a scalar and the coefficients of the lagged differences, the elements of the $\boldsymbol{\Phi}_j^{*\prime}s$, all decay at the same rate. Since $\mathbf{k}'\mathbf{z} = (\overline{p}^* + \overline{q})/(\overline{p}^* + \overline{q} + 1)$,

$$\boldsymbol{\Phi}_j^* = -\left(1/\mathbf{k}'\mathbf{z}\right)\left(1 - \mathbf{k}'z\right)^j\mathbf{z}\mathbf{k}' = -\left(\overline{p}^* + \overline{q} + 1\right)^{-j}\overline{\sigma}_{\varepsilon}^2\mathbf{z}\mathbf{z}'\boldsymbol{\Sigma}_{\varepsilon}^{-1}, \quad j = 1, 2, \ldots.$$

Furthermore,

$$\boldsymbol{\Phi}(1) = -\boldsymbol{\Phi}^* = \mathbf{I} - \left(1/\mathbf{k}'\mathbf{z}\right)\mathbf{z}\mathbf{k}' = \mathbf{I} - \overline{\sigma}_{\varepsilon}^2\mathbf{z}\mathbf{z}'\boldsymbol{\Sigma}_{\varepsilon}^{-1}. \tag{117}$$

If w_k is the weight attached to y_k in forming the mean, that is w_k is the kth element of the vector $\bar{\sigma}_\varepsilon^2 \mathbf{z}' \boldsymbol{\Sigma}_\varepsilon^{-1}$, the ith equation in the VECM can be expressed[12] as

$$\Delta y_{it} = \delta_i - \left(y_{i,t-1} - z_i \,\bar{\bar{y}}_{t-1}\right) - z_i \sum_{k=1}^{N} w_k \sum_{j=1}^{\infty} (-\bar{\theta})^j \,\Delta y_{k,t-j} + v_{it} \tag{118}$$

where δ_i is a constant, $\bar{\theta} = -1/(\bar{p}^* + \bar{q} + 1)$ depends on $\bar{q}$ and the $v_{it}'s$ are serially uncorrelated disturbances. The terms $y_{i,t-1} - z_i \bar{\bar{y}}_{t-1}$ can also be expressed as $N-1$ co-integrating vectors weighted by the elements of the last $N-1$ columns of $\boldsymbol{\Phi}^*$. *The most interesting point to emerge from this representation is that the (exponential) decay of the weights attached to lagged differences is the same for all variables in each equation.*

The single common trends model illustrates the implications of using a VAR or VECM as an approximating model. It has already been noted that an autoregression can be a very poor approximation to a random walk plus noise model, particularly if the signal–noise ratio, q, is small. In a multivariate model the problems are compounded. Thus, ignoring $\bar{\boldsymbol{\mu}}$ and $\beta^\dagger$, a model with a single common trend contains N parameters in addition to the parameters in $\boldsymbol{\Sigma}_\varepsilon$. The VECM has a disturbance covariance matrix with the same number of parameters as $\boldsymbol{\Sigma}_\varepsilon$. However the error correction matrix $\boldsymbol{\Phi}^*$ is $N \times N$ and on top of this a sufficient number of lagged differences, with $N \times N$ parameter matrices, $\boldsymbol{\Phi}_j^*$, must be used to give a reasonable approximation.

7.4. Convergence

STMs have recently been adapted to model converging economies and to produce forecasts that take account of convergence. Before describing these models it is first necessary to discuss balanced growth.

7.4.1. Balanced growth, stability and convergence

The *balanced growth* UC model is a special case of (96):

$$\mathbf{y}_t = \mathbf{i}\mu_t^\dagger + \boldsymbol{\alpha} + \boldsymbol{\psi}_t + \boldsymbol{\varepsilon}_t, \quad t = 1, \ldots, T \tag{119}$$

where $\mu_t^\dagger$ is a univariate local linear trend, $\mathbf{i}$ is a vector of ones, and $\boldsymbol{\alpha}$ is an $N \times 1$ vector of constants. Although there may be differences in the level of the trend in each series, the slopes are the same, irrespective of whether they are fixed or stochastic.

A balanced growth model implies that the series have a stable relationship over time. This means that there is a full rank $(N-1) \times N$ matrix, $\mathbf{D}$, with the property that $\mathbf{Di} = \mathbf{0}$, thereby rendering $\mathbf{Dy}_t$ jointly stationary. If the series are stationary in first differences, balanced growth may be incorporated in a vector error correction model (VECM) of the form (109) by letting $\mathbf{A} = \mathbf{D}$ and $\mathbf{A}_\perp = \mathbf{i}$. The system has a single

[12] In the univariate case $\bar{\bar{y}}_t = y_t$ and so (118) reduces to the (unstandardized) EWMA of differences, (37).

unit root, guaranteed by the fact that $\mathbf{Di} = \mathbf{0}$. The constants in $\boldsymbol{\delta}$ contain information on the common slope, β, and on the differences in the levels of the series, as contained in the vector $\boldsymbol{\alpha}$. These differences might be parameterized with respect to the contrasts in $\mathbf{Dy}_{t-1}$. For example if $\mathbf{Dy}_t$ has elements $y_{it} - y_{i+1,t}$, $i = 1, \ldots, N-1$, then α_i, the ith element of the $(N-1) \times 1$ vector $\boldsymbol{\alpha}$, is the gap between y_i and y_{i+1}. In any case, $\boldsymbol{\delta} = (\mathbf{I} - \sum_{j=1}^{p} \boldsymbol{\Phi}_j^*)\mathbf{i}\beta - \boldsymbol{\Gamma\alpha}$. The matrix $\boldsymbol{\Gamma}$ contains $N(N-1)$ free parameters and these may be estimated efficiently by OLS applied to each equation in turn. However, there is no guarantee that the estimate of $\boldsymbol{\Gamma}$ will be such that the model is stable.

7.4.2. Convergence models

A multivariate convergence model may be set up as

$$\mathbf{y}_t = \boldsymbol{\alpha} + \beta\mathbf{i}t + \boldsymbol{\mu}_t + \boldsymbol{\psi}_t + \boldsymbol{\varepsilon}_t, \quad t = 1, \ldots, T \tag{120}$$

with $\boldsymbol{\psi}_t$ and $\boldsymbol{\varepsilon}_t$ defined as (96) and

$$\boldsymbol{\mu}_t = \boldsymbol{\Phi}\boldsymbol{\mu}_{t-1} + \boldsymbol{\eta}_t, \quad \operatorname{Var}(\boldsymbol{\eta}_t) = \boldsymbol{\Sigma}_\eta. \tag{121}$$

Each row of $\boldsymbol{\Phi}$ sums to unity, $\boldsymbol{\Phi}\mathbf{i} = \mathbf{i}$. Thus setting λ to one in $(\boldsymbol{\Phi} - \lambda\mathbf{I})\mathbf{i} = \mathbf{0}$, shows that $\boldsymbol{\Phi}$ has an eigenvalue of one with a corresponding eigenvector consisting of ones. The other roots of $\boldsymbol{\Phi}$ are obtained by solving $|\boldsymbol{\Phi} - \lambda\mathbf{I}| = 0$; they should have modulus less than one for convergence.

If we write

$$\bar{\boldsymbol{\phi}}'\boldsymbol{\mu}_t = \bar{\boldsymbol{\phi}}'\boldsymbol{\Phi}\boldsymbol{\mu}_{t-1} + \bar{\boldsymbol{\phi}}'\boldsymbol{\eta}_t$$

it is clear that the $N \times 1$ vector of weights, $\bar{\boldsymbol{\phi}}$, which gives a random walk must be such that $\bar{\boldsymbol{\phi}}'(\boldsymbol{\Phi} - \mathbf{I}) = \mathbf{0}'$. Since the roots of $\boldsymbol{\Phi}'$ are the same as those of $\boldsymbol{\Phi}$, it follows from writing $\boldsymbol{\Phi}\bar{\boldsymbol{\phi}}' = \bar{\boldsymbol{\phi}}'$ that $\bar{\boldsymbol{\phi}}$ is the eigenvector of $\boldsymbol{\Phi}'$ corresponding to its unit root. This random walk, $\bar{\mu}_{\phi t} = \bar{\boldsymbol{\phi}}'\boldsymbol{\mu}_t$, is a common trend in the sense that it yields the common growth path to which all the economies converge. This is because $\lim_{j\to\infty} \boldsymbol{\Phi}^j = \mathbf{i}\bar{\boldsymbol{\phi}}'$. The common trend for the observations is a random walk with drift, β.

The *homogeneous* model has $\boldsymbol{\Phi} = \phi\mathbf{I} + (1-\phi)\mathbf{i}\bar{\boldsymbol{\phi}}'$, where $\mathbf{i}$ is an $N \times 1$ vector of ones, ϕ is a scalar convergence parameter and $\bar{\boldsymbol{\phi}}$ is an $N \times 1$ vector of parameters with the property that $\bar{\boldsymbol{\phi}}'\mathbf{i} = 1$. (It is straightforward to confirm that $\bar{\boldsymbol{\phi}}$ is the eigenvector of $\boldsymbol{\Phi}'$ corresponding to the unit root). The likelihood function is maximized numerically with respect to ϕ and the elements of $\bar{\boldsymbol{\phi}}$, denoted $\bar{\phi}_i$, $i = 1, \ldots, N$; the $\boldsymbol{\mu}_t$ vector is initialized with a diffuse prior. It is assumed that $0 \leqslant \phi \leqslant 1$, with $\phi = 1$ indicating no convergence. The $\bar{\phi}_i's$ are constrained to lie between zero and one and to sum to one.

In a homogeneous model, each trend can be decomposed into the common trend and a convergence component. The vector of convergence components defined by is $\boldsymbol{\mu}_t^\dagger = \boldsymbol{\mu}_t - \mathbf{i}\bar{\mu}_{\phi t}$ and it is easily seen that

$$\boldsymbol{\mu}_t^\dagger = \phi\boldsymbol{\mu}_{t-1}^\dagger + \boldsymbol{\eta}_t^\dagger, \quad t = 1, \ldots, T \tag{122}$$

where $\boldsymbol{\eta}_t^{\dagger} = \boldsymbol{\eta}_t - \mathbf{i}\bar{\eta}_{\phi t}$. The error correction form for each series

$$\Delta\mu_{it}^{\dagger} = (\phi - 1)\mu_{i,t-1}^{\dagger} + \eta_{it}^{\dagger}, \quad i = 1, \ldots, N,$$

shows that its relative growth rate depends on the gap between it and the common trend. Substituting (122) into (120) gives

$$\mathbf{y}_t = \boldsymbol{\alpha} + \beta\mathbf{i}t + \mathbf{i}\bar{\mu}_{\phi t} + \boldsymbol{\mu}_t^{\dagger} + \boldsymbol{\psi}_t + \boldsymbol{\varepsilon}_t, \quad t = 1, \ldots, T.$$

Once convergence has taken place, the model is of the balanced growth form, (119), but with an additional stationary component $\boldsymbol{\mu}_t^{\dagger}$.

The smooth homogeneous convergence model is

$$\mathbf{y}_t = \boldsymbol{\alpha} + \boldsymbol{\mu}_t + \boldsymbol{\psi}_t + \boldsymbol{\varepsilon}_t, \quad t = 1, \ldots, T \tag{123}$$

and

$$\boldsymbol{\mu}_t = \boldsymbol{\Phi}\boldsymbol{\mu}_{t-1} + \boldsymbol{\beta}_{t-1}, \quad \boldsymbol{\beta}_t = \boldsymbol{\Phi}\boldsymbol{\beta}_{t-1} + \boldsymbol{\zeta}_t, \; \mathrm{Var}(\boldsymbol{\zeta}_t) = \boldsymbol{\Sigma}_{\zeta}$$

with $\boldsymbol{\Phi} = \phi\mathbf{I} + (1-\phi)\mathbf{i}\bar{\boldsymbol{\phi}}'$ as before. Using scalar notation to write the model in terms of the common trend, $\bar{\mu}_{\phi,t}$, and convergence processes, $\mu_{it}^{\dagger} = \mu_{it} - \bar{\mu}_{\phi,t}$, $i = 1, \ldots, N$, yields

$$y_{it} = \alpha_i + \bar{\mu}_{\phi,t} + \mu_{it}^{\dagger} + \psi_{it} + \varepsilon_{it}, \quad i = 1, \ldots, N \tag{124}$$

where $\Sigma\alpha_i = 0$, the common trend is

$$\bar{\mu}_{\phi,t} = \bar{\mu}_{\phi,t-1} + \bar{\beta}_{\phi,t-1}, \quad \bar{\beta}_{\phi,t} = \bar{\beta}_{\phi,t-1} + \bar{\zeta}_{\phi,t}$$

and the convergence components are

$$\mu_{it}^{\dagger} = \phi\mu_{i,t-1}^{\dagger} + \beta_{it}^{\dagger}, \quad \beta_{it}^{\dagger} = \phi\beta_{i,t-1}^{\dagger} + \zeta_{it}^{\dagger}, \quad i = 1, \ldots, N.$$

The convergence components can be given a second-order error correction representation as in Section 2.8. The forecasts converge to those of a smooth common trend, but in doing so they may exhibit temporary divergence.

US regions. Carvalho and Harvey (2005) fit a smooth, homogeneous absolute convergence model, (124) with $\alpha_i = 0$, $i = 1, \ldots, N$, to annual series of six US regions. (NE and ME were excluded as they follow growth paths that, especially for the last two decades, seem to be diverging from the growth paths of the other regions.) The similar cycle parameters were estimated to be $\rho = 0.79$ and $2\pi/\lambda = 8.0$ years, while the estimate of ϕ was 0.889 and the weights, $\bar{\phi}_i$, were such that the common trend is basically constructed by weighting Great Lakes two-thirds and Plains one third. The model not only allows a separation into trends and cycles but also separates out the long-run balanced growth path from the transitional (converging) regional dynamics, thus permitting a characterization of convergence stylized facts. Figure 10 shows the forecasts of the convergence components for the six regional series over a twenty year

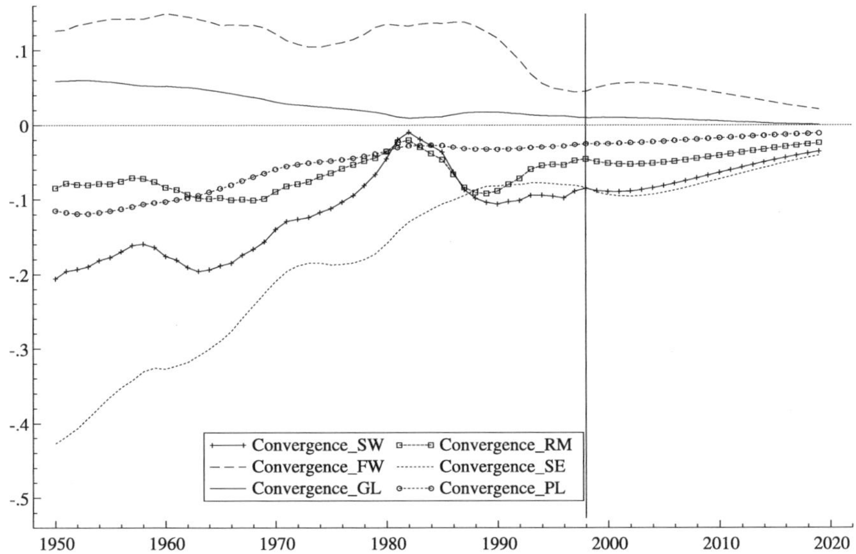

Figure 10. Forecasts for convergence components in US regions.

horizon (2000–2019). The striking feature of this figure is not the eventual convergence, but rather the prediction of divergence in the short run. Thus, although Plains and Great Lakes converge rapidly to the growth path of the common trend, which is hardly surprising given the composition of the common trend, the Far West, Rocky Mountains, South East and South West are all expected to widen their income gap, relative to the common trend, during the first five years of the forecast period. Only then do they resume their convergence towards the common trend and even then with noticeable differences in dynamics. This temporary divergence is a feature of the smooth convergence model; the second-order error correction specification not only admits slower changes but also, when the convergence process stalls, allows for divergence in the short run.

7.5. *Forecasting and nowcasting with auxiliary series*

The use of an auxiliary series that is a coincident or leading indicator yields potential gains for nowcasting and forecasting. Our analysis will be based on bivariate models. We will take one series, the first, to be the target series while the second is the related series. With nowcasting our concern is with the reduction in the MSE in estimating the level and the slope. We then examine how this translates into gains for forecasting. The emphasis is somewhat different from that in Chapter 16 by Marcellino in this Handbook where the concern is with the information to be gleaned from a large number of series.

We will concentrate on the local linear trend model, that is

$$\mathbf{y}_t = \boldsymbol{\mu}_t + \boldsymbol{\varepsilon}_t, \quad \boldsymbol{\varepsilon}_t \sim NID(0, \boldsymbol{\Sigma}_\varepsilon), \; t = 1, \ldots, T \tag{125}$$

where $\mathbf{y}_t$ and all the other vectors are 2×1 and $\boldsymbol{\mu}_t$ is as in (97). It is useful to write the covariance matrices of $\boldsymbol{\eta}_t$ as

$$\boldsymbol{\Sigma}_\eta = \begin{bmatrix} \sigma_{1\eta}^2 & \rho_\eta \sigma_{1\eta}\sigma_{2\eta} \\ \rho_\eta \sigma_{1\eta}\sigma_{2\eta} & \sigma_{2\eta}^2 \end{bmatrix} \tag{126}$$

where ρ_η is the correlation and similarly for the other disturbance covariance matrices, where the correlations will be ρ_ε and ρ_ζ.

When $\rho_\zeta = \pm 1$ there is then only one source of stochastic movement in the two slopes. This is the *common slopes* model. We can write

$$\beta_{2t} = \overline{\beta} + \theta \beta_{1t}, \quad t = 1, \ldots, T \tag{127}$$

where $\theta = \operatorname{sgn}(\rho_\zeta)\sigma_{2\zeta}/\sigma_{1\zeta}$ and $\overline{\beta}$ is a constant. When $\overline{\beta} = 0$, the model has *proportional slopes*. If, furthermore, θ is equal to one, that is $\sigma_{2\zeta} = \sigma_{1\zeta}$ and ρ_ζ positive, there are *identical slopes*.

The series in a common slopes model are *co-integrated* of order (2, 1). Thus, although both y_{1t} and y_{2t} require second differencing to make them stationary, there is a linear combination of first differences which is stationary. If, in addition, $\rho_\eta = \pm 1$, and, furthermore, $\sigma_{2\eta}/\sigma_{1\eta} = \sigma_{2\zeta}/\sigma_{1\zeta}$, then the series are CI(2,2), meaning that there is a linear combination of the observations themselves which is stationary. These conditions mean that $\boldsymbol{\Sigma}_\zeta$ is proportional to $\boldsymbol{\Sigma}_\eta$, which is a special case of what Koopman et al. (2000) call *trend homogeneity*.

7.5.1. *Coincident (concurrent) indicators*

In order to gain some insight into the potential gains from using a coincident indicator for nowcasting and forecasting, consider the local level model, that is (125) without the vector of slopes, $\boldsymbol{\beta}_t$. The MSE matrix of predictions is given by a straightforward generalization of (15), namely

$$\operatorname{MSE}(\widetilde{\mathbf{y}}_{T+l|T}) = \mathbf{P}_T + l\boldsymbol{\Sigma}_\eta + \boldsymbol{\Sigma}_\varepsilon, \quad l = 1, 2, \ldots.$$

The gains arise from $\mathbf{P}_T$ as the current level is estimated more precisely. However, $\mathbf{P}_T$ will tend to be dominated by the uncertainty in the level as the lead time increases.

Assuming the target series to be the first series, interest centres on $\operatorname{RMSE}(\widetilde{\mu}_{1T})$. It might be thought that high correlation between the disturbances in the two series necessarily leads to big reductions in this RMSE. However, this need not be the case. If $\boldsymbol{\Sigma}_\eta = q\boldsymbol{\Sigma}_\varepsilon$, where q is a positive scalar, the model as a whole is homogeneous, and there is no gain from a bivariate model (except in the estimation of the factors of proportionality). This is because the bivariate filter is the same as the univariate filter; see Harvey (1989, pp. 435–442). As a simple illustration, consider a model with $\sigma_{2\varepsilon} = \sigma_{1\varepsilon}$ and $q = 0.5$. RMSEs were calculated from the steady-state $\mathbf{P}$ matrix for various combinations of ρ_ε and ρ_η. With $\rho_\varepsilon = 0.8$, $\operatorname{RMSE}(\widetilde{\mu}_{1T})$ relative to that obtained in the univariate model is 0.94, 1 and 0.97 for ρ_η equal to 0, 0.8 and 1 respectively. Thus there is no gain under homogeneity and there is less reduction in RMSE when the levels are perfectly correlated compared with when they are uncorrelated. The biggest gain in precision is when $\rho_\varepsilon = -1$ and $\rho_\eta = 1$. In fact if the levels are identical, $(y_{1t} + y_{2t})/2$ estimates the level exactly. When $\rho_\varepsilon = 0$, the relative RMSEs are 1, 0.93 and 0.80 for ρ_η equal to 0, 0.8 and 1 respectively.

Observations on a related series can also be used to get more accurate estimates of the underlying growth rate in a target series and hence more accurate forecasts. For example, when the target series contains an irregular component but the related series does not, there is always a reduction in RMSE$(\widetilde{\beta}_{1T})$ from using the related series (unless the related series is completely deterministic). Further analysis of potential gains can be found in Harvey and Chung (2000).

Labour Force Survey. The challenge posed by combining quarterly survey data on unemployment with the monthly claimant count was described in the introduction. The appropriate model for the monthly CC series, y_{2t}, is a local linear trend with no irregular component. The monthly model for the LFS series is similar, except that the observations contain a survey sampling error as described in Section 2.5. A bivariate model with these features can be handled within the state space framework even if the LFS observations are only available every quarter or, as was the case before 1992, every year. A glance at Figure 1 suggests that the underlying trends in the two series are not the same. However, such divergence does not mean that the CC series contains no usable information. For example it is plausible that the underlying slopes of the two series move closely together even though the levels show a tendency to drift apart. In terms of model (125) this corresponds to a high correlation, ρ_ζ, between the stochastic slopes, accompanied by a much lower correlation for the levels, ρ_η. The analysis at the start of this subsection indicates that such a combination could lead to a considerable gain in the precision with which the underlying change in ILO unemployment is estimated. Models were estimated using monthly CC observations from 1971 together with quarterly LFS observations from May 1992 and annual observations from 1984. The last observations are in August 1998. The proportional slopes model is the preferred one. The weighting functions are shown in Figure 11.

Output gap. Kuttner (1994) uses a bivariate model for constructing an estimate of the output gap by combining the equation for the trend-cycle decomposition of GDP, y_t, in (28) with a Phillips curve effect that relates inflation to the lagged change in GDP and its cycle, ψ_t, that is,

$$\Delta p_t = \mu_p + \gamma \Delta y_{t-1} + \beta \psi_{t-1} + u_t$$

where p_t is the logarithm of the price level, μ_p is a constant and u_t is a stationary process. Planas and Rossi (2004) extend this idea further and examine the implications for detecting turning points. Harvey, Trimbur and van Dijk (2006) propose a variation in which Δy_{t-1} is dropped from the inflation equation and μ_p is stochastic.

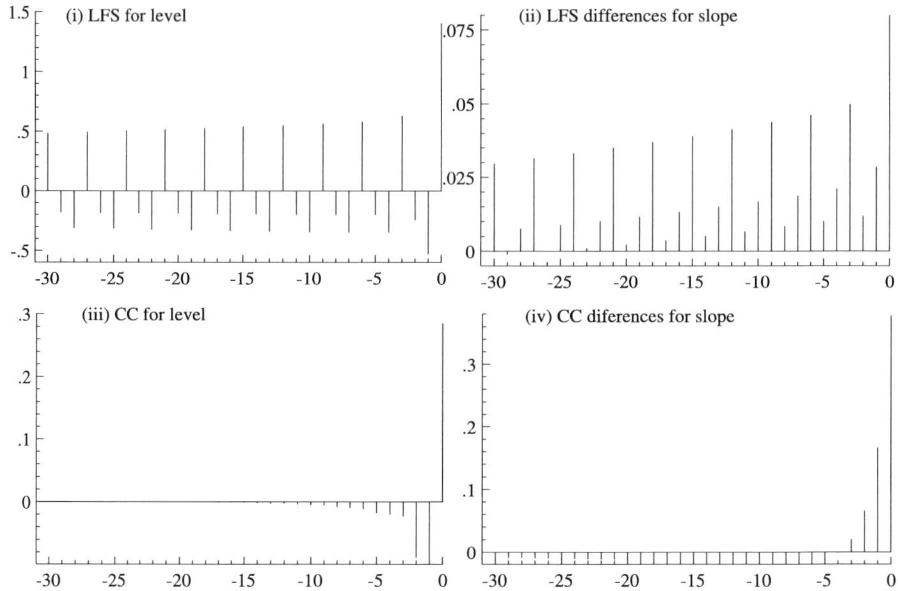

Figure 11. Weights applied to levels and differences of LFS and CC in estimating the current underlying change in LFS.

7.5.2. *Delayed observations and leading indicators*

Suppose that the first series is observed with a delay. We can then use the second series to get a better estimate of the first series and its underlying level than could be obtained by univariate forecasting. For the local level, the measurement equation at time T is

$$y_{2,T} = (0\ 1)\boldsymbol{\mu}_T + \varepsilon_{2,T}$$

and applying the KF we find

$$m_{1,T} = m_{1,T|T-1} + \frac{p_{1,2,T|T-1}}{p_{2,T|T-1} + \sigma_{\varepsilon 2}^2}\left(y_{2,T} - \widetilde{y}_{2,T|T-1}\right)$$

where, for example, $p_{1,2,T|T-1}$ is the element of $\mathbf{P}_{T|T-1}$ in row one, column two. The estimator of $y_{1,T}$ is given by the same expression, though the MSE's are different. In the homogeneous case it can be shown that the MSE is multiplied by $1-\rho^2$, where ρ is the correlation between the disturbances; see Harvey (1989, p. 467). The analysis of leading indicators is essentially the same.

7.5.3. *Preliminary observations and data revisions*

The optimal use of different vintages of observations in constructing the best estimate of a series, or its underlying level, at a particular date is an example of nowcasting; see

Harvey (1989, pp. 337–341) and Chapter 17 by Croushore in this Handbook. Using a state space approach, Patterson (1995) provides recent evidence on UK consumers' expenditure and concludes (p. 54) that "...preliminary vintages are not efficient forecasts of the final vintage".

Benchmarking can be regarded as another example of nowcasting in which monthly or quarterly observations collected over the year are readjusted so as to be consistent with the annual total obtained from another source such as a survey; see Durbin and Quenneville (1997). The state space treatment is similar to that of data revisions.

8. Continuous time

A continuous time model is more fundamental than one in discrete time. For many variables, the process generating the observations can be regarded as a continuous one even though the observations themselves are only made at discrete intervals. Indeed a good deal of the theory in economics and finance is based on continuous time models.

There are also strong statistical arguments for working with a continuous time model. Apart from providing an elegant solution to the problem of irregularly spaced observations, a continuous time model has the attraction of not being tied to the time interval at which the observations happen to be made. One of the consequences is that, for flow variables, the parameter space is more extensive than it typically would be for an analogous discrete time model. The continuous time formulation is also attractive for forecasting flow variables, particularly when cumulative predictions are to be made over a variable lead time.

Only univariate time series will be considered here. We will suppose that observations are spaced at irregular intervals. The τth observation will be denoted y_τ, for $\tau = 1, \ldots, T$, and t_τ will denote the time at which it is made, with $t_0 = 0$. The time between observations will be denoted by $\delta_\tau = t_\tau - t_{\tau-1}$.

As with discrete time models the state space form provides a general framework within which estimation and prediction may be carried out. The first subsection shows how a continuous time transition equation implies a discrete time transition equation at the observation points. The state space treatment for stocks and flows is then set out.

8.1. Transition equations

The continuous time analogue of the time-invariant discrete time transition equation is

$$\mathrm{d}\boldsymbol{\alpha}(t) = \mathbf{A}\boldsymbol{\alpha}(t)\,\mathrm{d}t + \mathbf{R}\mathbf{Q}^{1/2}\,\mathrm{d}\mathbf{W}_\eta(t) \tag{128}$$

where the $\mathbf{A}$ and $\mathbf{R}$ are $m \times m$ and $m \times g$, respectively, and may be functions of hyperparameters, $\mathbf{W}_\eta(t)$ is a standard multivariate Wiener process and $\mathbf{Q}$ is a $g \times g$ psd matrix.

The treatment of continuous time models hinges on the solution to the differential equations in (128). By defining $\boldsymbol{\alpha}_\tau$ as $\boldsymbol{\alpha}(t_\tau)$ for $\tau = 1, \ldots, T$, we are able to establish the discrete time transition equation,

$$\boldsymbol{\alpha}_\tau = \mathbf{T}_\tau \boldsymbol{\alpha}_{\tau-1} + \boldsymbol{\eta}_\tau, \quad \tau = 1, \ldots, T \tag{129}$$

where

$$\mathbf{T}_\tau = \exp(\mathbf{A}\delta_\tau) = \mathbf{I} + \mathbf{A}\delta_\tau + \frac{1}{2!}\mathbf{A}^2\delta_\tau^2 + \frac{1}{3!}\mathbf{A}^3\delta_\tau^3 + \cdots \tag{130}$$

and $\boldsymbol{\eta}_\tau$ is a multivariate white-noise disturbance term with zero and covariance matrix

$$\mathbf{Q}_\tau = \int_0^{\delta_\tau} \mathrm{e}^{\mathbf{A}(\delta_\tau - s)} \mathbf{RQR}' \mathrm{e}^{\mathbf{A}'(\delta_\tau - s)} \, \mathrm{d}s. \tag{131}$$

The condition for $\boldsymbol{\alpha}(t)$ to be stationary is that the real parts of the characteristic roots of $\mathbf{A}$ should be negative. This translates into the discrete time condition that the roots of $\mathbf{T} = \exp(\mathbf{A})$ should lie outside the unit circle. If $\boldsymbol{\alpha}(t)$ is stationary, the mean of $\boldsymbol{\alpha}(t)$ is zero and the covariance matrix is

$$\operatorname{Var}\big[\boldsymbol{\alpha}(t)\big] = \int_{-\infty}^{0} \mathrm{e}^{-\mathbf{A}s} \mathbf{RQR}' \mathrm{e}^{-\mathbf{A}'s} \, \mathrm{d}s. \tag{132}$$

The initial conditions for $\boldsymbol{\alpha}(t_0)$ are therefore $\mathbf{a}_{1|0} = \mathbf{0}$ and $\mathbf{P}_{1|0} = \operatorname{Var}[\boldsymbol{\alpha}(t)]$.

The main structural components are formulated in continuous time in the following way.

Trend: In the local level model, the level component, $\mu(t)$, is defined by $\mathrm{d}\mu(t) = \sigma_\eta \, \mathrm{d}W_\eta(t)$, where $W_\eta(t)$ is a standard Wiener process and σ_η is a non-negative parameter. Thus the increment $\mathrm{d}\mu(t)$ has mean zero and variance $\sigma_\eta^2 \, \mathrm{d}t$.

The linear trend component is

$$\begin{bmatrix} \mathrm{d}\mu(t) \\ \mathrm{d}\beta(t) \end{bmatrix} = \begin{bmatrix} 0 & 1 \\ 0 & 0 \end{bmatrix} \begin{bmatrix} \mu(t)\, \mathrm{d}t \\ \beta(t)\, \mathrm{d}t \end{bmatrix} + \begin{bmatrix} \sigma_\eta \, \mathrm{d}W_\eta(t) \\ \sigma_\zeta \, \mathrm{d}W_\zeta(t) \end{bmatrix} \tag{133}$$

where $W_\eta(t)$ and $W_\zeta(t)$ are mutually independent Wiener processes.

Cycle: The continuous cycle is

$$\begin{bmatrix} \mathrm{d}\psi(t) \\ \mathrm{d}\psi^*(t) \end{bmatrix} = \begin{bmatrix} \log\rho & \lambda_c \\ -\lambda_c & \log\rho \end{bmatrix} \begin{bmatrix} \psi(t)\, \mathrm{d}t \\ \psi^*(t)\, \mathrm{d}t \end{bmatrix} + \begin{bmatrix} \sigma_\kappa \, \mathrm{d}W_\kappa(t) \\ \sigma_\kappa \, \mathrm{d}W_\kappa^*(t) \end{bmatrix} \tag{134}$$

where $W_\kappa(t)$ and $W_\kappa^*(t)$ are mutually independent Wiener processes and σ_κ, ρ and λ_c are parameters, the latter being the frequency of the cycle. The characteristic roots of the matrix containing ρ and λ_c are $\log\rho \pm i\lambda_c$, so the condition for $\psi(t)$ to be a stationary process is $\rho < 1$.

Seasonal: The continuous time seasonal model is the sum of a suitable number of trigonometric components, $\gamma_j(t)$, generated by processes of the form (134) with ρ equal to unity and λ_c set equal to the appropriate seasonal frequency λ_j for $j = 1, \ldots, [s/2]$.

8.2. Stock variables

The discrete state space form for a stock variable generated by a continuous time process consists of the transition equation (129) together with the measurement equation

$$y_\tau = \mathbf{z}'\boldsymbol{\alpha}(t_\tau) + \varepsilon_\tau = \mathbf{z}'\boldsymbol{\alpha}_\tau + \varepsilon_\tau, \quad \tau = 1, \ldots, T \tag{135}$$

where ε_τ is a white-noise disturbance term with mean zero and variance σ_ε^2 which is uncorrelated with integrals of $\boldsymbol{\eta}(t)$ in all time periods. The Kalman filter can therefore be applied in a standard way. The discrete time model is time-invariant for equally spaced observations, in which case it is usually convenient to set δ_τ equal to unity. In a Gaussian model, estimation can proceed as in discrete time models since, even with irregularly spaced observations, the construction of the likelihood function can proceed via the prediction error decomposition.

8.2.1. Structural time series models

The continuous time components defined earlier can be combined to produce a continuous time structural model. As in the discrete case, the components are usually assumed to be mutually independent. Hence the **A** and **Q** matrices are block diagonal and so the discrete time components can be evaluated separately.

Trend: For a stock observed at times t_τ, $\tau = 1, \ldots, T$, it follows almost immediately that if the level component is Brownian motion then

$$\mu_\tau = \mu_{\tau-1} + \eta_\tau, \quad \mathrm{Var}(\eta_\tau) = \delta_\tau \sigma_\eta^2 \tag{136}$$

since

$$\eta_\tau = \mu(t_\tau) - \mu(t_{\tau-1}) = \sigma_\eta \int_{t_{\tau-1}}^{t_\tau} \mathrm{d}W_\eta(t) = \sigma_\eta\big(W_\eta(t_\tau) - W_\eta(t_{\tau-1})\big).$$

The discrete model is therefore a random walk for equally spaced observations. If the observation at time τ is made up of $\mu(t_\tau)$ plus a white noise disturbance term, ε_τ, the discrete time measurement equation can be written

$$y_\tau = \mu_\tau + \varepsilon_\tau, \quad \mathrm{Var}(\varepsilon_\tau) = \sigma_\varepsilon^2, \ \tau = 1, \ldots, T \tag{137}$$

and the set-up corresponds exactly to the familiar random walk plus noise model with signal–noise ratio $q_\delta = \delta\sigma_\eta^2/\sigma_\varepsilon^2 = \delta q$.

For the local linear trend model

$$\begin{bmatrix} \mu_\tau \\ \beta_\tau \end{bmatrix} = \begin{bmatrix} 1 & \delta_\tau \\ 0 & 1 \end{bmatrix} \begin{bmatrix} \mu_{\tau-1} \\ \beta_{\tau-1} \end{bmatrix} + \begin{bmatrix} \eta_\tau \\ \zeta_\tau \end{bmatrix}. \tag{138}$$

In view of the simple structure of the matrix exponential, the evaluation of the covariance matrix of the discrete time disturbances can be carried out directly, yielding

$$\operatorname{Var}\begin{bmatrix}\eta_\tau\\ \zeta_\tau\end{bmatrix} = \delta_\tau\begin{bmatrix}\sigma_\eta^2 + \frac{1}{3}\delta_\tau^2\sigma_\zeta^2 & \vdots & \frac{1}{2}\delta_\tau\sigma_\zeta^2\\ \cdots\cdots\cdots\cdots & \vdots & \cdots\cdots\\ \frac{1}{2}\delta_\tau\sigma_\zeta^2 & \vdots & \sigma_\zeta^2\end{bmatrix} \tag{139}$$

When δ_τ is equal to unity, the transition equation is of the same form as the discrete time local linear trend (17). However, (139) shows that independence for the continuous time disturbances implies that the corresponding discrete time disturbances are correlated.

When $\sigma_\eta^2 = 0$, signal extraction with this model yields a cubic spline. Harvey and Koopman (2000) argue that this is a good way of carrying out nonlinear regression. The fact that a model is used means that the problem of making forecasts from a cubic spline is solved.

Cycle: For the cycle model, use of the matrix exponential definition together with the power series expansions for the cosine and sine functions gives the discrete time model

$$\begin{bmatrix}\psi_\tau\\ \psi_\tau^*\end{bmatrix} = \rho^\delta\begin{bmatrix}\cos\lambda_c\delta_\tau & \sin\lambda_c\delta_\tau\\ -\sin\lambda_c\delta_\tau & \cos\lambda_c\delta_\tau\end{bmatrix}\begin{bmatrix}\psi_{\tau-1}\\ \psi_{\tau-1}^*\end{bmatrix} + \begin{bmatrix}\kappa_\tau\\ \kappa_\tau^*\end{bmatrix}. \tag{140}$$

When δ_τ equals one, the transition matrix corresponds exactly to the transition matrix of the discrete time cyclical component. Specifying that $\kappa(t)$ and $\kappa^*(t)$ be independent of each other with equal variances implies that

$$\operatorname{Var}\begin{bmatrix}\kappa_\tau\\ \kappa_\tau^*\end{bmatrix} = \left(\sigma_\kappa^2/\log\rho^{-2}\right)\left(1-\rho^{2\delta_\tau}\right)\mathbf{I}.$$

If $\rho = 1$, the covariance matrix is simply $\sigma_\kappa^2\delta_\tau\mathbf{I}$.

8.2.2. *Prediction*

In the general model of (128), the optimal predictor of the state vector for any positive lead time, l, is given by the forecast function

$$\mathbf{a}(t_T + l \mid T) = e^{\mathbf{A}l}\mathbf{a}_T \tag{141}$$

with associated MSE matrix

$$\mathbf{P}(t_T + l \mid T) = \mathbf{T}_l\mathbf{P}_T\mathbf{T}_l' + \mathbf{R}\mathbf{Q}_l\mathbf{R}', \quad l > 0 \tag{142}$$

where $\mathbf{T}_l$ and $\mathbf{Q}_l$ are, respectively (130) and (131) evaluated with δ_τ set equal to l.

The forecast function for the systematic part of the series,

$$\bar{y}(t) = \mathbf{z}'\boldsymbol{\alpha}(t) \tag{143}$$

can also be expressed as a continuous function of l, namely,

$$\widetilde{y}(t_T + l \mid T) = \mathbf{z}' \mathrm{e}^{\mathbf{A}l} \mathbf{a}_T.$$

The forecast of an observation made at time $t_T + l$, is

$$\widetilde{y}_{T+1|T} = \widetilde{y}(t_T + l \mid T) \tag{144}$$

where the observation to be forecast has been classified as the one indexed $\tau = T + 1$; its MSE is

$$\mathrm{MSE}\big(\widetilde{y}_{T+1|T}\big) = \mathbf{z}'\mathbf{P}(t_T + l \mid T)\mathbf{z} + \sigma_\varepsilon^2.$$

The evaluation of forecast functions for the various structural models is relatively straightforward. In general they take the same form as for the corresponding discrete time models. Thus the local level model has a forecast function

$$\widetilde{y}(t_T + l \mid T) = m(t_T + l \mid T) = m_T$$

and the MSE of the forecast of the $(T + 1)$-th observation, at time $t_T + l$, is

$$\mathrm{MSE}\big(\widetilde{y}_{T+1|T}\big) = p_T + l\sigma_\eta^2 + \sigma_\varepsilon^2$$

which is exactly the same form as (15).

8.3. Flow variables

For a flow

$$y_\tau = \int_0^{\delta_\tau} \mathbf{z}'\boldsymbol{\alpha}(t_{\tau-1} + r) + \sigma_\varepsilon \int_0^{\delta_\tau} \mathrm{d}W_\varepsilon(t_{\tau-1} + r), \quad \tau = 1, \ldots, T \tag{145}$$

where $W_\varepsilon(t)$ is independent of the Brownian motion driving the transition equation. Thus the irregular component is cumulated continuously whereas in the stock case it only comes into play when an observation is made.

The key feature in the treatment of flow variables in continuous time is the introduction of a cumulator variable, $y^f(t)$, into the state space model. The cumulator variable for the series at time t_τ is equal to the observation, y_τ, for $\tau = 1, \ldots, T$, that is $y^f(t_\tau) = y_\tau$. The result is an augmented state space system

$$\begin{aligned} \begin{bmatrix} \boldsymbol{\alpha}_\tau \\ y_\tau \end{bmatrix} &= \begin{bmatrix} \mathrm{e}^{\mathbf{A}\delta} & 0 \\ \mathbf{z}'\mathbf{W}(\delta_\tau) & 0 \end{bmatrix} \begin{bmatrix} \boldsymbol{\alpha}_{\tau-1} \\ y_{\tau-1} \end{bmatrix} + \begin{bmatrix} \mathbf{I} & \mathbf{0} \\ \mathbf{0}' & \mathbf{z}' \end{bmatrix} \begin{bmatrix} \boldsymbol{\eta}_\tau \\ \boldsymbol{\eta}_\tau^f \end{bmatrix} + \begin{bmatrix} \mathbf{0} \\ \varepsilon_\tau^f \end{bmatrix}, \\ y_\tau &= [\mathbf{0}' \;\; 1] \begin{bmatrix} \boldsymbol{\alpha}_\tau \\ y_\tau \end{bmatrix}, \qquad \tau = 1, \ldots, T \end{aligned} \tag{146}$$

with $\mathrm{Var}(\varepsilon_\tau^f) = \delta_\tau \sigma_\varepsilon^2$,

$$\mathbf{W}(r) = \int_0^r \mathrm{e}^{\mathbf{A}s}\, \mathrm{d}s \tag{147}$$

and

$$\operatorname{Var}\begin{bmatrix}\boldsymbol{\eta}_\tau\\ \boldsymbol{\eta}_\tau^f\end{bmatrix}=\int_0^{\delta_\tau}\begin{bmatrix}e^{\mathbf{A}r}\mathbf{RQR}'e^{\mathbf{A}'r} & \vdots & e^{\mathbf{A}r}\mathbf{RQR}'\mathbf{W}'(r)\\ \cdots\cdots\cdots\cdots & \vdots & \cdots\cdots\\ \mathbf{W}(r)\mathbf{RQR}'e^{\mathbf{A}'r} & \vdots & \mathbf{W}(r)\mathbf{RQR}'\mathbf{W}'(r)\end{bmatrix}=\mathbf{Q}_\tau^\dagger.$$

Maximum likelihood estimators of the hyperparameters can be constructed via the prediction error decomposition by running the Kalman filter on (146). No additional starting value problems are caused by bringing the cumulator variable into the state vector as $y^f(t_0)=0$.

An alternative way of approaching the problem is not to augment the state vector, as such, but to treat the equation

$$y_\tau=\mathbf{z}'\mathbf{W}(\delta_\tau)\boldsymbol{\alpha}_{\tau-1}+\mathbf{z}'\boldsymbol{\eta}_\tau^f+\varepsilon_\tau^f \tag{148}$$

as a measurement equation. Redefining $\boldsymbol{\alpha}_{\tau-1}$ as $\boldsymbol{\alpha}_\tau^*$ enables this equation to be written as

$$y_\tau=\mathbf{z}_\tau'\boldsymbol{\alpha}_\tau^*+\varepsilon_\tau,\qquad \tau=1,\ldots,T \tag{149}$$

where $\mathbf{z}_\tau'=\mathbf{z}'\mathbf{W}(\delta_\tau)$ and $\varepsilon_\tau=\mathbf{z}'\boldsymbol{\eta}_\tau^f+\varepsilon_\tau^f$. The corresponding transition equation is

$$\boldsymbol{\alpha}_{\tau+1}^*=\mathbf{T}_{\tau+1}\boldsymbol{\alpha}_\tau^*+\boldsymbol{\eta}_\tau,\qquad \tau=1,\ldots,T \tag{150}$$

where $\mathbf{T}_{\tau+1}=\exp(\mathbf{A}\delta_\tau)$. Taken together these two equations are a system of the form (53) and (55) with the measurement equation disturbance, ε_τ, and the transition equation disturbance, $\boldsymbol{\eta}_\tau$, correlated. The covariance matrix of $[\boldsymbol{\eta}_\tau'\ \varepsilon_\tau]'$ is given by

$$\operatorname{Var}\begin{bmatrix}\boldsymbol{\eta}_\tau\\ \varepsilon_\tau\end{bmatrix}=\begin{bmatrix}\mathbf{Q}_\tau & \mathbf{g}_\tau\\ \mathbf{g}_\tau' & h_\tau\end{bmatrix}=\begin{bmatrix}\mathbf{I} & \mathbf{0}\\ \mathbf{0}' & \mathbf{z}'\end{bmatrix}\mathbf{Q}_\tau^\dagger\begin{bmatrix}\mathbf{I} & \mathbf{0}'\\ \mathbf{0} & \mathbf{z}\end{bmatrix}+\begin{bmatrix}\mathbf{0} & \mathbf{0}\\ \mathbf{0} & \delta_\tau\sigma_\varepsilon^2\end{bmatrix}. \tag{151}$$

The modified version of the Kalman filter needed to handle such systems is described in Harvey (1989, Section 3.2.4). It is possible to find a SSF in which the measurement error is uncorrelated with the state disturbances, but this is at the price of introducing a moving average into the state disturbances; see Bergstrom (1984) and Chambers and McGarry (2002, p. 395).

The various matrix exponential expressions that need to be computed for the flow variable are relatively easy to evaluate for trend and seasonal components in STMs.

8.3.1. Prediction

In making predictions for a flow it is necessary to distinguish between the total accumulated effect from time t_τ to time $t_\tau+l$ and the amount of the flow in a single time period ending at time $t_\tau+l$. The latter concept corresponds to the usual idea of prediction in a discrete model.

Cumulative predictions. Let $y^f(t_T + l)$ denote the cumulative flow from the end of the sample to time $t_T + l$. In terms of the state space model of (146) this quantity is y_{T+1} with δ_{T+1} set equal to l. The optimal predictor, $\tilde{y}^f(t_T + l \mid T)$, can therefore be obtained directly from the Kalman filter as $\tilde{y}_{T+1|T}$. In fact the resulting expression gives the forecast function which we can write as

$$\tilde{y}^f(t_T + l \mid T) = \mathbf{z}'\mathbf{W}(l)\mathbf{a}_T, \quad l \geqslant 0 \tag{152}$$

with

$$\text{MSE}\big[\tilde{y}^f(t_T + l \mid T)\big] = \mathbf{z}'\mathbf{W}(l)\mathbf{P}_T\mathbf{W}'(l)\mathbf{z} + \mathbf{z}'\text{Var}\big(\boldsymbol{\eta}_\tau^f\big)\mathbf{z} + \text{Var}\big(\varepsilon_{T+1}^f\big). \tag{153}$$

For the local linear trend,

$$\tilde{y}^f(t_T + l \mid T) = l m_T + \frac{1}{2}l^2 b_T, \quad l \geqslant 0$$

with

$$\begin{aligned}\text{MSE}\big[\tilde{y}^f(t_T + l \mid T)\big] &= l^2 p_T^{(1,1)} + l^3 p_T^{(1,2)} + \frac{1}{4}l^4 p_T^{(2,2)} + \frac{1}{3}l^3\sigma_\eta^2 \\ &\quad + \frac{1}{20}l^5\sigma_\zeta^2 + l\sigma_\varepsilon^2\end{aligned} \tag{154}$$

where $p_T^{(i,j)}$ is the (i, j)th element of $\mathbf{P}_T$. Because the forecasts from a linear trend are being cumulated, the result is a quadratic. Similarly, the forecast for the local level, $l m_T$, is linear.

Predictions over the unit interval. Predictions over the unit interval emerge quite naturally from the state space form, (146), as the predictions of $y_{T+l}, l = 1, 2, \ldots,$ with δ_{T+l} set equal to unity for all l. Thus,

$$\tilde{y}_{T+l|T} = \mathbf{z}'\mathbf{W}(1)\mathbf{a}_{T+l-1|T}, \quad l = 1, 2, \ldots \tag{155}$$

with

$$\mathbf{a}_{T+l-1|T} = \mathrm{e}^{A(l-1)}\mathbf{a}_T, \quad l = 1, 2, \ldots. \tag{156}$$

The forecast function for the state vector is therefore of the same form as in the corresponding stock variable model. The presence of the term $\mathbf{W}(1)$ in (155) leads to a slight modification when these forecasts are translated into a prediction for the series itself. For STMs, the forecast functions are not too different from the corresponding discrete time forecast functions. However, an interesting feature is that pattern of weighting functions is somewhat more general. For example, for a continuous time local level, the MA parameter in the ARIMA(0, 1, 1) reduced form can take values up to 0.268 and the smoothing constant in the EWMA used to form the forecasts is in the range 0 to 1.268.

8.3.2. Cumulative predictions over a variable lead time

In some applications, the lead time itself can be regarded as a random variable. This happens, for example, in inventory control problems where an order is put in to meet demand, but the delivery time is uncertain. In such situations it may be useful to determine the unconditional distribution of the flow from the current point in time, that is

$$p(y_T^f) = \int_0^\infty p\big(y^f(t_T + l \mid T\big)p(l)\,\mathrm{d}l \tag{157}$$

where $p(l)$ is the p.d.f. of the lead time and $p(y^f(t_T + l \mid T))$ is the distribution of $y^f(t_T + l)$ conditional on the information at time T. In a Gaussian model, the mean of $y^f(t_T + l)$ is given by (152), while its variance is the same as the expression for the MSE of $y^f(t_T + l)$ given in (153). Although it may be difficult to derive the full unconditional distribution of y_T^f, expressions for the mean and variance of this distribution may be obtained for the principal structural time series models. In the context of inventory control, the unconditional mean might be the demand expected in the period before a new delivery arrives.

The mean of the unconditional distribution of y_T^f is

$$E\big(y_T^f\big) = E\big[\widetilde{y}^f(t_T + l \mid T)\big] \tag{158}$$

where the expectation is with respect to the distribution of the lead time. Similarly, the unconditional variance is

$$\mathrm{Var}\big(y_T^f\big) = E\big[\widetilde{y}^f(t_T + l \mid T)\big]^2 - \big[E\big(\widetilde{y}_T^f\big)\big]^2 \tag{159}$$

where the second raw moment of y_T^f can be obtained as

$$E\big[\widetilde{y}^f(t_T + l \mid T)\big]^2 = \mathrm{MSE}\big[\widetilde{y}^f(t_T + l \mid T)\big] + \big[\widetilde{y}^f(t_T + l \mid T)\big]^2.$$

The expressions for the mean and variance of y_T^f depend on the moments of the distribution of the lead time. This can be illustrated by the local level model. Let the jth raw moment of this distribution be denoted by μ'_j, with the mean abbreviated to μ. Then, by specializing (154),

$$E\big(y_T^f\big) = E(lm_T) = E(l)m_T = \mu m_T$$

and

$$\mathrm{Var}\big(y_T^f\big) = m_T^2\,\mathrm{Var}(l) + \mu\sigma_\varepsilon^2 + \mu'_2 p_T + \frac{1}{3}\mu'_3\sigma_\eta^2. \tag{160}$$

The first two terms are the standard formulae found in the operational research literature, corresponding to a situation in which σ_η^2 is zero and the (constant) mean is known. The third term allows for the estimation of the mean, which now may or may not be constant, while the fourth term allows for the movements in the mean that take place beyond the current time period.

The extension to the local linear trend and trigonometric seasonal components is dealt with in Harvey and Snyder (1990). As regards the lead time distribution, it may be possible to estimate moments from past observations. Alternatively, a particular distribution may be assumed. Snyder (1984) argues that the gamma distribution has been found to work well in practice.

9. Nonlinear and non-Gaussian models

In the *linear state space* form set out at the beginning of Section 6 the system matrices are non-stochastic and the disturbances are all white noise. The system is rather flexible in that the system matrices can vary over time. The additional assumption that the disturbances and initial state vector are normally distributed ensures that we have a *linear model,* that is, one in which the conditional means (the optimal estimates) of future observations and components are linear functions of the observations and all other characteristics of the conditional distributions are independent of the observations. If there is only one disturbance term, as in an ARIMA model, then serial independence of the disturbances is sufficient for the model to be linear, but with unobserved components this is not usually the case.

Non-linearities can be introduced into state space models in a variety of ways. A completely general formulation is laid out in the first subsection below, but more tractable classes of models are obtained by focussing on different sources of non-linearity. In the first place, the time-variation in the system matrices may be endogenous. This opens up a wide range of possibilities for modelling with the stochastic system matrices incorporating *feedback* in that they depend on past observations or combinations of observations. The Kalman filter can still be applied when the models are conditionally Gaussian, as described in Section 9.2. A second source of nonlinearity arises in an obvious way when the measurement and/or transition equations have a nonlinear functional form. Finally the model may be *non-Gaussian*. The state space may still be linear as for example when the measurement equation has disturbances generated by a t-distribution. More fundamentally non-normality may be intrinsic to the data. Thus the observations may be count data in which the number of events occurring in each time period is recorded. If these numbers are small, a normal approximation is unreasonable and in order to be data-admissible the model should explicitly take account of the fact that the observations must be non-negative integers. A more extreme example is when the data are dichotomous and can take one of only two values, zero and one. The structural approach to time series model-building attempts to take such data characteristics into account.

Count data models are usually based on distributions like the Poisson and negative binomial. Thus the non-Gaussianity implies a nonlinear measurement equation that must somehow be combined with a mechanism that allows the mean of the distribution to change over time. Section 9.3.1 sets out a class of models which deal with non-Gaussian distributions for the observations by means of conjugate filters. However, while these filters are analytic, the range of dynamic effects that can be handled is limited. A more general class of models is considered in Section 9.3.2. The statistical treatment of such models depends on applying computer intensive methods. Considerable progress has been made in recent years in both a Bayesian and classical framework.

When the state variables are discrete, a whole class of models can be built up based on Markov chains. Thus there is intrinsic non-normality in the transition equations and this may be combined with feedback effects. Analytic filters are possible in some cases such as the autoregressive models introduced by Hamilton (1989).

In setting up nonlinear models, there is often a choice between what Cox calls 'parameter driven' models, based on a latent or unobserved process, and 'observation driven' models in which the starting point is a one-step ahead predictive distribution. As a general rule, the properties of parameter driven models are easier to derive, but observation driven models have the advantage that the likelihood function is immediately available. This survey concentrates on parameter driven models, though it is interesting that some models, such as the conjugate ones of Section 9.3.1, belong to both classes.

9.1. General state space model

In the general formulation of a state space model, the distribution of the observations is specified conditional on the current state and past observations, that is,

$$p(\mathbf{y}_t \mid \boldsymbol{\alpha}_t, \mathbf{Y}_{t-1}) \tag{161}$$

where $\mathbf{Y}_{t-1} = \{\mathbf{y}_{t-1}, \mathbf{y}_{t-2}, \ldots\}$. Similarly the distribution of the current state is specified conditional on the previous state and observations, so that

$$p(\boldsymbol{\alpha}_t \mid \boldsymbol{\alpha}_{t-1}, \mathbf{Y}_{t-1}). \tag{162}$$

The initial distribution of the state, $p(\boldsymbol{\alpha}_0)$ is also specified. In a linear Gaussian model the conditional distributions in (161) and (162) are characterized by their first two moments and so they are specified by the measurement and transition equations.

Filtering: The statistical treatment of the general state space model requires the derivation of a recursion for $p(\boldsymbol{\alpha}_t \mid \mathbf{Y}_t)$, the distribution of the state vector conditional on the information at time t. Suppose this is given at time $t-1$. The distribution of $\boldsymbol{\alpha}_t$ conditional on $\mathbf{Y}_{t-1}$ is

$$p(\boldsymbol{\alpha}_t \mid \mathbf{Y}_{t-1}) = \int_{-\infty}^{\infty} p(\boldsymbol{\alpha}_t, \boldsymbol{\alpha}_{t-1} \mid \mathbf{Y}_{t-1})\, \mathrm{d}\boldsymbol{\alpha}_{t-1}$$

but the right-hand side may be rearranged as

$$p(\boldsymbol{\alpha}_t \mid \mathbf{Y}_{t-1}) = \int_{-\infty}^{\infty} p(\boldsymbol{\alpha}_t \mid \boldsymbol{\alpha}_{t-1}, \mathbf{Y}_{t-1}) p(\boldsymbol{\alpha}_{t-1} \mid \mathbf{Y}_{t-1})\, \mathrm{d}\boldsymbol{\alpha}_{t-1}. \tag{163}$$

The conditional distribution $p(\boldsymbol{\alpha}_t \mid \boldsymbol{\alpha}_{t-1}, \mathbf{Y}_{t-1})$ is given by (162) and so $p(\boldsymbol{\alpha}_t \mid \mathbf{Y}_{t-1})$ may, in principle, be obtained from $p(\boldsymbol{\alpha}_{t-1} \mid \mathbf{Y}_{t-1})$.

As regards updating,

$$\begin{aligned} p(\boldsymbol{\alpha}_t \mid \mathbf{Y}_t) = p(\boldsymbol{\alpha}_t \mid \mathbf{y}_t, \mathbf{Y}_{t-1}) &= \frac{p(\boldsymbol{\alpha}_t, \mathbf{y}_t \mid \mathbf{Y}_{t-1})}{p(\mathbf{y}_t \mid \mathbf{Y}_{t-1})} \\ &= \frac{p(\mathbf{y}_t \mid \boldsymbol{\alpha}_t, \mathbf{Y}_{t-1})p(\boldsymbol{\alpha}_t \mid \mathbf{Y}_{t-1})}{p(\mathbf{y}_t \mid \mathbf{Y}_{t-1})} \end{aligned} \tag{164}$$

where

$$p(\mathbf{y}_t \mid \mathbf{Y}_{t-1}) = \int_{-\infty}^{\infty} p(\mathbf{y}_t \mid \boldsymbol{\alpha}_t, \mathbf{Y}_{t-1}) p(\boldsymbol{\alpha}_t \mid \mathbf{Y}_{t-1})\, \mathrm{d}\boldsymbol{\alpha}_t. \tag{165}$$

The likelihood function may be constructed as the product of the predictive distributions, (165), as in (68).

Prediction: Prediction is effected by repeated application of (163), starting from $p(\boldsymbol{\alpha}_T \mid \mathbf{Y}_T)$, to give $p(\boldsymbol{\alpha}_{T+l} \mid \mathbf{Y}_T)$. The conditional distribution of y_{T+l} is then obtained by evaluating

$$p(\mathbf{y}_{T+l} \mid \mathbf{Y}_T) = \int_{-\infty}^{\infty} p(\mathbf{y}_{T+l} \mid \boldsymbol{\alpha}_{T+l}, \mathbf{Y}_T) p(\boldsymbol{\alpha}_{T+l} \mid \mathbf{Y}_T)\, \mathrm{d}\boldsymbol{\alpha}_{T+l}. \tag{166}$$

An alternative route is based on noting that the *predictive* distribution of $\mathbf{y}_{T+l}$ for $l > 1$ is given by

$$p(\mathbf{y}_{T+l} \mid \mathbf{Y}_T) = \int \cdots \int \prod_{j=1}^{l} p(\mathbf{y}_{T+j} \mid \mathbf{Y}_{T+j-1})\, \mathrm{d}\mathbf{y}_{T+j} \ldots \mathrm{d}\mathbf{y}_{T+l-1}. \tag{167}$$

This expression follows by observing that the joint distribution of the future observations may be written in terms of conditional distributions, that is

$$p(\mathbf{y}_{T+l}, \mathbf{y}_{T+l-1}, \ldots, \mathbf{y}_{T+1} \mid \mathbf{Y}_T) = \prod_{j=1}^{l} p(\mathbf{y}_{T+j} \mid \mathbf{Y}_{T+j-1}).$$

The predictive distribution of y_{T+l} is then obtained as a marginal distribution by integrating out $\mathbf{y}_{T+1}$ to $\mathbf{y}_{T+l-1}$. The usual point forecast is the conditional mean

$$E(\mathbf{y}_{T+l} \mid \mathbf{Y}_T) = \underset{T}{E}(\mathbf{y}_{T+l}) = \int_{-\infty}^{\infty} \mathbf{y}_{T+l}\, p(\mathbf{y}_{T+l} \mid \mathbf{Y}_T)\, \mathrm{d}\mathbf{y}_{T+l} \tag{168}$$

as this is the minimum mean square estimate. Other point estimates may be constructed. In particular the maximum *a posteriori* estimate is the mode of the conditional distribution. However, once we move away from normality, there is a case for expressing forecasts in terms of the whole of the predictive distribution.

The general filtering expressions may be difficult to solve analytically. Linear Gaussian models are an obvious exception and tractable solutions are possible in a number of other cases. Of particular importance is the class of conditionally Gaussian models described in the next subsection and the conjugate filters for count and qualitative observations developed in the subsection afterwards. Where an analytic solution is not available, Kitagawa (1987) has suggested using numerical methods to evaluate the various densities. The main drawback with this approach is the computational requirement: this can be considerable if a reasonable degree of accuracy is to be achieved.

9.2. Conditionally Gaussian models

A conditionally Gaussian state space model may be written as

$$\mathbf{y}_t = \mathbf{Z}_t(\mathbf{Y}_{t-1})\boldsymbol{\alpha}_t + \mathbf{d}_t(\mathbf{Y}_{t-1}) + \boldsymbol{\varepsilon}_t, \quad \boldsymbol{\varepsilon}_t \mid \mathbf{Y}_{t-1} \sim N\big(\mathbf{0}, \mathbf{H}_t(\mathbf{Y}_{t-1})\big), \tag{169}$$

$$\begin{aligned}\boldsymbol{\alpha}_t &= \mathbf{T}_t(\mathbf{Y}_{t-1})\boldsymbol{\alpha}_{t-1} + \mathbf{c}_t(\mathbf{Y}_{t-1}) + \mathbf{R}_t(\mathbf{Y}_{t-1})\boldsymbol{\eta}_t,\\ &\quad \boldsymbol{\eta}_t \mid \mathbf{Y}_{t-1} \sim N\big(\mathbf{0}, \mathbf{Q}_t(\mathbf{Y}_{t-1})\big)\end{aligned} \tag{170}$$

with $\boldsymbol{\alpha}_0 \sim N(\mathbf{a}_0, \mathbf{P}_0)$. Even though the system matrices may depend on observations up to and including $\mathbf{y}_{t-1}$, they may be regarded as being fixed once we are at time $t-1$. Hence the derivation of the Kalman filter goes through exactly as in the linear model with $\mathbf{a}_{t|t-1}$ and $\mathbf{P}_{t|t-1}$ now interpreted as the mean and covariance matrix of the distribution of $\boldsymbol{\alpha}_t$ conditional on the information at time $t-1$. However, since the conditional mean of $\boldsymbol{\alpha}_t$ will no longer be a linear function of the observations, it will be denoted by $\widetilde{\boldsymbol{\alpha}}_{t|t-1}$ rather than by $\mathbf{a}_{t|t-1}$. When $\widetilde{\boldsymbol{\alpha}}_{t|t-1}$ is viewed as an estimator of $\boldsymbol{\alpha}_t$, then $\mathbf{P}_{t|t-1}$ can be regarded as its conditional error covariance, or MSE, matrix. Since $\mathbf{P}_{t|t-1}$ will now depend on the particular realization of observations in the sample, it is no longer an unconditional error covariance matrix as it was in the linear case.

The system matrices will usually contain unknown parameters, $\boldsymbol{\psi}$. However, since the distribution of $\mathbf{y}_t$, conditional on $\mathbf{Y}_{t-1}$, is normal for all $t = 1, \ldots, T$, the likelihood function can be constructed from the predictive errors, as in (95).

The predictive distribution of $\mathbf{y}_{T+l}$ will not usually be normal for $l > 1$. Furthermore it is not usually possible to determine the form of the distribution. Evaluating conditional moments tends to be easier, though whether it is a feasible proposition depends on the way in which past observations enter into the system matrices. At the least one would hope to be able to use the law of iterated expectations to evaluate the conditional expectations of future observations thereby obtaining their MMSEs.

9.3. Count data and qualitative observations

Count data models are usually based on distributions such as the Poisson or negative binomial. If the means of these distributions are constant, or can be modelled in terms of observable variables, then estimation is relatively easy; see, for example, the book on generalized linear models (GLIM) by McCullagh and Nelder (1983). The essence of a time series model, however, is that the mean of a series cannot be modelled in terms of observable variables, so has to be captured by some stochastic mechanism. The structural approach explicitly takes into account the notion that there may be two sources of randomness, one affecting the underlying mean and the other coming from the distribution of the observations around that mean. Thus one can consider setting up a model in which the distribution of an observation conditional on the mean is Poisson or negative binomial, while the mean itself evolves as a stochastic process that is always positive. The same ideas can be used to handle qualitative variables.

9.3.1. Models with conjugate filters

The essence of the conjugate filter approach is to formulate a mechanism that allows the distribution of the underlying level to be updated as new observations become available and at the same time to produce a predictive distribution of the next observation. The solution to the problem rests on the use of natural-conjugate distributions of the type used in Bayesian statistics. This allows the formulation of models for count and qualitative data that are analogous to the random walk plus noise model in that they allow the underlying level of the process to change over time, but in a way that is implicit rather than explicit. By introducing a hyperparameter, ω, into these local level models, past observations are discounted in making forecasts of future observations. Indeed it transpires that in all cases the predictions can be constructed by an EWMA, which is exactly what happens in the random walk plus noise model under the normality assumption. Although the models draw on Bayesian techniques, the approach is can still be seen as classical as the likelihood function can be constructed from the predictive distributions and used as the basis for estimating ω. Furthermore the approach is open to the kind of model-fitting methodology used for linear Gaussian models.

The technique can be illustrated with the model devised for observations drawn from a Poisson distribution. Let

$$p(y_t \mid \mu_t) = \frac{\mu_t^{y_t} \mathrm{e}^{-\mu_t}}{y_t!}, \qquad t = 1, \ldots, T. \tag{171}$$

The conjugate prior for a Poisson distribution is the gamma distribution. Let $p(\mu_{t-1} \mid Y_{t-1})$ denote the p.d.f. of μ_{t-1} conditional on the information at time $t-1$. Suppose that this distribution is gamma, that is

$$p(\mu; a, b) = \frac{\mathrm{e}^{-b\mu}\mu^{a-1}}{\Gamma(a)b^{-a}}, \qquad a, b > 0$$

with $\mu = \mu_{t-1}, a = a_{t-1}$ and $b = b_{t-1}$ where a_{t-1} and b_{t-1} are computed from the first $t-1$ observations, Y_{t-1}. In the random walk plus noise with normally distributed observations, $\mu_{t-1} \sim N(m_{t-1}, p_{t-1})$ at time $t-1$ implies that $\mu_{t-1} \sim N(m_{t-1}, p_{t-1} + \sigma_\eta^2)$ at time $t-1$. In other words the mean of $\mu_t \mid Y_{t-1}$ is the same as that of $\mu_{t-1} \mid Y_{t-1}$ but the variance increases. The same effect can be induced in the gamma distribution by multiplying a and b by a factor less than one. We therefore suppose that $p(\mu_t \mid Y_{t-1})$

follows a gamma distribution with parameters $a_{t|t-1}$ and $b_{t|t-1}$ such that

$$a_{t|t-1} = \omega a_{t-1} \quad \text{and} \quad b_{t|t-1} = \omega b_{t-1} \tag{172}$$

and $0 < \omega \leqslant 1$. Then

$$E(\mu_t \mid Y_{t-1}) = \frac{a_{t|t-1}}{b_{t|t-1}} = \frac{a_{t-1}}{b_{t-1}} = E(\mu_{t-1} \mid Y_{t-1})$$

while

$$\operatorname{Var}(\mu_t \mid Y_{t-1}) = \frac{a_{t|t-1}}{b^2_{t|t-1}} = \omega^{-1}\operatorname{Var}(\mu_{t-1} \mid Y_{t-1}).$$

The stochastic mechanism governing the transition of μ_{t-1} to μ_t is therefore defined implicitly rather than explicitly. However, it is possible to show that it is formally equivalent to a multiplicative transition equation of the form

$$\mu_t = \omega^{-1}\mu_{t-1}\eta_t$$

where η_t has a beta distribution with parameters ωa_{t-1} and $(1-\omega)a_{t-1}$; see the discussion in Smith and Miller (1986).

Once the observation y_t becomes available, the posterior distribution, $p(\mu_t \mid Y_t)$, is obtained by evaluating an expression similar to (164). This yields a gamma distribution with parameters

$$a_t = a_{t|t-1} + y_t \quad \text{and} \quad b_t = b_{t|t-1} + 1. \tag{173}$$

The initial prior gamma distribution, that is the distribution of μ_t at time $t = 0$, tends to become diffuse, or non-informative, as $a, b \to 0$, although it is actually degenerate at $a = b = 0$ with $\Pr(\mu = 0) = 1$. However, none of this prevents the recursions for a and b being initialized at $t = 0$ and $a_0 = b_0 = 0$. A proper distribution for μ_t is then obtained at time $t = \tau$ where τ is the index of the first non-zero observation. It follows that, conditional on Y_τ, the joint density of the observations $y_{\tau+1}, \ldots, y_T$ can be constructed as the product of the predictive distributions. For Poisson observations and a gamma prior, the predictive distribution is a negative binomial distribution, that is,

$$p(y_t \mid Y_{t-1}) = \frac{\Gamma(a_{t|t-1} + y_t)}{\Gamma(y_t + 1)\Gamma(a_{t|t-1})} b_{t|t-1}^{a_{t|t-1}} (1 + b_{t|t-1})^{-(a_{t|t-1}+y_t)}. \tag{174}$$

Hence the log-likelihood function can easily constructed and then maximized with respect to the unknown hyperparameter ω.

It follows from the properties of the negative binomial that the mean of the predictive distribution of y_{T+1} is

$$E(y_{T+1} \mid Y_T) = a_{T+1|T}/b_{T+1|T} = a_T/b_T = \sum_{j=0}^{T-1} \omega^j y_{T-j} \Big/ \sum_{j=0}^{T-1} \omega^j \tag{175}$$

the last equality coming from repeated substitution with (172) and (173). In large samples the denominator of (175) is approximately equal to $1/(1-\omega)$ when $\omega < 1$ and the weights decline exponentially, as in (7) with $\lambda = 1 - \omega$. When $\omega = 1$, the right-hand side of (175), is equal to the sample mean; it is reassuring that this is the solution given by setting a_0 and b_0 equal to zero.

The l-step-ahead predictive distribution at time T is given by

$$p(y_{T+l} \mid Y_T) = \int_0^\infty p(y_{T+l} \mid \mu_{T+l})p(\mu_{T+l} \mid Y_T)\,\mathrm{d}\mu_{T+l}.$$

It could be argued that the assumption embodied in (172) suggests that $p(\mu_{T+l} \mid Y_T)$ has a gamma distribution with parameters $\omega^l a_T$ and $\omega^l b_T$. This would mean the predictive distribution for y_{T+l} was negative binomial with a and b given by $\omega^l a_T$ and $\omega^l b_T$ in the formulae above. Unfortunately the evolution that this implies for μ_t is not consistent with what would occur if observations were made at times $T+1, T+2, \ldots, T+l-1$. In the latter case, the distribution of y_{T+l} at time T is

$$p(y_{T+l} \mid Y_T) = \sum_{y_{T+l-1}} \cdots \sum_{y_{T+1}} \prod_{j=1}^{l} p(y_{T+j} \mid Y_{T+j-1}). \tag{176}$$

This is the analogue of (166) for discrete observations. It is difficult to derive a closed form expression for $p(y_{T+l|T})$ from (176) for $l > 1$ but it can, in principle, be evaluated numerically. Note, however, by the law of iterated expectations, $E(y_{T+l} \mid Y_T) = a_T/b_T$ for $l = 1, 2, 3, \ldots$, so the mean of the predictive distribution is the same for all lead times, just as in the Gaussian random walk plus noise.

Goals scored by England against Scotland. Harvey and Fernandes (1989) modelled the number of goals scored by England in international football matches played against Scotland in Glasgow up 1987. Estimation of the Poisson-gamma model gives $\widetilde{\omega} = 0.844$. The forecast is 0.82; the full one-step-ahead predictive distribution is shown in Table 2. (For the record, England won the 1989 match, two-nil.)

Similar filters may be constructed for the binomial distribution, in which case the conjugate prior is the beta distribution and the predictive distribution is the beta-binomial, and the negative binomial for which the conjugate prior is again the beta distribution and the predictive distribution is the beta-Pascal. Exponential distributions fit into the same

Table 2
Predictive probability distribution of goals in next match.

Number of goals					
0	1	2	3	4	>4
0.471	0.326	0.138	0.046	0.013	0.005

framework with gamma conjugate distributions and Pareto predictive distributions. In all cases the predicted level is an EWMA.

Boat race. The Oxford–Cambridge boat race provides an example of modelling qualitative variables by using the filter for the binomial distribution. Ignoring the dead heat of 1877, there were 130 boat races up to and including 1985. We denote a win for Oxford as one, and a win for Cambridge as zero. The runs test clearly indicates serial correlation and fitting the local Bernoulli model by ML gives an estimate of ω of 0.866. This results in an estimate of the probability of Oxford winning a future race of 0.833. The high probability is a reflection of the fact that Oxford won all the races over the previous ten years. Updating the data to 2000 gives a dramatic change as Cambridge were dominant in the 1990s. Despite Oxford winning in 2000, the estimate of the probability of Oxford winning future races falls to 0.42. Further updating can be carried out[13] very easily since the probability of Oxford winning is given by an EWMA. Note that because the data are binary, the distribution of the forecasts is just binomial (rather than beta-binomial) and this distribution is the same for any lead time.

A criticism of the above class of forecasting procedures is that when simulated the observations tend to go to zero. Specifically, if $\omega < 1$, $\mu_t \to 0$ almost surely, as $t \to \infty$; see Grunwald, Hamza and Hyndman (1997). Nevertheless for a given data set, fitting such a model gives a sensible weighting pattern – an EWMA – for the mean of the predictive distribution. It was argued in the opening section that this is the purpose of formulating a time series model. The fact that a model may not generate data sets with desirable properties is unfortunate but not fatal.

Explanatory variables can be introduced into these local level models via the kind of link functions that appear in GLIM models. Time trends and seasonal effects can be included as special cases. The framework does not extend to allowing these effects to be stochastic, as is typically the case in linear structural models. This may not be a serious restriction. Even with data on continuous variables, it is not unusual to find that the slope and seasonal effects are close to being deterministic. With count and qualitative data it seems even less likely that the observations will provide enough information to pick up changes in the slope and seasonal effects over time.

9.3.2. *Exponential family models with explicit transition equations*

The exponential family of distributions contains many of the distributions used for modelling count and quantitative data. For a multivariate series

$$p(\mathbf{y}_t \mid \boldsymbol{\theta}_t) = \exp\{\mathbf{y}_t'\boldsymbol{\theta}_t - b_t(\boldsymbol{\theta}_t) + c(\mathbf{y}_t)\}, \quad t = 1, \ldots, T$$

where $\boldsymbol{\theta}_t$ is an $N \times 1$ vector of 'signals', $b_t(\boldsymbol{\theta}_t)$ is a twice differentiable function of $\boldsymbol{\theta}_t$ and $c(\mathbf{y}_t)$ is a function of $\mathbf{y}_t$ only. The $\boldsymbol{\theta}_t$ vector is related to the mean of the distribution

[13] Cambridge won in 2001 and 2004, Oxford in 2002 and 2003; see www.theboatrace.org/therace/history

by a link function, as in GLIM models. For example when the observations are supposed to come from a univariate Poisson distribution with mean λ_t we set $\exp(\theta_t) = \lambda_t$. By letting $\boldsymbol{\theta}_t$ depend on a state vector that changes over time, it is possible to allow the distribution of the observations to depend on stochastic components other than the level. Dependence of $\boldsymbol{\theta}_t$ on past observations may also be countenanced, so that

$$p(\mathbf{y}_t \mid \boldsymbol{\theta}_t) = p(\mathbf{y}_t \mid \boldsymbol{\alpha}_t, \mathbf{Y}_{t-1})$$

where $\boldsymbol{\alpha}_t$ is a state vector. Explanatory variables could also be included. Unlike the models of the previous subsection, a transitional distribution is explicitly specified rather than being formed implicitly by the demands of conjugacy. The simplest option is to let $\boldsymbol{\theta}_t = \mathbf{Z}_t\boldsymbol{\alpha}_t$ and have $\boldsymbol{\alpha}_t$ generated by a linear transition equation. The statistical treatment is by simulation methods. Shephard and Pitt (1997) base their approach on Markov chain Monte Carlo (MCMC) while Durbin and Koopman (2001) use importance sampling and antithetic variables. Both techniques can also be applied in a Bayesian framework. A full discussion can be found in Durbin and Koopman (2001).

Van drivers. Durbin and Koopman (2001, pp. 230–233) estimate a Poisson model for monthly data on van drivers killed in road accidents in Great Britain. However, they are able to allow the seasonal component to be stochastic. (A stochastic slope could also have been included but the case for employing a slope of any kind is weak.) Thus the signal is taken to be

$$\theta_t = \mu_t + \gamma_t + \lambda w_t$$

where μ_t is a random walk and w_t is the seat belt intervention variable. The estimate of σ_ω^2 is, in fact, zero so the seasonal component turns out to be fixed after all. The estimated reduction in van drivers killed is 24.3% which is not far from the 24.1% obtained by Harvey and Fernandes (1989) using the conjugate filter.

Boat race. Durbin and Koopman (2001, p. 237) allow the probability of an Oxford win, π_t, to change over time, but remain in the range zero to one by taking the link function for the Bernouilli (binary) distribution to be a logit. Thus they set $\pi_t = \exp(\theta_t)/(1 + \exp(\theta_t))$ and let θ_t follow a random walk.

9.4. Heavy-tailed distributions and robustness

Simulation techniques of the kind alluded to in the previous subsection, are relatively easy to use when the measurement and transition equations are linear but the disturbances are non-Gaussian. Allowing the disturbances to have heavy-tailed distributions provides a robust method of dealing with outliers and structural breaks. While outliers and breaks can be dealt with ex post by dummy variables, only a robust model offers a viable solution to coping with them in the future.

9.4.1. Outliers

Allowing ε_t to have a heavy-tailed distribution, such as Student's t, provides a robust method of dealing with outliers; see Meinhold and Singpurwalla (1989). This is to be contrasted with an approach where the aim is to try to detect outliers and then to remove them by treating them as missing or modeling them by an intervention. An outlier is defined as an observation that is inconsistent with the model. By employing a heavy-tailed distribution, such observations are consistent with the model whereas with a Gaussian distribution they would not be. Treating an outlier as though it were a missing observation effectively says that it contains no useful information. This is rarely the case except, perhaps, when an observation has been recorded incorrectly.

Gas consumption in the UK. Estimating a Gaussian BSM for gas consumption produces a rather unappealing wobble in the seasonal component at the time North Sea gas was introduced in 1970. Durbin and Koopman (2001, pp. 233–235) allow the irregular to follow a t-distribution and estimate its degrees of freedom to be 13. The robust treatment of the atypical observations in 1970 produces a more satisfactory seasonal pattern around that time.

Another example of the application of robust methods is the seasonal adjustment paper of Bruce and Jurke (1996).

In small samples it may prove difficult to estimate the degrees of freedom. A reasonable solution then is to impose a value, such as six, that is able to handle outliers. Other heavy tailed distributions may also be used; Durbin and Koopman (2001, p. 184) suggest mixtures of normals and the general error distribution.

9.4.2. Structural breaks

Clements and Hendry (2003, p. 305) conclude that "...shifts in deterministic terms (intercepts and linear trends) are the major source of forecast failure". However, unless breaks within the sample are associated with some clearly defined event, such as a new law, dealing with them by dummy variables may not be the best way to proceed. In many situations matters are rarely clear cut in that the researcher does not know the location of breaks or indeed how many there may be. When it comes to forecasting matters are even worse.

The argument for modelling breaks by dummy variables is at its most extreme in the advocacy of piecewise linear trends, that is deterministic trends subject to changes in slope modelled as in Section 4.1. This is to be contrasted with a stochastic trend where there are small random breaks at all points in time. Of course, stochastic trends can easily be combined with deterministic structural breaks. However, if the presence and location of potential breaks are not known *a priori* there is a strong argument for using heavy-tailed distributions in the transition equation to accommodate them. Such breaks are not deterministic and their size is a matter of degree rather than kind. From the forecasting point of view this makes much more sense: a future break is virtually never deterministic – indeed the idea that its location and size might be known in advance is extremely optimistic. A robust model, on the other hand, takes account of the possibility of future breaks in its computation of MSEs and in the way it adapts to new observations.

9.5. *Switching regimes*

The observations in a time series may sometimes be generated by different mechanisms at different points in time. When this happens, the series is subject to *switching regimes*. If the points at which the regime changes can be determined directly from currently available information, the Kalman filter provides the basis for a statistical treatment. The first subsection below gives simple examples involving endogenously determined changes. If the regime is not directly observable but is known to change according to a Markov process we have *hidden Markov chain* models, as described in the book by MacDonald and Zucchini (1997). Models of this kind are described in latter subsections.

9.5.1. *Observable breaks in structure*

If changes in regime are known to take place at particular points in time, the SSF is time-varying but the model is linear. The construction of a likelihood function still proceeds via the prediction error decomposition, the only difference being that there are more parameters to estimate. Changes in the past can easily be allowed for in this way.

The point at which a regime changes may be endogenous to the model, in which case it becomes nonlinear. Thus it is possible to have a finite number of regimes each with a different set of hyperparameters. If the signal as to which regime holds depends on past values of the observations, the model can be set up so as to be conditionally Gaussian. Two possible models spring to mind. The first is a two-regime model in which the regime is determined by the sign of Δy_{t-1}. The second is a *threshold* model, in which the regime depends on whether or not y_t has crossed a certain threshold value in the previous period. More generally, the switch may depend on the estimate of the state based in information at time $t-1$. Such a model is still conditionally Gaussian and allows a fair degree of flexibility in model formulation.

Business cycles. In work on the business cycle, it has often been observed that the downward movement into a recession proceeds at a more rapid rate than the subsequent recovery. This suggests some modification to the cyclical components in structural models formulated for macroeconomic time series. A switch from one frequency to another can be made endogenous to the system by letting

$$\lambda_c = \begin{cases} \lambda_1 & \text{if } \widetilde{\psi}_{t|t-1} - \widetilde{\psi}_{t-1} > 0, \\ \lambda_2 & \text{if } \widetilde{\psi}_{t|t-1} - \widetilde{\psi}_{t-1} \leqslant 0 \end{cases}$$

where $\widetilde{\psi}_{t|t-1}$ and $\widetilde{\psi}_{t-1}$ are the MMSEs of the cyclical component based on the information at time $t-1$. A positive value of $\widetilde{\psi}_{t|t-1} - \widetilde{\psi}_{t-1}$ indicates that the cycle is in an upswing and hence λ_1 will be set to a smaller value than λ_2. In other words the period in the upswing is larger. Unfortunately the filtered cycle tends to be rather volatile, resulting in too many switches. A better rule might be to average changes over several periods using smoothed estimates, that is to use $\widetilde{\psi}_{t|t-1} - \widetilde{\psi}_{t-m|t-1} = \sum_{j=0}^{m-1} \Delta\widetilde{\psi}_{t-j|t-1}$.

9.5.2. Markov chains

Markov chains can be used to model the dynamics of binary data, that is, $y_t = 0$ or 1 for $t = 1, \ldots, T$. The movement from one state, or *regime*, to another is governed by transition probabilities. In a Markov chain these probabilities depend only on the current state. Thus if $y_{t-1} = 1$, $\Pr(y_t = 1) = \pi_1$ and $\Pr(y_t = 0) = 1 - \pi_1$, while if $y_{t-1} = 0$, $\Pr(y_t = 0) = \pi_0$ and $\Pr(y_t = 1) = 1 - \pi_0$. This provokes an interesting contrast with the EWMA that results from the conjugate filter model.[14]

The above ideas may be extended to situations where there is more than one state. The Markov chain operates as before, with a probability specified for moving from any of the states at time $t - 1$ to any other state at time t.

9.5.3. Markov chain switching models

A general state space model was set up at the beginning of this section by specifying a distribution for each observation conditional on the state vector, $\boldsymbol{\alpha}_t$, together with a distribution of $\boldsymbol{\alpha}_t$ conditional on $\boldsymbol{\alpha}_{t-1}$. The filter and smoother were written down for continuous state variables. The concern here is with a single state variable that is discrete. The filter presented below is the same as the filter for a continuous state, except that integration is replaced by summation. The series is assumed to be univariate.

The state variable takes the values $1, 2, \ldots, m$, and these values represent each of m different regimes. (In the previous subsection, the term 'state' was used where here we use regime; the use of 'state' for the value of the state variable could be confusing here.) The transition mechanism is a Markov process which specifies $\Pr(\alpha_t = i \mid \alpha_{t-1} = j)$ for $i, j = 1, \ldots, m$. Given probabilities of being in each of the regimes at time $t - 1$, the corresponding probabilities in the next time period are

$$\Pr(\alpha_t = i \mid Y_{t-1}) = \sum_{j=1}^{m} \Pr(\alpha_t = i \mid \alpha_{t-1} = j) \Pr(\alpha_{t-1} = j \mid Y_{t-1}),$$
$$i = 1, 2, \ldots, m,$$

and the conditional PDF of y_t is a mixture of distributions given by

$$p(y_t \mid Y_{t-1}) = \sum_{j=1}^{m} p(y_t \mid \alpha_t = j) \Pr(\alpha_t = j \mid Y_{t-1}) \tag{177}$$

[14] Having said that it should be noted that the Markov chain transition probabilities may be allowed to evolve over time in the same way as a single probability can be allowed to change in a conjugate binomial model; see Harvey (1989, p. 355).

where $p(y_t \mid \alpha_t = j)$ is the distribution of y_t in regime j. As regards updating

$$\Pr(\alpha_t = i \mid Y_t) = \frac{p(y_t \mid \alpha_t = i) \cdot \Pr(\alpha_t = i \mid Y_{t-1})}{p(y_t \mid Y_{t-1})}, \qquad i = 1, 2, \ldots, m.$$

Given initial conditions for the probability that α_t is equal to each of its m values at time zero, the filter can be run to produce the probability of being in a given regime at the end of the sample. Predictions of future observations can then be made. If $\mathbf{M}$ denotes the transition matrix with (i, j)th element equal to $\Pr(\alpha_t = i \mid \alpha_{t-1} = j)$ and $\mathbf{p}_{t|t-k}$ is the $m \times 1$ vector with ith element $\Pr(\alpha_t = i \mid Y_{t-k})$, $k = 0, 1, 2, \ldots$, then

$$\mathbf{p}_{T+l|T} = \mathbf{M}^l \mathbf{p}_{T|T}, \quad l = 1, 2, \ldots$$

and so

$$p(y_{T+l} \mid Y_T) = \sum_{j=1}^{m} p(y_{T+l} \mid \alpha_{T+l} = j) \Pr(\alpha_{T+l} = j \mid Y_T). \tag{178}$$

The likelihood function can be constructed from the one-step predictive distributions (177). The unknown parameters consist of the transition probabilities in the matrix $\mathbf{M}$ and the parameters in the measurement equation distributions, $p(y_t \mid \alpha_t = j)$, $j = 1, \ldots, m$.

The above state space form may be extended by allowing the distribution of y_t to be conditional on past observations as well as on the current state. It may also depend on past regimes, so the current state becomes a vector containing the state variables in previous time periods. This may be expressed by writing the state vector at time t as $\boldsymbol{\alpha}_t = (s_t, s_{t-1}, \ldots, s_{t-p})'$, where s_t is the state variable at time t.

In the model of Hamilton (1989), the observations are generated by an AR(p) process of the form

$$y_t = \mu(s_t) + \phi_1\big[y_{t-1} - \mu(s_{t-1})\big] + \cdots + \phi_p\big[y_{t-p} - \mu(s_{t-p})\big] + \varepsilon_t \tag{179}$$

where $\varepsilon_t \sim NID(0, \sigma^2)$. Thus the expected value of y_t, denoted $\mu(s_t)$, varies according to the regime, and it is the value appropriate to the corresponding lag on y_t that enters into the equation. Hence the distribution of y_t is conditional on s_t and s_{t-1} to s_{t-p} as well as on y_{t-1} to y_{t-p}. The filter of the previous subsection can still be applied although the summation must now be over all values of the $p + 1$ state variables in α_t. An exact filter is possible here because the time series model in (179) is an autoregression. The is no such analytic solution for an ARMA or structural time series model. As a result simulation methods have to be used as in Kim and Nelson (1999) and Luginbuhl and de Vos (1999).

10. Stochastic volatility

It is now well established that while financial variables such as stock returns are serially uncorrelated over time, their squares are not. The most common way of modelling this serial correlation in volatility is by means of the GARCH class in which it is assumed that the conditional variance of the observations is an exact function of the squares of past observations and previous variances. An alternative approach is to model volatility as an unobserved component in the variance. This leads to the class of *stochastic volatility* (SV) models. The topic is covered Chapter 15 by Andersen et al. in this Handbook so the treatment here will be brief. Earlier reviews of the literature are to be found in Taylor (1994) and Ghysels, Harvey and Renault (1996), while the edited volume by Shephard (2005) contains many of the important papers.

The stochastic volatility model has two attractions. The first is that it is the natural discrete time analogue (though it is only an approximation) of the continuous time model used in work on option pricing; see Hull and White (1987) and the review by Hang (1998). The second is that its statistical properties are relatively easy to determine and extensions, such as the introduction of seasonal components, are easily handled. The disadvantage with respect to the conditional variance models of the GARCH class is that whereas GARCH can be estimated by maximum likelihood, the full treatment of an SV model requires the use of computer intensive methods such as MCMC and importance sampling. However, these methods are now quite rapid and it would be wrong to rule out SV models on the grounds that they make unreasonably heavy computational demands.

10.1. Basic specification and properties

The basic discrete time SV model for a demeaned series of returns, y_t, may be written as

$$y_t = \sigma_t \varepsilon_t = \sigma \mathrm{e}^{0.5 h_t} \varepsilon_t, \quad \varepsilon_t \sim IID(0, 1), \ t = 1, \dots, T \tag{180}$$

where σ is a scale parameter and h_t is a stationary first-order autoregressive process, that is,

$$h_{t+1} = \phi h_t + \eta_t, \quad \eta_t \sim IID\big(0, \sigma_\eta^2\big) \tag{181}$$

where η_t is a disturbance term which may or may not be correlated with ε_t. If ε_t and η_t are allowed to be correlated with each other, the model can pick up the kind of asymmetric behaviour which is often found in stock prices.

The following properties of the SV model hold even if ε_t and η_t are contemporaneously correlated. Firstly y_t is a martingale difference. Secondly, stationarity of h_t implies stationarity of y_t. Thirdly, if η_t is normally distributed, terms involving exponents of h_t may be evaluated using properties of the lognormal distribution. Thus, the variance of y_t can be found and its kurtosis shown to be $\kappa_\varepsilon \exp(\sigma_h^2) > \kappa_\varepsilon$ where κ_ε is the kurtosis of ε_t. Similarly, the autocorrelations of powers of the absolute value of y_t, and its logarithm, can be derived; see Ghysels, Harvey and Renault (1996).

10.2. Estimation

Squaring the observations in (180) and taking logarithms gives

$$\log y_t^2 = \omega + h_t + \xi_t \tag{182}$$

where $\xi_t = \log \varepsilon_t^2 - E \log \varepsilon_t^2$, and $\omega = \log \sigma^2 + E \log \varepsilon_t^2$, so that ξ_t has zero mean by construction. If ε_t has a t_ν-distribution, it can be shown that the moments of ξ_t exist even if the distribution of ε_t is Cauchy, that is $\nu = 1$. In fact in this case ξ_t is symmetric with excess kurtosis two, compared with excess kurtosis four and a highly skewed distribution when ε_t is Gaussian.

The transformed observations, the $\log y_t^{2\prime}s$, can be used to construct a linear state space model. The measurement equation is (182) while (181) is the transition equation. The quasi maximum likelihood (QML) estimators of the parameters ϕ, σ_η^2 and the variance of ξ_t, σ_ξ^2, are obtained by treating ξ_t and η_t as though they were normal in the linear SSF and maximizing the prediction error decomposition form of the likelihood obtained via the Kalman filter; see Harvey, Ruiz and Shephard (1994). Harvey and Shephard (1996) show how the linear state space form can be modified so as to deal with an asymmetric model. The QML method is relatively easy to apply and, even though it is not efficient, it provides a reasonable alternative if the sample size is not too small; see Yu (2005).

Simulation based methods of estimation, such as Markov chain Monte Carlo and efficient method of moments, are discussed at some length in Chapter 15 by Andersen et al. in this Handbook. Important references include Jacquier, Polson and Rossi (1994, p. 416), Kim, Shephard and Chib (1998), Watanabe (1999) and Durbin and Koopman (2000).

10.3. Comparison with GARCH

The GARCH(1, 1) model has been applied extensively to financial time series. The variance in $y_t = \sigma_t \varepsilon_t$ is assumed to depend on the variance and squared observation in the previous time period. Thus,

$$\sigma_t^2 = \gamma + \alpha y_{t-1}^2 + \beta \sigma_{t-1}^2, \quad t = 1, \ldots, T. \tag{183}$$

The GARCH(1, 1) model displays similar properties to the SV model, particularly if ϕ is close to one (in which case $\alpha + \beta$ is also close to one). Jacquier, Polson and Rossi (1994, p. 373) present a graph of the correlogram of the squared weekly returns of a portfolio on the New York Stock Exchange together with the ACFs implied by fitting SV and GARCH(1, 1) models. The main difference in the ACFs seems to show up most at lag one with the ACF implied by the SV model being closer to the sample values.

The Gaussian SV model displays excess kurtosis even if ϕ is zero since y_t is a mixture of distributions. The σ_η^2 parameter governs the degree of mixing independently of the degree of smoothness of the variance evolution. This is not the case with a GARCH model where the degree of kurtosis is tied to the roots of the variance equation, α and β in the case of GARCH(1, 1). Hence, it is very often necessary to use a non-Gaussian distribution for ε_t to capture the high kurtosis typically found in a financial time series. Kim, Shephard and Chib (1998) present strong evidence against the use of the Gaussian GARCH, but find GARCH-t and Gaussian SV to be similar. In the exchange rate data they conclude on p. 384 that the two models "... fit the data more or less equally well". Further evidence on kurtosis is in Carnero, Pena and Ruiz (2004).

Fleming and Kirby (2003) compare the forecasting performance of GARCH and SV models. They conclude that "... GARCH models produce less precise forecasts ...", but go on to observe that "... in the simulations, it is not clear that the performance differences are large enough to be economically meaningful". On the other hand, Section 5.5 of Chapter 1 by Geweke and Whiteman in this Handbook describes a decision theoretic application, concerned with foreign currency hedging, in which there are clear advantages to using the SV model.

10.4. Multivariate models

The multivariate model corresponding to (180) assumes that each series is generated by a model of the form

$$y_{it} = \sigma_i \varepsilon_{it} e^{0.5 h_{it}}, \quad t = 1, \ldots, T \tag{184}$$

with the covariance (correlation) matrix of the vector $\boldsymbol{\varepsilon}_t = (\varepsilon_{1t}, \ldots, \varepsilon_{Nt})'$ being denoted by $\boldsymbol{\Sigma}_\varepsilon$. The vector of volatilities, $\mathbf{h}_t$, follows a VAR(1) process, that is,

$$\mathbf{h}_{t+1} = \boldsymbol{\Phi}\mathbf{h}_t + \boldsymbol{\eta}_t, \quad \boldsymbol{\eta}_t \sim IID(\mathbf{0}, \boldsymbol{\Sigma}_\eta).$$

This specification allows the movements in volatility to be correlated across different series via $\boldsymbol{\Sigma}_\eta$. Interactions can be picked up by the off-diagonal elements of $\boldsymbol{\Phi}$. A simple nonstationary model is obtained by assuming that the volatilities follow a multivariate random walk, that is $\boldsymbol{\Phi} = \mathbf{I}$. If $\boldsymbol{\Sigma}_\eta$ is singular, of rank $K < N$, there are only K components in volatility, that is each h_{it} in (184) is a linear combination of $K < N$ common trends. Harvey, Ruiz and Shephard (1994) apply the nonstationary model to four exchange rates and find just two common factors driving volatility. Other ways of incorporating factor structures into multivariate models are described in Andersen et al. Chapter 15 in this Handbook.

11. Conclusions

The principal structural time series models can be regarded as regression models in which the explanatory variables are functions of time and the parameters are time-varying. As such they provide a model based method of forecasting with an implicit weighting scheme that takes account of the properties of the time series and its salient features. The simplest procedures coincide with ad hoc methods that typically do well in forecasting competitions. For example the exponentially weighted moving average is rationalized by a random walk plus noise, though once non-Gaussian models are brought into the picture, exponentially weighting can also be shown to be appropriate for distributions such as the Poisson and binomial.

Because of the interpretation in terms of components of interest, model selection of structural time series models does not rely on correlograms and related statistical devices. This is important, since it means that the models chosen are typically more robust to changes in structure as well as being less susceptible to the distortions caused by sampling error. Furthermore, plausible models can be selected in situations where the observations are subject to data irregularities. Once a model has been chosen, problems like missing observations are easily handled within the state space framework. Indeed, even irregularly spaced observations are easily dealt with as the principal structural time series models can be set up in continuous time and the implied discrete time state space form derived.

The structural time series model framework can be adapted to produce forecasts – and 'nowcasts' – for a target series taking account of the information in an auxiliary series – possibly at a different sampling interval. Again the freedom from the model selection procedures needed for autoregressive-integrated-moving average models and the flexibility afforded by the state space form is of crucial importance.

As well as drawing attention to some of the attractions of structural time series models, the chapter has also set out some basic results for the state space form and derived some formulae linking models that can be put in this form with autoregressive integrated moving average and autoregressive representations. In a multivariate context, the vector error correction representation of a common trends structural time series model is obtained.

Finally, it is pointed out how recent advances in computer intensive methods have opened up the way to dealing with non-Gaussian and nonlinear models. Such models may be motivated in a variety of ways: for example by the need to fit heavy tailed distributions in order to handle outliers and structural breaks in a robust fashion or by a complex nonlinear functional form suggested by economic theory.

Acknowledgements

I would like to thank Fabio Busetti, David Dickey, Siem Koopman, Ralph Snyder, Allan Timmermann, Thomas Trimbur and participants at the San Diego conference in April 2004 for helpful comments on earlier drafts. The material in the chapter also provided the basis for a plenary session at the 24th International Symposium of Forecasting in Sydney in July 2004 and the L. Solari lecture at the University of Geneva in November 2004. The results in Section 7.3 on the VECM representation of the common trends model were presented at the EMM conference in Alghero, Sardinia in September, 2004 and I'm grateful to Soren Johansen and other participants for their comments.

References

Anderson, B.D.O., Moore, J.B. (1979). Optimal Filtering. Prentice-Hall, Englewood Cliffs, NJ.

Andrews, R.C. (1994). "Forecasting performance of structural time series models". Journal of Business and Economic Statistics 12, 237–252.

Assimakopoulos, V., Nikolopoulos, K. (2000). "The theta model: A decomposition approach to forecasting". International Journal of Forecasting 16, 521–530.

Bazen, S., Marimoutou, V. (2002). "Looking for a needle in a haystack? A re-examination of the time series relationship between teenage employment and minimum wages in the United States". Oxford Bulletin of Economics and Statistics 64, 699–725.

Bergstrom, A.R. (1984). "Continuous time stochastic models and issues of aggregation over time". In: Griliches, Z., Intriligator, M. (Eds.), Handbook of Econometrics, vol. 2. North-Holland, Amsterdam, pp. 1145–1212.

Box, G.E.P., Jenkins, G.M. (1976). Time Series Analysis: Forecasting and Control, revised ed. Holden-Day, San Francisco.

Box, G.E.P., Pierce, D.A., Newbold, P. (1987). "Estimating trend and growth rates in seasonal time series". Journal of the American Statistical Association 82, 276–282.

Brown, R.G. (1963). Smoothing, Forecasting and Prediction. Prentice-Hall, Englewood Cliffs, NJ.

Bruce, A.G., Jurke, S.R. (1996). "Non-Gaussian seasonal adjustment: X-12-ARIMA versus robust structural models". Journal of Forecasting 15, 305–328.

Burridge, P., Wallis, K.F. (1988). "Prediction theory for autoregressive-moving average processes". Econometric Reviews 7, 65–69.

Busetti, F., Harvey, A.C. (2003). "Seasonality tests". Journal of Business and Economic Statistics 21, 420–436.

Canova, F., Hansen, B.E. (1995). "Are seasonal patterns constant over time? A test for seasonal stability". Journal of Business and Economic Statistics 13, 237–252.

Carnero, M.A., Pena, D., Ruiz, E. (2004). "Persistence and kurtosis in GARCH and stochastic volatility models". Journal of Financial Econometrics 2, 319–342.

Carter, C.K., Kohn, R. (1994). "On Gibbs sampling for state space models". Biometrika 81, 541–553.

Carvalho, V.M., Harvey, A.C. (2005). "Growth, cycles and convergence in US regional time series". International Journal of Forecasting 21, 667–686.

Chambers, M.J., McGarry, J. (2002). "Modeling cyclical behaviour with differential–difference equations in an unobserved components framework". Econometric Theory 18, 387–419.

Chatfield, C., Koehler, A.B., Ord, J.K., Snyder, R.D. (2001). "A new look at models for exponential smoothing". The Statistician 50, 147–159.

Chow, G.C. (1984). "Random and changing coefficient models". In: Griliches, Z., Intriligator, M. (Eds.), Handbook of Econometrics, vol. 2. North-Holland, Amsterdam, pp. 1213–1245.

Clements, M.P., Hendry, D.F. (1998). Forecasting Economic Time Series. Cambridge University Press, Cambridge.

Clements, M.P., Hendry, D.F. (2003). "Economic forecasting: Some lessons from recent research". Economic Modelling 20, 301–329.

Dagum, E.B., Quenneville, B., Sutradhar, B. (1992). "Trading-day multiple regression models with random parameters". International Statistical Review 60, 57–73.

Davidson, J., Hendry, D.F., Srba, F., Yeo, S. (1978). "Econometric modelling of the aggregate time-series relationship between consumers' expenditure and income in the United Kingdom". Economic Journal 88, 661–692.

de Jong, P., Shephard, N. (1995). "The simulation smoother for time series models". Biometrika 82, 339–350.

Durbin, J., Quenneville, B. (1997). "Benchmarking by state space models". International Statistical Review 65, 23–48.

Durbin, J., Koopman, S.J. (2000). "Time series analysis of non-Gaussian observations based on state-space models from both classical and Bayesian perspectives (with discussion)". Journal of Royal Statistical Society, Series B 62, 3–56.

Durbin, J., Koopman, S.J. (2001). Time Series Analysis by State Space Methods. Oxford University Press, Oxford.

Durbin, J., Koopman, S.J. (2002). "A simple and efficient simulation smoother for state space time series models". Biometrika 89, 603–616.

Engle, R.F. (1978). "Estimating structural models of seasonality". In: Zellner, A. (Ed.), Seasonal Analysis of Economic Time Series. Bureau of the Census, Washington, DC, pp. 281–308.

Engle, R., Kozicki, S. (1993). "Testing for common features". Journal of Business and Economic Statistics 11, 369–380.

Fleming, J., Kirby, C. (2003). "A closer look at the relation between GARCH and stochastic autoregressive volatility". Journal of Financial Econometrics 1, 365–419.

Franses, P.H., Papp, R. (2004). Periodic Time Series Models. Oxford University Press, Oxford.

Frühwirth-Schnatter, S. (1994). "Data augmentation and dynamic linear models". Journal of Time Series Analysis 15, 183–202.

Frühwirth-Schnatter, S. (2004). "Efficient Bayesian parameter estimation". In: Harvey, A.C., et al. (Eds.), State Space and Unobserved Component Models. Cambridge University Press, Cambridge, pp. 123–151.

Fuller, W.A. (1996). Introduction to Statistical Time Series, second ed. Wiley, New York.

Ghysels, E., Harvey, A.C., Renault, E. (1996). "Stochastic volatility". In: Maddala, G.S., Rao, C.R. (Eds.), Handbook of Statistics, vol. 14. Elsevier, Amsterdam, pp. 119–192.

Grunwald, G.K., Hamza, K., Hyndman, R.J. (1997). "Some properties and generalizations of non-negative Bayesian time series models". Journal of the Royal Statistical Society, Series B 59, 615–626.

Hamilton, J.D. (1989). "A new approach to the economic analysis of nonstationary time series and the business cycle". Econometrica 57, 357–384.

Hang, J.J. (1998). "Stochastic volatility and option pricing". In: Knight, J., Satchell, S. (Eds.), Forecasting Volatility. Butterworth-Heinemann, Oxford, pp. 47–96.

Hannan, E.J., Terrell, R.D., Tuckwell, N. (1970). "The seasonal adjustment of economic time series". International Economic Review 11, 24–52.

Harrison, P.J., Stevens, C.F. (1976). "Bayesian forecasting". Journal of the Royal Statistical Society, Series B 38, 205–247.

Harvey, A.C. (1984). "A unified view of statistical forecasting procedures (with discussion)". Journal of Forecasting 3, 245–283.

Harvey, A.C. (1989). Forecasting, Structural Time Series Models and Kalman Filter. Cambridge University Press, Cambridge.

Harvey, A.C. (2001). "Testing in unobserved components models". Journal of Forecasting 20, 1–19.

Harvey, A.C., Chung, C.-H. (2000). "Estimating the underlying change in unemployment in the UK (with discussion)". Journal of the Royal Statistical Society, Series A 163, 303–339.

Harvey, A.C., de Rossi, G. (2005). "Signal extraction". In: Patterson, K., Mills, T.C. (Eds.), Palgrave Handbook of Econometrics, vol. 1. Palgrave MacMillan, Basingstoke, pp. 970–1000.

Harvey, A.C., Fernandes, C. (1989). "Time series models for count data or qualitative observations". Journal of Business and Economic Statistics 7, 409–422.

Harvey, A.C., Jaeger, A. (1993). "Detrending, stylized facts and the business cycle". Journal of Applied Econometrics 8, 231–247.

Harvey, A.C., Koopman, S.J. (1992). "Diagnostic checking of unobserved components time series models". Journal of Business and Economic Statistics 10, 377–389.

Harvey, A.C., Koopman, S.J. (1993). "Forecasting hourly electricity demand using time-varying splines". Journal of American Statistical Association 88, 1228–1236.

Harvey, A.C., Koopman, S.J. (2000). "Signal extraction and the formulation of unobserved components models". Econometrics Journal 3, 84–107.

Harvey, A.C., Koopman, S.J., Riani, M. (1997). "The modeling and seasonal adjustment of weekly observations". Journal of Business and Economic Statistics 15, 354–368.

Harvey, A.C., Ruiz, E., Shephard, N. (1994). "Multivariate stochastic variance models". Review of Economic Studies 61, 247–264.

Harvey, A.C., Scott, A. (1994). "Seasonality in dynamic regression models". Economic Journal 104, 1324–1345.
Harvey, A.C., Shephard, N. (1996). "Estimation of an asymmetric stochastic volatility model for asset returns". Journal of Business and Economic Statistics 14, 429–434.
Harvey, A.C., Snyder, R.D. (1990). "Structural time series models in inventory control". International Journal of Forecasting 6, 187–198.
Harvey, A.C., Todd, P.H.J. (1983). "Forecasting economic time series with structural and Box–Jenkins models (with discussion)". Journal of Business and Economic Statistics 1, 299–315.
Harvey, A.C., Trimbur, T. (2003). "General model-based filters for extracting cycles and trends in economic time series". Review of Economics and Statistics 85, 244–255.
Harvey, A.C., Trimbur, T., van Dijk, H. (2006). "Trends and cycles in economic time series: A Bayesian approach". Journal of Econometrics. In press.
Hillmer, S.C. (1982). "Forecasting time series with trading day variation". Journal of Forecasting 1, 385–395.
Hillmer, S.C., Tiao, G.C. (1982). "An ARIMA-model-based approach to seasonal adjustment". Journal of the American Statistical Association 77, 63–70.
Hipel, R.W., McLeod, A.I. (1994). Time Series Modelling of Water Resources and Environmental Systems. Developments in Water Science, vol. 45. Elsevier, Amsterdam.
Holt, C.C. (1957). "Forecasting seasonals and trends by exponentially weighted moving averages". ONR Research Memorandum 52, Carnegie Institute of Technology, Pittsburgh, PA.
Hull, J., White, A. (1987). "The pricing of options on assets with stochastic volatilities". Journal of Finance 42, 281–300.
Hyndman, R.J., Billah, B. (2003). "Unmasking the Theta method". International Journal of Forecasting 19, 287–290.
Ionescu, V., Oara, C., Weiss, M. (1997). "General matrix pencil techniques for the solution of algebraic Riccati equations: A unified approach". IEEE Transactions in Automatic Control 42, 1085–1097.
Jacquier, E., Polson, N.G., Rossi, P.E. (1994). "Bayesian analysis of stochastic volatility models (with discussion)". Journal of Business and Economic Statistics 12, 371–417.
Johansen, S. (1995). Likelihood-Based Inference in Co-Integrated Vector Autoregressive Models. Oxford University Press, Oxford.
Johnston, F.R., Harrison, P.J. (1986). "The variance of lead time demand". Journal of the Operational Research Society 37, 303–308.
Jones, R.H. (1993). Longitudinal Data with Serial Correlation: A State Space Approach. Chapman and Hall, London.
Kalman, R.E. (1960). "A new approach to linear filtering and prediction problems". Journal of Basic Engineering, Transactions ASME. Series D 82, 35–45.
Kim, C.J., Nelson, C. (1999). State-Space Models with Regime-Switching. MIT Press, Cambridge, MA.
Kim, S., Shephard, N.S., Chib, S. (1998). "Stochastic volatility: Likelihood inference and comparison with ARCH models". Review of Economic Studies 65, 361–393.
Kitagawa, G. (1987). "Non-Gaussian state space modeling of nonstationary time series (with discussion)". Journal of the American Statistical Association 82, 1032–1063.
Kitagawa, G., Gersch, W. (1996). Smoothness Priors Analysis of Time Series. Springer-Verlag, Berlin.
Koop, G., van Dijk, H.K. (2000). "Testing for integration using evolving trend and seasonals models: A Bayesian approach". Journal of Econometrics 97, 261–291.
Koopman, S.J., Harvey, A.C. (2003). "Computing observation weights for signal extraction and filtering". Journal of Economic Dynamics and Control 27, 1317–1333.
Koopman, S.J., Harvey, A.C., Doornik, J.A., Shephard, N. (2000). "STAMP 6.0 Structural Time Series Analyser, Modeller and Predictor". Timberlake Consultants Ltd., London.
Kozicki, S. (1999). "Multivariate detrending under common trend restrictions: Implications for business cycle research". Journal of Economic Dynamics and Control 23, 997–1028.
Krane, S., Wascher, W. (1999). "The cyclical sensitivity of seasonality in U.S. employment". Journal of Monetary Economics 44, 523–553.

Kuttner, K.N. (1994). "Estimating potential output as a latent variable". Journal of Business and Economic Statistics 12, 361–368.

Lenten, L.J.A., Moosa, I.A. (1999). "Modelling the trend and seasonality in the consumption of alcoholic beverages in the United Kingdom". Applied Economics 31, 795–804.

Luginbuhl, R., de Vos, A. (1999). "Bayesian analysis of an unobserved components time series model of GDP with Markov-switching and time-varying growths". Journal of Business and Economic Statistics 17, 456–465.

MacDonald, I.L., Zucchini, W. (1997). Hidden Markov Chains and other Models for Discrete-Valued Time Series. Chapman and Hall, London.

Makridakis, S., Hibon, M. (2000). "The M3-competitions: Results, conclusions and implications". International Journal of Forecasting 16, 451–476.

Maravall, A. (1985). "On structural time series models and the characterization of components". Journal of Business and Economic Statistics 3, 350–355.

McCullagh, P., Nelder, J.A. (1983). Generalised Linear Models. Chapman and Hall, London.

Meinhold, R.J., Singpurwalla, N.D. (1989). "Robustification of Kalman filter models". Journal of the American Statistical Association 84, 479–486.

Moosa, I.A., Kennedy, P. (1998). "Modelling seasonality in the Australian consumption function". Australian Economic Papers 37, 88–102.

Morley, J.C., Nelson, C.R., Zivot, E. (2003). "Why are Beveridge–Nelson and unobserved components decompositions of GDP so different?". Review of Economic and Statistics 85, 235–244.

Muth, J.F. (1960). "Optimal properties of exponentially weighted forecasts". Journal of the American Statistical Association 55, 299–305.

Nerlove, M., Wage, S. (1964). "On the optimality of adaptive forecasting". Management Science 10, 207–229.

Nerlove, M., Grether, D.M., Carvalho, J.L. (1979). Analysis of Economic Time Series. Academic Press, New York.

Nicholls, D.F., Pagan, A.R. (1985). "Varying coefficient regression". In: Hannan, E.J., Krishnaiah, P.R., Rao, M.M. (Eds.), Handbook of Statistics, vol. 5. North-Holland, Amsterdam, pp. 413–450.

Ord, J.K., Koehler, A.B., Snyder, R.D. (1997). "Estimation and prediction for a class of dynamic nonlinear statistical model". Journal of the American Statistical Association 92, 1621–1629.

Osborn, D.R., Smith, J.R. (1989). "The performance of periodic autoregressive models in forecasting U.K. consumption". Journal of Business and Economic Statistics 7, 117–127.

Patterson, K.D. (1995). "An integrated model of the date measurement and data generation processes with an application to consumers' expenditure". Economic Journal 105, 54–76.

Pfeffermann, D. (1991). "Estimation and seasonal adjustment of population means using data from repeated surveys". Journal of Business and Economic Statistics 9, 163–175.

Planas, C., Rossi, A. (2004). "Can inflation data improve the real-time reliability of output gap estimates?". Journal of Applied Econometrics 19, 121–133.

Proietti, T. (1998). "Seasonal heteroscedasticity and trends". Journal of Forecasting 17, 1–17.

Proietti, T. (2000). "Comparing seasonal components for structural time series models". International Journal of Forecasting 16, 247–260.

Quenneville, B., Singh, A.C. (2000). "Bayesian prediction MSE for state space models with estimated parameters". Journal of Time Series Analysis 21, 219–236.

Rosenberg, B. (1973). "Random coefficient models: The analysis of a cross-section of time series by stochastically convergent parameter regression". Annals of Economic and Social Measurement 2, 399–428.

Schweppe, F. (1965). "Evaluation of likelihood functions for Gaussian signals". IEEE Transactions on Information Theory 11, 61–70.

Shephard, N. (2005). Stochastic Volatility. Oxford University Press, Oxford.

Shephard, N., Pitt, M.K. (1997). "Likelihood analysis of non-Gaussian measurement time series". Biometrika 84, 653–667.

Smith, R.L., Miller, J.E. (1986). "A non-Gaussian state space model and application to prediction of records". Journal of the Royal Statistical Society, Series B 48, 79–88.

Snyder, R.D. (1984). "Inventory control with the Gamma probability distribution". European Journal of Operational Research 17, 373–381.

Stoffer, D., Wall, K. (2004). "Resampling in state space models". In: Harvey, A.C., Koopman, S.J., Shephard, N. (Eds.), State Space and Unobserved Component Models. Cambridge University Press, Cambridge, pp. 171–202.

Taylor, S.J. (1994). "Modelling stochastic volatility". Mathematical Finance 4, 183–204.

Trimbur, T. (2006). "Properties of higher order stochastic cycles". Journal of Time Series Analysis 27, 1–17.

Visser, H., Molenaar, J. (1995). "Trend estimation and regression analysis in climatological time series: An application of structural time series models and the Kalman filter". Journal of Climate 8, 969–979.

Watanabe, T. (1999). "A non-linear filtering approach to stochastic volatility models with an application to daily stock returns". Journal of Applied Econometrics 14, 101–121.

Wells, C. (1996). The Kalman Filter in Finance. Kluwer Academic Publishers, Dordrecht.

West, M., Harrison, P.J. (1989). Bayesian Forecasting and Dynamic Models. Springer-Verlag, New York.

Winters, P.R. (1960). "Forecasting sales by exponentially weighted moving averages". Management Science 6, 324–342.

Young, P. (1984). Recursive Estimation and Time-Series Analysis. Springer-Verlag, Berlin.

Yu, J. (2005). "On leverage in a stochastic volatility model". Journal of Econometrics 127, 165–178.

Chapter 8

FORECASTING ECONOMIC VARIABLES WITH NONLINEAR MODELS

TIMO TERÄSVIRTA

Stockholm School of Economics

Contents

Handbook of Economic Forecasting, Volume 1
Edited by Graham Elliott, Clive W.J. Granger and Allan Timmermann

DOI: 10.1016/S1574-0706(05)01008-6

Abstract

The topic of this chapter is forecasting with nonlinear models. First, a number of well-known nonlinear models are introduced and their properties discussed. These include the smooth transition regression model, the switching regression model whose univariate counterpart is called threshold autoregressive model, the Markov-switching or hidden Markov regression model, the artificial neural network model, and a couple of other models.

Many of these nonlinear models nest a linear model. For this reason, it is advisable to test linearity before estimating the nonlinear model one thinks will fit the data. A number of linearity tests are discussed. These form a part of model specification: the remaining steps of nonlinear model building are parameter estimation and evaluation that are also briefly considered.

There are two possibilities of generating forecasts from nonlinear models. Sometimes it is possible to use analytical formulas as in linear models. In many other cases, however, forecasts more than one periods ahead have to be generated numerically. Methods for doing that are presented and compared.

The accuracy of point forecasts can be compared using various criteria and statistical tests. Some of these tests have the property that they are not applicable when one of the two models under comparison nests the other one. Tests that have been developed in order to work in this situation are described.

The chapter also contains a simulation study showing how, in some situations, forecasts from a correctly specified nonlinear model may be inferior to ones from a certain linear model.

There exist relatively large studies in which the forecasting performance of nonlinear models is compared with that of linear models using actual macroeconomic series. Main features of some such studies are briefly presented and lessons from them described. In general, no dominant nonlinear (or linear) model has emerged.

Keywords

forecast comparison, nonlinear modelling, neural network, smooth transition regression, switching regression, Markov switching, threshold autoregression

JEL classification: C22, C45, C51, C52, C53

1. Introduction

In recent years, nonlinear models have become more common in empirical economics than they were a few decades ago. This trend has brought with it an increased interest in forecasting economic variables with nonlinear models: for recent accounts of this topic, see Tsay (2002) and Clements, Franses and Swanson (2004). Nonlinear forecasting has also been discussed in books on nonlinear economic modelling such as Granger and Teräsvirta (1993, Chapter 9) and Franses and van Dijk (2000). More specific surveys include Zhang, Patuwo and Hu (1998) on forecasting (not only economic forecasting) with neural network models and Lundbergh and Teräsvirta (2002) who consider forecasting with smooth transition autoregressive models. Ramsey (1996) discusses difficulties in forecasting economic variables with nonlinear models. Large-scale comparisons of the forecasting performance of linear and nonlinear models have appeared in the literature; see Stock and Watson (1999), Marcellino (2002) and Teräsvirta, van Dijk and Medeiros (2005) for examples. There is also a growing literature consisting of forecast comparisons that involve a rather limited number of time series and nonlinear models as well as comparisons entirely based on simulated series.

There exist an unlimited amount of nonlinear models, and it is not possible to cover all developments in this survey. The considerations are restricted to parametric nonlinear models, which excludes forecasting with nonparametric models. For information on nonparametric forecasting, the reader is referred to Fan and Yao (2003). Besides, only a small number of frequently applied parametric nonlinear models are discussed here. It is also worth mentioning that the interest is solely focused on stochastic models. This excludes deterministic processes such as chaotic ones. This is motivated by the fact that chaos is a less useful concept in economics than it is in natural sciences. Another area of forecasting with nonlinear models that is not covered here is volatility forecasting. The reader is referred to Andersen, Bollerslev and Christoffersen (2006) and the survey by Poon and Granger (2003).

The plan of the chapter is the following. In Section 2, a number of parametric nonlinear models are presented and their properties briefly discussed. Section 3 is devoted to strategies of building certain types of nonlinear models. In Section 4 the focus shifts to forecasting, more specifically, to different methods of obtaining multistep forecasts. Combining forecasts is also briefly mentioned. Problems in and ways of comparing the accuracy of point forecasts from linear and nonlinear models is considered in Section 5, and a specific simulated example of such a comparison in Section 6. Empirical forecast comparisons form the topic of Section 7, and Section 8 contains final remarks.

2. Nonlinear models

2.1. General

Regime-switching has been a popular idea in economic applications of nonlinear models. The data-generating process to be modelled is perceived as a linear process that switches between a number of regimes according to some rule. For example, it may be argued that the dynamic properties of the growth rate of the volume of industrial production or gross national product process are different in recessions and expansions. As another example, changes in government policy may instigate switches in regime.

These two examples are different in nature. In the former case, it may be assumed that nonlinearity is in fact controlled by an observable variable such as a lag of the growth rate. In the latter one, an observable indicator for regime switches may not exist. This feature will lead to a family of nonlinear models different from the previous one.

In this chapter we present a small number of special cases of the nonlinear dynamic regression model. These are rather general models in the sense that they have not been designed for testing a particular economic theory proposition or describing economic behaviour in a particular situation. They share this property with the dynamic linear model. No clear-cut rules for choosing a particular nonlinear family exist, but the previous examples suggest that in some cases, choices may be made *a priori*. Estimated models can, however, be compared *ex post*. In theory, nonnested tests offer such a possibility, but applying them in the nonlinear context is more demanding that in the linear framework, and few, if any, examples of that exist in the literature. Model selection criteria are sometimes used for the purpose as well as post-sample forecasting comparisons. It appears that successful model building, that is, a systematic search to find a model that fits the data well, is only possible within a well-defined family of nonlinear models. The family of autoregressive – moving average models constitutes a classic linear example; see Box and Jenkins (1970). Nonlinear model building is discussed in Section 3.

2.2. Nonlinear dynamic regression model

A general nonlinear dynamic model with an additive noise component can be defined as follows:

$$y_t = f(\mathbf{z}_t; \boldsymbol{\theta}) + \varepsilon_t \tag{1}$$

where $\mathbf{z}_t = (\mathbf{w}_t', \mathbf{x}_t')'$ is a vector of explanatory variables, $\mathbf{w}_t = (1, y_{t-1}, \ldots, y_{t-p})'$, and the vector of strongly exogenous variables $\mathbf{x}_t = (x_{1t}, \ldots, x_{kt})'$. Furthermore, $\varepsilon_t \sim \text{iid}(0, \sigma^2)$. It is assumed that y_t is a stationary process. Nonstationary nonlinear processes will not be considered in this survey. Many of the models discussed in this section are special cases of (1) that have been popular in forecasting applications. Moving average models and models with stochastic coefficients, an example of so-called doubly stochastic models, will also be briefly highlighted.

Strict stationarity of (1) may be investigated using the theory of Markov chains. Tong (1990, Chapter 4) contains a discussion of the relevant theory. Under a condition concerning the starting distribution, geometric ergodicity of a Markov chain implies strict stationarity of the same chain, and a set of conditions for geometric ergodicity are given. These results can be used for investigating strict stationarity in special cases of (1), as the model can be expressed as a $(p + 1)$-dimensional Markov chain. As an example

[Example 4.3 in Tong (1990)], consider the following modification of the exponential smooth transition autoregressive (ESTAR) model to be discussed in the next section:

$$\begin{aligned} y_t &= \sum_{j=1}^{p} \left[\phi_j y_{t-j} + \theta_j y_{t-j}\left(1 - \exp\{-\gamma y_{t-j}^2\}\right)\right] + \varepsilon_t \\ &= \sum_{j=1}^{p} \left[(\phi_j + \theta_j) y_{t-j} - \theta_j y_{t-j} \exp\{-\gamma y_{t-j}^2\}\right] + \varepsilon_t \end{aligned} \tag{2}$$

where $\{\varepsilon_t\} \sim \text{iid}(0, \sigma^2)$. It can be shown that (2) is geometrically ergodic if the roots of $1 - \sum_{j=1}^{p}(\phi_j + \theta_j)L^j$ lie outside the unit circle. This result partly relies on the additive structure of this model. In fact, it is not known whether the same condition holds for the following, more common but non-additive, ESTAR model:

$$y_t = \sum_{j=1}^{p} \left[\phi_j y_{t-j} + \theta_j y_{t-j}\left(1 - \exp\{-\gamma y_{t-d}^2\}\right)\right] + \varepsilon_t, \quad \gamma > 0$$

where $d > 0$ and $p > 1$.

As another example, consider the first-order self-exciting threshold autoregressive (SETAR) model (see Section 2.4)

$$y_t = \phi_{11} y_{t-1} I(y_{t-1} \leqslant c) + \phi_{12} y_{t-1} I(y_{t-1} > c) + \varepsilon_t$$

where $I(A)$ is an indicator function: $I(A) = 1$ when event A occurs; zero otherwise. A necessary and sufficient condition for this SETAR process to be geometrically ergodic is $\phi_{11} < 1$, $\phi_{12} < 1$ and $\phi_{11}\phi_{12} < 1$. For higher-order models, normally only sufficient conditions exist, and for many interesting models these conditions are quite restrictive. An example will be given in Section 2.4.

2.3. Smooth transition regression model

The smooth transition regression (STR) model originated in the work of Bacon and Watts (1971). These authors considered two regression lines and devised a model in which the transition from one line to the other is smooth. They used the hyperbolic tangent function to characterize the transition. This function is close to both the normal cumulative distribution function and the logistic function. Maddala (1977, p. 396) in fact recommended the use of the logistic function as transition function, and this has become the prevailing standard; see, for example, Teräsvirta (1998). In general terms we can define the STR model as follows:

$$\begin{aligned} y_t &= \boldsymbol{\phi}' \mathbf{z}_t + \boldsymbol{\theta}' \mathbf{z}_t G(\gamma, \mathbf{c}, s_t) + \varepsilon_t \\ &= \{\boldsymbol{\phi} + \boldsymbol{\theta} G(\gamma, \mathbf{c}, s_t)\}' \mathbf{z}_t + \varepsilon_t, \quad t = 1, \ldots, T \end{aligned} \tag{3}$$

where $\mathbf{z}_t$ is defined as in (1), $\boldsymbol{\phi} = (\phi_0, \phi_1, \ldots, \phi_m)'$ and $\boldsymbol{\theta} = (\theta_0, \theta_1, \ldots, \theta_m)'$ are parameter vectors, and $\varepsilon_t \sim \text{iid}(0, \sigma^2)$. In the transition function $G(\gamma, \mathbf{c}, s_t)$, γ is the slope parameter and $\mathbf{c} = (c_1, \ldots, c_K)'$ a vector of location parameters, $c_1 \leqslant \cdots \leqslant c_K$. The transition function is a bounded function of the transition variable s_t, continuous everywhere in the parameter space for any value of s_t. The last expression in (3) indicates that the model can be interpreted as a linear model with stochastic time-varying coefficients $\boldsymbol{\phi} + \boldsymbol{\theta} G(\gamma, \mathbf{c}, s_t)$ where s_t controls the time-variation. The logistic transition function has the general form

$$G(\gamma, \mathbf{c}, s_t) = \left(1 + \exp\left\{-\gamma \prod_{k=1}^{K} (s_t - c_k)\right\}\right)^{-1}, \quad \gamma > 0 \tag{4}$$

where $\gamma > 0$ is an identifying restriction. Equation (3) jointly with (4) defines the logistic STR (LSTR) model. The most common choices for K are $K = 1$ and $K = 2$. For $K = 1$, the parameters $\boldsymbol{\phi} + \boldsymbol{\theta} G(\gamma, \mathbf{c}, s_t)$ change monotonically as a function of s_t from $\boldsymbol{\phi}$ to $\boldsymbol{\phi}+\boldsymbol{\theta}$. For $K = 2$, they change symmetrically around the mid-point $(c_1+c_2)/2$ where this logistic function attains its minimum value. The minimum lies between zero and $1/2$. It reaches zero when $\gamma \to \infty$ and equals $1/2$ when $c_1 = c_2$ and $\gamma < \infty$. Slope parameter γ controls the slope and c_1 and c_2 the location of the transition function.

The LSTR model with $K = 1$ (LSTR1 model) is capable of characterizing asymmetric behaviour. As an example, suppose that s_t measures the phase of the business cycle. Then the LSTR1 model can describe processes whose dynamic properties are different in expansions from what they are in recessions, and the transition from one extreme regime to the other is smooth. The LSTR2 model is appropriate in situations where the local dynamic behaviour of the process is similar at both large and small values of s_t and different in the middle.

When $\gamma = 0$, the transition function $G(\gamma, \mathbf{c}, s_t) \equiv 1/2$ so that STR model (3) nests a linear model. At the other end, when $\gamma \to \infty$ the LSTR1 model approaches the switching regression (SR) model, see Section 2.4, with two regimes and $\sigma_1^2 = \sigma_2^2$. When $\gamma \to \infty$ in the LSTR2 model, the result is a switching regression model with three regimes such that the outer regimes are identical and the mid-regime different from the other two.

Another variant of the LSTR2 model is the exponential STR (ESTR, in the univariate case ESTAR) model in which the transition function

$$G(\gamma, c, s_t) = 1 - \exp\{-\gamma (s_t - c)^2\}, \quad \gamma > 0. \tag{5}$$

This transition function is an approximation to (4) with $K = 2$ and $c_1 = c_2$. When $\gamma \to \infty$, however, $G(\gamma, c, s_t) = 1$ for $s_t \neq c$, in which case equation (3) is linear except at a single point. Equation (3) with (5) has been a popular tool in investigations of the validity of the purchasing power parity (PPP) hypothesis; see for example the survey by Taylor and Sarno (2002).

In practice, the transition variable s_t is a stochastic variable and very often an element of $\mathbf{z}_t$. It can also be a linear combination of several variables. A special case, $s_t = t$, yields a linear model with deterministically changing parameters. Such a model has a role to play, among other things, in testing parameter constancy, see Section 2.7.

When $\mathbf{x}_t$ is absent from (3) and $s_t = y_{t-d}$ or $s_t = \Delta y_{t-d}$, $d > 0$, the STR model becomes a univariate smooth transition autoregressive (STAR) model. The logistic STAR (LSTAR) model was introduced in the time series literature by Chan and Tong (1986) who used the density of the normal distribution as the transition function. The exponential STAR (ESTAR) model appeared already in Haggan and Ozaki (1981). Later, Teräsvirta (1994) defined a family of STAR models that included both the LSTAR and the ESTAR model and devised a data-driven modelling strategy with the aim of, among other things, helping the user to choose between these two alternatives.

Investigating the PPP hypothesis is just one of many applications of the STR and STAR models to economic data. Univariate STAR models have been frequently applied in modelling asymmetric behaviour of macroeconomic variables such as industrial production and unemployment rate, or nonlinear behaviour of inflation. In fact, many different nonlinear models have been fitted to unemployment rates; see Proietti (2003) for references. As to STR models, several examples of the its use in modelling money demand such as Teräsvirta and Eliasson (2001) can be found in the literature. Venetis, Paya and Peel (2003) recently applied the model to a much investigated topic: usefulness of the interest rate spread in predicting output growth. The list of applications could be made longer.

2.4. *Switching regression and threshold autoregressive model*

The standard switching regression model is piecewise linear, and it is defined as follows:

$$y_t = \sum_{j=1}^{r+1} (\boldsymbol{\phi}'_j \mathbf{z}_t + \varepsilon_{jt}) I(c_{j-1} < s_t \leqslant c_j) \tag{6}$$

where $\mathbf{z}_t = (\mathbf{w}'_t, \mathbf{x}'_t)'$ is defined as before, s_t is a switching variable, usually assumed to be a continuous random variable, $c_0, c_1, \ldots, c_{r+1}$ are threshold parameters, $c_0 = -\infty$, $c_{r+1} = +\infty$. Furthermore, $\varepsilon_{jt} \sim \text{iid}(0, \sigma_j^2)$, $j = 1, \ldots, r$. It is seen that (6) is a piecewise linear model whose switch-points, however, are generally unknown. A popular alternative in practice is the two-regime SR model

$$y_t = (\boldsymbol{\phi}'_1 \mathbf{z}_t + \varepsilon_{1t}) I(s_t \leqslant c_1) + (\boldsymbol{\phi}'_2 \mathbf{z}_t + \varepsilon_{2t}) \{1 - I(s_t \leqslant c_1)\}. \tag{7}$$

It is a special case of the STR model (3) with $K = 1$ in (4).

When $\mathbf{x}_t$ is absent and $s_t = y_{t-d}$, $d > 0$, (6) becomes the self-exciting threshold autoregressive (SETAR) model. The SETAR model has been widely applied in economics. A comprehensive account of the model and its statistical properties can be found in Tong (1990). A two-regime SETAR model is a special case of the LSTAR1 model when the slope parameter $\gamma \to \infty$.

A special case of the SETAR model itself, suggested by Enders and Granger (1998) and called the momentum-TAR model, is the one with two regimes and $s_t = \Delta y_{t-d}$. This model may be used to characterize processes in which the asymmetry lies in growth rates: as an example, the growth of the series when it occurs may be rapid but the return to a lower level slow.

It was mentioned in Section 2.2 that stationarity conditions for higher-order models can often be quite restrictive. As an example, consider the univariate SETAR model of order p, that is, $\mathbf{x}_t \equiv \mathbf{0}$ and $\boldsymbol{\phi}_j = (1, \phi_{j1}, \ldots, \phi_{jp})'$ in (6). Chan (1993) contains a sufficient condition for this model to be stationary. It has the form

$$\max_i \sum_{j=1}^{p} |\phi_{ji}| < 1.$$

For $p = 1$ the condition becomes $\max_i |\phi_{1i}| < 1$, which is already in this simple case a more restrictive condition than the necessary and sufficient condition presented in Section 2.2.

The SETAR model has also been a popular tool in investigating the PPP hypothesis; see the survey by Taylor and Sarno (2002). Like the STAR model, the SETAR model has been widely applied to modelling asymmetries in macroeconomic series. It is often argued that the US interest rate processes have more than one regime, and SETAR models have been fitted to these series, see Pfann, Schotman and Tschernig (1996) for an example. These models have also been applied to modelling exchange rates as in Henry, Olekalns and Summers (2001) who were, among other things, interested in the effect of the East-Asian 1997–1998 currency crisis on the Australian dollar.

2.5. Markov-switching model

In the switching regression model (6), the switching variable is an observable continuous variable. It may also be an unobservable variable that obtains a finite number of discrete values and is independent of y_t at all lags, as in Lindgren (1978). Such a model may be called the Markov-switching or hidden Markov regression model, and it is defined by the following equation:

$$y_t = \sum_{j=1}^{r} \boldsymbol{\alpha}'_j \mathbf{z}_t I(s_t = j) + \varepsilon_t \tag{8}$$

where $\{s_t\}$ follows a Markov chain, often of order one. If the order equals one, the conditional probability of the event $s_t = i$ given s_{t-k}, $k = 1, 2, \ldots,$ is only dependent on s_{t-1} and equals

$$\Pr\{s_t = i | s_{t-1} = j\} = p_{ij}, \quad i, j = 1, \ldots, r \tag{9}$$

such that $\sum_{i=1}^{r} p_{ij} = 1$. The transition probabilities p_{ij} are unknown and have to be estimated from the data. The error process ε_t is often assumed not to be dependent on the 'regime' or the value of s_t, but the model may be generalized to incorporate that possibility. In its univariate form, $\mathbf{z}_t = \mathbf{w}_t$, model (8) with transition probabilities (9) has been called the suddenly changing autoregressive (SCAR) model; see Tyssedal and Tjøstheim (1988).

There is a Markov-switching autoregressive model, proposed by Hamilton (1989), that is more common in econometric applications than the SCAR model. In this model, the intercept is time-varying and determined by the value of the latent variable s_t and its lags. It has the form

$$y_t = \mu_{s_t} + \sum_{j=1}^{p} \alpha_j (y_{t-j} - \mu_{s_{t-j}}) + \varepsilon_t \tag{10}$$

where the behaviour of s_t is defined by (9), and $\mu_{s_t} = \mu^{(i)}$ for $s_t = i$, such that $\mu^{(i)} \neq \mu^{(j)}$, $i \neq j$. For identification reasons, y_{t-j} and $\mu_{s_{t-j}}$ in (10) share the same coefficient. The stochastic intercept of this model, $\mu_{s_t} - \sum_{j=1}^{p} \alpha_j \mu_{s_{t-j}}$, thus can obtain r^{p+1} different values, and this gives the model the desired flexibility. A comprehensive discussion of Markov-switching models can be found in Hamilton (1994, Chapter 22).

Markov-switching models can be applied when the data can be conveniently thought of as having been generated by a model with different regimes such that the regime changes do not have an observable or quantifiable cause. They may also be used when data on the switching variable is not available and no suitable proxy can be found. This is one of the reasons why Markov-switching models have been fitted to interest rate series, where changes in monetary policy have been a motivation for adopting this approach. Modelling asymmetries in macroeconomic series has, as in the case of SETAR and STAR models, been another area of application; see Hamilton (1989) who fitted a Markov-switching model of type (10) to the post World War II quarterly US GNP series. Tyssedal and Tjøstheim (1988) fitted a three-regime SCAR model to a daily IBM stock return series originally analyzed in Box and Jenkins (1970).

2.6. *Artificial neural network model*

Modelling various processes and phenomena, including economic ones, using artificial neural network (ANN) models has become quite popular. Many textbooks have been written about these models, see, for example, Fine (1999) or Haykin (1999). A detailed treatment can be found in White (2006), whereas the discussion here is restricted to the simplest single-equation case, which is the so-called "single hidden-layer" model. It has the following form:

$$y_t = \boldsymbol{\beta}_0' \mathbf{z}_t + \sum_{j=1}^{q} \beta_j G(\boldsymbol{\gamma}_j' \mathbf{z}_t) + \varepsilon_t \tag{11}$$

where y_t is the output series, $\mathbf{z}_t = (1, y_{t-1}, \ldots, y_{t-p}, x_{1t}, \ldots, x_{kt})'$ is the vector of inputs, including the intercept and lagged values of the output, $\boldsymbol{\beta}_0' \mathbf{z}_t$ is a linear unit, and β_j, $j = 1, \ldots, q$, are parameters, called "connection strengths" in the neural network literature. Many neural network modellers exclude the linear unit altogether, but it is a useful component in time series applications. Furthermore, function $G(.)$ is a bounded function called "the squashing function" and $\boldsymbol{\gamma}_j$, $j = 1, \ldots, q$, are parameter vectors. Typical squashing functions are monotonically increasing ones such as the logistic function and the hyperbolic tangent function and thus have the same form as transition functions of STAR models. The so-called radial basis functions that resemble density functions are another possibility. The errors ε_t are often assumed iid$(0, \sigma^2)$. The term "hidden layer" refers to the structure of (11). While the output y_t and the input vector $\mathbf{z}_t$ are observed, the linear combination $\sum_{j=1}^{q} \beta_j G(\boldsymbol{\gamma}_j' \mathbf{z}_t)$ is not. It thus forms a hidden layer between the "output layer" y_t and "input layer" $\mathbf{z}_t$.

A theoretical argument used to motivate the use of ANN models is that they are universal approximators. Suppose that $y_t = H(\mathbf{z}_t)$, that is, there exists a functional relationship between y_t and $\mathbf{z}_t$. Then, under mild regularity conditions for H, there exists a positive integer $q \leqslant q_0 < \infty$ such that for an arbitrary $\delta > 0$, $|H(\mathbf{z}_t) - \sum_{j=1}^{q} \beta_j G(\boldsymbol{\gamma}_j' \mathbf{z}_t)| < \delta$. The importance of this result lies in the fact that q is finite, whereby any unknown function H can be approximated arbitrarily accurately by a linear combination of squashing functions $G(\boldsymbol{\gamma}_j' \mathbf{z}_t)$. This has been discussed in several papers including Cybenko (1989), Funahashi (1989), Hornik, Stinchcombe and White (1989) and White (1990).

A statistical property separating the artificial neural network model (11) from other nonlinear econometric models presented here is that it is only locally identified. It is seen from Equation (11) that the hidden units are exchangeable. For example, letting any $(\beta_i, \boldsymbol{\gamma}_i')'$ and $(\beta_j, \boldsymbol{\gamma}_j')'$, $i \neq j$, change places in the equation does not affect the value of the likelihood function. Thus for $q > 1$ there always exists more than one observationally equivalent parameterization, so that additional parameter restrictions are required for global identification. Furthermore, the sign of one element in each $\boldsymbol{\gamma}_j$, the first one, say, has to be fixed in advance to exclude observationally equivalent parameterizations. The identification restrictions are discussed, for example, in Hwang and Ding (1997).

The rich parameterization of ANN models makes the estimation of parameters difficult. Computationally feasible, yet effective, shortcuts are proposed and implemented in White (2006). Goffe, Ferrier and Rogers (1994) contains an example showing that simulated annealing, which is a heuristic estimation method, may be a powerful tool in estimating parameters of these models. ANN models have been fitted to various economic time series. Since the model is a universal approximator rather than one with parameters with economic interpretation, the purpose of fitting these models has mainly been forecasting. Examples of their performance in forecasting macroeconomic variables can be found in Section 7.3.

2.7. Time-varying regression model

A time-varying regression model is an STR model in which the transition variable $s_t = t$. It can thus be defined as follows:

$$y_t = \boldsymbol{\phi}' \mathbf{z}_t + \boldsymbol{\theta}' \mathbf{z}_t G(\gamma, \mathbf{c}, t) + \varepsilon_t, \quad t = 1, \ldots, T \tag{12}$$

where the transition function

$$G(\gamma, \mathbf{c}, s_t) = \left(1 + \exp\left\{-\gamma \prod_{k=1}^{K} (t - c_k)\right\}\right)^{-1}, \quad \gamma > 0. \tag{13}$$

When $K = 1$ and $\gamma \to \infty$ in (13), Equation (12) represents a linear dynamic regression model with a break in parameters at $t = c_1$. It can be generalized to a model with several transitions:

$$y_t = \boldsymbol{\phi}'\mathbf{z}_t + \sum_{j=1}^{r} \boldsymbol{\theta}_j'\mathbf{z}_t G_j(\gamma_j, \mathbf{c}_j, t) + \varepsilon_t, \quad t = 1, \ldots, T \tag{14}$$

where transition functions G_j typically have the form (13) with $K = 1$. When $\gamma_j \to \infty$, $j = 1, \ldots, r$, in (14), the model becomes a linear model with multiple breaks. Specifying such models has recently received plenty of attention; see, for example, Bai and Perron (1998, 2003) and Banerjee and Urga (2005). In principle, these models should be preferable to linear models without breaks because the forecasts are generated from the most recent specification instead of an average one, which is the case if the breaks are ignored. In practice, the number of break-points and their locations have to be estimated from the data, which makes this suggestion less straightforward. Even if this difficulty is ignored, it may be optimal to use pre-break observations in forecasting. The reason is that while the one-step-ahead forecast based on post-break data is unbiased (if the model is correctly specified), it may have a large variance. The mean square error of the forecast may be reduced if the model is estimated by using at least some pre-break observations as well. This introduces bias but at the same time reduces the variance. For more information of this bias-variance trade-off, see Pesaran and Timmermann (2002).

Time-varying coefficients can also be stochastic:

$$y_t = \boldsymbol{\phi}_t'\mathbf{z}_t + \varepsilon_t, \quad t = 1, \ldots, T \tag{15}$$

where $\{\boldsymbol{\phi}_t\}$ is a sequence of random variables. In a large forecasting study, Marcellino (2002) assumed that $\{\boldsymbol{\phi}_t\}$ was a random walk, that is, $\{\Delta\boldsymbol{\phi}_t\}$ was a sequence of normal independent variables with zero mean and a known variance. This assumption is a testable alternative to parameter constancy; see Nyblom (1989). For the estimation of stochastic random coefficient models, the reader is referred to Harvey (2006). Another assumption, albeit a less popular one in practice, is that $\{\boldsymbol{\phi}_t\}$ follows a stationary vector autoregressive model. Parameter constancy in (15) may be tested against this alternative as well: see Watson and Engle (1985) and Lin and Teräsvirta (1999).

2.8. *Nonlinear moving average models*

Nonlinear autoregressive models have been quite popular among practitioners, but nonlinear moving average models have also been proposed in the literature. A rather general nonlinear moving average model of order q may be defined as follows:

$$y_t = f(\varepsilon_{t-1}, \varepsilon_{t-2}, \ldots, \varepsilon_{t-q}; \boldsymbol{\theta}) + \varepsilon_t$$

where $\{\varepsilon_t\} \sim \text{iid}(0, \sigma^2)$. A problem with these models is that their invertibility conditions may not be known, in which case the models cannot be used for forecasting. A common property of moving average models is that if the model is invertible, forecasts from it for more than q steps ahead equal the unconditional mean of y_t. Some nonlinear moving average models are linear in parameters, which makes forecasting with them easy in the sense that no numerical techniques are required when forecasting several steps ahead. As an example of a nonlinear moving average model, consider the asymmetric moving average (asMA) model of Wecker (1981). It has the form

$$y_t = \mu + \sum_{j=1}^{q} \theta_j \varepsilon_{t-j} + \sum_{j=1}^{q} \psi_j I(\varepsilon_{t-j} > 0)\varepsilon_{t-j} + \varepsilon_t \tag{16}$$

where $I(\varepsilon_{t-j} > 0) = 1$ when $\varepsilon_{t-j} > 0$ and zero otherwise, and $\{\varepsilon_t\} \sim \text{nid}(0, \sigma^2)$. This model has the property that the effects of a positive shock and a negative shock of the same sizes on y_t are not symmetric when $\psi_j \neq 0$ for at least one j, $j = 1, \ldots, q$.

Brännäs and De Gooijer (1994) extended (16) to contain a linear autoregressive part and called the model an autoregressive asymmetric moving average (ARasMA) model. The forecasts from an ARasMA model has the property that after q steps ahead they are identical to the forecasts from a linear AR model that has the same autoregressive parameters as the ARasMA model. This implies that the forecast densities more than q periods ahead are symmetric, unless the error distribution is asymmetric.

3. Building nonlinear models

Building nonlinear models comprises three stages. First, the structure of the model is specified, second, its parameters are estimated and third, the estimated model has to be evaluated before it is used for forecasting. The last stage is important because if the model does not satisfy in-sample evaluation criteria, it cannot be expected to produce accurate forecasts. Of course, good in-sample behaviour of a model is not synonymous with accurate forecasts, but in many cases it may at least be viewed as a necessary condition for obtaining such forecasts from the final model.

It may be argued, however, that the role of model building in constructing models for forecasting is diminishing because computations has become inexpensive. It is easy to estimate a possibly large number of models and combine the forecasts from them. This suggestion is related to thick modelling that Granger and Jeon (2004) recently discussed. A study where this has been a successful strategy will be discussed in Section 7.3.1. On the other hand, many popular nonlinear models such as the smooth transition or threshold autoregressive, or Markov switching models, nest a linear model and are unidentified if the data-generating process is linear. Fitting one of these models to linear series leads to inconsistent parameter estimates, and forecasts from the estimated model are bound to be bad. Combining these forecasts with others would not be a good idea. Testing linearity first, as a part of the modelling process, greatly reduces the probability of this alternative. Aspects of building smooth transition, threshold autoregressive, and Markov switching models will be briefly discussed below.

3.1. Testing linearity

Since many of the nonlinear models considered in this chapter nest a linear model, a short review of linearity testing may be useful. In order to illustrate the identification problem, consider the following nonlinear model:

$$y_t = \boldsymbol{\phi}'\mathbf{z}_t + \boldsymbol{\theta}'\mathbf{z}_t G(\boldsymbol{\gamma}; \mathbf{s}_t) + \varepsilon_t = \big(\boldsymbol{\phi} + \boldsymbol{\theta} G(\boldsymbol{\gamma}; \mathbf{s}_t)\big)'\mathbf{z}_t + \varepsilon_t \tag{17}$$

where $\mathbf{z}_t = (1, \widetilde{\mathbf{z}}_t')'$ is an $(m \times 1)$ vector of explanatory variables, some of which can be lags of y_t, and $\{\varepsilon_t\}$ is a white noise sequence with zero mean and $\mathsf{E}\varepsilon_t^2 = \sigma^2$. Depending on the definitions of $G(\boldsymbol{\gamma}; \mathbf{s}_t)$ and $\mathbf{s}_t$, (17) can represent an STR (STAR), SR (SETAR) or a Markov-switching model. The model is linear when $\boldsymbol{\theta} = \mathbf{0}$. When this is the case, parameter vector $\boldsymbol{\gamma}$ is not identified. It can take any value without the likelihood of the process being affected. Thus, estimating $\boldsymbol{\phi}, \boldsymbol{\theta}$ and $\boldsymbol{\gamma}$ consistently from (17) is not possible and for this reason, the standard asymptotic theory is not available.

The problem of testing a null hypothesis when the model is only identified under the alternative was first considered by Davies (1977). The general idea is the following. As discussed above, the model is identified when $\boldsymbol{\gamma}$ is known, and testing linearity of (17) is straightforward. Let $S_T(\boldsymbol{\gamma})$ be the corresponding test statistic whose large values are critical and define $\Gamma = \{\boldsymbol{\gamma}\colon \boldsymbol{\gamma} \in \Gamma\}$, the set of admissible values of $\boldsymbol{\gamma}$. When $\boldsymbol{\gamma}$ is unknown, the statistic is not operational because it is a function of $\boldsymbol{\gamma}$. Davies (1977) suggested that the problem be solved by defining another statistic $S_T = \sup_{\boldsymbol{\gamma} \in \boldsymbol{\Gamma}} S_T(\boldsymbol{\gamma})$ that is no longer a function of $\boldsymbol{\gamma}$. Its asymptotic null distribution does not generally have an analytic form, but Davies (1977) gives an approximation to it that holds under certain conditions, including the assumption that $S(\boldsymbol{\gamma}) = \operatorname{plim}_{T\to\infty} S_T(\boldsymbol{\gamma})$ has a derivative. This, however, is not the case in SR and SETAR models. Other choices of test statistic include the average:

$$S_T = \operatorname{ave} S_T(\boldsymbol{\gamma}) = \int_\Gamma S_T(\boldsymbol{\gamma})\, \mathrm{d}W(\boldsymbol{\gamma}) \tag{18}$$

where $W(\boldsymbol{\gamma})$ is a weight function defined by the user such that $\int_\Gamma W(\boldsymbol{\gamma})\, \mathrm{d}\boldsymbol{\gamma} = 1$. Another choice is the exponential:

$$\exp S_T = \ln\bigg(\int_\Gamma \exp\big\{(1/2)S_T(\boldsymbol{\gamma})\big\}\, \mathrm{d}W(\boldsymbol{\gamma})\bigg), \tag{19}$$

see Andrews and Ploberger (1994).

Hansen (1996) shows how to obtain asymptotic critical values for these statistics by simulation under rather general conditions. Given the observations $(y_t, \mathbf{z}_t)$, $t = 1, \ldots, T$, the log-likelihood of (17) has the form

$$L_T(\boldsymbol{\psi}) = c - (T/2)\ln\sigma^2 - \big(1/2\sigma^2\big)\sum_{t=1}^{T}\big\{y_t - \boldsymbol{\phi}'\mathbf{z}_t - \boldsymbol{\theta}'\mathbf{z}_t G(\boldsymbol{\gamma}; \mathbf{s}_t)\big\}^2$$

$\boldsymbol{\psi} = (\boldsymbol{\phi}', \boldsymbol{\theta}')'$. Assuming $\boldsymbol{\gamma}$ known, the average score for the parameters in the conditional mean equals

$$\mathbf{s}_T(\boldsymbol{\psi}, \boldsymbol{\gamma}) = \left(\sigma^2 T\right)^{-1} \sum_{t=1}^{T} \left(\mathbf{z}_t \otimes \left[1 \; G(\boldsymbol{\gamma}; \mathbf{s}_t)\right]'\right)\varepsilon_t. \tag{20}$$

Lagrange multiplier and Wald tests can be defined using (20) in the usual way. The LM test statistic equals

$$S_T^{\mathrm{LM}}(\boldsymbol{\gamma}) = T\mathbf{s}_T\left(\widetilde{\boldsymbol{\psi}}, \boldsymbol{\gamma}\right)' \widetilde{\mathbf{I}}_T\left(\widetilde{\boldsymbol{\psi}}, \boldsymbol{\gamma}\right)^{-1} \mathbf{s}_T\left(\widetilde{\boldsymbol{\psi}}, \boldsymbol{\gamma}\right)$$

where $\widetilde{\boldsymbol{\psi}}$ is the maximum likelihood estimator of $\boldsymbol{\psi}$ under H_0 and $\widetilde{\mathbf{I}}_T(\widetilde{\boldsymbol{\psi}}, \boldsymbol{\gamma})$ is a consistent estimator of the population information matrix $\mathbf{I}(\boldsymbol{\psi}, \boldsymbol{\gamma})$. An empirical distribution of $S_T^{\mathrm{LM}}(\boldsymbol{\gamma})$ is obtained by simulation as follows:

1. Generate T observations $\varepsilon_t^{(j)}$, $t = 1, \ldots, T$, for each $j = 1, \ldots, J$ from a normal $(0, \widetilde{\sigma}^2)$ distribution, JT observations in all.
2. Compute $\mathbf{s}_T^{(j)}(\boldsymbol{\psi}, \boldsymbol{\gamma}_a) = T^{-1} \sum_{t=1}^{T} (\mathbf{z}_t \otimes [1 \; G(\boldsymbol{\gamma}_a; \mathbf{s}_t)]')u_t^{(j)}$ where $\boldsymbol{\gamma}_a \in \Gamma_A \subset \Gamma$.
3. Set $S_T^{\mathrm{LM}(j)}(\boldsymbol{\gamma}_a) = T\mathbf{s}_T^{(j)}(\widetilde{\boldsymbol{\psi}}, \boldsymbol{\gamma}_a)' \widetilde{\mathbf{I}}_T^{(j)}(\widetilde{\boldsymbol{\psi}}, \boldsymbol{\gamma}_a)^{-1} \mathbf{s}_T^{(j)}(\widetilde{\boldsymbol{\psi}}, \boldsymbol{\gamma}_a)$.
4. Compute $S_T^{\mathrm{LM}(j)}$ from $S_T^{\mathrm{LM}(j)}(\boldsymbol{\gamma}_a)$, $a = 1, \ldots, A$.

Carrying out these steps once gives a simulated value of the statistic. By repeating them J times one generates a random sample $\{S_T^{\mathrm{LM}(1)}, \ldots, S_T^{\mathrm{LM}(J)}\}$ from the null distribution of S_T^{LM}. If the value of S_T^{LM} obtained directly from the sample exceeds the $100(1 - \alpha)\%$ quantile of the empirical distribution, the null hypothesis is rejected at (approximately) significance level α. The power of the test depends on the quality of the approximation Γ_A. Hansen (1996) applied this technique to testing linearity against the two-regime threshold autoregressive model. The empirical distribution may also be obtained by bootstrapping the residuals of the null model.

There is another way of handling the identification problem that is applicable in the context of STR models. Instead of approximating the unknown distribution of a test statistic it is possible to approximate the conditional log-likelihood or the nonlinear model in such a way that the identification problem is circumvented. See Luukkonen, Saikkonen and Teräsvirta (1988), Granger and Teräsvirta (1993) and Teräsvirta (1994) for discussion. Define $\boldsymbol{\gamma} = (\gamma_1, \boldsymbol{\gamma}_2')'$ in (17) and assume that $G(\gamma_1, \boldsymbol{\gamma}_2; \mathbf{s}_t) \equiv 0$ for $\gamma_1 = 0$. Assume, furthermore, that $G(\gamma_1, \boldsymbol{\gamma}_2; \mathbf{s}_t)$ is at least k times continuously differentiable for all values of $\mathbf{s}_t$ and $\boldsymbol{\gamma}$.

It is now possible to approximate the transition function by a Taylor expansion and circumvent the identification problem. First note that due to lack of identification, the linearity hypothesis can also be expressed as H_0: $\gamma_1 = 0$. Function G is approximated locally around the null hypothesis as follows:

$$G(\gamma_1, \boldsymbol{\gamma}_2; \mathbf{s}_t) = \sum_{j=1}^{k} \left(\gamma_1^j / j!\right)\delta_j(\mathbf{s}_t) + R_k(\gamma_1, \boldsymbol{\gamma}_2; \mathbf{s}_t) \tag{21}$$

where $\delta_j(\mathbf{s}_t) = \frac{\partial^j}{\partial \gamma_1^j} G(\gamma_1, \boldsymbol{\gamma}_2; \mathbf{s}_t)|_{\gamma_1=0}$, $j = 1, \ldots, k$. Replacing G in (17) by (21) yields, after reparameterization,

$$y_t = \boldsymbol{\phi}'\mathbf{z}_t + \sum_{j=1}^{k} \boldsymbol{\theta}_j(\gamma_1)'\mathbf{z}_t \delta_j(\mathbf{s}_t) + \varepsilon_t^* \tag{22}$$

where the parameter vectors $\boldsymbol{\theta}_j(\gamma_1) = 0$ for $\gamma_1 = 0$, and the error term $\varepsilon_t^* = \varepsilon_t + \boldsymbol{\theta}'\mathbf{z}_t R_k(\gamma_1, \boldsymbol{\gamma}_2; \mathbf{s}_t)$. The original null hypothesis can now be restated as H_0': $\boldsymbol{\theta}_j(\gamma_1) = 0$, $j = 1, \ldots, k$. It is a linear hypothesis in a linear model and can thus be tested using standard asymptotic theory, because under the null hypothesis $\varepsilon_t^* = \varepsilon_t$. Note, however, that this requires the existence of $\mathsf{E}\delta_j(\mathbf{s}_t)^2 \mathbf{z}_t \mathbf{z}_t'$. The auxiliary regression (22) can be viewed as a result of a trade-off in which information about the structural form of the alternative model is exchanged against a larger null hypothesis and standard asymptotic theory.

As an example, consider the STR model (3) and (4) and assume $K = 1$ in (4). It is a special case of (17) where $\gamma_2 = c$ and

$$G(\gamma_1, c; s_t) = \left(1 + \exp\{-\gamma_1(s_t - c)\}\right)^{-1}, \quad \gamma_1 > 0. \tag{23}$$

When $\gamma_1 = 0$, $G(\gamma_1, c; s_t) \equiv 1/2$. The first-order Taylor expansion of the transition function around $\gamma_1 = 0$ is

$$T(\gamma_1; s_t) = (1/2) - (\gamma_1/4)(s_t - c) + R_1(\gamma_1; s_t). \tag{24}$$

Substituting (24) for (23) in (17) yields, after reparameterization,

$$y_t = (\boldsymbol{\phi}_0^*)'\mathbf{z}_t + (\boldsymbol{\phi}_1^*)'\mathbf{z}_t s_t + \varepsilon_t^* \tag{25}$$

where $\boldsymbol{\phi}_1^* = \gamma_1 \bar{\boldsymbol{\phi}}_1^*$ such that $\bar{\boldsymbol{\phi}}_1^* \neq \mathbf{0}$. The transformed null hypothesis is thus H_0': $\boldsymbol{\phi}_1^* = \mathbf{0}$. Under this hypothesis and assuming that $\mathsf{E}s_t^2 \mathbf{z}_t \mathbf{z}_t'$ exists, the resulting LM statistic has an asymptotic χ^2 distribution with m degrees of freedom. This computationally simple test also has power against SR model, but Hansen's test that is designed directly against that alternative, is of course the more powerful of the two.

3.2. Building STR models

The STR model nests a linear regression model and is not identified when the data-generating process is the linear model. For this reason, a natural first step in building STR models is testing linearity against STR. There exists a data-based modelling strategy that consists of the three stages already mentioned: specification, estimation, and evaluation. It is described, among others, in Teräsvirta (1998), see also van Dijk, Teräsvirta and Franses (2002) or Teräsvirta (2004). Specification consists of testing linearity and, if rejected, determining the transition variable s_t. This is done using testing linearity against STR models with different transition variables. In the univariate case, determining the transition variable amounts to choosing the lag y_{t-d}. The decision to select the type of the STR model (LSTR1 or LSTR2) is also made at the specification stage and is based on the results of a short sequence of tests within an auxiliary regression that is used for testing linearity; see Teräsvirta (1998) for details.

Specification is partly intertwined with estimation, because the model may be reduced by setting coefficients to zero according to some rule and re-estimating the reduced model. This implies that one begins with a large STR model and then continues 'from general to specific'. At the evaluation stage the estimated STR model is subjected to misspecification tests such as tests of no error autocorrelation, no autoregressive conditional heteroskedasticity, no remaining nonlinearity and parameter constancy. The tests are described in Teräsvirta (1998). A model that passes the in-sample tests can be used for out-of-sample forecasting.

The presence of unidentified nuisance parameters is also a problem in misspecification testing. The alternatives to the STR model in tests of no remaining nonlinearity and parameter constancy are not identified when the null hypothesis is valid. The identification problem is again circumvented using a Taylor series expansion. In fact, the linearity test applied at the specification stage can be viewed as a special case of the misspecification test of no remaining nonlinearity.

It may be mentioned that Medeiros, Teräsvirta and Rech (2006) constructed a similar strategy for modelling with neural networks. There the specification stage involves, except testing linearity, selecting the variables and the number of hidden units. Teräsvirta, Lin and Granger (1993) presented a linearity test against the neural network model using the Taylor series expansion idea; for a different approach, see Lee, White and Granger (1993).

In some forecasting experiments, STAR models have been fitted to data without first testing linearity, and assuming the structure of the model known in advance. As already discussed, this should lead to forecasts that are inferior to forecasts obtained from models that have been specified using data. The reason is that if the data-generating process is linear, the parameters of the STR or STAR model are not estimated consistently. This in turn must have a negative effect on forecasts, compared to models obtained by a specification strategy in which linearity is tested before attempting to build an STR or STAR model.

3.3. Building switching regression models

The switching regression model shares with the STR model the property that it nests a linear regression model and is not identified when the nested model generates the observations. This suggests that a first step in specifying the switching regression model or the threshold autoregressive model should be testing linearity. In other words, one would begin by choosing between one and two regimes in (6). When this is done, it is usually assumed that the error variances in different regimes are the same: $\sigma_j^2 \equiv \sigma^2$, $j = 1, \ldots, r$.

More generally, the specification stage consists of selecting both the switching variable s_t and determining the number of regimes. There are several ways of determining the number of regimes. Hansen (1999) suggested a sequential testing approach to the problem. He discussed the SETAR model, but his considerations apply to the multivariate model as well. Hansen (1999) suggested a likelihood ratio test for this situation and showed how inference can be conducted using an empirical null distribution of the test statistic generated by the bootstrap. Applied sequentially and starting from a linear model, Hansen's empirical-distribution based likelihood ratio test can in principle be used for selecting the number of regimes in a SETAR model.

The test has excellent size and power properties as a linearity test, but it does not always work as well as a sequential test in the SETAR case. Suppose that the true model has three regimes, and Hansen's test is used for testing two regimes against three. Then it may happen that the estimated model with two regimes generates explosive realizations, although the data-generating process with three regimes is stationary. This causes problems in bootstrapping the test statistic under the null hypothesis. If the model is a static switching regression model, this problem does not occur.

Gonzalo and Pitarakis (2002) designed a technique based on model selection criteria. The number of regimes is chosen sequentially. Expanding the model by adding another regime is discontinued when the value of the model selection criterion, such as BIC, does not decrease any more. A drawback of this technique is that the significance level of each individual comparison (j regimes vs. $j+1$) is a function of the size of the model and cannot be controlled by the model builder. This is due to the fact that the size of the penalty in the model selection criterion is a function of the number of parameters in the two models under comparison.

Recently, Strikholm and Teräsvirta (2005) suggested approximating the threshold autoregressive model by a multiple STAR model with a large fixed value for the slope parameter γ. The idea is then to first apply the linearity test and then the test of no remaining nonlinearity sequentially to find the number of regimes. This gives the modeller an approximate control over the significance level, and the technique appears to work reasonably well in simulations. Selecting the switching variable s_t can be incorporated into every one of these three approaches; see, for example, Hansen (1999).

Estimation of parameters is carried out by forming a grid of values for the threshold parameter, estimating the remaining parameters conditionally on this value for each value in the grid and minimizing the sum of squared errors.

The likelihood ratio test of Hansen (1999) can be regarded as a misspecification test of the estimated model. The estimated model can also be tested following the suggestion by Eitrheim and Teräsvirta (1996) that is related to the ideas in Strikholm and Teräsvirta (2005). One can re-estimate the threshold autoregressive model as a STAR model with a large fixed γ and apply misspecification tests developed for the STAR model. Naturally, in this case there is no asymptotic distribution theory for these tests but they may nevertheless serve as useful indicators of misspecification. Tong (1990, Section 5.6) discusses ways of checking the adequacy of estimated nonlinear models that also apply to SETAR models.

3.4. Building Markov-switching regression models

The MS regression model has a structure similar to the previous models in the sense that it nests a linear model, and the model is not identified under linearity. In that case the transition probabilities are unidentified nuisance parameters. The first stage of building MS regression models should therefore be testing linearity. Nevertheless, this is very rarely the case in practice. An obvious reason is that testing linearity against the MS-AR alternative is computationally demanding. Applying the general theory of Hansen (1996) to this testing problem would require more computations than it does when the alternative is a threshold autoregressive model. Garcia (1998) offers an alternative that is computationally less demanding but does not appear to be in common use. Most practitioners fix the number of regimes in advance, and the most common choice appears to be two regimes. For an exception to this practice, see Li and Xu (2002).

Estimation of Markov-switching models is more complicated than estimation of models described in previous sections. This is because the model contains two unobservable processes: the Markov chain indicating the regime and the error process ε_t. Hamilton (1993) and Hamilton (1994, Chapter 22), among others, discussed maximum likelihood estimation of parameters in this framework.

Misspecification tests exist for the evaluation of Markov-switching models. The tests proposed in Hamilton (1996) are Lagrange multiplier tests. If the model is a regression model, a test may be constructed for testing whether there is autocorrelation or ARCH effects in the process or whether a higher-order Markov chain would be necessary to adequately characterize the dynamic behaviour of the switching process.

Breunig, Najarian and Pagan (2003) consider other types of tests and give examples of their use. These include consistency tests for finding out whether assumptions made in constructing the Markov-switching model are compatible with the data. Furthermore, they discuss encompassing tests that are used to check whether a parameter of some auxiliary model can be encompassed by the estimated Markov-switching model. The authors also emphasize the use of informal graphical methods in checking the validity of the specification. These methods can be applied to other nonlinear models as well.

4. Forecasting with nonlinear models

4.1. Analytical point forecasts

For some nonlinear models, forecasts for more than one period ahead can be obtained analytically. This is true for many nonlinear moving average models that are linear in parameters. As an example, consider the asymmetric moving average model (16), assume that it is invertible, and set $q = 2$ for simplicity. The optimal point forecast one period ahead equals

$$y_{t+1|t} = \mathsf{E}\{y_{t+1}|\mathcal{F}_t\} = \mu + \theta_1\varepsilon_t + \theta_2\varepsilon_{t-1} + \psi_1 I(\varepsilon_t > 0)\varepsilon_t + \psi_2 I(\varepsilon_{t-1} > 0)\varepsilon_{t-1}$$

and two periods ahead

$$y_{t+2|t} = \mathsf{E}\{y_{t+2}|\mathcal{F}_t\} = \mu + \theta_2\varepsilon_t + \psi_1 \mathsf{E}I(\varepsilon_{t+1} > 0)\varepsilon_{t+1} + \psi_2 I(\varepsilon_t > 0)\varepsilon_t.$$

For example, if $\varepsilon_t \sim \text{nid}(0, \sigma^2)$, then $\mathsf{E}I(\varepsilon_t > 0)\varepsilon_t = (\sigma^2/2)\sqrt{\pi/2}$. For more than two periods ahead, the forecast is simply the unconditional mean of y_t:

$$\mathsf{E}y_t = \mu + (\psi_1 + \psi_2)\mathsf{E}I(\varepsilon_t > 0)\varepsilon_t$$

exactly as in the case of a linear MA(2) model.

Another nonlinear model from which forecasts can be obtained using analytical expressions is the Markov-switching model. Consider model (8) and suppose that the exogenous variables are generated by the following linear model:

$$\mathbf{x}_{t+1} = \mathbf{A}\mathbf{x}_t + \boldsymbol{\eta}_{t+1}. \tag{26}$$

The conditional expectation of y_{t+1}, given the information up until t from (8), has the form

$$\begin{aligned}\mathsf{E}\{y_{t+1}|\mathbf{x}_t, \mathbf{w}_t\} &= \mathsf{E}\left[\sum_{j=1}^{r}\{y_{t+1}|\mathbf{x}_t, \mathbf{w}_t, s_{t+1} = j\}\right]\Pr\{s_{t+1} = j|\mathbf{x}_t, \mathbf{w}_t\} \\ &= \sum_{j=1}^{r} p_{j,t+1}\left(\boldsymbol{\alpha}'_{1j}\mathbf{A}\mathbf{x}_t + \boldsymbol{\alpha}'_{2j}\mathbf{w}_t\right)\end{aligned}$$

where $p_{j,t+1} = \Pr\{s_{t+1} = j|\mathbf{x}_t, \mathbf{w}_t\}$, is the conditional probability of the process being in state j at time $t+1$ given the past observable information. Then the forecast of y_{t+1} given $\mathbf{x}_t$ and $\mathbf{w}_t$ and involving the forecasts of $p_{j,t+1}$ becomes

$$y_{t+1|t} = \sum_{j=1}^{r} p_{j,t+1|t}\left(\boldsymbol{\alpha}'_{1j}\mathbf{A}\mathbf{x}_t + \boldsymbol{\alpha}'_{2j}\mathbf{w}_t\right). \tag{27}$$

In (27), $p_{j,t+1|t} = \Pr\{s_{t+1} = j|\mathbf{x}_t, \mathbf{w}_t\}$ is a forecast of $p_{j,t+1}$ from $\mathbf{p}'_{t+1|t} = \mathbf{p}'_t\mathbf{P}$ where $\mathbf{p}_t = (p_{1,t}, \ldots, p_{r,t})'$ with $p_{j,t} = \Pr\{s_t = j|\mathbf{x}_t, \mathbf{w}_t\}$, $j = 1, \ldots, r$, and $\mathbf{P} = [p_{ij}]$ is the matrix of transition probabilities defined in (9).

Generally, the forecast for $h \geqslant 2$ steps ahead has the following form:

$$y_{t+h|t} = \sum_{j=1}^{r} p_{j,t+h|t}\left(\boldsymbol{\alpha}'_{1j}\mathbf{A}^h\mathbf{x}_t + \boldsymbol{\alpha}'_{2j}\mathbf{w}^*_{t+h-1}\right)$$

where the forecasts $p_{j,t+h|t}$ of the regime probabilities are obtained from the relationship $\mathbf{p}'_{t+h|t} = \mathbf{p}'_t\mathbf{P}^h$ with $\mathbf{p}_{t+h|t} = (p_{1,t+h|t}, \ldots, p_{r,t+h|t})'$ and $\mathbf{w}^*_{t+h-1} = (y_{t+h-1|t}, \ldots, y_{t+1|t}, y_t, \ldots, y_{t-p+h-1})'$, $h \geqslant 2$.

As a simple example, consider the first-order autoregressive MS or SCAR model with two regimes

$$y_t = \sum_{j=1}^{2}(\phi_{0j} + \phi_{1j}y_{t-1})I(s_t = j) + \varepsilon_t \tag{28}$$

where $\varepsilon_t \sim \text{nid}(0, \sigma^2)$. From (28) it follows that the one-step-ahead forecast equals

$$y_{t+1|t} = \mathsf{E}\{y_{t+1}|y_t\} = \mathbf{p}_t'\mathbf{P}\boldsymbol{\phi}_0 + \mathbf{p}_t'\mathbf{P}\boldsymbol{\phi}_1 y_t$$

where $\boldsymbol{\phi}_j = (\phi_{j1}, \phi_{j2})'$, $j = 0, 1$. For two steps ahead, one obtains

$$\begin{aligned} y_{t+2|t} &= \mathbf{p}_t'\mathbf{P}^2\boldsymbol{\phi}_0 + \mathbf{p}_t'\mathbf{P}^2\boldsymbol{\phi}_1 y_{t+1|t} \\ &= \mathbf{p}_t'\mathbf{P}^2\boldsymbol{\phi}_0 + (\mathbf{p}_t'\mathbf{P}^2\boldsymbol{\phi}_1)(\mathbf{p}_t'\mathbf{P}\boldsymbol{\phi}_0) + (\mathbf{p}_t'\mathbf{P}^2\boldsymbol{\phi}_1)(\mathbf{p}_t'\mathbf{P}\boldsymbol{\phi}_1)y_t. \end{aligned}$$

Generally, the h-step ahead forecast, $h \geqslant 2$, has the form

$$y_{t+h|t} = \mathbf{p}_t'\mathbf{P}^h\boldsymbol{\phi}_0 + \sum_{i=0}^{h-2}\left(\prod_{j=0}^{i}\mathbf{p}_t'\mathbf{P}^{h-j}\boldsymbol{\phi}_1\right)\mathbf{p}_t'\mathbf{P}^{h-i-1}\boldsymbol{\phi}_0 + \left(\prod_{j=1}^{h}\mathbf{p}_t'\mathbf{P}^j\boldsymbol{\phi}_1\right)y_t.$$

Thus all forecasts can be obtained analytically by a sequence of linear operations. This is a direct consequence of the fact that the regimes in (8) are linear in parameters. If they were not, the situation would be different. This would also be the case if the exogenous variables were generated by a nonlinear process instead of the linear model (26). Forecasting in such situations will be considered next.

4.2. Numerical techniques in forecasting

Forecasting for more than one period ahead with nonlinear models such as the STR or SR model requires numerical techniques. Granger and Teräsvirta (1993, Chapter 9), Lundbergh and Teräsvirta (2002), Franses and van Dijk (2000) and Fan and Yao (2003), among others, discuss ways of obtaining such forecasts. In the following discussion, it is assumed that the nonlinear model is correctly specified. In practice, this is not the case. Recursive forecasting that will be considered here may therefore lead to rather inaccurate forecasts if the model is badly misspecified. Evaluation of estimated models by misspecification tests and other means before forecasting with them is therefore important.

Consider the following simple nonlinear model

$$y_t = g(\mathbf{x}_{t-1}; \boldsymbol{\theta}) + \varepsilon_t \tag{29}$$

where $\varepsilon_t \sim \text{iid}(0, \sigma^2)$ and $\mathbf{x}_t$ is a $(k \times 1)$ vector of exogenous variables. Forecasting one period ahead does not pose any problem, for the forecast

$$y_{t+1|t} = \mathsf{E}(y_{t+1}|\mathbf{x}_t) = g(\mathbf{x}_t; \boldsymbol{\theta}).$$

We bypass an extra complication by assuming that $\boldsymbol{\theta}$ is known, which means that the uncertainty from the estimation of parameters is ignored. Forecasting two steps ahead is already a more complicated affair because we have to work out $\mathsf{E}(y_{t+2}|\mathbf{x}_t)$. Suppose we can forecast $\mathbf{x}_{t+1}$ from the linear first-order vector autoregressive model

$$\mathbf{x}_{t+1} = \mathbf{A}\mathbf{x}_t + \boldsymbol{\eta}_{t+1} \tag{30}$$

where $\boldsymbol{\eta}_t = (\eta_{1t}, \ldots, \eta_{kt})' \sim \text{iid}(\mathbf{0}, \boldsymbol{\Sigma}_\eta)$. The one-step-ahead forecast of $\mathbf{x}_{t+1}$ is $\mathbf{x}_{t+1|t} = \mathbf{A}\mathbf{x}_t$. This yields

$$\begin{aligned} y_{t+2|t} &= \mathsf{E}(y_{t+2}|\mathbf{x}_t) = \mathsf{E}g(\mathbf{A}\mathbf{x}_t + \boldsymbol{\eta}_{t+1}; \boldsymbol{\theta}) \\ &= \int_{\eta_1} \cdots \int_{\eta_k} g(\mathbf{A}\mathbf{x}_t + \boldsymbol{\eta}_{t+1}; \boldsymbol{\theta})\, \mathrm{d}F(\eta_1, \ldots, \eta_k) \end{aligned} \tag{31}$$

which is a k-fold integral and where $F(\eta_1, \ldots, \eta_k)$ is the joint cumulative distribution function of $\boldsymbol{\eta}_t$. Even in the simple case where $\mathbf{x}_t = (y_t, \ldots, y_{t-p+1})'$ one has to integrate out the error term ε_t from the expected value $\mathsf{E}(y_{t+2}|\mathbf{x}_t)$. It is possible, however, to ignore the error term and just use

$$y^S_{t+2|t} = g(\mathbf{x}_{t+1|t}; \boldsymbol{\theta})$$

which Tong (1990) calls the 'skeleton' forecast. This method, while easy to apply, yields, however, a biased forecast for y_{t+2}. It may lead to substantial losses of efficiency; see Lin and Granger (1994) for simulation evidence of this.

On the other hand, numerical integration of (31) is tedious. Granger and Teräsvirta (1993) call this method of obtaining the forecast the exact method, as opposed to two numerical techniques that can be used to approximate the integral in (31). One of them is based on simulation, the other one on bootstrapping the residuals $\{\widehat{\boldsymbol{\eta}}_t\}$ of the estimated equation (30) or the residuals $\{\widehat{\varepsilon}_t\}$ of the estimated model (29) in the univariate case. In the latter case the parameter estimates thus do have a role to play, but the additional uncertainty of the forecasts arising from the estimation of the model is not accounted for.

The simulation approach requires that a distributional assumption is made about the errors $\boldsymbol{\eta}_t$. One draws a sample of N independent error vectors $\{\boldsymbol{\eta}^{(1)}_{t+1}, \ldots, \boldsymbol{\eta}^{(N)}_{t+1}\}$ from this distribution and computes the Monte Carlo forecast

$$y^{MC}_{t+2|t} = (1/N) \sum_{i=1}^{N} g\bigl(\mathbf{x}_{t+1|t} + \boldsymbol{\eta}^{(i)}_{t+1}; \boldsymbol{\theta}\bigr). \tag{32}$$

The bootstrap forecast is similar to (32) and has the form

$$y^{B}_{t+2|t} = (1/N_B) \sum_{i=1}^{N_B} g\bigl(\mathbf{x}_{t+1|t} + \widehat{\boldsymbol{\eta}}^{(i)}_{t+1}; \boldsymbol{\theta}\bigr) \tag{33}$$

where the errors $\{\widehat{\boldsymbol{\eta}}^{(1)}_{t+1}, \ldots, \widehat{\boldsymbol{\eta}}^{(N_B)}_{t+1}\}$ have been obtained by drawing them from the set of estimated residuals of model (30) with replacement. The difference between (32) and (33) is that the former is based on an assumption about the distribution of $\boldsymbol{\eta}_{t+1}$, whereas the latter does not make use of a distributional assumption. It requires, however, that the error vectors are assumed independent.

This generalizes to longer forecast horizons: For example,

$$y_{t+3|t} = \mathsf{E}(y_{t+3}|\mathbf{x}_t) = \mathsf{E}\bigl\{g(\mathbf{x}_{t+2}; \boldsymbol{\theta})|\mathbf{x}_t\bigr\}$$

$$= \mathsf{E}\{g(\mathbf{A}\mathbf{x}_{t+1} + \boldsymbol{\eta}_{t+2}; \boldsymbol{\theta})|\mathbf{x}_t\} = \mathsf{E}g(\mathbf{A}^2\mathbf{x}_t + \mathbf{A}\boldsymbol{\eta}_{t+1} + \boldsymbol{\eta}_{t+2}; \boldsymbol{\theta})$$
$$= \int_{\eta_1^{(2)}} \cdots \int_{\eta_k^{(2)}} \int_{\eta_1^{(1)}} \cdots \int_{\eta_k^{(1)}} g(\mathbf{A}^2\mathbf{x}_t + \mathbf{A}\boldsymbol{\eta}_{t+1} + \boldsymbol{\eta}_{t+2}; \boldsymbol{\theta})$$
$$\times \, \mathrm{d}F(\eta_1^{(1)}, \ldots, \eta_k^{(1)}, \eta_1^{(2)}, \ldots, \eta_k^{(2)})$$

which is a $2k$-fold integral. Calculation of this expectation by numerical integration may be a huge task, but simulation and bootstrap approaches are applicable. In the general case where one forecasts h steps ahead and wants to obtain the forecasts by simulation, one generates the random variables $\boldsymbol{\eta}_{t+1}^{(i)}, \ldots, \boldsymbol{\eta}_{t+h}^{(i)}$, $i = 1, \ldots, N$, and sequentially computes N forecasts for $y_{t+1|t}, \ldots, y_{t+h|t}$, $h \geqslant 2$. These are combined to a single point forecast for each of the time-points by simple averaging as in (32). Bootstrap-based forecasts can be computed in an analogous fashion.

If the model is univariate, the principles do not change. Consider, for simplicity, the following stable first-order autoregressive model:

$$y_t = g(y_{t-1}; \boldsymbol{\theta}) + \varepsilon_t \tag{34}$$

where $\{\varepsilon_t\}$ is a sequence of independent, identically distributed errors such that $\mathsf{E}\varepsilon_t = 0$ and $\mathsf{E}\varepsilon_t^2 = \sigma^2$. In that case,

$$y_{t+2|t} = \mathsf{E}[g(y_{t+1}; \boldsymbol{\theta}) + \varepsilon_{t+2}|y_t] = \mathsf{E}g(g(y_t; \boldsymbol{\theta}) + \varepsilon_{t+1}; \boldsymbol{\theta})$$
$$= \int_{\varepsilon} g(g(y_t; \boldsymbol{\theta}) + \varepsilon; \boldsymbol{\theta})\, \mathrm{d}F(\varepsilon). \tag{35}$$

The only important difference between (31) and (35) is that in the latter case, the error term that has to be integrated out is the error term of the autoregressive model (34). In the former case, the corresponding error term is the error term of the vector process (30), and the error term of (29) need not be simulated. For an example of a univariate case, see Lundbergh and Teräsvirta (2002).

It should be mentioned that there is an old strand of literature on forecasting from nonlinear static simultaneous-equation models in which the techniques just presented are discussed and applied. The structural equations of the model have the form

$$\mathbf{f}(\mathbf{y}_t, \mathbf{x}_t, \boldsymbol{\theta}) = \boldsymbol{\varepsilon}_t \tag{36}$$

where $\mathbf{f}$ is an $n \times 1$ vector of functions of the n endogenous variables $\mathbf{y}_t$, $\mathbf{x}_t$ is a vector of exogenous variables, $\{\boldsymbol{\varepsilon}_t\}$ a sequence of independent error vectors, and $\boldsymbol{\theta}$ the vector of parameters. It is assumed that (36) implicitly defines a unique inverse relationship

$$\mathbf{y}_t = \mathbf{g}(\boldsymbol{\varepsilon}_t, \mathbf{x}_t, \boldsymbol{\theta}).$$

There may not exist a closed form for $\mathbf{g}$ or the conditional mean and covariance matrix of $\mathbf{y}_t$. Given $\mathbf{x}_t = \mathbf{x}^0$, the task is to forecast $\mathbf{y}_t$. Different assumptions on $\boldsymbol{\varepsilon}_t$ lead to skeleton or "deterministic" forecasts, exact or "closed form" forecasts, or Monte Carlo forecasts; see Brown and Mariano (1984). The order of bias in these forecasts has been a topic of discussion, and Brown and Mariano showed that the order of bias in skeleton forecasts is O(1).

4.3. Forecasting using recursion formulas

It is also possible to compute forecasts numerically applying the Chapman–Kolmogorov equation that can be used for obtaining forecasts recursively by numerical integration. Consider the following stationary first-order nonlinear autoregressive model:

$$y_t = k(y_{t-1}; \boldsymbol{\theta}) + \varepsilon_t$$

where $\{\varepsilon_t\}$ is a sequence of iid$(0, \sigma^2)$ variables and that the conditional densities of the y_t are well-defined. Then a special case of the Chapman–Kolmogorov equation has the form [see, for example, Tong (1990, p. 346) or Franses and van Dijk (2000, pp. 119–120)]

$$f(y_{t+h}|y_t) = \int_{-\infty}^{\infty} f(y_{t+h}|y_{t+1}) f(y_{t+1}|y_t)\,\mathrm{d}y_{t+1}. \tag{37}$$

From (37) it follows that

$$y_{t+h|t} = \mathsf{E}\{y_{t+h}|y_t\} = \int_{-\infty}^{\infty} \mathsf{E}\{y_{t+h}|y_{t+1}\} f(y_{t+1}|y_t)\,\mathrm{d}y_{t+1} \tag{38}$$

which shows how $\mathsf{E}\{y_{t+h}|y_t\}$ may be obtained recursively. Consider the case $h = 2$. It should be noted that in (38), $f(y_{t+1}|y_t) = g(y_{t+1} - k(y_t; \boldsymbol{\theta})) = g(\varepsilon_{t+1})$. In order to calculate $f(y_{t+h}|y_t)$, one has to make an appropriate assumption about the error distribution $g(\varepsilon_{t+1})$. Since $\mathsf{E}\{y_{t+2}|y_{t+1}\} = k(y_{t+1}; \boldsymbol{\theta})$, the forecast

$$y_{t+2|t} = \mathsf{E}\{y_{t+2}|y_t\} = \int_{-\infty}^{\infty} k(y_{t+1}; \boldsymbol{\theta}) g\big(y_{t+1} - k(y_t; \boldsymbol{\theta})\big)\,\mathrm{d}y_{t+1} \tag{39}$$

is obtained from (39) by numerical integration. For $h > 2$, one has to make use of both (38) and (39). First, write

$$\mathsf{E}\{y_{t+3}|y_t\} = \int_{-\infty}^{\infty} k(y_{t+2}; \boldsymbol{\theta}) f(y_{t+2}|y_t)\,\mathrm{d}y_{t+2} \tag{40}$$

then obtain $f(y_{t+2}|y_t)$ from (37) where $h = 2$ and

$$f(y_{t+2}|y_{t+1}) = g\big(y_{t+2} - k(y_{t+1}; \boldsymbol{\theta})\big).$$

Finally, the forecast is obtained from (40) by numerical integration.

It is seen that this method is computationally demanding for large values of h. Simplifications to alleviate the computational burden exist, see De Gooijer and De Bruin (1998). The latter authors consider forecasting with SETAR models with the normal forecasting error (NFE) method. As an example, take the first-order SETAR model

$$\begin{aligned} y_t = {} & (\alpha_{01} + \alpha_{11} y_{t-1} + \varepsilon_{1t}) I(y_{t-1} < c) \\ & + (\alpha_{02} + \alpha_{12} y_{t-1} + \varepsilon_{2t}) I(y_{t-1} \geqslant c) \end{aligned} \tag{41}$$

where $\{\varepsilon_{jt}\} \sim \text{nid}(0, \sigma_j^2)$, $j = 1, 2$. For the SETAR model (41), the one-step-ahead minimum mean-square error forecast has the form

$$y_{t+1|t} = \mathsf{E}\{y_{t+1}|y_t < c\}I(y_t < c) + \mathsf{E}\{y_{t+1}|y_t \geqslant c\}I(y_t \geqslant c)$$

where $\mathsf{E}\{y_{t+1}|y_t < c\} = \alpha_{01} + \alpha_{11}y_t$ and $\mathsf{E}\{y_{t+1}|y_t \geqslant c\} = \alpha_{02} + \alpha_{12}y_t$. The corresponding forecast variance

$$\sigma_{t+1|t}^2 = \sigma_1^2 I(y_t < c) + \sigma_2^2 I(y_t \geqslant c).$$

From (41) it follows that the distribution of y_{t+1} given y_t is normal with mean $y_{t+1|t}$ and variance $\sigma_{t+1|t}^2$. Accordingly for $h \geqslant 2$, the conditional distribution of y_{t+h} given y_{t+h-1} is normal with mean $\alpha_{01} + \alpha_{11}y_{t+h-1}$ and variance σ_1^2 for $y_{t+h-1} < c$, and mean $\alpha_{02} + \alpha_{12}y_{t+h-1}$ and variance σ_2^2 for $y_{t+h-1} \geqslant c$. Let $z_{t+h-1|t} = (c - y_{t+h-1|t})/\sigma_{t+h-1|t}$ where $\sigma_{t+h-1|t}^2$ is the variance predicted for time $t+h-1$. De Gooijer and De Bruin (1998) show that the h-steps ahead forecast can be approximated by the following recursive formula:

$$\begin{aligned} y_{t+h|t} &= (\alpha_{01} + \alpha_{11}y_{t+h-1|t})\Phi(z_{t+h-1|t}) + (\alpha_{02} + \alpha_{12}y_{t+h-1|t})\Phi(-z_{t+h-1|t}) \\ &\quad - (\alpha_{11} - \alpha_{21})\sigma_{t+h-1|t}\phi(z_{t+h-1|t}) \end{aligned} \tag{42}$$

where $\Phi(x)$ is the cumulative distribution function of a standard normal variable x and $\phi(x)$ is the density function of x. The recursive formula for forecasting the variance is not reproduced here. The first two terms weight the regimes together: the weights are equal for $y_{t+h-1|t} = c$. The third term is a "correction term" that depends on the persistence of the regimes and the error variances. This technique can be generalized to higher-order SETAR models. De Gooijer and De Bruin (1998) report that the NFE method performs well when compared to the exact method described above, at least in the case where the error variances are relatively small. They recommend the method as being very quick and easy to apply.

It may be expected, however, that the use of the methods described in this subsection will lose in popularity when increased computational power makes the simulation-based approach both quick and cheap to use.

4.4. Accounting for estimation uncertainty

In Sections 4.1 and 4.2 it is assumed that the parameters are known. In practice, the unknown parameters are replaced by their estimates and recursive forecasts are obtained using these estimates. There are two ways of accounting for parameter uncertainty. It may be assumed that the (quasi) maximum likelihood estimator $\widehat{\boldsymbol{\theta}}$ of the parameter vector $\boldsymbol{\theta}$ has an asymptotic normal distribution, that is,

$$\sqrt{T}(\widehat{\boldsymbol{\theta}} - \boldsymbol{\theta}) \xrightarrow{D} \mathsf{N}(\mathbf{0}, \boldsymbol{\Sigma}).$$

One then draws a new estimate from the $\mathsf{N}(\widehat{\boldsymbol{\theta}}, T^{-1}\widehat{\boldsymbol{\Sigma}})$ distribution and repeats the forecasting exercise with them. For recursive forecasting in Section 4.2 this means repeating the calculations in (32) M times. Confidence intervals for forecasts can then be calculated from the MN individual forecasts. Another possibility is to re-estimate the parameters using data generated from the original estimated model by bootstrapping the residuals, call the estimated model $\mathcal{M}_B$. The residuals of $\mathcal{M}_B$ are then used to recalculate (33), and this procedure is repeated M times. This is a computationally intensive procedure and, besides, because the estimated models have to be evaluated (for example, explosive ones have to be discarded, so they do not distort the results), the total effort is substantial. When the forecasts are obtained analytically as in Section 4.1, the computational burden is less heavy because the replications to generate (32) or (33) are avoided.

4.5. Interval and density forecasts

Interval and density forecasts are obtained as a by-product of computing forecasts numerically. The replications form an empirical distribution that can be appropriately smoothed to give a smooth forecast density. For surveys, see Corradi and Swanson (2006) and Tay and Wallis (2002). As already mentioned, forecast densities obtained from nonlinear economic models may be asymmetric, which policy makers may find interesting. For example, if a density forecast of inflation is asymmetric suggesting that the error of the point forecast is more likely to be positive than negative, this may cause a policy response different from the opposite situation where the error is more likely to be negative than positive. The density may even be bi- or multimodal, although this may not be very likely in macroeconomic time series. For an example, see Lundbergh and Teräsvirta (2002), where the density forecast for the Australian unemployment rate four quarters ahead from an estimated STAR model, reported in Skalin and Teräsvirta (2002), shows some bimodality.

Density forecasts may be conveniently presented using fan charts; see Wallis (1999) and Lundbergh and Teräsvirta (2002) for examples. There are two ways of constructing fan charts. One, applied in Wallis (1999), is to base them on interquantile ranges. The other is to use highest density regions, see Hyndman (1996). The choice between these two depends on the forecaster's loss function. Note, however, that bi- or multimodal density forecasts are only visible in fan charts based on highest density regions.

Typically, the interval and density forecasts do not account for the estimation uncertainty, but see Corradi and Swanson (2006). Extending the considerations to do that when forecasting with nonlinear models would often be computationally very demanding. The reason is that estimating parameters of nonlinear models requires care (starting-values, convergence, etc.), and therefore simulations or bootstrapping involved could in many cases demand a large amount of both computational and human resources.

4.6. Combining forecasts

Forecast combination is a relevant topic in linear as well as in nonlinear forecasting. Combining nonlinear forecasts with forecasts from a linear model may sometimes lead to series of forecasts that are more robust (contain fewer extreme predictions) than forecasts from the nonlinear model. Following Granger and Bates (1969), the composite point forecast from models M_1 and M_2 is given by

$$\widehat{y}_{t+h|t}^{(1,2)} = (1-\lambda_t)\widehat{y}_{t+h|t}^{(1)} + \lambda_t \widehat{y}_{t+h|t}^{(2)} \tag{43}$$

where λ_t, $0 \leqslant \lambda_t \leqslant 1$, is the weight of the h-periods-ahead forecast $\widehat{y}_{t+h|t}^{(j)}$ of y_{t+h}. Suppose that the multi-period forecasts from these models are obtained numerically following the technique presented in Section 4.2. The same random numbers can be used to generate both forecasts, and combining the forecasts simply amounts to combining each realization from the two models. This means that each one of the N pairs of simulated forecasts from the two models is weighted into a single forecast using weights λ_t (model M_2) and $1-\lambda_t$ (model M_1). The empirical distribution of the N weighted forecasts is the combined density forecast from which one easily obtains the corresponding point forecast by averaging as discussed in Section 4.2.

Note that the weighting schemes themselves may be nonlinear functions of the past performance. This form of nonlinearity in forecasting is not discussed here, but see Deutsch, Granger and Teräsvirta (1994) for an application. The K-mean clustering approach to combining forecasts in Aiolfi and Timmermann (in press) is another example of a nonlinear weighting scheme. A detailed discussion of forecast combination and weighting schemes proposed in the literature can be found in Timmermann (2006).

4.7. Different models for different forecast horizons?

Multistep forecasting was discussed in Section 4.2 where it was argued that for most nonlinear models, multi-period forecasts have to be obtained numerically. While this is not nowadays computationally demanding, there may be other reasons for opting for analytically generated forecasts. They become obvious if one gives up the idea that the model assumed to generate the observations is the data-generating process. As already mentioned, if the model is misspecified, the forecasts from such a model are not likely to have any optimality properties, and another misspecified model may do a better job. The situation is illuminated by an example from Bhansali (2002). Suppose that at time T we want to forecast y_{T+2} from

$$y_t = \alpha y_{t-1} + \varepsilon_t \tag{44}$$

where $\mathsf{E}\varepsilon_t = 0$ and $\mathsf{E}\varepsilon_t\varepsilon_{t-j} = 0$, $j \neq 0$. Furthermore, y_T is assumed known. Then $y_{T+1|T} = \alpha y_T$ and $y_{T+2|T} = \alpha^2 y_T$, where $\alpha^2 y_T$ is the minimum mean square error forecast of y_{T+2} under the condition that (44) be the data-generating process. If this condition is not valid, the situation changes. It is also possible to forecast y_{T+2} directly from the model estimated by regressing y_t on y_{t-2}, the (theoretical) outcome being $y_{T+2|T}^* = \rho_2 y_T$ where $\rho_2 = \mathrm{corr}(y_t, y_{t-2})$. When model (44) is misspecified, $y_{T+2|T}^*$ obtained by the direct method may be preferred to $y_{T+2|T}$ in a linear least squares sense. The mean square errors of these two forecasts are equal if and only if $\alpha^2 = \rho_2$, that is, when the data-generating process is a linear AR(1)-process.

When this idea is applied to nonlinear models, the direct method has the advantage that no numerical generation of forecasts is necessary. The forecasts can be produced exactly as in the one-step-ahead case. A disadvantage is that a separate model has to be specified and estimated for each forecast horizon. Besides, these models are also misspecifications of the data-generating process. In their extensive studies of forecasting macroeconomic series with linear and nonlinear models, Stock and Watson (1999) and Marcellino (2002) have used this method. The interval and density forecasts obtained this way may sometimes differ from the ones generated recursively as discussed in Section 4.2. In forecasting more than one period ahead, the recursive techniques allow asymmetric forecast densities. On the other hand, if the error distribution of the 'direct forecast' model is assumed symmetric around zero, density forecasts from such a model will also be symmetric densities.

Which one of the two approaches produces more accurate point forecasts is an empirical matter. Lin and Granger (1994) study this question by simulation. Two nonlinear models, the first-order STAR and the sign model, are used to generate the data. The forecasts are generated in three ways. First, they are obtained from the estimated model assuming that the specification was known. Second, a neural network model is fitted to the generated series and the forecasts produced with it. Third, the forecasts are generated from a nonparametric model fitted to the series. The focus is on forecasting two periods ahead. On the one hand, the forecast accuracy measured by the mean square forecast error deteriorates compared to the iterative methods (32) and (33) when the forecasts two periods ahead are obtained from a 'direct' STAR or sign model, i.e., from a model in which the first lag is replaced by a second lag. On the other hand, the direct method works much better when the model used to produce the forecasts is a neural network or a nonparametric model.

A recent large-scale empirical study by Marcellino, Stock and Watson (2004) addresses the question of choosing an appropriate approach in a linear framework, using 171 monthly US macroeconomic time series and forecast horizons up to 24 months. The conclusion is that obtaining the multi-step forecasts from a single model is preferable to the use of direct models. This is true in particular for longer forecast horizons. A comparable study involving nonlinear time series models does not as yet seem to be available.

5. Forecast accuracy

5.1. *Comparing point forecasts*

A frequently-asked question in forecasting with nonlinear models has been whether they perform better than linear models. While many economic phenomena and models are nonlinear, they may be satisfactorily approximated by a linear model, and this makes the question relevant. A number of criteria, such as the root mean square forecast error (RMSFE) or mean absolute error (MAE), have been applied for the purpose.

It is also possible to test the null hypothesis that the forecasting performance of two models, measured in RMSFE or MAE or some other forecast error based criterion, is equally good against a one-sided alternative. This can be done for example by applying the Diebold–Mariano (DM) test; see Diebold and Mariano (1995) and Harvey, Leybourne and Newbold (1997). The test is not available, however, when one of the models nests the other. The reason is that when the data are generated from the smaller model, the forecasts are identical when the parameters are known. In this case the asymptotic distribution theory for the DM statistic no longer holds.

This problem is present in comparing linear and many nonlinear models, such as the STAR, SETAR or MS (SCAR) model, albeit in a different form. These models nest a linear model, but the nesting model is not identified when the smaller model has generated the observations. Thus, if the parameter uncertainty is accounted for, the asymptotic distribution of the DM statistic may depend on unknown nuisance parameters, and the standard distribution theory does not apply.

Solutions to the problem of nested models are discussed in detail in West (2006), and here the attention is merely drawn to two approaches. Recently, Corradi and Swanson (2002, 2004) have considered what they call a generic test of predictive accuracy. The forecasting performance of two models, a linear model (M_0) nested in a nonlinear model and the nonlinear model (M_1), is under test. Following Corradi and Swanson (2004), define the models as follows:

$$\mathsf{M}_0\colon \quad y_t = \phi_0 + \phi_1 y_{t-1} + \varepsilon_{0t}$$

where $(\phi_0, \phi_1)' = \arg\min_{(\phi_0,\phi_1)\in\boldsymbol{\Phi}} \mathsf{E}g(y_t - \phi_0 - \phi_1 y_{t-1})$. The alternative has the form

$$\mathsf{M}_1\colon \quad y_t = \phi_0(\boldsymbol{\gamma}) + \phi_1(\boldsymbol{\gamma}) y_{t-1} + \phi_2(\boldsymbol{\gamma}) G(\mathbf{w}_t; \boldsymbol{\gamma}) + \varepsilon_{1t} \tag{45}$$

where, setting $\boldsymbol{\phi}(\boldsymbol{\gamma}) = (\phi_0(\boldsymbol{\gamma}), \phi_1(\boldsymbol{\gamma}), \phi_2(\boldsymbol{\gamma}))'$,

$$\boldsymbol{\phi}(\boldsymbol{\gamma}) = \operatorname*{arg\,min}_{\boldsymbol{\phi}(\boldsymbol{\gamma})\in\boldsymbol{\Phi}(\boldsymbol{\gamma})} \mathsf{E}g\big(y_t - \phi_0(\boldsymbol{\gamma}) - \phi_1(\boldsymbol{\gamma}) y_{t-1} - \phi_2(\boldsymbol{\gamma}) G(\mathbf{w}_t; \boldsymbol{\gamma})\big).$$

Furthermore, $\boldsymbol{\gamma} \in \Gamma$ is a $d \times 1$ vector of nuisance parameters and Γ a compact subset of $\mathcal{R}^d$. The loss function is the same as the one used in the forecast comparison: for example the mean square error. The logistic function (4) may serve as an example of the nonlinear function $G(\mathbf{w}_t; \boldsymbol{\gamma})$ in (45).

The null hypothesis equals $\mathrm{H}_0\colon \mathsf{E}g(\varepsilon_{0,t+1}) = \mathsf{E}g(\varepsilon_{1,t+1})$, and the alternative is $\mathrm{H}_1\colon \mathsf{E}g(\varepsilon_{0,t+1}) > \mathsf{E}g(\varepsilon_{1,t+1})$. The null hypothesis corresponds to equal forecasting accuracy, which is achieved if $\phi_2(\boldsymbol{\gamma}) = 0$ for all $\boldsymbol{\gamma} \in \Gamma$. This allows restating the hypotheses as follows:

$$\begin{aligned} &H_0\colon \quad \phi_2(\boldsymbol{\gamma}) = 0 \quad \text{for all } \boldsymbol{\gamma} \in \Gamma, \\ &H_1\colon \quad \phi_2(\boldsymbol{\gamma}) \neq 0 \quad \text{for at least one } \boldsymbol{\gamma} \in \Gamma. \end{aligned} \tag{46}$$

Under this null hypothesis,

$$\mathsf{E}g'(\varepsilon_{0,t+1}) G(\mathbf{w}_t; \boldsymbol{\gamma}) = 0 \quad \text{for all } \boldsymbol{\gamma} \in \Gamma \tag{47}$$

where

$$g'(\varepsilon_{0,t}) = \frac{\partial g}{\partial \varepsilon_{0,t}} \frac{\partial \varepsilon_{0,t}}{\partial \boldsymbol{\phi}} = -\frac{\partial g}{\partial \varepsilon_{0,t}} \big(1, y_{t-1}, G(\mathbf{w}_{t-1}; \boldsymbol{\gamma})\big)'.$$

For example, if $g(\varepsilon) = \varepsilon^2$, then $\partial g/\partial \varepsilon = 2\varepsilon$. The values of $G(\mathbf{w}_t; \boldsymbol{\gamma})$ are obtained using a sufficiently fine grid. Now, Equation (47) suggests a conditional moment test of type Bierens (1990) for testing (46). Let

$$\widehat{\boldsymbol{\phi}}_T = (\widehat{\phi}_0, \widehat{\phi}_1)' = \arg\min_{\boldsymbol{\phi} \in \boldsymbol{\Phi}} T^{-1} \sum_{t=1}^{T} g(y_t - \phi_0 - \phi_1 y_{t-1})$$

and define $\widehat{\varepsilon}_{0,t+1|t} = y_{t+1} - \widehat{\boldsymbol{\phi}}_t' \mathbf{y}_t$ where $\mathbf{y}_t = (1, y_t)'$, for $t = T, T+1, \ldots, T-1$. The test statistic is

$$M_P = \int_{\Gamma} m_P(\boldsymbol{\gamma})^2 w(\boldsymbol{\gamma})\, \mathrm{d}\boldsymbol{\gamma} \tag{48}$$

where

$$m_P(\boldsymbol{\gamma}) = T^{-1/2} \sum_{t=T}^{T+P-1} g'\big(\widehat{\varepsilon}_{0,t+1|t}\big) G(\mathbf{z}_t; \boldsymbol{\gamma})$$

and the absolutely continuous weight function $w(\boldsymbol{\gamma}) \geqslant 0$ with $\int_{\Gamma} w(\boldsymbol{\gamma})\, \mathrm{d}\boldsymbol{\gamma} = 1$. The (nonstandard) asymptotic distribution theory for M_P is discussed in Corradi and Swanson (2002).

Statistic (48) does not answer the same question as the DM statistic. The latter can be used for investigating whether a given nonlinear model yields more accurate forecasts than a linear model not nested in it. The former answers a different question: "Does a given *family* of nonlinear models have a property such that one-step-ahead forecasts from models belonging to this family are more accurate than the corresponding forecasts from a linear model nested in it?"

Some forecasters who apply nonlinear models that nest a linear model begin by testing linearity against their nonlinear model. This practice is often encouraged; see, for example, Teräsvirta (1998). If one rejects the linearity hypothesis, then one should also reject (46), and an out-of-sample test would thus appear redundant. In practice it is possible, however, that (46) is not rejected although linearity is. This may be the case if the nonlinear model is misspecified, or there is a structural break or smooth parameter change in the prediction period, or this period is so short that the test is not sufficiently powerful. The role of out-of-sample tests in forecast evaluation compared to in-sample tests has been discussed in Inoue and Kilian (2004).

If one wants to consider the original question which the Diebold–Mariano test was designed to answer, a new test, recently developed by Giacomini and White (2003), is available. This is a test of conditional forecasting ability as opposed to most other tests including the Diebold–Mariano statistic that are tests of unconditional forecasting ability. The test is constructed under the assumption that the forecasts are obtained using a moving data window: the number of observations in the sample used for estimation does not increase over time. It is operational under rather mild conditions that allow heteroskedasticity. Suppose that there are two models M_1 and M_2 such that

$$\mathsf{M}_j:\quad y_t = f^{(j)}(\mathbf{w}_t;\boldsymbol{\theta}_j) + \varepsilon_{jt},\qquad j = 1, 2$$

where $\{\varepsilon_{jt}\}$ is a martingale difference sequence with respect to the information set $\mathcal{F}_{t-1}$. The null hypothesis is

$$\mathsf{E}\big[\big\{g_{t+\tau}\big(y_{t+\tau}, \widehat{f}_{mt}^{(1)}\big) - g_{t+\tau}\big(y_{t+\tau}, \widehat{f}_{mt}^{(2)}\big)\big\}|\mathcal{F}_{t-1}\big] = 0 \tag{49}$$

where $g_{t+\tau}(y_{t+\tau}, \widehat{f}_{mt}^{(j)})$ is the loss function, $\widehat{f}_{mt}^{(j)}$ is the τ-periods-ahead forecast for $y_{t+\tau}$ from model j estimated from the observations $t-m+1, \dots, t$. Assume now that there exist T observations, $t = 1, \dots, T$, and that forecasting is begun at $t = t_0 > m$. Then there will be $T_0 = T - \tau - t_0$ forecasts available for testing the null hypothesis.

Carrying out the test requires a test function $\mathbf{h}_t$ which is a $p \times 1$ vector. Under the null hypothesis, owing to the martingale difference property of the loss function difference,

$$\mathsf{E}\mathbf{h}_t \Delta g_{t+\tau} = \mathbf{0}$$

for all $\mathcal{F}$-measurable $p \times 1$ vectors $\mathbf{h}_t$. Bierens (1990) used a similar idea ($\Delta g_{t+\tau}$ replaced by a function of the error term ε_t) to construct a general model misspecification test. The choice of test function $\mathbf{h}_t$ is left to the user, and the power of the test depends on it. Assume now that $\tau = 1$. The GW test statistic has the form

$$S_{T_0,m} = T_0\left(T_0^{-1}\sum_{t=t_0}^{T_0}\mathbf{h}_t\Delta g_{t+\tau}\right)'\widehat{\boldsymbol{\Omega}}_{T_0}^{-1}\left(T_0^{-1}\sum_{t=t_0}^{T_0}\mathbf{h}_t\Delta g_{t+\tau}\right) \tag{50}$$

where $\widehat{\boldsymbol{\Omega}}_{T_0} = T_0^{-1}\sum_{t=t_0}^{T_0}(\Delta g_{t+\tau})^2\mathbf{h}_t\mathbf{h}_t'$ is a consistent estimator of the covariance matrix $\mathsf{E}(\Delta g_{t+\tau})^2\mathbf{h}_t\mathbf{h}_t'$. When $\tau > 1$, $\widehat{\boldsymbol{\Omega}}_{T_0}$ has to be modified to account for correlation in the forecast errors; see Giacomini and White (2003). Under the null hypothesis (49), the GW statistic (50) has an asymptotic χ^2-distribution with p degrees of freedom.

The GW test has not yet been applied to comparing the forecast ability of a linear model and a nonlinear model nested in it. Two things are important in applications. First, the estimation is based on a rolling window, but the size of the window may vary over time. Second, the outcome of the test depends on the choice of the test function $\mathbf{h}_t$. Elements of $\mathbf{h}_t$ not correlated with $\Delta g_{t+\tau}$ have a negative effect on the power of the test.

An important advantage with the GW test is that it can be applied to comparing methods for forecasting and not only models. The asymptotic distribution theory covers the situation where the specification of the model or models changes over time, which has sometimes been the case in practice. Swanson and White (1995, 1997a, 1997b) allow the specification to switch between a linear and a neural network model. In Teräsvirta, van Dijk and Medeiros (2005), switches between linear on the one hand and nonlinear specifications such as the AR-NN and STAR model on the other are an essential part of their forecasting exercise.

6. Lessons from a simulation study

Building nonlinear time series models is generally more difficult than constructing linear models. A main reason for building nonlinear models for forecasting must therefore be that they are expected to forecast better than linear models. It is not certain, however, that this is so. Many studies, some of which will be discussed later, indicate that in forecasting macroeconomic series, nonlinear models may not forecast better than linear ones. In this section we point out that sometimes this may be the case even when the nonlinear model is the data-generating process.

As an example, we briefly review a simulation study in Lundbergh and Teräsvirta (2002). The authors generate 10^6 observations from the following LSTAR model

$$y_t = -0.19 + 0.38\big(1 + \exp\{-10y_{t-1}\}\big)^{-1} + 0.9y_{t-1} + 0.4\varepsilon_t \tag{51}$$

where $\{\varepsilon_t\} \sim \mathrm{nid}(0,1)$. Model (51) may also be viewed as a special case of the neural network model (11) with a linear unit and a single hidden unit. The model has the property that the realization of 10^6 observations tends to fluctuate long periods around a local mean, either around -1.9 or 1.9. Occasionally, but not often, it switches from one 'regime' to the other, and the switches are relatively rapid. This is seen from Figure 1 that contains a realization of 2000 observations from (51). As a consequence of the swiftness of switches, model (51) is also nearly a special case of the SETAR model that Lanne and Saikkonen (2002) suggested for modelling strongly autocorrelated series.

The authors fit the model with the same parameters as in (51) to a large number of subseries of 1000 observations, estimate the parameters, and forecast recursively up to 20 periods ahead. The results are compared to forecasts obtained from first-order linear autoregressive models fitted to the same subseries. The measure of accuracy is the relative efficiency (RE) measure of Mincer and Zarnowitz (1969), that is, the ratio of the RMSFEs of the two forecasts. It turns out that the forecasts from the LSTAR model are more efficient than the ones from the linear model: the RE measure moves from about 0.96 (one period ahead forecasts) to about 0.85 (20 periods ahead). The forecasts are also obtained assuming that the parameters are known: in that case the RE measure lies below 0.8 (20 periods ahead), so having to estimate the parameters affects the forecast accuracy as may be expected.

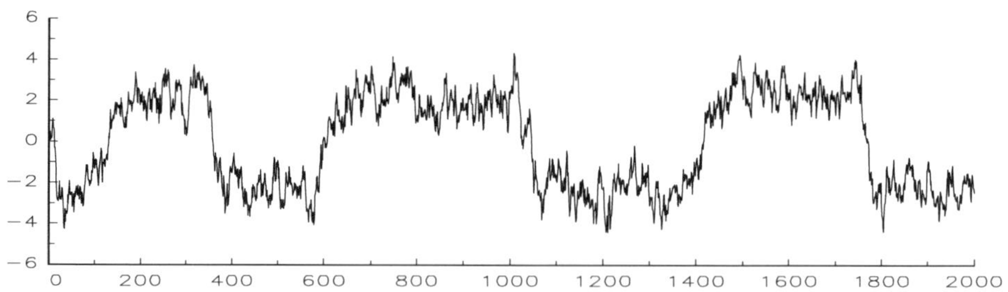

Figure 1. A realization of 2000 observations from model (51).

6. Lessons from a simulation study

Building nonlinear time series models is generally more difficult than constructing linear models. A main reason for building nonlinear models for forecasting must therefore be that they are expected to forecast better than linear models. It is not certain, however, that this is so. Many studies, some of which will be discussed later, indicate that in forecasting macroeconomic series, nonlinear models may not forecast better than linear ones. In this section we point out that sometimes this may be the case even when the nonlinear model is the data-generating process.

As an example, we briefly review a simulation study in Lundbergh and Teräsvirta (2002). The authors generate 10^6 observations from the following LSTAR model

$$y_t = -0.19 + 0.38\bigl(1 + \exp\{-10y_{t-1}\}\bigr)^{-1} + 0.9y_{t-1} + 0.4\varepsilon_t \tag{51}$$

where $\{\varepsilon_t\} \sim \text{nid}(0,1)$. Model (51) may also be viewed as a special case of the neural network model (11) with a linear unit and a single hidden unit. The model has the property that the realization of 10^6 observations tends to fluctuate long periods around a local mean, either around -1.9 or 1.9. Occasionally, but not often, it switches from one 'regime' to the other, and the switches are relatively rapid. This is seen from Figure 1 that contains a realization of 2000 observations from (51). As a consequence of the swiftness of switches, model (51) is also nearly a special case of the SETAR model that Lanne and Saikkonen (2002) suggested for modelling strongly autocorrelated series.

The authors fit the model with the same parameters as in (51) to a large number of subseries of 1000 observations, estimate the parameters, and forecast recursively up to 20 periods ahead. The results are compared to forecasts obtained from first-order linear autoregressive models fitted to the same subseries. The measure of accuracy is the relative efficiency (RE) measure of Mincer and Zarnowitz (1969), that is, the ratio of the RMSFEs of the two forecasts. It turns out that the forecasts from the LSTAR model are more efficient than the ones from the linear model: the RE measure moves from about 0.96 (one period ahead forecasts) to about 0.85 (20 periods ahead). The forecasts are also obtained assuming that the parameters are known: in that case the RE measure lies below 0.8 (20 periods ahead), so having to estimate the parameters affects the forecast accuracy as may be expected.

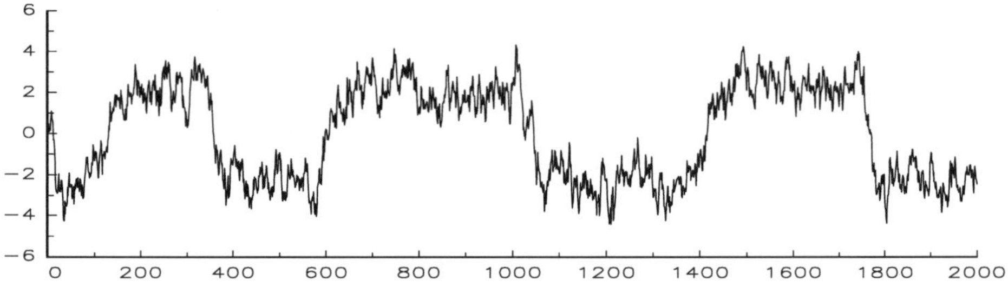

Figure 1. A realization of 2000 observations from model (51).

This is in fact not surprising, because the data-generating process is an LSTAR model. The authors were also interested in knowing how well this model forecasts when there is a large change in the value of the realization. This is defined as a change of at least equal to 0.2 in the absolute value of the transition function of (51). It is a rare occasion and occurs only in about 0.6% of the observations. The question was posed, because Montgomery et al. (1998) had shown that the nonlinear models of the US unemployment rate they considered performed better than the linear AR model when the unemployment increased rapidly but not elsewhere. Thus it was deemed interesting to study the occurrence of this phenomenon by simulation.

The results showed that the LSTAR model was better than the AR(1) model. The authors, however, also applied another benchmark, the first-order AR model for the differenced series, the ARI(1,1) model. This model was chosen as a benchmark because in the subseries of 1000 observations ending when a large change was observed, the unit root hypothesis, when tested using the augmented Dickey–Fuller test, was rarely rejected. A look at Figure 1 helps one understand why this is the case. Against the ARI(1,1) benchmark, the RE of the estimated LSTAR model was 0.95 at best, when forecasting three periods ahead, but RE exceeded unity for forecast horizons longer than 13 periods. There are at least two reasons for this outcome. First, since a large change in the series is a rare event, there is not very much evidence in the subseries of 1000 observations about the nonlinearity. Here, the difference between RE of the estimated model and the corresponding measure for the known model was greater than in the previous case, and RE of the latter model remained below unity for all forecast horizons. Second, as argued in Clements and Hendry (1999), differencing helps construct models that adapt more quickly to large shifts in the series than models built on undifferenced data. This adaptability is demonstrated in the experiment of Lundbergh and Teräsvirta (2002). A very basic example emphasizing the same thing can be found in Hendry and Clements (2003).

These results also show that a model builder who begins his task by testing the unit root hypothesis may often end up with a model that is quite different from the one obtained by someone beginning by first testing linearity. In the present case, the latter course is perfectly defendable, because the data-generating process is stationary. The prevailing paradigm, testing the unit root hypothesis first, may thus not always be appropriate when the possibility of a nonlinear data-generating process cannot be excluded. For a discussion of the relationship between unit roots and nonlinearity; see Elliott (2006).

7. Empirical forecast comparisons

7.1. Relevant issues

The purpose of many empirical economic forecast comparisons involving nonlinear models is to find out whether, for a given time series or a set of series, nonlinear models yield more accurate forecasts than linear models. In many cases, the answer appears to be negative, even when the nonlinear model in question fits the data better than the corresponding linear model. Reasons for this outcome have been discussed in the literature. One argument put forward is that nonlinear models may sometimes explain features in the data that do not occur very frequently. If these features are not present in the series during the period to be forecast, then there is no gain from using nonlinear models for generating the forecasts. This may be the case at least when the number of out-of-sample forecasts is relatively small; see for example Teräsvirta and Anderson (1992) for discussion.

Essentially the same argument is that the nonlinear model can only be expected to forecast better than a linear one in particular regimes. For example, a nonlinear model may be useful in forecasting the volume of industrial production in recessions but not expansions. Montgomery et al. (1998) forecast the quarterly US unemployment rate using a two-regime threshold autoregressive model (7) and a two-regime Markov switching autoregressive model (8). Both models, the SETAR model in particular, yield more accurate forecasts than the linear model when the forecasting origin lies in the recession. If it lies in the expansion, both models, now the MS-model in particular, perform clearly less well than the linear AR model. Considering Wolf's sunspot numbers, another nonlinear series, Tong and Moeanaddin (1988) showed that the values at the troughs of the sunspot cycle were forecast more accurately from a SETAR than from a linear model, whereas the reverse was true for the values around the peaks. An explanation to this finding may be that there is more variation over time in the height of the peaks than in the bottom value of the troughs.

Another potential reason for inferior performance of nonlinear models compared to linear ones is overfitting. A small example highlighting this possibility can be found in Granger and Teräsvirta (1991). The authors generated data from an STR model and fitted both a projection pursuit regression model [see Friedman and Stuetzle (1981)] and a linear model to the simulated series. When nonlinearity was strong (the error variance small), the projection pursuit approach led to more accurate forecasts than the linear model. When the evidence of nonlinearity was weak (the error variance large), the projection pursuit model overfitted, and the forecasts of the linear model were more accurate than the ones produced by the projection pursuit model. Careful modelling, including testing linearity before fitting a nonlinear model as discussed in Section 3, reduces the likelihood of overfitting.

From the discussion in Section 6 it is also clear that in some cases, when the time series are short, having to estimate the parameters as opposed to knowing them will erase the edge that a correctly specified nonlinear model has compared to a linear approximation. Another possibility is that even if linearity is rejected when tested, the nonlinear model fitted to the time series is misspecified to the extent that its forecasting performance does not match the performance of a linear model containing the same variables. This situation is even more likely to occur if a nonlinear model nesting a linear one is fitted to the data without first testing linearity.

Finally, Dacco and Satchell (1999) showed that in regime-switching models, the possibility of misclassifying an observation when forecasting may lead to the forecasts on the average being inferior to the one from a linear model, although a regime-switching model known to the forecaster generates the data. The criterion for forecast accuracy is the mean squared forecast error. The authors give analytic conditions for this to be the case and do it using simple Markov-switching and SETAR models as examples.

7.2. Comparing linear and nonlinear models

Comparisons of the forecasting performance of linear and nonlinear models have often included only a limited number of models and time series. To take an example, Montgomery et al. (1998) considered forecasts of the quarterly US civilian employment series from a univariate Markov-switching model of type (8) and a SETAR model. They separated expansions and contractions from each other and concluded that SETAR and Markov-switching models are useful in forecasting recessions, whereas they do not perform better than linear models during expansions. Clements and Krolzig (1998) study the forecasts from the Markov-switching autoregressive model of type (10) and a threshold autoregressive model when the series to be forecast is the quarterly US gross national product. The main conclusion of their study was that nonlinear models do not forecast better than linear ones when the criterion is the RMSFE. Similar conclusions were reached by Siliverstovs and van Dijk (2003), Boero and Marrocu (2002) and Sarantis (1999) for a variety of nonlinear models and economic time series. Bradley and Jansen (2004) obtained this outcome for a US excess stock return series, whereas there was evidence that nonlinear models, including a STAR model, yield more accurate forecasts for industrial production than the linear autoregressive model. Kilian and Taylor (2003) concluded that in forecasting nominal exchange rates, ESTAR models are superior to the random walk model, but only at long horizons, 2–3 years.

The RMSFE is a rather "academic" criterion for comparing forecasts. Granger and Pesaran (2000) emphasize the use of economic criteria that are based on the loss function of the forecaster. The loss function, in turn, is related to the decision problem at hand; for more discussion, see Granger and Machina (2006). In such comparisons, forecasts from nonlinear models may fare better than in RMSFE comparisons. Satchell and Timmermann (1995) focused on two loss functions: the MSFE and a payoff criterion based on the economic value of the forecast (forecasting the direction of change). When the MSFE increases, the probability of correctly forecasting the direction decreases if the forecast and the forecast error are independent. The authors showed that this need not be true when the forecast and the error are dependent of each other. They argued that this may often be the case for forecasts from nonlinear models.

Most forecast comparisons concern univariate or single-equation models. A recent exception is De Gooijer and Vidiella-i-Anguera (2004). The authors compared the forecasting performance of two bivariate threshold autoregressive models with cointegration with that of a linear bivariate vector error-correction model using two pairs of US macroeconomic series. For forecast comparisons, the RMSFE has to be generalized to the multivariate situation; see De Gooijer and Vidiella-i-Anguera (2004). The results indicated that the nonlinear models perform better than the linear one in an out-of-sample forecast exercise.

Some authors, including De Gooijer and Vidiella-i-Anguera (2004), have considered interval and density forecasts as well. The quality of such forecasts has typically been evaluated internally. For example, the assumed coverage probability of an interval forecast is compared to the observed coverage probability. This is a less than satisfactory approach when one wants to compare interval or density forecasts from different models. Corradi and Swanson (2006) survey tests developed for finding out which one of a set of misspecified models provides the most accurate interval or density forecasts. Since this is a very recent area of interest, there are hardly any applications yet of these tests to nonlinear models.

7.3. *Large forecast comparisons*

7.3.1. *Forecasting with a separate model for each forecast horizon*

As discussed in Section 4, there are two ways of constructing multiperiod forecasts. One may use a single model for each forecast horizon or construct a separate model for each forecast horizon. In the former alternative, generating the forecasts may be computationally demanding if the number of variables to be forecast and the number of forecast horizons is large. In the latter, specifying and estimating the models may require a large amount of work, whereas forecasting is simple. In this section the focus is on a number of large studies that involve nonlinear models and several forecast horizons and in which separate models are constructed for each forecast horizon. Perhaps the most extensive such study is the one by Stock and Watson (1999). Other examples include Marcellino (2002) and Marcellino (2004). Stock and Watson (1999) forecast 215 monthly US macroeconomic variables, whereas Marcellino (2002) and Marcellino (2004) considered macroeconomic variables of the countries of the European Union.

The study of Stock and Watson (1999) involved two types of nonlinear models: a "tightly parameterized" model which was the LSTAR model of Section 2.3 and a "loosely parameterized" one, which was the autoregressive neural network model. The authors experimented with two families of AR-NN models: one with a single hidden layer, see (11), and a more general family with two hidden layers. Various linear autoregressive models were included as well as models of exponential smoothing. Several methods of combining forecasts were included in comparisons. All told, the number of models or methods to forecast each series was 63.

The models were either completely specified in advance or the number of lags was specified using AIC or BIC. Two types of models were considered. Either the variables were in levels:

$$y_{t+h} = f_L(y_t, y_{t-1}, \ldots, y_{t-p+1}) + \varepsilon_t^L$$

where $h = 1, 6$ or 12, or they were in differences:

$$y_{t+h} - y_t = f_D(\Delta y_t, \Delta y_{t-1}, \ldots, \Delta y_{t-p+1}) + \varepsilon_t^D.$$

The experiment included several values of p. The series were forecast every month starting after a startup period of 120 observations. The last observation in all series was 1996(12), and for most series the first observation was 1959(1). The models were re-estimated and, in the case of combined forecasts, the weights of the individual models recalculated every month. The insanity filter that the authors called trimming of forecasts was applied. The purpose of the filter was to make the process better mimic the behaviour of a true forecaster.

The 215 time series covered most types of macroeconomic series from production, consumption, money and credit series to stock returns. The series that originally contained seasonality were seasonally adjusted.

The forecasting methods were ranked according to several criteria. A general conclusion was that the nonlinear models did not perform better than the linear ones. In one comparison, the 63 different models and methods were ranked on forecast performance using three different loss functions, the absolute forecast errors raised to the power one, two, or three, and the three forecast horizons. The best ANN forecast had rank around 10, whereas the best STAR model typically had rank around 20. The combined forecasts topped all rankings, and, interestingly, combined forecasts of nonlinear models only were always ranked one or two. The best linear models were better than the STAR models and, at longer horizons than one month, better than the ANN models. The no-change model was ranked among the bottom two in all rankings showing that all models had at least some relevance as forecasting tools.

A remarkable result, already evident from the previous comments, was that combining the forecasts from all nonlinear models generated forecasts that were among the most accurate in rankings. They were among the top five in 53% (models in levels) and 51% (models in differences) of all cases when forecasting one month ahead. This was by far the highest fraction of all methods compared. In forecasting six and twelve months ahead, these percentages were lower but still between 30% and 34%. At these horizons, the combinations involving all linear models had a comparable performance. All single models were left far behind. Thus a general conclusion from the study of Stock and Watson is that there is some exploitable nonlinearity in the series under consideration, but that it is too diffuse to be captured by a single nonlinear model.

Marcellino (2002) reported results on forecasting 480 variables representing the economies of the twelve countries of the European Monetary Union. The monthly time series were shorter than the series in Stock and Watson (1999), which was compensated for by a greater number of series. There were 58 models but, unlike Stock and Watson, Marcellino did not consider combining forecasts from them. In addition to linear models, neural network models and logistic STAR models were included in the study. A novelty, compared to Stock and Watson (1999), was that a set of time-varying autoregressive models of type (15) was included in the comparisons.

The results were based on rankings of models' performance measured using loss functions based on absolute forecast errors now raised to five powers from one to three in steps of 0.5. Neither neural network nor LSTAR models appeared in the overall top-10. But then, both the fraction of neural network models and LSTAR models that appeared in top-10 rankings for individual series was greater than the same fraction for linear methods or time-varying AR models. This, together with other results in the paper, suggests that nonlinear models in many cases work very well, but they can also relatively often perform rather poorly.

Marcellino (2002) also singled out three 'key economic variables': the growth rate of industrial production, the unemployment rate and the inflation measured by the consumer price index. Ranking models within these three categories showed that industrial production was best forecast by linear models. But then, in forecasting the unemployment rate, both the LSTAR and neural network models, as well as the time-varying AR model, had top rankings. For example, for the three-month horizon, two LSTAR models occupied the one-two ranks for all five loss functions (other ranks were not reported). This may not be completely surprising since many European unemployment rate series are distinctly asymmetric; see, for example, Skalin and Teräsvirta (2002) for discussion based on quarterly series. As to the inflation rate, the results were a mixture of the ones for the other two key variables.

These studies suggest some answers to the question of whether nonlinear models perform better than linear ones in forecasting macroeconomic series. The results in Stock and Watson (1999) indicate that using a large number of nonlinear models and combining forecasts from them is much better than using single nonlinear models. It also seems that this way of exploiting nonlinearity may lead to better forecasting performance than what is achieved by linear models. Marcellino (2002) did not consider this possibility. His results, based on individual models, suggest that nonlinear models are uneven performers but that they can do well in some types of macroeconomic series such as unemployment rates.

7.3.2. Forecasting with the same model for each forecast horizon

As discussed in Section 4, it is possible to obtain forecasts for several periods ahead recursively from a single model. This is the approach adopted in Teräsvirta, van Dijk and Medeiros (2005). The main question posed in that paper was whether careful modelling improves forecast accuracy compared to models with a fixed specification that remains unchanged over time. In the case of nonlinear models this implied testing linearity first and choosing a nonlinear model only if linearity is rejected. The lag structure of the nonlinear model was also determined from the data. The authors considered seven monthly macroeconomic variables of the G7 countries. They were industrial production, unemployment, volume of exports, volume of imports, inflation, narrow money, and short-term interest rate. Most series started in January 1960 and were available up to December 2000. The series were seasonally adjusted with the exception of the CPI inflation and the short-term interest rate. As in Stock and Watson (1999), the series were forecast every month. In order to keep the human effort and computational burdens at manageable levels, the models were only respecified every 12 months.

The models considered were the linear autoregressive model, the LSTAR model and the single hidden-layer feedforward neural network model. The results showed that there were series for which linearity was never rejected. Rejections, using LM-type tests, were somewhat more frequent against LSTAR than against the neural network model. The interest rate series, the inflation rate and the unemployment rate were most systematically nonlinear when linearity was tested against STAR. In order to find out whether modelling was a useful idea, the investigation also included a set of models with a predetermined form and lag structure.

Results were reported for four forecast horizons: 1, 3, 6 and 12 months. They indicated that careful modelling does improve the accuracy of forecasts compared to selecting fixed nonlinear models. The loss function was the root mean square error. The LSTAR model turned out to be the best model overall, better than the linear or neural network model, which was not the case in Stock and Watson (1999) or Marcellino (2002). The LSTAR model did not, however, dominate the others. There were series/country pairs for which other models performed clearly better than the STAR model. Nevertheless, as in Marcellino (2002), the LSTAR model did well in forecasting the unemployment rate.

The results on neural network models suggested the need for model evaluation: a closer scrutiny found some of the estimated models to be explosive, which led to inferior multi-step forecasts. This fact emphasizes the need for model evaluation before forecasting. For practical reasons, this phase of model building has been neglected in large studies such as the ones discussed in this section.

The results in Teräsvirta, van Dijk and Medeiros (2005) are not directly comparable to the ones in Stock and Watson (1999) or Marcellino (2002) because the forecasts in the former paper have been generated recursively from a single model for all forecast horizons. The time series used in these three papers have not been the same either. Nevertheless, put together the results strengthen the view that nonlinear models are a useful tool in macroeconomic forecasting.

8. Final remarks

This chapter contains a presentation of a number of frequently applied nonlinear models and shows how forecasts can be generated from them. Since such forecasts are typically obtained numerically when the same model is used for forecasting several periods ahead, forecast generation automatically yields not only point but interval and density forecasts as well. The latter are important because they contain more information than the pure point forecasts which, unfortunately, often are the only ones reported in publications. It is also sometimes argued that the strength of the nonlinear forecasting lies in density forecasts, whereas comparisons of point forecasts often show no substantial difference in performance between individual linear and nonlinear models. Results from large studies reported in Section 7.3 indicate that forecasts from linear models may be more robust than the ones from nonlinear models. In some cases the nonlinear models clearly outperform the linear ones, but in other occasions they may be strongly inferior to the latter.

It appears that nonlinear models may have a fair chance of generating accurate forecasts if the number of observations for specifying the model and estimating its parameters is large. This is due to the fact, discussed in Lundbergh and Teräsvirta (2002), that potential gains from forecasting with nonlinear models can be strongly reduced because of parameter estimation. A recent simulation-based paper by Psaradakis and Spagnolo (2005), where the observations are generated by a bivariate nonlinear system, either a threshold model or a Markov-switching one, with linear cointegration, strengthens this impression. In some cases, even when the data-generating process is nonlinear and the model is correctly specified, the linear model yields more accurate forecasts than the correct nonlinear one with estimated parameters. Short time series are thus a disadvantage, but the results also suggest that sufficient attention should be paid to estimation techniques. This is certainly true for neural network models that contain a large number of parameters. Recent developments in this area include White (2006).

In the nonlinear framework, the question of iterative vs. direct forecasts requires more research. Simulations reported in Lin and Granger (1994) suggest that the direct method is not a useful alternative when the data-generating process is a nonlinear model such as the STAR model, and a direct STAR model is fitted to the data for forecasting more than one period ahead. The direct method works better when the model used to produce the forecasts is a neural network model. This may not be surprising because the neural network model is a flexible functional form. Whether direct nonlinear models generate more accurate forecasts than direct linear ones when the data-generating process is nonlinear, is a topic for further research.

An encouraging feature is, however, that there is evidence of combination of a large number of nonlinear models leading to point forecasts that are superior to forecasts from linear models. Thus it may be concluded that while the form of nonlinearity in macroeconomic time series may be difficult to usefully capture with single models, there is hope for improving forecasting accuracy by combining information from several nonlinear models. This suggests that parametric nonlinear models will remain important in forecasting economic variables.

Acknowledgements

Financial support from Jan Wallander's and Tom Hedelius's Foundation, Grant No. J02-35, is gratefully acknowledged. Discussions with Clive Granger have been very helpful. I also wish to thank three anonymous referees, Marcelo Medeiros and Dick van Dijk for useful comments but retain responsibility for any errors and shortcomings in this work.

References

Aiolfi, M., Timmermann, A. (in press). "Persistence in forecasting performance and conditional combination strategies". Journal of Econometrics.

Andersen, T.G., Bollerslev, T., Christoffersen, P.F., Diebold, F.X. (2006). "Volatility and correlation forecasting". In: Elliott, G., Granger, C.W.J., Timmermann, A. (Eds.), Handbook of Economic Forecasting. Elsevier, Amsterdam, pp. 777–878. Chapter 15 in this volume.

Andrews, D.W.K., Ploberger, W. (1994). "Optimal tests when a nuisance parameter is present only under the alternative". Econometrica 62, 1383–1414.

Bacon, D.W., Watts, D.G. (1971). "Estimating the transition between two intersecting straight lines". Biometrika 58, 525–534.

Bai, J., Perron, P. (1998). "Estimating and testing linear models with multiple structural changes". Econometrica 66, 47–78.

Bai, J., Perron, P. (2003). "Computation and analysis of multiple structural change models". Journal of Applied Econometrics 18, 1–22.

Banerjee, A., Urga, G. (2005). "Modelling structural breaks, long memory and stock market volatility: An overview". Journal of Econometrics 129, 1–34.

Bhansali, R.J. (2002). "Multi-step forecasting". In: Clements, M.P., Hendry, D.F. (Eds.), A Companion to Economic Forecasting. Blackwell, Oxford, pp. 206–221.

Bierens, H.J. (1990). "A consistent conditional moment test of functional form". Econometrica 58, 1443–1458.

Boero, G., Marrocu, E. (2002). "The performance of non-linear exchange rate models: A forecasting comparison". Journal of Forecasting 21, 513–542.

Box, G.E.P., Jenkins, G.M. (1970). Time Series Analysis, Forecasting and Control. Holden-Day, San Francisco.

Bradley, M.D., Jansen, D.W. (2004). "Forecasting with a nonlinear dynamic model of stock returns and industrial production". International Journal of Forecasting 20, 321–342.

Brännäs, K., De Gooijer, J.G. (1994). "Autoregressive-asymmetric moving average model for business cycle data". Journal of Forecasting 13, 529–544.

Breunig, R., Najarian, S., Pagan, A. (2003). "Specification testing of Markov switching models". Oxford Bulletin of Economics and Statistics 65, 703–725.

Brown, B.W., Mariano, R.S. (1984). "Residual-based procedures for prediction and estimation in a nonlinear simultaneous system". Econometrica 52, 321–343.

Chan, K.S. (1993). "Consistency and limiting distribution of the least squares estimator of a threshold autoregressive model". Annals of Statistics 21, 520–533.

Chan, K.S., Tong, H. (1986). "On estimating thresholds in autoregressive models". Journal of Time Series Analysis 7, 178–190.

Clements, M.P., Franses, P.H., Swanson, N.R. (2004). "Forecasting economic and financial time-series with non-linear models". International Journal of Forecasting 20, 169–183.

Clements, M.P., Hendry, D.F. (1999). Forecasting Non-stationary Economic Time Series. MIT Press, Cambridge, MA.

Clements, M.P., Krolzig, H.-M. (1998). "A comparison of the forecast performance of Markov-switching and threshold autoregressive models of US GNP". Econometrics Journal 1, C47–C75.

Corradi, V., Swanson, N.R. (2002). "A consistent test for non-linear out of sample predictive accuracy". Journal of Econometrics 110, 353–381.

Corradi, V., Swanson, N.R. (2004). "Some recent developments in predictive accuracy testing with nested models and (generic) nonlinear alternatives". International Journal of Forecasting 20, 185–199.

Corradi, V., Swanson, N.R. (2006). "Predictive density evaluation". In: Elliott, G., Granger, C.W.J., Timmermann, A. (Eds.), Handbook of Economic Forecasting. Elsevier, Amsterdam, pp. 197–284. Chapter 5 in this volume.

Cybenko, G. (1989). "Approximation by superposition of sigmoidal functions". Mathematics of Control, Signals, and Systems 2, 303–314.

Dacco, R., Satchell, S. (1999). "Why do regime-switching models forecast so badly?". Journal of Forecasting 18, 1–16.

Davies, R.B. (1977). "Hypothesis testing when a nuisance parameter is present only under the alternative". Biometrika 64, 247–254.

De Gooijer, J.G., De Bruin, P.T. (1998). "On forecasting SETAR processes". Statistics and Probability Letters 37, 7–14.

De Gooijer, J.G., Vidiella-i-Anguera, A. (2004). "Forecasting threshold cointegrated systems". International Journal of Forecasting 20, 237–253.

Deutsch, M., Granger, C.W.J., Teräsvirta, T. (1994). "The combination of forecasts using changing weights". International Journal of Forecasting 10, 47–57.

Diebold, F.X., Mariano, R.S. (1995). "Comparing predictive accuracy". Journal of Business and Economic Statistics 13, 253–263.

Eitrheim, Ø., Teräsvirta, T. (1996). "Testing the adequacy of smooth transition autoregressive models". Journal of Econometrics 74, 59–75.

Elliott, G. (2006). "Forecasting with trending data". In: Elliott, G., Granger, C.W.J., Timmermann, A. (Eds.), Handbook of Economic Forecasting. Elsevier, Amsterdam, pp. 555–603. Chapter 11 in this volume.

Enders, W., Granger, C.W.J. (1998). "Unit-root tests and asymmetric adjustment with an example using the term structure of interest rates". Journal of Business and Economic Statistics 16, 304–311.

Fan, J., Yao, Q. (2003). Nonlinear Time Series. Nonparametric and Parametric Methods. Springer, New York.

Fine, T.L. (1999). Feedforward Neural Network Methodology. Springer, Berlin.

Franses, P.H., van Dijk, D. (2000). Non-Linear Time Series Models in Empirical Finance. Cambridge University Press, Cambridge.

Friedman, J.H., Stuetzle, W. (1981). "Projection pursuit regression". Journal of the American Statistical Association 76, 817–823.

Funahashi, K. (1989). "On the approximate realization of continuous mappings by neural networks". Neural Networks 2, 183–192.

Garcia, R. (1998). "Asymptotic null distribution of the likelihood ratio test in Markov switching models". International Economic Review 39, 763–788.

Giacomini, R., White, H. (2003). "Tests of conditional predictive ability". Working Paper 2003-09, Department of Economics, University of California, San Diego.

Goffe, W.L., Ferrier, G.D., Rogers, J. (1994). "Global optimization of statistical functions with simulated annealing". Journal of Econometrics 60, 65–99.

Gonzalo, J., Pitarakis, J.-Y. (2002). "Estimation and model selection based inference in single and multiple threshold models". Journal of Econometrics 110, 319–352.

Granger, C.W.J., Bates, J. (1969). "The combination of forecasts". Operations Research Quarterly 20, 451–468.

Granger, C.W.J., Jeon, Y. (2004). "Thick modeling". Economic Modelling 21, 323–343.

Granger, C.W.J., Machina, M.J. (2006). "Forecasting and decision theory". In: Elliott, G., Granger, C.W.J., Timmermann, A. (Eds.), Handbook of Economic Forecasting. Elsevier, Amsterdam, pp. 81–98. Chapter 2 in this volume.

Granger, C.W.J., Pesaran, M.H. (2000). "Economic and statistical measures of forecast accuracy". Journal of Forecasting 19, 537–560.

Granger, C.W.J., Teräsvirta, T. (1991). "Experiments in modeling nonlinear relationships between time series". In: Casdagli, M., Eubank, S. (Eds.), Nonlinear Modeling and Forecasting. Addison-Wesley, Redwood City, pp. 189–197.

Granger, C.W.J., Teräsvirta, T. (1993). Modelling Nonlinear Economic Relationships. Oxford University Press, Oxford.

Haggan, V., Ozaki, T. (1981). "Modelling non-linear random vibrations using an amplitude-dependent autoregressive time series model". Biometrika 68, 189–196.

Hamilton, J.D. (1989). "A new approach to the economic analysis of nonstationary time series and the business cycle". Econometrica 57, 357–384.

Hamilton, J.D. (1993). "Estimation, inference and forecasting of time series subject to changes in regime". In: Maddala, G.S., Rao, C.R., Vinod, H.R. (Eds.), Handbook of Statistics, vol. 11. Elsevier, Amsterdam, pp. 231–260.

Hamilton, J.D. (1994). Time Series Analysis. Princeton University Press, Princeton, NJ.

Hamilton, J.D. (1996). "Specification testing in Markov-switching time-series models". Journal of Econometrics 70, 127–157.

Hansen, B.E. (1996). "Inference when a nuisance parameter is not identified under the null hypothesis". Econometrica 64, 413–430.

Hansen, B.E. (1999). "Testing for linearity". Journal of Economic Surveys 13, 551–576.

Harvey, A.C. (2006). "Forecasting with unobserved components time series models". In: Elliott, G., Granger, C.W.J., Timmermann, A. (Eds.), Handbook of Economic Forecasting. Elsevier, Amsterdam. Chapter 7 in this volume.

Harvey, D., Leybourne, S., Newbold, P. (1997). "Testing the equality of prediction mean squared errors". International Journal of Forecasting 13, 281–291.

Haykin, S. (1999). Neural Networks. A Comprehensive Foundation, Second ed. Prentice-Hall, Upper Saddle River, NJ.

Hendry, D.F., Clements, M.P. (2003). "Economic forecasting: Some lessons from recent research". Economic Modelling 20, 301–329.

Henry, O.T., Olekalns, N., Summers, P.M. (2001). "Exchange rate instability: A threshold autoregressive approach". Economic Record 77, 160–166.

Hornik, K., Stinchcombe, M., White, H. (1989). "Multi-layer feedforward networks are universal approximators". Neural Networks 2, 359–366.

Hwang, J.T.G., Ding, A.A. (1997). "Prediction intervals for artificial neural networks". Journal of the American Statistical Association 92, 109–125.

Hyndman, R.J. (1996). "Computing and graphing highest density regions". The American Statistician 50, 120–126.

Inoue, A., Kilian, L. (2004). "In-sample or out-of-sample tests of predictability: Which one should we use?". Econometric Reviews 23, 371–402.

Kilian, L., Taylor, M.P. (2003). "Why is it so difficult to beat the random walk forecast of exchange rates?". Journal of International Economics 60, 85–107.

Lanne, M., Saikkonen, P. (2002). "Threshold autoregressions for strongly autocorrelated time series". Journal of Business and Economic Statistics 20, 282–289.

Lee, T.-H., White, H., Granger, C.W.J. (1993). "Testing for neglected nonlinearity in time series models: A comparison of neural network methods and alternative tests". Journal of Econometrics 56, 269–290.

Li, H., Xu, Y. (2002). "Short rate dynamics and regime shifts". Working Paper, Johnson Graduate School of Management, Cornell University.

Lin, C.-F., Teräsvirta, T. (1999). "Testing parameter constancy in linear models against stochastic stationary parameters". Journal of Econometrics 90, 193–213.

Lin, J.-L., Granger, C.W.J. (1994). "Forecasting from non-linear models in practice". Journal of Forecasting 13, 1–9.

Lindgren, G. (1978). "Markov regime models for mixed distributions and switching regressions". Scandinavian Journal of Statistics 5, 81–91.

Lundbergh, S., Teräsvirta, T. (2002). "Forecasting with smooth transition autoregressive models". In: Clements, M.P., Hendry, D.F. (Eds.), A Companion to Economic Forecasting. Blackwell, Oxford, pp. 485–509.

Luukkonen, R., Saikkonen, P., Teräsvirta, T. (1988). "Testing linearity against smooth transition autoregressive models". Biometrika 75, 491–499.

Maddala, D.S. (1977). Econometrics. McGraw-Hill, New York.

Marcellino, M. (2002). "Instability and non-linearity in the EMU". Discussion Paper No. 3312, Centre for Economic Policy Research.

Marcellino, M. (2004). "Forecasting EMU macroeconomic variables". International Journal of Forecasting 20, 359–372.

Marcellino, M., Stock, J.H., Watson, M.W. (2004). "A comparison of direct and iterated multistep AR methods for forecasting economic time series". Working Paper.

Medeiros, M.C., Teräsvirta, T., Rech, G. (2006). "Building neural network models for time series: A statistical approach". Journal of Forecasting 25, 49–75.

Mincer, J., Zarnowitz, V. (1969). "The evaluation of economic forecasts". In: Mincer, J. (Ed.), Economic Forecasts and Expectations. National Bureau of Economic Research, New York.

Montgomery, A.L., Zarnowitz, V., Tsay, R.S., Tiao, G.C. (1998). "Forecasting the U.S. unemployment rate". Journal of the American Statistical Association 93, 478–493.

Nyblom, J. (1989). "Testing for the constancy of parameters over time". Journal of the American Statistical Association 84, 223–230.

Pesaran, M.H., Timmermann, A. (2002). "Model instability and choice of observation window". Working Paper.

Pfann, G.A., Schotman, P.C., Tschernig, R. (1996). "Nonlinear interest rate dynamics and implications for term structure". Journal of Econometrics 74, 149–176.

Poon, S.H., Granger, C.W.J. (2003). "Forecasting volatility in financial markets". Journal of Economic Literature 41, 478–539.

Proietti, T. (2003). "Forecasting the US unemployment rate". Computational Statistics and Data Analysis 42, 451–476.

Psaradakis, Z., Spagnolo, F. (2005). "Forecast performance of nonlinear error-correction models with multiple regimes". Journal of Forecasting 24, 119–138.

Ramsey, J.B. (1996). "If nonlinear models cannot forecast, what use are they?". Studies in Nonlinear Dynamics and Forecasting 1, 65–86.

Sarantis, N. (1999). "Modelling non-linearities in real effective exchange rates". Journal of International Money and Finance 18, 27–45.

Satchell, S., Timmermann, A. (1995). "An assessment of the economic value of non-linear foreign exchange rate forecasts". Journal of Forecasting 14, 477–497.

Siliverstovs, B., van Dijk, D. (2003). "Forecasting industrial production with linear, nonlinear, and structural change models". Econometric Institute Report EI 2003-16, Erasmus University Rotterdam.

Skalin, J., Teräsvirta, T. (2002). "Modeling asymmetries and moving equilibria in unemployment rates". Macroeconomic Dynamics 6, 202–241.

Stock, J.H., Watson, M.W. (1999). "A comparison of linear and nonlinear univariate models for forecasting macroeconomic time series". In: Engle, R.F., White, H. (Eds.), Cointegration, Causality and Forecasting. A Festschrift in Honour of Clive W.J. Granger. Oxford University Press, Oxford, pp. 1–44.

Strikholm, B., Teräsvirta, T. (2005). "Determining the number of regimes in a threshold autoregressive model using smooth transition autoregressions". Working Paper 578, Stockholm School of Economics.

Swanson, N.R., White, H. (1995). "A model-selection approach to assessing the information in the term structure using linear models and artificial neural networks". Journal of Business and Economic Statistics 13, 265–275.

Swanson, N.R., White, H. (1997a). "Forecasting economic time series using flexible versus fixed specification and linear versus nonlinear econometric models". International Journal of Forecasting 13, 439–461.

Swanson, N.R., White, H. (1997b). "A model selection approach to real-time macroeconomic forecasting using linear models and artificial neural networks". Review of Economic and Statistics 79, 540–550.

Tay, A.S., Wallis, K.F. (2002). "Density forecasting: A survey". In: Clements, M.P., Hendry, D.F. (Eds.), A Companion to Economic Forecasting. Blackwell, Oxford, pp. 45–68.

Taylor, M.P., Sarno, L. (2002). "Purchasing power parity and the real exchange rate". International Monetary Fund Staff Papers 49, 65–105.

Teräsvirta, T. (1994). "Specification, estimation, and evaluation of smooth transition autoregressive models". Journal of the American Statistical Association 89, 208–218.

Teräsvirta, T. (1998). "Modeling economic relationships with smooth transition regressions". In: Ullah, A., Giles, D.E. (Eds.), Handbook of Applied Economic Statistics. Dekker, New York, pp. 507–552.

Teräsvirta, T. (2004). "Nonlinear smooth transition modeling". In: Lütkepohl, H., Krätzig, M. (Eds.), Applied Time Series Econometrics. Cambridge University Press, Cambridge, pp. 222–242.

Teräsvirta, T., Anderson, H.M. (1992). "Characterizing nonlinearities in business cycles using smooth transition autoregressive models". Journal of Applied Econometrics 7, S119–S136.

Teräsvirta, T., Eliasson, A.-C. (2001). "Non-linear error correction and the UK demand for broad money, 1878–1993". Journal of Applied Econometrics 16, 277–288.

Teräsvirta, T., Lin, C.-F., Granger, C.W.J. (1993). "Power of the neural network linearity test". Journal of Time Series Analysis 14, 309–323.

Teräsvirta, T., van Dijk, D., Medeiros, M.C. (2005). "Smooth transition autoregressions, neural networks, and linear models in forecasting macroeconomic time series: A re-examination". International Journal of Forecasting 21, 755–774.

Timmermann, A. (2006). "Forecast combinations". In: Elliott, G., Granger, C.W.J., Timmermann, A. (Eds.), Handbook of Economic Forecasting. Elsevier, Amsterdam, pp. 135–196. Chapter 4 in this volume.

Tong, H. (1990). Non-Linear Time Series. A Dynamical System Approach. Oxford University Press, Oxford.

Tong, H., Moeanaddin, R. (1988). "On multi-step nonlinear least squares prediction". The Statistician 37, 101–110.

Tsay, R.S. (2002). "Nonlinear models and forecasting". In: Clements, M.P., Hendry, D.F. (Eds.), A Companion to Economic Forecasting. Blackwell, Oxford, pp. 453–484.

Tyssedal, J.S., Tjøstheim, D. (1988). "An autoregressive model with suddenly changing parameters". Applied Statistics 37, 353–369.

van Dijk, D., Teräsvirta, T., Franses, P.H. (2002). "Smooth transition autoregressive models – a survey of recent developments". Econometric Reviews 21, 1–47.

Venetis, I.A., Paya, I., Peel, D.A. (2003). "Re-examination of the predictability of economic activity using the yield spread: A nonlinear approach". International Review of Economics and Finance 12, 187–206.

Wallis, K.F. (1999). "Asymmetric density forecasts of inflation and the Bank of England's fan chart". National Institute Economic Review 167, 106–112.

Watson, M.W., Engle, R.F. (1985). "Testing for regression coefficient stability with a stationary AR(1) alternative". Review of Economics and Statistics 67, 341–346.

Wecker, W.E. (1981). "Asymmetric time series". Journal of the American Statistical Association 76, 16–21.

West, K.D. (2006). "Forecast evaluation". In: Elliott, G., Granger, C.W.J., Timmermann, A. (Eds.), Handbook of Economic Forecasting. Elsevier, Amsterdam, pp. 99–134. Chapter 3 in this volume.

White, H. (1990). "Connectionist nonparametric regression: Multilayer feedforward networks can learn arbitrary mappings". Neural Networks 3, 535–550.

White, H. (2006). "Approximate nonlinear forecasting methods". In: Elliott, G., Granger, C.W.J., Timmermann, A. (Eds.), Handbook of Economic Forecasting. Elsevier, Amsterdam, pp. 459–512. Chapter 9 in this volume.

Zhang, G., Patuwo, B.E., Hu, M.Y. (1998). "Forecasting with artificial neural networks: The state of the art". International Journal of Forecasting 14, 35–62.

Chapter 9

APPROXIMATE NONLINEAR FORECASTING METHODS

HALBERT WHITE

Department of Economics, UC San Diego

Contents

Handbook of Economic Forecasting, Volume 1
Edited by Graham Elliott, Clive W.J. Granger and Allan Timmermann

DOI: 10.1016/S1574-0706(05)01009-8

Abstract

We review key aspects of forecasting using nonlinear models. Because economic models are typically misspecified, the resulting forecasts provide only an approximation to the best possible forecast. Although it is in principle possible to obtain superior approximations to the optimal forecast using nonlinear methods, there are some potentially serious practical challenges. Primary among these are computational difficulties, the dangers of overfit, and potential difficulties of interpretation. In this chapter we discuss these issues in detail. Then we propose and illustrate the use of a new family of methods (QuickNet) that achieves the benefits of using a forecasting model that is nonlinear in the predictors while avoiding or mitigating the other challenges to the use of nonlinear forecasting methods.

Keywords

prediction, misspecification, approximation, nonlinear methods, highly nonlinear methods, artificial neural networks, ridgelets, forecast explanation, model selection, QuickNet

JEL classification: C13, C14, C20, C45, C51, C43

1. Introduction

In this chapter we focus on obtaining a point forecast or prediction of a "target variable" Y_t given a $k \times 1$ vector of "predictors" X_t (with k a finite integer). For simplicity, we take Y_t to be a scalar. Typically, X_t is known or observed prior to the realization of Y_t, so the "t" subscript on X_t designates the observation index for which a prediction is to be made, rather than the time period in which X_t is first observed. The discussion to follow does not strictly require this time precedence, although we proceed with this convention implicit. Thus, in a typical time-series application, X_t may contain lagged values of Y_t, as well as values of other variables known prior to time t.

Although we use the generic observation index t throughout, it is important to stress that our discussion applies quite broadly, and not just to pure time-series forecasting. An increasingly important use of prediction models involves cross-section or panel data. In these applications, Y_t denotes the outcome variable for a generic individual t and X_t denotes predictors for the individual's outcome, observable prior to the outcome. Once the prediction model has been constructed using the available cross-section or panel data, it is then used to evaluate new cases whose outcomes are unknown.

For example, banks or other financial institutions now use prediction models extensively to forecast whether a new applicant for credit will be a good risk or not. If the prediction is favorable, then credit will be granted; otherwise, the application may be denied or referred for further review. These prediction models are built using cross-section or panel data collected by the firm itself and/or purchased from third party vendors. These data sets contain observations on individual attributes X_t, corresponding to information on the application, as well as subsequent outcome information Y_t, such as late payment or default. The reader may find it helpful to keep such applications in mind in what follows so as not to fall into the trap of interpreting the following discussion too narrowly.

Because of our focus on these broader applications of forecasting, we shall not delve very deeply into the purely time-series aspects of the subject. Fortunately, Chapter 8 in this volume by Teräsvirta (2006) contains an excellent treatment of these issues. In particular, there are a number of interesting and important issues that arise when considering multi-step-ahead time-series forecasts, as opposed to single-step-ahead forecasts. In time-series application of the results here, we implicitly operate with the convention that multi-step forecasts are constructed using the direct approach in which a different forecast model is constructed for each forecast horizon. The reader is urged to consult Teräsvirta's chapter for a wealth of time-series material complementary to the present chapter.

There is a vast array of methods for producing point forecasts, but for convenience, simplicity, and practical relevance we restrict our discussion to point forecasts constructed as approximations to the conditional expectation (mean) of Y_t given X_t,

$$\mu(X_t) \equiv E(Y_t|X_t).$$

It is well known that $\mu(X_t)$ provides the best possible prediction of Y_t given X_t in terms of prediction mean squared error (PMSE), provided Y_t has finite variance. That is, the function μ solves the problem

$$\min_{m \in \mathcal{M}} E\big[\big(Y_t - m(X_t)\big)^2\big], \tag{1}$$

where $\mathcal{M}$ is the collection of functions m of X_t having finite variance, and E is the expectation taken with respect to the joint distribution of Y_t and X_t.

By restricting attention to forecasts based on the conditional mean, we neglect forecasts that arise from the use of loss functions other than PMSE, such as prediction mean absolute error, which yields predictions based on the conditional median, or its asymmetric analogs, which yield predictions based on conditional quantiles [e.g., Koenker and Basset (1978), Kim and White (2003)]. Although we provide no further explicit discussion here, the methods we describe for obtaining PMSE-based forecasts do have immediate analogs for other such important loss functions.

Our focus on PMSE leads naturally to methods of least-squares estimation, which underlie the vast majority of forecasting applications, providing our discussion with its intended practical relevance.

If μ were known, then we could finish our exposition here in short order: μ provides the PMSE-optimal method for constructing forecasts and that is that. Or, if we knew the conditional distribution of Y_t given X_t, then μ would again be known, as it can be obtained from this distribution. Typically, however, we do not have this knowledge. Confronted with such ignorance, forecasters typically proceed by specifying a *model* for μ, that is, a collection $\mathcal{M}$ (note our notation above) of functions of X_t. If μ belongs to $\mathcal{M}$, then we say the model is "correctly specified". (So, for example, if Y_t has finite variance, then the model $\mathcal{M}$ of functions m of X_t having finite variance is correctly specified, as μ is in fact such a function.) If $\mathcal{M}$ is sufficiently restricted that μ does not belong to $\mathcal{M}$, then we say that the model is "misspecified".

Here we adopt the pragmatic view that either out of convenience or ignorance (typically both) we work with a misspecified model for μ. By taking $\mathcal{M}$ to be as specified in (1), we can generally avoid misspecification, but this is not necessarily convenient, as the generality of this choice poses special challenges for statistical estimation. (This choice for $\mathcal{M}$ leads to nonparametric methods of statistical estimation.) Restricting $\mathcal{M}$ leads to more convenient estimation procedures, and it is especially convenient, as we do here, to work with parametric models for μ. Unfortunately, we rarely have enough information about μ to correctly specify a parametric model for it.

When one's goal is to make predictions, the use of a misspecified model is by no means fatal. Our predictions will not be as good as they would be if μ were accessible, but to the extent that we can approximate μ more or less well, then our predictions will still be more or less accurate. As we discuss below, any model $\mathcal{M}$ provides us with a means of approximating μ, and it is for this reason that we declared above that our focus will be on "forecasts constructed as approximations" to μ. The challenge then is to choose $\mathcal{M}$ suitably, where by "suitably", we mean in such a way as to conveniently provide a good approximation to μ. Our discussion to follow elaborates our notions of convenience and goodness of approximation.

2. Linearity and nonlinearity

2.1. Linearity

Parametric models are models whose elements are indexed by a finite-dimensional parameter vector. An important and familiar example is the linear parametric model. This model is generated by the function $l(x,\beta) \equiv x'\beta$. We call β a "parameter vector", and, as β conforms with the predictors (represented here by x), we have β belonging to the "parameter space" $\mathcal{R}^k$, k-dimensional real Euclidean space. The *linear parametric model* is then the collection of functions

$$\mathcal{L} \equiv \{m : \mathcal{R}^k \to \mathcal{R} \mid m(x) = l(x,\beta) \equiv x'\beta,\ \beta \in \mathcal{R}^k\}.$$

We call the function l the "model parameterization", or simply the "parameterization". We see here that each model element $l(\cdot,\beta)$ of $\mathcal{L}$ is a linear function of x. It is standard to set the first element of x to the constant unity, so in fact $l(\cdot,\beta)$ is an *affine* function of the nonconstant elements of x. For simplicity, we nevertheless refer to $l(\cdot,\beta)$ in this context as "linear in x", and we call forecasts based on a parameterization linear in the predictors a "linear forecast".

For fixed x, the parameterization $l(x,\cdot)$ is also linear in the parameters. In discussing linearity or nonlinearity of the parameterization (equivalently, of the parametric model), it is important generally to specify to whether one is referring to the predictors x or to the parameters β. Here, however, this doesn't matter, as we have linearity either way.

Solving problem (1) with $\mathcal{M} = \mathcal{L}$, that is, solving

$$\min_{m \in \mathcal{L}} E\big[\big(Y_t - m(X_t)\big)^2\big],$$

yields $l(\cdot,\beta^*)$, where

$$\beta^* = \arg\min_{\beta \in \mathcal{R}^k} E\big[\big(Y_t - X_t'\beta\big)^2\big]. \tag{2}$$

We call β^* the "PMSE-optimal coefficient vector". This delivers not only the best forecast for Y_t given X_t based on the linear model $\mathcal{L}$, but also the *optimal linear approximation* to μ, as discussed by White (1980).

To establish this optimal approximation property, observe that

$$\begin{aligned} E\big[\big(Y_t - X_t'\beta\big)^2\big] &= E\big[\big(Y_t - \mu(X_t) + \mu(X_t) - X_t'\beta\big)^2\big] \\ &= E\big[\big(Y_t - \mu(X_t)\big)^2\big] + E\big[\big(\mu(X_t) - X_t'\beta\big)^2\big] \\ &\quad + 2E\big[\big(Y_t - \mu(X_t)\big)\big(\mu(X_t) - X_t'\beta\big)\big] \end{aligned}$$

$$= E\big[\big(Y_t - \mu(X_t)\big)^2\big] + E\big[\big(\mu(X_t) - X_t'\beta\big)^2\big].$$

The final equality follows from the fact that for all β

$$\begin{aligned} E\big[\big(Y_t - \mu(X_t)\big)\big(\mu(X_t) - X_t'\beta\big)\big] &= E\big[E\big[\big(Y_t - \mu(X_t)\big)\big(\mu(X_t) - X_t'\beta\big) \mid X_t\big]\big] \\ &= E\big[E\big[\big(Y_t - \mu(X_t)\big) \mid X_t\big]\big(\mu(X_t) - X_t'\beta\big)\big] \\ &= 0, \end{aligned}$$

because $E[(Y_t - \mu(X_t)) \mid X_t] = 0$. Thus,

$$\begin{aligned} E\big[\big(Y_t - X_t'\beta\big)^2\big] &= E\big[\big(Y_t - \mu(X_t)\big)^2\big] + E\big[\big(\mu(X_t) - X_t'\beta\big)^2\big] \\ &= \sigma_*^2 + \int \big(\mu(x) - x'\beta\big)^2 \, \mathrm{d}H(x), \end{aligned} \tag{3}$$

where $\mathrm{d}H$ denotes the joint density of X_t and σ_*^2 denotes the "pure PMSE", $\sigma_*^2 \equiv E[(Y_t - \mu(X_t))^2]$.

From (3) we see that the PMSE can be decomposed into two components, the pure PMSE σ_*^2, associated with the best possible prediction (that based on μ), and the *approximation mean squared error* (AMSE), $\int (\mu(x) - x'\beta)^2 \, \mathrm{d}H(x)$, for $x'\beta$ as an approximation to $\mu(x)$. The AMSE is *weighted* by $\mathrm{d}H$, the joint density of X_t, so that the squared approximation error is more heavily weighted in regions where X_t is likely to be observed and less heavily weighted in areas where X_t is less likely to be observed. This weighting forces the optimal approximation to be better in more frequently observed regions of the distribution of X_t, at the cost of being less accurate in less frequently observed regions of the distribution of X_t.

It follows that to minimize PMSE it is necessary and sufficient to minimize AMSE. That is, because β^* minimizes PMSE, it also satisfies

$$\beta^* = \arg\min_{\beta \in \mathcal{R}^k} \int \big(\mu(x) - x'\beta\big)^2 \, \mathrm{d}H(x).$$

This shows that β^* is the vector delivering the best possible approximation of the form $x'\beta$ to the PMSE-best predictor $\mu(x)$ of Y_t given $X_t = x$, where the approximation is best in the sense of AMSE. For brevity, we refer to this as the "optimal approximation property".

Note that AMSE is nonnegative. It is minimized at zero if and only if for some β_o, $\mu(x) = x'\beta_o$ (a.s.-H), that is, if and only if $\mathcal{L}$ is correctly specified. In this case, $\beta^* = \beta_o$.

An especially convenient property of β^* is that it can be represented in closed form. The first order conditions for β^* from problem (2) can be written as

$$E\big(X_t X_t'\big)\beta^* - E(X_t Y_t) = 0.$$

Define $M \equiv E(X_t X_t')$ and $L \equiv E(X_t Y_t)$. If M is nonsingular then we can solve for β^* to obtain the desired closed form expression

$$\beta^* = M^{-1} L.$$

The optimal point forecast based on the linear model $\mathcal{L}$ given predictors X_t is then given simply by

$$Y_t^* = l(X_t, \beta^*) = X_t'\beta^*.$$

In forecasting applications we typically have a sample of data that we view as representative of the underlying population distribution generating the data (the joint distribution of Y_t and X_t), but the population distribution is itself unknown. Typically, we do not even know the expectations M and L required to compute β^*, so the optimal point forecast Y_t^* is also unknown. Nevertheless, we can obtain a computationally convenient estimator of β^* from the sample data using the "plug-in principle". That is, we replace the unknown M and L by sample analogs $\hat{M} \equiv \frac{1}{n}\sum_{t=1}^{n} X_t X_t' = X'X/n$ and $\hat{L} \equiv \frac{1}{n}\sum_{t=1}^{n} X_t Y_t = X'Y/n$, where X is the $n \times k$ matrix with rows X_t', Y is the $n \times 1$ vector with elements Y_t, and n is the number of sample observations available for estimation. This yields the estimator

$$\hat{\beta} \equiv \hat{M}^{-1}\hat{L},$$

which we immediately recognize to be the ordinary least squares (OLS) estimator.

To keep the scope of our discussion tightly focused on the more practical aspects of the subject at hand, we shall not pay close attention to technical conditions underlying the statistical properties of $\hat{\beta}$ or the other estimators we discuss, and we will not state formal theorems here. Nevertheless, any claimed properties of the methods discussed here can be established under mild regularity conditions relevant for practical applications. In particular, under conditions ensuring that the law of large numbers holds (i.e., $\hat{M} \to M$ a.s., $\hat{L} \to L$ a.s.), it follows that as $n \to \infty$, $\hat{\beta} \to \beta^*$ a.s., that is, $\hat{\beta}$ consistently estimates β^*. Asymptotic normality can also be straightforwardly established for $\hat{\beta}$ under conditions sufficient to ensure the applicability of a suitable central limit theorem. [See White (2001, Chapters 2–5) for treatment of these issues.]

For clarity and notational simplicity, we operate throughout with the implicit understanding that the underlying regularity conditions ensure that our data are generated by an essentially stationary process that has suitably controlled dependence. For cross-section or panel data, it suffices that the observations are independent and identically distributed (i.i.d.). In time series applications, stationarity is compatible with considerable dependence, so we implicitly permit only as much dependence as is compatible with the availability of suitable asymptotic distribution theory. Our discussion thus applies straightforwardly to unit root time-series processes after first differencing or other suitable transformations, such as those relevant for cointegrated processes. For simplicity, we leave explicit discussion of these cases aside here. Relaxing the implicit stationarity assumption to accommodate heterogeneity in the data generating process is straightforward, but the notation necessary to handle this relaxation is more cumbersome than is justified here.

Returning to our main focus, we can now define the point forecast based on the linear model $\mathcal{L}$ using $\hat{\beta}$ for an *out-of-sample* predictor vector, say X_{n+1}. This is computed simply as

$$\hat{Y}_{n+1} = X'_{n+1}\hat{\beta}.$$

We italicized "out-of-sample" just now to emphasize the fact that in applications, forecasts are usually constructed based on predictors X_{n+1} not in the estimation sample, as the associated target variable (Y_{n+1}) is not available until after X_{n+1} is observed, as we discussed at the outset. The point of the forecasting exercise is to reduce our uncertainty about the as yet unavailable Y_{n+1}.

2.2. *Nonlinearity*

A nonlinear parametric model is generated from a nonlinear parameterization. For this, let ℓ be a finite integer and let the parameter space Θ be a subset of $\mathcal{R}^{\ell}$. Let f be a function mapping $\mathcal{R}^k \times \Theta$ into $\mathcal{R}$. This generates the parametric model

$$\mathcal{N} \equiv \{m : \mathcal{R}^k \to \mathcal{R} \mid m(x) = f(x, \theta), \theta \in \Theta\}.$$

The parameterization f (equivalently, the parametric model $\mathcal{N}$) can be nonlinear in the predictors only, nonlinear in the parameters only, or nonlinear in both. Models that are nonlinear in the predictors are of particular interest here, so for convenience we call the forecasts arising from such models "nonlinear forecasts". For now, we keep our discussion at the general level and later pay more particular attention to the special cases.

Completely parallel to our discussion of linear models, we have that solving problem (1) with $\mathcal{M} = \mathcal{N}$, that is, solving

$$\min_{m \in \mathcal{N}} E\big[\big(Y_t - m(X_t)\big)^2\big]$$

yields the optimal forecasting function $f(\cdot, \theta^*)$, where

$$\theta^* = \arg\min_{\theta \in \Theta} E\big[\big(Y_t - f(X_t, \theta)\big)^2\big]. \tag{4}$$

Here θ^* is the PMSE-optimal coefficient vector. This delivers not only the best forecast for Y_t given X_t based on the nonlinear model $\mathcal{N}$, but also the optimal *nonlinear* approximation to μ [see, e.g., White (1981)]. Now we have

$$\theta^* = \arg\min_{\theta \in \Theta} \int \big(\mu(x) - f(x, \theta)\big)^2 \, \mathrm{d}H(x).$$

The demonstration is completely parallel to that for β^*, simply replacing $x'\beta$ with $f(x, \theta)$. Now θ^* is the vector delivering the best possible approximation of the form $f(x, \theta)$ to the PMSE-best predictor $\mu(x)$ of Y_t given $X_t = x$, where, as before, the approximation is best in the sense of AMSE, where the weight is again $\mathrm{d}H$, the density of the X_t's.

The optimal point forecast based on the nonlinear model $\mathcal{N}$ given predictors X_t is thus given explicitly by

$$Y_t^* = f\big(X_t, \theta^*\big).$$

The advantage of using a nonlinear model $\mathcal{N}$ is that nonlinearity in the predictors can afford greater flexibility and thus, in principle, greater forecast accuracy. Provided the nonlinear model nests the linear model (i.e., $\mathcal{L} \subset \mathcal{N}$), it follows that

$$\min_{m \in \mathcal{N}} E\big[\big(Y_t - m(X_t)\big)^2\big] \leqslant \min_{m \in \mathcal{L}} E\big[\big(Y_t - m(X_t)\big)^2\big],$$

that is, the best PMSE for the nonlinear model is always at least as good as the best PMSE for the linear model. (The same relation also necessarily holds for AMSE.) A simple means of ensuring that $\mathcal{N}$ nests $\mathcal{L}$ is to include a linear component in f, for example, by specifying

$$f(x, \theta) = x'\alpha + g(x, \beta),$$

where g is some function nonlinear in the predictors.

Against the advantage of theoretically better forecast accuracy, using a nonlinear model has a number of potentially serious disadvantages relative to linear models: (1) the associated estimators can be much more difficult to compute; (2) nonlinear models can easily overfit the sample data, leading to inferior performance in practice; and (3) the resulting forecasts may appear more difficult to interpret. It follows that the more appealing nonlinear methods will be those that retain the advantage of flexibility but that mitigate or eliminate these disadvantages relative to linear models. We now discuss considerations involved in constructing forecasts with these properties.

3. Linear, nonlinear, and highly nonlinear approximation

When a parameterization is nonlinear in the parameters, there generally does not exist a closed form expression for the PMSE-optimal coefficient vector θ^*. One can nevertheless apply the plug-in principle in such cases to construct a potentially useful estimator $\hat{\theta}$ by solving the sample analog of the optimization problem (4) defining θ^*, which yields

$$\hat{\theta} \equiv \arg\min_{\theta \in \Theta} \frac{1}{n} \sum_{t=1}^{n} \big(Y_t - f(X_t, \theta)\big)^2.$$

The point forecast based on the nonlinear model $\mathcal{N}$ using $\hat{\theta}$ for an out-of-sample predictor vector X_{n+1}, is computed simply as

$$\hat{Y}_{n+1} = f\big(X_{n+1}, \hat{\theta}\big).$$

The challenge posed by attempting to use $\hat{\theta}$ is that its computation generally requires an iterative algorithm that may require considerable fine-tuning and that may or may not behave well, in that the algorithm may or may not converge, and, even with considerable effort, the algorithm may well converge to a local optimum instead of to the desired global optimum. These are the computational difficulties alluded to above.

As the advantage of flexibility arises entirely from nonlinearity in the predictors and the computational challenges arise entirely from nonlinearity in the parameters, it makes sense to restrict attention to parameterizations that are "series functions" of the form

$$f(x,\theta) = x'\alpha + \sum_{j=1}^{q} \psi_j(x)\beta_j, \tag{5}$$

where q is some finite integer and the "basis functions" ψ_j are nonlinear functions of x. This provides a parameterization nonlinear in x, but linear in the parameters $\theta \equiv (\alpha', \beta')'$, $\beta \equiv (\beta_1, \ldots, \beta_q)'$, thus delivering flexibility while simultaneously eliminating the computational challenges arising from nonlinearity in the parameters. The method of OLS can now deliver the desired sample estimator $\hat{\theta}$ for θ^*.

Restricting attention to parameterizations having the form (5) thus reduces the problem of choosing a forecasting model to the problem of jointly choosing the basis functions ψ_j and their number, q. With the problem framed in this way, an important next question is, "What choices of basis functions are available, and when should one prefer one choice to another?"

There is a vast range of possible choices of basis functions; below we mention some of the leading possibilities. Choosing among these depends not only on the properties of the basis functions, but also on one's prior knowledge about μ, and one's empirical knowledge about μ, that is, the data.

Certain broad requirements help narrow the field. First, given that our objective is to obtain as good an approximation to μ as possible, a necessary property for any choice of basis functions is that this choice should yield an increasingly better approximation to μ as q increases. Formally, this is the requirement that the span (the set of all linear combinations) of the basis functions $\{\psi_j, j = 1, 2, \ldots\}$ should be dense in the function space inhabited by μ. Here, this space is $\mathcal{M} \equiv L_2(\mathcal{R}^{k-1}, \mathrm{d}H)$, the separable Hilbert space of functions m on $\mathcal{R}^{k-1}$ for which $\int m(x)^2\,\mathrm{d}H(x)$ is finite. (Recall that x contains the constant unity, so there are only $k-1$ variables.) Second, given that we are fundamentally constrained by the amount of data available, it is also necessary that the basis functions should deliver a good approximation using as small a value for q as possible.

Although the denseness requirement narrows the field somewhat, there is still an overwhelming variety of choices for $\{\psi_j\}$ that have this property. Familiar examples are algebraic polynomials in x of degree dependent on j, and in particular the related special polynomials, such as Bernstein, Chebyshev, or Hermite, etc.; and trigonometric polynomials in x, that is, sines and cosines of linear combinations of x corresponding to pre-specified (multi-)frequencies, delivering Fourier series. Further, one can combine different families, as in Gallant's (1981) flexible Fourier form, which includes polynomials of first and second order, together with sine and cosine terms for a range of frequencies.

Important and powerful extensions of the algebraic polynomials are the classes of piecewise polynomials and splines [e.g., Wahba and Wold (1975), Wahba (1990)]. Well-known types of splines are linear splines, cubic splines, and B-splines.

The basis functions for the examples given so far are either orthogonal or can be made so with straightforward modifications. Orthogonality is not a necessary requirement, however. A particularly powerful class of basis functions that need not be orthogonal is the class of "wavelets", introduced by Daubechies (1988, 1992). These have the form $\psi_j(x) = \Psi(A_j(x))$, where Ψ is a "mother wavelet", a given function satisfying certain specific conditions, and $A_j(x)$ is an affine function of x that shifts and rescales x according to a specified dyadic schedule analogous to the frequencies of Fourier analysis. For a treatment of wavelets from an economics perspective, see Gencay, Selchuk and Whitcher (2001).

Recall that a vector space is *linear* if (among other things) for any two elements of the space f and g, all linear combinations $af + bg$ also belong to the space, where a and b are any real numbers. All of the basis functions mentioned so far define spaces of functions $g_q(x, \beta) \equiv \sum_{j=1}^{q} \psi_j(x)\beta_j$ that are linear in this sense, as taking a linear combination of two elements of this space gives

$$a\left[\sum_{j=1}^{q} \psi_j(x)\beta_j\right] + b\left[\sum_{j=1}^{q} \psi_j(x)\gamma_j\right] = \sum_{j=1}^{q} \psi_j(x)[a\beta_j + b\gamma_j],$$

which is again a linear combination of the first q of the ψ_j's.

Significantly, the second requirement mentioned above, namely that the basis should deliver a good approximation using as small a value for q as possible, suggests that we might obtain a better approximation by *not* restricting ourselves to the functions $g_q(x, \beta)$, which force the inclusion of the ψ_j's in a strict order (e.g., zero order polynomials first, followed by first order polynomials, followed by second order polynomials, and so on), but instead consider functions of the form

$$g_\Lambda(x, \beta) \equiv \sum_{j \in \Lambda} \psi_j(x)\beta_j,$$

where Λ is a set of natural numbers ("indexes") containing at most q elements, not necessarily the integers $1, \ldots, q$. The functions g_Λ are more flexible than the functions g_q, in that g_Λ admits g_q as a special case. The key idea is that by suitably choosing which basis functions to use in any given instance, one may obtain a better approximation for a given number of terms q.

The functions g_Λ define a *nonlinear* space of functions, in that linear combinations of the form $ag_\Lambda + bg_K$, where K also has q elements, generally have up to $2q$ terms, and are therefore not contained in the space of q-term linear combinations of the ψ_j's. Consequently, functions of the form g_Λ are called *nonlinear approximations* in the approximation theory literature. Note that the nonlinearity referred to here is the nonlinearity of the function spaces defined by the functions g_Λ. For given Λ, these functions are still linear in the parameters β_j, which preserves their appeal for us here.

Recent developments in the approximation theory literature have provided considerable insight into the question of which functions are better approximated using linear approximation (functions of the form g_q), and which functions are better approximated using nonlinear approximation (functions of the form g_Λ). The survey of DeVore (1998) is especially comprehensive and deep, providing a rich catalog of results permitting a comparison of these approaches. Given sufficient a priori knowledge about the function of interest, μ, DeVore's results may help one decide which approach to take.

To gain some of the flavor of the issues and results treated by DeVore (1998) that are relevant in the present context, consider the following approximation root mean squared errors:

$$\sigma_q(\mu, \psi) \equiv \inf_{\beta}\left[\int \left(\mu(x) - g_q(x, \beta)\right)^2 \mathrm{d}H(x)\right]^{1/2},$$

$$\sigma_\Lambda(\mu, \psi) \equiv \inf_{\Lambda,\beta}\left[\int \left(\mu(x) - g_\Lambda(x, \beta)\right)^2 \mathrm{d}H(x)\right]^{1/2}.$$

These are, for linear and nonlinear approximation respectively, the best possible approximation root mean squared errors (RMSEs) using $q\psi_j$'s. (For simplicity, we are ignoring the linear term $x'\alpha$ previously made explicit; alternatively, imagine we have absorbed it into μ.) DeVore devotes primary attention to one of the central issues of approximation theory, the "degree of approximation" question: "Given a positive real number a, for what functions μ does the degree of approximation (as measured here by the above approximation RMSE's) behave as $O(q^{-a})$?" Clearly, the larger is a, the more quickly the approximation improves with q.

In general, the answer to the degree of approximation question depends on the smoothness and dimensionality $(k - 1)$ of μ, quantified in precisely the right ways. For linear approximation, the smoothness conditions typically involve the existence of a number of derivatives of μ and the finiteness of their moments (e.g., second moments), such that more smoothness and smaller dimensionality yield quicker approximation. The answer also depends on the particular choice of the ψ_j's; suffice it to say that the details can be quite involved.

In the nonlinear case, familiar notions of smoothness in terms of derivatives generally no longer provide the necessary guidance. To describe the smoothness notion relevant in this context, suppose for simplicity that $\{\psi_j\}$ forms an orthonormal basis for the Hilbert space in which μ lives. Then the optimal coefficients β_j^* are given by

$$\beta_j^* = \int \psi_j(x)\mu(x)\,\mathrm{d}H(x).$$

As DeVore (1998, p. 135) states, "smoothness for [nonlinear] approximation should be viewed as *decay of the coefficients with respect to the basis* [i.e., the β_j^*'s]" (emphasis added). In particular, let $\tau = 1/(a+1/2)$. Then according to DeVore (1998, Theorem 4) $\sigma_\Lambda(\mu, \psi) = O(q^{-a})$ if and only if there exists a finite constant M such that $\#\{j\colon \beta_j^* > z\} \leqslant M^\tau z^{-\tau}$. For example, $\sigma_\Lambda(\mu, \psi) = O(q^{-1/2})$ if for some M we have $\#\{j\colon \beta_j^* > z\} \leqslant Mz^{-1}$.

An important and striking aspect of this view of smoothness is that it is *relative to the basis*. A function that is not at all smooth with respect to one basis may be quite smooth with respect to another. Another striking feature of results of this sort is that the dimensionality of μ no longer plays an explicit role, seemingly suggesting that nonlinear approximation may somehow hold in abeyance the "curse of dimensionality" (the inability to well approximate functions in high-dimensional spaces without inordinate amounts of data). A more precise interpretation of this situation seems to be that smoothness with respect to the basis also incorporates dimensionality, such that a given decay rate for the optimal coefficients is a stronger condition in higher dimensions.

In some cases, theory alone can inform us about the choice of basis functions. For example, it turns out, as DeVore (1998, p. 106) discusses, that with respect to nonlinear approximation, rational polynomials have approximation properties essentially equivalent to those of piecewise polynomials. In this sense, there is nothing to gain or lose in selecting one of these bases over another. In other cases, the helpfulness of the theory in choosing a basis depends on having quite specific knowledge about μ, for example, that it is very smooth (in the familiar sense) in some places and very rough in others or that it has singularities or discontinuities. For example, Dekel and Leviatan (2003) show that in this sense, wavelet approximations do not perform well in capturing singularities along curves, whereas nonlinear piecewise polynomial approximations do.

Usually, however, we economists have little prior knowledge about the familiar smoothness properties of μ, let alone their smoothness with respect to any given basis. As a practical matter, then, it may make sense to consider a collection of different bases, and let the data guide us to the best choice. Such a collection of bases is called a *library*. An example is the wavelet packet library proposed by Coifman and Wickerhauser (1992).

Alternatively, one can choose the ψ_j's from any suitable subset of the Hilbert space. Such a subset is called a *dictionary*; the idea is once again to let the data help decide which elements of the dictionary to select. Artificial neural networks (ANNs) are an example of a dictionary, generated by letting $\psi_j(x) = \Psi(x'\gamma_j)$ for a given "activation function" Ψ, such as the logistic cdf ($\Psi(z) = 1/(1 + \exp(-z))$), and with γ_j any element of $\mathcal{R}^k$. For a discussion of artificial neural networks from an econometric perspective, see Kuan and White (1994). Trippi and Turban (1992) contains a collection of papers applying ANNs to economics and finance.

Approximating a function μ using a library or dictionary is called *highly nonlinear approximation*, as not only is there the nonlinearity associated with choosing q basis functions, but there is the further choice of the basis itself or of the elements of the dictionary. Section 8 of DeVore's (1998) comprehensive survey is devoted to a discussion of the so far somewhat fragmentary degree of approximation results for approximations of this sort. Nevertheless, some powerful results are available. Specifically, for sufficiently rich dictionaries $\mathcal{D}$ (e.g., artificial neural networks as above), DeVore and Temlyakov (1996) show [see DeVore (1998, Theorem 7)] that for $a \geqslant \frac{1}{2}$ and sufficiently smooth functions μ

$$\sigma_q(\mu, \mathcal{D}) \leqslant C_a q^{-a},$$

where C_a is a constant quantifying the smoothness of μ relative to the dictionary, and, analogous to the case of nonlinear approximation, we define

$$\sigma_q(\mu, \mathcal{D}) \equiv \inf_{D,\beta}\left[\int \left(\mu(x) - g_D(x,\beta)\right)^2 \mathrm{d}H(x)\right]^{1/2},$$

$$g_D(x,\beta) \equiv \sum_{\psi_j \in D} \psi_j(x)\beta_j,$$

where D is a q element subset of $\mathcal{D}$. DeVore and Temlyakov's result generalizes an earlier result for $a = \frac{1}{2}$ of Maurey [see Pisier (1980)]. Jones (1992) provides a "greedy algorithm" and a "relaxed greedy algorithm" achieving $a = \frac{1}{2}$ for a specific dictionary and class of functions μ, and DeVore (1998) discusses further related algorithms.

The cases discussed so far by no means exhaust the possibilities. Among other notable choices for the ψ_j's relevant in economics are radial basis functions [Powell (1987), Lendasse et al. (2003)] and ridgelets [Candes (1998, 1999a, 1999b, 2003)].

Radial basis functions arise by taking

$$\psi_j(x) = \Psi\left(p_2(x,\gamma_j)\right),$$

where $p_2(x,\gamma_j)$ is a polynomial of (at most) degree 2 in x with coefficients γ_j, and Ψ is typically taken to be such that, with the indicated choice of p_2, (x,γ_j), $\Psi(p_2(x,\gamma_j))$ is proportional to a density function. Standard radial basis functions treat the γ_j's as free parameters, and restrict $p_2(x,\gamma_j)$ to have the form

$$p_2(x,\gamma_j) = -(x-\gamma_{1j})'\gamma_{2j}(x-\gamma_{1j})/2,$$

where $\gamma_j \equiv (\gamma_{1j}', \gamma_{2j}')'$, so that γ_{1j} acts as a centering vector, and γ_{2j} is a $k \times k$ symmetric positive semi-definite matrix acting to scale the departures of x from γ_{1j}. A common choice for Ψ is $\Psi = \exp$, which delivers $\Psi(p_2(x,\gamma_j))$ proportional to the multivariate normal density with mean γ_{1j} and with γ_{2j} a suitable generalized inverse of a given covariance matrix. Thus, standard radial basis functions have the form of a linear combination of multivariate densities, accommodating a mixture of densities as a special case. Treating the γ_j's as free parameters, we may view the radial basis functions as a dictionary, as defined above.

Candes's ridgelets can be thought of as a very carefully constructed special case of ANNs. Ridgelets arise by taking

$$\psi_j(x) = \gamma_{1j}^{-1/2}\Psi\left(\left[\tilde{x}'\gamma_{2j} - \gamma_{0j}\right]/\gamma_{1j}\right),$$

where $\tilde{x}$ denotes the vector of nonconstant elements of x (i.e., $x = (1, \tilde{x}')'$), γ_{0j} is real, $\gamma_{1j} > 0$, and γ_{2j} belongs to $\mathcal{S}^{k-2}$, the unit sphere in $\mathcal{R}^{k-1}$. The activation function Ψ is taken to belong to the space of rapidly decreasing functions (Schwartz space, a subset of C^{∞}) and to satisfy a specific admissibility property on its Fourier transform [see Candles (1999a, Definition 1)], essentially equivalent to the moment conditions

$$\int z^j \Psi(z)\,\mathrm{d}z = 0, \quad j = 0, \ldots, k/2 - 1.$$

This condition ensures that Ψ oscillates, has zero average value, zero average slope, etc. For example, $\Psi = D^h\phi$, the hth derivative of the standard normal density ϕ, is readily verified to be admissible with $h = k/2$.

The admissibility of the activation function has a number of concrete benefits, but the chief benefit for present purposes is that it leads to the explicit specification of a countable sequence $\{\gamma_j = (\gamma_{0j}, \gamma_{1j}, \gamma_{2j}')'\}$ such that any function f square integrable on a compact set has an *exact* representation of the form

$$f(x) \equiv \sum_{j=1}^{\infty} \psi_j(x)\beta_j^*.$$

The representing coefficients β_j^* are such that good approximations can be obtained using $g_q(x, \beta)$ or $g_\Lambda(x, \beta)$ as above. In this sense, the ridgelet dictionary that arises by letting the γ_j's be free parameters (as in the usual ANN approach) can be reduced to a countable subset that delivers a basis with appealing properties.

As Candes (1999b) shows, ridgelets turn out to be optimal for representing otherwise smooth multivariate functions that may exhibit linear singularities, achieving a rate of approximation of $O(q^{-a})$ with $a = s/(k-1)$, provided the sth derivatives of f exist and are square integrable. This is in sharp contrast to Fourier series or wavelets, which can be badly behaved in the presence of singularities. Candes (2003) provides an extensive discussion of the properties of ridgelet regression estimators, and, in particular, certain shrinkage estimators based on thresholding coefficients from a ridgelet regression. (By thresholding is meant setting to zero estimated coefficients whose magnitude does not exceed some pre-specified value.) In particular, Candes (2003) discusses the superiority in multivariate contexts of ridgelet methods to kernel smoothing and wavelet thresholding methods.

In DeVore's (1998) survey, Candes's papers, and the references cited there, the interested reader can find a wealth of further material describing the approximation properties of a wide variety of different choices for the ψ_j's. From a practical standpoint, however, these results do not yield hard and fast prescriptions about how to choose the ψ_j's, especially in the circumstances commonly faced by economists, where one may have little prior information about the smoothness of the function of interest. Nevertheless, certain helpful suggestions emerge. Specifically:

(i) nonlinear approximations are an appealing alternative to linear approximations;
(ii) using a library or dictionary of basis functions may prove useful;
(iii) ANNs, and ridgelets in particular, may prove useful.

These suggestions are simply things to try. In any given instance, the data must be the final arbiter of how well any particular approach works. In the next section, we provide a concrete example of how these suggestions may be put into practice and how they interact with other practical concerns.

4. Artificial neural networks

4.1. General considerations

In the previous section, we introduced artificial neural networks (ANNs) as an example of an approximation dictionary supporting highly nonlinear approximation. In this section, we consider ANNs in greater detail. Our attention is motivated not only by their flexibility and the fact that many powerful approximation methods can be viewed as special cases of ANNs (e.g., Fourier series, wavelets, and ridgelets), but also by two further reasons. First, ANNs have become increasingly popular in economic applications. Second, despite their increasing popularity, the application of ANNs in economics and other fields has often run into serious stumbling blocks, precisely reflecting the three key challenges to the use of nonlinear methods articulated at the outset. In this section we explore some further properties of ANNs that may help in mitigating or eliminating some of these obstacles, permitting both their more successful practical application and a more informed assessment of their relative usefulness.

Artificial neural networks comprise a family of flexible functional forms posited by cognitive scientists attempting to understand the behavior of biological neural systems. Kuan and White (1994) provide a discussion of their origins and an econometric perspective. Our focus here is on the ANNs introduced above, that is, the class of "single hidden layer feedforward networks", which have the functional form

$$f(x,\theta) = x'\alpha + \sum_{j=1}^{q} \Psi(x'\gamma_j)\beta_j, \tag{6}$$

where Ψ is a given activation function, and $\theta \equiv (\alpha', \beta', \gamma')'$, $\beta \equiv (\beta_1, \ldots, \beta_q)'$, $\gamma \equiv (\gamma_1', \ldots, \gamma_q')'$. $\Psi(x'\gamma_j)$ is called the "activation" of "hidden unit" j.

Except for the case of ridgelets, ANNs generally take the γ_j's to be free parameters, resulting in a parameterization nonlinear in the parameters, with all the attendant computational challenges that we would like to avoid. Indeed, these difficulties have been formalized by Jones (1997) and Vu (1998), who prove that optimizing such an ANN is an NP-hard problem. It turns out, however, that by suitably choosing the activation function Ψ, it is possible to retain the flexibility of ANNs without requiring the γ_j's to be free parameters and without necessarily imposing the ridgelet activation function or schedule of γ_j values, which can be somewhat cumbersome to implement in higher dimensions.

This possibility is a consequence of results of Stinchcombe and White (1998) ("SW"), as foreshadowed in earlier results of Bierens (1990). Taking advantage of these results leads to parametric models that are nonlinear in the predictors, with the attendant advantages of flexibility, and linear in the parameters, with the attendant advantages of computational convenience. These computational advantages create the possibility of mitigating the difficulties formalized by Jones (1997) and Vu (1998). We first take up the results of SW that create these opportunities and then describe a method for exploiting them for forecasting purposes. Subsequently, we perform some numerical experiments that shed light on the extent to which the resulting methods may succeed in avoiding the documented difficulties of nonlinearly parameterized ANNs.

4.2. Generically comprehensively revealing activation functions

In work proposing new specification tests with the property of consistency (that is, the property of having power against model misspecification of any form) Bierens (1990) proved a powerful and remarkable result. This result states essentially that for any random variable ε_t and random vector X_t, under general conditions $E(\varepsilon_t \mid X_t) \neq 0$ with nonzero probability implies $E(\exp(X_t'\gamma)\varepsilon_t) \neq 0$ for almost every $\gamma \in \Gamma$, where Γ is any nonempty compact set. Applying this result to the present context with $\varepsilon_t = Y_t - f(X_t, \theta^*)$, Bierens's result implies that if (with nonzero probability)

$$E\big(Y_t - f\big(X_t, \theta^*\big) \mid X_t\big) = \mu(X_t) - f\big(X_t, \theta^*\big) \neq 0,$$

then for almost every $\gamma \in \Gamma$ we have

$$E\big(\exp\big(X_t'\gamma\big)\big(Y_t - f\big(X_t, \theta^*\big)\big)\big) \neq 0.$$

That is, if the model $\mathcal{N}$ is misspecified, then the prediction error $\varepsilon_t = Y_t - f(X_t, \theta^*)$ resulting from the use of model $\mathcal{N}$ is correlated with $\exp(X_t'\gamma)$ for essentially any choice of γ. Bierens exploits this fact to construct a specification test based on a choice for γ that maximizes the sample correlation between $\exp(X_t'\gamma)$ and the sample prediction error $\hat{\varepsilon}_t = Y_t - f(X_t, \hat{\theta})$.

Stinchcombe and White (1998) show that Bierens's (1990) result holds more generally, with the exponential function replaced by any Ψ belonging to the class of *generically comprehensively revealing* (GCR) functions. These functions are "comprehensively revealing" in the sense that they can reveal arbitrary model misspecifications ($\mu(X_t) - f(X_t, \theta^*) \neq 0$ with nonzero probability); they are generic in the sense that almost any choice for γ will reveal the misspecification.

An important class of functions that SW demonstrate to be GCR is the class of non-polynomial real analytic functions (functions that are everywhere locally given by a convergent power series), such as the logistic cumulative distribution function (cdf) or the hyperbolic tangent function, tanh. Among other things, SW show how the GCR functions can be used to test for misspecification in ways that parallel Bierens's procedures for the regression context, but that also extend to specification testing beyond the regression context, such as testing for equality of distributions.

Here, we exploit SW's results for a different purpose, namely to obtain flexible parameterizations nonlinear in predictors and linear in parameters. To proceed, we represent a q hidden unit ANN more explicitly as

$$f_q\big(x, \theta_q^*\big) = x'\alpha_q^* + \sum_{j=1}^{q} \Psi\big(x'\gamma_j^*\big)\beta_{qj}^*,$$

where Ψ is GCR, and we let

$$\varepsilon_t = Y_t - f_q\big(x, \theta_q^*\big).$$

If, with nonzero probability, $\mu(X_t) - f_q(x, \theta_q^*) \neq 0$, then for almost every $\gamma \in \Gamma$ we have

$$E\big(\Psi\big(X_t'\gamma\big)\varepsilon_t\big) \neq 0.$$

As Γ is compact, we can pick γ_{q+1}^* such that

$$\big|\mathrm{corr}\big(\Psi\big(X_t'\gamma_{q+1}^*\big), \varepsilon_t\big)\big| \geqslant \big|\mathrm{corr}\big(\Psi\big(X_t'\gamma\big), \varepsilon_t\big)\big|$$

for all $\gamma \in \Gamma$, where $\mathrm{corr}(\cdot, \cdot)$ denotes the correlation of the indicated variables. Let Γ_m be a finite subset of Γ having m elements whose neighborhoods cover Γ. With Ψ chosen to be continuous, the continuity of the correlation operator then ensures that, with m sufficiently large, one can achieve correlations nearly as great as by optimizing over Γ by instead optimizing over Γ_m. Thus one can avoid full optimization over Γ at potentially small cost by instead picking $\gamma_{q+1}^* \in \Gamma_m$ such that

$$\big|\mathrm{corr}\big(\Psi\big(X_t'\gamma_{q+1}^*\big), \varepsilon_t\big)\big| \geqslant \big|\mathrm{corr}\big(\Psi\big(X_t'\gamma\big), \varepsilon_t\big)\big|$$

for all $\gamma \in \Gamma_m$. This suggests a process of adding hidden units in a stepwise manner, stopping when $|\mathrm{corr}(\Psi(X_t'\gamma_{q+1}^*), \varepsilon_t)|$ (or some other suitable measure of the predictive value of the marginal hidden unit) is sufficiently small.

5. QuickNet

We now propose a family of algorithms based on these considerations that can work well in practice, called "QuickNet". The algorithm requires specifying *a priori* a maximum number of hidden units, say $\bar{q}$, a GCR activation function Ψ, an integer m specifying the cardinality of Γ_m, and a method for choosing the subsets Γ_m.

In practice, initially choosing $\bar{q}$ to be on the order of 10 or 20 seems to work well; if the results indicate there is additional predictability not captured using $\bar{q}$ hidden units, this limit can always be relaxed. (For concreteness and simplicity, suppose for now that $\bar{q} < \infty$. More generally, one may take $\bar{q} = \bar{q}_n$, with $\bar{q}_n \to \infty$ as $n \to \infty$.) A common choice for Ψ is the logistic cdf, $\Psi(z) = 1/(1 + \exp(-z))$. Ridgelet activation functions are also an appealing option.

Choosing m to be 500–1000 often works well with Γ_m consisting of a range of values (chosen either deterministically or, especially with more than a few predictors, randomly) such that the norm of γ is neither too small nor too large. As we discuss in greater detail below, when the norm of γ is too small, $\Psi(X_t'\gamma)$ is approximately linear in X_t, whereas when the norm of γ is too large, $\Psi(X_t'\gamma)$ can become approximately constant in X_t, both situations to be avoided. This is true not only for the logistic cdf but also for many other nonlinear choices for Ψ. In any given instance, one can experiment with these choices to observe the sensitivity or robustness of the method to these choices.

Our approach also requires a method for selecting the appropriate degree of model complexity, so as to avoid overfitting, the second of the key challenges to the use of nonlinear models identified above. For concreteness, we first specify a prototypical member of the QuickNet family using cross-validated mean squared error (CVMSE) for this purpose. Below, we also briefly discuss possibilities other than CVMSE.

5.1. A prototype QuickNet algorithm

We now specify a prototype QuickNet algorithm. The specification of this section is generic, in that for succinctness we do not provide details on the construction of Γ_m or the computation of CVMSE. We provide further specifics on these aspects of the algorithm in Sections 5.2 and 5.3.

Our prototypical QuickNet algorithm is a form of relaxed greedy algorithm consisting of the following steps:

Step 0: Compute $\hat{\alpha}_0$ and $\hat{\varepsilon}_{0t}$ $(t = 1, \dots, n)$ by OLS: $\hat{\alpha}_0 = (X'X)^{-1}X'Y$, $\hat{\varepsilon}_{0t} = Y_t - X_t'\hat{\alpha}_0$.
Compute CVMSE(0) (cross-validated mean squared error for Step 0; details are provided below), and set $q = 1$.

Step 1a: Pick Γ_m, and find $\hat{\gamma}_q$ such that

$$\hat{\gamma}_q = \arg\max_{\gamma \in \Gamma_m} \left[\hat{r}\left(\Psi\left(X_t'\gamma\right), \hat{\varepsilon}_{q-1,t}\right)\right]^2,$$

where $\hat{r}$ denotes the sample correlation between the indicated random variables. To perform this maximization, one simply regresses $\hat{\varepsilon}_{q-1,t}$ on a constant and $\Psi(X_t'\gamma)$ for each $\gamma \in \Gamma_m$, and picks as $\hat{\gamma}_q$ the γ that yields the largest R^2.

Step 1b: Compute $\hat{\alpha}_q, \hat{\beta}_q \equiv (\hat{\beta}_{q1}, \dots, \hat{\beta}_{qq})'$ by OLS, regressing Y_t on X_t and $\Psi(X_t'\hat{\gamma}_j)$, $j = 1, \dots, q$, and compute $\hat{\varepsilon}_{qt}$ $(t = 1, \dots, n)$ as

$$\hat{\varepsilon}_{qt} = Y_t - X_t'\hat{\alpha}_q - \sum_{j=1}^{q} \Psi\left(X_t'\hat{\gamma}_j\right)\hat{\beta}_{qj}.$$

Compute CVMSE(q) and set $q = q + 1$. If $q > \bar{q}$, stop. Otherwise, return to Step 1a.

Step 2: Pick $\hat{q}$ such that

$$\hat{q} = \arg\min_{q \in \{1,\dots,\bar{q}\}} \text{CVMSE}(q),$$

and set the estimated parameters to be those associated with $\hat{q}$:

$$\hat{\theta}_{\hat{q}} \equiv \left(\hat{\alpha}_{\hat{q}}', \hat{\beta}_{\hat{q}}', \hat{\gamma}_1', \dots, \hat{\gamma}_{\hat{q}}'\right)'.$$

Step 3 (Optional): Perform nonlinear least squares for Y_t using the functional form

$$f_{\hat{q}}(x, \theta_{\hat{q}}) = x'\alpha + \sum_{j=1}^{\hat{q}} \Psi(x'\gamma_j)\beta_j,$$

starting the nonlinear iterations at $\hat{\theta}_{\hat{q}}$.

For convenience in what follows, we let $\hat{\theta}$ denote the parameter estimates obtained via this QuickNet algorithm (or any other members of the family, discussed below).

QuickNet's most obvious virtue is its computational simplicity. Steps 0–2 involve only OLS regression; this is essentially a consequence of exploiting the linearity of f_q in α and β. Although a potentially large number (m) of regressions are involved in Step 1a, these regressions only involve a single regressor plus a constant. These can be computed so quickly that this is not a significant concern. Moreover, the user has full control (through specification of m) over how intense a search is performed in Step 1a.

The only computational headache posed by using OLS in Steps 0–2 results from multicollinearity, but this can easily be avoided by taking proper care to select predictors X_t at the outset that vary sufficiently independently (little, if any, predictive power is lost in so doing), and by avoiding (either *ex ante* or *ex post*) any choice of γ in Step 1a that results in too little sample variation in $\Psi(X_t'\gamma)$. (See Section 5.2 below for more on this issue.) Consequently, execution of Steps 0–2 of QuickNet can be fast, justifying our name for the algorithm.

Above, we referred to QuickNet as a form of relaxed greedy algorithm. QuickNet is a greedy algorithm, because in Step 1a it searches for a single best additional term. The usual greedy algorithms add one term at a time, but specify full optimization over γ. In contrast, by restricting attention to Γ_m, QuickNet greatly simplifies computation, and by using a GCR activation function Ψ, QuickNet ensures that the risk of missing predictively useful nonlinearities is small. QuickNet is a relaxed greedy algorithm because it permits full adjustment of the estimated coefficients of all the previously included terms, permitting it to take full predictive advantage of these terms as the algorithm proceeds. In contrast, typical relaxed greedy algorithms permit only modest adjustment in the relative contributions of the existing and added terms.

The optional Step 3 involves an optimization nonlinear in parameters, so here one may seem to lose the computational simplicity motivating our algorithm design. In fact, however, Steps 0–2 set the stage for a relatively simple computational exercise in Step 3. A main problem in the brute-force nonlinear optimization of ANN models is, for given q, finding a good (near global optimum) value for θ, as the objective function is typically nonconvex in nasty ways. Further, the larger is q, the more difficult this becomes and the easier it is to get stuck at relatively poor local optima. Typically, the optimization bogs down fairly early on (with the best fits seen for relatively small values of q), preventing the model from taking advantage of its true flexibility. (Our example in Section 7 illustrates these issues.)

In contrast, $\hat{\theta}$ produced by Steps 0–2 of QuickNet typically delivers much better fit than estimates produced by brute-force nonlinear optimization, so that local optimization in the neighborhood of $\hat{\theta}$ produces a potentially useful refinement of $\hat{\theta}$. Moreover, the required computations are particularly simple, as optimization is done only with a fixed number $\hat{q}$ of hidden units, and the iterations of the nonlinear optimization can be computed as a sequence of OLS regressions. Whether or not the refinements of Step 3 are helpful can be assessed using the CVMSE. If CVMSE improves after Step 3, one can use the refined estimate; otherwise one can use the unrefined (Step 2) estimate.

5.2. Constructing Γ_m

The proper choice of Γ_m in Step 1a can make a significant difference in QuickNet's performance. The primary consideration in choosing Γ_m is to avoid choices that will result in candidate hidden unit activations that are collinear with previously included predictors, as such candidate hidden units will tend to be uncorrelated with the prediction errors, $\hat{\varepsilon}_{q-1,t}$ and therefore have little marginal predictive power. As previously included predictors will typically include the original X_t's, particular care should be taken to avoid choosing Γ_m so that it contains elements $\Psi(X_t'\gamma)$ that are either approximately constant or approximately proportional to $X_t'\gamma$.

To see what this entails in a simple setting, consider the case of logistic cdf activation function Ψ and a single predictor, $\widetilde{X}_t$, having mean zero. We denote a candidate nonlinear predictor as $\Psi(\gamma_1\widetilde{X}_t + \gamma_0)$. If γ_0 is chosen to be large in absolute value relative to $\gamma_1\widetilde{X}_t$, then $\Psi(\gamma_1\widetilde{X}_t + \gamma_0)$ behaves approximately as $\Psi(\gamma_0)$, that is, it is roughly constant. To avoid this, γ_0 can be chosen to be roughly the same order of magnitude as $\mathrm{sd}(\gamma_1\widetilde{X}_t)$, the standard deviation of $\gamma_1\widetilde{X}_t$. On the other hand, suppose γ_1 is chosen to be small relative to $\mathrm{sd}(\widetilde{X}_t)$. Then $\Psi(\gamma_1\widetilde{X}_t + \gamma_0)$ varies approximately proportionately to $\gamma_1\widetilde{X}_t + \gamma_0$. To avoid this, γ_1 should be chosen to be at least of the order of magnitude of $\mathrm{sd}(\widetilde{X}_t)$.

A simple way to ensure these properties is to pick γ_0 and γ_1 randomly, independently of each other and of $\widetilde{X}_t$. We can pick γ_1 to be positive, with a range spanning modest multiples of $\mathrm{sd}(\widetilde{X}_t)$ and pick γ_0 to have mean zero, with a variance that is roughly comparable to that of $\gamma_1\widetilde{X}_t$. The lack of nonnegative values for γ_1 is of no consequence here, given that Ψ is monotone. Randomly drawing m such choices for (γ_0, γ_1) thus delivers a set Γ_m that will be unlikely to contain elements that are either approximately constant or collinear with the included predictors. With these precautions, the elements of Γ_m are nonlinear functions of $\widetilde{X}_t$ and, as can be shown, are generically not linearly dependent on other functions of $\widetilde{X}_t$, such as previously included linear or nonlinear predictors. Choosing Γ_m in this way thus generates a plausibly useful collection of candidate nonlinear predictors.

In the multivariate case, similar considerations operate. Here, however, we replace $\gamma_1\widetilde{X}_t$ with $\gamma_1(\widetilde{X}_t'\gamma_2)$, where γ_2 is a direction vector, that is, a vector on $\mathcal{S}^{k-2}$, the unit sphere in $\mathcal{R}^{k-1}$, as in Candes's ridgelet parameterization. Now the magnitude of γ_0 should be comparable to $\mathrm{sd}(\gamma_1(\widetilde{X}_t'\gamma_2))$, and the magnitude of γ_1 should be chosen to be at least of the order of magnitude of $\mathrm{sd}(\widetilde{X}_t'\gamma_2)$. One can proceed by picking a direction γ_2 on the unit sphere (e.g., $\gamma_2 = \mathcal{Z}/(\mathcal{Z}'\mathcal{Z})^{1/2}$ is distributed uniformly on the unit sphere, provided $\mathcal{Z}$ is $(k-1)$-variate unit normal). Then chose γ_1 to be positive, with a range spanning modest multiples of $\mathrm{sd}(\widetilde{X}_t'\gamma_2)$ and pick γ_0 to have mean zero, with a variance that is roughly comparable to that of $\gamma_1(\widetilde{X}_t'\gamma_2)$. Drawing m such choices for $(\gamma_0, \gamma_1, \gamma_2')$ thus delivers a set Γ_m that will be unlikely to contain elements that are either approximately constant or collinear with the included predictors, just as in the univariate case.

These considerations are not specific to the logistic cdf activation Ψ, but operate generally. The key is to avoid choosing a Γ_m that contains elements that are either approximately constant or proportional to the included predictors. The strategies just described are broadly useful for this purpose and can be fine tuned for any particular choice of activation function.

5.3. Controlling overfit

The advantageous flexibility of nonlinear modeling is also responsible for the second key challenge noted above to the use nonlinear forecasting models, namely the danger of over-fitting the data. Our prototype QuickNet uses cross-validation to choose the meta-parameter q indexing model complexity, thereby attempting to control the tendency of such flexible models to overfit the sample data. This is a common method, with a long history in statistical and econometric applications. Numerous other members of the QuickNet family can be constructed by replacing CVMSE with alternate measures of model fit, such as AIC [Akaike (1970, 1973)], C_p [Mallows (1973)], BIC [Schwarz (1978), Hannan and Quinn (1979)], Minimum Description Length (MDL) [Rissanen (1978)], Generalized Cross-Validation (GCV) [Craven and Wahba (1979)], and others. We have specified CVMSE for concreteness and simplicity in our prototype, but, as results of Shao (1993, 1997) establish, the family members formed by using alternate model selection criteria in place of CVMSE have equivalent asymptotic properties under specific conditions, as discussed further below.

The simplest form of cross-validation is "delete 1" cross-validation [Allen (1974), Stone (1974, 1976)] which computes CVMSE as

$$\mathrm{CVMSE}_{(1)}(q) = \frac{1}{n}\sum_{t=1}^{n} \hat{\varepsilon}^2_{qt(-t)},$$

where $\hat{\varepsilon}_{qt(-t)}$ is the prediction error for observation t computed using estimators $\hat{\alpha}_{0(-t)}$ and $\hat{\beta}_{qj(-t)}$, $j = 1, \ldots, q$, obtained by omitting observation t from the sample, that is,

$$\hat{\varepsilon}_{qt(-t)} = Y_t - X_t'\hat{\alpha}_{0(-t)} - \sum_{j=1}^{q} \Psi\bigl(X_t'\hat{\gamma}_j\bigr)\hat{\beta}_{qj(-t)}.$$

Alternatively, one can calculate the "delete d" cross-validated mean squared error, $\mathrm{CVMSE}_{(d)}$ [Geisser (1975)]. For this, let S be a collection of N subsets s of $\{1, \ldots, n\}$

containing d elements. Let $\hat{\varepsilon}_{qt(-s)}$ be the prediction error for observation t computed using estimators $\hat{\alpha}_{0(-s)}$ and $\hat{\beta}_{qj(-s)}$, $j = 1, \ldots, q$, obtained by omitting observations in the set s from the estimation sample. Then $\text{CVMSE}_{(d)}$ is computed as

$$\text{CVMSE}_{(d)}(q) = \frac{1}{hN} \sum_{s \in S} \sum_{t \in s} \hat{\varepsilon}^2_{qt(-s)}.$$

Shao (1993, 1997) analyzes the model selection performance of these cross-validation measures and relates their performance to the other well-known model selection procedures in a context that accommodates cross-section but not time-series data. Shao (1993, 1997) gives general conditions establishing that given model selection procedures are either "consistent" or "asymptotically loss efficient". A consistent procedure is one that selects the best q term (now $q = q_n$) approximation with probability approaching one as n increases. An asymptotically loss efficient procedure is one that selects a model such that the ratio of the sample mean squared error of the selected q term model to that of the truly best q term model approaches one in probability. Consistency of selection is a stronger property than asymptotic loss efficiency.

The performance of the various procedures depends crucially on whether the model is misspecified (Shao's "Class 1") or correctly specified (Shao's "Class 2"). Given our focus on misspecified models, Class 1 is that directly relevant here, but the comparison with performance under Class 2 is nevertheless of interest. Put succinctly, Shao (1997) show that for Class 1 under general conditions, $\text{CVMSE}_{(1)}$ is consistent for model selection, as is $\text{CVMSE}_{(d)}$, provided $d/n \to 0$ [Shao (1997, Theorem 4; see also p. 234)]. These methods behave asymptotically equivalently to AIC, GCV, and Mallows' C_p. Further, for Class 1, $\text{CVMSE}_{(d)}$ is asymptotically loss efficient given $d/n \to 1$ and $q/(n-d) \to 0$ [Shao (1997, Theorem 5)]. With these weaker conditions on d, $\text{CVMSE}_{(d)}$ behaves asymptotically equivalently to BIC.

In contrast, for Class 2 (correctly specified models) in which the correct specification is not unique (e.g., there are terms whose optimal coefficients are zero), under Shao's conditions, $\text{CVMSE}_{(1)}$ and its equivalents (AIC, GCV, C_p) are asymptotically loss efficient but not consistent, as they tend to select more terms than necessary. In contrast, $\text{CVMSE}_{(d)}$ is consistent provided $d/n \to 1$ and $q/(n-d) \to 0$, as is BIC [Shao (1997, Theorem 5)]. The interested reader is referred to Shao (1993, 1997) and to the discussion following Shao (1997) for details and additional guidance and insight.

Given these properties, it may be useful as a practical procedure in cross-section applications to compute $\text{CVMSE}_{(d)}$ for a substantial range of values of d to identify an interval of values of d for which the model selected is relatively stable, and use that model for forecasting purposes.

In cross-section applications, the subsets of observations s used for cross-validation can be populated by selecting observations at random from the estimation data. In time series applications, however, adjacent observations are typically stochastically dependent, so random selection of observations is no longer appropriate. Instead, cross-validation observations should be obtained by removing blocks of contiguous observations in order to preserve the dependence structure of the data. A straightforward analog of $\text{CVMSE}_{(d)}$ is "h-block" cross-validation [Burman, Chow and Nolan (1994)], whose objective function CVMSE_h can be expressed as

$$\text{CVMSE}_h(q) = \frac{1}{n}\sum_{t=1}^{n}\hat{\varepsilon}^2_{qt(-t:h)},$$

where $\hat{\varepsilon}_{qt(-t:h)}$ is the prediction error for observation t computed using estimators $\hat{\alpha}_{0(-t:h)}$ and $\hat{\beta}_{qj(-t:h)}$, $j = 1, \ldots, q$, obtained by omitting a block of h observations on either side of observation t from the estimation sample, that is,

$$\hat{\varepsilon}_{qt(-t:h)} = Y_t - X_t'\hat{\alpha}_{0(-t:h)} - \sum_{j=1}^{q}\Psi\big(X_t'\hat{\gamma}_j\big)\hat{\beta}_{qj(-t:h)}.$$

Racine (2000) shows that with data dependence typical of economic time series, CVMSE_h is inconsistent for model selection in the sense of Shao (1993, 1997). An important contributor to this inconsistency, not present in the framework of Shao (1993, 1997), is the dependence between the observations of the omitted blocks and the remaining observations.

As an alternative, Racine (2000) introduces a provably consistent model selection method for Shao's Class 2 (correctly specified) case that he calls "hv-block" cross-validation. In this method, for given t one removes v "validation" observations on either side of that observation (a block of $n_v = 2v + 1$ observations) and computes the mean-squared error for this validation block using estimates obtained from a sample that omits not only the validation block, but also an additional block of h observations on either side of the validation block. Estimation for a given t is thus performed for a set of $n_e = n - 2h - 2v - 1$ observations. (The size of the estimation set is somewhat different for t near 1 or near n.)

One obtains CVMSE_{hv} by averaging the CVMSE for each validation block over all $n - 2v$ available validation blocks, indexed by $t = v + 1, \ldots, n - v$. With suitable choice of h [e.g., $h = \text{int}(n^{1/4})$, as suggested by Racine (2000)], this approach can be proven to induce sufficient independence between the validation block and the remaining observations to ensure consistent variable selection. Although Racine (2000) finds that $h = \text{int}(n^{1/4})$ appears to work well in practice, practical choice of h is still an interesting area warranting further research.

Mathematically, we can represent CVMSE_{hv} as

$$\text{CVMSE}_{hv}(q) = \frac{1}{n-2v}\sum_{t=v+1}^{n-v}\left\{\frac{1}{n_v}\sum_{\tau=t-v}^{t+v}\hat{\varepsilon}^2_{q\tau(-t:h,v)}\right\}.$$

(Note that a typo appears in Racine's article; the first summation above must begin at $v + 1$, not v.) Here $\hat{\varepsilon}_{q\tau(-t:h,v)}$ is the prediction error for observation τ computed using estimators $\hat{\alpha}_{0(-t:h,v)}$ and $\hat{\beta}_{qj(-t:h:v)}$, $j = 1, \ldots, q$, obtained by omitting a block of $h+v$

observations on either side of observation t from the estimation sample, that is,

$$\hat{\varepsilon}_{q\tau(-t:h,v)} = Y_\tau - X'_\tau \hat{\alpha}_{0(-t:h,v)} - \sum_{j=1}^{q} \Psi\big(X'_\tau \hat{\gamma}_j\big)\hat{\beta}_{qj(-t:h:v)}.$$

Racine shows that CVMSE_{hv} leads to consistent variable selection for Shao's Class 2 case by taking h to be sufficiently large (controlling dependence) and taking

$$v = \frac{n - \text{int}(n^\delta) - 2h - 1}{2},$$

where $\text{int}(n^\delta)$ denotes the integer part of n^δ, and δ is chosen such that $\ln(\bar{q})/\ln(n) < \delta < 1$. In some simulations, Racine observes good performance taking $h = \text{int}(n^\gamma)$ with $\gamma = 0.25$ and $\delta = 0.5$. Observe that analogous to the requirement $d/n \to 1$ in Shao's Class 2 case, Racine's choice analogously leads to $2v/n \to 1$.

Although Racine does not provide results for Shao's Class 1 (misspecified) case, it is quite plausible that for Class 1, asymptotic loss efficiency holds with the behavior for h and v as specified above, and that consistency of selection holds with h as above and with $v/n \to 0$, parallel to Shao's requirements for Class 1. In any case, the performance of Racine's hv-block bootstrap generally and in QuickNet in particular is an appealing topic for further investigation. Some evidence on this point emerges in our examples of Section 7.

Although hv-block cross-validation appears conceptually straightforward, one may have concerns about the computational effort involved, in that, as just described, on the order of n^2 calculations are required. Nevertheless, as Racine (1997) shows, there are computational shortcuts for block cross-validation of linear models that make this exercise quite feasible, reducing the computations to order nh^2, a very considerable savings. (In fact, this can be further reduced to order n.) For models nonlinear in the parameters the same shortcuts are not available, so not only are the required computations of order n^2, but the computational challenges posed by nonconvexities and nonconvergence are further exacerbated by a factor of approximately n. This provides another very strong motivation for working with models linear in the parameters. We comment further on the challenges posed by models nonlinear in the parameters when we discuss our empirical examples in Section 7.

The results described in this section are asymptotic results. For example, for Shao's results, $q = q_n$ may depend explicitly on n, with $q_n \to \infty$, provided $q_n/(n-d) \to 0$. In our discussion of previous sections, we have taken $q \leqslant \bar{q} < \infty$, but this has been simply for convenience. Letting $\bar{q} = \bar{q}_n$ such that $\bar{q}_n \to \infty$ with suitable restrictions on the rate at which $\bar{q}_n$ diverges, one can obtain formal results describing the asymptotic behavior of the resulting nonparametric estimators via the method of sieves. The interested reader is referred to Chen (2005) for an extensive survey of sieve methods.

Before concluding this section, we briefly discuss some potentially useful variants of the prototype algorithm specified above. One obvious possibility is to use CVMSE_{hv} to select the linear predictors in Step 0, and then to select more than one hidden unit term in each iteration of Step 1, replacing the search for the maximally correlated hidden unit term with a more extensive variable selection procedure based on CVMSE_{hv}.

By replacing CVMSE with AIC, C_p, GCV, or other consistent methods for controlling model complexity, one can easily generate other potentially appealing members of the QuickNet family, as noted above. It is also of interest to consider the use of more recently developed methods for automated model building, such as PcGets [Hendry and Krolzig (2001)] and RETINA [Perez-Amaral, Gallo and White (2003, 2005)]. Using either (or both) of these approaches in Step 1 results in methods that can select multiple hidden unit terms at each iteration of Step 1. In these members of the QuickNet family, there is no need for Step 2; one simply iterates Step 1 until no further hidden unit terms are selected.

Related to these QuickNet family members are methods that use multiple hypothesis testing to control the family-wise error rate [FWER, see Westfall and Young (1993)], the false discovery rate [FDR, Benjamini (1995) and Williams (2003)], the false discovery proportion [FDP, see Lehmann and Romano (2005)] in selecting linear predictors in Step 0 and multiple hidden unit terms at each iteration of Step 1. [In so doing, care must be taken to use specification-robust standard errors, such as those of Gonçalves and White (2005).] Again, Step 2 is unnecessary; the algorithm stops when no further hidden unit terms are selected.

6. Interpretational issues

The third challenge identified above to the use of nonlinear forecasts is the apparent difficulty of interpreting the resulting forecasts. This is perhaps an issue not so much of difficulty, but rather an issue more of familiarity. Linear models are familiar and comfortable to most practitioners, whereas nonlinear models are less so. Practitioners may thus feel comfortable interpreting linear forecasts, but somewhat adrift interpreting nonlinear forecasts.

The comfort many practitioners feel with interpreting linear forecasts is not necessarily well founded, however. Forecasts from a linear model are commonly interpreted on the basis of the estimated coefficients of the model, using a standard interpretation for these estimates, namely that any given coefficient estimate is the estimate of the *ceteris paribus* effect of that coefficient's associated variable, that is, the effect of that variable holding all other variables constant. The forecast is then the net result of all of the competing effects of the variables in the model.

Unfortunately, this interpretation has validity in only in highly specialized circumstances that are far removed from the context of most economic forecasting applications. Specifically, this interpretation can be justified essentially only in ideal circumstances where the predictors are error-free measures of variables causally related to the target variable, the linear model constitutes a correct specification of the causal relationship, the observations used for estimation have been generated in such a way that unobservable causal factors vary independently of the observable causal variables, and the forecaster (or some other agency) has, independently of the unobservable causal factors, *set* the values of the predictors that form the basis for the current forecast.

The familiar interpretation would fail if even one of these ideal conditions failed; however, in most economic forecasting contexts, none of these conditions hold. In almost all cases, the predictors are error-laden measurements of variables that may or may not be causally related to the target variable, so there is no necessary causal relationship pertinent to the forecasting exercise at hand. At most, there is a predictive relationship, embodied here by the conditional mean μ, and the model for this predictive relationship (either linear or nonlinear) is, as we have acknowledged above, typically misspecified. Moreover, the observations used for estimation have been generated outside the forecaster's (or any other sole agency's) control, as have the values of the predictors for the current forecast.

Faced with this reality, the familiar and comfortable interpretation thought to be available for linear forecasts cannot credibly be maintained. How, then, should one interpret forecasts, whether based on linear or nonlinear models? We proceed to give detailed answers to this question. *Ex post*, we hope the answers will appear to be obvious. Nevertheless, given the frequent objection to nonlinear models on the grounds that they are difficult to interpret, it appears to be worth some effort to show that there is nothing particularly difficult or mysterious about nonlinear forecasts: the interpretation of both linear and nonlinear forecasts is essentially similar. Further, our discussion highlights some important practical issues and methods that can be critical to the successful use of nonlinear models for forecasting.

6.1. *Interpreting approximation-based forecasts*

There are several layers available in the interpretation of our forecasts. The first and most direct interpretation is that developed in Sections 1 and 2 above: our forecasts are optimal approximations to the MSE-optimal prediction of the target variable given the predictors, namely the conditional mean. The approximation occurs on two levels. One is a functional approximation arising from the likely misspecification of the parameterized model. The other is a statistical approximation arising from our use of sample distributions instead of population distributions. This interpretation is *identical* for both linear and nonlinear models.

In the familiar, comfortable, and untenable interpretation for linear forecasts described above, the meaning of the estimated coefficients endows the forecast with its interpretation. Here the situation is precisely opposite: the interpretation of the forecast gives the estimated coefficients their meaning: the estimated coefficients are simply those that deliver the optimal approximation, whether linear or nonlinear.

6.2. *Explaining remarkable forecast outcomes*

It is, however, possible to go further and to explain *why* a forecast takes a particular value, in a manner parallel to the explanation afforded by the familiar linear interpretation when it validly applies. As we shall shortly see, this understanding obtains in a manner that is highly parallel for the linear and nonlinear cases, although the greater flexibility in the nonlinear case does lead to some additional nuances.

To explore this next layer of interpretation, we begin by identifying the circumstance to be explained. We first consider the circumstance that a forecast outcome is in some sense remarkable. For example, we may be interested answering the question, "Why is our forecast quite different than the simple expectation of our target variable?"

When put this way, the answer quickly becomes obvious. Nevertheless, it is helpful to consider this question in a little detail, from both the population and the sample point of view. This leads not only to useful insights but also to some important practical procedures. We begin with the population view for clarity and simplicity. The understanding obtained here then provides a basis for understanding the sample situation.

6.2.1. Population-based forecast explanation

Because our forecasts are generated by our parameterization, for the population setting we are interested in understanding how the difference

$$\delta^*(X_t) \equiv f(X_t, \theta^*) - \bar{\mu}$$

arises, where $\bar{\mu}$ is the unconditional mean of the target variable, $\bar{\mu} \equiv E(Y_t)$. If this difference is large or otherwise unusual, then there is some explaining to do and otherwise not.

We distinguish between values that, when viewed unconditionally, are unusual and values that are extreme. We provide a formal definition of these concepts below. For now, it suffices to work with the heuristic understanding that extreme values are particularly large magnitude values of either sign and that unusual values are not necessarily extreme, but (unconditionally) have low probability density. (Consider a bimodal density with well separated modes – values lying between the modes may be unusual although not extreme in the usual sense.) Extreme values may well be unusual, but are not necessarily so. For convenience, we call values that are either extreme or unusual "remarkable".

Put this way, the explanation for remarkable forecasts outcomes clearly lies in the conditioning. That is, what would otherwise be remarkable is no longer remarkable (indeed, is least remarkable in a precise sense), once one accounts for the conditioning. Two aspects of the conditioning are involved: the behavior of X_t (that is, the conditions underlying the conditioning) and the properties of $f^*(\cdot) \equiv f(\cdot, \theta^*)$ (the conditioning relationship and our approximation to it).

With regard to the properties of f^*, for present purposes it is more relevant to distinguish between parameterizations monotone or nonmonotone in the predictors than to distinguish between parameterizations linear or nonlinear in the predictors. We say that f^* is monotone if f^* is (weakly) monotone in each of its arguments (as is true if $f^*(X_t)$ is in fact linear in X_t); we say that f^* is nonmonotone if f^* is not monotone (either strongly or weakly) in at least one of its arguments.

If f^* is monotone, remarkable values of $\delta^*(X_t)$ must arise from remarkable values of X_t. The converse is not true, as remarkable values of different elements of X_t can cancel one another out and yield unremarkable values for $\delta^*(X_t)$.

If f^* is not monotone, then extreme values of $\delta^*(X_t)$ may or may not arise from extreme values of X_t. Values for $\delta^*(X_t)$ that are unusual but not extreme must arise from unusual values for X_t, but the converse is not true, as nonmonotonicities permit unusual values for X_t to nevertheless result in common values for $\delta^*(X_t)$.

From these considerations, it follows that insight into the genesis of a particular instance of $\delta^*(X_t)$ can be gained by comparing $\delta^*(X_t)$ to its distribution and X_t to its distribution, and observing whether one, both, or neither of these exhibits unconditionally extreme or unusual values.

There is thus a variety of distinct cases, with differing interpretations. As the monotonicity of f^* is either known a priori (as in the linear case) or in principle ascertainable given θ^* (or its estimate, as below), it is both practical and convenient to partition the cases according to whether or not f^* is monotone. We have the following straightforward taxonomy.

Explanatory taxonomy of prediction

Case I: *f^* monotone*

A. $\delta^*(X_t)$ not remarkable and X_t not remarkable:
Nothing remarkable to explain.

B. $\delta^*(X_t)$ not remarkable and X_t remarkable:
Remarkable values for X_t cancel out to produce an unremarkable forecast.

C. $\delta^*(X_t)$ remarkable and X_t not remarkable:
Ruled out.

D. $\delta^*(X_t)$ remarkable and X_t remarkable:
Remarkable forecast explained by remarkable values for predictors.

Case II: *f^* not monotone*

A. $\delta^*(X_t)$ not remarkable and X_t not remarkable:
Nothing remarkable to explain.

B. $\delta^*(X_t)$ not remarkable and X_t remarkable:
Either remarkable values for X_t cancel out to produce an unremarkable forecast, or (perhaps more likely) nonmonotonicities operate to produce an unremarkable forecast.

C.1 $\delta^*(X_t)$ unusual but not extreme and X_t not remarkable:
Ruled out.

C.2 $\delta^*(X_t)$ extreme and X_t not remarkable:
Extreme forecast explained by nonmonotonicities.

D.1 $\delta^*(X_t)$ unusual but not extreme and X_t unusual but not extreme:
Unusual forecast explained by unusual predictors.

D.2 $\delta^*(X_t)$ unusual but not extreme and X_t extreme:
Unusual forecast explained by nonmonotonicities.

D.3 $\delta^*(X_t)$ extreme and X_t unusual but not extreme:
Extreme forecast explained by nonmonotonicities.

D.4 $\delta^*(X_t)$ extreme and X_t extreme:
Extreme forecast explained by extreme predictors.

In assessing which interpretation applies, one first determines whether or not f^* is monotone and then assesses whether $\delta^*(X_t)$ is extreme or unusual relative to its unconditional distribution, and similarly for X_t. In the population setting this can be done using the respective probability density functions. In the sample setting, these densities are not available, so appropriate sample statistics must be brought to bear. We discuss some useful approaches below.

We also remind ourselves that when unusual values for X_t underlie a given forecast, then the approximation $f^*(X_t)$ to $\mu(X_t)$ is necessarily less accurate by construction. (Recall that AMSE weighs the approximation squared error by $\mathrm{d}H$, the joint density of X_t.) This affects interpretations I.B, I.D, II.B, and II.D.

6.2.2. Sample-based forecast explanation

In practice, we observe only a sample from the underlying population, not the population itself. Consequently, we replace the unknown population value θ^* with an estimator $\hat{\theta}$, and the circumstance to be explained is the difference

$$\hat{\delta}(X_{n+1}) \equiv f\big(X_{n+1}, \hat{\theta}\big) - \overline{Y}$$

between our point forecast $f(X_{n+1}, \hat{\theta})$ and the sample mean $\overline{Y} \equiv \frac{1}{n}\sum_{t=1}^{n} Y_t$, which provides a consistent estimator of the population mean $\bar{\mu}$. Note that the generic observation index t used for the predictors in our discussion of the population situation has now been replaced with the out-of-sample index $n+1$, to emphasize the out-of-sample nature of the forecast.

The taxonomy above remains identical, however, simply replacing population objects with their sample analogs, that is, by replacing f^* with $\hat{f}(\cdot) = f(\cdot, \hat{\theta})$, δ^* with $\hat{\delta}$, and the generic X_t with the out-of-sample X_{n+1}. With these replacements, we have the sample version of the Explanatory Taxonomy of Prediction. There is no need to state this explicitly.

In forecasting applications, one may be interested in explaining the outcomes of one or just a few predictions, or one may have a relatively large number of predictions (a hold-out sample) that one is potentially interested in explaining. In the former situation, the sample relevant for the explanation is the estimation sample; this is the only available basis for comparison in this case. In the latter situation, the hold-out sample is that relevant for comparison, as it is the behavior of the predictors in the hold-out sample that is responsible for the behavior of the forecast outcomes.

Application of our taxonomy thus requires practical methods for identifying extreme and unusual observations relative either to the estimation or to the hold-out sample. The issues are identical in either case, but for concreteness, it is convenient to think in terms of the hold-out sample in what follows.

One way to proceed is to make use of estimates of the unconditional densities of Y_t and X_t. As Y_t is univariate, there are many methods available to estimate this density effectively, both parametric and nonparametric. Typically X_t is multivariate, and it is more challenging to estimate this multivariate distribution without making strong assumptions. Li and Racine (2003) give a discussion of the issues involved and a particularly appealing practical approach to estimating the density of multivariate X_t.

Given density estimates, one can make the taxonomy operational by defining precisely what is meant by "extreme" and "unusual" in terms of these densities. For example, one may define "α-extreme" values as those lying outside the smallest connected region containing no more than probability mass $1-\alpha$. Similarly one may define α-unusual values as those lying in the largest region of the support containing no more than probability mass α.

Methods involving probability density estimates can be computationally intense, so it is also useful to have more "quick and dirty" methods available that identify extreme and unusual values according to specific criteria. For random scalars such as Y_t or $\hat{f}$, it is often sufficient to rank order the sample values and declare any values in the upper or lower $\alpha/2$ tails to be α-extreme. A quick and dirty way to identify extreme values of random vectors such as X_t is to construct a sample norm $Z_t = \|X_t\|$ such as

$$\|X_t\| = \left[(X_t - \overline{X})'\hat{\Sigma}^{-1}(X_t - \overline{X})\right]^{1/2},$$

where $\overline{X}$ is the sample mean of the X_t's and $\hat{\Sigma}$ is the sample covariance of the X_t's. The α-extreme values can be taken to be those that lie in the upper α tail of the sample distribution of the scalar Z_t.

Even more simply, one can examine the predictors individually, as remarkable values for the predictors individually are sufficient but not necessary for remarkable values for the predictors jointly. Thus, one can examine the standardized values of the individual predictors for extremes. Unusual values of the individual predictors can often be identified on the basis of the spacing between their order statistics, or, equivalently, on the average distance to a specified number of neighbors. This latter approach of computing the average distance to a specified number of neighbors may also work well in identifying unusual values of random vectors X_t.

An interesting and important phenomenon that can and does occur in practice is that nonlinear forecasts can be so remarkable as to be crazy. Swanson and White (1995) observed such behavior in their study of forecasts based on ANNs and applied an "insanity filter" to deal with such cases. Swanson and White's insanity filter labels forecasts as "insane" if they are sufficiently extreme and replaces insane forecasts with the unconditional mean. An alternative procedure is to replace insane forecasts with a forecast from a less flexible model, such as a linear forecast.

Our explanatory taxonomy explains insane forecasts as special cases of II.C.2, II.D.3 and II.D.4; nonmonotonicities are involved in the first two cases, and both nonmonotonicities and extreme values of the predictors can be involved in the last case.

Users of nonlinear forecasts should constantly be aware of the possibility of remarkable and, particularly, insane forecasts, and have methods ready for their detection and replacement, such as the insanity filter of Swanson and White (1995) or some variant.

6.3. Explaining adverse forecast outcomes

A third layer of interpretational issues impacting both linear and nonlinear forecasts concerns "reasons" and "reason codes". The application of sophisticated prediction models is increasing in a variety of consumer-oriented industries, such as consumer credit, mortgage lending, and insurance. In these applications, a broad array of regulations governs the use of such models. In particular, when prediction models are used to approve or deny applicants credit or other services or products, the applicant typically has a legal right to an explanation of the reason for the adverse decision. Usually these explanations take the form of one or more reasons, typically expressed in the form of "reason codes" that provide specific grounds for denial (e.g., "too many credit lines", "too many late payments", etc.).

In this context, concern about the difficulty of interpreting nonlinear forecasts translates into a concern about how to generate reasons and reason codes from such forecasts. Again, these concerns are perhaps due not so much to the difficulty of generating meaningful reason codes from nonlinear forecasts, but due rather to a lack of experience with such forecasts. In fact, there are a variety of straightforward methods for generating reasons and reason codes from nonlinear forecasting models. We now discuss briefly a straightforward approach for generating these from either linear or nonlinear forecasts. As the application areas for reasons and reason codes almost always involve cross-section or panel data, it should be understood that the approach described below is targeted specifically to such data. Analogous methods may be applicable to time-series data, but we leave their discussion aside here.

As in the previous section, we specify the circumstance to be explained, which is now an adverse forecast outcome. In our example, this is a rejection or denial of an application for a consumer service or product. For concreteness, consider an application for credit. Commonly in this context, approval or denial may be based on attaining a sufficient "credit score", which is often a prediction from a forecasting model based on admissible applicant characteristics. If the credit score is below a specified cut-off level, the application will be denied. Thus, the circumstance to be explained is a forecast outcome that lies below a given target threshold.

A sound conceptual basis for explaining a denial is to provide a reasonable alternative set of applicant characteristics that would have generated the opposite outcome, an approval. (For example, "had there not been so many late payments in the credit file, the application would have been approved".) The notion of reasonableness can be formally expressed in a satisfactory way in circumstances where the predictors take values in a metric space, so that there is a well-defined notion of distance between predictor values. Given this, reasonableness can be equated to distance in the metric (although some metrics may be more appropriate in a given context than others). The explanation for the adverse outcome can now be formally specified as the fact that the predictors (e.g., applicant attributes) differ from the closest set of predictor values that generates the favorable outcome.

This approach, while conceptually appealing, may present challenges in applications. One set of challenges arises from the fact that predictors are often categorical in practice, and it may or may not be easy to embed categorical predictors in a metric space. Another set of challenges arises from the fact that even when metrics can be applied, they can, if not wisely chosen, generate explanations that may invoke differences in every predictor. As the forecast may depend on potentially dozens of variables, the resultant explanation may be unsatisfying in the extreme.

The solution to these challenges is to apply a metric that is closely and carefully tied to the context of interest. When properly done, this makes it possible to generate a prioritized list of reasons for the adverse outcome (which can then be translated into prioritized reason codes) that is based on the univariate distance of specific relevant predictors from alternative values that generate favorable outcomes. To implement this approach, it suffices to suitably perturb each of the relevant predictors in turn and observe the behavior of the forecast outcome.

Clearly, this approach is equally applicable to linear or nonlinear forecasts. For continuous predictors, one increases or decreases each predictor until the outcome reaches the target threshold. For binary predictors, one "flips" the observed predictor to its complementary value and observes whether the forecast outcome exceeds the target threshold. For categorical predictors, one perturbs the observed category to each of its possible values and observes for which (if any) categories the outcome exceeds the target threshold.

If this process generates one or more perturbations that move the outcome past the target threshold, then these perturbations represent sufficient reasons for denial. We call these "sufficient perturbations" to indicate that if the predictor had been different in the specified way, then the score would have been sufficient for an approval. The sufficient perturbations can then be prioritized, and corresponding reasons and reason codes prioritized accordingly.

When this univariate perturbation approach fails to generate any sufficient perturbations, one can proceed to identify joint perturbations that can together move the forecast outcome past the target threshold. A variety of approaches can be specified, but we leave these aside so as not to stray too far from our primary focus here.

Whether one uses a univariate or joint perturbation approach, one must next prioritize the perturbations. Here the chosen metric plays a critical role, as this is what measures the closeness of the perturbation to the observed value for the individual. Specifying a metric may be relatively straightforward for continuous predictors, as here one can, for example, measure the number of (unconditional) standard deviations between the observed and sufficient perturbed values. One can then prioritize the perturbations in order of increasing distance in these univariate metrics.

A straightforward way to prioritize binary/categorical variables is in order of the closeness to the threshold delivered by the perturbation. Those perturbations that deliver scores closer to the threshold can then be assigned top priority. This makes sense, however, as long as perturbations that make the outcome closer to the threshold are in some sense "easier" or more accessible to the applicant. Here again the underlying metric plays a crucial role, and domain expertise must play a central role in specifying this.

Given that domain expertise is inevitably required for achieving sensible prioritizations (especially as between continuous and binary/categorical predictors), we do not delve into further detail here. Instead, we emphasize that this perturbation approach to the explanation of adverse forecast outcomes applies equally well to both linear and nonlinear forecasting models. Moreover, the considerations underlying prioritization of reasons are identical in either instance. Given these identities, there is no necessary interpretational basis with respect to reasons and reason codes for preferring linear over nonlinear forecasts.

7. Empirical examples

7.1. Estimating nonlinear forecasting models

In order to illustrate some of the ideas and methods discussed in the previous sections, we now present two empirical examples, one using real data and another using simulated data.

We first discuss a forecasting exercise in which the target variable to be predicted is the one day percentage return on the S&P 500 index. Thus,

$$Y_t = 100(P_t - P_{t-1})/P_{t-1},$$

where P_t is the closing index value on day t for the S&P 500. As predictor variables X_t, we choose three lags of Y_t, three lags of $|Y_t|$ (a measure of volatility), and three lags of the daily range expressed in percentage terms,

$$R_t = 100(Hi_t - Lo_t)/Lo_t,$$

where Hi_t is the maximum value of the index on day t and Lo_t is the minimum value of the index on day t. R_t thus provides another measure of market volatility. With these choices we have

$$X_t = \left(Y_{t-1}, Y_{t-2}, Y_{t-3}, |Y_{t-1}|, |Y_{t-2}|, |Y_{t-3}|, R_{t-1}, R_{t-2}, R_{t-3}\right)'.$$

We do not expect to be able to predict S&P 500 daily returns well, if at all, as standard theories of market efficiency imply that excess returns in this index should not be predictable using publicly available information, provided that, as is plausible for this index, transactions costs and nonsynchronous trading effects do not induce serial correlation in the log first differences of the price index and that time-variations in risk premia are small at the daily horizon [cf. Timmermann and Granger (2004)]. Indeed, concerted attempts to find evidence against this hypothesis have found none [see, e.g., Sullivan, Timmermann and White (1999)]. For simplicity, we do not adjust our daily returns for the risk free rate of return, so we will not formally address the efficient markets hypothesis here. Rather, our emphasis is on examining the relative behavior of the different nonlinear forecasting methods discussed above in a challenging environment.

Of course, any evidence of predictability found in the raw daily returns would certainly be interesting: even perfect predictions of variation in the risk free rate would result in extremely low prediction r-squares, as the daily risk free rate is on the order of 0.015% with miniscule variation over our sample compared to the variation in daily returns. Even if there is in fact no predictability in the data, examining the performance of various methods reveals their ability to capture patterns in the data. As predictability hinges on whether these patterns persist outside the estimation sample, applying our methods to this challenging example thus reveals the necessary capability of a given method to capture patterns, together with that method's ability to assess whether the patterns captured are "real" (present outside the estimation data) or not.

Our data set consists of daily S&P 500 index values for a period beginning on July 22, 1996 and ending on July 21, 2004. Data were obtained from http://finance.yahoo.com. We reserved the data from July 22, 2003 through July 21, 2004 for out-of-sample evaluation. Dropping the first four observations needed to construct the three required lags leaves 2008 observations in the data set, with $n = 1{,}755$ observations in the estimation sample and 253 observations in the evaluation hold-out sample.

For all of our experiments we use hv-block cross-validation, with $v = 672$ chosen proportional to $n^{1/2}$ and $h = 7 = \text{int}(n^{1/4})$, as recommended by Racine (2000). Our particular choice for v was made after a little experimentation showed stable model selection behavior. The choice for h is certainly adequate, given the lack of appreciable dependence exhibited by the data.

For our first experiment, we use a version of standard Newton–Raphson-based NLS to estimate the coefficients of ANN models for models with from zero to $\bar{q} = 50$ hidden units, using the logistic cdf activation function. We first fit a linear model (zero hidden units) and then add hidden units one at a time until 50 hidden units have been included. For a given number of hidden units, we select starting values for the hidden unit coefficients at random and from there perform Newton–Raphson iteration.

This first approach represents a naïve brute force approach to estimating the ANN parameter values, and, as the model is nonlinear in parameters, we experience (as expected) difficulties in obtaining convergence. Moreover, these become more frequent as more complex models are estimated. In fact, the frequency with which convergence problems arise is sufficient to encourage use of the following modest stratagem: for a given number of hidden units, if convergence is not achieved (as measured by a sufficiently small change in the value of the NLS objective function), then the hidden unit coefficients are frozen at the best values found by NLS and OLS is then applied to estimate the corresponding hidden-to-output coefficients (the β's). In fact, we find it helpful to apply this final step regardless of whether convergence is achieved by NLS. This is useful not only because one usually observes improvement in the objective function using this last step, but also because it facilitates a feasible computation of an approximation to the cross-validated MSE.

Although we touched on this issue only briefly above, it is now necessary to confront head-on the challenges for cross-validation posed by models nonlinear in the parameters. This challenge is that in order to compute exactly the cross-validated MSE associated with any given nonlinear model, one must compute the NLS parameter estimates obtained by holding out each required validation block of observations. There are roughly as many validation blocks as there are observations (thousands here). This multiplies by the number of validation blocks the difficulties presented by the convergence problems encountered in a single NLS optimization over the entire estimation data set. Even if this did not present a logistical quagmire (which it surely does), this also requires a huge increase in the required computations (a factor of approximately 1700 here). Some means of approximating the cross-validated MSE is thus required.

Here we adopt the expedient of viewing the hidden unit coefficients obtained by the initial NLS on the estimation set as identifying potentially useful predictive transforms of the underlying variables and hold these fixed in cross-validation. Thus we only need to re-compute the hidden-to-output coefficients by OLS for each validation block. As mentioned above, this can be done in a highly computationally efficient manner using Racine's (1997) feasible block cross-validation method. This might well result in overly optimistic cross-validated estimates of MSE, but without some such approximation, the exercise is not feasible. (The exercise avoiding such approximations might be feasible on a supercomputer, but, as we see shortly, this brute force NLS approach is dominated by QuickNet, so the effort is not likely justified.)

Table 1 reports a subset of the results for this first exercise. Here we report two summary measures of goodness of fit: mean squared error (MSE) and r-squared (R^2).

We report these measures for the estimation sample, the cross-validation sample (CV), and the hold-out sample (Hold-Out). For the estimation sample, R^2 is the standard multiple correlation coefficient. For the cross-validation sample, R^2 is computed as one minus the ratio of the cross-validated MSE to the estimation sample variance of the dependent variable. For the hold-out sample, R^2 is computed as one minus the ratio of the hold-out MSE to the hold-out sample variance of the dependent variable about the *estimation sample mean* of the dependent variable. Thus, we can observe negative values for the CV and Hold-Out R^2's. A positive value for the Hold-Out R^2 indicates that the out-of-sample predictive performance for the estimated model is better than that afforded by the simple constant prediction provided by the estimation sample mean of the dependent variable.

From Table 1 we see that, as expected, the estimation R^2 is never very large, ranging from a low of about 0.0089 to a high of about 0.0315. For the full experiment, the greatest estimation sample R^2 is about 0.0647, occurring with 50 hidden units (not shown). This apparently good performance is belied by the uniformly negative CV R^2's. Although the best CV R^2 or MSE (indicated by "*") identifies the model with the best Hold-Out R^2 (indicated by "^"), that is, the model with only linear predictors (zero hidden units), this model has a negative Hold-Out R^2, indicating that it does not even

Table 1
S&P 500: Naive nonlinear least squares – Logistic

Summary goodness of fit						
Hidden units	Estimation MSE	CV MSE	Hold-out MSE	Estimation R-squared	CV R-squared	Hold-out R-squared
0	1.67890	1.79932*	0.55548	0.00886	−0.06223	−0.03016^,*
1	1.67819	1.79965	0.56183	0.00928	−0.06242	−0.04194
2	1.67458	1.79955	0.57721	0.01141	−0.06236	−0.07046
3	1.67707	1.81529	0.55925	0.00994	−0.07166	−0.03715
4	1.65754	1.83507	0.58907	0.02147	−0.08333	−0.09245
5	1.64420	1.86859	0.57978	0.02935	−0.10312	−0.07522
6	1.67122	1.86478	0.55448	0.01340	−0.10087	−0.02831
7	1.66337	1.89032	0.56545	0.01803	−0.11595	−0.04865
8	1.66138	1.86556	0.59504	0.01921	−0.10134	−0.10353
9	1.65662	1.90687	0.56750	0.02202	−0.12572	−0.05245
10	1.66970	1.94597	0.56098	0.01429	−0.14880	−0.04037
11	1.64669	1.87287	0.58445	0.02788	−0.10565	−0.08390
12	1.65209	1.85557	0.55982	0.02469	−0.09544	−0.03822
13	1.64594	2.03215	0.56302	0.02832	−0.19968	−0.04415
14	1.64064	1.91624	0.58246	0.03145	−0.13125	−0.08020
15	1.64342	2.00411	0.57788	0.02981	−0.18313	−0.07170
16	1.65963	2.00244	0.57707	0.02024	−0.18214	−0.07021
17	1.65444	2.05466	0.58594	0.02330	−0.21297	−0.08665
18	1.64254	1.98832	0.60214	0.03033	−0.17381	−0.11670
19	1.65228	2.01295	0.59406	0.02458	−0.18835	−0.10172
20	1.64575	2.09084	0.60126	0.02843	−0.23432	−0.11506

perform as well as using the estimation sample mean as a predictor in the hold-out sample.

This unimpressive prediction performance is entirely expected, given our earlier discussion of the implications of the efficient market hypothesis, but what might not have been expected is the erratic behavior we see in the estimation sample MSEs. We see that as we consider increasingly flexible models, we do not observe increasingly better in-sample fits. Instead, the fit first improves for hidden units one and two, then worsens for hidden unit three, then at hidden units four and five improves dramatically, then worsens for hidden unit six, and so on, bouncing around here and there. Such behavior will not be surprising to those with prior ANN experience, but it can be disconcerting to those not previously inoculated.

The erratic behavior we have just observed is in fact a direct consequence of the challenging nonconvexity of the NLS objective function induced by the nonlinearity in parameters of the ANN model, coupled with our choice of a new set of random starting values for the coefficients at each hidden unit addition. This behavior directly reflects and illustrates the challenges posed by parameter nonlinearity pointed out earlier.

Table 2
S&P 500: Modified nonlinear least squares – Logistic

			Summary goodness of fit			
Hidden units	Estimation MSE	CV MSE	Hold-out MSE	Estimation R-squared	CV R-squared	Hold-out R-squared
0	1.67890	1.79932*	0.55548	0.00886	−0.06223	−0.03016^,*
1	1.67819	1.79965	0.56183	0.00928	−0.06242	−0.04194
2	1.67813	1.80647	0.56221	0.00932	−0.06645	−0.04264
3	1.67290	1.80611	0.58417	0.01241	−0.06623	−0.08338
4	1.67166	1.84150	0.58922	0.01314	−0.08713	−0.09274
5	1.67024	1.84690	0.59676	0.01398	−0.09032	−0.10673
6	1.67010	1.84711	0.59660	0.01406	−0.09044	−0.10642
7	1.66877	1.85188	0.59627	0.01484	−0.09326	−0.10582
8	1.66782	1.85215	0.59292	0.01541	−0.09341	−0.09961
9	1.66752	1.89321	0.59516	0.01558	−0.11766	−0.10375
10	1.66726	1.93842	0.59673	0.01573	−0.14434	−0.10666
11	1.66305	1.94770	0.59417	0.01822	−0.14982	−0.10193
12	1.65801	1.95322	0.58804	0.02119	−0.15308	−0.09056
13	1.65795	1.96126	0.58773	0.02123	−0.15783	−0.08998
14	1.65734	1.96638	0.58533	0.02159	−0.16085	−0.08552
15	1.65599	1.98448	0.58592	0.02239	−0.17153	−0.08662
16	1.65548	2.00899	0.58556	0.02269	−0.18601	−0.08595
17	1.65527	2.01352	0.58510	0.02281	−0.18868	−0.08509
18	1.65451	2.02145	0.58404	0.02326	−0.19336	−0.08313
19	1.65397	2.02584	0.58254	0.02358	−0.19595	−0.08035
20	1.65397	2.02583	0.58254	0.02358	−0.19595	−0.08036

This erratic estimation performance opens the possibility that the observed poor predictive performance could be due not to the inherent unpredictability of the target variable, but rather to the poor estimation job done by the brute force NLS approach. We next investigate the consequences of using a modified NLS that is designed to eliminate this erratic behavior. This modified NLS method picks initial values for the coefficients at each stage in a manner designed to yield increasingly better in-sample fits as flexibility increases. We simply use as initial values the final values found for the coefficients in the previous stage and select new initial coefficients at random only for the new hidden unit added at that stage; this implements a simple homotopy method.

We present the results of this next exercise in Table 2. Now we see that the in-sample MSE's behave as expected, decreasing nicely as flexibility increases. On the other hand, whereas our naïve brute force approach found a solution with only five hidden units delivering an estimation sample R^2 of 0.0293, this second approach requires 30 hidden units (not reported here) to achieve a comparable in-sample fit. Once again we have the best CV performance occurring with zero hidden units, corresponding to the best (but negative) out-of-sample R^2. Clearly, this modification to naïve brute force NLS does not resolve the question of whether the so far unimpressive results could be due to poor

Table 3
S&P 500: QuickNet – Logistic

Summary goodness of fit						
Hidden units	Estimation MSE	CV MSE	Hold-out MSE	Estimation R-squared	CV R-squared	Hold-out R-squared
0	1.67890	1.79932	0.55548	0.00886	−0.06223	−0.03016^
1	1.66180	1.79907	0.55916	0.01896	−0.06208	−0.03699
2	1.65123	1.78741	0.55726	0.02520	−0.05520	−0.03346
3	1.63153	1.76889	0.61121	0.03683	−0.04427	−0.13352
4	1.62336	1.76625	0.60269	0.04165	−0.04271	−0.11772
5	1.61769	1.77087	0.60690	0.04500	−0.04543	−0.12552
6	1.60716	1.76750	0.62050	0.05121	−0.04344	−0.15075
7	1.59857	1.75783	0.61638	0.05629	−0.03773	−0.14310
8	1.59297	1.76191	0.61259	0.05959	−0.04014	−0.13609
9	1.58653	1.75298	0.63545	0.06339	−0.03487	−0.17848
10	1.58100	1.75481	0.64401	0.06666	−0.03595	−0.19436
11	1.57871	1.75054*	0.64341	0.06801	−0.03343	−0.19323*
12	1.57364	1.75662	0.65497	0.07100	−0.03702	−0.21467
13	1.56924	1.76587	0.64614	0.07360	−0.04248	−0.19830
14	1.56483	1.76621	0.65012	0.07621	−0.04268	−0.20567
15	1.55869	1.76868	0.64660	0.07983	−0.04414	−0.19915
16	1.55063	1.78549	0.64260	0.08459	−0.05406	−0.19173
17	1.54289	1.78510	0.65037	0.08915	−0.05383	−0.20614
18	1.53846	1.78166	0.65182	0.09177	−0.05180	−0.20883
19	1.53587	1.80860	0.64796	0.09330	−0.06771	−0.20167
20	1.53230	1.81120	0.64651	0.09541	−0.06924	−0.19899

estimation performance, as the estimation performance of the naïve method is better, even if more erratic. Can QuickNet provide a solution?

Table 3 reports the results of applying QuickNet to our S&P 500 data, again with the logistic cdf activation function. At each iteration of Step 1, we selected the best of $m = 500$ candidate units and applied cross-validation using OLS, taking the hidden unit coefficients as given. Here we see much better performance in the CV and estimation samples than we saw in either of the two NLS approaches. The estimation sample MSEs decrease monotonically, as we should expect. Further, we see CV MSE first decreasing and then increasing as one would like, identifying an optimal complexity of eleven hidden units for the nonlinear model. The estimation sample R^2 for this CV-best model is 0.0634, much better than the value of 0.0293 found by the CV-best model in Table 1, and the CV MSE is now 1.751, much better than the corresponding best CV MSE of 1.800 found in Table 1.

Thus QuickNet does a much better job of fitting the data, in terms of both estimation and cross-validation measures. It is also much faster. Apart from the computation time required for cross-validation, which is comparable between the methods, QuickNet required 30.90 seconds to arrive at its solution, whereas naïve NLS required 600.30

seconds and modified NLS required 561.46 seconds respectively to obtain inferior solutions in terms of estimation and cross-validated fit.

Another interesting piece of evidence related to the flexibility of ANNs and the relative fitting capabilities of the different methods applied here is that QuickNet delivered a maximum estimation R^2 of 0.1727, compared to 0.0647 for naïve NLS and 0.0553 for modified NLS, with 50 hidden units (not shown) generating each of these values. Comparing these and other results, it is clear that QuickNet rapidly delivers much better sample fits for given degrees of model complexity, just as it was designed to do.

A serious difficulty remains, however: the CV-best model identified by QuickNet is not at all a good model for the hold-out data, performing quite poorly. It is thus important to warn that even with a principled attempt to avoid overfit via cross-validation, there is no guarantee that the CV-best model will perform well in real-world hold-out data. One possible explanation for this is that, even with cross-validation, the sheer flexibility of ANNs somehow makes them prone to over-fitting the data, viewed from the perspective of pure hold-out data.

Another strong possibility is that real world hold-out data can differ from the estimation (and thus cross-validation) data in important ways. If the relationship between the target variable and its predictors changes between the estimation and hold-out data, then even if we have found a good prediction model using the estimation data, there is no reason for that model to be useful on the hold-out data, where a different predictive relationship may hold. A possible response to handling such situations is to proceed recursively for each out-of-sample observation, refitting the model as each new observation becomes available. For simplicity, we leave aside an investigation of such methods here.

This example underscores the usefulness of an out-of-sample evaluation of predictive performance. Our results illustrate that it can be quite dangerous to simply trust that the predictive relationship of interest is sufficiently stable to permit building a model useful for even a modest post-sample time frame.

Below we investigate the behavior of our methods in a less ambiguous environment, using artificial data to ensure (1) that there is in fact a nonlinear relationship to be uncovered, and (2) that the predictive relationship in the hold-out data is identical to that in the estimation data. Before turning to these results, however, we examine two alternatives to the standard logistic ANN applied so far. The first alternative is a ridgelet ANN, and the second is a nonneural network method that uses the familiar algebraic polynomials. The purpose of these experiments is to compare the standard ANN approach with a promising but less familiar ANN method and to contrast the ANN approaches with a more familiar benchmark.

In Table 4, we present an experiment identical to that of Table 3, except that instead of using the standard logistic cdf activation function, we instead use the ridgelet activation function

$$\Psi(z) = D^5\phi(z) = \left(-z^5 + 10z^3 - 15z\right)\phi(z).$$

Table 4
S&P 500: QuickNet – Ridgelet

Summary goodness of fit						
Hidden units	Estimation MSE	CV MSE	Hold-out MSE	Estimation R-squared	CV R-squared	Hold-out R-squared
0	1.67890	1.79932	0.55548	0.00886	−0.06223	−0.03016^
1	1.66861	1.79555	0.56961	0.01494	−0.06000	−0.05636
2	1.66080	1.78798	0.59077	0.01955	−0.05553	−0.09561
3	1.65142	1.78114	0.59605	0.02509	−0.05150	−0.10540
4	1.63519	1.79177	0.59107	0.03467	−0.05777	−0.09617
5	1.62747	1.78463	0.60156	0.03922	−0.05356	−0.11561
6	1.61933	1.77995	0.61657	0.04403	−0.05079	−0.14346
7	1.60872	1.77598	0.64556	0.05029	−0.04845	−0.19723
8	1.59657	1.76742	0.67802	0.05747	−0.04339	−0.25742
9	1.58620	1.76409	0.70122	0.06358	−0.04143	−0.30045
10	1.57463	1.76207	0.72377	0.07042	−0.04023	−0.34226
⋮	⋮	⋮	⋮	⋮	⋮	⋮
36	1.35532	1.65232	0.87676	0.19989	0.02456	−0.62600
37	1.34989	1.65332	0.88115	0.20309	0.02396	−0.63414
38	1.34144	1.65063	0.88568	0.20808	0.02555	−0.64253
39	1.33741	1.64768*	0.88580	0.21046	0.02729	−0.64277*
40	1.33291	1.65941	0.88432	0.21312	0.02037	−0.64001
41	1.32711	1.65571	0.89149	0.21654	0.02255	−0.65331
42	1.32098	1.65407	0.89831	0.22016	0.02352	−0.66596
43	1.31413	1.66000	0.90193	0.22420	0.02002	−0.67268
44	1.30282	1.65042	0.91420	0.23088	0.02568	−0.69543
45	1.29695	1.65575	0.91205	0.23434	0.02253	−0.69144
46	1.29116	1.65312	0.91696	0.23776	0.02408	−0.70056
47	1.28461	1.65054	0.90577	0.24163	0.02560	−0.67980
48	1.27684	1.64873	0.92609	0.24622	0.02667	−0.71748
49	1.27043	1.65199	0.94510	0.25000	0.02475	−0.75273
50	1.26459	1.64845	0.95154	0.25345	0.02684	−0.76468

The choice of $h = 5$ is dictated by the fact that $k = 10$ for the present example. As this is a nonpolynomial analytic activation function, it is also GCR, so we may expect QuickNet to perform well in sample. We emphasize that we are simply performing QuickNet with a ridgelet activation function and are not implementing any estimation procedure specified by Candes. The results given here thus do not necessarily put ridgelets in their best light, but are nevertheless of interest as they do indicate what can be achieved with some fairly simple procedures.

Examining Table 4, we see results qualitatively similar to those for the logistic cdf activation function, but with the features noted there even more pronounced. Specifically, the estimation sample fit improves with additional complexity, but even more quickly, suggesting that the ridgelets are even more successful at fitting the estimation sample

Table 5
S&P 500: QuickNet – Polynomial

	Summary goodness of fit					
Hidden units	Estimation MSE	CV MSE	Hold-out MSE	Estimation R-squared	CV R-squared	Hold-out R-squared
0	1.67890	1.79932*	0.55548	0.00886	−0.06223	−0.03016^,*
1	1.65446	1.81835	0.56226	0.02329	−0.07346	−0.04274
2	1.64104	1.80630	0.56455	0.03121	−0.06635	−0.04698
3	1.62964	2.56943	0.56291	0.03794	−0.51686	−0.04394
4	1.62598	2.67543	0.56242	0.04011	−0.57944	−0.04304
5	1.62234	2.81905	0.56188	0.04225	−0.66422	−0.04203
6	1.61654	3.57609	0.56654	0.04568	−1.11114	−0.05068
7	1.60293	3.79118	0.56974	0.05371	−1.23812	−0.05661
8	1.59820	3.86937	0.56716	0.05650	−1.28428	−0.05183
9	1.59449	4.01195	0.56530	0.05870	−1.36845	−0.04837
10	1.58759	6.92957	0.56664	0.06277	−3.09087	−0.05086
11	1.58411	7.55240	0.56159	0.06482	−3.45855	−0.04150
12	1.58229	7.56162	0.56250	0.06590	−3.46400	−0.04318
13	1.57722	8.71949	0.56481	0.06889	−4.14755	−0.04747
14	1.57068	9.11945	0.56922	0.07275	−4.38366	−0.05565
15	1.56755	8.98026	0.57053	0.07460	−4.30149	−0.05807
16	1.56073	6.66135	0.57268	0.07862	−2.93253	−0.06206
17	1.55548	6.57781	0.56465	0.08172	−2.88321	−0.04717
18	1.55177	6.53618	0.56305	0.08392	−2.85863	−0.04420
19	1.54951	7.45435	0.56129	0.08525	−3.40067	−0.04094
20	1.54512	7.24081	0.57165	0.08784	−3.27461	−0.06015

data patterns. The estimation sample R^2 reaches a maximum of 0.2534 for 50 hidden units, an almost 50% increase over the best value for the logistic. The best CV performance occurs with 39 hidden units, with a CV R^2 that is actually positive (0.0273). As good as this performance is on the estimation and CV data, however, it is quite bad on the hold-out data. The Hold-out R^2 with 39 ridgelet units is -0.643, reinforcing our comments above about the possible mismatch between the estimation predictive relationship and the importance of hold-out sample evaluation.

In recent work, Hahn (1998) and Hirano and Imbens (2001) have suggested using algebraic polynomials for nonparametric estimation of certain conditional expectations arising in the estimation of causal effects. These polynomials thus represent a familiar and interesting benchmark against which to contrast our previous ANN results. In Table 5 we report the results of nonlinear approximation using algebraic polynomials, performed in a manner analogous to QuickNet. The estimation algorithm is identical, except that instead of randomly choosing m candidate hidden units as before, we now randomly choose m candidate monomials from which to construct polynomials.

For concreteness and to control erratic behavior that can result from the use of polynomials of too high a degree, we restrict ourselves to polynomials of degree less than or equal to 4. As before, we always include linear terms, so we randomly select candidate monomials of degree between 2 and 4. The candidates were chosen as follows. First, we randomly selected the degree of the candidate monomial such that degrees 2, 3, and 4 had equal (1/3) probabilities of selection. Let the randomly chosen degree be denoted d. Then we randomly selected d indexes with replacement from the set $\{1, \ldots, 9\}$ and constructed the candidate monomial by multiplying together the variables corresponding to the selected indexes.

The results of Table 5 are interesting in several respects. First, we see that although the estimation fits improve as additional terms are added, the improvement is nowhere near as rapid as it is for the ANN approaches. Even with 50 terms, the estimation R^2 only reaches 0.1422 (not shown). Most striking, however, is the extremely erratic behavior of the CV MSE. This bounces around, but generally trends up, reaching values as high as 41. As a consequence, the CV MSE ends up identifying the simple linear model as best, with its negative Hold-out R^2. The erratic behavior of the CV MSE is traceable to extreme variation in the distributions of the included monomials. (Standard deviations can range from 2 to 150; moreover, simple rescaling cannot cure the problem, as the associated regression coefficients essentially undo any rescaling.) This variation causes the OLS estimates, which are highly sensitive to leverage points, to vary wildly in the cross-validation exercise, creating large CV errors and effectively rendering CV MSE useless as an indicator of which polynomial model to select.

Our experiments so far have revealed some interesting properties of our methods, but because of the extremely challenging real-world forecasting environment to which they have been applied, we have not really been able to observe anything of their relative forecasting ability. To investigate the behavior of our methods in a more controlled environment, we now discuss a second set of experiments using artificial data in which we ensure (1) that there is in fact a nonlinear relationship to be uncovered, and (2) that the predictive relationship in the hold-out data is identical to that in the estimation data.

We achieve these goals by generating artificial estimation data according to the nonlinear relationship

$$Y_t^* = a\big(f_q\big(X_t, \theta_q^*\big) + 0.1\varepsilon_t\big),$$

with $q = 4$, where $X_t = (Y_{t-1}, Y_{t-2}, Y_{t-3}, |Y_{t-1}|, |Y_{t-2}|, |Y_{t-3}|, R_{t-1}, R_{t-2}, R_{t-3})'$, as in the original estimation data (note that X_t contains lags of the original Y_t and not lags of Y_t^*). In particular, we take Ψ to be the logistic cdf and set

$$f_q\big(x, \theta_q^*\big) = x'\alpha_q^* + \sum_{j=1}^{q} \Psi\big(x'\gamma_j^*\big)\beta_{qj}^*,$$

where $\varepsilon_t = Y_t - f_q(x, \theta_q^*)$, and with θ_q^* obtained by applying QuickNet (logistic) to the original estimation data with four hidden units. We choose a to ensure that Y_t^* exhibits the same unconditional standard deviation in the simulated data as it does in the actual data. The result is an artificial series of returns that contains an "amplified" nonlinear signal relative to the noise constituted by ε_t. We generate hold-out data according to the

Table 6
Artificial data: Ideal specification

Summary goodness of fit						
Hidden units	Estimation MSE	CV MSE	Hold-out MSE	Estimation R-squared	CV R-squared	Hold-out R-squared
0	1.30098	1.58077	0.99298	0.23196	0.06679	0.06664
1	1.12885	1.19004	0.83977	0.33359	0.29746	0.21065
2	0.81753	0.86963	0.67849	0.51737	0.48662	0.36225
3	0.66176	0.70360	0.63142	0.60933	0.58463	0.40649
4	0.43081	0.45147*	0.45279	0.74567	0.73348	0.57439^,*

same relationship using the actual X_t's, but now with ε_t generated as i.i.d. normal with mean zero and standard deviation equal to that of the errors in the estimation sample. The maximum possible hold-out sample R^2 turns out to be 0.574, which occurs when the model uses precisely the right set of coefficients for each of the four hidden units. The relationship is decidedly nonlinear, as using a linear predictor alone delivers a Hold-Out R^2 of only 0.0667. The results of applying the precisely right hidden units are presented in Table 6.

First we apply naïve NLS to these data, parallel to the results discussed of Table 1. Again we choose initial values for the coefficients at random. Given that the ideal hidden unit coefficients are located in a 40-dimensional space, there is little likelihood of stumbling upon these, so even though the model is in principle correctly specified for specifications with four or more hidden units, whatever results we obtain must be viewed as an approximation to an unknown nonlinear predictive relationship.

We report our naïve NLS results in Table 7. Here we again see the bouncing pattern of in-sample MSEs first seen in Table 1, but now the CV-best model containing eight hidden units also identifies a model that has locally superior hold-out sample performance. For the CV-best model, the estimation sample R^2 is 0.6228, the CV sample R^2 is 0.5405, and the Hold-Out R^2 is 0.3914. We also include in Table 7 the model that has the best Hold-Out R^2, which has 49 hidden units. For this model the Hold-Out R^2 is 0.4700; however, the CV sample R^2 is only 0.1750, so this even better model would not have appeared as a viable candidate. Despite this, these results are encouraging, in that now the ANN model identifies and delivers rather good predictive performance, both in and out of sample.

Table 8 displays the results using the modified NLS procedure parallel to Table 2. Now the estimation sample MSEs decline monotonically, but the CV MSEs never approach those seen in Table 7. The best CV R^2 is 0.4072, which corresponds to a Hold-Out R^2 of 0.286. The best Hold-Out R^2 of 0.3879 occurs with 41 hidden units, but again this would not have appeared as a viable candidate, as the corresponding CV R^2 is only 0.3251.

Table 7
Artificial data: Naive nonlinear least squares – Logistic

	Summary goodness of fit					
Hidden units	Estimation MSE	CV MSE	Hold-out MSE	Estimation R-squared	CV R-squared	Hold-out R-squared
0	1.30098	1.58077	0.99298	0.23196	0.06679	0.06664
1	1.30013	1.49201	0.99851	0.23247	0.11919	0.06144
2	1.25102	1.46083	0.93593	0.26146	0.13760	0.12026
3	1.25931	1.49946	0.93903	0.25657	0.11479	0.11735
4	1.14688	1.57175	0.92754	0.32294	0.07212	0.12815
5	1.24746	1.51200	0.93970	0.26356	0.10739	0.11672
6	1.23788	1.57817	0.96208	0.26922	0.06833	0.09569
7	1.10184	1.41418	0.86285	0.34953	0.16514	0.18895
8	0.63895	0.77829*	0.64743	0.62280	0.54054	0.39144*
9	1.07860	1.36222	0.83499	0.36325	0.19582	0.21514
10	1.17196	1.51568	0.89399	0.30814	0.10522	0.15968
11	1.01325	1.44063	0.73511	0.40183	0.14952	0.30902
12	1.04729	1.57122	0.89255	0.38174	0.07243	0.16104
13	1.16834	1.69258	0.92319	0.31027	0.00079	0.13224
14	0.97988	1.67652	0.85443	0.42153	0.01027	0.19687
15	1.17205	1.63191	0.83216	0.30808	0.03660	0.21780
16	1.02739	1.58299	0.77350	0.39348	0.06548	0.27294
17	1.07750	1.62341	0.84962	0.36390	0.04162	0.20140
18	0.97684	1.45189	0.72514	0.42333	0.14288	0.31840
19	1.01071	1.77567	0.75559	0.40333	−0.04827	0.28978
20	1.08027	2.20172	0.80205	0.36226	−0.29979	0.24610
⋮	⋮	⋮	⋮	⋮	⋮	⋮
49	0.72198	1.39742	0.56383	0.57378	0.17504	0.47002^

Next we examine the results obtained by QuickNet, parallel to the results of Table 3. In Table 9 we observe quite encouraging performance. The CV-best configuration has 33 hidden units, with a CV R^2 of 0.6484 and corresponding Hold-Out R^2 of 0.5430. This is quite close to the maximum possible value of 0.574 obtained by using precisely the right hidden units. Further, the true best hold-out performance has a Hold-Out R^2 of 0.5510 using 49 hidden units, not much different from that of the CV-best model. The corresponding CV R^2 is 0.6215, also not much different from that observed for the CV best model.

The required estimation time for QuickNet here is essentially identical to that reported above (about 31 seconds), but now naïve NLS takes 788.27 seconds and modified NLS requires 726.10 seconds.

In Table 10, we report the results of applying QuickNet with a ridgelet activation function. Given that the ridgelet basis is less smooth relative to our target function than the standard logistic ANN, which is ideally smooth in this sense, we should not expect

Table 8
Artificial data: Modified nonlinear least squares – Logistic

			Summary goodness of fit			
Hidden units	Estimation MSE	CV MSE	Hold-out MSE	Estimation R-squared	CV R-squared	Hold-out R-squared
0	1.30098	1.58077	0.99298	0.23196	0.06679	0.06664
1	1.30013	1.49201	0.99851	0.23247	0.11919	0.06144
2	1.30000	1.50625	1.00046	0.23255	0.11079	0.05961
3	0.91397	1.10375	0.84768	0.46044	0.34840	0.20321
4	0.86988	1.05591	0.80838	0.48647	0.37665	0.24016
5	0.85581	1.03175	0.80328	0.49478	0.39091	0.24495
6	0.85010	1.01461	0.80021	0.49815	0.40102	0.24783
7	0.84517	1.00845	0.79558	0.50105	0.40466	0.25219
8	0.83541	1.00419*	0.75910	0.50681	0.40718	0.28648*
9	0.80738	1.07768	0.75882	0.52336	0.36379	0.28674
10	0.79669	1.03882	0.73159	0.52967	0.38673	0.31233
11	0.79664	1.04495	0.73181	0.52971	0.38312	0.31213
12	0.79629	1.05454	0.72912	0.52991	0.37745	0.31466
13	0.79465	1.06053	0.72675	0.53088	0.37392	0.31688
14	0.78551	1.04599	0.71959	0.53628	0.38250	0.32361
15	0.78360	1.07676	0.72182	0.53740	0.36433	0.32152
16	0.76828	1.09929	0.70041	0.54645	0.35103	0.34165
17	0.76311	1.08872	0.70466	0.54950	0.35727	0.33765
18	0.76169	1.11237	0.70764	0.55034	0.34332	0.33484
19	0.76160	1.13083	0.70768	0.55039	0.33242	0.33481
20	0.76135	1.13034	0.70736	0.55054	0.33271	0.33511
⋮	⋮	⋮	⋮	⋮	⋮	⋮
41	0.68366	1.14326	0.65124	0.59640	0.32508	0.38786^

results as good as those seen in Table 9. Nevertheless, we observe quite good performance. The best CV MSE performance occurs with 50 hidden units, corresponding to a respectable hold-out R^2 of 0.471. Moreover, CV MSE appears to be trending downward, suggesting that additional terms could further improve performance.

Table 11 shows analogous results for the polynomial version of QuickNet. Again we see that additional polynomial terms do not improve in-sample fit as rapidly as do the ANN terms. We also again see the extremely erratic behavior of CV MSE, arising from precisely the same source as before, rendering CV MSE useless for polynomial model selection purposes. Interestingly, however, the hold-out R^2 of the better-performing models isn't bad, with a maximum value of 0.390. The challenge is that this model could never be identified using CV MSE.

We summarize these experiments with the following remarks. Compared to the familiar benchmark of algebraic polynomials, the use of ANNs appears to offer the ability to more quickly capture nonlinearities; and the alarmingly erratic behavior of

Table 9
Artificial data: QuickNet – Logistic

			Summary goodness of fit			
Hidden units	Estimation MSE	CV MSE	Hold-out MSE	Estimation R-squared	CV R-squared	Hold-out R-squared
0	1.30098	1.58077	0.99298	0.23196	0.06679	0.06664
1	1.21467	1.44012	0.93839	0.28292	0.14983	0.11795
2	1.00622	1.16190	0.86194	0.40598	0.31407	0.18982
3	0.87534	1.02132	0.81237	0.48324	0.39706	0.23641
4	0.82996	0.94456	0.71615	0.51004	0.44238	0.32685
5	0.79297	0.91595	0.67986	0.53187	0.45927	0.36096
6	0.76903	0.89458	0.67679	0.54600	0.47188	0.36384
7	0.72552	0.84374	0.62678	0.57169	0.50190	0.41085
8	0.68977	0.81835	0.58523	0.59280	0.51689	0.44991
9	0.66635	0.80670	0.55821	0.60662	0.52376	0.47530
10	0.63501	0.79596	0.55889	0.62512	0.53010	0.47466
⋮	⋮	⋮	⋮	⋮	⋮	⋮
29	0.49063	0.62450	0.49194	0.71036	0.63133	0.53759
30	0.47994	0.61135	0.49207	0.71667	0.63909	0.53747
31	0.47663	0.61293	0.48731	0.71862	0.63816	0.54195
32	0.47217	0.60931	0.48532	0.72125	0.64029	0.54382
33	0.46507	0.59559*	0.48624	0.72545	0.64840	0.54295*
34	0.46105	0.59797	0.48943	0.72782	0.64699	0.53995
35	0.45784	0.60633	0.48603	0.72971	0.64206	0.54315
36	0.45480	0.60412	0.48765	0.73151	0.64336	0.54163
37	0.45401	0.60424	0.48977	0.73198	0.64329	0.53964
⋮	⋮	⋮	⋮	⋮	⋮	⋮
49	0.43136	0.64107	0.47770	0.74535	0.62154	0.55098^

CV MSE for polynomials definitely serves as a cautionary note. In our controlled environment, QuickNet, either with logistic cdf or ridgelet activation function, performs well in rapidly extracting a reliable nonlinear predictive relationship. Naïve NLS is better than a simple linear forecast, as is modified NLS. The lackluster performance of the latter method does little to recommend it, however. Nor do the computational complexity, modest performance, and somewhat erratic behavior of naïve NLS support its routine use. The relatively good performance of QuickNet seen here suggests it is well worth application, further study, and refinement.

7.2. *Explaining forecast outcomes*

In this section we illustrate application of the explanatory taxonomy provided in Section 6.2. For conciseness, we restrict attention to examining the out-of-sample predictions made with the CV MSE-best nonlinear forecasting model corresponding to

Table 10
Artificial data: QuickNet – Ridgelet

Summary goodness of fit						
Hidden units	Estimation MSE	CV MSE	Hold-out MSE	Estimation R-squared	CV R-squared	Hold-out R-squared
0	1.30098	1.58077	0.99298	0.23196	0.06679	0.06664
1	1.22724	1.43273	0.87504	0.27550	0.15419	0.17750
2	1.17665	1.39998	0.83579	0.30537	0.17352	0.21439
3	1.09149	1.30517	0.75993	0.35564	0.22949	0.28570
4	0.98380	1.22154	0.75393	0.41922	0.27887	0.29134
5	0.88845	1.13625	0.73192	0.47550	0.32922	0.31203
6	0.85571	1.03044	0.71145	0.49483	0.39168	0.33126
7	0.83444	1.02006	0.69144	0.50739	0.39781	0.35008
8	0.81150	0.98440	0.64753	0.52093	0.41886	0.39135
9	0.78824	0.99417	0.67279	0.53467	0.41309	0.36761
10	0.77323	0.96053	0.70196	0.54352	0.43295	0.34018
⋮	⋮	⋮	⋮	⋮	⋮	⋮
27	0.56099	0.82982	0.55838	0.66882	0.51012	0.47515
28	0.55073	0.80588	0.53706	0.67488	0.52425	0.49518
29	0.54414	0.82178	0.51536	0.67877	0.51487	0.51559^
30	0.54103	0.81704	0.53229	0.68060	0.51766	0.49967
31	0.53545	0.80240	0.53970	0.68390	0.52630	0.49271
32	0.53222	0.80171	0.55080	0.68581	0.52671	0.48227
⋮	⋮	⋮	⋮	⋮	⋮	⋮
47	0.47173	0.75552	0.56503	0.72152	0.55398	0.46890
48	0.46773	0.74575	0.55972	0.72388	0.55975	0.47389
49	0.46531	0.73767	0.55892	0.72530	0.56452	0.47464
50	0.46239	0.73640*	0.56272	0.72703	0.56527	0.47107*

Table 9. This is an ANN with logistic cdf activation and 33 hidden units, achieving a hold-out R2 of 0.5493.

The first step in applying the taxonomy is to check whether the forecast function $\hat{f}$ is monotone or not. A simple way to check this is to examine the first partial derivatives of $\hat{f}$ with respect to the predictors, x, which we write $D\hat{f} = (D_1\hat{f}, \ldots, D_9\hat{f})$, $D_j\hat{f} \equiv \partial\hat{f}/\partial x_j$. If any of these derivatives change sign over the estimation or hold-out samples, then $\hat{f}$ is not monotone. Note that this is a necessary and not sufficient condition for monotonicity. In particular, if $\hat{f}$ is nonmonotone over regions not covered by the data, then this simple check will not signal nonmonotonicity. In such cases, further exploration of the forecast function may be required. In Table 12 we display summary statistics including the minimum and maximum values of the elements of $D\hat{f}$ over the hold-out sample. The nonmonotonicity is obvious from the differing signs of the maxima and minima. We are thus in Case II of the taxonomy.

Table 11
Artificial data: QuickNet – Polynomial

Summary goodness of fit						
Hidden units	Estimation MSE	CV MSE	Hold-out MSE	Estimation R-squared	CV R-squared	Hold-out R-squared
0	1.30098	1.58077	0.99298	0.23196	0.06679	0.06664
1	1.20939	1.42354*	0.96230	0.28604	0.15962	0.09547*
2	1.13967	1.54695	0.93570	0.32720	0.08676	0.12048
3	1.09208	2.26962	0.93592	0.35529	−0.33987	0.12027
4	1.03733	2.14800	0.89861	0.38761	−0.26807	0.15534
5	1.00583	4.26301	0.87986	0.40621	−1.51666	0.17297
6	0.98113	4.01405	0.86677	0.42079	−1.36969	0.18527
7	0.95294	3.34959	0.85683	0.43743	−0.97743	0.19461
8	0.93024	3.88817	0.86203	0.45083	−1.29538	0.18972
9	0.90701	4.35370	0.84558	0.46455	−1.57020	0.20519
10	0.89332	3.45478	0.84267	0.47263	−1.03953	0.20792
⋮	⋮	⋮	⋮	⋮	⋮	⋮
41	0.61881	15.22200	0.67752	0.63468	−7.98627	0.36316
42	0.61305	14.85660	0.67194	0.63809	−7.77057	0.36841
43	0.60894	15.82990	0.67470	0.64051	−8.34518	0.36581
44	0.60399	15.23310	0.67954	0.64344	−7.99283	0.36126
45	0.60117	13.93220	0.67664	0.64510	−7.22489	0.36399
46	0.59572	15.58510	0.66968	0.64832	−8.20064	0.37053
47	0.59303	15.63730	0.66592	0.64990	−8.23149	0.37407
48	0.58907	16.39490	0.65814	0.65224	−8.67874	0.38137
49	0.58607	15.33290	0.65483	0.65402	−8.05178	0.38448
50	0.58171	16.08150	0.64922	0.65659	−8.49372	0.38976^

Table 12
Hold-out sample: Summary statistics

Summary statistics for derivatives of prediction function									
	x_1	x_2	x_3	x_4	x_5	x_6	x_7	x_8	x_9
mean	−8.484	7.638	3.411	−7.371	−9.980	−8.375	0.538	−5.512	−12.267
sd	17.353	19.064	6.313	13.248	18.843	10.144	8.918	7.941	17.853
min	−155.752	−5.672	−6.355	−115.062	−168.269	−93.124	−9.563	−68.698	−156.821
max	3.785	166.042	51.985	2.084	4.331	0.219	70.775	3.177	2.722

Summary statistics for predictions and predictors										
	Prediction	x_1	x_2	x_3	x_4	x_5	x_6	x_7	x_8	x_9
mean	−0.111	0.046	0.048	0.043	0.580	0.582	0.586	1.009	1.010	1.013
sd	0.775	0.736	0.738	0.743	0.455	0.456	0.457	0.406	0.406	0.408
min	−2.658	−1.910	−1.910	−1.910	0.000	0.000	0.000	0.000	0.000	0.000
max	3.087	2.234	2.234	2.234	2.234	2.234	2.234	2.182	2.182	2.182

Table 13
Hold-out sample: Actual and standardized values of predictors

Order stat.	Prediction	x_1	x_2	x_3	x_4	x_5	x_6	x_7	x_8	x_9
253	3.087	−1.463	−0.577	−0.835	1.463	0.577	0.835	1.686	0.896	1.132
		−2.051	−0.847	−1.183	1.944	−0.010	0.545	1.668	−0.281	0.290
252	1.862	0.014	1.240	0.169	0.014	1.240	0.169	0.303	1.089	0.339
		−0.043	1.615	0.169	−1.243	1.444	−0.913	−1.738	0.193	−1.654
251	1.750	−0.815	−0.315	−1.043	0.815	0.315	1.043	1.093	0.523	1.583
		−1.170	−0.492	−1.463	0.517	−0.584	1.001	0.208	−1.198	1.397
2	−2.429	−0.077	0.167	0.766	0.077	0.167	0.766	1.008	1.965	0.786
		−0.167	0.161	0.973	−1.107	−0.909	0.394	−0.003	2.349	−0.559
1	−2.658	−0.762	−0.014	1.146	0.762	0.014	1.146	1.483	0.634	1.194
		−1.097	−0.084	1.484	0.400	−1.244	1.225	1.167	−0.925	0.444

Note: Actual values in first row, standardized values in second row.

The next step is to examine $\hat{\delta} = \hat{f} - \overline{Y}$ for remarkable values, that is, values that are either unusual or extreme. When one is considering a single out-of-sample prediction, the comparison must be done relative to the estimation data set. Here, however, we have a hold-out sample containing a relatively large number of observations, so we can conduct our examination relative to the hold-out data. For this, it is convenient to sort the hold-out observations in order of $\hat{\delta}$ (equivalently $\hat{f}$) and examine the distances between the order statistics. Large values for these distances identify potentially remarkable values. In this case we have that the largest values between order statistics occur only in the tail, so the only remarkable values are the extreme values. We are thus dealing with cases II.C.2, II.D.3, or II.D.4.

The taxonomy resolves the explanation once we determine whether the predictors are remarkable or not, and if remarkable in what way (unusual or extreme). The comparison data must be the estimation sample if there are only a few predictions, but given the relatively large hold-out sample here, we can assess the behavior of the predictors relative to the hold-out data. As mentioned in Section 6.2, a quick and dirty way to check for remarkable values is to consider each predictor separately. A check of the order statistic spacings for the individual predictors does not reveal unusual values in the hold-out data, so in Table 13 we present information bearing on whether or not the values of the predictors associated with the five most extreme $\hat{f}$'s are extreme. We provide both actual values and standardized values, in terms of (hold-out) standard deviations from the (hold-out) mean.

The largest and most extreme prediction ($\hat{f} = 3.0871$) has associated predictor values that are plausibly extreme: x_1 and x_4 are approximately two standard deviations from their hold-out sample means, and x_7 is at 1.67 standard deviations. This first example therefore is plausibly case II.D.4: an extreme forecast explained by extreme predictors. This classification is also plausible for examples 2 and 4, as predictors x_2,

x_7, and x_9 are moderately extreme for example 2 and predictor x_8 is extreme for example 4. On the other hand, the predictors for examples 3 and 5 do not appear to be particularly extreme. As we earlier found no evidence of unusual nonextreme predictors, these examples are plausibly classified as case II.C.2: extreme forecasts explained by nonmonotonicities.

It is worth emphasizing that the discussion of this section is not definitive, as we have illustrated our explanatory taxonomy using only the most easily applied tools. This is certainly relevant, as these tools are those most accessible to practitioners, and they afford a simple first cut at understanding particular outcomes. They are also helpful in identifying cases for which further analysis, and in particular application of more sophisticated tools, such as those involving multivariate density estimation, may be warranted.

8. Summary and concluding remarks

In this chapter, we have reviewed key aspects of forecasting using nonlinear models. In economics, any model, whether linear or nonlinear, is typically misspecified. Consequently, the resulting forecasts provide only an approximation to the best possible forecast. As we have seen, it is possible, at least in principle, to obtain superior approximations to the optimal forecast using a nonlinear approach. Against this possibility lie some potentially serious practical challenges. Primary among these are computational difficulties, the dangers of overfit, and potential difficulties of interpretation.

As we have seen, by focusing on models linear in the parameters and nonlinear in the predictors, it is possible to avoid the main computational difficulties and retain the benefits of the additional flexibility afforded by predictor nonlinearity. Further, use of nonlinear approximation, that is, using only the more important terms of a nonlinear series, can afford further advantages. There is a vast range of possible methods of this sort. Choice among these methods can be guided to only a modest degree by a priori knowledge. The remaining guidance must come from the data. Specifically, careful application of methods for controlling model complexity, such as Geisser's (1975) delete-*d* cross-validation for cross-section data or Racine's (2000) *hv*-block cross-validation for time-series data, is required in order to properly address the danger of overfit. A careful consideration of the interpretational issues shows that the difficulties there lie not so much with nonlinear models as with their relative unfamiliarity; as we have seen, the interpretational issues are either identical or highly parallel for linear and nonlinear approaches.

In our discussion here, we have paid particular attention to nonlinear models constructed using artificial neural networks (ANNs), using these to illustrate both the challenges to the use of nonlinear methods and effective solutions to these challenges. In particular, we propose QuickNet, an appealing family of algorithms for constructing nonlinear forecasts that retains the benefits of using a model nonlinear in the predictors while avoiding or mitigating the other challenges to the use of nonlinear forecasting models. In our limited example with artificial data, we saw some encouraging performance from QuickNet, both in terms of computational speed relative to more standard ANN methods and in terms of resulting forecasting performance relative to more familiar polynomial approximations. In our real-world data example, we also saw that building useful forecasting models can be quite challenging. There is no substitute for a thorough understanding of the strengths and weaknesses of the methods applied; nor can the importance of a thorough understanding of the domain being modeled be overemphasized.

Acknowledgements

The author is grateful for the comments and suggestions of the editors and three anonymous referees, which have led to substantial improvements over the initial draft. Any errors remain the author's responsibility.

References

Akaike, H. (1970). "Statistical predictor identification". Annals of the Institute of Statistical Mathematics 22, 203–217.

Akaike, H. (1973). "Information theory and an extension of the likelihood principle". In: Petrov, B.N., Csaki, F. (Eds.), Proceedings of the Second International Symposium of Information Theory. Akademiai Kiado, Budapest.

Allen, D. (1974). "The relationship between variable selection and data augmentation and a method for prediction". Technometrics 16, 125–127.

Benjamini, Y., Hochberg, Y. (1995). "Controlling the false discovery rate: A practical and powerful approach to multiple testing". Journal of the Royal Statistical Society, Series B 57, 289–300.

Burman, P., Chow, E., Nolan, D. (1994). "A cross validatory method for dependent data". Biometrika 81, 351–358.

Bierens, H. (1990). "A consistent conditional moment test of functional form". Econometrica 58, 1443–1458.

Candes, E. (1998). "Ridgelets: Theory and applications". Ph.D. Dissertation, Department of Statistics, Stanford University.

Candes, E. (1999a). "Harmonic analysis of neural networks". Applied and Computational Harmonic Analysis 6, 197–218.

Candes, E. (1999b). "On the representation of mutilated Sobolev functions". SIAM Journal of Mathematical Analysis 33, 2495–2509.

Candes, E. (2003). "Ridgelets: Estimating with ridge functions". Annals of Statistics 33, 1561–1599.

Chen, X. (2005). "Large sample sieve estimation of semi-nonparametric models". C.V. Starr Center Working Paper, New York University.

Coifman, R., Wickhauser, M. (1992). "Entropy based algorithms for best basis selection". IEEE Transactions on Information Theory 32, 712–718.

Craven, P., Wahba, G. (1979). "Smoothing noisy data with spline functions: Estimating the correct degree of smoothing by the method of generalized cross-validation". Numerical Mathematics 31, 377–403.

Daubechies, I. (1988). "Orthonormal bases of compactly supported wavelets". Communications in Pure and Applied Mathematics 41, 909–996.

Daubechies, I. (1992). Ten Lectures on Wavelets. SIAM, Philadelphia, PA.

Dekel, S., Leviatan, D. (2003). "Adaptive multivariate piecewise polynomial approximation". SPIE Proceedings 5207, 125–133.

DeVore, R. (1998). "Nonlinear approximation". Acta Numerica 7, 51–150.

DeVore, R., Temlyakov, V. (1996). "Some remarks on greedy algorithms". Advances in Computational Mathematics 5, 173–187.

Gallant, A.R. (1981). "On the bias in flexible functional forms and an essentially unbiased form: The Fourier flexible form". Journal of Econometrics 15, 211–245.

Geisser, S. (1975). "The predictive sample reuse method with applications". Journal of the American Statistical Association 70, 320–328.

Gencay, R., Selchuk, F., Whitcher, B. (2001). An Introduction to Wavelets and other Filtering Methods in Finance and Econometrics. Academic Press, New York.

Gonçalves, S., White, H. (2005). "Bootstrap standard error estimation for linear regressions". Journal of the American Statistical Association 100, 970–979.

Hahn, J. (1998). "On the role of the propensity score in efficient semiparametric estimation of average treatment effects". Econometrica 66, 315–331.

Hannan, E., Quinn, B. (1979). "The determination of the order of an autoregression". Journal of the Royal Statistical Society, Series B 41, 190–195.

Hendry, D.F., Krolzig, H.-M. (2001). Automatic Econometric Model Selection with PcGets. Timberlake Consultants Press, London.

Hirano, K., Imbens, G. (2001). "Estimation of causal effects using propensity score weighting: An application to right heart catheterization". Health Services & Outcomes Research 2, 259–278.

Jones, L.K. (1992). "A simple lemma on greedy approximation in Hilbert space and convergence rates for projection pursuit regression and neural network training". Annals of Statistics 20, 608–613.

Jones, L.K. (1997). "The computational intractability of training sigmoid neural networks". IEEE Transactions on Information Theory 43, 167–173.

Kim, T., White, H. (2003). "Estimation, inference, and specification testing for possibly misspecified quantile regressions". In: Fomby, T., Hill, R.C. (Eds.), Maximum Likelihood Estimation of Misspecified Models: Twenty Years Later. Elsevier, New York, pp. 107–132.

Koenker, R., Basset, G. (1978). "Regression quantiles". Econometrica 46, 33–50.

Kuan, C.-M., White, H. (1994). "Artificial neural networks: An econometric perspective". Econometric Reviews 13, 1–92.

Lehmann, E.L., Romano, J.P. (2005). "Generalizations of the familywise error rate". Annals of Statistics 33, 1138–1154.

Lendasse, A., Lee, J., de Bodt, E., Wertz, V., Verleysen, M. (2003). "Approximation by radial basis function networks: Application to option pricing". In: Lesage, C., Cottrell, M. (Eds.), Connectionist Approaches in Economics and Management Sciences. Kluwer, Amsterdam, pp. 203–214.

Li, Q., Racine, J. (2003). "Nonparametric estimation of distributions with categorical and continuous data". Journal of Multivariate Analysis 86, 266–292.

Mallows, C. (1973). "Some comments on C_p". Technometrics 15, 661–675.

Pérez-Amaral, T., Gallo, G.M., White, H. (2003). "A flexible tool for model building: The RElevant Transformation of the Inputs Network Approach (RETINA)". Oxford Bulletin of Economics and Statistics 65, 821–838.

Pérez-Amaral, T., Gallo, G.M., White, H. (2005). "A comparison of complementary automatic modeling methods: RETINA and PcGets". Econometric Theory 21, 262–277.

Pisier G. (1980). "Remarques sur un resultat non publie de B. Maurey". Seminaire d'Analyse Fonctionelle 1980–81, Ecole Polytechnique, Centre de Mathematiques, Palaiseau.

Powell, M. (1987). "Radial basis functions for multivariate interpolation: A review". In: Mason, J.C., Cox, M.G. (Eds.), Algorithms for Approximation. Oxford University Press, Oxford, pp. 143–167.

Racine, J. (1997). "Feasible cross-validatory model selection for general stationary processes". Journal of Applied Econometrics 12, 169–179.

Racine, J. (2000). "A consistent cross-validatory method for dependent data: *hv*-block cross-validation". Journal of Econometrics 99, 39–61.

Rissanen, J. (1978). "Modeling by shortest data description". Automatica 14, 465–471.
Schwarz, G. (1978). "Estimating the dimension of a model". Annals of Statistics 6, 461–464.
Shao, J. (1993). "Linear model selection by cross-validation". Journal of the American Statistical Association 88, 486–495.
Shao, J. (1997). "An asymptotic theory for linear model selection". Statistica Sinica 7, 221–264.
Stinchcombe, M., White, H. (1998). "Consistent specification testing with nuisance parameters present only under the alternative". Econometric Theory 14, 295–325.
Stone, M. (1974). "Cross-validatory choice and assessment of statistical predictions". Journal of the Royal Statistical Society, Series B 36, 111–147.
Stone, M. (1976). "An asymptotic equivalence of choice of model by cross-validation and Akaike's criterion". Journal of the Royal Statistical Society, Series B 39, 44–47.
Sullivan, R., Timmermann, A., White, H. (1999). "Data snooping, technical trading rule performance, and the bootstrap". Journal of Finance 54, 1647–1692.
Swanson, N., White, H. (1995). "A model selection approach to assessing the information in the term structure using linear models and artificial neural networks". Journal of Business and Economic Statistics 13, 265–276.
Teräsvirta, T. (2006). "Forecasting economic variables with nonlinear models". In: Elliott, G., Granger, C.W.J., Timmermann, A. (Eds.), Handbook of Economic Forecasting. Elsevier, Amsterdam. Chapter 8 in this volume.
Timmermann, A., Granger, C.W.J. (2004). "Efficient market hypothesis and forecasting". International Journal of Forecasting 20, 15–27.
Trippi, R., Turban, E. (1992). Neural Networks in Finance and Investing: Using Artificial Intelligence to Improve Real World Performance. McGraw-Hill, New York.
Vu, V.H. (1998). "On the infeasibility of training neural networks with small mean-squared error". IEEE Transactions on Information Theory 44, 2892–2900.
Wahba, G. (1990). Spline Models for Observational Data. SIAM, Philadelphia, PA.
Wahba, G., Wold, S. (1975). "A completely automatic French curve: Fitting spline functions by cross-validation". Communications in Statistics 4, 1–17.
Westfall, P., Young, S. (1993). Resampling-Based Multiple Testing: Examples and Methods for P-Value Adjustment. Wiley, New York.
White, H. (1980). "Using least squares to approximate unknown regression functions". International Economic Review 21, 149–170.
White, H. (1981). "Consequences and detection of misspecified nonlinear regression models". Journal of the American Statistical Association 76, 419–433.
White, H. (2001). Asymptotic Theory for Econometricians. Academic Press, San Diego, CA.
Williams, E. (2003). "Essays in multiple comparison testing". Ph.D. Dissertation, Department of Economics, University of California, San Diego, CA.

PART 3

FORECASTING WITH PARTICULAR DATA STRUCTURES

Chapter 10

FORECASTING WITH MANY PREDICTORS*

JAMES H. STOCK

Department of Economics, Harvard University and the National Bureau of Economic Research

MARK W. WATSON

Woodrow Wilson School and Department of Economics, Princeton University and the National Bureau of Economic Research

Contents

* We thank Jean Boivin, Serena Ng, Lucrezia Reichlin, Charles Whiteman and Jonathan Wright for helpful comments. This research was funded in part by NSF grant SBR-0214131.

Handbook of Economic Forecasting, Volume 1
Edited by Graham Elliott, Clive W.J. Granger and Allan Timmermann

DOI: 10.1016/S1574-0706(05)01010-4

Abstract

Historically, time series forecasts of economic variables have used only a handful of predictor variables, while forecasts based on a large number of predictors have been the province of judgmental forecasts and large structural econometric models. The past decade, however, has seen considerable progress in the development of time series forecasting methods that exploit many predictors, and this chapter surveys these methods. The first group of methods considered is forecast combination (forecast pooling), in which a single forecast is produced from a panel of many forecasts. The second group of methods is based on dynamic factor models, in which the comovements among a large number of economic variables are treated as arising from a small number of unobserved sources, or factors. In a dynamic factor model, estimates of the factors (which become increasingly precise as the number of series increases) can be used to forecast individual economic variables. The third group of methods is Bayesian model averaging, in which the forecasts from very many models, which differ in their constituent variables, are averaged based on the posterior probability assigned to each model. The chapter also discusses empirical Bayes methods, in which the hyperparameters of the priors are estimated. An empirical illustration applies these different methods to the problem of forecasting the growth rate of the U.S. index of industrial production with 130 predictor variables.

Keywords

forecast combining, dynamic factor models, principal components analysis, Bayesian model averaging, empirical Bayes forecasts, shrinkage forecasts

JEL classification: C32, C53, E17

1. Introduction

1.1. Many predictors: Opportunities and challenges

Academic work on macroeconomic modeling and economic forecasting historically has focused on models with only a handful of variables. In contrast, economists in business and government, whose job is to track the swings of the economy and to make forecasts that inform decision-makers in real time, have long examined a large number of variables. In the U.S., for example, literally thousands of potentially relevant time series are available on a monthly or quarterly basis. The fact that practitioners use many series when making their forecasts – despite the lack of academic guidance about how to proceed – suggests that these series have information content beyond that contained in the major macroeconomic aggregates. But if so, what are the best ways to extract this information and to use it for real-time forecasting?

This chapter surveys theoretical and empirical research on methods for forecasting economic time series variables using many predictors, where "many" can number from scores to hundreds or, perhaps, even more than one thousand. Improvements in computing and electronic data availability over the past ten years have finally made it practical to conduct research in this area, and the result has been the rapid development of a substantial body of theory and applications. This work already has had practical impact – economic indexes and forecasts based on many-predictor methods currently are being produced in real time both in the U.S. and in Europe – and research on promising new methods and applications continues.

Forecasting with many predictors provides the opportunity to exploit a much richer base of information than is conventionally used for time series forecasting. Another, less obvious (and less researched) opportunity is that using many predictors might provide some robustness against the structural instability that plagues low-dimensional forecasting. But these opportunities bring substantial challenges. Most notably, with many predictors come many parameters, which raises the specter of overwhelming the information in the data with estimation error. For example, suppose you have twenty years of monthly data on a series of interest, along with 100 predictors. A benchmark procedure might be using ordinary least squares (OLS) to estimate a regression with these 100 regressors. But this benchmark procedure is a poor choice. Formally, if the number of regressors is proportional to the sample size, the OLS forecasts are not first-order efficient, that is, they do not converge to the infeasible optimal forecast. Indeed, a forecaster who only used OLS would be driven to adopt a principle of parsimony so that his forecasts are not overwhelmed by estimation noise. Evidently, a key aspect of many-predictor forecasting is imposing enough structure so that estimation error is controlled (is asymptotically negligible) yet useful information is still extracted. Said differently, the challenge of many-predictor forecasting is to turn dimensionality from a curse into a blessing.

1.2. Coverage of this chapter

This chapter surveys methods for forecasting a single variable using many (n) predictors. Some of these methods extend techniques originally developed for the case that n is small. Small-n methods covered in other chapters in this Handbook are summarized only briefly before presenting their large-n extensions. We only consider linear forecasts, that is, forecasts that are linear in the predictors, because this has been the focus of almost all large-n research on economic forecasting to date.

We focus on methods that can exploit many predictors, where n is of the same order as the sample size. Consequently, we do not examine some methods that have been applied to moderately many variables, a score or so, but not more. In particular, we do not discuss vector autoregressive (VAR) models with moderately many variables [see Leeper, Sims and Zha (1996) for an application with $n = 18$]. Neither do we discuss complex model reduction/variable selection methods, such as is implemented in PC-GETS [see Hendry and Krolzig (1999) for an application with $n = 18$].

Much of the research on linear modeling when n is large has been undertaken by statisticians and biostatisticians, and is motivated by such diverse problems as predicting disease onset in individuals, modeling the effects of air pollution, and signal compression using wavelets. We survey these methodological developments as they pertain to economic forecasting, however we do not discuss empirical applications outside economics. Moreover, because our focus is on methods for forecasting, our discussion of empirical applications of large-n methods to macroeconomic problems other than forecasting is terse.

The chapter is organized by forecasting method. Section 2 establishes notation and reviews the pitfalls of standard forecasting methods when n is large. Section 3 focuses on forecast combining, also known as forecast pooling. Section 4 surveys dynamic factor models and forecasts based on principal components. Bayesian model averaging and Bayesian model selection are reviewed in Section 5, and empirical Bayes methods are surveyed in Section 6. Section 7 illustrates the use of these methods in an application to forecasting the Index of Industrial Production in the United States, and Section 8 concludes.

2. The forecasting environment and pitfalls of standard forecasting methods

This section presents the notation and assumptions used in this survey, then reviews some key shortcomings of the standard tools of OLS regression and information criterion model selection when there are many predictors.

2.1. Notation and assumptions

Let Y_t be the variable to be forecasted and let X_t be the $n \times 1$ vector of predictor variables. The h-step ahead value of the variable to be forecasted is denoted by Y^h_{t+h}.

For example, in Section 7 we consider forecasts of 3- and 6-month growth of the Index of Industrial Production. Let IP_t denote the value of the index in month t. Then the h-month growth of the index, at an annual rate of growth, is

$$Y_{t+h}^h = (1200/h)\ln(IP_{t+h}/IP_t), \tag{1}$$

where the factor $1200/h$ converts monthly decimal growth to annual percentage growth.

A forecast of Y_{t+h}^h at period t is denoted by $Y_{t+h|t}^h$, where the subscript $|t$ indicates that the forecast is made using data through date t. If there are multiple forecasts, as in forecast combining, the individual forecasts are denoted $Y_{i,t+h|t}^h$, where i runs over the m available forecasts.

The many-predictor literature has focused on the case that both X_t and Y_t are integrated of order zero (are $I(0)$). In practice this is implemented by suitable preliminary transformations arrived at by a combination of statistical pretests and expert judgment. In the case of IP, for example, unit root tests suggest that the logarithm of IP is well modeled as having a unit root, so that the appropriate transformation of IP is taking the log first difference (or, for h-step ahead forecasts, the hth difference of the logarithms, as in (1)).

Many of the formal theoretical results in the literature assume that X_t and Y_t have a stationary distribution, ruling out time variation. Unless stated otherwise, this assumption is maintained here, and we will highlight exceptions in which results admit some types of time variation. This limitation reflects a tension between the formal theoretical results and the hope that large-n forecasts might be robust to time variation.

Throughout, we assume that X_t has been standardized to have sample mean zero and sample variance one. This standardization is conventional in principal components analysis and matters mainly for that application, in which different forecasts would be produced were the predictors scaled using a different method, or were they left in their native units.

2.2. *Pitfalls of using standard forecasting methods when n is large*

OLS regression Consider the linear regression model

$$Y_{t+1} = \beta' X_t + \varepsilon_t, \tag{2}$$

where β is the $n \times 1$ coefficient vector and ε_t is an error term. Suppose for the moment that the regressors X_t have mean zero and are orthogonal with $T^{-1}\sum_{t=1}^T X_t X_t' = I_n$ (the $n \times n$ identity matrix), and that the regression error is i.i.d. $\mathrm{N}(0, \sigma_\varepsilon^2)$ and is independent of $\{X_t\}$. Then the OLS estimator of the ith coefficient, $\hat{\beta}_i$, is normally distributed, unbiased, has variance σ_ε^2/T, and is distributed independently of the other OLS coefficients. The forecast based on the OLS coefficients is $x'\hat{\beta}$, where x is the $n \times 1$ vector of values of the predictors used in the forecast. Assuming that x and $\hat{\beta}$ are independently distributed, conditional on x the forecast is distributed $\mathrm{N}(x'\beta, (x'x)\sigma_\varepsilon^2/T)$. Because $T^{-1}\sum_{t=1}^T X_t X_t' = I_n$, a typical value of X_t is $O_p(1)$, so a typical x vector used to construct a forecast will have norm of order $x'x = O_p(n)$. Thus let $x'x = cn$, where c is a constant. It follows that the forecast $x'\hat{\beta}$ is distributed $\mathrm{N}(x'\beta, c\sigma_\varepsilon^2(n/T))$. Thus, the forecast – which is unbiased under these assumptions – has a forecast error variance that is proportional to n/T. If n is small relative to T, then $E(x'\hat{\beta} - x'\beta)^2$ is small and OLS estimation error is negligible. If, however, n is large relative to T, then the contribution of OLS estimation error to the forecast does not vanish, no matter how large the sample size.

Although these calculations were done under the assumption of normal errors and strictly exogenous regressors, the general finding – that the contribution of OLS estimation error to the mean squared forecast error does not vanish as the sample size increases if n is proportional to T – holds more generally. Moreover, it is straightforward to devise examples in which the mean squared error of the OLS forecast using all the X's exceeds the mean squared error of using no X's at all; in other words, if n is large, using OLS can be (much) worse than simply forecasting Y by its unconditional mean.

These observations do not doom the quest for using information in many predictors to improve upon low-dimensional models; they simply point out that forecasts should not be made using the OLS estimator $\hat{\beta}$ when n is large. As Stein (1955) pointed out, under quadratic risk $(E[(\hat{\beta} - \beta)'(\hat{\beta} - \beta)])$, the OLS estimator is not admissible. James and Stein (1960) provided a shrinkage estimator that dominates the OLS estimator. Efron and Morris (1973) showed this estimator to be related to empirical Bayes estimators, an approach surveyed in Section 6 below.

Information criteria Reliance on information criteria, such as the Akaike information criterion (AIC) or Bayes information criterion (BIC), to select regressors poses two difficulties when n is large. The first is practical: when n is large, the number of models to evaluate is too large to enumerate, so finding the model that minimizes an information criterion is not computationally straightforward (however the methods discussed in Section 5 can be used). The second is substantive: the asymptotic theory of information criteria generally assumes that the number of models is fixed or grows at a very slow rate [e.g., Hannan and Deistler (1988)]. When n is of the same order as the sample size, as in the applications of interest, using model selection criteria can reduce the forecast error variance, relative to OLS, but in theory the methods described in the following sections are able to reduce this forecast error variance further. In fact, under certain assumptions those forecasts (unlike ones based on information criteria) can achieve first-order optimality, that is, they are as efficient as the infeasible forecasts based on the unknown parameter vector β.

3. Forecast combination

Forecast combination, also known as forecast pooling, is the combination of two or more individual forecasts from a panel of forecasts to produce a single, pooled forecast. The theory of combining forecasts was originally developed by Bates and Granger

(1969) for pooling forecasts from separate forecasters, whose forecasts may or may not be based on statistical models. In the context of forecasting using many predictors, the n individual forecasts comprising the panel are model-based forecasts based on n individual forecasting models, where each model uses a different predictor or set of predictors.

This section begins with a brief review of the forecast combination framework; for a more detailed treatment, see Chapter 4 in this Handbook by Timmermann. We then turn to various schemes for evaluating the combining weights that are appropriate when n – here, the number of forecasts to be combined – is large. The section concludes with a discussion of the main empirical findings in the literature.

3.1. Forecast combining setup and notation

Let $\{Y^h_{i,t+h|t}, \ i = 1, \ldots, n\}$ denote the panel of n forecasts. We focus on the case in which the n forecasts are based on the n individual predictors. For example, in the empirical work, $Y^h_{i,t+h|t}$ is the forecast of Y^h_{t+h} constructed using an autoregressive distributed lag (ADL) model involving lagged values of the ith element of X_t, although nothing in this subsection requires the individual forecast to have this structure.

We consider linear forecast combination, so that the pooled forecast is

$$Y^h_{t+h|t} = w_0 + \sum_{i=1}^{n} w_{it} Y^h_{i,t+h|t}, \tag{3}$$

where w_{it} is the weight on the ith forecast in period t.

As shown by Bates and Granger (1969), the weights in (3) that minimize the means squared forecast error are those given by the population projection of Y^h_{t+h} onto a constant and the individual forecasts. Often the constant is omitted, and in this case the constraint $\sum_{i=1}^{n} w_{it} = 1$ is imposed so that $Y^h_{t+h|t}$ is unbiased when each of the constituent forecasts is unbiased. As long as no one forecast is generated by the "true" model, the optimal combination forecast places weight on multiple forecasts. The minimum MSFE combining weights will be time-varying if the covariance matrices of $(Y^h_{t+h|t}, \{Y^h_{i,t+h|t}\})$ change over time.

In practice, these optimal weights are infeasible because these covariance matrices are unknown. Granger and Ramanathan (1984) suggested estimating the combining weights by OLS (or by restricted least squares if the constraints $w_{0t} = 0$ and $\sum_{i=1}^{n} w_{it} = 1$ are imposed). When n is large, however, one would expect regression estimates of the combining weights to perform poorly, simply because estimating a large number of parameters can introduce considerable sampling uncertainty. In fact, if n is proportional to the sample size, the OLS estimators are not consistent and combining using the OLS estimators does not achieve forecasts that are asymptotically first-order optimal. As a result, research on combining with large n has focused on methods which impose additional structure on the combining weights.

Forecast combining and structural shifts Compared with research on combination forecasting in a stationary environment, there has been little theoretical work on forecast combination when the individual models are nonstationary in the sense that they exhibit unstable parameters. One notable contribution is Hendry and Clements (2002), who examine simple mean combination forecasts when the individual models omit relevant variables and these variables are subject to out-of-sample mean shifts, which in turn induce intercept shifts in the individual misspecified forecasting models. Their calculations suggest that, for plausible ranges of parameter values, combining forecasts can offset the instability in the individual forecasts and in effect serves as an intercept correction.

3.2. *Large-n forecast combining methods*[1]

Simple combination forecasts Simple combination forecasts report a measure of the center of the distribution of the panel of forecasts. The equal-weighted, or average, forecast sets $w_{it} = 1/n$. Simple combination forecasts that are less sensitive to outliers than the average forecast are the median and the trimmed mean of the panel of forecasts.

Discounted MSFE weights Discounted MSFE forecasts compute the combination forecast as a weighted average of the individual forecasts, where the weights depend inversely on the historical performance of each individual forecast [cf. Diebold and Pauly (1987); Miller, Clemen and Winkler (1992) use discounted Bates–Granger (1969) weights]. The weight on the ith forecast depends inversely on its discounted MSFE:

$$w_{it} = m_{it}^{-1} \Big/ \sum_{j=1}^{n} m_{jt}^{-1}, \quad \text{where } m_{it} = \sum_{s=T_0}^{t-h} \rho^{t-h-s} \left(Y_{s+h}^{h} - \hat{Y}_{i,s+h|s}^{h}\right)^2, \tag{4}$$

where ρ is the discount factor.

Shrinkage forecasts Shrinkage forecasts entail shrinking the weights towards a value imposed a priori which is typically equal weighting. For example, Diebold and Pauly (1990) suggest shrinkage combining weights of the form

$$w_{it} = \lambda \hat{w}_{it} + (1 - \lambda)(1/n), \tag{5}$$

where $\hat{w}_{it}$ is the ith estimated coefficient from a recursive OLS regression of Y_{s+h}^{h} on $\hat{Y}_{1,s+h|s}^{h}, \ldots, \hat{Y}_{n,s+h|s}^{h}$ for $s = T_0, \ldots, t-h$ (no intercept), where T_0 is the first date for the forecast combining regressions and where λ controls the amount of shrinkage towards equal weighting. Shrinkage forecasts can be interpreted as a partial implementation of Bayesian model averaging (see Section 5).

[1] This discussion draws on Stock and Watson (2004a).

Time-varying parameter weights Time-varying parameter (TVP) weighting allows the weights to evolve as a stochastic process, thereby adapting to possible changes in the underlying covariances. For example, the weights can be modeled as evolving according to the random walk, $w_{it} = w_{it+1} + \eta_{it}$, where η_{it} is a disturbance that is serially uncorrelated, uncorrelated across i, and uncorrelated with the disturbance in the forecasting equation. Under these assumptions, the TVP combining weights can be estimated using the Kalman filter. This method is used by Sessions and Chatterjee (1989) and by LeSage and Magura (1992). LeSage and Magura (1992) also extend it to mixture models of the errors, but that extension did not improve upon the simpler Kalman filter approach in their empirical application.

A practical difficulty that arises with TVP combining is the determination of the magnitude of the time variation, that is, the variance of η_{it}. In principle, this variance can be estimated, however estimation of var(η_{it}) is difficult even when there are few regressors [cf. Stock and Watson (1998)].

Data requirements for these methods An important practical consideration is that these methods have different data requirements. The simple combination methods use only the contemporaneous forecasts, so forecasts can enter and leave the panel of forecasts. In contrast, methods that weight the constituent forecasts based on their historical performance require a historical track record for each forecast. The discounted MSFE methods can be implemented if there is historical forecast data, but the forecasts are available over differing subsamples (as would be the case if the individual X variables become available at different dates). In contrast, the TVP and shrinkage methods require a complete historical panel of forecasts, with all forecasts available at all dates.

3.3. Survey of the empirical literature

There is a vast empirical literature on forecast combining, and there are also a number of simulation studies that compare the performance of combining methods in controlled experiments. These studies are surveyed by Clemen (1989), Diebold and Lopez (1996), Newbold and Harvey (2002), and in Chapter 4 of this Handbook by Timmermann. Almost all of this literature considers the case that the number of forecasts to be combined is small, so these studies do not fall under the large-n brief of this survey. Still, there are two themes in this literature that are worth noting. First, combining methods typically outperform individual forecasts in the panel, often by a wide margin. Second, simple combining methods – the mean, trimmed mean, or median – often perform as well as or better than more sophisticated regression methods. This stylized fact has been called the "forecast combining puzzle", since extant statistical theories of combining methods suggest that in general it should be possible to improve upon simple combination forecasts.

The few forecast combining studies that consider large panels of forecasts include Figlewski (1983), Figlewski and Urich (1983), Chan, Stock and Watson (1999), Stock and Watson (2003, 2004a), Kitchen and Monaco (2003), and Aiolfi and Timmermann (2004). The studies by Figlewski (1983) and Figlewski and Urich (1983) use static factor models for forecast combining; they found that the factor model forecasts improved equal-weighted averages in one instance ($n = 33$ price forecasts) but not in another ($n = 20$ money supply forecasts). Further discussion of these papers is deferred to Section 4. Stock and Watson (2003, 2004b) examined pooled forecasts of output growth and inflation based on panels of up to 43 predictors for each of the G7 countries, where each forecast was based on an autoregressive distributed lag model with an individual X_t. They found that several combination methods consistently improved upon autoregressive forecasts; as in the studies with small n, simple combining methods performed well, in some cases producing the lowest mean squared forecast error. Kitchen and Monaco (2003) summarize the real time forecasting system used at the U.S. Treasury Department, which forecasts the current quarter's value of GDP by combining ADL forecasts made using 30 monthly predictors, where the combination weights depend on relative historical forecasting performance. They report substantial improvement over a benchmark AR model over the 1995–2003 sample period. Their system has the virtue of readily permitting within-quarter updating based on recently released data. Aiolfi and Timmermann (2004) consider time-varying combining weights which are nonlinear functions of the data. For example, they allow for instability by recursively sorting forecasts into reliable and unreliable categories, then computing combination forecasts with categories. Using the Stock–Watson (2003) data set, they report some improvements over simple combination forecasts.

4. Dynamic factor models and principal components analysis

Factor analysis and principal components analysis (PCA) are two longstanding methods for summarizing the main sources of variation and covariation among n variables. For a thorough treatment for the classical case that n is small, see Anderson (1984). These methods were originally developed for independently distributed random vectors. Factor models were extended to dynamic factor models by Geweke (1977), and PCA was extended to dynamic principal components analysis by Brillinger (1964).

This section discusses the use of these methods for forecasting with many predictors. Early applications of dynamic factor models (DFMs) to macroeconomic data suggested that a small number of factors can account for much of the observed variation of major economic aggregates [Sargent and Sims (1977), Stock and Watson (1989, 1991), Sargent (1989)]. If so, and if a forecaster were able to obtain accurate and precise estimates of these factors, then the task of forecasting using many predictors could be simplified substantially by using the estimated dynamic factors for forecasting, instead of using all n series themselves. As is discussed below, in theory the performance of estimators of the factors typically improves as n increases. Moreover, although factor analysis and PCA differ when n is small, their differences diminish as n increases; in fact, PCA (or dynamic PCA) can be used to construct consistent estimators of the factors in DFMs. These observations have spurred considerable recent interest in economic forecasting using the twin methods of DFMs and PCA.

This section begins by introducing the DFM, then turns to algorithms for estimation of the dynamic factors and for forecasting using these estimated factors. The section concludes with a brief review of the empirical literature on large-n forecasting with DFMs.

4.1. The dynamic factor model

The premise of the dynamic factor model is that the covariation among economic time series variables at leads and lags can be traced to a few underlying unobserved series, or factors. The disturbances to these factors might represent the major aggregate shocks to the economy, such as demand or supply shocks. Accordingly, DFMs express observed time series as a distributed lag of a small number of unobserved common factors, plus an idiosyncratic disturbance that itself might be serially correlated:

$$X_{it} = \lambda_i(\mathrm{L})' f_t + u_{it}, \quad i = 1, \ldots, n, \tag{6}$$

where f_t is the $q \times 1$ vector of unobserved factors, $\lambda_i(\mathrm{L})$ is a $q \times 1$ vector lag polynomial, called the "dynamic factor loadings", and u_{it} is the idiosyncratic disturbance. The factors and idiosyncratic disturbances are assumed to be uncorrelated at all leads and lags, that is, $E(f_t u_{is}) = 0$ for all i, s.

The unobserved factors are modeled (explicitly or implicitly) as following a linear dynamic process

$$\Gamma(\mathrm{L}) f_t = \eta_t, \tag{7}$$

where $\Gamma(\mathrm{L})$ is a matrix lag polynomial and η_t is a $q \times 1$ disturbance vector.

The DFM implies that the spectral density matrix of X_t can be written as the sum of two parts, one arising from the factors and the other arising from the idiosyncratic disturbance. Because F_t and u_t are uncorrelated at all leads and lags, the spectral density matrix of X_{it} at frequency ω is

$$S_{XX}(\omega) = \lambda(\mathrm{e}^{\mathrm{i}\omega}) S_{ff}(\omega) \lambda(\mathrm{e}^{-\mathrm{i}\omega})' + S_{uu}(\omega), \tag{8}$$

where $\lambda(z) = [\lambda_1(z) \ldots \lambda_n(z)]'$ and $S_{ff}(\omega)$ and $S_{uu}(\omega)$ are the spectral density matrices of f_t and u_t at frequency ω. This decomposition, which is due to Geweke (1977), is the frequency-domain counterpart of the variance decomposition of classical factor models.

In classical factor analysis, the factors are identified only up to multiplication by a nonsingular $q \times q$ matrix. In dynamic factor analysis, the factors are identified only up to multiplication by a nonsingular $q \times q$ matrix lag polynomial. This ambiguity can be resolved by imposing identifying restrictions, e.g., restrictions on the dynamic factor loadings and on $\Gamma(\mathrm{L})$. As in classical factor analysis, this identification problem makes it difficult to interpret the dynamic factors, but it is inconsequential for linear forecasting because all that is desired is the linear combination of the factors that produces the minimum mean squared forecast error.

Treatment of Y_t The variable to be forecasted, Y_t, can be handled in two different ways. The first is to include Y_t in the X_t vector and model it as part of the system (6) and (7). This approach is used when n is small and the DFM is estimated parametrically, as is discussed in Section 4.3. When n is large, however, computationally efficient nonparametric methods can be used to estimate the factors, in which case it is useful to treat the forecasting equation for Y_t as a single equation, not as a system.

The single forecasting equation for Y_t can be derived from (6). Augment X_t in that expression by Y_t, so that $Y_t = \lambda_Y(\mathrm{L})' f_t + u_{Yt}$, where $\{u_{Yt}\}$ is distributed independently of $\{f_t\}$ and $\{u_{it}\}$, $i = 1, \ldots, n$. Further suppose that u_{Yt} follows the autoregression, $\delta_Y(\mathrm{L})u_{Yt} = \nu_{Yt}$. Then $\delta_Y(\mathrm{L})Y_{t+1} = \delta_Y(\mathrm{L})'\lambda_Y(\mathrm{L}) f_{t+1} + \nu_{t+1}$ or $Y_{t+1} = \delta_Y(\mathrm{L})\lambda_Y(\mathrm{L})' f_{t+1} + \gamma(\mathrm{L})Y_t + \nu_{t+1}$, where $\gamma(\mathrm{L}) = \mathrm{L}^{-1}(1 - \delta_Y(\mathrm{L}))$. Thus $E[Y_{t+1} \mid X_t, Y_t, f_t, X_{t-1}, Y_{t-1}, f_{t-1}, \ldots] = E[\delta_Y(\mathrm{L})\lambda_Y(\mathrm{L})' f_{t+1} + \gamma(\mathrm{L})Y_t + \nu_{t+1} \mid Y_t, f_t, Y_{t-1}, f_{t-1}, \ldots] = \beta(\mathrm{L}) f_t + \gamma(\mathrm{L})Y_t$, where $\beta(\mathrm{L}) f_t = E[\delta_Y(\mathrm{L})\lambda_Y(\mathrm{L})' f_{t+1} \mid f_t, f_{t-1}, \ldots]$. Setting $Z_t = Y_t$, we thus have

$$Y_{t+1} = \beta(\mathrm{L}) f_t + \gamma(\mathrm{L})' Z_t + \varepsilon_{t+1}, \tag{9}$$

where $\varepsilon_{t+1} = \nu_{Yt+1} + (\delta_Y(\mathrm{L})\lambda_Y(\mathrm{L})' f_{t+1} - E[\delta_Y(\mathrm{L})\lambda_Y(\mathrm{L})' f_{t+1} \mid f_t, f_{t-1}, \ldots])$ has conditional mean zero given X_t, f_t, Y_t and their lags. We use the notation Z_t rather than Y_t for the regressor in (9) to generalize the equation somewhat so that observable predictors other than lagged Y_t can be included in the regression, for example, Z_t might include an observable variable that, in the forecaster's judgment, might be valuable for forecasting Y_{t+1} despite the inclusion of the factors and lags of the dependent variable.

Exact vs. approximate DFMs Chamberlain and Rothschild (1983) introduced a useful distinction between exact and approximate DFMs. In the *exact DFM*, the idiosyncratic terms are mutually uncorrelated, that is,

$$E(u_{it}u_{jt}) = 0 \quad \text{for } i \neq j. \tag{10}$$

The *approximate DFM* relaxes this assumption and allows for a limited amount of correlation among the idiosyncratic terms. The precise technical condition varies from paper to paper, but in general the condition limits the contribution of the idiosyncratic covariances to the total covariance of X as n gets large. For example, Stock and Watson (2002a) require that the average absolute covariances satisfy

$$\lim_{n\to\infty} n^{-1} \sum_{i=1}^{n} \sum_{j=1}^{n} \left| E(u_{it}u_{jt}) \right| < \infty. \tag{11}$$

There are two general approaches to the estimation of the dynamic factors, the first employing parametric estimation using an exact DFM and the second employing nonparametric methods, either PCA or dynamic PCA. We address these in turn.

4.2. DFM estimation by maximum likelihood

The initial applications of the DFM by Geweke's (1977) and Sargent and Sims (1977) focused on testing the restrictions implied by the exact DFM on the spectrum of X_t, that is, that its spectral density matrix has the factor structure (8), where S_{uu} is diagonal. If n is sufficiently larger than q (for example, if $q = 1$ and $n \geqslant 3$), the null hypothesis of an unrestricted spectral density matrix can be tested against the alternative of a DFM by testing the factor restrictions using an estimator of $S_{XX}(\omega)$. For fixed n, this estimator is asymptotically normal under the null hypothesis and the Wald test statistic has a chi-squared distribution. Although Sargent and Sims (1977) found evidence in favor of a reduced number of factors, their methods did not yield estimates of the factors and thus could not be used for forecasting.

With sufficient additional structure to ensure identification, the parameters of the DFM (6), (7) and (9) can be estimated by maximum likelihood, where the likelihood is computed using the Kalman filter, and the dynamic factors can be estimated using the Kalman smoother [Engle and Watson (1981), Stock and Watson (1989, 1991)]. Specifically, suppose that Y_t is included in X_t. Then make the following assumptions:

(1) the idiosyncratic terms follow a finite order AR model, $\delta_i(\mathrm{L})u_{it} = \nu_{it}$;
(2) $(\nu_{1t}, \ldots, \nu_{nt}, \eta_{1t}, \ldots, \eta_{qt})$ are i.i.d. normal and mutually independent;
(3) $\Gamma(\mathrm{L})$ has finite order with $\Gamma_0 = I_r$;
(4) $\lambda_i(\mathrm{L})$ is a lag polynomial of degree p; and
(5) $[\lambda'_{10} \ldots \lambda'_{q0}]' = I_q$.

Under these assumptions, the Gaussian likelihood can be constructed using the Kalman filter, and the parameters can be estimated by maximizing this likelihood.

One-step ahead forecasts Using the MLEs of the parameter vector, the time series of factors can be estimated using the Kalman smoother. Let $f_{t|T}$ and $u_{it|T}$, $i = 1, \ldots, n$, respectively denote the Kalman smoother estimates of the unobserved factors and idiosyncratic terms using the full data through time T. Suppose that the variable of interest is the final element of X_t. Then the one-step ahead forecast of the variable of interest at time $T + 1$ is $Y_{T+1|T} = X_{nT+1|T} = \hat{\lambda}_n(\mathrm{L})' f_{T|T} + u_{nT|T}$, where $\hat{\lambda}_n(\mathrm{L})$ is the MLE of $\lambda_n(\mathrm{L})$.[2]

h-step ahead forecasts Multistep ahead forecasts can be computed using either the iterated or the direct method. The iterated h-step ahead forecast is computed by solving the full DFM forward, which is done using the Kalman filter. The direct h-step ahead forecast is computed by projecting Y^h_{t+h} onto the estimated factors and observables, that is, by estimating $\beta_h(\mathrm{L})$ and $\gamma_h(\mathrm{L})$ in the equation

$$Y^h_{t+h} = \beta_h(\mathrm{L})' f_{t|t} + \gamma_h(\mathrm{L}) Y_t + \varepsilon^h_{t+h} \tag{12}$$

[2] Peña and Poncela (2004) provide an interpretation of forecasts based on the exact DFM as shrinkage forecasts.

(where $L^i f_{t/t} = f_{t-i/t}$) using data through period $T-h$. Consistent estimates of $\beta_h(L)$ and $\gamma_h(L)$ can be obtained by OLS because the signal extraction error $f_{t-i} - f_{t-i/t}$ is uncorrelated with $f_{t-j/t}$ and Y_{t-j} for $j \geqslant 0$. The forecast for period $T+h$ is then $\hat{\beta}_h(L)' f_{T|T} + \hat{\gamma}_h(L) Y_T$. The direct method suffers from the usual potential inefficiency of direct forecasts arising from the inefficient estimation of $\beta_h(L)$ and $\gamma_h(L)$, instead of basing the projections on the MLEs.

Successes and limitations Maximum likelihood has been used successfully to estimate the parameters of low-dimensional DFMs, which in turn have been used to estimate the factors and (among other things) to construct indexes of coincident and leading economic indicators. For example, Stock and Watson (1991) use this approach (with $n = 4$) to rationalize the U.S. Index of Coincident Indicators, previously maintained by the U.S. Department of Commerce and now produced the Conference Board. The method has also been used to construct regional indexes of coincident indexes, see Clayton-Matthews and Crone (2003). (For further discussion of DFMs and indexes of coincident and leading indicators, see Chapter 16 by Marcellino in this Handbook.) Quah and Sargent (1993) estimated a larger system ($n = 60$) by MLE. However, the underlying assumption of an exact factor model is a strong one. Moreover, the computational demands of maximizing the likelihood over the many parameters that arise when n is large are significant. Fortunately, when n is large, other methods are available for the consistent estimation of the factors in approximate DFMs.

4.3. DFM estimation by principal components analysis

If the lag polynomials $\lambda_i(L)$ and $\beta(L)$ have finite order p, then (6) and (9) can be written

$$X_t = \Lambda F_t + u_t, \tag{13}$$

$$Y_{t+1} = \beta' F_t + \gamma(L)' Z_t + \varepsilon_{t+1}, \tag{14}$$

where $F_t = [f_t' f_{t-1}' \cdots f_{t-p+1}']'$, $u_t = [u_{1t} \ldots u_{nt}]$, Λ is a matrix consisting of zeros and the coefficients of $\lambda_i(L)$, and β is a vector of parameters composed of the elements of $\beta(L)$. If the number of lags in β exceeds the number of lags in Λ, then the term $\beta' F_t$ in (14) can be replaced by a distributed lag of F_t.

Equations (13) and (14) rewrite the DFM as a static factor model, in which there are r static factors consisting of the current and lagged values of the q dynamic factors, where $r \leqslant pq$ (r will be strictly less than pq if one or more lagged dynamic factors are redundant). The representation (13) and (14) is called the static representation of the DFM.

Because F_t and u_t are uncorrelated at all leads and lags, the covariance matrix of X_t, Σ_{XX}, is the sum of two parts, one arising from the common factors and the other arising from the idiosyncratic disturbance:

$$\Sigma_{XX} = \Lambda \Sigma_{FF} \Lambda' + \Sigma_{uu}, \tag{15}$$

where Σ_{FF} and Σ_{uu} are the variance matrices of F_t and u_t. This is the usual variance decomposition of classical factor analysis.

When n is small, the standard methods of estimation of exact static factor models are to estimate Λ and Σ_{uu} by Gaussian maximum likelihood estimation or by method of moments [Anderson (1984)]. However, when n is large simpler methods are available. Under the assumptions that the eigenvalues of Σ_{uu} are $O(1)$ and $\Lambda'\Lambda$ is $O(n)$, the first r eigenvalues of Σ_{XX} are $O(N)$ and the remaining eigenvalues are $O(1)$. This suggests that the first r principal components of X can serve as estimators of Λ, which could in turn be used to estimate F_t. In fact, if Λ were known, then F_t could be estimated by $(\Lambda'\Lambda)^{-1}\Lambda'X_t$: by (13), $(\Lambda'\Lambda)^{-1}\Lambda'X_t = F_t + (\Lambda'\Lambda)^{-1}\Lambda'u_t$. Under the two assumptions, $\text{var}[(\Lambda'\Lambda)^{-1}\Lambda'u_t] = (\Lambda'\Lambda)^{-1}\Lambda'\Sigma_{uu}\Lambda(\Lambda'\Lambda)^{-1} = O(1/n)$, so that if Λ were known, F_t could be estimated precisely if n is sufficiently large.

More formally, by analogy to regression we can consider estimation of Λ and F_t by solving the nonlinear least-squares problem

$$\min_{F_1,\ldots,F_T,\Lambda} T^{-1}\sum_{t=1}^{T}(X_t - \Lambda F_t)'(X_t - \Lambda F_t) \tag{16}$$

subject to $\Lambda'\Lambda = I_r$. Note that this method treats $F_1, \ldots, F_T$ as fixed parameters to be estimated.[3] The first order conditions for maximizing (16) with respect to F_t shows that the estimators satisfy $\hat{F}_t = (\hat{\Lambda}'\hat{\Lambda})^{-1}\hat{\Lambda}'X_t$. Substituting this into the objective function yields the concentrated objective function, $T^{-1}\sum_{t=1}^{T} X_t'[I - \Lambda(\Lambda'\Lambda)^{-1}\Lambda]X_t$. Minimizing the concentrated objective function is equivalent to maximizing $\text{tr}\{(\Lambda'\Lambda)^{-1/2\prime}\Lambda'\hat{\Sigma}_{XX}\Lambda(\Lambda'\Lambda)^{-1/2}\}$, where $\hat{\Sigma}_{XX} = T^{-1}\sum_{t=1}^{T} X_t X_t'$. This in turn is equivalent to maximizing $\Lambda'\hat{\Sigma}_{XX}\Lambda$ subject to $\Lambda'\Lambda = I_r$, the solution to which is to set $\hat{\Lambda}$ to be the first r eigenvectors of $\hat{\Sigma}_{XX}$. The resulting estimator of the factors is $\hat{F}_t = \hat{\Lambda}'X_t$, which is the vector consisting of the first r principal components of X_t. The matrix $T^{-1}\sum_{t=1}^{T}\hat{F}_t\hat{F}_t'$ is diagonal with diagonal elements that equal the largest r ordered eigenvalues of $\hat{\Sigma}_{XX}$. The estimators $\{\hat{F}_t\}$ could be rescaled so that $T^{-1}\sum_{t=1}^{T}\hat{F}_t\hat{F}_t' = I_r$, however this is unnecessary if the only purpose is forecasting. We will refer to $\{\hat{F}_t\}$ as the PCA estimator of the factors in the static representation of the DFM.

PCA: large-n theoretical results Connor and Korajczyk (1986) show that the PCA estimators of the space spanned by the factors are pointwise consistent for T fixed and $n \to \infty$ in the approximate factor model, but do not provide formal arguments for n, $T \to \infty$. Ding and Hwang (1999) provide consistency results for PCA estimation of

[3] When $F_1, \ldots, F_T$ are treated as parameters to be estimated, the Gaussian likelihood for the classical factor model is unbounded, so the maximum likelihood estimator is undefined [see Anderson (1984)]. This difficulty does not arise in the least-squares problem (16), which has a global minimum (subject to the identification conditions discussed in this and the previous sections).

the classic exact factor model as $n, T \to \infty$, and Stock and Watson (2002a) show that, in the static form of the DFM, the space of the dynamic factors is consistently estimated by the principal components estimator as $n, T \to \infty$, with no further conditions on the relative rates of n or T. In addition, estimation of the coefficients of the forecasting equation by OLS, using the estimated factors as regressors, produces consistent estimates of $\beta(\mathrm{L})$ and $\gamma(\mathrm{L})$ and, consequently, forecasts that are first-order efficient, that is, they achieve the mean squared forecast error of the infeasible forecast based on the true coefficients and factors. Bai (2003) shows that the PCA estimator of the common component is asymptotically normal, converging at a rate of $\min(n^{1/2}, T^{1/2})$, even if u_t is serially correlated and/or heteroskedastic.

Some theory also exists, also under strong conditions, concerning the distribution of the largest eigenvalues of the sample covariance matrix of X_t. If n and T are fixed and X_t is i.i.d. $\mathrm{N}(0, \Sigma_{XX})$, then the principal components are distributed as those of a noncentral Wishart; see James (1964) and Anderson (1984). If n is fixed, $T \to \infty$, and the eigenvalues of Σ_{XX} are distinct, then the principal components are asymptotically normally distributed (they are continuous functions of $\hat{\Sigma}_{XX}$, which is itself asymptotically normally distributed). Johnstone (2001) [extended by El Karoui (2003)] shows that the largest eigenvalues of $\hat{\Sigma}_{XX}$ satisfy the Tracy–Widom law if $n, T \to \infty$, however these results apply to unscaled X_{it} (not divided by its sample standard deviation).

Weighted principal components Suppose for the moment that u_t is i.i.d. $\mathrm{N}(0, \Sigma_{uu})$ and that Σ_{uu} is known. Then by analogy to regression, one could modify (16) and consider the nonlinear generalized least-squares (GLS) problem

$$\min_{F_1,\dots,F_T,\Lambda} \sum_{t=1}^{T} (X_t - \Lambda F_t)' \Sigma_{uu}^{-1} (X_t - \Lambda F_t). \tag{17}$$

Evidently the weighting schemes in (16) and (17) differ. Because (17) corresponds to GLS when Σ_{uu} is known, there could be efficiency gains by using the estimator that solves (17) instead of the PCA estimator.

In applications, Σ_{uu} is unknown, so minimizing (17) is infeasible. However, Boivin and Ng (2003) and Forni et al. (2003b) have proposed feasible versions of (17). We shall call these weighted PCA estimators since they involve alternative weighting schemes in place of simply weighting by the inverse sample variances as does the PCA estimator (recall the notational convention that X_t has been standardized to have sample variance one). Jones (2001) proposed a weighted factor estimation algorithm which is closely related to weighted PCA estimation when n is large.

Because the exact factor model posits that Σ_{uu} is diagonal, a natural approach is to replace Σ_{uu} in (17) with an estimator that is diagonal, where the diagonal elements are estimators of the variance of the individual u_{it}'s. This approach is taken by Jones (2001) and Boivin and Ng (2003). Boivin and Ng (2003) consider several diagonal weighting schemes, including schemes that drop series that are highly correlated with others. One simple two-step weighting method, which Boivin and Ng (2003) found worked well in their empirical application to U.S. data, entails estimating the diagonal elements of Σ_{uu}

by the sample variances of the residuals from a preliminary regression of X_{it} onto a relatively large number of factors estimated by PCA.

Forni et al. (2003b) also consider two-step weighted PCA, where they estimated Σ_{uu} in (17) by the difference between $\hat{\Sigma}_{XX}$ and an estimator of the covariance matrix of the common component, where the latter estimator is based on a preliminary dynamic principal components analysis (dynamic PCA is discussed below). They consider both diagonal and nondiagonal estimators of Σ_{uu}. Like Boivin and Ng (2003), they find that weighted PCA can improve upon conventional PCA, with the gains depending on the particulars of the stochastic processes under study.

The weighted minimization problem (17) was motivated by the assumption that u_t is i.i.d. $N(0, \Sigma_{uu})$. In general, however, u_t will be serially correlated, in which case GLS entails an adjustment for this serial correlation. Stock and Watson (2005) propose an extension of weighted PCA in which a low-order autoregressive structure is assumed for u_t. Specifically, suppose that the diagonal filter $D(\mathrm{L})$ whitens u_t so that $D(\mathrm{L})u_t \equiv \tilde{u}_t$ is serially uncorrelated. Then the generalization of (17) is

$$\min_{D(\mathrm{L}), \tilde{F}_1, \ldots, \tilde{F}_T, \Lambda} \sum_{t=1}^{T} \left[D(\mathrm{L})X_t - \Lambda \tilde{F}_t\right]' \Sigma_{\tilde{u}\tilde{u}}^{-1} \left[D(\mathrm{L})X_t - \Lambda \tilde{F}_t\right], \tag{18}$$

where $\tilde{F}_t = D(\mathrm{L})F_t$ and $\Sigma_{\tilde{u}\tilde{u}} = E\tilde{u}_t\tilde{u}_t'$. Stock and Watson (2005) implement this with $\Sigma_{\tilde{u}\tilde{u}} = I_n$, so that the estimated factors are the principal components of the filtered series $D(\mathrm{L})X_t$. Estimation of $D(\mathrm{L})$ and $\{\tilde{F}_t\}$ can be done sequentially, iterating to convergence.

Factor estimation under model instability There are some theoretical results on the properties of PCA factor estimates when there is parameter instability. Stock and Watson (2002a) show that the PCA factor estimates are consistent even if there is some temporal instability in the factor loadings, as long as the temporal instability is sufficiently dissimilar from one series to the next. More broadly, because the precision of the factor estimates improves with n, it might be possible to compensate for short panels, which would be appropriate if there is parameter instability, by increasing the number of predictors. More work is needed on the properties of PCA and dynamic PCA estimators under model instability.

Determination of the number of factors At least two statistical methods are available for the determination of the number of factors when n is large. The first is to use model selection methods to estimate the number of factors that belong in the forecasting equation (14). Given an upper bound on the dimension and lags of F_t, Stock and Watson (2002a) show that this can be accomplished using an information criterion. Although the rate requirements for the information criteria in Stock and Watson (2002a) technically rule out the BIC, simulation results suggest that the BIC can perform well in the sample sizes typically found in macroeconomic forecasting applications.

The second approach is to estimate the number of factors entering the full DFM. Bai and Ng (2002) prove that the dimension of F_t can be estimated consistently for approximate DFMs that can be written in static form, using suitable information criteria which they provide. In principle, these two methods are complementary: a full set of factors could be chosen using the Bai–Ng method, and model selection could then be applied to the Y_t equation to select a subset of these for forecasting purposes.

h-step ahead forecasts Direct h-step ahead forecasts are produced by regressing Y^h_{t+h} against $\hat{F}_t$ and, possibly, lags of $\hat{F}_t$ and Y_t, then forecasting Y^h_{t+h}.

Iterated h-step ahead forecasts require specifying a subsidiary model of the dynamic process followed by F_t, which has heretofore not been required in the principal components method. One approach, proposed by Bernanke, Boivin and Eliasz (2005) models (Y_t, F_t) jointly as a VAR, which they term a factor-augmented VAR (FAVAR). They estimate this FAVAR using the PCA estimates of $\{F_t\}$. Although they use the estimated model for impulse response analysis, it could be used for forecasting by iterating the estimated FAVAR h steps ahead.

In a second approach to iterated multistep forecasts, Forni et al. (2003b) and Giannoni, Reichlin and Sala (2004) developed a modification of the FAVAR approach in which the shocks in the F_t equation in the VAR have reduced dimension. The motivation for this further restriction is that F_t contains lags of f_t. The resulting h-step forecasts are made by iterating the system forward using the Kalman filter.

4.4. DFM estimation by dynamic principal components analysis

The method of dynamic principal components was introduced by Brillinger (1964) and is described in detail in Brillinger's (1981) textbook. Static principal components entails finding the closest approximation to the covariance matrix of X_t among all covariance matrices of a given reduced rank. In contrast, dynamic principal components entails finding the closest approximation to the spectrum of X_t among all spectral density matrices of a given reduced rank.

Brillinger's (1981) estimation algorithm generalizes static PCA to the frequency domain. First, the spectral density of X_t is estimated using a consistent spectral density estimator, $\hat{S}_{XX}(\omega)$, at frequency ω. Next, the eigenvectors corresponding to the largest q eigenvalues of this (Hermitian) matrix are computed. The inverse Fourier transform of these eigenvectors yields estimators of the principal component time series using formulas given in Brillinger (1981, Chapter 9).

Forni et al. (2000, 2004) study the properties of this algorithm and the estimator of the common component of X_{it} in a DFM, $\lambda_i(\mathrm{L})' f_t$, when n is large. The advantages of this method, relative to parametric maximum likelihood, are that it allows for an approximate dynamic factor structure, and it does not require high-dimensional maximization when n is large. The advantage of this method, relative to static principal components, is that it admits a richer lag structure than the finite-order lag structure that led to (13).

Brillinger (1981) summarizes distributional results for dynamic PCA for the case that n is fixed and $T \to \infty$ (as in classic PCA, estimators are asymptotically normal because they are continuous functions of $\hat{S}_{XX}(\omega)$, which is asymptotically normal).

Forni et al. (2000) show that dynamic PCA provides pointwise consistent estimation of the common component as n and T both increase, and Forni et al. (2004) further show that this consistency holds if $n, T \to \infty$ and $n/T \to 0$. The latter condition suggests that some caution should be exercised in applications in which n is large relative to T, although further evidence on this is needed.

The time-domain estimates of the dynamic common components series are based on two-sided filters, so their implementation entails trimming the data at the start and end of the sample. Because dynamic PCA does not yield an estimator of the common component at the end of the sample, this method cannot be used for forecasting, although it can be used for historical analysis or [as is done by Forni et al. (2003b)] to provide a weighting matrix for subsequent use in weighted (static) PCA. Because the focus of this chapter is on forecasting, not historical analysis, we do not discuss dynamic principal components further.

4.5. *DFM estimation by Bayes methods*

Another approach to DFM estimation is to use Bayes methods. The difficulty with maximum likelihood estimation of the DFM when n is large is not that it is difficult to compute the likelihood, which can be evaluated fairly rapidly using the Kalman filter, but rather that it requires maximizing over a very large parameter vector. From a computational perspective, this suggests that perhaps averaging the likelihood with respect to some weighting function will be computationally more tractable than maximizing it; that is, Bayes methods might be offer substantial computational gains.

Otrok and Whiteman (1998), Kim and Nelson (1998), and Kose, Otrok and Whiteman (2003) develop Markov Chain Monte Carlo (MCMC) methods for sampling from the posterior distribution of dynamic factor models. The focus of these papers was inference about the parameters, historical episodes, and implied model dynamics, not forecasting. These methods also can be used for forecast construction (see Otrok, Silos and Whiteman (2003) and Chapter 1 by Geweke and Whiteman in this Handbook), however to date not enough is known to say whether this approach provides an improvement over PCA-type methods when n is large.

4.6. *Survey of the empirical literature*

There have been several empirical studies that have used estimated dynamic factors for forecasting. In two prescient but little-noticed papers, Figlewski (1983) ($n = 33$) and Figlewski and Urich (1983) ($n = 20$) considered combining forecasts from a panel of forecasts using a static factor model. Figlewski (1983) pointed out that, if forecasters are unbiased, then the factor model implied that the average forecast would converge in probability to the unobserved factor as n increases. Because some forecasters are better than others, the optimal factor-model combination (which should be close to but not equal to the largest weighted principle component) differs from equal weighting. In an application to a panel of $n = 33$ forecasters who participated in the Livingston price survey, with $T = 65$ survey dates, Figlewski (1983) found that using the optimal static factor model combination outperformed the simple weighted average. When Figlewski and Urich (1983) applied this methodology to a panel of $n = 20$ weekly forecasts of the money supply, however, they were unable to improve upon the simple weighted average forecast.

Recent studies on large-model forecasting have used pseudo-out-of-sample forecast methods (that is, recursive or rolling forecasts) to evaluate and to compare forecasts. Stock and Watson (1999) considered factor forecasts for U.S. inflation, where the factors were estimated by PCA from a panel of up to 147 monthly predictors. They found that the forecasts based on a single real factor generally had lower pseudo-out-of-sample forecast error than benchmark autoregressions and traditional Phillips-curve forecasts. Stock and Watson (2002b) found substantial forecasting improvements for real variables using dynamic factors estimated by PCA from a panel of up to 215 U.S. monthly predictors, a finding confirmed by Bernanke and Boivin (2003). Boivin and Ng (2003) compared forecasts using PCA and weighted PCA estimators of the factors, also for U.S. monthly data ($n = 147$). They found that weighted PCA forecasts tended to outperform PCA forecasts for real variables but not nominal variables.

There also have been applications of these methods to non-U.S. data. Forni et al. (2003b) focused on forecasting Euro-wide industrial production and inflation (HICP) using a short monthly data set (1987:2–2001:3) with very many predictors ($n = 447$). They considered both PCA and weighted PCA forecasts, where the weighted principal components were constructed using the dynamic PCA weighting method of Forni et al. (2003a). The PCA and weighted PCA forecasts performed similarly, and both exhibited modest improvements over the AR benchmark. Brisson, Campbell and Galbraith (2002) examined the performance factor-based forecasts of Canadian GDP and investment growth using two panels, one consisting of only Canadian data ($n = 66$) and one with both Canadian and U.S. data ($n = 133$), where the factors were estimated by PCA. They find that the factor-based forecasts improve substantially over benchmark models (autoregressions and some small time series models), but perform less well than the real-time OECD forecasts of these series. Using data for the UK, Artis, Banerjee and Marcellino (2001) found that 6 factors (estimated by PCA) explain 50% of the variation in their panel of 80 variables, and that factor-based forecasts could make substantial forecasting improvements for real variables, especially at longer horizons.

Practical implementation of DFM forecasting requires making many modeling decisions, notably to use PCA or weighted PCA, how to construct the weights if weighted PCA weights is used, and how to specify the forecasting equation. Existing theory provides limited guidance on these choices. Forni et al. (2003b) and Boivin and Ng (2005) provide simulation and empirical evidence comparing various DFM forecasting methods, and we provide some additional empirical comparisons are provided in Section 7 below.

DFM-based methods also have been used to construct real-time indexes of economic activity based on large cross sections. Two such indexes are now being produced and publicly released in real time. In the U.S., the Federal Reserve Bank of Chicago publishes the monthly Chicago Fed National Activity Index (CFNAI), where the index is the single factor estimated by PCA from a panel of 85 monthly real activity variables [Federal Reserve Bank of Chicago (undated)]. In Europe, the Centre for Economic Policy Research (CEPR) in London publishes the monthly European Coincident Index (EuroCOIN), where the index is the single dynamic factor estimated by weighted PCA from a panel of nearly 1000 economic time series for Eurozone countries [Altissimo et al. (2001)].

These methods also have been used for nonforecasting purposes, which we mention briefly although these are not the focus of this survey. Following Connor and Korajczyk (1986, 1988), there have been many applications in finance that use (static) factor model methods to estimate unobserved factors and, among other things, to test whether those unobserved factors are consistent with the arbitrage pricing theory; see Jones (2001) for a recent contribution and additional references. Forni and Reichlin (1998), Bernanke and Boivin (2003), Favero and Marcellino (2001), Bernanke, Boivin and Eliasz (2005), Giannoni, Reichlin and Sala (2002, 2004) and Forni et al. (2005) used estimated factors in an attempt better to approximate the true economic shocks and thereby to obtain improved estimates of impulse responses as variables. Another application, pursued by Favero and Marcellino (2001) and Favero, Marcellino and Neglia (2002), is to use lags of the estimated factors as instrumental variables, reflecting the hope that the factors might be stronger instruments than lagged observed variables. Kapetanios and Marcellino (2002) and Favero, Marcellino and Neglia (2002) compared PCA and dynamic PCA estimators of the dynamic factors. Generally speaking, the results are mixed, with neither method clearly dominating the other. A point stressed by Favero, Marcellino and Neglia (2002) is that the dynamic PCA methods estimate the factors by a two-sided filter, which makes it problematic, or even unsuitable, for applications in which strict timing is important, such as using the estimated factors in VARs or as instrumental variables. More research is needed before clear recommendation about which procedure is best for such applications.

5. Bayesian model averaging

Bayesian model averaging (BMA) can be thought of as a Bayesian approach to combination forecasting. In forecast combining, the forecast is a weighted average of the individual forecasts, where the weights can depend on some measure of the historical accuracy of the individual forecasts. This is also true for BMA, however in BMA the weights are computed as formal posterior probabilities that the models are correct. In addition, the individual forecasts in BMA are model-based and are the posterior means of the variable to be forecast, conditional on the selected model. Thus BMA extends forecast combining to a fully Bayesian setting, where the forecasts themselves are optimal Bayes forecasts, given the model (and some parametric priors). Importantly, recent research on BMA methods also has tackled the difficult computational problem in which the individual models can contain arbitrary subsets of the predictors X_t. Even if n is moderate, there are more models than can be computed exhaustively, yet by cleverly sampling the most likely models, BMA numerical methods are able to provide good approximations to the optimal combined posterior mean forecast.

The basic paradigm for BMA was laid out by Leamer (1978). In an early contribution in macroeconomic forecasting, Min and Zellner (1993) used BMA to forecast annual output growth in a panel of 18 countries, averaging over four different models. The area of BMA has been very active recently, mainly occurring outside economics. Work on BMA through the 1990s is surveyed by Hoeting et al. (1999) and their discussants, and Chapter 1 by Geweke and Whiteman in this Handbook contains a thorough discussion of Bayesian forecasting methods. In this section, we focus on BMA methods specifically developed for linear prediction with large n. This is the focus of Fernandez, Ley and Steel (2001a) [their application in Fernandez, Ley and Steel (2001b) is to growth regressions], and we draw heavily on their work in the next section.

This section first sets out the basic BMA setup, then turns to a discussion of the few empirical applications to date of BMA to economic forecasting with many predictors.

5.1. Fundamentals of Bayesian model averaging

In standard Bayesian analysis, the parameters of a given model are treated as random, distributed according to a prior distribution. In BMA, the binary variable indicating whether a given model is true also is treated as random and distributed according to some prior distribution.

Specifically, suppose that the distribution of Y_{t+1} conditional on X_t is given by one of K models, denoted by $M_1, \ldots, M_K$. We focus on the case that all the models are linear, so they differ by which subset of predictors X_t are contained in the model. Thus M_k specifies the list of indexes of X_t contained in model k. Let $\pi(M_k)$ denote the prior probability that the data are generated by model k, and let D_t denote the data set through date t. Then the predictive probability density for Y_{T+1} is

$$f(Y_{T+1} \mid D_T) = \sum_{k=1}^{K} f_k(Y_{T+1} \mid D_T) \Pr(M_k \mid D_T), \tag{19}$$

where $f_k(Y_{T+1} \mid D_T)$ is the predictive density of Y_{T+1} for model k and $\Pr(M_k \mid D_T)$ is the posterior probability of model k. This posterior probability is given by

$$\Pr(M_k \mid D_T) = \frac{\Pr(D_T \mid M_k)\pi(M_k)}{\sum_{i=1}^{K} \Pr(D_T \mid M_i)\pi(M_i)}, \tag{20}$$

where $\Pr(D_T \mid M_k)$ is given by

$$\Pr(D_T \mid M_k) = \int \Pr(D_T \mid \theta_k, M_k)\pi(\theta_k \mid M_k)\, \mathrm{d}\theta_k, \tag{21}$$

where θ_k is the vector of parameters in model k and $\pi(\theta_k \mid M_k)$ is the prior for the parameters in model k.

Under squared error loss, the optimal Bayes forecast is the posterior mean of Y_{T+1}, which we denote by $\tilde{Y}_{T+1|T}$. It follows from (19) that this posterior mean is

$$\tilde{Y}_{T+1|T} = \sum_{k=1}^{K} \Pr(M_k \mid D_T)\tilde{Y}_{M_k,T+1|T}, \tag{22}$$

where $\tilde{Y}_{M_k,T+1|T}$ is the posterior mean of Y_{T+1} for model M_k.

Comparison of (22) and (3) shows that BMA can be thought of as an extension of the Bates–Granger (1969) forecast combining setup, where the weights are determined by the posterior probabilities over the models, the forecasts are posterior means, and, because the individual forecasts are already conditional means, given the model, there is no constant term ($w_0 = 0$ in (3)).

These simple expressions mask considerable computational difficulties. If the set of models is allowed to be all possible subsets of the predictors X_t, then there are $K = 2^n$ possible models. Even with $n = 30$, this is several orders of magnitude more than is feasible to compute exhaustively. Thus the computational objective is to approximate the summation (22) while only evaluating a small subset of models. Achieving this objective requires a judicious choice of prior distributions and using appropriate numerical simulation methods.

Choice of priors Implementation of BMA requires choosing two sets of priors, the prior distribution of the parameters given the model and the prior probability of the model. In principle, the researcher could have prior beliefs about the values of specific parameters in specific models. In practice, however, given the large number of models this is rarely the case. In addition, given the large number of models to evaluate, there is a premium on using priors that are computationally convenient. These considerations lead to the use of priors that impose little prior information and that lead to posteriors (21) that are easy to evaluate quickly.

Fernandez, Ley and Steel (2001a) conducted a study of various priors that might usefully be applied in linear models with economic data and large n. Based on theoretical consideration and simulation results, they propose a benchmark set of priors for BMA in the linear model with large n. Let the kth model be

$$Y_{t+1} = X_t^{(k)\prime}\beta_k + Z_t'\gamma + \varepsilon_t, \tag{23}$$

where $X_t^{(k)}$ is the vector of predictors appearing in model k, Z_t is a vector of variables to be included in all models, β_k and γ are coefficient vectors, and ε_t is the error term. The analysis is simplified if the model-specific regressors $X_t^{(k)}$ are orthogonal to the common regressor Z_t, and this assumption is adopted throughout this section by taking $X_t^{(k)}$ to be the residuals from the projection of the original set of predictors onto Z_t. In applications to economic forecasting, because of serial correlation in Y_t, Z_t might include lagged values of Y that potentially appear in each model.

Following the rest of the literature on BMA in the linear model [cf. Hoeting et al. (1999)], Fernandez, Ley and Steel (2001a) assume that $\{X_t^{(k)}, Z_t\}$ is strictly exogenous and ε_t is i.i.d. $N(0, \sigma^2)$. In the notation of (21), $\theta_k = [\beta_k' \, \gamma' \, \sigma]'$. They suggest using conjugate priors, an uninformative prior for γ and σ^2 and Zellner's (1986) g-prior for β_k:

$$\pi(\gamma, \sigma \mid M_k) \propto 1/\sigma, \tag{24}$$

$$\pi(\beta_k \mid \sigma, M_k) = \mathrm{N}\left(0, \sigma^2\left(g \sum_{t=1}^{T} X_t^{(k)} X_t^{(k)\prime}\right)^{-1}\right). \tag{25}$$

With the priors (24) and (25), the conditional marginal likelihood $\Pr(D_T \mid M_k)$ in (21) is

$$\begin{aligned} &\Pr(Y_1, \ldots, Y_T \mid M_k) \\ &\quad = \text{const} \times a(g)^{\frac{1}{2}\#M_k}\left[a(g)SSR^R + \left(1 - a(g)\right)SSR_k^U\right]^{-\frac{1}{2}\mathrm{df}^R}, \end{aligned} \tag{26}$$

where $a(g) = g/(1+g)$, SSR^R is the sum of squared residuals of Y from the restricted OLS regression of Y_{t+1} on Z_t, SSR_k^U is the sum of squared residuals from the OLS regression of Y onto $(X_t^{(k)}, Z_t)$, $\#M_k$ is the dimension of $X_t^{(k)}$, df^R is the degrees of freedom of the restricted regression, and the constant is the same from one model to the next [see Raftery, Madigan and Hoeting (1997) and Fernandez, Ley and Steel (2001a)].

The prior model probability, $\pi(M_k)$, also needs to be specified. One choice for this prior is a multinomial distribution, where the probability is determined by the prior probability that an individual variable enters the model; see, for example, Koop and Potter (2004). If all the variables are deemed equally likely to enter and whether one variable enters the model is treated as independent of whether any other variable enters, then the prior probability for all models is the same and the term $\pi(\theta_k)$ drops out of the expressions. In this case, (22), (20) and (26) imply that

$$\begin{aligned} &\tilde{Y}_{T+1|T} = \sum_{k=1}^{K} w_k \tilde{Y}_{M_k,T+1|T}, \\ &\quad \text{where } w_k = \frac{a(g)^{\frac{1}{2}\#M_k}[1 + g^{-1}SSR_k^U/SSR^R]^{-\frac{1}{2}\mathrm{df}^R}}{\sum_{i=1}^{K} a(g)^{\frac{1}{2}\#M_i}[1 + g^{-1}SSR_i^U/SSR^R]^{-\frac{1}{2}\mathrm{df}^R}}. \end{aligned} \tag{27}$$

Three aspects of (27) bear emphasis. First, this expression links BMA and forecast combining: for the linear model with the g-prior and in which each model is given equal prior probability, the BMA forecast as a weighted average of the (Bayes) forecasts from the individual models, where the weighting factor depends on the reduction in the sum of squared residuals of model M_k, relative to the benchmark model that includes only Z_t.

Second, the weights in (27) (and the posterior (26)) penalize models with more parameters through the exponent $\#M_k/2$. This arises directly from the g-prior calculations and appears even though the derivation here places equal weight on all models. A further penalty could be placed on large models by letting $\pi(M_k)$ depend on $\#M_k$.

Third, the weights are based on the posterior (marginal likelihood) (26), which is conditional on $\{X_t^{(k)}, Z_t\}$. Conditioning on $\{X_t^{(k)}, Z_t\}$ is justified by the assumption that the regressors are strictly exogenous, an assumption we return to below.

The foregoing expressions depend upon the hyperparameter g. The choice of g determines the amount of shrinkage appears in the Bayes estimator of β_k, with higher values of g corresponding to greater shrinkage. Based on their simulation study, Fernandez, Ley and Steel (2001a) suggest $g = 1/\min(T, n^2)$. Alternatively, empirical Bayes methods could be used to estimate the value of g that provides the BMA forecasts with the best performance.

Computation of posterior over models If n exceeds 20 or 25, there are too many models to enumerate and the population summations in (27) cannot be evaluated directly. Instead, numerical algorithms have been developed to provide precise, yet numerically efficient, estimates of this the summation.

In principle, one could approximate the population mean in (27) by drawing a random sample of models, evaluating the weights and the posterior means for each forecast, and evaluating (27) using the sample averages, so the summations run over sampled models. In many applications, however, a large fraction of models might have posterior probability near zero, so this method is computationally inefficient. For this reason, a number of methods have been developed that permit accurate estimation of (27) using a relatively small sample of models. The key to these algorithms is cleverly deciding which models to sample with high probability. Clyde (1999a, 1999b) provides a survey of these methods. Two closely related methods are the stochastic search variable selection (SSVS) methods of George and McCulloch (1993, 1997) [also see Geweke (1996)] and the Markov chain Monte Carlo model composition (MC^3) algorithm of Madigan and York (1995); we briefly summarize the latter.

The MC^3 sampling scheme starts with a given model, say M_k. One of the n elements of X_t is chosen at random; a new model, $M_{k'}$, is defined by dropping that regressor if it appears in M_k, or adding it to M_k if it does not. The sampler moves from model M_k to $M_{k'}$ with probability $\min(1, B_{k,k'})$, where $B_{k,k'}$ is the Bayes ratio comparing the two models (which, with the g-prior, is computed using (26)). Following Fernandez, Ley and Steel (2001a), the summation (27) is estimated using the summands for the visited models.

Orthogonalized regressors The computational problem simplifies greatly if the regressors are orthogonal. For example, Koop and Potter (2004) transform X_t to its principal components, but in contrast to the DFM methods discussed in Section 3, all or a large number of the components are kept. This approach can be seen as an extension of the DFM methods in Section 4, where BIC or AIC model selection is replaced by BMA, where nonzero prior probability is placed on the higher principal components entering as predictors. In this sense, it is plausible to model the prior probability of the kth principle component entering as a declining function of k.

Computational details for BMA in linear models with orthogonal regressors and a g-prior are given in Clyde (1999a) and Clyde, Desimone and Parmigiani (1996). [As

Clyde, Desimone and Parmigiani (1996) point out, the method of orthogonalization is irrelevant when a g-prior is used, so weighted principal components can be used instead of standard PCA.] Let γ_j be a binary random variable indicating whether regressor j is in the model, and treat γ_j as independently (but not necessarily identically) distributed with prior probability $\pi_j = \Pr(\gamma_j = 1)$. Suppose that σ_ε^2 is known. Because the regressors are exogenous and the errors are normally distributed, the OLS estimators $\{\hat{\beta}_j\}$ are sufficient statistics. Because the regressors are orthogonal, γ_j, β_j and $\hat{\beta}_j$ are jointly independently distributed over j. Consequently, the posterior mean of β_j depends on the data only through $\hat{\beta}_j$ and is given by

$$E(\beta_j \mid \hat{\beta}_j, \sigma_\varepsilon^2) = a(g)\hat{\beta}_j \times \Pr(\gamma_j = 1 \mid \hat{\beta}_j, \sigma_\varepsilon^2), \tag{28}$$

where g is the g-prior parameter [Clyde (1999a, 1999b)]. Thus the weights in the BMA forecast can be computed analytically, eliminating the need for a stochastic sampling scheme to approximate (27). The expression (28) treats σ_ε^2 as known. The full BMA estimator can be computed by integrating over σ_ε^2, alternatively one could use a plug-in estimator of σ_ε^2 as suggested by Clyde (1999a, 1999b).

Bayesian model selection Bayesian model selection entails selecting the model with the highest posterior probability and using that model as the basis for forecasting; see the reviews by George (1999) and Chipman, George and McCulloch (2001). With suitable choice of priors, BMA can yield Bayesian model selection. For example, Fernandez, Ley and Steel (2001a) provide conditions on the choice of g as a function of k and T that produce consistent Bayesian model selection, in the sense that the posterior probability of the true model tends to one (the asymptotics hold the number of models K fixed as $T \to \infty$). In particular they show that, if $g = 1/T$ and the number of models K is held fixed, then the g-prior BMA method outlined above, with a flat prior over models, is asymptotically equivalent to model selection using the BIC.

Like other forms of model selection, Bayesian model selection might be expected to perform best when the number of models is small relative to the sample size. In the applications of interest in this survey, the number of models is very large and Bayesian model selection would be expected to share the problems of model selection more generally.

Extension to h-step ahead forecasts The algorithm outlined above does not extend to iterated multiperiod forecasts because the analysis is conditional on X and Z (models for X and Z are never estimated). Although the algorithm can be used to produce multiperiod forecasts, its derivation is inapplicable because the error term ε_t in (23) is modeled as i.i.d., whereas it would be MA($h-1$) if the dependent variable were Y_{t+h}^h, and the likelihood calculations leading to (27) no longer would be valid.

In principle, BMA could be extended to multiperiod forecasts by calculating the posterior using the correct likelihood with the MA($h-1$) error term, however the simplicity of the g-prior development would be lost and in any event this extension seems not to be in the literature. Instead, one could apply the formulas in (27), simply replacing Y_{t+1}

with Y^h_{t+h}; this approach is taken by Koop and Potter (2004), and although the formal BMA interpretation is lost the expressions provide an intuitively appealing alternative to the forecast combining methods of Section 3, in which only a single X appears in each model.

Extension to endogenous regressors Although the general theory of BMA does not require strict exogeneity, the calculations based on the g-prior leading to the average forecast (27) assume that $\{X_t, Z_t\}$ are strictly exogenous. This assumption is clearly false in a macro forecasting application. In practice, Z_t (if present) consists of lagged values of Y_t and one or two key variables that the forecaster "knows" to belong in the forecasting equation. Alternatively, if the regressor space has been orthogonalized, Z_t could consist of lagged Y_t and the first few one or two factors. In either case, Z is not strictly exogenous. In macroeconomic applications, X_t is not strictly exogenous either. For example, a typical application is forecasting output growth using many interest rates, measures of real activity, measures of wage and price inflation, etc.; these are predetermined and thus are valid predictors but X has a future path that is codetermined with output growth, so X is not strictly exogenous.

It is not clear how serious this critique is. On the one hand, the model-based posteriors leading to (27) evidently are not the true posteriors $\Pr(M_k \mid D_T)$ (the likelihood is fundamentally misspecified), so the elegant decision theoretic conclusion that BMA combining is the optimal Bayes predictor does not apply. On the other hand, the weights in (27) are simple and have considerable intuitive appeal as a competitor to forecast combining. Moreover, BMA methods provide computational tools for combining many models in which multiple predictors enter; this constitutes a major extension of forecast combining as discussed in Section 3, in which there were only n models, each containing a single predictor. From this perspective, BMA can be seen as a potentially useful extension of forecast combining, despite the inapplicability of the underlying theory.

5.2. *Survey of the empirical literature*

Aside from the contribution by Min and Zellner (1993), which used BMA methods to combine forecasts from one linear and one nonlinear model, the applications of BMA to economic forecasting have been quite recent.

Most of the applications have been to forecasting financial variables. Avramov (2002) applied BMA to the problem of forecasting monthly and quarterly returns on six different portfolios of U.S. stocks using $n = 14$ traditional predictors (the dividend yield, the default risk spread, the 90-day Treasury bill rate, etc.). Avramov (2002) finds that the BMA forecasts produce RMSFEs that are approximately two percent smaller than the random walk (efficient market) benchmark, in contrast to conventional information criteria forecasts, which have higher RMSFEs than the random walk benchmark. Cremers (2002) undertook a similar study with $n = 14$ predictors [there is partial overlap between Avramov's (2002) and Cremers' (2002) predictors] and found improvements in in-sample fit and pseudo-out-of-sample forecasting performance comparable to those found by Avramov (2002). Wright (2003) focuses on the problem of forecasting four exchange rates using $n = 10$ predictors, for a variety of values of g. For two of the currencies he studies, he finds pseudo-out-of-sample MSFE improvements of as much as 15% at longer horizons, relative to the random walk benchmark; for the other two currencies he studies, the improvements are much smaller or nonexistent. In all three of these studies, n has been sufficiently small that the authors were able to evaluate all possible models and simulation methods were not needed to evaluate (27).

We are aware of only two applications of BMA to forecasting macroeconomic aggregates. Koop and Potter (2004) focused on forecasting GDP and the change of inflation using $n = 142$ quarterly predictors, which they orthogonalized by transforming to principal components. They explored a number of different priors and found that priors that focused attention on the set of principal components that explained 99.9% of the variance of X provided the best results. Koop and Potter (2004) concluded that the BMA forecasts improve on benchmark AR(2) forecasts and on forecasts that used BIC-selected factors (although this evidence is weaker) at short horizons, but not at longer horizons. Wright (2004) considers forecasts of quarterly U.S. inflation using $n = 93$ predictors; he used the g-prior methodology above, except that he only considered models with one predictor, so there are only a total of n models under consideration. Despite ruling out models with multiple predictors, he found that BMA can improve upon the equal-weighted combination forecasts.

6. Empirical Bayes methods

The discussion of BMA in the previous section treats the priors as reflecting subjectively held a priori beliefs of the forecaster or client. Over time, however, different forecasters using the same BMA framework but different priors will produce different forecasts, and some of those forecasts will be better than others: the data can inform the choice of "priors" so that the priors chosen will perform well for forecasting. For example, in the context of the BMA model with prior probability π of including a variable and a g-prior for the coefficient conditional upon inclusion, the hyperparameters π and g both can be chosen, or estimated, based on the data.

This idea of using Bayes methods with an estimated, rather than subjective, prior distribution is the central idea of empirical Bayes estimation. In the many-predictor problem, because there are n predictors, one obtains many observations on the empirical distribution of the regression coefficients; this empirical distribution can in turn be used to find the prior (to estimate the prior) that comes as close as possible to producing a marginal distribution that matches the empirical distribution.

The method of empirical Bayes estimation dates to Robbins (1955, 1964), who introduced nonparametric empirical Bayes methods. Maritz and Lwin (1989), Carlin and Louis (1996), and Lehmann and Casella (1998, Section 4.6) provide monograph and textbook treatments of empirical Bayes methods. Recent contributions to the theory of empirical Bayes estimation in the linear model with orthogonal regressors include

George and Foster (2000) and Zhang (2003, 2005). For an early application of empirical Bayes methods to economic forecasting using VARs, see Doan, Litterman and Sims (1984).

This section lays out the basic structure of empirical Bayes estimation, as applied to the large-n linear forecasting problem. We focus on the case of orthogonalized regressors (the regressors are the principle components or weighted principle components). We defer discussion of empirical experience with large-n empirical Bayes macroeconomic forecasting to Section 7.

6.1. Empirical Bayes methods for large-n linear forecasting

The empirical Bayes model consists of the regression equation for the variable to be forecasted plus a specification of the priors. Throughout this section we focus on estimation with n orthogonalized regressors. In the empirical applications these regressors will be the factors, estimated by PCA, so we denote these regressors by the $n \times 1$ vector F_t, which we assume have been normalized so that $T^{-1}\sum_{t=1}^{T} F_t F_t' = I_n$. We assume that $n < T$ so all the principal components are nonzero; otherwise, n in this section would be replaced by $n' = \min(n, T)$. The starting point is the linear model

$$Y_{t+1} = \beta' F_t + \varepsilon_{t+1}, \tag{29}$$

where $\{F_t\}$ is treated as strictly exogenous. The vector of coefficients β is treated as being drawn from a prior distribution. Because the regressors are orthogonal, it is convenient to adopt a prior in which the elements of β are independently (although not necessarily identically) distributed, so that β_i has the prior distribution G_i, $i = 1, \dots, n$.

If the forecaster has a squared error loss function, then the Bayes risk of the forecast is minimized by using the Bayes estimator of β, which is the posterior mean. Suppose that the errors are i.i.d. $N(0, \sigma_\varepsilon^2)$, and for the moment suppose that σ_ε^2 is known. Conditional on β, the centered OLS estimators, $\{\hat{\beta}_i - \beta_i\}$, are i.i.d. $N(0, \sigma_\varepsilon^2/T)$; denote this conditional pdf by ϕ. Under these assumptions, the Bayes estimator of β_i is

$$\hat{\beta}_i^B = \frac{\int x\phi(\hat{\beta}_i - x)\,dG_i(x)}{\int \phi(\hat{\beta}_i - x)\,dG_i(x)} = \hat{\beta}_i + \sigma_\varepsilon^2 \ell_i(\hat{\beta}_i), \tag{30}$$

where $\ell_i(x) = d\ln(m_i(x))/dx$, where $m_i(x) = \int \phi(x - \beta)\,dG_i(\beta)$ is the marginal distribution of $\hat{\beta}_i$. The second expression in (30) is convenient because it represents the Bayes estimator as a function of the OLS estimator, σ_ε^2, and the score of the marginal distribution [see, for example, Maritz and Lwin (1989)].

Although the Bayes estimator minimizes the Bayes risk and is admissible, from a frequentist perspective it (and the Bayes forecast based on the predictive density) can have poor properties if the prior places most of its mass away from the true parameter value. The empirical Bayes solution to this criticism is to treat the prior as an unknown distribution to be estimated. To be concrete, suppose that the prior is the same for all i, that is, $G_i = G$ for all i. Then $\{\hat{\beta}_i\}$ constitute n i.i.d. draws from the marginal distribution m, which in turn depends on the prior G. Because the conditional distribution ϕ is known, this permits inference about G. In turn, the estimator of G can be used in (30) to compute the empirical Bayes estimator. The estimation of the prior can be done either parametrically or nonparametrically.

Parametric empirical Bayes The parametric empirical Bayes approach entails specifying a parametric prior distribution, $G_i(X; \theta)$, where θ is an unknown parameter vector that is common to all the priors. Then the marginal distribution of $\hat{\beta}_i$ is $m_i(x; \theta) = \int \phi(x - \beta)\,\mathrm{d}G_i(\beta; \theta)$. If $G_i = G$ for all i, then there are n i.i.d. observations on $\hat{\beta}_i$ from the marginal $m(x; \theta)$, and inference can proceed by maximum likelihood or by method of moments.

In the application at hand, where the regressors are the principal components, one might specify a prior with a spread that declines with i following some parametric structure. In this case, $\{\hat{\beta}_i\}$ constitute n independent draws from a heteroskedastic marginal distribution with parameterized heteroskedasticity, which again permits estimation of θ. Although the discussion has assumed that σ_ε^2 is known, it can be estimated consistently if $n, T \to \infty$ as long as $n/T \to \text{const} < 1$.

As a leading case, one could adopt the conjugate g-prior. An alternative approach to parameterizing G_i is to adopt a hierarchical prior. Clyde and George (2000) take this approach for wavelet transforms, as applied to signal compression, where the prior is allowed to vary depending on the wavelet level.

Nonparametric empirical Bayes The nonparametric empirical Bayes approach treats the prior as an unknown distribution. Suppose that the prior is the same (G) for all i, so that $\ell_i = \ell$ for all i. Then the second expression in (30) suggests the estimator

$$\hat{\beta}_i^{\mathrm{NEB}} = \hat{\beta}_i + \sigma_\varepsilon^2 \hat{\ell}(\hat{\beta}_i), \tag{31}$$

where $\hat{\ell}$ is an estimator of ℓ.

The virtue of the estimator (31) is that it does not require direct estimation of G; for this reason, Maritz and Lwin (1989) refer to it as a simple empirical Bayes estimator. Instead, the estimator (31) only requires estimation of the derivative of the log of the marginal likelihood, $\ell(x) = \mathrm{d}\ln(m_i(x))/\mathrm{d}x = (\mathrm{d}m(x)/\mathrm{d}x)/m(x)$. Nonparametric estimation of the score of i.i.d. random variables arises in other applications in statistics, in particular adaptive estimation, and has been extensively studied. Going into the details would take us beyond the scope of this survey, so instead the reader is referred to Maritz and Lwin (1989), Carlin and Louis (1996), and Bickel et al. (1993).

Optimality results Robbins (1955) considered nonparametric empirical Bayes estimation in the context of the compound decision problem, in which there are samples from each of n units, where the draws for the ith unit are from the same distribution, conditional on some parameters, and these parameters in turn obey some distribution G. The distribution G can be formally treated either as a prior, or simply as an unknown distribution describing the population of parameters across the different units. In this setting, given G, the estimator of the parameters that minimizes the Bayes risk is the

Bayes estimator. Robbins (1955, 1964) showed that it is possible to construct empirical Bayes estimators that are asymptotically optimal, that is, empirical Bayes estimators that achieve the Bayes risk based on the infeasible Bayes estimator using the true unknown distribution G as the number of units tends to infinity.

At a formal level, if $n/T \to c$, $0 < c < 1$, and if the true parameters β_i are in a $1/n^{1/2}$ neighborhood of zero, then the linear model with orthogonal regressors has a similar mathematical structure to the compound decision problem. Knox, Stock and Watson (2001) provide results about the asymptotic optimality of the parametric and nonparametric empirical Bayes estimators. They also provide conditions under which the empirical Bayes estimator (with a common prior G) is, asymptotically, the minimum risk equivariant estimator under the group that permutes the indexes of the regressors.

Extension to lagged endogenous regressors As in the methods of Sections 3–5, in practice it can be desirable to extend the linear regression model to include an additional set of regressors, Z_t, that the researcher has confidence belong in the model; the leading case is when Z_t consists of lags of Y_t. The key difference between Z_t and F_t is associated with the degree of certainty about the coefficients: Z_t are variables that the researcher believes to belong in the model with potentially large coefficients, whereas F_t is viewed as having potentially small coefficients. In principle a separate prior could be specified for the coefficients on Z_t. By analogy to the treatment in BMA, however, a simpler approach is to replace X_t and Y_{t+1} in the foregoing with the residuals from initial regressions of X_t and Y_{t+1} onto Z_t. The principal components F_t then can be computed using these residuals.

Extensions to endogenous regressors and multiperiod forecasts Like BMA, the theory for empirical Bayes estimation in the linear model was developed assuming that $\{X_t, Z_t\}$ are strictly exogenous. As was discussed in Section 5, this assumption is implausible in the macroeconomic forecasting. We are unaware of work that has extended empirical Bayes methods to the large-n linear forecasting model with regressors that are predetermined but not strictly exogenous.

7. Empirical illustration

This section illustrates the performance of these methods in an application to forecasting the growth rate of U.S. industrial production using $n = 130$ predictors. The results in this section are taken from Stock and Watson (2004a), which presents results for additional methods and for forecasts of other series.

7.1. Forecasting methods

The forecasting methods consist of univariate benchmark forecasts, and five categories of multivariate forecasts using all the predictors. All multistep ahead forecasts (including the univariate forecasts) were computed by the direct method, that is, using a single noniterated equation with dependent variable being the h-period growth in industrial production, Y_{t+h}^h, as defined in (1). All models include an intercept.

Univariate forecasts The benchmark model is an AR, with lag length selected by AIC (maximum lag $= 12$). Results are also presented for an AR(4).

OLS The OLS forecast is based on the OLS regression of Y_{t+h}^h onto X_t and four lags of Y_t.

Combination forecasts Three combination forecasts are reported. The first is the simple mean of the 130 forecasts based on autoregressive distributed lag (ADL) models with four lags each of X_t and Y_t. The second combination forecast is a weighted average, where the weights are computed using the expression implied by g-prior BMA, specifically, the weights are given by w_{it} in (27) with $g = 1$, where in this case the number of models K equals n [this second method is similar to one of several used by Wright (2004)].

DFM Three DFM forecasts are reported. Each is based on the regression of Y_{t+h}^h onto the first three factors and four lags of Y_t. The forecasts differ by the method of computing the factors. The first, denoted PCA(3, 4), estimates the factors by PCA. The second, denoted diagonal-weighted PCA(3, 4), estimates the factors by weighted PCA, where the weight matrix Σ_{uu} is diagonal, with diagonal element $\Sigma_{uu,ii}$ estimated by the difference between the corresponding diagonal elements of the sample covariance matrix of X_t and the dynamic principal components estimator of the covariance matrix of the common components, as proposed by Forni et al. (2003b). The third DFM forecast, denoted weighted PCA(3, 4) is similarly constructed, but also estimates the off-diagonal elements of Σ_{uu} analogously to the diagonal elements.

BMA Three BMA forecasts are reported. The first is BMA as outlined in section with correlated X's and $g = 1/T$. The second two are BMA using orthogonal factors computed using the formulas in Clyde (1999a) following Koop and Potter (2004), for two values of g, $g = 1/T$ and $g = 1$.

Empirical Bayes Two parametric empirical Bayes forecasts are reported. Both are implemented using the n principal components for the orthogonal regressors and using a common prior distribution G. The first empirical Bayes forecast uses the g-prior with mean zero, where g and σ_ε^2 are estimated from the OLS estimators and residuals. The second empirical Bayes forecast uses a mixed normal prior, in which $\beta_j = 0$ with probability $1 - \pi$ and is normally distributed, according to a g-prior with mean zero, with probability π. In this case, the parameters g, π, and the scale σ^2 are estimated from the OLS coefficients estimates, which allows for heteroskedasticity and autocorrelation in the regression error (the autocorrelation is induced by the overlapping observations in the direct multiperiod-ahead forecasts).

7.2. Data and comparison methodology

Data The data set consists of 131 monthly U.S. economic time series (industrial production plus 130 predictor variables) observed from 1959:1–2003:12. The data set is an updated version of the data set used in Stock and Watson (1999). The predictors include series in 14 categories: real output and income; employment and hours; real retail, manufacturing and trade sales; consumption; housing starts and sales; real inventories; orders; stock prices; exchange rates; interest rates and spreads; money and credit quantity aggregates; price indexes; average hourly earnings; and miscellaneous. The series were all transformed to be stationary by taking first or second differences, logarithms, or first or second differences of logarithms, following standard practice. The list of series and transformations are given in Stock and Watson (2004a).

Method for forecast comparisons All forecasts are pseudo-out-of-sample and were computed recursively (demeaning, standardization, model selection, and all model estimation, including any hyperparameter estimation, was done recursively). The period for forecast comparison is 1974:7–(2003:12-h). All regressions start in 1961:1, with earlier observations used for initial conditions. Forecast risk is evaluated using the mean squared forecast errors (MSFEs) over the forecast period, relative to the AR(AIC) benchmark.

7.3. Empirical results

The results are summarized in Table 1. These results are taken from Stock and Watson (2004a), which reports results for other variations on these methods and for more variables to be forecasted. Because the entries are MSFEs, relative to the AR(AIC) benchmark, entries less than one indicate a MSFE improvement over the AR(AIC) forecast. As indicated in the first row, the use of AIC to select the benchmark model is not particularly important for these results: the performance of an AR(4) and the AR(AIC) are nearly identical. More generally, the results in Table 1 are robust to changes in the details of forecast construction, for example, using an information criterion to select lag lengths.

It would be inappropriate to treat this comparison, using a single sample period and a single target variable, as a horse race that can determine which of these methods is "best". Still, the results in Table 1 suggest some broad conclusions. Most importantly, the results confirm that it is possible to make substantial improvements over the univariate benchmark if one uses appropriate methods for handling this large data set. At forecast horizons of one through six months, these forecasts can reduce the AR(AIC) benchmark by 15% to 33%. Moreover, as expected theoretically, the OLS forecast with all 130 predictors much performs much worse than the univariate benchmark.

As found in the research discussed in Section 4, the DFM forecasts using only a few factors – in this case, three – improve substantially upon the benchmark. For the forecasts of industrial production, there seems to be some benefit from computing the factors

Table 1
Forecasts of U.S. industrial production growth using 130 monthly predictors: Relative mean square forecast errors for various forecasting methods

Method	1	3	6	12
Univariate benchmarks				
AR(AIC)	1.00	1.00	1.00	1.00
AR(4)	0.99	1.00	0.99	0.99
Multivariate forecasts				
(1) OLS	1.78	1.45	2.27	2.39
(2) Combination forecasts				
Mean	0.95	0.93	0.87	0.87
SSR-weighted average	0.85	0.95	0.96	1.16
(3) DFM				
PCA(3, 4)	0.83	0.70	0.74	0.87
Diagonal weighted PC(3, 4)	0.83	0.73	0.83	0.96
Weighted PC(3, 4)	0.82	0.70	0.66	0.76
(4) BMA				
X's, $g = 1/T$	0.83	0.79	1.18	1.50
Principal components, $g = 1$	0.85	0.75	0.83	0.92
Principal components, $g = 1/T$	0.85	0.78	1.04	1.50
(5) Empirical Bayes				
Parametric/g-prior	1.00	1.04	1.56	1.92
Parametric/mixed normal prior	0.93	0.75	0.81	0.89

Notes: Entries are relative MSFEs, relative to the AR(AIC) benchmark. All forecasts are recursive (pseudo-out-of-sample), and the MSFEs were computed over the period 1974:7–(2003:12-h). The various columns correspond to forecasts of 1, 3, 6, and 12-month growth, where all the multiperiod forecasts were computed by direct (not iterated) methods. The forecasting methods are described in the text.

using weighted PCA rather than PCA, with the most consistent improvements arising from using the nondiagonal weighting scheme. Interestingly, nothing is gained by trying to exploit the information in the additional factors beyond the third using either BMA, applied to the PCA factors, or empirical Bayes methods. In addition, applying BMA to the original X's does not yield substantial improvements. Although simple mean averaging of individual ADL forecasts improves upon the autoregressive benchmark, the simple combination forecasts do not achieve the performance of the more sophisticated methods. The more complete analysis in Stock and Watson (2004a) shows that this interesting finding holds for other horizons and for forecasts of other U.S. series: low-dimensional forecasts using the first few PCA or weighted PCA estimators of the factors forecast as well or better than the methods like BMA that use many more factors.

A question of interest is how similar these different forecasting methods are. All the forecasts use information in lagged Y_t, but they differ in the way they handle information in X_t. One way to compare the treatment of X_t by two forecasting methods is to compare the partial correlations of the in-sample predicted values from the two methods, after controlling for lagged values of Y_t. Table 2 reports these partial corre-

Table 2
Partial correlations between large-n forecasts, given four lags of Y_t

Method	(1)	(2)	(3)	(4)	(5)	(6)	(7)	(8)	(9)	(10)
(1) Combination: mean	1.00									
(2) Combination: SSR-wtd	0.63	1.00								
(3) PCA(3, 4)	0.71	0.48	1.00							
(4) Diagonal wtd PC(3, 4)	0.66	0.56	0.90	1.00						
(5) Weighted PC(3, 4)	0.78	0.57	0.82	0.86	1.00					
(6) BMA/X's, $g = 1/T$	0.73	0.77	0.67	0.71	0.71	1.00				
(7) BMA/PC's, $g = 1$	0.76	0.61	0.62	0.61	0.72	0.82	1.00			
(8) BMA/PC's, $g = 1/T$	0.77	0.62	0.68	0.68	0.77	0.80	0.95	1.00		
(9) PEB/g-prior	0.68	0.56	0.52	0.50	0.60	0.77	0.97	0.85	1.00	
(10) PEB/mixed	0.79	0.63	0.70	0.70	0.80	0.82	0.96	0.99	0.87	1.00

Notes: The forecasting methods are defined in the text. Entries are the partial correlations between the in-sample predicted values from the different forecasting models, all estimated using Y_{t+1} as the dependent variable and computed over the full forecast period, where the partial correlations are computed using the residuals from the projections of the in-sample predicted values of the two forecasting methods being correlated onto four lagged values of Y_t.

lations for the methods in Table 1, based on full-sample one-step ahead regressions. The interesting feature of Table 2 is that the partial correlations among some of these methods is quite low, even for methods that have very similar MSFEs. For example, the PCA(3, 4) forecast and the BMA/X forecast with $g = 1/T$ both have relative MSFE of 0.83, but the partial correlation of their in-sample predicted values is only 0.67. This suggests that the forecasting methods in Table 2 imply substantially different weights on the original X_t data, which suggests that there could remain room for improvement upon the forecasting methods in Table 2.

8. Discussion

The past few years have seen considerable progress towards the goal of exploiting the wealth of data that is available for economic forecasting in real time. As the application to forecasting industrial production in Section 7 illustrates, these methods can make substantial improvements upon benchmark univariate models. Moreover, the empirical work discussed in this review makes the case that these forecasts improve not just upon autoregressive benchmarks, but upon standard multivariate forecasting models.

Despite this progress, the methods surveyed in this chapter are limited in at least three important respects, and work remains to be done. First, these methods are those that have been studied most intensively for economic forecasting, but they are not the only methods available. For example, Inoue and Kilian (2003) examine forecasts of U.S. inflation with $n = 26$ using bagging, a weighting scheme in which the weights are produced by bootstrapping forecasts based on pretest model selection. They report improvements over PCA factor forecasts based on these 26 predictors. As mentioned in the Introduction, Bayesian VARs are now capable of handling a score or more of predictors, and a potential advantage of Bayesian VARs is that they can produce iterated multistep forecasts. Also, there are alternative model selection methods in the statistics literature that have not yet been explored in economic forecasting applications, e.g., the LARS method [Efron et al. (2004)] or procedures to control the false discovery rate [Benjamini and Hochberg (1995)].

Second, all these forecasts are linear. Although the economic forecasting literature contains instances in which forecasts are improved by allowing for specific types of nonlinearity, introducing nonlinearities has the effect of dramatically increasing the dimensionality of the forecasting models. To the best of our knowledge, nonlinear forecasting with many predictors remains unexplored in economic applications.

Third, changes in the macroeconomy and in economic policy in general produces linear forecasting relations that are unstable, and indeed there is considerable empirical evidence of this type of nonstationarity in low-dimensional economic forecasting models [e.g., Clements and Hendry (1999), Stock and Watson (1996, 2003)]. This survey has discussed some theoretical arguments and empirical evidence suggesting that some of this instability can be mitigated by making high-dimensional forecasts: in a sense, the instability in individual forecasting relations might, in some cases, average out. But whether this is the case generally, and if so which forecasting methods are best able to mitigate this instability, largely remains unexplored.

References

Aiolfi, M., Timmermann, A. (2004). "Persistence in forecasting performance and conditional combination strategies". Journal of Econometrics. In press.

Altissimo, F., Bassanetti, A., Cristadoro, R., Forni, M., Lippi, M., Reichlin, L., Veronese, G. (2001). "The CEPR – Bank of Italy indicator". Bank of Italy. Manuscript.

Anderson, T.W. (1984). An Introduction to Multivariate Statistical Analysis, second ed. Wiley, New York.

Artis, M., Banerjee, A., Marcellino, M. (2001). "Factor forecasts for the UK". Bocconi University – IGIER. Manuscript.

Avramov, D. (2002). "Stock return predictability and model uncertainty". Journal of Financial Economics 64, 423–458.

Bai, J. (2003). "Inferential theory for factor models of large dimensions". Econometrica 71, 135–171.

Bai, J., Ng, S. (2002). "Determining the number of factors in approximate factor models". Econometrica 70, 191–221.

Bates, J.M., Granger, C.W.J. (1969). "The combination of forecasts". Operations Research Quarterly 20, 451–468.

Benjamini, Y., Hochberg, Y. (1995). "Controlling the false discovery rate: A practical and powerful approach to multiple testing". Journal of the Royal Statistical Society, Series B 57, 289–300.

Bernanke, B.S., Boivin, J. (2003). "Monetary policy in a data-rich environment". Journal of Monetary Economics 50, 525–546.

Bernanke, B.S., Boivin, J., Eliasz, P. (2005). "Measuring the effects of monetary policy: A factor-augmented vector autoregressive (FAVAR) approach". Quarterly Journal of Economics 120, 387–422.

Bickel, P., Klaassen, C.A.J., Ritov, Y., Wellner, J.A. (1993). "Efficient and Adaptive Estimation for Semiparametric Models". Johns Hopkins University Press, Baltimore, MD.

Boivin, J., Ng, S. (2003). "Are more data always better for factor analysis?" NBER. Working Paper No. 9829.

Boivin, J., Ng, S. (2005). "Understanding and comparing factor-based forecasts". NBER. Working Paper No. 11285.

Brillinger, D.R. (1964). "A frequency approach to the techniques of principal components, factor analysis and canonical variates in the case of stationary time series". Royal Statistical Society Conference, Cardiff Wales. Invited Paper. Available at http://stat-www.berkeley.edu/users/brill/papers.html.

Brillinger, D.R. (1981). "Time Series: Data Analysis and Theory", expanded ed. Holden-Day, San Francisco.

Brisson, M., Campbell, B., Galbraith, J.W. (2002). "Forecasting some low-predictability time series using diffusion indices". CIRANO. Manuscript.

Carlin, B., Louis, T.A. (1996). Bayes and Empirical Bayes Methods for Data Analysis. Monographs on Statistics and Probability, vol. 69. Chapman and Hall, Boca Raton.

Chamberlain, G., Rothschild, M. (1983). "Arbitrage factor structure, and mean-variance analysis of large asset markets". Econometrica 51, 1281–1304.

Chan, L., Stock, J.H., Watson, M. (1999). "A dynamic factor model framework for forecast combination". Spanish Economic Review 1, 91–121.

Chipman, H., George, E.I., McCulloch, R.E. (2001). The Practical Implementation of Bayesian Model Selection. IMS Lecture Notes Monograph Series, vol. 38. Institute of Mathematical Statistics.

Clayton-Matthews, A., Crone, T. (2003). "Consistent economic indexes for the 50 states". Federal Reserve Bank of Philadelphia. Manuscript.

Clemen, R.T. (1989). "Combining forecasts: A review and annotated bibliography". International Journal of Forecasting 5, 559–583.

Clements, M.P., Hendry, D.F. (1999). Forecasting Non-Stationary Economic Time Series. MIT Press, Cambridge, MA.

Clyde, M. (1999a). "Bayesian model averaging and model search strategies (with discussion)". In: Bernardo, J.M., Dawid, A.P., Berger, J.O., Smith, A.F.M. (Eds.), Bayesian Statistics, vol. 6. Oxford University Press, Oxford.

Clyde, M. (1999b). "Comment on 'Bayesian model averaging: A tutorial'". Statistical Science 14, 401–404.

Clyde, M., Desimone, H., Parmigiani, G. (1996). "Prediction via orthogonalized model mixing". Journal of the American Statistical Association 91, 1197–1208.

Clyde, M., George, E.I. (2000). "Flexible empirical Bayes estimation for wavelets". Journal of the Royal Statistical Society, Series B 62 (3), 681–698.

Connor, G., Korajczyk, R.A. (1986). "Performance measurement with the arbitrage pricing theory". Journal of Financial Economics 15, 373–394.

Connor, G., Korajczyk, R.A. (1988). "Risk and return in an equilibrium APT: Application of a new test methodology". Journal of Financial Economics 21, 255–289.

Cremers, K.J.M. (2002). "Stock return predictability: A Bayesian model selection perspective". The Review of Financial Studies 15, 1223–1249.

Diebold, F.X., Lopez, J.A. (1996). "Forecast evaluation and combination". In: Maddala, G.S., Rao, C.R. (Eds.), Handbook of Statistics, vol. 14. North-Holland, Amsterdam.

Diebold, F.X., Pauly, P. (1987). "Structural change and the combination of forecasts". Journal of Forecasting 6, 21–40.

Diebold, F.X., Pauly, P. (1990). "The use of prior information in forecast combination". International Journal of Forecasting 6, 503–508.

Ding, A.A., Hwang, J.T.G. (1999). "Prediction intervals, factor analysis models, and high-dimensional empirical linear prediction". Journal of the American Statistical Association 94, 446–455.

Doan, T., Litterman, R., Sims, C.A. (1984). "Forecasting and conditional projection using realistic prior distributions". Econometric Reviews 3, 1–100.

Efron, B., Morris, C. (1973). "Stein's estimation rule and its competitors – An empirical Bayes approach". Journal of the American Statistical Association 68, 117–130.

Efron, B., Hastie, T., Johnstone, I., Tibshirani, R. (2004). "Least angle regression". Annals of Statistics 32, 407–499.

El Karoui, N. (2003). "On the largest eigenvalue of Wishart matrices with identity covariance when n, p and $p/n \to \infty$". Stanford Statistics Department Technical Report 2003-25.

Engle, R.F., Watson, M.W. (1981). "A one-factor multivariate time series model of metropolitan wage rates". Journal of the American Statistical Association 76 (376), 774–781.

Favero, C.A., Marcellino, M. (2001). "Large datasets, small models and monetary policy in Europe". CEPR. Working Paper No. 3098.

Favero, C.A., Marcellino, M., Neglia, F. (2002). "Principal components at work: The empirical analysis of monetary policy with large datasets". Bocconi University. IGIER Working Paper No. 223.

Federal Reserve Bank of Chicago. "CFNAI background release". Available at http://www.chicagofed.org/economic_research_and_data/cfnai.cfm.

Fernandez, C., Ley, E., Steel, M.F.J. (2001a). "Benchmark priors for Bayesian model averaging". Journal of Econometrics 100, 381–427.

Fernandez, C., Ley, E., Steel, M.F.J. (2001b). "Model uncertainty in cross-country growth regressions". Journal of Applied Econometrics 16, 563–576.

Figlewski, S. (1983). "Optimal price forecasting using survey data". Review of Economics and Statistics 65, 813–836.

Figlewski, S., Urich, T. (1983). "Optimal aggregation of money supply forecasts: Accuracy, profitability and market efficiency". The Journal of Finance 28, 695–710.

Forni, M., Reichlin, L. (1998). "Let's get real: A dynamic factor analytical approach to disaggregated business cycle". Review of Economic Studies 65, 453–474.

Forni, M., Hallin, M., Lippi, M., Reichlin, L. (2000). "The generalized factor model: Identification and estimation". The Review of Economics and Statistics 82, 540–554.

Forni, M., Hallin, M., Lippi, M., Reichlin, L. (2003a). "Do financial variables help forecasting inflation and real activity in the EURO area?" Journal of Monetary Economics 50, 1243–1255.

Forni, M., Hallin, M., Lippi, M., Reichlin, L. (2003b). "The generalized dynamic factor model: One-sided estimation and forecasting". Manuscript.

Forni, M., Hallin, M., Lippi, M., Reichlin, L. (2004). "The generalized factor model: Consistency and rates". Journal of Econometrics 119, 231–255.

Forni, M., Giannoni, D., Lippi, M., Reichlin, L. (2005). "Opening the black box: Structural factor models with large cross-sections". Manuscript, University of Rome.

George, E.I. (1999). "Bayesian Model Selection". Encyclopedia of the Statistical Sciences Update, vol. 3. Wiley, New York.

George, E.I., Foster, D.P. (2000). "Calibration and empirical Bayes variable selection". Biometrika 87, 731–747.

George, E.I., McCulloch, R.E. (1993). "Variable selection via Gibbs sampling". Journal of the American Statistical Association 88, 881–889.

George, E.I., McCulloch, R.E. (1997). "Approaches for Bayesian variable selection". Statistica Sinica 7 (2), 339–373.

Geweke, J. (1977). "The dynamic factor analysis of economic time series". In: Aigner, D.J., Goldberger, A.S. (Eds.), Latent Variables in Socio-Economic Models. North-Holland, Amsterdam.

Geweke, J.F. (1996). "Variable selection and model comparison in regression". In: Berger, J.O., Bernardo, J.M., Dawid, A.P., Smith, A.F.M. (Eds.), Bayesian Statistics, vol. 5. Oxford University Press, Oxford, pp. 609–620.

Giannoni, D., Reichlin, L., Sala, L. (2002). "Tracking Greenspan: Systematic and unsystematic monetary policy revisited". ECARES. Manuscript.

Giannoni, D., Reichlin, L., Sala, L. (2004). "Monetary policy in real time". NBER Macroeconomics Annual 2004, 161–200.

Granger, C.W.J., Ramanathan, R. (1984). "Improved methods of combining forecasting". Journal of Forecasting 3, 197–204.

Hannan, E.J., Deistler, M. (1988). The Statistical Theory of Linear Systems. Wiley, New York.

Hendry, D.F., Clements, M.P. (2002). "Pooling of forecasts". Econometrics Journal 5, 1–26.

Hendry, D.F., Krolzig, H.-M. (1999). "Improving on 'Data mining reconsidered' by K.D. Hoover and S.J. Perez". Econometrics Journal 2, 41–58.

Hoeting, J.A., Madigan, D., Raftery, A.E., Volinsky, C.T. (1999). "Bayesian model averaging: A tutorial". Statistical Science 14, 382–417.

Inoue, A., Kilian, L. (2003). "Bagging time series models". North Carolina State University. Manuscript.

James, A.T. (1964). "Distributions of matrix variates and latent roots derived from normal samples". Annals of Mathematical Statistics 35, 475–501.

James, W., Stein, C. (1960). "Estimation with quadratic loss". Proceedings of the Fourth Berkeley Symposium on Mathematical Statistics and Probability 1, 361–379.

Johnstone, I.M. (2001). "On the distribution of the largest eigenvalue in principal component analysis". Annals of Statistics 29, 295–327.

Jones, C.S. (2001). "Extracting factors from heteroskedastic asset returns". Journal of Financial Economics 62, 293–325.

Kapetanios, G., Marcellino, M. (2002). "A comparison of estimation methods for dynamic factor models of large dimensions". Bocconi University – IGIER. Manuscript.

Kim, C.-J., Nelson, C.R. (1998). "Business cycle turning points, a new coincident index, and tests for duration dependence based on a dynamic factor model with regime switching". The Review of Economics and Statistics 80, 188–201.

Kitchen, J., Monaco, R. (2003). "The U.S. Treasury staff's real-time GDP forecast system". Business Economics, October.

Knox, T., Stock, J.H., Watson, M.W. (2001). "Empirical Bayes forecasts of one time series using many regressors". NBER. Technical Working Paper No. 269.

Koop, G., Potter, S. (2004). "Forecasting in dynamic factor models using Bayesian model averaging". Econometrics Journal 7, 550–565.

Kose, A., Otrok, C., Whiteman, C.H. (2003). "International business cycles: World, region, and country-specific factors". American Economic Review 93, 1216–1239.

Leamer, E.E. (1978). Specification Searches. Wiley, New York.

Leeper, E., Sims, C.A., Zha, T. (1996). "What does monetary policy do?" Brookings Papers on Economic Activity 2, 1–63.

Lehmann, E.L., Casella, G. (1998). Theory of Point Estimation, second ed. Springer-Verlag, New York.

LeSage, J.P., Magura, M. (1992). "A mixture-model approach to combining forecasts". Journal of Business and Economic Statistics 3, 445–452.

Madigan, D.M., York, J. (1995). "Bayesian graphical models for discrete data". International Statistical Review 63, 215–232.

Maritz, J.S., Lwin, T. (1989). Empirical Bayes Methods, second ed. Chapman and Hall, London.

Miller, C.M., Clemen, R.T., Winkler, R.L. (1992). "The effect of nonstationarity on combined forecasts". International Journal of Forecasting 7, 515–529.

Min, C., Zellner, A. (1993). "Bayesian and non-Bayesian methods for combining models and forecasts with applications to forecasting international growth rates". Journal of Econometrics 56, 89–118.

Newbold, P., Harvey, D.I. (2002). "Forecast combination and encompassing". In: Clements, M.P., Hendry, D.F. (Eds.), A Companion to Economic Forecasting. Blackwell Press, Oxford, pp. 268–283.

Otrok, C., Silos, P., Whiteman, C.H. (2003). "Bayesian dynamic factor models for large datasets: Measuring and forecasting macroeconomic data". University of Iowa. Manuscript.

Otrok, C., Whiteman, C.H. (1998). "Bayesian leading indicators: Measuring and predicting economic conditions in Iowa". International Economic Review 39, 997–1014.

Peña, D., Poncela, P. (2004). "Forecasting with nonstationary dynamic factor models". Journal of Econometrics 119, 291–321.

Quah, D., Sargent, T.J. (1993). "A dynamic index model for large cross sections". In: Stock, J.H., Watson, M.W. (Eds.), Business Cycles, Indicators, and Forecasting. University of Chicago Press for the NBER, Chicago. Chapter 7.

Raftery, A.E., Madigan, D., Hoeting, J.A. (1997). "Bayesian model averaging for linear regression models". Journal of the American Statistical Association 92, 179–191.

Robbins, H. (1955). "An empirical Bayes approach to statistics". Proceedings of the Third Berkeley Symposium on Mathematical Statistics and Probability 1, 157–164.

Robbins, H. (1964). "The empirical Bayes approach to statistical problems". Annals of Mathematical Statistics 35, 1–20.

Sargent, T.J. (1989). "Two models of measurements and the investment accelerator". The Journal of Political Economy 97, 251–287.

Sargent, T.J., Sims, C.A. (1977). "Business cycle modeling without pretending to have too much a priori economic theory". In: Sims, C., et al. (Eds.), New Methods in Business Cycle Research. Federal Reserve Bank of Minneapolis, Minneapolis.

Sessions, D.N., Chatterjee, S. (1989). "The combining of forecasts using recursive techniques with nonstationary weights". Journal of Forecasting 8, 239–251.

Stein, C. (1955). "Inadmissibility of the usual estimator for the mean of multivariate normal distribution". Proceedings of the Third Berkeley Symposium on Mathematical Statistics and Probability 1, 197–206.

Stock, J.H., Watson, M.W. (1989). "New indexes of coincident and leading economic indicators". NBER Macroeconomics Annual, 351–393.

Stock, J.H., Watson, M.W. (1991). "A probability model of the coincident economic indicators". In: Moore, G., Lahiri, K. (Eds.), The Leading Economic Indicators: New Approaches and Forecasting Records. Cambridge University Press, Cambridge, pp. 63–90.

Stock, J.H., Watson, M.W. (1996). "Evidence on structural instability in macroeconomic time series relations". Journal of Business and Economic Statistics 14, 11–30.

Stock, J.H., Watson, M.W. (1998). "Median unbiased estimation of coefficient variance in a time varying parameter model". Journal of the American Statistical Association 93, 349–358.

Stock, J.H., Watson, M.W. (1999). "Forecasting inflation". Journal of Monetary Economics 44, 293–335.

Stock, J.H., Watson, M.W. (2002a). "Macroeconomic forecasting using diffusion indexes". Journal of Business and Economic Statistics 20, 147–162.

Stock, J.H., Watson, M.W. (2002b). "Forecasting using principal components from a large number of predictors". Journal of the American Statistical Association 97, 1167–1179.

Stock, J.H., Watson, M.W. (2003). "Forecasting output and inflation: The role of asset prices". Journal of Economic Literature 41, 788–829.

Stock, J.H., Watson, M.W. (2004a). "An empirical comparison of methods for forecasting using many predictors". Manuscript.

Stock, J.H., Watson, M.W. (2004b). "Combination forecasts of output growth in a seven-country data set". Journal of Forecasting. In press.

Stock, J.H., Watson, M.W. (2005). "Implications of dynamic factor models for VAR analysis". Manuscript.

Wright, J.H. (2003). "Bayesian model averaging and exchange rate forecasts". Board of Governors of the Federal Reserve System. International Finance Discussion Paper No. 779.

Wright, J.H. (2004). "Forecasting inflation by Bayesian model averaging". Board of Governors of the Federal Reserve System. Manuscript.

Zellner, A. (1986). "On assessing prior distributions and Bayesian regression analysis with g-prior distributions". In: Goel, P.K., Zellner, A. (Eds.), Bayesian Inference and Decision Techniques: Essays in Honor of Bruno de Finietti. North-Holland, Amsterdam, pp. 233–243.

Zhang, C.-H. (2003). "Compound decision theory and empirical Bayes methods". Annals of Statistics 31, 379–390.

Zhang, C.-H. (2005). "General empirical Bayes wavelet methods and exactly adaptive minimax estimation". Annals of Statistics 33, 54–100.

Chapter 11

FORECASTING WITH TRENDING DATA

GRAHAM ELLIOTT

University of California

Contents

Handbook of Economic Forecasting, Volume 1
Edited by Graham Elliott, Clive W.J. Granger and Allan Timmermann

DOI: 10.1016/S1574-0706(05)01011-6

Abstract

This chapter examines the problems of dealing with trending type data when there is uncertainty over whether or not we really have unit roots in the data. This uncertainty is practical – for many macroeconomic and financial variables theory does not imply a unit root in the data however unit root tests fail to reject. This means that there may be a unit root or roots close to the unit circle. We first examine the differences between results using stationary predictors and nonstationary or near nonstationary predictors. Unconditionally, the contribution of parameter estimation error to expected loss is of the same order for stationary and nonstationary variables despite the faster convergence of the parameter estimates. However expected losses depend on true parameter values.

We then review univariate and multivariate forecasting in a framework where there is uncertainty over the trend. In univariate models we examine trade-offs between estimators in the short and long run. Estimation of parameters for most models dominates imposing a unit root. It is for these models that the effects of nuisance parameters in the models is clearest. For multivariate models we examine forecasting from cointegrating models as well as examine the effects of erroneously assuming cointegration. It is shown that inconclusive theoretical implications arise from the dependence of forecast performance on nuisance parameters. Depending on these nuisance parameters imposing cointegration can be more or less useful for different horizons. The problem of forecasting variables with trending regressors – for example, forecasting stock returns with the dividend–price ratio – is evaluated analytically. The literature on distortion in inference in such models is reviewed. Finally, forecast evaluation for these problems is discussed.

Keywords

unit root, cointegration, long run forecasts, local to unity

JEL classification: C13, C22, C32, C53

1. Introduction

In the seminal paper Granger (1966) showed that the majority of macroeconomic variables have a typical spectral shape dominated by a peak at low frequencies. From a time domain view this means that there is some relatively long run information in the current level of a variable, or alternately stated that there is some sort of 'trending' behavior in macroeconomic (and many financial) data that must be taken account of when modelling these variables.

The flip side of this finding is that there is exploitable information for forecasting, today's levels having a large amount of predictive power as to future levels of these variables. The difficulty that arises is being precise about what this trending behavior exactly is. By virtue of trends being slowly evolving by definition, in explaining the long run movements of the data there is simply not a lot of information in any dataset as to exactly how to specify this trend, nor is there a large amount of information available in any dataset for being able to distinguish between different models of the trend.

This chapter reviews the approaches to this problem in the econometric forecasting literature. In particular we examine attempts to evaluate the importance or lack thereof of particular assumptions on the nature of the trend. Intuitively we expect that the forecast horizon will be important. For longer horizons the long run behavior of the variable will become more important, which can be seen analytically. For the most part, the typical approach to the trending problem in practice has been to follow the Box and Jenkins (1970) approach of differencing the data, which amounts to the modelling of the apparent low frequency peak in the spectrum as being a zero frequency phenomenon. Thus the majority of the work has been in considering the imposition of unit roots at various parts of the model. We will follow this approach, examining the effects of such assumptions.

Since reasonable alternative specifications must be 'close' to models with unit roots, it follows directly to concern ourselves with models that are close on some metric to the unit root model. The relevant metric is the ability of tests to distinguish between the models of the trend – if tests can easily distinguish the models then there is no uncertainty over the form of the model and hence no trade-off to consider. However the set of models for this is extremely large, and for most of the models little analytic work has been done. To this end we concentrate on linear models with near unit roots. We exclude breaks, which are covered in Chapter 12 by Clements and Hendry in this Handbook. Also excluded are nonlinear persistent models, such as threshold models, smooth transition autoregressive models. Finally, more recently a literature has developed on fractional differencing, providing an alternative model to the near unit root model through the addition of a greater range of dynamic behavior. We do not consider these models either as the literature on forecasting with such models is still in early development.

Throughout, we are motivated by some general 'stylized' facts that accompany the professions experience with forecasting macroeconomic and financial variables. The first is the phenomenon of our inability in many cases to do better than the 'unit root forecast', i.e. our inability to say much more in forecasting a future outcome than giving today's value. This most notoriously arises in foreign exchange rates [the seminal paper is Meese and Rogoff (1983)] where changes in the exchange rate have not been easily forecast except at quite distant horizons. In multivariate situations as well imposition of unit roots (or the imposition of near unit roots such as in the Litterman vector autoregressions (VARs)) tend to perform better than models estimated in levels. The second is that for many difficult to forecast variables, such as the exchange rate or stock returns, predictors that appear to be useful tend to display trending behavior and also seem to result in unstable forecasting rules. The third is that despite the promise that cointegration would result in much better forecasts, evidence is decidedly mixed and Monte Carlo evidence is ambiguous.

We first consider the differences and similarities of including nonstationary (or near nonstationary) covariates in the forecasting model. This is undertaken in the next section. Many of the issues are well known from the literature on estimation of these models, and the results for forecasting follow directly. Considering the average forecasting behavior over many replications of the data, which is relevant for understanding the output of Monte Carlo studies, we show that inclusion of trending data has a similar order effect in terms of estimation error as including stationary series, despite the faster rate of convergence of the coefficients. Unlike the stationary case, however, the effect depends on the true value of the coefficients rather than being uniform across the parameter space.

The third section focusses on the univariate forecasting problem. It is in this, the simplest of models, that the effects of the various nuisance parameters that arise can be most easily examined. It is also the easiest model in which to examine the effect of the forecast horizon. The section also discusses the ideas behind conditional versus unconditional (on past data) approaches and the issues that arise.

Given the general lack of discomfort the profession has with imposing unit roots, cointegration becomes an important concept for multivariate models. We analyze the features of taking cointegration into account when forecasting in section three. In particular we seek to explain the disparate findings in both Monte Carlo studies and with using real data. Different studies have suggested different roles for the knowledge of cointegration at different frequencies, results that can be explained by the nuisance parameters of the models chosen to a large extent.

We then return to the ideas that we are unsure of the trending behavior, examining 'near' cointegrating models where either the covariates do not have an exact unit root or the cointegrating vector itself is trending. These are both theoretically and empirically common issues when it comes to using cointegrating methods and modelling multivariate models.

In section five we examine the trending 'mismatch' models where trending variables are employed to forecast variables that do not have any obvious trending behavior. This encompasses many forecasting models used in practice.

In a very brief section six we review issues revolving around forecast evaluation. This has not been a very developed subject and hence the review is short. We also briefly review other attempts at modelling trending behavior.

2. Model specification and estimation

We first develop a number of general points regarding the problem of forecasting with nonstationary or near nonstationary variables and highlight the differences and similarities in forecasting when all of the variables are stationary and when they exhibit some form of trending behavior.

Define Z_t to be deterministic terms, W_t to be variables that display trending behavior and V_t to be variables that are clearly stationary. First consider a linear forecasting regression when the variable set is limited to $\{V_t\}$. Consider the linear forecasting regression

$$y_{t+1} = \beta V_t + u_{t+1},$$

where throughout β will refer to an unknown parameter vector in keeping with the context of the discussion and $\hat{\beta}$ refers to an estimate of this unknown parameter vector using data up to time T. The expected one step ahead forecast loss from estimating this model is given by

$$EL\big(y_{T+1} - \hat{\beta}' V_T\big) = EL\big(u_{T+1} - T^{-1/2}\big\{T^{1/2}\big(\hat{\beta} - \beta\big)' V_T\big\}\big).$$

The expected loss then depends on the loss function as well as the estimator. In the case of mean-square error (MSE) and ordinary least squares (OLS) estimates (denoted by subscript OLS), this can be asymptotically approximated to a second order term as

$$E\big(y_{T+1} - \hat{\beta}'_{\mathrm{OLS}} V_T\big)^2 \approx \sigma_u^2\big(1 + mT^{-1}\big),$$

where m is the dimension of V_t. The asymptotic approximation follows from mean of the term $T\sigma_u^{-2}(\hat{\beta}_{\mathrm{OLS}} - \beta)' V_T V_T (\hat{\beta}_{\mathrm{OLS}} - \beta)$ being fairly well approximated by the mean of a χ_m^2 random variable over repeated draws of $\{y_t, V_t\}_1^{T+1}$. (If the variables V_T are lagged dependent variables the above approximation is not the best available, it is well known that in such cases the OLS coefficients have an additional small bias which is ignored here.) The first point to notice is that the term involving the estimated coefficients disappears at rate T for the MSE loss function, or more generally adds a term that disappears at rate $T^{1/2}$ inside the loss function. The second point is that this is independent of β, and hence there are no issues in thinking about the differences in 'risk' of using OLS for various possible parameterizations of the models. Third, this result is not dependent on the variance covariance matrix of the regressors. When we include nonstationary or nearly nonstationary regressors, we will see that the last two of these results disappear, however the first – against often stated intuition – remains the same.

Before we can consider the addition of trending regressors to the forecasting model, we first must define what this means. As noted in the introduction, this chapter does not explicitly examine breaks in coefficients. For the purposes of most of the chapter, we will consider nonstationary models where there is a unit root in the autoregressive representation of the variable. Nearly nonstationary models will be ones where the largest root of the autoregressive process, denoted by ρ, is 'close' to one. To be clear, we require a definition of close.

A reasonable definition of what we would mean by 'close to one' is values for ρ that are difficult to distinguish from one. Consider a situation where ρ is sufficiently far from one that standard tests for a unit root would reject always, i.e. with probability one. In such cases, there we clearly have no uncertainty over whether or not the variable is trending or not – it isn't. Further, treating variables with such little persistence as being 'stationary' does not create any great errors. The situation where we would consider that there is uncertainty over whether or not the data is trending, i.e. whether or not we can easily reject a unit root in the data, is the range of values for ρ where tests have difficulty distinguishing between this value of ρ and one. Since a larger number of observations helps us pin down this parameter more precisely, the range over ρ for which we have uncertainly shrinks as the sample size grows.

Thus we can obtain the relevant range, as a function of the number of observations, through examining the local power functions of unit root tests. Local power is obtained by these tests for ρ shrinking towards one at rate T, i.e. for local alternatives of the form $\rho = 1 - \gamma/T$ for γ fixed. We will use these local to unity asymptotics to evaluate asymptotic properties of the methods below. This makes ρ dependent on T, however we will suppress this notation. It should be understood that any model we consider has a fixed value for ρ, which will be understood for any sample size using asymptotic results for the corresponding value for γ given T.

It still remains to ascertain the relevant values for γ and hence pairs (ρ, T). It is well known that our ability to distinguish unit roots from those less than one depends on a number of factors including the initialization of the process and the specification of the deterministic terms. From Stock (1994) the relevant ranges can be read from his Figure 2 (pp. 2774–2775) for various tests and configurations of the deterministic component when initial conditions are set to zero effectively, when a mean is included the range for γ over which there is uncertainty is from zero to about $\gamma = 20$. When a time trend is included uncertainty is greater, the relevant uncertain range is from zero to about $\gamma = 30$. Larger initial conditions extend the range over γ for which tests have difficulty distinguishing the root from one [see Müller and Elliott (2003)]. For these models approximating functions of sample averages with normal distributions is not appropriate and instead these processes will be better approximated through applications of the Functional Central Limit Theorem.

Having determined what we mean by trending regressors, we can now turn to evaluating the similarities and difference with the stationary covariate models. We first split the trending and stationary covariates, as well as introduce the deterministics (as is familiar in the study of the asymptotic behavior of trending regressors when there are deterministic terms, these terms play a large role through altering the asymptotic behavior of the coefficients on the trending covariates). The model can be written

$$y_{t+1} = \beta_1' W_t + \beta_2' V_t + u_{1t},$$

where we recall that W_t are the trending covariates and V_t are the stationary covariates. In a linear regression the coefficients on variables with a unit root converge at the faster rate of T. [For the case of unit roots in a general regression framework, see Phillips and Durlauf (1986) and Sims, Stock and Watson (1990), the similar results for the local to unity case follow directly, see Elliott (1998).] We can write the loss from using OLS estimates of the linear model as

$$\begin{aligned} &L\big(y_{T+1} - \hat{\beta}_{1,\mathrm{OLS}}' W_T - \hat{\beta}_{2,\mathrm{OLS}}' V_T\big) \\ &\quad = L\big(u_{T+1} - T^{-1/2}\big[T\big(\hat{\beta}_{1,\mathrm{OLS}} - \beta_1\big)' T^{-1/2} W_T + T^{1/2}\big(\hat{\beta}_{2,\mathrm{OLS}} - \beta_2\big)' V_T\big]\big), \end{aligned}$$

where $T^{-1/2} W_T$ and V_T are $O_p(1)$. Notice that for the trending covariates we divide each of the trending regressors by the square root of T. But this is precisely the rate at which they diverge, and hence these too are $O_p(1)$ variables.

Now consider the three points above. First, standard intuition suggests that when we mix stationary and nonstationary (or nearly nonstationary) variables we can to some extent be less concerned with the parameter estimation on the nonstationary terms as they disappear at the faster rate of T as the sample size increases, hence they are an order of magnitude smaller than the coefficients on the stationary terms, at least asymptotically. However this is not true – the variables they multiply in the loss function grow at exactly this rate faster than the stationary covariates, so in the end they all end up making a contribution of the same order to the loss function. For MSE loss, this is that the terms disappear at rate T regardless of whether they are stationary or nonstationary (or deterministic, which was not shown here but follows by the same math).

Now consider the second and third points. The OLS coefficients $T(\hat{\beta}_{1,\mathrm{OLS}} - \beta_1)$ converge to nonstandard distributions which depend on the model through the local to unity parameter γ as well as other nuisance parameters of the model. The form depends on the specifics of the model, precise examples of this for various models will be given below. In the MSE loss case, terms such as $E[T(\hat{\beta}_{1,\mathrm{OLS}} - \beta_1)' W_T W_T' (\hat{\beta}_{1,\mathrm{OLS}} - \beta_1)]$ appear in the expected mean-square error.

Hence not only is the additional component to the expected loss when parameters are estimated now not well approximated by the number of parameters divided by T but it depends on γ through the expected value of the nonstandard term. Thus the OLS risk is now dependent on the true model, and one must think about what the true model is to evaluate what the OLS risk would be. This is in stark contrast to the stationary case. Finally, it also depends on the covariates themselves, since they also affect this nonstandard distribution and hence its expected value. The nature and dimension of any deterministic terms will additionally affect the risk through affecting this term. As is common in the nonstationary literature, whilst definitive statements can be made actual calculations will be special to the precise nature of the model and the properties of the regressors. The upshot is that it is not true that we can ignore the effects of the trending regressors asymptotically when evaluating expected loss because of their fast rate of convergence, and that the precise effects will vary from specification to specification.

This understanding drives the approach of the following. First, we will ignore for the most part the existence and effect of 'obviously' stationary covariates in the models. The main exception is the inclusion of error correction terms, which are closely related to the nonstationary terms and become part of the story. Second, we will proceed with a number of 'canonical' models – since the results differ from specification to specification it is more informative to analyze a few standard models closely.

A final general point refers to loss functions. Numerical results for trade-offs and evaluation of the effects of different methods for dealing with the trends will obviously depend on the loss function chosen. The typical loss function chosen in this literature is that of mean-square error (MSE). If the h step ahead forecast error conditional on information available at time t is denoted $e_{t+h|t}$ this is simply $E[e_{t+h|t}^2]$. In the case of multivariate models, multivariate versions of MSE have been examined. In this case the h step ahead forecast error is a vector and the analog to univariate MSE is $E[e'_{t+h|t}Ke_{t+h|t}]$ for some matrix of weights K. Notice that for each different choice of K we would have a different weighting of the forecast errors in each equation of the model and hence a different loss function, resulting in numerical evaluations of any choices over modelling to depend on K. Some authors have considered this a weakness of this loss function but clearly it is simply a feature of the reality that different loss functions necessarily lead to different outcomes precisely because they reflect different choices of what is important in the forecasting process. We will avoid this multivariate problem by simply choosing to evaluate a single equation from any multivariate problem.

There has also been some criticism of the use of the univariate MSE loss function in problems where there is a choice over whether or not the dependent variable is written in levels or differences. Consider an h step ahead forecast of y_t and assume that the forecast is conditional on information at time t. Now we can always write $y_{T+h} = y_T + \sum_{i=1}^{h} \Delta y_{t+i}$. So for any loss function, including the MSE, that is a function of the forecast errors only we have that

$$\begin{aligned} L(e_{t+h}) &= L(y_{t+h} - y_{t+h,t}) \\ &= L\left(y_t + \sum_{i=1}^{h} \Delta y_{t+i} - y_t + \sum_{i=1}^{h} \Delta y_{t+i,t}\right) \\ &= L\left(\sum_{i=1}^{h} (\Delta y_{t+i} - \Delta y_{t+i,t})\right) \end{aligned}$$

and so the forecast error can be written equivalently in the level or the sum of differences. Thus there is no implication for the choice of the loss function when we consider the two equivalent expressions of the forecast error.[1] We will refer to forecasting y_{T+h} and $y_{T+h} - y_T$ as being the same thing given that we will always assume that y_T is in the forecasters information set.

3. Univariate models

The simplest model in which to examine the issues, and hence the most examined model in the literature, is the univariate model. Even in this model results depend on a large variety of nuisance parameters. Consider the model

$$\begin{aligned} y_t &= \phi z_t + u_t, \quad t = 1, \ldots, T, \\ (1 - \rho L)u_t &= v_t, \quad t = 2, \ldots, T, \\ u_1 &= \xi, \end{aligned} \tag{1}$$

where z_t are strictly exogenous deterministic terms and ξ is the 'initial' condition. We will allow additional serial correlation through $v_t = c(L)\varepsilon_t$ where ε_t is a mean zero white noise term with variance σ_ε^2. The lag polynomial describing the dynamic behavior of y_t has been factored so that $\rho = 1 - \gamma/T$ corresponds to the largest root of the polynomial, and we assume that $c(L)$ is one summable.

Any result is going to depend on the specifics of the problem, i.e. results will depend on the exact model, in particular the nuisance parameters of the problem. In the literature on estimation and testing for unit roots it is well known that various nuisance parameters affect the asymptotic approximations to estimators and test statistics. There as here nuisance parameters such as the specification of the deterministic part of the model and the treatment of the initial condition affect results. The extent to which there are additional stationary dynamics in the model has a lesser effect. For the deterministic component we consider $z_t = 1$ and $z_t = (1, t)$ – the mean and time trend cases, respectively. For the initial condition we follow Müller and Elliott (2003) in modelling this term asymptotically as $\xi = \alpha\omega(2\gamma)^{-1/2}T^{1/2}$ where $\omega^2 = c(1)^2\sigma_\varepsilon^2$ and the rate $T^{1/2}$ results in this term being of the same order as the stochastic part of the model asymptotically. A choice of $\alpha = 1$ here corresponds to drawing the initial condition from its unconditional distribution.[2] Under these conditions we have

[1] Clements and Hendry (1993) and (1998, pp. 69–70) argue that the MSFE does not allow valid comparisons of forecast performance for predictions across models in levels or changes when $h > 1$. Note though that, conditional on time T dated information in both cases, they compare the levels loss of $E[y_{T+h} - y_T]^2$ with the difference loss of $E[y_{T+h} - y_{T+h-1}]^2$ which are two different objects, differing by the remaining $h - 1$ changes in y_t.

[2] It is common in Monte Carlo analysis to generate pseudo time series to be longer than the desired sample size and then drop early values in order to remove the effects of the initial condition. This, if sufficient observations are dropped, is the same as using the unconditional distribution. Notice though that α remains important – it is not possible to remove the effects of the initial condition for these models.

$$T^{-1/2}(u_{[Ts]}) \Rightarrow \omega M(s) = \begin{cases} \omega W(s) & \text{for } \gamma = 0, \\ \omega\alpha e^{-\gamma s}(2\gamma)^{-1/2} + \omega \int_0^s e^{-\gamma(s-\lambda)}\,dW(\lambda) & \text{else,} \end{cases} \tag{2}$$

where $W(\cdot)$ is a standard univariate Brownian motion. Also note that for $\gamma > 0$,

$$\begin{aligned} E\left[M(s)\right]^2 &= \alpha^2 e^{-2\gamma s}/(2\gamma) + \left(1 - e^{-2\gamma s}\right)/(2\gamma) \\ &= (\alpha^2 - 1)e^{-2\gamma s}/(2\gamma) + 1/(2\gamma), \end{aligned}$$

which will be used for approximating the MSE below.

If we knew that $\rho = 1$ then the variable has a unit root and forecasting would proceed using the model in first differences, following the Box and Jenkins (1970) approach. The idea that we know there is an exact unit root in a data series is not really relevant in practice. Theory rarely suggests a unit root in a data series, and even when we can obtain theoretical justification for a unit root it is typically a special case model [examples include the Hall (1978) model for consumption being a random walk, also results that suggest stock prices are random walks]. For most applications a potentially more reasonable approach both empirically and theoretically would be to consider models where $\rho \leqslant 1$ and there is uncertainty over its exact value. Thus there will be a trade-off between gains of imposing the unit root when it is close to being true and gains to estimation when we are away from this range of models.

A first step in considering how to forecast in this situation is to consider the cost of treating near unit root variables as though they have unit roots for the purposes of forecasting. To make any headway analytically we must simplify dramatically the models to show the effects. We first remove serial correlation.

In the case of the model in (1) and $c(L) = 1$,

$$\begin{aligned} y_{T+h} - y_T &= \varepsilon_{T+h} + \rho\varepsilon_{T+h-1} + \cdots + \rho^{h-1}\varepsilon_{T+1} + \left(\rho^h - 1\right)\left(y_T - \phi' z_T\right) \\ &\quad + \phi'(z_{T+h} - z_T) \\ &= \sum_{i=1}^{h} \rho^{h-i}\varepsilon_{T+i} + \left(\rho^h - 1\right)\left(y_T - \phi' z_T\right) + \phi'(z_{T+h} - z_T). \end{aligned}$$

Given that largest root ρ describes the stochastic trend in the data, it seems reasonable that the effects will depend on the forecast horizon. In the short run mistakes in estimating the trend will differ greatly from when we forecast further into the future. As this is the case, we will take these two sets of horizons separately.

A number of papers have examined these models analytically with reference to forecasting behavior. Magnus and Pesaran (1989) examine the model (1) where $z_t = 1$ with normal errors and $c(1) = 1$ and establish the exact unconditional distribution of the forecast error $y_{T+h} - y_T$ for various assumptions on the initial condition. Banerjee (2001) examines this same model for various initial values focussing on the impact of the nuisance parameters on MSE error using exact results. Some of the results given below are large sample analogs to these results. Clements and Hendry (2001) follow Sampson (1991) in examining the trade-off between models that impose the unit root and those that do not for forecasting in both short and long horizons with the model in (1) when $z_t = (1, t)$ and $c(L) = 1$ where also their model without a unit root sets $\rho = 0$. In all but the very smallest sample sizes these models are very different in the sense described above – i.e. the models are easily distinguishable by tests – so their analytic results cover a different set of comparisons to the ones presented here. Stock (1996) examines forecasting with the models in (1) for long horizons, examining the trade-offs between imposing the unit root or not as well as characterizing the unconditional forecast errors. Kemp (1999) provides large sample analogs to the Magnus and Pesaran (1989) results for long forecast horizons.

3.1. Short horizons

Suppose that we are considering imposing a unit root when we know the root is relatively close to one. Taking the mean case $\phi = \mu$ and considering a one step ahead forecast, we have that imposing a unit root leads to the forecast y_T of y_{T+h} (where imposing the unit root in the mean model annihilates the constant term in the forecasting equation). Contrast this to the optimal forecast based on past observations, i.e. we would use as a forecast $\mu + \rho^h(y_T - \mu)$. These differ by $(\rho^h - 1)(y_T - \mu)$ and hence the difference between forecasts assuming a unit root versus using the correct model will be large if either the root is far from one or the current level of the variable is far from its mean.

One reason to conclude that the 'unit root' is hard to beat in an autoregression is that this term is likely to be small on average, so even knowing the true model is unlikely to yield economically significant gains in the forecast when the forecasting horizon is short. The main reason follows directly from the term $(\rho^h - 1)(y_T - \mu)$ – for a large effect we require that $(\rho^h - 1)$ is large but as the root ρ gets further from one the distribution of $(y_T - \mu)$ becomes more tightly distributed about zero.

We can obtain an idea of the size of these affects analytically. In the case where $z_t = 1$, the unconditional MSE loss for a h step ahead forecast where h is small relative to the sample size is given by

$$\begin{aligned} E[y_{T+h} - y_T]^2 &= E\big[\varepsilon_{T+h} + \rho\varepsilon_{T+h-1} + \cdots + \rho^{h-1}\varepsilon_{T+1} + (\rho^h - 1)(y_T - \mu)\big]^2 \\ &= E\big[\varepsilon_{T+1} + \rho\varepsilon_{T+h-1} + \cdots + \rho^{h-1}\varepsilon_{T+1}\big]^2 \\ &\quad + T^{-1}\big\{T^2(\rho^h - 1)^2\big\}E\big[T^{-1}(y_T - \mu)^2\big]. \end{aligned}$$

The first order term is due to the unpredictable future innovations. Focussing on the second order term, we can approximate the term inside the expectations by its limit and after then taking expectations this term can be approximated by

$$\sigma_\varepsilon^{-2}T^2(\rho^h - 1)^2 E\big[T^{-1}(y_T - \mu)^2\big] \approx 0.5h^2\gamma(\alpha^2 - 1)\mathrm{e}^{-2\gamma} + \frac{h^2\gamma}{2}. \tag{3}$$

As γ increases, the term involving $\mathrm{e}^{-2\gamma}$ gets small fast and hence this term can be ignored. The first point to note then is that this leaves the result as basically linear in γ –

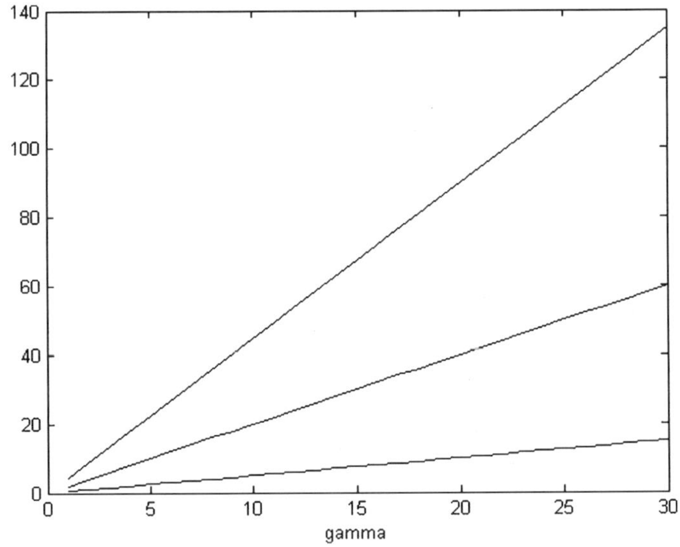

Figure 1. Evaluation of (3) for $h = 1, 2, 3$ in ascending order.

the loss as we expect is rising as the imposition of the unit root becomes less sensible and the result here shows that the effect is linear in the misspecification. The second point to note is that the slope of this linear effect is $h^2/2$, so is getting large faster and faster for any $\rho < 1$ the larger is the prediction horizon. This is also as we expect, if there is mean reversion then the further out we look the more likely it is that the variable has moved towards its mean and hence the larger the loss from giving a 'no change' forecast. The effect is increasing in h, i.e. given γ the marginal effect of a predicting an extra period ahead is $h\gamma$, which is larger the more mean reverting the data and larger the prediction horizon. The third point is that the effect of the initial condition is negligible in terms of the cost of imposing the unit root,[3] as it appears in the term multiplied by $e^{-2\gamma}$. Further, in the case where we use the unconditional distribution for the initial condition, i.e. $\alpha = 1$, these terms drop completely. For $\alpha \neq 1$ there will be some minor effects for very small γ.

The magnitude of the effects are pictured in Figure 1. This figure graphs the effect of this extra term as a function of the local to unity parameter for $h = 1, 2, 3$ and $\alpha = 1$. Steeper curves correspond to longer forecast horizons. Consider a forecasting problem where there are 100 observations available, and suppose that the true value for ρ was 0.9. This corresponds to $\gamma = 10$. Reading off the figure (or equivalently from the expression above) this corresponds to values of this additional term of 5, 20 and 45. Dividing these by the order of the term, i.e. 100, we have that the additional loss in MSE

[3] Banerjee (2001) shows this result using exact results for the distribution under normality.

as a percentage for the unpredictable component is of the order 5%, 10% and 15% of the size of the unpredictable component, respectively (since the size of the unpredictable component of the forecast error rises almost linearly in the forecast horizon when h is small).

When we include a time trend in the model, the model with the imposed unit root has a drift. An obvious estimator of the drift is the mean of the differenced series, denoted by $\hat{\tau}$. Hence the forecast MSE when a unit root is imposed is now

$$\begin{aligned}
&E[y_{T+1} - y_T - h\hat{\tau}]^2 \\
&\quad \cong E\big[\varepsilon_{T+h} + \rho\varepsilon_{T+h-1} + \cdots + \rho^{h-1}\varepsilon_{T+1} \\
&\qquad + T^{-1/2}\big\{T\big(\rho^h - 1\big) + h\big\}(y_T - \mu - \tau T) - hT^{-1/2}u_1\big]^2 \\
&\quad = E\big[\varepsilon_{T+h} + \rho\varepsilon_{T+h-1} + \cdots + \rho^{h-1}\varepsilon_{T+1}\big]^2 \\
&\qquad + T^{-1}E\big[\big\{T\big(\rho^h - 1\big) + h\big\}^2 T^{-1/2}(y_T - \mu - \tau T) - hT^{-1/2}u_1\big]^2.
\end{aligned}$$

Again, focussing on the second part of the term we have

$$\begin{aligned}
&\sigma_\varepsilon^{-2}E\big[\big\{T\big(\rho^h - 1\big) + h\big\}^2 T^{-1/2}(y_T - \mu - \tau T) - hT^{-1/2}u_1\big]^2 \\
&\quad \approx h^2\big[(1+\gamma)^2\big\{\big(\alpha^2 - 1\big)\mathrm{e}^{-2\gamma}/(2\gamma) + 1/(2\gamma)\big\} \\
&\qquad + \alpha^2/(2\gamma) - (1+\gamma)\mathrm{e}^{-\gamma}/\gamma\big]. \qquad (4)
\end{aligned}$$

Again the first term is essentially negligible, disappearing quickly as γ departs from zero, and equals zero as in the mean case when $\alpha = 1$. The last term, multiplied by $\mathrm{e}^{-\gamma}/\gamma$ also disappears fairly rapidly as γ gets larger. Focussing then on the last line of the previous expression, we can examine issues relevant to the imposition of a unit root on the forecast. First, as γ gets large the effect on the loss is larger than that for the constant only case. There are additional effects on the cost here, which is strictly positive for all horizons and initial values. The additional term arises due to the estimation of the slope of the time trend. As in the previous case, the longer the forecast horizon the larger the cost. The marginal effect of increasing the forecast horizon is also larger. Finally, unlike the model with only a constant, here the initial condition does have an effect, not only on the above effects but also on its own through the term $\alpha^2/2\gamma$. This term is decreasing the more distant the root is from one, however will have a nonnegligible effect for very roots close to one. The results are pictured in Figure 2 for $h = 1$, 2 and 3. These differential effects are shown by reporting in Figure 2 the expected loss term for both $\alpha = 1$ (solid lines) and for $\alpha = 0$ (accompanying dashed line).

The above results were for the model without any serial correlation. The presence of serial correlation alters the effects shown above, and in general these effects are complicated for short horizon forecasts. To see what happens, consider extending the model to allow the error terms to follow an MA(1), i.e. consider $c(L) = 1 + \psi L$. In the case where there is a constant only in the equation, we have that

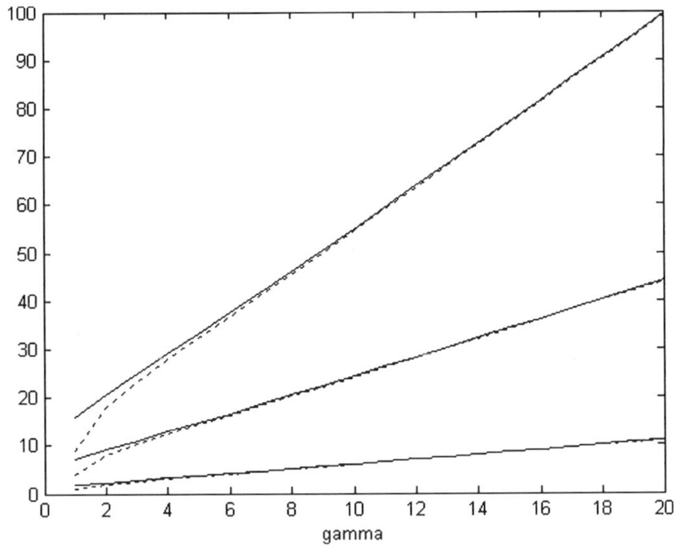

Figure 2. Evaluation of term in (4) for $h = 1, 2, 3$ in ascending order. Solid lines for $a = 1$ and dotted lines for $a = 0$.

$$\begin{aligned} y_{T+h} - y_T = {} & \left(\varepsilon_{T+h} + (\rho + \psi)\varepsilon_{T+h-1} + \cdots + \rho^{h-2}(\rho + \psi)\varepsilon_{T+1}\right) \\ & + \left[\left(\rho^h - 1\right)(y_T - \mu) + \rho^{h-1}\psi\varepsilon_T\right], \end{aligned}$$

where the first bracketed term is the unpredictable component and the second term in square brackets is the optimal prediction model. The need to estimate the coefficient on ε_T is not affected to the first order by the uncertainty over the value for ρ, hence this adds a term approximately equal to σ_ε^2/T to the MSE. In addition to this effect there are two other effects here – the first being that the variance of the unpredictable part changes and the second being that the unconditional variance of the term $(\rho^h - 1)(y_T - \mu)$ changes. Through the usual calculations and noting that now $T^{-1/2}y_{[T.]} \Rightarrow (1 + \psi)^2\sigma_\varepsilon^2 M(\cdot)$ we have the expression for the MSE

$$\begin{aligned} E[y_{T+h} - y_T]^2 \simeq \sigma_\varepsilon^2 \Bigg(& 1 + (h-1)(1+\psi)^2 \\ & + T^{-1}\left[(1+\psi)^2\left\{0.5h^2\gamma\left(\alpha^2 - 1\right)e^{-2\gamma} + \frac{h^2\gamma}{2}\right\} + 1\right]\Bigg). \end{aligned}$$

A few points can be made using this expression. First, when $h = 1$ there is an additional wedge in the size of the effect of not knowing the root relative to the variance of the unpredictable error. This wedge is $(1 + \psi)^2$ and comes through the difference between the variance of ε_t and the long run variance of $(1 - \rho L)y_t$, which are no longer the same in the model with serial correlation. We can see how various values for ψ will then change the cost of imposing the unit root. For $\psi < 0$ the MA component reduces the variation in the level of y_T, and imposing the root is less costly in this situation. Mathematically this comes through $(1+\psi)^2 < 1$. Positive MA terms exacerbate the cost. As h gets larger the differential scaling effect becomes relatively smaller, and the trade-off becomes similar to the results given earlier with the replacement of the variance of the shocks with the long run variance.

The costs of imposing coefficients that are near zero to zero needs to be compared to the problems of estimating these coefficients. It is clear that for ρ very close to one that imposition of a unit root will improve forecasts, but what 'very close' means here is an empirical question, depending on the properties of the estimators themselves. There is no obvious optimal estimator for ρ in these models. The typical asymptotic optimality result when $|\rho| < 1$ for the OLS estimator for ρ, denoted $\hat{\rho}_{\mathrm{OLS}}$, arises from a comparison of its pointwise asymptotic normal distribution compared to lower bounds for other consistent asymptotic normal estimators for ρ. Given that for the sample sizes and likely values for ρ we are considering here the OLS estimator has a distribution that is not even remotely close to being normal, comparisons between estimators based on this asymptotic approximation are not going to be relevant. Because of this, many potential estimators can be suggested and have been suggested in the literature. Throughout the results here we will write $\hat{\rho}$ (and similarly for nuisance parameters) as a generic estimator.

In the case where a constant is included the forecast requires estimates for both μ and ρ. The forecast is $y_{T+h|T} = (\hat{\rho}^h - 1)(y_T - \hat{\mu})$ resulting in forecast errors equal to

$$y_{T+h} - y_{T+h|T} = \sum_{i=1}^{h} \rho^{h-i}\varepsilon_{T+i} + (\hat{\mu}-\mu)\big(\hat{\rho}^h - 1\big) + \big(\rho^h - \hat{\rho}^h\big)(y_T - \mu).$$

The term due to the estimation error can be written as

$$\begin{aligned}&(\hat{\mu}-\mu)\big(\hat{\rho}^h - 1\big) + \big(\rho^h - \hat{\rho}^h\big)(y_T - \mu)\\&\quad = T^{-1/2}\big\{T^{-1/2}(\hat{\mu}-\mu)T\big(\hat{\rho}^h - 1\big) + T\big(\rho^h - \hat{\rho}^h\big)T^{-1/2}(y_T - \mu)\big\},\end{aligned}$$

where $T^{-1/2}(\hat{\mu}-\mu)$, $T(\hat{\rho}^h - 1)$ and $T(\rho^h - \hat{\rho}^h)$ are all $O_p(1)$ for reasonable estimators of the mean and autoregressive term. Hence, as with imposing a unit root, the additional term in the MSE will be disappearing at rate T. The precise distributions of these terms depend on the estimators employed. They are quite involved, being nonlinear functions of a Brownian motion. As such the expected value of the square of this is difficult to evaluate analytically and whilst we can write down what this expression looks like no results have yet been presented for making these results useful apart from determining the nuisance parameters that remain important asymptotically.

A very large number of different methods for estimating $\hat{\rho}^h$ and $\hat{\mu}$ have been suggested (and in the more general case estimators for the coefficients in more general dynamic models). The most commonly employed estimator is the OLS estimator, where we note that the regression of y_t on its lag and a constant results in the constant term in this regression being an estimator for $(1-\rho)\mu$. Instead of OLS, Prais and

Winsten (1954) and Cochrane and Orcutt (1949) estimators have been used. Andrews (1993), Andrews and Chen (1994), Roy and Fuller (2001) and Stock (1991) have suggested median unbiased estimators. Many researchers have considered using unit root pretests [cf. Diebold and Kilian (2000)]. We can consider any pretest as simply an estimator, $\hat{\rho}_{\mathrm{PT}}$ which is the OLS estimator for samples where the pretest rejects and equal to one otherwise. Sanchez (2002) has suggested a shrinkage estimator which can be written as a nonlinear function of the OLS estimator. In addition to this set of regressors researchers making forecasts for multiple steps ahead can choose between estimating $\hat{\rho}$ and taking the hth power or directly estimating $\hat{\rho}^h$.

In terms of the coefficients on the deterministic terms, there are also a range of estimators one could employ. From results such as in Elliott, Rothenberg and Stock (1996) for the model with y_1 normal with mean zero and variance equal to the innovation variance we have that the maximum likelihood estimators (MLE) for μ given ρ is

$$\hat{\mu} = \frac{y_1 + (1-\rho)\sum_{t=2}^{T}(1-\rho L)y_t}{1 + (T-1)(1-\rho)^2}. \tag{5}$$

Canjels and Watson (1997) examined the properties of a number of feasible GLS estimators for this model. Ng and Vogelsang (2002) suggest using this type of GLS detrending and show gains over OLS. In combination with unit root pretests they are also able to show gains from using GLS detrending for forecasting in this setting.

As noted, for any of the combinations of estimators of ρ and μ taking expectations of the asymptotic approximation is not really feasible. Instead, the typical approach in the literature has been to examine this in Monte Carlo. Monte Carlo evidence tends to suggest that GLS estimates for the deterministic components results in better forecasts that OLS, and that estimators such as the Prais–Winsten, median unbiased estimators, and pretesting have the advantage over OLS estimation of ρ. However general conclusions over which estimator is best rely on how one trades off the different performances of the methods for different values for ρ.

To see the issues, we construct Monte Carlo results for a number of the leading methods suggested. For $T = 100$ and various choices for $\gamma = T(\rho - 1)$ in an AR(1) model with standard normal errors and the initial condition drawn so $\alpha = 1$ we estimated the one step ahead forecast MSE and averaged over 40,000 replications. Reported in Figure 3 is the average of the estimated part of the term that disappears at rate T. For stationary variables we expect this to be equal to the number of parameters estimated, i.e. 2. The methods included were imposing a unit root (the upward sloping solid line), OLS estimation for both the root and mean (relatively flat dotted line), unit root pretesting using the Dickey and Fuller (1979) method with nominal size 5% (the humped dashed line) and the Sanchez shrinkage method (dots and dashes). As shown theoretically above, the imposition of a unit root, whilst sensible if very close to a unit root, has a MSE that increases linearly in the local to unity parameter and hence can accompany relatively large losses. The OLS estimation technique, whilst loss depends on the local to unity parameter, does so only a little for roots quite close to one. The trade-off between imposing the root at one and estimating using OLS has the imposition of the root

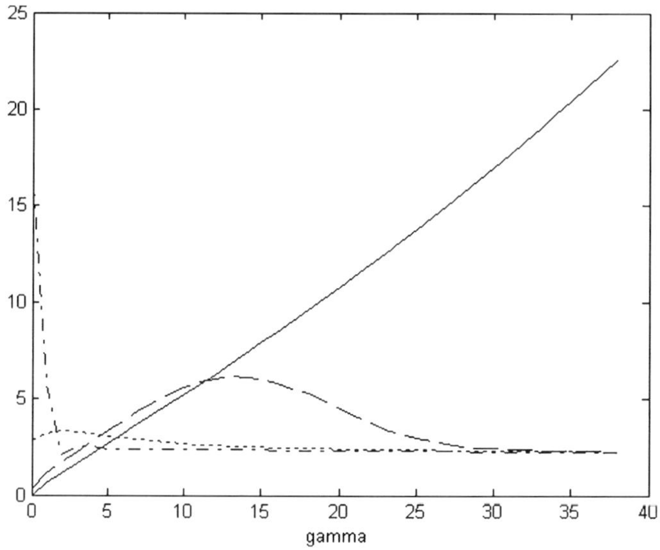

Figure 3. Relative effects of various estimated models in the mean case. The approaches are to impose a unit root (solid line), OLS (short dashes), DF pretest (long dashes) and Sanchez shrinkage (short and long dashes).

better only for $\gamma < 6$, i.e. for one hundred observations this is for roots of 0.94 or above. The pretest method works well at the 'ends', i.e. the low probability of rejecting a unit root at small values for γ means that it does well for such small values, imposing the truth or near to it, whilst because power eventually gets large it does as well as the OLS estimator for roots far from one. However the cost is at intermediate values – here the increase in average MSE is large as the power of the test is low. The Sanchez method does not do well for roots close to one, however does well away from one. Each method then embodies a different trade-off.

Apart from a rescaling of the y-axis, the results for h set to values greater than one but still small relative to the sample size result in almost identical pictures to that in Figure 3. For any moderate value for h the trade-offs occurs at the same local alternative.

Notice that any choice over which of the method to use in practice requires a weighting over the possible models, since no method uniformly dominates any other over the relevant parameter range. The commonly used 'differences' model of imposing the unit root cannot be beaten at $\gamma = 0$. Any pretest method to try and obtain the best of both worlds cannot possibly outperform the models it chooses between regardless of power if it controls size when $\gamma = 0$ as it will not choose this model with probability one and hence be inferior to imposing the unit root.

When a time trend is included the trade-off between the measures remains similar to that of the mean case qualitatively however the numbers differ. The results for the same experiment as in the mean case with $\alpha = 0$ are given in Figure 4 for the root imposed to one using the forecasting model $y_{T|T+1} = y_T + \hat{\tau}$, the model estimated by OLS and also

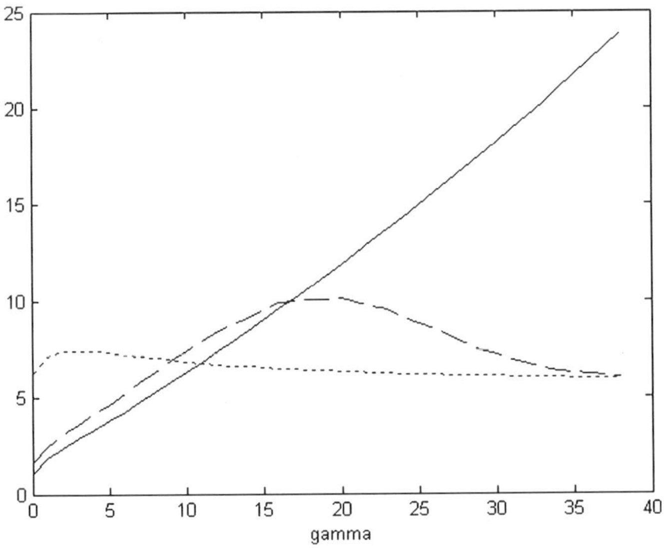

Figure 4. Relative effects of the imposed unit root (solid upward sloping line), OLS (short light dashes) and DF pretest (heavy dashes).

a hybrid approach using Dickey and Fuller t statistic pretesting with nominal size equal to 5%. As in the mean case, the use of OLS to estimate the forecasting model results in a relatively flat curve – the costs as a function of γ are varying but not much. Imposing the unit root on the forecasting model still requires that the drift term be estimated, so loss is not exactly zero at $\gamma = 0$ as in the mean case where no parameters are estimated. The value for γ for which estimation by OLS results in a lower MSE is larger than in the mean case. Here imposition of the root to zero performs better when $\gamma < 11$, so for $T = 100$ this is values for ρ of 0.9 or larger. The use of a pretest is also qualitatively similar to the mean case, however as might be expected the points where pretesting outperforms running the model in differences does differ. Here the value for which this is better is a value for γ of over 17 or so. The results presented here are close to their asymptotic counterparts, so these implications based on γ should extend relatively well to other sample sizes. Diebold and Kilian (2000) examine the trade-offs for this model in Monte Carlos for a number of choices of T and ρ. They note that for larger T the root needs to be closer to one for pretesting to dominate estimation of the model by OLS (their L model), which accords with the result here that this cutoff value is roughly a constant local alternative γ in h not too large. The value of pretesting – i.e. the models for which it helps – shrinks as T gets large. They also notice the 'ridge' where for near alternatives estimation dominates pretesting, however dismiss this as a small sample phenomenon. However asymptotically this region remains, there will be an interval for γ and hence ρ for which this is true for all sample sizes.

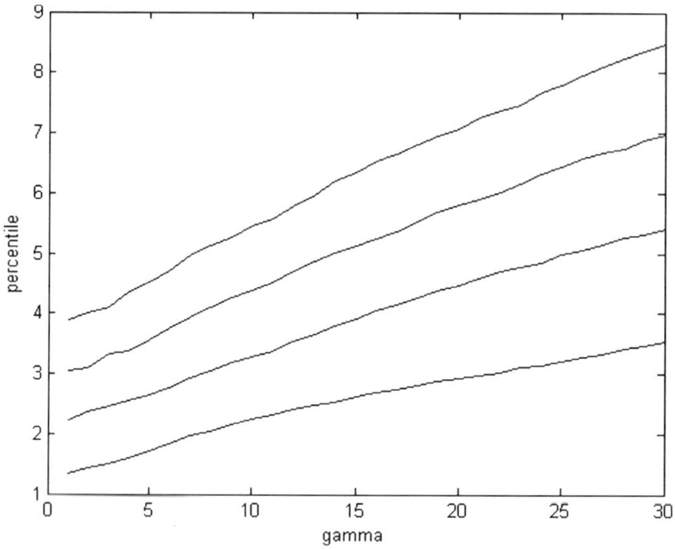

Figure 5. Percentiles of difference between OLS and Random Walk forecasts with $z_t = 1$, $h = 1$. Percentiles are for 20, 10, 5 and 2.5% in ascending order.

The 'value' of forecasts based on a unit root also is heightened by the corollary to the small size of the loss, namely that forecasts based on known parameters and forecasts based on imposing the unit root are highly correlated and hence their mistakes look very similar. We can evaluate the average size of the difference in the forecasts of the OLS and unit root models. In the case of no serial correlation the difference in h step ahead forecasts for the model with a mean is given by $(\hat{\rho}^h - 1)(y_T - \hat{\mu})$. Unconditionally this is symmetric around zero – whilst the first term pulls the estimated forecast towards the estimated mean the estimate of the mean ensures asymptotically that for every time this results in an underforecast when y_T is above its estimated mean there will be an equivalent situation where y_T is below its estimated mean. We can examine the percentiles of the limit result to evaluate the likely size of the differences between the forecasts for any (σ, T) pair. The term can be evaluated using a Monte Carlo experiment, the results for $h = 1$ and $h = 4$ are given in Figures 5 and 6, respectively, as a function of γ. To read the figures, note that the chance that the difference in forecasts scaled by multiplying by σ and dividing by $\sqrt{T}$ is between given percentiles is equal to the values given on the figure. Thus the difference between OLS and random walk one step ahead forecasts based on 100 observations when $\rho = 0.9$ has a 20% chance of being more than $2.4/\sqrt{100}$ or about one quarter of a standard deviation of the residual. Thus there is a sixty percent chance that the two forecasts differ by less than a quarter of a standard deviation of the shock in either direction. The effects are of course larger when $h = 4$, since there are more periods for which the two forecasts have time to diverge. However

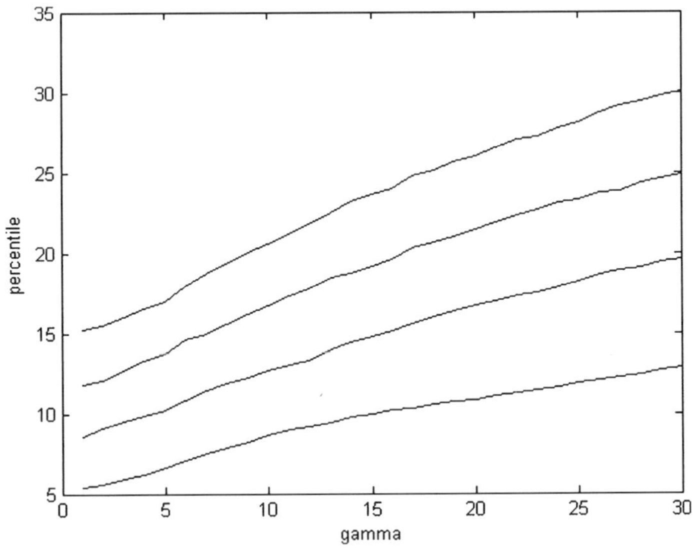

Figure 6. Percentiles of difference between OLS and Random Walk forecasts with $z_t = 1, h = 4$. Percentiles are for 20, 10, 5 and 2.5% in ascending order.

the difference is roughly h times as large, thus is of the same order of magnitude as the variance of the unpredictable component for a h step ahead forecast.

The above results present comparisons based on unconditional expected loss, as is typical in this literature. Such unconditional results are relevant for describing the outcomes of the typical Monte Carlo results in the literature, and may be relevant in describing a best procedure over many datasets, however may be less reasonable for those trying to choose a particular forecast model for a particular forecasting situation. For example, it is known that regardless of ρ the confidence interval for the forecast error in the unconditional case is in the case of normal innovations itself exactly normal [Magnus and Pesaran (1989)]. However this result arises from the normality of $y_T - \phi' z_T$ and the fact that the forecast error is an even function of the data. Alternatively put, the final observation $y_T - \phi' z_T$ is normally distributed, and this is weighted by values for the forecast model that are symmetrically distributed around zero so for every negative value there is a positive value. Hence overall we obtain a wide normal distribution. Phillips (1979) suggested conditioning on the observed y_T presented a method for constructing confidence intervals that condition on this final value of the data for the stationary case. Even in the simplest stationary case these confidence intervals are quite skewed and very different from the unconditional intervals. No results are available for the models considered here.

In practice we typically do not know $y_T - \phi' z_T$ since we do not know ϕ. For the best estimates for ϕ we have that $T^{-1/2}(y_T - \hat{\phi}' z_T)$ converges to a random variable and hence we cannot even consistently estimate this distance. But the sample is not completely uninformative of this distance, even though we have seen that the deviation of y_T from its mean impacts the cost of imposing a unit root. By extension it also matters in terms of evaluating which estimation procedure might be the one that minimizes loss conditional on the information in the sample regarding this distance. From a classical perspective, the literature has not attempted to use this information to construct a better forecast method. The Bayesian methods discussed in Chapter 1 by Geweke and Whiteman in this Handbook consider general versions of these models.

3.2. Long run forecasts

The issue of unit roots and cointegration has increasing relevance the further ahead we look in our forecasting problem. Intuitively we expect that 'getting the trend correct' will be more important the longer the forecast horizon. The problem of using lagged levels to predict changes at short horizons can be seen as one of an unbalanced regression – trying to predict a stationary change with a near nonstationary variable. At longer horizons this is not the case. One way to see mathematically that this is true is to consider the forecast h steps ahead in its telescoped form, i.e. through writing $y_{T+h} - y_T = \sum_{i=1}^{h} \Delta y_{T+i}$. For variables with behavior close to or equal to those of a unit root process, their change is close to a stationary variable. Hence if we let h get large, then the change we are going to forecast acts similarly to a partial sum of stationary variables, i.e. like an $I(1)$ process, and hence variables such as the current level of the variable that themselves resemble $I(1)$ processes may well explain their movement and hence be useful in forecasting for long horizons.

As earlier, in the case of an AR(1) model

$$y_{T+h} - y_T = \sum_{i=1}^{h} \rho^{h-i} \varepsilon_{T+i} + (\rho^h - 1)(y_T - \phi' z_T).$$

Before we saw that if we let h be fixed and let the sample size get large then the second term is overwhelmed by the first, effectively $(\rho^h - 1)$ becomes small as $(y_T - \mu)$ gets large, the overall effect being that the second term gets small whilst the unforecastable component is constant in size. It was this effect that picked up the intuition that getting the trend correct for short run forecasting is not so important. To approximate results for long run forecasting, consider allowing h get large as the sample size gets large, or more precisely let $h = [T\lambda]$ so the forecast horizon gets large at the same rate as the sample size. The parameter λ is fixed and is the ratio of the forecast horizon to the sample size. This approach to long run forecasting has been examined in a more general setup by Stock (1996) and Phillips (1998). Kemp (1999) and Turner (2004) examine the special univariate case discussed here.

For such a thought experiment, the first term $\sum_{i=1}^{h} \rho^{h-i} \varepsilon_{T+i} = \sum_{i=1}^{[T\lambda]} \rho^{[T\lambda]-i} \varepsilon_{T+i}$ is a partial sum and hence gets large as the sample size gets large. Further, since we have $\rho^h = (1 + \gamma/T)^{[T\lambda]} \approx \mathrm{e}^{\gamma\lambda}$ then $(\rho^h - 1)$ no longer becomes small and both terms have the same order asymptotically. More formally we have for $\rho = 1 - \gamma/T$ that in the case of a mean included in the model

$$T^{-1/2}(y_{T+h}-y_T) = T^{-1/2}\sum_{i=1}^{h}\rho^{h-i}\varepsilon_{T+i} + (\rho^h - 1)T^{-1/2}(y_T-\mu)$$
$$\Rightarrow \sigma_\varepsilon^2\{W_2(\lambda) + (\mathrm{e}^{-\gamma\lambda}-1)M(1)\},$$

where $W_2(\cdot)$ and $M(\cdot)$ are independent realizations of Ornstein Uhlenbeck processes where $M(\cdot)$ is defined in (2). It should be noted however that they are really independent (nonoverlapping) parts of the same process, and this expression could have been written in that form. There is no 'initial condition' effect in the first term because it necessarily starts from zero.

We can now easily consider the effect of wrongly imposing a unit root on this process in the forecasting model. The approximate scaled MSE for such an approach is given by

$$\begin{aligned} E[T^{-1}(y_{T+h}-y_T)^2] &\Rightarrow \sigma_\varepsilon^2 E\{W_2(\lambda) + (\mathrm{e}^{-\gamma\lambda}-1)M(1)\}^2 \\ &= \frac{\sigma_\varepsilon^2}{2\gamma}\{(1-\mathrm{e}^{-2\gamma\lambda}) + (\mathrm{e}^{-\gamma\lambda}-1)^2((\alpha^2-1)\mathrm{e}^{-2\gamma}+1)\} \\ &= \frac{\sigma_\varepsilon^2}{2\gamma}\{2-2\mathrm{e}^{-\gamma\lambda} + (\alpha^2-1)\mathrm{e}^{-2\gamma}(\mathrm{e}^{-\gamma\lambda}-1)^2\}. \end{aligned} \tag{6}$$

This expression can be evaluated to see the impact of different horizons and degrees of mean reversion and initial conditions. The effect of the initial condition follows directly from the equation. Since $\mathrm{e}^{-2\gamma}(\mathrm{e}^{-\gamma\lambda}-1)^2 > 0$ then $\alpha < 1$ corresponds to a decrease the expected MSE and $\alpha > 1$ an increase. This is nothing more than the observation made for short run forecasting that if y_T is relatively close to μ then the forecast error from using the wrong value for ρ is less than if $(y_T - \mu)$ is large. The greater is α the greater the weight on initial values far from zero and hence the greater the likelihood that y_T is far from μ.

Noting that the term that arises through the term $W_2(\lambda)$ is due to the unpredictable part, here we evaluate the term in (6) relative to the size of the variance of the unforecastable component. Figure 7 examines, for $\gamma = 1, 5$ and 10 in ascending order this term for various λ along the horizontal axis. A value of 1 indicates that the additional loss from imposing the random walk is zero, the proportion above one is the additional percentage loss due to this approximation. For γ large enough the term asymptotes to 2 as $\lambda \to 1$ – this means that the approximation cost attains a maximum at a value equal to the unpredictable component. For a prediction horizon half the sample size (so $\lambda = 0.5$) the loss when $\gamma = 1$ from assuming a unit root in the construction of the forecast is roughly 25% of the size of the unpredictable component.

As in the small h case when a time trend is included we must estimate the coefficient on this term. Using again the MLE assuming a unit root, denoted $\hat{\tau}$, we have that

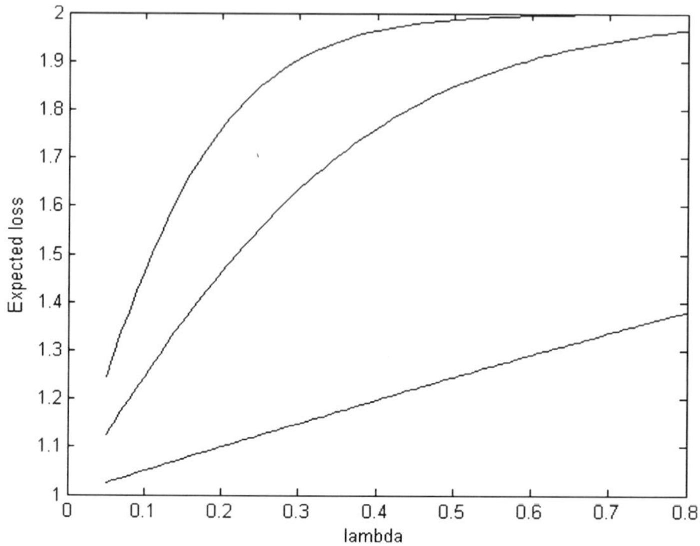

Figure 7. Ratio of MSE of unit root forecasting model to MSE of optimal forecast as a function of λ – mean case.

$$
\begin{aligned}
&T^{-1/2}(y_{T+h} - y_T - \hat{\tau} h) \\
&\quad = T^{-1/2}\sum_{i=1}^{h} \rho^{h-i}\varepsilon_{T+i} + (\rho^h - 1)T^{-1/2}(y_T - \phi' z_T) - T^{1/2}(\tau - \hat{\tau})(h/T) \\
&\quad \Rightarrow \sigma_\varepsilon^2\bigl\{W_2(\lambda) + (\mathrm{e}^{-\gamma\lambda} - 1)M(1) - \lambda\bigl(M(1) - M(0)\bigr)\bigr\}.
\end{aligned}
$$

Hence we have

$$
\begin{aligned}
&E\bigl[T^{-1}(y_{T+h} - y_T)^2\bigr] \\
&\quad \Rightarrow \sigma_\varepsilon^2 E\bigl\{W_2(\lambda) + (\mathrm{e}^{-\gamma\lambda} - 1)M(1) - \lambda\bigl(M(1) - M(0)\bigr)\bigr\}^2 \\
&\quad = \sigma_\varepsilon^2 E\bigl\{W_2(\lambda) + (\mathrm{e}^{-\gamma\lambda} - 1 - \lambda)M(1) + \lambda M(0)\bigr\}^2 \\
&\quad = \frac{\sigma_\varepsilon^2}{2\gamma}\bigl\{(1 - \mathrm{e}^{-2\gamma\lambda}) + (\mathrm{e}^{-\gamma\lambda} - 1 - \lambda)^2\bigl((\alpha^2 - 1)\mathrm{e}^{-2\gamma} + 1\bigr) + \lambda^2\alpha^2\bigr\} \\
&\quad = \frac{\sigma_\varepsilon^2}{2\gamma}\bigl\{1 + (1+\lambda)^2 + \lambda^2 a^2 - 2(1+\lambda)\mathrm{e}^{-\gamma\lambda} \\
&\qquad + (\alpha^2 - 1)\bigl((1+\lambda)^2\mathrm{e}^{-2\gamma} + \mathrm{e}^{-2\gamma(1+\lambda)} - 2(1+\lambda)\mathrm{e}^{-\gamma(2+\lambda)}\bigr)\bigr\}. \qquad (7)
\end{aligned}
$$

Here as in the case of a few periods ahead the initial condition does have an effect. Indeed, for γ large enough this term is $1 + (1+\lambda)^2 + \lambda^2 a^2$ and so the level at which this tops out depends on the initial condition. Further, this limit exists only as γ gets large and differs for each λ. The effects are shown for $\gamma = 1, 5$ and 10 in Figure 8, where the

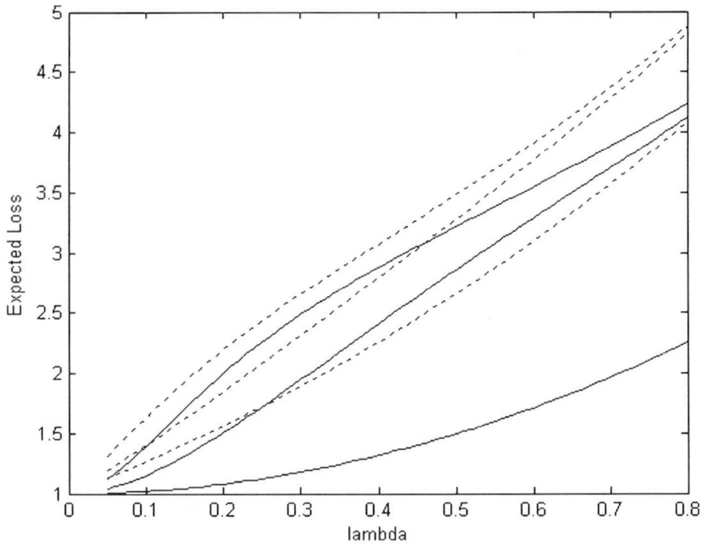

Figure 8. As per Figure 7 for Equation (7) where dashed lines are for $\alpha = 1$ and solid lines for $\alpha = 0$.

solid lines are for $\alpha = 0$ and the dashed lines for $\alpha = 1$. Curves that are higher are for larger γ. Here the effect of the unit root assumption, even though the trend coefficient is estimated and taken into account for the forecast, is much greater. The dependence of the asymptote on λ is shown to some extent through the upward sloping line for the larger values for γ. It is also noticeable that these asymptotes depend on the initial condition.

This trade-off must be matched with the effects of estimating the root and other nuisance parameters. To examine this, consider again the model without serial correlation. As before the forecast is given by

$$y_{T+h|T} = y_T + (\hat{\rho}^h - 1)(y_T - \hat{\phi}' z_T) + \hat{\phi}'(z_{T+h} - z_T).$$

In the case of a mean this yields a scaled forecast error

$$\begin{aligned} &T^{-1/2}(y_{T+h} - y_{T+h|T}) \\ &\quad = T^{-1/2}\varphi(\varepsilon_{T+h}, \ldots, \varepsilon_{T+1}) + (\rho^h - \hat{\rho}^h)T^{-1/2}(y_T - \mu) \\ &\quad\quad - (\hat{\rho}^h - 1)T^{-1/2}(\hat{\mu} - \mu) \\ &\quad \Rightarrow \sigma_\varepsilon^2\big(W_2(\lambda) + (\mathrm{e}^{\gamma\lambda} - \mathrm{e}^{\hat{\gamma}\lambda})M(1) - (\mathrm{e}^{\hat{\gamma}\lambda} - 1)\varphi\big), \end{aligned}$$

where $W_2(\lambda)$ and $M(1)$ are as before, $\hat{\gamma}$ is the limit distribution for $T(\hat{\rho} - 1)$ which differs across estimators for $\hat{\rho}$ and φ is the limit distribution for $T^{-1/2}(\hat{\mu} - \mu)$ which also differs over estimators. The latter two objects are in general functions of $M(\cdot)$ and are hence correlated with each other. The precise form of this expression depends on the limit results for the estimators.

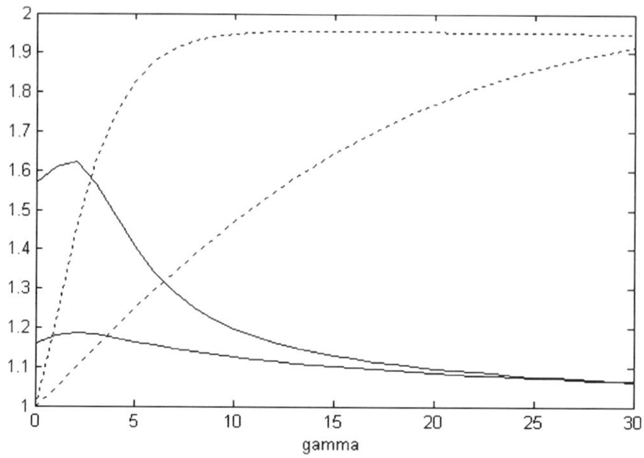

Figure 9. OLS versus imposed unit roots for the mean case at horizons $\lambda = 0.1$ and $\lambda = 0.5$. Dashed lines are the imposed unit root and solid lines for OLS.

As with the fixed horizon case, one can derive an analytic expression for the mean-square error as the mean of a complicated (i.e. nonlinear) function of Brownian motions [see Turner (2004) for the $\alpha = 0$ case] however these analytical results are difficult to evaluate. We can however evaluate this term for various initial conditions, degrees of mean reversion and forecast horizon length by Monte Carlo. Setting $T = 1000$ to approximate large sample results we report in Figure 9 the ratio of average squared loss of forecasts based on OLS estimates divided by the same object when the parameters of the model are known for various values for γ and $\lambda = 0.1$ and 0.5 with $\alpha = 0$ (solid lines, the curves closer to the x-axis are for $\lambda = 0.1$, in the case of $\alpha = 1$ the results are almost identical). Also plotted for comparison are the equivalent curves when the unit root is imposed (given by dashed lines). As for the fixed h case, for small enough γ it is better to impose the unit root. However estimation becomes a better approach on average for roots that accord with values for γ that are not very far from zero – values around $\gamma = 3$ or 4 for $\lambda = 0.5$ and 0.1, respectively. Combining this with the earlier results suggests that for values of $\gamma = 5$ or greater, which accords say with a root of 0.95 in a sample of 100 observations, that OLS should dominate the imposed unit root approach to forecasting. This is especially so for long horizon forecasting, as for large γ OLS strongly dominates imposing the root to one.

In the case of a trend this becomes $y_{T|T+h} = \hat{\rho}^h y_T + (1 - \hat{\rho}^h)\hat{\mu} + \hat{\tau}[T(1 - \hat{\rho}^h) + h]$ and the forecast error suitably scaled has the distribution

$$\begin{aligned}
&T^{-1/2}(y_{T+h} - y_{T+h|T}) \\
&\quad = T^{-1/2}\varphi(\varepsilon_{T+h}, \ldots, \varepsilon_{T+1}) + \left(\rho^h - \hat{\rho}^h\right)T^{-1/2}\left(y_T - \phi' z_t\right) \\
&\qquad - \left(\hat{\rho}^h - 1\right)T^{-1/2}(\hat{\mu} - \mu) - T^{1/2}(\hat{\tau} - \tau)\left[\left(1 - \hat{\rho}^h\right) + \lambda\right] \\
&\quad \Rightarrow \sigma_\varepsilon^2\left(W_2(\lambda) + \left(e^{\gamma\lambda} - e^{\hat{\gamma}\lambda}\right)M(1) - \left(e^{\hat{\gamma}\lambda} - 1\right)\varphi_1 + \left(1 + \lambda - e^{\hat{\gamma}\lambda}\right)\varphi_2\right),
\end{aligned}$$

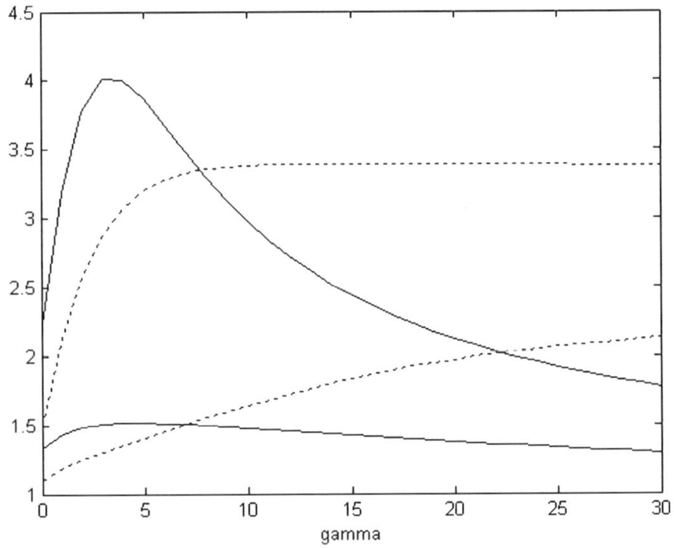

Figure 10. As per Figure 9 for the case of a mean and a trend.

where φ_1 is the limit distribution for $T^{-1/2}(\hat{\mu} - \mu)$ and φ_2 is the limit distribution for $T^{1/2}(\hat{\tau} - \tau)$. Again, the precise form of the limit result depends on the estimators.

The same Monte Carlo exercise as in Figure 9 is repeated for the case of a trend in Figure 10. Here we see that the costs of estimation when the root is very close to one is much greater, however as in the case with a mean only the trade-off is clearly strongly in favor of OLS estimation for larger roots. The point at which the curves cut – i.e. the point where OLS becomes better on average than imposing the root – is for a larger value for γ. This value is about $\gamma = 7$ for both horizons. Turner (2004) computes cutoff points for a wider array of λ.

There is little beyond Monte Carlo evidence on the issues of imposing the unit root (i.e. differencing always), estimating the root (i.e. levels always) and pretesting for a unit root (which will depend on the unit root test chosen). Diebold and Kilian (2000) provide Monte Carlo evidence using the Dickey and Fuller (1979) test as a pretest. Essentially, we have seen that the bias from estimating the root is larger the smaller the sample and the longer the horizon. This is precisely what is found in the Monte Carlo experiments. They also found little difference between imposing the unit root and pretesting for a unit root when the root is close to one, however pretesting dominates further from one. Hence they argue that pretesting always seems preferable to imposing the result. Stock (1996) more cautiously provides similar advice, suggesting pretests based on unit root tests of Elliott, Rothenberg and Stock (1996). All evidence was in terms of MSE unconditionally. Other researchers have run subsets of these Monte Carlo experiments [Clements and Hendry (1998), Campbell and Perron (1991)]. What is clear from the above calculations are two overall points. First, no method dominates everywhere, so the choice of what is best rests on the beliefs of what the model is likely to be. Second, the point at which estimation is preferred to imposition occurs for γ that are very close to zero in the sense that tests do not have great power of rejecting a unit root when estimating the root is the best practice.

Researchers have also applied the different models to data. Franses and Kleibergen (1996) examine the Nelson and Plosser (1982) data and find that imposing a unit root outperforms OLS estimation of the root in forecasting at both short and longer horizons (the longest horizons correspond to $\lambda = 0.1$). In practice, pretesting has appeared to 'work'. Stock and Watson (1999) examined many U.S. macroeconomic series and found that pretesting gave smaller out of sample MSE's on average.

4. Cointegration and short run forecasts

The above model can be extended to a vector of trending variables. Here the extreme cases of all unit roots and no unit roots are separated by the possibility that the variables may be cointegrated. The result of a series of variables being cointegrated means that there exist restrictions on the unrestricted VAR in levels of the variables, and so one would expect that imposing these restrictions will improve forecasts over not imposing them. The other implication that arises from the Granger Representation Theorem [Engle and Granger (1987)] is that the VAR in differences – which amounts to imposing too many restrictions on the model – is misspecified through the omission of the error correction term. It would seem that it would follow in a straightforward manner that the use of an error correction model will outperform both the levels and the differences models: the levels model being inferior because too many parameters are estimated and the differences model inferior because too few useful covariates are included. However the literature is divided on the usefulness of imposing cointegrating relationships on the forecasting model.

Christoffersen and Diebold (1998) examine a bivariate cointegrating model and show that the imposition of cointegration is useful at short horizons only. Engle and Yoo (1987) present a Monte Carlo for a similar model and find that a levels VAR does a little better at short horizons than the ECM model. Clements and Hendry (1995) provide general analytic results for forecast MSE in cointegrating models. An example of an empirical application using macroeconomic data is Hoffman and Rasche (1996) who find at short horizons that a VAR in differences outperforms a VECM or levels VAR for 5 of 6 series (inflation was the holdout). The latter two models were quite similar in forecast performance.

We will first investigate the 'classic' cointegrating model. By this we mean cointegrating models where it is clear that all the variables are $I(1)$ and that the cointegrating vectors are mean reverting enough that tests have probability one of detecting the correct cointegrating rank. There are a number of useful ways of writing down the cointegrating model so that the points we make are clear. The two most useful ones for our purposes here are the error correction form (ECM) and triangular form. These are simply rotations of the same model and hence for any of one form there exists a representation in the second form. The VAR in levels can be written as

$$W_t = A(L)W_{t-1} + u_t, \tag{8}$$

where W_t is an $nx1$ vector of $I(1)$ random variables. When there exist r cointegrating vectors $\beta' W_t = c_t$ the error correction model can be written as

$$\Phi(L)\big[I(1-L) - \alpha\beta' L\big]W_t = u_t,$$

where α, β are nxr and we have factored stationary dynamics in $\Phi(L)$ so $\Phi(1)$ has roots outside the unit circle. Comparing these equations we have $(A(1) - I_n) = \Phi(1)\alpha\beta'$. In this form we can differentiate the effects of the serial correlation and the impact matrix α. Rewriting in the usual form with use of the BN decomposition we have

$$\Delta W_t = \Phi(1)\alpha c_{t-1} + B(L)\,\Delta W_{t-1} + u_t.$$

Let y_t be the first element of the vector W_t and consider the usefulness in prediction that arises from including the error correction term c_{t-1} in the forecast of y_{t+h}. First think of the one step ahead forecast, which we get from taking the first equation in this system without regard to the remaining ones. From the one step ahead forecasting problem then the value of the ECM term is simply how useful variation in c_{t-1} is in explaining Δy_t. The value for forecasting depends on the parameter in front of the term in the model, i.e. the (1, 1) element of $\Phi(1)\alpha$ and also the variation in the error correction term itself. In general the relevant parameter here can be seen to be a function of the entire set of parameters that define the stationary serial correlation properties of the model ($\Phi(1)$ which is the sum of all of the lags) and the impact parameters α. Hence even in the one step ahead problem the usefulness of the cointegrating vector term the effect will depend on almost the entire model, which provides a clue as to the inability of Monte Carlo analysis to provide hard and fast rules as to the importance of imposing the cointegration restrictions.

When we consider forecasting more steps ahead, another critical feature will be the serial correlation in the error correction term c_t. If it were white noise then clearly it would only be able to predict the one step ahead change in y_t, and would be uninformative for forecasting $y_{t+h} - y_{t+h-1}$ for $h > 1$. Since the multiple step ahead forecast $y_{t+h} - y_t$ is simply the sum of the changes $y_{t+i} - y_{t+i-1}$ from $i = 1$ to h then it will have proportionally less and less impact on the forecast as the horizon grows. When this term is serially correlated however it will be able to explain the future changes, and hence will affect the trade-off between using this term and ignoring it. In order to establish properties of the error correction term, the triangular form of the model is useful. Normalize the cointegrating vector so that the cointegrating vector $\beta' = (I_r, -\theta')$ and define the matrix

$$K = \begin{pmatrix} I_r & -\theta' \\ 0 & I_{n-r} \end{pmatrix}.$$

Note that $Kz_t = (\beta' W_t, W'_{2t})$ where W_{2t} is the last $n - r$ elements of W_t and

$$K\alpha\beta' W_{t-1} = \begin{pmatrix} \beta'\alpha \\ \alpha_2 \end{pmatrix} \beta' W_{t-1}.$$

Premultiply the model by K (so that the leading term in the polynomial is the identity matrix as per convention) and we obtain

$$K\Phi(L)K^{-1}K\big[I(1-L) - \alpha\beta' L\big]W_t = Ku_t,$$

which can be rewritten

$$K\Phi(L)K^{-1}B(L)\begin{pmatrix} \beta' W_t \\ \Delta W_{2t} \end{pmatrix} = Ku_t, \tag{9}$$

where

$$B(L) = I + \begin{pmatrix} \alpha_1 - \theta\alpha_2 - I_r & 0 \\ \alpha_2 & 0 \end{pmatrix} L.$$

This form is useful as it allows us to think about the dynamics of the cointegrating vector c_t, which as we have stated will affect the usefulness of the cointegrating vector in forecasting future values of y. The dynamics of the error correction term are driven by the value of $\alpha_1 - \theta\alpha_2 - I_r$ and the roots of $\Phi(L)$ and will be influenced by a great many parameters in the model. This provides another reason for why Monte Carlo studies have proved to be inconclusive.

In order to show the various effects, it will be necessary to simplify the models considerably. We will examine a model without 'additional' serial correlation, i.e. one for which $\Phi(L) = I$. We also will let both y_t and $W_{2t} = x_t$ be univariate. This model is still rich enough for many different effects to be shown, and has been employed to examine the usefulness of cointegration in forecasting by a number of authors. The precise form of the model in its error correction form is

$$\begin{pmatrix} \Delta y_t \\ \Delta x_t \end{pmatrix} = \begin{pmatrix} \alpha_1 \\ \alpha_2 \end{pmatrix} \begin{pmatrix} 1 & -\theta \end{pmatrix} \begin{pmatrix} y_{t-1} \\ x_{t-1} \end{pmatrix} + \begin{pmatrix} u_{1t} \\ u_{2t} \end{pmatrix}. \tag{10}$$

This model under various parameterizations has been examined by Engle and Yoo (1987), Clements and Hendry (1995) and Christoffersen and Diebold (1998). In triangular form the model is

$$\begin{pmatrix} c_t \\ \Delta x_t \end{pmatrix} = \begin{pmatrix} \alpha_1 - \theta\alpha_2 + 1 & 0 \\ \alpha_2 & 0 \end{pmatrix} \begin{pmatrix} c_{t-1} \\ x_{t-1} \end{pmatrix} + \begin{pmatrix} u_{1t} - \theta u_{2t} \\ u_{2t} \end{pmatrix}.$$

The coefficient on the error correction term in the model for y_t is simply α_1, and the serial correlation properties for the error correction term is given by $\rho_c = \alpha_1 - \theta\alpha_2 + 1 = 1 + \beta'\alpha$. A restriction of course is that this term has roots outside the unit circle, and so this restricts possible values for β and α. Further, the variance of c_t also depends on the innovations to this variable which involve the entire variance covariance matrix of u_t as well as the cointegrating parameter. It should be clear that in thinking about the effect of various parameters on the value of including the cointegrating vector in the forecasting model controlled experiments will be difficult – changing a parameter involves a host of changes on the features of the model.

In considering h step ahead forecasts, we can recursively solve (10) to obtain

$$\begin{pmatrix} y_{T+h} - y_T \\ x_{T+h} - x_T \end{pmatrix} = \left(\sum_{i=1}^{h} \rho_c^{i-1}\right) \begin{pmatrix} \alpha_1 \\ \alpha_2 \end{pmatrix} (1 \quad -\theta) \begin{pmatrix} y_T \\ x_T \end{pmatrix} + \begin{pmatrix} \tilde{u}_{1T+h} \\ \tilde{u}_{2t+h} \end{pmatrix}, \tag{11}$$

where $\tilde{u}_{1T+h}$ and $\tilde{u}_{t+h}$ are unpredictable components. The result shows that the usefulness of the cointegrating vector for the h step ahead forecast depends on both the impact parameter α_1 as well as the serial correlation in the cointegrating vector ρ_c which is a function of the cointegrating vector as well as the impact parameter in both the equations. The larger the impact parameter, all else held equal, the greater the usefulness of the cointegrating vector term in constructing the forecast. The larger the root ρ_c also the larger the impact of this term.

These results give some insight as to the usefulness of the error correction term, and show that different Monte Carlo specifications may well give conflicting results simply through examining models with differing impact parameters and serial correlation properties of the error correction term. Consider the differences between the results[4] of Engle and Yoo (1987) and Christoffersen and Diebold (1998). Both papers are making the point that the error correction term is only relevant for shorter horizons, a point to which we will return. However Engle and Yoo (1987) claim that the error correction term is quite useful at moderate horizons, whereas Christoffersen and Diebold (1998) suggest that it is only at very short horizons that the term is useful. In the former model, the impact parameter is $\alpha_y = -0.4$ and $\rho_c = 0.4$. The impact parameter is of moderate size and so is the serial correlation, and so we would expect some reasonable usefulness of the term for moderate horizons. In Christoffersen and Diebold (1998), these coefficients are $\alpha_y = -1$ and $\rho_c = 0$. The large impact parameter ensures that the error correction term is very useful at very short horizons. However employing an error correction term that is not serially correlated also ensures that it will not be useful at moderate horizons. The differences really come down to the features of the model rather than providing a general notion for all error correction terms.

This analysis abstracted from estimation error. When the parameters of the model have to be estimated then the relative value of the error correction term is diminished on average through the usual effects of estimation error. The extra wrinkle over a standard analysis of this estimation error in stationary regression is that one must estimate the cointegrating vector (one must also estimate the impact parameters 'conditional' on

[4] Both these authors use the sum of squared forecast error for both equations in their comparisons. In the case of Engle and Yoo (1987) the error correction term is also useful in forecasting in the x equation, whereas it is not for the Christoffersen and Diebold (1998) experiment. This further exacerbates the magnitudes of the differences.

the cointegrating parameter estimate, however this effect is much lower order for standard cointegrating parameter estimators). We will not examine this carefully, however a few comments can be made. First, Clements and Hendry (1995) examine the Engle and Yoo (1987) model and show that using MLE's of the cointegrating vector outperforms the OLS estimator used in the former study. Indeed, at shorter horizons Engle and Yoo (1987) found that the unrestricted VAR outperformed the ECM even though the restrictions were valid.

It is clear that given sufficient observations, the consistency of the parameter estimates in the levels VAR means that asymptotically the cointegration feature of the model will still be apparent, which is to say that in the overidentified model is asymptotically equivalent to the true error correction model. In smaller samples there is the effect of some additional estimation error, and also the problem that the added variables are trending and hence have nonstandard distributions that are not centered on zero. This is the multivariate analog of the usual bias in univariate models on the lagged level term and disappears at the same rate, i.e. at rate T. Abidir, Kaddour and Tzavaliz (1999) examine this problem. In comparing the estimation error between the levels model and the error correction model many of the trade-offs are the same. However the estimation of the cointegrating vector can be important. Stock (1987) shows that the OLS estimator of the cointegrating vector has a large bias that also disappears at rate T. Whether or not this term will on average be large depends on a nuisance parameter of the error correction model, namely the zero frequency correlation between the shocks to the error correction term and the shocks to Δx_t. When this correlation is zero, OLS is the efficient estimator of the cointegrating vector and the bias is zero (in this case the OLS estimator is asymptotically mixed normal centered on the true cointegrating vector). However in the more likely case that this is nonzero, then OLS is asymptotically inefficient and other methods[5] are required to obtain this asymptotic mixed normality centered on the true vector. In part, this explains the results of Engle and Yoo (1987). The value for this spectral correlation in their study was -0.89, quite close to the bound of one and hence OLS is likely to provide very biased estimates of the cointegrating vector. It is in just such situations that efficient cointegrating vector estimation methods are likely to be useful, Clements and Hendry (1995) show in a Monte Carlo that indeed for this model specification there are noticeable gains.

The VAR in differences can be seen to omit regressors – the error correction terms – and hence suffers from not picking up the extra possible explanatory power of the regressors. Notice that as usual here the omitted variable bias that comes along with failing to include useful regressors is the forecasters friend – this omitted variable bias is picking up at least part of the omitted effect.

The usefulness of the cointegrating relationship fades as the horizon gets large. Indeed, eventually it has an arbitrarily small contribution compared to the unexplained

[5] There are many such methods. Johansen (1991) provided an estimator that was asymptotically efficient. Many other asymptotically equivalent methods are now available, see Watson (1994) for a review.

part of y_{T+h}. This is true of any stationary covariate in forecasting the level of an $I(1)$ series. Recalling that $y_{T+h} - y_t = \sum_{i=1}^{h}(y_{t+i} - y_{t+i-1})$ then as h gets large this sum of changes in y is getting large. Eventually the short memory nature of the stationary covariate is unable to predict the future period by period changes and hence becomes a very small proportion of the difference. Both Engle and Yoo (1987) and Christoffersen and Diebold (1998) make this point. This seems to be at odds with the idea that cointegration is a 'long run' concept, and hence should have something to say far in the future.

The answer is that the error correction model does impose something on the long run behavior of the variables, that they do not depart too far from their cointegrating relation. This is pointed out in Engle and Yoo (1987), as h gets large $\beta' W_{T+h,t}$ is bounded. Note that this is the forecast of c_{T+h}, which as is implicit in the triangular relation above bounded as ρ_c is between minus one and one. This feature of the error correction model may well be important in practice even when one is looking at horizons that are large enough so that the error correction term itself has little impact on the MSE of either of the individual variables. Suppose the forecaster is forecasting both variables in the model, and is called upon to justify a story behind why the forecasts are as they are. If they are forecasting variables that are cointegrated, then it is more reasonable that a sensible story can be told if the variables are not diverging from their long run relationship by too much.

5. Near cointegrating models

In any realistic problem we certainly do not know the location of unit roots in the model, and typically arrive at the model either through assumption or pretesting to determine the number of unit roots or 'rank', where the rank refers to the rank of $A(1) - I_n$ in Equation (8) and is equal to the number of variables minus the number of distinct unit roots. In the cases where this rank is not obvious, then we are uncertain as to the exact correct model for the trending behavior of the variables and can take this into account.

For many interesting examples, a feature of cointegrating models is the strong serial correlation in the cointegrating vector, i.e. we are unclear as to whether or not the variables are indeed cointegrated. Consider the forecasting of exchange rates. The real exchange rate can be written as a function of the nominal exchange rate less a price differential between the countries. This relationship is typically treated as a cointegrating vector, however there is a large literature checking whether there is a unit root in the real exchange rate despite the lack of support for such a proposition from any reasonable theory. Hence in a cointegrating model of nominal exchange rates and price differentials this real exchange rate term may or may not appear depending on whether we think it has a unit root (and hence cannot appear, there is no cointegration) or is simply highly persistent.

Alternatively, we are often fairly sure that certain 'great ratios' in the parlance of Watson (1994) are stationary however we are unsure if the underlying variables themselves have unit roots. For example, the consumption income ratio is certainly bounded and does not wander around too much, however we are uncertain if there really is a unit root in income and consumption. In forecasting interest rates we are sure that the interest rate differential is stationary (although it is typically persistent), however the unit root model for an interest rate seems unlikely to be true but yet tests for the root being one often fail to reject.

Both of these possible models represent different deviations from the cointegrated model. The first suggests more unit roots in the model, the competitor model being closer to having differences everywhere. For example, in the bivariate model with one potential cointegrating vector, the nearest model to a highly persistent cointegrating vector would be a model with both variables in differences. The second suggests fewer unit roots in the model. In the bivariate case the model would be in levels. We will examine both, similar issues arise.

For the first of these models, consider Equation (9),

$$\begin{pmatrix} \beta' W_t \\ \Delta W_{2t} \end{pmatrix} = \begin{pmatrix} \beta'\alpha + I_r \\ \alpha_2 \end{pmatrix} \beta' W_{t-1} + K\Phi(L)^{-1} u_t,$$

where the largest roots of the system for the cointegrating vectors $\beta' W_t$ are determined by the value for $\beta'\alpha + I_r$. For models where there are cointegrating vectors that are have near unit roots this means that eigen values of this term are close to one. The trending behavior of the cointegrating vectors thus depend on a number of parameters of the model. Also, trending behavior of the cointegrating vectors feeds back into the process for ΔW_{2t}. In a standard framework we would require that W_{2t} be $I(1)$. However, if $\beta' W_t$ is near $I(1)$ and $\Delta W_{2t} = \alpha_2 \beta' W_t + \text{noise}$, then we would require that $\alpha_2 = 0$ for this term to be $I(1)$. If $\alpha_2 \neq 0$, then W_{2t} will be near $I(2)$. Hence under the former case the regression becomes

$$\begin{pmatrix} \beta' W_t \\ \Delta W_t \end{pmatrix} = \begin{pmatrix} \alpha_1 + I_r \\ 0 \end{pmatrix} \beta' W_t + K\Phi(L)^{-1} u_t$$

and $\beta' W_t$ having a trend is $\alpha_1 + I_r$ having roots close to one.

In the special case of a bivariate model with one possible cointegrating vector the autoregressive coefficient is given by $\rho_c = \alpha_1 + 1$. Hence modelling ρ_c to be local to one is equivalent to modelling $\alpha_1 = -\gamma/T$. The model without additional serial correlation becomes

$$\begin{pmatrix} \Delta c_t \\ \Delta x_t \end{pmatrix} = \begin{pmatrix} \rho_c - 1 & 0 \\ 0 & 0 \end{pmatrix} \begin{pmatrix} c_{t-1} \\ x_{t-1} \end{pmatrix} + \begin{pmatrix} u_{1t} - \theta u_{2t} \\ u_{2t} \end{pmatrix}$$

in triangular form and

$$\begin{pmatrix} \Delta y_t \\ \Delta x_t \end{pmatrix} = \begin{pmatrix} \rho_c - 1 \\ 0 \end{pmatrix} \begin{pmatrix} 1 & -\theta \end{pmatrix} \begin{pmatrix} y_{t-1} \\ x_{t-1} \end{pmatrix} + \begin{pmatrix} u_{1t} \\ u_{2t} \end{pmatrix}$$

in the error correction form. We will thus focus on the simplified model for the object of focus

$$\Delta y_t = (\rho_c - 1)c_{t-1} + u_{1t} \tag{12}$$

as the forecasting model.

The model where we set ρ_c to unity here as an approximation results in the forecast equal to the no change forecast, i.e. $y_{T+h|T} = y_T$. Thus the unconditional forecast error is given by

$$E\left[y_{T+1} - y_T^f\right]^2 = E\left[(u_{1T+1}) - (\rho - 1)(y_T - \theta x_T)\right]^2$$
$$\approx \sigma_1^2\left(1 + T^{-1}\left\{\frac{\sigma_c^2}{\sigma_1^2}\right\}\frac{\gamma(1 - e^{-2\gamma})}{2}\right),$$

where $\sigma_1^2 = \text{var}(u_{1t})$ and $\sigma_c^2 = \text{var}(u_{1t} - \theta u_{2t})$ is the variance of the shocks driving the cointegrating vector. This is similar to the result in the univariate model forecast when we use a random walk forecast, with the addition of the component $\{\sigma_c^2/\sigma_1^2\}$ which alters the effect of imposing the unit root. This ratio shows that the result depends greatly on the ratio of the variance of the cointegrating vector vis a vis the variance of the shock to y_t. When this ratio is small, which is to say that when the cointegrating relationship varies little compared to the variation in Δy_t, then the impact of ignoring the cointegrating vector is small for one step ahead forecasts. This makes intuitive sense – in such cases the cointegrating vector does not much depart from its mean and so has little predictive power in determining what happens to the path of y_t.

That the loss from imposing a unit root here – which amounts to running the model in differences instead of including an error correction term – depends on the size of the shocks to the cointegrating vector relative to the shocks driving the variable to be forecast means that the trade-off between estimation of the model and imposing the root will vary with this correlation. This adds yet another factor that would drive the choice between imposing the unit root or estimating it. When the ratio is unity, the results are identical to the univariate near unit root problem. Different choices for the correlation between u_{1t} and u_{2t} will result in different ratios and different trade-offs. Figure 11 plots, for $\{\sigma_c^2/\sigma_1^2\} = 0.56$ and 1 and $T = 100$ the average one step ahead MSE of the forecast error for both the imposition of the unit root and also the model where the regression (12) is run with a constant in the model and these OLS coefficients used to construct the forecast. In this model the cointegrating vector is assumed known with little loss as the estimation error on this term has a lower order effect.

The figure graphs the MSE relative to the model with all coefficients known to γ on the horizontal axis. The relatively flat solid line gives the OLS MSE forecast results for both models – there is no real difference between the results for each model. The steepest upward sloping line (long and short dashes) gives results for the unit root imposed model where $\sigma_c^2/\sigma_1^2 = 1$, these results are comparable to the $h = 1$ case in Figure 1 (the asymptotic results suggest a slightly smaller effect than this small sample simulation). The flatter curve corresponds to $\sigma_c^2/\sigma_1^2 < 1$ for the cointegrating vector chosen here ($\theta = 1$) and so the effect of erroneously imposing a unit root is smaller. However this ratio could also be larger, making the effect greater than the usual unit root model. The result depends on the values of the nuisance parameters. This model is however highly stylized. More complicated dynamics can make the coefficient on the cointegrating vector larger or smaller, hence changing the relevant size of the effect.

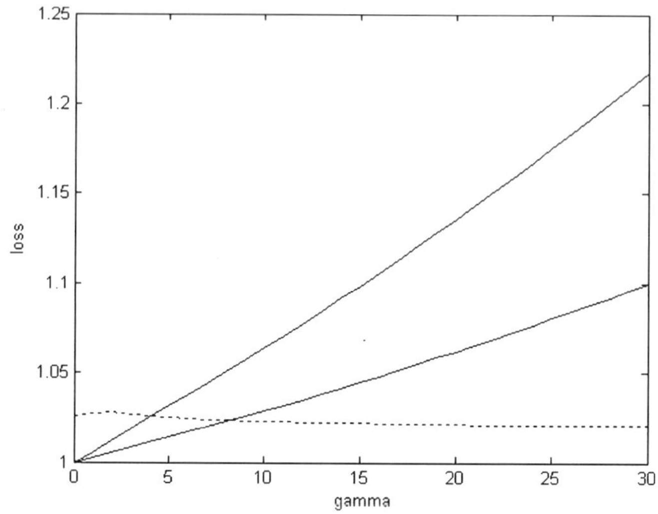

Figure 11. The upward sloping lines show loss from imposing a unit root for $\sigma_1^{-2}\sigma_c^2 = 0.56$ and 1 for steeper curves, respectively. The dashed line gives the results for OLS estimation (both models).

In the alternate case, where we are sure the cointegrating vector does not have too much persistence however we are unsure if there are unit roots in the underlying data, the model is close to one in differences. This can be seen in the general case from the general VAR form

$$W_t = A(L)W_{t-1} + u_t,$$
$$\Delta W_t = \big(A(1) - I_n\big)W_{t-1} + A^*(L)\,\Delta W_{t-1} + u_t$$

through using the Beveridge Nelson decomposition. Now let $\Psi = A(1) - I_n$ and consider the rotation

$$\begin{aligned}\Psi W_{t-1} &= \Psi K^{-1} K W_{t-1}\\ &= [\Psi_1, \Psi_2]\begin{pmatrix} I_r & \theta \\ 0 & I_{n-r}\end{pmatrix}\begin{pmatrix} I_r & \theta \\ 0 & I_{n-r}\end{pmatrix}\begin{pmatrix}\beta' W_t \\ W_{2t}\end{pmatrix}\\ &= \Psi_1\beta' W_{t-1} + (\Psi_2 + \theta\Psi_1)W_{2t-1},\end{aligned}$$

hence the model can be written as

$$\Delta W_t = \Psi_1\beta' W_{t-1} + (\Psi_2 + \theta\Psi_1)W_{2t-1} + A^*(L)\,\Delta W_{t-1} + u_t,$$

where the usual ECM arises if $(\Psi_2 + \theta\Psi_1)$ is zero. This is the zero restriction implicit in the cointegration model. Hence in the general case the 'near to unit root' of the right-hand side variables in the cointegrating framework is modelling this term to be near to zero.

This model has been analyzed in the context of long run forecasting in very general models by Stock (1996). To capture these ideas consider the triangular form for the model without serial correlation

$$\begin{pmatrix} y_t - \varphi' z_t - \theta x_t \\ (1-\rho_x L)(x_t - \phi' z_t) \end{pmatrix} = K u_t = \begin{pmatrix} u_{1t} - \theta u_{2t} \\ u_{2t} \end{pmatrix}$$

so we have $y_{T+h} = \varphi' z_{T+h} + \theta x_{T+h} + u_{1T+h} - \theta u_{2T+h}$. Combining this with the model of the dynamics of x_t gives the result for the forecast model. We have

$$\begin{aligned} &x_t = \phi z_t + u_{2t}^*, \quad t = 1, \dots, T, \\ &(1-\rho_x L)u_{2t}^* = u_{2t}, \quad t = 2, \dots, T, \\ &u_{21}^* = \xi, \end{aligned}$$

and so as

$$x_{T+h} - x_T = \sum_{i=1}^{h} \rho_x^{h-i} u_{2T+i} + (\rho^h - 1)(x_T - \phi' z_T) + \phi'(z_{T+h} - z_T),$$

then

$$\begin{aligned} y_{T+h} - y_T = {} & \theta\left(\sum_{i=1}^{h} \rho^{h-i} u_{2T+i} + (\rho^h - 1)(x_T - \phi' z_T) + \phi'(z_{T+h} - z_T)\right) \\ & - c_T + \varphi'(z_{T+h} - z_T) + u_{1T+h} - \theta u_{2T+h}. \end{aligned}$$

From this we can compute some distributional results.

If a unit root is assumed (cointegration 'wrongly' assumed) then the forecast is

$$\begin{aligned} y_{T+h|T}^{\mathrm{R}} - y_T &= \theta\phi'(z_{T+h} - z_T) - c_T + \varphi'(z_{T+h} - z_T) \\ &= (\theta\phi + \varphi)'(z_{T+h} - z_T) - c_T. \end{aligned}$$

In the case of a mean this is simply

$$y_{T+h|T}^{\mathrm{R}} - y_T = -(y_T - \varphi_1 - \gamma x_T)$$

and for a time trend it is

$$\begin{aligned} y_{T+h|T}^{\mathrm{R}} - y_T &= \theta\phi'(z_{T+h} - z_T) - c_T + \varphi'(z_{T+h} - z_T) \\ &= (\theta\phi_2 + \varphi_2)h - (y_T - \varphi_1 - \varphi_2 T - \theta x_T). \end{aligned}$$

If we do not impose the unit root we have the forecast model

$$\begin{aligned} y_{T+h|T}^{\mathrm{UR}} - y_T &= \theta(\rho^h - 1)(x_T - \phi' z_T) + \phi'(z_{T+h} - z_T) - c_T + \varphi'(z_{T+h} - z_T) \\ &= (\theta\phi + \varphi)'(z_{T+h} - z_T) - c_T - \theta(\rho^h - 1)(x_T - \phi' z_T). \end{aligned}$$

This allows us to understand the costs and benefits of imposition. The real discussion here is between imposing the unit root (modelling as a cointegrating model) and not imposing the unit root (modelling the variables in levels). Here the difference in the two forecasts is given by

$$y^{\mathrm{UR}}_{T+h|T} - y^{\mathrm{R}}_{T+h|T} = -\theta\left(\rho^h - 1\right)\left(x_T - \phi' z_T\right).$$

We have already examined such terms. Here the size of the effect is driven by the relative size of the shocks to the covariates and the shocks to the cointegrating vector, although the effect is the reverse of the previous model (in that model it was the cointegrating vector that is persistent, here it is the covariate). As before the effect is intuitively clear, if the shocks to the near nonstationary component are relatively small then x_T will be close to the mean and the effect is reduced. An extra wedge is driven into the effect by the cointegrating vector θ. A large value for this parameter implies that in the true model that x_t is an important predictor of y_{t+1}. The cointegrating term picks up part of this but not all, so ignoring the rest becomes costly.

As in the case of the near unit root cointegrating vector this model is quite stylized and models with a greater degree of dynamics will change the size of the results, however the general flavor remains.

6. Predicting noisy variables with trending regressors

In many problems the dependent variable itself displays no obvious trending behavior, however theoretically interesting covariates tend to exhibit some type of longer run trend. For many problems we might rule out unit roots for these covariates, however the trend is sufficiently strong that often tests for a unit root fail to reject and by implication standard asymptotic theory for stationary variables is unlikely to approximate well the distribution of the coefficient on the regressor. This leads to a number of problems similar to those examined in the models above.

To be concrete, consider the model

$$y_{1t} = \beta_0' z_t + \beta_1 y_{2t-1} + v_{1t} \tag{13}$$

which is to be used to predict y_{1t}. Further, suppose that y_{2t} is generated by the model in (1) in Section 3. The model for $v_t = [v_{1t}, v_{2t}]'$ is then $v_t = b^*(L)\eta_t^*$ where $E[\eta_t^* \eta_t^{*\prime}] = \Sigma$ where

$$\Sigma = \begin{pmatrix} \sigma_{11}^2 & \delta\sigma_{11}\sigma_{22} \\ \delta\sigma_{11}\sigma_{22} & \sigma_{22}^2 \end{pmatrix}$$

and

$$b^*(L) = \begin{pmatrix} 1 & 0 \\ 0 & c(L) \end{pmatrix}.$$

The assumption that v_{1t} is not serially correlated accords with the forecasting nature of this regression, if serial correlation were detected we would include lags of the dependent variable in the forecasting regression.

This regression has been used in many instances for forecasting. First, in finance a great deal of attention has been given to the possibility that stock market returns are predictable. In the context of (13) we have y_t being stock returns from period $t-1$ to t and y_{2t-1} is any predictor known at the time one must undertake the investment to earn the returns y_{1t}. Examples of predictors include dividend–price ratio, earnings to price ratios, interest rates or spreads [see, for example, Fama and French (1998), Campbell and Shiller (1988a, 1988b) Hodrick (1992)]. Yet each of these predictors tends to display large amounts of persistence despite the absence of any obvious persistence in returns [Stambaugh (1999)]. The model (13) also well describes the regression run at the heart of the 'forward market unbiasedness' puzzle first examined by Bilson (1981). Typically such a regression regresses the change in the spot exchange rate from time $t-1$ to t on the forward premium, defined as the forward exchange rate at time $t-1$ for a contract deliverable at time t less the spot rate at time $t-1$ (which through covered interest parity is simply the difference between the interest rates of the two currencies for a contract set at time $t-1$ and deliverable at time t). This can be recast as a forecasting problem through subtracting the forward premium from both sides, leaving the uncovered interest parity condition to mean that the difference between the realized spot rate and the forward rate should be unpredictable. However the forward premium is very persistent [Evans and Lewis (1995) argue that this term can appear quite persistent due to the risk premium appearing quite persistent]. The literature on this regression is huge. Froot and Thaler (1990) give a review. A third area that fits this regression is use of interest rates or the term structure of the interest rates to predict various macroeconomic and financial variables. Chen (1991) shows using standard methods that short run interest rates and the term structure are useful for predicting GNP.

There are a few 'stylized' facts about such prediction problems. First, in general the coefficient β often appears to be significantly different from one under the usual stationary asymptotic theory (i.e. the t statistic is outside the ± 2 bounds). Second, R^2 tends to be very small. Third, often the coefficient estimates seem to vary over subsamples more than standard stationary asymptotic theory might predict. Finally, these relationships have a tendency to 'break down' – often the in sample forecasting ability does not seem to translate to out of sample predictive ability. Models where β is equal to or close to zero and regressors that are nearly nonstationary combined with asymptotic theory that reflects this trending behavior in the predictor variable can to some extent account for all of these stylized facts.

The problem of inference on the OLS estimator $\hat{\beta}_1$ in (13) has been studied in both cases specific to particular regressions and also more generally. Stambaugh (1999) examines inference from a Bayesian viewpoint. Mankiw and Shapiro (1986), in the context of predicting changes in consumption with income, examined these types of regressions employing Monte Carlo methods to show that t statistics overreject the null hypothesis that $\beta = 0$ using conventional critical values. Elliott and Stock (1994) and Cavanagh, Elliott and Stock (1995) examined this model using local to unity asymptotic theory to understand this type of result. Jansson and Moriera (2006) provide methods to test this hypothesis.

First, consider the problem that the t statistic overrejects in the above regression. Elliott and Stock (1994) show that the asymptotic distribution of the t statistic testing the hypothesis that $\beta_1 = 0$ can be written as the weighted sum of a mixed normal and the usual Dickey and Fuller t statistic. Given that the latter is not well approximated by a normal, the failure of empirical size to equal nominal size will result when the weight on this nonstandard part of the distribution is nonzero.

To see the effect of regressing with a trending regressor we will rotate the error vector v_t through considering $\eta_t = Rv_t$ where

$$R = \begin{pmatrix} 1 & -\delta\frac{\sigma_{11}}{c(1)\sigma_{22}} \\ 0 & 1 \end{pmatrix}$$

so $\eta_{1t} = v_{1t} - \delta\frac{\sigma_{11}}{c(1)\sigma_{22}}v_{2t} = v_{1t} - \delta\frac{\sigma_{11}}{c(1)\sigma_{22}}\eta_{2t}$. This results in the spectral density of η_t at frequency zero scaled by 2π equal to $Rb^*(1)\Sigma b^*(1)R'$ which is equivalent to

$$\Omega = Rb^*(1)\Sigma b^*(1)R' = \begin{pmatrix} \sigma_{22}^2(1-\delta^2) & 0 \\ 0 & c(1)^2\sigma_{11}^2 \end{pmatrix}.$$

Now consider the regression

$$\begin{aligned} y_{1t} &= \beta_0' z_t + \beta_1 y_{1t-1} + v_{1t} \\ &= (\beta_0' + \phi')z_{t-1} + \beta_1\left(y_{2t-1} - \phi' z_{t-1}\right) + v_{1t} \\ &= \tilde{\beta}_0' z_{t-1} + \beta_1\left(y_{2t-1} - \phi' z_{t-1}\right) + v_{1t} \\ &= \beta' X_t + v_{1t}, \end{aligned}$$

where $\beta = (\tilde{\beta}_0', \beta_1)'$ and $X_t = (z_t', y_{1t-1} - \phi' z_{t-1})'$.

Typically OLS is used to examine this regression. We have that

$$\begin{aligned} \hat{\beta} - \beta &= \left(\sum_{t=2}^{T} X_t X_t'\right)^{-1} \sum_{t=2}^{T} X_t v_{2t} \\ &= \left(\sum_{t=2}^{T} X_t X_t'\right)^{-1} \sum_{t=2}^{T} X_t \eta_{2t} + \delta\frac{\sigma_{22}}{c(1)\sigma_{11}}\left(\sum_{t=2}^{T} X_t X_t'\right)^{-1} \sum_{t=2}^{T} X_t \eta_{1t} \end{aligned}$$

since $v_{2t} = \eta_{2t} + \delta\frac{\sigma_{22}}{c(1)\sigma_{11}}\eta_{1t}$. What we have done is rewritten the shock to the forecasting regression into orthogonal components describing the shock to the persistent regressor and the shock unrelated to y_{2t}.

To examine the asymptotic properties of the estimator, we require some additional assumptions. Jointly we can consider the vector of partial sums of η_t and we assume that this partial sum satisfies a functional central limit theorem (FCLT)

$$T^{-1/2}\sum_{t=1}^{[T.]} \eta_t \Rightarrow \Omega^{1/2}\begin{pmatrix} W_{2.1}(\cdot) \\ M(\cdot) \end{pmatrix},$$

where $M(\cdot)$ is as before and is asymptotically independent of the standard Brownian motion $W_{2.1}(\cdot)$.

Now the usefulness of the decomposition of the parameter estimator into two parts can be seen through examining what each of these terms look like asymptotically when suitably scaled. The first term, by virtue of η_{1t} being orthogonal to the entire history of x_t, will when suitably scaled have an asymptotic mixed normal distribution. The second term is exactly what we would obtain, apart from being multiplied at the front by $\delta \frac{\sigma_{22}}{\sigma_{11}}$, in the Dickey and Fuller (1979) regression of x_t on a constant and lagged dependent variable. Hence this term has the familiar nonstandard distribution from that regression when standardized in the same way as the first term. Also by virtue of the independence of η_{1t} and ε_{2t} each of these terms is asymptotically independent. Thus the limit distribution for the standardized coefficients is a weighted sum of a mixed normal and a Dickey and Fuller (1979) distribution, which will not be well approximated by a normal distribution.

Now consider the t statistic testing $\beta = 0$. The t statistic testing the hypothesis that $\beta_1 = 0$ when this is the null is typically employed to justify the regressors inclusion in the forecasting equation. This t statistic has an asymptotic distribution given by

$$t_{\hat{\beta}_1=0} \Rightarrow \left(1 - \delta^2\right)^{1/2} z^* + \delta \mathrm{DF},$$

where z^* is distributed as a standard normal and DF is the usual Dickey and Fuller t distribution when $c(1) = 1$ and $\gamma = 0$ and a variant of it otherwise. The actual distribution is

$$\mathrm{DF} = \frac{0.5(M^d(1)^2 - M^d(0)^2 - c(1)^2)}{\int M^d(s)\,\mathrm{d}s},$$

where $M^d(s)$ is the projection of $M(s)$ on the continuous analog of z_t. When $\gamma = 0$, $c(1) = 1$ and at least a constant term is included this is identical to the usual DF distribution with the appropriate order of deterministic terms. When $c(1)$ is not one we have an extra effect through the serial correlation [cf. Phillips (1987)].

The nuisance parameter that determines the weights, δ, is the correlation between the shocks driving the forecasting equation and the quasi difference of the covariate to be included in the forecasting regression. Hence asymptotically, this nuisance parameter along with the local to unity parameter describe the extent to which this test for inclusion over rejects.

The effect of the trending regressor on the type of R^2 we are likely to see in the forecasting regression (13) can be seen through the relationship between the t statistic and R^2 in the model where only a constant is included in the regression. In such models we have that the R^2 for the regression is approximately $T^{-1} t^2_{\beta_1=0}$. In the usual case of including a stationary regressor without predictive power we would expect that TR^2 is approximately the square of the t statistic testing exclusion of the regressor, i.e. is distributed as a χ^2_1 random variable, hence on average we expect R^2 to be T^{-1}. But in the case of a trending regressor $t^2_{\beta_1=0}$ will not be well approximated by a χ^2_1 as the

Table 1
Overrejection and R^2 as a function of endogeneity

		$\delta = 0.1$	0.3	0.5	0.7	0.9
0	% rej	0.058	0.075	0.103	0.135	0.165
	ave R^2	0.010	0.012	0.014	0.017	0.019
5	% rej	0.055	0.061	0.070	0.078	0.087
	ave R^2	0.010	0.011	0.011	0.012	0.013
10	% rej	0.055	0.058	0.062	0.066	0.071
	ave R^2	0.010	0.010	0.011	0.011	0.012
15	% rej	0.056	0.057	0.059	0.062	0.065
	ave R^2	0.010	0.010	0.011	0.011	0.011
20	% rej	0.055	0.057	0.059	0.060	0.063
	ave R^2	0.010	0.010	0.010	0.011	0.011

t statistic is not well approximated by a standard normal. On average the R^2 will be larger and because of the long tail of the DF distribution there is a larger chance of having relatively larger values for R^2. However, we still expect R^2 to be small most of the time even though the test of inclusion rejects.

The extent of overrejection and the average R^2 for various values of δ and γ are given in Table 1 for a test with nominal size equal to 5%. The sample size is $T = 100$ and zero initial condition for y_{1t} was employed.

The problem is larger the closer y_{1t} is to having a unit root and the larger is the long run correlation coefficient δ. For moderate values of δ, the effect is not great. The rejection rate numbers mask the fact that the $t_{\beta_1=0}$ statistics can on occasion be far from ± 2. A well-known property of the DF distribution is a long tail on the left-hand side of the distribution. The sum of these distributions will also have such a tail – for $\delta > 0$ it will be to the left of the mean and for $\delta > 0$ to the right. Hence some of these rejections can appear quite large using the asymptotic normal as an approximation to the limit distribution. This follows through to the types of values for R^2 we expect. Again, when γ is close to zero and δ is close to one the R^2 is twice what we expect on average, but still very small. Typically it will be larger than expected, but does not take on very large values. This conforms with the common finding of trending predictors appearing to be useful in the regression through entering the forecasting regression with statistically significant coefficients however they do not appear to pick up much of the variation in the variable to be predicted.

The trending behavior of the regressor can also explain greater than expected variability in the coefficient estimate. In essence, the typically reported standard error of the estimate based on asymptotic normality is not a relevant guide to the sampling variability of the estimator over repeated samples and hence expectations based on this will mislead. Alternatively, standard tests for breaks in coefficient estimates rely on the stationarity of the regressors, and hence are not appropriate for these types of regressions.

Hansen (2000) gives an analysis of break testing when the regressor is not well approximated by a stationary process and provides a bootstrap method for testing for breaks.

In all of the above, I have considered one step ahead forecasts. There are two approaches that have been employed for greater than one step ahead forecasts. The first is to consider the regression $y_{1t} = \beta_0' z_t + \beta_1 y_{2t-h} + \tilde{v}_{1t}$ as the model that generates the h step ahead forecast where $\tilde{v}_{1t}$ is the iterated error term. In this case results very similar to those given above apply.

A second version is to examine the forecastability of the cumulation of h steps of the variable to be forecast. The regression is

$$\sum_{i=1}^{h} y_{1t+i} = \beta_0' z_t + \beta_1 y_{2t} + \tilde{v}_{2t+h}.$$

Notice that for large enough h this cumulation will act like a trending variable, and hence greatly increase the chance that such a regression is really a spurious regression. Thus when y_{2t} has a unit root or near unit root behavior the distribution of $\hat{\beta}_1$ will be more like that of a spurious regression, and hence give the appearance of predictability even when there is none there. Unlike the results above, this can be true even if the variable is strictly exogenous. These results can be formalized analytically through considering the asymptotic thought experiment that $h = [\lambda T]$ as in Section 3 above. Valkenov (2003) explicitly examines this type of regression for $z_t = 1$ and general serial correlation in the predictor and shows the spurious regression result analytically.

Finally, there is a strong link between these models and those of Section 5 above. Compare Equation (12) and the regression examined in this section. Renaming the dependent variable in (12) as y_{2t} and the 'cointegrating' vector y_{1t} we have the model of this section.

7. Forecast evaluation with unit or near unit roots

A number of issues arise here. In this handbook West examines issues in forecast evaluation when the model is stationary. Here, when the data have unit root or near unit root behavior then this must be taken into account when conducting the tests. It will also affect the properties of constructed variables such as average loss depending on the model. Alternatively, other possibilities arise in forecast evaluation. The literature that extends these results to use of nonstationary data is much less well developed.

7.1. *Evaluating and comparing expected losses*

The natural comparison between forecasting procedures is to compare the procedures based on 'holdout' samples – use a portion of the sample to estimate the models and a portion of the sample to evaluate them. The relevant statistic becomes the average 'out of sample' loss. We can consider the evaluation of any forecasting model where either (or both) the outcome variable and the covariates used in the forecast might have unit roots or near unit roots. The difficulty that typically arises for examining sample averages and estimator behavior when the variables are not obviously stationary is that central limit theorems do not apply. The result is that these sample averages tend to converge to nonstandard distributions that depend on nuisance parameters, and this must be taken into account when comparing out of sample average MSE's as well as in understanding the sampling error in any given average MSE.

Throughout this section we follow the majority of the (stationary) literature and consider a sampling scheme where the T observations are split between a model estimation sample consisting of the observations $t = 1, \dots, T_1$, and an evaluation sample $t = T_1 + 1, \dots, T$. For asymptotic results we allow both samples to get large, defining $\kappa = T_1/T$. Further, we will allow the forecast horizon h to remain large as T increases, we set $h/T = \lambda$. We are thus examining approximations to situations where the forecast horizon is substantial compared to the sample available. These results are comparable to the long run forecasting results of the earlier sections.

As an example of how the sample average of out of sample forecast errors converges to a nonstandard distribution dependent on nuisance parameters, we can examine the simple univariate model of Section 3. In the mean case the forecast of y_{t+h} at time t is simply y_t and so the average forecast error for the holdout sample is

$$\mathrm{MSE}(h) = \frac{1}{T - T_1 - h} \sum_{t=T_1+1}^{T-h} (y_{t+h} - y_t)^2.$$

Now allowing $T(\rho - 1) = -\gamma$ then using the FCLT and continuous mapping theorem we have that after rescaling by T^{-1} then

$$\begin{aligned} T^{-1}\mathrm{MSE}(h) &= \frac{T}{T - T_1 - h} T^{-1} \sum_{t=T_1+1}^{T-h} \left(T^{-1/2} y_{t+h} - T^{-1/2} y_t\right)^2 \\ &\Rightarrow \sigma_\varepsilon^2 \frac{1}{1 - \lambda - \kappa} \int_\kappa^{1-\lambda} \left(M(s+\lambda) - M(s)\right)^2 \mathrm{d}s. \end{aligned}$$

The additional scaling by T gives some hint to understanding the output of average out of sample forecast errors. The raw average of out of sample forecast errors gets larger as the sample size increases. Thus interpreting directly this average as the likely forecast error using the model to forecast the next h periods is misleading. However on rescaling, it can be considered in this way. In the case where the initial value for the process y_t comes from its unconditional distribution, i.e. $\alpha = 1$, the limit distribution has a mean that is exactly the expected value for the expected MSE of a single h step ahead forecast.

When the largest root is estimated these expressions become even more complicated functions of Brownian motions, and as earlier become very difficult to examine analytically.

When the forecasting model is complicated further, by the addition of extra variables in the forecasting model, asymptotic approximations for average out of sample forecast error become even more complicated, typically depending on all the nuisance parameters of the model. Corradi, Swanson and Olivetti (2001) extend results to the cointegrated case where the rank of cointegration is known. In such models the variables that enter the regressions are stationary, and the same results as for stationary regression arise so long as loss is quadratic or the out of sample proportion grows at a slower rate than the in sample proportion (i.e. κ converges to one). Rossi (2005) provides analytical results for comparing models where all variables have near unit roots against the random walk model, along with methods for dealing with the nuisance parameter problem.

7.2. Orthogonality and unbiasedness regressions

Consider the basic orthogonality regression for differentiable loss functions, i.e. the regression

$$L'(e_{t+h}) = \beta' X_t + \varepsilon_{t+h}$$

(where X_t includes any information known at the time the forecast is made and $L'(\cdot)$ is the first derivative of the loss function) and we wish to test the hypothesis H_0: $\beta = 0$. If some or all of the variables in X_t are integrated or near integrated, then this affects the sampling distribution of the parameter estimates and the corresponding hypothesis tests.

This arises in practice in a number of instances. We have earlier noted that one popular choice for X_t, namely the forecast itself, has been used in testing what is known as 'unbiasedness' of the forecasts. In the case of MSE loss, where $L'(e_{t+h}) = e_{t+h}/2$ then unbiasedness means that on average the forecast is equal to the outcome. This can be done in the context of the regression above using

$$y_{t+h} - y_{t,t+h} = \beta_0 + \beta_1 y_{t+h,t} + \varepsilon_{t+h}.$$

If the series to be forecast is integrated or near integrated, then the predictor in this regression will have these properties and standard asymptotic theory for conducting this test does not apply.

Another case might be a situation where we want to construct a test that has power against a small nonstationary component in the forecast error. Including only stationary variables in X_t would not give any power in that direction, and hence one may wish to include a nonstationary variable. Finally, many variables that are suggested in theory to be potentially correlated with outcomes may exhibit large amounts of persistence. Such variables include interest rates etc. Again, in these situations we need to account for the different sampling behavior.

If the variables X_t can be neatly split (in a known way) between variables with unit roots and variables without and it is known how many cointegrating vectors there are amongst the unit root variables, then the framework of the regression fits that of Sims, Stock and Watson (1990). Under their assumptions the OLS coefficient vector $\hat{\beta}$ converges to a nonstandard distribution which involves functions of Brownian motions and normal variates. The distribution depends on nuisance parameters and standard tabulation of critical values is basically infeasible (the number of dimensions would be large). As a consequence, finding the critical values for the joint test of orthogonality is quite difficult.

This problem is of course equivalent to that of the previous section when it comes to distribution theory for $\hat{\beta}$ and consequently on testing this parameter. The same issues arise. Thus orthogonality tests with integrated or near integrated regressors are problematic, even without thinking about the construction of the forecast errors. Failure to realize the impacts of these correlations on the hypothesis test (i.e. proceeding as if the t statistics had asymptotic normal distributions or that the F statistics have asymptotic chi-square distributions) results in overrejection. Further, there is no simple method for constructing the alternate distributions, especially when there is uncertainty over whether or not there is a unit root in the regressor [see Cavanagh, Elliott and Stock (1995)].

Additional issues also arise when X_t includes the forecast or other constructed variables. In the stationary case results are available for various construction schemes (see Chapter 3 by West in this Handbook). These results will not in general carry over to the problem here.

7.3. *Cointegration of forecasts and outcomes*

An implication of good forecasting when outcomes are trending would be that forecasts and outcomes of the variable of interest would have a difference that is not trending. In this sense, if the outcomes have a unit root then we would expect forecasts and outcomes to be cointegrated. This has led some researchers to examine whether or not the forecasts made in practice are indeed cointegrated with the variable being forecast. The expected cointegrating vector is $\beta = (1, -1)'$, implying that the forecast error is stationary. This has been undertaken for exchange rates [Liu and Maddala (1992)] and macroeconomic data [Aggarwal, Mohanty and Song (1995)]. In the context of macroeconomic forecasts, Cheung and Chinn (1999) also relax the cointegrating vector assumption that the coefficients are known and estimate these coefficients.

The requirement that forecasts be cointegrated with outcomes is a very weak requirement. Note that the forecasters information set includes the current value of the outcome variable. Since the current value of the outcome variable is trivially cointegrated with the future outcome variable to be forecast (they differ by the change, which is stationary) then the forecaster has a simple observable forecast that satisfies the requirement that the forecast and outcome variable be cointegrated. This also means that forecasts generated by adding any stationary component to the current level of the variable will also satisfy the requirement of cointegration between the forecasts and the outcome. Thus even forecasts of the change that are uncorrelated with the actual change provided they are stationary will result in cointegration between forecasts and outcomes.

We can also imagine what happens under the null hypothesis of no cointegration. Under the null, forecast errors are $I(1)$ and hence become arbitrarily far from zero with probability one. It is hard to imagine that a forecaster would stick with such a method when the forecast becomes further from the current value of the outcome than typical changes in the outcome variable would suggest are plausible.

That this weak requirement obviously holds in many cases has not meant that the hypothesis has not been rejected. As with all testing situations, one must consider the test a joint test of the proposition being examined and the assumptions under which the test is derived. Given the unlikely event that forecasts and outcomes are truly becoming arbitrarily far apart, as would be suggested by a lack of cointegration, perhaps the problem is in the assumption that the trend is correctly characterized by a unit root. In the context of hypothesis testing on the β parameters Elliott (1998) shows that near unit roots causes major size distortions for tests on this parameter vector.

Overall, these tests are not likely to shed much light on the usefulness of forecasts.

8. Conclusion

Making general statements as to how to proceed with forecasting when there is trending behavior is difficult due to the strong dependence of the results on a myriad of nuisance parameters of the problem – extent of deterministic terms, initial values and descriptions of serial correlation. This becomes even more true when the model is multivariate, since there are many more combinations of nuisance parameters that can either reduce or enhance the value of estimation over imposition of unit roots.

Theoretically though a number of points arise. First, except for roots quite close to one estimation should outperform imposition of unit roots in terms of MSE error. Indeed, since estimation results in bounded MSE over reasonable regions of uncertainty over the parameter space whereas imposition of unit roots can result in very large losses it would seem to be the conservative approach would be to estimate the parameters if we are uncertain as to their values. This goes almost entirely against current practice and findings with real data. Two possibilities arise immediately. First, the models for which under which the theory above is useful are not good models of the data and hence the theoretical size of the trade-offs are different. Second, there are features of real data that, although the above models are reasonable, they affect the estimators in ways ignored by the models here and so when parameters are estimated large errors make the results less appropriate. Given that tests designed to distinguish between various models are not powerful enough to rule out the models considered here, it is unlikely that these other functions of the data – evaluations of forecast performance – will show the differences between the models.

For multivariate models the differences are exacerbated in most cases. Theory shows that imposing cointegration on the problem when true is still unlikely to help at longer horizons despite its nature as a long run restriction on the data. A number of authors have sought to characterize this issue as not one of imposing cointegration but imposing the correct number of unit roots on the model, however these are of course equivalent. It is true however that it is the estimation of the roots that can cause MSE to be larger, they can be poorly estimated in small samples. More directly though is that the trade-offs are similar in nature to the univariate model. Risk is bounded when the parameters are estimated.

Finally, it is not surprising that there is a short horizon/long horizon dichotomy in the forecasting of variables when the covariates display trending behavior. In the short run we are relating a trending variable to a nontrending one, and it is difficult to write down such a model where the trending covariate is going to explain a lot of the nontrending outcome. At longer horizons though the long run prediction becomes the sum of stationary increments, allowing trending covariates a greater opportunity of being correlated with the outcome to be forecast.

In part a great deal of the answer probably lies in the high correlation between the forecasts that arise from various assumptions and also the unconditional nature of the results of the literature. On the first point, given the data the differences just tend not to be huge and hence imposing the root and modelling the variables in differences not greatly costly in most samples, imposing unit roots just makes for a simpler modelling exercise. This type of conditional result has not been greatly examined in the literature. Things brings the second point – for what practical forecasting problems does the unconditional, i.e. averaging over lots of data sets, best practice become relevant? This too has not been looked at deeply in the literature. When the current variable is far from its deterministic component, estimating the root (which typically means using a mean reverting model) and imposing the unit root (which stops mean reversion) have a bigger impact in the sense that they generate very different forecasts. The modelling of the trending nature becomes very important in these cases even though on average it appears less important because we average over these cases as well as the more likely case that the current level of the variable is close to its deterministic component.

References

Abidir, K., Kaddour, H., Tzavaliz, E. (1999). "The influence of VAR dimensions on estimator biases". Econometrica 67, 163–181.

Aggarwal, R., Mohanty, S., Song, F. (1995). "Are survey forecasts of macroeconomic variables rational?" Journal of Business 68, 99–119.

Andrews, D. (1993). "Exactly median-unbiased estimation of first order autoregressive/unit root models". Econometrica 61, 139–165.

Andrews, D., Chen, Y.H. (1994). "Approximately median-unbiased estimation of autoregressive models". Journal of Business and Economics Statistics 12, 187–204.

Banerjee, A. (2001). "Sensitivity of univariate AR(1) time series forecasts near the unit root". Journal of Forecasting 20, 203–229.

Bilson, J. (1981). "The 'speculative efficiency' hypothesis". Journal of Business 54, 435–452.

Box, G., Jenkins, G. (1970). Time Series Analysis: Forecasting and Control. Holden-Day, San Francisco.

Campbell, J., Perron, P. (1991). "Pitfalls and opportunities: What macroeconomists should know about unit roots". NBER Macroeconomics Annual, 141–201.

Campbell, J., Shiller, R. (1988a). "The dividend–price ratio and expectations of future dividends". Review of Financial Studies 1, 195–228.

Campbell, J., Shiller, R. (1988b). "Stock prices, earnings and expected dividends". Journal of Finance 43, 661–676.

Canjels, E., Watson, M. (1997). "Estimating deterministic trends in the presence of serially correlated errors". Review of Economics and Statistics 79, 184–200.

Cavanagh, C., Elliott, G., Stock, J. (1995). "Inference in models with nearly integrated regressors". Econometric Theory 11, 11231–11247.

Chen, N. (1991). "Financial investment opportunities and the macroeconomy". Journal of Finance 46, 495–514.

Cheung, Y.-W., Chinn, M. (1999). "Are macroeconomic forecasts informative? Cointegration evidence from the ASA-NBER surveys". NBER Discussion Paper 6926.

Christoffersen, P., Diebold, F. (1998). "Cointegration and long-horizon forecasting". Journal of Business and Economic Statistics 16, 450–458.

Clements, M., Hendry, D. (1993). "On the limitations of comparing mean square forecast errors". Journal of Forecasting 12, 617–637.

Clements, M., Hendry, D. (1995). "Forecasting in cointegrated systems". Journal of Applied Econometrics 11, 495–517.

Clements, M., Hendry, D. (1998). Forecasting Economic Time Series. Cambridge University Press, Cambridge, MA.

Clements, M., Hendry, D. (2001). "Forecasting with difference-stationary and trend-stationary models". Econometrics Journal 4, s1–s19.

Cochrane, D., Orcutt, G. (1949). "Applications of least squares regression to relationships containing autocorrelated error terms". Journal of the American Statistical Association 44, 32–61.

Corradi, V., Swanson, N.R., Olivetti, C. (2001). "Predictive ability with cointegrated variables". Journal of Econometrics 104, 315–358.

Dickey, D., Fuller, W. (1979). "Distribution of the estimators for autoregressive time series with a unit root". Journal of the American Statistical Association 74, 427–431.

Diebold, F., Kilian, L. (2000). "Unit-root tests are useful for selecting forecasting models". Journal of Business and Economic Statistics 18, 265–273.

Elliott, G. (1998). "The robustness of cointegration methods when regressors almost have unit roots". Econometrica 66, 149–158.

Elliott, G., Rothenberg, T., Stock, J. (1996). "Efficient tests for and autoregressive unit root". Econometrica 64, 813–836.

Elliott, G., Stock, J. (1994). "Inference in models with nearly integrated regressors". Econometric Theory 11, 1131–1147.

Engle, R., Granger, C. (1987). "Co-integration and error correction: Representation, estimation, and testing". Econometrica 55, 251–276.

Engle, R., Yoo, B. (1987). "Forecasting and testing in co-integrated systems". Journal of Econometrics 35, 143–159.

Evans, M., Lewis, K. (1995). "Do long-term swings in the dollar affect estimates on the risk premium?" Review of Financial Studies 8, 709–742.

Fama, E., French, F. (1998). "Dividend yields and expected stock returns". Journal of Financial Economics 35, 143–159.

Franses, P., Kleibergen, F. (1996). "Unit roots in the Nelson–Plosser data: Do they matter for forecasting". International Journal of Forecasting 12, 283–288.

Froot, K., Thaler, R. (1990). "Anomalies: Foreign exchange". Journal of Economic Perspective 4, 179–192.

Granger, C. (1966). "The typical spectral shape of and economic variable". Econometrica 34, 150–161.

Hall, R. (1978). "Stochastic implications of the life-cycle-permanent income hypothesis: Theory and evidence". Journal of Political Economy 86, 971–988.

Hansen, B. (2000). "Testing for structural change in conditional models". Journal of Econometrics 97, 93–115.

Hodrick, R. (1992). "Dividend yields and expected stock returns: Alternative procedures for inference measurement". Review of Financial Studies 5, 357–386.

Hoffman, D., Rasche, R. (1996). "Assessing forecast performance in a cointegrated system". Journal of Applied Econometrics 11, 495–516.

Jansson, M., Moriera, M. (2006). "Optimal inference in regression models with nearly integrated regressors". Econometrica. In press.

Johansen, S. (1991). "Estimation and hypothesis testing of cointegrating vectors in Gaussian vector autoregressive models". Econometrica 59, 1551–1580.

Kemp, G. (1999). "The behavior of forecast errors from a nearly integrated $I(1)$ model as both the sample size and forecast horizon gets large". Econometric Theory 15, 238–256.

Liu, T., Maddala, G. (1992). "Rationality of survey data and tests for market efficiency in the foreign exchange markets". Journal of International Money and Finance 11, 366–381.

Magnus, J., Pesaran, B. (1989). "The exact multi-period mean-square forecast error for the first-order autoregressive model with an intercept". Journal of Econometrics 42, 238–256.

Mankiw, N., Shapiro, M. (1986). "Do we reject too often: Small sample properties of tests of rational expectations models". Economic Letters 20, 139–145.

Meese, R., Rogoff, K. (1983). "Empirical exchange rate models of the seventies: Do they fit out of sample?" Journal of International Economics 14, 3–24.

Müller, U., Elliott, G. (2003). "Tests for unit roots and the initial observation". Econometrica 71, 1269–1286.

Nelson, C., Plosser, C. (1982). "Trends and random walks in macroeconomic time series: Some evidence and implications". Journal of Monetary Economics 10, 139–162.

Ng, S., Vogelsang, T. (2002). "Forecasting dynamic time series in the presence of deterministic components". Econometrics Journal 5, 196–224.

Phillips, P.C.B. (1979). "The sampling distribution of forecasts from a first order autoregression". Journal of Econometrics 9, 241–261.

Phillips, P.C.B. (1987). "Time series regression with a unit root". Econometrica 55, 277–302.

Phillips, P.C.B. (1998). "Impulse response and forecast error variance asymptotics in nonstationary VARs". Journal of Econometrics 83, 21–56.

Phillips, P.C.B., Durlauf, S.N. (1986). "Multiple time series regression with integrated processes". Review of Economic Studies 52, 473–495.

Prais, S., Winsten, C.B. (1954). "Trend estimators and serial correlation". Cowles Foundation Discussion Paper 383.

Rossi, B. (2005). "Testing long-horizon predictive ability with high persistence, and the Meese–Rogoff puzzle". International Economic Review 46, 61–92.

Roy, A., Fuller, W. (2001). "Estimation for autoregressive time series with a root near one". Journal of Business and Economic Studies 19, 482–493.

Sampson, M. (1991). "The effect of parameter uncertainty on forecast variances and confidence intervals for unit root and trend stationary time series models". Journal of Applied Econometrics 6, 67–76.

Sanchez, I. (2002). "Efficient forecasting in nearly non-stationary processes". Journal of Forecasting 21, 1–26.

Sims, C., Stock, J., Watson, M. (1990). "Inference in linear time series models with some unit roots". Econometrica 58, 113–144.

Stambaugh, R. (1999). "Predictive regressions". Journal of Financial Economics 54, 375–421.

Stock, J.H. (1987). "Asymptotic properties of least squares estimators of cointegrating vectors". Econometrica 55, 1035–1056.

Stock, J.H. (1991). "Confidence intervals for the largest autoregressive root in U.S. macroeconomic time series". Journal of Monetary Economics 28, 435–459.

Stock, J.H. (1994). "Unit roots, structural breaks and trends". In: Engle, R., McFadden, D. (Eds.), Handbook of Econometrics, vol. 4. Elsevier, Amsterdam, pp. 2740–2841.

Stock, J.H. (1996). "VAR, error correction and pretest forecasts at long horizons". Oxford Bulletin of Economics and Statistics 58, 685–701.

Stock, J.H., Watson, M.W. (1999). "A comparison of linear and nonlinear univariate models for forecasting macroeconomic time series". In: Engle, R., White, H. (Eds.), Cointegration, Causality and Forecasting: A Festschrift for Clive W.J. Granger. Oxford University Press, Oxford, pp. 1–44.

Turner, J. (2004). "Local to unity, long horizon forecasting thresholds for model selection in the AR(1)". Journal of Forecasting 23, 513–539.

Valkenov, R. (2003). "Long horizon regressions: Theoretical results and applications". Journal of Financial Economics 68, 201–232.

Watson, M. (1994). "Vector autoregression and cointegration". In: Engle, R., McFadden, D. (Eds.), Handbook of Econometrics, vol. 4. Elsevier, Amsterdam, pp. 2843–2915.

Chapter 12

FORECASTING WITH BREAKS

MICHAEL P. CLEMENTS

Department of Economics, University of Warwick

DAVID F. HENDRY

Economics Department, University of Oxford

Contents

Handbook of Economic Forecasting, Volume 1
Edited by Graham Elliott, Clive W.J. Granger and Allan Timmermann

DOI: 10.1016/S1574-0706(05)01012-8

Abstract

A structural break is viewed as a permanent change in the parameter vector of a model. Using taxonomies of all sources of forecast errors for both conditional mean and conditional variance processes, we consider the impacts of breaks and their relevance in forecasting models: (a) where the breaks occur after forecasts are announced; and (b) where they occur in-sample and hence pre-forecasting. The impact on forecasts depends on which features of the models are non-constant. Different models and methods are shown to fare differently in the face of breaks. While structural breaks induce an instability in some parameters of a particular model, the consequences for forecasting are specific to the type of break and form of model. We present a detailed analysis for cointegrated VARs, given the popularity of such models in econometrics.

We also consider the detection of breaks, and how to handle breaks in a forecasting context, including ad hoc forecasting devices and the choice of the estimation period. Finally, we contrast the impact of structural break non-constancies with non-constancies due to non-linearity. The main focus is on macro-economic, rather than finance, data, and on forecast biases, rather than higher moments. Nevertheless, we show the relevance of some of the key results for variance processes. An empirical exercise 'forecasts' UK unemployment after three major historical crises.

Keywords

economic forecasting, structural breaks, break detection, cointegration, non-linear models

JEL classification: C530

1. Introduction

A structural break is a permanent change in the parameter vector of a model. We consider the case where such breaks are exogenous, in the sense that they were determined by events outside the model under study: we also usually assume that such breaks were unanticipated given the historical data up to that point. We do rule out multiple breaks, but because breaks are exogenous, each is treated as permanent. To the extent that breaks are predictable, action can be taken to mitigate the effects we show will otherwise occur. The main exception to this characterization of breaks will be our discussion of non-linear models which attempt to anticipate some shifts.

Using taxonomies of all sources of forecast errors, we consider the impacts of breaks and their relevance in forecasting models:

(a) where the breaks occur after forecasts are announced; and
(b) where they are in-sample and occurred pre-forecasting, focusing on breaks close to the forecast origin.

New generic (model-free) forecast-error taxonomies are developed to highlight what can happen in general. It transpires that it matters greatly what features actually break (e.g., coefficients of stochastic, or of deterministic, variables, or of other aspects of the model, such as error variances). Also, there are major differences in the effects of these different forms of breaks on different forecasting methods, in that some devices are robust, and others non-robust, to various pre-forecasting breaks. Thus, although structural breaks induce an instability in some parameters of a particular model, the consequences for forecasting are specific to the type of break and form of model. This allows us to account for the majority of the findings reported in the major 'forecasting competitions' literature. Later, we consider how to detect, and how to handle, breaks, and the impact of sample size thereon. We will mainly focus on macro-economic data, rather than finance data where typically one has a much larger sample size. Finally, because the most serious consequences of unanticipated breaks are on forecast biases, we mainly consider first moment effects, although we also note the effects of breaks in variance processes.

Our chapter builds on a great deal of previous research into forecasting in the face of structural breaks, and tangentially on related literatures about: forecasting models and methods; forecast evaluation; sources and effects of breaks; their detection; and ultimately on estimation and inference in econometric models. Most of these topics have been thoroughly addressed in previous Handbooks [see Griliches and Intriligator (1983, 1984, 1986), Engle and McFadden (1994), and Heckman and Leamer (2004)], and compendia on forecasting [see, e.g., Armstrong (2001) and Clements and Hendry (2002a)], so to keep the coverage of references within reasonable bounds we assume the reader refers to those sources inter alia.

As an example of a process subject to a structural break, consider the data generating process (DGP) given by the structural change model of, e.g., Andrews (1993):

$$y_t = (\mu_0 + \alpha_1 y_{t-1} + \cdots + \alpha_p y_{t-p}) \\ + (\mu_0^* + \alpha_1^* y_{t-1} + \cdots + \alpha_p^* y_{t-p}) s_t + \varepsilon_t, \tag{1}$$

where $\varepsilon_t \sim \mathsf{IID}[0, \sigma_\varepsilon^2]$ (that is, Independently, Identically Distributed, mean zero, variance σ_ε^2), and s_t is the indicator variable, $s_t \equiv 1_{(t>\tau)}$ which equals 1 when $t > \tau$ and zero when $t \leqslant \tau$. We focus on breaks in the conditional mean parameters, and usually ignore changes in the variance of the disturbance, as suggested by the form of (1). A constant-parameter pth-order autoregression (AR(p)) for y_t of the form

$$y_t = \mu_{0,1} + \alpha_{1,1} y_{t-1} + \cdots + \alpha_{p,1} y_{t-p} + v_t \tag{2}$$

would experience a structural break because the parameter vector shifts. Let $\boldsymbol{\phi} = (\mu_0\ \alpha_1 \ldots \alpha_p)'$, $\boldsymbol{\phi}^* = (\mu_0^*\ \alpha_1^* \ldots \alpha_p^*)'$ and $\boldsymbol{\phi}_1 = (\mu_{0,1}\ \alpha_{1,1} \ldots \alpha_{p,1})'$. Then the AR($p$) model parameters are $\boldsymbol{\phi}_1 = \boldsymbol{\phi}$ for $t \leqslant \tau$, but $\boldsymbol{\phi}_1 = \boldsymbol{\phi} + \boldsymbol{\phi}^*$ for $t > \tau$ (in Section 5, we briefly review testing for structural change when τ is unknown). If instead, the AR(p) were extended to include terms which interacted the existing regressors with a step dummy D_t defined by $D_t = s_t = 1_{(t>\tau)}$, the extended model (letting $\mathbf{x}_t = (1\ y_{t-1} \ldots y_{t-p})'$)

$$y_t = \boldsymbol{\phi}_{1,d}' \mathbf{x}_t + \boldsymbol{\phi}_{2,d}' \mathbf{x}_t D_t + v_{t,d} \tag{3}$$

exhibits extended parameter constancy – $(\boldsymbol{\phi}_{1,d}'\ \boldsymbol{\phi}_{2,d}') = (\boldsymbol{\phi}'\ \boldsymbol{\phi}^{*\prime})$ for all $t = 1, \ldots, T$, matching the DGP [see, e.g., Hendry (1996)]. Whether a model experiences a structural break is as much a property of the model as of the DGP.

As a description of the process determining $\{y_t\}$, Equation (1) is incomplete, as the cause of the shift in the parameter vector from $\boldsymbol{\phi}$ to $\boldsymbol{\phi} + \boldsymbol{\phi}^*$ is left unexplained. Following Bontemps and Mizon (2003), Equation (1) could be thought of as the 'local' DGP (LDGP) for $\{y_t\}$ – namely, the DGP for $\{y_t\}$ given only the variables being modeled (here, just the history of y_t). The original AR(p) model is mis-specified for the LDGP because of the structural change. A fully-fledged DGP would include the reason for the shift at time τ. Empirically, the forecast performance of any model such as (2) will depend on its relationship to the DGP. By adopting a 'model' such as (1) for the LDGP, we are assuming that the correspondence between the LDGP and DGP is close enough to sustain an empirically relevant analysis of forecasting. Put another way, knowledge of the factors responsible for the parameter instability is not essential in order to study the impact of the resulting structural breaks on the forecast performance of models such as (2).

LDGPs in economics will usually be multivariate and more complicated than (1), so to obtain results of some generality, the next section develops a 'model-free' taxonomy of errors for conditional first-moment forecasts. This highlights the sources of biases in forecasts. The taxonomy is then applied to forecasts from a vector autoregression (VAR). Section 3 presents a forecast-error taxonomy for conditional second-moment forecasts based on standard econometric volatility models. Section 4 derives the properties of forecasts for a cointegrated VAR, where it is assumed that the break occurs at the very end of the in-sample period, and so does not affect the models' parameter estimates.

Alternatively, any in-sample breaks have been detected and modeled. Section 5 considers the detection of in-sample breaks, and Section 6 the selection of the optimal window of data for model estimation as well as model specification more generally in the presence of in-sample breaks. Section 7 looks at a number of ad hoc forecasting methods, and assesses their performance in the face of breaks. When there are breaks, forecasting methods which adapt quickly following the break are most likely to avoid making systematic forecast errors. Section 8 contrasts breaks as permanent changes with non-constancies due to neglected non-linearities, from the perspectives of discriminating between the two, and for forecasting. Section 9 reports an empirical forecasting exercise for UK unemployment after three crises, namely the post-world-war double-decades of 1919–1938 and 1948–1967, and the post oil-crisis double-decade 1975–1994, to examine the forecasts of unemployment that would have been made by various devices: it also reports post-model-selection forecasts over 1992–2001, a decade which witnessed the ejection of the UK from the exchange-rate mechanism at its commencement. Section 10 briefly concludes. Two Appendices A and B, respectively, provide derivations for the taxonomy Equation (10) and for Section 4.3.

2. Forecast-error taxonomies

2.1. General (model-free) forecast-error taxonomy

In this section, a new general forecast-error taxonomy is developed to unify the discussion of the various sources of forecast error, and to highlight the effects of structural breaks on the properties of forecasts. The taxonomy distinguishes between breaks affecting 'deterministic' and 'stochastic' variables, both in-sample and out-of-sample, as well as delineating other possible sources of forecast error, including model mis-specification and parameter-estimation uncertainty, which might interact with breaks.

Consider a vector of n stochastic variables $\{\mathbf{x}_t\}$, where the joint density of $\mathbf{x}_t$ at time t is $\mathsf{D}_{\mathbf{x}_t}(\mathbf{x}_t \mid \mathbf{X}_{t-1}^1, \mathbf{q}_t)$, conditional on information $\mathbf{X}_{t-1}^1 = (\mathbf{x}_1, \ldots, \mathbf{x}_{t-1})$, where $\mathbf{q}_t$ denotes the relevant deterministic factors (such as intercepts, trends, and indicators). The densities are time dated to make explicit that they may be changing over time. The object of the exercise is to forecast $\mathbf{x}_{T+h}$ over forecast horizons $h = 1, \ldots, H$, from a forecast origin at T. A dynamic model $\mathsf{M}_{\mathbf{x}_t}[\mathbf{x}_t \mid \mathbf{X}_{t-1}^{t-s}, \tilde{\mathbf{q}}_t, \boldsymbol{\theta}_t]$, with deterministic terms $\tilde{\mathbf{q}}_t$, lag length s, and implicit stochastic specification defined by its parameters $\boldsymbol{\theta}_t$, is fitted over the sample $t = 1, \ldots, T$ to produce a forecast sequence $\{\hat{\mathbf{x}}_{T+h|T}\}$. Parameter estimates are a function of the observables, represented by:

$$\hat{\boldsymbol{\theta}}_{(T)} = \mathbf{f}_T\big(\widetilde{\mathbf{X}}_T^1, \widetilde{\mathbf{Q}}_T^1\big), \tag{4}$$

where $\widetilde{\mathbf{X}}$ denotes the measured data and $\widetilde{\mathbf{Q}}_T^1$ the in-sample set of deterministic terms which need not coincide with $\mathbf{Q}_T^1$. The subscript on $\hat{\boldsymbol{\theta}}_{(T)}$ in (4) represents the influence of sample size on the estimate, whereas that on $\boldsymbol{\theta}_t$ in $\mathsf{M}_{\mathbf{x}_t}[\cdot]$ denotes that the derived parameters of the model may alter over time (perhaps reflected in changed estimates).

Let $\boldsymbol{\theta}_{e,(T)} = \mathsf{E}_T[\hat{\boldsymbol{\theta}}_{(T)}]$ (where that exists). As shown in Clements and Hendry (2002b), it is convenient, and without loss of generality, to map changes in the parameters of deterministic terms into changes in those terms, and we do so throughout.

Since future values of the deterministic terms are 'known', but those of stochastic variables are unknown, the form of the function determining the forecasts will depend on the horizon

$$\hat{\mathbf{x}}_{T+h|T} = \mathbf{g}_h\big(\widetilde{\mathbf{X}}_T^{T-s+1}, \widetilde{\mathbf{Q}}_{T+h}^{T}, \hat{\boldsymbol{\theta}}_{(T)}\big). \tag{5}$$

In (5), $\widetilde{\mathbf{X}}_T^{T-s+1}$ enters up to the forecast origin, which might be less well measured than earlier data; see, e.g., [Wallis (1993)].[1] The model will generally be a mis-specified representation of the LDGP for any of a large number of reasons, even when designed to be congruent [see Hendry (1995, p. 365)].

The forecast errors of the model are given by $\mathbf{e}_{T+h|T} = \mathbf{x}_{T+h} - \hat{\mathbf{x}}_{T+h|T}$ with expected value

$$\mathsf{E}_{T+h}\big[\mathbf{e}_{T+h|T} \mid \mathbf{X}_T^1, \{\mathbf{Q}^{**}\}_{T+h}^1\big], \tag{6}$$

where we allow that the LDGP deterministic factors (from which the model's deterministic factors $\widetilde{\mathbf{Q}}_{T+h}^{T}$ are derived) are subject to in-sample shifts as well as forecast period shifts, denoted by $**$ as follows. If we let τ date an in-sample shift ($1 < \tau < T$), the LDGP deterministic factors are denoted by $\{\mathbf{Q}^{**}\}_{T+h}^1 = [\mathbf{Q}_\tau^1, \{\mathbf{Q}^*\}_T^{\tau+1}, \{\mathbf{Q}^{**}\}_{T+h}^{T+1}]$. Thus, the pre-shift in-sample period is $1, \ldots, \tau$, the post-shift in-sample period is $\tau + 1, \ldots, T$, and the forecast period is $T + 1, \ldots, T + h$, where we allow for the possibility of a shift at T. Absences of $**$ and $*$ indicate that forecast and in-sample period shifts did not occur. Thus, $\{\mathbf{Q}^*\}_T^{\tau+1} = \mathbf{Q}_T^{\tau+1}$ implies no in-sample shifts, denoted by $\mathbf{Q}_T^1$, and the absence of shifts both in-sample and during the forecast period gives $\mathbf{Q}_{T+h}^1$. Let $\{\mathbf{Q}^*\}_{T+h}^1 = [\mathbf{Q}_\tau^1, \{\mathbf{Q}^*\}_{T+H}^{\tau+1}]$ refer to an in-sample shift, but no subsequent forecast-period shifts. The deterministic factors $\widetilde{\mathbf{Q}}_T^1$ in the model may also be mis-specified in-sample when the LDGP deterministic factors are given by $\mathbf{Q}_T^1$ ('conventional' mis-specification). Of more interest, perhaps, is the case when the mis-specification is induced by an in-sample shift not being modeled. This notation reflects the important role that shifts in deterministic terms play in forecast failure, defined as a significant deterioration in forecast performance relative to the anticipated outcome, usually based on the historical performance of a model.

We define the forecast error from the LDGP as

$$\boldsymbol{\varepsilon}_{T+h|T} = \mathbf{x}_{T+h} - \mathsf{E}_{T+h}\big[\mathbf{x}_{T+h} \mid \mathbf{X}_T^1, \{\mathbf{Q}^{**}\}_{T+h}^1\big]. \tag{7}$$

By construction, this is the forecast error from using a correctly-specified model of the mean of $\mathsf{D}_{\mathbf{x}_t}(\mathbf{x}_t \mid \mathbf{X}_{t-1}^1, \mathbf{q}_t)$, where any structural change (in, or out, of sample) is known and incorporated, and the model parameters are known (with no estimation error). It

[1] The dependence of $\hat{\boldsymbol{\theta}}_{(T)}$ on the forecast origin is ignored below.

follows that $\mathsf{E}_{T+h}[\boldsymbol{\varepsilon}_{T+h|T} \mid \mathbf{X}_T^1, \{\mathbf{Q}^{**}\}_{T+h}^1] = \mathbf{0}$, so that $\boldsymbol{\varepsilon}_{T+h|T}$ is an innovation against all available information. Practical interest, though, lies in the model forecast error, $\mathbf{e}_{T+h|T} = \mathbf{x}_{T+h} - \hat{\mathbf{x}}_{T+h|T}$. The model forecast error is related to $\boldsymbol{\varepsilon}_{T+h|T}$ as given below, where we also separately delineate the sources of error due to structural change and mis-specification, etc.

$$
\begin{aligned}
\mathbf{e}_{T+h|T} &= \mathbf{x}_{T+h} - \hat{\mathbf{x}}_{T+h|T} \\
&= \left(\mathsf{E}_{T+h}\left[\mathbf{x}_{T+h} \mid \mathbf{X}_T^1, \{\mathbf{Q}^{**}\}_{T+h}^1\right] - \mathsf{E}_{T+h}\left[\mathbf{x}_{T+h} \mid \mathbf{X}_T^1, \{\mathbf{Q}^{*}\}_{T+h}^1\right]\right) && \text{(T1)} \\
&\quad + \left(\mathsf{E}_{T+h}\left[\mathbf{x}_{T+h} \mid \mathbf{X}_T^1, \{\mathbf{Q}^{*}\}_{T+h}^1\right] - \mathsf{E}_{T}\left[\mathbf{x}_{T+h} \mid \mathbf{X}_T^1, \{\mathbf{Q}^{*}\}_{T+h}^1\right]\right) && \text{(T2)} \\
&\quad + \left(\mathsf{E}_{T}\left[\mathbf{x}_{T+h} \mid \mathbf{X}_T^1, \{\mathbf{Q}^{*}\}_{T+h}^1\right] - \mathsf{E}_{T}\left[\mathbf{x}_{T+h} \mid \mathbf{X}_T^1, \widetilde{\mathbf{Q}}_{T+h}^1\right]\right) && \text{(T3)} \\
&\quad + \left(\mathsf{E}_{T}\left[\mathbf{x}_{T+h} \mid \mathbf{X}_T^1, \widetilde{\mathbf{Q}}_{T+h}^1\right] - \mathsf{E}_{T}\left[\mathbf{x}_{T+h} \mid \mathbf{X}_T^{T-s+1}, \widetilde{\mathbf{Q}}_{T+h}^1, \boldsymbol{\theta}_{e,(T)}\right]\right) && \text{(T4)} \\
&\quad + \left(\mathsf{E}_{T}\left[\mathbf{x}_{T+h} \mid \mathbf{X}_T^{T-s+1}, \widetilde{\mathbf{Q}}_{T+h}^1, \boldsymbol{\theta}_{e,(T)}\right]\right. \\
&\qquad \left. - \mathsf{E}_{T}\left[\mathbf{x}_{T+h} \mid \widetilde{\mathbf{X}}_T^{T-s+1}, \widetilde{\mathbf{Q}}_{T+h}^1, \boldsymbol{\theta}_{e,(T)}\right]\right) && \text{(T5)} \\
&\quad + \left(\mathsf{E}_{T}\left[\mathbf{x}_{T+h} \mid \widetilde{\mathbf{X}}_T^{T-s+1}, \widetilde{\mathbf{Q}}_{T+h}^1, \boldsymbol{\theta}_{e,(T)}\right] - \mathbf{g}_h\left(\widetilde{\mathbf{X}}_T^{T-s+1}, \widetilde{\mathbf{Q}}_{T+h}^1, \hat{\boldsymbol{\theta}}_{(T)}\right)\right) && \text{(T6)} \\
&\quad + \boldsymbol{\varepsilon}_{T+h|T}. && \text{(T7)}
\end{aligned}
\tag{8}
$$

The first two error components arise from structural change affecting deterministic (T1) and stochastic (T2) components respectively over the forecast horizon. The third (T3) arises from model mis-specification of the deterministic factors, both induced by failing to model in-sample shifts and 'conventional' mis-specification. Next, (T4) arises from mis-specification of the stochastic components, including lag length. (T5) and (T6) denote forecast error components resulting from data measurement errors, especially forecast-origin inaccuracy, and estimation uncertainty, respectively, and the last row (T7) is the LDGP innovation forecast error, which is the smallest achievable in this class.

Then (T1) is zero if $\{\mathbf{Q}^{**}\}_{T+h}^1 = \{\mathbf{Q}^{*}\}_{T+h}^1$, which corresponds to no forecast-period deterministic shifts (conditional on all in-sample shifts being correctly modeled). In general the converse also holds – (T1) being zero entails no deterministic shifts. Thus, a unique inference seems possible as to when (T1) is zero (no deterministic shifts), or non-zero (deterministic shifts).

Next, when $\mathsf{E}_{T+h}[\cdot] = \mathsf{E}_T[\cdot]$, so there are no stochastic breaks over the forecast horizon, entailing that the future distributions coincide with that at the forecast origin, then (T2) is zero. Unlike (T1), the terms in (T2) could be zero despite stochastic breaks, providing such breaks affected only mean-zero terms. Thus, no unique inference is feasible if (T2) is zero, though a non-zero value indicates a change. However, other moments would be affected in the first case.

When all the in-sample deterministic terms, including all shifts in the LDGP, are correctly specified, so $\widetilde{\mathbf{Q}}_{T+h}^1 = \{\mathbf{Q}^{*}\}_{T+h}^1$, then (T3) is zero. Conversely, when (T3) is zero, then $\widetilde{\mathbf{Q}}_{T+h}^1$ must have correctly captured in-sample shifts in deterministic terms, perhaps because there were none. When (T3) is non-zero, the in-sample deterministic factors may be mis-specified because of shifts, but this mistake ought to be detectable. However, (T3) being non-zero may also reflect 'conventional' deterministic mis-specifications. This type of mistake corresponds to omitting relevant deterministic terms, such as an intercept, seasonal dummy, or trend, and while detectable by an appropriately directed test, also has implications for forecasting when not corrected.

For correct stochastic specification, so $\boldsymbol{\theta}_{e,(T)}$ correctly summarizes the effects of $\mathbf{X}_T^1$, then (T4) is zero, but again the converse is false – (T4) can be zero in mis-specified models. A well-known example is approximating a high-order autoregressive LDGP for mean zero data with symmetrically distributed errors, by a first-order autoregression, where forecasts are nevertheless unbiased as discussed below for a VAR.

Next, when the data are accurate (especially important at the forecast origin), so $\widetilde{\mathbf{X}} = \mathbf{X}$, then (T5) is zero, but the converse is not entailed: (T5) can be zero just because the data are mean zero.

Continuing, (T6) concerns the estimation error, and arises when $\hat{\boldsymbol{\theta}}_{(T)}$ does not coincide with $\boldsymbol{\theta}_{e,(T)}$. Biases in estimation could, but need not, induce such an effect to be systematic, as might non-linearities in models or LDGPs. When estimated parameters have zero variances, so $\hat{\mathbf{x}}_{T+h|T} = \mathsf{E}_T[\mathbf{x}_{T+h} \mid \cdot, \boldsymbol{\theta}_{e,(T)}]$, then (T6) is zero, and conversely (except for events of probability zero). Otherwise, its main impacts will be on variance terms.

The final term (T7), $\boldsymbol{\varepsilon}_{T+h|T}$, is unlikely to be zero in any social science, although it will have a zero mean by construction, and be unpredictable from the past of the information in use. As with (T6), the main practical impact is through forecast error variances.

The taxonomy in (8) includes elements for the seven main sources of forecast error, partitioning these by whether or not the corresponding expectation is zero. However, several salient features stand out. First, the key distinction between whether the expectations in question are zero or non-zero. In the former case, forecasts will not be systematically biased, and the main impact of any changes or mis-specifications is on higher moments, especially forecast error variances. Conversely, if a non-zero mean error results from any source, systematic forecast errors will ensue. Secondly, and a consequence of the previous remark, some breaks will be easily detected because at whatever point in time they happened, 'in-sample forecasts' immediately after a change will be poor. Equally, others may be hard to detect because they have no impact on the mean forecast errors. Thirdly, the impacts of any transformations of a model on its forecast errors depend on which mistakes have occurred. For example, it is often argued that differencing doubles the forecast-error variance: this is certainly true of $\boldsymbol{\varepsilon}_{T+h|T}$, but is not true in general for $\mathbf{e}_{T+h|T}$. Indeed, it is possible in some circumstances to reduce the forecast-error variance by differencing; see, e.g., Hendry (2005). Finally, the taxonomy applies to any model form, but to clarify some of its implications, we turn to its application to the forecast errors from a VAR.

2.2. VAR model forecast-error taxonomy

We illustrate with a first-order VAR, and for convenience assume the absence of in-sample breaks so that the VAR is initially correctly specified. We also assume that the $n \times 1$ vector of variables $\mathbf{y}_t$ is an I(0) transformation of the original variables $\mathbf{x}_t$: Section 4.1 considers systems of cointegrated I(1) variables. Thus,

$$\mathbf{y}_t = \boldsymbol{\phi} + \boldsymbol{\Pi}\mathbf{y}_{t-1} + \boldsymbol{\epsilon}_t,$$

with $\boldsymbol{\epsilon}_t \sim \mathsf{IN}_n[\mathbf{0}, \boldsymbol{\Omega}_\epsilon]$, for an in-sample period $t = 1, \ldots, T$. The unconditional mean of $\mathbf{y}_t$ is $\mathsf{E}[\mathbf{y}_t] = (\mathbf{I}_n - \boldsymbol{\Pi})^{-1}\boldsymbol{\phi} \equiv \boldsymbol{\varphi}$, and hence the VAR(1) can be written as

$$\mathbf{y}_t - \boldsymbol{\varphi} = \boldsymbol{\Pi}(\mathbf{y}_{t-1} - \boldsymbol{\varphi}) + \boldsymbol{\epsilon}_t.$$

The h-step ahead forecasts conditional upon period T are given by, for $h = 1, \ldots, H$,

$$\hat{\mathbf{y}}_{T+h} - \hat{\boldsymbol{\varphi}} = \widehat{\boldsymbol{\Pi}}(\hat{\mathbf{y}}_{T+h-1} - \hat{\boldsymbol{\varphi}}) = \widehat{\boldsymbol{\Pi}}^h(\hat{\mathbf{y}}_T - \hat{\boldsymbol{\varphi}}), \tag{9}$$

where $\hat{\boldsymbol{\varphi}} = (\mathbf{I}_n - \widehat{\boldsymbol{\Pi}})^{-1}\hat{\boldsymbol{\phi}}$, and '^'s denote estimators for parameters, and forecasts for random variables. After the forecasts have been made at time T, $(\boldsymbol{\phi}, \boldsymbol{\Pi})$ change to $(\boldsymbol{\phi}^*, \boldsymbol{\Pi}^*)$, where $\boldsymbol{\Pi}^*$ still has all its eigenvalues less than unity in absolute value, so the process remains I(0). But from $T + 1$ onwards, the data are generated by

$$\begin{aligned}\mathbf{y}_{T+h} &= \boldsymbol{\varphi}^* + \boldsymbol{\Pi}^*(\mathbf{y}_{T+h-1} - \boldsymbol{\varphi}^*) + \boldsymbol{\epsilon}_{T+h} \\ &= \boldsymbol{\varphi}^* + (\boldsymbol{\Pi}^*)^h(\mathbf{y}_T - \boldsymbol{\varphi}^*) + \sum_{i=0}^{h-1}(\boldsymbol{\Pi}^*)^i\boldsymbol{\epsilon}_{T+h-i},\end{aligned}$$

so both the slope and the intercept may alter. The forecast-error taxonomy for $\hat{\boldsymbol{\epsilon}}_{T+h|T} = \mathbf{y}_{T+h} - \hat{\mathbf{y}}_{T+h|T}$ is then given by

$$\begin{aligned}\hat{\boldsymbol{\epsilon}}_{T+h|T} \simeq\, &(\mathbf{I}_n - (\boldsymbol{\Pi}^*)^h)(\boldsymbol{\varphi}^* - \boldsymbol{\varphi}) && \text{(ia) equilibrium-mean change} \\ &+ ((\boldsymbol{\Pi}^*)^h - \boldsymbol{\Pi}^h)(\mathbf{y}_T - \boldsymbol{\varphi}) && \text{(ib) slope change} \\ &+ (\mathbf{I}_n - \boldsymbol{\Pi}_p^h)(\boldsymbol{\varphi} - \boldsymbol{\varphi}_p) && \text{(iia) equilibrium-mean mis-specification} \\ &+ (\boldsymbol{\Pi}^h - \boldsymbol{\Pi}_p^h)(\mathbf{y}_T - \boldsymbol{\varphi}) && \text{(iib) slope mis-specification} \\ &+ (\boldsymbol{\Pi}_p^h + \mathbf{C}_h)(\mathbf{y}_T - \hat{\mathbf{y}}_T) && \text{(iii) forecast-origin uncertainty} \\ &- (\mathbf{I}_n - \boldsymbol{\Pi}_p^h)(\hat{\boldsymbol{\varphi}} - \boldsymbol{\varphi}_p) && \text{(iva) equilibrium-mean estimation} \\ &- \mathbf{F}_h(\widehat{\boldsymbol{\Pi}} - \boldsymbol{\Pi}_p)^\nu && \text{(ivb) slope estimation} \\ &+ \textstyle\sum_{i=0}^{h-1}(\boldsymbol{\Pi}^*)^i\boldsymbol{\epsilon}_{T+h-i} && \text{(v) error accumulation.}\end{aligned} \tag{10}$$

The matrices $\mathbf{C}_h$ and $\mathbf{F}_h$ are complicated functions of the whole-sample data, the method of estimation, and the forecast-horizon, defined in (A.1) and (A.2) below – see, e.g., Calzolari (1981). $(\cdot)^\nu$ denotes column vectoring, and the subscript p denotes a plim (expected values could be used where these exist). Details of the derivations are given in Clements and Hendry (1999, Chapter 2.9) and are noted for convenience in Appendix A.

This taxonomy conflates some of the distinctions in the general formulation above (e.g., mis-specification of deterministic terms other than intercepts) and distinguishes others (equilibrium-mean and slope estimation effects). Thus, the model mis-specification terms (iia) and (iib) may result from unmodeled in-sample structural change, as in the general taxonomy, but may also arise from the omission of relevant variables, or the imposition of invalid restrictions.

In (10), terms involving $\mathbf{y}_T - \boldsymbol{\varphi}$ have zero expectations even under changed parameters (e.g., (ib) and (iib)). Moreover, for symmetrically-distributed shocks, biases in $\widehat{\boldsymbol{\Pi}}$ for $\boldsymbol{\Pi}$ will not induce biased forecasts [see, e.g., Malinvaud (1970), Fuller and Hasza (1980), Hoque, Magnus and Pesaran (1988), and Clements and Hendry (1998) for related results]. The $\boldsymbol{\epsilon}_{T+h}$ have zero means by construction. Consequently, the primary sources of systematic forecast failure are (ia), (iia), (iii), and (iva). However, on ex post evaluation, (iii) will be removed, and in congruent models with freely-estimated intercepts and correctly modeled in-sample breaks, (iia) and (iva) will be zero on average. That leaves changes to the 'equilibrium mean' $\boldsymbol{\varphi}$ (not necessarily the intercept $\boldsymbol{\phi}$ in a model, as seen in (10)), as the primary source of systematic forecast error; see Hendry (2000) for a detailed analysis.

3. Breaks in variance

3.1. Conditional variance processes

The autoregressive conditional heteroskedasticity (ARCH) model of Engle (1982), and its generalizations, are commonly used to model time-varying conditional processes; see, inter alia, Engle and Bollerslev (1987), Bollerslev, Chou and Kroner (1992), and Shephard (1996); and Bera and Higgins (1993) and Baillie and Bollerslev (1992) on forecasting. The forecast-error taxonomy construct can be applied to variance processes. We show that ARCH and GARCH models can in general be solved for long-run variances, so like VARs, are a member of the equilibrium-correction class. Issues to do with the constancy of the long-run variance are then discussed.

The simplest ARCH(1) model for the conditional variance of u_t is $u_t = \eta_t \sigma_t$, where η_t is a standard normal random variable and

$$\sigma_t^2 = \omega + \alpha u_{t-1}^2, \tag{11}$$

where $\omega, \alpha > 0$. Letting $\sigma_t^2 = u_t^2 - v_t$, substituting in (11) gives

$$u_t^2 = \omega + \alpha u_{t-1}^2 + v_t. \tag{12}$$

From $v_t = u_t^2 - \sigma_t^2 = \sigma_t^2(\eta_t^2 - 1)$, $\mathsf{E}[v_t \mid \mathbf{Y}_{t-1}] = \sigma_t^2 \mathsf{E}[(\eta_t^2 - 1) \mid \mathbf{Y}_{t-1}] = 0$, so that the disturbance term $\{v_t\}$ in the AR(1) model (12) is uncorrelated with the regressor, as required. From the AR(1) representation, the condition for covariance stationarity of $\{u_t^2\}$ is $|\alpha| < 1$, whence

$$\mathsf{E}[u_t^2] = \omega + \alpha \mathsf{E}[u_{t-1}^2],$$

and so the unconditional variance is

$$\sigma^2 \equiv \mathsf{E}[u_t^2] = \frac{\omega}{1-\alpha}.$$

Substituting for ω in (11) gives the equilibrium-correction form

$$\sigma_t^2 - \sigma^2 = \alpha(u_{t-1}^2 - \sigma^2).$$

More generally, for an ARCH(p), $p > 1$,

$$\sigma_t^2 = \omega + \alpha_1 u_{t-1}^2 + \alpha_2 u_{t-2}^2 + \cdots + \alpha_p u_{t-p}^2 \tag{13}$$

provided the roots of $(1 - \alpha_1 z - \alpha_2 z^2 + \cdots + \alpha_p z^p) = 0$ lie outside the unit circle, we can write

$$\sigma_t^2 - \sigma^2 = \alpha_1(u_{t-1}^2 - \sigma^2) + \alpha_2(u_{t-2}^2 - \sigma^2) + \cdots + \alpha_p(u_{t-p}^2 - \sigma^2), \tag{14}$$

where

$$\sigma^2 \equiv \mathsf{E}[u_t^2] = \frac{\omega}{1 - \alpha_1 - \cdots - \alpha_p}.$$

The generalized ARCH [GARCH; see, e.g., Bollerslev (1986)] process

$$\sigma_t^2 = \omega + \alpha u_{t-1}^2 + \beta \sigma_{t-1}^2 \tag{15}$$

also has a long-run solution. The GARCH(1, 1) implies an ARMA(1, 1) for $\{u_t^2\}$. Letting $\sigma_t^2 = u_t^2 - v_t$, substitution into (15) gives

$$u_t^2 = \omega + (\alpha + \beta)u_{t-1}^2 + v_t - \beta v_{t-1}. \tag{16}$$

The process is stationary provided $\alpha + \beta < 1$. When that condition holds

$$\sigma^2 \equiv \mathsf{E}[u_t^2] = \frac{\omega}{1 - (\alpha + \beta)},$$

and combining the equations for σ_t^2 and σ^2 for the GARCH(1, 1) delivers

$$\sigma_t^2 - \sigma^2 = \alpha(u_{t-1}^2 - \sigma^2) + \beta(\sigma_{t-1}^2 - \sigma^2). \tag{17}$$

Thus, the conditional variance responds to the previous period's disequilibria between the conditional variance and the long-run variance and between the squared disturbance and the long-run variance, exhibiting equilibrium-correction type behavior.

3.2. GARCH model forecast-error taxonomy

As it is an equilibrium-correction model, the GARCH(1, 1) is not robust to shifts in σ^2, but may be resilient to shifts in ω, α and β which leave σ^2 unaltered. As an alternative to (17), express the process as

$$\sigma_t^2 = \sigma^2 + \alpha\left(u_{t-1}^2 - \sigma_{t-1}^2\right) + (\alpha + \beta)\left(\sigma_{t-1}^2 - \sigma^2\right). \tag{18}$$

In either (17) or (18), α and β multiply zero-mean terms provided σ^2 is unchanged by any shifts in these parameters. The forecast of next period's volatility based on (18) is given by

$$\hat{\sigma}_{T+1|T}^2 = \hat{\sigma}^2 + \hat{\alpha}\left(\hat{u}_T^2 - \hat{\sigma}_T^2\right) + \left(\hat{\alpha} + \hat{\beta}\right)\left(\hat{\sigma}_T^2 - \hat{\sigma}^2\right) \tag{19}$$

recognizing that $\{\alpha, \beta, \sigma^2\}$ will be replaced by in-sample estimates. The '^' on u_T denotes this term is the residual from modeling the conditional mean. When there is little dependence in the mean of the series, such as when $\{u_t\}$ is a financial returns series sampled at a high-frequency, u_T is the observed data series and replaces $\hat{u}_T$ (barring data measurement errors).

Then (19) confronts every problem noted above for forecasts of means: potential breaks in σ^2, α, β, mis-specification of the variance evolution (perhaps an incorrect functional form), estimation uncertainty, etc. The 1-step ahead forecast-error taxonomy takes the following form after a shift in ω, α, β to $\omega^*, \alpha^*, \beta^*$ at T to:

$$\sigma_{T+1}^2 = \sigma^{2*} + \alpha^*\left(u_T^2 - \sigma_T^2\right) + \left(\alpha^* + \beta^*\right)\left(\sigma_T^2 - \sigma^{2*}\right),$$

so that letting the subscript p denote the plim:

$$\begin{aligned}
\sigma_{T+1}^2 - \hat{\sigma}_{T+1|T}^2 \\
= {} & \left(1 - \left(\alpha^* + \beta^*\right)\right)\left(\sigma^{2*} - \sigma^2\right) && \text{[1] long-run mean shift} \\
& + \left(1 - \left(\hat{\alpha} + \hat{\beta}\right)\right)\left(\sigma^2 - \sigma_p^2\right) && \text{[2] long-run mean inconsistency} \\
& + \left(1 - \left(\hat{\alpha} + \hat{\beta}\right)\right)\left(\sigma_p^2 - \hat{\sigma}^2\right) && \text{[3] long-run mean variability} \\
& + \left(\alpha^* - \alpha\right)\left(u_T^2 - \sigma_T^2\right) && \text{[4] } \alpha \text{ shift} \\
& + \left(\alpha - \alpha_p\right)\left(u_T^2 - \sigma_T^2\right) && \text{[5] } \alpha \text{ inconsistency} \\
& + \left(\alpha_p - \hat{\alpha}\right)\left(u_T^2 - \sigma_T^2\right) && \text{[6] } \alpha \text{ variability} \\
& + \hat{\alpha}\left(u_T^2 - \mathsf{E}_T\left[\hat{u}_T^2\right]\right) && \text{[7] impact inconsistency} \\
& + \hat{\alpha}\left(\mathsf{E}_T\left[\hat{u}_T^2\right] - \hat{u}_T^2\right) && \text{[8] impact variability} \\
& + \left[\left(\alpha^* + \beta^*\right) - (\alpha + \beta)\right]\left(\sigma_T^2 - \sigma^2\right) && \text{[9] variance shift} \\
& + \left[(\alpha + \beta) - \left(\alpha_p + \beta_p\right)\right]\left(\sigma_T^2 - \sigma^2\right) && \text{[10] variance inconsistency} \\
& + \left[\left(\alpha_p + \beta_p\right) - \left(\hat{\alpha} + \hat{\beta}\right)\right]\left(\sigma_T^2 - \sigma^2\right) && \text{[11] variance variability} \\
& + \hat{\beta}\left(\sigma_T^2 - \mathsf{E}_T\left[\hat{\sigma}_T^2\right]\right) && \text{[12] } \sigma_T^2 \text{ inconsistency} \\
& + \hat{\beta}\left(\mathsf{E}_T\left[\hat{\sigma}_T^2\right] - \hat{\sigma}_T^2\right) && \text{[13] } \sigma_T^2 \text{ variability.}
\end{aligned} \tag{20}$$

The first term is zero only if no shift occurs in the long-run variance and the second only if a consistent in-sample estimate is obtained. However, the next four terms are zero on average, although the seventh possibly is not. This pattern then repeats, since the next block of four terms again is zero on average, with the penultimate term possibly non-zero, and the last zero on average. As with the earlier forecast error taxonomy, shifts in the mean seem pernicious, whereas those in the other parameters are much less serious contributors to forecast failure in variances. Indeed, even assuming a correct in-sample specification, so terms [2], [5], [7], [10], [12] all vanish, the main error components remain.

4. Forecasting when there are breaks

4.1. Cointegrated vector autoregressions

The general forecast-error taxonomy in Section 2.1 suggests that structural breaks in non-zero mean components are the primary cause of forecast biases. In this section, we examine the impact of breaks in VAR models of cointegrated I(1) variables, and also analyze models in first differences, because models of this type are commonplace in macroeconomic forecasting. The properties of forecasts made before and after the structural change has occurred are analyzed, where it is assumed that the break occurs close to the forecast origin. As a consequence, the comparisons are made holding the models' parameters constant. The effects of in-sample breaks are identified in the forecast-error taxonomies, and are analyzed in Section 6, where the choice of data window for model estimation is considered. Forecasting in cointegrated VARs (in the absence of breaks) is discussed by Engle and Yoo (1987), Clements and Hendry (1995), Lin and Tsay (1996), and Christoffersen and Diebold (1998), while Clements and Hendry (1996) (on which this section is based) allow for breaks.

The VAR is a closed system so that all non-deterministic variables are forecast within the system. The vector of all n variables is denoted by $\mathbf{x}_t$ and the VAR is assumed to be first-order for convenience:

$$\mathbf{x}_t = \boldsymbol{\tau}_0 + \boldsymbol{\tau}_1 t + \boldsymbol{\Upsilon}\mathbf{x}_{t-1} + \boldsymbol{\nu}_t, \tag{21}$$

where $\boldsymbol{\nu}_t \sim \mathsf{IN}_n[\mathbf{0}, \boldsymbol{\Omega}]$, and $\boldsymbol{\tau}_0$ and $\boldsymbol{\tau}_1$ are the vectors of intercepts and coefficients on the time trend, respectively. The system is assumed to be integrated, and to satisfy $r < n$ cointegration relations such that [see, for example, Johansen (1988)]

$$\boldsymbol{\Upsilon} = \mathbf{I}_n + \boldsymbol{\alpha}\boldsymbol{\beta}',$$

where $\boldsymbol{\alpha}$ and $\boldsymbol{\beta}$ are $n \times r$ matrices of rank r. Then (21) can be reparametrized as a vector equilibrium-correction model (VECM)

$$\Delta\mathbf{x}_t = \boldsymbol{\tau}_0 + \boldsymbol{\tau}_1 t + \boldsymbol{\alpha}\boldsymbol{\beta}'\mathbf{x}_{t-1} + \boldsymbol{\nu}_t. \tag{22}$$

Assuming that $n > r > 0$, the vector $\mathbf{x}_t$ consists of I(1) variables of which r linear combinations are I(0). The deterministic components of the stochastic variables $\mathbf{x}_t$ depend on $\boldsymbol{\alpha}$, $\boldsymbol{\tau}_0$ and $\boldsymbol{\tau}_1$. Following Johansen (1994), we can decompose $\boldsymbol{\tau}_0 + \boldsymbol{\tau}_1 t$ as

$$\boldsymbol{\tau}_0 + \boldsymbol{\tau}_1 t = \boldsymbol{\alpha}_\perp \boldsymbol{\zeta}_0 - \boldsymbol{\alpha}\boldsymbol{\lambda}_0 - \boldsymbol{\alpha}\boldsymbol{\lambda}_1 t + \boldsymbol{\alpha}_\perp \boldsymbol{\zeta}_1 t, \tag{23}$$

where $\boldsymbol{\lambda}_i = -(\boldsymbol{\alpha}'\boldsymbol{\alpha})^{-1}\boldsymbol{\alpha}'\boldsymbol{\tau}_i$ and $\boldsymbol{\zeta}_i = (\boldsymbol{\alpha}'_\perp\boldsymbol{\alpha}_\perp)^{-1}\boldsymbol{\alpha}'_\perp\boldsymbol{\tau}_i$ with $\boldsymbol{\alpha}'\boldsymbol{\alpha}_\perp = \mathbf{0}$, so that $\boldsymbol{\alpha}\boldsymbol{\lambda}_i$ and $\boldsymbol{\alpha}_\perp\boldsymbol{\zeta}_i$ are orthogonal by construction. The condition that $\boldsymbol{\alpha}_\perp\boldsymbol{\zeta}_1 = \mathbf{0}$ rules out quadratic trends in the levels of the variables, and we obtain

$$\Delta\mathbf{x}_t = \boldsymbol{\alpha}_\perp\boldsymbol{\zeta}_0 + \boldsymbol{\alpha}\left(\boldsymbol{\beta}'\mathbf{x}_{t-1} - \boldsymbol{\lambda}_0 - \boldsymbol{\lambda}_1 t\right) + \boldsymbol{\nu}_t. \tag{24}$$

It is sometimes more convenient to parameterize the deterministic terms so that the system growth rate $\boldsymbol{\gamma} = \mathsf{E}[\Delta\mathbf{x}_t]$ is explicit, so in the following we will adopt

$$\Delta\mathbf{x}_t = \boldsymbol{\gamma} + \boldsymbol{\alpha}\left(\boldsymbol{\beta}'\mathbf{x}_{t-1} - \boldsymbol{\mu}_0 - \boldsymbol{\mu}_1 t\right) + \boldsymbol{\nu}_t, \tag{25}$$

where one can show that $\boldsymbol{\gamma} = \boldsymbol{\alpha}_\perp\boldsymbol{\zeta}_0 + \boldsymbol{\alpha}\boldsymbol{\psi}$, $\boldsymbol{\mu}_0 = \boldsymbol{\psi} + \boldsymbol{\lambda}_0$ and $\boldsymbol{\mu}_1 = \boldsymbol{\lambda}_1$ with $\boldsymbol{\psi} = (\boldsymbol{\beta}'\boldsymbol{\alpha})^{-1}(\boldsymbol{\lambda}_1 - \boldsymbol{\beta}'\boldsymbol{\alpha}_\perp\boldsymbol{\zeta}_0)$ and $\boldsymbol{\beta}'\boldsymbol{\gamma} = \boldsymbol{\mu}_1$.

Finally, a VAR in differences (DVAR) may be used, which within sample is misspecified relative to the VECM unless $r = 0$. The simplest is

$$\Delta\mathbf{x}_t = \boldsymbol{\gamma} + \boldsymbol{\eta}_t, \tag{26}$$

so when $\boldsymbol{\alpha} = \mathbf{0}$, the VECM and DVAR coincide. In practice, lagged $\Delta\mathbf{x}_t$ may be used to approximate the omitted cointegrating vectors.

4.2. VECM forecast errors

We now consider dynamic forecasts and their errors under structural change, abstracting from the other sources of error identified in the taxonomy, such as parameter-estimation error. A number of authors have looked at the effects of parameter estimation on forecast-error moments [including, inter alia, Schmidt (1974, 1977), Calzolari (1981, 1987), Bianchi and Calzolari (1982), and Lütkepohl (1991)]. The j-step ahead forecasts for the levels of the process given by $\hat{\mathbf{x}}_{T+j|T} = \mathsf{E}_T[\mathbf{x}_{T+j} \mid \mathbf{x}_T]$ for $j = 1, \ldots, H$ are

$$\hat{\mathbf{x}}_{T+j|T} = \boldsymbol{\tau}_0 + \boldsymbol{\tau}_1(T + j) + \boldsymbol{\Upsilon}\hat{\mathbf{x}}_{T+j-1|T} = \sum_{i=0}^{j-1} \boldsymbol{\Upsilon}^i \boldsymbol{\tau}(i) + \boldsymbol{\Upsilon}^j \mathbf{x}_T, \tag{27}$$

where we let $\boldsymbol{\tau}_0 + \boldsymbol{\tau}_1(T + j - i) = \boldsymbol{\tau}(i)$ for notational convenience, with forecast errors $\hat{\boldsymbol{\nu}}_{T+j|T} = \mathbf{x}_{T+j} - \hat{\mathbf{x}}_{T+j|T}$. Consider a one-off change of $(\boldsymbol{\tau}_0 : \boldsymbol{\tau}_1 : \boldsymbol{\Upsilon})$ to $(\boldsymbol{\tau}_0^* : \boldsymbol{\tau}_1^* : \boldsymbol{\Upsilon}^*)$ which occurs either at period T (before the forecast is made) or at period $T + 1$ (after the forecast is made), but with the variance, autocorrelation, and distribution of the disturbance term remaining unaltered. Then the data generated by the process for the next H periods is given by

$$\mathbf{x}_{T+j} = \boldsymbol{\tau}_0^* + \boldsymbol{\tau}_1^*(T + j) + \boldsymbol{\Upsilon}^*\mathbf{x}_{T+j-1} + \boldsymbol{\nu}_{T+j}$$

$$= \sum_{i=0}^{j-1} (\boldsymbol{\Upsilon}^*)^i \boldsymbol{\tau}^*(i) + \sum_{i=0}^{j-1} (\boldsymbol{\Upsilon}^*)^i \boldsymbol{\nu}_{T+j-i} + (\boldsymbol{\Upsilon}^*)^j \mathbf{x}_T. \tag{28}$$

Thus, the j-step ahead forecast error can be written as

$$\hat{\boldsymbol{\nu}}_{T+j|T} = \left(\sum_{i=0}^{j-1} (\boldsymbol{\Upsilon}^*)^i \boldsymbol{\tau}^*(i) - \sum_{i=0}^{j-1} \boldsymbol{\Upsilon}^i \boldsymbol{\tau}(i) \right) + \sum_{i=0}^{j-1} (\boldsymbol{\Upsilon}^*)^i \boldsymbol{\nu}_{T+j-i}$$
$$+ \left((\boldsymbol{\Upsilon}^*)^j - \boldsymbol{\Upsilon}^j \right) \mathbf{x}_T. \tag{29}$$

The expectation of the j-step forecast error conditional on $\mathbf{x}_T$ is

$$\mathsf{E}\left[\hat{\boldsymbol{\nu}}_{T+j|T} \mid \mathbf{x}_T \right] = \left(\sum_{i=0}^{j-1} (\boldsymbol{\Upsilon}^*)^i \boldsymbol{\tau}^*(i) - \sum_{i=0}^{j-1} \boldsymbol{\Upsilon}^i \boldsymbol{\tau}(i) \right) + \left((\boldsymbol{\Upsilon}^*)^j - \boldsymbol{\Upsilon}^j \right) \mathbf{x}_T \tag{30}$$

so that the conditional forecast error variance is

$$\mathsf{V}\left[\hat{\boldsymbol{\nu}}_{T+j|T} \mid \mathbf{x}_T \right] = \sum_{i=0}^{j-1} (\boldsymbol{\Upsilon}^*)^i \boldsymbol{\Omega} (\boldsymbol{\Upsilon}^*)^{i\prime}.$$

We now consider a number of special cases where only the deterministic components change. With the assumption that $\boldsymbol{\Upsilon}^* = \boldsymbol{\Upsilon}$, we obtain

$$\begin{aligned}
\mathsf{E}[\hat{\boldsymbol{\nu}}_{T+j|T}] &= \mathsf{E}[\hat{\boldsymbol{\nu}}_{T+j|T} \mid \mathbf{x}_T] \\
&= \sum_{i=0}^{j-1} \boldsymbol{\Upsilon}^i \left(\left[\boldsymbol{\tau}_0^* + \boldsymbol{\tau}_1^* (T+j-i) \right] - \left[\boldsymbol{\tau}_0 + \boldsymbol{\tau}_1 (T+j-i) \right] \right) \\
&= \sum_{i=0}^{j-1} \boldsymbol{\Upsilon}^i \left[(\boldsymbol{\gamma}^* - \boldsymbol{\gamma}) + \boldsymbol{\alpha} (\boldsymbol{\mu}_0 - \boldsymbol{\mu}_0^*) + \boldsymbol{\alpha} (\boldsymbol{\mu}_1 - \boldsymbol{\mu}_1^*)(T+j-i) \right],
\end{aligned} \tag{31}$$

so that the conditional and unconditional biases are the same. The bias is increasing in j due to the shift in $\boldsymbol{\gamma}$ (the first term in square brackets) whereas the impacts of the shifts in $\boldsymbol{\mu}_0$ and $\boldsymbol{\mu}_1$ eventually level off because

$$\lim_{i \to \infty} \boldsymbol{\Upsilon}^i = \mathbf{I}_n - \boldsymbol{\alpha} (\boldsymbol{\beta}' \boldsymbol{\alpha})^{-1} \boldsymbol{\beta}' \equiv \mathbf{K},$$

and $\mathbf{K}\boldsymbol{\alpha} = \mathbf{0}$. When the linear trend is absent and the constant term can be restricted to the cointegrating space (i.e., $\boldsymbol{\tau}_1 = \mathbf{0}$ and $\boldsymbol{\zeta}_0 = \mathbf{0}$, which implies $\boldsymbol{\lambda}_1 = \mathbf{0}$ and therefore $\boldsymbol{\mu}_1 = \boldsymbol{\gamma} = \mathbf{0}$), then only the second term appears, and the bias is $O(1)$ in j. The formulation in (31) assumes that $\boldsymbol{\Upsilon}$, and therefore the cointegrating space, remains unaltered. Moreover, the coefficient on the linear trend alters but still lies in the cointegrating space. Otherwise, after the structural break, $\mathbf{x}_t$ would be propelled by quadratic trends.

4.3. DVAR forecast errors

Consider the forecasts from a simplified DVAR. Forecasts from the DVAR for $\Delta\mathbf{x}_t$ are defined by setting $\Delta\mathbf{x}_{T+j}$ equal to the population growth rate $\boldsymbol{\gamma}$,

$$\Delta\tilde{\mathbf{x}}_{T+j} = \boldsymbol{\gamma} \tag{32}$$

so that j-step ahead forecasts of the level of the process are obtained by integrating (32) from the initial condition $\mathbf{x}_T$,

$$\tilde{\mathbf{x}}_{T+j} = \tilde{\mathbf{x}}_{T+j-1} + \boldsymbol{\gamma} = \mathbf{x}_T + j\boldsymbol{\gamma} \quad \text{for } j = 1, \ldots, H. \tag{33}$$

When $\boldsymbol{\Upsilon}$ is unchanged over the forecast period, the expected value of the conditional j-step ahead forecast error $\tilde{\boldsymbol{\nu}}_{T+j|T}$ is

$$\mathsf{E}[\tilde{\boldsymbol{\nu}}_{T+j|T} \mid \mathbf{x}_T] = \sum_{i=0}^{j-1} \boldsymbol{\Upsilon}^i \left[\boldsymbol{\tau}_0^* + \boldsymbol{\tau}_1^*(T + j - i)\right] - j\boldsymbol{\gamma} + \left(\boldsymbol{\Upsilon}^j - \mathbf{I}_n\right)\mathbf{x}_T. \tag{34}$$

By averaging over $\mathbf{x}_T$ we obtain the unconditional bias $\mathsf{E}[\tilde{\boldsymbol{\nu}}_{T+j}]$.

Appendix B records the algebra for the derivation of (35):

$$\mathsf{E}[\tilde{\boldsymbol{\nu}}_{T+j|T}] = j\left(\boldsymbol{\gamma}^* - \boldsymbol{\gamma}\right) + \mathbf{A}_j\boldsymbol{\alpha}\left[\left(\boldsymbol{\mu}_0^a - \boldsymbol{\mu}_0^*\right) - \boldsymbol{\beta}'\left(\boldsymbol{\gamma}^* - \boldsymbol{\gamma}^a\right)(T + 1)\right]. \tag{35}$$

In the same notation, the VECM results from (31) are

$$\mathsf{E}[\hat{\boldsymbol{\nu}}_{T+j|T}] = j\left(\boldsymbol{\gamma}^* - \boldsymbol{\gamma}\right) + \mathbf{A}_j\boldsymbol{\alpha}\left[\left(\boldsymbol{\mu}_0 - \boldsymbol{\mu}_0^*\right) - \boldsymbol{\beta}'\left(\boldsymbol{\gamma}^* - \boldsymbol{\gamma}\right)(T + 1)\right]. \tag{36}$$

Thus, (36) and (35) coincide when $\boldsymbol{\mu}_0^a = \boldsymbol{\mu}_0$, and $\boldsymbol{\gamma}^a = \boldsymbol{\gamma}$ as will occur if either there is no structural change, or the change occurs after the start of the forecast period.

4.4. Forecast biases under location shifts

We now consider a number of interesting special cases of (35) and (36) which highlight the behavior of the DVAR and VECM under shifts in the deterministic terms. Viewing $(\boldsymbol{\tau}_0, \boldsymbol{\tau}_1)$ as the primary parameters, we can map changes in these parameters to changes in $(\boldsymbol{\gamma}, \boldsymbol{\mu}_0, \boldsymbol{\mu}_1)$ via the orthogonal decomposition into $(\boldsymbol{\zeta}_0, \boldsymbol{\lambda}_0, \boldsymbol{\lambda}_1)$. The interdependencies can be summarized as $\boldsymbol{\gamma}(\boldsymbol{\zeta}_0, \boldsymbol{\lambda}_1)$, $\boldsymbol{\mu}_0(\boldsymbol{\zeta}_0, \boldsymbol{\lambda}_0, \boldsymbol{\lambda}_1)$, $\boldsymbol{\mu}_1(\boldsymbol{\lambda}_1)$.

Case I: $\boldsymbol{\tau}_0^* = \boldsymbol{\tau}_0$, $\boldsymbol{\tau}_1^* = \boldsymbol{\tau}_1$. In the absence of structural change, $\boldsymbol{\mu}_0^a = \boldsymbol{\mu}_0$ and $\boldsymbol{\gamma}^a = \boldsymbol{\gamma}$ and so

$$\mathsf{E}[\hat{\boldsymbol{\nu}}_{T+j|T}] = \mathsf{E}[\tilde{\boldsymbol{\nu}}_{T+j|T}] = \mathbf{0} \tag{37}$$

as is evident from (35) and (36). The omission of the stationary I(0) linear combinations does not render the DVAR forecasts biased.

Case II: $\boldsymbol{\tau}_0^* \neq \boldsymbol{\tau}_0$, $\boldsymbol{\tau}_1^* = \boldsymbol{\tau}_1$, but $\boldsymbol{\zeta}_0^* = \boldsymbol{\zeta}_0$. Then $\boldsymbol{\mu}_0^* \neq \boldsymbol{\mu}_0$ but $\boldsymbol{\gamma}^* = \boldsymbol{\gamma}$:

$$\mathsf{E}[\hat{\boldsymbol{\nu}}_{T+j|T}] = \mathbf{A}_j\boldsymbol{\alpha}\left(\boldsymbol{\mu}_0 - \boldsymbol{\mu}_0^*\right), \tag{38}$$

$$\mathsf{E}[\tilde{\boldsymbol{\nu}}_{T+j|T}] = \mathbf{A}_j \boldsymbol{\alpha}(\boldsymbol{\mu}_0^a - \boldsymbol{\mu}_0^*). \tag{39}$$

The biases are equal if $\boldsymbol{\mu}_0^a = \boldsymbol{\mu}_0$; i.e., the break is after the forecast origin. However, $\mathsf{E}[\tilde{\boldsymbol{\nu}}_{T+j}] = \mathbf{0}$ when $\boldsymbol{\mu}_0^a = \boldsymbol{\mu}_0^*$, and hence the DVAR is unbiased when the break occurs prior to the commencement of forecasting. In this example the component of the constant term orthogonal to $\boldsymbol{\alpha}$ ($\boldsymbol{\zeta}_0$) is unchanged, so that the growth rate is unaffected.

Case III: $\boldsymbol{\tau}_0^* \neq \boldsymbol{\tau}_0$, $\boldsymbol{\tau}_1^* = \boldsymbol{\tau}_1$ (as in Case II), but now $\boldsymbol{\lambda}_0^* = \boldsymbol{\lambda}_0$ which implies $\boldsymbol{\zeta}_0^* \neq \boldsymbol{\zeta}_0$ and therefore $\boldsymbol{\mu}_0^* \neq \boldsymbol{\mu}_0$ and $\boldsymbol{\gamma}^* \neq \boldsymbol{\gamma}$. However, $\boldsymbol{\beta}'\boldsymbol{\gamma}^* = \boldsymbol{\beta}'\boldsymbol{\gamma}$ holds (because $\boldsymbol{\tau}_1^* = \boldsymbol{\tau}_1$) so that

$$\mathsf{E}[\hat{\boldsymbol{\nu}}_{T+j|T}] = j(\boldsymbol{\gamma}^* - \boldsymbol{\gamma}) + \mathbf{A}_j \boldsymbol{\alpha}(\boldsymbol{\mu}_0 - \boldsymbol{\mu}_0^*), \tag{40}$$

$$\mathsf{E}[\tilde{\boldsymbol{\nu}}_{T+j|T}] = j(\boldsymbol{\gamma}^* - \boldsymbol{\gamma}) + \mathbf{A}_j \boldsymbol{\alpha}(\boldsymbol{\mu}_0^a - \boldsymbol{\mu}_0^*). \tag{41}$$

Consequently, the errors coincide when $\boldsymbol{\mu}_0^a = \boldsymbol{\mu}_0$, but differ when $\boldsymbol{\mu}_0^a = \boldsymbol{\mu}_0^*$.

Case IV: $\boldsymbol{\tau}_0^* = \boldsymbol{\tau}_0$, $\boldsymbol{\tau}_1^* \neq \boldsymbol{\tau}_1$. All of $\boldsymbol{\mu}_0$, $\boldsymbol{\mu}_1$ and $\boldsymbol{\gamma}$ change. If $\boldsymbol{\beta}'\boldsymbol{\gamma}^* \neq \boldsymbol{\beta}'\boldsymbol{\gamma}$ then we have (35) and (36), and otherwise the biases of Case III.

4.5. Forecast biases when there are changes in the autoregressive parameters

By way of contrast, changes in autoregressive parameters that do not induce changes in means are relatively benign for forecasts of first moments. Consider the VECM forecast errors given by (29) when $\mathsf{E}[\mathbf{x}_t] = \mathbf{0}$ for all t, so that $\boldsymbol{\tau}_0 = \boldsymbol{\tau}_0^* = \boldsymbol{\tau}_1 = \boldsymbol{\tau}_1^* = \mathbf{0}$ in (21):

$$\hat{\boldsymbol{\nu}}_{T+j|T} = \sum_{i=0}^{j-1} \boldsymbol{\Upsilon}^{*i} \boldsymbol{\nu}_{T+j-i} + (\boldsymbol{\Upsilon}^{*j} - \boldsymbol{\Upsilon}^j)\mathbf{x}_T. \tag{42}$$

The forecasts are unconditionally unbiased, $\mathsf{E}[\hat{\boldsymbol{\nu}}_{T+j|T}] = \mathbf{0}$, and the effect of the break is manifest in higher forecast error variances

$$\mathsf{V}[\hat{\boldsymbol{\nu}}_{T+j|T} \mid \mathbf{x}_T] = \sum_{i=0}^{j-1} \boldsymbol{\Upsilon}^{*i} \boldsymbol{\Omega} \boldsymbol{\Upsilon}^{*i\prime} + (\boldsymbol{\Upsilon}^{*j} - \boldsymbol{\Upsilon}^j)\mathbf{x}_T\mathbf{x}_T'(\boldsymbol{\Upsilon}^{*j} - \boldsymbol{\Upsilon}^j)'.$$

The DVAR model forecasts are also unconditionally unbiased, from

$$\tilde{\boldsymbol{\nu}}_{T+j|T} = \sum_{i=0}^{j-1} \boldsymbol{\Upsilon}^{*i} \boldsymbol{\nu}_{T+j-i} + (\boldsymbol{\Upsilon}^{*j} - \mathbf{I}_n)\mathbf{x}_T,$$

since $\mathsf{E}[\tilde{\boldsymbol{\nu}}_{T+j|T}] = \mathbf{0}$ provided $\mathsf{E}[\mathbf{x}_T] = \mathbf{0}$.

When $\mathsf{E}[\mathbf{x}_T] \neq \mathbf{0}$, but is the same before and after the break (as when changes in the autoregressive parameters are offset by changes in intercepts) both models' forecast errors are unconditionally unbiased.

4.6. Univariate models

The results for $n = 1$ follow immediately as a special case of (21):

$$x_t = \tau_0 + \tau_1 t + \Upsilon x_{t-1} + \nu_t. \tag{43}$$

The forecasts from (43) and the 'unit-root' model $x_t = x_{t-1} + \gamma + \upsilon_t$ are unconditionally unbiased when Υ shifts provided $\mathsf{E}[x_t] = 0$ (requiring $\tau_0 = \tau_1 = 0$). When $\tau_1 = 0$, the unit-root model forecasts remain unbiased when τ_0 shifts provided the shift occurs prior to forecasting, demonstrating the greater adaptability of the unit-root model. As in the multivariate setting, the break is assumed not to affect the model parameters (so that γ is taken to equal its population value of zero).

5. Detection of breaks

5.1. Tests for structural change

In this section, we briefly review testing for structural change or non-constancy in the parameters of time-series regressions. There is a large literature on testing for structural change. See, for example, Stock (1994) for a review. Two useful distinctions can be drawn: whether the putative break point is known, and whether the change in the parameters is governed by a stochastic process. Section 8 considers tests against the alternative of non-linearity.

For a known break date, the traditional method of testing for a one-time change in the model's parameters is the Chow (1960) test. That is, in the model

$$y_t = \alpha_1 y_{t-1} + \cdots + \alpha_p y_{t-p} + \varepsilon_t \tag{44}$$

when the alternative is a one-off change:

$$\mathsf{H}_1(\pi)\colon \boldsymbol{\alpha} = \begin{cases} \boldsymbol{\alpha}_1(\pi) & \text{for } t = 1, 2, \ldots, \pi T, \\ \boldsymbol{\alpha}_2(\pi) & \text{for } t = \pi T + 1, \ldots, T, \end{cases}$$

where $\boldsymbol{\alpha}' = (\alpha_1\ \alpha_2 \ldots \alpha_p)$, $\pi \in (0, 1)$, a test of parameter constancy can be implemented as an LM, Wald or LR test, all of which are asymptotically equivalent. For example, the Wald test has the form

$$\mathsf{F}_T(\pi) = \frac{RSS_{1,T} - (RSS_{1,\pi T} + RSS_{\pi T+1,T})}{(RSS_{1,\pi T} + RSS_{\pi T+1,T})/(T - 2p)},$$

where $RSS_{1,T}$ is the 'restricted' residual sum of squares from estimating the model on all the observations, $RSS_{1,\pi T}$ is the residual sum of squares from estimating the model on observations 1 to πT, etc. These tests also apply when the model is not purely autoregressive but contains other explanatory variables, although for $\mathsf{F}_T(\pi)$ to be asymptotically chi-squared all the variables need to be $\mathsf{I}(0)$ in general.

When the break is not assumed known a priori, the testing procedure cannot take the break date π as given. The testing procedure is then non-standard, because π is identified under the alternative hypothesis but not under the null [Davies (1977, 1987)]. Quandt (1960) suggested taking the maximal $\mathsf{F}_T(\pi)$ over a range of values of $\pi \in \Pi$, for Π a pre-specified subset of (0, 1). Andrews (1993) extended this approach to non-linear models, and Andrews and Ploberger (1994) considered the 'average' and 'exponential' test statistics. The asymptotic distributions are tabulated by Andrews (1993), and depend on p and Π. Diebold and Chen (1996) consider bootstrap approximations to the finite-sample distributions.

Andrews (1993) shows that the sup tests have power against a broader range of alternatives than $\mathsf{H}_1(\pi)$, but will not have high power against 'structural change' caused by the omission of a stationary variable. For example, suppose the DGP is a stationary AR(2):

$$y_t = \alpha_1 y_{t-1} + \alpha_2 y_{t-2} + \varepsilon_t$$

and the null is $\phi_{1,t} = \phi_{1,0}$ for all t in the model $y_t = \phi_{1,t} y_{t-1} + \varepsilon_t$, versus H_1^*: $\phi_{1,t}$ varies with t. The omission of the second lag can be viewed as causing structural change in the model each period, but this will not be detectable as the model is stationary under the alternative for all $t = 1, \ldots, T$. Stochastic forms of model mis-specification of this sort were shown in Section 2.1 not to cause forecast bias.

In addition, Bai and Perron (1998) consider testing for multiple structural breaks, and Bai, Lumsdaine and Stock (1998) consider testing and estimating break dates when the breaks are common to a number of time series. Hendry, Johansen and Santos (2004) propose testing for this form of non-constancy by adding a complete set of impulse indicators to a model using a two-step process, and establish the null distribution in a location-scale IID distribution.

Tests for structural change can also be based on recursive coefficient estimates and recursive residuals. The CUSUM test of Brown, Durbin and Evans (1975) is based on the cumulation of the sequence of 1-step forecast errors obtained by recursively estimating the model. As shown by Krämer, Ploberger and Alt (1988) and discussed by Stock (1994), the CUSUM test only has local asymptotic power against breaks in non-zero mean regressors. Therefore, CUSUM test rejections are likely to signal more specific forms of change than the sup tests. Unlike sup tests, CUSUM tests will not have good local asymptotic power against $\mathsf{H}_1(\pi)$ when (44) does not contain an intercept (so that y_t is zero-mean).

As well as testing for 'non-stochastic' structural change, one can test for randomly time-varying coefficients. Nyblom (1989) tests against the alternative that the coefficients follow a random walk, and Breusch and Pagan (1979) against the alternative that the coefficients are random draws from a distribution with a constant mean and finite variance.

From a forecasting perspective, in-sample tests of parameter instability may be used in a number of ways. The finding of instability may guide the selection of the window of data to be used for model estimation, or lead to the use of rolling windows of observations to allow for gradual change, or to the adoption of more flexible models, as discussed in Sections 6 and 7.

As argued by Chu, Stinchcombe and White (1996), the 'one shot' tests discussed so far may not be ideal in a real-time forecasting context as new data accrue. The tests are designed to detect breaks on a given historical sample of a fixed size. Repeated application of the tests as new data becomes available, or repeated application retrospectively moving through the historical period, will result in the asymptotic size of the sequence of tests approaching one if the null rejection frequency is held constant. Chu, Stinchcombe and White (1996, p. 1047) illustrate with reference to the Ploberger, Krämer and Kontrus (1989) retrospective fluctuation test. In the simplest case that $\{Y_t\}$ is an independent sequence, the null of 'stability in mean' is H_0: $\mathsf{E}[Y_t] = 0, t = 1, 2, \ldots$ versus H_1: $\mathsf{E}[Y_t] \neq 0$ for some t. For a given n,

$$FL_n = \max_{k<n} \sigma_0^{-1} \sqrt{n}(k/n) \left| \frac{1}{k} \sum_{t=1}^{k} y_t \right|$$

is compared to a critical value c determined from the hitting probability of a Brownian motion. But if FL_n is implemented sequentially for $n+1, n+2, \ldots$ then the probability of a type 1 error is one asymptotically. Similarly if a Chow test is repeatedly calculated every time new observations become available.

Chu, Stinchcombe and White (1996) suggest monitoring procedures for CUSUM and parameter fluctuation tests where the critical values are specified as boundary functions such that they are crossed with the prescribed probability under H_0. The CUSUM implementation is as follows. Define

$$\widetilde{Q}_n^m = \hat{\sigma}^{-1} \sum_{i=m}^{m+n} \omega_i,$$

where m is the end of the historical period, so that monitoring starts at $m+1$, and $n \geqslant 1$. The ω_i are the recursive residuals, $\omega_i = \hat{\varepsilon}_i / \sqrt{\upsilon_i}$, where $\hat{\varepsilon}_i = y_i - \mathbf{x}_i' \hat{\boldsymbol{\beta}}_{i-1}$, and

$$\upsilon_i = 1 + \mathbf{x}_i' \left(\sum_{j=1}^{i-1} \mathbf{x}_j \mathbf{x}_j' \right)^{-1} \mathbf{x}_i,$$

with

$$\hat{\boldsymbol{\beta}}_i = \left(\sum_{j=1}^{i} \mathbf{x}_j \mathbf{x}_j' \right)^{-1} \left(\sum_{j=1}^{i} \mathbf{x}_j y_j \right),$$

for the model

$$y_t = \mathbf{x}_t' \boldsymbol{\beta} + \varepsilon_t,$$

where $\mathbf{x}_t$ is $k \times 1$, say, and $\mathbf{X}_j = (\mathbf{x}_1 \ldots \mathbf{x}_j)$, etc. $\hat{\sigma}^2$ is a consistent estimator of $\mathsf{E}[\varepsilon_t^2] = \sigma^2$. The boundary is given by

$$\sqrt{n+m-k}\sqrt{c+\ln\left(\frac{n+m-k}{m-k}\right)}$$

(where c depends on the size of the test). Hence, beginning with $n = 1$, $|\widetilde{Q}_n^m|$ is compared to the boundary, and so on for $n = 2$, $n = 3$, etc. until $|\widetilde{Q}_n^m|$ crosses the boundary, signalling a rejection of the null hypothesis H_0: $\boldsymbol{\beta}_t = \boldsymbol{\beta}$ for $t = n+1, n+2, \ldots$. As for the one-shot tests, rejection of the null may lead to an attempt to revise the model or the adoption of a more 'adaptable' model.

5.2. Testing for level shifts in ARMA models

In addition to the tests for structural change in regression models, the literature on the detection of outliers and level shifts in ARMA models [following on from Box and Jenkins (1976)] is relevant from a forecasting perspective; see, inter alia, Tsay (1986, 1988), Chen and Tiao (1990), Chen and Liu (1993), Balke (1993), Junttila (2001), and Sánchez and Peña (2003). In this tradition, ARMA models are viewed as being composed of a 'regular component' and possibly a component which represents anomalous exogenous shifts. The latter can be either outliers or permanent shifts in the level of the process. The focus of the literature is on the problems caused by outliers and level shifts on the identification and estimation of the ARMA model, viz., the regular component of the model. The correct identification of level shifts will have an important bearing on forecast performance. Methods of identifying the type and estimating the timing of the exogenous shifts are aimed at 'correcting' the time series prior to estimating the ARMA model, and often follow an iterative procedure. That is, the exogenous shifts are determined conditional on a given ARMA model, the data are then corrected and the ARMA model re-estimated, etc.; see Tsay (1988) [Balke (1993) provides a refinement] and Chen and Liu (1993) for an approach that jointly estimates the ARMA model and exogenous shifts.

Given an ARMA model

$$y_t = f(t) + \left[\theta(L)/\phi(L)\right]\varepsilon_t,$$

where $\varepsilon_t \sim \mathsf{IN}[0, \sigma_\varepsilon^2]$, $\theta(L) = 1 - \theta_1 L - \cdots - \theta_q L^q$, $\phi(L) = 1 - \phi_1 L - \cdots - \phi_p L^p$, then $[\theta(L)/\phi(L)]\varepsilon_t$ is the regular component. For a single exogenous shift, let

$$f(t) = \omega_0\left[\frac{\omega(L)}{\delta(L)}\right]\xi_t^{(d)},$$

where $\xi_t^{(d)} = 1$ when $t = d$ and $\xi_t^{(d)} = 0$ when $t \neq d$. The lag polynomials $\omega(L)$ and $\delta(L)$ define the type of exogenous event. $\omega(L)/\delta(L) = 1$ corresponds to an additive outlier (AO), whereby y_d is ω_0 higher than would be the case were the exogenous component absent. When $\omega(L)/\delta(L) = \theta(L)/\phi(L)$, we have an innovation outlier (IO).

The model can be written as

$$y_t = \frac{\theta(L)}{\phi(L)}\bigl(\varepsilon_t + \omega_0 \xi_t^{(d)}\bigr),$$

corresponding to the period d innovation being drawn from a Gaussian distribution with mean ω_0. Of particular interest from a forecasting perspective is when $\omega(L)/\delta(L) = (1 - L)^{-1}$, which represents a permanent level shift (LS):

$$\begin{aligned} y_t &= \bigl[\theta(L)/\phi(L)\bigr]\varepsilon_t, & t < d,\\ y_t - \omega_0 &= \bigl[\theta(L)/\phi(L)\bigr]\varepsilon_t, & t \geqslant d. \end{aligned}$$

Letting $\pi(L) = \phi(L)/\theta(L)$, we obtain the following residual series for the three specifications of $f(t)$:

$$\begin{aligned} &\text{IO:} \quad e_t = \pi(L)y_t = \omega_0 \xi_t^{(d)} + \varepsilon_t,\\ &\text{AO:} \quad e_t = \pi(L)y_t = \omega_0 \pi(L)\xi_t^{(d)} + \varepsilon_t,\\ &\text{LS:} \quad e_t = \pi(L)y_t = \omega_0 \pi(L)(1 - L)^{-1}\xi_t^{(d)} + \varepsilon_t. \end{aligned}$$

Hence the least-squares estimate of an IO at $t = d$ can be obtained by regressing e_t on $\xi_t^{(d)}$: this yields $\hat{\omega}_{0,\mathrm{IO}} = e_t$. Similarly, the least-squares estimate of an AO at $t = d$ can be obtained by regressing e_t on a variable that is zero for $t < d$, 1 for $t = d$, $-\pi_k$ for $t = d + k$, $k > 1$, to give $\hat{\omega}_{0,\mathrm{AO}}$. Similarly for LS.

The standardized statistics:

$$\begin{aligned} &\text{IOs:} \quad \tau_{\mathrm{IO}}(d) = \hat{\omega}_{0,\mathrm{IO}}(d)/\hat{\sigma}_\varepsilon,\\ &\text{AOs:} \quad \tau_{\mathrm{AO}}(d) = \bigl(\hat{\omega}_{0,\mathrm{AO}}(d)/\hat{\sigma}_\varepsilon\bigr)\sqrt{\textstyle\sum_{t=d}^{T}\bigl(\pi(L)\xi_t^{(d)}\bigr)^2},\\ &\text{LSs:} \quad \tau_{\mathrm{LS}}(d) = \bigl(\hat{\omega}_{0,\mathrm{LS}}(d)/\hat{\sigma}_\varepsilon\bigr)\sqrt{\textstyle\sum_{t=d}^{T}\bigl(\pi(L)(1 - L)^{-1}\xi_t^{(d)}\bigr)^2} \end{aligned}$$

are discussed by Chan and Wei (1988) and Tsay (1988). They have approximately normal distributions. Given that d is unknown, as is the type of the shift, the suggestion is to take:

$$\tau_{\max} = \max\{\tau_{\mathrm{IO},\max}, \tau_{\mathrm{AO},\max}, \tau_{\mathrm{LS},\max}\},$$

where $\tau_{j,\max} = \max_{1 \leqslant d \leqslant T}\{\tau_j(d)\}$, and compare this to a pre-specified critical value. Exceedance implies an exogenous shift has occurred.

As $\phi(L)$ and $\theta(L)$ are unknown, these tests require a pre-estimate of the ARMA model. Balke (1993) notes that when level shifts are present, the initial ARMA model will be mis-specified, and that this may lead to level shifts being identified as IOs, as well as reducing the power of the tests of LS.

Suppose $\phi(L) = 1 - \phi L$ and $\theta(L) = 1$, so that we have an AR(1), then in the presence of an unmodeled level shift of size μ at time d, the estimate of ϕ is inconsistent:

$$\operatorname*{plim}_{T\to\infty} \hat{\phi} = \phi + \left[\frac{(1-\phi)\mu^2(T-d)d/T^2}{\sigma_\varepsilon^2/(1-\phi^2) + \mu^2(T-d)d/T^2}\right]; \tag{45}$$

see, e.g., Rappoport and Reichlin (1989), Reichlin (1989), Chen and Tiao (1990), Perron (1990), and Hendry and Neale (1991). Neglected structural breaks will give the appearance of unit roots. Balke (1993) shows that the expected value of the $\tau_{\mathrm{LS}}(d)$ statistic will be substantially reduced for many combinations of values of the underlying parameters, leading to a reduction in power.

The consequences for forecast performance are less clear-cut. The failure to detect structural breaks in the mean of the series will be mitigated to some extent by the induced 'random-walk-like' property of the estimated ARMA model. An empirical study by Junttila (2001) finds that intervention dummies do not result in the expected gains in terms of forecast performance when applied to a model of Finnish inflation.

With this background, we turn to detecting the breaks themselves when these occur in-sample.

6. Model estimation and specification

6.1. Determination of estimation sample for a fixed specification

We assume that the break date is known, and consider the choice of the estimation sample. In practice the break date will need to be estimated, and this will often be given as a by-product of testing for a break at an unknown date, using one of the procedures reviewed in Section 5. The remaining model parameters are estimated, and forecasts generated, conditional on the estimated break point(s); see, e.g., Bai and Perron (1998).[2] Consequently, the properties of the forecast errors will depend on the pre-test for the break date. In the absence of formal frequentist analyses of this problem, we act as if the break date were known.[3]

Suppose the DGP is given by

$$y_{t+1} = 1_{(t\leqslant\tau)}\boldsymbol{\beta}_1'\mathbf{x}_t + (1 - 1_{(t\leqslant\tau)})\boldsymbol{\beta}_2'\mathbf{x}_t + u_{t+1} \tag{46}$$

so that the pre-break observations are $t = 1, \ldots, \tau$, and the post-break $t = \tau+1, \ldots, T$. There is a one-off change in all the slope parameters and the disturbance variance, from σ_1^2 to σ_2^2.

[2] In the context of assessing the predictability of stock market returns, Pesaran and Timmermann (2002a) choose an estimation window by determining the time of the most recent break using reversed ordered CUSUM tests. The authors also determine the latest break using the method in Bai and Perron (1998).

[3] Pastor and Stambaugh (2001) adopt a Bayesian approach that incorporates uncertainty about the locations of the breaks, so their analysis does not treat estimates of breakpoints as true values and condition upon them.

First, we suppose that the explanatory variables are strongly exogenous. Pesaran and Timmermann (2002b) consider the choice of m, the first observation for the model estimation period, where $m = \tau + 1$ corresponds to only using post-break observations. Let $\mathbf{X}_{m,T}$ be the $(T - m + 1) \times k$ matrix of observations on the k explanatory variables for the periods m to T (inclusive), $\mathbf{Q}_{m,T} = \mathbf{X}'_{m,T}\mathbf{X}_{m,T}$, and $\mathbf{Y}_{m,T}$ and $\mathbf{u}_{m,T}$ contain the latest $T - m + 1$ observations on y and u, respectively. The OLS estimator of $\boldsymbol{\beta}$ in

$$\mathbf{Y}_{m,T} = \mathbf{X}_{m,T}\boldsymbol{\beta}(m) + \mathbf{v}_{m,T}$$

is given by

$$\begin{aligned}
\hat{\boldsymbol{\beta}}_T(m) &= \mathbf{Q}_{m,T}^{-1}\mathbf{X}'_{m,T}\mathbf{Y}_{m,T} \\
&= \mathbf{Q}_{m,T}^{-1}\left(\mathbf{X}'_{m,\tau} : \mathbf{X}'_{\tau+1,T}\right)\begin{pmatrix}\mathbf{Y}_{m,\tau} \\ \mathbf{Y}_{\tau+1,T}\end{pmatrix} \\
&= \mathbf{Q}_{m,T}^{-1}\mathbf{Q}_{m,\tau}\boldsymbol{\beta}_1 + \mathbf{Q}_{m,T}^{-1}\mathbf{Q}_{\tau+1,T}\boldsymbol{\beta}_2 + \mathbf{Q}_{m,T}^{-1}\mathbf{X}'_{m,T}\mathbf{u}_{m,T},
\end{aligned}$$

where, e.g., $\mathbf{Q}_{m,\tau}$ is the second moment matrix formed from $\mathbf{X}_{m,\tau}$, etc. Thus $\hat{\boldsymbol{\beta}}_T(m)$ is a weighted average of the pre and post-break parameter vectors. The forecast error is

$$\begin{aligned}
e_{T+1} &= y_{T+1} - \hat{\boldsymbol{\beta}}_T(m)'\mathbf{x}_T \\
&= u_{T+1} + (\boldsymbol{\beta}_2 - \boldsymbol{\beta}_1)'\mathbf{Q}_{m,\tau}\mathbf{Q}_{m,T}^{-1}\mathbf{x}_T - \mathbf{u}'_{m,T}\mathbf{X}_{m,T}\mathbf{Q}_{m,T}^{-1}\mathbf{x}_T,
\end{aligned} \tag{47}$$

where the second term is the bias that results from using pre-break observations, which depends on the size of the shift $\boldsymbol{\delta}_\beta = (\boldsymbol{\beta}_2 - \boldsymbol{\beta}_1)$, amongst other things. The conditional MSFE is

$$\begin{aligned}
\mathsf{E}\left[e_{T+1}^2 \mid \mathcal{I}_T\right] = \sigma_2^2 &+ \left(\boldsymbol{\delta}'_\beta\mathbf{Q}_{m,\tau}\mathbf{Q}_{m,T}^{-1}\mathbf{x}_T\right)^2 \\
&+ \mathbf{x}'_T\mathbf{Q}_{m,T}^{-1}\mathbf{X}'_{m,T}\mathbf{D}_{m,T}\mathbf{X}_{m,T}\mathbf{Q}_{m,T}^{-1}\mathbf{x}_T,
\end{aligned} \tag{48}$$

where $\mathbf{D}_{m,T} = \mathsf{E}[\mathbf{u}_{m,T}\mathbf{u}'_{m,T}]$, a diagonal matrix with σ_1^2 in the first $\tau - m + 1$ elements, and σ_2^2 in the remainder. When $\sigma_2^2 = \sigma_1^2 = \sigma^2$ (say), $\mathbf{D}_{m,T}$ is proportional to the identity matrix, and the conditional MSFE simplifies to

$$\mathsf{E}\left[e_{T+1}^2 \mid \mathcal{I}_T\right] = \sigma^2 + \left(\boldsymbol{\delta}'_\beta\mathbf{Q}_{m,\tau}\mathbf{Q}_{m,T}^{-1}\mathbf{x}_T\right)^2 + \sigma^2\mathbf{x}'_T\mathbf{Q}_{m,T}^{-1}\mathbf{x}_T.$$

Using only post-break observations corresponds to setting $m = \tau + 1$. Since $\mathbf{Q}_{m,\tau} = \mathbf{0}$ when $m > \tau$, from (48) we obtain

$$\mathsf{E}\left[e_{T+1}^2 \mid \mathcal{I}_T\right] = \sigma_2^2 + \sigma_2^2\left(\mathbf{x}'_T\mathbf{Q}_{\tau+1,T}^{-1}\mathbf{x}_T\right)$$

since $\mathbf{D}_{\tau+1,T} = \sigma_2^2\mathbf{I}_{T-\tau}$.

Pesaran and Timmermann (2002b) consider $k = 1$ so that

$$e_{T+1} = u_{T+1} + (\beta_2 - \beta_1)\theta_m x_T - v_m x_T, \tag{49}$$

where

$$\theta_m = \frac{Q_{m,\tau}}{Q_{m,T}} = \frac{\sum_{t=m}^{\tau} x_{t-1}^2}{\sum_{t=m}^{T} x_{t-1}^2} \quad \text{and} \quad v_m = \mathbf{u}'_{m,T}\mathbf{X}_{m,T}Q_{m,T}^{-1} = \frac{\sum_{t=m}^{T} u_t x_{t-1}}{\sum_{t=m}^{T} x_{t-1}^2}.$$

Then the conditional MSFE has a more readily interpretable form:

$$\mathsf{E}\left[e_{T+1}^2 \mid \mathcal{I}_T\right] = \sigma_2^2 + \sigma_2^2 x_T^2 \left(\sigma_2^2 \delta_\beta^2 \theta_m^2 + \frac{\psi\theta_m + 1}{\sum_{t=m}^{T} x_{t-1}^2}\right),$$

where $\psi = (\sigma_1^2 - \sigma_2^2)/\sigma_2^2$. So decreasing m (including more pre-break observations) increases θ_m and therefore the squared bias (via $\sigma_2^2\delta_\beta^2\theta_m^2$) but the overall effect on the MSFE is unclear.

Including some pre-break observations is more likely to lower the MSFE the smaller the break, $|\delta_\beta|$; when the variability increases after the break period, $\sigma_2^2 > \sigma_1^2$, and the fewer the number of post-break observations (the shorter the distance $T - \tau$). Given that it is optimal to set $m < \tau + 1$, the optimal window size m^* is chose to satisfy

$$m^* = \underset{m=1,\ldots,\tau+1}{\operatorname{argmin}} \left\{\mathsf{E}\left[e_{T+1}^2 \mid \mathcal{I}_T\right]\right\}.$$

Unconditionally (i.e., on average across all values of x_t) the forecasts are unbiased for all m when $\mathsf{E}[x_t] = 0$. From (49):

$$\mathsf{E}[e_{T+1} \mid \mathcal{I}_T] = (\beta_2 - \beta_1)\theta_m x_T - v_m x_T \tag{50}$$

so that

$$\mathsf{E}[e_{T+1}] = \mathsf{E}\big(\mathsf{E}[e_{T+1} \mid \mathcal{I}_T]\big) = (\beta_2 - \beta_1)\theta_m \mathsf{E}[x_T] - v_m \mathsf{E}[x_T] = 0. \tag{51}$$

The unconditional MSFE is given by

$$\mathsf{E}\left[e_{T+1}^2\right] = \sigma^2 + \omega^2(\beta_2 - \beta_1)^2 \frac{\nu_1(\nu_1 + 2)}{\nu(\nu + 2)} + \frac{\sigma^2}{\nu - 2}$$

for conditional mean breaks ($\sigma_1^2 = \sigma_2^2 = \sigma^2$) with zero-mean regressors, and where $\mathsf{E}[x_t^2] = \omega^2$ and $\nu_1 = \tau - m + 1$, $\nu = T - m + 1$.

The assumption that $\mathbf{x}_t$ is distributed independently of all the disturbances $\{u_t,\ t = 1, \ldots, T\}$ does not hold for autoregressive models. The forecast error remains unconditionally unbiased when the regressors are zero-mean, as is evident with $\mathsf{E}[x_t] = 0$ in the case of $k = 1$ depicted in Equation (51), and consistent with the forecast-error taxonomy in Section 2.1. Pesaran and Timmermann (2003) show that including pre-break observations is more likely to improve forecasting performance than in the case of fixed regressors because of the finite small-sample biases in the estimates of the parameters of autoregressive models. They conclude that employing an expanding window of data may often be as good as employing a rolling window when there are breaks. Including pre-break observations is more likely to reduce MSFEs when the degree of persistence of the AR process declines after the break, and when the mean of the process is unaffected. A reduction in the degree of persistence may favor the use of pre-break observations by offsetting the small-sample bias. The small-sample bias of the AR parameter in the AR(1) model is negative:

$$\mathsf{E}[\hat{\beta}_1] - \beta_1 = \frac{-(1+3\beta_1)}{T} + O(T^{-3/2})$$

so that the estimate of β_1 based on post-break observations is on average below the true value. The inclusion of pre-break observations will induce a positive bias (relative to the true post-break value, β_2). When the regressors are fixed, finite-sample biases are absent and the inclusion of pre-break observations will cause bias, other things being equal. Also see Chong (2001).

6.2. Updating

Rather than assuming that the break has occurred some time in the past, suppose that the change happens close to the time that the forecasts are made, and may be of a continuous nature. In these circumstances, parameter estimates held fixed for a sequence of forecast origins will gradually depart from the underlying LDGP approximation. A moving window seeks to offset that difficulty by excluding distant observations, whereas updating seeks to 'chase' the changing parameters: more flexibly, 'updating' could allow for re-selecting the model specification as well as re-estimating its parameters. Alternatively, the model's parameters may be allowed to 'drift'. An assumption sometimes made in the empirical macro literature is that VAR parameters evolve as driftless random walks (with zero-mean, constant-variance Gaussian innovations) subject to constraints that rule out the parameters drifting into non-stationary regions [see Cogley and Sargent (2001, 2005) for recent examples]. In modeling the equity premium, Pastor and Stambaugh (2001) allow for parameter change by specifying a process that alternates between 'stable' and 'transition' regimes. In their Bayesian approach, the timing of the break points that define the regimes is uncertain, but the use of prior beliefs based on economics (e.g., the relationship between the equity premium and volatility, and with price changes) allows the current equity premium to be estimated. The next section notes some other approaches where older observations are down weighted, or when only the last few data points play a role in the forecast (as with double-differenced devices).

Here we note that there is evidence of the benefits of jointly re-selecting the model specification and re-estimating its resulting parameters in Phillips (1994, 1995, 1996), Schiff and Phillips (2000), and Swanson and White (1997), for example. However, Stock and Watson (1996) find that the forecasting gains from time-varying coefficient models appear to be rather modest. In a constant parameter world, estimation efficiency dictates that all available information should be incorporated, so updating as new data accrue is natural. Moreover, following a location shift, re-selection could allow an additional unit root to be estimated to eliminate the break, and thereby reduce systematic forecast failure, as noted at the end of Section 5.2; also see Osborn (2002, pp. 420–421) for a related discussion in a seasonal context.

7. Ad hoc forecasting devices

When there are structural breaks, forecasting methods which adapt quickly following the break are most likely to avoid making systematic forecast errors in sequential real-time forecasting. Using the tests for structural change discussed in Section 5, Stock and Watson (1996) find evidence of widespread instability in the postwar US univariate and bivariate macroeconomic relations that they study. A number of authors have noted that empirical-accuracy studies of univariate time-series forecasting models and methods often favor ad hoc forecasting devices over properly specified statistical models [in this context, often the ARMA models of Box and Jenkins (1976)].[4] One explanation is the failure of the assumption of parameter constancy, and the greater adaptivity of the forecasting devices. Various types of exponential smoothing (ES), such as damped trend ES [see Gardner and McKenzie (1985)], tend to be competitive with ARMA models, although it can be shown that ES only corresponds to the optimal forecasting device for a specific ARMA model, namely the ARIMA(0, 1, 1) [see, for example, Harvey (1992, Chapter 2)]. In this section, we consider a number of ad hoc forecasting methods and assess their performance when there are breaks. The roles of parameter estimation updating, rolling windows and time-varying parameter models have been considered in Sections 6.1 and 6.2.

7.1. Exponential smoothing

We discuss exponential smoothing for variance processes, but the points made are equally relevant for forecasting conditional means. The ARMA(1, 1) equation for u_t^2 for the GARCH(1, 1) indicates that the forecast function will be closely related to exponential smoothing. Equation (17) has the interpretation that the conditional variance will exceed the long-run (or unconditional) variance if last period's squared returns exceed the long-run variance and/or if last period's conditional variance exceeds the unconditional. Some straightforward algebra shows that the long-horizon forecasts approach σ^2. Writing (17) for σ_{T+j}^2, we have

$$\begin{aligned}\sigma_{T+j}^2 - \sigma^2 &= \alpha\left(u_{T+j-1}^2 - \sigma^2\right) + \beta\left(\sigma_{T+j-1}^2 - \sigma^2\right)\\ &= \alpha\left(\sigma_{T+j-1}^2 \boldsymbol{\nu}_{T+j-1}^2 - \sigma^2\right) + \beta\left(\sigma_{T+j-1}^2 - \sigma^2\right).\end{aligned}$$

Taking conditional expectations

$$\begin{aligned}\sigma_{T+j|T}^2 - \sigma^2 &= \alpha\left(\mathsf{E}\left[\sigma_{T+j-1}^2 \boldsymbol{\nu}_{T+j-1}^2 \mid \mathbf{Y}_T\right] - \sigma^2\right) + \beta\left(\mathsf{E}\left[\sigma_{T+j-1}^2 \mid \mathbf{Y}_T\right] - \sigma^2\right)\\ &= (\alpha+\beta)\left(\mathsf{E}\left[\sigma_{T+j-1}^2 \mid \mathbf{Y}_T\right] - \sigma^2\right)\end{aligned}$$

[4] One of the earliest studies was Newbold and Granger (1974). Fildes and Makridakis (1995) and Fildes and Ord (2002) report on the subsequent 'M-competitions', Makridakis and Hibon (2000) present the latest 'M-competition', and a number of commentaries appear in *International Journal of Forecasting* 17.

using

$$\mathsf{E}\big[\sigma_{T+j-1}^2 \boldsymbol{\nu}_{T+j-1}^2 \mid \mathbf{Y}_T\big] = \mathsf{E}\big[\sigma_{T+j-1}^2 \mid \mathbf{Y}_T\big]\mathsf{E}\big[\boldsymbol{\nu}_{T+j-1}^2 \mid \mathbf{Y}_T\big] = \mathsf{E}\big[\sigma_{T+j-1}^2 \mid \mathbf{Y}_T\big],$$

for $j > 2$. By backward substitution ($j > 0$),

$$\begin{aligned}\sigma_{T+j|T}^2 - \sigma^2 &= (\alpha + \beta)^{j-1}\big(\sigma_{T+1}^2 - \sigma^2\big) \\ &= (\alpha + \beta)^{j-1}\big[\alpha\big(u_T^2 - \sigma^2\big) + \beta\big(\sigma_T^2 - \sigma^2\big)\big]\end{aligned} \tag{52}$$

(given $\mathsf{E}[\sigma_{T+1}^2 \mid \mathbf{Y}_T] = \sigma_{T+1}^2$). Therefore $\sigma_{T+j|T}^2 \to \sigma^2$ as $j \to \infty$.

Contrast the EWMA formula for forecasting $T + 1$ based on $\mathbf{Y}_T$:

$$\begin{aligned}\tilde{\sigma}_{T+1|T}^2 &= \frac{1}{\sum_{s=0}^{\infty} \lambda^s}\big(u_T^2 + \lambda u_{T-1}^2 + \lambda^2 u_{T-2}^2 + \cdots\big) \\ &= (1 - \lambda)\sum_{s=0}^{\infty} \lambda^s u_{T-s}^2,\end{aligned} \tag{53}$$

where $\lambda \in (0, 1)$, so the largest weight is given to the most recent squared return, $(1-\lambda)$, and thereafter the weights decline exponentially. Rearranging gives

$$\tilde{\sigma}_{T+1|T}^2 = u_T^2 + \lambda\big(\tilde{\sigma}_{T|T-1}^2 - u_T^2\big).$$

The forecast is equal to the squared return plus/minus the difference between the estimate of the current-period variance and the squared return. Exponential smoothing corresponds to a restricted GARCH(1, 1) model with $\omega = 0$ and $\alpha + \beta = (1 - \lambda) + \lambda = 1$. From a forecasting perspective, these restrictions give rise to an ARIMA(0, 1, 1) for u_t^2 (see (16)). As an integrated process, the latest volatility estimate is extrapolated, and there is no mean-reversion. Thus the exponential smoother will be more robust than the GARCH(1, 1) model's forecasts to breaks in σ^2 when λ is close to zero: there is no tendency for a sequence of 1-step forecasts to move toward a long-run variance. When σ^2 is constant (i.e., when there are no breaks in the long-run level of volatility) and the conditional variance follows an 'equilibrium' GARCH process, this will be undesirable, but in the presence of shifts in σ^2 may avoid the systematic forecast errors from a GARCH model correcting to an inappropriate equilibrium.

Empirically, the estimated value of $\alpha + \beta$ in (15) is often found to be close to 1, and estimates of ω close to 0. $\alpha + \beta = 1$ gives rise to the Integrated GARCH (IGARCH) model. The IGARCH model may arise through the neglect of structural breaks in GARCH models, paralleling the impact of shifts in autoregressive models of means, as summarized in (45). For a number of daily stock return series, Lamoureux and Lastrapes (1990) test standard GARCH models against GARCH models which allow for structural change through the introduction of a number of dummy variables, although Maddala and Li (1996) question the validity of their bootstrap tests.

7.2. Intercept corrections

The widespread use of some macro-econometric forecasting practices, such as intercept corrections (or residual adjustments), can be justified by structural change. Published forecasts based on large-scale macro-econometric models often include adjustments for the influence of anticipated events that are not explicitly incorporated in the specification of the model. But in addition, as long ago as Marris (1954), the 'mechanistic' adherence to models in the generation of forecasts when the economic system changes was questioned. The importance of adjusting purely model-based forecasts has been recognized by a number of authors [see, inter alia, Theil (1961, p. 57), Klein (1971), Klein, Howrey and MacCarthy (1974), and the sequence of reviews by the UK ESRC Macroeconomic Modelling Bureau in Wallis et al. (1984, 1985, 1986, 1987), Turner (1990), and Wallis and Whitley (1991)]. Improvements in forecast performance after intercept correction (IC) have been documented by Wallis et al. (1986, Table 4.8, 1987, Figures 4.3 and 4.4) and Wallis and Whitley (1991), inter alia.

To illustrate the effects of IC on the properties of forecasts, consider the simplest adjustment to the VECM forecasts in Section 4.2, whereby the period T residual $\hat{\boldsymbol{\nu}}_T = \mathbf{x}_T - \hat{\mathbf{x}}_T = (\boldsymbol{\tau}_0^* - \boldsymbol{\tau}_0) + (\boldsymbol{\tau}_1^* - \boldsymbol{\tau}_1)T + \boldsymbol{\nu}_T$ is used to adjust subsequent forecasts. Thus, the adjusted forecasts are given by

$$\dot{\mathbf{x}}_{T+h} = \boldsymbol{\tau}_0 + \boldsymbol{\tau}_1(T+h) + \boldsymbol{\Upsilon}\dot{\mathbf{x}}_{T+h-1} + \hat{\boldsymbol{\nu}}_T, \tag{54}$$

where $\dot{\mathbf{x}}_T = \mathbf{x}_T$, so that

$$\dot{\mathbf{x}}_{T+h} = \hat{\mathbf{x}}_{T+h} + \sum_{i=0}^{h-1} \boldsymbol{\Upsilon}^i \hat{\boldsymbol{\nu}}_T = \hat{\mathbf{x}}_{T+h} + \mathbf{A}_h \hat{\boldsymbol{\nu}}_T. \tag{55}$$

Letting $\hat{\boldsymbol{\nu}}_{T+h}$ denote the h-step ahead forecast error of the unadjusted forecast, $\hat{\boldsymbol{\nu}}_{T+h} = \mathbf{x}_{T+h} - \hat{\mathbf{x}}_{T+h}$, the conditional (and unconditional) expectation of the adjusted-forecast error is

$$\mathsf{E}[\dot{\boldsymbol{\nu}}_{T+h} \mid \mathbf{x}_T] = \mathsf{E}[\hat{\boldsymbol{\nu}}_{T+h} - \mathbf{A}_h \hat{\boldsymbol{\nu}}_T] = [h\mathbf{A}_h - \mathbf{D}_h](\boldsymbol{\tau}_1^* - \boldsymbol{\tau}_1), \tag{56}$$

where we have used

$$\mathsf{E}[\hat{\boldsymbol{\nu}}_T] = (\boldsymbol{\tau}_0^* - \boldsymbol{\tau}_0) + (\boldsymbol{\tau}_1^* - \boldsymbol{\tau}_1)T.$$

The adjustment strategy yields unbiased forecasts when $\boldsymbol{\tau}_1^* = \boldsymbol{\tau}_1$ irrespective of any shift in $\boldsymbol{\tau}_0$. Even if the process remains unchanged there is no penalty in terms of bias from intercept correcting. The cost of intercept correcting is in terms of increased uncertainty. The forecast error variance for the type of IC discussed here is

$$\mathsf{V}[\dot{\boldsymbol{\nu}}_{T+h}] = 2\mathsf{V}[\hat{\boldsymbol{\nu}}_{T+h}] + \sum_{j=0}^{h-1}\sum_{i=0}^{h-1} \boldsymbol{\Upsilon}^j \boldsymbol{\Omega} \boldsymbol{\Upsilon}^{i\prime}, \quad j \neq i, \tag{57}$$

which is more than double the conditional expectation forecast error variance, $\mathsf{V}[\hat{\boldsymbol{v}}_{T+h} \mid \mathbf{x}_T]$. Clearly, there is a bias-variance trade-off: bias can be reduced at the cost of an inflated forecast-error variance. Notice also that the second term in (57) is of the order of h^2, so that this trade-off should be more favorable to intercept correcting at short horizons. Furthermore, basing ICs on averages of recent errors (rather than the period T error alone) may provide more accurate estimates of the break and reduce the inflation of the forecast-error variance. For a sufficiently large change in $\boldsymbol{\tau}_0$, the adjusted forecasts will be more accurate than those of unadjusted forecasts on squared-error loss measures. Detailed analyses of ICs can be found in Clements and Hendry (1996, 1998, Chapter 8, 1999, Chapter 6).

7.3. *Differencing*

Section 4.3 considered the forecast performance of a DVAR relative to a VECM when there were location shifts in the underlying process. Those two models are related by the DVAR omitting the disequilibrium feedback of the VECM, rather than by a differencing operator transforming the model used to forecast [see, e.g., Davidson et al. (1978)]. For shifts in the equilibrium mean at the end of the estimation sample, the DVAR could outperform the VECM. Nevertheless, both models were susceptible to shifts in the growth rate. Thus, a natural development is to consider differencing once more, to obtain a DDVAR and a DVECM, neither of which includes any deterministic terms when linear deterministic trends are the highest needed to characterize data.

The detailed algebra is presented in Hendry (2005), who shows that the simplest double-differenced forecasting device, namely:

$$\Delta^2 \mathbf{x}_{T+1|T} = \mathbf{0} \tag{58}$$

can outperform in a range of circumstances, especially if the VECM omits important explanatory variables and experiences location shifts. Indeed, the forecast-error variance of (58) need not be doubled by differencing, and could even be less than that of the VECM, so (58) would outperform in both mean and variance. In that setting, the DVECM will also do well, as (in the simplest case again) it augments (58) by $\boldsymbol{\alpha}\boldsymbol{\beta}'\Delta\mathbf{x}_{T-1}$ which transpires to be the most important observable component missing in (58), provided the parameters $\boldsymbol{\alpha}$ and $\boldsymbol{\beta}$ do not change. For example, consider (25) when $\boldsymbol{\mu}_1 = \mathbf{0}$, then differencing all the terms in the VECM but retaining their parameter estimates unaltered delivers

$$\Delta^2 \mathbf{x}_t = \Delta\boldsymbol{\gamma} + \boldsymbol{\alpha}\Delta\left(\boldsymbol{\beta}'\mathbf{x}_{t-1} - \boldsymbol{\mu}_0\right) + \boldsymbol{\xi}_t = \boldsymbol{\alpha}\boldsymbol{\beta}'\Delta\mathbf{x}_{t-1} + \boldsymbol{\xi}_t. \tag{59}$$

Then (59) has no deterministic terms, so does not equilibrium correct, thereby reducing the risks attached to forecasting after breaks. Although it will produce noisy forecasts, smoothed variants are easily formulated. When there are no locations shifts, the 'insurance' of differencing must worsen forecast accuracy and precision, but if location shifts occur, differencing will pay.

7.4. Pooling

Forecast pooling is a venerable ad hoc method of improving forecasts; see, inter alia, Bates and Granger (1969), Newbold and Granger (1974), Granger (1989), and Clements and Galvão (2005); Diebold and Lopez (1996) and Newbold and Harvey (2002) provide surveys, and Clemen (1989) an annotated bibliography. Combining individual forecasts of the same event has often been found to deliver a smaller MSFE than any of the individual forecasts. Simple rules for combining forecasts, such as averages, tend to work as well as more elaborate rules based on past forecasting performance; see Stock and Watson (1999) and Fildes and Ord (2002). Hendry and Clements (2004) suggest that such an outcome may sometimes result from location shifts in the DGP differentially affecting different models at different times. After each break, some previously well-performing model does badly, certainly much worse than the combined forecast, so eventually the combined forecast dominates on MSFE, even though at each point in time, it was never the best.

An improved approach might be obtained by trying to predict which device is most likely to forecast best at the relevant horizon, but the unpredictable nature of many breaks makes its success unlikely – unless the breaks themselves can be forecast. In particular, during quiescent periods, the DDV will do poorly, yet will prove a robust predictor when a sudden change eventuates. Indeed, encompassing tests across models would reveal the DDV to be dominated over 'normal' periods, so it cannot be established that dominated models should be excluded from the pooling combination.

Extensions to combining density and interval forecasts have been proposed by, e.g., Granger, White and Kamstra (1989), Taylor and Bunn (1998), Wallis (2005), and Hall and Mitchell (2005), inter alia.

8. Non-linear models

In previous sections, we have considered structural breaks in parametric linear dynamic models. The break is viewed as a permanent change in the value of the parameter vector. Non-linear models are characterized by dynamic properties that vary between two or more regimes, or states, in a way that is endogenously determined by the model. For example, non-linear models have been used extensively in empirical macroeconomics to capture differences in dynamic behavior between the expansion and contraction phases of the business cycle, and have also been applied to financial time series [see, inter alia, Albert and Chib (1993), Diebold, Lee and Weinbach (1994), Goodwin (1993), Hamilton (1994), Kähler and Marnet (1994), Kim (1994), Krolzig and Lütkepohl (1995), Krolzig (1997), Lam (1990), McCulloch and Tsay (1994), Phillips (1991), Potter (1995), and Tiao and Tsay (1994), as well as the collections edited by Barnett et al. (2000), and Hamilton and Raj (2002)]. Treating a number of episodes of parameter instability in a time series as non-random events representing permanent changes in the model will have different implications for characterizing and understanding the behavior of the time series, as well as for forecasting, compared to treating the time series as being governed by a non-linear model. Forecasts from non-linear models will depend on the phase of the business cycle and will incorporate the possibility of a switch in regime during the period being forecast, while forecasts from structural break models imply no such changes during the future.[5]

Given the possibility of parameter instability due to non-linearities, the tests of parameter instability in linear dynamic models (reviewed in Section 5) will be misleading if non-linearities cause rejections. Similarly, tests of non-linearities against the null of a linear model may be driven by structural instabilities. Carrasco (2002) addresses these issues, and we outline some of her main findings in Section 8.1. Noting the difficulties of comparing non-linear and structural break models directly using classical techniques, Koop and Potter (2000) advocate a Bayesian approach.

In Section 8.2, we compare forecasts from a non-linear model with those from a structural break model.

8.1. *Testing for non-linearity and structural change*

The structural change (SC) and two non-linear regime-switching models can be cast in a common framework as

$$\begin{aligned} y_t = {} & (\mu_0 + \alpha_1 y_{t-1} + \cdots + \alpha_p y_{t-p}) \\ & + \left(\mu_0^* + \alpha_1^* y_{t-1} + \cdots + \alpha_p^* y_{t-p}\right) s_t + \varepsilon_t, \end{aligned} \tag{60}$$

where ε_t is $\mathsf{IID}[0, \sigma^2]$ and s_t is the indicator variable. When $s_t = 1$ $(t \geqslant \tau)$, we have an SC model in which potentially all the mean parameters undergo a one-off change at some exogenous date, τ. The first non-linear model is the Markov-switching model (MS). In the MS model, s_t is an unobservable and exogenously determined Markov chain. In the 2-regime case, s_t takes the values of 1 and 0, defined by the transition probabilities

$$p_{ij} = \Pr(s_{t+1} = j \mid s_t = i), \quad \sum_{j=0}^{1} p_{ij} = 1, \ \forall i, j \in \{0, 1\}. \tag{61}$$

The assumption of fixed transition probabilities p_{ij} can be relaxed [see, e.g., Diebold, Rudebusch and Sichel (1993), Diebold, Lee and Weinbach (1994), Filardo (1994), Lahiri and Wang (1994), and Durland and McCurdy (1994)] and the model can be generalized to allow more than two states [e.g., Clements and Krolzig (1998, 2003)].

The second non-linear model is a self-exciting threshold autoregressive model [SETAR; see, e.g., Tong (1983, 1995)] for which $s_t = 1_{(y_{t-d} \leqslant r)}$, where d is a posi-

[5] Pesaran, Pettenuzzo and Timmermann (2004) use a Bayesian approach to allow for structural breaks over the forecast period when a variable has been subject to a number of distinct regimes in the past. Longer horizon forecasts tend to be generated from parameters drawn from the 'meta distribution' rather than those that characterize the latest regime.

tive integer. That is, the regime depends on the value of the process d periods earlier relative to a threshold r.

In Section 5, we noted that testing for a structural break is complicated by the structural break date τ being unknown – the timing of the change is a nuisance parameter which is unidentified under the null that $[\mu_0^* \; \alpha_1^* \; \ldots \; \alpha_p^*]' = \mathbf{0}$. For both the MS and SETAR models, there are also nuisance parameters which are unidentified under the null of linearity. For the MS model, these are the transition probabilities $\{p_{ij}\}$, and for the SETAR model, the value of the threshold, r. Testing procedures for non-linear models against the null of linearity have been developed by Chan (1990, 1991), Hansen (1992, 1996a), Garcia (1998), and Hansen (1996b).

The main findings of Carrasco (2002) can be summarized as:

(a) Tests of SC will have no power when the process is stationary, as in the case of the MS and SETAR models [see Andrews (1993)] – this is demonstrated for the 'sup' tests.

(b) Tests of SETAR non-linearity will have asymptotic power of one when the process is SC or MS (or SETAR), but only power against local alternatives which are $T^{1/4}$, rather than the usual $T^{1/2}$.

Thus, tests of SC will not be useful in detecting parameter instability due to non-linearity, whilst testing for SETAR non-linearity might be viewed as a portmanteau pre-test of instability. Tests of SETAR non-linearity will not be able to detect small changes.

8.2. Non-linear model forecasts

Of the two non-linear models, only the MS model minimum MSFE predictor can be derived analytically, and we focus on forecasting with this model.[6] To make matters concrete, consider the original Hamilton (1989) model of the US business cycle. This posits a fourth-order ($p = 4$) autoregression for the quarterly percentage change in US real GNP $\{y_t\}$ from 1953 to 1984:

$$y_t - \mu(s_t) = \alpha_1\big(y_{t-1} - \mu(s_{t-1})\big) + \cdots + \alpha_4\big(y_{t-4} - \mu(s_{t-4})\big) + u_t, \tag{62}$$

where $\varepsilon_t \sim \mathsf{IN}[0, \sigma_\varepsilon^2]$ and

$$\mu(s_t) = \begin{cases} \mu_1 > 0 & \text{if } s_t = 1 \text{ ('expansion' or 'boom')}, \\ \mu_0 < 0 & \text{if } s_t = 0 \text{ ('contraction' or 'recession')}. \end{cases} \tag{63}$$

[6] Exact analytical solutions are not available for multi-period forecasts from SETAR models. Exact numerical solutions require sequences of numerical integrations [see, e.g., Tong (1995, §4.2.4 and §6.2)] based on the Chapman–Kolmogorov relation. As an alternative, one might use Monte Carlo or bootstrapping [e.g., Tiao and Tsay (1994) and Clements and Smith (1999)], particularly for high-order autoregressions, or the normal forecast-error method (NFE) suggested by Al-Qassam and Lane (1989) for the exponential-autoregressive model, and adapted by De Gooijer and De Bruin (1997) to forecasting with SETAR models. See also Chapter 8 by Teräsvirta in this Handbook.

Relative to (60), $[\alpha_1^* \ \dots \ \alpha_p^*] = \mathbf{0}$ so that the autoregressive dynamics are constant across regimes, and when $p = 0$ (no autoregressive dynamics) $\mu_0 + \mu_0^*$ in (60) is equal to μ_1. The model (62) has a switching mean rather than intercept, so that for $p > 0$ the correspondence between the two sets of 'deterministic' terms is more complicated. Maximum likelihood estimation of the model is by the EM algorithm [see Hamilton (1990)].[7]

To obtain the minimum MSFE h-step predictor, we take the conditional expectation of y_{T+h} given $\mathbf{Y}_T = \{y_T, y_{T-1}, \dots\}$. Letting $\hat{y}_{T+j|T} = \mathsf{E}[y_{T+j} \mid \mathbf{Y}_T]$ gives rise to the recursion

$$\hat{y}_{T+h|T} = \hat{\mu}_{T+h|T} + \sum_{k=1}^{4} \alpha_k (\hat{y}_{T+h-k|T} - \hat{\mu}_{T+h-k|T}) \tag{64}$$

with $\hat{y}_{T+h|T} = y_{T+h}$ for $h \leqslant 0$ and where the predicted mean is given by

$$\hat{\mu}_{T+h|T} = \sum_{j=1}^{2} \mu_j \Pr(s_{T+h} = j \mid \mathbf{Y}_T). \tag{65}$$

The predicted regime probabilities

$$\Pr(s_{T+h} = j \mid \mathbf{Y}_T) = \sum_{i=0}^{1} \Pr(s_{T+h} = j \mid s_T = i) \Pr(s_T = i \mid \mathbf{Y}_T)$$

only depend on the transition probabilities $\Pr(s_{T+h} = j \mid s_{T+h-1} = i) = p_{ij}, i, j = 0, 1$, and the filtered regime probabilities $\Pr(s_T = i \mid \mathbf{Y}_T)$ [see, e.g., Hamilton (1989, 1990, 1993, 1994) for details].

The optimal predictor of the MS-AR model is linear in the last p observations and the last regime inference. The optimal forecasting rule becomes linear in the limit when $\Pr(s_t \mid s_{t-1}) = \Pr(s_t)$ for $s_t, s_{t-1} = 0, 1$, since then $\Pr(s_{T+h} = j \mid \mathbf{Y}_T) = \Pr(s_t = j)$ and from (65), $\hat{\mu}_{T+h} = \mu_y$, the unconditional mean of y_t. Then

$$\hat{y}_{T+h|T} = \mu_y + \sum_{k=1}^{4} \alpha_k (\hat{y}_{T+h-k|T} - \mu_y), \tag{66}$$

so to a first approximation, apart from differences arising from parameter estimation, forecasts will match those from linear autoregressive models.

Further insight can be obtained by writing the MS process $y_t - \mu(s_t)$ as the sum of two independent processes:

$$y_t - \mu_y = \mu_t + z_t,$$

[7] The EM algorithm of Dempster, Laird and Rubin (1977) is used because the observable time series depends on the s_t, which are unobservable stochastic variables.

such that $\mathsf{E}[\mu_t] = \mathsf{E}[z_t] = 0$. Assuming $p = 1$ for convenience, z_t is

$$z_t = \alpha z_{t-1} + \epsilon_t, \quad \epsilon_t \sim \mathsf{IN}\big[0, \sigma_\epsilon^2\big],$$

a linear autoregression with Gaussian disturbances. μ_t represents the contribution of the Markov chain:

$$\mu_t = (\mu_2 - \mu_1)\zeta_t,$$

where $\zeta_t = 1 - \Pr(s_t = 0)$ if $s_t = 0$ and $-\Pr(s_t = 0)$ otherwise. $\Pr(s_t = 0) = p_{10}/(p_{10} + p_{01})$ is the unconditional probability of regime 0. Using the autoregressive representation of a Markov chain:

$$\zeta_t = (p_{11} + p_{00} - 1)\zeta_{t-1} + v_t,$$

then predictions of the hidden Markov chain are given by

$$\hat{\zeta}_{T+h|T} = (p_{11} + p_{00} - 1)^h \hat{\zeta}_{T|T},$$

where $\hat{\zeta}_{T|T} = \mathsf{E}[\zeta_T \mid \mathbf{Y}_T] = \Pr(s_T = 0 \mid \mathbf{Y}_T) - \Pr(s_T = 0)$ is the filtered probability $\Pr(s_T = 0 \mid \mathbf{Y}_T)$ of being in regime 0 corrected for the unconditional probability. Thus $\hat{y}_{T+h|T} - \mu_y$ can be written as

$$\begin{aligned}
\hat{y}_{T+h|T} - \mu_y &= \hat{\mu}_{T+h|T} + \hat{z}_{T+h|T} \\
&= (\mu_0 - \mu_1)(p_{00} + p_{11} - 1)^h \hat{\zeta}_{T|T} \\
&\quad + \alpha^h\big[y_T - \mu_y - (\mu_0 - \mu_1)\hat{\zeta}_{T|T}\big] \\
&= \alpha^h(y_T - \mu_y) + (\mu_0 - \mu_1)\big[(p_{00} + p_{11} - 1)^h - \alpha^h\big]\hat{\zeta}_{T|T}. \qquad (67)
\end{aligned}$$

This expression shows how the difference between the MS model forecasts and forecasts from a linear model depends on a number of characteristics such as the persistence of $\{s_t\}$. Specifically, the first term is the optimal prediction rule for a linear model. The contribution of the Markov regime-switching structure is given by the term multiplied by $\hat{\zeta}_{T|T}$, where $\hat{\zeta}_{T|T}$ contains the information about the most recent regime at the time the forecast is made. Thus, the contribution of the non-linear part of (67) to the overall forecast depends on both the magnitude of the regime shifts, $|\mu_0 - \mu_1|$, and on the persistence of regime shifts $p_{00} + p_{11} - 1$ relative to the persistence of the Gaussian process, given by α.

8.3. Empirical evidence

There are a large number of studies comparing the forecast performance of linear and non-linear models. There is little evidence for the superiority of non-linear models across the board. For example, Stock and Watson (1999) compare smooth-transition models [see, e.g., Teräsvirta (1994)], neural nets [e.g., White (1992)], and linear autoregressive models for 215 US macro time series, and find mixed evidence – the non-linear models sometimes record small gains at short horizons, but at longer horizons the linear models are preferred. Swanson and White (1997) forecast nine US macro series using a variety of fixed-specification linear and non-linear models, as well as flexible specifications of these which allow the specification to vary as the in-sample period is extended. They find little improvement from allowing for non-linearity within the flexible-specification approach.

Other studies focus on a few series, of which US output growth is one of the most popular. For example, Potter (1995) and Tiao and Tsay (1994) find that the forecast performance of the SETAR model relative to a linear model is markedly improved when the comparison is made in terms of how well the models forecast when the economy is in recession. The reason is easily understood. Since a majority of the sample data points (approximately 78%) fall in the upper regime, the linear AR(2) model will be largely determined by these points, and will closely match the upper-regime SETAR model. Thus the forecast performance of the two models will be broadly similar when the economy is in the expansionary phase of the business cycle. However, to the extent that the data points in the lower regime are characterized by a different process, there will be gains to the SETAR model during the contractionary phase.

Clements and Krolzig (1998) use (67) to explain why MS models of post war US output growth [such as those of Hamilton (1989)] do not forecast markedly more accurately than linear autoregressions. Namely, they find that $p_{00} + p_{11} - 1 = 0.65$ in their study, and that the largest root of the AR polynomial is 0.64. Because $p_{00} + p_{11} - 1 \simeq \alpha$ in (67), the conditional expectation collapses to a linear prediction rule.

9. Forecasting UK unemployment after three crises

The times at which causal-model based forecasts are most valuable are when considerable change occurs. Unfortunately, that is precisely when causal models are most likely to suffer forecast failure, and robust forecasting devices to outperform, at least relatively. We are not suggesting that prior to any major change, some methods are better at anticipating such shifts, nor that anyone could forecast the unpredictable: what we are concerned with is that even some time after a shift, many model types, in particular members of the equilibrium-correction class, will systematically mis-forecast.

To highlight this property, we consider three salient periods, namely the post-world-war double-decades of 1919–1938 and 1948–1967, and the post oil-crisis double-decade 1975–1994, to examine forecasts of the UK unemployment rate (denoted $U_{r,t}$). Figure 1 records the historical time-series of $U_{r,t}$ from 1875 to 2001 within which our three episodes lie. The data are discussed in detail in Hendry (2001), and the 'structural' equation for unemployment is taken from that paper.

The dramatically different epochs pre World War I (panel a), inter war (b), post World War II (c), and post the oil crisis (d) are obvious visually as each panel unfolds. In (b) there is an upward mean shift in 1920–1940. Panel (c) shows a downward mean shift and lower variance for 1940–1980. In the last panel there is an upward mean shift and higher

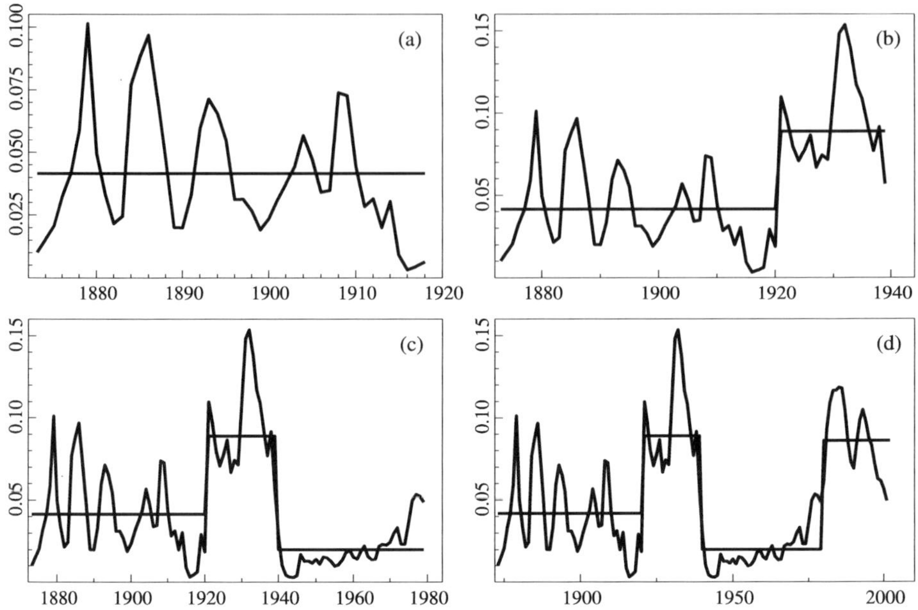

Figure 1. Shifts in unemployment.

variance from 1980 onwards. The unemployment rate time series seems distinctly non-stationary from shifts in both mean and variance at different times, but equally does not seem to have a unit root, albeit there is considerable persistence. Figure 2a records the changes in the unemployment rate.

The difficulty in forecasting after the three breaks is only partly because the preceding empirical evidence offers little guidance as to the subsequent behavior of the time series at each episode, since some 'naive' methods do not have great problems after breaks. Rather, it is the lack of adaptability of a forecasting device which seems to be the culprit.

The model derives the disequilibrium unemployment rate (denoted U_t^d) as a positive function of the difference between $U_{r,t}$ and the real interest rate $(R_{l,t} - \Delta p_t)$ minus the real growth rate (Δy_t). Then $U_{r,t}$ and $(R_{l,t} - \Delta p_t - \Delta y_t) = R_t^r$ are 'cointegrated' [using the PcGive test, $t_c = -3.9^{**}$; see Banerjee and Hendry (1992) and Ericsson and MacKinnon (2002)], or more probably, co-breaking [see Clements and Hendry (1999) and Hendry and Massmann (2006)]. Figure 2b plots the time series of R_t^r. The derived excess-demand for labor measure, U_t^d, is the long-run solution from an AD(2, 1) of $U_{r,t}$ on R_t^r with $\hat{\sigma} = 0.012$, namely,

$$U_t^d = U_{r,t} - \underset{(0.01)}{0.05} - \underset{(0.22)}{0.82} R_t^r, \qquad (68)$$

$$T = 1875\text{–}2001.$$

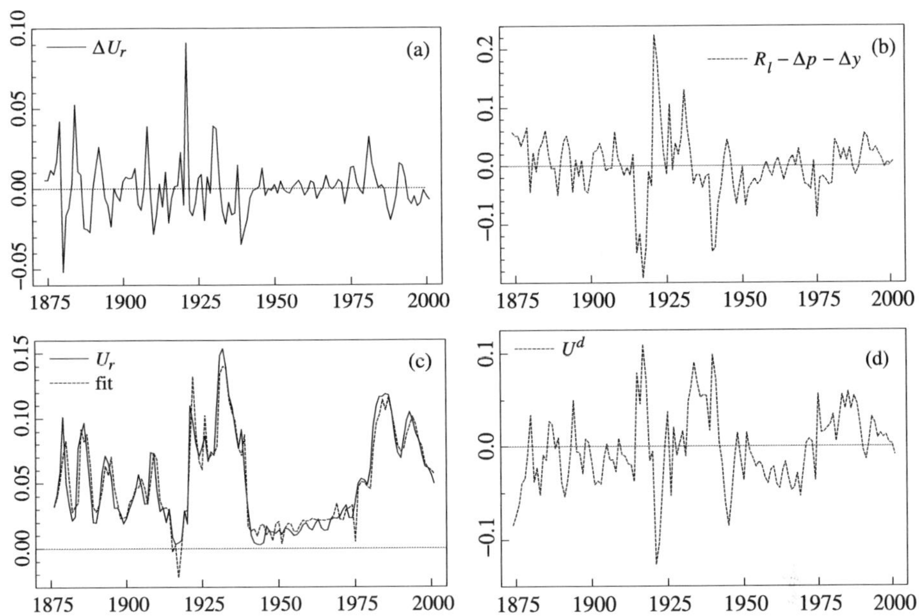

Figure 2. Unemployment with fitted values, $(R_{l,t} - \Delta p_t - \Delta y_t)$, and excess demand for labor.

The derived mean equilibrium unemployment is slightly above the historical sample average of 4.8%. U_t^d is recorded in Figure 2d.

Technically, given (68), a forecasting model for $U_{r,t}$ becomes a four-dimensional system for $U_{r,t}$, $R_{l,t}$, Δp_t, and Δy_t, but these in turn depend on other variables, rapidly leading to a large system. Instead, since the primary interest is illustrating forecasts from the equation for unemployment, we have chosen just to model $U_{r,t}$ and R_t^r as a bivariate VAR, with the restrictions implied by that formulation. That system was converted to an equilibrium-correction model (VECM) with the long-run solution given by (68) and $R^r = 0$. The full-sample FIML estimates from PcGive [see Hendry and Doornik (2001)] till 1991 were

$$\begin{aligned}
\Delta U_{r,t} &= \underset{(0.07)}{0.24}\Delta R_t^r - \underset{(0.037)}{0.14}U_{t-1}^d + \underset{(0.078)}{0.16}\Delta U_{r,t-1},\\
\Delta R_t^r &= -\underset{(0.077)}{0.43}R_{t-1}^r,\\
\hat{\sigma}_{U_r} &= 1.27\%, \quad \hat{\sigma}_{R^r} = 4.65\%, \quad T = 1875\text{–}1991,\\
\chi^2_{\text{nd}}(4) &= 76.2^{**}, \quad \mathsf{F}_{\text{ar}}(8, 218) = 0.81, \quad \mathsf{F}_{\text{het}}(27, 298) = 1.17.
\end{aligned} \tag{69}$$

In (69), $\hat{\sigma}$ denotes the residual standard deviation, and coefficient standard errors are shown in parentheses. The diagnostic tests are of the form $\mathsf{F}_j(k, T - l)$ which denotes an approximate F-test against the alternative hypothesis j for: second-order vector serial correlation [F_{ar}, see Guilkey (1974)] vector heteroskedasticity [$\mathsf{F}_{\mathrm{het}}$, see White (1980)]; and a chi-squared test for joint normality [$\chi^2_{\mathrm{nd}}(4)$, see Doornik and Hansen (1994)]. $*$ and $**$ denote significance at the 5% and 1% levels, respectively. All coefficients are significant with sensible signs and magnitudes, and the first equation is close to the OLS estimated model used in Hendry (2001). The likelihood ratio test of over-identifying restrictions of the VECM against the initial VAR yielded $\chi^2_{\mathrm{Id}}(8) = 2.09$. Figure 2c records the fitted values from the dynamic model in (69).

9.1. Forecasting 1992–2001

We begin with genuine ex ante forecasts. Since the model was selected from the sample $T = 1875$–1991, there are 10 new annual observations available since publication that can be used for forecast evaluation. This decade is picked purely because it is the last; there was in fact one major event, albeit not quite on the scale of the other three episodes to be considered, namely the ejection of the UK from the exchange rate mechanism (ERM) in the autumn of 1992, just at the forecast origin. Nevertheless, by historical standards the period transpired to be benign, and almost any method would have avoided forecast failure over this sample, including those considered here. In fact, the 1-step forecast test over 10 periods for (69), denoted $\mathsf{F}_{\mathrm{Chow}}$ [see Chow (1960)], delivered $\mathsf{F}_{\mathrm{Chow}}(20, 114) = 0.15$, consistent with parameter constancy over the post-selection decade. Figure 3 shows the graphical output for 1-step and 10-step forecasts

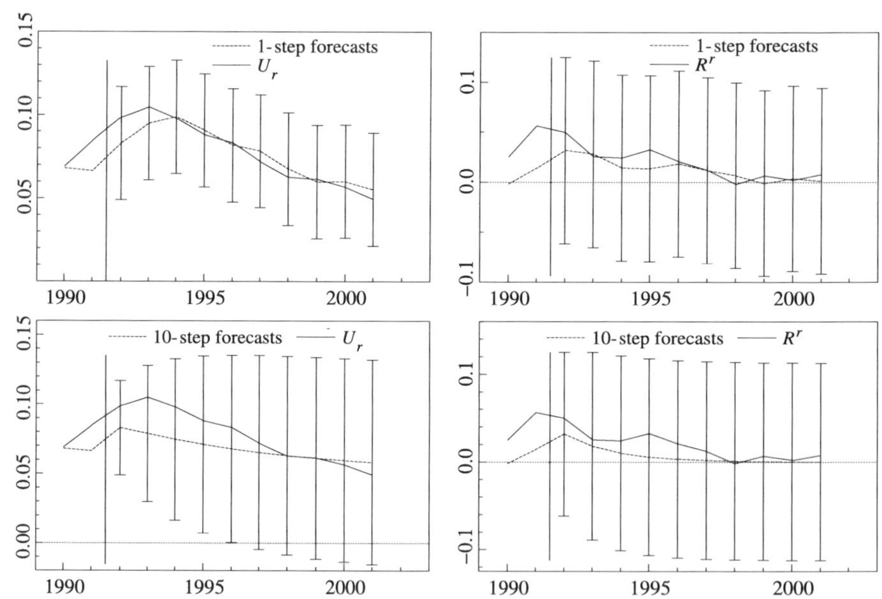

Figure 3. VECM 1-step and 10-step forecasts of $U_{r,t}$ and R^r_t, 1992–2001.

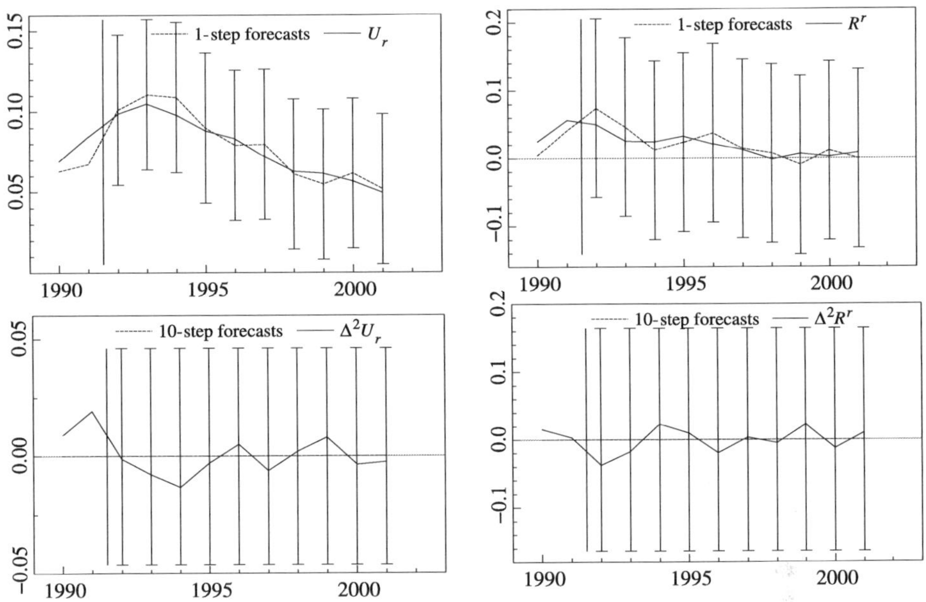

Figure 4. DVECM 1-step forecasts of $U_{r,t}$, R_t^r, and 10-step forecasts of $\Delta^2 U_{r,t}$, $\Delta^2 R_t^r$, 1992–2001.

of $U_{r,t}$ and R_t^r over 1992–2001. As can be seen, all the outcomes lie well inside the interval forecasts (shown as $\pm 2\hat{\sigma}_f$) for both sets of forecasts. Notice the equilibrium-correction behavior manifest in the 10-step forecasts, as U_r converges to 0.05 and R^r to 0: such must occur, independently of the outcomes for $U_{r,t}$ and R_t^r.

On all these criteria, the outcome is successful on the out-of-selection-sample evaluation. While far from definitive, as shown in Clements and Hendry (2005), these results demonstrate that the model merits its more intensive scrutiny over the three salient historical episodes.

By way of comparison, we also record the corresponding forecasts from the differenced models discussed in Section 7.3. First, we consider the VECM (denoted DVECM) which maintains the parameter estimates, but differences all the variables [see Hendry (2005)]. Figure 4 shows the graphical output for 1-step forecasts of $U_{r,t}$ and R_t^r and the 10-step forecasts of $\Delta^2 U_{r,t}$ and $\Delta^2 R_t^r$ over 1992–2001 (throughout, the interval forecasts for multi-step forecasts from mis-specified models are not adjusted for the – unknown – mis-specification). In fact, there was little discernible difference between the forecasts produced by the DVECM and those from a double-difference VAR [DDVAR, see Clements and Hendry (1999) and Section 7.3].

The 1-step forecasts are close to those from the VECM, but the entailed multi-step levels forecasts from the DVECM are poor, as the rise in unemployment prior to the forecast origin turns to a fall throughout the remainder of the period, but the forecasts continue to rise: there is no free lunch when insuring against forecast failure.

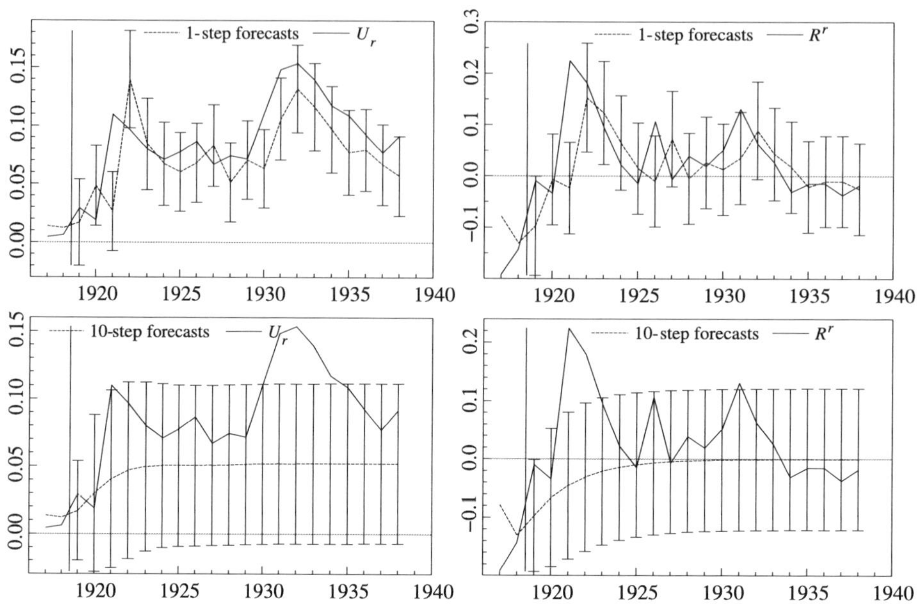

Figure 5. VECM 1-step and 10-step forecasts of $U_{r,t}$ and R_t^r, 1919–1938.

9.2. *Forecasting 1919–1938*

Over this sample, $\mathsf{F}_{\text{Chow}}(40, 41) = 2.81^{**}$, strongly rejecting the model re-estimated, but not re-selected, up to 1918. The graphs in Figure 5 confirm the forecast failure, for both 1-step and 10-step forecasts of $U_{r,t}$ and R_t^r. As well as missing the post-World-War I dramatic rise in unemployment, there is systematic under-forecasting throughout the Great Depression period, consistent with failing to forecast the substantial increase in R_t^r on both occasions. Nevertheless, the results are far from catastrophic in the face of such a large, systematic, and historically unprecedented, rise in unemployment.

Again using our comparator of the DVECM, Figure 6 shows the 1-step forecasts, with a longer historical sample to highlight the substantial forecast-period change (the entailed multi-step levels' forecasts are poor). Despite the noticeable level shift in $U_{r,t}$, the differenced model forecasts are only a little better initially, overshooting badly after the initial rise, but perform well over the Great Depression, which is forecasting long after the earlier break. $\mathsf{F}_{\text{Chow}}(40, 42) = 2.12^{**}$ is slightly smaller overall despite the initial 'bounce'.

9.3. *Forecasting 1948–1967*

The model copes well with the post-World-War II low level of unemployment, with $\mathsf{F}_{\text{Chow}}(40, 70) = 0.16$, with the outcomes shown in Figure 7. However, there is sys-

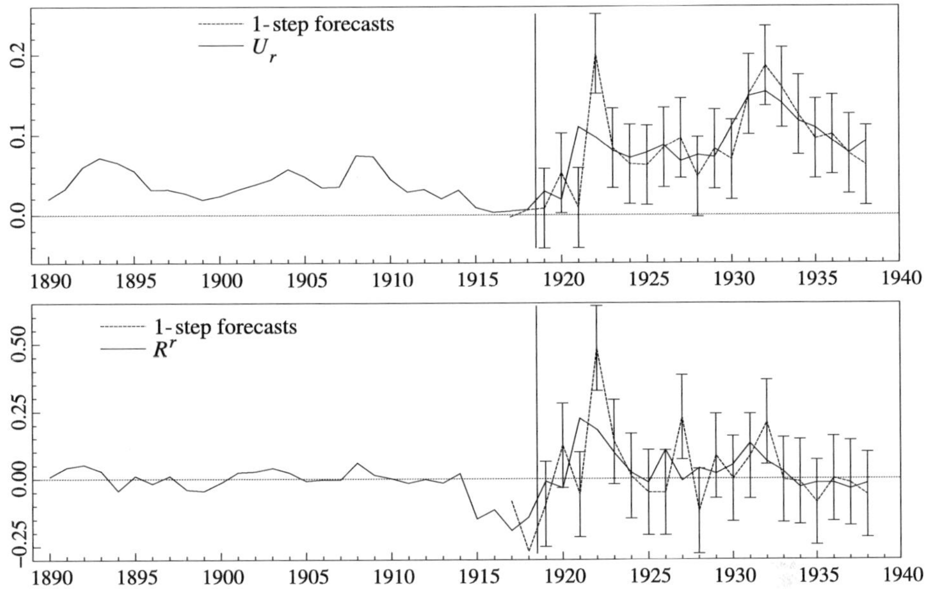

Figure 6. DVECM 1-step forecasts of $U_{r,t}$ and R_t^r, 1919–1938.

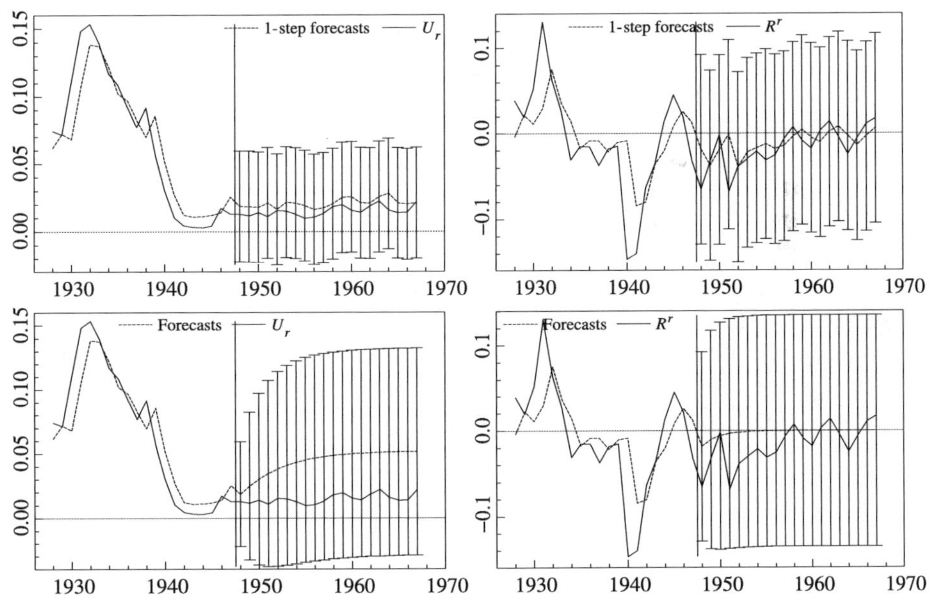

Figure 7. VECM 1-step and 10-step forecasts of $U_{r,t}$ and R_t^r, 1948–1967.

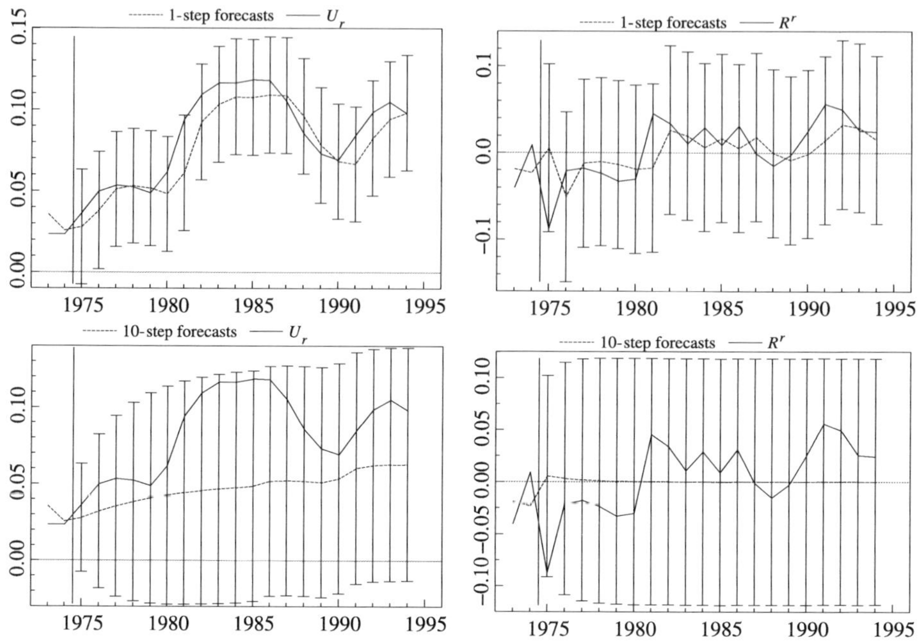

Figure 8. VECM 1-step and 10-step forecasts of $U_{r,t}$ and R_t^r, 1975–1994.

tematic over-forecasting of the level of unemployment, unsurprisingly given its exceptionally low level. The graph here emphasizes the equilibrium-correction behavior of U_r converging to 0.05 even though the outcome is now centered around 1.5%. The DVECM delivers $\mathsf{F}_{\text{Chow}}(40, 71) = 0.12$ so is closely similar. The forecasts are also little different, although the forecast intervals are somewhat wider.

9.4. *Forecasting 1975–1994*

Finally, after the first oil crisis, we find $\mathsf{F}_{\text{Chow}}(40, 97) = 0.61$, so surprisingly no forecast failure results, although the outcomes are poor as Figure 8 shows for both 1-step and 10-step forecasts of $U_{r,t}$ and R_t^r. There is systematic under-forecasting of the level of unemployment, but the trend is correctly discerned as upwards. Over this period, $\mathsf{F}_{\text{Chow}}(40, 98) = 0.53$ for the DVECM, so again there is little impact from removing the equilibrium-correction term.

9.5. *Overview*

Despite the manifest non-stationarity of the UK unemployment rate over the last century and a quarter, with location and variance shifts evident in the historical data, the empirical forecasting models considered here only suffered forecast failure occasionally, although they were often systematically adrift, under- or over-forecasting. The differenced VECM did not perform much better even when the VECM failed. A possible explanation may be the absence of deterministic components from the VECM in (69) other than that embedded in the long-run for unemployment. Since $\hat{\sigma}_{U_r} = 1.27\%$, a 95% forecast interval spans just over 5% points of unemployment so larger shifts are needed to reject the model.

It is difficult to imagine how well real-time forecasting might have performed historically: the large rise in unemployment during 1919–1920 seems to have been unanticipated at the time, and induced real hardship, leading to considerable social unrest. Conversely, while the Beveridge Report (Social Insurance and Allied Services, HMSO, 1942, followed by his Full Employment in a Free Society and The Economics of Full Employment, both in 1944) essentially mandated UK Governments to keep a low level of unemployment using Keynesian policies, nevertheless the outturn of 1.5% on average over 1946–1966 was unprecedented. And the Thatcher reforms of 1979 led to an unexpectedly large upturn in unemployment, commensurate with inter-war levels. Since the historical period delivered many unanticipated 'structural breaks', across many very different policy regimes (from the Gold Standard, floating, Bretton Woods currency pegs, back to a 'dirty' floating – just to note exchange-rate regimes), overall, the forecasting performance of the unemployment model considered here is really quite creditable.

10. Concluding remarks

Structural breaks in the form of unforeseen location shifts are likely to lead to systematic forecast biases. Other factors matter, as shown in the various taxonomies of forecast errors above, but breaks play a dominant role. The vast majority of forecasting models in regular use are members of the equilibrium-correction class, including VARs, VECMs, and DSGEs, as well as many popular models of conditional variance processes. Other types of models might be more robust to breaks. We have also noted issues to do with the choice of estimation sample, and the updating of the models' parameter estimates and of the model specification, as possible ways of mitigating the effects of some types of breaks. Some ad hoc forecasting devices exhibit greater adaptability than standard models, which may account for their successes in empirical forecasting competitions. Finally, we have contrasted non-constancies due to breaks with those due to non-linearities.

Appendix A: Taxonomy derivations for Equation (10)

We let $\boldsymbol{\delta}_{\varphi} = \hat{\boldsymbol{\varphi}} - \boldsymbol{\varphi}_p$, where $\boldsymbol{\varphi}_p = (\mathbf{I}_n - \boldsymbol{\Pi}_p)^{-1}\boldsymbol{\phi}_p$, $\boldsymbol{\delta}_{\Pi} = \widehat{\boldsymbol{\Pi}} - \boldsymbol{\Pi}_p$, and $\hat{\mathbf{y}}_T - \mathbf{y}_T = \boldsymbol{\delta}_y$.

First, we use the approximation:

$$\widehat{\boldsymbol{\Pi}}^h = (\boldsymbol{\Pi}_p + \boldsymbol{\delta}_{\Pi})^h \simeq \boldsymbol{\Pi}_p^h + \sum_{i=0}^{h-1} \boldsymbol{\Pi}_p^i \boldsymbol{\delta}_{\Pi} \boldsymbol{\Pi}_p^{h-i-1} \doteq \boldsymbol{\Pi}_p^h + \mathbf{C}_h. \tag{A.1}$$

Let $(\cdot)^\nu$ denote a vectorizing operator which stacks the columns of an $m \times n$ matrix $\mathbf{A}$ in an $mn \times 1$ vector $\mathbf{a}$, after which $(\mathbf{a})^\nu = \mathbf{a}$. Also, let $\otimes$ be the associated Kronecker product, so that when $\mathbf{B}$ is $p \times q$, then $\mathbf{A} \otimes \mathbf{B}$ is an $mp \times nq$ matrix of the form $\{b_{ij}\mathbf{A}\}$. Consequently, when $\mathbf{ABC}$ is defined,

$$(\mathbf{ABC})^\nu = \left(\mathbf{A} \otimes \mathbf{C}'\right)\mathbf{B}^\nu.$$

Using these, from (A.1),

$$\begin{aligned}\mathbf{C}_h(\mathbf{y}_T - \boldsymbol{\varphi}_p) &= \left(\mathbf{C}_h(\mathbf{y}_T - \boldsymbol{\varphi}_p)\right)^\nu \\ &= \left(\sum_{i=0}^{h-1} \boldsymbol{\Pi}_p^i \otimes (\mathbf{y}_T - \boldsymbol{\varphi}_p)'\boldsymbol{\Pi}_p^{h-i-1\prime}\right)\boldsymbol{\delta}_\Pi^\nu \\ &\triangleq \mathbf{F}_h\boldsymbol{\delta}_\Pi^\nu. \end{aligned} \tag{A.2}$$

To highlight components due to different effects (parameter change, estimation inconsistency, and estimation uncertainty), we decompose the term $(\boldsymbol{\Pi}^*)^h(\mathbf{y}_T - \boldsymbol{\varphi}^*)$ into

$$\left(\boldsymbol{\Pi}^*\right)^h\left(\mathbf{y}_T - \boldsymbol{\varphi}^*\right) = \left(\boldsymbol{\Pi}^*\right)^h(\mathbf{y}_T - \boldsymbol{\varphi}) + \left(\boldsymbol{\Pi}^*\right)^h\left(\boldsymbol{\varphi} - \boldsymbol{\varphi}^*\right),$$

whereas $\widehat{\boldsymbol{\Pi}}^h(\hat{\mathbf{y}}_T - \hat{\boldsymbol{\varphi}})$ equals

$$\begin{aligned}&\left(\boldsymbol{\Pi}_p^h + \mathbf{C}_h\right)\boldsymbol{\delta}_y - (\hat{\boldsymbol{\varphi}} - \boldsymbol{\varphi}_p) + (\mathbf{y}_T - \boldsymbol{\varphi}_p) \\ &\quad = \left(\boldsymbol{\Pi}_p^h + \mathbf{C}_h\right)\boldsymbol{\delta}_y - \left(\boldsymbol{\Pi}_p^h + \mathbf{C}_h\right)\boldsymbol{\delta}_\varphi + \left(\boldsymbol{\Pi}_p^h + \mathbf{C}_h\right)(\mathbf{y}_T - \boldsymbol{\varphi}_p) \\ &\quad \triangleq \left(\boldsymbol{\Pi}_p^h + \mathbf{C}_h\right)\boldsymbol{\delta}_y - \left(\boldsymbol{\Pi}_p^h + \mathbf{C}_h\right)\boldsymbol{\delta}_\varphi + \mathbf{F}_h\boldsymbol{\delta}_\Pi^\nu + \boldsymbol{\Pi}_p^h(\mathbf{y}_T - \boldsymbol{\varphi}) - \boldsymbol{\Pi}_p^h(\boldsymbol{\varphi}_p - \boldsymbol{\varphi}).\end{aligned}$$

Thus, $(\boldsymbol{\Pi}^*)^h(\mathbf{y}_T - \boldsymbol{\varphi}^*) - \widehat{\boldsymbol{\Pi}}^h(\hat{\mathbf{y}}_T - \hat{\boldsymbol{\varphi}})$ yields

$$\begin{aligned}&\left(\left(\boldsymbol{\Pi}^*\right)^h - \boldsymbol{\Pi}_p^h\right)(\mathbf{y}_T - \boldsymbol{\varphi}) - \mathbf{F}_h\boldsymbol{\delta}_\Pi^\nu - \left(\boldsymbol{\Pi}_p^h + \mathbf{C}_h\right)\boldsymbol{\delta}_y \\ &\quad - \left(\boldsymbol{\Pi}^*\right)^h\left(\boldsymbol{\varphi}^* - \boldsymbol{\varphi}\right) + \boldsymbol{\Pi}_p^h(\boldsymbol{\varphi}_p - \boldsymbol{\varphi}) + \left(\boldsymbol{\Pi}_p^h + \mathbf{C}_h\right)\boldsymbol{\delta}_\varphi.\end{aligned} \tag{A.3}$$

The interaction $\mathbf{C}_h\boldsymbol{\delta}_\varphi$ is like a 'covariance', but is omitted from the table. Hence (A.3) becomes

$$\begin{aligned}&\left(\left(\boldsymbol{\Pi}^*\right)^h - \boldsymbol{\Pi}^h\right)(\mathbf{y}_T - \boldsymbol{\varphi}) + \left(\boldsymbol{\Pi}^h - \boldsymbol{\Pi}_p^h\right)(\mathbf{y}_T - \boldsymbol{\varphi}) \\ &\quad - \left(\boldsymbol{\Pi}^*\right)^h\left(\boldsymbol{\varphi}^* - \boldsymbol{\varphi}\right) + \boldsymbol{\Pi}_p^h(\boldsymbol{\varphi}_p - \boldsymbol{\varphi}) \\ &\quad - \left(\boldsymbol{\Pi}_p^h + \mathbf{C}_h\right)\boldsymbol{\delta}_y - \mathbf{F}_h\boldsymbol{\delta}_\Pi^\nu + \boldsymbol{\Pi}_p^h\boldsymbol{\delta}_\varphi.\end{aligned}$$

The first and third rows have expectations of zero, so the second row collects the 'non-central' terms.

Finally, for the term $\boldsymbol{\varphi}^* - \hat{\boldsymbol{\varphi}}$ we have (on the same principle):

$$\left(\boldsymbol{\varphi}^* - \boldsymbol{\varphi}\right) + (\boldsymbol{\varphi} - \boldsymbol{\varphi}_p) - \boldsymbol{\delta}_\varphi.$$

Appendix B: Derivations for Section 4.3

Since $\boldsymbol{\Upsilon} = \mathbf{I}_n + \boldsymbol{\alpha\beta}'$, for $j > 0$,

$$\boldsymbol{\Upsilon}^j = (\mathbf{I}_n + \boldsymbol{\alpha\beta}')^j = \boldsymbol{\Upsilon}^{j-1}(\mathbf{I}_n + \boldsymbol{\alpha\beta}') = \boldsymbol{\Upsilon}^{j-1} + \boldsymbol{\Upsilon}^{j-1}\boldsymbol{\alpha\beta}' = \cdots$$
$$= \mathbf{I}_n + \sum_{i=0}^{j-1} \boldsymbol{\Upsilon}^i \boldsymbol{\alpha\beta}', \tag{B.1}$$

so

$$(\boldsymbol{\Upsilon}^j - \mathbf{I}_n) = \sum_{i=0}^{j-1} \boldsymbol{\Upsilon}^i \boldsymbol{\alpha\beta}' = \mathbf{A}_j \boldsymbol{\alpha\beta}' \tag{B.2}$$

defines $\mathbf{A}_j = \sum_{i=0}^{j-1} \boldsymbol{\Upsilon}^i$. Thus,

$$\mathsf{E}[(\boldsymbol{\Upsilon}^j - \mathbf{I}_n)\mathbf{w}_T] = \mathbf{A}_j \boldsymbol{\alpha} \mathsf{E}[\boldsymbol{\beta}'\mathbf{x}_T] = \mathbf{A}_j \boldsymbol{\alpha} \boldsymbol{f}_T, \tag{B.3}$$

where $\mathbf{f}_T = \mathsf{E}[\boldsymbol{\beta}'\mathbf{x}_T] = \boldsymbol{\mu}_0^a + \boldsymbol{\beta}'\boldsymbol{\gamma}^a(T+1)$, say, where the values of $\boldsymbol{\mu}_0^a = \boldsymbol{\mu}_0$ and $\boldsymbol{\gamma}^a = \boldsymbol{\gamma}$ if the change occurs after period T, and $\boldsymbol{\mu}_0^a = \boldsymbol{\mu}_0^*$ and $\boldsymbol{\gamma}^a = \boldsymbol{\gamma}^*$ if the change occurs before period T.

Substituting from (B.3) into (34):

$$\mathsf{E}[\tilde{\boldsymbol{\nu}}_{T+j}] = \sum_{i=0}^{j-1} \boldsymbol{\Upsilon}^i [\boldsymbol{\gamma}^* - \boldsymbol{\alpha\mu}_0^* - \boldsymbol{\alpha\mu}_1^*(T+j-i)] - j\boldsymbol{\gamma} + \mathbf{A}_j \boldsymbol{\alpha} \boldsymbol{f}_T. \tag{B.4}$$

From (B.1), as $\boldsymbol{\Upsilon}^i = \mathbf{I}_n + \mathbf{A}_i \boldsymbol{\alpha\beta}'$,

$$\mathbf{A}_j = \sum_{k=0}^{j-1} \boldsymbol{\Upsilon}^k = \sum_{k=0}^{j-1} (\mathbf{I}_n + \mathbf{A}_k \boldsymbol{\alpha\beta}') = j\mathbf{I}_n + \left(\sum_{k=0}^{j-1} \mathbf{A}_k\right)\boldsymbol{\alpha\beta}' = j\mathbf{I}_n + \mathbf{B}_j \boldsymbol{\alpha\beta}'. \tag{B.5}$$

Thus from (B.4), since $\boldsymbol{\beta}'\boldsymbol{\gamma} = \boldsymbol{\mu}_1$ and $\boldsymbol{\beta}'\boldsymbol{\gamma}^* = \boldsymbol{\mu}_1^*$,

$$\begin{aligned}
\mathsf{E}[\tilde{\boldsymbol{\nu}}_{T+j}] &= \mathbf{A}_j\boldsymbol{\gamma}^* - \mathbf{A}_j\boldsymbol{\alpha\mu}_0^* - \mathbf{A}_j\boldsymbol{\alpha\beta}'\boldsymbol{\gamma}^*(T+j) + \sum_{i=1}^{j-1} i\boldsymbol{\Upsilon}^i\boldsymbol{\alpha\beta}'\boldsymbol{\gamma}^* - j\boldsymbol{\gamma} \\
&\quad + \mathbf{A}_j\boldsymbol{\alpha}\boldsymbol{f}_T \\
&= j(\boldsymbol{\gamma}^* - \boldsymbol{\gamma}) + \mathbf{A}_j\boldsymbol{\alpha}\boldsymbol{f}_T - \boldsymbol{\mu}_0^* - \boldsymbol{\beta}'\boldsymbol{\gamma}^*T \\
&\quad + \left(\sum_{i=1}^{j-1} i\boldsymbol{\Upsilon}^i - j\mathbf{A}_j + \mathbf{B}_j\right)\boldsymbol{\alpha\beta}'\boldsymbol{\gamma}^* \\
&= j(\boldsymbol{\gamma}^* - \boldsymbol{\gamma}) + \mathbf{A}_j\boldsymbol{\alpha}(\boldsymbol{\mu}_0^a - \boldsymbol{\mu}_0^* - \boldsymbol{\beta}'[\boldsymbol{\gamma}^* - \boldsymbol{\gamma}^a](T+1)) \\
&\quad + \mathbf{C}_j\boldsymbol{\alpha\beta}'\boldsymbol{\gamma}^*,
\end{aligned} \tag{B.6}$$

where $\mathbf{C}_j = (\mathbf{D}_j + \mathbf{B}_j - (j-1)\mathbf{A}_j)$ when $\mathbf{D}_j = \sum_{i=1}^{j-1} i\boldsymbol{\Upsilon}^i$. However, $\mathbf{C}_j\boldsymbol{\alpha}\boldsymbol{\beta}' = \mathbf{0}$ as follows. Since $\boldsymbol{\Upsilon}^j = \mathbf{I}_n + \mathbf{A}_j\boldsymbol{\alpha}\boldsymbol{\beta}'$ from (B.2), then

$$j\mathbf{A}_j\boldsymbol{\alpha}\boldsymbol{\beta}' = j\boldsymbol{\Upsilon}^j - j\mathbf{I}_n,$$

and so eliminating $j\mathbf{I}_n$ using (B.5):

$$(\mathbf{B}_j - j\mathbf{A}_j)\boldsymbol{\alpha}\boldsymbol{\beta}' = \mathbf{A}_j - j\boldsymbol{\Upsilon}^j.$$

Also,

$$\mathbf{D}_j = \sum_{i=1}^{j} i\boldsymbol{\Upsilon}^i - j\boldsymbol{\Upsilon}^j = \sum_{i=1}^{j} \boldsymbol{\Upsilon}^i - j\boldsymbol{\Upsilon}^j + \left(\sum_{i=1}^{j-1} i\boldsymbol{\Upsilon}^i\right)\boldsymbol{\Upsilon} = \mathbf{A}_j\boldsymbol{\Upsilon} - j\boldsymbol{\Upsilon}^j + \mathbf{D}_j\boldsymbol{\Upsilon}.$$

Since $\boldsymbol{\Upsilon} = \mathbf{I}_n + \boldsymbol{\alpha}\boldsymbol{\beta}'$,

$$\mathbf{D}_j\boldsymbol{\alpha}\boldsymbol{\beta}' = j\boldsymbol{\Upsilon}^j - \mathbf{A}_j - \mathbf{A}_j\boldsymbol{\alpha}\boldsymbol{\beta}'.$$

Combining these results,

$$\begin{aligned}\mathbf{C}_j\boldsymbol{\alpha}\boldsymbol{\beta}' &= \big(\mathbf{D}_j + \mathbf{B}_j - (j-1)\mathbf{A}_j\big)\boldsymbol{\alpha}\boldsymbol{\beta}' \\ &= j\boldsymbol{\Upsilon}^j - \mathbf{A}_j - \mathbf{A}_j\boldsymbol{\alpha}\boldsymbol{\beta}' + \mathbf{A}_j - j\boldsymbol{\Upsilon}^j + \mathbf{A}_j\boldsymbol{\alpha}\boldsymbol{\beta}' = \mathbf{0}.\end{aligned} \tag{B.7}$$

References

Al-Qassam, M.S., Lane, J.A. (1989). "Forecasting exponential autoregressive models of order 1". Journal of Time Series Analysis 10, 95–113.

Albert, J., Chib, S. (1993). "Bayes inference via Gibbs sampling of autoregressive time series subject to Markov mean and variance shifts". Journal of Business and Economic Statistics 11, 1–16.

Andrews, D.W.K. (1993). "Tests for parameter instability and structural change with unknown change point". Econometrica 61, 821–856.

Andrews, D.W.K., Ploberger, W. (1994). "Optimal tests when a nuisance parameter is present only under the alternative". Econometrica 62, 1383–1414.

Armstrong, J.S. (Ed.) (2001). Principles of Forecasting. Kluwer Academic, Boston.

Bai, J., Lumsdaine, R.L., Stock, J.H. (1998). "Testing for and dating common breaks in multivariate time series". Review of Economics and Statistics 63, 395–432.

Bai, J., Perron, P. (1998). "Estimating and testing linear models with multiple structural changes". Econometrica 66, 47–78.

Baillie, R.T., Bollerslev, T. (1992). "Prediction in dynamic models with time-dependent conditional variances". Journal of Econometrics 52, 91–113.

Balke, N.S. (1993). "Detecting level shifts in time series". Journal of Business and Economic Statistics 11, 81–92.

Banerjee, A., Hendry, D.F. (1992). "Testing integration and cointegration: An overview". Oxford Bulletin of Economics and Statistics 54, 225–255.

Barnett, W.A., Hendry, D.F., Hylleberg, S., et al. (Eds.) (2000). Nonlinear Econometric Modeling in Time Series Analysis. Cambridge University Press, Cambridge.

Bates, J.M., Granger, C.W.J. (1969). "The combination of forecasts". Operations Research Quarterly 20, 451–468. Reprinted in: Mills, T.C. (Ed.) (1999). Economic Forecasting. Edward Elgar.

Bera, A.K., Higgins, M.L. (1993). "ARCH models: Properties, estimation and testing". Journal of Economic Surveys 7, 305–366.

Bianchi, C., Calzolari, G. (1982). "Evaluating forecast uncertainty due to errors in estimated coefficients: Empirical comparison of alternative methods". In: Chow, G.C., Corsi, P. (Eds.), Evaluating the Reliability of Macro-Economic Models. Wiley, New York. Chapter 13.

Bollerslev, T. (1986). "Generalised autoregressive conditional heteroskedasticity". Journal of Econometrics 51, 307–327.

Bollerslev, T., Chou, R.S., Kroner, K.F. (1992). "ARCH modelling in finance – A review of the theory and empirical evidence". Journal of Econometrics 52, 5–59.

Bontemps, C., Mizon, G.E. (2003). "Congruence and encompassing". In: Stigum, B.P. (Ed.), Econometrics and the Philosophy of Economics. Princeton University Press, Princeton, pp. 354–378.

Box, G.E.P., Jenkins, G.M. (1976). Time Series Analysis, Forecasting and Control. Holden-Day, San Francisco. First published 1970.

Breusch, T.S., Pagan, A.R. (1979). "A simple test for heteroscedasticity and random coefficient variation". Econometrica 47, 1287–1294.

Brown, R.L., Durbin, J., Evans, J.M. (1975). "Techniques for testing the constancy of regression relationships over time (with discussion)". Journal of the Royal Statistical Society B 37, 149–192.

Calzolari, G. (1981). "A note on the variance of ex post forecasts in econometric models". Econometrica 49, 1593–1596.

Calzolari, G. (1987). "Forecast variance in dynamic simulation of simultaneous equations models". Econometrica 55, 1473–1476.

Carrasco, M. (2002). "Misspecified structural change, threshold, and Markov switching models". Journal of Econometrics 109, 239–273.

Chan, K.S. (1990). "Testing for threshold autoregression". The Annals of Statistics 18, 1886–1894.

Chan, K.S. (1991). "Percentage points of likelihood ratio tests for threshold autoregression". Journal of the Royal Statistical Society, Series B 53, 691–696.

Chan, N.H., Wei, C.Z. (1988). "Limiting distributions of least squares estimates of unstable autoregressive processes". Annals of Statistics 16, 367–401.

Chen, C., Liu, L.-M. (1993). "Joint estimation of model parameters and outlier effects in time series". Journal of the American Statistical Association 88, 284–297.

Chen, C., Tiao, G.C. (1990). "Random level-shift time series models, ARIMA approximations and level-shift detection". Journal of Business and Economic Statistics 8, 83–97.

Chong, T. (2001). "Structural change in AR(1) models". Econometric Theory 17, 87–155.

Chow, G.C. (1960). "Tests of equality between sets of coefficients in two linear regressions". Econometrica 28, 591–605.

Christoffersen, P.F., Diebold, F.X. (1998). "Cointegration and long-horizon forecasting". Journal of Business and Economic Statistics 16, 450–458.

Chu, C.S., Stinchcombe, M., White, H. (1996). "Monitoring structural change". Econometrica 64, 1045–1065.

Clemen, R.T. (1989). "Combining forecasts: A review and annotated bibliography". International Journal of Forecasting 5, 559–583. Reprinted in: Mills, T.C. (Ed.) (1999). Economic Forecasting. Edward Elgar.

Clements, M.P., Galvão, A.B. (2005). "Combining predictors and combining information in modelling: Forecasting US recession probabilities and output growth". In: Milas, C., Rothman, P., van Dijk, D. (Eds.), Nonlinear Time Series Analysis of Business Cycles. Contributions to Economic Analysis Series. Elsevier. In press.

Clements, M.P., Hendry, D.F. (1995). "Forecasting in cointegrated systems". Journal of Applied Econometrics 10, 127–146. Reprinted in: Mills, T.C. (Ed.) (1999). Economic Forecasting. Edward Elgar.

Clements, M.P., Hendry, D.F. (1996). "Intercept corrections and structural change". Journal of Applied Econometrics 11, 475–494.

Clements, M.P., Hendry, D.F. (1998). Forecasting Economic Time Series: The Marshall Lectures on Economic Forecasting. Cambridge University Press, Cambridge.

Clements, M.P., Hendry, D.F. (1999). Forecasting Non-Stationary Economic Time Series. MIT Press, Cambridge, MA.

Clements, M.P., Hendry, D.F. (Eds.) (2002a). A Companion to Economic Forecasting. Blackwells, Oxford.

Clements, M.P., Hendry, D.F. (2002b). "Explaining forecast failure in macroeconomics". In: Clements and Hendry (2002a), pp. 539–571.

Clements, M.P., Hendry, D.F. (2005). "Evaluating a model by forecast performance". Oxford Bulletin of Economics and Statistics 67, 931–956.

Clements, M.P., Krolzig, H.-M. (1998). "A comparison of the forecast performance of Markov-switching and threshold autoregressive models of US GNP". Econometrics Journal 1, 47–75.

Clements, M.P., Krolzig, H.-M. (2003). "Business cycle asymmetries: Characterisation and testing based on Markov-switching autoregressions". Journal of Business and Economic Statistics 21, 196–211.

Clements, M.P., Smith, J. (1999). "A Monte Carlo study of the forecasting performance of empirical SETAR models". Journal of Applied Econometrics 14, 124–141.

Cogley, T., Sargent, T.J. (2001). "Evolving post World War II inflation dynamics". NBER Macroeconomics Annual 16, 331–373.

Cogley, T., Sargent, T.J. (2005). "Drifts and volatilities: Monetary policies and outcomes in the post World War II US". Review of Economic Dynamics 8, 262–302.

Davidson, J.E.H., Hendry, D.F., Srba, F., Yeo, J.S. (1978). "Econometric modelling of the aggregate time-series relationship between consumers' expenditure and income in the United Kingdom". Economic Journal 88, 661–692. Reprinted in: Hendry, D.F. (1993). Econometrics: Alchemy or Science? Blackwell Publishers, Oxford and Oxford University Press, 2000.

Davies, R.B. (1977). "Hypothesis testing when a nuisance parameter is present only under the alternative". Biometrika 64, 247–254.

Davies, R.B. (1987). "Hypothesis testing when a nuisance parameter is present only under the alternative". Biometrika 74, 33–43.

De Gooijer, J.G., De Bruin, P. (1997). "On SETAR forecasting". Statistics and Probability Letters 37, 7–14.

Dempster, A.P., Laird, N.M., Rubin, D.B. (1977). "Maximum likelihood estimation from incomplete data via the EM algorithm". Journal of the Royal Statistical Society, Series B 39, 1–38.

Diebold, F.X., Chen, C. (1996). "Testing structural stability with endogenous breakpoint: A size comparison of analytic and bootstrap procedures". Journal of Econometrics 70, 221–241.

Diebold, F.X., Lee, J.H., Weinbach, G.C. (1994). "Regime switching with time-varying transition probabilities". In: Hargreaves, C. (Ed.), Non-Stationary Time-Series Analyses and Cointegration. Oxford University Press, Oxford, pp. 283–302.

Diebold, F.X., Lopez, J.A. (1996). "Forecast evaluation and combination". In: Maddala, G.S., Rao, C.R. (Eds.), Handbook of Statistics, vol. 14. North-Holland, Amsterdam, pp. 241–268.

Diebold, F.X., Rudebusch, G.D., Sichel, D.E. (1993). "Further evidence on business cycle duration dependence". In: Stock, J., Watson, M. (Eds.), Business Cycles Indicators, and Forecasting. University of Chicago Press and NBER, Chicago, pp. 255–280.

Doornik, J.A., Hansen, H. (1994). "A practical test for univariate and multivariate normality". Discussion Paper, Nuffield College.

Durland, J.M., McCurdy, T.H. (1994). "Duration dependent transitions in a Markov model of U.S. GNP growth". Journal of Business and Economic Statistics 12, 279–288.

Engle, R.F. (1982). "Autoregressive conditional heteroscedasticity, with estimates of the variance of United Kingdom inflation". Econometrica 50, 987–1007.

Engle, R.F., Bollerslev, T. (1987). "Modelling the persistence of conditional variances". Econometric Reviews 5, 1–50.

Engle, R.F., McFadden, D. (Eds.) (1994). Handbook of Econometrics, vol. 4. Elsevier Science, North-Holland, Amsterdam.

Engle, R.F., Yoo, B.S. (1987). "Forecasting and testing in co-integrated systems". Journal of Econometrics 35, 143–159.

Ericsson, N.R., MacKinnon, J.G. (2002). "Distributions of error correction tests for cointegration". Econometrics Journal 5, 285–318.

Filardo, A.J. (1994). "Business cycle phases and their transitional dynamics". Journal of Business and Economic Statistics 12, 299–308.

Fildes, R.A., Makridakis, S. (1995). "The impact of empirical accuracy studies on time series analysis and forecasting". International Statistical Review 63, 289–308.

Fildes, R.A., Ord, K. (2002). "Forecasting competitions – Their role in improving forecasting practice and research". In: Clements and Hendry (2002a), pp. 322–253.

Fuller, W.A., Hasza, D.P. (1980). "Predictors for the first-order autoregressive process". Journal of Econometrics 13, 139–157.

Garcia, R. (1998). "Asymptotic null distribution of the likelihood ratio test in Markov switching models". International Economic Review 39, 763–788.

Gardner, E.S., McKenzie, E. (1985). "Forecasting trends in time series". Management Science 31, 1237–1246.

Goodwin, T.H. (1993). "Business-cycle analysis with a Markov-switching model". Journal of Business and Economic Statistics 11, 331–339.

Granger, C.W.J. (1989). "Combining forecasts – Twenty years later". Journal of Forecasting 8, 167–173.

Granger, C.W.J., White, H., Kamstra, M. (1989). "Interval forecasting: An analysis based upon ARCH-quantile estimators". Journal of Econometrics 40, 87–96.

Griliches, Z., Intriligator, M.D. (Eds.) (1983). Handbook of Econometrics, vol. 1. North-Holland, Amsterdam.

Griliches, Z., Intriligator, M.D. (Eds.) (1984). Handbook of Econometrics, vol. 2. North-Holland, Amsterdam.

Griliches, Z., Intriligator, M.D. (Eds.) (1986). Handbook of Econometrics, vol. 3. North-Holland, Amsterdam.

Guilkey, D.K. (1974). "Alternative tests for a first order vector autoregressive error specification". Journal of Econometrics 2, 95–104.

Hall, S., Mitchell, J. (2005). "Evaluating, comparing and combining density forecasts using the KLIC with an application to the Bank of England and NIESRC fan charts of inflation". Oxford Bulletin of Economics and Statistics 67, 995–1033.

Hamilton, J.D. (1989). "A new approach to the economic analysis of nonstationary time series and the business cycle". Econometrica 57, 357–384.

Hamilton, J.D. (1990). "Analysis of time series subject to changes in regime". Journal of Econometrics 45, 39–70.

Hamilton, J.D. (1993). "Estimation, inference, and forecasting of time series subject to changes in regime". In: Maddala, G.S., Rao, C.R., Vinod, H.D. (Eds.), Handbook of Statistics, vol. 11. North-Holland, Amsterdam.

Hamilton, J.D. (1994). Time Series Analysis. Princeton University Press, Princeton.

Hamilton, J.D., Raj, B. (Eds.) (2002). Advances in Markov-Switching Models. Applications in Business Cycle Research and Finance. Physica-Verlag, New York.

Hansen, B.E. (1992). "The likelihood ratio test under nonstandard conditions: Testing the Markov switching model of GNP". Journal of Applied Econometrics 7, S61–S82.

Hansen, B.E. (1996a). "Erratum: The likelihood ratio test under nonstandard conditions: Testing the Markov switching model of GNP". Journal of Applied Econometrics 11, 195–198.

Hansen, B.E. (1996b). "Inference when a nuisance parameter is not identified under the null hypothesis". Econometrica 64, 413–430.

Harvey, A.C. (1992). Forecasting, Structural Time Series Models and the Kalman Filter. Cambridge University Press, Cambridge.

Heckman, J.J., Leamer, E.E. (Eds.) (2004). Handbook of Econometrics, vol. 5. Elsevier Science, North-Holland, Amsterdam.

Hendry, D.F. (1995). Dynamic Econometrics. Oxford University Press, Oxford.

Hendry, D.F. (1996). "On the constancy of time-series econometric equations". Economic and Social Review 27, 401–422.

Hendry, D.F. (2000). "On detectable and non-detectable structural change". Structural Change and Economic Dynamics 11, 45–65. Reprinted in: Hagemann, H., Landesman, M., Scazzieri, R. (Eds.) (2002). The Economics of Structural Change. Edward Elgar, Cheltenham.

Hendry, D.F. (2001). "Modelling UK inflation, 1875–1991". Journal of Applied Econometrics 16, 255–275.

Hendry, D.F. (2005). "Robustifying forecasts from equilibrium-correction models". Special Issue in Honor of Clive Granger, Journal of Econometrics. In press.

Hendry, D.F., Clements, M.P. (2004). "Pooling of forecasts". The Econometrics Journal 7, 1–31.

Hendry, D.F., Doornik, J.A. (2001). Empirical Econometric Modelling Using PcGive 10, vol. I. Timberlake Consultants Press, London.

Hendry, D.F., Johansen, S., Santos, C. (2004). "Selecting a regression saturated by indicators". Unpublished Paper, Economics Department, University of Oxford.

Hendry, D.F., Massmann, M. (2006). "Co-breaking: Recent advances and a synopsis of the literature". Journal of Business and Economic Statistics. In press.

Hendry, D.F., Neale, A.J. (1991). "A Monte Carlo study of the effects of structural breaks on tests for unit roots". In: Hackl, P., Westlund, A.H. (Eds.), Economic Structural Change, Analysis and Forecasting. Springer-Verlag, Berlin, pp. 95–119.

Hoque, A., Magnus, J.R., Pesaran, B. (1988). "The exact multi-period mean-square forecast error for the first-order autoregressive model". Journal of Econometrics 39, 327–346.

Johansen, S. (1988). "Statistical analysis of cointegration vectors". Journal of Economic Dynamics and Control 12, 231–254. Reprinted in: Engle, R.F., Granger, C.W.J. (Eds.) (1991). Long-Run Economic Relationships. Oxford University Press, Oxford, pp. 131–152.

Johansen, S. (1994). "The role of the constant and linear terms in cointegration analysis of nonstationary variables". Econometric Reviews 13, 205–229.

Junttila, J. (2001). "Structural breaks, ARIMA model and Finnish inflation forecasts". International Journal of Forecasting 17, 207–230.

Kähler, J., Marnet, V. (1994). "Markov-switching models for exchange rate dynamics and the pricing of foreign-currency options". In: Kähler, J., Kugler, P. (Eds.), Econometric Analysis of Financial Markets. Physica Verlag, Heidelberg.

Kim, C.J. (1994). "Dynamic linear models with Markov-switching". Journal of Econometrics 60, 1–22.

Klein, L.R. (1971). An Essay on the Theory of Economic Prediction. Markham Publishing Company, Chicago.

Klein, L.R., Howrey, E.P., MacCarthy, M.D. (1974). "Notes on testing the predictive performance of econometric models". International Economic Review 15, 366–383.

Koop, G., Potter, S.M. (2000). "Nonlinearity, structural breaks, or outliers in economic time series". In Barnett et al. (2000), pp. 61–78.

Krämer, W., Ploberger, W., Alt, R. (1988). "Testing for structural change in dynamic models". Econometrica 56, 1355–1369.

Krolzig, H.-M. (1997). Markov Switching Vector Autoregressions: Modelling, Statistical Inference and Application to Business Cycle Analysis. Lecture Notes in Economics and Mathematical Systems, vol. 454. Springer-Verlag, Berlin.

Krolzig, H.-M., Lütkepohl, H. (1995). "Konjunkturanalyse mit Markov-regimewechselmodellen". In: Oppenländer, K.H. (Ed.), Konjunkturindikatoren. Fakten, Analysen, Verwendung. München Wien, Oldenbourg, pp. 177–196.

Lahiri, K., Wang, J.G. (1994). "Predicting cyclical turning points with leading index in a Markov switching model". Journal of Forecasting 13, 245–263.

Lam, P.-S. (1990). "The Hamilton model with a general autoregressive component. Estimation and comparison with other models of economic time series". Journal of Monetary Economics 26, 409–432.

Lamoureux, C.G., Lastrapes, W.D. (1990). "Persistence in variance, structural change, and the GARCH model". Journal of Business and Economic Statistics 8, 225–234.

Lin, J.-L., Tsay, R.S. (1996). "Co-integration constraint and forecasting: An empirical examination". Journal of Applied Econometrics 11, 519–538.

Lütkepohl, H. (1991). Introduction to Multiple Time Series Analysis. Springer-Verlag, New York.

Maddala, G.S., Li, H. (1996). "Bootstrap based tests in financial models". In: Maddala, G.S., Rao, C.R. (Eds.), Handbook of Statistics, vol. 14. North-Holland, Amsterdam, pp. 463–488.

Makridakis, S., Hibon, M. (2000). "The M3-competition: Results, conclusions and implications". International Journal of Forecasting 16, 451–476.

Malinvaud, E. (1970). Statistical Methods of Econometrics, second ed. North-Holland, Amsterdam.

Marris, R.L. (1954). "The position of economics and economists in the Government Machine: A comparative critique of the United Kingdom and the Netherlands". Economic Journal 64, 759–783.

McCulloch, R.E., Tsay, R.S. (1994). "Bayesian analysis of autoregressive time series via the Gibbs sampler". Journal of Time Series Analysis 15, 235–250.

Newbold, P., Granger, C.W.J. (1974). "Experience with forecasting univariate time series and the combination of forecasts". Journal of the Royal Statistical Society A 137, 131–146.

Newbold, P., Harvey, D.I. (2002). "Forecasting combination and encompassing". In: Clements, M.P., Hendry, D.F. (Eds.), A Companion to Economic Forecasting. Blackwells, Oxford, pp. 268–283.

Nyblom, J. (1989). "Testing for the constancy of parameters over time". Journal of the American Statistical Association 84, 223–230.

Osborn, D. (2002). "Unit root versus deterministic representations of seasonality for forecasting". In: Clements, M.P., Hendry, D.F. (Eds.), A Companion to Economic Forecasting. Blackwells, Oxford, pp. 409–431.

Pastor, L., Stambaugh, R.F. (2001). "The equity premium and structural breaks". Journal of Finance 56, 1207–1239.

Perron, P. (1990). "Testing for a unit root in a time series with a changing mean". Journal of Business and Economic Statistics 8, 153–162.

Pesaran, M.H., Pettenuzzo, D., Timmermann, A. (2004). "Forecasting time series subject to multiple structural breaks". Mimeo, University of Cambridge and UCSD.

Pesaran, M.H., Timmermann, A. (2002a). "Market timing and return prediction under model instability". Journal of Empirical Finance 9, 495–510.

Pesaran, M.H., Timmermann, A. (2002b). "Model instability and choice of observation window". Mimeo, University of Cambridge.

Pesaran, M.H., Timmermann, A. (2003). "Small sample properties of forecasts from autoregressive models under structural breaks". Journal of Econometrics. In press.

Phillips, K. (1991). "A two-country model of stochastic output with changes in regime". Journal of International Economics 31, 121–142.

Phillips, P.C.B. (1994). "Bayes models and forecasts of Australian macroeconomic time series". In: Hargreaves, C. (Ed.), Non-Stationary Time-Series Analyses and Cointegration. Oxford University Press, Oxford.

Phillips, P.C.B. (1995). "Automated forecasts of Asia-Pacific economic activity". Asia-Pacific Economic Review 1, 92–102.

Phillips, P.C.B. (1996). "Econometric model determination". Econometrica 64, 763–812.

Ploberger, W., Krämer, W., Kontrus, K. (1989). "A new test for structural stability in the linear regression model". Journal of Econometrics 40, 307–318.

Potter, S. (1995). "A nonlinear approach to US GNP". Journal of Applied Econometrics 10, 109–125.

Quandt, R.E. (1960). "Tests of the hypothesis that a linear regression system obeys two separate regimes". Journal of the American Statistical Association 55, 324–330.

Rappoport, P., Reichlin, L. (1989). "Segmented trends and non-stationary time series". Economic Journal 99, 168–177.

Reichlin, L. (1989). "Structural change and unit root econometrics". Economics Letters 31, 231–233.

Sánchez, M.J., Peña, D. (2003). "The identification of multiple outliers in ARIMA models". Communications in Statistics: Theory and Methods 32, 1265–1287.

Schiff, A.F., Phillips, P.C.B. (2000). "Forecasting New Zealand's real GDP". New Zealand Economic Papers 34, 159–182.

Schmidt, P. (1974). "The asymptotic distribution of forecasts in the dynamic simulation of an econometric model". Econometrica 42, 303–309.

Schmidt, P. (1977). "Some small sample evidence on the distribution of dynamic simulation forecasts". Econometrica 45, 97–105.

Shephard, N. (1996). "Statistical aspects of ARCH and stochastic volatility". In: Cox, D.R., Hinkley, D.V., Barndorff-Nielsen, O.E. (Eds.), Time Series Models: In Econometrics, Finance and other Fields. Chapman and Hall, London, pp. 1–67.

Stock, J.H. (1994). "Unit roots, structural breaks and trends". In: Engle, R.F., McFadden, D.L. (Eds.), Handbook of Econometrics. North-Holland, Amsterdam, pp. 2739–2841.

Stock, J.H., Watson, M.W. (1996). "Evidence on structural instability in macroeconomic time series relations". Journal of Business and Economic Statistics 14, 11–30.

Stock, J.H., Watson, M.W. (1999). "A comparison of linear and nonlinear univariate models for forecasting macroeconomic time series". In: Engle, R.F., White, H. (Eds.), Cointegration, Causality and Forecasting: A Festschrift in Honour of Clive Granger. Oxford University Press, Oxford, pp. 1–44.

Swanson, N.R., White, H. (1997). "Forecasting economic time series using flexible versus fixed specification and linear versus nonlinear econometric models". International Journal of Forecasting 13, 439–462.

Taylor, J.W., Bunn, D.W. (1998). "Combining forecast quantiles using quantile regression: Investigating the derived weights, estimator bias and imposing constraints". Journal of Applied Statistics 25, 193–206.

Teräsvirta, T. (1994). "Specification, estimation and evaluation of smooth transition autoregressive models". Journal of the American Statistical Association 89, 208–218.

Theil, H. (1961). Economic Forecasts and Policy, second ed. North-Holland, Amsterdam.

Tiao, G.C., Tsay, R.S. (1994). "Some advances in non-linear and adaptive modelling in time-series". Journal of Forecasting 13, 109–131.

Tong, H. (1983). Threshold Models in Non-Linear Time Series Analysis. Springer-Verlag, New York.

Tong, H. (1995). Non-Linear Time Series. A Dynamical System Approach. Clarendon Press, Oxford. First published 1990.

Tsay, R.S. (1986). "Time-series model specification in the presence of outliers". Journal of the American Statistical Association 81, 132–141.

Tsay, R.S. (1988). "Outliers, level shifts and variance changes in time series". Journal of Forecasting 7, 1–20.

Turner, D.S. (1990). "The role of judgement in macroeconomic forecasting". Journal of Forecasting 9, 315–345.

Wallis, K.F. (1993). "Comparing macroeconometric models: A review article". Economica 60, 225–237.

Wallis, K.F. (2005). "Combining density and interval forecasts: A modest proposal". Oxford Bulletin of Economics and Statistics 67, 983–994.

Wallis, K.F., Whitley, J.D. (1991). "Sources of error in forecasts and expectations: UK economic models 1984–88". Journal of Forecasting 10, 231–253.

Wallis, K.F., Andrews, M.J., Bell, D.N.F., Fisher, P.G., Whitley, J.D. (1984). Models of the UK Economy, A Review by the ESRC Macroeconomic Modelling Bureau. Oxford University Press, Oxford.

Wallis, K.F., Andrews, M.J., Bell, D.N.F., Fisher, P.G., Whitley, J.D. (1985). Models of the UK Economy, A Second Review by the ESRC Macroeconomic Modelling Bureau. Oxford University Press, Oxford.

Wallis, K.F., Andrews, M.J., Fisher, P.G., Longbottom, J., Whitley, J.D. (1986). Models of the UK Economy: A Third Review by the ESRC Macroeconomic Modelling Bureau. Oxford University Press, Oxford.

Wallis, K.F., Fisher, P.G., Longbottom, J., Turner, D.S., Whitley, J.D. (1987). Models of the UK Economy: A Fourth Review by the ESRC Macroeconomic Modelling Bureau. Oxford University Press, Oxford.

White, H. (1980). "A heteroskedastic-consistent covariance matrix estimator and a direct test for heteroskedasticity". Econometrica 48, 817–838.

White, H. (1992). Artificial Neural Networks: Approximation and Learning Theory. Oxford University Press, Oxford.

Chapter 13

FORECASTING SEASONAL TIME SERIES

ERIC GHYSELS

Department of Economics, University of North Carolina

DENISE R. OSBORN

School of Economic Studies, University of Manchester

PAULO M.M. RODRIGUES

Faculty of Economics, University of Algarve

Contents

Handbook of Economic Forecasting, Volume 1
Edited by Graham Elliott, Clive W.J. Granger and Allan Timmermann

DOI: 10.1016/S1574-0706(05)01013-X

Abstract

This chapter reviews the principal methods used by researchers when forecasting seasonal time series. In addition, the often overlooked implications of forecasting and feedback for seasonal adjustment are discussed. After an introduction in Section 1, Section 2 examines traditional univariate linear models, including methods based on SARIMA models, seasonally integrated models and deterministic seasonality models. As well as examining how forecasts are computed in each case, the forecast implications of misspecifying the class of model (deterministic versus nonstationary stochastic) are considered. The linear analysis concludes with a discussion of the nature and implications of cointegration in the context of forecasting seasonal time series, including merging short-term seasonal forecasts with those from long-term (nonseasonal) models.

Periodic (or seasonally varying parameter) models, which often arise from theoretical models of economic decision-making, are examined in Section 3. As periodic models may be highly parameterized, their value for forecasting can be open to question. In this context, modelling procedures for periodic models are critically examined, as well as procedures for forecasting.

Section 3 discusses less traditional models, specifically nonlinear seasonal models and models for seasonality in variance. Such nonlinear models primarily concentrate on interactions between seasonality and the business cycle, either using a threshold specification to capture changing seasonality over the business cycle or through regime transition probabilities being seasonally varying in a Markov switching framework. Seasonality heteroskedasticity is considered for financial time series, including deterministic versus stochastic seasonality, periodic GARCH and periodic stochastic volatility models for daily or intra-daily series.

Economists typically consider that seasonal adjustment rids their analysis of the "nuisance" of seasonality. Section 5 shows this to be false. Forecasting seasonal time series is an inherent part of seasonal adjustment and, further, decisions based on seasonally adjusted data affect future outcomes, which destroys the assumed orthogonality between seasonal and nonseasonal components of time series.

Keywords

seasonality, seasonal adjustment, forecasting with seasonal models, nonstationarity, nonlinearity, seasonal cointegration models, periodic models, seasonality in variance

JEL classification: C22, C32, C53

1. Introduction

Although seasonality is a dominant feature of month-to-month or quarter-to-quarter fluctuations in economic time series [Beaulieu and Miron (1992), Miron (1996), Franses (1996)], it has typically been viewed as of limited interest by economists, who generally use seasonally adjusted data for modelling and forecasting. This contrasts with the perspective of the economic agent, who makes (say) production or consumption decisions in a seasonal context [Ghysels (1988, 1994a), Osborn (1988)].

In this chapter, we study forecasting of seasonal time series and its impact on seasonal adjustment. The bulk of our discussion relates to the former issue, where we assume that the (unadjusted) value of a seasonal series is to be forecast, so that modelling the seasonal pattern itself is a central issue. In this discussion, we view seasonal movements as an inherent feature of economic time series which should be integrated into the econometric modelling and forecasting exercise. Hence, we do not consider seasonality as a separable component in the unobserved components methodology, which is discussed in Chapter 7 in this Handbook [see Harvey (2006)]. Nevertheless, such unobserved components models do enter our discussion, since they are the basis of official seasonal adjustment. Our focus is then not on the seasonal models themselves, but rather on how forecasts of seasonal time series enter the adjustment process and, consequently, influence subsequent decisions. Indeed, the discussion here reinforces our position that seasonal and nonseasonal components are effectively inseparable.

Seasonality is the periodic and largely repetitive pattern that is observed in time series data over the course of a year. As such, it is largely predictable. A generally agreed definition of seasonality in the context of economics is provided by Hylleberg (1992, p. 4) as follows: "*Seasonality is the systematic, although not necessarily regular, intra-year movement caused by the changes of weather, the calendar, and timing of decisions, directly or indirectly through the production and consumption decisions made by the agents of the economy. These decisions are influenced by endowments, the expectations and preferences of the agents, and the production techniques available in the economy.*" This definition implies that seasonality is not necessarily fixed over time, despite the fact that the calendar does not change. Thus, for example, the impact of Christmas on consumption or of the summer holiday period on production may evolve over time, despite the timing of Christmas and the summer remaining fixed.

Intra-year observations on most economic time series are typically available at quarterly or monthly frequencies, so our discussion concentrates on these frequencies. We follow the literature in referring to each intra-year observation as relating to a "season", by which we mean an individual month or quarter. Financial time series are often observed at higher frequencies, such as daily or hourly and methods analogous to those discussed here can be applied when forecasting the patterns of financial time series that are associated with the calendar, such as days of the week or intradaily patterns. However, specific issues arise in forecasting financial time series, which is not the topic of the present chapter.

In common with much of the forecasting literature, our discussion assumes that the forecaster aims to minimize the mean-square forecast error (MSFE). As shown by Whittle (1963) in a linear model context, the optimal (minimum MSFE) forecast is given by the expected value of the future observation y_{T+h} conditional on the information set, $y_1, \ldots, y_T$, available at time T, namely

$$\widehat{y}_{T+h|T} = E(y_{T+h}|y_1, \ldots, y_T). \tag{1}$$

However, the specific form of $\widehat{y}_{T+h|T}$ depends on the model assumed to be the data generating process (DGP).

When considering the optimal forecast, the treatment of seasonality may be expected to be especially important for short-run forecasts, more specifically forecasts for horizons h that are less than one year. Denoting the number of observations per year as S, then this points to $h = 1, \ldots, S-1$ as being of particular interest. Since $h = S$ is a one-year ahead forecast, and seasonality is typically irrelevant over the horizon of a year, seasonality may have a smaller role to play here than at shorter horizons. Seasonality obviously once again comes into play for horizons $h = S+1, \ldots, 2S-1$ and at subsequent horizons that do not correspond to an integral number of years.

Nevertheless, the role of seasonality should not automatically be ignored for forecasts at horizons of an integral number of years. If seasonality is changing, then a model that captures this changing seasonal pattern should yield more accurate forecasts at these horizons than one that ignores it.

This chapter is structured as follows. In Section 2 we briefly introduce the widely-used classes of univariate SARIMA and deterministic seasonality models and show how these are used for forecasting purposes. Moreover, an analysis on forecasting with misspecified seasonal models is presented. This section also discusses Seasonal Cointegration, including the use of Seasonal Cointegration Models for forecasting purposes, and presents the main conclusions of forecasting comparisons that have appeared in the literature. The idea of merging short- and long-run forecasts, put forward by Engle, Granger and Hallman (1989), is also discussed.

Section 3 discusses the less familiar periodic models where parameters change over the season; such models often arise from economic theories in a seasonal context. We analyze forecasting with these models, including the impact of neglecting periodic parameter variation and we discuss proposals for more parsimonious periodic specifications that may improve forecast accuracy. Periodic cointegration is also considered and an overview of the few existing results of forecast performance of periodic models is presented.

In Section 4 we move to recent developments in modelling seasonal data, specifically nonlinear seasonal models and models that account for seasonality in volatility. Nonlinear models include those of the threshold and Markov switching types, where the focus is on capturing business cycle features in addition to seasonality in the conditional mean. On the other hand, seasonality in variance is important in finance; for instance, Martens, Chang and Taylor (2002) show that explicitly modelling intraday seasonality improves out-of-sample forecasting performance.

The final substantive section of this chapter turns to the interactions of seasonality and seasonal adjustment, which is important due to the great demand for seasonally adjusted data. This section demonstrates that such adjustment is not separable from forecasting the seasonal series. Further, we discuss the feedback from seasonal adjustment to seasonality that exists when the actions of policymakers are considered.

In addition to general conclusions, Section 6 draws some implications from the chapter that are relevant to the selection of a forecasting model in a seasonal context.

2. Linear models

Most empirical models applied when forecasting economic time series are linear in parameters, for which the model can be written as

$$y_{Sn+s} = \mu_{Sn+s} + x_{Sn+s}, \tag{2}$$

$$\phi(L)x_{Sn+s} = u_{Sn+s} \tag{3}$$

where y_{Sn+s} ($s = 1, \dots, S, n = 0, \dots, T - 1$) represents the observable variable in season (e.g., month or quarter) s of year n, the polynomial $\phi(L)$ contains any unit roots in y_{Sn+s} and will be specified in the following subsections according to the model being discussed, L represents the conventional lag operator, $L^k x_{Sn+s} \equiv x_{Sn+s-k}$, $k = 0, 1, \dots,$ the driving shocks $\{u_{Sn+s}\}$ of (3) are assumed to follow an ARMA(p, q), $0 \leqslant p, q < \infty$ process, such as, $\beta(L)u_{Sn+s} = \theta(L)\varepsilon_{Sn+s}$, where the roots of $\beta(z) \equiv 1 - \sum_{j=1}^{p} \beta_j z^j = 0$ and $\theta(z) \equiv 1 - \sum_{j=1}^{q} \theta_j z^j = 0$ lie outside the unit circle, $|z| = 1$, with $\varepsilon_{Sn+s} \sim \text{iid}(0, \sigma^2)$. The term μ_{Sn+s} represents a deterministic kernel which will be assumed to be either (i) a set of seasonal means, i.e., $\sum_{s=1}^{S} \delta_s D_{s,Sn+s}$ where $D_{i,Sn+s}$ is a dummy variable taking value 1 in season i and zero elsewhere, or (ii) a set of seasonals with a (nonseasonal) time trend, i.e., $\sum_{s=1}^{S} \delta_s D_{s,Sn+s} + \tau(Sn+s)$. In general, the second of these is more plausible for economic time series, since it allows the underlying level of the series to trend over time, whereas $\mu_{Sn+s} = \delta_s$ implies a constant underlying level, except for seasonal variation.

When considering forecasts, we use T to denote the total (observed) sample size, with forecasts required for the future period $T + h$ for $h = 1, 2, \dots$.

Linear seasonal forecasting models differ essentially in their assumptions about the presence of unit roots in $\phi(L)$. The two most common forms of seasonal models in empirical economics are seasonally integrated models and models with deterministic seasonality. However, seasonal autoregressive integrated moving average (SARIMA) models retain an important role as a forecasting benchmark. Each of these three models and their associated forecasts are discussed in a separate subsection below.

2.1. SARIMA model

When working with nonstationary seasonal data, both annual changes and the changes between adjacent seasons are important concepts. This motivated Box and Jenkins

(1970) to propose the SARIMA model

$$\beta(L)(1-L)\big(1-L^S\big)y_{Sn+s} = \theta(L)\varepsilon_{Sn+s} \tag{4}$$

which results from specifying $\phi(L) = \Delta_1\Delta_S = (1-L)(1-L^S)$ in (3). It is worth noting that the imposition of $\Delta_1\Delta_S$ annihilates the deterministic variables (seasonal means and time trend) of (2), so that these do not appear in (4). The filter $(1-L^S)$ captures the tendency for the value of the series for a particular season to be highly correlated with the value for the same season a year earlier, while $(1-L)$ can be motivated as capturing the nonstationary nonseasonal stochastic component. This model is often found in textbooks, see for instance Brockwell and Davis (1991, pp. 320–326) and Harvey (1993, pp. 134–137). Franses (1996, pp. 42–46) fits SARIMA models to various real macroeconomic time series.

An important characteristic of model (4) is the imposition of unit roots at all seasonal frequencies, as well as two unit roots at the zero frequency. This occurs as $(1-L)(1-L^S) = (1-L)^2(1+L+L^2+\cdots+L^{S-1})$, where $(1-L)^2$ relates to the zero frequency while the moving annual sum $(1+L+L^2+\cdots+L^{S-1})$ implies unit roots at the seasonal frequencies (see the discussion below for seasonally integrated models). However, the empirical literature does not provide much evidence favoring the presence of two zero frequency unit roots in observed time series [see, e.g., Osborn (1990) and Hylleberg, Jørgensen and Sørensen (1993)], which suggests that the SARIMA model is overdifferenced. Although these models may seem empirically implausible, they can be successful in forecasting due to their parsimonious nature.

More specifically, the special case of (4) where

$$(1-L)\big(1-L^S\big)y_{Sn+s} = (1-\theta_1 L)\big(1-\theta_S L^S\big)\varepsilon_{Sn+s} \tag{5}$$

with $|\theta_1| < 1$, $|\theta_S| < 1$ retains an important position. This is known as the airline model because Box and Jenkins (1970) found it appropriate for monthly airline passenger data. Subsequently, the model has been shown to provide robust forecasts for many observed seasonal time series, and hence it often provides a benchmark for forecast accuracy comparisons.

2.1.1. Forecasting with SARIMA models

Given that ε_{T+h} is assumed to be iid$(0, \sigma^2)$, and if all parameters are known, the optimal (minimum MSFE) h-step ahead forecast of $\Delta_1\Delta_S y_{T+h}$ for the airline model (5) is, from (1),

$$\begin{aligned}\Delta_1\Delta_S\widehat{y}_{T+h|T} = {} & -\theta_1 E(\varepsilon_{T+h-1}|y_1,\ldots,y_T) - \theta_S E(\varepsilon_{T+h-S}|y_1,\ldots,y_T) \\ & + \theta_1\theta_S E(\varepsilon_{T+h-S-1}|y_1,\ldots,y_T), \quad h \geqslant 1\end{aligned} \tag{6}$$

where $E(\varepsilon_{T+h-i}|y_1,\ldots,y_T) = 0$ if $h > i$ and $E(\varepsilon_{T+h-i}|y_1,\ldots,y_T) = \varepsilon_{T+h-i}$ if $h \leqslant i$. Corresponding expressions can be derived for forecasts from other ARIMA models. In practice, of course, estimated parameters are used in generating these forecast values.

Forecasts of y_{T+h} for a SARIMA model can be obtained from the identity

$$E(y_{T+h}|y_1,\ldots,y_T) = E(y_{T+h-1}|y_1,\ldots,y_T) + E(y_{T+h-S}|y_1,\ldots,y_T) - E(y_{T+h-S-1}|y_1,\ldots,y_T) + \Delta_1\Delta_S\widehat{y}_{T+h|T}. \tag{7}$$

Clearly, $E(y_{T+h-i}|y_1,\ldots,y_T) = y_{T+h-i}$ for $h \leqslant i$, and forecasts $E(y_{T+h-i}|y_1,\ldots,y_T)$ for $h > i$ required on the right-hand side of (7) can be generated recursively for $h = 1, 2, \ldots$.

In this linear model context, optimal forecasts of other linear transformations of y_{T+h} can be obtained from these; for example, $\Delta_1\widehat{y}_{T+h} = \widehat{y}_{T+h} - \widehat{y}_{T+h-1}$ and $\Delta_S\widehat{y}_{T+h} = \widehat{y}_{T+h} - \widehat{y}_{T+h-S}$. In the special case of the airline model, (6) implies that $\Delta_1\Delta_S\widehat{y}_{T+h|T} = 0$ for $h > S+1$, and hence $\Delta_1\widehat{y}_{T+h|T} = \Delta_1\widehat{y}_{T+h-S|T}$ and $\Delta_S\widehat{y}_{T+h|T} = \Delta_S\widehat{y}_{T+h-1|T}$ at these horizons; see also Clements and Hendry (1997) and Osborn (2002). Therefore, when applied to forecasts for $h > S+1$, the airline model delivers a "same change" forecast, both when considered over a year and also over a single period compared to the corresponding period of the previous year.

2.2. Seasonally integrated model

Stochastic seasonality can arise through the stationary ARMA components $\beta(L)$ and $\theta(L)$ of u_{Sn+s} in (3). The case of stationary seasonality is treated in the next subsection, in conjunction with deterministic seasonality. Here we examine nonstationary stochastic seasonality where $\phi(L) = 1 - L^S = \Delta_S$ in (2). However, in contrast to the SARIMA model, the seasonally integrated model imposes only a single unit root at the zero frequency. Application of annual differencing to (2) yields

$$\beta(L)\Delta_S y_{Sn+s} = \beta(1)S\tau + \theta(L)\varepsilon_{Sn+s} \tag{8}$$

since $\Delta_S\mu_{Sn+s} = S\tau$. Thus, the seasonally integrated process of (8) has a common annual drift, $\beta(1)S\tau$, across seasons. Notice that the underlying seasonal means μ_{Sn+s} are not observed, since the seasonally varying component $\sum_{s=1}^{S}\delta_s D_{s,Sn+s}$ is annihilated by seasonal (that is, annual) differencing. In practical applications in economics, it is typically assumed that the stochastic process is of the autoregressive form, so that $\theta(L) = 1$.

As a result of the influential work of Box and Jenkins (1970), seasonal differencing has been a popular approach when modelling and forecasting seasonal time series. Note, however, that a time series on which seasonal differencing $(1 - L^S)$ needs to be applied to obtain stationarity has S roots on the unit circle. This can be seen by factorizing $(1 - L^S)$ into its evenly spaced roots, $\mathrm{e}^{\pm \mathrm{i}(2\pi k/S)}$ $(k = 0, 1, \ldots, S-1)$ on the unit circle, that is, $(1-L^S) = (1-L)(1+L)\prod_{k=1}^{S^*}(1-2\cos\eta_k L+L^2) = (1-L)(1+L+\cdots+L^{S-1})$ where $S^* = \mathrm{int}[(S-1)/2]$, int[.] is the integer part of the expression in brackets and $\eta_k \in (0,\pi)$. The real positive unit root, $+1$, relates to the long-run or zero frequency, and hence is often referred to as nonseasonal, while the remaining $(S-1)$ roots represent seasonal unit roots that occur at frequencies η_k (the unit root at frequency π is known as the Nyquist frequency root and the complex roots as the harmonics). A seasonally integrated process y_{Sn+s} has unbounded spectral density at each seasonal frequency due to the presence of these unit roots.

From an economic point of view, nonstationary seasonality can be controversial because the values over different seasons are not cointegrated and hence can move in any direction in relation to each other, so that "*winter can become summer*". This appears to have been first noted by Osborn (1993). Thus, the use of seasonal differences, as in (8) or through the multiplicative filter as in (4), makes rather strong assumptions about the stochastic properties of the time series under analysis. It has, therefore, become common practice to examine the nature of the stochastic seasonal properties of the data via seasonal unit root tests. In particular, Hylleberg, Engle, Granger and Yoo [HEGY] (1990) propose a test for the null hypothesis of seasonal integration in quarterly data, which is a seasonal generalization of the Dickey–Fuller [DF] (1979) test. The HEGY procedure has since been extended to the monthly case by Beaulieu and Miron (1993) and Taylor (1998), and was generalized to any periodicity S, by Smith and Taylor (1999).[1]

2.2.1. *Testing for seasonal unit roots*

Following HEGY and Smith and Taylor (1999), *inter alia*, the regression-based approach to testing for seasonal unit roots implied by $\phi(L) = 1 - L^S$ can be considered in two stages. First, the OLS de-meaned series $\widetilde{x}_{Sn+s} = y_{Sn+s} - \hat{\mu}_{Sn+s}$ is obtained, where $\hat{\mu}_{Sn+s}$ is the fitted value from the OLS regression of y_{Sn+s} on an appropriate set of deterministic variables. Provided μ_{Sn+s} is not estimated under an overly restrictive case, the resulting unit root tests will be exact invariant to the parameters characterizing the mean function μ_{Sn+s}; see Burridge and Taylor (2001).

Following Smith and Taylor (1999), $\phi(L)$ in (3) is then linearized around the seasonal unit roots $\exp(\pm \mathrm{i}2\pi k/S)$, $k = 0, \ldots, [S/2]$, so that the auxiliary regression equation

$$\begin{aligned}\Delta_S \widetilde{x}_{Sn+s} &= \pi_0 \widetilde{x}_{0,Sn+s-1} + \pi_{S/2} \widetilde{x}_{S/2,Sn+s-1} \\ &\quad + \sum_{k=1}^{S^*} \left(\pi_{\alpha,k} \widetilde{x}^{\alpha}_{k,Sn+s-1} + \pi_{\beta,k} \widetilde{x}^{\beta}_{k,Sn+s-1} \right) \\ &\quad + \sum_{j=1}^{p^*} \beta_j^* \Delta_S \widetilde{x}_{Sn+s-j} + \varepsilon_{Sn+s} \end{aligned} \tag{9}$$

is obtained. The regressors are linear transformations of $\widetilde{x}_{Sn+s}$, namely

$$\widetilde{x}_{0,Sn+s} \equiv \sum_{j=0}^{S-1} \widetilde{x}_{Sn+s-j}, \qquad \widetilde{x}_{S/2,Sn+s} \equiv \sum_{j=0}^{S-1} \cos\big[(j+1)\pi\big] \widetilde{x}_{Sn+s-j},$$

[1] Numerous other seasonal unit root tests have been developed; see *inter alia* Breitung and Franses (1998), Busetti and Harvey (2003), Canova and Hansen (1995), Dickey, Hasza and Fuller (1984), Ghysels, Lee and Noh (1994), Hylleberg (1995), Osborn et al. (1988), Rodrigues (2002), Rodrigues and Taylor (2004a, 2004b) and Taylor (2002, 2003). However, in practical applications, the HEGY test is still the most widely applied.

$$\widetilde{x}^{\alpha}_{k,Sn+s} \equiv \sum_{j=0}^{S-1} \cos\big[(j+1)\omega_k\big]\widetilde{x}_{Sn+s-j},$$

$$\widetilde{x}^{\beta}_{k,Sn+s} \equiv -\sum_{j=0}^{S-1} \sin\big[(j+1)\omega_k\big]\widetilde{x}_{Sn+s-j}, \tag{10}$$

with $k = 1, \ldots, S^*$, $S^* = \text{int}[(S-1)/2]$. For example, in the quarterly case, $S = 4$, the relevant transformations are:

$$\widetilde{x}_{0,Sn+s} \equiv \big(1 + L + L^2 + L^3\big)\widetilde{x}_{Sn+s}, \qquad \widetilde{x}_{2,Sn+s} \equiv -\big(1 - L + L^2 - L^3\big)\widetilde{x}_{Sn+s},$$
$$\widetilde{x}^{\alpha}_{1,Sn+s} \equiv \widetilde{x}_{1,Sn+s-1} = -L\big(1 - L^2\big)\widetilde{x}_{Sn+s},$$
$$\widetilde{x}^{\beta}_{1,Sn+s} \equiv \widetilde{x}_{1,Sn+s} = -\big(1 - L^2\big)\widetilde{x}_{Sn+s}. \tag{11}$$

The regression (9) can be estimated over observations $Sn + s = p^* + S + 1, \ldots, T$, with $\pi_{S/2}\widetilde{x}_{S/2,Sn+s-1}$ omitted if S is odd. Note also that the autoregressive order p^* used must be sufficiently large to satisfactorily account for any autocorrelation, including any moving average component in (8).

The presence of unit roots implies exclusion restrictions for π_0, $\pi_{k,\alpha}$, $\pi_{k,\beta}$, $k = 1, \ldots, S^*$, and $\pi_{S/2}$ (S even), while the overall null hypothesis of seasonal integration implies all these are zero. To test seasonal integration against stationarity at one or more of the seasonal or nonseasonal frequencies, HEGY suggest using: t_0 (left-sided) for the exclusion of $\widetilde{x}_{0,Sn+s-1}$; $t_{S/2}$ (left-sided) for the exclusion of $\widetilde{x}_{S/2,Sn+s-1}$ (S even); F_k for the exclusion of *both* $\widetilde{x}^{\alpha}_{k,Sn+s-1}$ and $\widetilde{x}^{\beta}_{k,Sn+s-1}$, $k = 1, \ldots, S^*$. These tests examine the potential unit roots separately at each of the zero and seasonal frequencies, raising issues of the significance level for the overall test (Dickey, 1993). Consequently, Ghysels, Lee and Noh (1994), also consider joint frequency OLS F-statistics. Specifically $F_{1\ldots[S/2]}$ tests for the presence of all seasonal unit roots by testing for the exclusion of $\widetilde{x}_{S/2,Sn+s-1}$ (S even) and $\{\widetilde{x}^{\alpha}_{k,Sn+s-1}, \widetilde{x}^{\beta}_{k,Sn+s-1}\}_{k=1}^{S^*}$, while $F_{0\ldots[S/2]}$ examines the overall null hypothesis of seasonal integration, by testing for the exclusion of $\widetilde{x}_{0,Sn+s-1}$, $\widetilde{x}_{S/2,Sn+s-1}$ (S even), and $\{\widetilde{x}^{\alpha}_{k,Sn+s-1}, \widetilde{x}^{\beta}_{k,Sn+s-1}\}_{k=1}^{S^*}$ in (9). These joint tests are further considered by Taylor (1998) and Smith and Taylor (1998, 1999).

Empirical evidence regarding seasonal integration in quarterly data is obtained by (among others) HEGY, Lee and Siklos (1997), Hylleberg, Jørgensen and Sørensen (1993), Mills and Mills (1992), Osborn (1990) and Otto and Wirjanto (1990). The monthly case has been examined relatively infrequently, but relevant studies include Beaulieu and Miron (1993), Franses (1991) and Rodrigues and Osborn (1999). Overall, however, there is little evidence that the seasonal properties of the data justify application of the Δ_s filter for economic time series. Despite this, Clements and Hendry (1997) argue that the seasonally integrated model is useful for forecasting, because the seasonal differencing filter makes the forecasts robust to structural breaks in seasonality.[2]

[2] Along slightly different lines it is also worth noting that Ghysels and Perron (1996) show that traditional seasonal adjustment filters also mask structural breaks in nonseasonal patterns.

On the other hand, Kawasaki and Franses (2004) find that imposing individual seasonal unit roots on the basis of model selection criteria generally improves one-step ahead forecasts for monthly industrial production in OECD countries.

2.2.2. Forecasting with seasonally integrated models

As they are linear, forecasts from seasonally integrated models are generated in an analogous way to SARIMA models. Assuming all parameters are known and there is no moving average component (i.e., $\theta(L) = 1$), the optimal forecast is given by

$$\begin{aligned}\Delta_S \widehat{y}_{T+h|T} &= \beta(1) S\tau + \sum_{i=1}^{p} \beta_i E(\Delta_S y_{T+h-i} | y_1, \dots, y_T) \\ &= \beta(1) S\tau + \sum_{i=1}^{p} \beta_i \Delta_S \widehat{y}_{T+h-i|T} \qquad (12)\end{aligned}$$

where $\Delta_S \widehat{y}_{T+h-i|T} = \widehat{y}_{T+h-i|T} - \widehat{y}_{T+h-i-S|T}$ and $\widehat{y}_{T+h-S|T} = y_{T+h-S}$ for $h - S \leqslant 0$, with forecasts generated recursively for $h = 1, 2, \dots$.

As noted by Ghysels and Osborn (2001) and Osborn (2002, p. 414), forecasts for other transformations can be easily obtained. For instance, the level and first difference forecasts can be derived as

$$\widehat{y}_{T+h|T} = \Delta_S \widehat{y}_{T+h|T} + \widehat{y}_{T-S+h|T} \qquad (13)$$

and

$$\begin{aligned}\Delta_1 \widehat{y}_{T+h|T} &= \widehat{y}_{T+h|T} - \widehat{y}_{T+h-1|T} \\ &= \Delta_S \widehat{y}_{T+h} - (\Delta_1 \widehat{y}_{T+h-1} + \cdots + \Delta_1 \widehat{y}_{T+h-(S-1)}), \qquad (14)\end{aligned}$$

respectively.

2.3. Deterministic seasonality model

Seasonality has often been perceived as a phenomenon that generates peaks and troughs within a particular season, year after year. This type of effect is well described by deterministic variables leading to what is conventionally referred to as *deterministic seasonality*. Thus, models frequently encountered in applied economics often explicitly allow for seasonal means. Assuming the stochastic component x_{Sn+s} of y_{Sn+s} is stationary, then $\phi(L) = 1$ and (2)/(3) implies

$$\beta(L) y_{Sn+s} = \sum_{i=1}^{S} \beta(L) \mu_{Sn+s} + \theta(L) \varepsilon_{Sn+s} \qquad (15)$$

where ε_{Sn+s} is again a zero mean white noise process. For simplicity of exposition, and in line with usual empirical practice, we assume the absence of moving average components, i.e., $\theta(L) = 1$. Note, however, that stationary stochastic seasonality may also enter through $\beta(L)$.

Although the model in (15) assumes a stationary stochastic process, it is common, for most economic time series, to find evidence favouring a zero frequency unit root. Then $\phi(L) = 1 - L$ plays a role and the deterministic seasonality model is

$$\beta(L)\Delta_1 y_{Sn+s} = \sum_{s=1}^{S} \beta(L)\Delta_1 \mu_{Sn+s} + \varepsilon_{Sn+s} \tag{16}$$

where $\Delta_1 \mu_{Sn+s} = \mu_{Sn+s} - \mu_{Sn+s-1}$, so that (only) the change in the seasonal mean is identified.

Seasonal dummies are frequently employed in empirical work within a linear regression framework to represent seasonal effects [see, for example, Barsky and Miron (1989), Beaulieu, Mackie-Mason and Miron (1992), and Miron (1996)]. One advantage of considering seasonality as deterministic lies in the simplicity with which it can be handled. However, consideration should be given to various potential problems that can occur when treating a seasonal pattern as purely deterministic. Indeed, spurious deterministic seasonality emerges when seasonal unit roots present in the data are neglected [Abeysinghe (1991, 1994), Franses, Hylleberg and Lee (1995), and Lopes (1999)]. On the other hand, however, Ghysels, Lee and Siklos (1993) and Rodrigues (2000) establish that, for some purposes, (15) or (16) can represent a valid approach even with seasonally integrated data, provided the model is adequately augmented to take account of any seasonal unit roots potentially present in the data.

The core of the deterministic seasonality model is the seasonal mean effects, namely μ_{Sn+s} and $\Delta_1\mu_{Sn+s}$, for (15) and (16), respectively. However, there are a number of (equivalent) different ways that these may be represented, whose usefulness depends on the context. Therefore, we discuss this first. For simplicity, we assume the form of (15) is used and refer to μ_{Sn+s}. However, corresponding comments apply to $\Delta_1\mu_{Sn+s}$ in (16).

2.3.1. Representations of the seasonal mean

When $\mu_{Sn+s} = \sum_{s=1}^{S} \delta_s D_{s,Sn+s}$, the mean relating to each season is constant over time, with $\mu_{Sn+s} = \mu_s = \delta_s$ ($n = 1, 2, \dots, s = 1, 2, \dots, S$). This is a conditional mean, in the sense that $\mu_{Sn+s} = E[y_{Sn+s} | t = Sn + s]$ depends on the season s. Since all seasons appear with the same frequency over a year, the corresponding unconditional mean is $E(y_{Sn+s}) = \mu = (1/S)\sum_{s=1}^{S} \mu_s$. Although binary seasonal dummy variables, $D_{s,Sn+s}$, are often used to capture the seasonal means, this form has the disadvantage of not separately identifying the unconditional mean of the series.

Equivalently to the conventional representation based on $D_{s,Sn+s}$, we can identify the unconditional mean through the representation

$$\mu_{Sn+s} = \mu + \sum_{s=1}^{S} \delta_s^* D_{s,Sn+s}^* \tag{17}$$

where the dummy variables $D^*_{s,Sn+s}$ are constrained to sum to zero over the year, $\sum_{s=1}^{S} D^*_{s,Sn+s} = 0$. To avoid exact multicollinearity, only $S-1$ such dummy variables can be included, together with the intercept, in a regression context. The constraint that these variables sum to zero then implies the parameter restriction $\sum_{s=1}^{S} \delta^*_s = 0$, from which the coefficient on the omitted dummy variable can be retrieved. One specific form of such dummies is the so-called centered seasonal dummy variables, which are defined as $D^*_{s,Sn+s} = D_{s,Sn+s} - (1/S)\sum_{s=1}^{S} D_{s,Sn+s}$.[3] Nevertheless, care in interpretation is necessary in (17), as the interpretation of δ^*_s depends on the definition of $D^*_{s,Sn+s}$. For example, the coefficients of $D^*_{s,Sn+s} = D_{s,Sn+s} - (1/S)\sum_{s=1}^{S} D_{s,Sn+s}$ do not have a straightforward seasonal mean deviation interpretation.

A specific form sometimes used for (17) relates the dummy variables to the seasonal frequencies considered above for seasonally integrated models, resulting in the trigonometric representation [see, for example, Harvey (1993, 1994), or Ghysels and Osborn (2001)]

$$\mu_{Sn+s} = \mu + \sum_{j=1}^{S^{**}} \left(\gamma_j \cos \lambda_{jSn+s} + \gamma^*_j \sin \lambda_{jSn+s}\right) \tag{18}$$

where $S^{**} = \mathrm{int}[S/2]$, and $\lambda_{jt} = \frac{2\pi j}{S}$, $j = 1, \ldots, S^{**}$. When S is even, the sine term is dropped for $j = S/2$; the number of trigonometric coefficients (γ_j, γ^*_j) is always $S-1$.

The above comments carry over to the case when a time trend is included. For example, the use of dummies which are restricted to sum to zero with a (constant) trend implies that we can write

$$\mu_{Sn+s} = \mu + \tau(Sn+s) + \sum_{s=1}^{S} \delta^*_s D^*_{s,Sn+s} \tag{19}$$

with unconditional overall mean $E(y_{Sn+s}) = \mu + \tau(Sn+s)$.

2.3.2. Forecasting with deterministic seasonal models

Due to the prevalence of nonseasonal unit roots in economic time series, consider the model of (16), which has forecast function for $\widehat{y}_{T+h|T}$ given by

$$\widehat{y}_{T+h|T} = \widehat{y}_{T+h-1|T} + \beta(1)\tau + \sum_{i=1}^{S} \beta(L)\Delta_1\delta_i D_{iT+h} + \sum_{j=1}^{p} \beta_j \Delta_1 \widehat{y}_{T+h-j|T} \tag{20}$$

when $\mu_{Sn+s} = \sum_{s=1}^{S} \delta_s D_{s,Sn+s} + \tau(Sn+s)$, and, as above, $\widehat{y}_{T+h-i|T} = y_{T+h-i|T}$ for $h < i$. Once again, forecasts are calculated recursively for $h = 1, 2, \ldots$ and since the

[3] These centered seasonal dummy variables are often offered as an alternative representation to conventional zero/one dummies in time series computer packages, including RATS and PcFiml.

model is linear, forecasts of other linear functions, such as $\Delta_S \widehat{y}_{T+h|T}$ can be obtained using forecast values from (20).

With $\beta(L) = 1$ and assuming $T = NS$ for simplicity, the forecast function for y_{T+h} obtained from (20) is

$$\widehat{y}_{T+h|T} = y_T + h\tau + \sum_{i=1}^{h} (\delta_i - \delta_{i-1}). \tag{21}$$

When h is a multiple of S, it is easy to see that deterministic seasonality becomes irrelevant in this expression, because the change in a purely deterministic seasonal pattern over a year is necessarily zero.

2.4. Forecasting with misspecified seasonal models

From the above discussion, it is clear that various linear models have been proposed, and are widely used, to forecast seasonal time series. In this subsection we consider the implications of using each of the three forecasting models presented above when the true DGP is a seasonal random walk or a deterministic seasonal model. These DGPs are considered because they are the simplest processes which encapsulate the key notions of nonstationary stochastic seasonality and deterministic seasonality. We first present some analytical results for forecasting with misspecified models, followed by the results of a Monte Carlo analysis.

2.4.1. Seasonal random walk

The seasonal random walk DGP is

$$y_{Sn+s} = y_{S(n-1)+s} + \varepsilon_{Sn+s}, \qquad \varepsilon_{Sn+s} \sim \mathrm{iid}(0, \sigma^2). \tag{22}$$

When this seasonally integrated model is correctly specified, the one-step ahead MSFE is $E[(y_{T+1} - \widehat{y}_{T+1|T})^2] = E[(y_{T+1-S} + \varepsilon_{T+1} - y_{T+1-S})^2] = \sigma^2$.

Consider, however, applying the deterministic seasonality model (16), where the zero frequency nonstationarity is recognized and modelling is undertaken after first differencing. The relevant DGP (22) has no trend, and hence we specify $\tau = 0$. Assume a researcher naively applies the model $\Delta_1 y_{Sn+s} = \sum_{i=1}^{S} \Delta_1 \delta_i D_{i,Sn+s} + \upsilon_{Sn+s}$ with no augmentation, but (wrongly) assumes υ to be iid. Due to the presence of nonstationary stochastic seasonality, the estimated dummy variable coefficients do not asymptotically converge to constants. Although analytical results do not appear to have been derived for the resulting forecasts, we anticipate that the MSFE will converge to a degenerate distribution due to neglected nonstationarity.

On the other hand, if the dynamics are adequately augmented, then serial correlation is accounted for and the consistency of the parameter estimates is guaranteed. More specifically, the DGP (22) can be written as

$$\Delta_1 y_{Sn+s} = -\Delta_1 y_{Sn+s-1} - \Delta_1 y_{Sn+s-2} - \cdots - \Delta_1 y_{Sn+s+1-S} + \varepsilon_{Sn+s} \tag{23}$$

and, since these autoregressive coefficients are estimated consistently, the one-step ahead forecasts are asymptotically given by $\Delta_1 \widehat{y}_{T+1|T} = -\Delta_1 y_T - \Delta_1 y_{T-1} - \cdots - \Delta_1 y_{T-S+2}$. Therefore, augmenting with $S-1$ lags of the dependent variable [see Ghysels, Lee and Siklos (1993) and Rodrigues (2000)] asymptotically implies $E[(y_{T+1} - \widehat{y}_{T+1|T})^2] = E(y_{T+1-S} + \varepsilon_{T+1} - (y_T - \Delta_1 y_T - \Delta_1 y_{T-1} - \cdots - \Delta_1 y_{T-S+2}))^2] = E[(y_{T+1-S} + \varepsilon_{T+1} - y_{T+1-S})^2] = \sigma^2$. If fewer than $S-1$ lags of the dependent variable ($\Delta_1 y_{Sn+s}$) are used, then neglected nonstationarity remains and the MSFE is anticipated to be degenerate, as in the naive case.

Turning to the SARIMA model, note that the DGP (22) can be written as

$$\Delta_1 \Delta_S y_{Sn+s} = \Delta_1 \varepsilon_{Sn+s} = \upsilon_{Sn+s} \tag{24}$$

where υ_{Sn+s} here is a noninvertible moving average process, with variance $E[(\upsilon_{Sn+s})^2] = 2\sigma^2$. Again supposing that the naive forecaster assumes υ_{Sn+s} is iid, then, using (7),

$$\begin{aligned} &E\big[(y_{T+1} - \widehat{y}_{T+1|T})^2\big] \\ &\quad = \big[\big((y_{T+1-S} + \varepsilon_{T+1}) - (y_{T+1-S} + \Delta_S y_T + \Delta_1 \Delta_S \widehat{y}_{T+1|T})\big)^2\big] \\ &\quad = E\big[(\varepsilon_{T+1} - \Delta_S y_T)^2\big] \\ &\quad = E\big[(\varepsilon_{T+1} - \varepsilon_T)^2\big] = 2\sigma^2 \end{aligned}$$

where our naive forecaster uses $\Delta_1 \Delta_S \widehat{y}_{T+1|T} = 0$ based on iid υ_{Sn+s}. This represents an extreme case, since in practice we anticipate that some account would be taken of the autocorrelation inherent in (24). Nevertheless, it is indicative of potential forecasting problems from using an overdifferenced model, which implies the presence of noninvertible moving average unit roots that cannot be well approximated by finite order AR polynomials.

2.4.2. *Deterministic seasonal AR(1)*

Consider now a DGP of a random walk with deterministic seasonal effects, which is

$$y_{Sn+s} = y_{Sn+s-1} + \sum_{i=1}^{S} \delta_i^* D_{i,Sn+s} + \varepsilon_{Sn+s} \tag{25}$$

where $\delta_i^* = \delta_i - \delta_{i-1}$ and $\varepsilon_{Sn+s} \sim \text{iid}(0, \sigma^2)$. As usual, the one-step ahead MSFE is $E[(y_{T+1} - \widehat{y}_{T+1|T})^2] = \sigma^2$ when $\widehat{y}_{T+1}$ is forecast from the correctly specified model (25), so that $\widehat{y}_{T+1|T} = y_T + \sum_{i=1}^{S} \delta_i^* D_{i,T+1}$.

If the seasonally integrated model (12) is adopted for forecasting, application of the differencing filter eliminates the deterministic seasonality and induces artificial moving average autocorrelation, since

$$\Delta_S y_{Sn+s} = \delta + S(L)\varepsilon_{Sn+s} = \delta + \upsilon_{Sn+s} \tag{26}$$

where $\delta = \sum_{i=1}^{S} \delta_i^*$, $S(L) = 1 + L + \cdots + L^{S-1}$ and here the disturbance $\upsilon_{Sn+s} = S(L)\varepsilon_{Sn+s}$ is a noninvertible moving average process, with moving average unit roots at each of the seasonal frequencies. However, even if this autocorrelation is not accounted for, δ in (26) can be consistently estimated. Although we would again expect a forecaster to recognize the presence of autocorrelation, the noninvertible moving average process cannot be approximated through the usual practice of autoregressive augmentation. Hence, as an extreme case, we again examine the consequences of a naive researcher assuming υ_{Sn+s} to be iid. Now, using the representation considered in (13) to derive the level forecast from a seasonally integrated model, it follows that

$$E\big(y_{T+1} - \widehat{y}_{T+1|T}\big)^2 = E\left[\left(y_T + \sum_{i=1}^{S} \delta_i^* D_{i,T+1} + \varepsilon_{T+1}\right) - \big(y_{T+1-S} + \Delta_S \widehat{y}_{T+1|T}\big)\right]^2$$

with $y_{T+1-S} = y_{T-S} + \sum_{i=1}^{S} \delta_i^* D_{i,T+1-S} + \varepsilon_{T+1-S}$. Note that although the seasonally integrated model apparently makes no allowance for the deterministic seasonality in the DGP, this deterministic seasonality is also present in the past observation y_{T+1-S} on which the forecast is based. Hence, since $D_{i,T+1} = D_{i,T+1-S}$, the deterministic seasonality cancels between y_T and y_{T-S}, so that

$$\begin{aligned} E\big[\big(y_{T+1} - \widehat{y}_{T+1|T}\big)^2\big] &= E\big[(y_T + \varepsilon_{T+1}) - (y_{T-S} + \varepsilon_{T+1-S})\big]^2 \\ &= E\big[(y_T - y_{T-S} - \delta + \varepsilon_{T+1} - \varepsilon_{T+1-S})^2\big] \\ &= E\big[\big((\varepsilon_T + \varepsilon_{T-1} + \cdots + \varepsilon_{T-S+1}) + \varepsilon_{T+1} - \varepsilon_{T+1-S}\big)^2\big] \\ &= E\big[(\varepsilon_{T+1} + \varepsilon_T + \cdots + \varepsilon_{T-S+2})^2\big] = S\sigma^2 \end{aligned}$$

as, from (26), the naive forecaster uses $\Delta_S \widehat{y}_{T+1} = \delta$. The result also uses (26) to substitute for $y_T - y_{T-S}$. Thus, as a consequence of seasonal overdifferencing, the MSFE increases proportionally to the periodicity of the data. This MSFE effect can, however, be reduced if the overdifferencing is (partially) accounted for through augmentation.

Now consider the use of the SARIMA model when the data is in fact generated by (25). Although

$$\Delta_1 \Delta_S y_{Sn+s} = \Delta_S \varepsilon_{Sn+s} \tag{27}$$

we again consider the naive forecaster who assumes $\upsilon_{Sn+s} = \Delta_S \varepsilon_{Sn+s}$ is iid. Using (7), and noting from (27) that the forecaster uses $\Delta_1 \Delta_S \widehat{y}_{T+1} = 0$, it follows that

$$\begin{aligned} E\big[\big(y_{T+1} - \widehat{y}_{T+1|T}\big)^2\big] &= E\left[\left(y_T + \sum_{i=1}^{S} \delta_i^* D_{i,T+1} + \varepsilon_{T+1} - y_{T+1-S} + \Delta_S y_T\right)^2\right] \\ &= E\big[(\varepsilon_{T+1} - \varepsilon_{T+1-S})^2\big] = 2\sigma^2. \end{aligned}$$

Once again, the deterministic seasonal pattern is taken into account indirectly, through the implicit dependence of the forecast on the past observed value y_{T+1-S} that incorporates the deterministic seasonal effects. Curiously, although the degree of overdifferencing is higher in the SARIMA than in the seasonally integrated model, the MSFE is smaller in the former case.

As already noted, our analysis here does not take account of either augmentation or parameter estimation and hence these results or misspecified models may be considered "worst case" scenarios. It is also worth noting that when seasonally integrated or SARIMA models are used for forecasting a deterministic seasonality DGP, then fewer parameters might be estimated in practice than required in the true DGP. This greater parsimony may outweigh the advantages of using the correct specification and hence it is plausible that a misspecified model could, in particular cases and in moderate or small samples, yield lower MSFE. These issues are investigated in the next subsection through a Monte Carlo analysis.

2.4.3. *Monte Carlo analysis*

This Monte Carlo analysis complements the results of the previous subsection, allowing for augmentation and estimation uncertainty. In all experiments, 10000 replications are used with a maximum lag order considered of $p\max = 8$, the lag selection based on Ng and Perron (1995). Forecasts are performed for horizons $h = 1, \dots, 8$, in samples of $T = 100$, 200 and 400 observations. The tables below report results for $h = 1$ and $h = 8$.

Forecasts are generated using the following three types of models:

$$M_1\colon\quad \Delta_1\Delta_4 y_{4n+s} = \sum_{i=1}^{p_1} \phi_{1,i}\Delta_1\Delta_4 y_{4n+s-i} + \varepsilon_{1,4n+s},$$

$$M_2\colon\quad \Delta_4 y_{4n+s} = \sum_{i=1}^{p_2} \phi_{2,i}\Delta_4 y_{4n+s-i} + \varepsilon_{2,4n+s},$$

$$M_3\colon\quad \Delta_1 y_{4n+s} = \sum_{k=1}^{4} \delta_k D_{k,4n+s} + \sum_{i=1}^{p_3} \phi_{3,i}\Delta_1 y_{4n+s-i} + \varepsilon_{3,4n+s}.$$

The first DGP is the seasonal autoregressive process

$$y_{Sn+s} = \rho y_{S(n-1)+s} + \varepsilon_{Sn+s} \tag{28}$$

where $\varepsilon_{Sn+s} \sim \text{niid}(0, 1)$ and $\rho = \{1, 0.9, 0.8\}$.

Panels (a) to (c) of Table 1 indicate that as one moves from $\rho = 1$ into the stationarity region ($\rho = 0.9$, $\rho = 0.8$) the one-step ahead ($h = 1$) empirical MSFE deteriorates for all forecasting models. For $h = 8$, a similar phenomenon occurs for M_1 and M_2, however M_3 shows some improvement. This behavior is presumably related to the greater degree of overdifferencing imposed by models M_1 and M_2, compared to M_3.

When $\rho = 1$, panel (a) indicates that model M_2 (which considers the correct degree of differencing) yields lower MSFE for both $h = 1$ and $h = 8$ than M_1 and M_3. This advantage for M_2 carries over in relation to M_1 even when $\rho < 1$. However, in panel (c),

Table 1
MSFE when the DGP is (28)

		(a) $\rho = 1$			(b) $\rho = 0.9$			(c) $\rho = 0.8$		
h	T	M_1	M_2	M_3	M_1	M_2	M_3	M_1	M_2	M_3
1	100	1.270	1.035	1.136	1.347	1.091	1.165	1.420	1.156	1.174
	200	1.182	1.014	1.057	1.254	1.068	1.074	1.324	1.123	1.087
	400	1.150	1.020	1.041	1.225	1.074	1.044	1.294	1.123	1.058
8	100	2.019	1.530	1.737	2.113	1.554	1.682	2.189	1.579	1.585
	200	1.933	1.528	1.637	2.016	1.551	1.562	2.084	1.564	1.483
	400	1.858	1.504	1.554	1.942	1.533	1.485	2.006	1.537	1.421
					Average number of lags					
	100	5.79	1.21	3.64	5.76	1.25	3.65	5.81	1.39	3.71
	200	6.98	1.21	3.64	6.94	1.30	3.67	6.95	1.57	3.79
	400	7.65	1.21	3.62	7.67	1.38	3.70	7.68	1.88	3.97

as one moves further into the stationarity region ($\rho = 0.8$) the performance of M_3 is superior to M_2 for sample sizes $T = 200$ and $T = 400$.

Our simple analysis of the previous subsection shows that M_3 should (asymptotically and with augmentation) yield the same forecasts as M_2 for the seasonal random walk of panel (a), but less accurate forecasts are anticipated from M_1 in this case. Our Monte Carlo results verify the practical impact of that analysis. Interestingly, the autoregressive order selected remains relatively stable across the three autoregressive scenarios considered ($\rho = 1, 0.9, 0.8$). Indeed, in this and other respects, the "close to nonstationary" DGPs have similar forecast implications as the nonstationary random walk.

The second DGP considered in this simulation is the first order autoregressive process with deterministic seasonality,

$$y_{Sn+s} = \sum_{i=1}^{S} \delta_i D_{i,Sn+s} + x_{Sn+s}, \tag{29}$$

$$x_{Sn+s} = \rho x_{Sn+s-1} + \varepsilon_{Sn+s} \tag{30}$$

where $\varepsilon_{Sn+s} \sim \text{niid}(0, 1)$, $\rho = \{1, 0.9, 0.8\}$ and $(\delta_1, \delta_2, \delta_3, \delta_4) = (-1, 1, -1, 1)$. Here M_3 provides the correct DGP when $\rho = 1$.

Table 2 shows that (as anticipated) M_3 outperforms M_1 and M_2 when $\rho = 1$, and this carries over to $\rho = 0.9, 0.8$ when $h = 1$. It is also unsurprising that M_3 yields lowest MSFE for $h = 8$ when this is the true DGP in panel (a). Although our previous analysis indicates that M_2 should perform worse than M_1 in this case when the models are not augmented, in practice these models have similar performance when $h = 1$ and M_2 is superior at $h = 8$. The superiority of M_3 also applies when $\rho = 0.9$. However, despite greater overdifferencing, M_2 outperforms M_3 at $h = 8$ when $\rho = 0.8$. In this case, the estimation of additional parameters in M_3 appears to have an adverse effect on forecast

Table 2
MSFE when the DGP is (29) and (30)

		(a) $\rho = 1$			(b) $\rho = 0.9$			(c) $\rho = 0.8$		
h	T	M_1	M_2	M_3	M_1	M_2	M_3	M_1	M_2	M_3
1	100	1.426	1.445	1.084	1.542	1.472	1.151	1.626	1.488	1.210
	200	1.370	1.357	1.032	1.478	1.387	1.092	1.550	1.401	1.145
	400	1.371	1.378	1.030	1.472	1.402	1.077	1.538	1.416	1.120
8	100	7.106	5.354	4.864	6.831	4.073	3.993	5.907	3.121	3.246
	200	7.138	5.078	4.726	6.854	3.926	3.887	5.864	3.030	3.139
	400	7.064	4.910	4.577	6.774	3.839	3.771	5.785	2.986	3.003
					Average number of lags					
	100	2.64	4.07	0.80	2.68	4.22	1.00	2.86	4.27	1.48
	200	2.70	4.34	0.78	2.76	4.46	1.24	3.16	4.49	2.36
	400	2.71	4.48	0.76	2.81	4.53	1.72	3.62	4.53	4.02

accuracy, compared with M_2. In this context, note that the number of lags used in M_3 is increasing as one moves into the stationarity region.

One striking finding of the results in Tables 1 and 2 is that M_2 and M_3 have similar forecast performance at the longer forecast horizon of $h = 8$, or two years. In this sense, the specification of seasonality as being of the nonstationary stochastic or deterministic form may not be of great concern when forecasting. However, the two zero frequency unit roots imposed by the SARIMA model M_1 (and not present in the DGP) leads to forecasts at this non-seasonal horizon which are substantially worse than those of the other two models.

At one-step-ahead horizon, if it is unclear whether the process has zero and seasonal unit roots, our results indicate that the use of the deterministic seasonality model with augmentation may be a more flexible tool than the seasonally integrated model.

2.5. Seasonal cointegration

The univariate models addressed in the earlier subsections are often adequate when short-run forecasts are required. However, multivariate models allow additional information to be utilized and may be expected to improve forecast accuracy. In the context of nonstationary economic variables, cointegration restrictions can be particularly important. There is a vast literature on the forecasting performance of cointegrated models, including Ahn and Reinsel (1994), Clements and Hendry (1993), Lin and Tsay (1996) and Christoffersen and Diebold (1998). The last of these, in particular, shows that the incorporation of cointegration restrictions generally leads to improved long-run forecasts.

Despite the vast literature concerning cointegration, that relating specifically to the seasonal context is very limited. This is partly explained by the lack of evidence for the presence of the full set of seasonal unit roots in economic time series. If seasonality is of the deterministic form, with nonstationarity confined to the zero frequency, then conventional cointegration analysis is applicable, provided that seasonal dummy variables are included where appropriate. Nevertheless, seasonal differencing is sometimes required and it is important to investigate whether cointegration applies also to the seasonal frequency, as well as to the conventional long-run (at the zero frequency). When seasonal cointegration applies, we again anticipate that the use of these restrictions should improve forecast performance.

2.5.1. Notion of seasonal cointegration

To introduce the concept, now let y_{Sn+s} be a vector of seasonally integrated time series. For expositional purposes, consider the quarterly ($S = 4$) case

$$\Delta_4 y_{4n+s} = \eta_{4n+s} \tag{31}$$

where η_{4n+s} is a zero mean stationary and invertible vector stochastic process. Given the vector of seasonally integrated time series, linear combinations may exist that cancel out corresponding seasonal (as well as zero frequency) unit roots. The concept of seasonal cointegration is formalized by Engle, Granger and Hallman (1989), Hylleberg, Engle, Granger and Yoo [HEGY] (1990) and Engle et al. (1993). Based on HEGY, the error-correction representation of a quarterly seasonally cointegrated vector is[4]

$$\begin{aligned}\beta(L)\Delta_4 y_{4n+s} &= \alpha_0 b_0' y_{0,4n+s-1} + \alpha_{11} b_{11}' y_{1,4n+s-1} + \alpha_{12} b_{12}' y_{1,4n+s-2} \\ &\quad + \alpha_2 b_2' y_{2,4n+s-1} + \varepsilon_{4n+s}\end{aligned} \tag{32}$$

where ε_{4n+s} is an iid process, with covariance matrix $E[\varepsilon_{4n+s}\varepsilon_{4n+s}'] = \Sigma$ and each element of the vector $y_{i,4n+s}$ ($i = 0, 1, 2$) is defined through the transformations of (11). Since each element of y_{4n+s} exhibits nonstationarity at the zero and the two seasonal frequencies (π, $\pi/2$), cointegration may apply at each of these frequencies. Indeed, in general, the rank as well as the coefficients of the cointegrating vectors may differ over these frequencies.

The matrix b_0 of (32) contains the linear combinations that eliminate the zero frequency unit root (+1) from the individual $I(1)$ series of $y_{0,4n+s}$. Similarly, b_2 cancels the Nyquist frequency unit root (−1), i.e., the nonstationary biannual cycle present in $y_{2,4n+s}$. The coefficient matrices α_0 and α_2 represent the adjustment coefficients for the variables of the system to the cointegrating relationships at the zero and biannual frequencies, respectively. For the annual cycle corresponding to the complex pair of unit roots $\pm i$, the situation is more complex, leading to two terms in (32). The fact that the cointegrating relations (b_{12}', b_{11}') and adjustment matrices $(\alpha_{12}, \alpha_{11})$ relate to two lags of $y_{1,4n+s}$ is called polynomial cointegration by Lee (1992).

Residual-based tests for the null hypothesis of no seasonal cointegration are discussed by Engle et al. (1993) in the setup of single equation regression models, while Hassler

[4] The generalization for seasonality at any frequency is discussed in Johansen and Schaumburg (1999).

and Rodrigues (2004) provide an empirically more appealing approach. Lee (1992) developed the first system approach to testing for seasonal cointegration, extending the analysis of Johansen (1988) to this case. However, Lee assumes $\alpha_{11}b'_{11} = 0$, which Johansen and Schaumburg (1999) argue is restrictive and they provide a more general treatment.

2.5.2. Cointegration and seasonal cointegration

Other representations may shed light on issues associated with forecasting and seasonal cointegration. Using definitions (11), (32) can be rewritten as

$$\begin{aligned}\beta(L)\Delta_4 y_{4n+s} &= \Pi_1 y_{4n+s-1} + \Pi_2 y_{4n+s-2} + \Pi_3 y_{4n+s-3} \\ &\quad + \Pi_4 y_{4(n-1)+s} + \varepsilon_{4n+s}\end{aligned} \tag{33}$$

where the matrices Π_i $(i = 1, 2, 3, 4)$ are given by

$$\begin{aligned}\Pi_1 &= \alpha_0 b'_0 - \alpha_2 b'_2 - \alpha_{11} b'_{11}, \quad \Pi_2 = \alpha_0 b'_0 + \alpha_2 b'_2 - \alpha_{12} b'_{12}, \\ \Pi_3 &= \alpha_0 b'_0 - \alpha_2 b'_2 + \alpha_{11} b'_{11}, \quad \Pi_4 = \alpha_0 b'_0 + \alpha_2 b'_2 + \alpha_{12} b'_{12}.\end{aligned} \tag{34}$$

Thus, seasonal cointegration implies that the annual change adjusts to y_{4n+s-i} at lags $i = 1, 2, 3, 4$, with (in general) distinct coefficient matrices at each lag; see also Osborn (1993).

Since seasonal cointegration is considered relatively infrequently, it is natural to ask what are the implications of undertaking a conventional cointegration analysis in the presence of seasonal cointegration. From (33) we can write, assuming $\beta(L) = 1$ for simplicity, that,

$$\begin{aligned}\Delta_1 y_{4n+s} &= (\Pi_1 - I) y_{4n+s-1} + \Pi_2 y_{4n+s-2} + \Pi_3 y_{4n+s-3} \\ &\quad + (\Pi_4 + I) y_{4n+s-4} + \varepsilon_{4n+s} \\ &= (\Pi_1 + \Pi_2 + \Pi_3 + \Pi_4) y_{4n+s-1} - (\Pi_2 + \Pi_3 + \Pi_4 + I)\Delta_1 y_{4n+s-1} \\ &\quad - (\Pi_3 + \Pi_4 + I)\Delta_1 y_{4n+s-2} + (\Pi_4 + I)\Delta_1 y_{4n+s-3} + \varepsilon_{4n+s}.\end{aligned} \tag{35}$$

Thus (provided that the ECM is adequately augmented with at least three lags of the vector of first differences), a conventional cointegration analysis implies (35), where the matrix coefficient on the lagged level y_{4n+s-1} is $\Pi_1 + \Pi_2 + \Pi_3 + \Pi_4$. However, it is easy to see from (34) that

$$\Pi_1 + \Pi_2 + \Pi_3 + \Pi_4 = 4\alpha_0 b'_0, \tag{36}$$

so that a conventional cointegration analysis should uncover the zero frequency cointegrating relationships. Although the cointegrating relationships at seasonal frequencies do not explicitly enter the cointegration considered in (36), these will be reflected in the coefficients for the lagged first difference variables, as implied by (35). This generalizes the univariate result of Ghysels, Lee and Noh (1994), that a conventional Dickey–Fuller test remains applicable in the context of seasonal unit roots, provided that the test regression is sufficiently augmented.

2.5.3. Forecasting with seasonal cointegration models

The handling of deterministic components in seasonal cointegration is discussed by Franses and Kunst (1999). In particular, the seasonal dummy variable coefficients need to be restricted to the (seasonal) cointegrating space if seasonal trends are not to be induced in the forecast series.

However, to focus on seasonal cointegration, we continue to ignore deterministic terms. The optimal forecast in a seasonally cointegrated system can then be obtained from (33) as

$$\Delta_4 \widehat{y}_{T+h|T} = \Pi_1 \widehat{y}_{T+h-1|T} + \Pi_2 \widehat{y}_{T+h-2|T} + \Pi_3 \widehat{y}_{T+h-3|T} + \Pi_4 \widehat{y}_{T+h-4|T} + \sum_{i=1}^{p} \beta_i \Delta_4 \widehat{y}_{T+h-i|T} \tag{37}$$

where, analogously to the univariate case, $\widehat{y}_{T+h|T} = E[y_{T+h}|y_1, \ldots, y_T] = \widehat{y}_{T+h-4|T} + \Delta_4 \widehat{y}_{T+h|T}$ is computed recursively for $h = 1, 2, \ldots$. As this is a linear system, optimal forecasts of another linear transformation, such as $\Delta_1 \widehat{y}_{T+h}$, are obtained by applying the required linear transformation to the forecasts generated by (37).

For one-step ahead forecasts ($h = 1$), it is straightforward to see that the matrix MSFE for this system is

$$E\big[\big(y_{T+1} - \widehat{y}_{T+1|T}\big)\big(y_{T+1} - \widehat{y}_{T+1|T}\big)'\big] = E\big[\varepsilon_{T+1}\varepsilon_{T+1}'\big] = \Sigma.$$

To consider longer horizons, we take the case of $h = 2$ and assume $\beta(L) = 1$ for simplicity. Forecasting from the seasonally cointegrated system then implies

$$\begin{aligned} &E\big[\big(y_{T+2} - \widehat{y}_{T+2|T}\big)\big(y_{T+2} - \widehat{y}_{T+2|T}\big)'\big] \\ &\quad = E\big[\big\{\Pi_1\big(y_{T+1} - \widehat{y}_{T+1|T}\big) + \varepsilon_{T+2}\big\}\big\{\Pi_1\big(y_{T+1} - \widehat{y}_{T+1|T}\big) + \varepsilon_{T+2}\big\}'\big] \\ &\quad = \Pi_1 \Sigma \Pi_1' + \Sigma \end{aligned} \tag{38}$$

with $\Pi_1 = (\alpha_0 b_0' - \alpha_{11} b_{11}' - \alpha_2 b_2')$. Therefore, cointegration at the seasonal frequencies plays a role here, in addition to cointegration at the zero frequency.

If the conventional ECM representation (35) is used, then (allowing for the augmentation required even when $\beta(L) = 1$) identical expressions to those just obtained result for the matrix MSFE, due to the equivalence established above between the seasonal and the conventional ECM representations.

When forecasting seasonal time series, and following the seminal paper of Davidson et al. (1978), a common approach is to model the annual differences with cointegration applied at the annual lag. Such a model is

$$\beta^*(L)\Delta_4 y_{4n+s} = \Pi y_{4(n-1)+s} + v_{4n+s} \tag{39}$$

where $\beta^*(L)$ is a polynomial in L and v_{4n+s} is assumed to be vector white noise. If the DGP is given by the seasonally cointegrated model, rearranging (23) yields

$$\beta(L)\Delta_4 y_{4n+s} = (\Pi_1 + \Pi_2 + \Pi_3 + \Pi_4) y_{4(n-1)+s} + \Pi_1 \Delta_1 y_{4n+s-1}$$

$$+ (\Pi_1 + \Pi_2)\Delta_1 y_{4n+s-2} + (\Pi_1 + \Pi_2 + \Pi_3)\Delta_1 y_{4n+s-3} + \varepsilon_{4n+s}. \tag{40}$$

As with conventional cointegration modelling in first differences, the long run zero frequency cointegrating relationships may be uncovered by such an analysis, through $\Pi_1 + \Pi_2 + \Pi_3 + \Pi_4 = \Pi = 4\alpha_0 b_0'$. However, the autoregressive augmentation in $\Delta_4 y_{4n+s}$ adopted in (39) implies overdifferencing compared with the first difference terms on the right-hand side of (40), and hence is unlikely (in general) to provide a good approximation to the coefficients of $\Delta_1 y_{4n+s-i}$ of (40). Indeed, the model based on (39) is valid only when $\Pi_1 = \Pi_2 = \Pi_3 = 0$.

Therefore, if a researcher wishes to avoid issues concerned with seasonal cointegration when such cointegration may be present, it is preferable to use a conventional VECM (with sufficient augmentation) than to consider an annual difference specification such as (39).

2.5.4. Forecast comparisons

Few papers examine forecasts for seasonally cointegrated models for observed economic time series against the obvious competitors of conventional vector error-correction models and VAR models in first differences. In one such comparison, Kunst (1993) finds that accounting for seasonal cointegration generally provides limited improvements, whereas Reimers (1997) finds seasonal cointegration models produce relatively more accurate forecasts when longer forecast horizons are considered. Kunst and Franses (1998) show that restricting seasonal dummies in seasonal cointegration yields better forecasts in most cases they consider, which is confirmed by Löf and Lyhagen (2002). From a Monte Carlo study, Lyhagen and Löf (2003) conclude that use of the seasonal cointegration model provides a more robust forecast performance than models based on pre-testing for unit roots at the zero and seasonal frequencies.

Our review above of cointegration and seasonal cointegration suggests that, in the presence of seasonal cointegration, conventional cointegration modelling will uncover zero frequency cointegration. Since seasonality is essentially an intra-year phenomenon, it may be anticipated that zero frequency cointegration may be relatively more important than seasonal cointegration at longer forecast horizons. This may explain the findings of Kunst (1993) and Reimers (1997) that conventional cointegration models often forecast relatively well in comparison with seasonal cointegration. Our analysis also suggests that a model based on (40) should not, in general, be used for forecasting, since it does not allow for the possible presence of cointegration at the seasonal frequencies.

2.6. Merging short- and long-run forecasts

In many practical contexts, distinct models are used to generate forecasts at long and short horizons. Indeed, long-run models may incorporate factors such as technical progress, which are largely irrelevant when forecasting at a horizon of (say) less than a year. In an interesting paper Engle, Granger and Hallman (1989) discuss merging short- and long-run forecasting models. They suggest that when considering a (single) variable y_{Sn+s}, one can think of models generating the short- and long-run forecasts as approximating different parts of the DGP, and hence these models may have different specifications with non-overlapping sets of explanatory variables. For instance, if y_{Sn+s} is monthly demand for electricity (as considered by Engle, Granger and Hallman), the short-run model may concentrate on rapidly changing variables, including strongly seasonal ones (e.g., temperature and weather variables), whereas the long-run model assimilates slowly moving variables, such as population characteristics, appliance stock and efficiencies or local output. To employ all the variables in the short-run model is too complex and the long-run explanatory variables may not be significant when estimation is by minimization of the one-month forecast variance.

Following Engle, Granger and Hallman (1989), consider $y_{Sn+s} \sim I(1)$ which is cointegrated with variables of the $I(1)$ vector x_{Sn+s} such that $z_{Sn+s} = y_{Sn+s} - \alpha_1' x_{Sn+s}$ is stationary. The true DGP is

$$\Delta_1 y_{Sn+s} = \delta - \gamma z_{Sn+s-1} + \beta' w_{Sn+s} + \varepsilon_{Sn+s}, \tag{41}$$

where w_{Sn+s} is a vector of $I(0)$ variables that can include lags of $\Delta_1 y_{Sn+s}$. Three forecasting models can be considered: the complete true model given by (41), the long-run forecasting model of $y_{Sn+s} = \alpha_0 + \alpha_1' x_{Sn+s} + \eta_{Sn+s}$ and the short-run forecasting model that omits the error-correction term z_{Sn+s-1}. For convenience, we assume that annual forecasts are produced from the long-run model, while forecasts of seasonal (e.g., monthly or quarterly) values are produced by the short-run model.

If all data are available at a seasonal periodicity and the DGP is known, one-step forecasts can be found using (41) as

$$\widehat{y}_{T+1|T} = \delta - (1+\gamma) y_T + \gamma \alpha_1' x_T + \beta' \widehat{w}_{T+1|T}. \tag{42}$$

Given forecasts of x and w, multi-step forecasts $\widehat{y}_{T+h|T}$ can be obtained by iterating (42) to the required horizon. For forecasting a particular season, the long-run forecasts of w_{Sn+s} are constants (their mean for that season) and the DGP implies the long-run forecast

$$\widehat{y}_{T+h|T} \approx \alpha_1' \widehat{x}_{T+h|T} + c \tag{43}$$

where c is a (seasonally varying) constant. Annual forecasts from (43) will be produced by aggregating over seasons, which removes seasonal effects in c. Consequently, the long-run forecasting model should produce annual forecasts similar to those from (43) using the DGP. Similarly, although the short-run forecasting model omits the error-correction term z_{Sn+s}, it will be anticipated to produce similar forecasts to (42), since season-to-season fluctuations will dominate short-run forecasts.

Due to the unlikely availability of long-run data at the seasonal frequency, the complete model (41) is unattainable in practice. Essentially, Engle, Granger and Hallman (1989) propose that the forecasts from the long-run and short-run models be combined to produce an approximation to this DGP. Although not discussed in detail by Engle, Granger and Hallman (1989), long-run forecasts may be made at the annual frequency and then interpolated to seasonal values, in order to provide forecasts approximating those from (41).

In this set-up, the long-run model includes annual variables and has nothing to say about seasonality. By design, cointegration relates only to the zero frequency. Seasonality is allocated entirely to the short-run and is modelled through the deterministic component and the forecasts $\widehat{w}_{T+h|T}$ of the stationary variables. Rather surprisingly, this approach to forecasting appears almost entirely unexplored in subsequent literature, with issues of seasonal cointegration playing a more prominent role. This is unfortunate, since (as noted in the previous subsection) there is little evidence that seasonal cointegration improves forecast accuracy and, in any case, can be allowed for by including sufficient lags of the relevant variables in the dynamics of the model. In contrast, the approach of Engle, Granger and Hallman (1989) allows information available only at an annual frequency to play a role in capturing the long-run, and such information is not considered when the researcher focuses on seasonal cointegration.

3. Periodic models

Periodic models provide another approach to modelling and forecasting seasonal time series. These models are more general than those discussed in the previous section in allowing all parameters to vary across the seasons of a year. Periodic models can be useful in capturing economic situations where agents show distinct seasonal characteristics, such as seasonally varying utility of consumption [Osborn (1988)]. Within economics, periodic models usually take an autoregressive form and are known as PAR (periodic autoregressive) models.

Important developments in this field, have been made by, *inter alia*, Pagano (1978), Troutman (1979), Gladyshev (1961), Osborn (1991), Franses (1994) and Boswijk and Franses (1996). Applications of PAR models include, for example, Birchenhall et al. (1989), Novales and Flores de Fruto (1997), Franses and Romijn (1993), Herwartz (1997), Osborn and Smith (1989) and Wells (1997).

3.1. *Overview of PAR models*

A univariate PAR(p) model can be written as

$$y_{Sn+s} = \sum_{j=1}^{S} \big[\mu_j + \tau_j(Sn+s)\big] D_{j,Sn+s} + x_{Sn+s}, \tag{44}$$

$$x_{Sn+s} = \sum_{j=1}^{S} \sum_{i=1}^{p_j} \phi_{ij} D_{j,Sn+s} x_{Sn+s-i} + \varepsilon_{Sn+s} \tag{45}$$

where (as in the previous section) S represents the periodicity of the data, while here p_j is the order of the autoregressive component for season j, $p = \max(p_1, \ldots, p_S)$, $D_{j,Sn+s}$ is again a seasonal dummy that is equal to 1 in season j and zero otherwise, and $\varepsilon_{Sn+s} \sim \mathrm{iid}(0, \sigma_s^2)$. The PAR model of (44)–(45) requires a total of $(3S + \sum_{j=1}^{S} p_j)$ parameters to be estimated. This basic model can be extended by including periodic moving average terms [Tiao and Grupe (1980), Lütkepohl (1991)].

Note that this process is nonstationary in the sense that the variances and covariances are time-varying within the year. However, considered as a vector process over the S seasons, stationarity implies that these intra-year variances and covariances remain constant over years, $n = 0, 1, 2, \ldots$. It is this vector stationarity concept that is appropriate for PAR processes.

Substituting from (45) into (44), the model for season s is

$$\phi_s(L) y_{Sn+s} = \phi_s(L)\bigl[\mu_s + \tau_s(Sn + s)\bigr] + \varepsilon_{Sn+s} \tag{46}$$

where $\phi_j(L) = 1 - \phi_{1j} L - \cdots - \phi_{p_j,j} L^{p_j}$. Alternatively, following Boswijk and Franses (1996), the model for season s can be represented as

$$(1 - \alpha_s L) y_{Sn+s} = \delta_s + \omega_s(Sn + s) + \sum_{k=1}^{p-1} \beta_{ks}(1 - \alpha_{s-k} L) y_{Sn+s-k} + \varepsilon_{Sn+s} \tag{47}$$

where $\alpha_{s-Sm} = \alpha_s$ for $s = 1, \ldots, S$, $m = 1, 2, \ldots$ and $\beta_j(L)$ is a $(p_j - 1)$-order polynomial in L. Although the parameterization of (47) is useful, it should also be appreciated that the factorization of $\phi_s(L)$ implied in (47) is not, in general, unique [del Barrio Castro and Osborn (2004)]. Nevertheless, this parameterization is useful when the unit root properties of y_{Sn+s} are isolated in $(1 - \alpha_s L)$. In particular, the process is said to be periodically integrated if

$$\prod_{s=1}^{S} \alpha_s = 1, \tag{48}$$

with the stochastic part of $(1 - \alpha_s L) y_{Sn+s}$ being stationary. In this case, (48) serves to identify the parameters of (47) and the model is referred to as a periodic integrated autoregressive (PIAR) model. To distinguish periodic integration from conventional (nonperiodic) integration, we require that not all $\alpha_s = 1$ in (48).

An important consequence of periodic integration is that such series cannot be decomposed into distinct seasonal and trend components; see Franses (1996, Chapter 8). An alternative possibility to the PIAR process is a conventional unit root process with periodic stationary dynamics, such as

$$\beta_s(L) \Delta_1 y_{Sn+s} = \delta_s + \varepsilon_{Sn+s}. \tag{49}$$

As discussed below, (47) and (49) have quite different forecast implications for the future pattern of the trend.

3.2. Modelling procedure

The crucial issues for modelling a potentially periodic process are deciding whether the process is, indeed, periodic and deciding the appropriate order p for the PAR.

3.2.1. Testing for periodic variation and unit roots

Two approaches can be considered to the inter-related issues of testing for the presence of periodic coefficient variation.

(a) Test the nonperiodic (constant autoregressive coefficient) null hypothesis

$$H_0\colon \quad \phi_{ij} = \phi_i, \quad j = 1, \dots, S, i = 1, \dots, p \tag{50}$$

against the alternative of a periodic model using a χ^2 or F test (the latter might be preferred unless the number of years of data is large). This is conducted using an OLS estimation of (44) and, as no unit root restriction is involved, its validity does not depend on stationarity [Boswijk and Franses (1996)].

(b) Estimate a nonperiodic model and apply a diagnostic test for periodic autocorrelation to the residuals [Franses (1996, pp. 101–102)]. Further, Franses (1996) argues that neglected parameter variations may surface in the variance of the residual process, so that a test for periodic heteroskedasticity can be considered, by regressing the squared residuals on seasonal dummy variables [see also del Barrio Castro and Osborn (2004)]. These can again be conducted using conventional distributions.

Following a test for periodic coefficient variation, such as (50), unit root properties may be examined. Boswijk and Franses (1996) develop a generalization of the Dickey–Fuller unit root t-test statistic applicable in a periodic context. Conditional on the presence of a unit root, they also discuss testing the restriction $\alpha_s = 1$ in (47), with this latter test being a test of restrictions that can be applied using the conventional χ^2 or F-distribution. When the restrictions $\alpha_s = 1$ are valid, the process can be written as (49) above. Ghysels, Hall and Lee (1996) also propose a test for seasonal integration in the context of a periodic process.

3.2.2. Order selection

The order selection of the autoregressive component of the PAR model is obviously important. Indeed, because the number of autoregressive coefficients required is (in general) pS, this may be considered to be more crucial in this context than for the linear AR models of the previous section.

Order specification is frequently based on an information criterion. Franses and Paap (1994) find that the Schwarz Information Criterion (SIC) performs better for order selection in periodic models than the Akaike Information Criterion (AIC). This is, perhaps, unsurprising in that AIC leads to more highly parameterized models, which may be considered overparameterized in the periodic context. Franses and Paap (1994) recommend backing up the SIC strategy that selects p by F-tests for $\phi_{i,p+1} = 0, i = 1, \ldots, S$. Having established the PAR order, the null hypothesis of nonperiodicity (50) is then examined.

If used without restrictions, a PAR model tends to be highly parameterized, and the application of restrictions may yield improved forecast accuracy. Some of the model reduction strategies that can be considered are:

- Allow different autoregressive orders p_j for each season, $j = 1, \ldots, S$, with possible follow-up elimination of intermediate regressors by an information criterion or using statistical significance.
- Employ common parameters for across seasons. Rodrigues and Gouveia (2004) specify a PAR model for monthly data based on $S = 3$ seasons. In the same vein, Novales and Flores de Fruto (1997) propose grouping similar seasons into blocks to reduce the number of periodic parameters to be estimated.
- Reduce the number of parameters by using short Fourier series [Jones and Brelsford (1968), Lund et al. (1995)]. Such Fourier reductions are particularly useful when changes in the correlation structure over seasons are not abrupt.
- Use a layered approach, where a "first layer" removes the periodic autocorrelation in the series, while a "second layer" has an ARMA(p, q) representation [Bloomfield, Hurd and Lund (1994)].

3.3. Forecasting with univariate PAR models

Perhaps the simplest representation of a PAR model for forecasting purposes is (47), from which the h-step forecast is given by

$$\begin{aligned}\widehat{y}_{T+h|T} &= \alpha_s \widehat{y}_{T+h-1|T} + \delta_s + \omega_s(T+h) \\ &\quad + \sum_{k=1}^{p-1} \beta_{ks}\bigl(\widehat{y}_{T+h-k|T} - \alpha_{s-k}\widehat{y}_{T+h-k-1|T}\bigr) \end{aligned} \tag{51}$$

when $T+h$ falls in season s. This expression can be iterated for $h = 1, 2, \ldots$. Assuming a unit root PAR process, we can distinguish the forecasting implications of y being periodically integrated (with $\prod_{i=1}^{S} \alpha_i = 1$, but not all $\alpha_s = 1$) and an $I(1)$ process ($\alpha_s = 1, s = 1, \ldots, S$).

To discuss the essential features of the $I(1)$ case, an order $p = 2$ is sufficient. A key feature for forecasting nonstationary processes is the implications for the deterministic component. In this specific case, $\phi_s(L) = (1-L)(1-\beta_s L)$, so that (46) and (47) imply

$$\begin{aligned}\delta_s + \omega_s(T+h) &= (1-L)(1-\beta_s L)\bigl[\mu_s + \tau_s(T+h)\bigr] \\ &= \Delta\mu_s - \beta_s\Delta\mu_{s-1} + \tau_s(T+h) - (1+\beta_s)\tau_{s-1}(T+h-1) \\ &\quad + \beta_s\tau_{s-2}(T+h-2)\end{aligned}$$

and hence

$$\delta_s = \Delta\mu_s - \beta_s\Delta\mu_{s-1} + \tau_{s-1} + \beta_s\tau_{s-1} - 2\beta_s\tau_{s-2},$$

$$\omega_s = \tau_s - (1 + \beta_s)\tau_{s-1} + \beta_s \tau_{s-2}.$$

Excluding specific cases of interaction[5] between values of τ_s and β_s, the restriction $\omega_s = 0$, $s = 1, \ldots, S$ in (51) implies $\tau_s = \tau$, so that the forecasts for the seasons do not diverge as the forecast horizon increases. With this restriction, the intercept

$$\delta_s = \Delta\mu_s - \beta_s \Delta\mu_{s-1} + (1 - \beta_s)\tau$$

implies a deterministic seasonal pattern in the forecasts. Indeed, in the special case that $\beta_s = \beta$, $s = 1, \ldots, S$, this becomes the forecast for a deterministic seasonal process with a stationary AR(1) component.

The above discussion shows that a stationary periodic autoregression in an $I(1)$ process does not essentially alter the characteristics of the forecasts, compared with an $I(1)$ process with deterministic seasonality. We now turn attention to the case of periodic integration.

In a PIAR process, the important feature is the periodic nonstationarity, and hence we gain sufficient generality for our discussion by considering $\phi_s(L) = 1 - \alpha_s L$. In this case, (51) becomes

$$\widehat{y}_{T+h|T} = \alpha_s \widehat{y}_{T+h-1|T} + \delta_s + \omega_s(T + h) \tag{52}$$

for which (46) implies

$$\begin{aligned}\delta_s + \omega_s(T + h) &= (1 - \alpha_s L)\big[\mu_s + \tau_s(T + h)\big] \\ &= \mu_s - \alpha_s \mu_{s-1} + \tau_s(T + h) - \alpha_s \tau_{s-1}(T + h - 1)\end{aligned}$$

and hence

$$\begin{aligned}\delta_s &= \mu_s - \alpha_s \mu_{s-1} + \alpha_s \tau_{s-1}, \\ \omega_s &= \tau_s - \alpha_s \tau_{s-1}.\end{aligned}$$

Here imposition of $\omega_s = 0$ $(s = 1, \ldots, S)$ implies $\tau_s - \alpha_s \tau_{s-1} = 0$, and hence $\tau_s \neq \tau_{s-1}$ in (44) for at least one s, since the periodic integrated process requires not all $\alpha_s = 1$. Therefore, forecasts exhibiting distinct trends over the S seasons are a natural consequence of a PIAR specification, whether or not an explicit trend is included in (52). A forecaster adopting a PIAR model needs to appreciate this.

However, allowing $\omega_s \neq 0$ in (52) enables the underlying trend in $\widehat{y}_{T+h|T}$ to be constant over seasons. Specifically, $\tau_s = \tau$ $(s = 1, \ldots, S)$ requires $\omega_s = (1 - \alpha_s)\tau$, which implies an intercept in (52) whose value is restricted over $s = 1, \ldots, S$. The interpretation is that the trend in the periodic difference $(1 - \alpha_s L)\widehat{y}_{T+h|T}$ must counteract the diverging trends that would otherwise arise in the forecasts $\widehat{y}_{T+h|T}$ over seasons; see Paap and Franses (1999) or Ghysels and Osborn (2001, pp. 155–156). An important implication is that if forecasts with diverging trends over seasons are implausible, then a constant (nonzero) trend can be achieved through the imposition of appropriate restrictions on the trend terms in the forecast function for the PIAR model.

[5] Stationarity for the periodic component here requires only $|\beta_1 \beta_2 \cdots \beta_S| < 1$.

3.4. Forecasting with misspecified models

Despite their theoretical attractions in some economic contexts, periodic models are not widely used for forecasting in economics. Therefore, it is relevant to consider the implications of applying an ARMA forecasting model to periodic GDP. This question is studied by Osborn (1991), building on Tiao and Grupe (1980).

It is clear from (44) and (45) that the autocovariances of a stationary PAR process differ over seasons. Denoting the autocovariance for season s at lag k by $\gamma_{sk} = E(x_{Sn+s}x_{Sn+s-k})$, the overall mean autocovariance at lag k is

$$\gamma_k = \frac{1}{S}\sum_{s=1}^{S}\gamma_{sk}. \tag{53}$$

When an ARMA model is fitted, asymptotically it must account for all nonzero autocovariances γ_k, $k = 0, 1, 2, \ldots$. Using (53), Tiao and Grupe (1980) and Osborn (1991) show that the implied ARMA model fitted to a PAR(p) process has, in general, a purely seasonal autoregressive operator of order p, together with a potentially high order moving average.

As a simple case, consider a purely stochastic PAR(1) process for $S = 2$ seasons per year, so that

$$\begin{aligned} x_{Sn+s} &= \phi_s x_{Sn+s-1} + \varepsilon_{Sn+s} \\ &= \phi_1\phi_2 x_{Sn+s-2} + \varepsilon_{Sn+s} + \phi_{s-1}\varepsilon_{Sn+s-1}, \quad s = 1, 2 \end{aligned} \tag{54}$$

where white noise ε_{Sn+s} has $E(\varepsilon^2_{Sn+s}) = \sigma^2_s$ and $\phi_0 = \phi_2$. The corresponding misspecified ARMA model that accounts for the autocovariances (53) effectively takes a form of average across the two processes in (54) to yield

$$x_{Sn+s} = \phi_1\phi_2 x_{Sn+s-2} + u_{Sn+s} + \theta u_{Sn+s-1} \tag{55}$$

where u_{Sn+s} has autocovariances $\gamma_k = 0$ for all lags $k = 1, 2 \ldots$. From known results concerning the accuracy of forecasting using aggregate and disaggregate series, the MSFE at any horizon h using the (aggregate) ARMA representation (54) must be at least as large as the mean MSFE over seasons for the true (disaggregate) PAR(1) process.

As in the analysis of misspecified processes in the discussion of linear models in the previous section, these results take no account of estimation effects. To the extent that, in practice, periodic models require the estimation of more coefficients than ARMA ones, the theoretical forecasting advantage of the former over the latter for a true periodic DGP will not necessarily carry over when observed data are employed.

3.5. Periodic cointegration

Periodic cointegration relates to cointegration between individual processes that are either periodically integrated or seasonally integrated. To concentrate on the essential issues, we consider periodic cointegration between the univariate nonstationary process y_{Sn+s} and the vector nonstationary process x_{Sn+s} as implying that

$$z_{Sn+s} = y_{Sn+s} - \alpha_s' x_{Sn+s}, \quad s = 1, \ldots, S, \tag{56}$$

is a (possibly periodic) stationary process, with not all vectors α_s equal over $s = 1, \ldots, S$. The additional complications of so-called partial periodic cointegration will not be considered. We also note that there has been much confusion in the literature on periodic processes relating to types of cointegration that can apply. These issues are discussed by Ghysels and Osborn (2001, pp. 168–171).

In both theoretical developments and empirical applications, the most popular single equation periodic cointegration model [PCM] has the form:

$$\begin{aligned}\Delta_S y_{Sn+s} = {} & \sum_{s=1}^{S} \mu_s D_{s,Sn+s} + \sum_{s=1}^{S} \lambda_s D_{s,Sn+s} \big(y_{Sn+s-S} - \alpha_s' x_{Sn+s-S} \big) \\ & + \sum_{k=1}^{p} \phi_k \Delta_S y_{Sn+s-k} + \sum_{k=0}^{p} \delta_k' \Delta_S x_{Sn+s-k} + \varepsilon_{Sn+s}\end{aligned} \tag{57}$$

where y_{Sn+s} is the variable of specific interest, x_{Sn+s} is a vector of weakly exogenous explanatory variables and ε_{Sn+s} is white noise. Here λ_s and α_s' are seasonally varying adjustment and long-run parameters, respectively; the specification of (57) could allow the disturbance variance to vary over seasons. As discussed by Ghysels and Osborn (2001, p. 171) this specification implicitly assumes that the individual variables of y_{Sn+s}, x_{Sn+s} are seasonally integrated, rather than periodically integrated.

Boswijk and Franses (1995) develop a Wald test for periodic cointegration through the unrestricted model

$$\begin{aligned}\Delta_S y_{Sn+s} = {} & \sum_{s=1}^{S} \mu_s D_{s,Sn+s} + \sum_{s=1}^{S} \big(\delta_{1s} D_{s,Sn+s} y_{Sn+s-S} + \delta_{2s}' D_{s,Sn+s} x_{Sn+s-4} \big) \\ & + \sum_{k=1}^{p} \beta_k \Delta_S y_{Sn+s-k} + \sum_{k=0}^{p} \tau_k' \Delta_S x_{Sn+s-k} + \varepsilon_{Sn+s}\end{aligned} \tag{58}$$

where under cointegration $\delta_{1s} = \lambda_s$ and $\delta_{2s} = -\alpha_s' \lambda_s$. Defining $\delta_s = (\delta_{1s}, \delta_{2s}')'$ and $\delta = (\delta_1', \delta_2', \ldots, \delta_S')'$, the null hypothesis of no cointegration in any season is given by H_0: $\delta = 0$. Because cointegration for one season s does not necessarily imply cointegration for all $s = 1, \ldots, S$, the alternative hypothesis H_1: $\delta \neq 0$ implies cointegration for at least one s. Relevant critical values for the quarterly case are given in Boswijk and Franses (1995), who also consider testing whether cointegration applies in individual seasons and whether cointegration is nonperiodic.

Since periodic cointegration is typically applied in contexts that implicitly assume seasonally integrated variables, it seems obvious that the possibility of seasonal cointegration should also be considered. Although Franses (1993, 1995) and Ghysels and

Osborn (2001, pp. 174–176) make some progress towards a testing strategy to distinguish between periodic and seasonal cointegration, this issue has yet to be fully worked out in the literature.

When the periodic ECM model of (57) is used for forecasting, a separate model is (of course) required to forecast the weakly exogenous variables in x.

3.6. Empirical forecast comparisons

Empirical studies of the forecast performance of periodic models for economic variables are mixed. Osborn and Smith (1989) find that periodic models produce more accurate forecasts than nonperiodic ones for the major components of quarterly UK consumers expenditure. However, although Wells (1997) finds evidence of periodic coefficient variation in a number of US time series, these models do not consistently produce improved forecast accuracy compared with nonperiodic specifications. In investigating the forecasting performance of PAR models, Rodrigues and Gouveia (2004) observe that using parsimonious periodic autoregressive models, with fewer separate "seasons" modelled than indicated by the periodicity of the data, presents a clear advantage in forecasting performance over other models. When examining forecast performance for observed UK macroeconomic time series, Novales and Flores de Fruto (1997) draw a similar conclusion.

As noted in our previous discussion, the role of deterministic variables is important in periodic models. Using the same series as Osborn and Smith (1989), Franses and Paap (2002) consider taking explicit account of the appropriate form of deterministic variables in PAR models and adopt encompassing tests to formally evaluate forecast performance.

Relatively few studies consider the forecast performance of periodic cointegration models. However, Herwartz (1997) finds little evidence that such models improve accuracy for forecasting consumption in various countries, compared with constant parameter specifications. In comparing various vector systems, Löf and Franses (2001) conclude that models based on seasonal differences generally produce more accurate forecasts than those based on first differences or periodic specifications.

In view of their generally unimpressive performance in empirical forecast comparisons to date, it seems plausible that parsimonious approaches to periodic ECM modelling may be required for forecasting, since an unrestricted version of (57) may imply a large number of parameters to be estimated. Further, as noted in the previous section, there has been some confusion in the literature about the situations in which periodic cointegration can apply and there is no clear testing strategy to distinguish between seasonal and periodic cointegration. Clarification of these issues may help to indicate the circumstances in which periodic specifications yield improved forecast accuracy over nonperiodic models.

4. Other specifications

The previous sections have examined linear models and periodic models, where the latter can be viewed as linear models with a structure that changes with the season. The simplest models to specify and estimate are linear (time-invariant) ones. However, there is no *a priori* reason why seasonal structures should be linear and time-invariant. The preferences of economic agents may change over time or institutional changes may occur that cause the seasonal pattern in economic variables to alter in a systematic way over time or in relation to underlying economic conditions, such as the business cycle.

In recent years a burgeoning literature has examined the role of nonlinear models for economic modelling. Although much of this literature takes the context as being nonseasonal, a few studies have also examined these issues for seasonal time series. Nevertheless, an understanding of the nature of change over time is a fundamental prerequisite for accurate forecasting.

The present section first considers nonlinear threshold and Markov switching time series models, before turning to a notion of seasonality different from that discussed in previous sections, namely seasonality in variance. Consider for expository purposes the general model,

$$y_{Sn+s} = \mu_{Sn+s} + \xi_{Sn+s} + x_{Sn+s}, \tag{59}$$

$$\psi(L)x_{Sn+s} = \varepsilon_{Sn+s} \tag{60}$$

where μ_{Sn+s} and ξ_{Sn+s} represent deterministic variables which will be presented in detail in the following sections, $\varepsilon_{Sn+s} \sim \Gamma(0, h_t)$, Γ is a probability distribution and h_t represents the assumed variance which can be constant over time or time varying.

In the following section we start to look at nonlinear models and the implications of seasonality in the mean, which will be introduced through μ_{Sn+s} and ξ_{Sn+s}, considering that the errors are i.i.d. $N(0, \sigma^2)$; and in Section 4.2 proceed to investigate the modelling of seasonality in variance, considering that the errors follow GARCH or stochastic volatility type behaviour and allowing for the seasonal behavior in volatility to be deterministic and stochastic.

4.1. Nonlinear models

Although many different types of nonlinear models have been proposed, perhaps those used in a seasonal context are of the threshold or regime-switching types. In both cases, the relationship is assumed to be linear within a regime. These nonlinear models focus on the interaction between seasonality and the business cycle, since Ghysels (1994b), Canova and Ghysels (1994), Matas-Mir and Osborn (2004) and others have shown that these are interrelated.

4.1.1. Threshold seasonal models

In this class of models, the regimes are defined by the values of some variable in relation to specific thresholds, with the transition between regimes being either abrupt or smooth. To distinguish these, the former are referred to as threshold autoregressive (TAR) models, while the latter are known as smooth transition autoregressive (STAR) models. Threshold models have been applied to seasonal growth in output, with the annual output growth used as the business cycle indicator.

Cecchitti and Kashyap (1996) provide some theoretical basis for an interaction between seasonality and the business cycle, by outlining an economic model of seasonality in production over the business cycle. Since firms may hit capacity restrictions when production is high, they will reallocate production to the usually slack summer months near business cycle peaks.

Motivated by this hypothesis, Matas-Mir and Osborn (2004) consider the seasonal TAR model for monthly data given as

$$\begin{aligned}\Delta_1 y_{Sn+s} = {} & \mu_0 + \eta_0 I_{Sn+s} + \tau_0(Sn+s) \\ & + \sum_{j=1}^{S}\big[\mu_j^* + \eta_j^* I_{Sn+s} + \tau_j^*(Sn+s)\big] D^*_{j,Sn+s} \\ & + \sum_{i=1}^{p} \phi_i \Delta_1 y_{Sn+s-i} + \varepsilon_{Sn+s} \qquad (61)\end{aligned}$$

where $S = 12$, $\varepsilon_{Sn+s} \sim \text{iid}(0, \sigma^2)$, $D^*_{j,Sn+s}$ is a seasonal dummy variable and the regime indicator I_{Sn+s} is defined in terms of a threshold value r for the lagged annual change in y. Note that this model results from (59) and (60) by considering that $\mu_{Sn+s} = \delta_0+\gamma_0(Sn+s)+\sum_{j=1}^{S}[\delta_j+\gamma_j(Sn+s)]D_{j,Sn+s}$, $\xi_{Sn+s} = [\alpha_0+\sum_{j=1}^{S}\alpha_j D_{j,Sn+s}]I_{Sn+s}$ and $\psi(L) = \phi(L)\Delta_1$ is a polynomial of order $p+1$. The nonlinear specification of (61) allows the overall intercept and the deterministic seasonality to change with the regime, but (for reasons of parsimony) not the dynamics. Systematic changes in seasonality are permitted through the inclusion of seasonal trends. Matas-Mir and Osborn (2004) find support for the seasonal nonlinearities in (61) for around 30 percent of the industrial production series they analyze for OECD countries.

A related STAR specification is employed by van Dijk, Strikholm and Terasvirta (2003). However, rather than using a threshold specification which results from the use of the indicator function I_{Sn+s}, these authors specify the transition between regimes using the logistic function

$$G_i(\varphi_{it}) = \big[1 + \exp\{-\gamma_i(\varphi_{it} - c_i)/\sigma_{s_{it}}\}\big]^{-1}, \quad \gamma_i > 0 \qquad (62)$$

for a transition variable φ_{it}. In fact, they allow two such transition functions ($i = 1, 2$) when modelling the quarterly change in industrial production for G7 countries, with one transition variable being the lagged annual change ($\varphi_{1t} = \Delta_4 y_{t-d}$ for some delay d), which can be associated with the business cycle, and the other transition variable being time ($\varphi_{2t} = t$). Potentially all coefficients, relating to both the seasonal dummy variables and the autoregressive dynamics are allowed to change with the regime. These authors conclude that changes in the seasonal pattern associated with the time transition are more important than those associated with the business cycle.

In a nonseasonal context, Clements and Smith (1999) investigate the multi-step forecast performance of TAR models via empirical MSFEs and show that these models perform significantly better than linear models particularly in cases when the forecast origin covers a recession period. It is notable that recessions have fewer observations than expansions, so that their forecasting advantage appears to be in atypical periods.

There has been little empirical investigation of the forecast accuracy of nonlinear seasonal threshold models for observed series. The principal available study is Franses and van Dijk (2005), who consider various models of seasonality and nonlinearity for quarterly industrial production for 18 OECD countries. They find that, in general, linear models perform best at short horizons, while nonlinear models with more elaborate seasonal specifications are preferred at longer horizons.

4.1.2. Periodic Markov switching regime models

Another approach to model the potential interaction between seasonal and business cycles is through periodic Markov switching regime models. Special cases of this class include the (aperiodic) switching regime models considered by Hamilton (1989, 1990), among many others. Ghysels (1991, 1994b, 1997) presented a periodic Markov switching structure which was used to investigate the nonuniformity over months of the distribution of the NBER business cycle turning points for the US. The discussion here, which is based on Ghysels (2000) and Ghysels, Bac and Chevet (2003), will focus first on a simplified illustrative example to present some of the key features and elements of interest. The main purpose is to provide intuition for the basic insights. In particular, one can map periodic Markov switching regime models into their linear representations. Through the linear representation one is able to show that hidden periodicities are left unexploited and can potentially improve forecast performance.

Consider a univariate time series process, again denoted $\{y_{Sn+s}\}$. It will typically represent a growth rate of, say, GNP. Moreover, for the moment, it will be assumed the series does not exhibit seasonality in the mean (possibly because it was seasonally adjusted) and let $\{y_{Sn+s}\}$ be generated by the following stochastic structure:

$$\big(y_{Sn+s} - \mu\big[(i_{Sn+s}, \mathbf{v})\big]\big) = \phi\big(y_{Sn+s-1} - \mu\big[(i_{Sn+s-1}, \mathbf{v} - \mathbf{1})\big]\big) + \varepsilon_{Sn+s} \tag{63}$$

where $|\phi| < 1$, ε_t is i.i.d. $N(0, \sigma^2)$ and $\mu[\cdot]$ represents an intercept shift function. If $\mu \equiv \bar{\mu}$, i.e., a constant, then (63) is a standard linear stationary Gaussian AR(1) model. Instead, following Hamilton (1989), we assume that the intercept changes according to a Markovian switching regime model. However, in (63) we have $x_t \equiv (i_t, \mathbf{v})$, namely, the state of the world is described by a stochastic switching regime process $\{i_t\}$ and a seasonal indicator process $\mathbf{v}$. The $\{i_{Sn+s}\}$ and $\{\mathbf{v}\}$ processes interact in the following way, such that for $i_{Sn+s} \in \{0, 1\}$:[6]

$$\begin{array}{c|cc} & 0 & 1 \\ \hline 0 & q(\mathbf{v}) & 1-q(\mathbf{v}) \\ 1 & 1-p(\mathbf{v}) & p(\mathbf{v}) \end{array} \tag{64}$$

where the transition probabilities $q(\cdot)$ and $p(\cdot)$ are allowed to change with the season. When $p(\cdot) = \bar{p}$ and $q(\cdot) = \bar{q}$, we obtain the standard homogeneous Markov chain model considered by Hamilton. However, if for at least one season the transition probability matrix differs, we have a situation where a regime shift will be more or less likely depending on the time of the year. Since $i_{Sn+s} \in \{0, 1\}$, consider the mean shift function:

$$\mu[(i_t, \mathbf{v})] = \alpha_0 + \alpha_1 i_{Sn+s}, \quad \alpha_1 > 0. \tag{65}$$

Hence, the process $\{y_{Sn+s}\}$ has a mean shift α_0 in state 1 ($i_{Sn+s} = 0$) and $\alpha_0 + \alpha_1$ in state 2. These above equations are a version of Hamilton's model with a periodic stochastic switching process. If state 1 with low mean drift is called a recession and state 2 an expansion, then we stay in a recession or move to an expansion with a probability scheme that depends on the season.

The structure presented so far is relatively simple, yet as we shall see, some interesting dynamics and subtle interdependencies emerge. It is worth comparing the AR(1) model with a periodic Markovian stochastic switching regime structure and the more conventional linear ARMA processes as well as periodic ARMA models. Let us perhaps start by briefly explaining intuitively what drives the connections between the different models. The model with y_{Sn+s} typically representing a growth series, is covariance stationary under suitable regularity conditions discussed in Ghysels (2000). Consequently, the process has a linear Wold MA representation. Yet, the time series model provides a relatively parsimonious structure which determines nonlinearly predictable MA innovations. In fact, there are two layers beneath the Wold MA representation. One layer relates to *hidden periodicities*, as described in Tiao and Grupe (1980) or Hansen and Sargent (1993), for instance. Typically, such hidden periodicities can be uncovered via augmentation of the state space with the augmented system having a linear representation. However, the periodic switching regime model imposes *further structure* even after the hidden periodicities are uncovered. Indeed, there is a second layer which makes the innovations of the augmented system nonlinearly predictable. Hence, the model has nonlinearly predictable innovations and features of hidden periodicities combined.

To develop this more explicitly, let us first note that the switching regime process $\{i_{Sn+s}\}$ admits the following AR(1) representation:

$$i_{Sn+s} = \left[1 - q(\mathbf{v}_t)\right] + \lambda(\mathbf{v}_t) i_{t-1} + v_{Sn+s}(\mathbf{v}) \tag{66}$$

[6] In order to avoid too cumbersome notation, we did not introduce a separate notation for the theoretical representation of stochastic processes and their actual realizations.

where $\lambda(\cdot) \in \{\lambda^1, \dots, \lambda^S\}$ with $\lambda(\mathbf{v}) \equiv -1 + p(\mathbf{v}) + q(\mathbf{v}) = \lambda^s$ for $\mathbf{v} = \mathbf{v}$. Moreover, conditional on $i_{t-1} = 1$,

$$v_{Sn+s}(\mathbf{v}) = \begin{cases} (1 - p(\mathbf{v})) & \text{with probability } p(\mathbf{v}), \\ -p(\mathbf{v}) & \text{with probability } 1 - p(\mathbf{v}_t) \end{cases} \tag{67}$$

while conditional on $i_{t-1} = 0$,

$$v_{Sn+s}(\mathbf{v}) = \begin{cases} -(1 - q(\mathbf{v})) & \text{with probability } q(\mathbf{v}), \\ q(\mathbf{v}) & \text{with probability } 1 - q(\mathbf{v}_t). \end{cases} \tag{68}$$

Equation (66) is a periodic AR(1) model where all the parameters, including those governing the error process, may take on different values every season. Of course, this is a different way of saying that the "state-of-the-world" is not only described by $\{i_{Sn+s}\}$ but also $\{\mathbf{v}\}$. While (66) resembles the periodic ARMA models which were discussed by Tiao and Grupe (1980), Osborn (1991) and Hansen and Sargent (1993), among others, it is also fundamentally different in many respects. The most obvious difference is that the innovation process has a discrete distribution.

The linear time invariant representation for the stochastic switching regime process i_{Sn+s} is a finite order ARMA process, as we shall explain shortly. One should note that the process will certainly not be represented by an AR(1) process as it will not be Markovian in such a straightforward way when it is expressed by a univariate AR(1) process, since part of the state space is "missing". A more formal argument can be derived directly from the analysis in Tiao and Grupe (1980) and Osborn (1991).[7] The periodic nature of autoregressive coefficients pushes the seasonality into annual lags of the AR polynomial and substantially complicates the MA component.

Ultimately, we are interested in the time series properties of $\{y_{Sn+s}\}$. Since

$$y_{Sn+s} = \alpha_0 + \alpha_1 i_{Sn+s} + (1 - \phi L)^{-1} \varepsilon_{Sn+s}, \tag{69}$$

and ε_{Sn+s} was assumed Gaussian and independent, we can simply view $\{y_{Sn+s}\}$ as the sum of two independent unobserved processes: namely, $\{i_{Sn+s}\}$ and the process $(1 - \phi L)^{-1} \varepsilon_{Sn+s}$. Clearly, all the features just described about the $\{i_{Sn+s}\}$ process will be translated into similar features inherited by the observed process y_{Sn+s}, while y_{Sn+s} has the following linear time series representation:

$$w_y(z) = \alpha_1^2 w_i(z) + 1/\big[(1 - \phi z)\big(1 - \phi z^{-1}\big)\big]\sigma^2/2\pi. \tag{70}$$

This linear representation has hidden periodic properties and a stacked skip sampled version of the $(1 - \phi L)^{-1} \varepsilon_{Sn+s}$ process. Finally, the vector representation obtained as such would inherit the nonlinear predictable features of $\{i_{Sn+s}\}$.

[7] Osborn (1991) establishes a link between periodic processes and contemporaneous aggregation and uses it to show that the periodic process must have an average forecast MSE at least as small as that of its univariate time invariant counterpart. A similar result for periodic hazard models and scoring rules for predictions is discussed in Ghysels (1993).

Let us briefly return to (69). We observe that the linear representation has seasonal mean shifts that appear as a "deterministic seasonal" in the univariate representation of y_{Sn+s}. Hence, besides the spectral density properties in (70), which may or may not show peaks at the seasonal frequency, we note that periodic Markov switching produces seasonal mean shifts in the univariate representation. This result is, of course, quite interesting since intrinsically we have a purely random stochastic process with occasional mean shifts. The fact that we obtain something that resembles a deterministic seasonal simply comes from the unequal propensity to switch regime (and hence mean) during some seasons of the year.

4.2. Seasonality in variance

So far our analysis has concentrated on models which account for seasonality in the conditional mean only, however a different concept of considerable interest, particularly in the finance literature, is the notion of seasonality in the variance. There is both seasonal heteroskedasticity in daily data and intra-daily data. For daily data, see for instance Tsiakas (2004b). For intra-daily see, e.g., Andersen and Bollerslev (1997). In a recent paper, Martens, Chang and Taylor (2002) present evidence which shows that explicitly modelling intraday seasonality improves out-of-sample forecasting performance; see also Andersen, Bollerslev and Lange (1999).

The notation needs to be slightly generalized in order to handle intra-daily seasonality. In principle we could have three subscripts, like for instance m, s, and n, referring to the mth intra-day observation in 'season' s (e.g., week s) in year n. Most often we will only use m and T, the latter being the total sample. Moreover, since seasonality is often based on daily observations we will often use d as a subscript to refer to a particular day (with m intra-daily observations).

In order to investigate whether out-of-sample forecasting is improved when using seasonal methods, Martens, Chang and Taylor (2002) consider a conventional t-distribution GARCH(1,1) model as benchmark

$$\begin{aligned} r_t &= \mu + \varepsilon_t, \\ \varepsilon_t | \Psi_{t-1} &\sim D(0, h_t), \\ h_t &= \omega + \alpha\varepsilon_{t-1}^2 + \beta h_{t-1} \end{aligned}$$

where Ψ_{t-1} corresponds to the information set available at time $t-1$ and D represents a scaled t-distribution. In this context, the out-of-sample variance forecast is given by

$$\widehat{h}_{T+1} = \widehat{\omega} + \widehat{\alpha}\varepsilon_T^2 + \widehat{\beta} h_T. \tag{71}$$

As Martens, Chang and Taylor (2002) also indicate, for GARCH models with conditional scaled *t-distributions* with υ degrees of freedom, the expected absolute return is given by

$$E|r_{T+1}| = 2\frac{\sqrt{\upsilon - 2}}{\sqrt{\pi}} \frac{\Gamma[(\upsilon + 1)/2]}{\Gamma[\upsilon/2](\upsilon - 1)} \sqrt{\widehat{h}_{T+1}}$$

where Γ is the gamma-function.

However, as pointed out by Andersen and Bollerslev (1997, p. 125), standard ARCH modelling implies a geometric decay in the autocorrelation structure and cannot accommodate strong regular cyclical patterns. In order to overcome this problem, Andersen and Bollerslev suggest a simple specification of interaction between the pronounced intraday periodicity and the strong daily conditional heteroskedasticity as

$$r_t = \sum_{m=1}^{M} r_{t,m} = \sigma_t \frac{1}{M^{1/2}} \sum_{m=1}^{M} \upsilon_m Z_{t,m} \tag{72}$$

where r_t denotes the daily continuous compounded return calculated from the M uncorrelated intraday components $r_{t,m}$, σ_t denotes the conditional volatility factor for day t, υ_m represents the deterministic intraday pattern and $Z_{t,m} \sim \text{iid}(0, 1)$, which is assumed to be independent of the daily volatility process $\{\sigma_t\}$. Both volatility components must be non-negative, i.e., $\sigma_t > 0$ a.s. for all t and $\upsilon_m > 0$ for all m.

4.2.1. Simple estimators of seasonal variances

In order to take into account the intradaily seasonal pattern, Taylor and Xu (1997) consider for each intraday period the average of the squared returns over all trading days, i.e., the variance estimate is given as

$$\upsilon_m^2 = \frac{1}{D} \sum_{t=1}^{N} r_{t,m}^2, \quad n = 1, \ldots, M \tag{73}$$

where N is the number of days. An alternative is to use

$$\upsilon_{d,m}^2 = \frac{1}{M_d} \sum_{k \in T_d} r_{k,m}^2$$

where T_d is the set of daily time indexes that share the same day of the week as time index d, and M_d is the number of time indexes in T_d. Note that this approach, in contrast to (73), takes into account the day of the week. Following the assumption that volatility is the product of seasonal volatility and a time-varying nonseasonal component as in (72), the seasonal variances can be computed as

$$\upsilon_{d,m}^2 = \exp\left[\frac{1}{M_d} \sum_{k \in T_d} \ln\left((r_{k,m} - \bar{r})^2\right)\right]$$

where $\bar{r}$ is the overall mean taken over all returns.

The purpose of estimating these seasonal variances is to scale the returns,

$$\tilde{r}_t \equiv \tilde{r}_{d,m} \equiv \frac{r_{d,m}}{\upsilon_{d,m}}$$

in order to estimate a conventional GARCH(1,1) model for the scaled returns, and hence, forecasts of $\widetilde{h}_{T+1}$ can be obtained in the conventional way as in (71). To transform the volatility forecasts for the scaled returns into volatility forecasts for the original returns, Martens, Chang and Taylor (2002) suggest multiplying the volatility forecasts by the appropriate estimate of the seasonal standard deviation, $v_{d,m}$.

4.2.2. Flexible Fourier form

The Flexible Fourier Form (FFF) [see Gallant (1981)] is a different approach to capture deterministic intraday volatility pattern; see *inter alia* Andersen and Bollerslev (1997, p. 152) and Beltratti and Morana (1999). Andersen and Bollerslev assume that the intraday returns are given as

$$r_{d,m} = E(r_{d,m}) + \frac{\sigma_d v_{d,m} Z_{d,m}}{M^{1/2}} \tag{74}$$

where $E(r_{d,m})$ denotes the unconditional mean and $Z_{d,m} \sim \text{iid}(0, 1)$. From (74) they define the variable

$$x_{d,m} \equiv 2\ln\big[\big|r_{d,m} - E(r_{d,m})\big|\big] - \ln\sigma_d^2 + \ln M = \ln v_{d,m}^2 + \ln Z_{d,m}^2.$$

Replacing $E(r_{d,m})$ by the sample average of all intraday returns and σ_d by an estimate from a daily volatility model, $\widehat{x}_{d,m}$ is obtained. Treating $\widehat{x}_{d,m}$ as dependent variable, the seasonal pattern is obtained by OLS as

$$\widehat{\widehat{x}}_{d,m} \equiv \sum_{j=0}^{J} \sigma_d^j \Bigg[\mu_{0j} + \mu_{1j}\frac{m}{M_1} + \mu_{2j}\frac{n^2}{M_2} + \sum_{i=1}^{l} \lambda_{ij} I_{t=d_t} + \sum_{i=1}^{p}\left(\gamma_{ij}\cos\frac{2\pi i n}{M} + \delta_{ij}\sin\frac{2\pi i n}{M}\right)\Bigg],$$

where $M_1 = (M+1)/2$ and $M_2 = (M+1)(M+2)/6$ are normalizing constants and p is set equal to four. Each of the corresponding $J+1$ FFFs are parameterized by a quadratic component (the terms with μ coefficients) and a number of sinusoids. Moreover, it may be advantageous to include time-specific dummies for applications in which some intraday intervals do not fit well within the overall regular periodic pattern (the λ coefficients).

Hence, once $\widehat{\widehat{x}}_{d,m}$ is estimated, the intraday seasonal volatility pattern can be determined as [see Martens, Chang and Taylor (2002)],

$$\widehat{v}_{d,m} = \exp\big(\widehat{\widehat{x}}_{d,m}/2\big)$$

or alternatively [as suggested by Andersen and Bollerslev (1997, p. 153)],

$$\widehat{v}_{d,m} = \frac{T\exp(\widehat{\widehat{x}}_{d,m}/2)}{\sum_{d=1}^{[T/M]}\sum_{n=1}^{M}\exp(\widehat{\widehat{x}}_{d,m}/2)}$$

which results from the normalization $\sum_{d=1}^{[T/M]} \sum_{n=1}^{M} v_{d,m} \equiv 1$, where $[T/M]$ represents the number of trading days in the sample.

4.2.3. Stochastic seasonal pattern

The previous two subsections assume that the observed seasonal pattern is deterministic. However, there may be no reason that justifies daily or weekly seasonal behavior in volatility as deterministic. Beltratti and Morana (1999) provide, among other things, a comparison between deterministic and stochastic models for the filtering of high frequency returns. In particular, the deterministic seasonal model of Andersen and Bollerslev (1997), described in the previous subsection, is compared with a model resulting from the application of the structural methodology developed by Harvey (1994).

The model proposed by Beltratti and Morana (1999) is an extension of one introduced by Harvey, Ruiz and Shephard (1994), who apply a stochastic volatility model based on the structural time series approach to analyze daily exchange rate returns. This methodology is extended by Payne (1996) to incorporate an intra-day fixed seasonal component, whereas Beltratti and Morana (1999) extend it further to accommodate stochastic intra-daily cyclical components, as

$$r_{t,m} = \bar{r}_{t,m} + \sigma_{t,m}\varepsilon_{t,m} = \bar{r}_{t,m} + \sigma\varepsilon_{t,m} \exp\left(\frac{\mu_{t,m} + h_{t,m} + c_{t,m}}{2}\right) \tag{75}$$

for $t = 1, \ldots, T$, $n = 1, \ldots, M$; and where σ is a scale factor, $\varepsilon_{t,m} \sim \text{iid}(0, 1)$, $\mu_{t,m}$ is the non-stationary volatility component given as $\mu_{t,m} = \mu_{t,m-1} + \xi_{t,m}$, $\xi_{t,m} \sim \text{nid}(0, \sigma_{\xi}^2)$, $h_{t,m}$ is the stochastic stationary acyclic volatility component, $h_{t,m} = \phi h_{t,m-1} + \vartheta_{t,m}$, $\vartheta_{t,m} \sim \text{nid}(0, \sigma_{\vartheta}^2)$, $|\phi| < 1$, c_t is the cyclical volatility component and $\bar{r}_{t,m} = E[r_{t,m}]$.

As suggested by Beltratti and Morana, squaring both sides and taking logs, allows (75) to be rewritten as,

$$\ln\bigl(|r_{t,m} - \bar{r}_{t,m}|\bigr)^2 = \ln\left[\sigma\varepsilon_{t,m} \exp\left(\frac{\mu_{t,m} + h_{t,m} + c_{t,m}}{2}\right)\right]^2,$$

that is,

$$2\ln|r_{t,m} - \bar{r}_{t,m}| = \iota + \mu_{t,m} + h_{t,m} + c_{t,m} + w_{t,m}$$

where $\iota = \ln\sigma^2 + E[\ln\varepsilon_{t,m}^2]$ and $w_{t,m} = \ln\varepsilon_{t,m}^2 - E[\ln\varepsilon_{t,m}^2]$.

The c_t component is broken into a number of cycles corresponding to the fundamental daily frequency and its intra-daily harmonics, i.e., $c_{t,m} = \sum_{i=1}^{2} c_{i,t,m}$. Beltratti and Morana model the fundamental daily frequency, $c_{1,t,m}$, as stochastic while its harmonics, $c_{2,t,m}$, as deterministic. In other words, following Harvey (1994), the stochastic cyclical component, $c_{1,t,m}$, is considered in state space form as

$$c_{1,t,m} = \begin{bmatrix} \psi_{1,t,m} \\ \psi_{1,t,m}^* \end{bmatrix} = \rho \begin{bmatrix} \cos\lambda & \sin\lambda \\ -\sin\lambda & \cos\lambda \end{bmatrix} \begin{bmatrix} \psi_{1,t,m-1} \\ \psi_{1,t,m-1}^* \end{bmatrix} + \begin{bmatrix} \kappa_{1,t,m} \\ \kappa_{1,t,m}^* \end{bmatrix}$$

where $0 \leqslant \rho \leqslant 1$ is a damping factor and $\kappa_{1,t,m} \sim \text{nid}(0, \sigma_{1,\kappa}^2)$ and $\kappa_{1,t,m}^* \sim \text{nid}(0, \sigma_{1,\kappa}^{*2})$ are white noise disturbances with $Cov(\kappa_{1,t,m}, \kappa_{1,t,m}^*) = 0$. Whereas, $c_{2,t,m}$ is modelled using a flexible Fourier form as

$$c_{2,t,m} = \mu_1 \frac{m}{M_1} + \mu_2 \frac{n^2}{M_2} + \sum_{i=2}^{p} (\delta_{ci} \cos i\lambda n + \delta_{si} \sin i\lambda n).$$

It can be observed from the specification of these components that this model encompasses that of Andersen and Bollerslev (1997).

One advantage of this state space formulation results from the possibility that the various components may be estimated simultaneously. One important conclusion that comes out of the empirical evaluation of this model, is that it presents some superior results when compared with the models that treat seasonality as strictly deterministic; for more details see Beltratti and Morana (1999).

4.2.4. *Periodic GARCH models*

In the previous section we dealt with intra-daily returns data. Here we return to daily returns and to daily measures of volatility. An approach to seasonality considered by Bollerslev and Ghysels (1996) is the periodic GARCH (P-GARCH) model which is explicitly designed to capture (daily) seasonal time variation in the second-order moments; see also Ghysels and Osborn (2001, pp. 194–198). The P-GARCH includes all GARCH models in which hourly dummies, for example, are used in the variance equation.

Extending the information set Ψ_{t-1} with a process defining the stage of the periodic cycle at each point, say to Ψ_{t-1}^s, the P-GARCH model is defined as,

$$\begin{aligned} r_t &= \mu + \varepsilon_t, \\ \varepsilon_t | \Psi_{t-1}^s &\sim D(0, h_t), \\ h_t &= \omega_{s(t)} + \alpha_{s(t)} \varepsilon_{t-1}^2 + \beta_{s(t)} h_{t-1} \end{aligned} \tag{76}$$

where $s(t)$ refers to the stage of the periodic cycle at time t. The periodic cycle of interest here is a repetitive cycle covering one week. Notice that there is resemblance with the periodic models discussed in Section 3.

The P-GARCH model is potentially more efficient than the methods described earlier. These methods [with the exception of Beltratti and Morana (1999)] first estimate the seasonals, and after deseasonalizing the returns, estimate the volatility of these adjusted returns. The P-GARCH model on the other hand, allows for simultaneous estimation of the seasonal effects and the remaining time-varying volatility.

As indicated by Ghysels and Osborn (2001, p. 195) in the existing ARCH literature, the modelling of non-trading day effects has typically been limited to $\omega_{s(t)}$, whereas (76) allows for a much richer dynamic structure. However, some caution is necessary as discussed in Section 3 for the PAR models, in order to avoid overparameterization.

Moreover, as suggested by Martens, Chang and Taylor (2002), one can consider the parameters $\omega_{s(t)}$ in (76) in such a way that they represent: (a) the average absolute/square returns (e.g., 240 dummies) or (b) the FFF. Martens, Chang and Taylor (2002) consider the second approach allowing for only one FFF for the entire week instead of separate FFF for each day of the week.

4.2.5. Periodic stochastic volatility models

Another popular class of models is the so-called stochastic volatility models [see, e.g., Ghysels, Harvey and Renault (1996) for further discussion]. In a recent paper Tsiakas (2004a) presents the periodic stochastic volatility (PSV) model. Models of stochastic volatility have been used extensively in the finance literature. Like GARCH-type models, stochastic volatility models are designed to capture the persistent and predictable component of daily volatility, however in contrast with GARCH models the assumption of a stochastic second moment introduces an additional source of risk.

The benchmark model considered by Tsiakas (2004a) is the conventional stochastic volatility model given as,

$$y_t = \alpha + \rho y_{t-1} + \eta_t \tag{77}$$

and

$$\eta_t = \varepsilon_t \upsilon_t, \qquad \varepsilon_t \sim \text{nid}(0, 1)$$

where the persistence of the stochastic conditional volatility υ_t is captured by the latent log-variance process h_t, which is modelled as a dynamic Gaussian variable

$$\upsilon_t = \exp(h_t/2)$$

and

$$h_t = \mu + \beta' X_t + \phi(h_{t-1} - \mu) + \sigma \varrho_t, \qquad \varrho_t \sim \text{nid}(0, 1). \tag{78}$$

Note that in this framework ε_t and ϱ_t are assumed to be independent and that returns and their volatility are stationary, i.e., $|\rho| < 1$ and $|\phi| < 1$, respectively.

Tsiakas (2004a) introduces a PSV model in which the constants (levels) in both the conditional mean and the conditional variances are generalized to account for day of the week, holiday (non-trading day) and month of the year effects.

5. Forecasting, seasonal adjustment and feedback

The greatest demand for forecasting seasonal time series is a direct consequence of removing seasonal components. The process, called seasonal adjustment, aims to filter raw data such that seasonal fluctuations disappear from the series. Various procedures exist and Ghysels and Osborn (2001, Chapter 4) provide details regarding the most commonly used, including the U.S. Census Bureau X-11 method and its recent upgrade, the X-12-ARIMA program and the TRAMO/SEATS procedure.

We cover three issues in this section. The first subsection discusses how forecasting seasonal time series is deeply embedded in the process of seasonal adjustment. The second handles forecasting of seasonally adjusted series and the final subsection deals with feedback and control.

5.1. Seasonal adjustment and forecasting

The foundation of seasonal adjustment procedures is the decomposition of a series into a trend cycle, and seasonal and irregular components. Typically a series y_t is decomposed into the *product* of a trend cycle y_t^{tc}, seasonal y_t^s, and irregular y_t^i. However, assuming the use of logarithms, we can consider the additive decomposition

$$y_t = y_t^{tc} + y_t^s + y_t^i. \tag{79}$$

Other decompositions exist [see Ghysels and Osborn (2001), Hylleberg (1986)], yet the above decomposition has been the focus of most of the academic research. Seasonal adjustment filters are two-sided, involving both leads and lags. The linear X-11 filter will serve the purpose here as illustrative example to explain the role of forecasting.[8] The linear approximation to the monthly X-11 filter is:

$$\begin{aligned}\nu_{X-11}^{M}(L) &= 1 - SM_C(L)M_2(L)\{1 - HM(L)[1 - SM_C(L)M_1(L)SM_C(L)]\} \\ &= 1 - SM_C(L)M_2(L) + SM_C(L)M_2(L)HM(L) \\ &\quad - SM_C^3(L)M_1(L)M_2(L)HM(L) + SM_C^3(L)M_1(L)M_2(L),\end{aligned} \tag{80}$$

where $SM_C(L) \equiv 1 - SM(L)$, a centered thirteen-term MA filter, namely $SM(L) \equiv (1/24)(1 + L)(1 + L + \cdots + L^{11})L^{-6}$, $M_1(L) \equiv (1/9)(L^S + 1 + L^{-S})^2$ with $S = 12$. A similar filter is the "3 × 5" seasonal moving average filter $M_2(L) \equiv (1/15)(\sum_{j=-1}^{1} L^{jS})(\sum_{j=-2}^{2} L^{jS})$ again with $S = 12$. The procedure also involves a $(2H + 1)$-term Henderson moving average filter $HM(L)$ [see Ghysels and Osborn (2001) the default value is $H = 6$, yielding a thirteen-term Henderson moving average filter].

The monthly X-11 filter has roughly 5 years of leads and lags. The original X-11 seasonal adjustment procedure consisted of an array of asymmetric filters that complemented the two-sided symmetric filter. There was a separate filter for each scenario of missing observations, starting with a concurrent adjustment filter when on past data and none of the future data. Each of the asymmetric filters, when compared to the symmetric filter, implicitly defined a forecasting model for the missing observations in the data. Unfortunately, these different asymmetric filters implied inconsistent forecasting

[8] The question whether seasonal adjustment procedures are, at least approximately, linear data transformations is investigated by Young (1968) and Ghysels, Granger and Siklos (1996).

models across time. To eliminate this inconsistency, a major improvement was designed and implemented by Statistics Canada and called X-11-ARIMA [Dagum (1980)] that had the ability to extend time series with forecasts and backcasts from ARIMA models prior to seasonal adjustment. As a result, the symmetric filter was always used and any missing observations were filled in with an ARIMA model-based prediction. Its main advantage was smaller revisions of seasonally adjusted series as future data became available [see, e.g., Bobbitt and Otto (1990)]. The U.S. Census Bureau also proceeded in 1998 to major improvements of the X-11 procedure. These changes were so important that they prompted the release of what is called X-12-ARIMA. Findley et al. (1998) provide a very detailed description of the new improved capabilities of the X-12-ARIMA procedure. It encompasses the improvements of Statistics Canada's X-11-ARIMA and encapsulates it with a front end regARIMA program, which handles regression and ARIMA models, and a set of diagnostics, which enhance the appraisal of the output from the original X-11-ARIMA. The regARIMA program has a set of built-in regressors for the monthly case [listed in Table 2 of Findley et al. (1998)]. They include a constant trend, deterministic seasonal effects, trading-day effects (for both stock and flow variables), length-of-month variables, leap year, Easter holiday, Labor day, and Thanksgiving dummy variables as well as additive outlier, level shift, and temporary ramp regressors.

Goméz and Maravall (1996) succeeded in building a seasonal adjustment package using signal extraction principles. The package consists of two programs, namely TRAMO (Time Series Regression with ARIMA Noise, Missing observations, and Outliers) and SEATS (Signal Extraction in ARIMA Time Series). The TRAMO program fulfills the role of preadjustment, very much like regARIMA does for X-12-ARIMA adjustment. Hence, it performs adjustments for outliers, trading-day effects, and other types of intervention analysis [following Box and Tiao (1975)].

This brief description of the two major seasonal adjustment programs reveals an important fact: seasonal adjustment involves forecasting seasonal time series. The models that are used in practice are the univariate ARIMA models described in Section 2.

5.2. *Forecasting and seasonal adjustment*

Like it or not, many applied time series studies involve forecasting seasonally adjusted series. However, as noted in the previous subsection, pre-filtered data are predicted in the process of adjustment and this raises several issues. Further, due to the use of two-sided filters, seasonal adjustment of historical data involves the use of future values. Many economic theories rest on the behavioral assumption of rational expectations, or at least are very careful regarding the information set available to agents. In this regard the use of seasonally adjusted series may be problematic.

An issue rarely discussed in the literature is that forecasting seasonally adjusted series, should at least in principle be linked to the forecasting exercise that is embedded in the seasonal adjustment process. In the previous subsection we noted that since adjustment filters are two-sided, future realizations of the raw series have to be predicted.

Implicitly one therefore has a prediction model for the non-seasonal components y_t^{tc} and irregular y_t^i appearing in Equation (79). For example, how many unit roots is y_t^{tc} assumed to have when seasonal adjustment procedures are applied, and is the same assumption used when subsequently seasonally adjusted series are predicted? One might also think that the same time series model either implicitly or explicitly used for $y_t^{tc} + y_t^i$ should be subsequently used to predict the seasonally adjusted series. Unfortunately that is not the case, since the seasonally adjusted series equals $y_t^{tc} + y_t^i + e_t$, where the latter is an extraction error, i.e., the error between the true non-seasonal and its estimate. However, this raises another question scantly discussed in the literature. A time series model for $y_t^{tc} + y_t^i$, embedded in the seasonal adjustment procedure, namely used to predict future raw data, and a time series model for e_t, (properties often known and determined by the extraction filter), implies a model for $y_t^{tc} + y_t^i + e_t$. To the best of our knowledge applied time series studies never follow a strategy that borrows the non-seasonal component model used by statistical agencies and adds the stochastic properties of the extraction error to determine the prediction model for the seasonally adjusted series. Consequently, the model specification by statistical agencies in the course of seasonal adjusting a series is never taken into account when the adjusted series are actually used in forecasting exercises. Hence, seasonal adjustment and forecasting seasonally adjusted series are completely independent. In principle this ought not to be the case.

To conclude this subsection, it should be noted, however, that in some circumstances the filtering procedure is irrelevant and therefore the issues discussed in the previous paragraph are also irrelevant. The context is that of linear regression models with linear (seasonal adjustment) filters. This setting was originally studied by Sims (1974) and Wallis (1974), who considered regression models without lagged dependent variables; i.e., the classical regression. They showed that OLS estimators are consistent whenever all the series are filtered by the same filter. Hence, if all the series are adjusted by, say the linear X-11 filter, then there are no biases resulting from filtering. Absence of bias implies that point forecasts will not be affected by filtering, when such forecasts are based on regression models. In other words, the filter design is irrelevant as long as the same filter is used across all series. However, although parameter estimates remain asymptotically unbiased, it should be noted that residuals feature autocorrelation induced by filtering. The presence of autocorrelation should in principle be taken into account in terms of forecasting. In this sense, despite the invariance of OLS estimation to linear filtering, we should note that there remains an issue of residual autocorrelation.

5.3. *Seasonal adjustment and feedback*

While the topic of this Handbook is 'forecasting', it should be noted that in many circumstances, economic forecasts feed back into decisions and affect future outcomes. This is a situation of 'control', rather than 'forecasting', since the prediction needs to take into account its effect on future outcomes. Very little is said about the topic in this Handbook, and we would like to conclude this chapter with a discussion of the topic in the context of seasonal adjustment. The material draws on Ghysels (1987), who studies seasonal extraction in the presence of feedback in the context of monetary policy.

Monetary authorities often target nonseasonal components of economic time series, and for illustrative purpose Ghysels (1987) considers the case of monetary aggregates being targeted. A policy aimed at controlling the nonseasonal component of a time series can be studied as a linear quadratic optimal control problem in which observations are contaminated by seasonal noise (recall Equation (79)). The usual seasonal adjustment procedures assume however, that the future outcomes of the nonseasonal component are unaffected by today's monetary policy decisions. This is the typical forecasting situation discussed in the previous subsections. Statistical agencies compute future forecasts of raw series in order to seasonally adjusted economic time series. The latter are then used by policy makers, whose actions affect future outcomes. Hence, from a control point of view, one cannot separate the policy decision from the filtering problem, in this case the seasonal adjustment filter.

The optimal filter derived by Ghysels (1987) in the context of a monetary policy example is very different from X-11 or any of the other standard adjustment procedures. This implies that the use of (1) a model-based approach, as in SEATS/TRAMO, (2) a X-11-ARIMA or X-12-ARIMA procedure is suboptimal. In fact, the decomposition emerging from a linear quadratic control model is nonorthogonal because of the feedback. The traditional seasonal adjustment procedure start from an orthogonal decomposition. Note that the dependence across seasonal and nonseasonal components is in part determined by the monetary policy rule. The degree to which traditional adjustment procedures fall short of being optimal is difficult to judge [see, however, Ghysels (1987), for further discussion].

6. Conclusion

In this chapter, we present a comprehensive overview of models and approaches that have been used in the literature to account for seasonal (periodic) patterns in economic and financial data, relevant to forecasting context. We group seasonal time series models into four categories: conventional univariate linear (deterministic and ARMA) models, seasonal cointegration, periodic models and other specifications. Each is discussed in a separate section. A final substantive section is devoted to forecasting and seasonal adjustment.

The ordering of our discussion is based on the popularity of the methods presented, starting with the ones most frequently used in the literature and ending with recently proposed methods that are yet to achieve wide usage. It is also obvious that methods based on nonlinear models or examining seasonality in high frequency financial series generally require more observations than the simpler methods discussed earlier.

Our discussion above does not attempt to provide general advice to a user as to what method(s) should be used in practice. Ultimately, the choice of method is data-driven and depends on the context under analysis. However, two general points arise from our discussion that are relevant to this issue.

Firstly, the length of available data will influence the choice of method. Indeed, the relative lack of success to date of periodic models in forecasting may be due to the number of parameters that (in an unrestricted form) they can require. Indeed, simple deterministic (dummy variable) models may, in many situations, take account of the sufficient important features of seasonality for practical forecasting purposes.

Secondly, however, we would like to emphasize that the seasonal properties of the specific series under analysis is a crucial factor to be considered. Indeed, our Monte Carlo analysis in Section 2 establishes that correctly accounting for the nature of seasonality can improve forecast performance. Therefore, testing of the data should be undertaken prior to forecasting. In our context, such tests include seasonal unit root tests and tests for periodic parameter variation. Although commonly ignored, we also recommend extending these tests to consider seasonality in variance. If sufficient data are available, tests for nonlinearity might also be undertaken. While we are skeptical that nonlinear seasonal models will yield substantial improvements to forecast accuracy for economic time series at the present time, high frequency financial time series may offer scope for such improvements.

It is clear that further research to assess the relevance of applying more complex models would offer new insights, particularly in the context of models discussed in Sections 3 and 4. Such models are typically designed to capture specific features of the data, and a forecaster needs to be able to assess both the importance of these features for the data under study and the likely impact of the additional complexity (including the number of parameters estimated) on forecast accuracy.

Developments on the interactions between seasonality and forecasting, in particular in the context of the nonlinear and volatility models discussed in Section 4, are important areas of work for future consideration. Indeed, as discussed in Section 5, such issues arise even when seasonally adjusted data are used for forecasting.

References

Abeysinghe, T. (1991). "Inappropriate use of seasonal dummies in regression". Economic Letters 36, 175–179.

Abeysinghe, T. (1994). "Deterministic seasonal models and spurious regressions". Journal of Econometrics 61, 259–272.

Ahn, S.K., Reinsel, G.C. (1994). "Estimation of partially non-stationary vector autoregressive models with seasonal behavior". Journal of Econometrics 62, 317–350.

Andersen, T.G., Bollerslev, T. (1997). "Intraday periodicity and volatility persistence in financial markets". Journal of Empirical Finance 4, 115–158.

Andersen, T.G., Bollerslev, T., Lange, S. (1999). "Forecasting financial market volatility: Sample frequency vis-a-vis forecast horizon". Journal of Empirical Finance 6, 457–477.

Barsky, R.B., Miron, J.A. (1989). "The seasonal cycle and the business cycle". Journal of Political Economy 97, 503–535.

Beaulieu, J.J., Mackie-Mason, J.K., Miron, J.A. (1992). "Why do countries and industries with large seasonal cycles also have large business cycles?". Quarterly Journal of Economics 107, 621–656.

Beaulieu, J.J., Miron, J.A. (1992). "A cross country comparison of seasonal cycles and business cycles". Economic Journal 102, 772–788.

Beaulieu, J.J., Miron, J.A. (1993). "Seasonal unit roots in aggregate U.S. data". Journal of Econometrics 55, 305–328.

Beltratti, A., Morana, C. (1999). "Computing value-at-risk with high-frequency data". Journal of Empirical Finance 6, 431–455.

Birchenhall, C.R., Bladen-Hovell, R.C., Chui, A.P.L., Osborn, D.R., Smith, J.P. (1989). "A seasonal model of consumption". Economic Journal 99, 837–843.

Bloomfield, P., Hurd, H.L., Lund, R.B. (1994). "Periodic correlation in stratospheric ozone data". Journal of Time Series Analysis 15, 127–150.

Bobbitt, L., Otto, M.C. (1990). "Effects of forecasts on the revisions of seasonally adjusted values using the X-11 seasonal adjustment procedure". In: Proceedings of the Business and Economic Statistics Section. American Statistical Association, Alexandria, pp. 449–453.

Bollerslev, T., Ghysels, E. (1996). "Periodic autoregressive conditional heteroscedasticity". Journal of Business and Economic Statistics 14, 139–151.

Boswijk, H.P., Franses, P.H. (1995). "Periodic cointegration: Representation and inference". Review of Economics and Statistics 77, 436–454.

Boswijk, H.P., Franses, P.H. (1996). "Unit roots in periodic autoregressions". Journal of Time Series Analysis 17, 221–245.

Box, G.E.P., Jenkins, G.M. (1970). Time Series Analysis: Forecasting and Control. Holden-Day, San Francisco.

Box, G.E.P., Tiao, G.C. (1975). "Intervention analysis with applications to economic and environmental problems". Journal of the American Statistical Association 70, 70–79.

Breitung, J., Franses, P.H. (1998). "On Phillips–Perron type tests for seasonal unit roots". Econometric Theory 14, 200–221.

Brockwell, P.J., Davis, R.A. (1991). Time Series: Theory and Methods, second ed. Springer-Verlag, New York.

Burridge, P., Taylor, A.M.R. (2001). "On the properties of regression-based tests for seasonal unit roots in the presence of higher-order serial correlation". Journal of Business and Economic Statistics 19, 374–379.

Busetti, F., Harvey, A. (2003). "Seasonality tests". Journal of Business and Economic Statistics 21, 420–436.

Canova, F., Ghysels, E. (1994). "Changes in seasonal patterns: Are they cyclical?". Journal of Economic Dynamics and Control 18, 1143–1171.

Canova, F., Hansen, B.E. (1995). "Are seasonal patterns constant over time? A test for seasonal stability". Journal of Business and Economic Statistics 13, 237–252.

Cecchitti, S., Kashyap, A. (1996). "International cycles". European Economic Review 40, 331–360.

Christoffersen, P.F., Diebold, F.X. (1998). "Cointegration and long-horizon forecasting". Journal of Business and Economic Statistics 16, 450–458.

Clements, M.P., Hendry, D.F. (1993). "On the limitations of comparing mean square forecast errors". Journal of Forecasting 12, 617–637.

Clements, M.P., Smith, J. (1999). "A Monte Carlo study of the forecasting performance of empirical SETAR models". Journal of Applied Econometrics 14, 123–141.

Clements, M.P., Hendry, D.F. (1997). "An empirical study of seasonal unit roots in forecasting". International Journal of Forecasting 13, 341–356.

Dagum, E.B. (1980). "The X-11-ARIMA seasonal adjustment method". Report 12-564E, Statistics Canada, Ottawa.

Davidson, J.E.H., Hendry, D.F., Srba, F., Yeo, S. (1978). "Econometric modelling of the aggregate time series relationship between consumers' expenditure income in the United Kingdom". Economic Journal 88, 661–692.

del Barrio Castro, T., Osborn, D.R. (2004). "The consequences of seasonal adjustment for periodic autoregressive processes". Econometrics Journal 7, 307–321.

Dickey, D.A. (1993). "Discussion: Seasonal unit roots in aggregate U.S. data". Journal of Econometrics 55, 329–331.

Dickey, D.A., Fuller, W.A. (1979). "Distribution of the estimators for autoregressive time series with a unit root". Journal of the American Statistical Association 74, 427–431.

Dickey, D.A., Hasza, D.P., Fuller, W.A. (1984). "Testing for unit roots in seasonal time series". Journal of the American Statistical Association 79, 355–367.

Engle, R.F., Granger, C.W.J., Hallman, J.J. (1989). "Merging short- and long-run forecasts: An application of seasonal cointegration to monthly electricity sales forecasting". Journal of Econometrics 40, 45–62.

Engle, R.F., Granger, C.W.J., Hylleberg, S., Lee, H.S. (1993). "Seasonal cointegration: The Japanese consumption function". Journal of Econometrics 55, 275–298.

Findley, D.F., Monsell, B.C., Bell, W.R., Otto, M.C., Chen, B.-C. (1998). "New capabilities and methods of the X-12-ARIMA seasonal-adjustment program". Journal of Business and Economic Statistics 16, 127–177 (with discussion).

Franses, P.H. (1991). "Seasonality, nonstationarity and the forecasting of monthly time series". International Journal of Forecasting 7, 199–208.

Franses, P.H. (1993). "A method to select between periodic cointegration and seasonal cointegration". Economics Letters 41, 7–10.

Franses, P.H. (1994). "A multivariate approach to modeling univariate seasonal time series". Journal of Econometrics 63, 133–151.

Franses, P.H. (1995). "A vector of quarters representation for bivariate time-series". Econometric Reviews 14, 55–63.

Franses, P.H. (1996). Periodicity and Stochastic Trends in Economic Time Series. Oxford University Press, Oxford.

Franses, P.H., Hylleberg, S., Lee, H.S. (1995). "Spurious deterministic seasonality". Economics Letters 48, 249–256.

Franses, P.H., Kunst, R.M. (1999). "On the role of seasonal intercepts in seasonal cointegration". Oxford Bulletin of Economics and Statistics 61, 409–434.

Franses, P.H., Paap, R. (1994). "Model selection in periodic autoregressions". Oxford Bulletin of Economics and Statistics 56, 421–439.

Franses, P.H., Paap, R. (2002). "Forecasting with periodic autoregressive time series models". In: Clements, M.P., Hendry, D.F. (Eds.), A Companion to Economic Forecasting. Basil Blackwell, Oxford, pp. 432–452, Chapter 19.

Franses, P.H., Romijn, G. (1993). "Periodic integration in quarterly UK macroeconomic variables". International Journal of Forecasting 9, 467–476.

Franses, P.H., van Dijk, D. (2005). "The forecasting performance of various models for seasonality and nonlinearity for quarterly industrial production". International Journal of Forecasting 21, 87–105.

Gallant, A.R. (1981). "On the bias in flexible functional forms and an essentially unbiased form: The Fourier flexible form". Journal of Econometrics 15, 211–245.

Ghysels, E. (1987). "Seasonal extraction in the presence of feedback". Journal of the Business and Economic Statistics 5, 191–194. Reprinted in: Hylleberg, S. (Ed.), Modelling Seasonality. Oxford University Press, 1992, pp. 181–192.

Ghysels, E. (1988). "A study towards a dynamic theory of seasonality for economic time series". Journal of the American Statistical Association 83, 168–172. Reprinted in: Hylleberg, S. (Ed.), Modelling Seasonality. Oxford University Press, 1992, pp. 181–192.

Ghysels, E. (1991). "Are business cycle turning points uniformly distributed throughout the year?". Discussion Paper No. 3891, C.R.D.E., Université de Montréal.

Ghysels, E. (1993). "On scoring asymmetric periodic probability models of turning point forecasts". Journal of Forecasting 12, 227–238.

Ghysels, E. (1994a). "On the economics and econometrics of seasonality". In: Sims, C.A. (Ed.), Advances in Econometrics – Sixth World Congress. Cambridge University Press, Cambridge, pp. 257–316.

Ghysels, E. (1994b). "On the periodic structure of the business cycle". Journal of Business and Economic Statistics 12, 289–298.

Ghysels, E. (1997). "On seasonality and business cycle durations: A nonparametric investigation". Journal of Econometrics 79, 269–290.

Ghysels, E. (2000). "A time series model with periodic stochastic regime switching, Part I: Theory". Macroeconomic Dynamics 4, 467–486.

Ghysels, E., Bac, C., Chevet, J.-M. (2003). "A time series model with periodic stochastic regime switching, Part II: Applications to 16th and 17th Century grain prices". Macroeconomic Dynamics 5, 32–55.

Ghysels, E., Granger, C.W.J., Siklos, P. (1996). "Is seasonal adjustment a linear or nonlinear data filtering process?". Journal of Business and Economic Statistics 14, 374–386 (with discussion). Reprinted in: Newbold, P., Leybourne, S.J. (Eds.), Recent Developments in Time Series. Edward Elgar, 2003, and reprinted in: Essays in Econometrics: Collected Papers of Clive W.J. Granger, vol. 1. Cambridge University Press, 2001.

Ghysels, E., Hall, A., Lee, H.S. (1996). "On periodic structures and testing for seasonal unit roots". Journal of the American Statistical Association 91, 1551–1559.

Ghysels, E., Harvey, A., Renault, E. (1996). "Stochastic volatility". In: Statistical Methods in Finance. In: Maddala, G.S., Rao, C.R. (Eds.), Handbook of Statistics, vol. 14. North-Holland, Amsterdam.

Ghysels, E., Lee, H.S., Noh, J. (1994). "Testing for unit roots in seasonal time series: Some theoretical extensions and a Monte Carlo investigation". Journal of Econometrics 62, 415–442.

Ghysels, E., Lee, H.S., Siklos, P.L. (1993). "On the (mis)specification of seasonality and its consequences: An empirical investigation with US data". Empirical Economics 18, 747–760.

Ghysels, E., Osborn, D.R. (2001). The Econometric Analysis of Seasonal Time Series. Cambridge University Press, Cambridge.

Ghysels, E., Perron, P. (1996). "The effect of linear filters on dynamic time series with structural change". Journal of Econometrics 70, 69–97.

Gladyshev, E.G. (1961). "Periodically correlated random sequences". Soviet Mathematics 2, 385–388.

Goméz, V., Maravall, A. (1996). "Programs TRAMO and SEATS, instructions for the user (beta version: September 1996)". Working Paper 9628, Bank of Spain.

Hamilton, J.D. (1989). "A new approach to the economic analysis of nonstationary time series and the business cycle". Econometrica 57, 357–384.

Hamilton, J.D. (1990). "Analysis of time series subject to changes in regime". Journal of Econometrics 45, 39–70.

Hansen, L.P., Sargent, T.J. (1993). "Seasonality and approximation errors in rational expectations models". Journal of Econometrics 55, 21–56.

Harvey, A.C. (1993). Time Series Models. Harvester Wheatsheaf.

Harvey, A.C. (1994). Forecasting, Structural Time Series Models and the Kalman Filter. Cambridge University Press.

Harvey, A.C. (2006). "Unobserved components models". In: Elliott, G., Granger, C.W.J., Timmermann, A. (Eds.), Handbook of Economic Forecasting. Elsevier, Amsterdam. Chapter 7 in this volume.

Harvey, A.C., Ruiz, E., Shephard, N. (1994). "Multivariate stochastic variance models". Review of Economic Studies 61, 247–264.

Hassler, U., Rodrigues, P.M.M. (2004). "Residual-based tests against seasonal cointegration". Mimeo, Faculty of Economics, University of Algarve.

Herwartz, H. (1997). "Performance of periodic error correction models in forecasting consumption data". International Journal of Forecasting 13, 421–431.

Hylleberg, S. (1986). Seasonality in Regression. Academic Press.

Hylleberg, S. (1992). Modelling Seasonality. Oxford University Press.

Hylleberg, S. (1995). "Tests for seasonal unit roots: General to specific or specific to general?". Journal of Econometrics 69, 5–25.

Hylleberg, S., Jørgensen, C., Sørensen, N.K. (1993). "Seasonality in macroeconomic time series". Empirical Economics 18, 321–335.

Hylleberg, S., Engle, R.F., Granger, C.W.J., Yoo, B.S. (1990). "Seasonal integration and cointegration". Journal of Econometrics 44, 215–238.

Johansen, S. (1988). "Statistical analysis of cointegration vectors". Journal of Economic Dynamics and Control, 231–254.

Johansen, S., Schaumburg, E. (1999). "Likelihood analysis of seasonal cointegration". Journal of Econometrics 88, 301–339.

Jones, R.H., Brelsford, W.M. (1968). "Time series with periodic structure". Biometrika 54, 403–407.

Kawasaki, Y., Franses, P.H. (2004). "Do seasonal unit roots matter for forecasting monthly industrial production?". Journal of Forecasting 23, 77–88.

Kunst, R.M. (1993). "Seasonal cointegration in macroeconomic systems: Case studies for small and large European countries". Review of Economics and Statistics 78, 325–330.

Kunst, R.M., Franses, P.H. (1998). "The impact of seasonal constants on forecasting seasonally cointegrated time series". Journal of Forecasting 17, 109–124.

Lee, H.S. (1992). "Maximum likelihood inference on cointegration and seasonal cointegration". Journal of Econometrics 54, 1–49.

Lee, H.S., Siklos, P.L. (1997). "The role of seasonality in economic time series: Reinterpreting money-output causality in U.S. data". International Journal of Forecasting 13, 381–391.

Lin, J., Tsay, R. (1996). "Cointegration constraint and forecasting: An empirical examination". Journal of Applied Econometrics 11, 519–538.

Löf, M., Franses, P.H. (2001). "On forecasting cointegrated seasonal time series". International Journal of Forecasting 17, 607–621.

Löf, M., Lyhagen, J. (2002). "Forecasting performance of seasonal cointegration models". International Journal of Forecasting 18, 31–44.

Lopes, A.C.B.S. (1999). "Spurious deterministic seasonality and autocorrelation corrections with quarterly data: Further Monte Carlo results". Empirical Economics 24, 341–359.

Lund, R.B., Hurd, H., Bloomfield, P., Smith, R.L. (1995). "Climatological time series with periodic correlation". Journal of Climate 11, 2787–2809.

Lütkepohl, H. (1991). Introduction to Multiple Time Series Analysis. Springer-Verlag, Berlin.

Lyhagen, J., Löf, M. (2003). "On seasonal error correction when the process include different numbers of unit roots". SSE/EFI Working Paper, Series in Economics and Finance, 0418.

Martens, M., Chang, Y., Taylor, S.J. (2002). "A comparison of seasonal adjustment methods when forecasting intraday volatility". Journal of Financial Research 2, 283–299.

Matas-Mir, A., Osborn, D.R. (2004). "Does seasonality change over the business cycle? An investigation using monthly industrial production series". European Economic Review 48, 1309–1332.

Mills, T.C., Mills, A.G. (1992). "Modelling the seasonal patterns in UK macroeconomic time series". Journal of the Royal Statistical Society, Series A 155, 61–75.

Miron, J.A. (1996). The Economics of Seasonal Cycles. MIT Press.

Ng, S., Perron, P. (1995). "Unit root tests in ARMA models with data-dependent methods for the selection of the truncation lag". Journal of American Statistical Society 90, 268–281.

Novales, A., Flores de Fruto, R. (1997). "Forecasting with periodic models: A comparison with time invariant coefficient models". International Journal of Forecasting 13, 393–405.

Osborn, D.R. (1988). "Seasonality and habit persistence in a life-cycle model of consumption". Journal of Applied Econometrics, 255–266. Reprinted in: Hylleberg, S. (Ed.), Modelling Seasonality. Oxford University Press, 1992, pp. 193–208.

Osborn, D.R. (1990). "A survey of seasonality in UK macroeconomic variables". International Journal of Forecasting 6, 327–336.

Osborn, D.R. (1991). "The implications of periodically varying coefficients for seasonal time-series processes". Journal of Econometrics 48, 373–384.

Osborn, D.R. (1993). "Discussion on seasonal cointegration: The Japanese consumption function". Journal of Econometrics 55, 299–303.

Osborn, D.R. (2002). "Unit-root versus deterministic representations of seasonality for forecasting". In: Clements, M.P., Hendry, D.F. (Eds.), A Companion to Economic Forecasting. Blackwell Publishers.

Osborn, D.R., Chui, A.P.L., Smith, J.P., Birchenhall, C.R. (1988). "Seasonality and the order of integration for consumption". Oxford Bulletin of Economics and Statistics 50, 361–377. Reprinted in: Hylleberg, S. (Ed.), Modelling Seasonality. Oxford University Press, 1992, pp. 449–466.

Osborn, D.R., Smith, J.P. (1989). "The performance of periodic autoregressive models in forecasting seasonal UK consumption". Journal of Business and Economic Statistics 7, 1117–1127.

Otto, G., Wirjanto, T. (1990). "Seasonal unit root tests on Canadian macroeconomic time series". Economics Letters 34, 117–120.

Paap, R., Franses, P.H. (1999). "On trends and constants in periodic autoregressions". Econometric Reviews 18, 271–286.

Pagano, M. (1978). "On periodic and multiple autoregressions". Annals of Statistics 6, 1310–1317.

Payne, R. (1996). "Announcement effects and seasonality in the intraday foreign exchange market". Financial Markets Group Discussion Paper 238, London School of Economics.

Reimers, H.-E. (1997). "Seasonal cointegration analysis of German consumption function". Empirical Economics 22, 205–231.

Rodrigues, P.M.M. (2000). "A note on the application of DF test to seasonal data". Statistics and Probability Letters 47, 171–175.

Rodrigues, P.M.M. (2002). "On LM-type tests for seasonal unit roots in quarterly data". Econometrics Journal 5, 176–195.

Rodrigues, P.M.M., Gouveia, P.M.D.C. (2004). "An application of PAR models for tourism forecasting". Tourism Economics 10, 281–303.

Rodrigues, P.M.M., Osborn, D.R. (1999). "Performance of seasonal unit root tests for monthly data". Journal of Applied Statistics 26, 985–1004.

Rodrigues, P.M.M., Taylor, A.M.R. (2004a). "Alternative estimators and unit root tests for seasonal autoregressive processes". Journal of Econometrics 120, 35–73.

Rodrigues, P.M.M., Taylor, A.M.R. (2004b). "Efficient tests of the seasonal unit root hypothesis". Working Paper, Department of Economics, European University Institute.

Sims, C.A. (1974). "Seasonality in regression". Journal of the American Statistical Association 69, 618–626.

Smith, R.J., Taylor, A.M.R. (1998). "Additional critical values and asymptotic representations for seasonal unit root tests". Journal of Econometrics 85, 269–288.

Smith, R.J., Taylor, A.M.R. (1999). "Likelihood ration tests for seasonal unit roots". Journal of Time Series Analysis 20, 453–476.

Taylor, A.M.R. (1998). "Additional critical values and asymptotic representations for monthly seasonal unit root tests". Journal of Time Series Analysis 19, 349–368.

Taylor, A.M.R. (2002). "Regression-based unit root tests with recursive mean adjustment for seasonal and nonseasonal time series". Journal of Business and Economic Statistics 20, 269–281.

Taylor, A.M.R. (2003). "Robust stationarity tests in seasonal time series processes". Journal of Business and Economic Statistics 21, 156–163.

Taylor, S.J., Xu, X. (1997). "The incremental volatility information in one million foreign exchange quotations". Journal of Empirical Finance 4, 317–340.

Tiao, G.C., Grupe, M.R. (1980). "Hidden periodic autoregressive moving average models in time series data". Biometrika 67, 365–373.

Troutman, B.M. (1979). "Some results in periodic autoregression". Biometrika 66, 219–228.

Tsiakas, I. (2004a). "Periodic stochastic volatility and fat tails". Working Paper, Warwick Business School, UK.

Tsiakas, I. (2004b). "Is seasonal heteroscedasticity real? An international perspective". Working Paper, Warwick Business School, UK.

van Dijk, D., Strikholm, B., Terasvirta, T. (2003). "The effects of institutional and technological change and business cycle fluctuations on seasonal patterns in quarterly industrial production series". Econometrics Journal 6, 79–98.

Wallis, K.F. (1974). "Seasonal adjustment and relations between variables". Journal of the American Statistical Association 69, 18–32.

Wells, J.M. (1997). "Business cycles, seasonal cycles, and common trends". Journal of Macroeconomics 19, 443–469.

Whittle, P. (1963). Prediction and Regulation. English University Press, London.

Young, A.H. (1968). "Linear approximation to the census and BLS seasonal adjustment methods". Journal of the American Statistical Association 63, 445–471.

PART 4

APPLICATIONS OF FORECASTING METHODS

Chapter 14

SURVEY EXPECTATIONS

M. HASHEM PESARAN

University of Cambridge and USC

MARTIN WEALE

National Institute of Economic and Social Research

Contents

Handbook of Economic Forecasting, Volume 1
Edited by Graham Elliott, Clive W.J. Granger and Allan Timmermann

DOI: 10.1016/S1574-0706(05)01014-1

Abstract

This paper focuses on survey expectations and discusses their uses for testing and modelling of expectations. Alternative models of expectations formation are reviewed and the importance of allowing for heterogeneity of expectations is emphasized. A weak form of the rational expectations hypothesis which focuses on average expectations rather than individual expectations is advanced. Other models of expectations formation, such as the adaptive expectations hypothesis, are briefly discussed. Testable implications of rational and extrapolative models of expectations are reviewed and the importance of the loss function for the interpretation of the test results is discussed. The paper then provides an account of the various surveys of expectations, reviews alternative methods of quantifying the qualitative surveys, and discusses the use of aggregate and individual survey responses in the analysis of expectations and for forecasting.

Keywords

models of expectations formation, survey data, heterogeneity, tests of rational expectations

JEL classification: C40, C50, C53, C80

1. Introduction

Expectations formation is an integral part of the decision making process by households, firms, as well as the private and public institutions. At the theoretical level the rational expectations hypothesis as advanced by Muth (1961) has gained general acceptance as the dominant model of expectations formation. It provides a fully theory-consistent framework where subjective expectations of individual decision makers are set to their objective counterparts, assuming a known true underlying economic model. Expectations can be in the form of point expectations, or could concern the whole conditional probability distribution of the future values of the variables that influence individual decisions, namely probability or density expectations. Point expectations would be sufficient in the case of linear-quadratic decision problems where the utility (or cost) functions are quadratic and the constraints linear. For more general decision problems density expectations might be required.

From an empirical viewpoint, expectations formation is closely linked to point and density forecasting and as such is subject to data and model uncertainty. Assuming that individual decision makers know the true model of the economy is no more credible than claiming that economic forecasts made using econometric models will be free of systematic bias and informational inefficiencies. This has led many investigators to explore the development of a weaker form of the rational expectations hypothesis that allows for model uncertainty and learning.[1] In this process experimental and survey data on expectations play an important role in providing better insights into how expectations are formed. There is now a substantial literature on survey expectations. Experimental data on expectations are also becoming increasingly available and are particularly important for development of a better understanding of how learning takes place in the expectations formation process.

As with many areas of applied econometrics, initial studies of survey data on expectations tended to focus on the properties of aggregate summaries of survey findings, and their role in aggregate time-series models. The first study of individual responses was published in 1983 and much of the more recent work has been focused on this. Obviously, when a survey covers expectations of individual experience, such as firm's sales or a consumer's income, it is desirable to assess the survey data in the light of the subsequent outcome for the individual. This allows an assessment of the reported expectations in a manner which is not possible using only time-series aggregates but it requires some form of panel data set. Even where a survey collects information on expectations of some macro-economic aggregate, such as the rate of inflation, it is likely that analysis of individual responses will provide richer and more convincing

[1] Evans and Honkapohja (2001) provide an excellent account of recent developments of expectations formation models subject to learning.

conclusions than would be found from the time-series analysis of aggregated responses alone.

This paper focuses on the analysis of survey expectations at the individual and at the aggregate levels and discusses their uses in forecasting and for testing and modelling of expectations. Most expectations data are concerned with point expectations, although some attempts have been made to elicit density expectations, in particular expectations of second order moments. Survey data are often compiled in the form of qualitative responses and their conversion into quantitative measures might be needed. The elicitation process embodied in the survey techniques also presents further problems for the use of survey expectations. Since respondents tend to lack proper economic incentives when answering survey questions about their expectations, the responses might not be sufficiently accurate or reliable. Finally, survey expectations tend to cover relatively short horizons, typically 1–12 months, and their use in long-term forecasting or impulse response analysis will be limited, and would require augmenting the survey data with a formal expectations formation model for generation of longer term expectations, beyond the horizon of the survey data. The literature on these and on a number of other related issues is covered. In particular, we consider the evidence on the use of survey expectations in forecasting. The question of interest would be to see if expectations data when used as supplementary variables in forecasting models would lead to better forecasting performance. We note that many expectational surveys also collect information about the recent past. Such data are potentially useful for "nowcasting" because they are typically made available earlier than the "hard" official data to which they are supposed to relate. While their study falls outside a synthesis of work on survey measures of expectations, and is not discussed here, it is worth noting that many of the methods used to analyze and test survey data about expectations of the future also apply with little or no modification, to analysis of these retrospective data. In some circumstances, as we discuss in Section 3.3, they may be required to assess the performance of surveys about expectations of the future.

While we focus on survey expectations rather than the forecasting properties of particular statistical or econometric models, it is worth emphasizing that the distinction is more apparent than real. Some surveys collate the forecasts of professional forecasters, and it is likely that at least some of these are generated by formal forecasting models and forecasting processes of various types. Even where information on such expectations is collected from the public at large, such expectations may be closely informed by the published forecasts of professional forecasters. There are some circumstances where it is, however, unlikely that formal models are implied. If consumers are asked about their expectations of their own incomes, while these may be influenced by forecasts for the macro-economy, they are unlikely to be solely the outcome of formal forecasting procedures. When businesses are asked about how they expect their own sales or prices to change, the same is likely to be true. The ambiguity of the distinction and the fact that some important issues are raised by surveys which collect information from professional analysts and forecasters does mean, however, that we give some consideration to such surveys as well as to those which are likely to reflect expectations rather than forecasts.

Our review covers four separate but closely related topics and is therefore organized in four distinct parts set out in Sections 2, 3, 4 and 5. In Section 2 we address the question of concepts and models of expectations formation. Section 3 looks at the development of measures of expectations including issues arising in the quantification of qualitative measures of expectations. Section 4 considers the use of survey expectations in forecasting, and Section 5 considers how survey data are used in testing theories with particular emphasis on models of expectations formation. Conclusions follow.

We begin Section 2 by introducing some of the basic concepts and the various models of expectations formation advanced in the literature. In Section 2.1 we introduce the rational expectations hypothesis and discuss the importance of allowing for heterogeneity of expectations in relating theory to survey expectations. To this end a weak form of the rational expectations hypothesis, which focuses on average expectations rather than individual expectations, is advanced. Other models of expectations formation, such as the adaptive expectations hypothesis, are briefly reviewed in Section 2.2. In Section 2.3 we discuss some of the issues involved in testing models of expectations. Section 2.4 further considers the optimality of survey forecasts in the case where loss functions are asymmetric.

The introductory subsection to Section 3 provides a historical account of the development of surveys of expectations. As noted above, many of these surveys collect qualitative data; Section 3.1 considers ways of quantifying these qualitative expectations paying attention to both the use of aggregated data from these surveys and to the use of individual responses. In Section 3.2 we discuss different ways of providing and interpreting information on uncertainty to complement qualitative or quantitative information on expectations. In Section 3.3 we discuss the analysis of individual rather than aggregated responses to surveys about expectations.

The focus of Section 4 is on the uses of survey data in producing economic forecasts. In Section 4.1 we discuss the use of survey data in the context of forecast combination as a means of using disparate forecasts to produce a more accurate compromise forecast. Section 4.2 considers how they can be used to indicate the uncertainty of forecasts and in Section 4.3 we discuss the use of qualitative surveys to produce forecasts of quantitative macro-economic aggregates.

Methods of testing models of expectation formation, discussed in Section 5 are split between analysis based on the results of quantitative surveys of expectations in Section 5.1 and the analysis of qualitative disaggregated data in Section 5.2. A substantial range of econometric issues arises in both cases. Perhaps not surprisingly more attention has been paid to the former than to the latter although, since many of the high-frequency expectations surveys are qualitative in form, the second area is likely to develop in importance.

2. Concepts and models of expectations formation

Expectations are subjectively held beliefs by individuals about uncertain future outcomes or the beliefs of other individuals in the market place.[2] How expectations are formed, and whether they lend themselves to mathematical representations have been the subject of considerable debate and discussions. The answers vary and depend on the nature and the source of uncertainty that surrounds a particular decision. Knight (1921) distinguishes between 'true uncertainty' and 'risk' and argues that under the former it is not possible to reduce the uncertainty and expectations to 'an objective quantitatively determined probability' (p. 321). Pesaran (1987) makes a distinction between exogenous and behavioural uncertainty and argues that the former is more likely to lend itself to formal probabilistic analysis. In this review we focus on situations where individual expectations can be formalized.

Denote individual i's point expectations of a k dimensional vector of future variables, say $\mathbf{x}_{t+1}$, formed with respect to the information set, Ω_{it}, by $E_i(\mathbf{x}_{t+1} \mid \Omega_{it})$. Similarly, let $f_i(\mathbf{x}_{t+1} \mid \Omega_{it})$ be individual i's density expectations, so that

$$E_i(\mathbf{x}_{t+1} \mid \Omega_{it}) = \int \mathbf{x}_{t+1} f_i(\mathbf{x}_{t+1} \mid \Omega_{it})\, d\mathbf{x}_t.$$

Individual i's belief about individual j's expectations of $\mathbf{x}_{t+1}$ may also be written as

$$E_i\big[E_j(\mathbf{x}_{t+1} \mid \Omega_{jt}) \mid \Omega_{it}\big].$$

Clearly, higher order expectations can be similarly defined but will not be pursued here.

In general, point expectations of the same variable could differ considerably across individuals, due to differences in Ω_{it} (information disparity), and differences in the subjective probability densities, $f_i(.)$ (belief disparity). The two sources of expectations heterogeneity are closely related and could be re-inforcing. Information disparities could initiate and maintain disparities in beliefs, whilst differences in beliefs could lead to information disparities when information processing is costly.[3]

Alternative models of expectations formation provide different characterizations of the way subjective beliefs and objective reality are related. At one extreme lies the rational expectations hypothesis of Muth (1961) that postulates the coincidence of the two concepts, and is contrasted with the Knightian view that denies any specific links between expectations and reality. In what follows we provide an overview of the alternative models, confining ourselves to expectations formation models that lend themselves to statistical formalizations.

[2] It is also possible for individuals to form expectations of present or past events about which they are not fully informed. This is related to "nowcasting" or "backcasting" in the forecasting literature mentioned above.

[3] Models of rationally heterogeneous expectations are discussed, for example, in Evans and Ramey (1992), Brock and Hommes (1997) and Branch (2002). See also Section 5.1.5 for discussion of evidence on expectations heterogeneity.

2.1. The rational expectations hypothesis

For a formal representation of the rational expectations hypothesis (REH), as set out by Muth, we first decompose the individual specific information sets, Ω_{it}, into a *public information* set Ψ_t, and an individual-specific *private information* set Φ_{it} such that

$$\Omega_{it} = \Psi_t \cup \Phi_{it},$$

for $i = 1, 2, \dots, N$. Further, we assume that the 'objective' probability density function of $\mathbf{x}_{t+1}$ is given by $f(\mathbf{x}_{t+1} \mid \Psi_t)$. Then the REH postulates that

$$\mathrm{H_{REH}}: \quad f_i(\mathbf{x}_{t+1} \mid \Omega_{it}) = f(\mathbf{x}_{t+1} \mid \Psi_t), \quad \text{for all } i. \tag{1}$$

Under the Muthian notion of the REH, private information plays no role in the expectations formation process, and expectations are fully efficient with respect to the public information, Ψ_t. In the case of point expectations, the optimality of the REH is captured by the "orthogonality" condition

$$E(\boldsymbol{\xi}_{t+1} \mid S_t) = \mathbf{0}, \tag{2}$$

where $\boldsymbol{\xi}_{t+1}$ is the error of expectations defined by

$$\boldsymbol{\xi}_{t+1} = \mathbf{x}_{t+1} - E(\mathbf{x}_{t+1} \mid \Psi_t), \tag{3}$$

and $S_t \subseteq \Psi_t$, is a subset of Ψ_t. The orthogonality condition (2) in turn implies that, under the REH, expectations errors have zero means and are serially uncorrelated. It does not, for example, require the expectations errors to be conditionally or unconditionally homoskedastic. From a formal mathematical perspective, it states that under the REH (in the sense of Muth) expectations errors form a martingale difference process with respect to the non-decreasing information set available to the agent at the time expectations are formed. In what follows we shall use the term 'orthogonality condition' and the 'martingale property' of the expectations errors interchangeably. The orthogonality condition is often used to test the informational efficiency of survey expectations. But as we shall see it is neither necessary nor sufficient for rationality of expectations if individual expectations are formed as optimal forecasts with respect to general cost functions under incomplete learning.

Also, the common knowledge assumptions that underlie the rationality of individual expectations in the Muthian sense is rather restrictive, and has been relaxed in the literature where different notions of the rational expectations equilibria are defined and implemented under asymmetric and heterogeneous information. See, for example, Radner (1979), Grossman and Stiglitz (1980), Hellwig (1980) and Milgrom (1981), just to mention some of the early important contributions.

In advancing the REH, Muth (1961) was in fact fully aware of the importance of allowing for cross section heterogeneity of expectations.[4] One of his aims in proposing the REH was to explain the following stylized facts observed using expectations data:

[4] Pigou (1927) and Keynes (1936) had already emphasized the role of heterogeneity of information and beliefs across agents for the analysis of financial markets.

1. Averages of expectations in an industry are more accurate than naive models and as accurate as elaborate equation systems, although there are considerable cross-sectional differences of opinion.
2. Reported expectations generally underestimate the extent of changes that actually take place [Muth (1961, p. 316)].

One of the main reasons for the prevalence of the homogeneous version of the rational expectations hypothesis given by (1) has been the conceptual and technical difficulties of dealing with rational expectations models under heterogeneous information.[5] Early attempts to allow for heterogeneous information in rational expectations models include Lucas (1973), Townsend (1978) and Townsend (1983). More recent developments are surveyed by Hommes (2006) who argues that an important paradigm shift is occurring in economics and finance from a representative rational agent model towards heterogeneous agent models. Analysis of heterogeneous rational expectations models invariably involves the "infinite regress in expectations" problem that arises as agents need to forecast the forecasts of others. A number of different solution strategies have been proposed in the literature which in different ways limit the scope of possible solutions. For example, Binder and Pesaran (1998) establish that a unique solution results if it is assumed that each agent bases her/his forecasts of others only on the information set that is common knowledge, Ψ_t.

When the heterogeneous rational expectations model has a unique solution, expectations errors of individual agents continue to satisfy the usual orthogonality conditions. However, unlike in models under homogeneous information, the average expectations error across decision makers, defined as $\boldsymbol{\xi}_{t+1} = \mathbf{x}_{t+1} - \sum_{i=1}^{N} w_{it} E(\mathbf{x}_{t+1} \mid \Omega_{it})$ is generally not orthogonal with respect to the individual decision makers' information sets, where w_{it} is the weight attached to the ith individual in forming the average expectations measure. Seen from this perspective a weaker form of the REH that focuses on 'average' expectations might be more desirable. Consider the average density expectations computed over N individuals

$$\bar{f}_w(\mathbf{x}_{t+1} \mid \Omega_t) = \sum_{i=1}^{N} w_{it} f_i(\mathbf{x}_{t+1} \mid \Omega_{it}). \tag{4}$$

The average form of the REH can then be postulated as

$$\overline{\mathrm{H}}_{\mathrm{REH}}: \quad \bar{f}_w(\mathbf{x}_{t+1} \mid \Omega_t) = f(\mathbf{x}_{t+1} \mid \Psi_t), \tag{5}$$

where $\Omega_t = \bigcup_{i=1}^{N} \Omega_{it}$, and w_{it} are non-negative weights that satisfy the conditions:

$$\sum_{i=1}^{N} w_{it} = 1, \quad \sum_{i=1}^{N} w_{it}^2 = O\left(\frac{1}{N}\right). \tag{6}$$

[5] For example, as recently acknowledged by Mankiw, Reis and Wolfers (2004), the fact that expectations are not the same across individuals is routinely ignored in the macroeconomic literature.

In terms of point expectations, the average form of the REH holds if

$$\overline{E}_w(\mathbf{x}_{t+1} \mid \Omega_t) = \sum_{i=1}^{N} w_{it} E_i(\mathbf{x}_{t+1} \mid \Omega_{it}) = E(\mathbf{x}_{t+1} \mid \Psi_t), \tag{7}$$

which is much weaker than the REH and allows for a considerable degree of heterogeneity of individual expectations.

This version of the REH is, for example, compatible with systematic errors of expectations being present at the individual level. Suppose that individual expectations can be decomposed as

$$E_i(\mathbf{x}_{t+1} \mid \Omega_{it}) = \mathbf{H}_i E(\mathbf{x}_{t+1} \mid \Psi_t) + \mathbf{u}_{it}, \tag{8}$$

where $\mathbf{H}_i$ is a $k \times k$ matrix of fixed constants, and $\mathbf{u}_{it}$, $i = 1, 2, \ldots, N$, are the individual-specific components. The individual expectations errors are now given by

$$\boldsymbol{\xi}_{i,t+1} = \mathbf{x}_{t+1} - E_i(\mathbf{x}_{t+1} \mid \Omega_{it}) = \boldsymbol{\xi}_{t+1} + (\mathbf{I}_k - \mathbf{H}_i)E(\mathbf{x}_{t+1} \mid \Psi_t) - \mathbf{u}_{it},$$

where $\mathbf{I}_k$ is an identity matrix of order k. Clearly, this does not satisfy the REH if $\mathbf{H}_i \neq \mathbf{I}_k$, and/or $\mathbf{u}_{it}$ are, for example, serially correlated. Using the weights w_{it}, the average expectations errors are now given by

$$\bar{\boldsymbol{\xi}}_{w,t+1} = \boldsymbol{\xi}_{t+1} + \left(\mathbf{I}_k - \overline{\mathbf{H}}_w\right)E(\mathbf{x}_{t+1} \mid \Psi_t) - \bar{\mathbf{u}}_{wt},$$

where

$$\bar{\boldsymbol{\xi}}_{w,t+1} = \sum_{i=1}^{N} w_{it}\boldsymbol{\xi}_{i,t+1}, \quad \overline{\mathbf{H}}_{wt} = \sum_{i=1}^{N} w_{it}\mathbf{H}_i, \quad \bar{\mathbf{u}}_{wt} = \sum_{i=1}^{N} w_{it}\mathbf{u}_{it}.$$

The conditions under which average expectations are 'rational' are much less restrictive as compared to the conditions required for the rationality of individual expectations. A set of sufficient conditions for the rationality of average expectations is given by

1. N is sufficiently large.
2. $\mathbf{u}_{it}$ are distributed independently across i, and for each i they are covariance stationary.
3. The weights, w_{it}, satisfy the conditions in (6) and are distributed independently of $\mathbf{u}_{jt}$, for all i and j.
4. $\mathbf{H}_i$ are distributed independently of w_{it} and across i with mean $\mathbf{I}_k$ and finite second order moments.

Under these conditions (for each t) we have[6]

$$\bar{\boldsymbol{\xi}}_{w,t+1} \overset{\text{q.m.}}{\rightarrow} \boldsymbol{\xi}_{t+1}, \quad \text{as } N \rightarrow \infty,$$

[6] For a proof, see Pesaran (2004, Appendix A).

where $\overset{\text{q.m.}}{\to}$ denotes convergence in quadratic means. Therefore, average, 'consensus' or market rationality can hold even if the underlying individual expectations are non-rational in the sense of Muth.[7] The above conditions allow for a high degree of heterogeneity of expectations, and are compatible with individual expectations errors being biased and serially correlated As we shall see this result is particularly relevant to tests of the REH that are based on survey responses.

2.2. *Extrapolative models of expectations formation*

In addition to the REH, a wide variety of expectations formation models has been advanced in the literature with differing degrees of informational requirements. Most of these models fall under the "extrapolative" category, where point expectations are determined by weighted averages of past realizations. A general extrapolative formula is given by

$$E_i(\mathbf{x}_{t+1} \mid \Omega_{it}) = \sum_{s=0}^{\infty} \mathbf{\Phi}_{is}\mathbf{x}_{t-s}, \tag{9}$$

where the coefficient matrices, $\mathbf{\Phi}_{is}$, are assumed to be absolute summable subject to the adding up condition

$$\sum_{s=0}^{\infty} \mathbf{\Phi}_{is} = \mathbf{I}_k. \tag{10}$$

This condition ensures that *unconditionally* expectations and observations have the same means. For example, suppose that $\mathbf{x}_t$ follows the first-order stationary autoregressive process (unknown to the individuals)

$$\mathbf{x}_t = \boldsymbol{\mu} + \mathbf{\Psi}\mathbf{x}_{t-1} + \boldsymbol{\varepsilon}_t,$$

where all eigenvalues of $\mathbf{\Psi}$ lie inside the unit circle. It is then easily seen that

$$E\big[E_i(\mathbf{x}_{t+1} \mid \Omega_{it})\big] = \left(\sum_{s=0}^{\infty} \mathbf{\Phi}_{is}\right)(\mathbf{I}_k - \mathbf{\Psi})^{-1}\boldsymbol{\mu},$$

and under the adding up condition, (10), yields, $E[E_i(\mathbf{x}_{t+1} \mid \Omega_{it})] = E(\mathbf{x}_t) = (\mathbf{I}_k - \mathbf{\Psi})^{-1}\boldsymbol{\mu}$. Under (10), time averages of extrapolative expectations will be the same as the sample mean of the underlying processes, an implication that can be tested using quantitative survey expectations, if available.

[7] The term consensus forecasts or expectations was popularized by Joseph Livingston, the founder of the Livingston Survey in the U.S. See Section 3 for further details and references.

The average (or consensus) version of the extrapolative hypothesis derived using the weights, w_{it} defined by (6), has also the extrapolative form

$$\bar{E}(\mathbf{x}_{t+1} \mid S_t) = \sum_{s=0}^{\infty} \bar{\mathbf{\Phi}}_{st}\mathbf{x}_{t-s}, \tag{11}$$

where S_t contains $\mathbf{x}_t, \mathbf{x}_{t-1}, \ldots; w_{1t}, w_{2t}, \ldots$ and

$$\bar{\mathbf{\Phi}}_{st} = \sum_{i=1}^{N} w_{it}\mathbf{\Phi}_{is}.$$

It is clear that under extrapolative expectations individual expectations need not be homogeneous and could follow a number of different processes all of which are special cases of the general extrapolative scheme. Once again, under the adding up condition (10), $E[\bar{E}(\mathbf{x}_{t+1} \mid S_t)] = E(\mathbf{x}_t)$, so long as $\sum_{i=1}^{N} w_{it} = 1$.

2.2.1. *Static models of expectations*

The simplest form of an extrapolative model is the static expectations model considered by Keynes (1936). In its basic form it is defined by

$$E_i(\mathbf{x}_{t+1} \mid \Omega_{it}) = \bar{E}(\mathbf{x}_{t+1} \mid S_t) = \mathbf{x}_t,$$

and is optimal (in the mean squared error sense) if $\mathbf{x}_t$ follows a pure random walk model. A more recent version of this model, used in the case of integrated processes is given by

$$\bar{E}(\mathbf{x}_{t+1} \mid S_t) = \mathbf{x}_t + \Delta\mathbf{x}_t,$$

which is applicable when $\Delta\mathbf{x}_{t+1}$ follows a random walk. This latter specification has the advantage of being robust to shifts in the unconditional mean of the $\mathbf{x}_t$ processes. Neither of these specifications, however, allows for any form of adaptation to the changing nature of the underlying time series.

2.2.2. *Return to normality models*

A simple generalization of the static model that takes account of the evolution of the underlying processes is the 'mean-reverting' or the 'return to normality' model defined by

$$\bar{E}(\mathbf{x}_{t+1} \mid S_t) = (\mathbf{I}_k - \mathbf{\Lambda})\mathbf{x}_t + \mathbf{\Lambda}\mathbf{x}_t^*, \tag{12}$$

where $\mathbf{\Lambda}$ is a non-negative definite matrix, and $\mathbf{x}_t^*$ represents the 'normal' or 'the long-run equilibrium' level of $\mathbf{x}_t$. In this formulation, expectations are adjusted downward if $\mathbf{x}_t$ is above its normal level and *vice versa* if $\mathbf{x}_t$ is below its normal level. Different specifications of $\mathbf{x}_t^*$ can be considered. For example, assuming

$$\mathbf{x}_t^* = (\mathbf{I}_k - \mathbf{W})\mathbf{x}_t + \mathbf{W}\mathbf{x}_{t-1},$$

yields the regressive expectations model

$$\overline{E}(\mathbf{x}_{t+1} \mid S_t) = (\mathbf{I}_k - \mathbf{\Lambda}\mathbf{W})\mathbf{x}_t + \mathbf{\Lambda}\mathbf{W}\mathbf{x}_{t-1},$$

where $\mathbf{W}$ is a weighting matrix.

2.2.3. Adaptive expectations model

This is the most prominent form of extrapolative expectations, and can be obtained from the general extrapolative formula, (11), by setting

$$\mathbf{\Phi}_s = \mathbf{\Gamma}(\mathbf{I}_k - \mathbf{\Gamma})^s, \quad s = 0, 1, \ldots$$

and assuming that all eigenvalues of $\mathbf{I}_k - \mathbf{\Gamma}$ line inside the unit circle. Alternatively, the adaptive expectations model can be obtained from the return to normality model (12), by setting

$$\mathbf{x}_t^* = (\mathbf{I} - \mathbf{W})\mathbf{x}_t + \mathbf{W}\overline{E}(\mathbf{x}_t \mid S_{t-1}),$$

which yields the familiar representation

$$\overline{E}(\mathbf{x}_{t+1} \mid S_t) - \overline{E}(\mathbf{x}_t \mid S_{t-1}) = \mathbf{\Gamma}\big[\mathbf{x}_t - \overline{E}(\mathbf{x}_t \mid S_{t-1})\big]. \tag{13}$$

Higher order versions of the adaptive expectations model have also been employed in the analysis of expectations data. A general rth order vector adaptive model is given by

$$\overline{E}(\mathbf{x}_{t+1} \mid S_t) - \overline{E}(\mathbf{x}_t \mid S_{t-1}) = \sum_{j=0}^{r-1} \mathbf{\Psi}_j\big[\mathbf{x}_{t-j} - \overline{E}(\mathbf{x}_{t-j} \mid S_{t-j-1})\big]. \tag{14}$$

Under this model expectations are revised in line with past errors of expectations. In the present multivariate setting, past expectations errors of all variables can potentially affect the extent to which expectations of a single variable are revised. Univariate adaptive expectations models can be derived by restricting $\mathbf{\Psi}_j$ to be diagonal for all j.

The univariate version of the adaptive expectations model was introduced into economics by Koyck (1954) in a study of investment, by Cagan (1956) in a study of money demand in conditions of hyper-inflation and by Nerlove (1958) in a study of the cobweb cycle. Adaptive expectations were also used extensively in empirical studies of consumption and the Phillips curve prior to the ascendancy of the REH in early 1970s.

In general, adaptive expectations need not be informationally efficient, and expectations errors generated by adaptive schemes could be serially correlated. Originally, the adaptive expectations hypothesis was advanced as a plausible 'rule of thumb' for updating and revising expectations, without claiming that it will be optimal. Muth (1960) was the first to show that the adaptive expectations hypothesis is optimal (in the sense of yielding minimum mean squared forecast errors) only if the process generating $\mathbf{x}_{t+1}$ has the following integrated, first-order moving average representation (IMA(1)):

$$\Delta \mathbf{x}_{t+1} = \boldsymbol{\varepsilon}_{t+1} - (\mathbf{I}_k - \boldsymbol{\Gamma})\boldsymbol{\varepsilon}_t, \quad \boldsymbol{\varepsilon}_{t+1}|S_t \sim IID(\mathbf{0}, \boldsymbol{\Sigma}_{\varepsilon}).$$

In general, adaptive expectations need not be optimal and could perform particularly poorly when the underlying processes are subject to structural breaks.

2.2.4. Error-learning models

The adaptive expectations hypothesis is concerned with one-step ahead expectations, and how they are updated, but it can be readily generalized to deal with expectations formed over longer horizons. Denoting the h-step ahead expectations by $\bar{E}(\mathbf{x}_{t+h} \mid S_t)$, the error-learning model is given by

$$\bar{E}(\mathbf{x}_{t+h} \mid S_t) - \bar{E}(\mathbf{x}_{t+h} \mid S_{t-1}) = \boldsymbol{\Gamma}_h\big[\mathbf{x}_t - \bar{E}(\mathbf{x}_t \mid S_{t-1})\big], \tag{15}$$

which for $h = 1$ reduces to the simple adaptive expectations scheme. The error-learning model states that the revision to expectations of $\mathbf{x}_{t+h}$ over the period $t - 1$ to t is proportional to the current error of expectations. Different expectations formation models can be obtained assuming different patterns for the revision coefficients $\boldsymbol{\Gamma}_h$. Error-learning models have been proposed in the literature by Meiselman (1962), Mincer and Zarnowitz (1969) and Frenkel (1975) and reduce to the adaptive expectations model if the revision coefficients, $\boldsymbol{\Gamma}_h$, are restricted to be the same across different horizons. Mincer and Zarnowitz (1969) show that the revision coefficients are related to the weights $\boldsymbol{\Phi}_j$ in the general extrapolations formula via the following recursive relations:

$$\boldsymbol{\Gamma}_h = \sum_{j=0}^{h-1} \boldsymbol{\Phi}_j \boldsymbol{\Gamma}_{h-1-j}, \quad h = 1, 2, \ldots, \tag{16}$$

when $\boldsymbol{\Gamma}_0 = \mathbf{I}_k$. They demonstrate that the revision coefficients will be falling (rising) when the weights $\boldsymbol{\Phi}_j$ decline (rise) more than exponentially. The error-correction and the general extrapolation model are algebraically equivalent, but the former is particularly convenient when survey data are available on expectations over different horizons.

2.3. Testable implications of expectations formation models

Broadly speaking there are two general approaches to testing expectations formation models: 'direct' tests that make use of survey data on expectations, and 'indirect' tests that focus on cross-equation parametric restrictions of the expectations formation models when combined with a particular parametric economic model. The direct approach is applicable to testing the REH as well as the extrapolative models, whilst the indirect approach has been used primarily in testing of the REH. Given the focus of this paper we shall confine our discussion to direct tests.

2.3.1. Testing the REH

Suppose that quantitative expectations of $\mathbf{x}_{t+h}$ are available on individuals, $i = 1, 2, \ldots, N$, formed at time $t = 1, 2, \ldots, T$, over different horizons, $h = 1, 2, \ldots, H$, and denote these by ${}_t\mathbf{x}^e_{i,t+h}$. In the case of many surveys only qualitative responses are available and they need to be converted into quantitative measures, a topic that we return to in Section 3.1. The realizations, $\mathbf{x}_{t+h}$, are often subject to data revisions that might not have been known to the individuals when forming their expectations. The agent's loss function might not be quadratic. These issues will be addressed in subsequent sections. For the time being, we abstract from data revisions and conversion errors and suppose that ${}_t\mathbf{x}^e_{i,t+h}$ and the associated expectations errors

$$\boldsymbol{\xi}_{i,t+h} = \mathbf{x}_{t+h} - {}_t\mathbf{x}^e_{i,t+h}, \tag{17}$$

are observed free of measurement errors. Under this idealized set up the test of the REH can proceed by testing the orthogonality condition, (2), applied to the individual expectations errors, $\boldsymbol{\xi}_{i,t+h}$, assuming that

$${}_t\mathbf{x}^e_{i,t+h} = E_i(\mathbf{x}_{t+h} \mid \Omega_{it}) = \int \mathbf{x}_{t+h} f_i(\mathbf{x}_{t+h} \mid \Omega_{it}) d\mathbf{x}_t, \tag{18}$$

namely that survey responses and mathematical expectations of the individual's density expectations are identical. The orthogonality condition applied to the individual expectations errors may now be written as

$$E_i\left(\mathbf{x}_{t+h} - {}_t\mathbf{x}^e_{i,t+h} \mid S_{it}\right) = \mathbf{0}, \quad \text{for } i = 1, 2, \ldots, N \text{ and } h = 1, 2, \ldots, H, \tag{19}$$

namely expectations errors (at all horizons) form martingale difference processes with respect to the information set S_{it}, where S_{it} could contain any sub-set of the public information set, Ψ_t, specifically $\mathbf{x}_t, \mathbf{x}_{t-1}, \mathbf{x}_{t-2}, \ldots$, and the past values of individual-specific expectations, ${}_{t-\ell}\mathbf{x}^e_{i,t+h-\ell}$, $\ell = 1, 2, \ldots$. Information on other individuals' expectations, ${}_{t-\ell}\mathbf{x}^e_{j,t+h-\ell}$ for $j \neq i$ should not be included in S_{it} unless they are specifically supplied to the individual respondents being surveyed. In such a case the test encompasses the concept that the explanatory power of a rational forecast cannot be enhanced by the use of information provided by any other forecast [Fair and Shiller (1990), Bonham and Dacy (1991)]. A test of unbiasedness of the rational expectations can be carried out by including a vector of unity, $\boldsymbol{\tau} = (1, 1, \ldots, 1)'$ amongst the elements of S_{it}. As noted earlier, the REH does not impose any restrictions on conditional or unconditional volatilities of the expectations errors, so long as the underlying losses are quadratic in those errors.

The REH can also be tested using the time consistency property of mathematical expectations, so long as at least two survey expectations are available for the same target dates (i.e. $H \geqslant 2$). The subjective expectations, $E_i(\mathbf{x}_{t+h} \mid S_{i,t+\ell})$ formed at time $t + \ell$ for period $t + h$ $(h > \ell)$ are said to be consistent if expectations of $E_i(\mathbf{x}_{t+h} \mid S_{i,t+\ell})$ formed at time t are equal to $E_i(\mathbf{x}_{t+h} | S_{it})$ for all ℓ. See Pesaran (1989) and Froot and Ito (1990). Clearly, expectations formed rationally also satisfy the consistency property, and in particular

$$E_i\left[E_i(\mathbf{x}_{t+h} \mid S_{i,t+1}) \mid S_{it}\right] = E_i(\mathbf{x}_{t+h} \mid S_{it}).$$

Therefore, under (18)

$$E_i\left[\left({}_{t+1}\mathbf{x}^e_{i,t+h} - {}_t\mathbf{x}^e_{i,t+h}\right) \mid S_{it}\right] = \mathbf{0},$$

which for the same target date, t, can be written as

$$E_i\left[\left({}_{t-h+1}\mathbf{x}^e_{it} - {}_{t-h}\mathbf{x}^e_{it}\right) \mid S_{i,t-h}\right] = \mathbf{0}, \quad \text{for } h = 2, 3, \ldots, H. \tag{20}$$

Namely revisions in expectations of $\mathbf{x}_t$ over the period $t - h$ to $t - h + 1$ must be informationally efficient. As compared to the standard orthogonality conditions (19), the orthogonality conditions in (20) have the added advantage that they do not necessarily require data on realizations, and are therefore likely to be more robust to data revisions. Davies and Lahiri (1995) utilize these conditions in their analysis of the Blue Chip Survey of Professional Forecasts and in a later paper [Davies and Lahiri (1999)] they study the Survey of Professional Forecasters.

Average versions of (19) and (20) can also be considered, namely

$$\bar{E}\left(\mathbf{x}_{t+h} - {}_t\bar{\mathbf{x}}^e_{t+h} \mid S_t\right) = \mathbf{0}, \quad \text{for } h = 1, 2, \ldots, H, \tag{21}$$

where

$${}_t\bar{\mathbf{x}}^e_{t+h} = \sum_{i=1}^{N} w_{it}\, {}_t\mathbf{x}^e_{i,t+h}, \tag{22}$$

and $S_t \subseteq \Psi_t$. Similarly,

$$E\left[\left({}_{t-h+1}\bar{\mathbf{x}}^e_t - {}_{t-h}\bar{\mathbf{x}}^e_t\right) \mid S_{t-h}\right] = \mathbf{0}, \quad \text{for } h = 2, 3, \ldots, H. \tag{23}$$

In using these conditions special care needs to be exercised in the choice of S_{t-h}. For example, inclusion of past average expectations, ${}_{t-h}\bar{\mathbf{x}}^e_t, {}_{t-h-1}\bar{\mathbf{x}}^e_t, \ldots$ in S_{t-h} might not be valid if information on average expectations were not publicly released.[8] But in testing the rationality of individual expectations it would be valid to include past expectations of the individual under consideration in her/his information set, S_{it}.

2.3.2. *Testing extrapolative models*

In their most general formulation, as set out in (9), the extrapolative models have only a limited number of testable implications; the most important of which is the linearity of the relationship postulated between expectations, $\bar{E}(\mathbf{x}_{t+1} \mid S_t)$, and $\mathbf{x}_t, \mathbf{x}_{t-1}, \ldots$. Important testable implications, however, follow if it is further assumed that extrapolative

[8] The same issue also arises in panel tests of the REH where past average expectations are included as regressors in a panel of individual expectations. For a related critique see Bonham and Cohen (2001).

expectations must also satisfy the time consistency property discussed above. The time consistency of expectations requires that

$$\overline{E}\{\overline{E}(\mathbf{x}_{t+1} \mid S_t) \mid S_{t-1}\} = \overline{E}(\mathbf{x}_{t+1} \mid S_{t-1}),$$

and is much less restrictive than the orthogonality condition applied to the forecast errors. Under time consistency and using (11) we have

$$\overline{E}(\mathbf{x}_{t+1} \mid S_{t-1}) = \mathbf{\Phi}_0 \overline{E}(\mathbf{x}_t \mid S_{t-1}) + \sum_{s=1}^{\infty} \mathbf{\Phi}_s \mathbf{x}_{t-s},$$

and hence

$$\overline{E}(\mathbf{x}_{t+1} \mid S_t) - \overline{E}(\mathbf{x}_{t+1} \mid S_{t-1}) = \mathbf{\Phi}_0\big[\mathbf{x}_t - \overline{E}(\mathbf{x}_t \mid S_{t-1})\big].$$

When losses are quadratic in expectations errors, under time consistency the survey expectations would then satisfy the relationships

$${}_t\bar{\mathbf{x}}^e_{t+1} - {}_{t-1}\bar{\mathbf{x}}^e_{t+1} = \mathbf{\Phi}_0\big(\mathbf{x}_t - {}_{t-1}\bar{\mathbf{x}}^e_t\big), \tag{24}$$

which state that revisions to expectations of $\mathbf{x}_{t+1}$ over the period $t-1$ to t should depend only on the expectations errors and not on $\mathbf{x}_t$ or its lagged values. Under asymmetrical losses expectations revisions would also depend on revisions to expected volatilities, and the time consistency of the extrapolative expectations can be tested only if direct observations on expected volatilities are available. The new testable implications discussed in Patton and Timmermann (2004) are also relevant here.

Relation (24) also shows that extrapolative expectations could still suffer from systematic errors, even if they satisfy the time consistency property. Finally, using the results (15) and (16) obtained for the error learning models, time consistency implications of the extrapolation models can be readily extended to expectations formed at time t and time $t-1$ for higher order horizons, $h > 1$.

As noted earlier, direct tests of time consistency of expectations require survey data on expectations of the same target date formed at two different previous dates at the minimum. In cases where such multiple observations are not available, it seems meaningful to test only particular formulations of the extrapolation models such as the mean-reverting or the adaptive hypothesis. Testable implications of the finite-order adaptive models are discussed further in Pesaran (1985) and Pesaran (1987, Chapter 9) where an empirical analysis of the formation of inflation expectations in British manufacturing industries is provided.

2.4. *Testing the optimality of survey forecasts under asymmetric losses*

The two orthogonality conditions, (19) and (20), are based on the assumption that individual forecast responses are the same as conditional mathematical expectations. See (18). This assumption is, however, valid if forecasts are made with respect to loss functions that are quadratic in forecast errors and does not hold in more general settings where the loss function is non-quadratic or asymmetric. Properties of optimal forecasts under general loss functions are discussed in Patton and Timmermann (2004) where new testable implications are also established. Asymmetric losses can arise in practice for a number of different reasons, such as institutional constraints, or non-linear effects in economic decisions. In a recent paper Elliott, Komunjer and Timmermann (2003) even argue that "on economic grounds one would, if anything, typically expect asymmetric losses".[9] Once the symmetric loss function is abandoned, as shown by Zellner (1986), optimal forecasts need not be unbiased.[10] This point is easily illustrated with respect to the LINEX function introduced by Varian (1975), and used by Zellner (1986) in a Bayesian context. The LINEX function has the following simple form

$$\varphi_i(\xi_{i,t+1}) = \frac{2}{\alpha_i^2}\left[\exp(\alpha_i \xi_{i,t+1}) - \alpha_i \xi_{i,t+1} - 1\right],$$

where $\xi_{i,t+1}$ is the forecast error defined by (17). To simplify the exposition we assume here that $\xi_{i,t+1}$ is a scalar. For this loss function the optimal forecast is given by[11]

$${}_t x_{i,t+h}^e = \alpha_i^{-1} \log\left\{E_i\left(\exp(\alpha_i x_{t+h}) \mid \Omega_{it}\right)\right\}.$$

In the case where individual ith conditional expected density of x_{t+h} is normal we have

$${}_t x_{i,t+h}^e = E_i(x_{t+h} \mid \Omega_{it}) + \left(\frac{\alpha_i}{2}\right) V_i(x_{t+h} \mid \Omega_{it}),$$

where $V_i(x_{t+h} \mid \Omega_{it})$ is the conditional variance of individual ith expected density. The degree of asymmetry of the cost function is measured by α_i. When $\alpha_i > 0$, under-predicting is more costly than over-predicting, and the reverse is true when $\alpha_i < 0$. This is reflected in the optimal forecasts ${}_t x_{i,t+h}^e$, that exceeds $E_i(x_{t+h} \mid \Omega_{it})$ when $\alpha_i < 0$ and falls below it when $\alpha_i > 0$.

It is interesting that qualitatively similar results can be obtained for other seemingly different loss functions. A simple example is the so-called "Lin-Lin" function:

$$C_i(\xi_{i,t+1}) = a_i \xi_{i,t+1} I(\xi_{i,t+1}) - b_i \xi_{i,t+1} I(-\xi_{i,t+1}), \tag{25}$$

where $a_i, b_i > 0$, and $I(A)$ is an indicator variable that takes the value of unity if $A > 0$ and zero otherwise. The relative cost of over and under-prediction is determined by a_i and b_i. For example, under-predicting is more costly if $a_i > b_i$. The optimal forecast for this loss function is given by

$${}_t x_{i,t+h}^e = \arg\min_{x^*}\left\{E_i\left[C_i\left(x_{t+h} - x^*\right) \mid \Omega_{it}\right]\right\}.$$

[9] In a related paper, Elliott and Timmermann (2005) consider the reverse of the rationality testing problem and derive conditions under which the parameters of an assumed loss function can be estimated from the forecast responses and the associated realizations assuming that the forecasters are rational.

[10] For further discussion, see Batchelor and Zarkesh (2000), Granger and Pesaran (2000) and Elliott, Komunjer and Timmermann (2003).

[11] For a derivation, see Granger and Pesaran (2000).

Since the Lin-Lin function is not differentiable a general closed form solution does not seem possible. But, assuming that $x_{t+h} \mid \Omega_{it}$ is normally distributed the following simple solution can be obtained:[12]

$$ {}_t x^e_{i,t+h} = E_i(x_{t+h} \mid \Omega_{it}) + \kappa_i \sigma_i(x_{t+h} \mid \Omega_{it}), $$

where

$$ \sigma_i(x_{t+h} \mid \Omega_{it}) = \sqrt{V_i(x_{t+h} \mid \Omega_{it})}, \qquad \kappa_i = \Phi^{-1}\left(\frac{a_i}{a_i + b_i}\right), $$

and $\Phi^{-1}(\cdot)$ is the inverse cumulative distribution function of a standard normal variate. The similarity of the solutions under the LINEX and the Lin-Lin cost functions is striking, although the quantitative nature of the adjustments for the asymmetries differs. Not surprisingly, under symmetrical losses, $a_i = b_i$ and $\kappa_i = \Phi^{-1}(1/2) = 0$, otherwise, $\kappa_i > 0$ if $a_i > b_i$ and *vice versa*. Namely, it is optimal to over-predict if the cost of over-prediction (b_i) is low relative to the cost of under-prediction (a_i). The size of the forecast bias, $\kappa_i \sigma_i(x_{t+h} \mid \Omega_{it})$, depends on $a_i/(a_i + b_i)$ as well as the expected volatility. Therefore, under asymmetric cost functions, the standard orthogonality condition (19) is not satisfied, and in general we might expect $E_i(\xi_{i,t+h} \mid \Omega_{it})$ to vary with $\sigma_i(x_{t+h} \mid \Omega_{it})$. The exact nature of this relationship depends on the assumed loss function, and tests of rationality need to be conducted in relation to suitable restrictions on the expected density functions and not just their first moments. At the individual level, valid tests of the 'rationality' hypothesis require survey observations of forecast volatilities as well as of mean forecasts. Only in the special case where forecast volatilities are not time varying, a test of informational efficiency of individual forecasts can be carried out without such additional observations. In the homoskedastic case where $\sigma_i(x_{t+h} \mid \Omega_{it}) = \sigma_{ih}$, the relevant orthogonality condition to be tested is given by

$$ E_i\left(x_{t+h} - {}_t x^e_{i,t+h} \mid S_{it}\right) = d_{ih}, $$

where d_{ih} is given by $-(\alpha_i/2)\sigma^2_{ih}$ in the case of the LINEX loss function and by $-\kappa_i \sigma_{ih}$ in the case of the Lin-Lin function. In this case, although biased survey expectations no longer constitute evidence against rationality, statistical significance of time varying elements of S_{it} as regressors does provide evidence against rationality.

The orthogonality conditions, (20), based on the time consistency property can also be used under asymmetrical losses. For example, for the Lin-Lin loss function we have

$$ E_i\left[\left(x_t - {}_{t-h+1} x^e_{it}\right) \mid \Omega_{i,t-h+1}\right] = -\kappa_i \sigma_i(x_t \mid \Omega_{i,t-h+1}), $$
$$ E_i\left[\left(x_t - {}_{t-h+1} x^e_{it}\right) \mid \Omega_{i,t-h}\right] = -\kappa_i \sigma_i(x_t \mid \Omega_{i,t-h}), $$

[12] See Christoffersen and Diebold (1997). An alternative derivation is provided in Appendix A.

and hence

$$E_i\left({}_{t-h+1}x_{it}^e - {}_{t-h}x_{it}^e \mid S_{i,t-h}\right)$$
$$= -\kappa_i\left\{E\left[\sigma_i(x_t \mid \Omega_{i,t-h+1}) \mid S_{i,t-h}\right] - E\left[\sigma_i(x_t \mid \Omega_{i,t-h}) \mid S_{i,t-h}\right]\right\}.$$

Once again, if $\sigma_i(x_{t+h} \mid \Omega_{it}) = \sigma_{ih}$ we have

$$E_i\left({}_{t-h+1}x_{it}^e - {}_{t-h}\, x_{it}^e \mid S_{i,t-h}\right) = -\kappa_i(\sigma_{i,h-1} - \sigma_{ih}),$$

and the rationality of expectations can be conducted with respect to the time-varying components of $S_{i,t-h}$.

Similarly modified orthogonality conditions can also be obtained for the consensus forecasts, when $\sigma_i(x_{t+h} \mid \Omega_{it}) = \sigma_{ih}$. Specifically, we have

$$E_i\left(x_{t+h} - {}_t\bar{x}_{t+h}^e \mid S_{it}\right) = \bar{d}_h,$$

and

$$E_i\left({}_{t-h+1}\bar{x}_t^e - {}_{t-h}\, \bar{x}_t^e \mid S_{t-h}\right) = \bar{d}_{h-1} - \bar{d}_h,$$

where $\bar{d}_h = \sum_{i=1}^N w_i d_{ih}$.

In the more general case where expected volatilities are time varying, tests of rationality based on survey expectations also require information on individual or average expected volatilities, $\sigma_i(x_{t+h} \mid \Omega_{it})$. Direct measurement of $\sigma_i(x_{t+h} \mid \Omega_{it})$ based on survey expectations have been considered by Demetriades (1989), Batchelor and Jonung (1989), Dasgupta and Lahiri (1993) and Batchelor and Zarkesh (2000). But with the exception of Batchelor and Zarkesh (2000), these studies are primarily concerned with the cross section variance of expectations over different respondents, rather than $\sigma_i(x_{t+h} \mid \Omega_{it})$, an issue which we discuss further in Section 4.2 in the context of the forecasts of event probabilities collated by the Survey of Professional Forecasters. An empirical analysis of the relationship between expectations errors and expected volatilities could be of interest both for shedding lights on the importance of asymmetries in the loss functions, as well as for providing a more robust framework for orthogonality testing. With direct observations on $\sigma_i(x_{t+h} \mid \Omega_{it})$, say ${}_t\sigma_{i,t+1}^e$, one could run regressions of $x_{t+h} - {}_tx_{i,t+h}^e$ on ${}_t\sigma_{i,t+1}^e$ and other variables in Ω_{it}, for example $\mathbf{x}_t, \mathbf{x}_{t-1}, \ldots$. Under rational expectations with asymmetric losses, only the coefficient of ${}_t\sigma_{i,t+1}^e$ should be statistically significant in this regression. Similar tests based on the time consistency conditions can also be developed.

3. Measurement of expectations: History and developments

The collection of data on future expectations of individuals has its roots in the development of survey methodology as a means of compiling data in the years before the Second World War. Use of sample surveys made it possible to collect information on a range of topics which could not be covered by administrative sources and full enumeration censuses; it was natural that these began to extend themselves to covering questions about the future as well as the past. It also has to be said that interest in measuring expectations was likely only after economists had started to understand the importance expectations of future events as determinants of the current decisions. This was a process which began in the 1920s with discussions on the nature of risk and uncertainty [Knight (1921)], expanded in the 1930s through Keynes' contributions and has continued to develop ever since.

The earliest systematic attempt to collect information on expectations which we have been able to trace was a study carried out in 1944 by the United States' Department of Agriculture. This was a survey of consumer expectations attempting to measure consumer sentiment [Katona (1975)] with the latter calculated by aggregating the categorical answers provided to a variety of questions; the survey has been widely imitated. Dominitz and Manski (2005) present a statistical analysis of the way in which the sentiment indicator is produced. Currently the survey is run by the University of Michigan and is known as the Michigan Survey, with many other similar surveys conducted across OECD countries so as to provide up to date information on consumer expectations. Questions on expectations are also sometimes included in panel surveys. The British Household Panel Survey is one such example which asks questions such as whether households expect their financial positions to improve or worsen over the coming year. Such surveys, as well as offering an insight into how such expectations may be formed, do of course make it possible to assess whether, or how far, such expectations are well-founded by comparing the experiences of individual households with their prior expectations.

A key aspect of the Michigan Survey, and of many other more recent surveys, is that some of its questions ask for qualitative responses. Consumers are not asked to say what they think their income next week or next year will be, by what percentage they expect it to change from their current income or even to provide a range in which they expect the change in their income to lie. Instead they are simply asked to provide a qualitative indication of whether they expect to be better off or worse off. That this structure has been widely copied, in surveys of both consumers and businesses is perhaps an indication that it is easier to obtain reliable responses to qualitative questions of this sort than to more precise questions. In other words there is believed to be some sort of trade-off between the loss of information consequent on qualitative questions of this sort and the costs in terms of response rate and therefore possible bias from asking more precise questions. It may also be that the answers to more precise questions yield more precise but not necessarily more accurate answers (the truth elicitation problem). For either reason the consequence is that a key research issue in the use of expectational data is handling the link between the qualitative data and the quantitative variables which indicate the outcomes of business and consumer decisions and experiences. It is also the case that some surveys which collect qualitative information on the future also collect qualitative information on the past; the question of linking these latter data to quantitative variables also arises and many of the questions are the same as those arising in the interpretation of prospective qualitative data.

Household surveys were later complemented with business surveys on the state of economic activity. In the period before the Second World War a number of countries produced reports on the state of business. These do not, however, appear to have collected any formal indicators of sentiment. The United States inquiry into the state of business developed into the Institute of Supply Management survey. This asks firms a range of questions about the state of business including the level of order books and capacity utilization. It does not ask either about what is expected to happen in the future or about firms' experiences of the very recent past. However, the Institut für Wirtschaftsforschung (IFO, now CESifo) in Munich in 1948 started to ask manufacturing firms questions about their expectations of output growth and price increase in the near future as well as questions about recent movement of these variables. They also included a question about firms' expectations of the evolution of the business environment. The sort of questions present in the Institute of Supply Management survey were also covered.

This survey structure has since been adopted by other countries. For example, the Confederation of British Industry (CBI) began to ask similar questions of the UK manufacturing sector in 1958 and has continued to do so ever since. The Tankan surveys cover similar grounds in Japan. Policy-makers and financial economists often rely on the results of these surveys as indicators of both past and future short-term movements of the economic variables. There has, moreover, gradually been a recognition that similar methods can be used to cover other aspects of the economy; in the European Union, EU-sponsored surveys now cover industrial production, construction, retail sales and other services.

Another type of survey expectations has also been initiated in the United States. In 1946 a journalist, Joseph Livingston started to ask a number of economists their expectations of inflation over the coming year and the coming five years. Quantitative rather than qualitative survey data were collected, relating not to expectations of individual experiences but regarding the macro-economy as a whole. Although people are being asked to produce forecasts in both cases, the performance of forecasts about individual experiences can be verified satisfactorily only if data are collected on how the circumstances of the individuals actually evolve over time. The performance of the second type of forecast can, by contrast, be verified by direct comparisons with realized macroeconomic data.

The exercise gave rise to what has become known as the Livingston Survey [Croushore (1997), Thomas (1999)] and has broadened in scope to collect information on expectations about a range of economic variables including consumer and wholesale prices, the Standard and Poor's industrial share price index, real and nominal GNP (now GDP), corporate profits and the unemployment rate from a number of economists. It is the oldest continuous survey of economists' expectations and is now conducted by the Federal Reserve Bank of Philadelphia.

In contrast to the consumer expectations questions, these respondents were expected to provide point estimates of their expectations. No doubt this was more practical than with the consumer expectations survey because the respondents were practising economists and therefore might be assumed to be more capable of and more comfortable with providing quantitative answers to the questions. With a survey of this type it is possible to calculate not only the mean but also the standard deviation of the responses. The mean, though appealing as a representation of the consensus, is unlikely to be the best prediction generated from the individual forecasts.

Other surveys of macroeconomic forecasts include the Philadelphia Fed's Survey of Professional Forecasters,[13] the Blue Chip Survey of Professional Forecasters, and the National Association of Business Economists (NABE) surveys; they are produced quarterly and consist of annual forecasts for many macroeconomic variables.[14] The Goldsmith–Nagan Bond and Money Market Letter provides an aggregation of forecasts of the yield on 3-month US Treasury Bills and other key interest rates from 30–40 analysts. Interest rates, unlike many of the variables considered in the Livingston Survey are typically inputs to rather than outputs of macro-economic models and forecasts. In that sense the survey is probably reporting judgements as to how individual expectations might differ from the pattern implied by the yield curve rather than the outcome of a more formal forecasting process.

To the extent that there is a difference between opinions and formal forecasts produced by some sort of forecasting model, this not made clear in the information collected in the Livingston Survey. The Survey of Blue Chip Forecasters, on the other hand focuses on organizations making use of formal forecasting models. As always it is unclear how far the forecasts generated by the latter are the products of the models rather than the judgements of the forecasters producing them. But this survey, too, indicates the range of opinion of forecasters and means and standard deviations can be computed from it.

The Survey of Professional Forecasters asks respondents to provide probabilities that key variables will fall into particular ranges, instead of simply asking forecasters to provide their forecasts. This does, therefore, make available serious information on the degree of uncertainty as perceived by individual forecasters. The production and assessment of these forecasts is discussed elsewhere in this volume. A range of other surveys [Manski (2004)] also asks questions about event probabilities from households and individuals about their perceptions of the probabilities of events which affect them, such as job loss,[15] life expectancy[16] and future income.[17] We discuss the importance of these subsequently in Section 4.2.

[13] This was formerly conducted by the American Statistical Association (ASA) and the National Bureau of Economic Research (NBER). It was known as the ASA/NBER survey.

[14] The variables included in the Survey of Professional Forecasters and other details are described in Croushore (1993).

[15] U.S. Survey of Economic Expectations [Dominitz and Manski (1997a, 1997b)].

[16] U.S. Health and Retirement Survey [Juster and Suzman (1995), Hurd and McGarry (2002)].

[17] Italy's Survey of Household Income and Wealth [Guiso, Japelli and Terlizzese (1992), Guiso, Japelli and Pistaferri (2002)], the Netherlands' VSB Panel Survey [Das and Donkers (1999)], the US Survey of Economic Expectations [Dominitz and Manski (1997a, 1997b)] and the U.S. Survey of Consumers [Dominitz and Manski (2003, 2004)].

Surveys similar to these exist for other countries although few collect information on individual perceptions of uncertainty. Consensus Forecasts collates forecasts produced for a number of different countries and Isiklar, Lahiri and Loungani (2005) use the average of the forecasts for each country as a basis for an analysis of forecast revision. In the UK, HM Treasury publishes its own compilation of independent economic forecasts. The Zentrum für Europäische Wirtschaftsforschung (ZEW) collects data on the views of "financial experts" about the German economy's prospects. We provide a summary of key surveys in Table 1. A list of key references is presented in Appendix B.

To the extent that the surveys report forecasts produced as a result of some forecasting process, it is questionable how far such forecasts actually represent anyone's expectations, at least in a formal sense. Sometimes they are constructed to show what will happen if a policy which is not expected to be followed is actually followed. Thus the forecasts produced by the UK's Monetary Policy Committee are usually based on two interest rate assumptions. The first is that interest rates are held constant for two years and the second that they follow the pattern implied by the yield curve. Both of these assumptions may be inconsistent with the Monetary Policy Committee's view of the economic situation. There is the separate question of whether such forecasts contain predictive power over and above that of the direct quantitative and qualitative information mentioned above; and the weaker question of whether the predictive power of such forecasts can be enhanced by combining them with official and other data sets based on past realizations. Obviously the answer to the latter depends in part on whether and how forecasters use such information in the production of their forecasts.

A third category of information on expectations is implied by prices of financial assets. Subject to concerns over risk premia which are widely discussed (and never completely resolved) long-term interest rates are an average of expected future short-term interest rates, so that financial institutions are able to publish the future short-term rates implied by them. Forward exchange rates and commodity prices have to be regarded as expectations of future spot prices. In the case of the foreign exchange markets arbitrage, which should reinforce the role of futures prices as market expectations, is possible at very low cost. In the case of commodities which are perishable or expensive to store there is less reason to expect arbitrage to ensure that the future price is a clearly defined market expectation. Such markets have existed for many years, but since 1981 we have started to see the introduction of index-linked government debt. With the assumption that the difference between the yield on nominal and indexed debt represents expected inflation, it becomes possible to deduce a market series for expectations of inflation in each period for which future values can be estimated for both nominal and real interest rates. When using such estimates it must be remembered that the markets for indexed debt are often rather thin and that, at least historically, the range of available securities has been small, reducing the accuracy with which future real interest rates can be predicted. The development of options markets has meant that it is possible to infer estimates of interest rate uncertainty from options prices. The markets for options in indexed debt have, however, not yet developed to the point at which it is possible to infer a measure of the uncertainty of expected inflation.

Table 1
A selected list of sources for survey data

Institution	Country/ Region	Web link	Availability Free?	Qualitative/ Quantitative	Notes
European Commission Business and Consumer Surveys	European Union	http://www.europa.eu.int/comm/economy_finance/indicators/businessandconsumersurveys_en.htm	Yes	Qualitative	Business and consumer data on expectations and experience
IFO Business Survey (now CESifo)	Germany	http://www.cesifo-group.de/portal/page?_pageid=36,34759&_dad=portal&_schema=PORTAL		Both	Provides data on business expectations and experience
Tankan	Japan	http://www.boj.or.jp/en/stat/tk/tk.htm	Yes	Both	Qualitative business data. Quantitative forecasts of profit and loss accounts
Consensus Economics	Most of the World excluding Africa and parts of Asia	http://www.consensuseconomics.com		Quantitative	Collates economics forecasts
Confederation of British Industry	UK	http://www.cbi.org.uk/ndbs/content.nsf/b80e12d0cd1cd37c802567bb00491cbf/2f172e85d0508cea80256e20003e95c6?OpenDocument		Qualitative	Provides data on business expectations and experience
HM Treasury Survey of UK Forecasters	UK	http://www.hm-treasury.gov.uk/economic_data_and_tools/forecast_for_the_uk_economy/data_forecasts_index.cfm	Yes	Quantitative	Collates economics forecasts
Blue Chip Economic Indicators	US. Limited information on other countries	http://www.aspenpublishers.com/bluechip.asp	Yes	Quantitative	Collates economic forecasts
Institute of Supply Management (formerly National Association Purchasing Managers)	USA	http://www.ism.ws/ISMReport/index.cfm		Qualitative	Does not collect data on expectations or forecasts
Livingston Survey	USA	http://www.phil.frb.org/econ/liv/index.html	Yes	Quantitative	Covers inflation expectations
Survey of Consumers University of Michigan	USA	http://www.sca.isr.umich.edu/main.php		Both	Data on consumer expectations and experience
Survey of Professional Forecasters	USA	http://www.phil.frb.org/econ/spf/index.html	Yes	Quantitative	Collates economic forecasts. Includes indicators of forecast density functions

We now proceed to a discussion of the quantification of qualitative survey data. This then allows us to discuss the empirical issues concerning alternative models of expectations formation.

3.1. Quantification and analysis of qualitative survey data

Consider a survey that asks a sample of N_t respondents (firms or households) whether they expect a variable, $x_{i,t+1}$ (if it is specific to respondent i), or x_{t+1} (if it is a macro-economic variable) to "go up" ($u^e_{i,t+1}$), "stay the same" ($s^e_{i,t+1}$), or "go down" ($d^e_{i,t+1}$) relative to the previous period.[18] The number of respondents could vary over time and tends to differ markedly across sample surveys. The individual responses, $u^e_{i,t+1}$, $s^e_{i,t+1}$ and $d^e_{i,t+1}$ formed at time t, are often aggregated (with appropriate weights) into proportions of respondents expecting a rise, no change or a fall, typically denoted by U^e_{t+1}, S^e_{t+1} and D^e_{t+1}, respectively. A number of procedures have been suggested in the literature for converting these proportions into aggregate measures of expectations.[19] We shall consider two of these methods in some detail and briefly discuss their extensions and further developments. The conversion techniques can be applied to aggregation of responses that concern an individual-specific variable such as the output growth or price change of a particular firm. They can also be applied when respondents are asked questions regarding the same common variable, typically macro-economic variables such as the inflation, GDP growth or exchange rates. The main conversion techniques are:

1. The probability approach of Carlson and Parkin (1975).
2. The regression approach of Pesaran (1984) and Pesaran (1987).[20]

Although motivated in different ways, the two approaches are shown to share a common foundation. We consider each approach in turn.[21]

3.1.1. The probability approach

This approach was first employed by Theil (1952) to motivate the use by Anderson (1952) of the so-called "balance statistic" ($U^e_{t+1} - D^e_{t+1}$) as a method of quantification of qualitative survey observations. The balance statistic, up to a scalar factor, provides an accurate measure of the average expected, or actual, change in the variable in question if the average percentage change anticipated by those reporting a rise is opposite in sign

[18] To simplify the notations we have suppressed the left-side t subscript of ${}_tu^e_{i,t+1}$, ${}_ts^e_{i,t+1}$, etc.

[19] Nardo (2003) provides a useful survey of the issues surrounding quantification of qualitative expectations.

[20] A related procedure is the reverse-regression approach advanced by Cunningham, Smith and Weale (1998) and Mitchell, Smith and Weale (2002), which we shall also be discussed briefly later.

[21] The exposition draws on Pesaran (1987) and Mitchell, Smith and Weale (2002). For alternative reviews and extensions of the probability and regression approaches see Wren-Lewis (1985) and Smith and McAleer (1995).

but equal in absolute size to the average percentage change of those reporting a fall, and if these percentages do not change over time.

The probability approach relaxes this restrictive assumption, and instead assumes that responses by the ith respondent about the future values of x_{it} (say the ith firm's output) are based on her/his subjective probability density function conditional on the available information. Denote this subjective probability density function by $f_i(x_{i,t+1} \mid \Omega_{it})$. It is assumed that the responses are constructed in the following manner:

- if ${}_t x^e_{i,t+1} \geqslant b_{it}$ respondent i expects a "rise" in output; $u^e_{i,t+1} = 1$, $d^e_{i,t+1} = s^e_{i,t+1} = 0$,
- if ${}_t x^e_{i,t+1} \leqslant -a_{it}$ respondent i expects a "fall" in output; $d^e_{i,t+1} = 1$, $u^e_{i,t+1} = s^e_{i,t+1} = 0$,
- if $-a_{it} < {}_t x^e_{i,t+1} < b_{it}$ respondent i expects "no change" in output; $s^e_{i,t+1} = 1$, $u^e_{i,t+1} = d^e_{i,t+1} = 0$,

where as before ${}_t x^e_{i,t+1} = E(x_{i,t+1} \mid \Omega_{it})$ and $(-a_{it}, b_{it})$ is known as the indifference interval for given positive values, a_{it} and b_{it}, that define perceptions of falls and rises in output.

It is clear that, in general, it will not be possible to derive the individual expectations, ${}_t x^e_{i,t+1}$, from the qualitative observations, $u^e_{i,t+1}$ and $d^e_{i,t+1}$.[22] The best that can be hoped for is to obtain an average expectations measure. Suppose that individual expectations, ${}_t x^e_{i,t+1}$, can be viewed as independent draws from a common distribution, represented by the density function, $g({}_t x^e_{i,t+1})$, with mean ${}_t x^e_{t+1}$ and the standard deviation, ${}_t \sigma^e_{t+1}$. Further assume that the perception thresholds a_{it} and b_{it} are symmetric and fixed both across respondents and over time, $a_{it} = b_{it} = \lambda$, $\forall i, t$. Then the percentage of respondents reporting rises and falls by U^e_{t+1} and D^e_{t+1}, respectively, converge to the associated population values (for a sufficiently large N_t),

$$U^e_{t+1} \xrightarrow{p} \Pr({}_t x^e_{i,t+1} \geqslant \lambda) = 1 - G_{t+1}(\lambda), \quad \text{as } N_t \to \infty, \tag{26}$$

$$D^e_{t+1} \xrightarrow{p} \Pr({}_t x^e_{i,t+1} \leqslant -\lambda) = G_{t+1}(-\lambda), \quad \text{as } N_t \to \infty, \tag{27}$$

where $G_{t+1}(\cdot)$ is the cumulative density function of $g({}_t x^e_{i,t+1})$, assumed common across i. Then, conditional on a particular value for λ and a specific form for the aggregate density function, ${}_t x^e_{t+1} = E_c({}_t x^e_{i,t+1})$ can be derived in terms of U^e_{t+1} and D^e_{t+1}. Notice that expectations are taken with respect to the cross section distribution of individual expectations. It is also important to note that $({}_t \sigma^e_{t+1})^2 = E_c[{}_t x^e_{i,t+1} - E_c({}_t x^e_{i,t+1})]^2$ is a cross section variance and measures the cross section dispersion of individual expectations and should not be confused with the volatility of individual expectations that could be denoted by $V(x_{i,t+1} \mid \Omega_{it})$. ${}_t \sigma^e_{t+1}$ is best viewed as a measure of discord or disagreement across agents, whilst $V(x_{i,t+1} \mid \Omega_{it})$ represents the extent to which the ith individual is uncertain about his/her future point expectations.

[22] Note that $s^e_{i,t+1} = 1 - u^e_{i,t+1} - d^e_{i,t+1}$.

The accuracy of the probability approach clearly depends on its underlying assumptions and the value of N_t. As the Monte Carlo experiments carried out by Löffler (1999) show the sampling error of the probability approach can be considerable when N_t is not sufficiently large, even if distributional assumptions are satisfied. It is, therefore, important that estimates of ${}_t x^e_{t+1}$ based U^e_{t+1} and D^e_{t+1} are used with care, and with due allowance for possible measurement errors involved.[23] Jeong and Maddala (1991) use the generalized method of moments to deal with the question of measurement error. Cunningham, Smith and Weale (1998) and Mitchell, Smith and Weale (2002) apply the method of reverse regression to address the same problem. This is discussed further in Section 3.1.3. Ivaldi (1992) considers the question of measurement error when analyzing responses of individual firms.

The traditional approach of Carlson and Parkin (1975) assumes the cross section density of ${}_t x^e_{i,t+1}$ to be normal. From (26) and (27)

$$1 - U^e_{t+1} = \Phi\left(\frac{\lambda - {}_t x^e_{t+1}}{{}_t\sigma^e_{t+1}}\right), \tag{28}$$

$$D^e_{t+1} = \Phi\left(\frac{-\lambda - {}_t x^e_{t+1}}{{}_t\sigma^e_{t+1}}\right), \tag{29}$$

where $\Phi(.)$ is the cumulative distribution function of a standard normal variate. Using (28) and (29) we note that

$$r^e_{t+1} = \Phi^{-1}\left(1 - U^e_{t+1}\right) = \frac{\lambda - {}_t x^e_{t+1}}{{}_t\sigma^e_{t+1}}, \tag{30}$$

$$f^e_{t+1} = \Phi^{-1}\left(D^e_{t+1}\right) = \frac{-\lambda - {}_t x^e_{t+1}}{{}_t\sigma^e_{t+1}}, \tag{31}$$

where r^e_{t+1} can be calculated as the abscissa of the standard normal distribution corresponding to the cumulative probability of $(1 - U^e_{t+1})$, and f^e_{t+1} is the abscissa corresponding to D^e_{t+1}. Other distributions such as logistic and the Student t distribution have also been used in the literature. See, for example, Batchelor (1981).

We can solve for ${}_t x^e_{t+1}$ and ${}_t\sigma^e_{t+1}$

$${}_t x^e_{t+1} = \lambda\left(\frac{f^e_{t+1} + r^e_{t+1}}{f^e_{t+1} - r^e_{t+1}}\right), \tag{32}$$

and

$${}_t\sigma^e_{t+1} = \frac{2\lambda}{r^e_{t+1} - f^e_{t+1}}. \tag{33}$$

[23] Measurement errors in survey expectations and their implications for testing of expectations formation models are discussed, for example, in Pesaran (1987), Jeong and Maddala (1991), Jeong and Maddala (1996) and Rich, Raymond and Butler (1993).

This leaves only λ unknown. Alternative approaches to the estimation of λ have been proposed in the literature. Carlson and Parkin assume unbiasedness of generated expectations over the sample period, $t = 1, \ldots, T$ and estimate λ by

$$\hat{\lambda} = \left(\sum_{t=1}^{T} x_t\right) \Big/ \left(\sum_{t=1}^{T} \left(\frac{f_t^e + r_t^e}{f_t^e - r_t^e}\right)\right),$$

where x_t is the realization of the variable under consideration. For alternatives see *inter alia* Batchelor (1981), Batchelor (1982), Pesaran (1984) and Wren-Lewis (1985). Since λ is a constant its role is merely to scale ${}_t x_{t+1}^e$.

Further discussions of the Carlson and Parkin estimator of ${}_t x_{t+1}^e$ can be found in Fishe and Lahiri (1981), Batchelor and Orr (1988) and Dasgupta and Lahiri (1992). There is, however, one key aspect of it which has not received much attention. The method essentially exploits the fact that when data are presented in the trichotomous classification, there are two independent proportions which result from this. The normal distribution is fully specified by two parameters, its mean and its variance. Thus Carlson and Parkin use the two degrees of freedom present in the reported proportions to determine the two parameters of the normal distribution. If the survey were dichotomous – reporting only people who expected rises and those who expected falls, then it would be possible to deduce only one of the parameters, typically the mean by assuming that the variance is constant at some known value.

A problem also arises if the survey covers more than three categories – for example if it asks firms to classify their expectations or experiences into one of five categories, a sharp rise, a modest rise, no change, a modest fall or a sharp fall. Taking a time series of such a survey it is impossible to assume that the thresholds are constant over time; the most that can be done is to set out some minimand, for example making the thresholds in each individual period as close as possible to the sample mean. The regression approach which follows is unaffected by this problem.

3.1.2. The regression approach

Consider the aggregate variable x_t as a weighted average of the variables associated with the individual respondents (cf. (22))

$$ {}_t\bar{x}_{t+1}^e = \sum_{i=1}^{N_t} w_{it}\, {}_t x_{i,t+1}^e, \tag{34}$$

where w_{it} is the weight of the ith respondent which is typically set to $1/N_t$. Suppose now that at time t respondents are grouped according to whether they reported an expectation of a rise or a fall. Denote the two groups by $\mathcal{U}_{t+1}$ and $\mathcal{D}_{t+1}$ and rewrite (34) equivalently as

$$ {}_t\bar{x}_{t+1}^e = \sum_{i\in\mathcal{U}_{t+1}} w_{it}^+ {}_t x_{i,t+1}^{e+} + \sum_{i\in\mathcal{D}_{t+1}} w_{it}^- {}_t x_{i,t+1}^{e-}, \tag{35}$$

where the superscripts + and − denote the respondent expecting an increase and a decrease, respectively. From the survey we do not have exact quantitative information on $x_{i,t+1}^{e+}$ and ${}_t x_{i,t+1}^{e-}$. Following Pesaran (1984), suppose that

$$x_{i,t+1}^{e+} = \alpha + v_{i\alpha} \quad \text{and} \quad {}_t x_{i,t+1}^{e-} = -\beta + v_{i\beta}, \tag{36}$$

where $\alpha, \beta > 0$ and $v_{i\alpha}$ and $v_{i\beta}$ are independently distributed across i with zero means and variances σ_α^2 and σ_β^2. Assume that these variances are sufficiently small and the distributions of $v_{i\alpha}$ and $v_{i\beta}$ are appropriately truncated so that $x_{i,t+1}^{e+} > 0$ and ${}_t x_{i,t+1}^{e-} < 0$ for all i and t. Using these in (35) we have (for sufficiently large elements in $\mathcal{U}_{t+1}$ and $\mathcal{D}_{t+1}$)[24]

$${}_t\bar{x}_{t+1}^e \approx \alpha \sum_{i \in \mathcal{U}_{t+1}} w_{it}^+ - \beta \sum_{i \in \mathcal{D}_{t+1}} w_{it}^-, \tag{37}$$

or simply

$${}_t\bar{x}_{t+1}^e \approx \alpha U_{t+1}^e - \beta D_{t+1}^e, \tag{38}$$

where U_{t+1}^e and D_{t+1}^e are the (appropriately weighted) proportion of firms that reported an expected rise and fall, respectively, and α and β are unknown positive parameters. The balance statistic, $U_{t+1}^e - D_{t+1}^e$ advocated by Anderson (1952) and Theil (1952) is a special case of (38) where $a = \beta = 1$. Pesaran (1984) allows for possible asymmetries and non-linearities in the relationship that relates ${}_t\bar{x}_{t+1}^e$ to U_{t+1}^e and D_{t+1}^e. The unknown parameters are estimated by linear or non-linear regressions (as deemed appropriate) of the realized values of x_t (the average underlying variable) on past realizations U_t and D_t, corresponding to the expected proportions U_{t+1}^e and D_{t+1}^e, respectively. As noted above, this approach can be straigthtforwardly extended if the survey provides information on more than two categories.

3.1.3. Other conversion techniques – further developments and extensions

There have been a number of related contributions that construct models in which parameters can vary over time. For example Kanoh and Li (1990) use a logistic model to explain the proportions giving each of three categorical responses to a question about expected inflation in Japan. They assume that expected inflation is a linear function of current and past inflation. A model in which the parameters are time-varying is preferred to one in which they are not. Smith and McAleer (1995) suggest that the thresholds in Carlson and Parkin's model might be varying over time, assuming that they are subject to both permanent shocks and short-term shocks which are uncorrelated over time.

[24] Recent evidence on price changes in European economies suggest that on average out of every 100 price changes 60 relate to price rises and the remaining 40 to price falls. There is also a remarkable symmetry in the average sizes of price rises and price falls. These and other important findings of the Inflation Persistence Network (sponsored by the European Central Bank) are summarized in Gadzinski and Orlandi (2004).

The model is then estimated using a Kalman filter technique finding that the time-series model is preferred to the standard model.

Cunningham, Smith and Weale (1998) and Mitchell, Smith and Weale (2002) relate survey responses to official data by regressing the proportions of firms reporting rises and falls on the official data. Cunningham, Smith and Weale (1998), however, take the view that the survey data represent some transformation of the underlying latent variable with an additional error term added on arising for perception and measurement reasons. For this reason it may seem more appropriate to estimate regression equations which explain observed proportions, U_{t+1}^e and D_{t+1}^e (or U_t and D_t) rather than explaining output by the survey aggregates. This means that estimates of the variable represented by the survey have to be derived by inverting each regression equation. Since the number of independent regression equations is equal to the number of categories less one, there are this number of separate estimates of the variable of interest produced. Since, however, the covariance of the vector of these distinct estimates can be estimated from the standard properties of regression equations, it is possible to produce a variance-weighted mean of the different estimates to give a best estimate of the variable of interest [Stone, Champernowne and Meade (1942)].

Mitchell, Smith and Weale (2002) extend this technique using the CBI survey data. Instead of explaining the two survey proportions (the proportion reporting or expecting a rise in output and the proportion reporting or expecting a fall) they look at the proportions reporting/expecting rises or falls as proportions of those who had reported/expected rises, no change or falls in the previous period.[25] This creates a system of six equations which can be estimated in the same way. Mitchell, Smith and Weale describe this as a semi-disaggregate approach. They find evidence suggesting that the thresholds which underpin both the regression and the reverse regression models, are functions of the responses in the previous period. While there is some evidence of serial correlation in the relevant aggregate regressions, the evidence for this is much weaker in the six semi-disaggregate regressions suggesting that the apparent serial correlation may result from a failure to take account of the dependence of thresholds on previous responses. The semi-disaggregate approach gives a better within-sample fit than does the aggregate approach which Cunningham et al. find outperformed the usual regression approach.

3.2. Measurement of expectations uncertainty

In Section 3.1.1 we discussed alternative methods of obtaining an estimate of cross section mean and dispersion of individual expectations, and it was noted that the dispersion measures of the type defined by (33), do not necessarily measure the uncertainty faced by individual respondents when forming their expectations. To measure expectations

[25] These variables are not published but can, of course, be constructed from access to the firms' individual responses.

uncertainty one needs further survey measurements where respondents are explicitly asked about the degree of confidence they attach to their point expectations. There are only a few surveys that address this issue of expectations uncertainty.

Surveys sometimes collect qualitative data on uncertainty. For example the CBI survey asks respondents to indicate whether their investment plans are constrained by demand uncertainty. Here respondents are being asked to report if they are influenced by the second moment of their own sales growth. The impact of this could be substantial even if there were very little difference between both the experience and the point expectations of the individual respondents. With some modifications the approach set out in Section 3.1.1 can be used to analyze these data.

There the analysis relied on the assumption that the underlying latent variable was normally distributed, which is clearly not appropriate for quantification of higher order moments of expected probability distributions.

Mitchell, Mouratidis and Weale (2005) istead assume that individual experiences of uncertainty can be represented by the square of a random normally distributed variable. With the assumptions that each individual experience is drawn from a $\chi^2(1)$ distribution and that there is a common threshold for shocks above which respondents report the situation as uncertain, they are able to produce an index of underlying uncertainty which is unique down to a time-invariant scaling factor.

In other cases, as we have noted above, surveys ask respondents to provide probabilities that variables will lie in particular ranges. In this case the variance of the expectation can be estimated by fitting an appropriate density function to the event probabilities provided by the respondents [Dominitz and Manski (1997b), Dominitz (1998)].

3.3. Analysis of individual responses

The previous sections discuss ways of quantifying aggregated responses, such as the proportion of respondents expecting a rise or a fall in the variable in question so as to be able to make use of them either in interpreting the results of the surveys in real time or in the more general use of such surveys in applied macro analysis. As we noted in the introduction, however, analysis of individual responses, particularly in a panel context, is generally more satisfactory.

A number of surveys, such as the CBI survey, ask respondents to provide categorical information about some variable of interest, both *ex ante* and *ex post*. Where these surveys are conducted from samples drawn afresh on each occasion there is little that can be done beyond exploring the link between the *ex ante* data and future growth or the *ex post* data and past growth using one of the methods discussed in Section 3.1. But where the data are collected from a panel so that it is possible to keep track of the expectations and outcomes as reported by individual respondents, then it becomes possible to explore whether respondents' expectations are consistent with rationality according to a number of different definitions.

Nerlove (1983) was one of the first to discuss the problem of exploring the relationship between individuals' expectations and the associated realizations using two-way tables of categorical data. Obviously this can be used to explore association between any pairs of variables. The most obvious comparison is that between reports of expectations for period t made in period $t-1$ and the subsequent out-turns reported *ex post* for period t. One may also explore the relationship between expected or reported price rises and expected or reported output growth, or the way in which expectations are linked to past realizations. Gourieroux and Pradel (1986), Ivaldi (1992) and Das and Donkers (1999) discuss ways of testing the rationality of expectations in such data.

In order to explore these issues further we first recap and extend our notation. Suppose that there are m (taken to be an odd number) possible categories and respondent i is asked to report *ex ante* which category is relevant to his/her expectation, ${}_tx^e_{i,t+1}$, formed at the end of period t of the variable whose outcome, $x_{i,t+1}$ is realized in period $t+1$. The mid-category, $(m+1)/2$ is taken as the "no-change" category.

1. The prediction is denoted by the discrete random variables $y^e_{i,t+1,j}$, $j = 1, 2, \ldots, m$, where

$$
{}_ty^e_{i,t+1,j} = \begin{cases} 1 & \text{if } c^e_{j-1} < {}_tx^e_{i,t+1} \leqslant c^e_j, \\ 0 & \text{otherwise.} \end{cases} \tag{39}
$$

2. The outcome is denoted by the discrete random variable $y_{i,t+1,j}$, $j = 1, 2, \ldots, m$, defined similarly as

$$
y_{i,t+1,j} = \begin{cases} 1 & \text{if } c_{j-1} < x_{i,t+1} \leqslant c_j, \\ 0 & \text{otherwise.} \end{cases}
$$

We follow convention and assume $\{c^e_0, c_0\} = -\infty$ and $\{c^e_m, c_m\} = \infty$. Let

$$
p^e_j = \Pr({}_ty^e_{i,t+1,j} = 1); \quad p_j = \Pr(y_{i,t+1,j} = 1),
$$

and

$$
p_{jk} = \Pr({}_ty^e_{i,t+1,j} = 1 \mid y_{i,t+1,k} = 1),
$$

and assume that p^e_j, p_j and p_{jk} are invariant across i and t, and denote the estimates of these probabilities by $\hat{p}^e_j$, $\hat{p}_j$ and $\hat{p}_{jk}$, respectively. Under this set up $\hat{p}^e_j$, $\hat{p}_j$ and $\hat{p}_{jk}$ can be computed consistently from the *ex ante* and *ex post* responses, assuming that individual responses are independent draws from a common multivariate distribution.

If positive and negative surprises are equally likely, then it would not be surprising to find a substantial number of respondents expecting no change. On the other hand if everyone subsequently experiences a sizable shock, very few people will report an out-turn of no change. The French and German surveys of past and expected future output growth (Germany) or past and expected future demand (France) certainly exhibit this feature with more expectations than subsequent responses falling in the no change category. Thus we generally observe $p^e_{(m+1)/2} > p_{(m+1)/2}$.

Suppose now that the aim is to derive forecasts of the proportion of observations that fall in a given category, j, which we denote by p^*_j. By Bayes theorem and using the above notation

$$p_j^* = \sum_{k=1}^{m} p_k p_{jk}.$$

In general, the conditional probabilities, p_{jk}, are not known and need to be estimated. Nerlove suggests estimating p_{jk} using past observations of the relationship between forecasts and out-turns. This is, however, subject to a number of problems. The most important of these is probably that past relationships between expectations and out-turns have been affected by macro-economic shocks. If the effects of these can be removed or averaged out, then the relationship is more likely to be satisfactory. Not surprisingly, the move from p_j^e to p_j^* disperses the responses from the centre to the extremes of the distribution. Nerlove then uses measures of association suggested by Goodman and Kruskal (1979) to identify patterns in the two-way tables looking at links between expectations and previous out-turns and errors in previous out-turns in order to explore how quickly expectations are influenced by the past, as well as the link between expectations and the out-turns described by them. While a number of interactions are identified, the exercise suffers from the problem that it does not actually offer a means of exploring the performance of different expectational models, except in the most general of terms.

Gourieroux and Pradel (1986) prove that, for expectations to be rational it must be that $p_{kk} > \max_{j \neq k} p_{jk}$, for $k = 1, 2, \ldots, m$. Ivaldi (1992) notes that a test of rationality based on Gourieroux and Pradel's criterion is likely to lack power and instead proposes a two-step estimation method based on a latent variable model where in the first step, using the theory of polychoric correlations, the correlation matrix of the latent variables is estimated, and in the second step, under certain exact identifying assumptions, the estimated correlation coefficients are used to obtain consistent estimates of the underlying parameters of the latent variable model. This estimation approach is applied to business surveys of French manufacturing industry conducted by INSÉE that ask firms about their expectations of output growth and the subsequent out-turns over four periods of three successive surveys during 1984–1985 (giving two estimates of the relationship between expectation and out-turn in each period). The hypothesis of rational expectations is rejected in five out of eight cases. However, Ivaldi argues that the test tends to over-reject when samples are large and therefore the case against rationality is weaker than these findings suggest. The data, however, pass an efficiency test in that he can accept the hypothesis that the influence of out-turns up to period t on the expectation for $t + 1$ is the same as that on the out-turn for period $t + 1$.

Das and Donkers (1999) point out that the respondents are not given precise instructions about how to respond to the questions. There are a number of possible answers that individuals might give to a question about what they expect to happen. For example, they might report the category in which lies the mean, the median or the mode and with a skewed probability distribution these will differ. Using the multivariate normal distribution as the limiting case of the polynomial distribution Das and Donkers (1999) show that, if the expectations reported are those of the mode and if the *ex post* responses are drawn from the same distribution

$$\sqrt{\frac{N_k}{2\hat{p}_{kk}}}\left(\hat{p}_{kk} - \hat{p}_{jk}\right) \longrightarrow N(0, 1),$$

where N_k is the number of realizations that fall in the kth category. We note that the modal assumption is awkward in the situation where the density function is symmetric and the central category has low probability because the range $[c_{(m+1)/2}, c_{(m-1)/2})$ is small.

Where the reported category k is that in which the median value of the underlying variable lies, then the most one can say is that

$$\sum_{j=k+1}^{m} p_{jk} \leqslant 0.5 \quad \text{and} \quad \sum_{j=1}^{k-1} p_{jk} \leqslant 0.5,$$

which can again be tested using the normal distribution. If, however respondents report their mean values, then Das and Donkers (1999) point out that without information on the underlying variable and the thresholds, it is impossible to test whether the initial expectations are consistent with the underlying distribution.

4. Uses of survey data in forecasting

Both qualitative and quantitative survey data on expectations could be potentially important in forecasting, either on their own or in conjunction with other variables. Concern about the future is widespread and the demand for forecasts is obvious. Where expectational data are quantitative, as with the Livingston survey, their interpretation seems equally obvious. Users nevertheless, are likely to be interested in whether they have any predictive power. With qualitative data the same question arises but with the additional complication that the performance of any indicator is bound to depend on the econometric methods used to carry out the conversions.

Obviously in most circumstances survey data are not the only means of forecasting available. Unless other methods (such as time series methods) have no predictive power, it is likely that good forecasts will involve either the addition of survey data to time series models or the use of forecast combination techniques to combine forecasts arising from surveys with those generated by time-series techniques.

4.1. Forecast combination

It is generally, and not surprisingly, found that combinations of forecasts produced by different bodies tend to be more accurate than forecasts produced by any individual. Granger and Ramanathan (1984) show that, when the covariance structure of the forecasting errors is stable, then the regression coefficients of an equation explaining the out-turn in terms of the disparate forecasts provides the optimal combination of the different forecasts. Clearly, the forecasts thus combined can be of different types and from different sources. Thus it is perfectly possible to combine forecasts such as those presented in the Survey of Professional Forecasters with those generated using similar approaches by public bodies such as the Federal Reserve Board and those which are the expectations of 'experts' rather than properly worked out forecasts as such. A recent development of work of this type is provided by Elliott and Timmermann (2005). They show that the framework provided by a switching model offers a means of forecast combination better than the traditional approach. They also compare their results with other methods using time-varying weights [Zellner, Hong and Min (1991), Deutsch, Granger and Teräsvirta (1994)].

4.2. Indicating uncertainty

Economists and policy-makers need to take an interest not only in expected future values but also in the uncertainty that surrounds such expectations. As we noted above, there is no reason to believe that the cross dispersion of point estimates is a good indication of the uncertainty perceived by individual respondents. Survey data can, in principle, provide information about subjective uncertainty as well as about some form of point expectations. The topic is ignored in many surveys and not given much emphasis in others. As we have noted above, the CBI survey does, however, ask respondents whether their investment plans are limited by uncertainty about demand. This is plainly a question about second moments which provides information about subjective views of uncertainty and, given an appropriate quantification method, can be used to represent the latter. We have already discussed means of doing this in Section 3.2; it remains to be implemented.

There have, however, been a small number of attempts to infer income uncertainty in surveys of consumers. Thus Guiso, Japelli and Terlizzese (1992) asked respondents to provide probabilities for inflation in twelve months time and "your opinion about labour earnings or pensions [growth] twelve months from now" falling into particular ranges, with the probabilities being designed to sum to one (p. 332). These questions were included in the 1989 Survey of Household Income and Wealth run by the Bank of Italy.

Dominitz and Manski (1997b) designed a survey specifically to elucidate information on income uncertainty, as part of the University of Wisconsin's Survey of Economic Expectations and thereby produced an indication of subjective income uncertainty of households. They concluded that the best way of collecting data on the subjective distribution was to ask people the probabilities that their incomes over the next twelve months would be below each of four thresholds, with the thresholds chosen in the light of reported realized income. Respondents were also asked to report the lowest and highest possible amounts their household incomes might be. Subsequent analysis of these data [Dominitz (1998)] suggests that the measures of expectation which can be reconstituted from these density functions are reasonably good guides to out-turns [Dominitz (2001)], and that the estimates of uncertainty thus derived correlate reasonably well with measures deduced from the Panel Survey of Income Dynamics on the basis of the forecast performance of time-series models of incomes. On the basis mainly of these findings Manski (2004) is optimistic about the ability of surveys of this type to collect information on expectations and plans of individuals.

Rather more work has been done on the data collected in surveys of economists expectations/forecasts of macro-economic variables, with particular use being made of the event probabilities collated by the Survey of Professional Forecasters. Zarnowitz and Lambros (1987) and Lahiri, Teigland and Zaporowski (1988) use this survey to compare the dispersion of point forecasts of inflation and real GNP growth produced by economic forecasters in the United States with the uncertainty that individual forecasters report for their forecasts. Zarnowitz and Lambros (1987) find that the dispersion of point forecasts understates the uncertainty of the predictive probability distribution, with some evidence that high inflation is associated with uncertainty about inflation. Confirmation of the importance of this distinction is provided by the observation that, while the average variance of forecasters' individual distributions has little influence in an equation for the real rate of interest, the average measures of skewness and kurtosis seemed to have a significant depressing influence on interest rates.

Bomberger (1996) suggested, comparing the dispersion of forecasts in the Livingston survey with variance estimates of inflation generated by ARCH/GARCH processes, that there was a close relationship between the two, although the latter was around four times the former. This work was criticized by Rich and Butler (1998) with a defence by Bomberger (1999). The reader is, however left with the feeling that there is something unsatisfactory in using the dispersion if an arbitrary scaling factor is required to relate it to a suitable statistical measure. This malaise persists even if as Bomberger claims, the scaling factor is stable over the period he considered. Giordani and Söderlind (2003), looking again at the results of the Survey of Professional Forecasters, extend Bomberger's analysis. They derive three measures of uncertainty, (i) disagreement or dispersion of point forecasts, (ii) the average of the estimated standard deviations of the individual forecasts (calculated from the event probabilities presented in the Survey), and (iii) a measure of the aggregate variance derived by aggregating the individual event probabilities to produce an aggregate probability density function. They report a correlation between measures (i) and (ii) of 0.60 when looking at inflation with a correlation of 0.44 when they consider output. The correlations between (i) and (iii) are 0.75 in both cases. From these results they argue that "disagreement is a fairly good proxy for other measures" despite the fact that it accounts for at most just over half of the variation in the other measures. However, they find that estimates of uncertainty generated by time-series GARCH methods do not match those generated from the survey data. Lahiri and Liu (2005) explore the changes in the pattern of the individual density forecasts presented in the survey. They find less persistence in the uncertainty associated with each individual forecast than studies based on aggregate data suggest and also that past forecast error has little influence on reported forecast uncertainty. Engelberg, Manski and Williams (2006) cast further doubt on Bomberger's conclusions. The area is clearly an important area for further research.

4.3. Aggregated data from qualitative surveys

Despite the apparent advantages in using quantified surveys, qualitative surveys are widespread and considerable attention is paid to them in the real-time economic debate. It is therefore important also to consider at their performance as measures of the state of the macro-economy.

4.3.1. Forecasting: Output growth

As we have noted, qualitative surveys typically include questions about output prospects. As is clear from Section 3.1, the method of analysis is essentially the same as that used to analyze responses to questions about past output movements. However, the relevant survey response in period t is aligned to the actual out-turn in period $t+1$ rather than anything which is known in period t. Obviously when applying the reverse regression approach due attention has to be made of the fact that future output is unknown at the time the survey is carried out, and an appropriate form of GMM such as instrumental variables must be used to deal with this.

There is a wide range of studies addressing the capacity of prospective survey questions to anticipate output movements. We discuss these before considering work on anticipating inflationary expectations and predicting future price movements.

Öller (1990) finds balance statistics useful as a means of identifying cyclical turning points in economic data. Entorf (1993) finds, however, looking at the question in the IFO survey about expected future business conditions (rather than the expected output of the respondent itself) that the proportion of respondents expecting business conditions to worsen is a better predictor of future output changes than is the balance statistic. Cunningham, Smith and Weale (1998) examining surveys from the United Kingdom also find that use of the balance statistic results in loss of information. Smith and McAleer (1995) use the survey collected by the Confederation of Australian Industries to explore the capacity of six questions to predict future movements in five variables, output, employment, prices, stocks of finished goods and overtime working. Here we focus on the results obtained on output, discussing price movements in the next section. The survey is of form similar to those discussed above, with categorical responses for 'up', 'same', 'down' and a small 'not available' category. The authors explore the performance of different methods of quantifying the surveys and also test whether expectations are rational, by exploring whether expectational errors are orthogonal to expectations themselves (see Section 2.3). The performance of the models is assessed only in-sample over the period, 1966Q2–1989Q2. In-sample the best-performing model is the time-varying parameters model with a root mean square error lower than that of the probability model and an ARIMA(2,1,0) model. Obviously the time-varying parameters model has fewer degrees of freedom left than the probability model. Driver and Urga (2004) by contrast, looking at out of sample performance for the UK find that a regression model based on the balance statistic offers the best out of sample performance for interpreting retrospective data about output, investment and employment.

The best-performing model was therefore different from that found for the retrospective analysis of the UK by Cunningham, Smith and Weale (1998). Comparison of these studies indicates that generalization about which method of quantification works best is not possible. Although both Smith and McAleer (1995) and Driver and Urga (2004) compare various approaches over long periods, they do not consider whether for the series they investigate the performance ranking of the conversion procedures remain stable across different sub-periods or variables.

There have been a number of other studies looking at the performance of these prospective measures of economic performance, often published by the bodies which produce the indicators themselves. But in most cases they do not go beyond the general question of whether the indicators have some ability to fit the data. Rahiala and Teräsvirta (1993) consider the role of business surveys in predicting output growth in metal and engineering industries in Finland and Sweden. Bergström (1995) explores the link between manufacturing output and a range of business surveys in Sweden, and Madsen (1993) studies the predictive power of production expectations in eight OECD countries. Klein and Moore (1991) look at the capacity of diffusion indices[26] constructed from the National Association of Purchasing Managers' Surveys in the United States to predict turning points of the United States economy. Hild (2002) uses the method of principal components to explore the inter-relationships between variables in the French survey, but does not concern himself with the fact that polychoric correlations should be used to evaluate the principal components while Bouton and Erkel-Rousse (2002) look at the information contained in qualitative data on the service sector for France. Gregoir and Lenglart (2000) use the survey to derive a coincident indicator based on a two-state Markov process. Parigi and Schlitzer (1995) consider forecasts of the Italian business cycle.

4.3.2. Forecasting: Inflation

As we have noted above, the question of the link between expectational data and inflation has received more attention than that between expectational data and output movements, partly because of the importance attached to inflationary expectations in a number of macroeconomic models such as the expectations-augmented Philips curve and the assumption that a real interest rate can be derived by deducting inflationary expectations from the nominal interest rate. Thus both Carlson and Parkin (1975) and Pesaran (1984) developed their models with specific reference to inflation expectations. We address the performance of qualitative and quantitative expectations data in the context of models and theories in the next section. Here we focus on the capacity of both types of expectations data to anticipate inflation, at least to some extent.

[26] Diffusion indices offer a means of combining a number of different but related indicators. They show the proportion of indicators registering a rise rather than a fall in whatever variable each indicator happens to report.

Looking first at qualitative data Lee (1994) uses the probability method to explore the link between firms' expectations of price and cost increases and the response to the retrospective questions about the same variables. He studies the period 1972Q2 to 1989Q4 which covered the very rapid price increases of the 1970s and the much lower rate of price increase, particularly from 1983 onwards. He carries out his analysis for the nine subsectors of manufacturing identified by the CBI survey as well as for the manufacturing sector as a whole. He is able to reject the hypothesis that there was a unit root in unanticipated inflation of output prices for all sectors except electrical engineering on the basis of an ADF(4) test statistic. Even for electrical engineering the test statistic of -2.35 makes it likely that the process is I(0) rather than I(1). He finds that expectations are conservative in that changes in the actual rate of price increase are only partially reflected in changes in the expected rate of price increase. Moreover, a test for rationality of expectations (see Section 2.1) suggests that the expectational error can be explained by information available at the time the expectations are formed; in other words expectations are not rational. The variables used to explain the errors are manufacturing output price increases, manufacturing materials cost increases, manufacturing wage costs, the change in the exchange rate, the growth of total output, the growth of the money stock and the aggregate unemployment rate all lagged one quarter. Only for the chemical industry can the hypothesis of rationality be accepted at a 5% significance level. He also finds that the "conversion errors" the difference between actual price increases and those deduced from the qualitative survey are explained to some extent by the variables used to explain the expectational errors. This raises the possibility that the rejection of rationality of expectations is a consequence of some flaw in the conversion process rather than a defect with the expectations themselves. If the expectational errors are corrected for the conversion errors, then the position is more mixed, with the rational expectations hypothesis rejected for five out of nine sectors. Compared to the retrospective and prospective studies of output growth mentioned above, this takes us further because it actually points to a failing of a particular conversion method – that the conversion errors are predictable in terms of known variables – rather than simply offering a comment on the performance of different methods.

4.3.3. *Forecasting: Consumer sentiment and consumer spending*

As we noted in Section 3, the first surveys to collect information on expectations were the studies of consumer sentiment. Dominitz and Manski (1997b) provide a brief account of early attempts to assess their value. They explain how the surveys acquired a poor reputation because they seemed to have little capacity to explain future consumption. Early econometric studies [Tobin (1959), Adams (1964)] use methods which would now be regarded as unsuitable – such as estimation of relationships between variables which are probably I(1) – without exploring issues of co-integration and dynamic adjustment.

The value of these surveys was questioned by Federal Reserve Consultant Committee on Consumer Survey Statistics (1955) leading to a response from Katona (1957). Juster

(1964) also thought their value was limited and Dominitz and Manski (1997b) conclude that this interchange left most economists with the feeling that qualitative expectational survey data were of limited use. Nevertheless, the Michigan Survey has continued and the European Union supports the collection of similar data in its member states, perhaps because Praet and Vuchelen (1984) find that they have some power to predict future movements in aggregate consumption. We save our discussion of more recent work on disaggregated data for Section 5.2.2 below.

5. Uses of survey data in testing theories: Evidence on rationality of expectations

An obvious role for expectational data is in the testing of models of the way in which expectations are formed. Market mechanisms which might penalize people who form their expectations 'inefficiently' are likely to be weak or could take a long time to work. Thus given a number of competing models of the way in which people might actually form expectations, such as those discussed in Section 2, it is possible to use actual measures of expected future out-turns to try to distinguish between different expectations formation models.

In many cases economic theories refer to the influence of expected future events on current behaviour. Where there is no independent measure of expectations, then it is impossible to test the theory independently of the assumption made about the way in which people form their expectations. It is not possible to test this assumption independently of the model of behaviour consequent on that assumption. Independent measures of expected future values mean that it is possible to test theories contingent only on the assumption that the expectational data do in fact represent people's or firms' expectations of the future.

Two examples can make this clear. The life-cycle model of consumer behaviour leads to the conclusion that, at any age, people who have an expectation of a rapidly rising income are likely to have lower asset levels than those who do not. If one makes an assumption that people's expectations of future income growth are based on some particular model (such as reversion to the mean for their cohort appropriately adjusted for individual characteristics such as education level), then it is possible to explore this question. But if expectations are in fact different, then the model may be rejected for the wrong reasons. Information from individual households on their own expectations of how their financial situations are likely to develop allows a cleaner assessment of the model in question.

Another obvious example where survey data on expectations can be used for testing a theory concerns the role of uncertainty in influencing investment. The direction of the influence of uncertainty depends on a number of factors [Caballero (1991)]. But, unless there is a direct measure of uncertainty available, it is almost impossible to test the theory independently of the assumption made about the determinants of uncertainty.

Manski (2004) discusses many other examples and similarly concludes:

> "Economists have long been hostile to subjective data. Caution is prudent, but hostility is not warranted. The empirical evidence cited in this article shows that, by and large, persons respond informatively to questions eliciting probabilistic expectations for personally significant events. We have learned enough for me to recommend, with some confidence, that economists should abandon their antipathy to measurement of expectations. The unattractive alternative to measurement is to make unsubstantiated assumptions." (p. 1370)

In the remainder of this part we shall focus on the use of survey expectations for testing the expectations formation process in economics and finance. We begin with an overview of the studies that use quantitative (or quantified) survey responses, before turning to studies that base their analysis directly on qualitative responses.

5.1. Analysis of quantified surveys, econometric issues and findings

On the face of it exploration of the results of quantified surveys is straightforward. Numerical forecasts or expectations can be compared *ex post* with numerical out-turns and tests of the orthogonality conditions, as discussed in Section 2.3, can be explored as tests for rationality. One is also in a position to explore questions of non-linearity. There are, nevertheless, a number of important econometric considerations which need to be taken into account in carrying out such tests.

5.1.1. Simple tests of expectations formation: Rationality in the financial markets

As we have noted above, some surveys cover the expectations of people involved in financial markets. Dominguez (1986), looking at a survey run by Money Market Services Inc. of thirty people involved in the foreign exchange markets, tests the hypothesis that expectations were rational. She has weekly data for the period 1983–1985 for the exchange rates of the US$ against Sterling, the Deutsche Mark, the Swiss Franc and the Yen and looks at the subperiods 1983–1984 and 1984–1985, using one-week and two-week non-overlapping observations. She rejects the hypothesis of rationality at least a 5% significance level in all the cases she examined. Over longer horizons she rejects rationality at three months but not at one month. Frankel and Froot (1987b) continue with the same theme, looking at the exchange rate expectations of people involved in the foreign exchange markets and comparing them with out-turns over the period 1976–1985. They find that expectations are relatively inelastic and that expectational errors can often be explained statistically by past forecasting errors. Thus the people they surveyed could be described as slow to learn. Nevertheless, the nature of the departure of expectations from the pattern implied by rationality depends on the period under consideration. Elliott and Ito (1999) find that, although survey data for the Yen/US$ rate are worse than random-walk predictions in terms of mean-square error, they can identify a profitable trading rule based on subjective forecasts compared to the forward rate;

the profits are, however, very variable. Takagi (1991) presents a survey of literature on survey measures of foreign exchange expectations.

The studies by Dominguez (1986) and Frankel and Froot (1987b) are time-series analyses applied to the median response in each period of the relevant sample. Elliott and Ito (1999) look at the mean, minimum and maximum of the reported responses in each period. We consider the issue of heterogeneity in more detail in Section 5.1.5.

There is also the question whether and how far the departure from rationality can be explained in terms of a risk premium, either constant or varying over time, rather than systematic errors in expectations. We explore this in Section 5.1.4.

5.1.2. *Testing rationality with aggregates and in panels*

Tests of rationality and analysis of expectations formation have been carried out using the mean of the forecasts produced by a number of different forecasters, e.g., Pesando (1975), Friedman (1980), Brown and Maital (1981) and Caskey (1985). While these can report on the rationality of the mean they cannot imply anything about the rationality of individual forecasts [Keane and Runkle (1990), Bonham and Cohen (2001)]. It is perfectly possible that the different forecasts have offsetting biases with the mean of these biases being zero or some value not significantly different from zero. Thus the conclusion that the mean is unbiased (or more generally orthogonal to the information set) does not make it possible to draw any similar conclusion about the individual expectations/forecasts.

But it is also possible that the hypothesis of rationality might be rejected for the aggregate when it is in fact true of all of the individuals, at least if the individual forecasts are produced using both private and public information as Figlewski and Wachtel (1983) make clear. We have, in Section 2.1 distinguished the public information set, Ψ_t from the private information set available to agent i, Φ_{it}. Suppose that $\mathbf{y}_t \in \Psi_t$ and $\mathbf{z}_{it} \in \Phi_{it}$, for $i = 1, 2, \ldots, N$, such that

$$E(\mathbf{z}_{it} \mid \Phi_{jt}) = \begin{cases} \mathbf{z}_{it} & \text{if } i = j, \\ 0 & \text{if } i \neq j, \end{cases}$$

and assume that each individual forms her/his expectations based on the same data generating process given by

$$x_{t+1} = \boldsymbol{\gamma}'\mathbf{y}_t + N^{-1}\sum_{j=1}^{N} \boldsymbol{\delta}'_j \mathbf{z}_{jt} + \varepsilon_{t+1},$$

where ε_{t+1} are martingale processes with respect to the individual information sets, $\Omega_{it} = \Psi_t \cup \Phi_{it}$. Under this set up individual i's expectations are given by

$${}_t x^e_{i,t+1} = \boldsymbol{\gamma}'\mathbf{y}_t + N^{-1}\boldsymbol{\delta}'_i \mathbf{z}_{it},$$

and by construction the individual expectations errors

$$x_{t+1} - {}_t x^e_{i,t+1} = N^{-1} \sum_{j=1,\ j\neq i}^{N} \boldsymbol{\delta}'_j \mathbf{z}_{jt} + \varepsilon_{t+1},$$

form martingale processes with respect to Ω_{it}, namely $E(x_{t+1} - {}_t x^e_{i,t+1} \mid \Omega_{it}) = 0$.

Consider now the expectations errors associated with mean or consensus forecasts, ${}_t\bar{x}^e_{t+1} = N^{-1}\sum_{i=1}^N {}_t x^e_{i,t+1}$, and note that

$$\eta_{t+1} = x_{t+1} - {}_t\bar{x}^e_{t+1} = \left(1 - \frac{1}{N}\right)\bar{z}_t + \varepsilon_{t+1},$$

where $\bar{z}_t = N^{-1}\sum_{i=1}^N \boldsymbol{\delta}'_i \mathbf{z}_{it}$. Therefore, since ${}_t\bar{x}^e_{t+1} = \boldsymbol{\gamma}'\mathbf{y}_t + N^{-1}\bar{z}_t$, the orthogonality regression often carried out using the consensus forecasts:

$$x_{t+1} - {}_t\bar{x}^e_{t+1} = \alpha + \beta_t \bar{x}^e_{t+1} + u_{t+1}, \tag{40}$$

is likely to yield a biased inference for a given $N > 1$. In other words the hypothesis of rationality, requiring $\alpha = \beta = 0$ may be rejected even when true. Figlewski and Wachtel (1983) refer to this as the private information bias.

If the mean forecast is unsuitable as a variable with which to explore rationality, use of panel regression for this problem might not be satisfactory either. Consider the panel version of (40),

$$x_{t+1} - {}_t\bar{x}^e_{i,t+1} = \alpha_i + \beta_{it} x^e_{i,t+1} + u_{i,t+1}. \tag{41}$$

If the regression equation errors are correlated across forecasters, so that $Cov(u_{i,t+1}, u_{j,t+1}) \neq 0$ when $i \neq j$, then estimating the equations jointly for all forecasters as a seemingly unrelated set of regression equations will deliver estimates of the parameters more efficient than those found by Ordinary Least Squares. But, as authors such as Pesaran and Smith (1995) have pointed out in other contexts, the restrictions $\alpha_i = \alpha$, $\beta_i = \beta$ for all i should not be imposed without being tested. If the restrictions (described as micro-homogeneity) can be accepted then regression (40) produces consistent estimates of α and β. If these restrictions do not hold, then all of the forecasters cannot be producing rational forecasts, so the consensus equation cannot be given any meaningful interpretation.

Having made these observations Bonham and Cohen (2001) develop a GMM extension of the seemingly unrelated regression approach of Zellner (1962) in order to explore rationality in the forecasts reported in the Survey of Professional Forecasters. They find that they reject micro-homogeneity in most cases with the implication that the REH needs to be tested at the level of individual forecasters, albeit taking account of the increased efficiency offered by system methods.

5.1.3. Three-dimensional panels

The work discussed above looks at the analysis of a panel of forecasts in which each forecaster predicts a variable or variables of interest over the same given horizon. But Davies and Lahiri (1995) point out that in many cases forecasters produce forecasts for a number of different future target dates (horizons). At any date they are likely to forecast GDP growth in the current year, the next year and possibly even in the year after that. Thus any panel of forecasts has a third dimension given by the horizon of the forecasts. Davies and Lahiri develop a GMM method for exploiting this third dimension; obviously its importance lies in the fact that there is likely to be a correlation in the forecast errors of forecasts produced by any particular forecaster for the same variable at two different horizons. People who are optimistic about GDP growth in the near future are likely to be optimistic also in the more distant future. The three-dimensional panel analysis takes account of this.

5.1.4. Asymmetries or bias

Froot and Frankel (1989) use survey data as measures of expectations to the explore whether the apparent inefficiency in the foreign exchange market which they observed, can be attributed to expectations not being rational or to the presence of a risk premium. They reject the hypothesis that none of the bias is due to systematic expectational errors, and cannot reject the hypothesis that it is entirely due to this cause. They also cannot reject the hypothesis that the risk premium is constant. MacDonald (2000) surveys more recent work in the same vein and discusses work on bond and equity markets. A general finding in bond markets is that term premia are non-zero and tend to rise with time to maturity. They also appear to be time-varying and related to the level of interest rates. There is also evidence of systematic bias in the US stock market [Abou and Prat (1995)]. Macdonald draws attention to the heterogeneity of expectations across market participants, evidence for the latter being the scale of trading in financial markets.

As we noted in Section 2.4, in the presence of asymmetric loss functions, the optimal forecast is different from the expectation. Since the loss function has to be assumed invariant over time if it is to be of any analytical use, the offset arising from an asymmetric loss function can be distinguished from bias only if the second moment of the process driving the variable of interest changes over time. If the variance of the variable forecast is constant it is not possible to distinguish bias from the effect of asymmetry, but if it follows some time-series process, it should be possible to distinguish the two.

Batchelor and Peel (1998) exploit this to test for the effects of asymmetric loss functions in the forecasts of 3-month yields on US Treasury Bills contained in the Goldsmith–Nagan Bond and Money Market Letter. They fit a GARCH process to the variance of the interest rate around its expected value, and assume that the individuals using the forecast have a Lin-Lin loss function (Section 2.4). They apply the analysis to the mean of the forecasts reported in the survey despite the criticisms of the use of the mean identified above. The Lin-Lin loss function provides a framework indicating how they should expect the offset of the interest rate forecast from its expectation to vary over time. Batchelor and Peel find that, although the GARCH process is poorly defined and does not enter into the equation testing forecast performance with a statistically significant coefficient, its presence in the regression equation means that one is able to accept the joint hypothesis that the forecast is linked to the outcome with unit coefficient and zero bias. It is, of course, not clear how much weight should be placed on this finding, but the analysis does suggest that there is some point in looking for the consequences of asymmetries for optimal forecasts when the variances of the variables forecasted follow a GARCH process.

Elliott, Komunjer and Timmermann (2003) devise an alternative method of testing jointly the hypothesis that forecasts are rational and that offsets from expected values are the consequence of asymmetric loss functions. They use the forecasts of money GDP growth collated by the Survey of Professional Forecasters and assess the individual forecasts reported there instead of the mean of these. Estimating Equation (41), they reject the hypothesis of rationality at the 5% level for twenty-nine participants out of the ninety-eight in the panel.

They then propose a generalized form of the Lin-Lin loss function. In their alternative a forecaster's utility is assumed to be a non-linear function of the forecast error. The function is constructed in two stages, with utility linked to a non-linear function of the absolute forecast error by means of a constant absolute risk aversion utility function, with the Lin-Lin function arising when risk-aversion is absent. It is, however, assumed that the embarrassment arising from a positive forecast error differs from that associated with a negative forecast error giving a degree of asymmetry. Appropriate choice of parameters means that the specification is flexible over whether under-forecasting is more or less embarrassing than over-forecasting. The resulting loss function has the form

$$L_i(e_{i,t+1}) = \big\{\alpha + (1-2\alpha)I(-e_{i,t+1})\big\}e^{p}_{i,t+1}, \tag{42}$$

where $e_{i,t+1} = x_{t+1} - {}_tx^*_{i,t+1}$ denotes the difference between the outcome and the forecast, ${}_tx^*_{it+1}$, which is of course no longer equal to the expectation, and $I()$ is the indicator function which takes the value 1 when its argument is zero or positive and 0 otherwise. $p = 1$ and $0 < \alpha < 1$ deliver the Lin-Lin function.

The authors show that OLS estimates of β_i in Equation (41) are biased when the true loss function is given by (42) and that the distribution of β_i is also affected. It follows that the F-test used to explore the hypothesis of rationality is also affected, with the limiting case, as the number of observations rises without limit, being given by a non-central χ^2 distribution. If the parameters of the loss function are known it is possible to correct the standard tests, and ensure that the hypothesis of rationality can be appropriately tested. Even where these are unknown the question can be explored using GMM estimation and the J-test for over-identification.

When the joint hypothesis of symmetry and rationality is tested (setting $p = 2$), this is rejected for 34/98 forecasters at a 5% level. However once asymmetry is allowed rationality is rejected only for four forecasters at the same significance level; such a rejection rate could surely be regarded as the outcome of chance.

Patton and Timmermann (2004) develop a flexible approach designed to allow for the possibility that different forecasters have different loss functions. This leads to testable implications of optimality even if the loss functions of the forecasters are unknown. They explore the consensus (i.e. mean) forecasts published by the Survey of Professional Forecasters for inflation and output growth (GNP growth before 1992) for 1983–2003. They find evidence of suboptimality against quadratic loss functions but not against alternative loss functions for both variables. Their work supports the idea that the loss functions of inflation forecasters are asymmetric except at low levels of inflation.

5.1.5. Heterogeneity of expectations

Many studies allow for the possibility that some individuals may be rational and others may not. But they do not look at the mechanisms by which the irrational individuals might form their expectations.

Four papers explore this issue.[27] Ito (1990) looks at expectations of foreign exchange rates, using a survey run by the Japan Centre for International Finance, which, unlike the studies mentioned above [Dominguez (1986), Frankel and Froot (1987b)] provides individual responses. He finds clear evidence for the presence of individual effects which are invariant over time and that these are related to the trades of the relevant respondents. Thus exporters tend to anticipate a yen depreciation while importers anticipate an appreciation, a process described by Ito as 'wishful thinking'. These individual effects are due to fixed effects rather than different time-series responses to past data. As with the earlier work, rationality of expectations is generally rejected. So too is consistency of the form described in Section 2.3. Frankel and Froot (1987a, 1987b, 1990a, 1990b), Allen and Taylor (1990) and Ito (1990) also show that at short horizons traders tend to use extrapolative chartist rules, whilst at longer horizons they tend to use more mean reverting rules based on fundamentals.

Dominitz and Manski (2005) present summary statistics for heterogeneity of expectations about equity prices. Respondents to the Michigan Survey were asked how much they thought a mutual fund (unit trust) investment would rise over the coming year and what they thought were the chances it would rise in nominal and real terms. The Survey interviews most respondents twice. The authors classify respondents into three types, those who expect the market to follow a random walk, those who expect recent rates of return to persist and those who anticipate mean reversion. The Michigan Survey suggests that where people are interviewed twice only 15% of the population can be thus

[27] In an interesting paper, Kurz (2001) also provide evidence on the heterogeneity of forecasts across the private agents and the Staff of the Federal Reserve Bank in the U.S., and explores its implications for the analysis of rational beliefs, as developed earlier in Kurz (1994).

categorized. It finds that young people tend to be more optimistic than old people about the stock market, that men are more optimistic than women and that optimism increases with education. The other two papers we consider explore expectations formation in more detail.

Carroll (2003) draws on an epidemiological framework to model how households form their expectations. He models the evolution of households' inflationary expectations as reported in the Michigan Survey with the assumption that households gradually form their views from news reports and that these in turn absorb the views of people whose trade is forecasting as represented in the Survey of Professional Forecasters. The diffusion process is, however, slow, because neither the journalists writing news stories nor the people reading them give undivided attention to the matter of updating their inflationary expectations. Even if the expectations of professional forecasters are rational this means that expectations of households will be slow to change. Carroll finds that the Michigan Survey has a mean square error almost twice that of the Survey of Professional Forecasters and also that the former has a much lower capacity than the latter to predict inflation in equations which also allow for the effects of lagged dependent variables. The Michigan Survey adds nothing significant to an equation which includes the results of the Survey of Professional Forecasters but the opposite is not true. Indeed the professional forecasts Granger-cause household expectations but household expectations do not seem to Granger-cause professional forecasts.

Carroll assumes that there is a unit root or near unit root in the inflation rate – a proposition which is true for some countries with some policy regimes but which is unlikely to be true for monetary areas with clear public inflation targets – and finds that the pattern by which Michigan Survey expectations are updated from those of professional forecasters is consistent with a simple diffusion process similar to that by which epidemics spread. There is, however, a constant term in the regression equation which implies some sort of residual view about the inflation rate – or at least that there is an element in household expectations which may be very slow indeed to change. Carroll also finds that during periods of intense news coverage the gap between household expectations and those of professional forecasters narrows faster than when inflation is out of the news. This of course does not, in itself demonstrate that heavy news coverage leads to the faster updating; it may simply be that when inflation matters more people pay more attention to it. Nevertheless it is consistent with a view that dissemination occurs from professional forecasters through news media to households.

In a second paper, Branch (2004) explores the heterogeneity of inflation expectations as measured by the Michigan Survey that covers the expectations reported by individuals rather than by professional forecasters. He considers the period from January 1977 to December 1993 and, although the survey interviews each respondent twice with a lag of six months, he treats each monthly observation as a cross-section and does not exploit the panel structure of the data set. Unlike earlier work on testing expectations which sought to understand the determination of the mean forecast, Branch explores the dispersion of survey responses and investigates the characteristics of statistical processes which might account for that dispersion. With an average of just under seven hundred responses each month, the probability density that underlies the forecasts is well-populated and it is possible to explore structures more complicated than distributions such as the normal density.

The framework he uses is a mixture of three normal distributions. However, instead of extending the methods surveyed by Hartley (1978) to find the parameters of each distribution and the weight attached to each in each period, he imposes strong assumptions on the choice of the models used to generate the means of each distribution from three relatively simple specifications; first naive expectations where expected inflation of the ith respondent, π_{it}^e, is set equal to π_{t-1}, the lagged realized of inflation, secondly adaptive expectations (with the adaption coefficient determined by least squares over the data as a whole), and thirdly a forecast generated from a vector autoregression. Branch assumes that the proportion of respondents using each of the three forecasting mechanism depends on the 'success', W_{jt}, associated with the choice of the jth forecast for $j = 1, 2, 3$. Success is calculated as the sum of a constant term specific to each of the three methods (C_j, $j = 1, 2, 3$), and a mean square error term, $MSE_{j,t}$, calculated as an exponential decay process applied to current and past mean square errors

$$MSE_{jt} = (1 - \delta)MSE_{j,t-1} + \delta(\pi_{it}^e - \pi_t)^2,$$

with

$$W_{jt} = -(MSE_{jt} + C_j). \tag{43}$$

The probability that an individual uses method j, n_{jt} is then given by a restricted logistic function as

$$n_{jt} = \frac{e^{-\beta W_{jt}}}{\sum_j e^{-\beta W_{jt}}}. \tag{44}$$

Given the series of forecasts produced by the three methods and the standard deviation of the disturbance around each point forecast added on to each point forecast by the individual who uses that forecasting method, it is then possible to calculate the cost associated with each method and thus the proportion of respondents who "should" use this means of forecasting. Branch assumes that the standard deviation of the disturbance is time invariant and is also the same for each of these three forecasting methods. He then finds that, conditional on the underlying structure he has imposed, the model 'fits' the data, with the proportions of respondents using each of the three forecasting methods consistent with (43) and (44) and that one can reject the hypothesis that only one of the forecasting methods is used.

The evidence presented shows that heterogeneity of expectations in itself does not contradict the rationality hypothesis in that people choose between forecasting methods depending on their performance and their cost, and different individual could end up using different forecasting models depending on their particular circumstances. The results do not, however, provide a full test of 'rationality' of the individual choices since in reality the respondents could have faced many other model choices not considered by

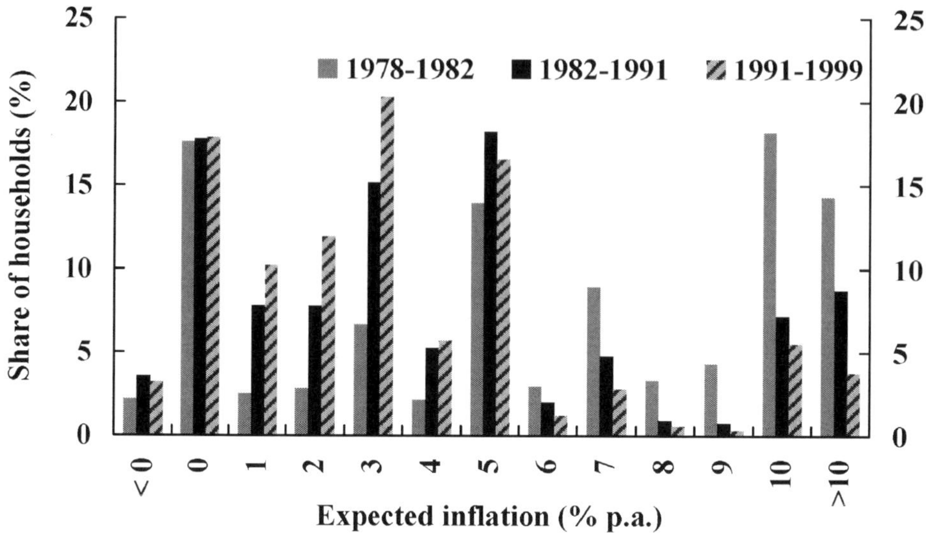

Figure 1. The density function of inflation expectations as identified in the Michigan Survey.

Branch. Also there is no reason to believe that the same set of models will be considered by all respondents at all times. Testing 'rationality' in the presence of heterogeneity and information processing costs poses new problems, very much along the lines discussed in Pesaran and Timmermann (1995) and Pesaran and Timmermann (2005) on the use sequential (recursive) modelling in finance.

Nevertheless, an examination of the raw data raises a number of further questions which might be addressed. In Figure 1 we show the density of inflation expectations in the United States as reported by the Michigan Survey. The densities are shown averaged for three sub-periods, 1978–1981, 1981–1991 and 1991–1999, and are reproduced from Bryan and Palmqvist (2004). As they point out, there is a clear clustering of inflationary expectations, with 0% p.a., 3% p.a. and 5% p.a. being popular answers in the 1990s. Thus there is a question whether in fact many of the respondents are simply providing categorical data. This observation and its implications for the analysis of expectations remain to be investigated.

5.2. *Analysis of disaggregate qualitative data*

The studies surveyed above all, in various forms, provide interpretations of aggregated qualitative data. One might imagine, however, that both in terms of extracting an aggregate signal from the data and in studying expectations more generally, that there would be substantial gains from the use of individual responses and especially where the latter are available in panel form. The main obstacle to their use is that the data are typically not collected by public sector bodies and records are often not maintained to the standards which might be expected in the public sector. We are, however, able to identify a number of studies which make use of disaggregate data collected in wide-ranging surveys.

5.2.1. Disaggregate analysis of expectations of inflation and output

Horvath, Nerlove and Wilson (1992) examine the rationality of expectations of price increases held by British firms, using the data from the CBI survey. We have drawn attention in Section 5.2 of what can and cannot be done using categorical data in a non-parametric framework. However, more detailed analysis is possible if one is prepared to make use of parametric models. The idea is to explore the relationship between the latent variables explaining the categorical responses to the questions about both expected future price movements and past price changes conditional on a set of exogenous variables, $\mathbf{z}_{t-1}$. For example, in the context of the following parametric model

$$x_{i,t+1} = \alpha_i + \beta_i \, {}_t x^e_{i,t+1} + \boldsymbol{\gamma}'_i \mathbf{z}_{t-1} + \varepsilon_{i,t+1},$$

since only qualitative measurements are available on $x_{i,t+1}$ and ${}_t x^e_{i,t+1}$ it is necessary to infer the regression relationship from what can be deduced about the polychoric correlations of the latent variables [Olsson (1979)]. In order to identify the model so as to test the hypothesis of rationality it is necessary to make two further assumptions, first that expectations are on average correct over the period and secondly that the thresholds involved in the categorization of expectations are the same as those involved in the categorization of the out-turn ($c^p_j = c^r_j$ for all j). Having estimated their model in this way, the authors reject the restrictions required by rationality. Kukuk (1994) uses similar methods to explore the rationality of both inflation and output expectations in the IFO survey. He too rejects the hypothesis of rationality.

Mitchell, Smith and Weale (2005) address the question how one might produce aggregate indicators of expected output change from an analysis of the disaggregated qualitative responses to the CBI survey. They are therefore concerned with how to use the survey for forecasting purposes rather than testing any particular economic hypothesis. In essence therefore the issue they address is, that, while the conversion methods identified in Section 3.1 may be sensible ways of extracting aggregate signals from the surveys once they have been consolidated, they may not be the best method of using the survey if one has access to the individual responses. In other words, the conventional method of reporting the results may itself be inefficient if the survey is intended to be used to provide a macro-economic signal.

The method they used is applicable only to surveys which maintain a panel of respondents. On the basis of the past relationship between each respondent's answer and actual output change, they gave each firm a score. This score can be estimated non-parametrically, as simply the mean growth in output in those periods in which the firm gave the response in question. Alternatively a probit model can be estimated to link the firm's response to output change. Given an aggregate forecasting model for output growth (such as a time-series model) Bayes' theorem can be used to derive expected output growth conditional on the response of each firm.

To produce an estimate of aggregate output growth the mean of the individual scores is taken. Experience showed that the resulting series, although strongly correlated with output growth, is much less volatile and a regression equation is needed to align it against actual output growth. Out of sample testing of the approach suggests that it performs better than the more conventional methods based on the approaches discussed in Section 3.1. Nevertheless the results do not suggest that the survey is very informative as compared to a simple time-series model.

5.2.2. *Consumer expectations and spending decisions*

Das and Donkers (1999) study the answers given by households to questions about expected income growth collected in the Netherlands' Socio-Economic Panel. Using the methods of Section 5.2 they reject the hypothesis that the respondents have rational expectations about their future income growth. Respondents to the survey are asked to give one of five categorical responses to expectations of income growth over the coming twelve months and also to report in the same way actual income growth over the past twelve months. The categorical responses are: 'Strong decrease', 'Decrease', 'No change', 'Increase', and 'Strong increase'.

It is found that, for people who had expected a decrease the number actually experiencing no change is larger than those reporting a decrease *ex post* in all five of the years considered and that the difference is statistically significant in four of the five years. For those reporting category 'Strong decrease' *ex ante* the condition for rationality is violated in three of the five years but the violation is not statistically significant. For those reporting the last three categories the condition for rationality is not violated. Analysis on the assumption that the reported expectations are medians similarly leads to rejection of the assumption of rationality for those expecting categories one and two. Analysis of the means is disrupted by outliers and the authors imposed 5% upper and lower trims on the sample.

They explore the idea that expectations might be based on the means by using the actual incomes reported by the households, with a weak condition being that the means of *ex post* income growth for each *ex ante* category should be increasing in the categorical ordering. Although this condition is violated sometimes for categories one and five, the violation is not statistically significant. However real income growth was positive in three of the five years for those expecting a decline in income and in two of the years the growth was significantly above zero. This leads to the conclusion that, at least as reported in the survey from the Netherlands, expectations are not rational and tend to be excessively pessimistic. Thus greater ingenuity is needed to exploit the cross-section information contained in these data.

Souleles (2004) uses data from the Michigan Survey and explores whether the survey provides any information beyond that present in current consumption to predict future consumption. The problem he faces is that the Michigan Survey does not collect data on actual consumption and he deals with this problem by imputing information on expectations from the Michigan Survey to the United States Consumer Expenditure Survey; the latter collects consumption data from households four times in a year, providing information on spending in four quarterly periods.

Thus a discrete choice model is fitted to the Michigan Survey data to explain household responses by demographic data and income with the effects of age and income being allowed to vary over time, although no formal tests are presented for parameter stability. Given the model parameters it is possible to impute the underlying continuous variables being the responses to each of the five questions. It is then possible to explore the augmented Euler equation for consumption

$$\Delta \ln c_{i,t+1} = \boldsymbol{\beta}_0' \mathbf{d}_t + \boldsymbol{\beta}_1' \mathbf{w}_{i,t+1} + \beta_2 \hat{q}_{it} + \eta_{i,t+1},$$

where $\mathbf{d}_t$ is a full set of month dummies, $\mathbf{w}_{i,t+1}$ includes the age of the household head and changes in the number of adults and children and $\hat{q}_{it}$ is the fitted value of the latent expectational variable imputed to household i in period t. Note that the augmentation of the Euler equation to include demographic variables in an *ad hoc* fashion is done frequently in micro-econometric studies of household spending. In fact, although changes in household size should be expected to influence the change in household consumption, the impact of the former is specified very tightly in the population-augmented Euler equation; the restrictions implied by economic theory are rarely tested. Also the econometric specification imposes slope homogeneity which could bias the estimates.

The survey asks about past income growth and expectations of future income growth. An underlying latent variable can also be fitted to these as a function of time and demographic characteristics. It then becomes possible to work out the revision to the underlying latent variable for each household; the life-cycle model suggests that expectational errors such as these should also be expected to have an impact on consumption growth and that, too can be tested.

The study finds that non-durable consumption growth is sensitive to a number of indicators from the Michigan Survey, both the expectation and realization of the financial position, business conditions over five years, expected income growth and expected inflation. Some of these variables may be standing in for real interest rates, omitted from the Euler equation but the study does offer *prima facie* evidence that current consumption is not a sufficient statistic for future consumption. There is also evidence that consumption growth is sensitive to expectational errors although, somewhat surprisingly, errors in expectations of future income do not seem to play a role.

This study sheds light on the link between consumer sentiment, expectations and spending growth. While its research method is innovative, it has less to say than Branch (2004) on the mechanisms by which expectations are formed. Readers are therefore unable to judge why or how far the apparent inadequacy of the Euler equation model is associated with the failure of households to make efficient predictions of the future.

6. Conclusions

The collection of data on expectations about both macro-economic variables and individual experiences provides a means of exploring mechanisms of expectations formation, linking theory to expectation and identifying the forecasting power of those expectations. A number of important issues arise. First of all there is the important question: what is the nature of expectations and how do they relate to any particular loss function? Secondly, how are expectations formed and to what extent do people learn from experience? Thirdly, what is the relationship between assumptions standard to economic theory and expectations formation in practice? Finally, how far can expectational data enhance the performance of conventional forecasting methods such as time-series models.

The studies we have discussed have identified many of these questions to some extent. However, it remains the case that the analysis of individual responses to such surveys, and in particular to those which collect only qualitative information, is underdeveloped. We expect that, as this literature develops, it will yield further valuable insights about the way people form expectations and the link between those expectations and subsequent reality. Most studies have focused on point expectations, although studies which look at the Survey of Professional Forecasters do often also consider the information provided on the density function of expectations. By contrast there has been very little work done on qualitative information on uncertainty even though surveys such as the CBI survey have collected such data for many years. This appears to be another vein likely to yield interesting results.

The utility of many of the data sets is limited by the fact that they are collected as cross-sections rather than panels; such surveys are likely to be more informative if they are run as well-maintained panels even if this results in a reduction in sample size. For those surveys which collect expectational information from a large number of respondents (i.e. not usually those of the forecasts of professional economists) we have not been able to find much evidence of interplay between the design of the surveys and the analysis of the information that they collect. In many countries the use made of such surveys in key decisions such as interest rate setting, has increased considerably because of the perception that they provide rapid economic information. There does not yet, however, appear to be a science of rapid data collection relating the design of these surveys to the uses made of the data that they provide. Work on this topic is also likely to be of great value.

Separately there is the question how the surveys themselves might be expected to evolve. As the tools and computing power needed to analyze panels have developed so the value of surveys maintained as panels is likely to increase. At present some are and others are not, but there appears to be no consensus developing yet about the merits of maintaining a panel, even if it is one which rotates fairly rapidly. Secondly there is the issue of collecting event probabilities rather than or in addition to quantitative or qualitative expectations. Studies carried out to date suggest that such data are useful and one might expect that increasing attention will be paid to this by data collectors.

Acknowledgements

Helpful comments by two anonymous referees, Kajal Lahiri, James Mitchell and Ron Smith are gratefully acknowledged.

Appendix A: Derivation of optimal forecasts under a 'Lin-Lin' cost function

To simplify the notations we abstract from individual subscripts, i, and write the Lin-Lin cost function, (25) for $h = 1$ as:

$$C(\xi_{t+1}) = (a+b)\big(x_{t+1} - {}_t x^*_{t+1}\big) I\big(x_{t+1} - {}_t x^*_{t+1}\big) - b\big(x_{t+1} - {}_t x^*_{t+1}\big).$$

We also assume that

$$x_{t+1} \mid \Omega_t \sim N\big[E(x_{t+1} \mid \Omega_t), \sigma^2(x_{t+1} \mid \Omega_t)\big].$$

Under this assumption it is easily seen that

$$\begin{aligned} &E\big[\big(x_{t+1} - {}_t x^*_{t+1}\big) I\big(x_{t+1} - {}_t x^*_{t+1}\big) \mid \Omega_t\big] \\ &\quad = \sigma^2(x_{t+1} \mid \Omega_t) \int_{z=\mu_{t+1}}^{\infty} (z + \mu_{t+1})\phi(z)\,\mathrm{d}z, \end{aligned}$$

where $\phi(\cdot)$ is the probability density function of the standard normal variate, and

$$\mu_{t+1} = \frac{{}_t x^*_{t+1} - E(x_{t+1} \mid \Omega_t)}{\sigma(x_{t+1} \mid \Omega_t)}.$$

Hence,

$$\begin{aligned} &E\big[\big(x_{t+1} - x^*_{t+1}\big) I\big(x_{t+1} - x^*_{t+1}\big) \mid \Omega_t\big] \\ &\quad = \sigma(x_{t+1} \mid \Omega_t)\big\{\phi(\mu_{t+1}) - \mu_{t+1}\big(1 - \Phi(\mu_{t+1})\big)\big\}, \end{aligned}$$

where $\Phi(\cdot)$ is the cumulative distribution function of a standard normal variate. Therefore,

$$E\big[C(\xi_{t+1}) \mid \Omega_t\big] = (a+b)\sigma(x_{t+1} \mid \Omega_t)\big\{\phi(\mu_{t+1}) + \mu_{t+1}\big[\Phi(\mu_{t+1}) - \theta\big]\big\}, \quad \text{(A.1)}$$

where $\theta = a/(a+b)$. The first-order condition for minimization of the expected cost function is given by

$$\frac{\delta E_x[C(\xi_{t+1})]}{\delta \mu_{t+1}} = (a+b)\sigma(x_{t+1} \mid \Omega_t)\big[\Phi(\mu_{t+1}) - \theta\big],$$

and $E_x[C(\xi_{t+1})]$ is globally minimized for

$$\mu^*_{t+1} = \Phi^{-1}(\theta), \quad \text{(A.2)}$$

and hence the optimal forecast, ${}_t x^*_{t+1}$, is given by

$$ {}_t x^*_{t+1} = E(x_{t+1} \mid \Omega_t) + \sigma(x_{t+1} \mid \Omega_t)\Phi^{-1}\left(\frac{a}{a+b}\right). $$

Also, using (A.2) in (A.1), the expected loss evaluated at ${}_t x^*_{t+1}$ can be obtained as

$$ E^*\left[C(\xi_{t+1}) \mid \Omega_t\right] = (a+b)\sigma(x_{t+1} \mid \Omega_t)\phi\left[\Phi^{-1}(\theta)\right], $$

which is proportional to expected volatility. The expected cost of ignoring the asymmetric nature of the loss function when forming expectations is given by

$$ (a+b)\sigma(x_{t+1} \mid \Omega_t)\left\{\phi(0) - \phi\left[\Phi^{-1}(\theta)\right]\right\} \geqslant 0, $$

which is an increasing function of expected volatility.

Appendix B: References to the main sources of expectational data

1. CBI: Carlson and Parkin (1975), Cunningham, Smith and Weale (1998), Demetriades (1989), Driver and Urga (2004), Horvath, Nerlove and Wilson (1992), Lee (1994), Mitchell, Smith and Weale (2002, 2005), Pesaran (1984, 1985, 1987), Wren-Lewis (1985).
2. IFO: Anderson (1952), Entorf (1993), Hüfner and Schröder (2002), Kukuk (1994), Nerlove (1983), Scholer, Schlemper and Ehlgen (1993a, 1993b), Theil (1952).
3. INSEE: Bouton and Erkel-Rousse (2002), Gregoir and Lenglart (2000), Hild (2002), Ivaldi (1992), Nerlove (1983).
4. Livingston:[28] Bomberger (1996, 1999), Brown and Maital (1981), Caskey (1985), Croushore (1997), Figlewski and Wachtel (1981, 1983), Pesando (1975), Rich and Butler (1998), Thomas (1999).
5. Michigan: Adams (1964), Branch (2004), Bryan and Palmqvist (2004), Carroll (2003), Dominitz and Manski (1997b, 2004, 2005), Fishe and Lahiri (1981), Katona (1957, 1975), Maddala, Fishe and Lahiri (1983), Rich, Raymond and Butler (1993), Souleles (2004).
6. Institute of Supply Management: Dasgupta and Lahiri (1993), Klein and Moore (1991).
7. Survey of Professional Forecasters:[29] Bonham and Cohen (2001), Bonham and Dacy (1991), Croushore (1993), Davies and Lahiri (1999), Elliott, Komunjer and Timmermann (2005), Fair and Shiller (1990), Giordani and Söderlind (2003), Jeong and Maddala (1996), Keane and Runkle (1990), Lahiri, Teigland and Zaporowski (1988), Zarnowitz and Lambros (1987).

[28] A full bibliography can be found at http://www.phil.frb.org/econ/liv/livbib.html.

[29] A full bibliography can be found at http://www.phil.frb.org/econ/spf/spfbib.html.

8. Others: Bergström (1995), Davies and Lahiri (1995), Dominguez (1986), Frankel and Froot (1987b), Hüfner and Schröder (2002), Ito (1990), Kanoh and Li (1990), Kauppi, Lassila and Teräsvirta (1996), MacDonald (2000), Madsen (1993), Nerlove (1983), Öller (1990), Parigi and Schlitzer (1995), Praet (1985), Praet and Vuchelen (1984), Rahiala and Teräsvirta (1993), Smith and McAleer (1995), Tobin (1959).

References

Abou, A., Prat, G. (1995). "Formation des anticipations boursières". Journées de Microéconomie Appliqué 12, 1–33.

Adams, F. (1964). "Consumer attitudes, buying plans and purchases of durable goods: A principal components, time series approach". Review of Economics and Statistics 46, 346–355.

Allen, H., Taylor, M. (1990). "Charts, noise in fundamentals in the London foreign exchange market". The Economic Journal 100, 49–59.

Anderson, O. (1952). "The business test of the IFO – Institute for Economic Research, Munich, and its theoretical model". Review of the International Statistical Institute 20, 1–17.

Batchelor, R. (1981). "Aggregate expectation under the stable laws". Journal of Econometrics 16, 199–210.

Batchelor, R. (1982). "Expectations, output and inflation". European Economic Review 17, 1–25.

Batchelor, R., Jonung, L. (1989). "Cross-sectional evidence on the rationality of the means and variance of inflation expectations". In: Grunert, K., Ölander, F. (Eds.), Understanding Economic Behaviour. Reidel, Dordrecht, pp. 93–105.

Batchelor, R., Orr, A. (1988). "Inflation expectations revisited". Economica 55, 317–331.

Batchelor, R., Peel, D. (1998). "Rationality testing under asymmetric loss". Economics Letters 61, 49–54.

Batchelor, R., Zarkesh, F. (2000). "Variance rationality: A direct test". In: Gardes, F., Prat, G. (Eds.), Expectations in Goods and Financial Markets. Edward Elgar, London.

Bergström, R. (1995). "The relationship between manufacturing production and different business surveys in Sweden, 1968–1992". International Journal of Forecasting 11, 379–393.

Binder, M., Pesaran, M. (1998). "Decision making in the presence of heterogeneous information and social interactions". International Economic Review 39, 1027–1053.

Bomberger, W. (1996). "Disagreement as a measure of uncertainty". Journal of Money, Credit and Banking 31, 381–392.

Bomberger, W. (1999). "Disagreement and uncertainty". Journal of Money, Credit and Banking 31, 273–276.

Bonham, C., Cohen, R. (2001). "To aggregate, pool, or neither: Testing the rational expectations hypothesis using survey data". Journal of Business and Economic Statistics 19, 278–291.

Bonham, C., Dacy, D. (1991). "In search of a strictly rational forecast". Review of Economics and Statistics 73, 245–253.

Bouton, F., Erkel-Rousse, H. (2002). "Conjontures sectorielles et prévision à court terme de l'activité: L'apport de l'enquête de conjonture dans les services". Économie et Statistique 359–360, 35–68.

Branch, W. (2002). "Local convergence properties of a Cobweb model with rationally heterogeneous expectations". Journal of Economic Dynamics and Control 27 (1), 63–85.

Branch, W. (2004). "The theory of rationally heterogeneous expectations: Evidence from survey data on inflation expectations". Economic Journal 114, 592–621.

Brock, W., Hommes, C.H. (1997). "A rational route to randomness". Econometrica 65, 1059–1160.

Brown, B., Maital, S. (1981). "What do economists know? An empirical study of experts expectations". Econometrica 49, 491–504.

Bryan, M., Palmqvist, S. (2004). "Testing near-rationality using survey data". Sveriges Riksbank Working Paper No. 183.

Caballero, R.J. (1991). "On the sign of the investment–uncertainty relationship". American Economic Review 81 (1), 279–288.
Cagan, P. (1956). "The monetary dynamics of hyper-inflation". In: Friedman, M. (Ed.), Studies in the Quantity Theory of Money. University of Chicago Press, Chicago, pp. 25–117.
Carlson, J., Parkin, M. (1975). "Inflation expectations". Economica 42, 123–138.
Carroll, C. (2003). "Macro-economic expectations of households and professional forecasters". Quarterly Journal of Economics CXVIII, 269–298.
Caskey, J. (1985). "Modelling the formation of price expectations: A Bayesian approach". American Economic Review 75, 768–776.
Christoffersen, P., Diebold, F. (1997). "Optimal prediction under asymmetric loss". Econometric Theory 13, 808–817.
Croushore, D. (1993). "Introducing the Survey of Professional Forecasters". Federal Reserve Bank of Philadelphia Business Review, November/December, 3–13.
Croushore, D. (1997). "The Livingston Survey: Still useful after all these years". Federal Reserve Bank of Philadelphia Business Review, March/April, 15–26.
Cunningham, A., Smith, R., Weale, M. (1998). "Measurement errors and data estimation: The quantification of survey data". In: Begg, I.G., Henry, S.G.B. (Eds.), Applied Economics and Public Policy. Cambridge University Press, Cambridge, pp. 41–58.
Das, M., Donkers, B. (1999). "How certain are Dutch households about future income? An empirical analysis". Review of Income and Wealth 45, 325–338.
Dasgupta, S., Lahiri, K. (1992). "A comparative study of alternative methods of quantifying qualitative survey responses using NAPM data". Journal of Business and Economic Statistics 10, 391–400.
Dasgupta, S., Lahiri, K. (1993). "On the use of dispersion measures from NAPM surveys in business cycle forecasting". Journal of Forecasting 12, 239–253.
Davies, A., Lahiri, K. (1995). "A new framework for analyzing three-dimensional panel data". Journal of Econometrics 68, 205–227.
Davies, A., Lahiri, K. (1999). "Re-examining the rational expectations hypothesis using panel data on multi-period forecasts". In: Analysis of Panels and Limited Dependent Variable Models. Cambridge University Press, Cambridge, pp. 226–354.
Demetriades, P. (1989). "The relationship between the level and variability of inflation: Theory and evidence". Journal of Applied Econometrics 4, 239–250.
Deutsch, M., Granger, C., Terasvirta, T. (1994). "The combination of forecasts using changing weights". International Journal of Forecasting 10, 47–57.
Dominguez, K. (1986). "Are foreign exchange forecasts rational: New evidence from survey data". Economics Letters 21, 277–281.
Dominitz, J. (1998). "Earnings expectations, revisions and realizations". Review of Economics and Statistics LXXX, 374–388.
Dominitz, J. (2001). "Estimation of income expectations models using expectations and realization data". Journal of Econometrics 102, 165–195.
Dominitz, J., Manski, C. (1997a). "Perceptions of economic insecurity: Evidence from the survey of economic expectations". Public Opinion Quarterly 61, 261–287.
Dominitz, J., Manski, C. (1997b). "Using expectations data to study subjective income expectations". Journal of the American Statistical Association 92, 855–867.
Dominitz, J., Manski, C. (2003). "How should we measure consumer confidence (sentiment)?" National Bureau of Economic Research Working Paper 9926.
Dominitz, J., Manski, C. (2004). "How should we measure consumer confidence?" Journal of Economic Perspectives 18, 51–66.
Dominitz, J., Manski, C. (2005). "Measuring and interpreting expectations of equity returns". Mimeo.
Driver, C., Urga, G. (2004). "Transforming qualitative survey data: Performance comparisons for the UK". Oxford Bulletin of Economics and Statistics 66, 71–90.
Elliott, G., Komunjer, I., Timmermann, A. (2005). "Estimation and testing of forecast rationality under flexible loss". Review of Economic Studies.

Elliott, G., Ito, T. (1999). "Heterogeneous expectations and tests of efficiency in the yen/dollar forward exchange market". Journal of Monetary Economics 43, 435–456.

Elliott, G., Komunjer, I., Timmermann, A. (2003). "Biases in macroeconomic forecasts: Irrationality or asymmetric loss". Mimeo, UCSD.

Elliott, G., Timmermann, A. (2005). "Optimal forecast combination under regime switching". International Economic Review 46, 1081–1102.

Engelberg, J., Manski, C., Williams J. (2006). "Comparing the point predictions and subjective probability distributions of professional forecasters". Unpublished manuscript, www.faculty.econ.northweston.edu/faculty/manski/profesional_forecasters.pdf

Entorf, H. (1993). "Constructing leading indicators from non-balanced sectoral business survey series". International Journal of Forecasting 9, 211–225.

Evans, G., Honkapohja, S. (2001). Learning and Expectations in Macroeconomics. Princeton University Press, Princeton.

Evans, G., Ramey, G. (1992). "Expectation calculation and macroeconomic dynamics". American Economic Review 82, 207–224.

Fair, R., Shiller, R. (1990). "Comparing information in forecasts from econometric models". American Economic Review 80, 375–389.

Federal Reserve Consultant Committee on Consumer Survey Statistics. (1955). "Smithies Committee report". Hearings of the Sub-Committee on Economic Statistics of the Joint Committee on the Economic Report, 84th US Congress.

Figlewski, S., Wachtel, P. (1981). "The formation of inflationary expectations". Review of Economics and Statistics 63, 529–531.

Figlewski, S., Wachtel, P. (1983). "Rational expectations, informational efficiency and tests using survey data". Review of Economics and Statistics 65, 529–531.

Fishe, R., Lahiri, K. (1981). "On the estimation of inflationary expectations from qualitative responses". Journal of Econometrics 16, 89–102.

Frankel, J., Froot, K. (1987a). "Short-term and long-term expectations of the yen/dollar exchange rate: Evidence from survey data". Journal of the Japanese and International Economies 1, 249–274.

Frankel, J., Froot, K. (1987b). "Using survey data to test standard propositions regarding exchange rate expectations". American Economic Review 77, 133–153.

Frankel, J., Froot, K. (1990a). "Chartists, fundamentalists and the demand for dollars". In: Courakis, A.S., Taylor, M.P. (Eds.), Private Behaviour and Government Policy in Interdependent Economies. Oxford University Press, Oxford, pp. 73–126.

Frankel, J., Froot, K. (1990b). "The rationality of the foreign exchange rate. Chartists, fundamentalists and trading in the foreign exchange market". American Economic Review Papers and Proceedings 80, 181–185.

Frenkel, J. (1975). "Inflation and the formation of expectations". Journal of Monetary Economics 1, 403–421.

Friedman, B. (1980). "Survey evidence on the 'rationality' of interest rate expectations". Journal of Monetary Economics 6, 453–465.

Froot, K., Frankel, J. (1989). "Interpreting tests of forward discount bias using survey data on exchange rate expectations". Quarterly Journal of Economics CIV, 133–153.

Froot, K., Ito, T. (1990). "On the consistency of short-run and long-run exchange rate expectations". Journal of International Money and Finance 8, 487–510.

Gadzinski, G., Orlandi, F. (2004). "Inflation persistence in the European Union, the Euro area and the United States". European Central Bank Working Paper No 414, www.ecb.int/pub/pdf/scpwps/ecbwp414.pdf.

Giordani, P., Söderlind, P. (2003). "Inflation forecast uncertainty". European Economic Review 47, 1037–1061.

Goodman, L., Kruskal, W. (1979). Measures of Association for Cross-Classifications. Springer-Verlag, New York.

Gourieroux, C., Pradel, J. (1986). "Direct tests of the rational expectation hypothesis". European Economic Review 30, 265–284.

Granger, C., Pesaran, M. (2000). "A decision theoretic approach to forecast evaluation". In: Chan, W.S., Li, W.K., Tong, H. (Eds.), Statistics and Finance: An Interface. Imperial College Press, London, pp. 261–278.

Granger, C., Ramanathan, R. (1984). "Improved methods of combining forecasts". Journal of Forecasting 3, 197–204.

Gregoir, S., Lenglart, F. (2000). "Measuring the probability of a business cycle turning point by using a multivariate qualitative hidden Markov model". Journal of Forecasting 19 (2), 81–102.

Grossman, S., Stiglitz, J. (1980). "On the impossibility of informationally efficient markets". American Economic Review 70, 393–408.

Guiso, L., Japelli, T., Pistaferri, L. (2002). "An empirical analysis of earnings and unemployment risk". Journal of Business and Economic Statistics 20, 241–253.

Guiso, L., Japelli, T., Terlizzese, D. (1992). "Earnings uncertainty and precautionary saving". Journal of Monetary Economics 30, 307–337.

Hartley, M. (1978). "Comment on "Estimating mixtures of normal distributions and switching regressions" by Quandt and Ramsey". Journal of the American Statistical Association 73 (364), 738–741.

Hellwig, M. (1980). "On the aggregation of information in competitive markets". Journal of Economic Theory 22, 477–498.

Hild, F. (2002). "Une lecture enrichie des réponses aux enquêtes de conjoncture". Économie et Statistique 359–360, 13–33.

Hommes, C. (2006). "Heterogeneous agent models in economics and finance". In: Judd, K.L., Tesfatsion, L. (Eds.), Agent-Based Computational Economics. In: Handbook of Computational Economics, vol. 2. Elsevier Science, Amsterdam. In press.

Horvath, B., Nerlove, M., Wilson, D. (1992). "A reinterpretation of direct tests of forecast rationality using business survey data". In: Oppenländer, K., Poser, G. (Eds.), Business Cycle Analysis by Means of Economic Surveys, Part I. Avebury, Aldershot, pp. 131–152.

Hüfner, F., Schröder, M. (2002). "Prognosengehalt von ifo-Geschäftserwartungen und ZEW-Konjunkturerwartungen: ein ökonometrischer Vergleich". Jahrbücher für Nationalökonomie und Statistik 222/3, 316–336.

Hurd, M., McGarry, K. (2002). "Evaluation of the subjective probabilities of survival". Economic Journal 112, 66–985.

Isiklar, G., Lahiri, K., Loungani, P. (2005). "How quickly do forecasters incorporate news?" Department of Economics, Albany, USA.

Ito, T. (1990). "Foreign exchange expectations: Micro-survey data". American Economic Review 80, 434–449.

Ivaldi, M. (1992). "Survey evidence on the rationality of expectations". Journal of Applied Econometrics 7, 225–241.

Jeong, J., Maddala, G. (1991). "Measurement errors and tests for rationality". Journal of Business and Economic Statistics 9, 431–439.

Jeong, J., Maddala, G. (1996). "Testing the rationality of survey data using the weighted double-bootstrapped method of moments". Review of Economics and Statistics 78, 296–302.

Juster, T. (1964). Anticipations and Purchases. Princeton University Press, Princeton, USA.

Juster, T., Suzman, R. (1995). "An overview of the health and retirement study". Journal of Human Resources 30, S7–S56.

Kanoh, S., Li, Z. (1990). "A method of exploring the mechanism of inflation expectations based on qualitative survey data". Journal of Business and Economic Statistics 8, 395–403.

Katona, G. (1957). "Federal reserve board committee reports on consumer expectations and savings statistics". Review of Economics and Statistics 39, 40–46.

Katona, G. (1975). Psychological Economics. Elsevier, New York.

Kauppi, E., Lassila, J., Teräsvirta, T. (1996). "Short-term forecasting of industrial production with business survey data: Experience from Finland's Great Depression, 1990–1993". International Journal of Forecasting 12, 73–81.

Keane, M., Runkle, D. (1990). "Testing the rationality of price forecasts: New evidence from panel data". American Economic Review 80, 714–735.

Keynes, J. (1936). The General Theory of Employment, Interest and Money. Macmillan, London.
Klein, P., Moore, G. (1991). "Purchasing management survey data: Their value as leading indicators". In: Lahiri, K., Moore, G.H. (Eds.), Leading Economic Indicators: New Approaches and Forecasting Records. Cambridge University Press, Cambridge, pp. 403–428.
Knight, F. (1921). Risk, Uncertainty and Profit. Houghton, Mifflin & Co, New York.
Koyck, L. (1954). Distributed Lags and Investment Analysis. North-Holland, Amsterdam.
Kukuk, M. (1994). "Haben Unternehmer Rationale Erwartungen? Eine Empirische Untersuchung". Ifo-Studien 40, 111–125.
Kurz, M. (1994). "On the structure and diversity of rational beliefs". Economic Theory 4, 877–900.
Kurz, M. (2001). "Heterogenous forecasting and Federal Reserve information". Working Paper 02-002, Department of Economics, Stanford University.
Lahiri, K., Liu, F. (2005). "Modelling multi-period inflation uncertainty using a panel of density forecasts". Journal of Applied Econometrics. In press.
Lahiri, K., Teigland, C., Zaporowski, M. (1988). "Interest rates and subjective probability distribution of inflation forecasts". Journal of Money, Credit and Banking 20, 233–248.
Lee, K. (1994). "Formation of price and cost inflation expectations in British manufacturing: A multisectoral analysis". Economic Journal 104, 372–386.
Löffler, G. (1999). "Refining the Carlson–Parkin method". Economics Letters 64, 167–171.
Lucas, R. (1973). "Some international evidence on output-inflation trade-offs". American Economic Review 63, 326–344.
MacDonald, R. (2000). "Expectations formation and risk in three financial markets: Surveying what the surveys say". Journal of Economic Surveys 14, 69–100.
Maddala, G., Fishe, R., Lahiri, K. (1983). "A time-series analysis of popular expectations data on inflation and interest rates". In: Applied Time-series Analysis of Economic Data. US Census Bureau, Washington, pp. 278–290.
Madsen, J. (1993). "The predictive value of production expectations in manufacturing industry". Journal of Forecasting 12, 273–289.
Mankiw, N., Reis, R., Wolfers, J. (2004). "Disagreement about inflation expectations". NBER Working Paper No 9796.
Manski, C. (2004). "Measuring expectations". Econometrica 72, 1329–1376.
Meiselman, D. (1962). The Term Structure of Interest Rates. Prentice-Hall, Englewood Cliffs, NJ.
Milgrom, P. (1981). "Rational expectations, information acquisition, and competitive bidding". Econometrica 49, 921–943.
Mincer, J., Zarnowitz, V. (1969). "The evaluation of economic forecasts". In: Mincer, J. (Ed.), Economic Forecasts and Expectations. National Bureau of Economic Research, New York.
Mitchell, J., Mouratidis, K., Weale, M. (2005). "Uncertainty in UK manufacturing: Evidence from qualitative survey data". NIESR Discussion Paper No. 266, www.niesr.ac.uk/pubs/dp266.pdf
Mitchell, J., Smith, R., Weale, M. (2002). "Quantification of qualitative firm-level survey data". Economic Journal 112, C117–C135.
Mitchell, J., Smith, R., Weale, M. (2005). "Forecasting manufacturing output growth using firm-level survey data". Manchester School 73, 479–499.
Muth, J. (1960). "Optimal properties of exponentially-weighted forecasts". Journal of the American Statistical Association 55, 229–306.
Muth, J. (1961). "Rational expectations and the theory of price movements". Econometrica 29, 315–335.
Nardo, M. (2003). "The quantification of qualitative survey data: A critical assessment". Journal of Economic Surveys 17, 645–668.
Nerlove, M. (1958). "Adaptive expectations and cobweb phenomena". Quarterly Journal of Economics 72, 227–240.
Nerlove, M. (1983). "Expectations plans and realizations in theory and practice". Econometrica 51, 1251–1279.
Öller, L. (1990). "Forecasting the business cycle using survey data". International Journal of Forecasting 6, 453–461.

Olsson, U. (1979). "Maximum-likelihood estimation of the polychoric correlation coefficient". Psychometrika 44, 443–460.
Parigi, G., Schlitzer, G. (1995). "Quarterly forecasts of the Italian business cycle by means of monthly economic indicators". Journal of Forecasting 14, 117–141.
Patton, A., Timmermann, A. (2004). "Testable implications of forecast optimality". London School of Economics Mimeo.
Pesando, J. (1975). "A note on the rationality of the Livingston price expectations". Journal of Political Economy 83, 849–858.
Pesaran, M. (1984). "Expectations formation and macroeconomic modelling". In: Magrange, P., Muet, P. (Eds.), Contemporary Macroeconomic Modelling. Blackwell, Oxford, pp. 27–53.
Pesaran, M. (1985). "Formation of inflation expectations in British manufacturing industries". Economic Journal 95, 948–975.
Pesaran, M. (1987). The Limits to Rational Expectations. Basil Blackwell, Oxford.
Pesaran, M. (1989). "Consistency of short-term and long-term expectations". Journal of International Money and Finance 8, 511–520.
Pesaran, M. (2004). "Estimation and inference in large heterogeneous panels with multifactor error structure". CESifo Working Paper Series No 1331.
Pesaran, M., Smith, R. (1995). "Estimating long-run relationships from dynamic heterogeneous panels". Journal of Econometrics 68, 79–113.
Pesaran, M., Timmermann, A. (1995). "Predictability of stock returns: Robustness and economic significance". Journal of Finance 50, 1201–1228.
Pesaran, M., Timmermann, A. (2005). "Real time econometrics". Econometric Theory 21, 212–231.
Pigou, A. (1927). Industrial Fluctuations. Macmillan, London.
Praet, P. (1985). "Endogenizing consumers' expectations in four major EC countries". Journal of Economic Psychology 6, 255–269.
Praet, P., Vuchelen, J. (1984). "The contribution of EC consumer surveys in forecasting consumer expenditures; an econometric analysis for four major countries". Journal of Economic Psychology 5, 101–124.
Radner, R. (1979). "Rational expectations equilibrium: Generic existence and the information revealed by prices". Econometrica 47, 655–678.
Rahiala, M., Teräsvirta, T. (1993). "Business survey data in forecasting the output of the Swedish and Finnish metal and engineering industries: A Kalman filter approach". Journal of Forecasting 12, 255–271.
Rich, R., Butler, J. (1998). "Disagreement as a measure of uncertainty. A comment on Bomberger". Journal of Money, Credit and Banking 30, 411–419.
Rich, R., Raymond, J., Butler, J. (1993). "Testing for measurement errors in expectations from survey data. An instrumental variable approach". Economics Letters 43, 5–10.
Scholer, K., Schlemper, M., Ehlgen, J. (1993a). "Konjunkturindikatoren auf der Grundlage von Survey Daten – Teil I". Jahrbücher für Nationalökonomie und Statistik 212, 248–256.
Scholer, K., Schlemper, M., Ehlgen, J. (1993b). "Konjunkturindikatoren auf der Grundlage von Survey Daten – Teil II". Jahrbücher für Nationalökonomie und Statistik 212, 419–441.
Smith, J., McAleer, M. (1995). "Alternative procedures for converting qualitative response data to quantitative expectations: An application to Australian manufacturing". Journal of Applied Econometrics 10, 165–185.
Souleles, N.S. (2004). "Expectations, heterogeneous forecast errors and consumption: Micro evidence from the Michigan consumer sentiment surveys". Journal of Money, Credit and Banking 36, 39–72.
Stone, J., Champernowne, D., Meade, J. (1942). "The precision of national income estimates". Review of Economic Studies 9, 111–125.
Takagi, S. (1991). "Exchange rate expectations – A survey of survey studies". IMF Staff Papers 38, 156–183.
Theil, H. (1952). "On the time shape of economic microvariables and the Munich business test". Revue de l'Institute International de Statistique 20.
Thomas, L. (1999). "Survey measures of expected US inflation". Journal of Economic Perspectives 13, 125–144.
Tobin, J. (1959). "On the predictive value of consumer intentions and attitudes". Review of Economics and Statistics 41, 1–11.

Townsend, R. (1978). "Market anticipations, rational expectations, and Bayesian analysis". International Economic Review 19, 481–494.

Townsend, R. (1983). "Forecasting the forecasts of others". Journal of Political Economy 91, 546–588.

Varian, H. (1975). "A Bayesian approach to real estate assessment". In: Fienberg, S., Zellner, A. (Eds.), Studies in Bayesian Econometrics and Statistics in Honour of Leonard J. Savage. North-Holland, Amsterdam, pp. 195–208.

Wren-Lewis, S. (1985). "The quantification of survey data on expectations". National Institute Economic Review 113, 39–49.

Zarnowitz, V., Lambros, L.A. (1987). "Consensus and uncertainty in economic prediction". Journal of Political Economy 95, 591–621.

Zellner, A. (1962). "An efficient method of estimating seemingly unrelated regressions and tests for aggregation bias". Journal of the American Statistical Association 57, 348–368.

Zellner, A. (1986). "Biased predictors, rationality and the evaluation of forecasts". Economics Letters 21, 45–48.

Zellner, A., Hong, C., Min, C.-K. (1991). "Forecasting turning points in international output growth rates using Bayesian exponentially weighted autoregression time-varying parameter and pooling techniques". Journal of Econometrics 49, 275–304.

Chapter 15

VOLATILITY AND CORRELATION FORECASTING*

TORBEN G. ANDERSEN

Kellogg School of Management, Northwestern University, Evanston, IL 60208, and NBER
e-mail: t-andersen@kellogg.northwestern.edu

TIM BOLLERSLEV

Department of Economics, Duke University, Durham, NC 27708, and NBER
e-mail: boller@econ.duke.edu

PETER F. CHRISTOFFERSEN

Faculty of Management, McGill University, Montreal, Quebec, H3A 1G5, and CIRANO
e-mail: peter.christoffersen@mcgill.ca

FRANCIS X. DIEBOLD

Department of Economics, University of Pennsylvania, Philadelphia, PA 19104, and NBER
e-mail: fdiebold@sas.upenn.edu

Contents

* The work of Andersen, Bollerslev and Diebold was supported by grants from the U.S. National Science Foundation, and the work of Christoffersen was supported by FQRSC, SSHRC and IFM2. The authors gratefully acknowledge extremely helpful comments from two anonymous referees. The usual disclaimer applies.

Handbook of Economic Forecasting, Volume 1
Edited by Graham Elliott, Clive W.J. Granger and Allan Timmermann

DOI: 10.1016/S1574-0706(05)01015-3

Abstract

Volatility has been one of the most active and successful areas of research in time series econometrics and economic forecasting in recent decades. This chapter provides a selective survey of the most important theoretical developments and empirical insights to emerge from this burgeoning literature, with a distinct focus on forecasting applications. Volatility is inherently latent, and Section 1 begins with a brief intuitive account of various key volatility concepts. Section 2 then discusses a series of different economic situations in which volatility plays a crucial role, ranging from the use of volatility forecasts in portfolio allocation to density forecasting in risk management. Sections 3–5 present a variety of alternative procedures for univariate volatility modeling and forecasting based on the GARCH, stochastic volatility and realized volatility paradigms, respectively. Section 6 extends the discussion to the multivariate problem of forecasting conditional covariances and correlations, and Section 7 discusses volatility forecast evaluation methods in both univariate and multivariate cases. Section 8 concludes briefly.

Keywords

volatility modeling, covariance forecasting, GARCH, stochastic volatility, realized volatility

JEL classification: C1, C5, G1

1. Introduction

In everyday language, volatility refers to the fluctuations observed in some phenomenon over time. Within economics, it is used slightly more formally to describe, without a specific implied metric, the variability of the random (unforeseen) component of a time series. More precisely, or narrowly, in financial economics, volatility is often defined as the (instantaneous) standard deviation (or "sigma") of the random Wiener-driven component in a continuous-time diffusion model. Expressions such as the "implied volatility" from option prices rely on this terminology. In this chapter, we use the term volatility in the looser descriptive sense, characteristic of economics and econometrics, rather than the precise notion often implied in finance. Nonetheless, much of our discussion will be motivated by the need for forecasting the volatility of financial asset return series.

Return volatility is, of course, central to financial economics. Indeed, as noted by Campbell, Lo and MacKinlay (1997):

> " ... what distinguishes financial economics is the central role that uncertainty plays in both financial theory and its empirical implementation... Indeed in the absence of uncertainty, the problems of financial economics reduce to exercises in basic microeconomics" (p. 3).

This departure of finance from standard microeconomics is even more striking once one recognizes that volatility is inherently unobserved, or latent, and evolves stochastically through time. Not only is there nontrivial uncertainty to deal with in financial markets, but the level of uncertainty is latent. This imbues financial decision making with complications rarely contemplated within models of optimizing behavior in other areas of economics.

Depending on the data availability as well as the intended use of the model estimates and associated forecasts, volatility models are cast either in discrete time or continuous time. It is clear, however, that the trading and pricing of securities in many of today's liquid financial asset markets is evolving in a near continuous fashion throughout the trading day. As such, it is natural to think of the price and return series of financial assets as arising through discrete observations from an underlying continuous-time process. It is, however, in many situations useful – and indeed standard practice – to formulate the underlying model directly in discrete time, and we shall consider both approaches in the chapter. Formally, there is also no necessary contradiction between the two strategies, as it is always, in principle, possible to deduce the distributional implications for a price series observed only discretely from an underlying continuous-time model. At the same time, formulation and estimation of empirically realistic continuous-time models often presents formidable challenges. Thus, even though many of the popular discrete-time models in current use are not formally consistent with an underlying continuous-time price processes, they are typically much easier to deal with from an inferential perspective, and as such, discrete-time models and forecasting procedures remain the method of choice in most practical applications.

1.1. Basic notation and notions of volatility

We first introduce some notation that will allow us to formalize the discussion of the different models and volatility concepts considered throughout the chapter. As noted above, although it is often natural to think about the process being forecasted as evolving in continuous time, many of the key developments in volatility forecasting have been explicitly formulated in terms of models for discretely sampled observations. In the univariate case, with observations available at equally spaced discrete points in time, we shall refer to such a process as

$$y_t \equiv y(t), \quad t = 1, 2, \ldots, \tag{1.1}$$

where $y(t)$ in turn may be thought of as the underlying continuously evolving process. We shall assume throughout that the *conditional* second moments of the y_t process exist, and refer to the corresponding conditional mean and variance as

$$\mu_{t|t-1} = E[y_t \mid \mathcal{F}_{t-1}], \tag{1.2}$$

and

$$\sigma^2_{t|t-1} = \mathrm{Var}[y_t \mid \mathcal{F}_{t-1}] = E\big[(y_t - \mu_{t|t-1})^2 \mid \mathcal{F}_{t-1}\big], \tag{1.3}$$

respectively, where the information set, $\mathcal{F}_{t-1}$, is assumed to reflect all relevant information through time $t - 1$. Just as the conditional mean may differ from the unconditional mean by effectively incorporating the most recent information into the one-step-ahead forecasts, $\mu_{t|t-1} \neq E(y_t)$, so will the conditional variance in many applications in macroeconomics and finance, $\sigma^2_{t|t-1} \neq \mathrm{Var}(y_t)$. This difference between conditional and unconditional moments is, of course, what underlies the success of time series based forecasting procedures more generally. For notational simplicity we will focus our discussion on the univariate case, but many of the same ideas readily carry over to the multivariate case. In the case of vector processes, discussed in detail in Section 6, we shall use the notation Y_t, with the corresponding vector of conditional means denoted by $M_{t|t-1}$, and the conditional covariance matrix denote by $\Omega_{t|t-1}$.

As previously noted, most of the important developments and applications in volatility modeling and forecasting have come within financial economics. Thus, to help fix ideas, we focus on the case of return volatility modeling and forecasting in the remainder of this section. To facilitate subsequent discussions, it will sometimes prove convenient to refer to the corresponding "price" and "return" processes by the letters p and r, respectively. Specifically, let $p(t)$ denote the logarithmic price of an asset. The return over the discrete interval $[t - h, t]$, $h > 0$, is then given by

$$r(t, h) = p(t) - p(t - h). \tag{1.4}$$

When measuring the returns over one time unit, $h = 1$, indicating, say, daily returns, we will generally drop the second indicator, so that

$$r(t) \equiv r(t, 1) = p(t) - p(t - 1). \tag{1.5}$$

Also, for discrete-time models and procedures, we shall follow the convention set out above, indicating the timing of the returns by subscripts in lieu of parentheses,

$$r_t = p_t - p_{t-1}. \tag{1.6}$$

Similarly, we shall refer to the multivariate case involving vectors of returns by the upper case letter, R_t.

Consider the discretely sampled return process, r_t. This one-period return is readily decomposed into an expected conditional mean return and an innovation, where the latter may be expressed as a standardized white noise process scaled by the time-varying conditional volatility. Specifically, using the notation in Equations (1.2) and (1.3),

$$r_t = \mu_{t|t-1} + \varepsilon_t = \mu_{t|t-1} + \sigma_{t|t-1} z_t, \tag{1.7}$$

where z_t denotes a mean zero, variance one, serially uncorrelated disturbance (white noise) process. This is the decomposition and volatility concept underlying the popular, and empirically highly successful, ARCH and GARCH type models discussed in Section 3. One reason that this approach is very convenient and tractable is that – conditional on the null hypothesis that all relevant information is observed and the model correctly specified – the volatility is known, or predetermined, as of time $t-1$.

The assumption that all relevant information is observed and used in the formation of conditional expectations in accordance with the true model is obviously strong, but has powerful and very convenient implications. In contrast, if some relevant information is not directly observable, then it is only possible to exploit a genuine subset of the full information set, say $\Im_{t-1} \subset \mathcal{F}_{t-1}$. Under this scenario, the "true" conditional variance will be unobservable, even under correct model specification, and the volatility process becomes genuinely latent,

$$E\big[\big(r_t - E[r_t \mid \Im_{t-1}]\big)^2 \mid \Im_{t-1}\big] \neq \sigma^2_{t|t-1} \equiv E\big[\varepsilon_t^2 \mid \mathcal{F}_{t-1}\big].$$

Treating the volatility process as latent effectively transforms the volatility estimation problem into a filtering problem in which the "true" volatility cannot be determined exactly, but only extracted with some degree of error. This general line of reasoning is relevant for our discussion of stochastic volatility models in Section 4, and for the relationship between continuous and discrete-time modeling and forecasting procedures.

For now, however, we proceed under the convenient assumption that we are dealing with correctly specified models and the associated full information sets, so that the conditional first and second moments are directly observable and well specified. In this situation, the one-period-ahead volatility defined in (1.3) provides an unbiased estimate of the subsequent squared return innovation. Consequently, model specification and forecast evaluation tests can be constructed by comparing the realization of the squared return innovations to the corresponding one-step-ahead forecasts,

$$\varepsilon_t^2 = \sigma^2_{t|t-1} z_t^2 = \sigma^2_{t|t-1} + \sigma^2_{t|t-1}\big(z_t^2 - 1\big). \tag{1.8}$$

The second term on the right-hand side has mean zero, confirming the unbiasedness of the conditional variance. However, there is typically a large amount of noise in the one-period squared return innovations relative to the underlying volatility, as manifest by a large idiosyncratic error component governed by the variance of z_t^2. In fact, for daily or weekly return data, this variance term is an order of magnitude larger than the period-per-period variation in the volatility process. Hence, even if the conditional variance can be seen as the proper forecasts of the corresponding "realized volatility", as given by the squared return innovation, the latter provides a poor ex-post indicator of the actual volatility over the period, and would consequently not provide a very reliable way of judging the quality of the forecasts. We return to this point below.

Before doing so, however, it is useful to think of the returns as arising from an underlying continuous-time process. In particular, suppose that this underlying model involves a continuous sample path for the (logarithmic) price process. The return process may then, under general assumptions, be written in standard stochastic differential equation (sde) form as

$$\mathrm{d}p(t) = \mu(t)\,\mathrm{d}t + \sigma(t)\,\mathrm{d}W(t), \quad t \geqslant 0, \tag{1.9}$$

where $\mu(t)$ denotes the drift, $\sigma(t)$ refers to the point-in-time or spot volatility, and $W(t)$ denotes a standard Brownian motion. We will be more specific regarding the additional properties of these processes later on in the chapter. Intuitively, over (infinitesimal) small time intervals, Δ,

$$r(t,\Delta) \equiv p(t) - p(t-\Delta) \simeq \mu(t-\Delta)\cdot\Delta + \sigma(t-\Delta)\,\Delta W(t),$$

where $\Delta W(t) \equiv W(t) - W(t-\Delta) \sim N(0,\Delta)$. Of course, for $\Delta = 1$, and constant drift, $\mu(\tau) \equiv \mu_{t|t-1}$, and volatility, $\sigma(\tau) \equiv \sigma_{t|t-1}$, for $t-1 < \tau \leqslant t$, this reduces to the discrete-time return decomposition in (1.7) with the additional assumption that z_t is i.i.d. $N(0,1)$. Importantly, however, the drift, $\mu(t)$, and instantaneous volatility, $\sigma(t)$, for the continuous-time model in (1.9) need not be constant over the $[t-1,t]$ time interval, resulting in the general expression for the one-period return,

$$r(t) = p(t) - p(t-1) = \int_{t-1}^{t} \mu(s)\,\mathrm{d}s + \int_{t-1}^{t} \sigma(s)\,\mathrm{d}W(s). \tag{1.10}$$

The semblance between this representation and the previous one-period return for the discrete-time model in (1.7) is clear. The conditional mean and variance processes in the discrete formulation are replaced by the corresponding integrated (averaged) realizations of the (potentially stochastically time-varying) mean and variance process over the following period, with the return innovations driven by the continuously evolving standard Brownian motion. For full generality, the above continuous-time model can be extended with a jump process allowing for discontinuities in the price path, as discussed further in Section 4.

Intuitively, the volatility for the continuous-time process in (1.9) over $[t-1,t]$ is intimately related to the evolution of the diffusive coefficient, $\sigma(t)$, which is also known as the spot volatility. In fact, given the i.i.d. nature of the return innovations governed by the Brownian motion process, the return variation should be related to the cumulative (integrated) spot variance. It is, indeed, possible to formalize this intuition: the conditional return variation is linked closely and – under certain conditions in an ex-post sense – equal to the so-called integrated variance (volatility),

$$\mathrm{IV}(t) \equiv \int_{t-1}^{t} \sigma^2(s)\,\mathrm{d}s. \tag{1.11}$$

We provide more in-depth discussion and justification for this integrated volatility measure and its relationship to the conditional return distribution in Section 4. It is, however, straightforward to motivate the association through the approximate discrete return process, $r(t, \Delta)$, introduced above. If the variation in the drift is an order of magnitude less than the variation in the volatility over the $[t-1, t]$ time interval – which holds empirically over daily or weekly horizons and is consistent with a no-arbitrage condition – it follows, for small (infinitesimal) time intervals, Δ,

$$\mathrm{Var}\big(r(t) \mid \mathcal{F}_{t-1}\big) \simeq E\left[\sum_{j=1}^{1/\Delta} \sigma^2(t - j/\Delta) \cdot \Delta \,\middle|\, \mathcal{F}_{t-1}\right] \simeq E\big[\mathrm{IV}(t) \mid \mathcal{F}_{t-1}\big].$$

Hence, the integrated variance measure corresponds closely to the conditional variance, $\sigma^2_{t|t-1}$, for discretely sampled returns. It represents the realized volatility over the same one-period-ahead forecast horizon, and it simply reflects the cumulative impact of the spot volatility process over the return horizon. In other words, integrated variances are ex-post realizations that are directly comparable to ex-ante volatility forecasts. Moreover, in contrast to the one-period-ahead squared return innovations, which, as discussed in the context of (1.8), are plagued by large idiosyncratic errors, the integrated volatility measure is not distorted by error. As such, it serves as an ideal theoretical ex-post benchmark for assessing the quality of ex-ante volatility forecasts.

To more clearly illustrate these differences between the various volatility concepts, Figure 1 graphs the simulations from a continuous-time stochastic volatility process. The simulated model is designed to induce temporal dependencies consistent with the popular, and empirically successful, discrete-time GARCH(1, 1) model discussed in Section 3.[1] The top left panel displays sample path realization of the spot volatility or variance, $\sigma^2(t)$, over the 2500 "days" in the simulated sample. The top panel on the right shows the corresponding "daily" integrated volatility or variance, $\mathrm{IV}(t)$. The two bottom panels show the "optimal" one-step-ahead discrete-time GARCH(1, 1) forecasts, $\sigma^2_{t|t-1}$, along with the "daily" squared returns, r_t^2. A number of features in these displays are of interest. First, it is clear that even though the "daily" squared returns generally track

[1] The simulated continuous-time GARCH diffusion shown in Figure 1 is formally defined by $\mathrm{d}p(t) = \sigma(t)\,\mathrm{d}W_1(t)$ and $\mathrm{d}\sigma^2(t) = 0.035[0.636 - \sigma^2(t)]\,\mathrm{d}t + 0.144\sigma^2(t)\,\mathrm{d}W_2(t)$, where $W_1(t)$ and $W_2(t)$ denote two independent Brownian motions. The same model has previously been analyzed in Andersen and Bollerslev (1998a), Andersen, Bollerslev and Meddahi (2004, 2005), among others.

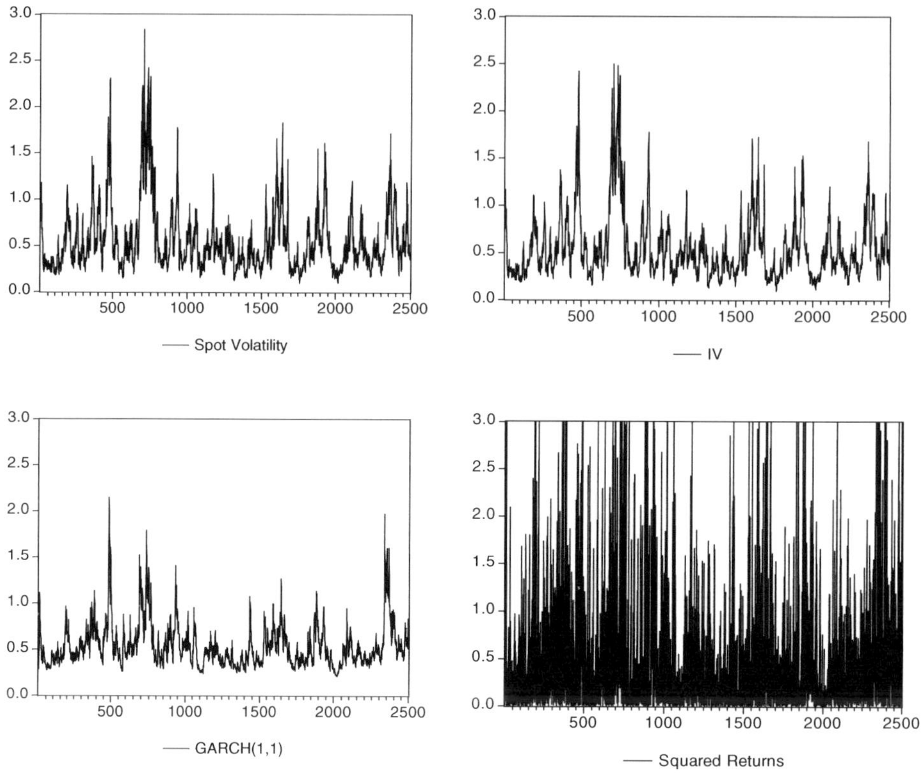

Figure 1. Different volatility concepts. We show the "daily" spot volatility, $\sigma^2(t)$, the integrated volatility, $\mathrm{IV}(t)$, the discrete-time GARCH based volatility forecasts, $\sigma^2_{t|t-1}$, and the corresponding squared returns, r_t^2, from a simulated continuous-time GARCH diffusion.

the overall level of the volatility in the first two panels, as an unbiased measure should, it is an extremely noisy proxy. Hence, a naive assessment of the quality of the GARCH based forecasts in the third panel based on a comparison with the ex-post squared returns in panel four invariable will suggest very poor forecast quality, despite the fact that by construction the GARCH based procedure is the "optimal" discrete-time forecast. We provide a much more detailed discussion of this issue in Section 7 below. Second, the integrated volatility provides a mildly smoothed version of the spot volatility process. Since the simulated series has a very persistent volatility component the differences are minor, but still readily identifiable. Third, the "optimal" discrete-time GARCH forecasts largely appear as smoothed versions of the spot and integrated volatility series. This is natural as forecasts, by construction, should be less variable than the corresponding ex-post realizations. Fourth, it is also transparent, however, that the GARCH based forecasts fail to perfectly capture the nature of the integrated volatility series. The largest spike in volatility (around the 700–750 "day" marks) is systematically underestimated by the GARCH forecasts while the last spike (around the 2300–2350 "day" marks) is exaggerated relative to the actual realizations. This reflects the fact that the volatility is not constant over the "day", and as such the (realized) integrated volatility is not equal to the (optimal) forecast from the discrete-time GARCH model which only utilizes the past "daily" return observations. Instead, there is a genuine random component to the volatility process as it evolves stochastically over the "trading day". As a result, the "daily" return observations do not convey all relevant information and the GARCH model simply cannot produce fully efficient forecasts compared to what is theoretically possible given higher frequency "intraday" data. At the same time, in practice it is not feasible to produce exact real-time measures of the integrated, let alone the spot, volatility, as the processes are latent and we only have a limited and discretely sampled set of return observations available, even for the most liquid asset markets. As such, an important theme addressed in more detail in Sections 4 and 5 below involves the construction of practical measures of ex-post realized volatility that mimic the properties of the integrated volatility series.

1.2. Final introductory remarks

This section has introduced some of the basic notation used in our subsequent discussion of the various volatility forecasting procedures and evaluation methods. Our initial account also emphasizes a few conceptual features and practical considerations. First, volatility forecasts and measurements are generally restricted to (nontrivial) discrete-time intervals, even if the underlying process may be thought of as evolving in continuous time. Second, differences between ARCH and stochastic volatility models may be seen as direct consequences of assumptions about the observable information set. Third, it is important to recognize the distinction between ex-ante forecasts and ex-post realizations. Only under simplifying – and unrealistic – assumptions are the two identical. Fourth, standard ex-post measurements of realized volatility are often hampered by large idiosyncratic components. The ideal measure is instead, in cases of general interest, given by the so-called integrated volatility. The relationships among the various concepts are clearly illustrated by the simulations in Figure 1.

The rest of the chapter unfolds as follows. Section 2 provides an initial motivating discussion of several practical uses of volatility forecasts. Sections 3–5 present a variety of alternative procedures for univariate volatility forecasting based on the GARCH, stochastic volatility and realized volatility paradigms, respectively. Section 6 extends the discussion to the multivariate problem of forecasting conditional covariances and correlations, and Section 7 discusses practical volatility forecast evaluation techniques. Section 8 concludes briefly.

2. Uses of volatility forecasts

This section surveys how volatility forecasts are used in practical applications along with applications in the academic literature. While the emphasis is on financial applications the discussion is kept at a general level. Thus, we do not yet assume a specific volatility forecasting model. The issues involved in specifying and estimating particular volatility forecasting models will be discussed in subsequent sections.

We will first discuss a number of general statistical forecasting applications where volatility dynamics are important. Then we will go into some detail on various applications in finance. Lastly we will briefly mention some applications in macroeconomics and in other disciplines.

2.1. Generic forecasting applications

For concreteness, assume that the future realization of the variable of interest can be written as a decomposition similar to the one already developed in Equation (1.7),

$$y_{t+1} = \mu_{t+1|t} + \sigma_{t+1|t} z_{t+1}, \qquad z_{t+1} \sim \text{i.i.d. } F, \tag{2.1}$$

where $\{y_{t+1}\}$ denotes a discrete-time real-valued univariate stochastic process, and F refers to the distribution of the zero-mean, unit-variance innovation, z_{t+1}. This representation is not entirely general as there could be higher-order conditional dependence in the innovations. Such higher-moment dynamics would complicate some of the results, but the qualitative insights would remain the same. Thus, to facilitate the presentation we continue our discussion of the different forecast usages under slightly less than full generality.

2.1.1. Point forecasting

We begin by defining the forecast loss function which maps the ex-ante forecasts $\hat{y}_{t+1|t}$ and the ex-post realization y_{t+1} into a loss value $L(y_{t+1}, \hat{y}_{t+1|t})$, which by assumption increases with the discrepancy between the realization and the forecast. The exact form of the loss function depends, of course, directly on the use of the forecast. However, in many situations the loss function may reasonably be written in the form of an additive error, $e_{t+1} \equiv y_{t+1} - \hat{y}_{t+1}$, as the argument, so that $L(y_{t+1}, \hat{y}_{t+1|t}) = L(e_{t+1})$. We will refer to this as the forecast error loss function.

In particular, under the symmetric quadratic forecast error loss function, which is implicitly used in many practical applications, the optimal point forecast is simply the conditional mean of the process, regardless of the shape of the conditional distribution. That is,

$$\hat{y}_{t+1|t} \equiv \operatorname*{Arg\,min}_{\hat{y}} E\big[(y_{t+1} - \hat{y})^2 \mid \mathcal{F}_t\big] = \mu_{t+1|t}.$$

Volatility forecasting is therefore irrelevant for calculating the optimal point forecast, unless the conditional mean depends directly on the conditional volatility. However, this exception is often the rule in finance, where the expected return generally involves some function of the volatility of market wide risk factors. Of course, as discussed further below, even if the conditional mean does not explicitly depend on the conditional volatility, volatility dynamics are still relevant for assessing the uncertainty of the point forecasts.

In general, when allowing for asymmetric loss functions, the volatility forecast will be a key part of the optimal forecast. Consider for example the asymmetric linear loss function,

$$L(e_{t+1}) = a|e_{t+1}|\mathbf{I}(e_{t+1} > 0) + b|e_{t+1}|\mathbf{I}(e_{t+1} \leqslant 0), \tag{2.2}$$

where $a, b > 0$, and $\mathbf{I}(\cdot)$ denotes the indicator function equal to zero or one depending on the validity of its argument. In this case positive and negative forecast errors have different weights (a and b, respectively) and thus different losses. Now the optimal forecast can be shown to be

$$\hat{y}_{t+1|t} = \mu_{t+1|t} + \sigma_{t+1|t} F^{-1}\bigl(a/(a+b)\bigr), \tag{2.3}$$

which obviously depends on the relative size of a and b. Importantly, the volatility plays a key role even in the absence of conditional mean dynamics. Only if $F^{-1}(a/(a+b)) = 0$ does the optimal forecast equal the conditional mean.

This example is part of a general set of results in Granger (1969) who shows that if the conditional distribution is symmetric (so that $F^{-1}(1/2) = 0$) and if the forecast error loss function is also symmetric (so that $a/(a+b) = 1/2$) but not necessarily quadratic, then the conditional mean is the optimal point forecast.

2.1.2. *Interval forecasting*

Constructing accurate interval forecasts around the conditional mean forecast for inflation was a leading application in Engle's (1982) seminal ARCH paper. An interval forecast consists of an upper and lower limit. One version of the interval forecast puts $p/2$ probability mass below and above the lower and upper limit, respectively. The interval forecast can then be written as

$$\hat{y}_{t+1|t} = \bigl\{\mu_{t+1|t} + \sigma_{t+1|t} F^{-1}(p/2), \mu_{t+1|t} + \sigma_{t+1|t} F^{-1}(1-p/2)\bigr\}. \tag{2.4}$$

Notice that the volatility forecast plays a key role again. Note also the direct link between the interval forecast and the optimal point forecast for the asymmetric linear loss function in (2.3).

2.1.3. *Probability forecasting including sign forecasting*

A forecaster may care about the variable of interest falling above or below a certain threshold value. As an example, consider a portfolio manager who might be interested in forecasting whether the return on a stock index will be larger than the known risk-free bond return. Another example might be a rating agency forecasting if the value of a firm's assets will end up above or below the value of its liabilities and thus trigger bankruptcy. Yet another example would be a central bank forecasting the probability of inflation – or perhaps an exchange rate – falling outside its target band. In general terms, if the concern is about a variable y_{t+1} ending up above some fixed (known) threshold, c, the loss function may be expressed as

$$L(y_{t+1}, \hat{y}_{t+1|t}) = \big(\mathbf{I}(y_{t+1} > c) - \hat{y}_{t+1|t}\big)^2. \tag{2.5}$$

Minimizing the expected loss by setting the first derivative equal to zero then readily yields

$$\begin{aligned} \hat{y}_{t+1|t} &= E\big[\mathbf{I}(y_{t+1} > c) \mid \mathcal{F}_t\big] = P(y_{t+1} > c \mid \mathcal{F}_t) \\ &= 1 - F\big((c - \mu_{t+1|t})/\sigma_{t+1|t}\big). \end{aligned} \tag{2.6}$$

Thus, volatility dynamics are immediately important for these types of probability forecasts, even if the conditional mean is constant and not equal to c; i.e., $c - \mu_{t+1|t} \neq 0$.

The important special case where $c = 0$ is sometimes referred to as sign forecasting. In this situation,

$$\hat{y}_{t+1|t} = 1 - F(-\mu_{t+1|t}/\sigma_{t+1|t}). \tag{2.7}$$

Hence, the volatility dynamics will affect the forecast as long as the conditional mean is not zero, or the conditional mean is not directly proportional to the standard deviation.

2.1.4. Density forecasting

In many applications the entire conditional density of the variable in question is of interest. That is, the forecast takes the form of a probability distribution function

$$\hat{y}_{t+1|t} = f_{t+1|t}(y) \equiv f(y_{t+1} = y \mid \mu_{t+1|t}, \sigma_{t+1|t}) = f(y_{t+1} = y \mid \mathcal{F}_t). \tag{2.8}$$

Of course, the probability density function may itself be time-varying, for example, due to time-varying conditional skewness or kurtosis, but as noted earlier for simplicity we rule out these higher order effects here.

Figure 2 shows two stylized density forecasts corresponding to a high and low volatility day, respectively. Notice that the mean outcome is identical (and positive) on the two days. However, on the high volatility day the occurrence of a large negative (or large positive) outcome is more likely. Notice also that the probability of a positive outcome (of any size) is smaller on the high volatility day than on the low volatility day. Thus, as discussed in the preceding sections, provided that the level of the volatility is forecastable, the figure indicates some degree of sign predictability, despite the constant mean.

2.2. Financial applications

The trade-off between risk and expected return, where risk is associated with some notion of price volatility, constitute one of the key concepts in modern finance. As such, measuring and forecasting volatility is arguably among the most important pursuits in empirical asset pricing finance and risk management.

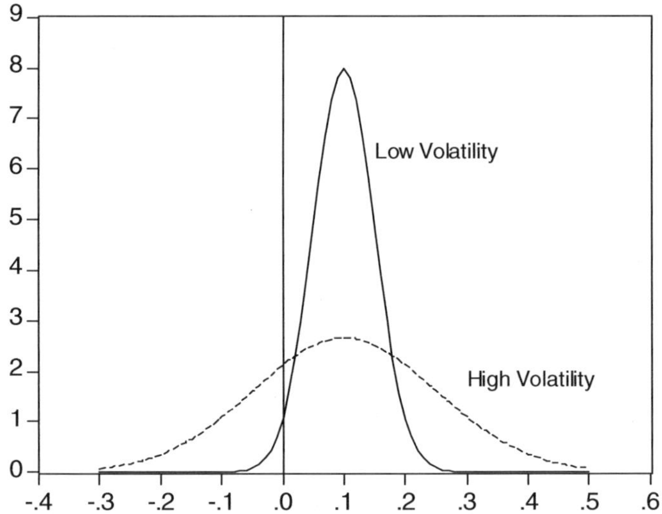

Figure 2. Density forecasts on high volatility and low volatility days. The figure shows two hypothetical return distributions for a low volatility (solid line) and high volatility (dashed line) day. The areas to the left of the vertical line represent the probability of a negative return.

2.2.1. *Risk management: Value-at-Risk (VaR) and Expected Shortfall (ES)*

Consider a portfolio of returns formed from a vector of N risky assets, R_{t+1}, with corresponding vector of portfolio weights, W_t. The portfolio return is defined as

$$r_{w,t+1} = \sum_{i=1}^{N} w_{i,t} r_{i,t+1} \equiv W_t' R_{t+1}, \tag{2.9}$$

where the w subscript refers to the fact that the portfolio distribution depends on the actual portfolio weights.

Financial risk managers often report the riskiness of the portfolio using the concept of Value-at-Risk (VaR) which is simply the quantile of the conditional portfolio distribution. If we model the portfolio returns directly as a univariate process,

$$r_{w,t+1} = \mu_{w,t+1|t} + \sigma_{w,t+1|t} z_{w,t+1}, \qquad z_{w,t+1} \sim \text{i.i.d. } F_w, \tag{2.10}$$

then the VaR is simply

$$\text{VaR}_{t+1|t}^{p} = \mu_{w,t+1|t} + \sigma_{w,t+1|t} F_w^{-1}(p). \tag{2.11}$$

This, of course, corresponds directly to the lower part of the interval forecast previously defined in Equation (2.4).

Figure 3 shows a typical simulated daily portfolio return time series with dynamic volatility (solid line). The short-dashed line, which tracks the lower range of the return,

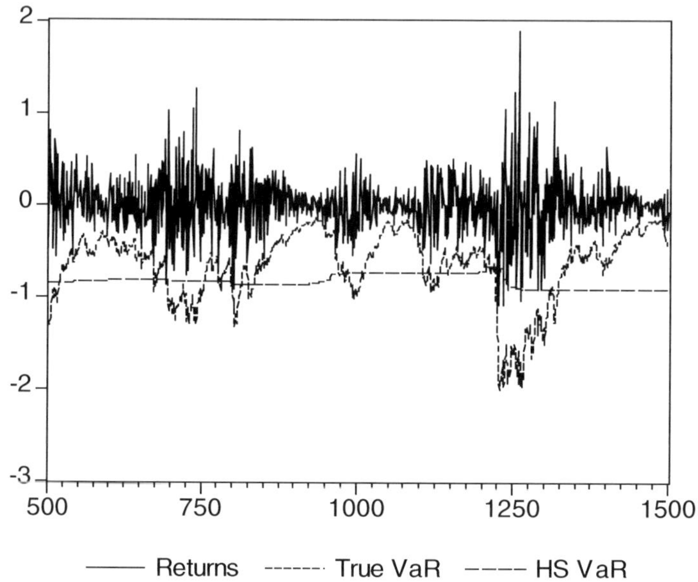

Figure 3. Simulated portfolio returns with dynamic volatility and historical simulation VaRs. The solid line shows a time series of typical simulated daily portfolio returns. The short-dashed line depicts the true one-day-ahead, 1% VaR. The long-dashed line gives the 1% VaR based on the so-called Historical Simulation (HS) technique and a 500-day moving window.

depicts the true 1-day, 1% VaR corresponding to the simulated portfolio return. Notice that the true VaR varies considerably over time and increases in magnitude during bursts in the portfolio volatility. The relatively sluggish long-dashed line calculates the VaR using the so-called Historical Simulation (HS) technique. This is a very popular approach in practice. Rather than explicitly modeling the volatility dynamics, the HS technique calculates the VaR as an empirical quantile based on a moving window of the most recent 250 or 500 days. The HS VaR in Figure 3 is calculated using a 500-day window. Notice how this HS VaR reacts very sluggishly to changes in the volatility, and generally is too large (in absolute value) when the volatility is low, and more importantly too small (in absolute value) when the volatility is high. Historical simulation thus underestimates the risk when the risk is high. This is clearly not a prudent risk management practice. As such, these systematic errors in the HS VaR clearly highlight the value of explicitly modeling volatility dynamics in financial risk management.

The VaR depicted in Figure 3 is a very popular risk-reporting measure in practice, but it obviously only depicts a very specific aspect of the risk; that is with probability p the loss will be at least the VaR. Unfortunately, the VaR measure says nothing about the expected magnitude of the loss on the days the VaR is breached.

Alternatively, the Expected Shortfall (ES) risk measure was designed to provide additional information about the tail of the distribution. It is defined as the expected loss on the days when losses are larger than the VaR. Specifically,

$$\mathrm{ES}_{t+1|t}^{p} \equiv E\big[r_{w,t+1} \mid r_{w,t+1} < \mathrm{VaR}_{t+1|t}^{p}\big] = \mu_{w,t+1|t} + \sigma_{w,t+1|t}\mathrm{EF}_{w}^{p}. \tag{2.12}$$

Again, it is possible to show that if $z_{w,t}$ is i.i.d., the multiplicative factor, EF_w^p, is constant and depends only on the shape of the distribution, F_w. Thus, the volatility dynamics plays a similar role in the ES risk measure as in the VaR in Equation (2.11).

The analysis above assumed a univariate portfolio return process specified as a function of the portfolio weights at any given time. Such an approach is useful for risk measurement but is not helpful, for example, for calculating optimal portfolio weights. If active risk management is warranted, say maximizing expected returns subject to a VaR constraint, then a multivariate model is needed. If we assume that each return is modeled separately then the vector of returns can be written as

$$R_{t+1} = M_{t+1|t} + \Omega_{t+1|t}^{1/2} Z_{t+1}, \qquad Z_{t+1} \sim \text{i.i.d. } F, \tag{2.13}$$

where $M_{t+1|t}$ and $\Omega_{t+1|t}$ denote the vector of conditional mean returns and the covariance matrix for the returns, respectively, and all of the elements in the vector random process, Z_t, are independent with mean zero and variance one. Consequently, the mean and the variance of the portfolio returns, $W_t' R_{t+1}$, may be expressed as

$$\mu_{w,t+1|t} = W_t' M_{t+1|t}, \qquad \sigma_{w,t+1|t}^2 = W_t' \Omega_{t+1|t} W_t. \tag{2.14}$$

In the case of the normal distribution, $Z_{t+1} \sim N(0, I)$, linear combinations of multivariate normal variables are themselves normally distributed, so that $r_{w,t+1} \equiv W_t' R_{t+1} \sim N(\mu_{w,t+1|t}, \sigma_{w,t+1|t}^2)$, but this aggregation property does not hold in general for other multivariate distributions. Hence, except in special cases, such as the multivariate normal, the VaR and ES measures are not known in closed form, and will have to be calculated using Monte Carlo simulation.

2.2.2. *Covariance risk: Time-varying betas and conditional Sharpe ratios*

The above discussion has focused on measuring the risk of a portfolio from purely statistical considerations. We now turn to a discussion of the more fundamental economic issue of the expected return on an asset given its risk profile. Assuming the absence of arbitrage opportunities a fundamental theorem in finance then proves the existence of a stochastic discount factor, say SDF_{t+1}, which can be used to price any asset, say I, via the conditional expectation

$$E\big[\mathrm{SDF}_{t+1}(1 + r_{i,t+1}) \mid \mathcal{F}_t\big] = 1. \tag{2.15}$$

In particular, the return on the risk free asset, which pays one dollar for sure the next period, must satisfy $1 + r_{f,t} = E[\mathrm{SDF}_{t+1} \mid \mathcal{F}_t]^{-1}$. It follows also directly from (2.15) that the expected excess return on any risky asset must be proportional to its covariance with the stochastic discount factor,

$$E[r_{i,t+1} - r_{f,t} \mid \mathcal{F}_t] = -(1 + r_{f,t}) \operatorname{Cov}(\mathrm{SDF}_{t+1}, r_{i,t+1} \mid \mathcal{F}_t). \tag{2.16}$$

Now, assuming that the stochastic discount factor is linearly related to the market return,

$$\mathrm{SDF}_{t+1} = a_t - b_t(1 + r_{M,t+1}), \tag{2.17}$$

it follows from $E[\mathrm{SDF}_{t+1}(1+r_{M,t+1}) \mid \mathcal{F}_t] = 1$ and $1+r_{f,t} = E[\mathrm{SDF}_{t+1} \mid \mathcal{F}_t]^{-1}$ that

$$\begin{aligned} a_t &= (1 + r_{f,t})^{-1} + b_t \mu_{M,t+1|t}, \\ b_t &= (1 + r_{f,t})^{-1}(\mu_{M,t+1|t} - r_{f,t})/\sigma^2_{M,t+1|t}, \end{aligned} \tag{2.18}$$

where $\mu_{M,t+1|t} \equiv E[1 + r_{M,t+1} \mid \mathcal{F}_t]$ and $\sigma^2_{M,t+1|t} \equiv \mathrm{Var}[r_{M,t+1} \mid \mathcal{F}_t]$. Notice that the dynamics in the moments of the market return (along with any dynamics in the risk-free rate) render the coefficients in the SDF time varying. Also, in parallel to the classic one-period CAPM model of Markowitz (1952) and Sharpe (1964), the *conditional* expected excess returns must satisfy the relation,

$$E[r_{i,t+1} - r_{f,t} \mid \mathcal{F}_t] = \beta_{i,t}(\mu_{M,t+1|t} - r_{f,t}), \tag{2.19}$$

where the *conditional* "beta" is defined by $\beta_{i,t} \equiv \mathrm{Cov}(r_{M,t+1}, r_{i,t+1} \mid \mathcal{F}_t)/\sigma^2_{M,t+1|t}$. Moreover, the expected risk adjusted return, also know as the *conditional* Sharpe ratio, equals

$$\begin{aligned} \mathrm{SR}_t &\equiv E[r_{i,t+1} - r_{f,t} \mid \mathcal{F}_t]/\,\mathrm{Var}(r_{i,t+1} \mid \mathcal{F}_t)^{1/2} \\ &= \mathrm{Corr}(r_{M,t+1}, r_{i,t+1} \mid \mathcal{F}_t)/\sigma_{M,t+1|t}. \end{aligned} \tag{2.20}$$

The simple asset pricing framework above illustrates how the expected return (raw and risk adjusted) on various assets will be driven by the mean and volatility dynamics of the overall market return as well as the dynamics of the covariance between the market and the individual assets. Covariance forecasting is thus at least as important as volatility forecasting in the context of financial asset pricing, and we discuss each in subsequent sections.

2.2.3. *Asset allocation with time-varying covariances*

The above CAPM model imposes a very restrictive structure on the covariance matrix of asset returns. In this section we instead assume a generic dynamic covariance matrix and study the optimization problem of an investor who constructs a portfolio of N risky assets by minimizing the portfolio variance subject to achieving a certain target portfolio return, μ_p.

Formally, the investor chooses a vector of portfolio weights, W_t, by solving the quadratic programming problem

$$\min W_t' \Omega_{t+1|t} W_t \quad \text{s.t. } W_t' M_{t+1|t} = \mu_p. \tag{2.21}$$

From the corresponding first order conditions, the resulting portfolio weights for the risky assets satisfy

$$W_t^* = \frac{\Omega_{t+1|t}^{-1} M_{t+1|t}}{M'_{t+1|t} \Omega_{t+1|t}^{-1} M_{t+1|t}} \mu_p, \tag{2.22}$$

with the optimal portfolio weight for the risk-free asset given by

$$w_{f,t}^* = 1 - \sum_{i=1}^{N} w_{i,t}^*. \tag{2.23}$$

Moreover, from (2.21) the portfolio Sharpe ratio equals

$$\mathrm{SR}_t = \mu_p \Big/ \sqrt{W_t^{*\prime} \Omega_{t+1|t} W_t^*}. \tag{2.24}$$

Just as in the CAPM pricing model discussed above, both volatility and covariance dynamics are clearly important for asset allocation. Notice also that even if we rule out exploitable conditional mean dynamics, the optimal portfolio weights would still be time-varying from the second moment dynamics alone.

2.2.4. *Option valuation with dynamic volatility*

The above tools are useful for the analysis of primitive securities with linear payoffs such as stocks, bonds, foreign exchange and futures contracts. Consider now instead a European call option which gives the owner the right but not the obligation to buy the underlying asset (say a stock or currency) on a future date, T, at a strike price, K. The option to exercise creates a nonlinear payoff which in turn requires a special set of tools for pricing and risk management.

In the Black–Scholes–Merton (BSM) option pricing model the returns are assumed to be normally distributed with constant volatility, σ, along with the possibility of (costless) continuous trading and a constant risk free rate, r_f. In this situation, the call price of an option equals

$$c_t = \mathrm{BSM}\big(s_t, \sigma^2, K, r_f, T\big) = s_t \Phi(d) - K \exp(-r_f T) \Phi\big(d - \sigma\sqrt{T}\,\big), \tag{2.25}$$

where s_t denotes the current price of the asset, $d = (\ln(s_t/K) + T(r_f + \sigma^2/2))/(\sigma\sqrt{T})$, and $\Phi(\cdot)$ refers to the cumulative normal distribution function.

Meanwhile, the constant volatility assumption in BSM causes systematic pricing errors when comparing the theoretical prices with actual market prices. One manifestation of this is the famous volatility-smiles which indicate systematic underpricing by the BSM model for in- or out-of-the-money options. The direction of these deviations, however, are readily explained by the presence of stochastic volatility, which creates fatter tails than the normal distribution, in turn increasing the value of in- and out-of-the-money options relative to the constant-volatility BSM model.

In response to this, Hull and White (1987) explicitly allow for an independent stochastic volatility factor in the process for the underlying asset return. Assuming that this additional volatility risk factor is not priced in equilibrium, the Hull–White call option price simply equals the expected BSM price, where the expectation is taken over the future integrated volatility. More specifically, defining the integrated volatility as the integral of the spot volatility during the remaining life of the option,

$$\mathrm{IV}(T,t)=\int_t^T \sigma^2(u)\,\mathrm{d}u,$$

where $\mathrm{IV}(T,t)=\mathrm{IV}(T)+\mathrm{IV}(T-1)+\cdots+\mathrm{IV}(t+1)$ generalizes the integrated variance concept from Equation (1.11) to a multi-period horizon in straightforward fashion. The Hull–White option valuation formula may then be succinctly written as

$$C_t=E\big[\mathrm{BSM}\big(\mathrm{IV}(T,t)\big)\mid \mathcal{F}_t\big]. \tag{2.26}$$

In discrete time, the integrated volatility may be approximated by the sum of the corresponding one-period conditional variances,

$$\mathrm{IV}(T,t)\approx\sum_{\tau=t}^{T-1}\sigma^2_{\tau+1|\tau}.$$

Several so-called realized volatility measures have also recently been proposed in the literature for (ex-post) approximating the integrated volatility. We will return to a much more detailed discussion of these measures in Sections 4 and 5 below.

Another related complication that arises in the pricing of equity options, in particular, stems from the apparent negative correlation between the returns and the volatility. This so-called leverage effect, as discussed further below, induces negative skewness in the return distribution and causes systematic asymmetric pricing errors in the BSM model.

Assuming a mean-reverting stochastic volatility process, Heston (1993) first developed an option pricing formula where the innovations to the returns and the volatility are correlated, and where the volatility risk is priced by the market. In contrast to the BSM setting, where an option can be hedged using a dynamically rebalanced stock and bond portfolio alone, in the Heston model an additional position must be taken in another option in order to hedge the volatility risk.

Relying on Heston's formulation, Fouque, Papanicolaou and Sircar (2000) show that the price may conveniently be expressed as

$$C_t=E\big[\mathrm{BSM}\big(\xi_{t,T}s_t,\big(1-\rho^2\big)\,\mathrm{IV}(T,t)\big)\mid \mathcal{F}_t\big], \tag{2.27}$$

where ρ refers to the (instantaneous) correlation between the returns and the volatility, and $\xi_{t,T}$ denotes a stochastic scaling factor determined by the volatility risk premium, with the property that $E[\xi_{t,T}\mid \mathcal{F}_t]=1$. Importantly, however, the integrated volatility remains the leading term as in the Hull–White valuation formula.

2.3. Volatility forecasting in fields outside finance

Although volatility modeling and forecasting has proved to be extremely useful in finance, the motivation behind Engle's (1982) original ARCH model was to provide a tool for measuring the dynamics of inflation uncertainty. Tools for modeling volatility dynamics have been applied in many other areas of economics and indeed in other areas of the social sciences, the natural sciences and even medicine. In the following we list a few recent papers in various fields showcasing the breath of current applications of volatility modeling and forecasting. It is by no means an exhaustive list but these papers can be consulted for further references.

Related to Engle's original work, the modeling of inflation uncertainty and its relationship with labor market variables has recently been studied by Rich and Tracy (2004). They corroborate earlier findings of an inverse relationship between desired labor contract durations and the level of inflation uncertainty. Analyzing the inflation and output forecasts from the Survey of Professional Forecasters, Giordani and Soderlind (2003) find that while each forecaster on average tends to underestimate uncertainty, the disagreement between forecasters provides a reasonable proxy for inflation and output uncertainty. The measurement of uncertainty also plays a crucial role in many microeconomic models. Meghir and Pistaferri (2004), for instance, estimate the conditional variance of income shocks at the microlevel and find strong evidence of temporal variance dynamics.

Lastrapes (1989) first analyzed the relationship between exchange rate volatility and U.S. monetary policy. In a more recent study, Ruge-Murcia (2004) developed a model of a central bank with asymmetric preferences for unemployment above versus below the natural rate. The model implies an inflation bias proportional to the conditional variance of unemployment. Empirically, the conditional variance of unemployment is found to be positively related to the rate of inflation. In another central banking application, Tse and Yip (2003) use volatility models to study the effect on changes in the Hong Kong currency board on interbank market rates.

Volatility modeling and forecasting methods have also found several interesting uses in agricultural economics. Ramirez and Fadiga (2003), for instance, find evidence of asymmetric volatility patterns in U.S. soybean, sorghum and wheat prices. Building on the earlier volatility spill-over models used in analyzing international financial market linkages in the papers by Engle, Ito and Lin (1990) and King, Sentana and Wadhwani (1994), Buguk, Hudson and Hanson (2003) have recently used similar methods in documenting strong price volatility spillovers in the supply-chain of fish production. The volatility in feeding material prices (e.g., soybeans) affects the volatility of fish feed prices which in turn affect fish farm price volatility and finally wholesale price volatility. Also, Barrett (1999) uses a GARCH model to study the effect of real exchange rate depreciations on stochastic producer prices in low-income agriculture.

The recent deregulation in the utilities sector has also prompted many new applications of volatility modeling of gas and power prices. Shawky, Marathe and Barrett (2003) use dynamic volatility models to determine the minimum variance hedge ratios for electricity futures. Linn and Zhu (2004) study the effect of natural gas storage report announcements on intraday volatility patterns in gas prices. They also find evidence of strong intraday patterns in natural gas price volatility. Battle and Barquin (2004) use a multivariate GARCH model to simulate gas and oil price paths, which in turn are shown to be useful for risk management in the wholesale electricity market.

In a related context, Taylor and Buizza (2003) use weather forecast uncertainty to model electricity demand uncertainty. The variability of wind measurements is found to be forecastable using GARCH models in Cripps and Dunsmuir (2003), while temperature forecasting with seasonal volatility dynamics is explored in Campbell and Diebold (2005). Marinova and McAleer (2003) model volatility dynamics in ecological patents.

In political science, Maestas and Preuhs (2000) suggest modeling political volatility broadly defined as periods of rapid and extreme change in political processes, while Gronke and Brehm (2002) use ARCH models to assess the dynamics of volatility in presidential approval ratings.

Volatility forecasting has recently found applications even in medicine. Ewing, Piette and Payne (2003) forecast time varying volatility in medical net discount rates which are in turn used to determine the present value of future medical costs. Also, Johnson, Elashoff and Harkema (2003) use a heteroskedastic time series process to model neuromuscular activation patterns in patients with spinal cord injuries, while Martin-Guerrero et al. (2003) use a dynamic volatility model to help determine the optimal EPO dosage for patients with secondary anemia.

2.4. Further reading

Point forecasting under general loss functions when allowing for dynamic volatility has been analyzed by Christoffersen and Diebold (1996, 1997). Patton and Timmermann (2004) have recently shown that under general specifications of the loss function, the optimal forecast error will have a conditional expected value that is a function of the conditional variance of the underlying process. Methods for incorporating time-varying volatility into interval forecasts are suggested in Granger, White and Kamstra (1989). Financial applications of probability forecasting techniques are considered in Christoffersen and Diebold (2003).

Financial risk management using dynamic volatility models is surveyed in Christoffersen (2003) and Jorion (2000). Berkowitz and O'Brien (2002), Pritsker (2001), and Barone-Adesi, Giannopoulos and Vosper (1999) explicitly document the value added from incorporating volatility dynamics into daily financial risk management systems.

Volatility forecasting at horizons beyond a few weeks is found to be difficult by West and Cho (1995) and Christoffersen and Diebold (2000). However, Brandt and Jones (2002) show that using intraday information improves the longer horizon forecasts considerably. Guidolin and Timmermann (2005a) uncover VaR dynamics at horizons of up to two years. Campbell (1987, 2003), Shanken (1990), Aït-Sahalia and Brandt (2001), Harvey (2001), Lettau and Ludvigson (2003) and Marquering and Verbeek (2004) find that interest rate spreads and financial ratios help predict volatility at longer horizons.

A general framework for conditional asset pricing allowing for time-varying betas is laid out in Cochrane (2001). Market timing arising from time-varying Sharpe ratios is analyzed in Whitelaw (1997), while volatility timing has been explicitly explored by Johannes, Polson and Stroud (2004). The relationship between time-varying volatility and return has been studied in Engle, Lilien and Robbins (1987), French, Schwert and Stambaugh (1987), Bollerslev, Engle and Wooldridge (1988), Bollerslev, Chou and Kroner (1992), Glosten, Jagannathan and Runkle (1993), among many others.

The value of modeling volatility dynamics for asset allocation in a single-period setting have been highlighted in the series of papers by Fleming, Kirby and Oestdiek (2001, 2003), with multi-period extensions considered by Wang (2004). The general topic of asset allocation under predictable returns is surveyed in Brandt (2005). Brandt (1999) and Aït-Sahalia and Brandt (2001) suggest portfolio allocation methods which do not require the specification of conditional moment dynamics.

The literature on option valuation allowing for volatility dynamics is very large and active. In addition to some of the key theoretical contributions mentioned above, noteworthy empirical studies based on continuous-time methods include Bakshi, Cao and Chen (1997), Bates (1996), Chernov and Ghysels (2000), Eraker (2004), Melino and Turnbull (1990), and Pan (2002). Recent discrete-time applications, building on the theoretical work of Duan (1995) and Heston (1993), can be found in Christoffersen and Jacobs (2004a, 2004b) and Heston and Nandi (2000).

3. GARCH volatility

The current interest in volatility modeling and forecasting was spurred by Engle's (1982) path breaking ARCH paper, which set out the basic idea of modeling and forecasting volatility as a time-varying function of current information. The GARCH class of models, of which the GARCH(1, 1) remains the workhorse, were subsequently introduced by Bollerslev (1986), and also discussed independently by Taylor (1986). These models, including their use in volatility forecasting, have been extensively surveyed elsewhere and we will not attempt yet another exhaustive survey here. Instead we will try to highlight some of the key features of the models which help explain their dominant role in practical empirical applications. We will concentrate on univariate formulations in this section, with the extension to multivariate GARCH-based covariance and correlation forecasting discussed in Section 6.

3.1. Rolling regressions and RiskMetrics

Rolling sample windows arguably provides the simplest way of incorporating actual data into the estimation of time-varying volatilities, or variances. In particular, consider the rolling sample variance based on the p most recent observations as of time t,

$$\hat{\sigma}_t^2 = p^{-1} \sum_{i=0}^{p-1} (y_{t-i} - \hat{\mu})^2 \equiv p^{-1} \sum_{i=0}^{p-1} \hat{\varepsilon}_{t-i}^2. \tag{3.1}$$

Interpreting $\hat{\sigma}_t^2$ as an estimate of the current variance of y_t, the value of p directly determines the variance-bias tradeoff of the estimator, with larger values of p reducing the variance but increasing the bias. For instance, in the empirical finance literature, it is quite common to rely on rolling samples of five-years of monthly data, corresponding to a value of $p = 60$, in estimating time varying-variances, covariances, and CAPM betas.

Instead of weighting each of the most recent p observations the same, the bias of the estimator may be reduced by assigning more weights to the most recent observations. An exponentially weighted moving average filter is commonly applied in doing so,

$$\hat{\sigma}_t^2 = \gamma(y_t - \hat{\mu})^2 + (1-\gamma)\hat{\sigma}_{t-1}^2 \equiv \gamma \sum_{i=1}^{\infty}(1-\gamma)^{i-1}\hat{\varepsilon}_{t-i}^2. \tag{3.2}$$

In practice, the sum will, of course, have to be truncated at $I = t - 1$. This is typically done by equating the pre-sample values to zero, and adjusting the finite sum by the corresponding multiplication factor $1/[1 - (1-\gamma)^t]$. Of course, for large values of t and $(1 - \gamma) < 1$, the effect of this truncation is inconsequential. This approach is exemplified by RiskMetrics [J.P. Morgan (1996)], which rely on a value of $\gamma = 0.06$ and $\mu \equiv 0$ in their construction of daily (monthly) volatility measures for wide range of different financial rates of returns.

Although it is possible to write down explicit models for y_t which would justify the rolling window approach and the exponential weighted moving average as the optimal estimators for the time-varying variances in the models, the expressions in (3.1) and (3.2) are more appropriately interpreted as data-driven filters. In this regard, the theoretical properties of both filters as methods for extracting consistent estimates of the current volatility as the sampling frequencies of the underlying observations increases over fixed-length time intervals – or what is commonly referred to as continuous record, or fill-in, asymptotics – has been extensively studied in a series of influential papers by Dan Nelson [these papers are collected in the edited volume of readings by Rossi (1996)].

It is difficult to contemplate optimal volatility forecasting without the notion of a model, or data generating process. Of course, density or VaR forecasting, as discussed in Section 2, is even more problematic. Nonetheless, the filters described above are often used in place of more formal model building procedures in the construction of h-period-ahead volatility forecasts by simply equating the future volatility of interest with the current filtered estimate,

$$\operatorname{Var}(y_{t+h} \mid \mathcal{F}_t) \equiv \sigma_{t+h|t}^2 \approx \hat{\sigma}_t^2. \tag{3.3}$$

In the context of forecasting the variance of multi-period returns, assuming that the corresponding one-period returns are serially uncorrelated so that the forecast equals the sum of the successive one-period variance forecasts, it follows then directly that

$$\operatorname{Var}(y_{t+k} + y_{t+k-1} + \cdots + y_{t+1} \mid \mathcal{F}_t) \equiv \sigma_{t:t+k|t}^2 \approx k\hat{\sigma}_t^2. \tag{3.4}$$

Hence, the multi-period return volatility scales with the forecast horizon, k. Although this approach is used quite frequently by finance practitioners it has, as discussed further below, a number of counterfactual implications. In contrast, the GARCH(1, 1) model, to which we now turn, provides empirically realistic mean-reverting volatility forecasts within a coherent and internally consistent, yet simple, modeling framework.

3.2. GARCH(1, 1)

In order to define the GARCH class of models, consider the decomposition of y_t into the one-step-ahead conditional mean, $\mu_{t|t-1} \equiv E(y_t \mid \mathcal{F}_{t-1})$, and variance, $\sigma^2_{t|t-1} \equiv \mathrm{Var}(y_t \mid \mathcal{F}_{t-1})$, in parallel to the expression in Equation (1.7) above,

$$y_t = \mu_{t|t-1} + \sigma_{t|t-1} z_t, \quad z_t \sim \text{i.i.d.}, \ E(z_t) = 0, \ \mathrm{Var}(z_t) = 1. \tag{3.5}$$

The GARCH(1, 1) model for the conditional variance is then defined by the recursive relationship,

$$\sigma^2_{t|t-1} = \omega + \alpha \varepsilon^2_{t-1} + \beta \sigma^2_{t-1|t-2}, \tag{3.6}$$

where $\varepsilon_t \equiv \sigma_{t|t-1} z_t$, and the parameters are restricted to be nonnegative, $\omega > 0, \alpha \geqslant 0$, $\beta \geqslant 0$, in order to ensure that the conditional variance remains positive for all realizations of the z_t process. The model is readily extended to higher order GARCH(p, q) models by including additional lagged squared innovations and/or conditional variances on the right-hand side of the equation.

By recursive substitution, the GARCH(1, 1) model may alternatively be expressed as an ARCH(∞) model,

$$\sigma^2_{t|t-1} = \omega(1-\beta)^{-1} + \alpha \sum_{i=1}^{\infty} \beta^{i-1} \varepsilon^2_{t-i}. \tag{3.7}$$

This obviously reduces to the exponentially weighted moving average filter in (3.2) for $\omega = 0$, $\alpha = \gamma$, and $\beta = 1 - \gamma$. The corresponding GARCH model in which $\alpha + \beta = 1$ is also sometimes referred to as an Integrated GARCH, or IGARCH(1, 1) model. Importantly, however, what sets the GARCH(1, 1) model, and more generally the ARCH class of models, apart from the filters discussed above is the notion of a data generating process embedded in the distributional assumptions for z_t. This means that the construction of optimal variance forecasts is a well-posed question within the context of the model.

In particular, it follows directly from the formulation of the model that the optimal, in a mean-square error sense, one-step ahead variance forecasts equals $\sigma^2_{t+1|t}$. Corresponding expressions for the longer run forecasts, $\sigma^2_{t+h|t}$ for $h > 1$, are also easily constructed by recursive procedures. To facilitate the presentation, assume that the conditional mean is constant and equal to zero, or $\mu_{t|t-1} = 0$, and that $\alpha + \beta < 1$ so that the unconditional variance of the process exists,

$$\sigma^2 = \omega(1 - \alpha - \beta)^{-1}. \tag{3.8}$$

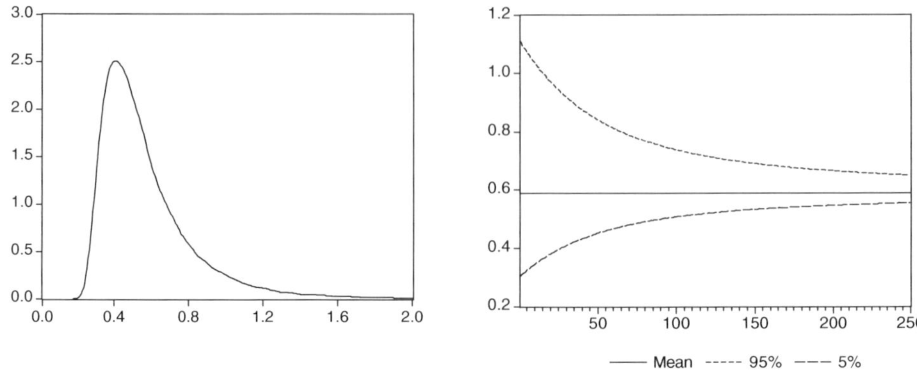

Figure 4. GARCH volatility term structure. The first panel shows the unconditional distribution of $\sigma^2_{t+1|t}$. The second panel shows the term-structure-of-variance, $k^{-1}\sigma^2_{t:t+k|t}$, for $\sigma^2_{t+1|t}$ equal to the mean, together with the fifth and the ninety-fifth percentiles in the unconditional distribution.

The h-step ahead forecast is then readily expressed as

$$\sigma^2_{t+h|t} = \sigma^2 + (\alpha + \beta)^{h-1}\big(\sigma^2_{t+1|t} - \sigma^2\big), \tag{3.9}$$

showing that the forecasts revert to the long-run unconditional variance at an exponential rate dictated by the value of $\alpha + \beta$.

Moreover, with serially uncorrelated returns, so that the conditional variance of the sum is equal to the sum of the conditional variances, the optimal forecast for the variance of the k-period return may be expressed as

$$\sigma^2_{t:t+k|t} = k\sigma^2 + \big(\sigma^2_{t+1|t} - \sigma^2\big)\big(1 - (\alpha + \beta)^k\big)(1 - \alpha - \beta)^{-1}. \tag{3.10}$$

Thus, the longer the forecast horizon (the higher the value of k), the less variable will be the forecast per unit time-interval. That is, the term-structure-of-variance, or $k^{-1}\sigma^2_{t:t+k|t}$, flattens with k.

To illustrate, consider Figure 4. The left-hand panel plots the unconditional distribution of $\sigma^2_{t+1|t}$ for the same GARCH(1, 1) model depicted in Figure 1. The mean of the distribution equals $\sigma^2 = 0.020(1 - 0.085 - 0.881)^{-1} \approx 0.588$, but there is obviously considerable variation around that value, with a much longer tail to the right. The panel on the right gives the corresponding term-structure for $k = 1, 2, \ldots, 250$, and $\sigma^2_{t+1|t}$ equal to the mean, five, and ninety-five percentiles in the unconditional distribution. The slope of the volatility-term-structure clearly flattens with the horizon. The figure also illustrates that the convergence to the long-run unconditional variance occurs much slower for a given percentage deviation of $\sigma^2_{t+1|t}$ above the median than for the same percentage deviation below the median.

To further illustrate the dynamics of the volatility-term structure, Figure 5 graphs $k^{-1}\sigma^2_{t:t+k|t}$ for $k = 1, 5, 22$ and 66, corresponding to daily, weekly, monthly and

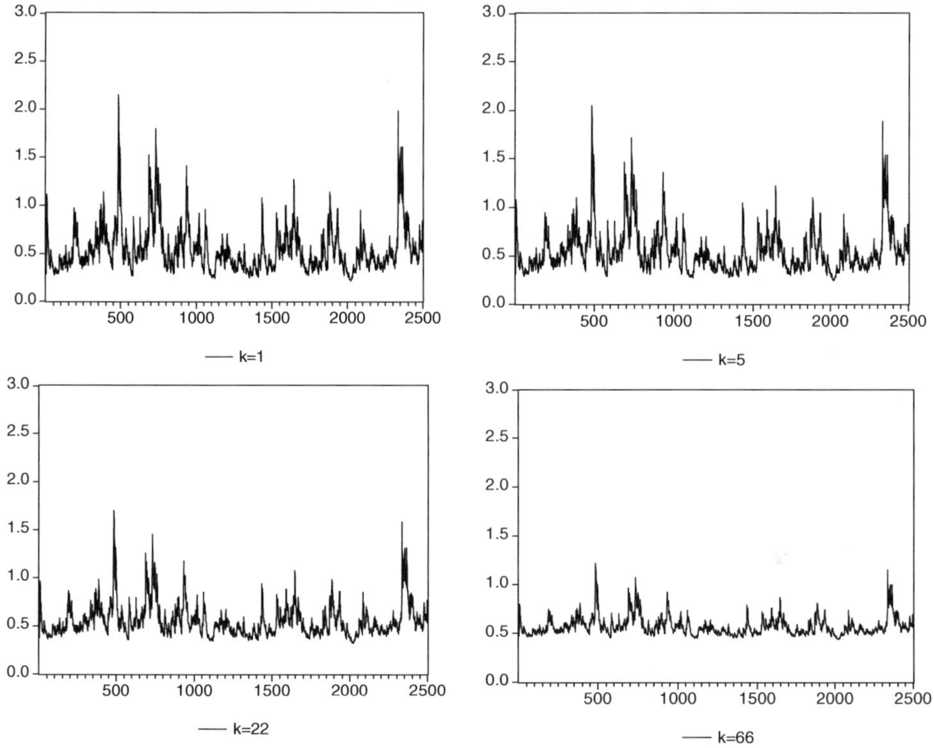

Figure 5. GARCH volatility forecasts and horizons. The four panels show the standardized "daily" GARCH(1, 1) volatility forecasts, $k^{-1}\sigma^2_{t:t+k|t}$, for horizons $k = 1, 5, 22, 66$.

quarterly forecast horizons, for the same $t = 1, 2, \ldots, 2500$ GARCH(1, 1) simulation sample depicted in Figure 1. Comparing the four different panels, the volatility-of the-volatility clearly diminishes with the forecast horizon.

It is also informative to compare and contrast the optimal GARCH(1, 1) volatility forecasts to the common empirical practice of horizon volatility scaling by k. In this regard, it follows directly from the expressions in (3.9) and (3.10) that

$$E\big(k\sigma^2_{t+1|t}\big) = k\sigma^2 = E\big(\sigma^2_{t:t+k|t}\big),$$

so that the level of the scaled volatility forecasts will be right on average. However, comparing the variance of the scaled k-period forecasts to the variance of the optimal forecast,

$$\begin{aligned}\mathrm{Var}\big(k\sigma^2_{t+1|t}\big) &= k^2\,\mathrm{Var}\big(\sigma^2_{t+1|t}\big) > \big(1-(\alpha+\beta)^k\big)^2(1-\alpha-\beta)^{-2}\,\mathrm{Var}\big(\sigma^2_{t+1|t}\big)\\ &= \mathrm{Var}\big(\sigma^2_{t:t+k|t}\big),\end{aligned}$$

it is obvious that by not accounting for the mean-reversion in the volatility, the scaled forecasts exaggerate the volatility-of-the-volatility relative to the true predictable variation. On tranquil days the scaled forecasts underestimate the true risk, while the risk is inflated on volatile days. Obviously not a very prudent risk management procedure.

This tendency for the horizon scaled forecasts to exhibit excessive variability is also directly evident from the term structure plots in Figure 5. Consider the optimal k-period ahead variance forecasts defined by k times the $k^{-1}\sigma_{t:t+k|t}^2$ series depicted in the last three panels. Contrasting these correct multi-step forecasts with their scaled counterparts defined by k times the $\sigma_{t+1|t}^2$ series in the first panel, it is obvious, that although both forecasts will be centered around the right unconditional value of $k\sigma^2$, the horizon scaled forecasts will result in too large "day-to-day" fluctuations. This is especially true for the longer run "monthly" ($k = 22$) and "quarterly" ($k = 66$) forecasts in the last two panels.

3.3. Asymmetries and "leverage" effects

The basic GARCH model discussed in the previous section assumes that positive and negative shocks of the same absolute magnitude will have the identical influence on the future conditional variances. In contrast, the volatility of aggregate equity index return, in particular, has been shown to respond asymmetrically to past negative and positive return shocks, with negative returns resulting in larger future volatilities. This asymmetry is generally referred to as a "leverage" effect, although it is now widely agreed that financial leverage alone cannot explain the magnitude of the effect, let alone the less pronounced asymmetry observed for individual equity returns. Alternatively, the asymmetry has also been attributed to a "volatility feedback" effect, whereby heightened volatility requires an increase in the future expected returns to compensate for the increased risk, in turn necessitating a drop in the current price to go along with the initial increase in the volatility. Regardless of the underlying economic explanation for the phenomenon, the three most commonly used GARCH formulations for describing this type of asymmetry are the GJR or Threshold GARCH (TGARCH) models of Glosten, Jagannathan and Runkle (1993) and Zakoïan (1994), the Asymmetric GARCH (AGARCH) model of Engle and Ng (1993), and the Exponential GARCH (EGARCH) model of Nelson (1991).

The conditional variance in the GJR(1, 1), or TGARCH(1, 1), model simply augments the standard GARCH(1, 1) formulation with an additional ARCH term conditional on the sign of the past innovation,

$$\sigma_{t|t-1}^2 = \omega + \alpha\varepsilon_{t-1}^2 + \gamma\varepsilon_{t-1}^2 I(\varepsilon_{t-1} < 0) + \beta\sigma_{t-1|t-2}^2, \tag{3.11}$$

where $I(\cdot)$ denotes the indicator function. It is immediately obvious that for $\gamma > 0$, past negative return shocks will have a larger impact on the future conditional variances. Mechanically, the calculation of multi-period variance forecast works exactly as for the standard symmetric GARCH model. In particular, assuming that

$$P\left(z_t \equiv \sigma_{t|t-1}^{-1}\varepsilon_t < 0\right) = 0.5,$$

it follows readily that

$$\sigma^2_{t+h|t} = \sigma^2 + (\alpha + 0.5\gamma + \beta)^{h-1}\big(\sigma^2_{t+1|t} - \sigma^2\big), \tag{3.12}$$

where the long-run, or unconditional variance, now equals

$$\sigma^2 = \omega(1 - \alpha - 0.5\gamma - \beta)^{-1}. \tag{3.13}$$

Although the forecasting formula looks almost identical to the one for the GARCH(1, 1) model in Equation (3.9), the inclusion of the asymmetric term may materially affect the forecasts by importantly altering the value of the current conditional variance, $\sigma^2_{t+1|t}$.

The news impact curve, defined by the functional relationship between $\sigma^2_{t|t-1}$ and ε_{t-1} holding all other variables constant, provides a simple way of characterizing the influence of the most recent shock on next periods conditional variance. In the standard GARCH model this curve is obviously quadratic around $\varepsilon_{t-1} = 0$, while the GJR model with $\gamma > 0$ has steeper slopes for negative values of ε_{t-1}. In contrast, the Asymmetric GARCH, or AGARCH(1, 1), model,

$$\sigma^2_{t|t-1} = \omega + \alpha(\varepsilon_{t-1} - \gamma)^2 + \beta\sigma^2_{t-1|t-2}, \tag{3.14}$$

shifts the center of the news impact curve from zero to γ, affording an alternative way of capturing asymmetric effects. The GJR and AGARCH model may also be combined to achieve even more flexible parametric formulations.

Instead of directly parameterizing the conditional variance, the EGARCH model is formulated in terms of the logarithm of the conditional variance, as in the EGARCH(1, 1) model,

$$\log\big(\sigma^2_{t|t-1}\big) = \omega + \alpha\big(|z_{t-1}| - E\big(|z_{t-1}|\big)\big) + \gamma z_{t-1} + \beta\log\big(\sigma^2_{t-1|t-2}\big), \tag{3.15}$$

where as previously defined, $z_t \equiv \sigma^{-1}_{t|t-1}\varepsilon_t$. As for the GARCH model, the EGARCH model is readily extended to higher order models by including additional lags on the right-hand side. The parameterization in terms of logarithms has the obvious advantage of avoiding nonnegativity constraints on the parameters, as the variance implied by the exponentiated logarithmic variance from the model is guaranteed to be positive. As in the GJR and AGARCH models above, values of $\gamma > 0$ in the EGARCH model directly captures the asymmetric response, or "leverage" effect. Meanwhile, because of the nondifferentiability with respect to z_{t-1} at zero, the EGARCH model is often somewhat more difficult to estimate and analyze numerically. From a forecasting perspective, the recursions defined by the EGARCH equation (3.15) readily deliver the optimal – in a mean-square error sense – forecast for the future logarithmic conditional variances, $E(\log(\sigma^2_{t+h}) \mid \mathcal{F}_t)$. However, in most applications the interest centers on point forecasts for σ^2_{t+h}, as opposed to $\log(\sigma^2_{t+h})$. Unfortunately, the transformation of the $E(\log(\sigma^2_{t+h}) \mid \mathcal{F}_t)$ forecasts to $E(\sigma^2_{t+h} \mid \mathcal{F}_t)$ generally depends on the entire h-step ahead forecast distribution, $f(y_{t+h} \mid \mathcal{F}_t)$. As discussed further in Section 3.6 below, this distribution is generally not available in closed-form, but it may be approximated by Monte Carlo simulations from the convolution of the corresponding h one-step-ahead predictive distributions implied by the z_t innovation process using numerical techniques. In contrast, the expression for $\sigma^2_{t+h|t}$ in Equation (3.12) for the GJR or TGARCH model is straightforward to implement, and only depends upon the assumption that $P(z_t < 0) = 0.5$.

3.4. Long memory and component structures

The GARCH, TGARCH, AGARCH, and EGARCH models discussed in the previous sections all imply that shocks to the volatility decay at an exponential rate. To illustrate, consider the GARCH(1, 1) model. It follows readily from Equation (3.9) that the impulse effect of a time-t shock on the forecast of the variance h period into the future is given by $\partial\sigma^2_{t+h|t}/\partial\varepsilon^2_t = \alpha(\alpha+\beta)^{h-1}$, or more generally

$$\partial\sigma^2_{t+h|t}/\partial\varepsilon^2_t = \kappa\delta^h, \tag{3.16}$$

where $0 < \delta < 1$. This exponential decay typically works well when forecasting over short horizons. However, numerous studies, including Ding, Granger and Engle (1993) and Andersen and Bollerslev (1997), have argued that the autocorrelations of squared and absolute returns decay at a much slower hyperbolic rate over longer lags. In the context of volatility forecasting using GARCH models parameterized in terms of ε^2_t, this suggests that better long term forecasts may be obtained by formulating the conditional variance in such a way that the impulse effect behaves as

$$\partial\sigma^2_{t+h|t}/\partial\varepsilon^2_t \approx \kappa h^\delta, \tag{3.17}$$

for large values of h, where again $0 < \delta < 1$. Several competing long-memory, or fractionally integrated, GARCH type models have been suggested in the literature to achieve this goal.

In the Fractionally Integrated FIGARCH(1, d, 1) model proposed by Baillie, Bollerslev and Mikkelsen (1996) the conditional variance is defined by

$$\sigma^2_{t|t-1} = \omega + \beta\sigma^2_{t-1|t-2} + \left[1 - \beta L - (1-\alpha L - \beta L)(1-L)^d\right]\varepsilon^2_t. \tag{3.18}$$

For $d = 0$ the model reduces to the standard GARCH(1, 1) model, but for values of $0 < d < 1$ shocks to the point volatility forecasts from the model will decay at a slow hyperbolic rate. The actual forecasts are most easily constructed by recursive substitution in

$$\sigma^2_{t+h|t+h-1} = \omega(1-\beta)^{-1} + \lambda(L)\sigma^2_{t+h-1|t+h-2}, \tag{3.19}$$

with $\sigma^2_{t+h|t+h-1} \equiv \varepsilon^2_t$ for $h < 0$, and the coefficients in $\lambda(L) \equiv 1 - (1-\beta L)^{-1}(1 - \alpha L - \beta L)(1-L)^d$ calculated from the recursions,

$$\lambda_1 = \alpha + d,$$
$$\lambda_j = \beta\lambda_{j-1} + \left[(j-1-d)j^{-1} - (\alpha+\beta)\right]\delta_{j-1}, \quad j = 2, 3, \ldots,$$

where $\delta_j \equiv \delta_{j-1}(j-1-d)j^{-1}$ refer to the coefficients in the MacLaurin series expansion of the fractional differencing operator, $(1-L)^d$. Higher order FIGARCH models, or volatility forecast filters, may be defined in an analogous fashion. Asymmetries are also easily introduced into the recursions by allowing for separate influences of past positive and negative innovations as in the GJR or TGARCH model. Fractional Integrated EGARCH, or FIEGARCH, models may be similarly defined by parameterizing the logarithmic conditional variance as a fractionally integrated distributed lag of past values.

An alternative, and often simpler, approach for capturing longer-run dependencies involves the use of component type structures. Granger (1980) first showed that the superposition of an infinite number of stationary AR(1) processes may result in a true long-memory process. In fact, there is a long history in statistics and time series econometrics for approximating long memory by the sum of a few individually short-memory components. This same idea has successfully been used in the context of volatility modeling by Engle and Lee (1999) among others.

In order to motivate the Component GARCH model of Engle and Lee (1999), rewrite the standard GARCH(1, 1) model in (3.6) as

$$\left(\sigma_{t|t-1}^2 - \sigma^2\right) = \alpha\left(\varepsilon_{t-1}^2 - \sigma^2\right) + \beta\left(\sigma_{t-1|t-2}^2 - \sigma^2\right), \tag{3.20}$$

where it is assumed that $\alpha + \beta < 1$, so that the model is covariance stationary and the long term forecasts converge to the long-run, or unconditional, variance $\sigma^2 = \omega(1-\alpha-\beta)^{-1}$. The component model then extends the basic GARCH model by explicitly allowing the long-term level to be time-varying,

$$\left(\sigma_{t|t-1}^2 - \zeta_t^2\right) = \alpha\left(\varepsilon_{t-1}^2 - \zeta_t^2\right) + \beta\left(\sigma_{t-1|t-2}^2 - \zeta_t^2\right), \tag{3.21}$$

with ζ_t^2 parameterized by the separate equation,

$$\zeta_t^2 = \omega + \rho\zeta_{t-1}^2 + \varphi\left(\varepsilon_{t-1}^2 - \sigma_{t-1|t-2}^2\right). \tag{3.22}$$

Hence, the transitory dynamics is governed by $\alpha + \beta$, while the long-run dependencies are described by $\rho > 0$. It is possible to show that for the model to be covariance stationary, and the unconditional variance to exist, the parameters must satisfy $(\alpha + \beta)(1-\rho) + \rho < 1$. Also, substituting the latter equation into the first, the model may be expressed as the restricted GARCH(2, 2) model,

$$\begin{aligned}\sigma_{t|t-1}^2 &= \omega(1-\alpha-\beta) + (\alpha+\varphi)\varepsilon_{t-1}^2 - \left(\varphi(\alpha+\beta) + \rho\alpha\right)\varepsilon_{t-2}^2 \\ &\quad + (\rho+\beta+\varphi)\sigma_{t-1|t-2}^2 + \left(\varphi(\alpha+\beta) - \rho\beta\right)\sigma_{t-2|t-3}^2.\end{aligned}$$

As for the GARCH(1, 1) model, volatility shocks therefore eventually dissipate at the exponential rate in Equation (3.15). However, for intermediate forecast horizons and values of ρ close to unity, the volatility forecasts from the component GARCH model will display approximate long memory.

To illustrate, consider Figure 6 which graphs the volatility impulse response function, $\partial\sigma_{t+h|t}^2/\partial\varepsilon_t^2$, $h = 1, 2, \ldots, 250$, for the RiskMetrics forecasts, the standard

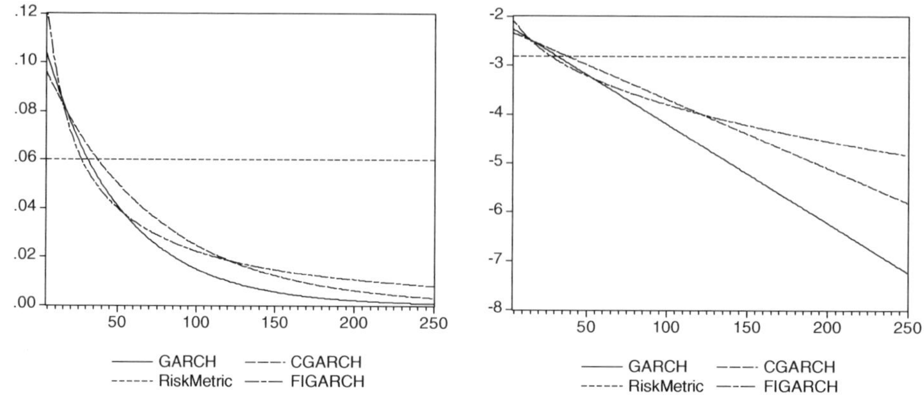

Figure 6. Volatility impulse response coefficients. The left panel graphs the volatility impulse response function, $\partial\sigma^2_{t+h|t}/\partial\varepsilon^2_t$, $h = 1, 2, \ldots, 250$, for the RiskMetrics forecasts, the standard GARCH(1, 1) model in (3.6), the FIGARCH(1, d, 1) model in (3.18), and the component GARCH model in (3.21) and (3.22). The right panel plots the corresponding logarithmic values.

GARCH(1, 1) model in (3.6), the FIGARCH(1, d, 1) model in (3.18), and the component GARCH model defined by (3.21) and (3.22). The parameters for the different GARCH models are calibrated to match the volatilities depicted in Figure 1. To facilitate comparisons and exaggerate the differences across models, the right-hand panel depicts the logarithm of the same impulse response coefficients. The RiskMetrics forecasts, corresponding to an IGARCH(1, 1) model with $\alpha = 0.06$, $\beta = 1 - \alpha = 0.94$ and $\omega = 0$, obviously results in infinitely persistent volatility shocks. In contrast, the impulse response coefficients associated with the GARCH(1, 1) forecasts die out at the exponential rate $(0.085+0.881)^h$, as manifest by the log-linear relationship in the right-hand panel. Although the component GARCH model also implies an exponential decay and therefore a log-linear relationship, it fairly closely matches the hyperbolic decay rate for the long-memory FIGARCH model for the first 125 steps. However, the two models clearly behave differently for forecasts further into the future. Whether these differences and potential gains in forecast accuracy over longer horizons are worth the extra complications associated with the implementation of a fractional integrated model obviously depends on the specific uses of the forecasts.

3.5. Parameter estimation

The values of the parameters in the GARCH models are, of course, not known in practice and will have to be estimated. By far the most commonly employed approach for doing so is Maximum Likelihood Estimation (MLE) under the additional assumption that the standardized innovations in Equation (3.5), $z_t \equiv \sigma^{-1}_{t|t-1}(y_t - \mu_{t|t-1})$, are i.i.d.

normally distributed, or equivalently that the conditional density for y_t takes the form,

$$f(y_t \mid \mathcal{F}_{t-1}) = (2\pi)^{-1/2}\sigma_{t|t-1}^{-1} \exp\bigl(-1/2\sigma_{t|t-1}^{-2}(y_t - \mu_{t|t-1})^2\bigr). \tag{3.23}$$

In particular, let θ denote the vector of unknown parameters entering the conditional mean and variance functions to be estimated. By standard recursive conditioning arguments, the log-likelihood function for the $y_T, y_{T-1}, \ldots, y_1$ sample is then simply given by the sum of the corresponding T logarithmic conditional densities,

$$\log L(\theta; y_T, \ldots, y_1)$$
$$= -\frac{T}{2}\log(2\pi) - \frac{1}{2}\sum_{t=1}^{T}\bigl[\log\sigma_{t|t-1}^2(\theta) - \sigma_{t|t-1}^{-2}(\theta)\bigl(y_t - \mu_{t|t-1}(\theta)\bigr)^2\bigr]. \tag{3.24}$$

The likelihood function obviously depends upon the parameters in a highly nonlinear fashion, and numerical optimization techniques are required in order to find the value of θ which maximizes the function, say $\hat{\theta}_T$. Also, to start up the recursions for calculating $\sigma_{t|t-1}^2(\theta)$, pre-sample values of the conditional variances and squared innovations are also generally required. If the model is stationary, these initial values may be fixed at their unconditional sample counterparts, without affecting the asymptotic distribution of the resulting estimates. Fortunately, there now exist numerous software packages for estimating all of the different GARCH formulations discussed above based upon this likelihood approach.

Importantly, provided that the model is correctly specified and satisfies a necessary set of technical regularity conditions, the estimates obtained by maximizing the function in (3.24) inherit the usual optimality properties associated with MLE, allowing for standard parameter inference based on an estimate of the corresponding information matrix. This same asymptotic distribution may also be used in incorporating the parameter estimation error uncertainty in the distribution of the volatility forecasts from the underlying model. However, this effect is typically ignored in practice, instead relying on a simple plugin approach using $\hat{\theta}_T$ in place of the true unknown parameters in the forecasting formulas. Of course, in many financial applications the size of the sample used in the parameter estimation phase is often very large compared to the horizon of the forecasts, so that the additional influence of the parameter estimation error is likely to be relatively minor compared to the inherent uncertainty in the forecasts from the model. Bayesian inference procedures can, of course, also be used in directly incorporating the parameter estimation error uncertainty in the model forecasts.

More importantly from a practical perspective, the log-likelihood function in Equation (3.24) employed in almost all software packages is based on the assumption that z_t is i.i.d. normally distributed. Although this assumption coupled with time-varying volatility implies that the unconditional distribution of y_t has fatter tails than the normal, this is typically not sufficient to account for all of the mass in the tails in the distributions of daily or weekly returns. Hence, the likelihood function is formally misspecified.

However, if the conditional mean and variance are correctly specified, the corresponding Quasi-Maximum Likelihood Estimates (QMLE) obtained under this auxiliary assumption of conditional normality will generally be consistent for the true value of θ. Moreover, asymptotically valid robust standard errors may be calculated from the so-called "sandwich-form" of the covariance matrix estimator, defined by the outer product of the gradients post- and pre-multiplied by the inverse of the usual information matrix estimator. Since the expressions for the future conditional variances for most of the GARCH models discussed above do not depend upon the actual distribution of z_t, as long as $E(z_t \mid \mathcal{F}_{t-1}) = 0$ and $E(z_t^2 \mid \mathcal{F}_{t-1}) = 1$, this means that asymptotically valid point volatility forecasts may be constructed from the conditionally normal QMLE for θ without fully specifying the distribution of z_t.

Still, the efficiency of the parameter estimates, and therefore the accuracy of the resulting point volatility forecasts obtained by simply substituting $\hat{\theta}_T$ in place of the unknown parameters in the forecasting formulas, may be improved by employing the correct conditional distribution of z_t. A standardized Student t distribution with degrees of freedom $\nu > 2$ often provides a good approximation to this distribution. Specifically,

$$f(y_t \mid \mathcal{F}_{t-1}) = \Gamma\left(\frac{\nu+1}{2}\right)\Gamma\left(\frac{\nu}{2}\right)^{-1}\left((\nu-2)\sigma_{t|t-1}^2\right)^{-1/2} \times \left(1+(\nu-2)^{-1}\sigma_{t|t-1}^{-2}(y_t-\mu_{t|t-1})^2\right)^{-(\nu+1)/2} \tag{3.25}$$

with the log-likelihood function given by the sum of the corresponding T logarithmic densities, and the degrees of freedom parameter ν estimated jointly with the other parameters of the model entering the conditional mean and variance functions. Note, that for $\nu \to \infty$ the distribution converges to the conditional normal density in (3.23). Of course, more flexible distributions allowing for both fat tails and asymmetries could be, and have been, employed as well. Additionally, semi-nonparametric procedures in which the parameters in $\mu_{t|t-1}(\theta)$ and $\sigma_{t|t-1}^2(\theta)$ are estimated sequentially on the basis of nonparametric kernel type estimates for the distribution of $\hat{z}_t$ have also been developed to enhance the efficiency of the parameter estimates relative to the conditionally normal QMLEs. From a forecasting perspective, however, the main advantage of these more complicated conditionally nonnormal estimation procedures lies not so much in the enhanced efficiency of the plugin point volatility forecasts, $\sigma_{T+h|T}^2(\hat{\theta}_T)$, but rather in their ability to better approximate the tails in the corresponding predictive distributions, $f(y_{T+h} \mid \mathcal{F}_T; \hat{\theta}_T)$. We next turn to a discussion of this type of density forecasting.

3.6. Fat tails and multi-period forecast distributions

The ARCH class of models directly specifies the one-step-ahead conditional mean and variance, $\mu_{t|t-1}$ and $\sigma_{t|t-1}^2$, as functions of the time $t-1$ information set, $\mathcal{F}_{t-1}$. As such, the one-period-ahead predictive density for y_t is directly determined by the distribution of z_t. In particular, assuming that z_t is i.i.d. standard normal,

$$f_z(z_t) = (2\pi)^{-1/2}\exp(-z_i/2),$$

the conditional density of y_t is then given by the expression in Equation (3.23) above, where the $\sigma_{t|t-1}^{-1}$ term is associated with the Jacobian of the transformation from z_t to y_t. Thus, in this situation, the one-period-ahead VaR at level p is readily calculated by $\mathrm{VaR}_{t+1|t}^{p} = \mu_{t+1|t} + \sigma_{t+1|t} F_z^{-1}(p)$, where $F_z^{-1}(p)$ equals the pth quantile in the standard normal distribution.

Meanwhile, as noted above the distributions of the standardized GARCH innovations often have fatter tails than the normal distribution. To accommodate this feature alternative conditional error distributions, such as the Student t distribution in Equation (3.25) discussed above, may be used in place of the normal density in Equation (3.23) in the construction of empirically more realistic predictive densities. In the context of quantile predictions, or VARs, this translates into multiplication factors, $F_z^{-1}(p)$, in excess of those for the normal distribution for small values of p. Of course, the exact value of $F_z^{-1}(p)$ will depend upon the specific parametric estimates for the distribution of z_t. Alternatively, the standardized in-sample residuals based on the simpler-to-implement QMLE for the parameters, say $\hat{z}_t \equiv \hat{\sigma}_{t|t-1}^{-1}(y_t - \hat{\mu}_{t|t-1})$, may be used in nonparametrically estimating the distribution of z_t, and in turn the quantiles, $\hat{F}_z^{-1}(p)$.

The procedures discussed above generally work well in approximating VARs within the main range of support of the distribution, say $0.01 < p < 0.99$. However, for quantiles in the very far left or right tail, it is not possible to meaningfully estimate $F_z^{-1}(p)$ without imposing some additional structure on the problem. Extreme Value Theory (EVT) provides a framework for doing so. In particular, it follows from EVT that under general conditions the tails of any admissible distribution must behave like those of the Generalized Pareto class of distributions. Hence, provided that z_t is i.i.d., the extreme quantiles in $f(y_{t+1} \mid \mathcal{F}_t)$ may be inferred exactly as above, using only the $[rT]$ smallest (largest) values of $\hat{z}_t$ in actually estimating the parameters of the corresponding extreme value distribution used in calculating $\hat{F}_z^{-1}(p)$. The fraction r of the full sample T used in this estimation dictates where the tails, and consequently the extreme value distribution, begin. In addition to standard MLE techniques, a number of simplified procedures, including the popular Hill estimator, are also available for estimating the required tail parameters.

The calculation of multi-period forecast distributions is more complicated. To facilitate the presentation, suppose that the information set defining the conditional one-step-ahead distribution, $f(y_{t+1} \mid \mathcal{F}_t)$, and consequently the conditional mean and variance, $\mu_{t+1|t}$ and $\sigma_{t+1|t}^2$, respectively, is restricted to current and past values of y_t. The multi-period-ahead predictive distribution is then formally defined by the convolution of the corresponding h one-step-ahead distributions,

$$f(y_{t+h} \mid \mathcal{F}_t) = \iint \cdots \int f(y_{t+h} \mid \mathcal{F}_{t+h-1}) f(y_{t+h-1} \mid \mathcal{F}_{t+h-2}) \cdots f(y_{t+1} \mid \mathcal{F}_t)\, \mathrm{d}y_{t+h-1}\, \mathrm{d}y_{t+h-2} \ldots \mathrm{d}y_{t+1}. \tag{3.26}$$

This multi-period mixture distribution generally has fatter tails than the underlying one-step-ahead distributions. In particular, assuming that the one-step-ahead distributions are conditionally normal as in (3.23) then, if the limiting value exists, the unconditional distribution, $f(y_t) = \lim_{h\to\infty} f(y_t \mid \mathcal{F}_{t-h})$, will be leptokurtic relative to the normal. This is, of course, entirely consistent with the unconditional distribution of most speculative returns having fatter tails than the normal. It is also worth noting that even though the conditional one-step-ahead predictive distributions, $f(y_{t+1} \mid \mathcal{F}_t)$, may be symmetric, if the conditional variance depends on the past values of y_t in an asymmetric fashion, as in the GJR, AGARCH or EGARCH models, the multi-step-ahead distribution, $f(y_{t+h} \mid \mathcal{F}_t)$, $h > 1$, will generally be asymmetric. Again, this is directly in line with the negative skewness observed in the unconditional distribution of most equity index return series.

Despite these general results, analytical expressions for the multi-period predictive density in (3.26) are not available in closed-form. However, numerical techniques may be used in recursively building up an estimate for the predictive distribution, by repeatedly drawing future values for $y_{t+j} = \mu_{t+j|t+j-1} + \sigma_{t+j|t+j-1} z_{t+j}$ based on the assumed parametric distribution $f_z(z_t)$, or by bootstrapping z_{t+j} from the in-sample distribution of the standardized residuals.

Alternatively, $f(y_{t+h} \mid \mathcal{F}_t)$ may be approximated by a time-invariant parametric or nonparametrically estimated distribution with conditional mean and variance, $\mu_{t+h|t} \equiv E(y_{t+j} \mid \mathcal{F}_t)$ and $\sigma^2_{t+h|t} \equiv \mathrm{Var}(y_{t+j} \mid \mathcal{F}_t)$, respectively. The multi-step conditional variance is readily calculated along the lines of the recursive prediction formulas discussed in the preceding sections. This approach obviously neglects any higher order dependencies implied by the convolution in (3.26). However, in contrast to the common approach of scaling which, as illustrated in Figure 5, may greatly exaggerate the volatility-of-the-volatility, the use of the correct multi-period conditional variance means that this relatively simple-to-implement approach for calculating multi-period predictive distributions usually works very well in practice.

The preceding discussion has focused on one or multi-period forecast distributions spanning the identical unit time interval as in the underlying GARCH model. However, as previously noted, in financial applications the forecast distribution of interest often involves the sum of y_{t+j} over multiple periods corresponding to the distribution of continuously compounded multi-period returns, say $y_{t:t+h} \equiv y_{t+h} + y_{t+h-1} + \cdots + y_{t+1}$. The same numerical techniques used in approximating $f(y_{t+h} \mid \mathcal{F}_t)$ by Monte Carlo simulations discussed above may, of course, be used in approximating the corresponding distribution of the sum, $f(y_{t:t+h} \mid \mathcal{F}_t)$.

Alternatively, assuming that the y_{t+j}'s are serially uncorrelated, as would be approximately true for most speculative returns over daily or weekly horizons, the conditional variance of $y_{t:t+h}$ is simply equal to the sum of the corresponding h variance forecasts,

$$\mathrm{Var}(y_{t:t+h} \mid \mathcal{F}_t) \equiv \sigma^2_{t:t+h|t} = \sigma^2_{t+h|t} + \sigma^2_{t+h-1|t} + \cdots + \sigma^2_{t+1|t}. \tag{3.27}$$

Thus, in this situation the conditional distribution of $y_{t:t+h}$ may be estimated on the basis of the corresponding in-sample standardized residuals, $\hat{z}_{t:t+h} \equiv \hat{\sigma}^{-1}_{t:t+h|t}(y_{t:t+h} - \hat{\mu}_{t:t+h|t})$. Now, if the underlying GARCH process for y_t is covariance stationary, we have $\lim_{h\to\infty} h^{-1}\mu_{t:t+h} = E(y_t)$ and $\lim_{h\to\infty} h^{-1}\sigma^2_{t:t+h} = \mathrm{Var}(y_t)$. Moreover, as shown by Diebold (1988), it follows from a version of the standard Central Limit

Theorem that $z_{t:t+h} \Rightarrow N(0, 1)$. Thus, volatility clustering disappears under temporal aggregation, and the unconditional return distributions will be increasingly better approximated by a normal distribution the longer the return horizons. This suggests that for longer-run forecasts, or moderately large values of h, the distribution of $z_{t:t+h}$ will be approximately normal. Consequently, the calculation of longer-run multi-period VARs may reasonably rely on the conventional quantiles from a standard normal probability table in place of $F_z^{-1}(p)$ in the formula $\text{VaR}^p_{t:t+h|t} = \mu_{t:t+h|t} + \sigma_{t:t+h|t} F_z^{-1}(p)$.

3.7. Further reading

The ARCH and GARCH class of models have been extensively surveyed elsewhere; see, e.g., review articles by Andersen and Bollerslev (1998b), Bollerslev, Chou and Kroner (1992), Bollerslev, Engle and Nelson (1994), Diebold (2004), Diebold and Lopez (1995), Engle (2001, 2004), Engle and Patton (2001), Pagan (1996), Palm (1996), and Shephard (1996). The models have now also become part of the standard toolbox discussed in econometrics and empirical oriented finance textbooks; see, e.g., Hamilton (1994), Mills (1993), Franses and van Dijk (2000), Gouriéroux and Jasiak (2001), Alexander (2001), Brooks (2002), Chan (2002), Tsay (2002), Christoffersen (2003), Enders (2004), and Taylor (2004). A series of the most influential early ARCH papers have been collected in Engle (1995). A fairly comprehensive list as well as forecast comparison of the most important parametric formulations are also provided in Hansen and Lunde (2005).

Several different econometric and statistical software packages are available for estimating all of the most standard univariate GARCH models, including EViews, PC-GIVE, Limdep, Microfit, RATS, S+, SAS, SHAZAM, and TSP. The open-ended matrix programming environments GAUSS, Matlab, and Ox also offer easy add-ons for GARCH estimation, while the NAG library and the UCSD Department of Economics website provide various Fortran based procedures and programs. Partial surveys and comparisons of some of these estimation packages and procedures are given in Brooks (1997), Brooks, Burke and Persand (2001), and McCullough and Renfro (1998).

The asymmetry, or "leverage" effect, directly motivating a number of the alternative GARCH formulations were first documented empirically by Black (1976) and Christie (1982). In addition to the papers by Nelson (1991), Engle and Ng (1993), Glosten, Jagannathan and Runkle (1993), and Zakoïan (1994) discussed in Section 3.3, other important studies on modeling and understanding the volatility asymmetry in the GARCH context include Campbell and Hentschel (1992), Hentschel (1995), and Bekaert and Wu (2000), while Engle (2001) provides an illustration of the importance of incorporating asymmetry in GARCH-based VaR calculations.

The long-memory FIGARCH model of Baillie, Bollerslev and Mikkelsen (1996) in Section 3.4 may be seen as a special case of the ARCH(∞) model in Robinson (1991). The FIGARCH model also encompasses the IGARCH model of Engle and Bollerslev (1986) for $d = 1$. However, even though the approach discussed here affords a convenient framework for generating point forecasts with long-memory dependencies, when viewed as a model the unconditional variance does not exist, and the FIGARCH class of models has been criticized accordingly by Giraitis, Kokoszka and Leipus (2000), among others. An alternative formulation which breaks the link between the conditions for second-order stationarity and long-memory dependencies have been proposed by Davidson (2004). Alternative long-memory GARCH formulations include the FIEGARCH model of Bollerslev and Mikkelsen (1996), and the model in Ding and Granger (1996) based on the superposition of an infinite number of ARCH models. In contrast, the component GARCH model in Engle and Lee (1999) and the related developments in Gallant, Hsu and Tauchen (1999) and Müller et al. (1997), is based on the mixture of only a few components; see also the earlier related results on modeling and forecasting long-run dynamic dependencies in the mean by O'Connell (1971) and Tiao and Tsay (1994). Meanwhile, Bollerslev and Mikkelsen (1999) have argued that when pricing very long-lived financial contracts, the fractionally integrated volatility approach can result in materially different prices from the ones implied by the more standard GARCH models with exponential decay. The multifractal models recently advocated by Calvet and Fisher (2002, 2004) afford another approach for incorporating long memory into volatility forecasting.

Long memory also has potential links to regimes and structural break in volatility. Diebold and Inoue (2001) argue that the apparent finding of long memory could be due to the existence of regime switching. Mikosch and Starica (2004) explicitly uses nonstationarity as a source of long memory in volatility. Structural breaks in volatility is considered by Andreou and Ghysels (2002), Lamoureux and Lastrapes (1990), Pastor and Stambaugh (2001), and Schwert (1989). Hamilton and Lin (1996) and Perez-Quiros and Timmermann (2000) study volatility across business cycle regimes. The connections between long memory and structural breaks are reviewed in Banerjee and Urga (2005); see also Chapter 12 by Clements and Hendry in this Handbook.

Early contributions concerning the probabilistic and statistical properties of GARCH models, as well as the MLE and QMLE techniques discussed in Section 3.5, include Bollerslev and Wooldridge (1992), Lee and Hansen (1994), Lumsdaine (1996), Nelson (1990), and Weiss (1986); for a survey of this literature see also Li, Ling and McAleer (2002). Bollerslev (1986) discusses conditions for existence of the second moment in the specific context of the GARCH model. Loretan and Phillips (1994) contains a more general discussion on the issue of covariance stationarity. Bayesian methods for estimating ARCH models were first implemented by Geweke (1989a) and they have since be developed further in Bauwens and Lubrano (1998, 1999). The GARCH-t model discussed in Section 3.5 was first introduced by Bollerslev (1987), while Nelson (1991) suggested the so-called Generalized Error Distribution (GED) for better approximating the distribution of the standardized innovations. Engle and Gonzalez-Rivera (1991) first proposed the use of kernel-based methods for nonparametrically estimating the conditional distribution, whereas McNeil and Frey (2000) relied on Extreme Value Theory (EVT) for estimating the uppermost tails in the conditional distribution; see also Embrechts, Klüppelberg and Mikosch (1997) for a general discussion of extreme value theory.

As discussed in Section 3.6, even if the one-step-ahead conditional distribution is known (by assumption), the corresponding multi-period distributions are not available in closed-form and are generally unknown. Some of the complications that arise in this situation have been discussed in Baillie and Bollerslev (1992), who also consider the use of a Cornish–Fisher expansion for approximating specific quantiles in the multi-step-ahead predictive distributions. Numerical techniques for calculating the predictive distributions based on importance sampling schemes were first implemented by Geweke (1989b). Other important results related to the distribution of temporally aggregated GARCH models include Drost and Nijman (1993), Drost and Werker (1996), and Meddahi and Renault (2004).

4. Stochastic volatility

This section introduces the general class of models labeled Stochastic Volatility (SV). In the widest sense of the term, SV models simply allow for a stochastic element in the time series evolution of the conditional variance process. For example, GARCH models are SV models. The more meaningful categorization, which we adopt here, is to contrast ARCH type models with *genuine* SV models. The latter explicitly includes an unobserved (nonmeasurable) shock to the return variance into the characterization of the volatility dynamics. In this scenario, the variance process becomes inherently latent so that – even conditional on all past information and perfect knowledge about the data generating process – we cannot recover the exact value of the current volatility state. The technical implication is that the volatility process is not measurable with respect to observable (past) information. Hence, the assessment of the volatility state at day t changes as contemporaneous or future information from days $t + j$, $j \geqslant 0$, is incorporated into the analysis. This perspective renders estimation of latent variables from past data alone (filtering) as well as from all available, including future, data (smoothing) useful. In contrast, GARCH models treat the conditional variance as observable given past information and, as discussed above, typically applies (quasi-) maximum likelihood techniques for inference, so smoothing has no role in that setting.

Despite these differences, the two model classes are closely related, and we consider them to be complementary rather than competitors. In fact, from a practical forecasting perspective it is hard to distinguish the performance of standard ARCH and SV models. Hence, even if one were to think that the SV framework is appealing, the fact that ARCH models typically are easier to estimate explains practitioners reliance on ARCH as the volatility forecasting tool of choice. Nonetheless, the development of powerful method of simulated moments, Markov Chain Monte Carlo (MCMC) and other simulation based procedures for estimation and forecasting of SV models may render them competitive with ARCH over time. Moreover, the development of the concept of realized volatility and the associated use of intraday data for volatility measurement, discussed in the next section, is naturally linked to the continuous-time SV framework of financial economics.

The literature on SV models is vast and rapidly growing, and excellent surveys are already available on the subject, e.g., Ghysels, Harvey and Renault (1996) and Shephard (1996, 2004). Consequently, we focus on providing an overview of the main approaches with particular emphasis on the generation of volatility forecasts within each type of model specification and inferential technique.

4.1. Model specification

Roughly speaking, there are two main perspectives behind the SV paradigm when used in the context of modeling financial rate of returns. Although both may be adapted to either setting, there are precedents for one type of reasoning to be implemented in discrete time and the other to be cast in continuous time. The first centers on the Mixture of Distributions Hypothesis (MDH), where returns are governed by an event time process that represents a transformation of the time clock in accordance with the intensity of price relevant news, dating back to Clark (1973). The second approach stems from financial economics where the price and volatility processes often are modeled separately via continuous sample path diffusions governed by stochastic differential equations. We briefly introduce these model classes and point out some of the similarities to ARCH models in terms of forecasting procedures. However, the presence of a latent volatility factor renders both the estimation and forecasting problem more complex for the SV models. We detail these issues in the following subsections.

4.1.1. The mixture-of-distributions hypothesis

Adopting the rational perspective that asset prices reflect the discounted value of future expected cash flows, such prices should react almost continuously to the myriad of news that arrive on a given trading day. Assuming that the number of news arrival is large, one may expect a central limit theory to apply and financial returns should be well approximated by a conditional normal distribution with the conditioning variable corresponding to the number of relevant news events. More generally, a number of other variables associated with the overall activity of the financial market such as the daily number of trades, the daily cumulative trading volume or the number of quotes may well be similarly related to the information flow in the market. These considerations inspire the following type of representation,

$$y_t = \mu_y s_t + \sigma_y s_t^{1/2} z_t, \tag{4.1}$$

where y_t is the market "activity" variable under consideration, s_t is the strictly positive process reflecting the intensity of relevant news arrivals, μ_y represents the mean response of the variable per news event, σ_y is a scale parameter, and z_t is i.i.d. $N(0, 1)$. Equivalently, this relationship may be written as

$$y_t | s_t \sim N\big(\mu_y s_t, \sigma_y^2 s_t\big). \tag{4.2}$$

This formulation constitutes a normal mixture model. If the s_t process is time-varying it induces a fat-tailed unconditional distribution, consistent with stylized facts for most return and trading volume series. Intuitively, days with high information flow display more price fluctuations and activity than days with fewer news releases. Moreover, if the s_t process is positively correlated, then shocks to the conditional mean and variance process for y_t will be persistent. This is consistent with the observed activity clustering in financial markets, where return volatility, trading volume, the number of transactions and quotes, the number of limit orders submitted to the market, etc., all display pronounced serial dependence.

The specification in (4.1) is analogous to the one-step-ahead decomposition given in Equation (3.5). The critical difference is that the formulation is endowed with a structural interpretation, implying that the mean and variance components cannot be observed prior to the trading day as the number of news arrivals is inherently random. In fact, it is usually assumed that the s_t process is unobserved by the econometrician, even during period t, so that the true mean and variance series are both latent. From a technical perspective this implies that we must distinguish between the full information set ($s_t \in \mathcal{F}_t$) and observable information ($s_t \notin \Im_t$). The latter property is a defining feature of the genuine volatility class. The inability to observe this important component of the MDH model complicates inference and forecasting procedures as discussed below.

In the case of short horizon return series, μ_y is close to negligible and can reasonably be ignored or simply fixed at a small constant value. Furthermore, if the mixing variable s_t is latent then the scaling parameter, σ_y, is not separately identified and may be fixed at unity. This produces the following return (innovation) model,

$$r_t = s_t^{1/2} z_t, \tag{4.3}$$

implying a simple normal-mixture representation,

$$r_t | s_t \sim N(0, s_t). \tag{4.4}$$

Both univariate models for returns of the form (4.4) or multivariate systems including a return variable along with other related market activity variables, such as trading volume or the number of transactions, are referred to as derived from the Mixture-of-Distributions Hypothesis (MDH).

The representation in (4.3) is of course directly comparable to that for the return innovation in Equation (3.5). It follows immediately that volatility forecasting is related to forecasts of the latent volatility factor given the observed information,

$$\mathrm{Var}(r_{t+h} \mid \Im_t) = E(s_{t+h} \mid \Im_t). \tag{4.5}$$

If some relevant information is not observed and thus not included in $\Im_t$, then the expression in (4.5) will generally not represent the actual conditional return variance, $E(s_{t+h} \mid \mathcal{F}_t)$. This point is readily seen through a specific example.

In particular, Taylor (1986) first introduced the log-SV model by adopting an autoregressive parameterization of the latent log-volatility (or information flow) variable,

$$\log s_{t+1} = \eta_0 + \eta_1 \log s_t + u_t, \quad u_t \sim \text{i.i.d.}\ \left(0, \sigma_u^2\right), \tag{4.6}$$

where the disturbance term may be correlated with the innovation in the return equation, that is, $\rho = \operatorname{corr}(u_t, z_t) \neq 0$. This particular representation, along with a Gaussian assumption on u_t, has been so widely adopted that it has come to be known as *the* stochastic volatility model. Note that, if ρ is negative, there is an asymmetric return-volatility relationship present in the model, akin to the "leverage effect" in the GJR and EGARCH models discussed in Section 3.3, so that negative return shocks induce higher future volatility than similar positive shocks. In fact, it is readily seen that the log-SV formulation in (4.6) generalizes the EGARCH(1, 1) model by considering the case,

$$u_t = \alpha\big(|z_t| - E|z_t|\big) + \gamma z_t, \tag{4.7}$$

where the parameters η_0 and η_1 correspond to ω and β in Equation (3.15), respectively. Under the null hypothesis of EGARCH(1, 1), the information set, $\Im_t$, includes past asset returns, and the idiosyncratic return innovation series, z_t, is effectively observable so likelihood based analysis is straightforward. However, if u_t is not (only) a function of z_t, i.e., Equation (4.7) no longer holds, then there are two sources of error in the system. In this more general case it is no longer possible to separately identify the underlying innovations to the return and volatility processes, nor the true underlying volatility state.

This above example illustrates both how any ARCH model may be seen as a special case of a corresponding SV model and how the defining feature of the genuine SV model may complicate forecasting, as the volatility state is unobserved. Obviously, in representations like (4.6), the current state of volatility is a critical ingredient for forecasts of future volatility. We expand on the tasks confronting estimation and volatility forecasting in this setting in Section 4.1.3.

There are, of course, an unlimited number of alternative specifications that may be entertained for the latent volatility process. However, Stochastic Autoregressive Volatility (SARV) of Andersen (1994) has proven particular convenient. The representation is again autoregressive,

$$v_t = \omega + \beta v_{t-1} + [\gamma + \alpha v_{t-1}]u_t, \tag{4.8}$$

where u_t denotes an i.i.d. sequence, and $s_t = g(v_t)$ links the dynamic evolution of the state variable to the stochastic variance factor in Equation (4.3). For example, for the log-SV model, $g(v_t) = \exp(v_t)$. Likewise, SV generalizations of the GARCH(1, 1) may be obtained via $g(v_t) = v_t$ and an SV extension of a GARCH model for the conditional standard deviation is produced by letting $g(v_t) = v_t^{1/2}$. Depending upon the specific transformation $g(\cdot)$ it may be necessary to impose additional (positivity) constraints on the innovation sequence u_t, or the parameters in (4.8). Even if inference on parameters can be done, moment based procedures do not produce estimates of the latent volatility process, so from a forecasting perspective the analysis must necessarily be supplemented with some method of approximating the sample path realization of the underlying state variables.

4.1.2. Continuous-time stochastic volatility models

The modeling of asset returns in continuous time stems from the financial economics literature where early contributions to portfolio selection by Merton (1969) and option pricing by Black and Scholes (1973) demonstrated the analytical power of the diffusion framework in handling dynamic asset allocation and pricing problems. The idea of casting these problems in a continuous-time diffusion context also has a remarkable precedent in Bachelier (1900).

Under weak regularity conditions, the general representation of an arbitrage-free asset price process is

$$\mathrm{d}p(t) = \mu(t)\,\mathrm{d}t + \sigma(t)\,\mathrm{d}W(t) + j(t)\,\mathrm{d}q(t), \quad t \in [0, T], \tag{4.9}$$

where $\mu(t)$ is a continuous, locally bounded variation process, the volatility process $\sigma(t)$ is strictly positive, $W(t)$ denotes a standard Brownian motion, $q(t)$ is a jump indicator taking the values zero (no jump) or unity (jump) and, finally, the $j(t)$ represents the size of the jump if one occurs at time t. [See, e.g., Andersen, Bollerslev and Diebold (2005) for further discussion.] The associated one-period return is

$$\begin{aligned} r(t) &= p(t) - p(t-1) \\ &= \int_{t-1}^{t} \mu(\tau)\,\mathrm{d}\tau + \int_{t-1}^{t} \sigma(\tau)\,\mathrm{d}W(\tau) + \sum_{t-1 \leqslant \tau < t} \kappa(\tau), \end{aligned} \tag{4.10}$$

where the last sum simply cumulates the impact of the jumps occurring over the period, as we define $\kappa(t) = j(t) \cdot \mathbf{I}(q(t) = 1)$, so that $\kappa(t)$ is zero everywhere except when a discrete jump occurs.

In this setting a formal ex-post measure of the return variability, derived from the theory of quadratic variation for semi-martingales, may be defined as

$$\mathrm{QV}(t) = \int_{t-1}^{t} \sigma^2(s)\,\mathrm{d}s + \sum_{t-1 < s \leqslant t} \kappa^2(s). \tag{4.11}$$

In the special case of a pure SV diffusion, the corresponding quantity reduces to the integrated variance, as already defined in Equation (1.11) in Section 1,

$$\mathrm{IV}(t) \equiv \int_{t-1}^{t} \sigma^2(s)\,\mathrm{d}s. \tag{4.12}$$

These return variability measures are naturally related to the return variance. In fact, for a pure SV diffusion (without jumps) where the volatility process, $\sigma(\tau)$, is independent of the Wiener process, $W(\tau)$, we have

$$r(t) \big| \{\mu(\tau), \sigma(\tau);\ t-1 \leqslant \tau \leqslant t\} \sim N\left(\int_{t-1}^{t} \mu(\tau)\,\mathrm{d}\tau, \int_{t-1}^{t} \sigma^2(\tau)\,\mathrm{d}\tau\right), \tag{4.13}$$

so the integrated variance *is* the true measure of the actual (ex-post) return variance in this context. Of course, if the conditional variance and mean processes evolve stochastically we cannot perfectly predict the future volatility, and we must instead form expectations based on the current information. For short horizons, the conditional mean variation is negligible and we may focus on the following type of forecasts, for a positive integer h,

$$\operatorname{Var}\bigl(r(t+h) \mid \Im_t\bigr) \approx E\left[\int_{t+h-1}^{t+h} \sigma^2(\tau)\,\mathrm{d}\tau \;\middle|\; \Im_t\right] \equiv E\bigl[\mathrm{IV}(t+h) \mid \Im_t\bigr]. \tag{4.14}$$

The expressions in (4.13) and (4.14) generalize the corresponding equations for discrete-time SV models in (4.4) and (4.5), respectively. Of course, the return variation arising from the conditional mean process may need to be accommodated as well over longer horizons. Nonetheless, the dominant term in the return variance forecast will invariably be associated with the expected integrated variance or, more generally, the expected quadratic variation. In simple continuous-time models, we may be able to derive closed-form expressions for these quantities, but in empirically realistic settings they are typically not available in analytic form and alternative procedures must be used. We discuss these issues in more detail below.

The initial diffusion models explored in the literature were not genuine SV diffusions but rather, with a view toward tractability, cast as special cases of the constant elasticity of variance (CEV) class of models,

$$\mathrm{d}p(t) = \bigl(\mu - \phi\bigl[p(t) - \mu\bigr]\bigr)\,\mathrm{d}t + \sigma p(t)^{\gamma}\,\mathrm{d}W(t), \quad t \in [0, T], \tag{4.15}$$

where $\phi \geqslant 0$ determines the strength of mean reversion toward the unconditional mean μ in the log-price process, while $\gamma \geqslant 0$ allows for conditional heteroskedasticity in the return process. Popular representations are obtained by specific parameter restrictions, e.g., the Geometric Brownian motion for $\phi = 0$ and $\gamma = 0$, the Vasicek model for $\gamma = 0$, and the Cox-Ingersoll and Ross (CIR) or square-root model for $\gamma = \frac{1}{2}$. These three special cases allow for a closed-form characterization of the likelihood, so the analysis is straightforward. Unfortunately, they are also typically inadequate in terms of capturing the volatility dynamics of asset returns. A useful class of extensions have been developed from the CIR model. In this model the instantaneous mean and variance processes are both affine functions of the log price. The affine model class extends the above representation with $\gamma = \frac{1}{2}$ to a multivariate setting with general affine conditional mean and variance specifications. The advantage is that a great deal of analytic tractability is retained while allowing for more general and empirically realistic dynamic features.

Many genuine SV representations of empirical interest fall outside of the affine class, however. For example, Hull and White (1987) develop a theory for option pricing under stochastic volatility using a model much in the spirit of Taylor's discrete-time log SV in Equation (4.6). With only a minor deviation from their representation, we may write it, for $t \in [0, T]$,

$$\begin{aligned} dp(t) &= \mu(t)\,dt + \sigma(t)\,dW(t), \\ d\log\sigma^2(t) &= \beta\big(\alpha - \log\sigma^2(t)\big)\,dt + v\,dW_\sigma(t). \end{aligned} \tag{4.16}$$

The strength of the mean reversion in (log) volatility is given by β and the volatility is governed by v. Positive but low values of β induces a pronounced volatility persistence, while large values of v increase the idiosyncratic variation in the volatility series. Furthermore, the log transform implies that the volatility of volatility rises with the level of volatility, even if v is time invariant. Finally, a negative correlation, $\rho < 0$, between the Wiener processes $W(t)$ and $W_\sigma(t)$ will induce an asymmetric return-volatility relationship in line with the leverage effect discussed earlier. As such, these features allow the representation in (4.16) to capture a number of stylized facts about asset return series quite parsimoniously.

Another popular nonaffine specification is the GARCH diffusion analyzed by Drost and Werker (1996). This representation can formally be shown to induce a GARCH type behavior for any discretely sampled price series and it is therefore a nice framework for eliciting and assessing information about the volatility process through data gathered at different sampling frequencies. This is also the process used in the construction of Figure 1. It takes the form

$$\begin{aligned} dp(t) &= \mu\,dt + \sigma(t)\,dW(t), \\ d\sigma^2(t) &= \beta\big(\alpha - \sigma^2(t)\big)\,dt + v\sigma^2(t)\,dW_\sigma(t), \end{aligned} \tag{4.17}$$

where the two Wiener processes are now independent.

The SV diffusions in (4.16) and (4.17) are but simple examples of the increasingly complex multi-factor (affine as well as nonaffine) jump-diffusions considered in the literature. Such models are hard to estimate by standard likelihood or method of moments techniques. This renders their use in forecasting particularly precarious. There is a need for both reliable parameter estimates and reliable extraction of the values for the underlying state variables. In particular, the current value of the state vector (and thus volatility) constitutes critical conditioning information for volatility prediction. The usefulness of such specifications for volatility forecasting is therefore directly linked to the availability of efficient inference methods for these models.

4.1.3. Estimation and forecasting issues in SV models

The incorporation of a latent volatility process in SV models has two main consequences. First, estimation cannot be performed through a direct application of maximum likelihood principles. Many alternative procedures will involve an efficiency loss relative to this benchmark so model parameter uncertainty may then be larger. Since forecasting is usually made conditional on point estimates for the parameters, this will tend to worsen the predictive ability of model based forecasts. Second, since the current state for volatility is not observed, there is an additional layer of uncertainty surrounding forecasts made conditional on the estimated state of volatility. We discuss these issues below and the following sections then review two alternative estimation and forecasting procedures developed, in part, to cope with these challenges.

Formally, the SV likelihood function is given as follows. Let the vector of return (innovations) and volatilities over $[0, T]$ be denoted by $\underline{r} = (r_1, \ldots, r_T)$ and $\underline{s} = (s_1, \ldots, s_T)$, respectively. Collecting the parameters in the vector θ, the probability density for the data given θ may then be written as

$$\begin{aligned} f(\underline{r}; \theta) &= \int f(\underline{r}, \underline{s}; \theta)\, \mathrm{d}\underline{s} = \prod_{t=1}^{T} f(r_t \mid \Im_{t-1}; \theta) \\ &= \prod_{t=1}^{T} \int f(r_t \mid s_t; \theta) f(s_t \mid \Im_{t-1}; \theta)\, \mathrm{d}s_t. \end{aligned} \tag{4.18}$$

For parametric discrete-time SV models, the conditional density $f(r_t \mid s_t, \theta)$ is typically known in closed form, but $f(s_t \mid \Im_{t-1}; \theta)$ is not available. Without being able to utilize this decomposition, we face an integration over the full unobserved volatility vector which is a T-dimensional object and generally not practical to compute given the serial dependence in the latent volatility process.

The initial response to these problems was to apply alternative estimation procedures. In his original treatment Taylor (1986) uses moment matching. Later, Andersen (1994) shows that it is feasible to estimate a broad class of discrete-time SV models through standard GMM procedures. However, this is not particularly efficient as the unconditional moments that may be expressed in closed form are quite different from the (efficient) score moments associated with the (infeasible) likelihood function. Another issue with GMM estimates is the need to extract estimates of the state variables if it is to serve as a basis for volatility forecasting. GMM does not provide any direct identification of the state variables, so this must be addressed in a second step. In that regard, the Kalman filter was often used. This technique allows for sequential estimation of parameters and latent state variables. As such, it provides a conceptual basis for the analysis, even if the basic Kalman filter is inadequate for general nonlinear and non-Gaussian SV models.

Nelson (1988) first suggested casting the SV estimation problem in a state space setting. We illustrate the approach for the simplest version of the log-SV model without a leverage effect, that is, $\rho = 0$ in (4.4) and (4.6). Now, squaring the expression in (4.3), takings logs and assuming Gaussian errors in the transition equation for the volatility state in Equation (4.6), it follows that

$$\begin{aligned} \log r_t^2 &= \log s_t + \log z_t^2, \quad z_t \sim \text{i.i.d. } N(0, 1), \\ \log s_{t+1} &= \eta_0 + \eta_1 \log s_t + u_t, \quad u_t \sim \text{i.i.d. } N\big(0, \sigma_u^2\big). \end{aligned}$$

To conform with standard notation, it is useful to consolidate the constant from the transition equation into the measurement equation for the log-squared return residual. Defining $h_t \equiv \log s_t$, we have

$$\log r_t^2 = \omega + h_t + \xi_t, \quad \xi_t \sim \text{i.i.d. } (0, 4.93),$$
$$h_{t+1} = \eta h_t + u_t, \quad u_t \sim \text{i.i.d. } N\big(0, \sigma_u^2\big), \tag{4.19}$$

where $\omega = \eta_0 + E(\log z_t^2) = \eta_0 - 1.27$, $\eta = \eta_1$, and ξ_t is a demeaned log χ^2 distributed error term. The system in (4.19) is given in the standard linear state space format. The top equation provides the measurement equation where the squared return is linearly related to the latent underlying volatility state and an i.i.d. skewed and heavy tailed error term. The bottom equation provides the transition equation for the model and is given as a first-order Gaussian autoregression.

The Kalman filter applies directly to (4.19) by assuming Gaussian errors; see, e.g., Harvey (1989, 2006). However, the resultant estimators of the state variables and the future observations are only minimum mean-squared error for estimators that are linear combinations of past $\log r_t^2$. Moreover, the non-Gaussian errors in the measurement equation implies that the exact likelihood cannot be obtained from the associated prediction errors. Nonetheless, the Kalman filter may be used in the construction of QMLEs of the model parameters for which asymptotically valid inference is available, even if these estimates generally are fairly inefficient. Arguably, the most important insight from the state space representation is instead the inspiration it has provided for the development of more efficient estimation and forecasting procedures through nonlinear filtering techniques.

The state space representation directly focuses attention on the task of making inference regarding the latent state vector, i.e., for SV models the question of what we can learn about the current state of volatility. A comprehensive answer is provided by the solution to the *filtering problem*, i.e., the distribution of the state vector given the current information set, $f(s_t \mid \Im_t; \theta)$. Typically, this distribution is critical in obtaining the one-step-ahead volatility forecast,

$$f(s_t \mid \Im_{t-1}; \theta) = \int f(s_t \mid s_{t-1}; \theta) f(s_{t-1} \mid \Im_{t-1}; \theta) \, \mathrm{d}s_{t-1}, \tag{4.20}$$

where the first term in the integral is obtained directly from the transition equation in the state space representation. Once the one-step-ahead distribution has been determined, the task of constructing multiple-step-ahead forecasts is analogous to the corresponding problem under ARCH models where multi-period forecasts also generally depend upon the full distributional characterization of the model. A unique feature of the SV model is instead the *smoothing problem*, related to ex-post inference regarding the in-sample volatility given the set of observed returns over the full sample, $f(s_t \mid \Im_T; \theta)$, where $t \leqslant T$. At the end of the sample, either the filtering or smoothing solution can serve as the basis for out-of-sample volatility forecasts (for h a positive integer),

$$f(s_{T+h} \mid \Im_T; \theta) = \int f(s_{T+h} \mid s_T; \theta) f(s_T \mid \Im_T; \theta) \, \mathrm{d}s_T, \tag{4.21}$$

where, again, given the solution for $h = 1$, the problem of determining the multi-period forecasts is analogous to the situation with multi-period ARCH-based forecasts discussed in Section 3.6.

As noted, all of these conditional volatility distributions may in theory be derived in closed form under the linear Gaussian state space representation via the Kalman filter. Unfortunately, even the simplest SV model contains some non-Gaussian and/or nonlinear elements. Hence, standard filtering methods provide, at best, approximate solutions and they have generally been found to perform poorly in this setting, in turn necessitating alternative more specialized filtering and smoothing techniques. Moreover, we have deliberately focused on the discrete-time case above. For the continuous-time SV models, the complications are more profound as even the discrete one-period return distribution conditional on the initial volatility state typically is not known in closed form. Hence, not only is the last term on the extreme right of Equation (4.18) unknown, but the first term is also intractable, further complicating likelihood-based analysis. We next review two recent approaches that promise efficient inference more generally and also provide ways of extracting reliable estimates of the latent volatility state needed for forecasting purposes.

4.2. Efficient method of simulated moments procedures for inference and forecasting

The Efficient Method of Moments (EMM) procedure is the prime example of a Method of Simulated Moments (MSM) approach that has the potential to deliver efficient inference and produce credible volatility forecasting for general SV models. The intuition behind EMM is that, by traditional likelihood theory, the scores (the derivative of the log likelihood with respect to the parameter vector) provide efficient estimating moments. In fact, maximum likelihood is simply a just-identified GMM estimator based on the score (moment) vector. Hence, intuitively, from an efficiency point of view, one would like to approximate the score vector when choosing the GMM moments. Since the likelihood of SV models is intractable, the approach is to utilize a semi-nonparametric approximation to the log likelihood estimated in a first step to produce the moments. Next, one seeks to match the approximating score moments with the corresponding moments from a long simulation of the SV model. Thus, the main requirement for applicability of EMM is that the model can be simulated effectively and the system is stationary so that the requisite moments can be computed by simple averaging from a simulation of the system. Again, this idea, like the MCMC approach discussed in the next section, is, of course, applicable more generally, but for concreteness we will focus on estimation and forecasting with SV models for financial rate of returns.

More formally, let the sample of discretely observed returns be given by $\underline{r} = (r_1, r_2, \ldots, r_T)$. Moreover, let x_{t-1} denote the vector of relevant conditioning variables for the log-likelihood function at time t, and let $\underline{x} = (x_0, x_1, \ldots, x_{T-1})$. For simplicity, we assume a long string of prior return observations are the only components of $\underline{x}$, but other predetermined variables from an extended dynamic representation of the system may be incorporated as well. In the terminology of Equation (4.18), the complication is that the likelihood contribution from the tth return is not available, that is, $f(r_t \mid \Im_{t-1}; \theta) \equiv f(r_t \mid x_{t-1}; \theta)$ is unknown. The proposal is to instead approximate this density by a flexible semi-nonparametric (SNP) estimate using the full data sample. Without going into specifics, an appropriate procedure may be developed to obtain a close approximation to this conditional density within a class of SNP densities which are analytically tractable and allow for explicit computation of the associated score vector. The leading term will typically consist of a GARCH type model. Essentially, the information regarding the probabilistic structure available from the data is being encoded into an empirically tractable SNP representation, so that, for a large enough sample, we have

$$g(r_t \mid x_{t-1}; \hat{\eta}_T) \approx f(r_t \mid \Im_{t-1}; \theta_0), \tag{4.22}$$

where $g(r_t \mid x_{t-1}; \hat{\eta}_T)$ denotes the fitted SNP density evaluated at the (pseudo) maximum likelihood estimate $\hat{\eta}_T$, and θ_0 denotes the true (unknown) parameter vector of the model generating the data under the null hypothesis. In general, the functional form of g is entirely different from the unknown f, and hence there is no direct compatibility between the two parameter vectors η and θ, although we require that the dimension of η is at least as large as that of θ. Notice how this SNP representation sidesteps the lack of a tractable expression for the likelihood contribution as given by the middle term in the likelihood expression in (4.18). Although the SNP density is not used for formal likelihood estimation, it is used to approximate the "efficient" score moments.

By construction, $\hat{\eta}_T$ satisfies a set of first order conditions for the pseudo log-likelihood function under the empirical measure induced by the data, that is, letting $\underline{r}_t = (r_t, x_{t-1})$, it holds that

$$\frac{1}{T}\sum_{t=1}^{T} \frac{\partial}{\partial \eta} \log g(r_t \mid x_{t-1}; \hat{\eta}_T) \equiv \frac{1}{T}\sum_{t=1}^{T} \psi_T(\underline{r}_t) = 0. \tag{4.23}$$

It is clear that (4.23) takes the form of (pseudo) score moments. This representation of the data through a set of (efficient) moment conditions is the key part of the "projection step" of EMM. The data structure has effectively been projected onto an analytically tractable class of SNP densities augmented, as appropriate, by a leading dynamic (GARCH) term.

Since we are working under the assumption that we have a good approximation to the underlying true conditional density, we would intuitively expect that, for T large,

$$E_{\theta_0}\big[\psi_T(\tilde{r})\big] \approx \frac{1}{M}\sum_{i=1}^{M} \psi_T(\underline{\tilde{r}}_i) \approx \frac{1}{T}\sum_{t=1}^{T} \psi_T(\underline{r}_t) = 0, \tag{4.24}$$

and any large artificial sample, $\underline{\tilde{r}} = (\tilde{r}_1, \tilde{r}_2, \ldots, \tilde{r}_N, \tilde{x}_0, \tilde{x}_1, \ldots, \tilde{x}_{M-1})$, generated by the same assumed (true) data generating process, $f(r_t \mid \Im_{t-1}; \theta_0)$, that is behind the observed return data, $\underline{r}$. These conjectures are formalized by Gallant and Tauchen (1996), who show how the pseudo score moments obtained in (4.23) by fixing $\hat{\eta}_T$ can serve as valid (and efficient) moment conditions for estimating the parameter of interest, θ. Since no analytic expression for the expectation on the extreme left in (4.24) is available, they propose a simulation estimator where the expectation is approximated arbitrarily well by a very large simulated sample moment ($M \gg T$) from the true underlying model. The ability to practically eliminate the simulation error renders the EMM estimator (in theory) independent of simulation size, M, but the uncertainty associated with the projection step, for which the sample size is constrained by the actual data, remains and the estimator, $\hat{\theta}_T$, is asymptotically normal with standard errors that reflects the estimation uncertainty in (4.23).

An obvious attraction of the EMM technique, beyond the potential for efficient inference, is that there are almost no restrictions on the underlying parametric model apart from stationarity and the ability to be able to simulate effectively from the model. This implies that the procedure can be used for continuous-time processes, even if we only observe a set of discretely sampled data. A seemingly important drawback, however, is the lack of any implied estimates of the underlying latent state variables which are critical for successful forecasting. Gallant and Tauchen (1998) provides a solution within the EMM setting through the so-called reprojection technique, but the procedure can be used more widely in parametric dynamic latent variable model estimated by other means as well.

Reprojection takes the parameter estimate of the system as given, i.e., the EMM estimator for θ in the current context. It is then feasible to generate arbitrarily long simulated series of observable and latent variables. These simulated series can be used for estimation of the conditional density via a SNP density function approximation as under the projection step described above. In other words, the identical procedure is exploited but now for a long simulated series from the null model rather than for the observed data sample. For illustration, let $\underline{\tilde{r}} = (\tilde{r}_1, \tilde{r}_2, \ldots, \tilde{r}_N, \tilde{x}_0, \tilde{x}_1, \ldots, \tilde{x}_{M-1})$ be a long simulated series from the null model, $f(r_i \mid \mathcal{F}_{i-1}; \hat{\theta}_T)$, where we condition on the EMM estimate. We may then utilize the SNP density estimate based on the simulated sample, $g(\tilde{r}_t \mid \tilde{x}_{t-1}; \tilde{\eta})$, in lieu of the unknown density for practical calculations, where the point estimate, $\tilde{\eta}$, is treated as independent of the sample size M since the estimation error is negligible for a sufficiently large simulated sample. In effect, the simulations integrate out the latent variables in the representation (4.5). Given the tractability of the SNP densities, we can now evaluate the one-step-ahead conditional mean and variance (or any other moments of interest) directly as a function of any observed history x_{t-1} by simply plugging into the SNP density estimate and perform the integration analytically – this is the reprojection step of recombining the SNP density with the actual data. Clearly, the corresponding multi-step ahead conditional density estimates can be constructed in an analogous fashion. Moreover, since the simulations also generate contemporaneous values for the latent state vectors we may similarly represent the conditional distributions of future latent state variables given the current and past observable variables through the SNP density approximation strategy,

$$f\big(\tilde{s}_{t+j} \mid \tilde{x}_t; \hat{\theta}_T\big) \approx g(\tilde{s}_{t+j} \mid \tilde{x}_t; \tilde{\eta}), \quad j \geqslant 0. \tag{4.25}$$

This allows for direct forecasts of conditional volatility and associated quantities in a genuine SV setting. As such, reprojection may be interpreted as a numerically intensive, simulation-based, nonlinear Kalman filtering technique, providing a practical solution to the filtering and forecasting problems in Equations (4.20) and (4.21).

4.3. Markov Chain Monte Carlo (MCMC) procedures for inference and forecasting

The MCMC method represents a Bayesian approach to the high-dimensional inference problem implicit in the expression for the likelihood given in Equation (4.18). The approach was advocated as particularly well suited for analysis of the discrete SV model by Jacquier, Polson and Rossi (1994). Beyond the standard Bayesian perspective of treating the model parameters as random variables rather than fixed coefficients, the main conceptual shift is that the entire latent state vector is treated as additional parameters. Hence, the main focus is on the joint distribution of the parameters and the vector of state variables, $\psi = (\theta, \underline{s})$, conditional on the data, $f(\psi \mid \underline{r})$, termed the posterior distribution. This density is extremely high dimensional and analytically intractable. The MCMC approach instead exploits that the joint distribution can be characterized fully through a set of associated conditional distributions where the density for a group of parameters, or even a single parameter, is expressed conditional on the remaining parameters. Concretely, let ψ_i denote the ith group of coefficients in ψ, and ψ_{-I} be the vector obtained from ψ by excluding the ith group of coefficients. The so-called Clifford–Hammersley theorem then implies that the following set of conditional distributions determines $f(\psi \mid \underline{r})$:

$$f(\psi_1 \mid \psi_{-1}, \underline{r}),\ f(\psi_2 \mid \psi_{-2}, \underline{r}),\ \ldots,\ f(\psi_k \mid \psi_{-k}, \underline{r}), \tag{4.26}$$

where, as described above, $\psi = (\psi_1, \psi_2, \ldots, \psi_k)$ is treated as k exclusive subsets of parameters.

The MCMC procedure starts by initializing $\psi = (\theta, \underline{s})$ through conditioning on the observed data, $\underline{r}$, and drawing ψ from the assumed prior distribution. Next, by combining the current draw for the parameter vector with the specified SV model dynamics and the observed returns, it is often feasible to draw the (group of) parameters sequentially conditional on the remainder of the system and cycle through the conditional densities in (4.26). A full run through the parameter vector is termed a sweep of the MCMC sampler. Some of these distributions may not be given in closed form and the draws may need to be extended through an accept–reject procedure termed a Metropolis–Hastings algorithm to ensure that the resulting Markov chain produces draws from the invariant joint posterior target distribution. If all the conditional distributions can be sampled directly we have a Gibbs sampler, but SV models often call for the two techniques to be used at different stages of the sweep, resulting in a hybrid MCMC algorithm. Typically, a large number of sweeps is necessary to overcome the serial dependence inherent in draws of any parameter from subsequent sweeps of the sampler. Once a long sample from the joint posterior distribution has been generated, inference on individual parameters and latent state variables can be done via the mode, mean and standard deviation of the posterior distribution, for example. Likewise, we can analyze properties of functions of the state variables directly using the posterior distribution.

A key advantage of the MCMC procedure is that the distribution of the latent state vector is obtained as an inherent part of the estimation. Moreover, the inference automatically accounts for the uncertainty regarding model parameters, θ. The resulting chain produces an elegant solution to the smoothing problem of determining $f(\underline{s} \mid \underline{r})$. Of course, from a forecasting perspective, the interest is in determining $f(s_{t+j} \mid \underline{x}_t)$, where the integer $j \geqslant 0$ and $\underline{x}_t = (r_1, r_2, \ldots, r_t)$, rather than $f(s_{t+j} \mid \underline{x}_T)$ which is generated by the MCMC procedure. Unfortunately, the filter related distribution, $f(s_{t+1} \mid \underline{x}_t)$, corresponds to the intractable term in Equation (4.18) that renders the likelihood estimation impractical for genuine SV models. The MCMC inference procedure succeeds by sidestepping the need to compute this quantity. However, given the economic import of the issue, recent research is actively seeking new effective ways for better handling the filtering problem within the MCMC framework.

For a discrete-time SV model, the possibility of filtering as well as sequential one-step-ahead volatility forecasting is linked to the feasibility of providing an effective scheme to generate a random sample from $f(s_{t+1} \mid \underline{x}_t, \theta)$ given an existing set of draws (or *particles*), $s_t^1, s_t^2, \ldots, s_t^N$, from the preceding distribution $f(s_t \mid \underline{x}_{t-1}, \theta)$. Such an algorithm is termed a *particle filter*. In order to recognize the significance of the particle filter, note that by Bayes' law,

$$f(s_{t+1} \mid \underline{x}_{t+1}, \theta) \propto f(r_{t+1} \mid s_{t+1}, \theta) f(s_{t+1} \mid \underline{x}_t, \theta). \tag{4.27}$$

The first distribution on the right-hand side is typically specified directly by the SV model, so the issue of determining the filtering distribution on the left-hand side is essentially equivalent to the task of obtaining the predictive distribution of the state variable on the extreme right. But given a large set of particles we can approximate the latter term in straightforward fashion,

$$\begin{aligned} f(s_{t+1} \mid \underline{x}_t, \theta) &= \int f(s_{t+1} \mid s_t, \theta) f(s_t \mid \underline{x}_t, \theta)\, \mathrm{d}s_t \\ &\approx \frac{1}{M} \sum_{j=1}^{M} f\bigl(s_{t+1} \mid s_t^j, \theta\bigr). \end{aligned} \tag{4.28}$$

This provides a direct solution to the latent state vector forecasting problem, that in turn can be plugged into (4.27) to provide a sequential update to the particle filter. This in essence is the MCMC answer to the filtering and out-of-sample forecasting problems in Equations (4.20) and (4.21). The main substantive problem is how to best sample from the last distribution in (4.28), as schemes which may appear natural can be very inefficient; see, e.g., the discussion and suggestions in Kim, Shephard and Chib (1998).

In summary, the MCMC approach works well for many problems of significant interest, but there are serious issues under scrutiny concerning the use of the technique for more complex settings. When applicable, it has some unique advantages such as providing a complete solution to the smoothing problem and accounting for inherent parameter estimation uncertainty. On the other hand, there are systems that are more amenable to analysis under EMM and the associated diagnostic tools and general reprojection procedures under EMM render it a formidable contender. It is remarkable that the issues of efficient forecasting and filtering within genuine SV models now has two attractive, albeit computationally intensive, solutions whereas just a few years ago no serious approach to the problem existed.

4.4. *Further reading*

The formal distinction between *genuine* stochastic volatility and ARCH models is developed in Andersen (1992); see also Fleming and Kirby (2003). An early advocate for the Mixture-of-Distributions-Hypothesis (MDH), beyond Clark (1973), is Praetz (1972) who shows that an i.i.d. mixture of a Gaussian term and an inverted Gamma distribution for the variance will produce Student t distributed returns. However, if the variance mixture is not linked to observed variables, the i.i.d. mixture is indistinguishable from a standard fat-tailed error distribution and the associated volatility process is not part of the genuinely stochastic volatility class.

Many alternative representations of the driving process s_t have been proposed. Clark (1973) observes that trading volume is highly correlated with return volatility and suggest that volume may serve as a good proxy for the "activity variable", s_t. Moreover, he finds volume to be approximately lognormal (unconditionally), suggesting a lognormal–normal mixture for the return distribution. One drawback of this formulation is that daily trading volume is assumed i.i.d. Not only is this counterfactual for trading volume, but it also implies that the return process is i.i.d. This is at odds with the strong empirical evidence of pronounced temporal dependence in return volatility. A number of natural extensions arise from the simple MDH. Tauchen and Pitts (1983) provide a more structural interpretation, as they develop a characterization of the joint distribution of the daily return and volume relationship governed by the underlying latent information flow s_t. However, partially for tractability, they retain the temporal independence of the information flow series. For early tests of the MDH model using high-frequency data [see, e.g., Harris (1986, 1987)], while the early return-volume literature is surveyed by Karpoff (1987). Gallant, Rossi and Tauchen (1992) provides an extensive study of the joint conditional distribution without imposing any MDH restrictions. Direct studies of the MDH include Lamoureux and Lastrapes (1994) and Richardson and Smith (1994). While the latter strongly rejects the standard MDH formulation, Andersen (1996) develops an alternative structurally based version of the hypothesis and finds the "modified" MDH to perform much better. Further refinements in the specification have been pursued by, e.g., Liesenfeld (1998, 2001) and Bollerslev and Jubinsky (1999). In principle, the use of additional nonreturn variables along with return data should enhance estimation efficiency and allow for a better assessment of current market conditions. On the other hand, it is far from obvious that structural modeling of complicated multivariate models will prove useful in a prediction context as even minor misspecification of the additional series in the system may impede forecast performance. In fact, there is no credible evidence yet that these models help improve volatility forecast performance, even if they have importantly enhanced our understanding of the qualitative functioning of financial markets.

SV diffusion models of the form analyzed by Hull and White (1987) were also proposed concurrently by Johnson and Shanno (1987), Scott (1987), and Wiggins (1987). An early specification and exploration of a pure jump continuous-time model is Merton (1976). Melino and Turnbull (1990) were among the first to estimate SV models via GMM. The log-SV model from (4.2)–(4.3) has emerged as a virtual testing ground for alternative inference procedures in this context. Andersen and Sørensen (1996) provide a systematic study of the choice of moments and weighting matrix for this particular model. The lack of efficiency is highlighted in Andersen, Chung and Sørensen (1999) where the identical model is estimated through the scores of an auxiliary model developed in accordance with the efficient method of moments (EMM) procedure. Another useful approach is to apply GMM to moment conditions in the spectral domain; see, e.g., Singleton (2001), Jiang and Knight (2002), and Chacko and Viceira (2003). Within the QMLE Kalman filter based approach, a leverage effect may be incorporated and allowance for the idiosyncratic return error to be conditionally Student t distributed can be made, as demonstrated by Harvey, Ruiz and Shephard (1994) and Harvey and Shephard (1996). Andersen and Sørensen (1997) provides an extensive discussion of the relative efficiency of QMLE and GMM for estimation of the discrete-time log-SV model. The issue of asymptotically optimal moment selection for GMM estimation from among absolute or log squared returns in the log-SV model has received a near definitive treatment in Dhaene and Vergote (2004). The standard log-SV model has also been estimated through a number of other techniques by among others Danielsson and Richard (1993), Danielsson (1994), Fridman and Harris (1998), Monfardini (1998), and Sandmann and Koopman (1998). Long memory in volatility as discussed in Section 3.4 can be similarly accommodated within an SV setting; see, e.g., Breidt, Crato and de Lima (1998), Harvey (1998), Comte and Renault (1998), and Deo and Hurvich (2001). Duffie, Pan and Singleton (2000) is a good reference for a general treatment of modeling with the so-called affine class of models, while Piazzesi (2005) provides a recent survey of these models with a view toward term structure applications.

EMM may be seen as a refinement of the Method of Simulated Moments (MSM) of Duffie and Singleton (1993), representing a particular choice of indirect inference criterion, or binding function, in the terminology of Gouriéroux, Monfort and Renault (1993). The approach also has precedents in Smith (1990, 1993). An early application of EMM techniques to the discrete-time SV model is Gallant, Hsieh and Tauchen (1997). Among the earliest papers using EMM for stochastic volatility models are Andersen and Lund (1997) and Gallant and Tauchen (1997). Extensions of the EMM approach to SV jump-diffusions are found in Andersen, Benzoni and Lund (2002) and Chernov et al. (2003). As a starting point for implementations of the EMM procedure, one may access general purpose EMM and SNP code from a web site maintained by A. Ronald Gallant and George E. Tauchen at Duke University at the link ftp.econ.duke.edu in the directories /pub/get/emm and /pub/arg/snp, respectively. In practical applications, it is often advantageous to further refine the SNP density approximations through specifically designed leading GARCH terms which parsimoneously capture the dependency structure in the specific data under investigation. The benefits of doing so is further discussed in Andersen and Lund (1997) and Andersen, Benzoni and Lund (2002).

The particle filter discussed above for the generation of filter estimates for the latent variables of interest within the standard SV model arguably provides a more versatile approach than the alternative importance sampling methods described by, e.g., Danielsson (1994) and Sandmann and Koopman (1998). The extension of the MCMC inference technique to a continuous-time setting is discussed in Elerian, Chib and Shephard (2001) and Eraker (2001). The latter also provides one of the first examples of MCMC estimation of an SV diffusion model, while Eraker, Johannes and Polson (2003) further introduces jumps in both prices and volatility. Johannes and Polson (2005) offer a recent comprehensive survey of the still ongoing research on the use of the MCMC approach in the general nonlinear jump-diffusion SV setting.

5. Realized volatility

The notion of realized volatility has at least two key distinct implications for practical volatility estimation and forecasting. The first relates to the measurement of realizations of the latent volatility process without the need to rely on an explicit model. As such, the realized volatility provides *the* natural benchmark for forecast evaluation purposes. The second relates to the possibility of modeling volatility directly through standard time series techniques with discretely sampled daily observations, while effectively exploiting the information in intraday high-frequency data.

5.1. The notion of realized volatility

The most fundamental feature of realized volatility is that it provides a consistent nonparametric estimate of the price variability that has transpired over a given discrete interval. Any log-price process subject to a no-arbitrage condition and weak auxiliary assumptions will constitute a semi-martingale that may be decomposed into a locally predictable mean component and a martingale with finite second moments. Within this class, there is a unique measure for the realized sample-path variation termed the quadratic variation. By construction the quadratic variation cumulates the intensity of the unexpected price changes over the specific horizon and it is thus a prime candidate for a formal volatility measure.

The intuition behind the use of realized volatility as a return variation measure is most readily conveyed within the popular continuous-time diffusion setting (4.9) obtained by ruling out jumps and thus reducing to the representation (1.7), reproduced here for convenience,

$$\mathrm{d}p(t) = \mu(t)\,\mathrm{d}t + \sigma(t)\,\mathrm{d}W(t), \qquad t \in [0, T]. \tag{5.1}$$

Applying a discretization of the process as in Section 1, we have for small $\Delta > 0$, that

$$r(t,\Delta) \equiv p(t) - p(t-\Delta) \simeq \mu(t-\Delta)\Delta + \sigma(t-\Delta)\,\Delta W(t), \tag{5.2}$$

where $\Delta W(t) \equiv W(t) - W(t-\Delta) \sim N(0,\Delta)$.

Over short intervals the squared return and the squared return innovation are closely related as both are largely determined by the idiosyncratic return component,

$$\begin{aligned} r^2(t,\Delta) &\simeq \mu^2(t-\Delta)\Delta^2 + 2\Delta\mu(t-\Delta)\sigma(t-\Delta)\,\Delta W(t) \\ &\quad + \sigma^2(t-\Delta)\big(\Delta W(t)\big)^2. \end{aligned} \tag{5.3}$$

In particular, the return variance is (approximately) equal to the expected squared return innovation,

$$\mathrm{Var}\big[r(t,\Delta) \mid \mathcal{F}_{t-\Delta}\big] \simeq E\big[r^2(t,\Delta) \mid \mathcal{F}_{t-\Delta}\big] \simeq \sigma^2(t-\Delta)\Delta. \tag{5.4}$$

This suggests that we may be able to measure the return volatility directly from the squared return observations. However, this feature is not of much direct use as the high-frequency returns have a large idiosyncratic component that induces a sizeable measurement error into the actual squared return relative to the underlying variance. Up to the dominant order in Δ,

$$\mathrm{Var}\big[r^2(t,\Delta) \mid \mathcal{F}_{t-\Delta}\big] \simeq 2\sigma^4(t-\Delta)\Delta^2, \tag{5.5}$$

where terms involving higher powers of Δ are ignored as they become negligible for small values of Δ. Thus, it follows that the "noise-to-signal" ratio in squared returns relative to the underlying volatility is of the same order as volatility itself,

$$\frac{\mathrm{Var}[r^2(t,\Delta) \mid \mathcal{F}_{t-\Delta}]}{E[r^2(t,\Delta) \mid \mathcal{F}_{t-\Delta}]} \simeq 2E\big[r^2(t,\Delta) \mid \mathcal{F}_{t-\Delta}\big]. \tag{5.6}$$

This relationship cannot be circumvented when only one (squared) return observation is used as a volatility proxy. Instead, by exploiting the fact that return innovations, under a no-arbitrage (semi-martingale) assumption, are serially uncorrelated to construct volatility measures for lower frequency returns we find, to dominant order in Δ,

$$\begin{aligned} \sum_{j=1}^{1/\Delta} E\big[r^2(t-1+j\cdot\Delta,\Delta) \mid \mathcal{F}_{t-1+j\cdot\Delta}\big] &\simeq \sum_{j=1}^{1/\Delta} \sigma^2(t-1+j\cdot\Delta)\cdot\Delta \\ &\simeq \int_{t-1}^{t} \sigma^2(s)\,\mathrm{d}s, \end{aligned} \tag{5.7}$$

where the last approximation stems from the sum converging to the corresponding integral as the size of Δ shrinks toward zero. Equation (5.7) generalizes (5.4) to the multi-period setting with the second approximation in (5.7) only being meaningful for Δ small.

The advantage of (5.7) is that the uncorrelated "measurement errors" have been effectively smoothed away to generate a much better noise-to-signal ratio. The expression in (5.5) may be extended in a similar manner to yield

$$\begin{aligned}\sum_{j=1}^{1/\Delta} \mathrm{Var}\big[r^2(t-1+j\cdot\Delta,\Delta) \mid \mathcal{F}_{t-1+j\cdot\Delta}\big] &\simeq 2\sum_{j=1}^{1/\Delta} \sigma^4(t-1+j\cdot\Delta)\cdot\Delta^2 \\ &\simeq 2\Delta\int_{t-1}^{t} \sigma^4(s)\,\mathrm{d}s. \end{aligned} \tag{5.8}$$

Consequently,

$$\begin{aligned}\frac{\sum_{j=1}^{1/\Delta} \mathrm{Var}[r^2(t-1+j\cdot\Delta,\Delta) \mid \mathcal{F}_{t-1+j\cdot\Delta}]}{\sum_{j=1}^{1/\Delta} E[r^2(t-1+j\cdot\Delta,\Delta) \mid \mathcal{F}_{t-1+j\cdot\Delta}]} &\simeq 2\Delta\frac{\int_{t-1}^{t}\sigma^4(s)\,\mathrm{d}s}{\int_{t-1}^{t}\sigma^2(s)\,\mathrm{d}s} \\ &\equiv 2\Delta\frac{\mathrm{IQ}(t)}{\mathrm{IV}(t)}, \end{aligned} \tag{5.9}$$

where the integrated quarticity is defined through the identity on the right-hand side of (5.9), with the integrated variance, $\mathrm{IV}(t)$, having previously been defined in (4.12).

The fact that the "noise-to-signal" ratio in (5.9) shrinks to zero with Δ suggests that high-frequency returns may be very useful for estimation of the underlying (integrated) volatility process. The notion of realized volatility is designed to take advantage of these features. Formally, realized volatility is defined as

$$\mathrm{RV}(t,\Delta) = \sum_{j=1}^{1/\Delta} r^2(t-1+j\cdot\Delta,\Delta). \tag{5.10}$$

Equation (5.8) suggests that realized volatility is consistent for the integrated volatility in the sense that finer and finer sampling of the intraday returns, $\Delta \to 0$, ultimately will annihilate the measurement error and, in the limit, realized volatility measures the latent integrated volatility perfectly, that is,

$$\mathrm{RV}(t,\Delta) \to \mathrm{IV}(t), \tag{5.11}$$

as $\Delta \to 0$. These arguments may indeed by formalized; see, e.g., the extended discussion in Andersen, Bollerslev and Diebold (2005). In reality, there is a definite lower bound on the return horizon that can be used productively for computation of the realized volatility, both because we only observe discretely sampled returns and, more important, market microstructure features such as discreteness of the price grid and bid–ask spreads induce gross violations of the semi-martingale property at the very highest return frequencies. This implies that we typically will be sampling returns at an intraday frequency that leaves a nonnegligible error term in the estimate of integrated volatility. It is natural to conjecture from (5.9) that asymptotically, as $\Delta \to 0$,

$$\sqrt{1/\Delta}\big[\mathrm{RV}(t,\Delta) - \mathrm{IV}(t)\big] \sim N\big(0, 2\cdot\mathrm{IQ}(t)\big), \tag{5.12}$$

which turns out to be true under quite general assumptions. Of course, the $\mathrm{IQ}(t)$ measure must be estimated as well for the above result to provide a practical tool for inference.

The distributional result in (5.12) and a feasible consistent estimator for $\mathrm{IQ}(t)$ based purely on intraday data have been provided by Barndorff-Nielsen and Shephard (2002, 2004b). It may further be shown that these measurement errors are approximately uncorrelated across consecutive periods which has important simplifying implications for time series modeling.

The consistency result in (5.11) extends to the general semi-martingale setting where the price path may display discontinuities due to jumps, as specified in Equation (4.9). The realized volatility will still converge in the continuous-record limit ($\Delta \to 0$) to the period-by-period quadratic variation of the semi-martingale. However, the quadratic variation is no longer identical to the integrated volatility but will also include the cumulative squared jumps,

$$\mathrm{RV}(t, \Delta) \to \mathrm{QV}(t) = \int_{t-1}^{t} \sigma^2(s)\, \mathrm{d}s + \sum_{t-1<s\leqslant t} \kappa^2(s). \tag{5.13}$$

A few comments are in order. First, $\mathrm{QV}(t)$ is best interpreted as the actual return variation that transpired over the period, and as such it is the natural target for realized volatility measurement. Second, $\mathrm{QV}(t)$ is the realization of a random variable which generally cannot be forecasted with certainty at time $t-1$. But it does represent the future realization that volatility forecasts for time t should be compared against. In other words, the quadratic variation constitutes *the* quantity of interest in volatility measurement and forecasting. Since the realizations of $\mathrm{QV}(t)$ are latent, it is natural to use the observed $\mathrm{RV}(t, \Delta)$ as a feasible proxy. Third, financial decision making is concerned with forecasts of volatility (or quadratic variation) rather than the $\mathrm{QV}(t)$ directly. Fourth, the identification of forecasts of return volatility with forecasts of quadratic variation is only approximate as it ignores variation in the process induced by innovations in the conditional mean process. Over short horizons the distinction is negligible, but for longer run volatility prediction (quarterly or annual) one may need to pay some attention to the discrepancy between the two quantities, as discussed at length in Andersen, Bollerslev and Diebold (2005).

The distribution theory for quadratic variation under the continuous sample path assumption has also been extended to cover cumulative absolute returns raised to an arbitrary power. The leading case involves cumulating the high-frequency absolute returns. These quantities display improved robustness properties relative to realized volatility as the impact of outliers are mitigated. Although the limiting quantity – the power variation – is not directly linked to the usual volatility measure of interest in finance, this concept has inspired further theoretical developments that has led to intriguing new nonparametric tests for the presence of jumps and the identification of the associated jump sizes; see, e.g., Barndorff-Nielsen and Shephard (2004a). Since the jumps may have very different intertemporal persistence characteristics than the diffusion volatility, explicit disentangling of the components of quadratic variation corresponding to jumps versus diffusion volatility can have important implications for volatility forecasting.

In summary, the notion of realized volatility represents a model-free approach to (continuous-record) consistent estimation of the quadratic return variation under general assumptions based primarily upon arbitrage-free financial markets. As such it allows us to harness the information inherent in high-frequency returns for assessment of lower frequency return volatility. It is thus *the* natural approach to measuring actual (ex-post) realized return variation over a given horizon. This perspective has now gained widespread acceptance in the literature, where alternative volatility forecast models are routinely assessed in terms of their ability to explain the distribution of subsequent realized volatility, as defined above.

5.2. Realized volatility modeling

The realized volatility is by construction an observed proxy for the underlying quadratic variation and the associated (measurement) errors are uncorrelated. This suggests a straightforward approach where the temporal features of the series are modeled through standard time series techniques, letting the data guide the choice of the appropriate distributional assumptions and the dynamic representation. This is akin to the standard procedure for modeling macroeconomic data where the underlying quantities are measured (most likely with a substantial degree of error) and then treated as directly observed variables.

The strategy of estimating time series models directly for realized volatility is advocated in a sequence of papers by Andersen et al. (2001a, 2001b, 2003). A striking finding is that the realized volatility series share fundamental statistical properties across different asset classes, time periods, and countries. The evidence points strongly toward a long-memory type of dependency in volatility. Moreover, the logarithmic realized volatility series is typically much closer to being homoskedastic and approximately unconditionally Gaussian. These features are readily captured through an ARFIMA$(p, d, 0)$ representation of the logarithmic realized volatility,

$$\Phi(L)(1 - L)^d \bigl(\log \mathrm{RV}(t, \Delta) - \mu_0\bigr) = u_t, \quad t = 1, 2, \ldots, T, \tag{5.14}$$

where $(1 - L)^d$ denotes the fractional differencing operator, $\Phi(L)$ is a polynomial lag operator accounting for standard autoregressive structure, μ_0 represents the unconditional mean of the logarithmic realized volatility, and u_t is a white noise error term that is (approximately) Gaussian. The coefficient d usually takes a value around 0.40, consistent with a stationary but highly persistent volatility process for which shocks only decay at a slow hyperbolic rate rather than the geometric rate associated with standard ARMA models or GARCH models for the conditional variance. Finally, the volatility of volatility is strongly increasing in the level of volatility as log-realized volatility is approximately homoskedastic. This is, of course, reminiscent of the log-SV and the EGARCH models.

A number of practical modeling issues have been sidestepped above. One is the choice of the sampling frequency at which the realized volatility measures are constructed. The early literature focused primarily on determining the highest intraday frequency at which the underlying returns satisfy the maintained semi-martingale assumption of being approximately uncorrelated. An early diagnostic along these lines termed the "volatility signature plot" was developed by Andersen et al. (1999, 2000), as discussed further in Section 7 below. A simple alternative is to apply standard ARMA filtering to the high-frequency returns in order to strip them of any "artificial" serial correlation induced by the market microstructure noise, and then proceed with the filtered uncorrelated returns in lieu of the raw high-frequency returns. While none of these procedures are optimal in a formal statistical sense, they both appear to work reasonable well in many practical situations. Meanwhile, a number of alternative more efficient sampling schemes under various assumptions about the market microstructure complications have recently been proposed in a series of interesting papers, and this is still very much ongoing research.

A second issue concerns the potential separation of jumps and diffusive volatility components in the realized volatility process. The theoretical basis for these procedures and some initial empirical work is presented in Barndorff-Nielsen and Shephard (2004a). The issue has been pursued empirically by Andersen, Bollerslev and Diebold (2003), who find compelling evidence that the diffusive volatility is much more persistent than the jump component. In fact, the jumps appear close to i.i.d., although the jumps in equity indices display some clustering, especially in the size of the jumps. This points to potentially important improvements in modeling and forecasting from this type of separation of the realized volatility into sudden discrete shifts in prices versus more permanent fluctuations in the intensity of the regular price movements. Empirically, this is in line with the evidence favoring non-Gaussian fat-tailed return innovations in ARCH models.

A third issue is the approach used to best accommodate the indications of "long memory". An alternative to fractional integration is to introduce several autoregressive volatility components into the model. As discussed in the context of the GARCH class of models in Section 3.4, if the different components display strong, but varying, degrees of persistence they may combine to produce a volatility dependency structure that is indistinguishable from long memory over even relatively long horizons.

5.3. Realized volatility forecasting

Forecasting is straightforward once the realized volatility has been cast within the traditional time series framework and the model parameters have been estimated. Since the driving variable is the realized volatility we no longer face a latent variable issue. This implies that standard methods for forecasting a time series within the ARFIMA framework is available; see, e.g., Beran (1994) for an introduction to models incorporating long-memory features. One-step-ahead minimum mean-squared error forecasts are readily produced, and within the linear Gaussian setting it is then legitimate to further condition on the forecast in order to iterate forward and produce multiple-step-ahead forecasts. There are a couple of caveats, however. First, as with most other volatility forecasting procedures, the forecasts are, of course, conditional on the point estimate for the model parameters. Second, if the model is formulated in terms of the logarithmic volatility then it is also log volatility that is being predicted through the usual forecast procedures. There is a practical problem of converting the forecast for log volatility into a "pure" volatility forecast as the expected value of the transformed variable depends not only on the expected log volatility, but on the entire multiple-step-ahead conditional distribution of log volatility. For short horizons this is not an issue as the requisite correction term usually is negligible, but for longer horizons adjustments may be necessary. This is similar to the issue that arise in the construction of forecast form the EGARCH model. As discussed in Section 3.6, the required correction term may be constructed by simulation based methods, but the preferred approach will depend on the application at hand and the distributional characteristics of the model. For additional inspiration on how to address such issues consult, e.g., Chapter 6 on ARMA forecasting methods by Lütkepohl (2006) in this handbook.

A few additional comments are in order. First, the evidence in Andersen, Bollerslev and Diebold (2005) indicates that the above approach has very good potential. The associated forecasts for foreign exchange rate volatility outperform a string of alternative candidate models from the literature. This is not a tautology as it should be preferable to generate the forecasts from the true underlying model rather than an ad hoc time series model estimated from period-by-period observations of realized volatility. In other words, if a GARCH diffusion is the true model then optimal forecasts would incorporate the restrictions implied by this model. However, the high-frequency volatility process is truly complex, possessing several periodic components, erratic short run dynamics and longer run persistence features that combined appear beyond reach of simple parametric models. The empirical evidence suggests that daily realized volatility serves as a simple, yet effective, aggregator of the volatility information inherent in the intraday data.

Second, there is an issue of how to compute realized volatility for a calendar period when the trading day is limited by an official closing. This problem is minor for the over-the-counter foreign exchange market where 24-hour trading is observed, but this is often not the case for equity or bond markets. For example, for a one-month-ahead equity volatility forecast there may only be twenty-two trading days with about six-and-a-half hours of trading per day. But the underlying price process is not stalled while the markets are closed. Oftentimes there will be substantial changes in prices between one market close and the subsequent opening, reflecting return volatility overnight and over the weekend. One solution is to simply rely on the intraday returns for a realized volatility measure over the trading day and then scale this quantity up by a factor that reflects the average ratio of volatility over the calendar day versus the trading day. This may work quite satisfactorily in practice, but it obviously ignores the close-to-open return for a given day entirely in constructing the realized volatility for that calendar day. Alternatively, the volatility of the close-to-open return may be modeled by a conventional GARCH type model.

Third, we have not discussed the preferred sampling frequency of intraday returns in situations where the underlying asset is relatively illiquid. If updated price observations are only available intermittently throughout the trading day, many high-frequency returns may have to be computed from prices or quotes earlier in the day. This brings up a couple of issues. One, the effective sampling frequency is lower than the one that we are trying to use for the realized volatility computation. Two, illiquid price series also tend to have larger bid–ask spreads and be more sensitive to random fluctuations in order flow, implying that the associated return series will contain a relatively large amount of noise. A simple response that will help alleviate both issues is to lower the sampling frequency. However, with the use of less intraday returns comes a larger measurement error in realized volatility, as evidenced by Equation (5.12). Nonetheless, for an illiquid asset it may only be possible to construct meaningful weekly rather than daily realized volatility measures from say half-hourly or hourly return observations rather than five-minute returns. Consequently, the intertemporal fluctuations are smoothed out so that the observed measure carries less information about the true state of the volatility at the end of the period. This, of course, can be critically important for accurate forecasting.

In sum, the use of the realized volatility measures for forecasting is still in its infancy and many issues must be explored in future work. However, it is clear that the use of intraday information has large potential to improve upon the performance of standard volatility forecast procedures based only on daily or lower frequency data. The realized volatility approach circumvents the need to model the intraday data directly and thus provides a great deal of simplification. Importantly, it seems to achieve this objective without sacrificing a lot of efficiency. For example, Andersen, Bollerslev and Meddahi (2004) find the time series approach built directly from the realized volatility measures to be very good approximations to the theoretically optimal procedures in a broad class of SV diffusion models that can be analyzed analytically through newly developed tools associated with the so-called Eigenfunction SV models of Meddahi (2001). Nonetheless, if the objective exclusively is volatility forecasting, some very recent work suggests that alternative intraday measures may carry even more empirically relevant information regarding future volatility, including the power variation measures constructed from cumulative absolute returns; see, e.g., Ghysels, Santa-Clara and Valkanov (2004). This likely reflects superior robustness features of absolute versus squared intraday returns, but verification of such conjectures awaits future research. The confluence of compelling empirical performance, novel econometric theory, the availability of ever more high-frequency data and computational power, and the importance of forecast performance for decision making render this approach fertile ground for new research.

5.4. *Further reading*

The realized volatility approach has a precedent in the use of cumulative daily squared returns as monthly volatility measures; see, e.g., French, Schwert and Stambaugh (1987) and Schwert (1989). Hsieh (1989) was among the first to informally apply this same procedure with high-frequency intraday returns, while Zhou (1996) provides one of the earliest formal assessments of the relationship between cumulative squared intraday returns and the underlying return variance, albeit in a highly stylized setting. The pioneering work by Olsen & Associates on the use of high-frequency data, as summarized in Dacorogna et al. (2001), also importantly paved the way for many of the more recent empirical developments in the realized volatility area.

The use of component structures and related autoregressive specifications for approximating long-memory dependencies within the realized volatility setting has been explored by Andersen, Bollerslev and Diebold (2003), Barndorff-Nielsen and Shephard (2001), Bollerslev and Wright (2001), and Corsi (2003), among others. The finite sample performance of alternative nonparametric tests for jumps based on the bipower variation measure introduced by Barndorff-Nielsen and Shephard (2004a) have been extensively analyzed by Huang and Tauchen (2004). Andersen, Bollerslev and Diebold (2003) demonstrate the importance of disentangling the components of quadratic variation corresponding to jumps versus diffusion volatility for volatility forecasting. The complexities involved in a direct high-frequency characterization of the volatility process is also illustrated by Andersen and Bollerslev (1998c).

Ways of incorporating noisy overnight returns into the daily realized volatility measure are discussed in Fleming, Kirby and Ostdiek (2003) and Hansen and Lunde (2004a). The related issue of measuring the integrated variance in the presence of market microstructure noise and how to best use all of the available high frequency data has been addressed in a rapidly growing recent literature. Corsi et al. (2001) argue for the use of exponential moving average filtering, similar to a standard MA(1) filter for the high-frequency returns, while other more recent procedures, including sub-sampling and ways of choosing the "optimal" sampling frequency, have been suggested and analyzed empirically by, e.g., Aït-Sahalia, Mykland and Zhang (2005), Bandi and Russell (2004), Barucci and Reno (2002), Bollen and Inder (2002), Curci and Corsi (2004), and Hansen and Lunde (2004b), among others. Some of these issues are discussed further in Section 7 below, where we also consider the robust alternative range based volatility estimator recently explored by Alizadeh, Brandt and Diebold (2002) for dynamic volatility modeling and forecasting.

Implied volatility provides yet another forward looking volatility measure. Implied volatilities are based on the market's forecasts of future volatilities extracted from the prices of options written on the asset of interest. As discussed in Section 2.2.4 above, using a specific option pricing formula, one may infer the expected integrated volatility of the underlying asset over the remaining time-to-maturity of the option. The main complication associated with the use of these procedures lies in the fact that the option prices also generally reflect a volatility risk premium in the realistic scenario where the volatility risk cannot be perfectly hedged; see, e.g., the discussion in Bollerslev and Zhou (2005). Nonetheless, many studies find options implied volatilities to provide useful information regarding the future volatility of the underlying asset. At the same time, the results pertaining to the forecast performance of implied volatilities are somewhat mixed, and there is still only limited evidence regarding the relative predictive power of implied volatilities versus the realized volatility procedures discussed above. Another issue is that many assets of interest do not have sufficiently active options markets that reliable implied volatilities can be computed on, say, a daily basis.

6. Multivariate volatility and correlation

The discussion in the preceding three sections has been focused almost exclusively on univariate forecasts. Yet, as discussed in Section 2, in many practical situations covariance and/or correlation forecasting plays an equal, if not even more important, role in the uses of volatility forecasts. Fortunately, many of the same ideas and procedures discussed in the context of univariate forecasts are easily adapted to the multivariate setting. However, two important complications arise in this setting, namely the imposition of sufficient conditions to ensure that the forecasts for the covariance matrix remain positive definite for all forecasting horizons, and, second, maintaining an empirically realistic yet parsimoniously parameterized model. We will organize our discussion of the various multivariate approaches with these key concerns in mind.

Before turning to this discussion, it is worth noting that in many situations, multivariate volatility modeling and forecasting may be conveniently sidestepped through the use of much-simpler-to-implement univariate procedures for appropriately transformed series. In particular, in the context of financial market volatility forecasting, consider the leading case involving the variance of a portfolio made up of N individual assets. In the notation of Section 2.2.1 above,

$$r_{w,t+1} = \sum_{i=1}^{N} w_{i,t} r_{i,t+1} \equiv w_t' R_{t+1}. \tag{6.1}$$

The conditional one-step-ahead variance of the portfolio equals

$$\sigma_{w,t+1|t}^2 = \sum_{i=1}^{N} \sum_{j=1}^{N} w_{i,t} w_{j,t} \{\Omega_{t+1|t}\}_{i,j} = w_t' \Omega_{t+1|t} w_t, \tag{6.2}$$

where $\Omega_{t+1|t}$ denotes the $N \times N$ covariance matrix for the returns. A forecast for the portfolio return variance based upon this representation therefore requires the construction of multivariate forecasts for the $\frac{1}{2}N(N+1)$ unique elements in the covariance matrix for the assets in the portfolio. Alternatively, define the univariate time series of artificial historical portfolio returns constructed on the basis of the weights for the current portfolio in place,

$$r_{w,\tau}^t \equiv w_t' R_\tau, \quad \tau = 1, 2, \ldots, t. \tag{6.3}$$

A univariate forecast for the variance of the returns on this artificially constructed portfolio indirectly ensures that the covariances among the individual assets receive exactly the same weight as in Equation (6.2). Note, that unless the portfolio weights for the actual portfolio in place are constantly rebalanced, the returns on this artificially constructed portfolio will generally differ from the actual portfolio returns, that is $r_{w,\tau}^t \equiv w_t' R_\tau \neq w_\tau' R_\tau \equiv r_{w,\tau}$ for $\tau \neq t$. As such, the construction of the variance forecasts for $r_{w,\tau}^t$ requires the estimation of a new (univariate) model each period to properly reflect the relevant portfolio composition in place at time t. Nonetheless, univariate volatility models are generally much easier to implement than their multivariate counterparts, so that this approach will typically be much less computationally demanding than the formulation of a satisfactory full scale multivariate volatility model for $\Omega_{t+1|t}$, especially for large values of N. Moreover, since the relative changes in the actual portfolio weights from one period to the next are likely to be small, good starting values for the parameters in the period-by-period univariate models are readily available from the estimates obtained in the previous period. Of course, this simplified approach also requires that historical returns for the different assets in the portfolio are actually available. If that is not the case, artificial historical prices could be constructed from a pricing model, or by matching the returns to those of other assets with similar characteristics; see, e.g., Andersen et al. (2005) for further discussion along these lines.

Meanwhile, as discussed in Sections 2.2.2 and 2.2.3, there are, of course, many situations in which forecasts for the covariances and/or correlations play a direct and important role in properly assessing and comparing the risks of different decisions or investment opportunities. We next turn to a discussion of some of the multivariate models and forecasting procedures available for doing so.

6.1. Exponential smoothing and RiskMetrics

The exponentially weighted moving average filter, championed by RiskMetrics, is arguable the most commonly applied approach among finance practitioners for estimating time-varying covariance matrices. Specifically, let $Y_t \equiv R_t$ denote the $N \times 1$ vector of asset returns. The estimate for the current covariance matrix is then defined by

$$\hat{\Omega}_t = \gamma Y_t Y_t' + (1-\gamma)\hat{\Omega}_{t-1} \equiv \gamma \sum_{i=1}^{\infty} (1-\gamma)^{i-1} Y_t Y_t'. \tag{6.4}$$

This directly parallels the earlier univariate definition in Equation (3.2), with the additional assumption that the mean of all the elements in Y_t is equal to zero. As in the univariate case, practical implementation is typically done by truncating the sum at $I = t-1$, scaling the finite sum by $1/[1-(1-\gamma)^t]$. This approach is obviously very simple to implement in any dimension N, involving only a single tuning parameter, γ, or by appealing to the values advocated by RiskMetrics (0.06 and 0.04 in the case of daily and monthly returns, respectively) no unknown parameters whatsoever. Moreover, the resulting covariance matrix estimates are guaranteed to be positive definite.

The simple one-parameter filter in (6.4) may, of course, be further refined by allowing for different decay rates for the different elements in $\hat{\Omega}_t$. Specifically, by using a smaller value of γ for the off-diagonal, or covariance, terms in $\hat{\Omega}_t$, the corresponding time-varying correlations,

$$\hat{\rho}_{ij,t} \equiv \frac{\{\hat{\Omega}_t\}_{ij}}{\{\hat{\Omega}_t\}_{ii}^{1/2}\{\hat{\Omega}_t\}_{jj}^{1/2}}, \tag{6.5}$$

will exhibit more persistent dynamic dependencies. This slower rate of decay for the correlations often provide a better characterization of the dependencies across assets.

Meanwhile, the h-period-ahead forecasts obtained by simply equating the future conditional covariance matrix with the current filtered estimate,

$$\operatorname{Var}(Y_{t+h} \mid \mathcal{F}_t) \equiv \Omega_{t+h|t} \approx \hat{\Omega}_t, \tag{6.6}$$

are plagued by the same counterfactual implications highlighted in the context of the corresponding univariate filter in Sections 3.1 and 3.2. In particular, assuming that the one-period returns are serially uncorrelated so that the forecast for the covariance matrix of the multi-period returns equals the sum of the successive one-period covariance forecasts,

$$\operatorname{Var}(Y_{t+k} + Y_{t+k-1} + \cdots + Y_{t+1} \mid \mathcal{F}_t) \equiv \Omega_{t:t+k|t} \approx k\hat{\Omega}_t, \tag{6.7}$$

the multi-period covariance matrix scales with the forecast horizon, k, rather than incorporating empirically more realistic mean-reversion. Moreover, it is difficult to contemplate the choice of the tuning parameter(s), γ, for the various elements in $\hat{\Omega}_t$ without a formal model. The multivariate GARCH class of models provides an answer to these problems by formally characterizing the temporal dependencies in the forecasts for the individual variances and covariances within a coherent statistical framework.

6.2. Multivariate GARCH models

The multivariate GARCH class of models was first introduced and estimated empirically by Bollerslev, Engle and Wooldridge (1988). Denoting the one-step-ahead conditional mean vector and covariance matrix for Y_t by $M_{t|t-1} \equiv E(Y_t \mid \mathcal{F}_{t-1})$ and $\Omega_{t|t-1} \equiv \operatorname{Var}(Y_t \mid \mathcal{F}_{t-1})$, respectively, the multivariate version of the decomposition in (3.5) may be expressed as

$$Y_t = M_{t|t-1} + \Omega_{t|t-1}^{1/2} Z_t, \quad Z_t \sim \text{i.i.d.},\ E(Z_t) = 0,\ \operatorname{Var}(Z_t) = I, \tag{6.8}$$

where Z_t now denotes a vector white noise process with unit variances. The square root of the $\Omega_{t|t-1}$ matrix is not unique, but any operator satisfying the condition that $\Omega_{t|t-1}^{1/2} \cdot \Omega_{t|t-1}^{1/2} \equiv \Omega_{t|t-1}$ will give rise to the same conditional covariance matrix.

The multivariate counterpart to the successful univariate GARCH(1, 1) model in (3.6) is now naturally defined by

$$\operatorname{vech}(\Omega_{t|t-1}) = C + A \operatorname{vech}\bigl(e_{t-1}e_{t-1}'\bigr) + B \operatorname{vech}(\Omega_{t-1|t-2}), \tag{6.9}$$

where $e_t \equiv \Omega_{t|t-1}^{1/2} Z_t$, $\operatorname{vech}(\cdot)$ denotes the operator that stacks the $\frac{1}{2}N(N+1)$ unique elements in the lower triangular part of a symmetric matrix into a $\frac{1}{2}N(N+1) \times 1$ vector, and the parameter matrices C, A, and B, are of dimensions $\frac{1}{2}N(N+1) \times 1$, $\frac{1}{2}N(N+1) \times \frac{1}{2}N(N+1)$, and $\frac{1}{2}N(N+1) \times \frac{1}{2}N(N+1)$, respectively. As in the univariate case, the GARCH(1, 1) model in (6.9) is readily extended to higher order models by including additional lagged terms on the right-hand side of the equation. Note, that for $N = 1$ the model in (6.9) is identical to formulation in (3.6), but for $N > 1$ each of the elements in the covariance matrix is allowed to depend (linearly) on all of the other lagged elements in the conditional covariance matrix as well as the cross products of all the lagged innovations.

The formulation in (6.9) could also easily be extended to allow for asymmetric influences of past negative and positive innovations, as in the GJR or TGARCH model in (3.11), by including the signed cross-products of the residuals on the right-hand side. The most straightforward generalization would be to simply include $\mathrm{vech}(\min\{e_{t-1}, 0\} \min\{e_{t-1}, 0\}')$, but other matrices involving the cross-products of $\max\{e_{t-1}, 0\}$ and/or $\min\{e_{t-1}, 0\}$ have proven important in some empirical applications. Of course, other exogenous explanatory variables could be included in a similar fashion.

Meanwhile, multi-step-ahead forecasts for the conditional variances and covariances from the linear model in (6.9) are readily generated by recursive substitution in the equation,

$$\begin{aligned}\mathrm{vech}(\Omega_{t+h|t+h-1}) &= C + A\,\mathrm{vech}(F_{t+h-1|t+h-2}) \\ &\quad + B\,\mathrm{vech}(\Omega_{t+h-1|t+h-2}),\end{aligned} \tag{6.10}$$

where by definition,

$$F_{t+h|t+h-1} \equiv e_{t+h}e'_{t+h}, \quad h \leqslant 0,$$

and

$$F_{t+h|t+h-1} \equiv \Omega_{t+h|t+h-1}, \quad h \geqslant 1.$$

These recursions, and their extensions to higher order models, are, of course, easy to implement on a computer. Also, provided that the norm of all the eigenvalues of $A + B$ are less than unity, the long-run forecasts for $\Omega_{t+h|t}$ will converge to the "unconditional covariance matrix" implied by the model, $(I - A - B)^{-1}C$, at the exponential rate of decay dictated by $(A + B)^h$. Again, these results directly mirror the univariate expressions in Equations (3.8) and (3.9).

Still, nothing guarantees that the "unconditional covariance matrix" implied by (6.9), $(I - A - B)^{-1}C$, is actually positive definite, nor that the recursion in (6.10) results in positive definite h-step ahead forecasts for the future covariance matrices. In fact, without imposing any additional restrictions on the C, A, and B parameter matrices, the forecasts for the covariance matrices will most likely not be positive definite. Also, the unrestricted GARCH(1, 1) formulation in (6.9) involves a total of $\frac{1}{2}N^4 + N^3 + N^2 + \frac{1}{2}N$ unique parameters. Thus, for $N = 5$ the model has 465 parameters, whereas for $N = 100$ there is a total of 51,010,050 parameters! Needless to say, estimation of this many free parameters isn't practically feasible. Thus, various simplifications designed to ensure positive definiteness and a more manageable number of parameters have been developed in the literature.

In the diagonal vech model the A and B matrices are both assumed to be diagonal, so that a particular element in the conditional covariance matrix only depends on its own lagged value and the corresponding cross product of the innovations. This model may alternatively be written in terms of Hadamard products, or element-by-element multiplication, as

$$\Omega_{t|t-1} = C + A \circ \left(e_{t-1}e'_{t-1}\right) + B \circ \Omega_{t-1|t-2}, \tag{6.11}$$

where C, A, and B now denote symmetric positive definite matrices of dimension $N \times N$. This model greatly reduces the number of free parameters to $3(N^2+N)/2$, and, importantly, covariance matrix forecasts generated from this model according to the recursions in (6.10) are guaranteed to be positive definite. However, the model remains prohibitively "expensive" in terms of parameters in large dimensions. For instance, for $N = 100$ there are still 15,150 free parameters in the unrestricted diagonal vech model.

A further dramatic simplification is obtained by restricting all of the elements in the A and B matrices in (6.11) to be the same,

$$\Omega_{t|t-1} = C + \alpha\left(e_{t-1}e'_{t-1}\right) + \beta\Omega_{t-1|t-2}. \tag{6.12}$$

This scalar diagonal multivariate GARCH representation mimics the RiskMetrics exponential smoother in Equation (6.4), except for the positive definite C matrix intercept, and the one additional smoothing parameter. Importantly however, provided that $\alpha + \beta < 1$, the unconditional covariance matrix implied by the model in (6.12) equals $\Omega = (1 - \alpha - \beta)^{-1}C$, and in parallel to the expression for the univariate GARCH(1, 1) model in Equation (3.9), the h-period forecasts mean reverts to Ω according to the formula,

$$\Omega_{t+h|t} = \Omega + (\alpha + \beta)^{h-1}(\Omega_{t+1|t} - \Omega).$$

This contrasts sharply with the RiskMetrics forecasts, which as previously noted show no mean reversion, with the counterfactual implication that the multi-period covariance forecasts for (approximately) serially uncorrelated returns scale with the forecast horizon. Of course, the scalar model in (6.12) could easily be refined to allow for different (slower) decay rates for the covariances by adding just one or two additional parameters to describe the off-diagonal elements. Still, the model is arguably too simplistic from an empirical perspective, and we will discuss other practically feasible multivariate models and forecasting procedures in the subsequent sections. Before doing so, however, we briefly discuss some of the basic principles and ideas involved in the estimation of multivariate GARCH models.

6.3. Multivariate GARCH estimation

Estimation and inference for multivariate GARCH models may formally proceed along the same lines as for the univariate models discussed in Section 3.5. In particular, assume that the conditional distribution of Y_t is multivariate normal with mean, $M_{t|t-1}$, and covariance matrix, $\Omega_{t|t-1}$. The log-likelihood function is given by the sum of the corresponding T logarithmic conditional normal densities,

$$\begin{aligned}\log L(\theta; Y_T, \ldots, Y_1) \\ = -\frac{TN}{2}\log(2\pi) \\ - \frac{1}{2}\sum_{t=1}^{T}\left[\log \Omega_{t|t-1}(\theta) - \left(Y_t - M_{t|t-1}(\theta)\right)' \Omega_{t|t-1}(\theta)^{-1}\left(Y_t - M_{t|t-1}(\theta)\right)\right],\end{aligned} \tag{6.13}$$

where we have highlighted the explicit dependence on the parameter vector, θ. Provided that the assumption of conditional normality is true and the parametric models for the mean and covariance matrices are correctly specified, the resulting estimates, say $\hat{\theta}_T$, will satisfy the usual optimality conditions associated with maximum likelihood. Moreover, even if the conditional normality assumption is violated, the resulting estimates may still be given a QMLE interpretation, with robust parameter inference based on the "sandwich-form" of the covariance matrix estimator, as discussed in Section 3.5.

Meanwhile, as discussed in Section 2, when constructing interval or VaR type forecasts, the whole conditional distribution becomes important. Thus, in parallel to the discussion in Sections 3.5 and 3.6, other multivariate conditional distributions may be used in place of the multivariate normal distributions underlying the likelihood function in (6.13). Different multivariate generalizations of the univariate fat-tailed Student t distribution in (3.24) have proved quite successful for many daily and weekly financial rate of returns.

The likelihood function in (6.13), or generalizations allowing for conditionally non-normal innovations, may in principle be maximized by any of a number of different numerical optimization techniques. However, even for moderate values of N, say $N \geqslant 5$, the dimensionality of the problem for the general model in (6.9) or the diagonal vech model in (6.11) renders the computations hopelessly demanding from a practical perspective. As previously noted, this lack of tractability motivates the more parsimonious parametric specifications discussed below.

An alternative approach for circumventing the curse-of-dimensionality within the context of the diagonal vech model has recently been advocated by Ledoit, Santa-Clara and Wolf (2003). Instead of estimating all of the elements in the C, A and B matrices jointly, inference in their Flex GARCH approach proceed by estimating separate bivariate models for all of the possible pairwise combinations of the N elements in Y_t. These individual matrix estimates are then "pasted" together to a full-dimensional model in such a way that the resulting $N \times N$ matrices in (6.11) are ensured to be positive definite.

Another practical approach for achieving more parsimonious and empirically meaningful multivariate GARCH forecasting models rely on so-called variance targeting techniques. Specifically, consider the general multivariate formulation in (6.9) obtained by replacing C with

$$C = (I - A - B)\,\mathrm{vech}(V), \tag{6.14}$$

where V denotes a positive definite matrix. Provided that the norm of all the eigenvalues for $A + B$ are less than unity, so that the inverse of $(I - A - B)$ exists, this reparameterization implies that the long-run forecasts for $\Omega_{t+h|t}$ will converge to V for $h \to \infty$. As such, variance targeting can help ensure that the long-run forecasts are well behaved. Of course, this doesn't reduce the number of unknown parameters in the model per se, as the long-run covariance matrix, V, must now be determined. However, an often employed approach is to fix V at the unconditional sample covariance matrix,

$$\hat{V} = \frac{1}{T}\sum_{t=1}^{T}\big(Y_t - \hat{M}_{t|t-1}\big)\big(Y_t - \hat{M}_{t|t-1}\big)',$$

where $\hat{M}_{t|t-1}$ denotes some first-stage estimate for the conditional mean. This estimation of V obviously introduces an additional source of parameter estimation error uncertainty, although the impact of this is typically ignored in practice when conducting inference about the other parameters entering the equation for the conditional covariance matrix.

6.4. Dynamic conditional correlations

One commonly applied approach for large scale dynamic covariance matrix modeling and forecasting is the Constant Conditional Correlation (CCC) model of Bollerslev (1990). Specifically, let $D_{t|t-1}$ denote the $N \times N$ diagonal matrix with the conditional standard deviations, or the square root of the diagonal elements in $\Omega_{t|t-1} \equiv \mathrm{Var}(Y_t \mid \mathcal{F}_{t-1})$, along the diagonal. The conditional covariance matrix may then be uniquely expressed in terms of the decomposition,

$$\Omega_{t|t-1} = D_{t|t-1}\Gamma_{t|t-1}D_{t|t-1}, \tag{6.15}$$

where $\Gamma_{t|t-1}$ denote the $N \times N$ matrix of conditional correlations. Of course, this decomposition does not result in any immediate simplifications from a modeling perspective, as the conditional correlation matrix must now be estimated. However, following Bollerslev (1990) and assuming that the temporal variation in the covariances are driven solely by the temporal variation in the corresponding conditional standard deviations, so that the conditional correlations are constant,

$$\Gamma_{t|t-1} \equiv \Gamma, \tag{6.16}$$

dramatically reduces the number of parameters in the model relative to the linear vech specifications discussed above. Moreover, this assumption also greatly simplifies the multivariate estimation problem, which may now proceed in two steps. In the first step N individual univariate GARCH models are estimated for each of the series in Y_t, resulting in an estimate for the diagonal matrix, $\hat{D}_{t|t-1}$. Then defining the $N \times 1$ vector of standardized residuals for each of the univariate series,

$$\hat{\varepsilon}_t \equiv \hat{D}_{t|t-1}^{-1}(Y_t - \hat{M}_{t|t-1}), \tag{6.17}$$

the elements in Γ may simply be estimated by the corresponding sample analogue,

$$\hat{\Gamma} = \frac{1}{T}\sum_{t=1}^{T} \hat{\varepsilon}_t \hat{\varepsilon}_t'. \tag{6.18}$$

Importantly, this estimate for Γ is guaranteed to be positive definite with ones along the diagonal and all of the other elements between minus one and one. In addition to being simple to implement, this approach therefore has the desirable feature that as long as the individual variances in $\hat{D}_{t|t-1}$ are positive, the resulting covariance matrices defined by (6.15) are guaranteed to be positive definite.

While the assumption of constant conditional correlations may often be a reasonable simplification over shorter time periods, it is arguable too simplistic in many situations of practical interest. To circumvent this, while retaining the key features of the decomposition in (6.15), Engle (2002) and Tse and Tsui (2002) have recently proposed a convenient framework for directly modeling any temporal dependencies in the conditional correlations. In the most basic version of the Dynamic Conditional Correlation (DCC) model of Engle (2002), the temporal variation in the conditional correlation is characterized by a simple scalar GARCH(1, 1) model, along the lines of (6.12), with the covariance matrix for the standardized residuals targeted at their unconditional value in (6.18). That is,

$$Q_{t|t-1} = (1-\alpha-\beta)\hat{\Gamma} + \alpha(\hat{\varepsilon}_{t-1}\hat{\varepsilon}_{t-1}') + \beta Q_{t-1|t-2}. \tag{6.19}$$

Although this recursion guarantees that the $Q_{t|t-1}$ matrices are positive definite, the individual elements are not necessarily between minus one and one. Thus, in order to arrive at an estimate for the conditional correlation matrix, the elements in $Q_{t|t-1}$ must be standardized, resulting in the following estimate for the ijth correlation:

$$\hat{\rho}_{ij,t} \equiv \{\hat{\Gamma}_{t|t-1}\}_{ij} = \frac{\{Q_t\}_{ij}}{\{Q_t\}_{ii}^{1/2}\{Q_t\}_{jj}^{1/2}}. \tag{6.20}$$

Like the CCC model, the DCC model is also relatively simple to implement in large dimensions, requiring only the estimation of N univariate models along with a choice of the two exponential smoothing parameters in (6.19).

Richer dynamic dependencies in the correlations could be incorporated in a similar manner, although this immediately raises some of the same complications involved in directly parameterizing $\Omega_{t|t-1}$. However, as formally shown in Engle and Sheppard (2001), the parameters in (6.19) characterizing the dynamic dependencies in $Q_{t|t-1}$, and in turn $\Gamma_{t|t-1}$, may be consistently estimated in a second step by maximizing the partial log-likelihood function,

$$\log L(\theta; Y_T, \ldots, Y_1)^* = -\frac{1}{2}\sum_{t=1}^{T}\left[\log\left|\Gamma_{t|t-1}(\theta)\right| - \hat{\varepsilon}_t'\Gamma_{t|t-1}(\theta)^{-1}\hat{\varepsilon}_t\right],$$

where $\hat{\varepsilon}_t$ refers to the first step estimates defined in (6.17). Of course, the standard errors for the resulting correlation parameter estimates must be adjusted to take account of the first stage estimation errors in $\hat{D}_{t|t-1}$. Extensions of the basic DCC structure in (6.19) and (6.20) along these lines allowing for greater flexibility in the dependencies in the correlations across different types of assets, asymmetries in the way in which the correlations respond to past negative and positive return innovations, regime switches in the correlations, to name but a few, are currently being actively explored by a number of researchers.

6.5. Multivariate stochastic volatility and factor models

An alternative approach for achieving a more manageable and parsimonious multivariate volatility forecasting model entails the use of factor structures. Factor structures are, of course, central to the field of finance, and the Arbitrage Pricing Theory (APT) in particular. Multivariate factor GARCH and stochastic volatility models were first analyzed by Diebold and Nerlove (1989) and Engle, Ng and Rothschild (1990). To illustrate, consider a simple one-factor model in which the commonality in the volatilities across the $N \times 1$ R_t vector of asset returns is driven by a single scalar factor, f_t,

$$R_t = a + bf_t + e_t, \tag{6.21}$$

where a and b denote $N \times 1$ parameter vectors, and e_t is assumed to be i.i.d. through time with covariance matrix Λ. This directly captures the idea that variances (and covariances) generally move together across assets. Now, assuming that the factor is conditionally heteroskedastic, with conditional variance denoted by $\sigma^2_{t|t-1} \equiv \mathrm{Var}(f_t \mid \mathcal{F}_{t-1})$, the conditional covariance matrix for R_t takes the form

$$\Omega_{t|t-1} \equiv \mathrm{Var}(R_t \mid \mathcal{F}_{t-1}) = bb'\sigma^2_{t|t-1} + \Lambda. \tag{6.22}$$

Compared to the unrestricted GARCH models discussed in Section 6.2, the factor GARCH representation greatly reduces the number of free parameters. Moreover, the conditional covariance matrix in (6.22) is guaranteed to be positive definite.

To further appreciate the implications of the factor representation, let b_i and λ_{ij} denote the ith and ijth element in b and Λ, respectively. It follows then directly from the expression in (6.22) that the conditional correlation between the ith and the jth observation is given by

$$\rho_{ij,t} \equiv \frac{b_i b_j \sigma^2_{t|t-1} + \lambda_{ij}}{(b_i^2 \sigma^2_{t|t-1} + \lambda_{ii})^{1/2} (b_j^2 \sigma^2_{t|t-1} + \lambda_{jj})^{1/2}}. \tag{6.23}$$

Thus, provided that the corresponding factor loadings are of the same sign, or $b_i b_j > 0$, the conditional correlation implied by the model will increase toward unity as the volatility of the factor increases. That is, there is an empirically realistic built-in volatility-in-correlation effect.

Importantly, multivariate conditional covariance matrix forecasts are also readily constructed from forecasts for the univariate factor variance. In particular, assuming that the vector of returns is serially uncorrelated, the conditional covariance matrix for the k-period continuously compounded returns is simply given by

$$\Omega_{t:t+k|t} \equiv \mathrm{Var}(R_{t+k} + \cdots + R_{t+1} \mid \mathcal{F}_t) = bb'\sigma^2_{t:t+k|t} + k\Lambda, \tag{6.24}$$

where $\sigma^2_{t:t+k|t} \equiv \mathrm{Var}(f_{t+k} + \cdots + f_{t+1} \mid \mathcal{F}_t)$. Further assuming that the factor is directly observable and that the conditional variance for f_t is specified in terms of the observable information set, $\mathcal{F}_{t-1}$, the forecasts for $\sigma^2_{t:t+k|t}$ may be constructed along the lines of the univariate GARCH class of models discussed in Section 3. If, on the other hand, the factor is latent or if the conditional variance for f_t is formulated in terms of unobservable information, $\Im_{t-1}$, one of the more intensive numerical procedures for the univariate stochastic volatility class of models discussed in Section 4 must be applied in calculating $\sigma^2_{t:t+k|t}$. Of course, the one-factor model in (6.21) could easily be extended to allow for multiple factors, resulting in obvious generalizations of the expressions in (6.22) and (6.24). As long as the number of factors remain small, the same appealing simplifications hold true.

Meanwhile, an obvious drawback from an empirical perspective to the simple factor model in (6.21) with homoskedastic innovations concerns the lack of heteroskedasticity in certain portfolios. Specifically, let $\Psi = \{\psi \mid \psi' b = 0,\ \psi \neq 0\}$ denote the set of $N \times 1$ vectors orthogonal to the vector of factor loadings, b. Any portfolio constructed from the N original assets with portfolio weights, $w = \psi/(\psi_1 + \cdots + \psi_N)$ where $\psi \in \Psi$, will then be homoskedastic,

$$\mathrm{Var}(r_{w,t} \mid \mathcal{F}_{t-1}) \equiv \mathrm{Var}\big(w' R_t \bigm| \mathcal{F}_{t-1}\big) = w'bb'w\sigma^2_{t|t-1} + w'\Lambda w = w'\Lambda w. \tag{6.25}$$

Similarly, the corresponding multi-period forecasts defined in (6.24) will also be time invariant. Yet, in applications with daily or weekly returns it is almost always impossible to construct portfolios which are void of volatility clustering effects. The inclusion of additional factors does not formally solve the problem. As long as the number of factors is less than N, the corresponding null-set Ψ is not empty. Of course, allowing the covariance matrix of the idiosyncratic innovations to be heteroskedastic would remedy this problem, but that then raises the issue of how to model the temporal variation in the $(N \times N)$-dimensional Λ_t matrix. One approach would be to include enough factors so that the Λ_t matrix may be assumed to be diagonal, only requiring the estimation of N univariate volatility models for the elements in e_t.

Whether the rank deficiency in the forecasts of the conditional covariance matrices from the basic factor structure and the counterfactual implication of no volatility clustering in certain portfolios discussed above should be a cause for concern ultimately depends upon the uses of the forecasts. However, it is clear that the reduction in the dimension of the problem to a few systematic risk factors may afford great computational simplifications in the context of large scale covariance matrix modeling and forecasting.

6.6. Realized covariances and correlations

The high-frequency data realized volatility approach for measuring, modeling and forecasting univariate volatilities outlined in Section 5 may be similarly adapted to modeling and forecasting covariances and correlations. To set out the basic idea, let $R(t, \Delta)$ denote the $N \times 1$ vector of logarithmic returns over the $[t - \Delta, t]$ time interval,

$$R(t, \Delta) \equiv P(t) - P(t - \Delta). \tag{6.26}$$

The $N \times N$ realized covariation matrix for the unit time interval, $[t - 1, t]$, is then formally defined by

$$\text{RCOV}(t, \Delta) = \sum_{j=1}^{1/\Delta} R(t - 1 + j \cdot \Delta, \Delta) R(t - 1 + j \cdot \Delta, \Delta)'. \tag{6.27}$$

This directly parallels the univariate definition in (5.10). Importantly, the realized covariation matrix is symmetric by construction, and as long as the returns are linearly independent and $N < 1/\Delta$, the matrix is guaranteed to be positive definite.

In order to more formally justify the realized covariation measure, suppose that the evolution of the $N \times 1$ vector price process may be described by the N-dimensional continuous-time diffusion,

$$\mathrm{d}P(t) = M(t)\,\mathrm{d}t + \Sigma(t)\,\mathrm{d}W(t), \quad t \in [0, T], \tag{6.28}$$

where $M(t)$ denotes the $N \times 1$ instantaneous drifts, $\Sigma(t)$ refer to the $N \times N$ instantaneous diffusion matrix, and $W(t)$ now denotes an $(N \times 1)$-dimensional vector of independent standard Brownian motions. Intuitively, for small values of $\Delta > 0$,

$$R(t, \Delta) \equiv P(t) - P(t - \Delta) \simeq M(t - \Delta)\Delta + \Sigma(t - \Delta)\,\Delta W(t), \tag{6.29}$$

where $\Delta W(t) \equiv W(t) - W(t - \Delta) \sim N(0, \Delta I_N)$. Of course, this latter expression directly mirrors the univariate equation (5.2). Now, using similar arguments to the ones in Section 5.1, it follows that the multivariate realized covariation in (6.27) will converge to the corresponding multivariate integrated covariation for finer and finer sampled high-frequency returns, or $\Delta \to 0$,

$$\text{RCOV}(t, \Delta) \to \int_{t-1}^{t} \Sigma(s)\Sigma(s)'\,\mathrm{d}s \equiv \text{ICOV}(t). \tag{6.30}$$

Again, by similar arguments to the ones in Section 5.1, the multivariate integrated covariation defined by the right-hand side of Equation (6.30) provides the true measure for the actual return variation and *covariation* that transpired over the $[t - 1, t]$ time interval. Also, extending the univariate results in (5.12), Barndorff-Nielsen and Shephard (2004b) have recently shown that the multivariate realized volatility errors, $\sqrt{1/\Delta}[\text{RCOV}(t, \Delta) - \text{ICOV}(t)]$, are approximately serially uncorrelated and asymptotically (for $\Delta \to 0$) distributed as a mixed normal with a random covariance matrix that may be estimated. Moreover following (5.13), the consistency of the realized covariation measure for the true quadratic covariation caries over to situations in which the vector price process contains jumps. As such, these theoretical results set the stage for multivariate volatility modeling and forecasting based on the realized covariation measures along the same lines as the univariate discussion in Sections 5.2 and 5.3.

In particular, treating the $\frac{1}{2}N(N+1) \times 1$ vector, vech[RCOV(t), Δ)], as a direct observation (with uncorrelated measurement errors) on the unique elements in the covariation matrix of interest, standard multivariate time series techniques may be used in jointly modeling the variances and the off-diagonal covariance elements. For instance, a simple VAR(1) forecasting model, analogues to the GARCH(1, 1) model in (6.9), may be specified as

$$\operatorname{vech}\bigl[\mathrm{RCOV}(t, \Delta)\bigr] = C + A \operatorname{vech}\bigl[\mathrm{RCOV}(t-1, \Delta)\bigr] + u_t, \tag{6.31}$$

where u_t denotes an $N \times 1$ vector white noise process. Of course, higher order dynamic dependencies could be included in a similar manner. Indeed, the results in Andersen et al. (2001b, 2003), suggest that for long-run forecasting it may be important to incorporate long-memory type dependencies in both variances and covariances. This could be accomplished through the use of a true multivariate fractional integrated model, or as previously discussed an approximating component type structure.

Even though RCOV(t, Δ) is positive definite by construction, nothing guarantees that the forecasts from an unrestricted multivariate time series model along the lines of the VAR(1) in (6.31) will result in positive definite covariance matrix forecasts. Hence, it may be desirable to utilize some of the more restrictive parameterizations for the multivariate GARCH models discussed in Section 6.2, to ensure positive definite covariance matrix forecasts. Nonetheless, replacing $\Omega_{t|t-1}$ with the directly observable RCOV(t, Δ), means that the parameters in the corresponding models may be estimated in a straightforward fashion using simple least squares, or some other easy-to-implement estimation method, rather than the much more numerically intensive multivariate MLE or QMLE estimation schemes.

Alternatively, an unrestricted model for the $\frac{1}{2}N(N+1)$ nonzero elements in the Cholesky decomposition, or lower triangular matrix square-root, of RCOV(t, Δ), could also be estimated. Of course, the nonlinear transformation involved in such a decomposition means that the corresponding matrix product of the forecasts from the model will generally not be unbiased for the elements in the covariation matrix itself. Following Andersen et al. (2003), sometimes it might also be possible to infer the covariances of interest from the variances of different cross-rates or portfolios through appropriately defined arbitrage conditions. In those situations forecasts for the covariances may therefore be constructed from a set of forecasting models for the corresponding variances, in turn avoiding directly modeling any covariances.

The realized covariation matrix in (6.27) may also be used in the construction of realized correlations, as in Andersen et al. (2001a, 2001b). These realized correlations could be modeled directly using standard time series techniques. However, the correlations are, of course, restricted to lie between minus one and one. Thus, to ensure that this constraint is not violated, it might be desirable to use the Fisher transform, $z = 0.5 \cdot \log[(1 + \rho)/(1 - \rho)]$, or some other similar transformation, to convert the support of the distribution for the correlations from $[-1, 1]$ to the whole real line. This is akin to the log transformation for the univariate realized volatilities employed in Equation (5.14). Meanwhile, there is some evidence that the dynamic dependencies in the correlations between many financial assets and markets are distinctly different from that of the corresponding variances and covariances, exhibiting occasional "correlation breakdowns". These types of dependencies may best be characterized by regime switching type models. Rather than modeling the correlations individually, the realized correlation matrix could also be used in place of $\hat{e}_t \hat{e}_t'$ in the DCC model in (6.19), or some generalization of that formulation, in jointly modeling all of the elements in the conditional correlation matrix.

The realized covariation and correlation measures discussed above are, of course, subject to the same market microstructure complications that plague the univariate realized volatility measures discussed in Section 5. In fact, some of the problems are accentuated with the possibility of nonsynchronous observations in two or more markets. Research on this important issues is still very much ongoing, and it is too early to draw any firm conclusions about the preferred method or sampling scheme to employ in the practical implementation of the realized covariation measures. Nonetheless, it is clear that the realized volatility approach afford a very convenient and powerful approach for effectively incorporating high-frequency financial data into both univariate and multivariate volatility modeling and forecasting.

6.7. Further reading

The use of historical pseudo returns as a convenient way of reducing the multivariate modeling problem to a univariate setting, as outlined in Section 6.1, is discussed at some length in Andersen et al. (2005). This same study also discusses the use of a smaller set of liquid base assets along with a factor structure as another computationally convenient way of reducing the dimension of time-varying covariance matrix forecasting for financial rate of returns.

The RiskMetrics, or exponential smoothing approach, for calculating covariances and associated Value-at-Risk measures is discussed extensively in Christoffersen (2003), Jorion (2000), and Zaffaroni (2004) among others. Following earlier work by DeSantis and Gerard (1997), empirically more realistic slower decay rates for the covariances in the context of exponential smoothing has been successfully implemented by DeSantis et al. (2003).

In addition to the many ARCH and GARCH survey papers and book treatments listed in Section 3, the multivariate GARCH class of models has recently been surveyed by Bauwens, Laurent and Rombouts (2006). A comparison of some of the available commercial software packages for the estimation of multivariate GARCH models is available in Brooks, Burke and Persand (2003). Conditions for the covariance matrix forecasts for the linear formulations discussed in Section 6.2 to be positive definite was first established by Engle and Kroner (1995), who also introduced the so-called BEKK parameterization. Asymmetries, or leverage effects, within this same class of models were subsequently studied by Kroner and Ng (1998). The bivariate EGARCH model of Braun, Nelson and Sunier (1995) and the recent matrix EGARCH model of Kawakatsu (2005) offer alternative ways of doing so. The multivariate GARCH QMLE procedures outlined in Section 6.3 were first discussed by Bollerslev and Wooldridge (1992), while Ling and McAleer (2003) provide a more recent account of some of the subsequent important theoretical developments. The use of a fat tailed multivariate Student t distribution in the estimation of multivariate GARCH models was first considered by Harvey, Ruiz and Sentana (1992); see also Bauwens and Laurent (2005) and Fiorentini, Sentana and Calzolari (2003) for more recent applications of alternative multivariate nonnormal distributions. Issues related to cross-sectional and temporal aggregation of multivariate GARCH and stochastic volatility models have been studied by Nijman and Sentana (1996) and Meddahi and Renault (2004).

Several empirical studies have documented important temporal dependencies in asset return correlations, including early contributions by Erb, Harvey and Viskanta (1994) and Longin and Solnik (1995) focusing on international equity returns. More recent work by Ang and Chen (2002) and Cappiello, Engle and Sheppard (2004) have emphasized the importance of explicitly incorporating asymmetries in the way in which the correlations respond to past negative and positive return shocks. Along these lines, Longin and Solnik (2001) report evidence in support of more pronounced dependencies following large (extreme) negative return innovations. A test for the assumption of constant conditional correlations underlying the CCC model discussed in Section 6.4 has been derived by Bera and Kim (2002). Recent work on extending the DCC model to allow for more flexible dynamic dependencies in the correlations, asymmetries in the responses to past negative and positive returns, as well as switches in the correlations across regimes, include Billio, Caporin and Gobbo (2003), Cappiello, Engle and Sheppard (2004), Franses and Hafner (2003), and Pelletier (2005). Guidolin and Timmermann (2005b) find large variations in the correlation between stock and bond returns across different market regimes defined as crash, slow growth, bull and recovery. Sheppard (2004) similarly finds evidence of business cycle frequency dynamics in conditional covariances.

The factor ARCH models proposed by Diebold and Nerlove (1989) and Engle, Ng and Rothschild (1990) have been used by Ng, Engle and Rothschild (1992) and Bollerslev and Engle (1993), among others, in modeling common persistence in conditional variances and covariances. Harvey, Ruiz and Shephard (1994) and King, Sentana and Wadhwani (1994) were among the first to estimate multivariate stochastic volatility models. More recent empirical studies and numerically efficient algorithms for the estimation of latent multivariate volatility structures include Aguilar and West (2000), Fiorentini, Sentana and Shephard (2004), and Liesenfeld and Richard (2003). Issues related to identification within heteroskedastic factor models have been studied by Sentana and Fiorentini (2001). A recent insightful discussion of the basic features of multivariate stochastic volatility factor models, along with a discussion of their origins, is provided in Shephard (2004). The multivariate Markov-switching multifractal model of Calvet, Fisher and Thompson (2005) may also be interpreted as a latent factor stochastic volatility model with a closed form likelihood. Other related relatively easy-to-implement multivariate approaches include the two-step Orthogonal GARCH model of Alexander (2001), in which the conditional covariance matrix is determined by univariate models for a (small) set of the largest (unconditional) principal components.

The realized volatility approach discussed in Section 6.6 affords a simple practically feasible way for covariance and correlation forecasting in situations when high-frequency data is available. The formal theory underpinning this approach in the multivariate setting has been spelled out in Andersen et al. (2003) and Barndorff-Nielsen and Shephard (2004b). A precursor to some of these results is provided by the alternative double asymptotic rolling regression based framework in Foster and Nelson (1996). The benefits of the realized volatility approach versus more conventional multivariate GARCH based forecasts in the context of asset allocation have been forcefully demonstrated by Fleming, Kirby and Ostdiek (2003). Meanwhile, the best way of actually implementing the realized covariation measures with high-frequency financial data subject to market microstructure frictions still remains very much of an open research question. In a very early paper, Epps (1979) first observed a dramatic drop in high-frequency based sample correlations among individual stock returns as the length of the return interval approached zero; see also Lundin, Dacorogna and Müller (1998). In addition to the many mostly univariate studies noted in Section 4, Martens (2003) provides a recent assessment and comparison of some of the existing ways for best alleviating the impact of market microstructure frictions in the multivariate setting, including the covariance matrix estimator of De Jong and Nijman (1997), the lead-lag adjustment of Scholes and Williams (1977), and the range-based covariance measure of Brandt and Diebold (2006).

The multivariate procedures discussed in this section are (obviously) not exhaustive of the literature. Other recent promising approaches for covariance and correlation forecasting include the use of copulas for conveniently linking univariate GARCH [e.g., Jondeau and Rockinger (2005) and Patton (2004)] or realized volatility models; the use of shrinkage to ensure positive definiteness in the estimation and forecasting of very large-dimensional covariance matrices [e.g., Jagannathan and Ma (2003) and Ledoit and Wolf (2003)]; and forecast model averaging techniques [e.g., Pesaran and Zaffaroni (2004)]. It remains to be seen which of these, if any, will be added to the standard multivariate volatility forecasting toolbox.

7. Evaluating volatility forecasts

The discussion up until this point has surveyed the most important univariate and multivariate volatility models and forecasting procedures in current use. This section gives an overview of some of the most useful methods available for volatility forecast evaluation. The methods introduced here can either be used by an external evaluator or by the forecaster him/herself as a diagnostic tool on the forecasting model. A more general discussion and review of the forecast evaluation literature can be found in Diebold and Lopez (1996) and Chapter 3 by West in this Handbook.

Below, we will first introduce a general loss function framework and then highlight the particular issues involved when forecasting volatility itself is the direct object of interest. We then discuss several other important forecasting situations where volatility dynamics are crucial, including Value-at-Risk, probability, and density forecasting.

7.1. Point forecast evaluation from general loss functions

Consider the general forecast loss function, $L(y_{t+1}, \hat{y}_{t+1|t})$, discussed in Section 2, in which the arguments are the univariate discrete-time real-valued stochastic variable, y_{t+1}, as well as its forecast, $\hat{y}_{t+1|t}$. From the optimization problem solved by the optimal forecast, $\hat{y}_{t+1|t}$ must satisfy the generic first order condition

$$E_t\left[\frac{\partial L(y_{t+1}, \hat{y}_{t+1|t})}{\partial \hat{y}}\right] = 0. \tag{7.1}$$

The partial derivative of the loss function – the term inside the conditional expectation – is sometimes referred to as the generalized forecast error. Realizations of this partial derivative should fluctuate unpredictably around zero, directly in line with the standard optimality condition that regular forecasts display uncorrelated prediction errors.

Specifically, consider the situation in which we observe a sequence of out-of-sample forecasts and subsequent realizations, $\{y_{t+1}, \hat{y}_{t+1|t}\}_{t=1}^{T}$. A natural diagnostic on (7.1) is then given by the simple regression version of the conditional expectation, that is

$$\frac{\partial L(y_{t+1}, \hat{y}_{t+1|t})}{\partial \hat{y}} = a + b' x_t + \varepsilon_{t+1}, \tag{7.2}$$

where x_t denotes a vector of candidate explanatory variables in the time t information set observed by the forecaster, $\mathcal{F}_t$, and b is a vector of regression coefficients. An appropriately calibrated forecast should then have $a = b = 0$, which can be tested using standard t- and F-tests properly robustified to allow for heteroskedasticity in the regression errors, ε_{t+1}. Intuitively, if a significant coefficient is obtained on a forecasting variable, which the forecaster should reasonably have known at time t, then the forecasting model is not optimal, as the variable in question could and should have been used to make the generalized forecast error variance lower than it actually is.

If the forecasts arise from a known well-specified statistical model with estimated parameters then the inherent parameter estimation error should ideally be accounted for. This can be done using the asymptotic results in West and McCracken (1998) or the finite sample Monte Carlo tests in Dufour (2004). However, external forecast evaluators may not have knowledge of the details of the underlying forecasting model (if one exists) in which case parameter estimation error uncertainty is not easily accounted for. Furthermore, in most financial applications the estimation sample is typically fairly large rendering the parameter estimation error relatively small compared with other potentially more serious model specification errors. In this case standard (heteroskedasticity robust) t-tests and F-tests may work reasonably well. Note also that in the case of, say, h-day forecasts from a daily model, the horizon overlap implies that the first $h - 1$ autocorrelations will not be equal to zero, and this must be allowed for in the regression.

As an example of the general framework in (7.2), consider the case of quadratic loss, $L(y_{t+1}, \hat{y}_{t+1|t}) = (y_{t+1} - \hat{y}_{t+1|t})^2$. In this situation

$$\frac{\partial L(y_{t+1}, \hat{y}_{t+1|t})}{\partial \hat{y}} = -2(y_{t+1} - \hat{y}_{t+1|t}), \tag{7.3}$$

which suggests the forecast evaluation regression

$$(y_{t+1} - \hat{y}_{t+1|t}) = a + b' x_t + \varepsilon_{t+1}. \tag{7.4}$$

While the choice of information variables to include in x_t is somewhat arbitrary, one obvious candidate does exist, namely the time t forecast itself. Following this idea and letting $x_t = \hat{y}_{t+1|t}$, results in the so-called Mincer and Zarnowitz (1969) regression, which can thus be viewed as a test of forecast optimality relative to a limited information set. We write

$$(y_{t+1} - \hat{y}_{t+1|t}) = a + b\hat{y}_{t+1|t} + \varepsilon_{t+1},$$

or equivalently

$$y_{t+1} = a + (b + 1)\hat{y}_{t+1|t} + \varepsilon_{t+1}. \tag{7.5}$$

Clearly the ex-ante forecast should not be able to explain the ex-post forecast error. For example, if b is significantly negative, and thus $(b + 1) < 1$, then the forecast is too volatile relative to the subsequent realization and the forecast should be scaled down.

It is often of interest to compare forecasts from different models, or forecasters. This is easily done by letting $x_t = [\hat{y}_{t+1|t}\ \hat{y}_{A,t+1|t}]$, where $\hat{y}_{A,t+1|t}$ denotes the alternative forecast. The forecast evaluation regression then takes the form,

$$y_{t+1} = a + (b + 1)\hat{y}_{t+1|t} + b_A \hat{y}_{A,t+1|t} + \varepsilon_{t+1}, \tag{7.6}$$

where a failure to reject the hypothesis that $b_A = 0$ implies that the additional information provided by the alternative forecast is not significant. Or, in other words, the benchmark forecast encompasses the alternative forecast.

7.2. Volatility forecast evaluation

The above discussion was cast at a general level. We now turn to the case in which volatility itself is the forecasting object of interest. Hence, $y_{t+1} \equiv \sigma^2_{t:t+1}$ now refers to some form of ex-post volatility measure, while $y_{t+1|t} \equiv \hat{\sigma}^2_{t:t+1|t}$ denotes the corresponding ex-ante volatility forecast.

The regression-based framework from above then suggests the general volatility forecast evaluation regression

$$\sigma^2_{t:t+1} - \hat{\sigma}^2_{t:t+1|t} = a + b' x_t + \varepsilon_{t+1}, \tag{7.7}$$

or as a special case the Mincer–Zarnowitz volatility regression

$$\sigma_{t:t+1}^2 = a + (b+1)\hat{\sigma}_{t:t+1|t}^2 + \varepsilon_{t+1},$$

where an optimal forecast would satisfy $a = b = 0$. Immediately, however, the question arises of how to actually measure the ex-post variance? As discussed at some length in Sections 1 and 5, the "true" variance, or volatility, is inherently unobservable, and we are faced with the challenge of having to rely on a proxy in order to assess the forecast quality.

The simplest proxy is the squared observation of the underlying variable, y_{t+1}^2, which, when the mean is zero, has the property of being (conditionally) unbiasedness, or $E_t[y_{t+1}^2] = \sigma_{t:t+1}^2$. Thus, the accuracy of the volatility forecasts could be assessed by the following simple regression:

$$y_{t+1}^2 = a + (b+1)\hat{\sigma}_{t:t+1|t}^2 + \varepsilon_{t+1}. \tag{7.8}$$

However, as illustrated by Figure 1, the squared observation typically provides a very noisy proxy for the true (latent) volatility process of interest. We are essentially estimating the variance each period using just a single observation, and the corresponding regression fit is inevitably very low, even if the volatility forecast is accurate. For instance, regressions of the form (7.8), using daily or weekly squared returns as the left-hand side independent variable, typically result in unspectacular R^2's of around 5–10%. We are seemingly stuck with an impossible task, namely to precisely assess the forecastability of something which is itself not observed.

Fortunately, Figure 1 and the accompanying discussion in Sections 1 and 5 suggest a workable solution to this conundrum. In financial applications observations are often available at very high frequencies. For instance, even if the forecaster is only interested in predicting volatility over daily or longer horizons, observations on the asset prices are often available at much finer intradaily sampling frequencies, say $1/\Delta \gg 1$ observations per "day" or unit time interval. Hence, in this situation following the discussion in Section 5.1, a proxy for the (latent) daily volatility may be calculated from the intradaily squared return as

$$\mathrm{RV}(t+1,\Delta) \equiv \sum_{j=1}^{1/\Delta} \bigl[p(t+j\cdot\Delta) - p\bigl(t+(j-1)\cdot\Delta\bigr)\bigr]^2.$$

The resulting forecast evaluation regression thus takes the form,

$$\mathrm{RV}(t+1,\Delta) = a + (b+1)\hat{\sigma}_{t:t+1|t}^2 + \varepsilon_{t+1}, \tag{7.9}$$

which coincides with (7.8) for $\Delta = 1$. However, in contrast to the low R^2's associated with (7.8), Andersen and Bollerslev (1998a) find that in liquid markets the R^2 of the regression in (7.9) can be as high as 50% for the very same volatility forecast that produces an R^2 of only 5–10% in the former regression! In other words, even a reasonably accurate volatility forecasting model will invariably appear to have a low degree of forecastability when evaluated on the basis of a noisy volatility proxy. Equally important, it will be difficult to detect a poor volatility forecasting model when a noisy volatility proxy is used.

Reliable high-frequency information is, of course, not available for all financial markets. Still, intra-day high and low prices, or quotes, are often available over long historical time periods. Under idealized conditions – a Geometric Brownian motion with a constant diffusive volatility σ – the expected value of the log range (the difference between the high and the low logarithmic price) over the unit time interval is directly related to volatility of the process by the equation

$$E\big[\big(\max\{p(\tau) \mid t \leqslant \tau < t+1\} - \min\{p(\tau) \mid t \leqslant \tau < t+1\}\big)^2\big]$$
$$= 4\log(2)\sigma^2. \tag{7.10}$$

Hence, a range-based proxy for the per-period volatility is naturally defined by

$$\sigma^2_{r,t:t+1} = \frac{1}{4\log(2)}$$
$$\times \big(\max\{p(\tau) \mid t \leqslant \tau < t+1\} - \min\{p(\tau) \mid t \leqslant \tau < t+1\}\big)^2. \tag{7.11}$$

It is readily seen that, under ideal conditions, this range-based volatility proxy is inferior to the realized variance measure constructed with a large number of intraday observations, or $\Delta \ll 1$. However, as previously discussed, a host of market microstructure and other complications often render practical situations less than ideal. Thus, even when high-frequency data are available, the range-based volatility forecast evaluation regression,

$$\sigma^2_{r,t:t+1} = a + (b+1)\hat{\sigma}^2_{t:t+1|t} + \varepsilon_{t+1}, \tag{7.12}$$

may still provide a useful robust alternative, or complement, to the realized volatility regression in (7.9).

To illustrate, consider Figure 7, which graphs a simulated geometric Brownian motion price process during a "24 hour" or "288 five-minute" period. The "fundamental", but unobserved, price process is given by the dashed line. In practice, however, we only observe this fundamental price plus a random bid–ask spread, as indicated by the jagged solid line in the figure. The figure conveys several important insights. First, notice that the squared daily return is small (close to zero) even though there are large within-day price fluctuations. As such, the true but unobserved volatility is fairly high, and poorly estimated by the daily squared return. Second, the bid–ask bounces effect introduces artificial volatility in the observed prices. As a result, realized volatilities based on very finely sampled high-frequency squared returns produce upward biased volatility measures. As previously discussed, it is, of course, possible to adjust for this bias, and several procedures for doing so have recently been proposed in the literature. Nonetheless, the figure highlights the dangers of using too small a value for Δ in the realized volatility estimation without accounting for the bid–ask spread effect.

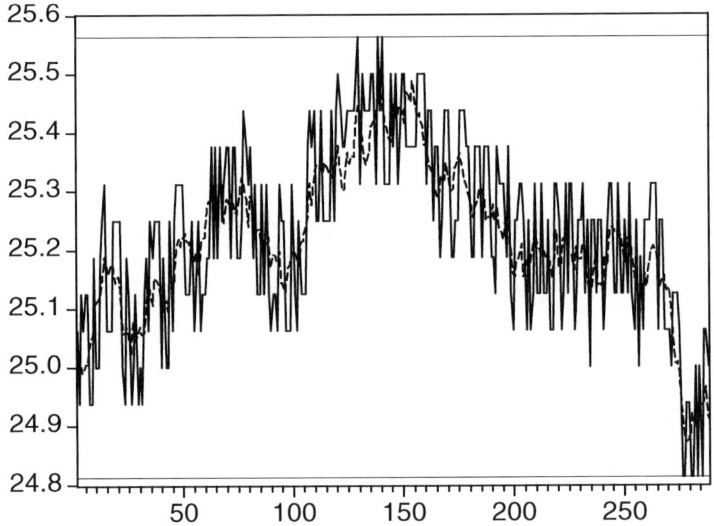

Figure 7. Simulated fundamental and observed intraday prices. The smooth dashed line represents the fundamental, but unobserved, simulated asset price. The jagged solid line solid represents the observed transaction prices reflecting bid or ask driven transactions. The two horizontal lines denote the min and max prices observed within the day.

Third, the bid–ask spread only affects the range-based measure (the difference between the two horizontal lines) twice as opposed to $1/\Delta$ times for every high-frequency return entering the realized volatility calculation. As such, the range affords a more robust (to market microstructure frictions) volatility measure. Meanwhile, an obvious drawback to the range-based volatility measure is that the multiplicative adjustment in Equation (7.11) only provides an unbiased measure for integrated volatility under the ideal, and empirically unrealistic, assumption of a geometric Brownian motion, and the "right" multiplication factor is generally unknown. Moreover, extensions to multivariate settings and covariance estimation is difficult to contemplate in the context of the range.

The preceding discussion highlights the need for tools to help in choosing the value of Δ in the realized volatility measure. To this end Andersen et al. (1999, 2000) first proposed the "volatility signature plot", as a simple indicative graphical tool. The signature plot provides a graphical representation of the realized volatility averaged over multiple days as a function of the sampling frequency, Δ, going from very high (say one-minute intervals) to low (say daily) frequencies. Recognizing that the bid–ask spread (and other frictions) generally bias the realized volatility measure, this suggests choosing the highest frequency possible for which the average realized volatility appears to have stabilized. To illustrate, Figure 8 shows a simulated example corresponding to the somewhat exaggerated market microstructure effects depicted in Figure 7. In this situation the plot suggests a sampling frequency of around "120 to 180 minutes" or "2 to

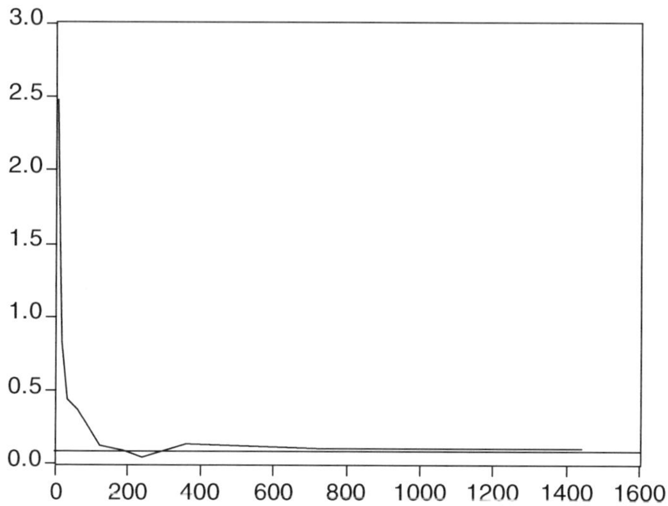

Figure 8. Volatility signature plot. The figure depicts the impact of the bid–ask spread for measuring realized volatility by showing the unconditional sample means for the realized volatilities as a function of the length of the return interval for the high-frequency data underlying the calculations. The simulated prices are subject to bid–ask bounce effects shown in Figure 7.

3 hours". Meanwhile, the actual empirical evidence for a host of actively traded assets indicate that fixing Δ somewhere between 5 and 15 minutes typically works well, but many other more refined procedures for eliminating the systematic bias in the simple realized volatility estimator are now also available.

7.3. Interval forecast and Value-at-Risk evaluation

We now discuss situations where the dynamic volatility constitutes an important part of the forecast, but the volatility itself is not the direct object of interest, leading examples of which include Value-at-Risk and probability forecasts. Specifically, consider the interval forecasts of the form discussion in Section 2,

$$\hat{y}_{t+1|t} \equiv \{\hat{y}^L_{t+1|t}, \hat{y}^U_{t+1|t}\}, \tag{7.13}$$

where the lower and upper parts of the interval forecast are defined so that there is a $(1 - p/2)$ probability of the ex-post realization falling below the lower interval and above the upper interval, respectively. In other words, the forecast promises that the ex-post outcome, y_{t+1}, will fall inside the ex-ante forecasted interval with conditional probability, p. This setting naturally suggests the definition of a zero–one indicator sequence taking the value one if the realization falls inside the predicted interval and zero otherwise. We denote this indicator by

$$I_{t+1} \equiv \mathbf{I}(\hat{y}^L_{t+1|t} < y_{t+1} < \hat{y}^U_{t+1|t}). \tag{7.14}$$

Thus, for a correctly specified conditional interval forecast the conditional probability satisfies

$$P(I_{t+1} \mid \mathcal{F}_t) = p,$$

which also equals the conditional expectation of the zero–one indicator sequence,

$$E(I_{t+1} \mid \mathcal{F}_t) = p \cdot 1 + (1 - p) \cdot 0 = p. \tag{7.15}$$

A general regression version of this conditional expectation is readily expressed as

$$I_{t+1} - p = a + b' x_t + \varepsilon_{t+1}, \tag{7.16}$$

where the joint hypothesis that $a = b = 0$ would be indicative of a correctly conditionally calibrated interval forecast series.

Since the construction of the interval forecast depends crucially on the forecasts for the underlying volatility, the set of information variables, x_t, could naturally include one or more volatility forecasts. The past value of the indicator sequence itself could also be included in the regression as an even easier and potentially effective choice of information variable. If the interval forecast ignores important volatility dynamics then the ex-post observations falling outside the ex-ante interval will cluster corresponding to periods of high volatility. In turn, this will induce serial dependence in the indicator sequence leading to a significantly positive b coefficient for $x_t = (I_t - p)$.

As noted in Section 2, the popular Value-at-Risk forecast corresponds directly to a one-sided interval forecast, and the regression in (7.16) can similarly be used to evaluate, or backtest, VARs. The indicator sequence in this case would simply be

$$I_{t+1} = \mathbf{I}\big(y_{t+1} < \mathrm{VaR}^{p}_{t+1|t}\big), \tag{7.17}$$

where y_{t+1} now refers to the ex-post portfolio return. Capturing clustering in the indicator series (and thus clustered VaR violations) is particularly important within the context of financial risk management. The occurrence of, say, three VaR violations in one week is more likely to cause financial distress than three violations scattered randomly throughout the year. Recognizing that clusters in VaR violations likely are induced by neglected volatility dynamics again highlights the importance of volatility modeling and forecasting in financial risk management.

7.4. *Probability forecast evaluation and market timing tests*

The interval and VaR forecasts discussed above correspond to quantiles (or thresholds) in the conditional distribution for a fixed and pre-specified probability of interest, p. In Section 2 we also considered probability forecasting in which the threshold of interest is pre-specified, with the probability of the random variable exceeding the threshold being forecasted. In this case the loss function is given by

$$L(y_{t+1}, \hat{y}_{t+1|t}) = \big(\mathbf{I}(y_{t+1} > c) - \hat{y}_{t+1|t}\big)^2, \tag{7.18}$$

where c denotes the threshold, and the optimal forecast equals

$$\hat{y}_{t+1|t} = P(y_{t+1} > c \mid \mathcal{F}_t).$$

The generalized forecast error follows directly from (7.3), $-2(\mathbf{I}(y_{t+1} > c) - \hat{y}_{t+1|t})$, resulting in the corresponding forecast evaluation regression

$$\mathbf{I}(y_{t+1} > c) - \hat{y}_{t+1|t} = a + b'x_t + \varepsilon_{t+1}, \tag{7.19}$$

where the hypothesis of probability forecast unbiasedness corresponds to $a = 0$ and $b = 0$. Again, the volatility forecast as well as the probability forecast itself would both be natural candidates for the vector of information variables. Notice also the similarity between the probability forecast evaluation regression in (7.19) and the interval forecast and VaR evaluation regression in (7.16).

The probability forecast evaluation framework above is closely related to tests for market timing in empirical finance. In market timing tests, y_{t+1} is the excess return on a risky asset and interest centers on forecasting the probability of a positive excess return, thus $c = 0$. In this regard, money managers are often interested in the correspondence between ex-ante probability forecasts which are larger than 0.5 and the occurrence of a positive excess return ex-post. In particular, suppose that a probability forecast larger than 0.5 triggers a long position in the risky asset and vice versa. The regression

$$\mathbf{I}(y_{t+1} > 0) = a + b\mathbf{I}(\hat{y}_{t+1|t} > 0.5) + \varepsilon_{t+1} \tag{7.20}$$

then provides a simple framework for evaluating the market timing ability in the forecasting model underlying the probability forecast, $\hat{y}_{t+1|t}$. Based on this regression it is also possible to show that $b = p_+ + p_- - 1$, where p_+ and p_- denote the probabilities of a correctly forecasted positive and negative return, respectively. A significantly positive b thus implies that either p_+ or p_- or both are significantly larger than 0.5.

7.5. *Density forecast evaluation*

The forecasts considered so far all predict certain aspects of the conditional distribution without necessarily fully specifying the distribution over the entire support. For many purposes, however, the entire predictive density is of interest, and tools for evaluating density forecasts are therefore needed. In Section 2 we explicitly defined the conditional density forecast as

$$\hat{y}_{t+1|t} = f_{t+1|t}(y) \equiv f(y_{t+1} = y \mid \mathcal{F}_t).$$

The Probability Integral Transform (PIT), defined as the probability of obtaining a value below the actual ex-post realization according to the ex-ante density forecast,

$$u_{t+1} \equiv \int_{-\infty}^{y_{t+1}} f_{t+1|t}(s)\,\mathrm{d}s, \tag{7.21}$$

provides a general framework for evaluating the predictive distribution. As the PIT variable is a probability, its support is necessarily between zero and one. Furthermore, if the density forecast is correctly specified, u_{t+1} must be i.i.d. uniformly distributed,

$$u_{t+1} \sim \text{i.i.d. } U(0, 1). \tag{7.22}$$

Intuitively, if the density forecast on average puts too little weight, say, in the left extreme of the support then a simple histogram of the PIT variable would not be flat but rather have too many observations close to zero. Thus, the PIT variable should be uniformly distributed. Furthermore, one should not be able to forecast at time t where in the forecasted density the realization will fall at time $t+1$. If one could, then that part of the density forecast is assigned too little weight at time t. Thus, the PIT variable should also be independent over time.

These considerations show that it is not sufficient to test whether the PIT variable is uniformly distributed on average. We also need conditional tests to properly assess whether the u_{t+1}'s are i.i.d. Testing for an i.i.d. uniform distribution is somewhat cumbersome due to the bounded support. Alternatively, one may more conveniently test for normality of the transformed PIT variable,

$$\tilde{u}_{t+1} \equiv \Phi^{-1}(u_{t+1}) \sim \text{i.i.d. } N(0, 1), \tag{7.23}$$

where $\Phi^{-1}(u)$ denotes the inverse cumulative density function of a standard normal variable.

In particular, the i.i.d. normal property in (7.23) implies that the conditional moment of any order j should equal the corresponding unconditional (constant) moment in the standard normal distribution, say μ_j. That is,

$$E\left[\tilde{u}_{t+1}^{j} \mid \mathcal{F}_t\right] - \mu_j = 0. \tag{7.24}$$

This in turn suggests a simple density forecast evaluation system of regressions

$$\tilde{u}_{t+1}^{j} - \mu_j = a_j + b_j' x_{j,t} + \varepsilon_{j,t+1}, \tag{7.25}$$

where j determines the order of the moment in question. For instance, testing the hypothesis that $a_j = b_j = 0$ for $j = 1, 2, 3, 4$ will assess if the first four conditional (noncentral) moments are constant and equal to their standard normal values.

Consider now the case where the density forecast specification underlying the forecast supposedly is known,

$$y_{t+1} = \mu_{t+1|t} + \sigma_{t+1|t} z_{t+1}, \quad z_{t+1} \sim \text{i.i.d. } F. \tag{7.26}$$

In this situation, it is possible to directly test the validity of the dynamic model specification for the innovations,

$$z_{t+1} = (y_{t+1} - \mu_{t+1|t})/\sigma_{t+1|t} \sim \text{i.i.d. } F. \tag{7.27}$$

The i.i.d. property is most directly and easily tested via the autocorrelations of various powers, j, of the standardized residuals, say $\mathrm{Corr}(z_t^j, z_{t-k}^j)$.

In particular, under the null hypothesis that the autocorrelations are zero at all lags, the Ljung–Box statistics for up to Kth order serial correlation,

$$\mathrm{LB}^j(K) \equiv T(T+2)\sum_{k=1}^{K}\mathrm{Corr}^2\big(z_t^j, z_{t-k}^j\big)\big/(T-k), \tag{7.28}$$

should be the realization of a chi-square distribution with K degrees of freedom. Of course, this K degree of freedom test ignores the fact that the parameters in the density forecasting model typically will have to be estimated. As noted in Section 7.1, refined test statistics as well as simulation based techniques are available to formally deal with this issue.

As previously noted, in most financial applications involving daily or weekly returns, it is reasonable to assume that $\mu_{t+1|t} \approx 0$, so that

$$z_{t+1}^2 \approx y_{t+1}^2/\sigma_{t+1|t}^2.$$

Thus, a dynamic variance model can readily be thought of as removing the dynamics from the squared observations. Misspecified variance dynamics are thus likely to show up as significant autocorrelations in z_{t+1}^2. This therefore suggests setting $j = 2$ in (7.28) and calculating the Ljung–Box test based on the autocorrelations of the squared innovations, $\mathrm{Corr}(z_t^2, z_{t-k}^2)$. This same Ljung–Box test procedure can, of course, also be used in testing for the absence of dynamic dependencies in the moments of the density forecast evaluation variable from (7.23), $\tilde{u}_{t+1}$.

7.6. Further reading

This section only scratches the surface on forecast evaluation. The properties and evaluation of point forecasts from general loss functions have recently been analyzed by Patton and Timmermann (2003, 2004). The statistical comparison of competing forecasts under general loss functions has been discussed by Diebold and Mariano (1995), Giacomini and White (2004), and West (1996). Forecast evaluation under mean-squared error loss is discussed in detail by West in Chapter 3 of this Handbook. Interval, quantile and Value-at-Risk forecast evaluation is developed further in Christoffersen (1998, 2003), Christoffersen, Hahn and Inoue (2001), Christoffersen and Pelletier (2004), Engle and Manganelli (2004), and Giacomini and Komunjer (2005). The evaluation of probability forecasts, sign forecasts and market timing techniques is surveyed in Breen, Glosten and Jagannathan (1989), Campbell, Lo and MacKinlay (1997, Chapter 2), and Christoffersen and Diebold (2003). Methods for density forecast evaluation are developed in Berkowitz (2001), Diebold, Gunther and Tay (1998), Giacomini (2002), and Hong (2000), as well as in Chapter 5 by Corradi and Swanson in this Handbook.

White (2000) provides a framework for assessing if the best forecasting model from a large set of potential models outperforms a given benchmark. Building on this idea, Hansen, Lunde and Nason (2003, 2005) develop a model confidence set approach for choosing the best volatility forecasting model.

Moreover, combining a number of volatility forecasts may be preferable to choosing a single best forecast. The general topic of forecast combination is discussed in detail in Chapter 4 by Timmermann in this Handbook. Volatility forecast combination has been found to work well in practice by Hu and Tsoukalas (1999).

Further discussion of volatility forecasting and forecast evaluation based on realized volatility measures can be found in Andersen and Bollerslev (1998a), Andersen, Bollerslev and Meddahi (2004, 2005), and Patton (2005). Andersen et al. (1999), Aït-Sahalia, Mykland and Zhang (2005), Bandi and Russel (2003, 2004), Bollen and Inder (2002), Curci and Corsi (2004), Hansen and Lunde (2004b), Martens (2003), and Zhang, Mykland and Aït-Sahalia (2005) all analyze the important choice of sampling frequency and/or the use of various sub-sampling and other corrective procedures in the practical construction of unbiased (and efficient) realized volatility measures. Alizadeh, Brandt and Diebold (2002) discuss the relative merits of realized and range-based volatility. For early work on the properties of range-based estimates, see Feller (1951) and Parkinson (1980).

Testing for normality of the transformed Probability Integral Transform (PIT) variable can be done in numerous ways. A couple of interesting recent procedures for testing dynamic models for correct distributional assumptions taking into account the parameter estimation error uncertainty are given by Bontemps and Meddahi (2005) and Duan (2003).

Several important topics were not explicitly discussed in this section. In the general forecasting area they include covariance and correlation forecast evaluation [see, e.g., Brandt and Diebold (2006)], as well as related multivariate density forecast evaluation [see, e.g., Diebold, Hahn and Tay (1999)]. In the area of financial forecast applications, we did not discuss the evaluation of time-varying betas [see, e.g., Ghysels (1998)], volatility-based asset allocation [see, e.g., Fleming, Kirby and Ostdiek (2001, 2003)], and option valuation models [see, e.g., Bates (2003) and Christoffersen and Jacobs (2004a, 2004b)], to mention some. Nonetheless, the general volatility forecast evaluation framework set out above is flexible enough so that it may easily be adapted to each of these more specific situations.

8. Concluding remarks

This chapter has focused on rigorous yet practical methods for volatility modeling and forecasting. The literature has obviously advanced rapidly and will almost surely continue to thrive for the foreseeable future, as key challenges remain at least partially open. Some of these, such as large-dimensional covariance matrix modeling and practical ways in which to best make use of the newly available ultra-high-frequency data have been touched upon.

Less obviously, and beyond the narrower realm of mathematical volatility models, the financial–econometric volatility literature has impacted the financial landscape in additional and important ways. Most notably, the newly-entrenched awareness of large time variation and high persistence in asset return volatility has led to the emergence of volatility as an asset class, with a variety of vehicles now available for taking positions exclusively in volatility. This contrasts with traditional options-based instruments, the value of which varies, for example, with the price of the underlying in addition to its volatility. The new vehicles include both exchange-traded products such as the Chicago Board Options Exchange's VIX volatility index, which depends directly on the one-month options implied volatility for the S&P500 aggregate market index, as well as more specialized over-the-counter volatility and covariance swaps, which are essentially futures contracts written on various realized volatility measures.

In addition to the obvious and traditional uses of such products, such as hedging volatility exposure associated with running an options book, important new uses in asset allocation environments are emerging, as portfolio managers add volatility to otherwise-standard portfolios. While large positions in volatility may be undesirable, because volatility reverts to a fixed mean and hence has zero expected return in the long-run, small positions can provide a valuable hedge against crisis episodes in which simultaneously plunging prices cause both correlations and volatilities to increase. This type of hedge, of course, can be very appealing in both private and central bank asset-management environments.

Although it would be an exaggeration to claim that the mathematical volatility forecasting models reviewed here are solely responsible for the emergence and deepening of financial volatility markets, the development of the models nevertheless provided (and continue to provide) a major push, the effects of which we predict will continue to evolve and resonate with financial market practice for many years to come.

References

Aguilar, O., West, M. (2000). "Bayesian dynamic factor models and variance matrix discounting for portfolio allocation". Journal of Business and Economic Statistics 18, 338–357.

Aït-Sahalia, Y., Brandt, M. (2001). "Variable selection for portfolio choice". Journal of Finance 56, 1297–1350.

Aït-Sahalia, Y., Mykland, P.A., Zhang, L. (2005). "How often to sample a continuous-time process in the presence of market microstructure noise". Review of Financial Studies 18, 351–416.

Alexander, C. (2001). Market Models: A Guide to Financial Data Analysis. Wiley, Chichester.

Alizadeh, S., Brandt, M.W., Diebold, F.X. (2002). "Range-based estimation of stochastic volatility models". Journal of Finance 57, 1047–1092.

Andersen, T.G. (1992). "Volatility". Working Paper, Finance Department, Kellogg School, Northwestern University.

Andersen, T.G. (1994). "Stochastic autoregressive volatility: A framework for volatility modeling". Mathematical Finance 4, 75–102.

Andersen, T.G. (1996). "Return volatility and trading volume: An information flow interpretation of stochastic volatility". Journal of Finance 51, 169–204.

Andersen, T.G., Benzoni, L., Lund, J. (2002). "An empirical investigation of continuous-time equity return models". Journal of Finance 57, 1239–1284.

Andersen, T.G., Bollerslev, T. (1997). "Heterogeneous information arrivals and return volatility dynamics: Uncovering the long-run in high frequency returns". Journal of Finance 52, 975–1005.

Andersen, T.G., Bollerslev, T. (1998a). "Answering the skeptics: Yes, standard volatility models do provide accurate forecasts". International Economic Review 39, 885–905.
Andersen, T.G., Bollerslev, T. (1998b). "ARCH and GARCH models". In: Kotz, S., Read, C.B., Banks, D.L. (Eds.), Encyclopedia of Statistical Sciences, vol. II. Wiley, New York.
Andersen, T.G., Bollerslev, T. (1998c). "DM–dollar volatility: Intraday activity patterns, macroeconomic announcements, and longer run dependencies". Journal of Finance 53, 219–265.
Andersen, T.G., Bollerslev, T., Diebold, F.X. (2003). "Some like it smooth and some like it rough: Untangling continuous and jump components in measuring, modeling and forecasting asset return volatility". Working Paper, Northwestern University, Duke University and University of Pennsylvania.
Andersen, T.G., Bollerslev, T., Diebold, F.X. (2005). "Parametric and nonparametric measurements of volatility". In: Aït-Sahalia, Y., Hansen, L.P. (Eds.), Handbook of Financial Econometrics. North-Holland, Amsterdam.
Andersen, T.G., Bollerslev, T., Meddahi, N. (2004). "Analytic evaluation of volatility forecasts". International Economic Review 45, 1079–1110.
Andersen, T.G., Bollerslev, T., Meddahi, N. (2005). "Correcting the errors: Volatility forecast evaluation using high-frequency data and realized volatilities". Econometrica 73, 279–296.
Andersen, T.G., Chung, H.J., Sørensen, B.E. (1999). "Efficient method of moments estimation of a stochastic volatility model: A Monte Carlo study". Journal of Econometrics 91, 61–87.
Andersen, T.G., Lund, J. (1997). "Estimating continuous-time stochastic volatility models of the short term interest rate diffusion". Journal of Econometrics 77, 343–377.
Andersen, T.G., Sørensen, B.E. (1996). "GMM estimation of a stochastic volatility model: A Monte Carlo study". Journal of Business and Economic Statistics 14, 328–352.
Andersen, T.G., Sørensen, B.E. (1997). "GMM and QML asymptotic standard deviations in stochastic volatility models: Comments on Ruiz (1994)". Journal of Econometrics 76, 397–403.
Andersen, T.G., Bollerslev, T., Diebold, F.X., Labys, P. (1999). "(Understanding, optimizing, using and forecasting) realized volatility and correlation". Working Paper, Northwestern University, Duke University and University of Pennsylvania.
Andersen, T.G., Bollerslev, T., Diebold, F.X., Labys, P. (2000). "Great realizations". Risk Magazine 18, 105–108.
Andersen, T.G., Bollerslev, T., Diebold, F.X., Ebens, H. (2001a). "The distribution of stock return volatility". Journal of Financial Economics 61, 43–76.
Andersen, T.G., Bollerslev, T., Diebold, F.X., Labys, P. (2001b). "The distribution of exchange rate volatility". Journal of the American Statistical Association 96, 42–55.
Andersen, T.G., Bollerslev, T., Diebold, F.X., Labys, P. (2003). "Modeling and forecasting realized volatility". Econometrica 71, 579–625.
Andersen, T.G., Bollerslev, T., Christoffersen, P.F., Diebold, F.X. (2005). "Practical volatility and correlation modeling for financial market risk management". In: Carey, M., Stulz, R. (Eds.), Risks of Financial Institutions. University of Chicago Press for National Bureau of Economic Research, Chicago.
Andreou, E., Ghysels, E. (2002). "Detecting multiple breaks in financial market volatility dynamics". Journal of Applied Econometrics 17, 579–600.
Ang, A., Chen, J. (2002). "Asymmetric correlation of equity portfolios". Journal of Financial Economics 63, 443–494.
Bachelier, L. (1900). "Théorie de la spéculation". Annales de l'Ecole Normale Supérieure 3. Gauthier-Villars, Paris. English translation in: Cootner, P.H. (Ed.), The Random Character of Stock Market Prices. MIT Press, Cambridge.
Baillie, R.T., Bollerslev, T. (1992). "Prediction in dynamic models with time dependent conditional variances". Journal of Econometrics 52, 91–113.
Baillie, R.T., Bollerslev, T., Mikkelsen, H.O. (1996). "Fractionally integrated generalized autoregressive conditional heteroskedasticity". Journal of Econometrics 74, 3–30.
Bakshi, G., Cao, C., Chen, Z. (1997). "Empirical performance of alternative option pricing models". Journal of Finance 52, 2003–2049.

Bandi, F., Russell, J.R. (2003). "Volatility or microstructure noise". Working Paper, University of Chicago.

Bandi, F., Russell, J.R. (2004). "Microstructure noise, realized variance, and optimal sampling". Working Paper, Graduate School of Business, University of Chicago.

Banerjee, A., Urga, G. (2005). "Modelling structural breaks, long memory and stock market volatility: An overview". Journal of Econometrics 129, 1–34.

Barndorff-Nielsen, O.E., Shephard, N. (2001). "Non-Gaussian Ornstein–Uhlenbeck-based models and some of their uses in financial economics". Journal of the Royal Statistical Society, Series B 63, 167–207.

Barndorff-Nielsen, O.E., Shephard, N. (2002). "Estimating quadratic variation using realised variance". Journal of Applied Econometrics 17, 457–477.

Barndorff-Nielsen, O.E., Shephard, N. (2004a). "Power and bipower variation with stochastic volatility and jumps". Journal of Financial Econometrics 2, 1–37.

Barndorff-Nielsen, O.E., Shephard, N. (2004b). "Econometric analysis of realized covariation: High frequency based covariance, regression and correlation in financial economics". Econometrica 72, 885–925.

Barone-Adesi, G., Giannopoulos, K., Vosper, L. (1999). "VaR without correlations for non-linear portfolios". Journal of Futures Markets 19, 583–602.

Barrett, C. (1999). "The effects of real exchange rate depreciation on stochastic producer prices in low-income agriculture". Agricultural Economics 20, 215–230.

Barucci, E., Reno, R. (2002). "On measuring volatility and the GARCH forecasting performance". Journal of International Financial Markets, Institutions and Money 12, 182–200.

Bates, D.S. (1996). "Jumps and stochastic volatility: Exchange rate processes implicit in Deutsche Mark options". Review of Financial Studies 9, 69–107.

Bates, D.S. (2003). "Empirical option pricing: A retrospection". Journal of Econometrics 116, 387–404.

Battle, C., Barquin, J. (2004). "Fuel prices scenario generation based on a multivariate GARCH model for risk analysis in a wholesale electricity market". International Journal of Electrical Power and Energy Systems 26, 273–280.

Bauwens, L., Laurent, S. (2005). "A new class of multivariate skew densities with application to GARCH models". Journal of Business and Economic Statistics 23, 346–354.

Bauwens, L., Laurent, S., Rombouts, J.V.K. (2006). "Multivariate GARCH models: A survey". Journal of Applied Econometrics. In press.

Bauwens, L., Lubrano, M. (1998). "Bayesian inference on GARCH models using the Gibbs sampler". The Econometrics Journal 1, 23–46.

Bauwens, L., Lubrano, M. (1999). Bayesian Dynamic Econometrics. Oxford University Press, Oxford.

Bekaert, G., Wu, G. (2000). "Asymmetric volatility and risk in equity markets". Review of Financial Studies 13, 1–42.

Bera, A.K., Kim, S. (2002). "Testing constancy of correlation and other specifications of the BGARCH model with an application to international equity returns". Journal of Empirical Finance 7, 305–362.

Beran, J. (1994). Statistics for Long-Memory Processes. Chapman and Hall, New York.

Berkowitz, J. (2001). "Testing density forecasts with applications to risk management". Journal of Business and Economic Statistics 19, 465–474.

Berkowitz, J., O'Brien, J. (2002). "How accurate are the value-at-risk models at commercial banks?" Journal of Finance 57, 1093–1112.

Billio, M., Caporin, M., Gobbo, M. (2003). "Block dynamic conditional correlation multivariate GARCH models". Working Paper, Università di Venezia.

Black, F. (1976). "Studies of stock market volatility changes". Proceedings of the American Statistical Association, Business and Economic Statistics Section, 177–181.

Black, F., Scholes, M. (1973). "The pricing of options and corporate liabilities". Journal of Political Economy 81, 637–654.

Bollen, B., Inder, B. (2002). "Estimating daily volatility in financial markets utilizing intraday data". Journal of Empirical Finance 9, 551–562.

Bollerslev, T. (1986). "Generalized autoregressive conditional heteroskedasticity". Journal of Econometrics 31, 307–327.

Bollerslev, T. (1987). "A conditionally heteroskedastic time series model for speculative prices and rates of return". Review of Economics and Statistics 69, 542–547.

Bollerslev, T. (1990). "Modeling the coherence in short-run nominal exchange rates: A multivariate generalized ARCH model". Review of Economics and Statistics 72, 498–505.

Bollerslev, T., Chou, R.Y., Kroner, K.F. (1992). "ARCH modeling in finance: A selective review of the theory and empirical evidence". Journal of Econometrics 52, 5–59.

Bollerslev, T., Engle, R.F. (1993). "Common persistence in conditional variances". Econometrica 61, 167–186.

Bollerslev, T., Engle, R.F., Nelson, D.B. (1994). "ARCH models". In: Engle, R.F., McFadden, D. (Eds.), Handbook of Econometrics, vol. IV. North-Holland, Amsterdam, pp. 2959–3038.

Bollerslev, T., Engle, R.F., Wooldridge, J.M. (1988). "A capital asset pricing model with time varying covariances". Journal of Political Economy 96, 116–131.

Bollerslev, T., Jubinsky, P.D. (1999). "Equity trading volume and volatility: Latent information arrivals and common long-run dependencies". Journal of Business and Economic Statistics 17, 9–21.

Bollerslev, T., Mikkelsen, H.O. (1996). "Modeling and pricing long memory in stock market volatility". Journal of Econometrics 73, 151–184.

Bollerslev, T., Mikkelsen, H.O. (1999). "Long-term equity anticipation securities and stock market volatility dynamics". Journal of Econometrics 92, 75–99.

Bollerslev, T., Wooldridge, J.M. (1992). "Quasi-maximum likelihood estimation and inference in dynamic models with time varying covariances". Econometric Reviews 11, 143–172.

Bollerslev, T., Wright, J.H. (2001). "Volatility forecasting, high-frequency data, and frequency domain inference". Review of Economic and Statistics 83, 596–602.

Bollerslev, T., Zhou, H. (2005). "Volatility puzzles: A simple framework for gauging return-volatility regressions". Journal of Econometrics. In press.

Bontemps, C., Meddahi, N. (2005). "Testing normality: A GMM approach". Journal of Econometrics 124, 149–186.

Brandt, M.W. (1999). "Estimating portfolio and consumption choice: A conditional Euler equations approach". Journal of Finance 54, 1609–1646.

Brandt, M.W. (2005). "Portfolio choice problems". In: Aït-Sahalia, Y., Hansen, L.P. (Eds.), Handbook of Financial Econometrics. North-Holland, Amsterdam.

Brandt, M.W., Diebold, F.X. (2006). "A no-arbitrage approach to range-based estimation of return covariances and correlations". Journal of Business 79, 61–74.

Brandt, M.W., Jones, C. (2002). "Volatility forecasting with range-based EGARCH models". Working Paper, The Wharton School, University of Pennsylvania.

Braun, P.A., Nelson, D.B., Sunier, A.M. (1995). "Good news, bad news, volatility, and betas". Journal of Finance 50, 1575–1603.

Breen, W., Glosten, L.R., Jagannathan, R. (1989). "Economic significance of predictable variations in stock index returns". Journal of Finance 44, 1177–1189.

Breidt, F.J., Crato, N., de Lima, P.F.J. (1998). "On the detection and estimation of long memory in stochastic volatility". Journal of Econometrics 83, 325–348.

Brooks, C. (1997). "GARCH modelling in finance: A review of the software options". The Economic Journal 107, 1271–1276.

Brooks, C. (2002). Introductory Econometrics for Finance. Cambridge University Press, Cambridge.

Brooks, C., Burke, S.P., Persand, G. (2001). "Benchmarks and the accuracy of GARCH model estimation". International Journal of Forecasting 17, 45–56.

Brooks, C., Burke, S.P., Persand, G. (2003). "Multivariate GARCH models: Software choice and estimation issues". Journal of Applied Econometrics 18, 725–734.

Buguk, C., Hudson, D., Hanson, T. (2003). "Price volatility spillover in agricultural markets: An examination of U.S. catfish markets". Journal of Agricultural and Resource Economics 28, 86–99.

Calvet, L., Fisher, A. (2002). "Multifractality in asset returns: Theory and evidence". Review of Economics and Statistics 84, 381–406.

Calvet, L., Fisher, A. (2004). "How to forecast long-run volatility: Regime switching and the estimation of multifractal processes". Journal of Financial Econometrics 2, 49–83.

Calvet, L.E., Fisher, A.J., Thompson, S.B. (2005). "Volatility comovement: A multifrequency approach". Journal of Econometrics. In press.

Campbell, J.Y. (1987). "Stock returns and the term structure". Journal of Financial Economics 18, 373–399.

Campbell, J.Y. (2003). "Consumption-based asset pricing". In: Constantinides, G.M., Harris, M., Stulz, R. (Eds.), Handbook of the Economics of Finance, vol. 1B. North-Holland, Amsterdam, pp. 803–888.

Campbell, J.Y., Hentschel, L. (1992). "No news is good news: An asymmetric model of changing volatility in stock returns". Journal of Financial Economics 31, 281–318.

Campbell, J.Y., Lo, A.W., MacKinlay, A.C. (1997). The Econometrics of Financial Markets. Princeton University Press, Princeton.

Campbell, S., Diebold, F.X. (2005). "Weather forecasting for weather derivatives". Journal of the American Statistical Association 100, 6–16.

Cappiello, L., Engle, R.F., Sheppard, K. (2004). "Asymmetric dynamic in the correlations of global equity and bond returns". Working Paper, NYU Stern School of Business.

Chacko, G., Viceira, L.M. (2003). "Spectral GMM estimation of continuous-time processes". Journal of Econometrics 116, 259–292.

Chan, N.H. (2002). Time Series: Applications to Finance. Wiley, New York.

Chernov, M., Ghysels, E. (2000). "A study towards a unified framework for the joint estimation of objective and risk neutral measures for the purpose of options valuation". Journal of Financial Economics 56, 407–458.

Chernov, M., Gallant, A.R., Ghysels, E., Tauchen, G.E. (2003). "Alternative models for stock price dynamics". Journal of Econometrics 116, 225–257.

Christie, A.A. (1982). "The stochastic behavior of common stock variances: Value, leverage and interest rate effects". Journal of Financial Economics 10, 407–432.

Christoffersen, P.F. (1998). "Evaluating interval forecasts". International Economic Review 39, 841–862.

Christoffersen, P.F. (2003). Elements of Financial Risk Management. Academic Press, San Diego.

Christoffersen, P.F., Diebold, F.X. (1996). "Further results on forecasting and model selection under asymmetric loss". Journal of Applied Econometrics 11, 561–572.

Christoffersen, P.F., Diebold, F.X. (1997). "Optimal prediction under asymmetric loss". Econometric Theory 13, 808–817.

Christoffersen, P.F., Diebold, F.X. (2000). "How relevant is volatility forecasting for financial risk management?" Review of Economics and Statistics 82, 12–22.

Christoffersen, P.F., Diebold, F.X. (2003). "Financial asset returns, direction-of-change forecasting, and volatility dynamics". NBER Working Paper 10009.

Christoffersen, P.F., Hahn, J., Inoue, A. (2001). "Testing and comparing value-at-risk measures". Journal of Empirical Finance 8, 325–342.

Christoffersen, P.F., Jacobs, K. (2004a). "The importance of the loss function in option valuation". Journal of Financial Economics 72, 291–318.

Christoffersen, P.F., Jacobs, K. (2004b). "Which GARCH model for option valuation?" Management Science 50, 1204–1221.

Christoffersen, P.F., Pelletier, D. (2004). "Backtesting value-at-risk: A duration-based approach". Journal of Financial Econometrics 2, 84–108.

Clark, P.K. (1973). "A subordinated stochastic process model with finite variance for speculative prices". Econometrica 41, 135–156.

Cochrane, J. (2001). Asset Pricing. Princeton University Press, Princeton.

Comte, F., Renault, E. (1998). "Long memory in continuous-time stochastic volatility models". Mathematical Finance 8, 291–323.

Corsi, F. (2003). "A simple long memory model of realized volatility". Working Paper, University of Southern Switzerland.

Corsi, F., Zumbach, G., Müller, U.A., Dacorogna, M. (2001). "Consistent high-precision volatility from high-frequency data". Economic Notes 30, 183–204.

Cripps, E., Dunsmuir, W.T.M. (2003). "Modeling the variability of Sydney Harbor wind measurements". Journal of Applied Meteorology 42, 1131–1138.

Curci, G., Corsi, F. (2004). "A discrete sine transform approach for realized volatility measurement". Working Paper, University of Pisa and University of Southern Switzerland.

Dacorogna, M.M., Müller, U.A., Nagler, R.J., Olsen, R.B., Pictet, O.V. (2001). An Introduction to High-Frequency Finance. Academic Press, San Diego.

Danielsson, J. (1994). "Stochastic volatility in asset prices: Estimation by simulated maximum likelihood". Journal of Econometrics 54, 375–400.

Danielsson, J., Richard, J.F. (1993). "Accelerated Gaussian importance sampler with application to dynamic latent variable models". Journal of Applied Econometrics 8, S153–S173.

Davidson, J. (2004). "Moment and memory properties of linear conditional heteroskedasticity models, and a new model". Journal of Business and Economic Statistics 22, 16–29.

De Jong, F., Nijman, T. (1997). "High frequency analysis of lead-lag relationships between financial markets". Journal of Empirical Finance 4, 259–277.

Deo, R., Hurvich, C. (2001). "On the log periodogram regression estimator of the memory parameter in long memory stochastic volatility models". Econometric Theory 17, 686–710.

DeSantis, G., Gerard, B. (1997). "International asset pricing and portfolio diversification with time-varying risk". Journal of Finance 52, 1881–1912.

DeSantis, G., Litterman, R., Vesval, A., Winkelmann, K. (2003). "Covariance matrix estimation". In: Litterman, R. (Ed.), Modern Investment Management: An Equilibrium Approach. Wiley, London.

Dhaene, G., Vergote, O. (2004). "Asymptotic results for GMM estimators of stochastic volatility models". Working Paper, Department of Economics, K.U. Leuven.

Diebold, F.X. (1988). Empirical Modeling of Exchange Rate Dynamics. Springer-Verlag, New York.

Diebold, F.X. (2004). "The Nobel memorial prize for Robert F. Engle". Scandinavian Journal of Economics 106, 165–185.

Diebold, F.X., Gunther, T., Tay, A. (1998). "Evaluating density forecasts, with applications to financial risk management". International Economic Review 39, 863–883.

Diebold, F.X., Hahn, J., Tay, A. (1999). "Multivariate density forecast evaluation and calibration in financial risk management: High-frequency returns on foreign exchange". Review of Economics and Statistics 81, 661–673.

Diebold, F.X., Inoue, A. (2001). "Long memory and regime switching". Journal of Econometrics 105, 131–159.

Diebold, F.X., Lopez, J. (1995). "Modeling volatility dynamics". In: Hoover, K. (Ed.), Macroeconometrics: Developments, Tensions and Prospects. Kluwer Academic, Boston, pp. 427–472.

Diebold, F.X., Lopez, J. (1996). "Forecast evaluation and combination". In: Maddala, G.S., Rao, C.R. (Eds.), Handbook of Statistics. North-Holland, Amsterdam, pp. 241–268.

Diebold, F.X., Mariano, R.S. (1995). "Comparing predictive accuracy". Journal of Business and Economic Statistics 13, 253–265.

Diebold, F.X., Nerlove, M. (1989). "The dynamics of exchange rate volatility: A multivariate latent factor ARCH model". Journal of Applied Econometrics 4, 1–21.

Ding, Z., Granger, C.W.J. (1996). "Modeling volatility persistence of speculative returns: A new approach". Journal of Econometrics 73, 185–215.

Ding, Z., Granger, C.W.J., Engle, R.F. (1993). "A long memory property of stock market returns and a new model". Journal of Empirical Finance 1, 83–106.

Drost, F.C., Nijman, T.E. (1993). "Temporal aggregation of GARCH processes". Econometrica 61, 909–927.

Drost, F.C., Werker, B.J.M. (1996). "Closing the GARCH gap: Continuous time GARCH modeling". Journal of Econometrics 74, 31–58.

Duan, J.-C. (1995). "The GARCH option pricing model". Mathematical Finance 5, 13–32.

Duan, J.-C. (2003). "A specification test for time series models by a normality transformation". Working Paper, Rotman School of Management, University of Toronto.

Duffie, D., Pan, J., Singleton, K.J. (2000). "Transform analysis and asset pricing for affine jump-diffusions". Econometrica 68, 1343–1376.

Duffie, D., Singleton, K.J. (1993). "Simulated moments estimation of Markov models of asset prices". Econometrica 61, 929–952.

Dufour, J.M. (2004). "Monte Carlo tests with nuisance parameters: A general approach to finite-sample inference and nonstandard asymptotics in econometrics". Working Paper, Université de Montréal.

Elerian, O., Chib, S., Shephard, N. (2001). "Likelihood inference for discretely observed nonlinear diffusions". Econometrica 69, 959–994.

Embrechts, P., Klüppelberg, C., Mikosch, T. (1997). Modelling Extremal Events for Insurance and Finance. Springer-Verlag, Berlin.

Enders, W. (2004). Applied Econometric Time Series. Wiley, Hoboken.

Engle, R.F. (1982). "Autoregressive conditional heteroskedasticity with estimates of the variance of UK inflation". Econometrica 50, 987–1008.

Engle, R.F. (1995). ARCH: Selected Readings. Oxford University Press, Oxford.

Engle, R.F. (2001). "GARCH 101: The use of ARCH/GARCH models in applied econometrics". Journal of Economic Perspectives 15, 157–168.

Engle, R.F. (2002). "Dynamic conditional correlation: A simple class of multivariate GARCH models". Journal of Business and Economic Statistics 20, 339–350.

Engle, R.F. (2004). "Nobel lecture. Risk and volatility: Econometric models and financial practice". American Economic Review 94, 405–420.

Engle, R.F., Bollerslev, T. (1986). "Modeling the persistence of conditional variances". Econometric Reviews 5, 1–50.

Engle, R.F., Gonzalez-Rivera, G. (1991). "Semiparametric ARCH models". Journal of Business and Economic Statistics 9, 345–360.

Engle, R.F., Ito, T., Lin, W.L. (1990). "Meteor showers or heat waves? Heteroskedastic intra-daily volatility in the foreign exchange market". Econometrica 58, 525–542.

Engle, R.F., Kroner, F.K. (1995). "Multivariate simultaneous generalized ARCH". Econometric Theory 11, 122–150.

Engle, R.F., Lee, G.G.J. (1999). "A permanent and transitory component model of stock return volatility". In: Engle, R.F., White, H. (Eds.), Cointegration, Causality, and Forecasting: A Festschrift in Honor of Clive W.J. Granger. Oxford University Press, Oxford, pp. 475–497.

Engle, R.F., Lilien, D.M., Robbins, R.P. (1987). "Estimating time varying risk premia in the term structure: The ARCH-M model". Econometrica 55, 391–407.

Engle, R.F., Manganelli, S. (2004). "CAViaR: Conditional autoregressive value at risk by regression quantiles". Journal of Business and Economic Statistics 22, 367–381.

Engle, R.F., Ng, V.K. (1993). "Measuring and testing the impact of news on volatility". Journal of Finance 48, 1749–1778.

Engle, R.F., Ng, V.K., Rothschild, M. (1990). "Asset pricing with a factor-ARCH covariance structure: Empirical estimates for treasury bills". Journal of Econometrics 45, 213–238.

Engle, R.F., Patton, A.J. (2001). "What good is a volatility model?" Quantitative Finance 1, 237–245.

Engle, R.F., Sheppard, K. (2001). "Theoretical and empirical properties of dynamic conditional correlation multivariate GARCH". Working Paper, NYU Stern School of Business.

Epps, T. (1979). "Comovements in stock prices in the very short run". Journal of the American Statistical Association 74, 291–298.

Eraker, B. (2001). "MCMC analysis of diffusions with applications to finance". Journal of Business and Economic Statistics 19, 177–191.

Eraker, B. (2004). "Do stock prices and volatility jump? Reconciling evidence from spot and option prices". Journal of Finance 59, 1367–1403.

Eraker, B., Johannes, M., Polson, N.G. (2003). "The impact of jumps in equity index volatility and returns". Journal of Finance 58, 1269–1300.

Erb, C., Harvey, C., Viskanta, T. (1994). "Forecasting international equity correlations". Financial Analysts Journal 50, 32–45.

Ewing, B.T., Piette, M.J., Payne, J.E. (2003). "Forecasting medical net discount rates". Journal of Risk and Insurance 70, 85–95.

Feller, W. (1951). "The asymptotic distribution of the range of sums of random variables". Annals of Mathematical Statistics 22, 427–432.

Fiorentini, G., Sentana, E., Calzolari, G. (2003). "Maximum likelihood estimation and inference in multivariate conditionally heteroskedastic dynamic regression models with Student-t innovations". Journal of Business and Economic Statistics 21, 532–546.

Fiorentini, G., Sentana, E., Shephard, N. (2004). "Likelihood-based estimation of latent generalized ARCH structures". Econometrica 72, 1481–1517.

Fleming, J., Kirby, C. (2003). "A closer look at the relation between GARCH and stochastic autoregressive volatility". Journal of Financial Econometrics 1, 365–419.

Fleming, J., Kirby, C., Ostdiek, B. (2001). "The economic value of volatility timing". Journal of Finance 56, 329–352.

Fleming, J., Kirby, C., Ostdiek, B. (2003). "The economic value of volatility timing using "realized" volatility". Journal of Financial Economics 67, 473–509.

Foster, D.P., Nelson, D.B. (1996). "Continuous record asymptotics for rolling sample variance estimators". Econometrica 64, 139–174.

Fouque, J.-P., Papanicolaou, G., Sircar, K.R. (2000). Derivatives in Financial Markets with Stochastic Volatility. Princeton University Press, Princeton.

Franses, P.H., Hafner, C. (2003). "A generalized dynamic conditional correlation model for many asset returns". Working Paper, Erasmus University, Rotterdam.

Franses, P.H., van Dijk, D. (2000). Non-Linear Time Series Models in Empirical Finance. Cambridge University Press, Cambridge.

French, K.R., Schwert, G.W., Stambaugh, R.F. (1987). "Expected stock returns and volatility". Journal of Financial Economics 19, 3–29.

Fridman, M., Harris, L. (1998). "A maximum likelihood approach for non-Gaussian stochastic volatility models". Journal of Business and Economic Statistics 16, 284–291.

Gallant, A.R., Hsieh, D.A., Tauchen, G.E. (1997). "Estimation of stochastic volatility models with diagnostics". Journal of Econometrics 81, 159–192.

Gallant, A.R., Hsu, C.T., Tauchen, G.E. (1999). "Using daily range data to calibrate volatility diffusions and extract the forward integrated variance". Review of Economics and Statistics 81, 617–631.

Gallant, A.R., Rossi, P.E., Tauchen, G.E. (1992). "Stock prices and volume". Review of Financial Studies 5, 199–242.

Gallant, A.R., Tauchen, G.E. (1996). "Which moments to match". Econometric Theory 12, 657–681.

Gallant, A.R., Tauchen, G.E. (1997). "Estimation of continuous-time models for stock returns and interest rates". Macroeconomic Dynamics 1, 135–168.

Gallant, A.R., Tauchen, G. (1998). "Reprojecting partially observed systems with application to interest rate diffusions". Journal of the American Statistical Association 93, 10–24.

Geweke, J. (1989a). "Bayesian inference in econometric models using Monte Carlo integration". Econometrica 57, 1317–1340.

Geweke, J. (1989b). "Exact predictive densities in linear models with ARCH disturbances". Journal of Econometrics 40, 63–86.

Ghysels, E. (1998). "On stable factor structures in the pricing of risk: Do time-varying betas help or hurt?" Journal of Finance 53, 549–573.

Ghysels, E., Harvey, A.C., Renault, E. (1996). "Stochastic volatility". In: Maddala, G.S., Rao, C.R. (Eds.), Handbook of Statistics, vol. 14. North-Holland, Amsterdam.

Ghysels, E., Santa-Clara, P., Valkanov, R. (2004). "Predicting volatility: Getting the most out of data sampled at different frequencies". Working Paper, University of North Carolina and University of California, Los Angeles.

Giacomini, R. (2002). "Comparing density forecasts via weighted likelihood ratio tests: Asymptotic and bootstrap methods". Boston College, Department of Economics Working Paper 583.

Giacomini, R., Komunjer, I. (2005). "Evaluation and combination of conditional quantile forecasts". Journal of Business and Economic Statistics 23, 416–431.

Giacomini, R., White, H. (2004). "Tests of conditional predictive ability". Working Paper, University of California, San Diego.

Giordani, P., Soderlind, P. (2003). "Inflation forecast uncertainty". European Economic Review 47, 1037–1059.

Giraitis, L., Kokoszka, P., Leipus, R. (2000). "Stationary ARCH models: Dependence structure and central limit theorem". Econometric Theory 16, 3–22.

Glosten, L.R., Jagannathan, R., Runkle, D. (1993). "On the relation between the expected value and the volatility of the nominal excess return on stocks". Journal of Finance 48, 1779–1801.

Gouriéroux, C., Jasiak, J. (2001). Financial Econometrics. Princeton University Press, Princeton.

Gouriéroux, C., Monfort, A., Renault, E. (1993). "Indirect inference". Journal of Applied Econometrics 8, S85–S118.

Granger, C.W.J. (1969). "Prediction with a generalized cost of error function". Operational Research Quarterly 20, 199–207.

Granger, C.W.J. (1980). "Long memory relationships and the aggregation of dynamic models". Journal of Econometrics 14, 227–238.

Granger, C.W.J., White, H., Kamstra, M. (1989). "Interval forecasting: An analysis based on ARCH-quantile estimators". Journal of Econometrics 40, 87–96.

Gronke, P., Brehm, J. (2002). "History, heterogeneity, and presidential approval: A modified ARCH approach". Electoral Studies 21, 425–452.

Guidolin, M., Timmermann, A. (2005a). "Term structure of risk under alternative specifications". Journal of Econometrics. In press.

Guidolin, M., Timmermann, A. (2005b). "An econometric model of nonlinear dynamics in the joint distribution of stock and bond returns". Journal of Applied Econometrics. In press.

Hamilton, J.D. (1994). Time Series Analysis. Princeton University Press, Princeton.

Hamilton, J.D., Lin, G. (1996). "Stock market volatility and the business cycle". Journal of Applied Econometrics 11, 573–593.

Hansen, P.R., Lunde, A. (2004a). "A realized variance for the whole day based on intermittent high-frequency data". Working Paper, Department of Economics, Stanford University.

Hansen, P.R., Lunde, A. (2004b). "An unbiased measure of realized variance". Working Paper, Department of Economics, Stanford University.

Hansen, P.R., Lunde, A. (2005). "A forecast comparison of volatility models: Does anything beat a GARCH(1, 1)?" Journal of Applied Econometrics 20, 873–889.

Hansen, P.R., Lunde, A., Nason, J.M. (2003). "Choosing the best volatility models: A model confidence set approach". Oxford Bulletin of Economics and Statistics 65, 839–861.

Hansen, P.R., Lunde, A., Nason, J.M. (2005). "Model confidence sets for forecasting models". Working Paper, Stanford University.

Harris, L. (1986). "Cross-security tests of the mixture of distributions hypothesis". Journal of Financial and Quantitative Analysis 21, 39–46.

Harris, L. (1987). "Transactions data tests of the mixture of distributions hypothesis". Journal of Financial and Quantitative Analysis 22, 127–141.

Harvey, A.C. (1989). Forecasting, Structural Time Series Models and the Kalman Filter. Cambridge University Press, Cambridge.

Harvey, A.C. (1998). "Long memory in stochastic volatility". In: Knight, J., Satchell, S. (Eds.), Forecasting Volatility in Financial Markets. Butterworth–Heineman, Oxford, pp. 307–320.

Harvey, A.C. (2006). "Forecasting with unobserved components time series models". In: Elliott, G., Granger, C.W.J., Timmermann, A. (Eds.), Handbook of Economic Forecasting. Elsevier, Amsterdam, pp. 327–412. This volume.

Harvey, A.C., Ruiz, E., Sentana, E. (1992). "Unobserved component time series models with ARCH disturbances". Journal of Econometrics 52, 129–157.

Harvey, A.C., Ruiz, E., Shephard, E. (1994). "Multivariate stochastic variance models". Review of Economic Studies 61, 247–264.

Harvey, A.C., Shephard, E. (1996). "Estimation of an asymmetric model of asset prices". Journal of Business and Economic Statistics 14, 429–434.

Harvey, C.R. (2001). "The specification of conditional expectations". Journal of Empirical Finance 8, 573–637.

Hentschel, L. (1995). "All in the family: Nesting symmetric and asymmetric GARCH models". Journal of Financial Economics 39, 71–104.

Heston, S.L. (1993). "A closed form solution for options with stochastic volatility, with applications to bond and currency options". Review of Financial Studies 6, 327–343.

Heston, S.L., Nandi, S. (2000). "A closed-form GARCH option valuation model". Review of Financial Studies 13, 585–625.

Hong, Y. (2000). "Evaluation of out-of-sample density forecasts with applications to stock prices". Working Paper, Department of Economics and Department of Statistical Science, Cornell University.

Hsieh, D.A. (1989). "Modeling heteroskedasticity in foreign exchange rates". Journal of Business and Economic Statistics 7, 307–317.

Hu, M., Tsoukalas, C. (1999). "Combining conditional volatility forecasts using neural networks: An application to the EMS exchange rates". Journal of International Financial Markets, Institutions and Money 9, 407–422.

Huang, X., Tauchen, G.E. (2004). "The relative contribution of jumps to total price variance". Working Paper, Duke University.

Hull, J., White, A. (1987). "The pricing of options on assets with stochastic volatilities". Journal of Finance 42, 281–300.

J.P. Morgan (1996). RiskMetrics, Technical Documents, fourth ed. New York.

Jacquier, E., Polson, N.G., Rossi, P.E. (1994). "Bayesian analysis of stochastic volatility models". Journal of Business and Economic Statistics 12, 371–389.

Jagannathan, R., Ma, T. (2003). "Risk reduction in large portfolios: Why imposing the wrong constraints helps". Journal of Finance 58, 1651–1684.

Jiang, G.J., Knight, J.L. (2002). "Efficient estimation of the continuous time stochastic volatility model via the empirical characteristic function". Journal of Business and Economic Statistics 20, 198–212.

Johannes, M., Polson, N.G. (2005). "MCMC methods for continuous-time financial econometrics". In: Aït-Sahalia, Y., Hansen, L.P. (Eds.), Handbook of Financial Econometrics. North-Holland, Amsterdam.

Johannes, M., Polson, N., Stroud, J. (2004). "Sequential optimal portfolio performance: Market and volatility timing". Working Paper, Columbia University, University of Pennsylvania, and University of Chicago.

Johnson, T.D., Elashoff, R.M., Harkema, S.J.A. (2003). "Bayesian change point analysis of electromyographic data: Detecting muscle activation patterns and associated applications". Biostatistics 4, 143–164.

Johnson, H., Shanno, D. (1987). "Option pricing when the variance is changing". Journal of Financial and Quantitative Analysis 22, 143–152.

Jondeau, E., Rockinger, M. (2005). "The copula-GARCH model of conditional dependence: An international stock market application". Journal of International Money and Finance. In press.

Jorion, P. (2000). Value at Risk: The New Benchmark for Managing Financial Risk. McGraw–Hill, New York.

Karpoff, J.M. (1987). "The relation between price changes and trading volume: A survey". Journal of Financial and Quantitative Analysis 22, 109–126.

Kawakatsu, H. (2005). "Matrix exponential GARCH". Journal of Econometrics. In press.

Kim, S., Shephard, N., Chib, S. (1998). "Stochastic volatility: Likelihood inference and comparison with ARCH models". Review of Economic Studies 65, 361–393.

King, M., Sentana, E., Wadhwani, S. (1994). "Volatility and links between national stock markets". Econometrica 62, 901–933.

Kroner, K.F., Ng, V.K. (1998). "Modelling asymmetric comovements of asset returns". Review of Financial Studies 11, 817–844.

Lamoureux, C.G., Lastrapes, W.D. (1990). "Persistence in variance, structural change, and the GARCH model". Journal of Business and Economic Statistics 8, 225–234.

Lamoureux, C.G., Lastrapes, W.D. (1994). "Endogenous trading volume and momentum in stock-return volatility". Journal of Business and Economic Statistics 14, 253–260.

Lastrapes, W.D. (1989). "Exchange rate volatility and US Monetary Policy: An ARCH application". Journal of Money, Credit and Banking 21, 66–77.

Ledoit, O., Santa-Clara, P., Wolf, M. (2003). "Flexible multivariate GARCH modeling with an application to international stock markets". Review of Economics and Statistics 85, 735–747.

Ledoit, O., Wolf, M. (2003). "Improved estimation of the covariance matrix of stock returns with an application to portfolio selection". Journal of Empirical Finance 10, 603–621.

Lee, S.W., Hansen, B.E. (1994). "Asymptotic theory for the GARCH(1, 1) quasi-maximum likelihood estimator". Econometric Theory 10, 29–52.

Lettau, M., Ludvigson, S. (2003). "Measuring and modeling variation in the risk-return tradeoff". Working Paper, New York University and NBER.

Li, W.K., Ling, S., McAleer, M. (2002). "Recent theoretical results for time series with GARCH errors". Journal of Economic Surveys 16, 245–269.

Liesenfeld, R. (1998). "Dynamic bivariate mixture models: Modeling the behavior of prices and trading volume". Journal of Business and Economic Statistics 16, 101–109.

Liesenfeld, R. (2001). "A generalized bivariate mixture model for stock price volatility and trading volume". Journal of Econometrics 104, 141–178.

Liesenfeld, R., Richard, J.F. (2003). "Univariate and multivariate stochastic volatility models: Estimation and diagnostics". Journal of Empirical Finance 10, 505–531.

Ling, S., McAleer, M. (2003). "Asymptotic theory for a vector ARMA-GARCH model". Econometric Theory 19, 280–310.

Linn, S.C., Zhu, Z. (2004). "Natural gas prices and the gas storage report: Public news and volatility in energy futures markets". Journal of Futures Markets 24, 283–313.

Longin, F., Solnik, B. (1995). "Is the correlation in international equity returns constant: 1970–1990?" Journal of International Money and Finance 14, 3–26.

Longin, F., Solnik, B. (2001). "Extreme correlation of international equity markets". Journal of Finance 56, 649–676.

Loretan, M., Phillips, P.C.B. (1994). "Testing covariance stationarity under moment condition failure with an application to stock returns". Journal of Empirical Finance 1, 211–248.

Lumsdaine, R.L. (1996). "Consistency and asymptotic normality of the quasi-maximum likelihood estimator in GARCH(1, 1) and covariance stationary GARCH(1, 1) models". Econometrica 64, 575–596.

Lundin, M., Dacorogna, M.M., Müller, U.A. (1998). "Correlation of high frequency financial time series". In: Lequeux, P. (Ed.), The Financial Markets Tick by Tick. Wiley, London.

Lütkepohl, H. (2006). "Forecasting with VARMA models". In: Elliott, G., Granger, C.W.J., Timmermann, A. (Eds.), Handbook of Economic Forecasting. Elsevier, Amsterdam, pp. 287–325. This volume.

Maestas, C., Preuhs, R. (2000). "Modeling volatility in political time series". Electoral Studies 19, 95–110.

Marinova, D., McAleer, M. (2003). "Modeling trends and volatility in ecological patents in the USA". Environmental Modelling and Software 18, 195–203.

Markowitz, H. (1952). "Portfolio selection". Journal of Finance 7, 77–91.

Marquering, W., Verbeek, M. (2004). "The economic value of predicting stock index returns and volatility". Journal of Financial and Quantitative Analysis 39, 407–429.

Martens, M. (2003). "Estimating unbiased and precise realized covariances". Working Paper, University of Rotterdam.

Martin-Guerrero, J.D., Camps-Valls, G., Soria-Olivas, E., Serrano-Lopez, A.J., Perez-Ruixo, J.J., Jimenez-Torres, N.V. (2003). "Dosage individualization of erythropoietin using a profile dependent support vector regression". IEEE Transactions on Biomedical Engineering 50, 1136–1142.

McCullough, B., Renfro, C. (1998). "Benchmarks and software standards: A case study of GARCH procedures". Journal of Economic and Social Measurement 25, 59–71.

McNeil, A.J., Frey, R. (2000). "Estimation of tail-related risk measures for heteroskedastic financial time series: An extreme value approach". Journal of Empirical Finance 7, 271–300.
Meddahi, N. (2001). "An eigenfunction approach for volatility modeling". Working Paper, University of Montréal.
Meddahi, N., Renault, E. (2004). "Temporal aggregation of volatility models". Journal of Econometrics 119, 355–379.
Meghir, C., Pistaferri, L. (2004). "Income variance dynamics and heterogeneity". Econometrica 72, 1–32.
Melino, A., Turnbull, S.M. (1990). "Pricing foreign currency options with stochastic volatility". Journal of Econometrics 45, 239–265.
Merton, R.C. (1969). "Lifetime portfolio selection under uncertainty: The continuous-time case". Review of Economics and Statistics 51, 247–257.
Merton, R.C. (1976). "Option pricing when underlying stock returns are discontinuous". Journal of Financial Economics 3, 125–144.
Mikosch, T., Starica, C. (2004). "Nonstationarities in financial time series, the long range dependence and the IGARCH effects". Review of Economics and Statistics 86, 378–390.
Mills, T.C. (1993). The Econometric Modelling of Financial Time Series. Cambridge University Press, Cambridge.
Mincer, J., Zarnowitz, V. (1969). "The evaluation of economic forecasts". In: Mincer, J. (Ed.), Economic Forecasts and Expectations. National Bureau of Economic Research, New York.
Monfardini, C. (1998). "Estimating stochastic volatility models through indirect inference". The Econometrics Journal 1, C113–C128.
Müller, U.A., Dacorogna, M.M., Davé, R.D., Olsen, R.B., Puctet, O.V., von Weizsäcker, J. (1997). "Volatilities of different time resolutions – Analyzing the dynamics of market components". Journal of Empirical Finance 4, 213–239.
Nelson, D.B. (1988). "Time series behavior of stock market volatility and returns". Ph.D. dissertation, MIT.
Nelson, D.B. (1990). "Stationarity and persistence in the GARCH(1, 1) model". Econometric Theory 6, 318–334.
Nelson, D.B. (1991). "Conditional heteroskedasticity in asset returns: A new approach". Econometrica 59, 347–370.
Nijman, T., Sentana, E. (1996). "Marginalization and contemporaneous aggregation in multivariate GARCH processes". Journal of Econometrics 71, 71–87.
Ng, V.K., Engle, R.F., Rothschild, M. (1992). "A multi-dynamic-factor model for stock returns". Journal of Econometrics 52, 245–266.
O'Connell, P.E. (1971). "A simple stochastic modelling of Hurst's law". Proceedings of International Symposium on Mathematical Models in Hydrology 1, 169–187.
Pagan, A. (1996). "The econometrics of financial markets". Journal of Empirical Finance 3, 15–102.
Palm, F. (1996). "GARCH models of volatility". In: Rao, C.R., Maddala, G.S. (Eds.), Handbook of Statistics, vol. 14. North-Holland, Amsterdam, pp. 209–240.
Pan, J. (2002). "The jump-risk premia implicit in options: Evidence from an integrated time-series study". Journal of Financial Economics 63, 3–50.
Parkinson, M. (1980). "The extreme value method for estimating the variance of the rate of returns". Journal of Business 53, 61–65.
Pastor, L., Stambaugh, R. (2001). "The Equity premium and structural breaks". Journal of Finance 56, 1207–1245.
Patton, A. (2004). "Modeling asymmetric exchange rate dependence". Working Paper, London School of Economics.
Patton, A. (2005). "Volatility forecast evaluation and comparison using imperfect volatility proxies". Working Paper, London School of Economics.
Patton, A., Timmermann, A. (2003). "Properties of optimal forecasts". CEPR Discussion Paper 4037.
Patton, A., Timmermann, A. (2004). "Testable implications of forecast optimality". Working Paper, London School of Economics and University of California at San Diego.

Pelletier, D. (2005). "Regime switching for dynamic correlations". Journal of Econometrics. In press.
Perez-Quiros, G., Timmermann, A. (2000). "Firm size and cyclical variations in stock returns". Journal of Finance 55, 1229–1262.
Pesaran, M.H., Zaffaroni, P. (2004). "Model averaging and value-at-risk based evaluation of large multi asset volatility models for risk management". Working Paper, Department of Economics, University of Cambridge.
Piazzesi, M. (2005). "Affine term structure models". In: Hansen, L.P., Aït-Sahalia, Y (Eds.), Handbook of Financial Econometrics. North-Holland, Amsterdam.
Praetz, P.D. (1972). "The distribution of share price changes". Journal of Business 45, 49–55.
Pritsker, M. (2001). "The hidden dangers of historical simulation". Working Paper, Federal Reserve Board.
Ramirez, O.A., Fadiga, M. (2003). "Forecasting agricultural commodity prices with asymmetric error GARCH models". Journal of Agricultural and Resource Economics 28, 71–85.
Rich, R., Tracy, J. (2004). "Uncertainty and labor contract durations". Review of Economics and Statistics 86, 270–287.
Richardson, M., Smith, T. (1994). "A direct test of the mixture of distributions hypothesis: Measuring the daily flow of information". Journal of Financial and Quantitative Analysis 29, 101–116.
Robinson, P.M. (1991). "Testing for strong serial correlation and dynamic conditional heteroskedasticity in multiple regression". Journal of Econometrics 47, 67–84.
Rossi, P.E. (1996). Modeling Stock Market Volatility: Bridging the Gap to Continuous Time. Academic Press, San Diego.
Ruge-Murcia, F.J. (2004). "The inflation bias when the central bank targets the natural rate of unemployment". European Economic Review 48, 91–107.
Sandmann, G., Koopman, S.J. (1998). "Estimation of stochastic volatility models through Monte Carlo maximum likelihood". Journal of Econometrics 87, 271–301.
Scholes, M., Williams, J. (1977). "Estimating betas from non-synchronous data". Journal of Financial Economics 5, 309–327.
Schwert, G.W. (1989). "Why does stock market volatility change over time?" Journal of Finance 44, 1115–1153.
Scott, L.O. (1987). "Option pricing when the variance changes randomly: Theory, estimation and an application". Journal of Financial and Quantitative Analysis 22, 419–438.
Sentana, E., Fiorentini, G. (2001). "Identification, estimation and testing of conditionally heteroskedastic factor models". Journal of Econometrics 102, 143–164.
Shanken, J.A. (1990). "Intertemporal asset pricing: An empirical investigation". Journal of Econometrics 45, 99–120.
Sharpe, W. (1964). "Capital asset prices – A theory of market equilibrium under conditions of risk". Journal of Finance 19, 425–442.
Shawky, M.A., Marathe, A., Barrett, C.L. (2003). "A first look at the empirical relation between spot and futures electricity prices in the United States". Journal of Futures Markets 23, 931–955.
Shephard, N. (1996). "Statistical aspects of ARCH and stochastic volatility models". In: Cox, D.R., Hinkley, D.V., Barndorff-Nielsen, O.E. (Eds.), Time Series Models in Econometrics, Finance and Other Fields. Chapman and Hall, London, pp. 1–67.
Shephard, N. (2004). Stochastic Volatility: Selected Readings. Oxford University Press, Oxford.
Sheppard, K. (2004). "Economic factors and the covariance of equity returns". Working Paper, University of California, San Diego.
Singleton, K.J. (2001). "Estimation of affine asset pricing models using the empirical characteristic function". Journal of Econometrics 102, 111–141.
Smith Jr., A.A. (1990). "Three essays on the solution and estimation of dynamic macroeconomic models". Ph.D. dissertation, Duke University.
Smith Jr., A.A. (1993). "Estimating nonlinear time-series models using simulated vector autoregressions". Journal of Applied Econometrics 8, S63–S84.
Tauchen, G., Pitts, M. (1983). "The price variability-volume relationship on speculative markets". Econometrica 51, 485–505.

Taylor, S.J. (1986). Modeling Financial Time Series. Wiley, Chichester.

Taylor, S.J. (2004). Asset Price Dynamics and Prediction. Princeton University Press, Princeton.

Taylor, J.W., Buizza, R. (2003). "Using weather ensemble predictions in electricity demand forecasting". International Journal of Forecasting 19, 57–70.

Tiao, G.C., Tsay, R.S. (1994). "Some advances in non-linear and adaptive modeling in time series". Journal of Forecasting 14, 109–131.

Tsay, R.S. (2002). Analysis of Financial Time Series. Wiley, New York.

Tse, Y.K., Tsui, A.K.C. (2002). "A multivariate GARCH model with time-varying correlations". Journal of Business and Economic Statistics 20, 351–362.

Tse, Y.K., Yip, P.S.L. (2003). "The impacts of Hong Kong's currency board reforms on the interbank market". Journal of Banking and Finance 27, 2273–2296.

Wang, L. (2004). "Investing when volatility fluctuates". Working Paper, The Wharton School and Singapore Management University.

Weiss, A.A. (1986). "Asymptotic theory for ARCH models: Estimation and testing". Econometric Theory 2, 107–131.

West, K.D. (1996). "Asymptotic inference about predictive ability". Econometrica 64, 1067–1084.

West, K.D., Cho, D. (1995). "The predictive ability of several models of exchange rate volatility". Journal of Econometrics 69, 367–391.

West, K.D., McCracken, M.W. (1998). "Regression-based tests of predictive ability". International Economic Review 39, 817–840.

White, H. (2000). "A reality check for data snooping". Econometrica 68, 1097–1127.

Whitelaw, R.F. (1997). "Time-varying Sharpe ratios and market timing". Working Paper, NYU, Stern School of Business.

Wiggins, J.B. (1987). "Option values under stochastic volatility: Theory and empirical estimates". Journal of Financial Economics 19, 351–372.

Zaffaroni, P. (2004). "Estimating and forecasting volatility with large scale models: Theoretical appraisal of professional practice". Working Paper, Banca d'Italia.

Zakoïan, J.-M. (1994). "Threshold heteroskedastic models". Journal of Economic Dynamics and Control 18, 931–955.

Zhang, L., Mykland, P.A., Aït-Sahalia, Y. (2005). "A tale of two time scales: Determining integrated volatility with noisy high-frequency data". Journal of the American Statistical Association 100, 1394–1411.

Zhou, B. (1996). "High-frequency data and volatility in foreign exchange rates". Journal of Business and Economic Statistics 14, 45–52.

Chapter 16

LEADING INDICATORS

MASSIMILIANO MARCELLINO*

IEP-Bocconi University, IGIER and CEPR
e-mail: massimiliano.marcellino@uni-bocconi.it

Contents

* I am grateful to two anonymous Referees, to participants at the Rady Conference on Economic Forecasting (UCSD) and to seminar participants at the Dutch Central Bank, University of Barcelona and Università Tor Vergata for useful comments on a previous draft; to Maximo Camacho, Jim Hamilton, Chang-Jin Kim, Charles Nelson, and Gabriel Perez-Quiros for sharing their code; to Ataman Ozyildirim at the Conference Board and Anirvan Banerji at ECRI for data and information; to Andrea Carriero and Alice Ghezzi for excellent research assistance; and to Nicola Scalzo for editorial assistance.

Handbook of Economic Forecasting, Volume 1
Edited by Graham Elliott, Clive W.J. Granger and Allan Timmermann

DOI: 10.1016/S1574-0706(05)01016-5

Abstract

In this chapter we provide a guide for the construction, use and evaluation of leading indicators, and an assessment of the most relevant recent developments in this field of economic forecasting. To begin with, we analyze the problem of indicator selection, choice of filtering methods, business cycle dating procedures to transform a continuous variable into a binary expansion/recession indicator, and methods for the construction of composite indexes. Next, we examine models and methods to transform the leading indicators into forecasts of the target variable. Finally, we consider the evaluation of the resulting leading indicator based forecasts, and review the recent literature on the forecasting performance of leading indicators.

Keywords

business cycles, leading indicators, coincident indicators, turning points, forecasting

JEL classification: E32, E37, C53

1. Introduction

Since the pioneering work of Mitchell and Burns (1938) and Burns and Mitchell (1946), leading indicators have attracted considerable attention, in particular by politicians and business people, who consider them as a useful tool for predicting future economic conditions. Economists and econometricians have developed more mixed feelings towards the leading indicators, starting with Koopmans' (1947) critique of the work of Burns and Mitchell, considered as an exercise in "measurement without theory". The resulting debate has stimulated the production of a vast literature that deals with the different aspects of the leading indicators, ranging from the choice and evaluation of the best indicators, possibly combined in composite indexes, to the development of more and more sophisticated methods to relate them to the target variable.

In this chapter we wish to provide a guide for the construction, use and evaluation of leading indicators and, more important, an assessment of the most relevant recent developments in this field of economic forecasting.

We start in Section 2 with a discussion of the choice of the target variable for the leading indicators, which can be a single variable, such as GDP or industrial production, or a composite coincident index, and the focus can be in anticipating either future values of the target or its turning points. We then evaluate the basic requirements for an economic variable to be a useful leading indicator, which can be summarized as:

(i) consistent timing (i.e., to systematically anticipate peaks and troughs in the target variable, possibly with a rather constant lead time);
(ii) conformity to the general business cycle (i.e., have good forecasting properties not only at peaks and troughs);
(iii) economic significance (i.e., being supported by economic theory either as possible causes of business cycles or, perhaps more importantly, as quickly reacting to negative or positive shocks);
(iv) statistical reliability of data collection (i.e., provide an accurate measure of the quantity of interest);
(v) prompt availability without major later revisions (i.e., being timely and regularly available for an early evaluation of the expected economic conditions, without requiring subsequent modifications of the initial statements);
(vi) smooth month to month changes (i.e., being free of major high frequency movements).

Once the choice of the target measure of aggregate activity and of the leading indicators is made, two issues emerge: first, the selection of the proper variable transformation, if any, and, second, the adoption of a dating rule that identifies the peaks and troughs in the series, and the associated expansionary and recessionary periods and their durations. The choice of the variable transformation is related to the two broad definitions of the cycle recognized in the literature, the so-called classical cycle and the growth or deviation cycle. In the case of the deviation cycle, the focus is on the deviations of the target variable from an appropriately defined trend rate of growth, while the classical cycle relies on the levels of the target variable. There is a large technical literature on variable transformation by filtering the data, and in Section 3 we review some of the key contributions in this area. We also compare alternative dating algorithms, highlighting their pros and cons.

In Section 4 we describe simple nonmodel based techniques for the construction of composite coincident or leading indexes. Basically, each component of the index should be carefully selected on the basis of the criteria mentioned above, properly filtered to enhance its business cycle characteristics, deal with seasonal adjustment and remove outliers, and standardized to make its amplitude similar or equal to that of the other index components. The components are then aggregated into the composite index using a certain weighting scheme, typically simple averaging.

From an econometric point of view, composite leading indexes constructed following the procedure sketched above are subject to several criticisms. For example, there is no explicit reference to the target variable in the construction of the composite leading index and the weighting scheme is fixed over time, with periodic revisions mostly due either to data issues, such as changes in the production process of an indicator, or to the past unsatisfactory performance of the index. The main counterpart of these problems is simplicity. Nonmodel based indexes are easy to build, easy to explain, and easy to interpret, which are very valuable assets, in particular for the general public and for policy-makers. Moreover, simplicity is often a plus also for forecasting.

Most of the issues raised for the nonmodel based approach to the construction of composite indexes are addressed by the model based procedures, which can be grouped into two main classes: dynamic factor models and Markov switching models.

Dynamic factor models were developed by Geweke (1977) and Sargent and Sims (1977), but their use became well known to most business cycle analysts after the publication of Stock and Watson's (1989) attempt to provide a formal probabilistic basis for Burns and Mitchell's coincident and leading indicators. The rationale of the approach is that a set of variables is driven by a limited number of common forces, and by idiosyncratic components that are uncorrelated across the variables under analysis. Stock and Watson (1989) estimated a coincident index of economic activity as the unobservable factor in a dynamic factor model for four coincident indicators: industrial production, real disposable income, hours of work and sales.

The main criticism Sims (1989) raised in his comment to Stock and Watson (1989) is the use of a constant parameter statistical model (estimated with classical rather than Bayesian methods). This comment relates to the old debate on the characterization of business cycles as extrinsic phenomena, i.e., generated by the arrival of external shocks propagated through a linear model, versus intrinsic phenomena, i.e., generated by the nonlinear development of the endogenous variables. The main problem with the latter view, at least implicitly supported also by Burns and Mitchell that treated expansions and recessions as two different periods, was the difficulty of casting it into a simple and testable statistical framework, an issue addressed by Hamilton (1989).

Hamilton's (1989) Markov switching model allows the growth rate of the variables (and possibly their dynamics) to depend on the status of the business cycle, which is modelled as a Markov chain. With respect to the factor model based analysis, there is again a single unobservable force underlying the evolution of the indicators but, first, it is discrete rather than continuous and, second, it does not directly affect or summarize the variables but rather indirectly determines their behavior that can change substantially over different phases of the cycle.

As in the case of Stock and Watson (1989), Hamilton (1989) has generated an impressive amount of subsequent research. Here it is worth mentioning the work by Diebold and Rudebusch (1996), which allows the parameters of the factor model in Stock and Watson (1989) to change over the business cycle according to a Markov process. Kim and Nelson (1998) estimated the same model but in a Bayesian framework using the Gibbs sampler, as detailed below, therefore addressing both of Sims' criticisms reported above. Unfortunately, both papers confine themselves to the construction of a coincident indicator and do not consider the issue of leading indicators.

In Sections 5 and 6 we review in detail the competing model based approaches to the construction of composite indexes and discuss their advantages and disadvantages.

In Section 7 we illustrate the practical implementation of the theoretical results by constructing and comparing a set of alternative indexes for the US. We find that all model based coincident indexes are in general very similar and close to the equal weighted ones. As a consequence, the estimation of the current economic condition is rather robust to the choice of method. The model based leading indexes are somewhat different from their nonmodel based counterparts. Their main advantage is that they are derived in a proper statistical framework that, for example, permits the computation of standard errors around the index, the unified treatment of data revisions and missing observations, and the possibility of using time-varying parameters.

In Section 8 we evaluate other approaches for forecasting using leading indicators. In particular, Section 8.1 deals with observed transition models, where the relationship between the target variable and the leading indicators can be made dependent on a set of observable variables, such as GDP growth or the interest rate. Section 8.2 considers neural network and nonparametric methods, where even less stringent hypotheses are imposed on the relationship between the leading indicators and their target. Section 8.3 focuses on the use of binary models for predicting business cycle phases, a topic that attracted considerable attention in the '90s, perhaps as a consequence of the influential study by Diebold and Rudebusch (1989). Finally, Section 8.4 analyzes forecast pooling procedures in the leading indicator context since, starting with the pioneering work of Bates and Granger (1969), it is well known that combining several forecasts can yield more accurate predictions than those of each of the individual forecasts.

In Section 9 we consider the methodological aspects of the evaluation of the forecasting performance of the leading indicators when used either in combination with simple rules to predict turning points [e.g., Vaccara and Zarnowitz (1978)], or as regressors in a model for (a continuous or discrete) target variable. We then discuss a set of empirical examples, to illustrate the theoretical concepts.

A review of the recent literature on the actual performance of leading indicators is contained in Section 10. Four main strands of research can be identified in this literature. First, the consequences of the use of real time information on the composite leading index and its components rather than the final releases. Second, the assessment of the relative performance of the new more sophisticated models for the coincident-leading indicators. Third, the evaluation of financial variables as leading indicators. Finally, the analysis of the behavior of the leading indicators during the two most recent US recessions as dated by the NBER, namely, July 1990–March 1991 and March 2001–November 2001.

To conclude, in Section 11 we summarize what we have learned about leading indicators in the recent past, and suggest directions for further research in this interesting and promising field of forecasting.

2. Selection of the target and leading variables

The starting point for the construction of leading indicators is the choice of the target variable, namely, the variable that the indicators are supposed to lead. Such a choice is discussed in the first subsection. Once the target variable is identified, the leading indicators have to be selected, and we discuss selection criteria in the second subsection.

2.1. Choice of target variable

Burns and Mitchell (1946, p. 3) proposed that:

> "... a cycle consists of expansions occurring at about the same time in many economic activities..."

Yet, later on in the same book (p. 72) they stated:

> "Aggregate activity can be given a definite meaning and made conceptually measurable by identifying it with gross national product."

These quotes underlie the two most common choices of target variable: either a single indicator that is closely related to GDP but available at the monthly level, or a composite index of coincident indicators.

GDP could provide a reliable summary of the current economic conditions if it were available on a monthly basis. Though both in the US and in Europe there is a growing interest in increasing the sampling frequency of GDP from quarterly to monthly, the current results are still too preliminary to rely on.

In the past, industrial production provided a good proxy for the fluctuations of GDP, and it is still currently monitored for example by the NBER business cycle dating committee and by the Conference Board in the US, in conjunction with other indicators. Yet, the ever rising share of services compared with the manufacturing, mining, gas and electric utility industries casts more and more doubts on the usefulness of IP as a single coincident indicator.

Another common indicator is the volume of sales of the manufacturing, wholesale and retail sectors, adjusted for price changes so as to proxy real total spending. Its main drawback, as in the case of IP, is its partial coverage of the economy.

A variable with a close to global coverage is real personal income less transfers, that underlies consumption decisions and aggregate spending. Yet, unusual productivity growth and favorable terms of trade can make income behave differently from payroll employment, the other most common indicator with economy wide coverage. More precisely, the monitored series is usually the number of employees on nonagricultural payrolls, whose changes reflect the net hiring (both permanent and transitory) and firing in the whole economy, with the exception of the smallest businesses and the agricultural sector.

Some authors focused on unemployment rather than employment, e.g., Boldin (1994) or Chin, Geweke and Miller (2000), on the grounds that the series is timely available and subject to minor revisions. Yet, typically unemployment is slightly lagging and not coincident.

Overall, it is difficult to identify a single variable that provides a good measure of current economic conditions, is available on a monthly basis, and is not subject to major later revisions. Therefore, it is preferable to consider combinations of several coincident indicators.

The monitoring of several coincident indicators can be done either informally, for example the NBER business cycle dating committee examines the joint evolution of IP, employment, sales and real disposable income [see, e.g., Hall et al. (2003)], or formally, by combining the indicators into a composite index. A composite coincident index can be constructed in a nonmodel based or in a model based framework, and we will review the main approaches within each category in Sections 4 and 5, respectively.

Once the target variable is defined, it may be necessary to emphasize its cyclical properties by applying proper filters, and/or to transform it into a binary expansion/recession indicator relying on a proper dating procedure. Both issues are discussed in Section 3.

2.2. *Choice of leading variables*

Since the pioneering work of Mitchell and Burns (1938), variable selection has rightly attracted considerable attention in the leading indicator literature; see, e.g., Zarnowitz and Boschan (1975a, 1975b) for a review of early procedures at the NBER and Department of Commerce. Moore and Shiskin (1967) formalized an often quoted scoring system [see, e.g., Boehm (2001), Phillips (1998–1999)], based mostly upon

(i) consistent timing as a leading indicator (i.e., to systematically anticipate peaks and troughs in the target variable, possibly with a rather constant lead time);
(ii) conformity to the general business cycle (i.e., have good forecasting properties not only at peaks and troughs);
(iii) economic significance (i.e., being supported by economic theory either as possible causes of business cycles or, perhaps more importantly, as quickly reacting to negative or positive shocks);
(iv) statistical reliability of data collection (i.e., provide an accurate measure of the quantity of interest);

(v) prompt availability without major later revisions (i.e., being timely and regularly available for an early evaluation of the expected economic conditions, without requiring subsequent modifications of the initial statements);
(vi) smooth month to month changes (i.e., being free of major high frequency movements).

Some of these properties can be formally evaluated at different levels of sophistication. In particular, the peak/trough dates of the target and candidate leading variables can be compared and used to evaluate whether the peak structure of the leading indicator systematically anticipated that of the coincident indicator, with a stable lead time (property (i)). An alternative procedure can be based on the statistical concordance of the binary expansion/recession indicators (resulting from the peak/trough dating) for the coincident and lagged leading variables, where the number of lags of the leading variable can be either fixed or chosen to maximize the concordance. A formal test for no concordance is defined below in Section 9.1. A third option is to run a logit/probit regression of the coincident expansion/recession binary indicator on the leading variable, evaluating the explanatory power of the latter. The major advantage of this procedure is that several leading indicators can be jointly considered to measure their partial contribution. Details on the implementation of this procedure are provided in Section 8.3.

To assess whether a leading indicator satisfies property (ii), conformity to the general business cycle, it is preferable to consider it and the target coincident index as continuous variables rather than transforming them into binary indicators. Then, the set of available techniques includes frequency domain procedures (such as the spectral coherence and the phase lead), and several time domain methods, ranging from Granger causality tests in multivariate linear models, to the evaluation of the marginal predictive content of the leading indicators in sophisticated nonlinear models, possibly with time varying parameters, see Sections 6 and 8 for details on these methods. Within the time domain framework it is also possible to consider a set of additional relevant issues such as the presence of cointegration between the coincident and leading indicators, the determination of the number lags of the leading variable, or the significance of duration dependence. We defer a discussion of these topics to Section 6.

Property (iii), economic significance, can be hardly formally measured, but it is quite important both to avoid the measurement without theory critique, e.g., Koopmans (1947), and to find indicators with stable leading characteristics. On the other hand, the lack of a commonly accepted theory of the origin of business cycles [see, e.g., Fuhrer and Schuh (1998)] makes it difficult to select a single indicator on the basis of its economic significance.

Properties (iv) and (v) have received considerable attention in recent years and, together with economic theory developments, underlie the more and more widespread use of financial variables as leading indicators (due to their exact measurability, prompt availability and absence of revisions), combined with the adoption of real-time datasets for the assessment of the performance of the indicators, see Section 10 for details on these issues. Time delays in the availability of leading indicators are particularly problematic for the construction of composite leading indexes, and have been treated differently in the literature and in practice. Either preliminary values of the composite indexes are constructed excluding the unavailable indicators and later revised, along the tradition of the NBER and later of the Department of Commerce and the Conference Board, or the unavailable observations are substituted with forecasts, as in the factor based approaches described in Section 6.2. The latter solution is receiving increasing favor also within the traditional methodology; see, e.g., McGuckin, Ozyildirim and Zarnowitz (2003). Within the factor based approaches the possibility of measurement error in the components of the leading index, due, e.g., to data revisions, can also be formally taken into account, as discussed in Section 5.1, but in practice the resulting composite indexes require later revisions as well. Yet, both for the traditional and for the more sophisticated methods, the revisions in the composite indexes due to the use of later releases of their components are minor.

The final property (vi), a smooth evolution in the leading indicator, can require a careful choice of variable transformations and/or filter. In particular, the filtering procedures discussed in Section 3 can be applied to enhance the business cycle characteristics of the leading indicators, and in general should be if the target variable is filtered. In general, they can provide improvements with respect to the standard choice of month to month differences of the leading indicator. Also, longer differences can be useful to capture sustained growth or lack of it [see, e.g., Birchenhall et al. (1999)] or differences with respect to the previous peak or trough to take into consideration the possible nonstationary variations of values at turning points [see, e.g., Chin, Geweke and Miller (2000)].

As in the case of the target variable, the use of a single leading indicator is dangerous because economic theory and experience teach that recessions can have different sources and characteristics. For example, the twin US recessions of the early '80s were mostly due to tight monetary policy, that of 1991 to a deterioration in the expectations climate because of the first Iraq war, and that of 2001 to the bursting of the stock market bubble and, more generally, to over-investment; see, e.g., Stock and Watson (2003b). In the Euro area, the three latest recessions according to the CEPR dating are also rather different, with the one in 1974 lasting only three quarters and characterized by synchronization across countries and coincident variables, as in 1992–1993 but contrary to the longer recession that started at the beginning of 1980 and lasted 11 quarters.

A combination of leading indicators into composite indexes can therefore be more useful in capturing the signals coming from different sectors of the economy. The construction of a composite index requires several steps and can be undertaken either in a nonmodel based framework or with reference to a specific econometric model of the evolution of the leading indicators, possibly jointly with the target variable. The two approaches are discussed in Sections 4 and 6, respectively.

3. Filtering and dating procedures

Once the choice of the target measure of aggregate activity (and possibly of the leading indicators) is made, two issues emerge: first the selection of the proper variable transformation, if any, and second the adoption of a dating rule that identifies the peaks and troughs in the series, and the associated expansionary and recessionary periods and their durations.

The choice of the variable transformation is related to the two broad definitions of the cycle recognized in the literature, the so-called classical cycle and the growth or deviation cycle. In the case of the deviation cycle, the focus is on the deviations of the rate of growth of the target variable from an appropriately defined trend rate of growth, while the classical cycle relies on the levels of the target variable.

Besides removing long term movements as in the deviation cycle, high frequency fluctuations can also be eliminated to obtain a filtered variable that satisfies the duration requirement in the original definition of Burns and Mitchell (1946, p. 3):

> "...in duration business cycles vary from more than one year to ten or twelve years; they are not divisible into shorter cycles of similar character with amplitudes approximating their own."

There is a large technical literature on methods of filtering the data. In line with the previous paragraph, Baxter and King (1999) argued that the ideal filter for cycle measurement must be customized to retain unaltered the amplitude of the business cycle periodic components, while removing high and low frequency components. This is known as a *band-pass* filter and, for example, when only cycles with frequency in the range 1.5–8 years are of interest, the theoretical frequency response function of the filter takes the rectangular form: $w(\omega) = \mathrm{I}(2\pi/(8s) \leqslant \omega \leqslant 2\pi/(1.5s))$, where $\mathrm{I}(\cdot)$ is the indicator function. Moreover, the phase displacement of the filter should always be zero, to preserve the timing of peaks and troughs; the latter requirement is satisfied by a symmetric filter.

Given the two business cycle frequencies, $\omega_{c1} = 2\pi/(8s)$ and $\omega_{c2} = 2\pi/(1.5s)$, the band-pass filter is

$$w_{\mathrm{bp}}(L) = \frac{\omega_{c2} - \omega_{c1}}{\pi} + \sum_{j=1}^{\infty} \frac{\sin(\omega_{c2} j) - \sin(\omega_{c1} j)}{\pi j} \left(L^j + L^{-j}\right). \tag{1}$$

Thus, the ideal band-pass filter exists and is unique, but it entails an infinite number of leads and lags, so in practice an approximation is required. Baxter and King (1999) showed that the K-terms approximation to the ideal filter (1) that is optimal in the sense of minimizing the integrated squared approximation error is simply (1) truncated at lag K. They proposed using a three year window, i.e., $K = 3s$, as a valid rule of thumb for macroeconomic time series. They also constrained the weights to sum up to zero, so that the resulting approximation is a detrending filter; see, e.g., Stock and Watson (1999a) for an application.

As an alternative, Christiano and Fitzgerald (2003) proposed to project the ideal filter on the available sample. If $c_t = w_{\mathrm{bp}}(L)x_t$ denotes the ideal cyclical component, their proposal is to consider $\hat{c}_t = E(c_t \mid x_1, \ldots, x_T)$, where x_t is given a parametric linear representation, e.g., an ARIMA model. They also found that for a wide class of macroeconomic time series the filter derived under the random walk assumption for x_t is feasible and handy.

Baxter and King (1999) did not consider the problem of estimating the cycle at the extremes of the available sample (the first and last three years), which is inconvenient for a real-time assessment of current business conditions. Christiano and Fitzgerald (2003) suggested to replace the out of sample missing observations by their best linear prediction under the random walk hypothesis. Yet, this can upweight the last and the first available observations.

As a third alternative, Artis, Marcellino and Proietti (2004, AMP) designed a bandpass filter as the difference of two Hodrick and Prescott (1997) detrending filters with parameters $\lambda = 1$ and $\lambda = 677.13$, where these values are selected to ensure that $\omega_{c1} = 2\pi/(8s)$ and $\omega_{c2} = 2\pi/(1.5s)$. The resulting estimates of the cycle are comparable to the Baxter and King cycle, although slightly noisier, without suffering from unavailability of the end of sample estimates.

Working with growth rates of the coincident variables rather than levels, a convention typically adopted for the derivation of composite indexes, corresponds to the application of a filter whose theoretical frequency response function increases monotonically, starting at zero at the zero frequency. Therefore, growth cycles and deviation cycles need not be very similar.

In early post-war decades, especially in Western Europe, growth was relatively persistent and absolute declines in output were comparatively rare; the growth or deviation cycle then seemed to be of more analytical value, especially as inflexions in the rate of growth of output could reasonably be related to fluctuations in the levels of employment and unemployment. In more recent decades, however, there have been a number of instances of absolute decline in output, and popular description at any rate has focussed more on the classical cycle. The concern that de-trending methods can affect the information content of the series in unwanted ways [see, e.g., Canova (1999)] has reinforced the case for examining the classical cycle. The relationships among the three types of cycles are analyzed in more details below, after defining the dating algorithms to identify peaks and troughs in the series and, possibly, transform it into a binary indicator.

In the US, the National Bureau of Economic Research (http://www.nber.org) provides a chronology of the classical business cycle since the early '20s, based on the consensus of a set of coincident indicators concerning production, employment, real income and real sales, that is widely accepted among economists and policy-makers; see, e.g., Moore and Zarnowitz (1986). A similar chronology has been recently proposed for the Euro area by the Center for Economic Policy Research (http://www.cepr.org), see Artis et al. (2003).

Since the procedure underlying the NBER dating is informal and subject to substantial delays in the announcement of the peak and trough dates (which is rational to avoid later revisions), several alternative methods have been put forward and tested on the basis of their ability to closely reproduce the NBER classification.

The simplest approach, often followed by practitioners, is to identify a recession with at least two quarters of negative real GDP growth. Yet, the resulting chronology differs with respect to the NBER in a number of occasions; see, e.g., Watson (1991) or Boldin (1994).

A more sophisticated procedure was developed by Bry and Boschan (1971) and further refined by Harding and Pagan (2002). In particular, for quarterly data on the log-difference of GDP or GNP (Δx_t), Harding and Pagan defined an expansion terminating sequence, ETS_t, and a recession terminating sequence, RTS_t, as follows:

$$\begin{aligned} \mathrm{ETS}_t &= \{(\Delta x_{t+1} < 0) \cap (\Delta\Delta x_{t+2} < 0)\}, \\ \mathrm{RTS}_t &= \{(\Delta x_{t+1} > 0) \cap (\Delta\Delta x_{t+2} > 0)\}. \end{aligned} \tag{2}$$

The former defines a candidate point for a peak in the classical business cycle, which terminates the expansion, whereas the latter defines a candidate for a trough. When compared with the NBER dating, usually there are only minor discrepancies. Stock and Watson (1989) adopted an even more complicated rule for identifying peaks and troughs in their composite coincident index.

Within the Markov Switching (MS) framework, discussed in details in Sections 5 and 6, a classification of the observations into two regimes is automatically produced by comparing the probability of being in a recession with a certain threshold, e.g., 0.50. The turning points are then easily obtained as the dates of switching from expansion to recession, or vice versa. Among others, Boldin (1994) reported encouraging results using an MS model for unemployment, and Layton (1996) for the ECRI coincident index. Chauvet and Piger (2003) also confirmed the positive results with a real-time dataset and for a more up-to-date sample period.

Harding and Pagan (2003) compared their nonparametric rule with the MS approach, and further insight can be gained from Hamilton's (2003) comments on the paper and the authors' rejoinder. While the nonparametric rule produces simple, replicable and robust results, it lacks a sound economic justification and cannot be used for probabilistic statements on the current status of the economy. On the other hand, the MS model provides a general statistical framework to analyze business cycle phenomena, but the requirement of a parametric specification introduces a subjective element into the analysis and can necessitate careful tailoring. Moreover, if the underlying model is linear, the MS recession indicator is not identified while pattern recognition works in any case.

AMP developed a dating algorithm based on the theory of Markov chains that retains the attractive features of the nonparametric methods, but allows the computation of the probability of being in a certain regime or of a phase switch. Moreover, the algorithm can be easily modified to introduce depth or amplitude restrictions, and to construct diffusion indices. Basically, the transition probabilities are scored according to the pattern in the series x_t rather than within a parametric MS model. The resulting chronology for the Euro area is very similar to the one proposed by the CEPR, and a similar result emerges for the US with respect to the NBER dating, with the exception of the last recession, see Section 7 below for details.

An alternative parametric procedure to compute the probability of being in a certain cyclical phase is to adopt a probit or logit model where the dependent variable is the

NBER expansion/recession classification, and the regressors are the coincident indicators. For example, Birchenhall et al. (1999) showed that the fit of a logit model is very good in sample when the four NBER coincident indicators are used. They also found that the logit model outperformed an MS alternative, while Layton and Katsuura (2001) obtained the opposite ranking in a slightly different context.

The in-sample estimated parameters from the logit or probit models can also be used in combination with future available values of the coincident indicators to predict the future status of the economy, which is useful, for example, to conduct a real time dating exercise because of the mentioned delays in the NBER announcements.

So far, in agreement with most of the literature, we have classified observations into two phases, recessions and expansions, which are delimited by peaks and troughs in economic activity. However, multiphase characterizations of the business cycle are not lacking in the literature: the popular definition due to Burns and Mitchell (1946) postulated four states: expansion, recession, contraction, recovery; see also Sichel (1994) for an ex-ante three phases characterization of the business cycle, Artis, Krolzig and Toro (2004) for an ex-post three-phases classification based on a model with Markov switching, and Layton and Katsuura (2001) for the use of multinomial logit models.

To conclude, having defined several alternative dating procedures, it is useful to return to the different notions of business cycle and recall a few basic facts about their dating, summarizing results in AMP.

First, neglecting duration ties, classical recessions (i.e., peak-trough dynamics in x_t), correspond to periods of prevailing negative growth, $\Delta x_t < 0$. In effect, negative growth is a sufficient, but not necessary, condition for a classical recession under the Bry and Boschan dating rule and later extensions. Periods of positive growth can be observed during a recession, provided that they are so short lived that they do not determine an exit from the recessionary state.

Second, turning points in x_t correspond to Δx_t crossing the zero line (from above zero if the turning point is a peak, from below in the presence of a trough in x_t). This is strictly true under the calculus rule, according to which $\Delta x_t < 0$ terminates the expansion.

Third, if x_t admits the log-additive decomposition, $x_t = \psi_t + \mu_t$, where ψ_t denotes the deviation cycle, then growth is in turn decomposed into cyclical and residual changes:

$$\Delta x_t = \Delta\psi_t + \Delta\mu_t.$$

Hence, assuming that $\Delta\mu_t$ is mostly due to growth in trend output, deviation cycle recessions correspond to periods of growth below potential growth, that is $\Delta x_t < \Delta\mu_t$. Using the same arguments, turning points correspond to Δx_t crossing $\Delta\mu_t$. When the sum of potential growth and cyclical growth is below zero, that is $\Delta\mu_t + \Delta\psi_t < 0$, a classical recession also occurs.

Finally, as an implication of the previous facts, classical recessions are always a subset of deviation cycle recessions, and there can be multiple classical recessionary episodes within a period of deviation cycle recessions. This suggests that an analysis of the deviation cycle can be more informative and relevant also from the economic policy point of view, even though more complicated because of the filtering issues related to the extraction of the deviation cycle.

4. Construction of nonmodel based composite indexes

In the nonmodel based framework for the construction of composite indexes, the first element is the selection of the index components. Each component should satisfy the criteria mentioned in Section 2. In addition, in the case of leading indexes, a balanced representation of all the sectors of the economy should be achieved, or at least of those more closely related to the target variable.

The second element is the transformation of the index components to deal with seasonal adjustment, outlier removal, treatment of measurement error in first releases of indicators subject to subsequent revision, and possibly forecast of unavailable most recent observations for some indicators. These adjustments can be implemented either in a univariate framework, mostly by exploiting univariate time series models for each indicator, or in a multivariate context. In addition, the transformed indicators should be made comparable to be included in a single index. Therefore, they are typically detrended (using different procedures such as differencing, regression on deterministic trends, or the application of more general band-pass filters), possibly smoothed to eliminate high frequency movements (using moving averages or, again, band pass filters), and standardized to make their amplitudes similar or equal.

The final element for the construction of a composite index is the choice of a weighting scheme. The typical choice, once the components have been standardized, is to give them equal weights. This seems a sensible averaging scheme in this context, unless there are particular reasons to give larger weights to specific variables or sectors, depending on the target variable or on additional information on the economic situation; see, e.g., Niemira and Klein (1994, Chapter 3) for details.

A clear illustration of the nonmodel based approach is provided by (a slightly simplified version of) the step-wise procedure implemented by the Conference Board, CB (previously by the Department of Commerce, DOC) to construct their composite coincident index (CCI), see www.conference-board.org for details.

First, for each individual indicator, x_{it}, month-to-month symmetric percentage changes (spc) are computed as $x_{it\_\text{spc}} = 200 * (x_{it} - x_{it-1})/(x_{it} + x_{it+1})$. Second, for each x_{it_spc} a volatility measure, v_i, is computed as the inverse of its standard deviation. Third, each x_{it_spc} is adjusted to equalize the volatility of the components, the standardization factor being $s_i = v_i / \sum_i v_i$. Fourth, the standardized components, $m_{it} = s_i x_{it\_\text{spc}}$, are summed together with equal weights, yielding $m_t = \sum_i m_{it}$. Fifth, the index in levels is computed as

$$\text{CCI}_t = \text{CCI}_{t-1} * (200 + m_t)/(200 - m_t) \tag{3}$$

with the starting condition

$$\mathrm{CCI}_1 = (200 + m_1)/(200 - m_1).$$

Finally, rebasing CCI to average 100 in 1996 yields the $\mathrm{CCI}_{\mathrm{CB}}$.

From an econometric point of view, composite leading indexes (CLI) constructed following the procedure sketched above are subject to several criticisms, some of which are derived in a formal framework in Emerson and Hendry (1996). First, even though the single indicators are typically chosen according to some formal or informal bivariate analysis of their relationship with the target variable, there is no explicit reference to the target variable in the construction of the CLI, e.g., in the choice of the weighting scheme. Second, the weighting scheme is fixed over time, with periodic revisions mostly due either to data issues, such as changes in the production process of an indicator, or to the past unsatisfactory performance of the index. Endogenously changing weights that track the possibly varying relevance of the single indicators over the business cycle and in the presence of particular types of shocks could produce better results, even though their derivation is difficult. Third, lagged values of the target variable are typically not included in the leading index, while there can be economic and statistical reasons underlying the persistence of the target variable that would favor such an inclusion. Fourth, lagged values of the single indicators are typically not used in the index, while they could provide relevant information, e.g., because not only does the point value of an indicator matter but also its evolution over a period of time is important for anticipating the future behavior of the target variable. Fifth, if some indicators and the target variable are cointegrated, the presence of short run deviations from the long run equilibrium could provide useful information on future movements of the target variable. Finally, since the index is a forecast for the target variable, standard errors should also be provided, but their derivation is virtually impossible in the nonmodel based context because of the lack of a formal relationship between the index and the target.

The main counterpart of these problems is simplicity. Nonmodel based indexes are easy to build, easy to explain, and easy to interpret, which are very valuable assets, in particular for the general public and for policy-makers. Moreover, simplicity is often a plus also for forecasting. With this method there is no estimation uncertainty, no major problems of overfitting, and the literature on forecast pooling suggests that equal weights work pretty well in practice [see, e.g., Stock and Watson (2003a)] even though here variables rather than forecasts are pooled.

Most of the issues raised for the nonmodel based composite indexes are addressed by the model based procedures described in the next two sections, which in turn are in general much more complicated and harder to understand for the general public. Therefore, while from the point of view of academic research and scientific background of the methods there is little to choose, practitioners may well decide to base their preferences on the practical forecasting performance of the two approaches to composite index construction.

5. Construction of model based composite coincident indexes

Within the model based approaches for the construction of a composite coincident index (CCI), two main methodologies have emerged: dynamic factor models and Markov switching models. In both cases there is a single unobservable force underlying the current status of the economy, but in the former approach this is a continuous variable, while in the latter it is a discrete variable that evolves according to a Markov chain. We now review these two methodologies, highlighting their pros and cons.

5.1. Factor based CCI

Dynamic factor models were developed by Geweke (1977) and Sargent and Sims (1977), but their use became well known to most business cycle analysts after the publication of Stock and Watson's (1989, SW) attempt to provide a formal probabilistic basis for Burns and Mitchell's coincident and leading indicators, with subsequent refinements of the methodology in Stock and Watson (1991, 1992). The rationale of the approach is that a set of variables is driven by a limited number of common forces and by idiosyncratic components that are either uncorrelated across the variables under analysis or in any case common to only a limited subset of them. The particular model that SW adopted is the following:

$$\Delta x_t = \beta + \gamma(L)\,\Delta C_t + u_t, \tag{4}$$

$$D(L)u_t = e_t, \tag{5}$$

$$\phi(L)\,\Delta C_t = \delta + v_t, \tag{6}$$

where x_t includes the (logs of the) four coincident variables used by the CB for their $\mathrm{CCI}_{\mathrm{CB}}$, the only difference being the use of hours of work instead of employment since the former provides a more direct measure of fluctuations in labor input. C_t is the single factor driving all variables, while u_t is the idiosyncratic component; Δ indicates the first difference operator, L is the lag operator and $\gamma(L)$, $D(L)$, $\phi(L)$ are, respectively, vector, matrix and scalar lag polynomials. SW used first differenced variables since unit root tests indicated that the coincident indexes were integrated, but not cointegrated. The model is identified by assuming that $D(L)$ is diagonal and e_t and v_t are mutually and serially uncorrelated at all leads and lags, which ensures that the common and the idiosyncratic components are uncorrelated. Moreover, ΔC_t should affect contemporaneously at least one coincident variable. Notice that the hypothesis of one factor, ΔC_t, does not mean that there is a unique source of aggregate fluctuations, but rather that different shocks have proportional dynamic effects on the variables.

For estimation, the model in (4)–(6) is augmented by the identity

$$C_{t-1} = \Delta C_{t-1} + C_{t-2}, \tag{7}$$

and cast into state-space form. The Kalman filter can then be used to write down the likelihood function, which is in turn maximized to obtain parameter and factor estimates, all the details are presented in Stock and Watson (1991).

A few additional comments are in order. First, the composite coincident index, $\mathrm{CCI}_{\mathrm{SW}t}$, is obtained through the Kalman filter as the minimum mean squared error linear estimator of C_t using information on the coincident variables up to period t. Hence, the procedure can be implemented in real time, conditional on the availability of data on the coincident variables. By using the Kalman smoother rather than the filter, it is possible to obtain end of period estimates of the state of the economy, i.e., $C_{t|T}$. Second, it is possible to obtain a direct measure of the contribution of each coincident indicator in x_t to the index by computing the response of the latter to a unit impulse in the former. Third, since data on some coincident indicator are published with delay, they can be treated as missing observations and estimated within the state-space framework. Moreover, the possibility of measurement error in the first releases of the coincident indicators can also be taken into consideration by adding an error term to the measurement equation. This is an important feature since data revisions are frequent and can be substantial, for example as testified by the revised US GDP growth rate data for 2001. Fourth, a particular time varying pattern in the parameters of the lag polynomials $D(L)$ and $\phi(L)$ can be allowed by using a time-varying transition matrix. Fifth, standard errors around the coincident index can be computed, even though they were not reported by SW.

The cyclical structure of $\mathrm{CCI}_{\mathrm{SW}}$ closely follows the NBER expansions and recessions, and the correlation of two quarters growth rates in $\mathrm{CCI}_{\mathrm{SW}}$ and real GDP was about 0.86 over the period 1959–1987. Stock and Watson (1991) also compared their $\mathrm{CCI}_{\mathrm{SW}}$ with the DOC's one, finding that the overall relative importance of the single indicators is roughly similar (but the weights are different since the latter index is made up of contemporaneous indicators only), the correlation of the levels of the composite indexes was close to 0.94, again over the period 1959–1987, and the coherence of their growth rates at business cycle frequency was even higher.

These findings provide support for the simple averaging methodology originated at the NBER and then further developed at the DOC and the CB, but they also question the practical usefulness of the SW's approach, which is substantially more complicated. Overall, the SW methodology, and more generally model based index construction, are worth their cost since they provide a proper statistical framework that, for example, permits the computation of standard errors around the composite index, the unified treatment of data revisions and missing observations, the possibility of using time-varying parameters and, as we will see in more detail in the next section, a coherent framework for the development of composite leading indexes.

A possible drawback of SW's procedure is that it requires an ex-ante classification of variables into coincident and leading or lagging, even though this is common practice in this literature, and it cannot be directly extended to analyze large datasets because of computational problems, see Section 6.2 for details. Forni et al. (2000, 2001, FHLR henceforth) proposed an alternative factor based methodology that addresses both issues, and applied it to the derivation of a composite coincident indicator for the Euro area. They analyzed a large set of macroeconomic time series for each country of the Euro area using a dynamic factor model, and decomposed each time series into a common and an idiosyncratic component, where the former is the part of the variable explained by common Euro area shocks, the latter by variable specific shocks. The $\mathrm{CCI}_{\mathrm{FHLR}}$ is obtained as a weighted average of the common components of the interpolated monthly GDP series for each country, where the weights are proportional to GDP, and takes into account both within and across-countries cross correlations.

More specifically, the model FHLR adopted is

$$x_{it} = b_i'(L)v_t + \xi_{it}, \quad i = 1, \ldots, N, \; t = 1, \ldots, T, \tag{8}$$

where x_{it} is a stationary univariate random variable, v_t is a $q \times 1$ vector of common shocks, $\chi_{it} = x_{it} - \xi_{it}$ is the common component of x_{it}, and ξ_{it} is its idiosyncratic component. The shock v_t is an orthonormal white noise process, so that $\mathrm{var}(v_{jt}) = 1$, $\mathrm{cov}(v_t, v_{t-k}) = 0$, and $\mathrm{cov}(v_{jt}, v_{st-k}) = 0$ for any $j \neq s$, t and k. $\xi_N = \{\xi_{1t}, \ldots, \xi_{Nt}\}'$ is a wide sense stationary process, and $\mathrm{cov}(\xi_{jt}, v_{st-k}) = 0$ for any j, s, t and k. $b_i(L)$ is a $q \times 1$ vector of square summable, bilateral filters, for any i. Notice that SW's factor model (4) is obtained as a particular case of (8) when there is one common shock ($q = 1$), $b_i(L) = \gamma_i(L)/\phi(L)$, and the idiosyncratic components are assumed to be orthogonal.

Grouping the variables into $x_{Nt} = \{x_{1t}, \ldots, x_{Nt}\}'$, FHLR also required x_{Nt} (and χ_{Nt}, ξ_{Nt} that are similarly defined) to have rational spectral density matrices, Σ_N^x, Σ_N^χ, and Σ_N^ξ, respectively. To achieve identification, they assumed that the first (largest) idiosyncratic dynamic eigenvalue, λ_{N1}^ξ, is uniformly bounded, and that the first (largest) q common dynamic eigenvalues, $\lambda_{N1}^\chi, \ldots, \lambda_{Nq}^\chi$, diverge when N increases, where dynamic eigenvalues are the eigenvalues of the spectral density matrix; see, e.g., Brillinger (1981, Chapter 9). In words, the former condition limits the effects of ξ_{it} on other cross-sectional units. The latter, instead, requires v_t to affect infinitely many units.

Assuming that the number of common shocks is known, FHLR suggested to estimate the common component of χ_{it}, $\hat{\chi}_{it}$, as the projection of x_{it} on past, present, and future dynamic principal components of all variables, and proved that, under mild conditions, $\hat{\chi}_{it}$ is a consistent estimator of χ_{it} when N and T diverge. Once the common component is estimated, the idiosyncratic one is obtained simply as a residual, namely, $\hat{\xi}_{it} = x_{it} - \hat{\chi}_{it}$.

To determine the number of factors, q, FHLR suggested to exploit two features of the model: (a) the average over frequencies of the first q dynamic eigenvalues diverges, while the average of the $(q + 1)$th does not; (b) there should be a big gap between the variance of x_{Nt} explained by the first q dynamic principal components and that explained by the $(q+1)$th principal component. As an alternative, an information criterion could be used, along the lines of Bai and Ng (2002).

The methodology was further refined by Altissimo et al. (2001) and Forni et al. (2003a) for real time implementation, and it is currently adopted to produce the CEPR's composite coincident indicator for the Euro area, Eurocoin (see www.cepr.org). In particular, they exploited the large cross-sectional dimension for forecasting indicators available with delay and for filtering out high frequency dynamics. Alternative coincident indexes for the Euro area following the SW methodology were proposed by

Proietti and Moauro (2004), while Carriero and Marcellino (2005) compared several methodologies, finding that they yield very similar results.

5.2. Markov switching based CCI

The main criticism Sims (1989) raised in his comment to Stock and Watson (1989) is the use of a constant parameter model (even though, as remarked above, their framework is flexible enough to allow for parameter variation), and a similar critique can be addressed to FHLR's method. Hamilton's (1989) Markov switching model is a powerful response to this criticism, since it allows the growth rate of the variables (and possibly their dynamics) to depend on the status of the business cycle. A basic version of the model can be written as

$$\Delta x_t = c_{s_t} + A_{s_t} \Delta x_{t-1} + u_t, \tag{9}$$

$$u_t \sim \text{i.i.d. } N(0, \Sigma), \tag{10}$$

where, as in (4), x_t includes the coincident variables under analysis (or a single composite index), while s_t measures the status of the business cycle, with $s_t = 1$ in recessions and $s_t = 0$ in expansions, and both the deterministic component and the dynamics can change over different business cycle phases. The binary state variable s_t is not observable, but the values of the coincident indicators provide information on it.

With respect to the factor model based analysis, there is again a single unobservable force underlying the evolution of the indicators but, first, it is discrete rather than continuous and, second, it does not directly affect or summarize the variables but rather indirectly determines their behavior that can change substantially over different phases of the cycle.

To close the model and estimate its parameters, an equation describing the behavior of s_t is required, and it cannot be of autoregressive form as (6) since s_t is a binary variable. Hamilton (1989) proposed to adopt the Markov switching (MS) model, where

$$\Pr(s_t = j \mid s_{t-1} = i) = p_{ij}, \tag{11}$$

as previously considered by Lindgren (1978) and Neftci (1982) in simpler contexts. For expositional purposes we stick to the two states hypothesis, though there is some empirical evidence that three states can further improve the specification, representing recession, high growth and normal growth; see, e.g., Kim and Murray (2002) for the US and Artis, Krolzig and Toro (2004) for the Euro area.

In our business cycle context, the quantity of special interest is an estimate of the unobservable current status of the economy and, assuming a mean square error loss function, the best estimator coincides with the conditional expectation of s_t given current and past information on x_t, which in turn is equivalent to the conditional probability

$$\zeta_{t|t} = \begin{pmatrix} \Pr(s_t = 0 \mid x_t, x_{t-1}, \ldots, x_1) \\ \Pr(s_t = 1 \mid x_t, x_{t-1}, \ldots, x_1) \end{pmatrix}. \tag{12}$$

Using simple probability rules, it follows that

$$\zeta_{t|t} = \begin{pmatrix} \frac{f(x_t \mid s_t=0,\ x_{t-1},\ldots,x_1)\Pr(s_t=0 \mid x_{t-1},\ldots,x_1)}{f(x_t \mid x_{t-1},\ldots,x_1)} \\ \frac{f(x_t \mid s_t=1,\ x_{t-1},\ldots,x_1)\Pr(s_t=1 \mid x_{t-1},\ldots,x_1)}{f(x_t \mid x_{t-1},\ldots,x_1)} \end{pmatrix}, \tag{13}$$

where

$$\begin{aligned}
&\Pr(s_t = i \mid x_{t-1}, \ldots, x_1) = \sum_{j=0}^{1} p_{ji} \Pr(s_{t-1} = j \mid x_{t-1}, \ldots, x_1), \\
&f(x_t \mid s_t = i,\ x_{t-1}, \ldots, x_1) \\
&\quad = \frac{1}{(2\pi)^{T/2}} |\Sigma|^{-1/2} \\
&\qquad \times \exp\bigl[-(\Delta x_t - c_i - A_i\, \Delta x_{t-1})' \Sigma^{-1} (\Delta x_t - c_i - A_i\, \Delta x_{t-1})/2\bigr], \\
&f(x_t, s_t = i \mid x_{t-1}, \ldots, x_1) \\
&\quad = f(x_t \mid s_t = i,\ x_{t-1}, \ldots, x_1) \Pr(s_t = i \mid x_{t-1}, \ldots, x_1), \\
&f(x_t \mid x_{t-1}, \ldots, x_1) = \sum_{j=0}^{1} f(x_t, s_t = j \mid x_{t-1}, \ldots, x_1), \quad i = 0, 1.
\end{aligned} \tag{14}$$

Hamilton (1994) or Krolzig (1997) provide additional details on these computations, and formulae to calculate $\zeta_{t|T}$, i.e., the smoothed estimator of the probability of being in a given status in period t. Notice also that the first and last rows of (14) provide, respectively, the probability of the state and the density of the variables conditional on past information only, that will be used in Section 6.3 in a related context for forecasting.

For comparison and since it is rather common in empirical applications [see, e.g., Niemira and Klein (1994) for the US and Artis et al. (1995) for the UK], it is useful to report Neftci's (1982) formula to compute the (posterior) probability of a turning point given the available data, as refined by Diebold and Rudebusch (1989). Defining

$$\Pi_t = \Pr(s_t = 1 \mid x_t, \ldots, x_1), \tag{15}$$

the formula is

$$\begin{aligned}
\Pi_t &= \frac{A_1}{B_1 + C_1}, \\
A_1 &= \bigl(\Pi_{t-1} + p_{01}(1 - \Pi_{t-1})\bigr) f(x_t \mid s_t = 1,\ x_{t-1}, \ldots, x_1), \\
B_1 &= \bigl(\Pi_{t-1} + p_{01}(1 - \Pi_{t-1})\bigr) f(x_t \mid s_t = 1,\ x_{t-1}, \ldots, x_1), \\
C_1 &= (1 - \Pi_{t-1})(1 - p_{01}) f(x_t \mid s_t = 0,\ x_{t-1}, \ldots, x_1).
\end{aligned} \tag{16}$$

The corresponding second element of $\zeta_{t|t}$ in (13) can be written as

$$\begin{aligned}
\Pi_t &= \frac{A_2}{B_2 + C_2}, \\
A_2 &= \big(\Pi_{t-1} - \Pi_{t-1} p_{01} + p_{01}(1 - \Pi_{t-1})\big) f(x_t \mid s_t = 1,\ x_{t-1}, \dots, x_1), \\
B_2 &= \big(\Pi_{t-1} - \Pi_{t-1} p_{01} + p_{01}(1 - \Pi_{t-1})\big) f(x_t \mid s_t = 1,\ x_{t-1}, \dots, x_1), \\
C_2 &= \big((1 - \Pi_{t-1})(1 - p_{01}) + \Pi_{t-1} p_{01}\big) f(x_t \mid s_t = 0,\ x_{t-1}, \dots, x_1).
\end{aligned} \tag{17}$$

Since in practice the probability of transition from expansion to recession, p_{01}, is very small [e.g., Diebold and Rudebusch (1989) set it at 0.02], the term $\Pi_{t-1} p_{01}$ is also very small and the two probabilities in (16) and (17) are very close. Yet, in general it is preferable to use the expression in (17) which is based on a more general model. Notice also that when $\Pi_t = 1$ the formula in (16) gives a constant value of 1 [e.g., Diebold and Rudebusch (1989) put an ad hoc upper bound of 0.95 for the value that enters the recursive formula], while this does not happen with (17).

The model in (9)–(11) can be extended in several dimensions, for example, to allow for more states and cointegration among the variables [see, e.g., Krolzig, Marcellino and Mizon (2002)] or time-varying probabilities as, e.g., in Diebold, Lee and Weinbach (1994) or Filardo (1994). The latter case is of special interest in our context when past values of the leading indicators, y, are the driving forces of the probabilities, as in Filardo (1994), who substituted (11) with

$$\Pr(s_t = i \mid s_{t-1} = j,\ x_{t-1}, \dots, x_1,\ y_{t-1}, \dots, y_1) = \frac{\exp(\theta y_{t-1})}{1 + \exp(\theta y_{t-1})}, \tag{18}$$

so that the first row of (14) should be modified into

$$\begin{aligned}
\Pr(s_t = i \mid x_{t-1}, \dots, x_1) = {} & \frac{\exp(\theta y_{t-1})}{1 + \exp(\theta y_{t-1})} \Pr(s_{t-1} = j \mid x_{t-1}, \dots, x_1) \\
& + \frac{1}{1 + \exp(\theta y_{t-1})} \Pr(s_{t-1} = i \mid x_{t-1}, \dots, x_1).
\end{aligned} \tag{19}$$

Another example is provided by Filardo and Gordon (1998), who used a probit model rather than a logistic specification for $\Pr(s_t = i \mid s_{t-1} = j,\ x_{t-1}, \dots,\ x_1,\ y_{t-1}, \dots, y_1)$, while Ravn and Sola (1999) warned against possible parameter instability of relationships such as (18). Raj (2002) provides a more detailed review of these and other extensions of the MS model.

Factor models and Markov switching specifications capture two complementary and fundamental features of business cycles, namely, the diffusion of slow-down and recovery across many series and the different behavior of several indicators in expansions and recessions. They are not only flexible and powerful statistical tools but can also be given sound justifications from an economic theory point of view; see, e.g., the overview in Diebold and Rudebusch (1996). The latter article represents also one of the earliest attempts to combine the two approaches, by allowing the factor underlying SW's model to evolve according to a Markov switching model. To provide support for their ideas, they fitted univariate and multivariate MS models to, respectively, the DOC's composite coincident indicator and its components, finding substantial evidence in favor of the MS specifications. Yet, they did not jointly estimate the factor MS model. Such a task was tackled by Chauvet (1998) and Kim and Yoo (1995), using an approximated maximum likelihood procedure developed by Kim (1994), and by Kim and Nelson (1998) and Filardo and Gordon (1999) using Gibbs sampler techniques introduced by Albert and Chib (1993a), Carter and Kohn (1994), and Shephard (1994).

In particular, Kim and Nelson (1998) substituted Equation (6) in SW's model with

$$\begin{aligned} &\phi(L)(\Delta C_t - \mu_{s_t} - \delta) = v_t, \\ &\mu_{s_t} = \mu_0 + \mu_1 s_t, \end{aligned} \tag{20}$$

where the transition probabilities are either constant or follow a probit specification. They compared the (posterior) regime probabilities from the factor MS model estimated with the four SW's components with those from a univariate MS model for IP, concluding that the former are much more closely related with the NBER expansion/recession classification. Yet, such a result is not surprising since Filardo (1994) showed that time-varying probabilities are needed for the univariate MS model to provide a close match with the NBER classification. When the original SW's model is estimated using the Gibbs sampling approach, the posterior distributions of the parameters are very close to those obtained using (20) instead of (6), the main difference being a slightly larger persistence of the estimated factor. Filardo and Gordon (1999), focusing on the 1990 recession, also found a similar performance of the standard and MS factor model, while a multivariate MS model with time-varying probabilities performed best during the recessionary part of 1990 (but not significantly better in the remaining months). Finally, Kim and Nelson (1998) also found a close similarity of their composite coincident indicator and the equal weighted DOC's one, with correlation in the growth rates above 0.98.

Finally, notice that if the probability of the states is time varying, e.g., as in (18), and the indicators in y_t include a measure of the length of the current recession (or expansion), it is possible to allow and test for duration dependence, namely, for whether the current or past length of a business cycle phase influences its future duration. The test is based on the statistical significance of the parameter associated with the duration indicator in an equation such as (18). Earlier studies using nonparametric techniques, such as Diebold and Rudebusch (1990) or Diebold, Rudebusch and Sichel (1993), detected positive duration dependence for recessions but not for expansions. Such a finding was basically confirmed by Durland and McCurdy (1994) using a semi-Markov model with duration depending only on calendar time, by Filardo and Gordon (1998) in a univariate Markov switching framework that also relates duration to macroeconomic variables, and by Kim and Nelson (1998) in their multivariate factor MS model. Therefore, another interesting question to be addressed in Sections 6 and 8 is whether leading indicators can be used to predict the duration of a business cycle phase.

In summary, no clear cut ranking of the multivariate model based approaches to CCI construction emerges, but the resulting indexes are in general very similar and close to the equal weighted ones, as we will see in the examples of Section 7. The positive aspect of this result is that estimation of the current economic condition is rather robust to the choice of method. Another implication is that pooling methods can be expected to yield no major improvements because of high correlation of all the indicators; see, e.g., Carriero and Marcellino (2005), but this is an issue that certainly deserves further investigation.

6. Construction of model based composite leading indexes

Leading indicators are hardly of any use without a rule to transform them into a forecast for the target variable. These rules range from simple nonparametric procedures that monitor the evolution of the leading indicator and transform it into a recession signal, e.g., the three-consecutive-declines in the CLI_{CB} rule [e.g., Vaccara and Zarnowitz (1978)], to sophisticated nonlinear models for the joint evolution of the leading indicators and the target variable, which can be used to predict growth rates, turning points, and expected duration of a certain business cycle phase. In this section we discuss the methods that are directly related to those reviewed in the previous section in the context of CCIs. In particular, Section 6.1 deals with linear models, Section 6.2 with factor based models, and Section 6.3 with Markov switching models. Examples are provided in the next section, while other approaches are considered in Section 8 below.

6.1. VAR based CLI

A linear VAR provides the simplest model based framework to understand the relationship between coincident and leading indicators, the construction of regression based composite leading indexes, the role of the latter in forecasting, and the consequences of invalid restrictions or unaccounted cointegration.

Let us group the m coincident indicators in the vector x_t, and the n leading indicators in y_t. For the moment, we assume that (x_t, y_t) is weakly stationary and its evolution is described by the VAR(1):

$$\begin{pmatrix} x_t \\ y_t \end{pmatrix} = \begin{pmatrix} c_x \\ c_y \end{pmatrix} + \begin{pmatrix} A & B \\ C & D \end{pmatrix} \begin{pmatrix} x_{t-1} \\ y_{t-1} \end{pmatrix} + \begin{pmatrix} e_{xt} \\ e_{yt} \end{pmatrix},$$
$$\begin{pmatrix} e_{xt} \\ e_{yt} \end{pmatrix} \sim \text{i.i.d.} \left(\begin{pmatrix} 0 \\ 0 \end{pmatrix}, \begin{pmatrix} \Sigma_{xx} & \Sigma_{xy} \\ \Sigma_{yx} & \Sigma_{yy} \end{pmatrix} \right). \tag{21}$$

It immediately follows that the expected value of x_{t+1} conditional on the past is

$$E(x_{t+1} \mid x_t, x_{t-1}, \ldots, y_t, y_{t-1}, \ldots) = c_x + Ax_t + By_t, \tag{22}$$

so that for y to be a useful set of leading indicators it must be $B \neq 0$. When $A \neq 0$, lagged values of the coincident variables also contain useful information for forecasting. Both hypotheses are easily testable and, in case both $A = 0$ and $B = 0$ are rejected, a composite regression based leading indicator for x_{t+1} (considered as a vector) can be constructed as

$$\mathrm{CLI1}_t = \hat{c}_x + \hat{A}x_t + \widehat{B}y_t, \tag{23}$$

where the $\hat{}$ indicates the OLS estimator. Standard errors around this CLI can be constructed using standard methods for VAR forecasts; see, e.g., Lütkepohl (2006). Moreover, recursive estimation of the model provides a convenient tool for continuous updating of the weights.

A similar procedure can be followed when the target variable is dated $t+h$ rather than t. For example, when $h=2$,

$$\begin{aligned}\mathrm{CLI1}_t^{h=2} &= \hat{c}_x + \hat{A}\hat{x}_{t+1|t} + \widehat{B}\hat{y}_{t+1|t} \\ &= \hat{c}_x + \hat{A}(\hat{c}_x + \hat{A}x_t + \widehat{B}y_t) + \widehat{B}(\hat{c}_y + \widehat{C}x_t + \widehat{D}y_t).\end{aligned} \tag{24}$$

As an alternative, the model in (21) can be rewritten as

$$\begin{pmatrix} x_t \\ y_t \end{pmatrix} = \begin{pmatrix} \tilde{c}_x \\ \tilde{c}_y \end{pmatrix} + \begin{pmatrix} \tilde{A} & \widetilde{B} \\ \widetilde{C} & \widetilde{D} \end{pmatrix} \begin{pmatrix} x_{t-h} \\ y_{t-h} \end{pmatrix} + \begin{pmatrix} \tilde{e}_{xt} \\ \tilde{e}_{yt} \end{pmatrix}, \tag{25}$$

where a $\tilde{}$ indicates that the new parameters are a combination of those in (21), and $\tilde{e}_{xt}$ and $\tilde{e}_{yt}$ are correlated of order $h-1$. Specifically,

$$\begin{aligned}\begin{pmatrix} \tilde{c}_x \\ \tilde{c}_y \end{pmatrix} &= \left(I + \begin{pmatrix} A & B \\ C & D \end{pmatrix} + \cdots + \begin{pmatrix} A & B \\ C & D \end{pmatrix}^{h-1}\right)\begin{pmatrix} c_x \\ c_y \end{pmatrix}, \\ \begin{pmatrix} \tilde{A} & \widetilde{B} \\ \widetilde{C} & \widetilde{D} \end{pmatrix} &= \begin{pmatrix} A & B \\ C & D \end{pmatrix}^{h}, \\ \begin{pmatrix} \tilde{e}_{xt} \\ \tilde{e}_{yt} \end{pmatrix} &= \left(I + \begin{pmatrix} A & B \\ C & D \end{pmatrix} + \cdots + \begin{pmatrix} A & B \\ C & D \end{pmatrix}^{h-1}\right)\begin{pmatrix} e_{xt} \\ e_{yt} \end{pmatrix}.\end{aligned} \tag{26}$$

The specification in (25) can be estimated by OLS, and the resulting CLI written as

$$\widetilde{\mathrm{CLI1}}_t^h = \hat{\tilde{c}}_x + \hat{\tilde{A}}x_t + \widehat{\widetilde{B}}y_t. \tag{27}$$

The main disadvantage of this latter method, often called dynamic estimation, is that a different model has to be specified for each forecast horizon h. On the other hand, no model is required for the leading indicators, and the estimators of the parameters in (25) can be more robust than those in (21) in the presence of mis-specification; see, e.g., Clements and Hendry (1996) for a theoretical discussion and Marcellino, Stock and Watson (2005) for an extensive empirical analysis of the two competing methods (showing that dynamic estimation is on average slightly worse than the iterated method for forecasting US macroeconomic time series). For the sake of simplicity, in the rest of the paper we will focus on $h=1$ whenever possible.

Consider now the case where the target variable is a composite coincident indicator,

$$\mathrm{CCI}_t = wx_t, \tag{28}$$

where w is a $1 \times m$ vector of weights as in Section 4. To construct a model based CLI for the CCI in (28) two routes are available. First, and more common, we could model CCI_t and y_t with a finite order VAR, say

$$\begin{pmatrix} \mathrm{CCI}_t \\ y_t \end{pmatrix} = \begin{pmatrix} d_{\mathrm{CCI}} \\ d_y \end{pmatrix} + \begin{pmatrix} e(L) & F(L) \\ g(L) & H(L) \end{pmatrix} \begin{pmatrix} \mathrm{CCI}_{t-1} \\ y_{t-1} \end{pmatrix} + \begin{pmatrix} u_{\mathrm{CCI}t} \\ u_{yt} \end{pmatrix}, \tag{29}$$

where L is the lag operator and the error process is white noise. Repeating the previous procedure, the composite leading index for $h = 1$ is

$$\mathrm{CLI2}_t = \hat{d}_{\mathrm{CCI}} + \hat{e}(L)\mathrm{CCI}_t + \widehat{F}(L)y_t. \tag{30}$$

Yet, in this case the VAR is only an approximation for the generating mechanism of (wx_t, y_t), since in general the latter should have an infinite number of lags or an MA component.

The alternative route is to stick to the model in (21), and construct the CLI as

$$\mathrm{CLI3}_t = w\mathrm{CLI1}_t, \tag{31}$$

namely, aggregate the composite leading indicators for each of the components of the CCI, using the same weights as in the CCI. Lütkepohl (1987) showed in a related context that in general aggregating the forecasts (CLI3) is preferable than forecasting the aggregate (CLI2) when the variables are generated by the model in (21), while this is not necessarily the case if the model in (21) is also an approximation and/or the x variables are subject to measurement error; see also Lütkepohl (2006). Stock and Watson (1992) overall found little difference in the performance of CLI2 and CLI3.

Both CLI2 and CLI3 are directly linked to the target variable, incorporate distributed lags of both the coincident and the leading variables (depending on the lag length of the VAR), the weights can be easily periodically updated using recursive estimation of the model, and standard errors around the point forecasts (or the whole distribution under a distributional assumption for the error process in the VAR) are readily available. Therefore, this simple linear model based procedure already addresses several of the main criticisms to the nonmodel based composite index construction, see Section 4.

In this context the dangers of using a simple average of the y variables as a composite leading index are also immediately evident, since the resulting index can provide an inefficient forecast of the CCI unless specific restrictions on the VAR coefficients in (21) are satisfied. In particular, indicating by i_n a $1 \times n$ vector with elements equal to $1/n$, the equal weight composite leading index

$$\mathrm{CLI}_{\mathrm{EW}t} = i_n y_t \tag{32}$$

is optimal and coincides with CLI3 if and only if

$$wc_x = 0, \quad wA = 0, \quad wB = i_n, \tag{33}$$

which imposes $1 + m + n$ restrictions on the parameters of the x equations in (21). In higher order VARs, the product of the weights w and the coefficients of longer lags of x and y in the x equations should also be equal to zero. Notice that these are all testable assumptions as long as $m + n$ is small enough with respect to the sample size to leave sufficient degrees of freedom for the VAR parameter estimation. For example, in the case of the Conference Board, $m + n = 14$ and monthly data are available for about 45 years for a total of more than 500 observations. Auerbach (1982) found that a regression based CLI in sample performed better than the equal weighted CLI_{CB} for industrial production and the unemployment rate, but not out of sample.

If the restrictions in (33) are not satisfied but it is desired to use in any case CLI_{EW} (or more generally a given CLI) to forecast the CCI, it can be possible to improve upon its performance by constructing a VAR for the two composite indexes CCI and CLI_{EW} $(wx_t, i_n y_t)$, say

$$\begin{pmatrix} \text{CCI}_t \\ \text{CLI}_{\text{EW}t} \end{pmatrix} = \begin{pmatrix} f_{\text{CCI}} \\ f_{\text{CLI}_{\text{EW}}} \end{pmatrix} + \begin{pmatrix} e(L) & f(L) \\ g(L) & h(L) \end{pmatrix} \begin{pmatrix} \text{CCI}_{t-1} \\ \text{CLI}_{\text{EW}t-1} \end{pmatrix} + \begin{pmatrix} v_{\text{CCI}t} \\ v_{\text{CLI}_{\text{EW}}t} \end{pmatrix} \tag{34}$$

and construct the new composite index as

$$\text{CLI4}_t = \hat{f}_{\text{CCI}} + \hat{e}(L)\text{CCI}_t + \hat{f}(L)\text{CLI}_{\text{EW}t}. \tag{35}$$

This is for example the methodology adopted by Koch and Rasche (1988), who analyzed a VAR for IP, as a coincident indicator, and the equal weighted DOC leading index. Since CLI4 has a dynamic structure and also exploits past information in the CCI, it can be expected to improve upon CLI_{EW}. Moreover, since the VAR in (34) is much more parsimonious than both (21) and (29), CLI4 could perform in practice even better than the other composite indexes, in particular in small samples.

A point that has not gained attention in the literature but can be of importance is the specification of the equations for the (single or composite) leading indicators. Actually, in all the models we have considered so far, the leading variables depend on lags of the coincident ones, which can be an unreliable assumption from an economic point of view. For example, the interest rate spread depends on future expected short term-interest rates and the stock market index on future expected profits and dividends, and these expectations are positively and highly correlated with the future expected overall economic conditions. Therefore, the leading variables could depend on future expected coincident variables rather than on their lags. For example, the equations for y_t in the model for (x_t, y_t) in (21) could be better specified as

$$y_t = c_y + Cx^e_{t+1|t-1} + Dy_{t-1} + e_{yt}, \tag{36}$$

where $x^e_{t+1|t-1}$ indicates the expectation of x_{t+1} conditional on information available in period $t - 1$. Combining these equations with those for x_t in (21), it is possible to obtain a closed form expression for $x^e_{t+1|t-1}$, which is

$$x^e_{t+1|t-1} = (I - BC)^{-1}\big(c_x + Ac_x + Bc_y + A^2x_{t-1} + (AB + BD)y_{t-1}\big). \tag{37}$$

Therefore, a VAR specification such as that in (21) can also be considered as a reduced form of a more general model where the leading variables depend on expected future coincident variables. A related issue is whether the coincident variables, x_t, could also depend on their future expected values, as it often results in new-Keynesian models; see, e.g., Walsh (2003). Yet, the empirical evidence in Fuhrer and Rudebusch (2004) provides little support for this hypothesis.

Another assumption we have maintained so far is that both the coincident and the leading variables are weakly stationary, while in practice it is likely that the behavior of most of these variables is closer to that of integrated process. Following Sims, Stock and Watson (1990), this is not problematic for consistent estimation of the parameters of VARs in levels such as (21), and therefore for the construction of the related CLIs, even though inference is complicated and, for example, hypotheses on the parameters such as those in (33) could not be tested using standard asymptotic distributions. An additional complication is that in this literature, when the indicators are I(1), the VAR models are typically specified in first differences rather than in levels, without prior testing for cointegration. Continuing the VAR(1) example, the adopted model would be

$$\begin{pmatrix} \Delta x_t \\ \Delta y_t \end{pmatrix} = \begin{pmatrix} c_x \\ c_y \end{pmatrix} + \begin{pmatrix} e_{xt} \\ e_{yt} \end{pmatrix}, \tag{38}$$

rather than possibly

$$\begin{aligned} \begin{pmatrix} \Delta x_t \\ \Delta y_t \end{pmatrix} &= \begin{pmatrix} c_x \\ c_y \end{pmatrix} - \left(\begin{pmatrix} I_m & 0 \\ 0 & I_n \end{pmatrix} - \begin{pmatrix} A & B \\ C & D \end{pmatrix} \right) \begin{pmatrix} x_{t-1} \\ y_{t-1} \end{pmatrix} + \begin{pmatrix} e_{xt} \\ e_{yt} \end{pmatrix} \\ &= \begin{pmatrix} c_x \\ c_y \end{pmatrix} - \alpha\beta' \begin{pmatrix} x_{t-1} \\ y_{t-1} \end{pmatrix} + \begin{pmatrix} e_{xt} \\ e_{yt} \end{pmatrix}, \end{aligned} \tag{39}$$

where β is the matrix of cointegrating coefficients and α contains the loadings of the error correction terms. As usual, omission of relevant variables yields biased estimators of the parameters of the included regressors, which can translate into biased and inefficient composite leading indicators. See Emerson and Hendry (1996) for additional details and generalizations and, e.g., Clements and Hendry (1999) for the consequences of omitting cointegrating relations when forecasting. As long as $m + n$ is small enough with respect to the sample size, the number and composition of the cointegrating vectors can be readily tested [see, e.g., Johansen (1988) for tests within the VAR framework], and the specification in (39) used as a basis to construct model based CLIs that also take cointegration into proper account. Hamilton and Perez-Quiros (1996) found cointegration to be important for improving the forecasting performance of the CLI_{DOC}.

Up to now we have implicitly assumed, as it is common in most of the literature that analyzes CCIs and CLIs within linear models, that the goal of the composite leading index is forecasting a continuous variable, the CCI. Yet, leading indicators were originally developed for forecasting business cycle turning points. Simulation based methods can be used to derive forecasts of a binary recession/expansion indicator, and these in turn can be exploited to forecast the probability that a recession will take place within, or at, a certain horizon.

Let us consider the model in (29) and assume that the parameters are known and the errors are normally distributed. Then, drawing random numbers from the joint distribution of the errors for period $t+1, \ldots, t+n$ and solving the model forward, it is possible to get a set of simulated values for $(\mathrm{CCI}_{t+1}, \Delta y_{t+1}), \ldots, (\mathrm{CCI}_{t+n}, \Delta y_{t+n})$. Repeating the exercise many times, a histogram of the realizations provides an approximation for the conditional distribution of $(\mathrm{CCI}_{t+1}, \Delta y_{t+1}), \ldots, (\mathrm{CCI}_{t+n}, \Delta y_{t+n})$ given the past. Given this distribution and a rule to transform the continuous variable CCI into a binary recession indicator, e.g., the three months negative growth rule, the probability that a given future observation can be classified as a recession is computed as the fraction of the relevant simulated future values of the CCI that satisfy the rule.

A related problem that could be addressed within this framework is forecasting the beginning of the next recession, which is given by the time index of the first observation that falls into a recessionary pattern. Assuming that in period t the economy is in expansion, the probability of a recession after q periods, i.e., in $t+q$, is equal to the probability that $\mathrm{CCI}_{t+1}, \ldots, \mathrm{CCI}_{t+q-1}$ belong to an expansionary pattern while CCI_{t+q} to a recessionary one.

The procedure can be easily extended to allow for parameter uncertainty by drawing parameter values from the distribution of the estimators rather than treating them as fixed. Normality of the errors is also not strictly required since resampling can be used; see, e.g., Wecker (1979), Kling (1987), and Fair (1993) for additional details and examples.

Bayesian techniques are also available for forecasting turning points in linear models, see, e.g., Geweke and Whiteman (2006). In particular, Zellner and Hong (1991) and Zellner, Hong and Gulati (1990) addressed the problem in a decision-theoretic framework, using fixed parameter AR models with leading indicators as exogenous regressors. In our notation, the model can be written as

$$x_t = z_t'\beta + u_t, \qquad u_t \sim \text{i.i.d. } N(0, \sigma^2), \tag{40}$$

where $z_t' = (x_{t-1}, y_{t-1})$, x_t is a univariate coincident variable or index, y_t is the $1 \times n$ vector of leading indicators, and β is a $k \times 1$ parameter vector, with $k = n + 1$.

Zellner, Hong and Gulati (1990) and Zellner, Hong and Min (1991) used annual data and declared a downturn (DT) in year $T+1$ if the annual growth rate observations satisfy

$$x_{T-2}, x_{T-1} < x_T > x_{T+1}, \tag{41}$$

while no downturn (NDT) happens if

$$x_{T-2}, x_{T-1} < x_T \leqslant x_{T+1}. \tag{42}$$

Similar definitions were proposed for upturns and no upturns.

The probability of a DT in $T+1$, p_{DT}, can be calculated as

$$p_{\mathrm{DT}} = \int_{-\infty}^{x_T} p(x_{T+1} \mid A_1, D_T)\,\mathrm{d}x_{T+1}, \tag{43}$$

where A_1 indicates the condition $(x_{T-2}, x_{T-1} < x_T)$, D_T denotes the past sample and prior information as of period T, and p is the predictive probability density function (pdf) defined as

$$p(x_{T+1} \mid D_T) = \int_\theta f(x_{T+1} \mid \theta, D_T)\pi(\theta \mid D_T)\,\mathrm{d}\theta, \tag{44}$$

where $f(x_{T+1} \mid \theta, D_T)$ is the pdf for x_{T+1} given the parameter vector $\theta = (\beta, \sigma^2)$ and D_T, while $\pi(\theta \mid D_T)$ is the posterior pdf for θ obtained by Bayes' Theorem.

The predictive pdf is constructed as follows. First, natural conjugate prior distributions are assumed for β and σ, namely, $p(\beta \mid \sigma) \sim N(0, \sigma^2 I \times 10^6)$ and $p(\sigma) \sim \mathrm{IG}(v_0 s_0)$, where IG stands for inverted gamma and v_0 and s_0 are very small numbers; see, e.g., Canova (2004, Chapter 9) for details. Second, at $t = 0$, the predictive pdf $p(x_1 \mid D_0)$ is a Student-t, namely, $t_{v_0} = (x_1 - z_1'\hat{\beta}_0)/s_0 a_0$ has a univariate Student-t density with v_0 degrees of freedom, where $a_0^2 = 1 + z_1' z_1 10^6$ and $\hat{\beta}_0 = 0$. Third, the posterior pdfs obtained period by period using the Bayes' Theorem are used to compute the period by period predictive pdfs. In particular, the predictive pdf for x_{T+1} is again Student-t and

$$t_{v_T} = \left(x_{T+1} - z_{T+1}'\hat{\beta}_T\right)/s_T a_T \tag{45}$$

has a univariate Student-t pdf with v_T degrees of freedom, where

$$\begin{aligned}
\hat{\beta}_T &= \hat{\beta}_{T-1} + \left(Z_{T-1}' Z_{T-1}\right)^{-1} z_T\left(x_T - z_T'\hat{\beta}_{T-1}\right)/\left[1 + z_T'(Z_T' Z_T)^{-1} z_T\right],\\
a_T^2 &= 1 + z_{T+1}'\left(Z_T' Z_T\right)^{-1} z_{T+1},\\
v_T &= v_{T-1} + 1,\\
v_T s_T^2 &= v_{T-1} s_{T-1} + \left(x_T - z_T'\hat{\beta}_T\right)^2 + \left(\hat{\beta}_T - \hat{\beta}_{T-1}\right)' Z_{T-1}' Z_{T-1}\left(\hat{\beta}_T - \hat{\beta}_{T-1}\right),
\end{aligned}$$

and $Z_T' = (z_T, z_{T-1}, \ldots, z_1)$. Therefore,

$$\Pr(x_{T+1} < x_T \mid D_T) = \Pr\left(t_{v_T} < \left(x_T - z_{T+1}'\hat{\beta}_T\right)/s_T a_T \mid D_T\right),$$

which can be analytically evaluated using the Student-t distribution with v_T degrees of freedom.

Finally, if the loss function is symmetric (i.e., the loss from wrongly predicting NDT in the case of DT is the same as predicting DT in the case of NDT), then a DT is predicted in period $T + 1$ if $p_{\mathrm{DT}} > 0.5$. Otherwise, the cut-off value depends on the loss structure, see also Section 8.3.

While the analysis in Zellner, Hong and Gulati (1990) is univariate, the theory for Bayesian VARs is also well developed, starting with Doan, Litterman and Sims (1984). A recent model in this class was developed by Zha (1998) for the Atlanta FED, and its performance in turning point forecasting is evaluated by Del Negro (2001). In this case the turning point probabilities are computed by simulations from the predictive pdf rather than analytically, in line with the procedure illustrated above in the classical context.

To conclude, a common problem of VAR models is their extensive parameterization, which prevents the analysis of large data sets. Canova and Ciccarelli (2001, 2003) proposed Bayesian techniques that partly overcome this problem, extending previous analysis by, e.g., Zellner, Hong and Min (1991), and providing applications to turning point forecasting; see Canova (2004, Chapter 10) for an overview. As an alternative, factor models can be employed, as we discuss in the next subsection.

6.2. Factor based CLI

The idea underlying Stock and Watson's (1989, SW) methodology for the construction of a CCI, namely that a single common force drives the evolution of several variables, can also be exploited to construct a CLI. In particular, if the single leading indicators are also driven by the (leads of the) same common force, then a linear combination of their present and past values can contain useful information for predicting the CCI.

To formalize the intuition above, following SW, Equation (6) in Section 5.1 is substituted with

$$\Delta C_t = \delta_C + \lambda_{CC}(L)\,\Delta C_{t-1} + \Lambda_{Cy}(L)\,\Delta y_{t-1} + v_{ct}. \tag{46}$$

and, to close the model, equations for the leading indicators are also added

$$\Delta y_t = \delta_y + \lambda_{yC}(L)\,\Delta C_{t-1} + \Lambda_{yy}(L)\,\Delta y_{t-1} + v_{yt}, \tag{47}$$

where v_{ct} and v_{yt} are i.i.d. and uncorrelated with the errors in (5).

The model in (4), (5), (46), (47) can be cast into state space form and estimated by maximum likelihood through the Kalman filter. SW adopted a simpler two-step procedure, where in the first step the model (4)–(6) is estimated, and in the second step the parameters of (46), (47) are obtained conditional on those in the first step. This procedure is robust to mis-specification of Equations (46), (47), in particular the estimated CCI coincides with that in Section 5.1, but it can be inefficient when either the whole model is correctly specified or, at least, the lags of the leading variables contain helpful information for estimating the current status of the economy. Notice also that the "forecasting" system (46), (47) is very similar to that in (29), the main difference being that here C_t is unobservable and therefore substituted with the estimate obtained in the first step of the procedure, which is CCI_{SW}. Another minor difference is that SW constrained the polynomials $\lambda_{yC}(L)$ and $\Lambda_{yy}(L)$ to eliminate higher order lags, while $\lambda_{CC}(L)$ and $\Lambda_{Cy}(L)$ are left unrestricted; see SW for the details on the lag length determination.

The SW composite leading index is constructed as

$$\text{CLI}_{\text{SW}} = \widehat{C}_{t+6|t} - C_{t|t}, \tag{48}$$

namely, it is a forecast of the 6-month growth rate in the CCI_{SW}, where the value in $t+6$ is forecasted and that in t is estimated. This is rather different from the NBER tradition, represented nowadays by the CLI_{CB} that, as mentioned, aims at leading turning points in the level of the CCI. Following the discussion in Section 3, focusing on growth rather than on levels can be more interesting in periods of prolonged expansions.

A few additional comments are in order about SW's procedure. First, the leading indicators should depend on expected future values of the coincident index rather than on its lags, so that a better specification for (47) is along the lines of (36). Yet, we have seen that in the reduced form of (36) the leading indicators depend on their own lags and on those of the coincident variables, and a similar comment holds in this case. Second, the issue of parameter constancy is perhaps even more relevant in this enlarged model, and in particular for forecasting. Actually, in a subsequent (1997) revision of the procedure, SW made the deterministic component of (46), δ_C, time varying; in particular, it evolves according to a random walk. Third, dynamic estimation of Equation (46) would avoid the need of (47). This would be particularly convenient in this framework where the dimension of y_t is rather large, and a single forecast horizon is considered, $h = 6$. Fourth, rather than directly forecasting the CCI_{SW}, the components of x_t could be forecasted and then aggregated into the composite index using the in sample weights, along the lines of (31). Fifth, while SW formally tested for lack of cointegration among the components of x_t, they did not do it among the elements of y_t, and of (x_t, y_t), namely, there could be omitted cointegrating relationships either among the leading indicators, or among them and the coincident indicators. Finally, the hypothesis of a single factor driving both the coincident and the leading indicators should be formally tested.

Otrok and Whiteman (1998) derived a Bayesian version of SW's CCI and CLI. As in the classical context, the main complication is the nonobservability of the latent factor. To address this issue, a step-wise procedure is adopted where the posterior distribution of all unknown parameters of the model is determined conditional on the latent factor, then the conditional distribution of the latent factor conditional on the data and the other parameters is derived, the joint posterior distribution for the parameters and the factor is sampled using a Markov Chain Monte Carlo procedure using the conditional distributions in the first two steps, and a similar route is followed to obtain the marginal predictive pdf of the factor, which is used in the construction of the leading indicator; see Otrok and Whiteman (1998), Kim and Nelson (1998), Filardo and Gordon (1999) for details and Canova (2004, Chapter 11) for an overview.

The SW's methodology could also be extended to exploit recent developments in the dynamic factor model literature. In particular, a factor model for all the potential leading indicators could be considered, and the estimated factors used to forecast the coincident index or its components. Let us sketch the steps of this approach, more details can be found in Stock and Watson (2006).

The model for the leading indicators in (47) can be replaced by

$$\Delta y_t = \Lambda f_t + \xi_t, \tag{49}$$

where the dimension of Δy_t can be very large, possibly larger than the number of observations (so that no sequential indicator selection procedure is needed), f_t is an $r \times 1$ vector of common factors (so that more than one factor can drive the indicators), and ξ_t is a vector containing the idiosyncratic component of each leading indicator. Precise moment conditions on f_t and ξ_t, and requirements on the loadings matrix Λ, are given in Stock and Watson (2002a, 2002b). Notice that f_t could contain contemporaneous and lagged values of factors, so that the model is truly dynamic even though the representation in (49) is static.

Though the model in (49) is a simple extension of that for the construction of SW's composite coincident index in (4), its estimation is complicated by the possibly very large number of parameters, that makes maximum likelihood computationally not feasible. Therefore, Stock and Watson (2002a, 2002b) defined the factor estimators, $\hat{f}_t$, as the minimizers of the objective function

$$V_{nT}(f, \Lambda) = \frac{1}{nT} \sum_{i=1}^{n} \sum_{t=1}^{T} (y_{it} - \Lambda_i f_t)^2. \tag{50}$$

It turns out that the optimal estimators of the factors are the r eigenvectors corresponding to the r largest eigenvalues of the $T \times T$ matrix $n^{-1} \sum_{i=1}^{n} \underline{y}_i \underline{y}_i'$, where $\underline{y}_i = (y_{i1}, \ldots, y_{iT})$, and these estimators converge in probability to the space spanned by the true factors f_t. See Bai (2003) for additional inferential results, Bai and Ng (2002) for results related to the choice of the number of factors, r, Boivin and Ng (2003) for issues related to the choice of the size of the dataset (i.e., the number of leading indicators in our case), and Kapetanios and Marcellino (2003) for an alternative (parametric) estimation procedure.

The factors driving the leading indicators, possibly coinciding with (leads of) those driving the coincident indicators, can be related to the coincident composite index by replacing Equation (46) with

$$\Delta C_t = \delta_C + \lambda_{CC}(L)\,\Delta C_{t-1} + \lambda_{Cy}(L) f_{t-1} + v_{ct}. \tag{51}$$

Another important result proved by Stock and Watson (2002a, 2002b) is that the factors in the equation above can be substituted by their estimated counterparts, $\hat{f}_t$, without (asymptotically) modifying the mean square forecast error; see also Bai and Ng (2003) for additional results.

A forecasting procedure based on the use of (49) and (51), produced good results for the components of the CCI_{SW}, Stock and Watson (2002a, 2002b), but also for predicting macroeconomic variables for the Euro area, the UK, and the Accession countries, see, respectively, Marcellino, Stock and Watson (2003), Artis, Banerjee and Marcellino (2005), and Banerjee, Marcellino and Masten (2005). Yet, in these studies the set of indicators for factor extraction was not restricted to those with leading properties, and the target variable was not the composite coincident index. Camba-Mendez et al. (2001) used only leading indicators on the largest European countries for factor extraction (estimating iteratively the factor model cast in state-space form), and confirmed the good forecasting performance of the estimated factors when inserted in a VAR for predicting GDP growth.

The alternative factor based approach by FHLR described in Section 5.1 can also be used to construct a CLI. The leading variables are endogenously determined using the phase delay of their common components with respect to CCI_{FHLR} (the weighted average of the common components of interpolated monthly GDP for Euro area countries). An equal weight average of the resulting leading variables is the CLI_{FHLR}. Future values of the CCI_{FHLR} are predicted with a VAR for CCI_{FHLR}, CLI_{FHLR}. Further refinements of the methodology are presented in Forni et al. (2003a), with applications in Forni et al. (2003b).

All the factor based methods we have considered up to now focus on predicting continuous variables. Therefore, as in the case of linear models, we now discuss how to forecast discrete variables related to business cycle dynamics. In particular, we review the final important contribution of SW, further refined in Stock and Watson (1992), namely, the construction of a pattern recognition algorithm for the identification of recessions, and the related approach for computing recession probabilities.

As mentioned in Section 3, a recession is broadly defined by the three Ds: duration, a recession should be long enough; depth, there should be a substantial slowdown in economic activity; and diffusion, such a slowdown should be common to most sectors of the economy. Diffusion requires several series or a composite index to be monitored, and SW were in favor of the latter option, using their CCI (which, we recall, in the cumulated estimate of ΔC_t in Equation (4)). Moreover, SW required a recession to be characterized by ΔC_t falling below a certain boundary value, b_{rt} (depth), for either (a) six consecutive months or (b) nine months with no more than one increase during the middle seven months (duration), where (b) is the same as requiring ΔC_t to follow for seven of nine consecutive months including the first and the last month. Expansions were treated symmetrically, with b_{et} being the counterpart of b_{rt}, and both b_{rt} and b_{et} were treated as i.i.d. normal random variables.

A particular month is classified as a recession if it falls in a recessionary pattern as defined above. In particular, suppose that it has to be decided whether month t belongs to a recessionary pattern. Because of the definition of a recessionary pattern, the longest span of time to be considered is given by $\Delta C_{t-8}, \ldots, \Delta C_{t-1}$ and $\Delta C_{t+1}, \ldots, \Delta C_{t+8}$. For example, it could be that ΔC_t is below the threshold b_{rt} and also $\Delta C_{t-i} < b_{rt-i}$ for $i = 1, \ldots, 5$; in this case the sequence $\Delta C_{t-5}, \ldots, \Delta C_t$ is sufficient to classify period t as a recession. But it could be that $\Delta C_{t-i} > b_{rt-i}$ for $i = 1, \ldots, 8$, $\Delta C_t < b_{rt}$, $\Delta C_{t+1} > b_{rt+1}$, and $\Delta C_{t+i} < b_{rt+i}$ for $i = 2, \ldots, 8$, which requires to consider the whole sequence of 17 periods $\Delta C_{t-8}, \ldots, \Delta C_t, \ldots, \Delta C_{t+8}$ to correctly classify period t as a recession. Notice also that the sequence for ΔC_t has to be compared with the corresponding sequence of thresholds, $b_{rt-8}, \ldots, b_{rt}, \ldots, b_{rt+8}$.

The binary recession indicator, R_t, takes the value 1 if ΔC_t belongs to a recessionary pattern, and 0 otherwise. The expansion indicator is defined symmetrically, but is also worth noting that the definition of recession is such that there can be observations that are classified neither as recessions nor as expansions. Also, there is no role for duration dependence or correlation, in the sense that the probability of recession is independent of the length of the current expansion or recession, and of past values of R_t.

The evaluation of the probability of recession in period $t + h$ conditional on information on the present and past of the CCI and of the leading indicators (and on the fact that $t + h$ belongs either to an expansionary or to a recessionary pattern), requires the integration of a 34-dimensional distribution, where 17 dimensions are due to the evaluation of an (estimated and forecasted) sequence for ΔC_t that spans 17 periods, and the remaining ones from integration with respect to the distribution of the threshold parameters. Stock and Watson (1992) described in details a simulation based procedure to perform numerically the integration, and reported results for their composite recession indicator, $\mathrm{CRI}_{\mathrm{SW}}$, that evaluates in real time the probability that the economy will be in a recession 6-months ahead.

Though a rule that transforms the $\mathrm{CRI}_{\mathrm{SW}}$ into a binary variable is not defined, high values of the $\mathrm{CRI}_{\mathrm{SW}}$ should be associated with realizations of recessions. Using the NBER dating as a benchmark, SW found the in-sample performance of the CRI quite satisfactory, as well as that of the CLI. Yet, out of sample, in the recessions of 1990 and 2001, both indicators failed to provide strong early warnings, an issue that is considered in more detail in Section 10.3.

To conclude, it is worth pointing out that the procedure underlying SW's CRI is not specific to their model. Given the definition of a recessionary pattern, any model that relates a CCI to a set of leading indicators or to a CLI can be used to compute the probability of recession in a given future period using the same simulation procedure as SW but drawing the random variables from the different model under analysis. The simplest case is when the model for the coincident indicator and the leading indexes is linear, which is the situation described at the end of the previous subsection.

6.3. Markov switching based CLI

The MS model introduced in Section 5.2 to define an intrinsic coincident index, and in Section 3 to date the business cycle, can also be exploited to evaluate the forecasting properties of a single or composite leading indicator. In particular, a simplified version of the model proposed by Hamilton and Perez-Quiros (1996) can be written as

$$\begin{aligned} \Delta x_t - c_{s_t} &= a(\Delta x_{t-1} - c_{s_{t-1}}) + b(\Delta y_{t-1} - d_{s_{t+r-1}}) + u_{xt}, \\ \Delta y_t - d_{s_{t+r}} &= c(\Delta x_{t-1} - c_{s_{t-1}}) + d(\Delta y_{t-1} - d_{s_{t+r-1}}) + u_{yt}, \\ u_t &= (u_{xt}, u_{yt})' \sim \text{i.i.d. } N(0, \Sigma), \end{aligned} \tag{52}$$

where x and y are univariate, s_t evolves according to the constant transition probability Markov chain defined in (11), and the leading characteristics of y are represented not only by its influence on future values of x but also by its being driven by future values of the state variable, s_{t+r}.

The main difference between (52) and the MS model used in Section 5.2, Equation (9), is the presence of lags and leads of the state variable. This requires to define a new state variable, s_t^*, such that

$$s_t^* = \begin{cases} 1 & \text{if } s_{t+r} = 1,\ s_{t+r-1} = 1,\ \ldots,\ s_{t-1} = 1, \\ 2 & \text{if } s_{t+r} = 0,\ s_{t+r-1} = 1,\ \ldots,\ s_{t-1} = 1, \\ 3 & \text{if } s_{t+r} = 1,\ s_{t+r-1} = 0,\ \ldots,\ s_{t-1} = 1, \\ \vdots & \qquad\qquad \vdots \\ 2^{r+2} & \text{if } s_{t+r} = 0,\ s_{t+r-1} = 0,\ \ldots,\ s_{t-1} = 0. \end{cases} \tag{53}$$

The transition probabilities of the Markov chain driving s_t^* can be derived from (11), and in the simplest case where $r = 1$ they are summarized by the matrix

$$P = \begin{pmatrix} p_{11} & 0 & 0 & 0 & p_{11} & 0 & 0 & 0 \\ p_{10} & 0 & 0 & 0 & p_{10} & 0 & 0 & 0 \\ 0 & p_{01} & 0 & 0 & 0 & p_{01} & 0 & 0 \\ 0 & p_{00} & 0 & 0 & 0 & p_{00} & 0 & 0 \\ 0 & 0 & p_{11} & 0 & 0 & 0 & p_{11} & 0 \\ 0 & 0 & p_{10} & 0 & 0 & 0 & p_{10} & 0 \\ 0 & 0 & 0 & p_{01} & 0 & 0 & 0 & p_{01} \\ 0 & 0 & 0 & p_{00} & 0 & 0 & 0 & p_{00} \end{pmatrix}, \tag{54}$$

whose ith, jth element corresponds to the probability that $s_t^* = i$ given that $s_{t-1}^* = j$.

The quantity of major interest is the probability that s_t^* assumes a certain value given the available information, namely,

$$\zeta_{t|t} = \begin{pmatrix} \Pr(s_t^* = 1 \mid x_t, x_{t-1}, \dots, x_1,\ y_t, y_{t-1}, \dots, y_1) \\ \Pr(s_t^* = 2 \mid x_t, x_{t-1}, \dots, x_1,\ y_t, y_{t-1}, \dots, y_1) \\ \vdots \\ \Pr(s_t^* = 2^{r+2} \mid x_t, x_{t-1}, \dots, x_1,\ y_t, y_{t-1}, \dots, y_1) \end{pmatrix}, \tag{55}$$

which is the counterpart of Equation (12) in this more general context. The vector $\zeta_{t|t}$ and the conditional density of future values of the variables given the past, $f(x_{t+1}, y_{t+1} \mid s_{t+1}^*, x_t, \dots, x_1,\ y_t, \dots, y_1)$, can be computed using the sequential procedure outlined in Section 5.2; see Hamilton and Perez-Quiros (1996) and Krolzig (2004) for details. The latter can be used for forecasting future values of the coincident variable, the former to evaluate the current status of the economy or to forecast its future status up to period $t + r$. For example, the probability of being in a recession today is given by the sum of the rows of $\zeta_{t|t}$ corresponding to those values of s_t^* characterized by $s_t = 1$, while the probability of being in a recession in period $t + r$ is given by the sum of the rows of $\zeta_{t|t}$ corresponding to those values of s_t^* characterized by $s_{t+r} = 1$. To make inference on states beyond period $t + r$, it is possible to use the formula

$$\zeta_{t+m|t} = P^m \zeta_{t|t}, \tag{56}$$

which is a direct extension of the first row of (14).

Hamilton and Perez-Quiros (1996) found that their model provides only a weak signal of recession in 1960, 1970 and 1990. Moreover, the evidence in favor of the nonlinear cyclical factor is weak and the forecasting gains for predicting GNP growth or its turning point are minor with respect to a linear VAR specification. Even weaker evidence in favor of the MS specification was found when a cointegrating relationship between GNP and lagged CLI is included in the model. The unsatisfactory performance of the MS model could be due to the hypothesis of constant probability of recessions, as in the univariate context; see, e.g., Filardo (1994). Evidence supporting this claim, based on the recession of 1990, is provided by Filardo and Gordon (1999).

Chauvet (1998) found a good performance also for the factor MS model in tracking the recession of 1990 using the proper version of $\zeta_{t|t}$ in that context. This is basically the only forecasting application of the factor MS models described in Section 2.1, so that further research is needed to close the gap. For example, SW's procedure for the CLI construction could be implemented using Kim and Nelson's (1998) MS version of the factor model, or a switching element could be introduced in the SW's VAR Equations (46) and (47).

The MS model can also be used to derive analytic forecasts of recession (or expansion) duration. Suppose that x_t follows the simpler MS model in (9)–(11) and that it is known that in period t the economy is in a recession, i.e., $s_t = 1$. Then,

$$\begin{aligned}
&\Pr(s_{t+1} = 1 \mid x_t, \dots, x_1) = p_{11}, \\
&\Pr(s_{t+2} = 1,\ s_{t+1} = 1 \mid x_t, \dots, x_1) \\
&\quad = \Pr(s_{t+2} = 1 \mid s_{t+1} = 1,\ x_t, \dots, x_1) \Pr(s_{t+1} = 1 \mid x_t, \dots, x_1) = p_{11}^2, \\
&\ \vdots
\end{aligned} \tag{57}$$

and the probability that the recession ends in period $t + n$ is

$$\Pr(s_{t+n} = 0,\ s_{t+n-1} = 1,\ \dots,\ s_{t+1} = 1 \mid x_t, \dots, x_1) = (1 - p_{11}) p_{11}^{n-1}. \tag{58}$$

Instead, if (11) is substituted with (18), i.e., the state probabilities are time-varying, then

$$\begin{aligned}
&\Pr(s_{t+n} = 0,\ s_{t+n-1} = 1,\ \dots,\ s_{t+1} = 1 \mid x_t, \dots, x_1) \\
&\quad = (1 - \hat{p}_{11,t+n}) \prod_{j=1}^{n-1} \hat{p}_{11,t+j}
\end{aligned} \tag{59}$$

with

$$\hat{p}_{11,t+j} = E\left(\frac{\exp(\theta y_{t+j-1})}{1 + \exp(\theta y_{t+j-1})} \,\middle|\, x_t, \dots, x_1,\ y_t, \dots, y_1 \right). \tag{60}$$

It follows that an estimator of the expected remaining duration of the recession, τ, in period t is given by

$$\hat{\tau} = E(\tau \mid s_t = 1) = \sum_{i=1}^{\infty} i (1 - \hat{p}_{11,t+i}) \prod_{j=1}^{i-1} \hat{p}_{11,t+j}, \tag{61}$$

which simplifies to

$$\hat{\tau} = E(\tau \mid s_t = 1) = \sum_{i=1}^{\infty} i (1 - p_{11}) p_{11}^{i-1}, \tag{62}$$

for constant probabilities. An interesting issue is therefore whether the leading indicators are useful to predict τ or not.

To conclude, Bayesian methods for the estimation of Markov switching models were developed by Albert and Chib (1993a), McCulloch and Tsay (1994), Filardo and Gordon (1994) and several other authors; see, e.g., Filardo and Gordon (1999) for a comparison of Bayesian linear, MS and factor models for coincident indicators, and Canova (2004, Chapter 11) for an overview. Yet, to the best of our knowledge, there are no applications to forecasting turning points with Bayesian MS models while, for example, a Bayesian replication of the Hamilton and Perez-Quiros (1996) exercise would be feasible and interesting.

7. Examples of composite coincident and leading indexes

In this section we provide empirical examples to illustrate some of the theoretical methods introduced so far. In particular, in the first subsection we compare several composite coincident indexes obtained with different methodologies, while in the second subsection we focus on leading indexes.

7.1. Alternative CCIs for the US

In Figure 1 we graph four composite coincident indexes for the US over the period 1959:1–2003:12: the Conference Board's equal weighted nonmodel based CCI, the

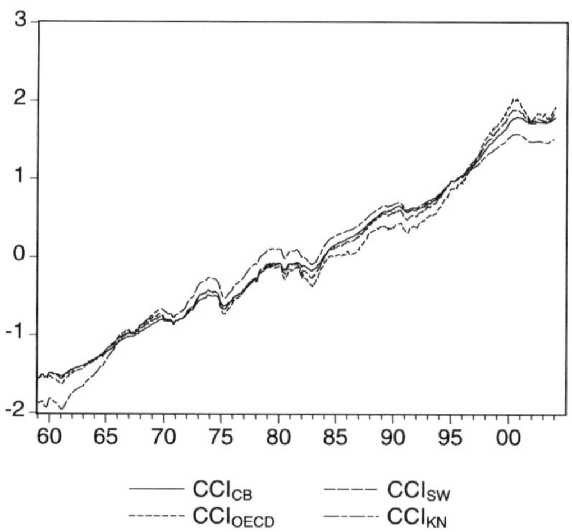

Figure 1. Composite coincident indexes. The figure reports the Conference Board's composite coincident indicator (CCI_{CB}), the OECD reference coincident series (CCI_{OECD}), Stock and Watson's coincident index (CCI_{SW}), and the coincident index derived from the four components in CCI_{CB} modeled with a dynamic factor model as in Kim and Nelson (1998) (CCI_{KN}). All indexes have been normalized to have zero mean and unit standard deviation.

Table 1
Correlation of composite coincident indexes (6-month percentage change)

	CCI_{CB}	CCI_{OECD}	CCI_{SW}	CCI_{KN}
CCI_{CB}	1			
CCI_{OECD}	0.941	1		
CCI_{SW}	0.979	0.969	1	
CCI_{KN}	0.943	0.916	0.947	1

Note: Common sample is 1970:01–2003:11.

OECD coincident reference series which is a transformation of IP, the Stock and Watson's (1989) factor model based CCI, and the Kim and Nelson's (1998) Bayesian MS factor model based CCI computed using the four coincident series combined in the CCI_{CB}. For the sake of comparability, all indexes are normalized to have zero mean and unit standard deviation.

The figure highlights the very similar behavior of all the CCIs, which in particular share the same pattern of peaks and troughs. The visual impression is confirmed by the correlations for the levels, and by those for the 6-month percentage changes reported in Table 1, the lowest value being 0.916 for CCI_{KN} and CCI_{OECD}. These values are in line with previous studies, see Section 5, and indicate that it is possible to achieve a close to complete agreement on the status of the economy.

In Figure 2 we consider dating the US classical and deviation cycles. In the upper panel we graph the CCI_{CB} and the NBER expansion/recession classification. The figure highlights that the NBER recessions virtually coincide with the peak-trough periods in the CCI_{CB}. In the middle panel we graph the CCI_{CB} and the expansion/recession classification resulting from the AMP dating. The results are virtually identical with respect to the NBER (see also the first two columns of Table 3), with the noticeable difference that AMP identifies a double dip at the beginning of the new century with recessions in 2000:10–2001:12 and 2002:7–2003:4 versus 2001:3–2001:11 for the NBER. In the lower panel of Figure 2 we graph the HP band pass filtered CCI_{CB}, described in Section 3, and the AMP dating for the resulting deviation cycle. As discussed in Section 3, the classical cycle recessions are a subset of those for the deviation cycle, since the latter capture periods of lower growth even if not associated with declines in the level of the CCI.

Finally, in Figure 3 we report the (filtered) probability of recessions computed with two methods. In the upper panel we graph the probabilities resulting from the Kim and Nelson's (1998) Bayesian MS factor model applied to the four coincident series combined in the CCI_{CB}. In the lower panel those from the AMP nonparametric MS approach applied to the CCI_{CB}. The results in the two panels are very similar, and the matching of peaks in these probabilities and NBER dated recessions is striking. The latter result supports the use of these methods for real-time dating of the business cycle. It is also worth noting that both methods attribute a probability close to 60% for a second

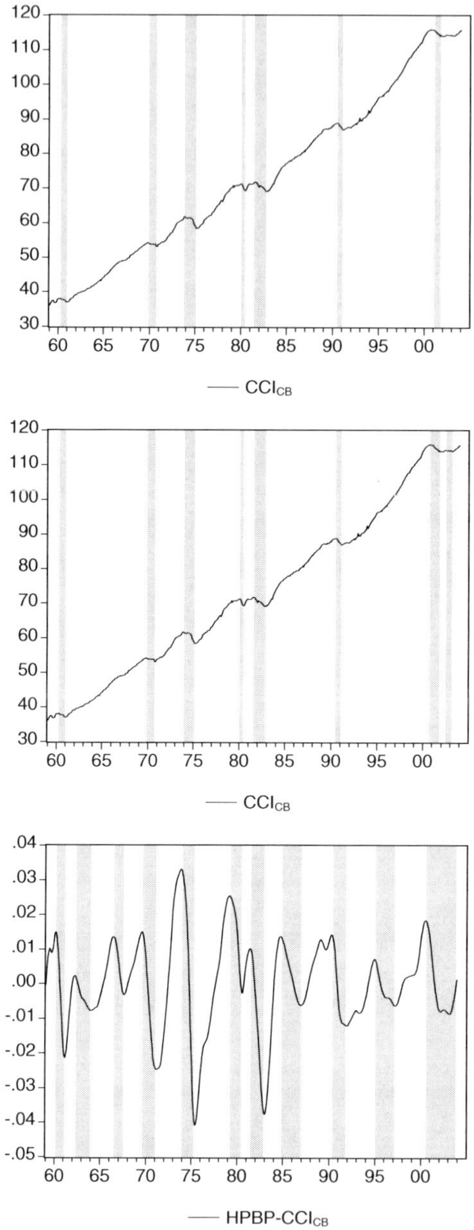

Figure 2. Classical and deviation cycles. Upper panel: CCI_{CB} and NBER dated recessions (shaded areas). Middle panel: CCI_{CB} and recessions dated with Artis, Marcellino and Proietti (2004) algorithm (shaded areas). Lower panel: HP-band pass filtered CCI_{CB} and recessions dated with Artis, Marcellino and Proietti (2004) algorithm (shaded areas).

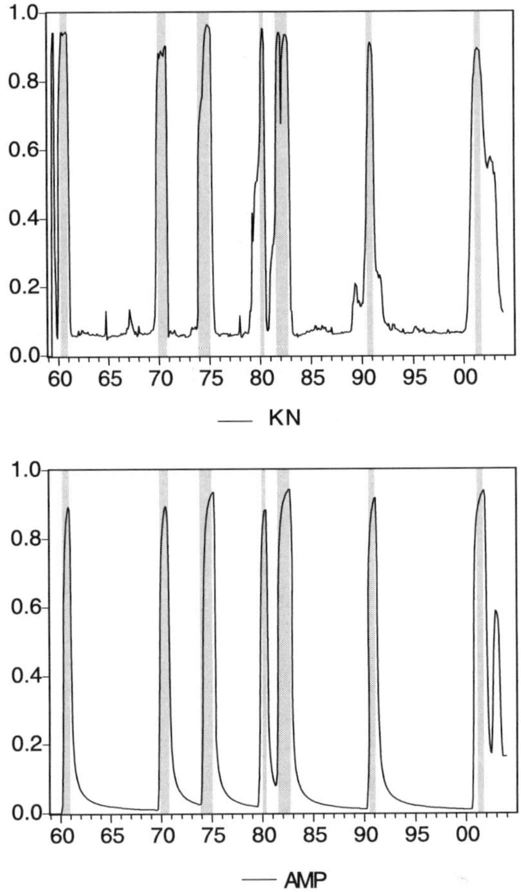

Figure 3. Probability of recession and NBER dated recessions. The upper panel reports the (filtered) probability of recession computed from a dynamic factor model for the four components in the CCI_{CB} using the Kim and Nelson's (1998) methodology. The lower panel reports the (filtered) probability of recession computed using the algorithm in Artis, Marcellino and Proietti (2004) applied to the CCI_{CB}. The shaded areas are the NBER dated recessions.

short recession at the beginning of the century, in line with the AMP dating reported in the middle panel of Figure 2 but in contrast with the NBER dating.

7.2. *Alternative CLIs for the US*

We start this subsection with an analysis of the indicator selection process for Stock and Watson's (1989, SW) model based composite leading index, described in detail in

Section 6.2, and of the construction of two nonmodel based indexes for the US produced by official agencies, the Conference Board, CLI_{CB}, and the OECD, CLI_{OECD}.

SW started with a rather large dataset of about 280 series, yet smaller than Mitchell and Burns' original selection of 487 candidate indicators. The series can be divided into ten groups: "measures of output and capacity utilization; consumption and sales; inventories and orders; money and credit quantity variables; interest rates and asset prices; exchange rates and foreign trade; employment, earnings and measures of the labor force; wages and prices; measures of government fiscal activity; and other variables", SW (p. 365).

The bivariate relationships between each indicator, properly transformed, and the growth of the CCI_{DOC} were evaluated using frequency domain techniques (the coherence and the phase lead), and time domain techniques (Granger causality tests and marginal predictive content for CCI_{DOC} beyond that of CLI_{DOC}). The choice of CCI_{DOC} rather than CCI_{SW} as the target variable can raise some doubts, but the latter was likely not developed yet at the time, and in addition the two composite coincident indexes are highly correlated. Some series were retained even if they performed poorly on the basis of the three criteria listed above, because either economic theory strongly supported their inclusion or they were part of the CLI_{DOC}. After this first screening, 55 variables remained in the list of candidate components of the composite leading index.

It is interesting that SW mentioned the possibility of using all the 55 series for the construction of an index, but abandoned the project for technical reasons (at the time construction of a time series model for all these variables was quite complicated) and because it would be difficult to evaluate the contribution of each component to the index. About ten years later, the methodology to address the former issue became available, see Stock and Watson (2002a, 2002b) and the discussion in Section 6.2 above, but the latter issue remains, the trade-off between parsimony and broad coverage of the index is still unresolved.

The second indicator selection phase is based on a step-wise regression procedure. The dependent variable is $CCI_{SWt+6} - CCI_{SWt}$, i.e., the six months growth rate in the SW composite coincident index, that is also the target variable for SW composite leading index, see Section 6.2. Different sets of variables (including their lags as selected by the AIC) are used as regressors, variables in each set are retained on the basis of their marginal explanatory power, the best variables in each original set are grouped into other sets of regressors, and the procedure is repeated until a small number of indicators remains in the list.

At the end, seven variables (and their lags) were included in the composite index, as listed in Table 1 in SW. They are:

(i) an index of new private housing authorized,
(ii) the growth rate of manufacturers' unfilled orders for durable goods industries,
(iii) the growth rate in a trade weighted nominal exchange rate,
(iv) the growth rate of part-time work in nonagricultural industries,
(v) the difference of the yield on constant-maturity portfolio of 10-years US treasury bonds,

(vi) the spread between interest rates on 6-months corporate paper and 6-months US treasury bills,

(vii) the spread between the yield on 10-years and 1-year US Treasury bonds.

The only change in the list so far took place in 1997, when the maturity in (vi) became 3 months. SW also discussed theoretical explanations for the inclusion of these variables (and exclusion of others). The most innovative variables in SW's CLI_{SW} are the financial spreads, whose forecasting ability became the focus of theoretical and empirical research in subsequent years. Yet, following an analysis of the performance of their CLI_{SW} during the 1990 recession, see Section 10.3, Stock and Watson (1992) also introduced a nonfinancial based index (CLI2_{SW}).

A potential problem of the extensive variable search underlying the final selection of index components, combined with parameter estimation, is overfitting. Yet, when SW checked the overall performance of their selection procedure using Monte Carlo simulations, the results were satisfactory. Even better results were obtained by Hendry and Krolzig (1999, 2001) for their automated model selection procedure, PcGets; see Banerjee and Marcellino (2005) for an application to leading indicator selection for the US.

A final point worth noting about SW's indicator selection procedure is the use of variable transformations. First, seasonally adjusted series are used. Second, a stationarity transformation is applied for the indicator to have similar properties as the target. Third, some series are smoothed because of high frequency noise, in particular, (ii)–(v) in the list above. The adopted filter is $f(L) = 1+2L+2L^2+L^3$. Such a filter is chosen with reference to the target variable, the 6-month growth of CCI, and to the use of first differenced indicators, since $f(L)(1-L)$ is a band-pass filter with gains concentrated at periods of four months to one year. Finally, if the most recent values of some of the seven indicators are not available, they are substituted with forecasts in order to be able to use as timely information as possible. Zarnowitz and Braun (1990), in their comment to SW, pointed out that smoothing the indicators contributes substantially to the good forecasting performance of SW's CLI, combined with the use of the most up-to-date information.

The practice of using forecasts when timely data are not available is now supported also for the CLI_{CB} [see McGuckin, Ozyildirim and Zarnowitz (2003)], but not yet implemented in the published version of the index. The latter is computed following the same steps as for the coincident index, the CCI_{CB} described in Section 4, but with a different choice of components. In particular, the single indicators combined in the index include average weekly hours, manufacturing; average weekly initial claims for unemployment insurance; manufacturers' new orders, consumer good and materials (in 1996$); vendor performance, slower deliveries diffusion index; manufacturers' new orders, nondefense capital goods; building permits, new private housing units; stock prices, 500 common stocks; money supply (in 1996$); interest rate spread, 10-year Treasury bond less federal funds; and the University of Michigan's index of consumer expectations.

This list originates from the original selection of Mitchell and Burns (1938), but only two variables passed the test of time: average weekly hours in the manufacturing sector and the Standard and Poor's stock index (that replaces the Dow Jones index of industrial common stock prices); see Moore (1983) for an historical perspective. Both variables are not included in the $\mathrm{CLI}_{\mathrm{SW}}$, since their marginal contribution in forecasting the 6-month growth of the $\mathrm{CCI}_{\mathrm{SW}}$ is not statistically significant. Other major differences in the components of the two composite leading indexes are the inclusion in $\mathrm{CLI}_{\mathrm{CB}}$ of M2 and of the index of consumer expectations (the relationship of M2 with the $\mathrm{CCI}_{\mathrm{SW}}$ is found to be unstable, while consumer expectations were added to $\mathrm{CLI}_{\mathrm{CB}}$ in the '90s so that the sample is too short for a significant evaluation of their role); and the exclusion from $\mathrm{CLI}_{\mathrm{CB}}$ of an exchange rate measure and of the growth in part time work (yet, the former has a small weight in the $\mathrm{CLI}_{\mathrm{SW}}$, while the latter is well proxied by the average weekly hours in manufacturing and the new claims for unemployment insurance).

The third CLI for the US we consider is the OECD composite short leading index, $\mathrm{CLI}_{\mathrm{OECD}}$ (see www.oecd.org). Several points are worth making. First, the target is represented by the turning points in the growth cycle of industrial production, where the trend component is estimated using a modified version of the phase average trend (PAT) method developed at the NBER [see Niemira and Klein (1994) for details], and the Bry and Boschan (1971) methodology is adopted for dating peaks and troughs. All of these choices are rather questionable, since industrial production is a lower and lower share of GDP (though still one of the most volatile components), theoretically sounder filters such as those discussed in Section 3 are available for detrending, and more sophisticated procedures are available for dating, see again Section 3. On the other hand, since the OECD computes the leading index for a wide variety of countries, simplicity and robustness are also relevant for them.

Second, the criteria for the selection of the components of the index are broadly in line with those listed in Section 2. The seven chosen indicators as listed in the OECD web site include dwellings started; net new orders for durable goods, share price index; consumer sentiment indicator; weekly hours of work, manufacturing; purchasing managers index; and the spread of interest rates. Overall, there is a strong similarity with the elements of the $\mathrm{CLI}_{\mathrm{CB}}$.

Third, as for $\mathrm{CLI}_{\mathrm{CB}}$, the components are first standardized and then aggregated with equal weights. More precisely, each indicator is detrended with the PAT method; smoothed according to its months for cyclical dominance (MCD) values to reduce irregularity; transformed to homogenize the cyclical amplitudes; standardized by subtracting the mean from the observed values and then dividing the resulting difference by the mean of the absolute values of the differences from the mean; and finally aggregated. When timely data for an indicator are not available, the indicator is not included in the preliminary release of the composite leading index.

Finally, the composite index is adjusted to ensure that its cyclical amplitude on average agrees with that of the detrended reference series. The trend restored version of the index is also computed and published, to get comparability with the IP series.

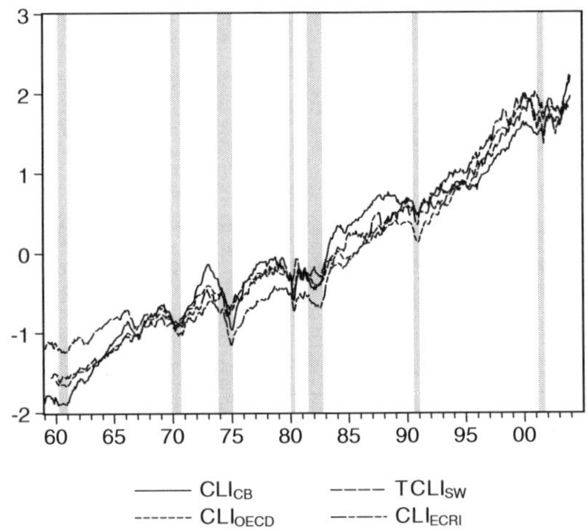

Figure 4. Composite leading indexes. The figure reports the Conference Board composite leading index (CLI_{CB}), the OECD leading index (CLI_{OECD}), a transformation of Stock and Watson's leading index ($TCLI_{SW}$, see text), the ECRI leading index (CLI_{ECRI}), and the NBER dated recessions (shaded areas). All indexes have been normalized to have zero mean and unit standard deviation.

A fourth CLI commonly monitored for the US is the Economic Cycle Research Institute's weekly leading index (see www.businesscycle.com). The precise parameters and procedural details underlying the construction of the CLI_{ECRI} are proprietary, the methodology is broadly described in Boschan and Banerji (1990).

In Figure 4 we graph the four composite leading indexes for the US we have described: the Conference Board's leading index (CLI_{CB}), the OECD leading index (CLI_{OECD}), the ECRI's weekly leading index (CLI_{ECRI}), and a transformation of Stock and Watson's (1989) composite leading index ($TCLI_{SW}$), their leading index plus their coincident index that yields a 6-month ahead forecast for the level of the coincident index, see Section 6.2. For comparability, all indexes are normalized to have zero mean and unit standard deviation. In the same figure we graph the NBER dated recessions (shaded areas).

Visual inspection suggests that the four indices move closely together, and their peaks anticipate NBER recessions. These issues are more formally evaluated in Tables 2 and 3. In Table 2 we report the correlations of the 6-month percentage changes of the four indices, which are indeed high, in particular when the '60s are excluded from the sample, the lowest value being 0.595 for CLI_{SW} and CLI_{ECRI}.

In Table 3 we present a descriptive analysis of the peak and trough structure of the four leading indexes (obtained with the AMP algorithm), compared either with the NBER dating or with the dating of the CCI_{CB} resulting from the AMP algorithm. The $TCLI_{SW}$ has the worst performance in terms of missed peaks and troughs, but it is worth recalling that the goal of the CLI_{SW} is not predicting turning points but the 6-month growth rate of the CCI_{SW}. The other three leading indexes missed no peaks or troughs,

Table 2
Correlation of composite leading indexes (6-month percentage change)

	CLI_{CB}	CLI_{OECD}	CLI_{SW}	CLI_{ECRI}
CLI_{CB}	1			
CLI_{OECD}	0.891	1		
CLI_{SW}	0.719	0.601	1	
CLI_{ECRI}	0.817	0.791	0.595	1

Note: Common sample is 1970:01–2003:11.

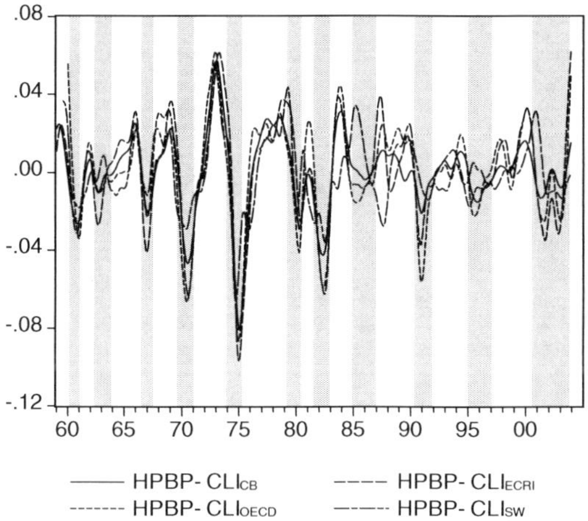

Figure 5. Filtered composite leading indexes with AMP dated recessions for deviation cycle of CCI_{CB}. The figure reports the HP-band pass filtered versions of the four CLIs in Figure 4, and the Artis, Marcellino and Proietti (2004) dating of the HP band pass filtered versions of the CCI_{CB} (shaded areas).

with the exception of the 2002 peak identified only by the AMP dating algorithm. Yet, they gave three false alarms, in 1966, 1984–1985, and 1994–1995. The average lead for recessions is about 9–10 months for all indexes (slightly shorter for $TCLI_{SW}$), but for expansions it drops to only 3–4 months for CLI_{OECD} and CLI_{ECRI}. Based on this descriptive analysis, the CLI_{CB} appears to yield the best overall leading performance. Yet, these results should be interpreted with care since they are obtained with the final release of the leading indicators rather than with real time data, see Section 10.1.

In Figure 5 we graph the HP band pass filtered versions of the four composite leading indexes, with the AMP deviation cycle dating (shaded areas). Again the series move closely together, slightly less so for the HPBP-$TCLI_{SW}$, and their peaks anticipate dated recessions.

Table 3
Classical cycles, dating of coincident and leading indexes

Peak						Trough					
Coincident		Leading (AMP)				Coincident		Leading (AMP)			
NBER	AMP	CB	OECD	ECRI	SW	NBER	AMP	CB	OECD	ECRI	SW
Apr 1960	May 1960	Jan 1959*	Jan 1960*	Jan 1959	Aug 1959*	Feb 1961	Feb 1961	Mar 1960	Dec 1960	Oct 1960	May 1960
				Jan 1962						Jun 1962	
		Apr 1966	Apr 1966	Apr 1966	Feb 1966			Dec 1966	Nov 1966	Dec 1966	Jul 1966
Dec 1969	Nov 1969	May 1969	Jan 1969	Jan 1969	**MISSING**	Nov 1970	Nov 1970	Apr 1970	Apr 1970	Jul 1970	**MISSING**
Nov 1973	Dec 1973	Feb 1973	Feb 1973	Jun 1973	Jan 1973	Mar 1975	Mar 1975	Jan 1975	Dec 1974	Jan 1975	Aug 1974
Jan 1980	Feb 1980	Nov 1978	Aug 1978	Nov 1978	Jun 1979	Jul 1980	Jul 1980	Apr 1980	Apr 1980	May 1980	Aug 1981
Jul 1981	Aug 1981	Nov 1980	Nov 1980	May 1981	**MISSING**	Nov 1982	Dec 1982	Jan 1982	Feb 1982	Aug 1982	**MISSING**
			Feb 1984		Oct 1985				Sep 1984		Jun 1986
		Jul 1988						Jun 1989			
Jul 1990	Jul 1990	Feb 1990	Mar 1990	Oct 1989	Feb 1990	Mar 1991	Mar 1991	Jan 1991	Dec 1990	Dec 1990	Jan 1991
		Nov 1994	Dec 1994					May 1995	Apr 1995		
				May 1998						Oct 1998	
Mar 2001	Oct 2000	Feb 2000	Feb 2000	Feb 2000	**MISSING**	Nov 2001	Dec 2001	Mar 2001	Oct 2001	Oct 2001	**MISSING**
	Jul 2002	**MISSING**	May 2002	**MISSING**	Feb 2002		Apr 2003	**MISSING**	**MISSING**	Apr 2003	**MISSING**

	Peak								Trough							
	NBER	AMP	NBER	AMP	NBER	AMP	NBER	AMP	NBER	AMP	NBER	AMP	NBER	AMP	NBER	AMP
Average lead	10	11	9	9	9	10	7	8	9	9	4	4	3	3	8	9
St. dev.	4.23	4.28	4.30	5.31	5.13	4.75	3.78	2.50	4.30	5.31	2.89	3.04	1.11	1	5.38	5.80
False alarms	3	3	3	3	3	3	2	2	3	3	3	3	3	3	2	2
Missing	0	1	0	0	0	1	2	4	0	1	0	0	0	1	3	4

Note: Shaded values are false alarms, 'MISSING' indicates a missed turning point. Leads longer than 18 months are considered false alarms. Negative leads are considered missed turning points. AMP: dating based on algorithm in Artis, Marcellino and Proietti (2004).

* indicates no previous available observation. Based on final release of data.

Table 4
Correlations of HP band pass filtered composite leading indexes

	HPBP-CLI_{CB}	HPBP-CLI_{OECD}	HPBP-CLI_{ECRI}	HPBP-CLI_{SW}
HPBP-CLI_{CB}	1			
HPBP-CLI_{OECD}	0.919	1		
HPBP-CLI_{ECRI}	0.906	0.882	1	
HPBP-CLI_{SW}	0.703	0.595	0.645	1

Note: Common sample is 1970:01–2003:11.

From Table 4, the HPBP-$TCLI_{SW}$ is the least correlated with the other indexes, correlation coefficients are in the range 0.60–0.70, while for the other three indexes the lowest correlation is 0.882.

From Table 5, the ranking of the indexes in terms of lead-time for peaks and troughs is similar to that in Table 3. In this case there is no official dating of the deviation cycle, so that we use the AMP algorithm applied to the HPBP-CCI_{CB} as a reference. The HPBP-CLI_{CB} confirms its good performance, with an average lead time of 7 months for recessions, 10 months for expansions, and just one missed signal and two false alarms. The HPBP-CLI_{ECRI} is a close second, while the HPBP-$TCLI_{SW}$ remains the worst, with 3–4 missed signals.

Finally, the overall good performance of the simple nonmodel based CLI_{CB} deserves further attention. We mentioned that it is obtained by cumulating, using the formula in (3), an equal weighted average of the one month symmetric percent changes of ten indicators. The weighted average happens to have a correlation of 0.960 with the first principal component of the ten members of the CLI_{CB}. The latter provides a nonparametric estimator for the factor in a dynamic factor model, see Section 6.2 and Stock and Watson (2002a, 2002b) for details. Therefore, the CLI_{CB} can also be considered as a good proxy for a factor model based composite leading indicator.

8. Other approaches for prediction with leading indicators

In this section we discuss other methods to transform leading indicators into a forecast for the target variable. In particular, Section 8.1 deals with observed transition models, Section 8.2 with neural network and nonparametric methods, Section 8.3 with binary models, and Section 8.4 with forecast pooling procedures. Examples are provided in the next section, after having defined formal evaluation criteria for leading indicator based forecasts.

8.1. Observed transition models

In the class of MS models described in Sections 5.2 and 6.3, the transition across states is abrupt and driven by an unobservable variable. As an alternative, in smooth transition (ST) models the parameters evolve over time at a certain speed, depending on the

Table 5
Deviations cycles, dating of coincident and leading indexes

Peak					Trough				
Coincident	Leading				Coincident	Leading			
CB	CB	OECD	ECRI	SW	CB	CB	OECD	ECRI	SW
Mar 1960	May 1959	Feb 1960	Jul 1959	Sep 1959	Mar 1961	Nov 1960	Jan 1961	Oct 1960	Jan 1961
May 1962	Jan 1962	Jan 1962	Dec 1961	**MISSING**	Jan 1964	Sep 1962	Nov 1962	Sep 1962	**MISSING**
				Apr 1963					May 1964
Jul 1967	Feb 1966	Mar 1966	Feb 1966	Jan 1967	Aug 1967	Feb 1967	Jan 1967	Dec 1966	Jan 1967
Aug 1969	Feb 1969	Dec 1968	Feb 1969	Dec 1967	Mar 1971	Jul 1970	Jun 1970	Aug 1970	Jun 1970
Dec 1973	Feb 1973	Jan 1973	May 1973	Jan 1973	Jun 1975	Feb 1975	Jan 1975	Jan 1975	Oct 1974
Mar 1979	Sep 1978	Sep 1978	Dec 1978	May 1979	Jul 1980	May 1982	Apr 1980	Jun 1982	Feb 1980
Jul 1981	**MISSING**	Mar 1981	**MISSING**	Sep 1980	Jan 1983	**MISSING**	May 1982	**MISSING**	Jun 1982
Nov 1984	Jan 1984	Dec 1983	Oct 1983	Apr 1985	Jan 1987	Jan 1986	May 1985	Oct 1985	Aug 1987
			Jun 1987					Apr 1988	
May 1990	Sep 1987	Aug 1987	Nov 1989	Jan 1990	Dec 1991	Dec 1990	Jan 1991	Nov 1990	Jul 1991
		Feb 1993					Jul 1993		
Jan 1995	Jun 1994	Jun 1994	Oct 1993	Jan 1994	Mar 1997	Nov 1995	Aug 1995	Feb 1995	Oct 1994
				Aug 1995					May 1997
		Nov 1997					Oct 1998		
Aug 2000	Jan 2000	Mar 2000	Mar 2000	Jan 2001	Dec 2003*	May 2001	Dec 2003*	Dec 2003*	Nov 2003*
	May 2002					Dec 2003*			
Aver. lead	7	6	7	8		10	7	10	6
St. dev.	2.28	3.21	3.80	3.25		4.67	4.03	4.47	2.31
False alarms	2	2	1	2		1	4	2	1
Missing	1	0	1	4		1	0	1	3

Note: Shaded values are false alarms, 'MISSING' indicates a missed turning point. Leads longer than 18 months are considered false alarms. Negative leads are considered missed turning points. AMP: dating based on algorithm in Artis, Marcellino and Proietti (2004).

* indicates last available observation. Based on final release of data.

behavior of observable variables. In particular, the ST-VAR, that generalizes the linear model in (21) can be written as

$$\begin{aligned}\Delta x_t &= c_x + A\,\Delta x_{t-1} + B\,\Delta y_{t-1} + (c_x + A\,\Delta x_{t-1} + B\Delta y_{t-1})F_x + u_{xt},\\ \Delta y_t &= c_y + C\Delta x_{t-1} + D\Delta y_{t-1} + (c_y + C\Delta x_{t-1} + D\Delta y_{t-1})F_y + u_{yt},\\ u_t &= (u_{xt}, u_{yt})' \sim \text{i.i.d. } N(0, \Sigma),\end{aligned} \tag{63}$$

where

$$F_x = \frac{\exp(\theta_0 + \theta_1 z_{t-1})}{1 + \exp(\theta_0 + \theta_1 z_{t-1})}, \qquad F_y = \frac{\exp(\phi_0 + \phi_1 z_{t-1})}{1 + \exp(\phi_0 + \phi_1 z_{t-1})}, \tag{64}$$

and z_{t-1} contains lags of x_t and y_t.

The smoothing parameters θ_1 and ϕ_1 regulate the shape of parameter change over time. When they are equal to zero, the model becomes linear, while for large values the model tends to a self-exciting threshold model [see, e.g., Potter (1995), Artis, Galvao and Marcellino (2003)], whose parameters change abruptly as in the MS case. In this sense the ST-VAR provides a flexible tool for modelling parameter change.

The transition function F_x is related to the probability of recession. In particular, when the values of z_{t-1} are much smaller than the threshold value, θ_0, the value of F_x gets close to zero, while large values lead to values of F_x close to one. This is a convenient feature in particular when F_x only depends on lags of y_t, since it provides direct evidence on the usefulness of the leading indicators to predict recessions. As an alternative, simulation methods as in Section 6.1 can be used to compute the probabilities of recession.

Details on the estimation and testing procedures for ST models, and extensions to deal with more than two regimes or time-varying parameters, are reviewed, e.g., by van Dijk, Teräsvirta and Franses (2002), while Teräsvirta (2006) focuses on the use of ST models in forecasting. In particular, as it is common with nonlinear models, forecasting more than one-step ahead requires the use of simulation techniques, unless dynamic estimation is used as, e.g., in Stock and Watson (1999b) or Marcellino (2003).

Univariate versions of the ST model using leading indicators as transition variables were analyzed by Granger, Teräsvirta and Anderson (1993), while Camacho (2004), Anderson and Vahid (2001), and Camacho and Perez-Quiros (2002) considered the VAR case. The latter authors found a significant change in the parameters only for the constant, in line with the MS specifications described in the previous subsection and with the time-varying constant introduced by SW to compute their CLI.

Finally, Bayesian techniques for the analysis of smooth transition models were developed by Lubrano (1995), and by Geweke and Terui (1993) and Chen and Lee (1995) for threshold models; see Canova (2004, Chapter 11) for an overview. Yet, there are no applications to forecasting using leading indicators.

8.2. Neural networks and nonparametric methods

The evidence reported so far, and that summarized in Section 10 below, is not sufficient to pin down the best parametric model to relate the leading to the coincident indicator, different sample periods or indicators can produce substantially different results. A possible remedy is to use artificial neural networks, which can provide a valid approximation to the generating mechanism of a vast class of nonlinear processes; see, e.g., Hornick, Stinchcombe and White (1989), and Swanson and White (1997), Stock and Watson (1999b), Marcellino (2003) for their use as forecasting devices.

In particular, Stock and Watson (1999b) considered two types of univariate neural network specifications. The single layer model with n_1 hidden units (and a linear component) is

$$x_t = \beta_0' z_t + \sum_{i=1}^{n_1} \gamma_{1i} g(\beta_{1i}' z_t) + e_t, \tag{65}$$

where $g(z)$ is the logistic function, i.e., $g(z) = 1/(1 + e^{-z})$, and z_t includes lags of the dependent variable. Notice that when $n_1 = 1$ the model reduces to a linear specification with a logistic smooth transition in the constant. A more complex model is the double layer feedforward neural network with n_1 and n_2 hidden units:

$$x_t = \beta_0' z_t + \sum_{j=1}^{n_2} \gamma_{2j} g\left(\sum_{i=1}^{n_1} \beta_{2ji} g(\beta_{1i}' z_t)\right) + e_t. \tag{66}$$

The parameters of (65) and (66) can be estimated by nonlinear least squares, and forecasts obtained by dynamic estimation.

While the studies using NN mentioned so far considered point forecasts, Qi (2001) focused on turning point prediction. The model she adopted is a simplified version of (66), namely,

$$r_t = g\left(\sum_{i=1}^{n_1} \beta_{2i} g(\beta_{1i}' z_t)\right) + e_t, \tag{67}$$

where z_t includes lagged leading indicators in order to evaluate their forecasting role, and r_t is a binary recession indicator. Actually, since $g(\cdot)$ is the logistic function, the predicted values from (67) are constrained to lie in the [0, 1] interval. As for (65) and (66), the model is estimated by nonlinear least squares, and dynamic estimation is adopted when forecasting.

An alternative way to tackle the uncertainty about the functional form of the relationship between leading and coincident indicators is to adopt a nonparametric specification, with the cost for the additional flexibility being the required simplicity of the model. Based on the results from the parametric models they evaluated, Camacho and Perez-Quiros (2002) suggested the specification,

$$x_t = m(y_{t-1}) + e_t, \tag{68}$$

estimated by means of the Nadaraya–Watson estimator; see also Härdle and Vieu (1992). Therefore,

$$\hat{x}_t = \left(\sum_{j=1}^{T} K\left(\frac{y_{t-1} - y_j}{h}\right) x_j\right) \Big/ \left(\sum_{j=1}^{T} K\left(\frac{y_{t-1} - y_j}{h}\right)\right), \tag{69}$$

where $K(\cdot)$ is the Gaussian kernel and the bandwidth h is selected by leave-one-out cross validation.

The model is used to predict recessions according to the two negative quarters rule. For example,

$$\Pr(x_{t+2} < 0,\ x_{t+1} < 0 \mid y_t) = \int_{y_{t+2}<0} \int_{y_{t+1}<0} f(x_{t+2}, x_{t+1} \mid y_t)\, \mathrm{d}x_{t+2}\, \mathrm{d}x_{t+1}, \tag{70}$$

and the densities are estimated using an adaptive kernel estimator; see Camacho and Perez-Quiros (2002) for details.

Another approach that imposes minimal structure on the leading-coincident indicator connection is the pattern recognition algorithm proposed by Keilis-Borok et al. (2000). The underlying idea is to monitor a set of leading indicators, comparing their values to a set of thresholds, and when a large fraction of the indicators rise above the threshold a recession alarm, A_t, is sent. Formally, the model is

$$A_t = \begin{cases} 1 & \text{if } \sum_{k=1}^{N} \Psi_{kt} \geqslant N - b, \\ 0 & \text{otherwise}, \end{cases} \tag{71}$$

where $\Psi_{kt} = 1$ if $y_{kt} \geqslant c_k$, and $\Psi_{kt} = 0$ otherwise. The salient features of this approach are the tight parameterization (only $N+1$ parameters, $b, c_1, \ldots, c_N$), which is in general a plus in forecasting, the transformation of the indicators into binary variables prior to their combination (from y_{kt} to Ψ_{kt} and then summed with equal weights), and the focus on the direct prediction of recessions, A_t is a $0/1$ variable.

Keilis-Borok et al. (2000) used 6 indicators: SW's CCI defined in Section 5.1 and five leading indicators, the interest rate spread, a short term interest rate, manufacturing and trade inventories, weekly initial claims for unemployment, and the index of help wanted advertising. They analyzed three different versions of the model in (71) where the parameters are either judgementally assigned or estimated by nonlinear least squares, with or without linear filtering of the indicators, finding that all versions perform comparably and satisfactory, producing (in a pseudo-out-of-sample context) an early warning of the five recessions over the period 1961 to 1990. Yet, the result should be interpreted with care because of the use of the finally released data and of the selection of the indicators using full sample information, consider, e.g., the use of the spread which was not common until the end of the '80s.

8.3. Binary models

In the models we have analyzed so far to relate coincident and leading indicators, the dependent variable is continuous, even though forecasts of business cycle turning points are feasible either directly (MS or ST models) or by means of simulation methods (linear or factor models). A simpler and more direct approach treats the business cycle phases as a binary variable, and models it using a logit or probit specification.

In particular, let us assume that the economy is in recession in period t, $R_t = 1$, if the unobservable variable s_t is larger than zero, where the evolution of s_t is governed by

$$s_t = \beta' y_{t-1} + e_t. \tag{72}$$

Therefore,

$$\Pr(R_t = 1) = \Pr(s_t > 0) = F(\beta' y_{t-1}), \tag{73}$$

where $F(\cdot)$ is either the cumulative normal distribution function (probit model), or the logistic function (logit model). The model can be estimated by maximum likelihood, and the estimated parameters combined with current values of the leading indicators to provide an estimate of the recession probability in period $t + 1$, i.e.,

$$\widehat{R}_{t+1} = \Pr(R_{t+1} = 1) = F(\hat{\beta}' y_t). \tag{74}$$

The logit model was adopted, e.g., by Stock and Watson (1991) and the probit model by Estrella and Mishkin (1998), while Birchenhall et al. (1999) provided a statistical justification for the former in a Bayesian context [on the latter, see also Zellner and Rossi (1984) and Albert and Chib (1993b)]. Binary models for European countries were investigated by Estrella and Mishkin (1997), Bernard and Gerlach (1998), Estrella, Rodrigues and Schich (2003), Birchenhall, Osborn and Sensier (2001), Osborn, Sensier and Simpson (2001), Moneta (2003).

Several points are worth discussing about the practical use of the probit or logit models for turning point prediction. First, often in practice the dating of R_t follows the NBER expansion/recession classification. Since there are substantial delays in the NBER's announcements, it is not known in period t whether the economy is in recession or not. Several solutions are available to overcome this problem. Either the model is estimated with data up to period $t - k$ and it is assumed that β remains constant in the remaining part of the sample; or R_t is substituted with an estimated value from an auxiliary binary model for the current status of the economy, e.g., using the coincident indicators as regressors [see, e.g., Birchenhall et al. (1999)] or one of the alternative methods for real-time dating of the cycle described in Section 2.2 is adopted.

Second, as in the case of dynamic estimation, a different model specification is required for each forecast horizon. For example, if an h-step ahead prediction is of interest, the model in (72) should be substituted with

$$s_t = \gamma_h' y_{t-h} + u_{t,h}. \tag{75}$$

This approach typically introduces serial correlation and heteroskedasticity into the error term $u_{t,h}$, so that the logit specification combined with nonlinear least-squares estimation and robust estimation of the standard errors of the parameters can be preferred over standard maximum likelihood estimation, compare, for example, (67) in the previous subsection which can be considered as a generalization of (75). Notice also that $\hat{\gamma}_h' y_{t-h}$ can be interpreted as an h-step ahead composite leading indicator. As an alternative, the model in (72) could be complemented with an auxiliary specification for y_t, say,

$$y_t = Ay_{t-1} + v_t \tag{76}$$

so that

$$\begin{aligned}\Pr(R_{t+h} = 1) = \Pr(s_{t+h} > 0) &= \Pr\big(\beta' A^{h-1} y_t + \eta_{t+h-1} + e_{t+h} > 0\big) \\ &= F_{\eta+e}\big(\beta' A^{h-1} y_t\big)\end{aligned} \tag{77}$$

with $\eta_{t+h-1} = \beta' v_{t+h-1} + \beta' A v_{t+h-2} + \cdots + \beta' A^{h-1} v_t$. In general, the derivation of $F_{\eta+e}(\cdot)$ is quite complicated, and the specification of the auxiliary model for y_t can introduce additional noise. Dueker (2005) extended and combined Equations (72) and (76) into

$$\begin{pmatrix} s_t \\ y_t \end{pmatrix} = \begin{pmatrix} a & B \\ c & D \end{pmatrix} \begin{pmatrix} s_{t-1} \\ y_{t-1} \end{pmatrix} + \begin{pmatrix} e_{st} \\ e_{yt} \end{pmatrix}, \tag{78}$$

which is referred to as Qual-VAR because of its similarity with the models considered in Section 6.1. The model composed of the equation for s_t alone is the dynamic ordered probit studied by Eichengreen, Watson and Grossman (1985), who derived its likelihood and the related maximum likelihood estimators. Adding the set of equations for y_t has the main advantage of closing the model for forecasting purposes. Moreover, Dueker (2005) showed that the model can be rather easily estimated using Gibbs sampling techniques, and Dueker and Wesche (2001) found sizeable forecasting gains with respect to the standard probit model, in particular during recessionary periods.

Third, the construction of the probability of a recession within a certain period, say $t+2$, is complicated within the binary model framework. The required probability is given by $\Pr(R_{t+1} = 0,\ R_{t+2} = 1) + \Pr(R_{t+1} = 1,\ R_{t+2} = 0) + \Pr(R_{t+1} = 1,\ R_{t+2} = 1)$. Then, either from (75),

$$\begin{aligned}\Pr(R_{t+1} = 1,\ R_{t+2} = 1) &= \Pr(s_{t+1} > 0,\ s_{t+2} > 0) \\ &= \Pr\big(u_{t+1,1} > -\gamma_1' y_t,\ u_{t+2,2} > -\gamma_2' y_t\big),\end{aligned} \tag{79}$$

or from (77),

$$\begin{aligned}&\Pr(R_{t+1} = 1,\ R_{t+2} = 1) = \Pr(s_{t+1} > 0,\ s_{t+2} > 0) \\ &\quad = \Pr\big(\beta' y_t + e_{t+1} > 0,\ \beta' A y_t + \beta' v_{t+1} + e_{t+2} > 0\big),\end{aligned} \tag{80}$$

and similar formulae apply for $\Pr(R_{t+1} = 0,\ R_{t+2} = 1)$ and $\Pr(R_{t+1} = 1,\ R_{t+2} = 0)$. As long as the joint distributions in (79) and (80) are equivalent to the product of the marginal ones, as in this case assuming that v_t are uncorrelated with e_t, and the error terms are i.i.d., an analytic solution can be found. For higher values of h simulation methods are required. For example, a system made up of the models resulting using Equation (75) for different values of h can be jointly estimated and used to simulate the probability values in (79). A similar approach can be used to compute the probability that an expansion (or a recession) will have a certain duration. A third, simpler alternative, is to define another binary variable directly linked to the event of interest, in this case,

$$R2_t = \begin{cases} 0 & \text{if no recession in period } t+1,\ t+2, \\ 1 & \text{if at least one recession in } t+1,\ t+2, \end{cases} \tag{81}$$

and then model $R2_t$ with a probit or logit specification as a function of indicators dated up to period $t-1$. The problem of this approach is that it is not consistent with the model for R_t in Equations (72), (73). The extent of the mis-specification should be evaluated in practice and weighted with the substantial simplification in the computations. A final, more promising, approach is simulation of the Qual-VAR model in (78), along the lines of the linear model in Section 6.1.

Fourth, an additional issue that deserves investigation is the stability of the parameters over time, and in particular across business cycle phases. Chin, Geweke and Miller (2000) proposed to estimate different parameters in expansions and recessions, using an exogenous classification of the states based on their definition of turning points. Dueker (1997, 2002) suggested to make the switching endogenous by making the parameters of (72) evolve according to a Markov chain. Both authors provided substantial evidence in favor of parameters instability.

Fifth, an alternative procedure to compute the probability of recession in period t consists of estimating logit or probit models for a set of coincident indicators, and then aggregating the resulting forecasts. The weights can be either those used to aggregate the indicators into a composite index, or they can be determined within a pooling context, as described in the next subsection.

Sixth, Pagan (2005) points out that the construction of the binary R_t indicator matters, since it can imply that the indicator is not i.i.d. as required by the standard probit or logit analysis.

Finally, as in the case of MS or ST models, the estimated probability of recession, $\hat{r}_{t+1}$, should be transformed into a 0/1 variable using a proper rule. The common choices are of the type $\hat{r}_t \geqslant c$ where c is either 0.5, a kind of uninformative Bayesian prior, or equal to the sample unconditional recession probability. Dueker (2002) suggested to make the cutoff values also regime dependent, say c_0 and c_1, and to compare the estimated probability with a weighted combination of c_0 and c_1 using the related regime probabilities. In general, as suggested, e.g., by Zellner, Hong and Gulati (1990) and analyzed in details by Lieli (2004), the cutoff should be a function of the preferences of the forecasters.

8.4. Pooling

Since the pioneering work of Bates and Granger (1969), it is well known that pooling several forecasts can yield a mean square forecast error (msfe) lower than that of each of the individual forecasts; see Timmermann (2006) for a comprehensive overview. Hence, rather than selecting a preferred forecasting model, it can be convenient to combine all the available forecasts, or at least some subsets.

Several pooling procedures are available. The three most common methods in practice are linear combination, with weights related to the msfe of each forecast [see, e.g., Granger and Ramanathan (1984)], median forecast selection, and predictive least squares, where a single model is chosen, but the selection is recursively updated at each forecasting round on the basis of the past forecasting performance.

Stock and Watson (1999b) and Marcellino (2004) presented a detailed study of the relative performance of these pooling methods, using a large dataset of, respectively, US and Euro area macroeconomic variables, and taking as basic forecasts those produced by a range of linear and nonlinear models. In general simple averaging with equal weights produces good results, more so for the US than for the Euro area. Stock and Watson (2003a) focused on the role of pooling for GDP growth forecasts in the G7 countries, using a larger variety of pooling methods, and dozens of models. They concluded that median and trimmed mean pooled forecasts produce a more stable forecasting performance than each of their component forecasts. Incidentally, they also found pooled forecasts to perform better than the factor based forecasts discussed in Section 6.2.

Camacho and Perez-Quiros (2002) focused on pooling leading indicator models, in particular they considered linear models, MS and ST models, probit specifications, and the nonparametric model described in Section 8.2, using regression based weights as suggested by Granger and Ramanathan (1984). Hence, the pooled forecast is obtained as

$$\hat{x}_{t+1|t} = w_1\hat{x}_{t+1|t,1} + w_2\hat{x}_{t+1|t,2} + \cdots + w_p\hat{x}_{t+1|t,p}, \tag{82}$$

and the weights, w_i, are obtained as the estimated coefficients from the linear regression

$$x_t = \omega_1\hat{x}_{t|t-1,1} + \omega_2\hat{x}_{t|t-1,2} + \cdots + \omega_p\hat{x}_{t|t-1,p} + u_t \tag{83}$$

which is estimated over a training sample using the forecasts from the single models to be pooled, $\hat{x}_{t|t-1,i}$, and the actual values of the target variable.

Camacho and Perez-Quiros (2002) evaluated the role of pooling not only for GDP growth forecasts but also for turning point prediction. The pooled recession probability is obtained as

$$\hat{r}_{t+1|t} = F(a_1\hat{r}_{t+1|t,1} + a_2\hat{r}_{t+1|t,2} + \cdots + a_p\hat{r}_{t+1|t,p}), \tag{84}$$

where $F(\cdot)$ is the cumulative distribution function of a normal variable, and the weights, a_i, are obtained as the estimated parameters in the probit regression

$$r_t = F(\alpha_1\hat{r}_{t|t-1,1} + \alpha_2\hat{r}_{t|t-1,2} + \cdots + \alpha_p\hat{r}_{t|t-1,p}) + e_t, \tag{85}$$

which is again estimated over a training sample using the recession probabilities from the single models to be pooled, $\hat{r}_{t|t-1,i}$, and the actual values of the recession indicator, r_t.

The pooling method described above was studied from a theoretical point of view by Li and Dorfman (1996) in a Bayesian context. A more standard Bayesian approach to forecast combination is the use of the posterior odds of each model as weights; see, e.g., Zellner and Min (1993). When all models have equal prior odds, this is equivalent to the use of the likelihood function value of each model as its weight in the pooled forecast.

9. Evaluation of leading indicators

In this section we deal with the evaluation of the forecasting performance of the leading indicators when used either in combination with simple rules to predict turning points, or as regressors in one of the models described in the previous sections to forecast either the growth rate of the target variable or its turning points. In the first subsection we consider methodological aspects while in the second subsection we discuss empirical examples.

9.1. Methodology

A first assessment of the goodness of leading indicators can be based on standard in-sample specification and mis-specification tests of the models that relate the indicators to the target variable.

The linear model in (21) provides the simplest framework to illustrate the issues. A first concern is whether it is a proper statistical model of the relationships among the coincident and the leading variables. This requires the estimated residuals to mimic the assumed i.i.d. characteristics of the errors, the parameters to be stable over time, and the absence of nonlinearity. Provided these hypotheses are not rejected, the model can be used to assess additional properties, such as Granger causality of the leading for the coincident indicators, or to evaluate the overall goodness of fit of the equations for the coincident variables (or for the composite coincident index). The model also offers a simple nesting framework to evaluate the relative merits of competing leading indicators, whose significance can be assessed by means of standard testing procedures. For a comprehensive analysis of the linear model see, e.g., Hendry (1995).

The three steps considered for the linear model, namely, evaluation of the goodness of the model from a statistical point of view, testing of hypotheses of interest on the parameters, and comparison with alternative specifications should be performed for each of the approaches listed in Sections 6 and 8. In particular, Hamilton and Raj (2002) and Raj (2002) provide up-to-date results for Markov-switching models, van Dijk, Teräsvirta and Franses (2002) for smooth transition models, while, e.g., Mizon and Marcellino (2006) present a general framework for model comparison.

Yet, in-sample analyses are more useful to highlight problems of a certain indicator or methodology than to provide empirical support in their favor, since they can be biased by over-fitting and related problems due to the use of the same data for model specification, estimation, and evaluation. A more sound appraisal of the leading indicators can be based on their out of sample performance, an additional reason for this being that forecasting is their main goal.

When the target is a continuous variable, such as the growth of a CCI over a certain period, standard forecast evaluation techniques can be used. In particular, the out-of-sample mean square forecast error (MSFE) or mean absolute error (MAE) provide standard summary measures of forecasting performance. Tests for equal forecast accuracy can be computed along the lines of Diebold and Mariano (1995), Clark and McCracken (2001), the standard errors around the MSFE of a model relative to a benchmark can be computed following West (1996), and tests for forecast encompassing can be constructed as in Clark and McCracken (2001). West (2006) provides an up-to-date survey of forecast evaluation techniques.

Moreover, as discussed in Section 6, simulation methods are often employed to compute the joint distribution of future values of the CCI to produce recession forecasts. Such a joint distribution can be evaluated using techniques developed in the density forecast literature; see, e.g., Corradi and Swanson (2006).

When the target variable, R_t, is a binary indicator while the (out of sample) forecast is a probability of recession, P_t, similar techniques can be used since the forecast error is a continuous time variable. For example, Diebold and Rudebusch (1989) defined the accuracy of the forecast as

$$\mathrm{QPS} = \frac{1}{T}\sum_{t=1}^{T} 2(P_t - R_t)^2, \tag{86}$$

where QPS stands for quadratic probability score, which is the counterpart of the MSFE. The range of QPS is [0, 2], with 0 for perfect accuracy. A similar loss function that assigns more weight to larger forecast errors is the log probability score,

$$\mathrm{LPS} = -\frac{1}{T}\sum_{t=1}^{T}\big((1 - R_t)\log(1 - P_t) + R_t \log P_t\big). \tag{87}$$

The range of LPS is $[0, \infty]$, with 0 for perfect accuracy.

Furthermore, Stock and Watson (1992) regressed $R_{t+k} - \mathrm{CRI}_{t+k|t}$, i.e., the difference of their indicator of recession and the composite recession index, on available information in period t, namely

$$R_{t+k} - \mathrm{CRI}_{t+k|t} = z_t\beta + e_t, \tag{88}$$

where the regressors in z_t are indicators included or excluded in SW's CLI. The error term in the above regression is heteroskedastic, because of the discrete nature of R_t, and serially correlated, because of the k-period ahead forecast horizon. Yet, robust t- and

F-statistics can be used to test the hypothesis of interest, $\beta = 0$, that is associated with correct model specification when z_t contains indicators included in the CLI, or with an efficient use of the information in the construction of the recession forecast when z_t contains indicators excluded from the CLI. Of course, the model in (88) can also be adopted when the dependent variable is a growth rate forecast error.

If the CRI or any probability of recession are transformed into a binary indicator, S_t, by choosing a threshold such that if the probability of recession increases beyond it then the indicator is assigned a value of one, the estimation method for the regression in (88) should be changed, since the dependent variable becomes discrete. In this case, a logistic or probit regression with appropriate corrections for the standard errors of the estimated coefficients would suit.

Contingency tables can also be used for a descriptive evaluation of the methodology in the case of binary forecasts and outcomes. They provide a summary of the percentage of correct predictions, missed signals (no prediction of slowdown when it takes place), and false alarms (prediction of slowdown when it does not take place). A more formal assessment can be based on a concordance index, defined as

$$I_{RS} = \frac{1}{T}\sum_{t=1}^{T}\left[R_t S_t + (1 - S_t)(1 - R_t)\right], \tag{89}$$

with values in the interval [0, 1], and 1 for perfect concordance. Under the assumption that S_t and R_t are independent, the estimate of the expected value of the concordance index is $2\overline{SR} = 1 - \overline{R} - \overline{S}$, where $\overline{R}$ and $\overline{S}$ are the averages of R_t and S_t. Subtracting this quantity from I_{RS} yields the mean-corrected concordance index [Harding and Pagan (2002, 2005)]:

$$I_{RS}^{*} = 2\frac{1}{T}\sum_{t=1}^{T}\left(S_t - \overline{S}\right)\left(R_t - \overline{R}\right). \tag{90}$$

AMP showed that under the null hypothesis of independence of S_t and R_t,

$$T^{1/2} I_{RS}^{*} \to N\left(0, 4\sigma^2\right), \quad \sigma^2 = \gamma_R(0)\gamma_S(0) + 2\sum_{\tau=1}^{\infty}\gamma_R(\tau)\gamma_S(\tau), \tag{91}$$

where $\gamma_S(\tau) = E[(S_t - E(S_t))(S_{t-\tau} - E(S_t))]$ and $\gamma_S(\tau)$ is defined accordingly. A consistent estimator of σ^2 is

$$\hat{\sigma}^2 = \hat{\gamma}_R(0)\hat{\gamma}_S(0) + 2\sum_{\tau=1}^{l}\left(1 - \frac{\tau}{T}\right)\hat{\gamma}_R(\tau)\hat{\gamma}_S(\tau), \tag{92}$$

where l is the truncation parameter and $\hat{\gamma}_R(\tau)$ and $\hat{\gamma}_S(\tau)$ are the sample counterparts of $\gamma_R(\tau)$ and $\gamma_S(\tau)$. As an alternative, Harding and Pagan (2002, 2005) proposed to regress R_t on S_t, and use a robust t-test to evaluate the significance of S_t.

Notice that since the predictive performance of the leading indicators can vary over expansions and recessions, and/or near turning points, it can be worth providing a separate evaluation of the models and the indicators over these subperiods, using any of the methods mentioned so far. The comparison should also be conducted at different forecast horizons, since the ability to provide early warnings is another important property for a leading indicator, though difficult to be formally assessed in a statistical framework.

A final comment concerns the choice of the loss function, that in all the forecast evaluation criteria considered so far is symmetric. Yet, when forecasting growth or a recession indicator typically the losses are greater in case of a missed signal than for a false alarm, for example, because policy-makers or firms cannot take timely counteracting measures. Moreover, false alarms can be due to the implementation of timely and effective policies as a reaction to the information in the leading indicators, or can signal major slowdowns that do not turn into recessions but can be of practical policy relevance. These considerations suggest that an asymmetric loss function could be a more proper choice, and in such a case using the methods summarized so far to evaluate a leading indicator based forecast or rank competing forecasts can be misleading. For example, a model can produce a higher loss than another model even if the former has a lower MSFE or MAE, the best forecast can be biased, or an indicator can be significant in (88) without reducing the loss; see, e.g., Artis and Marcellino (2001), Elliott, Komunjer and Timmermann (2003), Patton and Timmermann (2003), and Granger and Machina (2006) for an overview. More generally, the construction itself of the leading indicators and their inclusion in forecasting models should be driven by the loss function and, in case, take its asymmetry into proper account.

9.2. Examples

We now illustrate the methodology for model evaluation discussed in the previous subsection, using four empirical examples that involve some of the models reviewed in Sections 6 and 8.

The first application focuses on the use of linear models for the (one-month symmetric percent changes of the) CCI_{CB} and the CLI_{CB}. We focus on the following six specifications. A bivariate VAR for the CCI_{CB} and the CLI_{CB}, as in Equation (34). A univariate AR for the CCI_{CB}. A bivariate ECM for the CCI_{CB} and the CLI_{CB}, as in Equation (39), where one cointegrating vector is imposed and its coefficient recursively estimated. A VAR for the four components of the CCI_{CB} and the CLI_{CB}, as in Equation (29). A VAR for the CCI_{CB} and the ten components of the CLI_{CB}. Finally, a VAR for the four components of the CCI_{CB} and the ten components of the CLI_{CB}, as in Equation (21). Notice that most of these models are nonnested, except for the AR which is nested in some of the VARs, and for the bivariate VAR which is nested in the ECM.

The models are compared on the basis of their forecasting performance one and six month ahead over the period 1989:1–2003:12, which includes the two recessions of July 1990–March 1991 and March 2001–November 2001. The forecasts are computed recursively with the first estimation sample being 1959:1–1988:12 for one step ahead forecasts and 1959:1–1988:6 for six step ahead forecasts, using the final release of the indexes and their components. While the latter choice can bias the evaluation towards the usefulness of the leading indicators, this is not a major problem when the forecasting comparison excludes the '70s and '80s and when, as in our case, the interest focuses on the comparison of alternative models for the same vintage of data, see the next section for details. The lag length is chosen by BIC over the full sample. Recursive BIC selects smaller models for the initial samples, but their forecasting performance is slightly worse. The forecasts are computed using both the standard iterated method, and dynamic estimation (as described in Equation (25)).

The comparison is based on the MSE and MAE relative to the bivariate VAR for the CCI_{CB} and the CLI_{CB}. The Diebold and Mariano (1995) test for the statistical significance of the loss differentials is also computed. The results are reported in the upper panel of Table 6.

Five comments can be made. First, the simple AR model performs very well, there are some very minor gains from the VAR only six step ahead. This finding indicates that the lagged behavior of the CCI_{CB} contains useful information that should be included in a leading index. Second, taking cointegration into account does not improve the forecasting performance. Third, forecasting the four components of the CCI_{CB} and then aggregating the forecasts, as in Equation (31), decreases the MSE at both horizons, and the difference with respect to the bivariate VAR is significant one-step ahead. Fourth, disaggregation of the CLI_{CB} into its components is not useful, likely because of the resulting extensive parameterization of the VAR and the related increased estimation uncertainty. Finally, the ranking of iterated forecasts and dynamic estimation is not clear cut, but for the best performing VAR using the four components of the CCI_{CB} the standard iterated method decreases both the MSE and the MAE by about 10%.

In the middle and lower panels of Table 6 the comparison is repeated for, respectively, recessionary and expansionary periods. The most striking result is the major improvement of the ECM during recessions, for both forecast horizons. Yet, this finding should be interpreted with care since it is based on 18 observations only.

The second empirical example replicates and updates the analysis of Hamilton and Perez-Quiros (1996). They compared univariate and bivariate models, with and without Markov switching, for predicting one step ahead the turning points of (quarterly) GNP using the CLI_{CB} as a leading indicator, named CLI_{DOC} at that time. They found a minor role for switching (and for the use of real time data rather than final revisions), and instead a positive role for cointegration. Our first example highlighted that cointegration is not that relevant for forecasting during most of the recent period, and we wonder whether the role of switching has also changed. We use monthly data on the CCI_{CB} and the CLI_{CB}, with the same estimation and forecast sample as in the previous example. The turning point probabilities for the linear models are computed by simulations, as described at the end of Section 6.1, using a two consecutive negative growth rule to identify recessions. For the MS we use the filtered recession probabilities. We also add to the comparison a probit model where the NBER based expansion/recession indicator is regressed on six lags of the CLI_{CB}. The NBER based expansion/recession indicator is also the target for the linear and MS based forecasts, as in Hamilton and Perez-Quiros (1996).

Table 6
Forecast comparison of alternative VAR models for CCI_{CB} and CLI_{CB}

		1 step-ahead		6 step-ahead DYNAMIC		6 step-ahead ITERATED	
		Relative MSE	Relative MAE	Relative MSE	Relative MAE	Relative MSE	Relative MAE
				Whole sample			
CCI + CLI	VAR(2)	1	1	1	1	1	1
CCI	AR(2)	1.001	1.010	0.982	0.963*	1.063	1.032
CCI + CLI coint	VECM(2)	1.042	1.074*	1.067	1.052	1.115	1.100
4 comp. of CCI + CLI	VAR(2)	0.904**	0.976	0.975	0.973	0.854**	0.911**
CCI + 10 comp. of CLI	VAR(1)	1.158***	1.114***	1.035	1.017	1.133**	1.100***
4 comp. CCI + 10 comp. CLI	VAR(1)	0.995	1.029	1.090	1.035	0.913	0.967
	VAR(2)	0.075	0.186	0.079	0.216	0.075	0.201
				Recessions			
CCI + CLI	VAR(2)	1	1	1	1	1	1
CCI	AR(2)	0.988	0.975	0.949	0.940	1.303**	1.154**
CCI + CLI coint	VECM(2)	0.681***	0.774***	0.744	0.882	0.478***	0.626***
4 comp. of CCI + CLI	VAR(2)	0.703*	0.784**	0.825	0.879	0.504***	0.672***
CCI + 10 comp. of CLI	VAR(1)	1.095	1.009	1.151	1.131	1.274*	1.117
4 comp. CCI + 10 comp. CLI	VAR(1)	0.947	0.852	1.037	1.034	0.614***	0.714***
	VAR(2)	0.087	0.258	0.096	0.252	0.163	0.368
				Expansions			
CCI + CLI	VAR(2)	1	1	1	1	1	1
CCI	AR(2)	1.002	1.016	0.977	0.956*	0.997	1.005
CCI + CLI coint	VECM(2)	1.090*	1.123***	1.118	1.081	1.292***	1.206***
4 comp. of CCI + CLI	VAR(2)	0.931*	1.007	0.987	0.980	0.952	0.964
CCI + 10 comp. of CLI	VAR(1)	1.166***	1.132***	1.015	0.997	1.093*	1.096**
4 comp. CCI + 10 comp. CLI	VAR(1)	1.001	1.058	1.087	1.029	0.997	1.023
	VAR(2)	0.074	0.177	0.076	0.208	0.065	0.183

Note: Forecast sample is: 1989:1–2003:12. First estimation sample is 1959:1–1988:12 (for 1 step-ahead) or 1959:1–1988:6 (for 6 step-ahead), recursively updated. Lag length selection by BIC. MSE and MAE are mean square and absolute forecast error. VAR for CCI_{CB} and CLI_{CB} is benchmark.

*indicates significance at 10%,

**indicates significance at 5%,

***indicates significance at 1% of the Diebold–Mariano test for the null hypothesis of no significant difference in MSE or MAE with respect to the benchmark.

Table 7
Turning point predictions

Target	Model	Relative MSE	Relative MAE
NBER	univariate	1.0302	1.2685***
(1 step-ahead)	univariate MS	1.3417	1.0431
	bivariate	1.0020	1.0512
	bivariate MS	0.6095	0.4800***
	probit CLI_CB	1	1
	probit	0.0754	0.1711

Note: One-step ahead turning point forecasts for the NBER expansion/recession indicator. Linear and MS models [as in Hamilton and Perez-Quiros (1996)] for CCI_{CB} and CLI_{CB}. Six lags of CLI_{CB} are used in the probit model.
***indicates significance at 1% of the Diebold–Mariano test for the null hypothesis of no significant difference in MSE or MAE with respect to the benchmark.

In Table 7 we report the MSE and MAE for each model relative to the probit, where the MSE is just a linear transformation of the QPS criterion of Diebold and Rudebusch (1989, 1991a, 1991b) and the Diebold and Mariano (1995) test for the statistical significance of the loss differentials. The results indicate a clear preference for the bivariate MS model, with the probit a far second best, notwithstanding its direct use of the target series as dependent variable. The turning point probabilities for the five models are graphed in Figure 6, together with the NBER dated recessions (shaded areas). The figure highlights that the probit model misses completely the 2001 recession, while both MS models indicate it, and also provide sharper signals for the 1990–1991 recession. Yet, the univariate MS model also gives several false alarms.

Our third empirical application is a more detailed analysis of the probit model. In particular, we consider whether the other composite leading indexes discussed in Section 7.2, the CLI_{ECRI}, CLI_{OECD}, and CLI_{SW}, or the three-month ten-year spread on the treasury bill rates have a better predictive performance than the CLI_{CB}. The estimation and forecasting sample is as in the first empirical example, and the specification of the probit models is as in the second example, namely, six lags of each CLI are used as regressors (more specifically, the symmetric one month percentage changes for CLI_{CB} and the one month growth rates for the other CLIs). We also consider a sixth probit model where three lags of each of the five indicators are included as regressors.

From Table 8, the model with the five indexes is clearly favored for one-step ahead turning point forecasts of the NBER based expansion/recession indicator, with large and significant gains with respect to the benchmark, which is based on the CLI_{CB}. The second best is the ECRI indicator, followed by OECD and SW. Repeating the analysis for six month ahead forecasts, the gap across models shrinks, the term spread becomes the first or second best (depending on the use of MSE or MAE), and the combination of the five indexes remains a good choice. Moreover, the models based on these variables

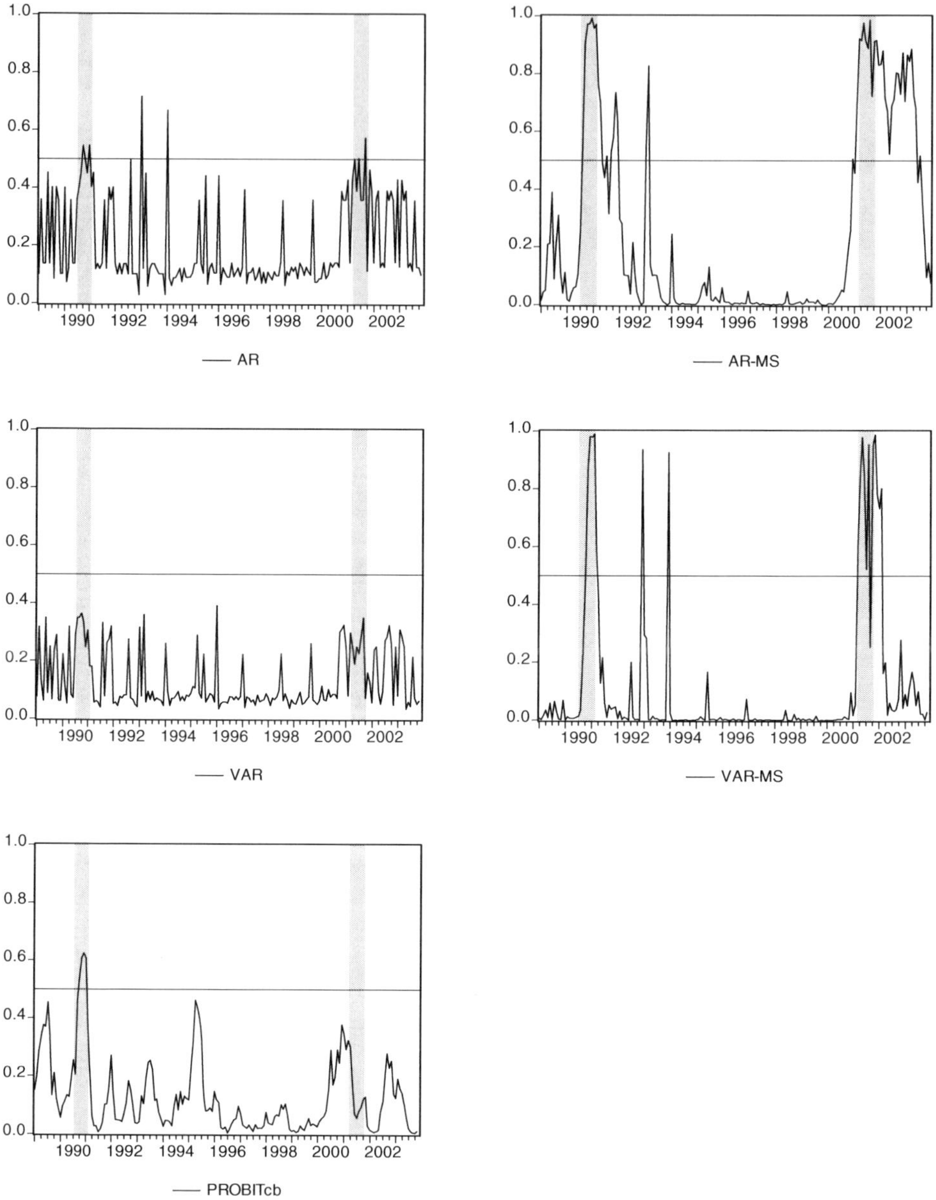

Figure 6. One month ahead recession probabilities. The models are those in Table 7. Shaded areas are NBER dated recessions.

Table 8
Forecasting performance of alternative CLIs using probit models for NBER recession/expansion classification

Target	Model	Relative MSE	Relative MAE
NBER	CLI_CB	1	1
(1 step-ahead)	CLI_SW	1.01	0.664***
	CLI_ECRI	0.588	0.597***
	CLI_OECD	0.719	0.714***
	termspread	0.952	0.937
	4 CLI + spread	0.565**	0.404***
NBER	CLI_CB	1	1
(6 step-ahead)	CLI_SW	1.085	0.956
	CLI_ECRI	0.888	0.948
	CLI_OECD	0.912	0.834**
	termspread	0.736**	0.726***
	4 CLI + spread	0.837**	0.692***
CLI_CB	1 step-ahead	0.073	0.169
	6 step-ahead	0.085	0.191

Note: Forecast sample is: 1989:1–2003:12. First estimation sample is 1959:1–1988:12, recursively updated. Fixed lag length: 6 lags for the first four models and 3 lags for the model with all four CLIs (see text for details). MSE and MAE are mean square and absolute forecast error. Probit model for CLI_{CB} is benchmark.
**indicates significance at 5%,
***indicates significance at 1% of the Diebold–Mariano test for the null hypothesis of no significant difference in MSE or MAE with respect to the benchmark.

(and also those using the ECRI and OECD indexes) provided early warnings for both recessions in the sample, see Figures 7 and 8.

The final empirical example we discuss evaluates the role of forecast combination as a tool for enhancing the predictive performance. In particular, we combine together the forecasts we have considered in each of the three previous examples, using either equal weights or the inverse of the MSEs obtained over the training sample 1985:1–1988:12. The results are reported in Table 9.

In the case of forecasts of the growth rate of the CCI_{CB}, upper panel, the pooled forecasts outperform most models but are slightly worse than the best performing single model, the VAR with the CLI_{CB} and the four components of the CCI_{CB} (compare with Table 6). The two forecast weighting schemes produce virtually identical results. For NBER turning point prediction, middle panel of Table 9, pooling linear and MS models cannot beat the best performing bivariate MS model (compare with Table 7), even when using the better performing equal weights for pooling or adding the probit model with the CLI_{CB} index as regressor into the forecast combination. Finally, also in the case of probit forecasts for the NBER turning points, lower panel of Table 9, a single model

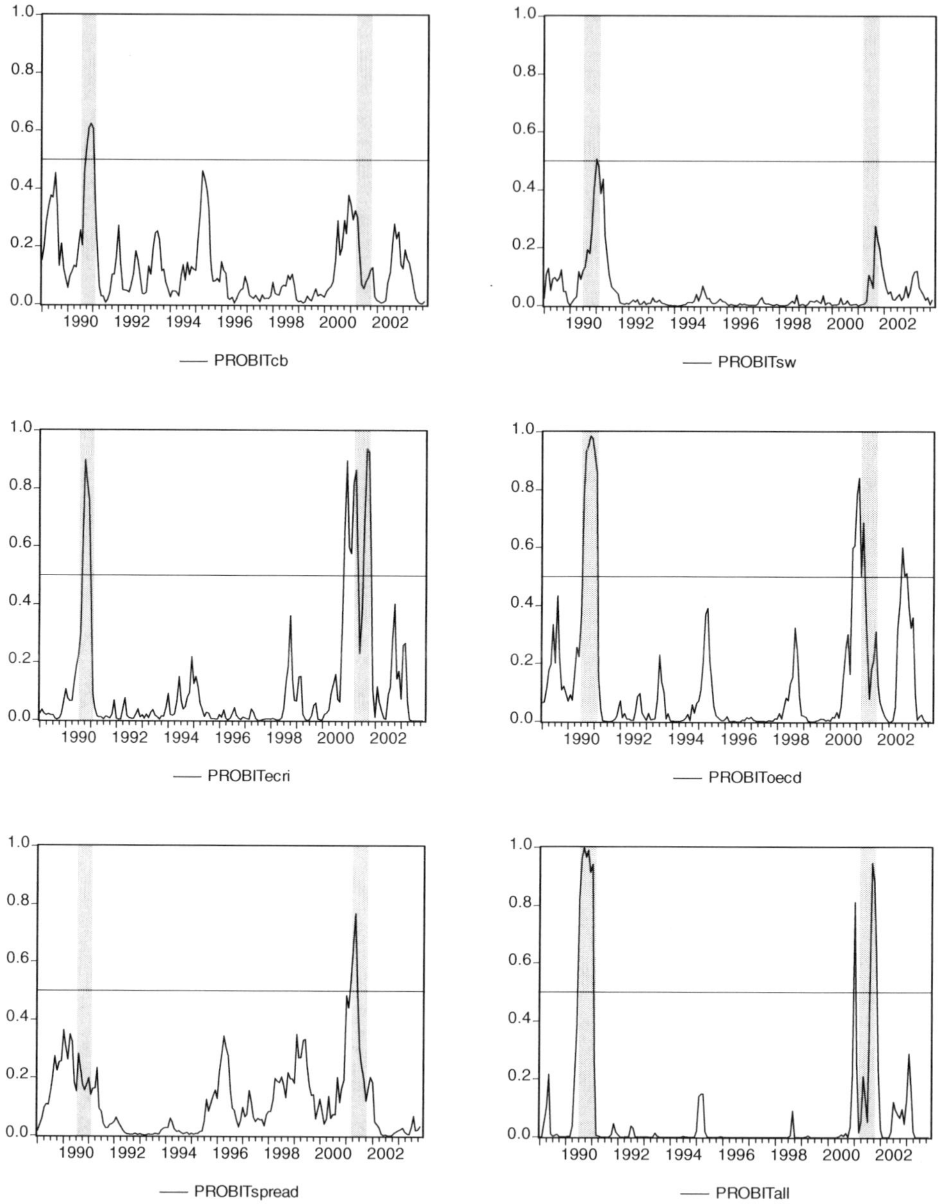

Figure 7. One month ahead recession probabilities for alternative probit models. The models are those in Table 8. Shaded areas are NBER dated recessions.

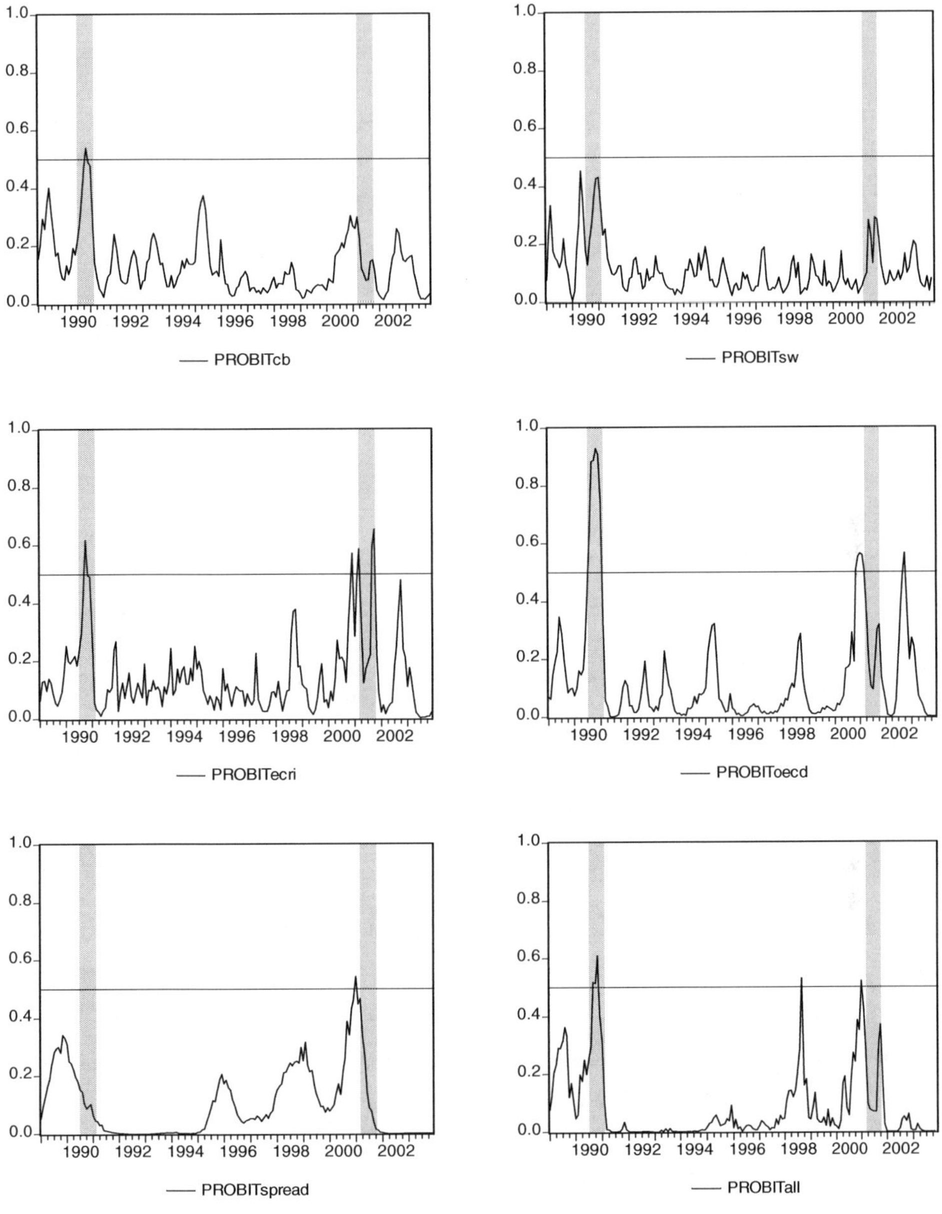

Figure 8. Six months ahead recession probabilities for alternative probit models. The models are those in Table 8. Shaded areas are NBER dated recessions.

Table 9
Evaluation of forecast pooling

Combine	Relative MSE	Relative MAE	Relative MSE	Relative MAE
	Predicting CCI_CB growth			
	MSE-weighted		Simple average	
6 linear models (1 month)	0.9474	0.9824	0.9418**	0.9781
6 linear models (6 month dynamic)	0.8873	0.9100	0.8863	0.9082
6 linear models (6 month iterated)	0.9352**	0.9776	0.9255**	0.9701
	Predicting NBER turning points			
	MSE-weighted		Simple average	
4 linear and MS models (1 month)	0.8683	1.1512	0.6676	0.9607
4 linear and MS models + probit (1 month)	0.8300	1.0989	0.6695	0.9686
	Predicting NBER turning points			
	MSE-weighted		Simple average	
5 single index PROBIT (1 month)	0.7423**	0.8028***	0.7014**	0.7844***
5 single index PROBIT + all (1 month)	0.6900**	0.7579***	0.6395**	0.7234***
5 single index PROBIT (6 months)	0.8863***	0.9069**	0.8667***	0.8956**
5 single index PROBIT + all (6 months)	0.8707***	0.8695***	0.8538***	0.8569***

Note: Forecast sample is 1989:1–2003:12. The forecasts pooled in the upper panel are from the six models in Table 6 and the benchmark is the VAR(2). The forecasts pooled in the middle panel are from the models in Table 7, including or excluding the probit, and the benchmark is the probit model with 6 lags of CLI_{CB} as regressor. The forecasts pooled in the lower panel are from the models in Table 8, including or excluding the probit with all indicators, and the benchmark is as in the middle panel.
**indicates significance at 5%,
***indicates significance at 1% of the Diebold–Mariano test for the null hypothesis of no significant difference in MSE or MAE with respect to the benchmark.

performs better than the pooled forecast for both one and six month horizons (compare Table 8), and equal weights slightly outperforms MSE based weights for pooling.

10. Review of the recent literature on the performance of leading indicators

Four main strands of research can be identified in the recent literature on the evaluation of the performance of leading indicators. First, the consequences of the use of real time information on the composite leading index and its components rather than the final releases. Second, the assessment of the relative performance of the new models for the coincident-leading indicators. Third, the evaluation of financial variables as leading indicators. Finally, the analysis of the behavior of the leading indicators during the two most recent US recessions as dated by the NBER, namely, July 1990–March 1991 and

March 2001–November 2001 [see, e.g., McNees (1991) for results on the previous recessions]. We now review in turn the main contributions in each field, grouping together the first two.

10.1. The performance of the new models with real time data

The importance of using real time data rather than final releases when evaluating the performance of the composite leading indicators was emphasized by Diebold and Rudebusch (1991a, 1991b). The rationale is that the composite indexes are periodically revised because of a variety of reasons including changes in data availability, timing or definition, modifications in the standardization factors, but also the past tracking performance of the index or some of its components; see Diebold and Rudebusch (1988), Swanson, Ghysels and Callan (1998) for an assessment of the revision process for the DOC-CB CLI, and Croushore (2006) for an updated overview on the use of real time data when forecasting. Therefore, an assessment of the usefulness of a composite leading index, even in a pseudo-real time framework but using the final release of the data, can yield biased results.

Diebold and Rudebusch (1991b) estimated a linear dynamic model for IP and the CLI, using dynamic estimation, and evaluated the marginal predictive content of the CLI in sample and recursively out of sample (for 1969–1988) using both finally and first released data for the CLI. While in the first two cases inclusion of the CLI in the model systematically reduces the MSFE, in the third one the results are not clear cut and depend on the lag-length and the forecast horizon. A similar finding emerges using the CCI instead of IP as the target variable, and when the Neftci's (1982) algorithm is adopted to predict turning points in IP [Diebold and Rudebusch (1991a)]. Instead, using an MS model for predicting turning points, Lahiri and Wang (1994) found the results to be rather robust to the use of historical or revised data on the DOC CLI.

Filardo (1999) analyzed the performance of simple rules of thumb applied to the CLI_{CB} and of the recession probabilities computed using Neftci's (1982) formula, a linear model, a probit model, and SW's CRI, using both final and first released data over the period 1977–1998. Overall, rules of thumb and the Neftci's formula applied to the CLI_{CB} performed poorly, better with ex-post data; probit and linear models were robust to the adoption of the real-time data, because of the use of mostly financial variables as regressors, while SW's CRI was not evaluated in real time. Since the models were not directly compared on the same grounds, a ranking is not feasible but, overall, the results point towards the importance of using real-time data for the CLI also over a different and more recent sample than Diebold and Rudebusch (1991a, 1991b).

Hamilton and Perez-Quiros (1996) evaluated the usefulness of the DOC-CB CLI using linear and MS VARs, with and without cointegration, finding that the best model for predicting GDP growth and turning points over the period 1975–1993 is the linear VAR (cointegration matters in sample but not out of sample), and in this framework the CLI appears to have predictive content also with real-time data. A similar conclusion emerged from the analysis of Camacho and Perez-Quiros (2002) for the period 1972–

1998, even though they found that nonlinearity matters, the MS model was the best in and out of sample. Even better is a combination of the MS model with the nonparametric forecast described in Section 8.2.

A few studies compared the models described in Sections 6 and 8 using the final release of the data. Notice that this is less problematic in comparative analyses than in single model evaluation since all the methods can be expected to be equally advantaged. Layton and Katsuura (2001) considered logit and probit models, and a Filardo (1994) type time-varying (static) MS model, using the ECRI coincident and leading indexes. The latter model performed best in a pseudo-real time evaluation exercise over the period 1979–1999, and was found to be quite useful in dating the business cycle in Layton (1998), confirming the findings in Filardo (1994). Instead, Birchenhall et al. (1999) found more support for the probit model than for the MS specification.

10.2. Financial variables as leading indicators

Though financial variables have a long history as leading indicators, e.g., Mitchell and Burns (1938) included the Dow Jones composite index of stock prices in their list of leading indicators for the US economy, a systematic evaluation of their forecasting performance started much later, in the '80s, and since then attracted increased attention.

Stock and Watson (2003b) reviewed over 90 articles dealing with the usefulness of financial indicators for predicting output growth (and inflation), and we refer to them and to Kozicki (1997) and Dotsey (1998) for details on single studies. They also provided their own evaluation using several indicators for the G7 countries and, on the basis of the survey and of their results, concluded that some asset prices have significant predictive content at some times in some countries, but it is not possible to find a single indicator with a consistently good performance for all countries and time periods. While pooling provided a partial solution to the instability problem, Stock and Watson (2003a) suggested that "... the challenge is to develop methods better geared to the intermittent and evolving nature of these predictive relations" (p. 4).

The evidence reported in the previous and next subsection indeed points towards the usefulness of models with time-varying parameters, and also confirms the necessity of a careful choice of the financial variables to be used as leading indicators and of a continuous monitoring of their performance. A rapid survey of the literature on the interest rate spreads provides a clear and valuable illustration and clarification for this statement.

As mentioned in Section 7.2, Stock and Watson (1989) included two spreads into their CLI, a paper-bill spread (the difference between the 6-month commercial paper rate and the 6-month Treasury bill rate) and a term spread (the difference between the 10-year and the 1-year Treasury bond rates).

The paper-bill spread tends to widen before a recession reflecting expectations of business bankruptcies, corporations' growing cash requirements near the peak of the business cycle, and tighter monetary policy (the paper rate rises because banks deny loans due to the restricted growth of bank reserves, so that potential borrowers seek funds in the commercial paper marker). Yet, the paper bill-spread could also change for other reasons unrelated to the business cycle, such as changes in the Treasury's debt management policy, or foreign central banks interventions in the exchange market since a large amount of their reserves in dollars are invested in Treasury bills; see, e.g., Friedman and Kuttner (1998), who found these reasons capable of explaining the bad leading performance of the paper-bill spread for the 1990–1991 recession, combined with the lack of a tighter monetary policy. The performance for the 2001 recession was also unsatisfactory, the spread was small and declining from August 2000 to the end of 2001, see also the next subsection.

The term spread has two components, expected changes in interest rates and the term premium for higher risk and/or lower liquidity. Therefore the commonly observed negative slope of the term structure prior to recession, i.e., long term rates becoming lower than short term ones, can be due either to lower expected short term rates (signaling expansionary monetary policy) or to lower term premia. Hamilton and Kim (2002) found both components to be relevant for forecasting output growth, with the former dominating at longer forecast horizons. The bad leading performance of the term spread for the 1990–1991 recession is also typically attributed to the lack of a tighter monetary policy in this specific occasion. The term spread became instead negative from June 2000 through March 2001, anticipating the recession of 2001, but the magnitude was so small by historical standards that, for example, SW's composite leading index did not signal the recession, see also the next subsection.

Gertler and Lown (2000) suggested to use the high-yield (junk)/AAA bond spread as a leading indicator, since it is less sensitive to monetary policy and provides a good proxy for the premium for external funds, i.e., for the difference between the costs of external funds and the opportunity costs of using internal funds. The premium for external funds moves countercyclically, since during expansions the borrowers' financial position typically improves, and this further fosters the aggregate activity; see, e.g., Bernanke and Gertler (1989) for a formalization of this final accelerator mechanism. Therefore, a widening high-yield spread signals a deterioration of economic conditions. Gertler and Lown (2000) found that after the mid '80s the high-yield spread had a better forecasting performance than both the paper-bill and the term spreads for the US GDP growth, also providing a warning for the 1990–1991 recession. Yet, as for the paper-bill spread, the high-yield spread can also change for reasons unrelated with the business cycle, such as confidence crises in emerging markets. In particular, Duca (1999) indicated that the widening of the spread prior to the 1990–1991 recession could be an accidental event related with the thrift crisis and the associated sale of junk bonds in an illiquid market.

A related question of interest is whether it is better to use a financial indicator in isolation or as a component of a composite index. Estrella and Mishkin (1998) ran probit regressions using the term-spread, the $\mathrm{CLI}_{\mathrm{CB}}$, the $\mathrm{CLI}_{\mathrm{SW}}$, and some of their components, concluding that both in sample and out of sample the spread yields the largest forecasting gains. Moreover, addition of other regressors is in general harmful, except for the NYSE index returns. Similar conclusions emerged from the analysis in Dueker

(1997), who also used more complicated versions of the probit model, allowing for dynamics and Markov switching parameters. Qi (2001) also obtained a similar finding using the neural network model described in Section 8.2. The CLI_{SW} was best at 1-quarter forecast horizon, but the term spread at 2- to 6-quarter horizon. Yet, she also detected substantial instability of the results over different decades, namely, the '70s, '80s, and '90s. Estrella, Rodrigues and Schich (2003) also found some instability for the US, more so when the dependent variable is the GDP growth rate than when it is a binary expansion/recession indicator.

Chauvet and Potter (2001) detected substantial instability also in the probit model when it is estimated with the Gibbs sampler. Moreover, the date of the break has a major role in determining the predictive performance of the spread, for example, the probability of a future recession are about 45% in December 2000 when no break is assumed but increase to 90% imposing a break in 1984. Unfortunately, there is considerable uncertainty about the break date, so that the posterior mean probability of recession across all break dates is 32% with a 95% interval covering basically the whole [0, 1] interval. Chauvet and Potter (2005) extended the basic probit model to allow for parameter instability, using a time-varying specification, and also for autocorrelated errors. Though the more complicated models performed better, along the lines of Dueker (1997), they provided a weaker signal of recession in 2001 in a real-time evaluation exercise.

Finally, positive results on the leading properties of the term spread and other financial variables for other countries were reported, e.g., by Davis and Henry (1994), Davis and Fagan (1997), Estrella and Mishkin (1997), Estrella, Rodrigues and Schich (2003), and Moneta (2003). Yet, Moneta (2003) found also for the Euro area a deterioration in the relative leading characteristics of the spread after the '80s, and an overall unsatisfactory performance in predicting the Euro area recession of the early '90s.

10.3. The 1990–1991 and 2001 US recessions

Stock and Watson (1993) conducted a detailed analysis of possible reasons for the failure of their CRI to produce early warnings of the 1990–1991 recession. They could not detect any signs of model failure or mis-specification and therefore concluded that the major problem was the peculiar origin of this recession compared with its predecessors, namely, a deterioration in the expectations climate followed by a drop in consumption. In such a case, the treasury bill yield curve, exchange rates, and partly IP provided wrong signals. Only three other leading indicators in their set gave moderate negative signals, part-time work, building permits and unfilled orders, but they were not sufficiently strong to offset the other indicators.

Phillips (1998–1999) compared the performance of the CRI_{SW}, and of the CLI_{CB} and the term spread, transformed into probabilities of recession using Neftci's (1982) formula, for forecasting the 1990–1991 recession using real time data. He found that the CLI_{CB} produced the best results. Moreover, the SW's index modified to allow for longer lags on the term and quality spreads worked better in sample but not for this recession.

Chauvet (1998) also used a real time dataset to produce recession forecasts from her dynamic MS factor model, and found that the filtered probability of recession peaked beyond 0.5 already at the beginning of 1990 and then in May of that year.

Filardo and Gordon (1999) contrasted a linear VAR model, an MS model with time-varying parameters, the SW's model, and an MS factor model with time-varying parameters, along the lines of Chauvet (1998). All models were estimated using Gibbs sampling techniques, and compared on the basis of the marginalized likelihoods and Bayes factors in 1990, as suggested by Geweke (1994), since these quantities are easily computed as a by-product of the estimation. They found that all models performed comparatively over the period January–June, but in the second part of the year, when the recession started, the MS model was ranked first, the VAR second, and the factor model third, with only minor differences between the two versions.

Filardo (2002), using the same models as in Filardo (1999) found that the two-month rule on the CLI_{CB} worked well in predicting the 2001 recession, but sent several false alarms in the '90s. A probit model with a 3-month forecast horizon and the term spread, corporate spread, S&P500 returns and the CLI_{CB} as regressors also worked well, predicting the beginning of the recession in January 2001 using a 50% rule. Instead, the CRI_{SW} did not perform well using a 50% rule, while SW's CRI-C (contemporaneous) worked better but was subject to large revisions.

Stock and Watson (2003a) analyzed in details the reasons for the poor performance of the CRI, concluding that is was mostly due to the particular origin of the recession (coming from the decline in stock prices and business investment), which is not properly reflected by most of the indicators in their CRI. In particular, the best indicators for the GDP growth rate were the term spread, the short term interest rate, the junk bond spread, stock prices, and new claims for unemployment. Notice that most of these variables are included in Filardo's (2002) probit models. Moreover, they found that pooled forecasts worked well, but less well than some single indicators in the list reported above.

Dueker (2005) found that his Qual-VAR predicted the timing of the 2001 recession quite well relative to the professional forecasters, while the evidence in Dueker and Wesche (2001) is more mixed. Dueker (2002) noticed that an MS-probit model with the CLI_{CB} as regressor worked also rather well in this occasion, providing a 6-month warning of the beginning of the recession (but not in the case of the previous recession).

Overall, some differences in the ranking of models and usefulness of the leading indicators emerged because of the choice of the specific coincident and leading variables, sample period, criteria of evaluation, etc. Yet, a few findings are rather robust. First, indicator selection and combination methods are important, and there is hardly a one fits all choice, even though financial variables and the equal weighted CLI_{CB} seem to have a good average performance. Second, the model that relates coincident and leading indicators also matters, and an MS feature is systematically helpful. Finally, pooling the forecasts produced good results whenever applied, even though there is only limited evidence as far as turning points are concerned.

11. What have we learned?

The experience of the last two recessions in the US confirmed that these are difficult events to predict, because the generating shocks and their propagation mechanism change from time to time, and there is a very limited sample to fit the more and more complex models that try to capture these time-varying features. Nonetheless, the recent literature on leading indicators provided several new useful insights for the prediction of growth rates and turning points of a target variable.

The first set of improvements is just in the definition of the target variable. In Section 5 we have seen that several formal procedures were developed to combine coincident indicators into a composite index, which is in general preferable to monitoring a single indicator because of its narrower coverage of the economy. In practice, the new model based CCIs are very similar to the old-style equal averages of the (standardized) coincident indicators, such as the CCI_{CB}, but they provide a sounder statistical framework for the use and evaluation of the CCIs. More sophisticated filtering procedures were also developed to emphasize the business cycle information in a CCI, as detailed in Section 3, even though substantial care should be exerted in their implementation to avoid phase shifts and other distortions. New methods were also developed for dating the peaks and troughs in either the classical or the deviation cycle. They closely reproduce the NBER dating for the US and the CEPR dating for the Euro area, but are more timely and can also provide a probabilistic measure of uncertainty around the dated turning points.

The second set of advances concerns the construction of leading indicators. While there was general agreement on the characteristics of a good leading indicator, such as consistent timing or conformity to the general business cycle, in Section 2 we have seen that there are now better methods to formally test the presence of these characteristics and assess their extent. Moreover, there were several developments in the construction of the composite leading indexes, ranging from taking into explicit account data problems such as missing values or measurement error, to an even more careful variable selection relying on new economic and statistical theories, combined with sounder statistical procedures for merging the individual leading indicators into a CLI, as described in Sections 6 and 7.

The third, and perhaps most important, set of enhancements is in the use of the leading indicators. In Sections 6 and 8 we have seen that simple rules to transform a CLI into a turning point forecast have been substituted with sophisticated nonlinear and time-varying models for the joint evolution of the coincident and leading indicators. Moreover, mainly using simulation-based techniques, it is now rather easy to use a model to produce both point and probability and duration forecasts.

The final set of improvements is in the evaluation of leading indicators. In Section 9 we have seen that formal statistical methods are now available to assess the forecasting performance of leading indicators, possibly combined with the use of real time data to prevent biased favorable results due to revisions in the composition of the CLIs. Moreover, the overview in Section 10 of the forecasting performance over the two most recent recessions in the US has provided some evidence in favor of the forecasting capabilities of CLIs, in particular when simple weighting procedures are applied to a rather large set of indicators, combined with sophisticated models for the resulting CLI and the target variable.

Notwithstanding the substantial progress in the recent years, there is still considerable scope for research in this area. For example, it might be useful to achieve a stronger consensus on the choice of the target variable, and in particular on whether the classical cycle is really the target of interest or a deviation cycle could provide more useful information. The collection of higher quality monthly series and the development of better methods to handle data irregularities also deserve attention. But the crucial element remains the selection of the leading variables, and of the weighting scheme for their combination into a CLI. Both choices should be made endogenous and frequently updated to react to the changing shocks that hit the economy, and further progress is required in this area. Forecast pooling could provide an easier method to obtain more robust predictions, but very limited evidence is available for turning point and duration forecasts. It is also worth mentioning that while in this chapter we have focused on real activity as the target variable, other choices are possible such as inflation or a stock market index [see, e.g., the contributions in Lahiri and Moore (1991)] and most of the developments we have surveyed could be usefully applied in these related contexts.

References

Albert, J., Chib, S. (1993a). "Bayesian analysis via Gibbs sampling of autoregressive time series subject to Markov mean and variance shifts". Journal of Business and Economic Statistics 11, 1–15.

Albert, J., Chib, S. (1993b). "Bayesian analysis of binary and polychotomous response data". Journal of the American Statistical Association 88, 669–679.

Altissimo, F., Bassanetti, A., Cristadoro, R., Forni, M., Lippi, M., Reichlin, L., Veronese, G. (2001). "Euro-Coin: A real time coincident indicator of the Euro area business cycle". CEPR Working Paper 3108.

Anderson, H.M., Vahid, F. (2001). "Predicting the probability of a recession with nonlinear autoregressive leading-indicator models". Macroeconomic Dynamics 5, 482–505.

Artis, M.J., Banerjee, A., Marcellino, M. (2005). "Factor forecasts for the UK". Journal of Forecasting. In press.

Artis, M.J., Galvao, A.B., Marcellino, M. (2003). "The transmission mechanism in a changing world". CEPR Working Paper No. 4014. Journal of Applied Econometrics. In press.

Artis, M.J., Krolzig, H.-M., Toro, J. (2004). "The European business cycle". Oxford Economic Papers 56 (1), 1–44.

Artis, M.J., Marcellino, M. (2001). "Fiscal forecasting: The track record of IMF, OECD and EC". Econometrics Journal 4, s20–s36.

Artis, M.J., Marcellino, M., Proietti, T. (2004). "Dating the Euro area business cycle". Oxford Bulletin of Economics and Statistics 66, 537–565.

Artis, M.J., Osborn, D., Bladen-Hovell, R., Smith, G., Zhang, W. (1995). "Turning point prediction for the UK using CSO leading indicators". Oxford Economic Papers 4, July.

Artis, M.J., Canova, F., Galí, J., Giavazzi, F., Portes, R., Reichlin, L., Uhlig, H., Weil, P. (2003). "Business cycle dating committee of the Centre for Economic Policy Research". CEPR.

Auerbach, A.J. (1982). "The index of leading indicators: "Measurement without theory", thirty-five years later". Review of Economics and Statistics 64 (4), 589–595.

Bai, J. (2003). "Inferential theory for factor models of large dimensions". Econometrica 71, 135–171.

Bai, J., Ng, S. (2002). "Determining the number of factors in approximate factor models". Econometrica 70 (1), 191–221.

Bai, J., Ng, S. (2003). "Confidence intervals for diffusion index forecasts with a large number of predictors". Working Paper, University of Michigan.

Banerjee, A.N., Marcellino, M. (2005). "Are there any reliable leading indicators for US inflation and GDP growth?" International Journal of Forecasting. In press.

Banerjee, A.N., Marcellino, M., Masten, I. (2005). "Forecasting macroeconomic variables for the accession countries". In: Artis, M., Banerjee, A., Marcellino, M. (Eds.), The European Enlargement: Prospects and Challenges. Cambridge University Press, Cambridge. In press.

Bates, J.M., Granger, C.W.J. (1969). "The combination of forecasts". Operations Research Quarterly 20, 451–468.

Baxter, M., King, R.G. (1999). "Measuring business cycles: Approximate band-pass filters for macroeconomic time series". Review of Economics and Statistics 81 (4), 575–593.

Bernanke, B.S., Gertler, M.L. (1989). "Agency costs, net worth, and business fluctuations". American Economic Review 79, 14–31.

Bernard, H., Gerlach, S. (1998). "Does the term structure predict recessions? The international evidence". International Journal of Finance and Economics 3, 195–215.

Birchenhall, C.R., Osborn, D.R., Sensier, M. (2001). "Predicting UK business cycle regimes". Scottish Journal of Political Economy 48 (2), 179–195.

Birchenhall, C.R., Jessen, H., Osborn, D.R., Simpson, P. (1999). "Predicting US business cycle regimes". Journal of Business and Economic Statistics 17 (3), 313–323.

Boehm, E.A. (2001). "The contribution of economic indicator analysis to understanding and forecasting business cycles". Indian Economic Review 36, 1–36.

Boivin, J., Ng, S. (2003). "Are more data always better for factor analysis". NBER Working Paper No. 9829. Journal of Econometrics. In press.

Boldin, M.D. (1994). "Dating turning points in the business cycle". Journal of Business 67 (1), 97–131.

Boschan, C., Banerji, A. (1990). "A reassessment of composite indexes". In: Klein, P.A. (Ed.), Analyzing Modern Business Cycles. M.E. Sharpe, Armonk, NY.

Brillinger, D.R. (1981). Time Series Data Analysis and Theory. Holt, Rinehart, and Winston, New York.

Bry, G., Boschan, C. (1971). "Cyclical analysis of time series: Selected procedures and computer programs". Technical Paper 20, NBER. Columbia University Press.

Burns, A.F., Mitchell, W.C. (1946). "Measuring business cycles". NBER Studies in Business Cycles No. 2, New York.

Camacho, M. (2004). "Vector smooth transition regression models for US GDP and the composite index of leading indicators". Journal of Forecasting 23 (3), 173–196.

Camacho, M., Perez-Quiros, G. (2002). "This is what the leading indicators lead". Journal of Applied Econometrics 17 (1), 61–80.

Camba-Mendez, G., Kapetanios, G., Smith, R.J., Weale, M.R. (2001). "An automatic leading indicator of economic activity: Forecasting GDP growth for European countries". Econometrics Journal 4 (1), S56–S90.

Canova, F. (1999). "Reference cycle and turning points: A sensitivity to detrending and classification rules". Economic Journal 112, 117–142.

Canova, F. (2004). Methods for Applied Macroeconomic Research. Princeton University Press. In press.

Canova, F., Ciccarelli, M. (2001). "Forecasting and turning point predictions in a Bayesian panel VAR model". Journal of Econometrics 120 (2), 327–359.

Canova, F., Ciccarelli, M. (2003). "Panel index VAR models: Specification, estimation, testing and leading indicators". CEPR Discussion Paper No. 4033.

Carriero, A., Marcellino, M. (2005). "Building composite coincident indicators for European countries". Mimeo, Bocconi University.

Carter, C.K., Kohn, R. (1994). "On Gibbs sampling for state space models". Biometrika 81, 541–555.

Chauvet, M. (1998). "An econometric characterization of business cycle dynamics with factor structure and regime switching". International Economic Review 39 (4), 969–996.
Chauvet, M., Piger, J.M. (2003). "Identifying business cycle turning points in real time". Federal Reserve Bank of St. Louis Review 85 (2), 13–26.
Chauvet, M., Potter, S. (2001). "Predicting a recession: Evidence from the yield curve in the presence of structural breaks". Economic Letters 77 (2), 245–253.
Chauvet, M., Potter, S. (2005). "Forecasting recessions using the yield curve". Journal of Forecasting 24 (2), 77–103.
Chen, C.W.S., Lee, J.C. (1995). "Bayesian inference of threshold autoregressive models". Journal of Time Series Analysis 16, 483–492.
Chin, D., Geweke, J., Miller, P. (2000). "Predicting turning points". Federal Reserve Bank of Minneapolis Staff Report No. 267.
Christiano, L., Fitzgerald, T. (2003). "The band pass filter". International Economic Review 44 (2), 435–465.
Clark, T.E., McCracken, M.W. (2001). "Test of equal forecast accuracy and encompassing for nested models". Journal of Econometrics 105, 85–100.
Clements, M.P., Hendry, D.F. (1996). "Multi-step estimation for forecasting". Oxford Bulletin of Economics and Statistics 58, 657–684.
Clements, M.P., Hendry, D.F. (1999). Forecasting Non-Stationary Economic Time Series. MIT Press, Cambridge, MA.
Corradi, V., Swanson, N.R. (2006). "Predictive density evaluation". In: Elliott, G., Granger, C.W.J., Timmermann, A. (Eds.), Handbook of Economic Forecasting. Elsevier, Amsterdam, pp. 197–284. Chapter 5 in this volume.
Croushore, D. (2006). "Forecasting with real-time macroeconomic data". In: Elliott, G., Granger, C.W.J., Timmermann, A. (Eds.), Handbook of Economic Forecasting. Elsevier, Amsterdam, pp. 961–982. Chapter 17 in this volume.
Davis, E.P., Fagan, G. (1997). "Are financial spreads useful indicators of future inflation and output growth in EU countries?" Journal of Applied Econometrics 12, 701–714.
Davis, E.P., Henry, S.G.B. (1994). "The use of financial spreads as indicator variables: Evidence for the United Kingdom and Germany". IMF Staff Papers 41, 517–525.
Del Negro, M. (2001). "Turn, turn, turn: Predicting turning points in economic activity". Federal Reserve Bank of Atlanta Economic Review 87.
Diebold, F.X., Lee, J.-H., Weinbach, G.C. (1994). "Regime switching with time-varying transition probabilities". In: Hargreaves, C. (Ed.), Non-Stationary Time-Series Analyses and Cointegration. Oxford University Press, Oxford, pp. 283–302.
Diebold, F.X., Mariano, R. (1995). "Comparing predictive accuracy". Journal of Business and Economic Statistics 13, 253–263.
Diebold, F.X., Rudebusch, G.D. (1988). "Stochastic properties of revisions in the index of leading indicators". In: Proceedings of the Business and Economic Statistics Section. American Statistical Association, pp. 712–717.
Diebold, F.X., Rudebusch, G.D. (1989). "Scoring the leading indicators". The Journal of Business 62 (3), 369–391.
Diebold, F.X., Rudebusch, G.D. (1990). "A nonparametric investigation of duration dependence in the American business cycle". Journal of Political Economy 98, 596–616.
Diebold, F.X., Rudebusch, G.D. (1991a). "Turning point prediction with the composite leading index: An ex ante analysis". In: Lahiri, K., Moore, G.H. (Eds.), Leading Economic Indicators: New Approaches and Forecasting Records. Cambridge University Press, Cambridge, UK, pp. 231–256.
Diebold, F.X., Rudebusch, G.D. (1991b). "Forecasting output with composite leading index: A real-time analysis". Journal of the American Statistical Association 86 (415), 603–610.
Diebold, F.X., Rudebusch, G.D. (1996). "Measuring business cycles: A modern perspective". The Review of Economics and Statistics 78 (1), 67–77.

Diebold, F.X., Rudebusch, G.D., Sichel, D.E. (1993). "Further evidence on business cycle duration dependence". In: Stock, J.H., Watson, M.W. (Eds.), Business Cycles, Indicators, and Forecasting. The University of Chicago Press, Chicago, pp. 255–280.

Doan, T., Litterman, R., Sims, C. (1984). "Forecasting and conditional projection using realistic prior distributions". Econometric Reviews 3, 1–100.

Dotsey, M. (1998). "The predictive content of the interest rate term spread for future economic growth". Federal Reserve Bank of Richmond Economic Quarterly 84 (3), 31–51.

Duca, J.V. (1999). "What credit market indicators tell us". Federal Reserve Bank of Dallas Economic and Financial Review 1999:Q3, 2–13.

Dueker, M.J. (1997). "Strengthening the case for the yield curve as a predictor of US recessions". Federal Reserve Bank of St. Louis Review 79 (2), 41–51.

Dueker, M.J. (2002). "Regime-dependent recession forecasts and the 2001 recession". Federal Reserve Bank of St. Louis Review 84 (6), 29–36.

Dueker, M.J. (2005). "Dynamic forecasts of qualitative variables: A Qual VAR model of US recessions". Journal of Business and Economic Statistics 23 (1), 96–104.

Dueker, M.J., Wesche, K. (2001). "Forecasting output with information from business cycle turning points: A qualitative variable VAR". Federal Reserve Bank of St. Louis Working Paper 2001-019B.

Durland, J.M., McCurdy, T.H. (1994). "Duration-dependent transitions in a Markov model of US GNP growth". Journal of Business and Economic Statistics 12, 279–288.

Eichengreen, B., Watson, M.W., Grossman, R.S. (1985). "Bank rate policy under the interwar gold standard". Economic Journal 95, 725–745.

Elliott, G., Komunjer, I., Timmermann, A. (2003). "Estimating loss function parameters". CEPR Discussion Papers No. 3821. Submitted Review of Economic Studies.

Emerson, R.A., Hendry, D.F. (1996). "An evaluation of forecasting using leading indicators". Journal of Forecasting 15, 271–291.

Estrella, A., Mishkin, F.S. (1997). "The predictive power of the term structure of interest rates in Europe and the United States: Implications for the European Central Bank". European Economic Review 41, 1375–1401.

Estrella, A., Mishkin, F.S. (1998). "Predicting US recessions: Financial variables as leading indicators". The Review of Economics and Statistics 80 (1), 45–61.

Estrella, A., Rodrigues, A.P., Schich, S. (2003). "How stable is the predictive power of the yield curve? Evidence from Germany and the United States". Review of Economics and Statistics 85 (3), 629–644.

Fair, R. (1993). "Estimating event probabilities from macroeconomic models using stochastic simulation". In: Stock, J.H., Watson, M.W. (Eds.), Business Cycles, Indicators, and Forecasting. The University of Chicago Press, Chicago, pp. 157–178.

Filardo, A.J. (1994). "Business cycle phases and their transitional dynamics". Journal of Business and Economic Statistics 12 (3), 299–308.

Filardo, A.J. (1999). "How reliable are recession prediction models?" Federal Reserve Bank of Kansas City Economic Review 84 (2), 35–55.

Filardo, A.J. (2002). "The 2001 US recession: What did recession prediction models tell us?" Paper prepared for a book honoring Geoffrey H. Moore, Bank for International Settlements.

Filardo, A.J., Gordon, S.F. (1994). "International co-movements of business cycles". Research Working Paper 94-11, Federal Reserve Bank of Kansas.

Filardo, A.J., Gordon, S.F. (1998). "Business cycle durations". Journal of Econometrics 85, 99–123.

Filardo, A.J., Gordon, S.F. (1999). "Business cycle turning points: Two empirical business cycle model approaches". In: Rothman, P. (Ed.), Nonlinear Time Series Analysis of Economic and Financial Data, vol. 1. Kluwer Academic, pp. 1–32. Chapter I.

Forni, M., Hallin, M., Lippi, M., Reichlin, L. (2000). "The generalized factor model: Identification and estimation". The Review of Economics and Statistics 82 (4), 540–554.

Forni, M., Hallin, M., Lippi, M., Reichlin, L. (2001). "Coincident and leading indicators for the Euro area". The Economic Journal 111 (May), C62–C85.

Forni, M., Hallin, M., Lippi, M., Reichlin, L. (2003a). "The generalized dynamic factor model: One-sided estimation and forecasting". Journal of the American Statistical Association. In press.

Forni, M., Hallin, M., Lippi, M., Reichlin, L. (2003b). "Do financial variables help forecasting inflation and real activity in the Euro area?" Journal of Monetary Economics 50, 1243–1255.

Friedman, B.M., Kuttner, K.N. (1998). "Indicator properties of the paper-bill spread: Lessons from recent experience". The Review of Economics and Statistics 80 (1), 34–44.

Fuhrer, J.C., Rudebusch, G.D. (2004). "Estimating the Euler equation for output". Journal of Monetary Economics 51 (September), 1133–1153.

Fuhrer, J.C., Schuh, S. (1998). "Beyond shocks: What causes business cycles? An overview". Proceedings from the Federal Reserve Bank of Boston Conference Series No. 42, pp. 1–31.

Gertler, M., Lown, C.S. (2000). "The information in the high yield bond spread for the business cycle: Evidence and some implications". NBER Working Paper Series No. 7549.

Geweke, J. (1977). "The dynamic factor analysis of economic time series". In: Aigner, D.J., Goldberger, A.S. (Eds.), Latent Variables in Socio-Economic Models. North-Holland, Amsterdam. Chapter 19.

Geweke, J. (1994). "Variable selection and model comparison in regression". In: Berger, J.O., Bernardo, J.M., Dawid, A.P., Smith, A.F.M. (Eds.), Proceedings of the Fifth Valencia International Meetings on Bayesian Statistics.

Geweke, J., Terui, N. (1993). "Bayesian threshold autoregressive models for nonlinear time series". Journal of Time Series Analysis 14, 441–455.

Geweke, J., Whiteman, C.H. (2006). "Bayesian forecasting". In: Elliott, G., Granger, C.W.J., Timmermann, A. (Eds.), The Handbook of Economic Forecasting. Elsevier, Amsterdam, pp. 3–80. Chapter 1 in this volume.

Granger, C.W.J., Machina, M.J. (2006). "Forecasting and decision theory". In: Elliott, G., Granger, C.W.J., Timmermann, A. (Eds.), The Handbook of Economic Forecasting. Elsevier, Amsterdam, pp. 81–98. Chapter 2 in this volume.

Granger, C.W.J., Ramanathan, R. (1984). "Improved methods of combining forecasts". Journal of Forecasting 3, 197–204.

Granger, C.W.J., Teräsvirta, T., Anderson, H.M. (1993). "Modelling nonlinearity over the business cycle". In: Stock, J.H., Watson, M.W. (Eds.), Business Cycles, Indicators, and Forecasting. The University of Chicago Press, Chicago, pp. 311–325.

Hall, R.E., Feldstein, M., Frankel, J., Gordon, R., Romer, C., Romer, D., Zarnowitz, V. (2003). "The NBER's recession dating procedure". Business Cycle Dating Committee, National Bureau of Economic Research.

Hamilton, J.D. (1989). "A new approach to the economic analysis of nonstationary time series and the business cycle". Econometrica 57, 357–384.

Hamilton, J.D. (1994). Time Series Analysis. Princeton University Press, Princeton.

Hamilton, J.D. (2003). "Comment on a comparison of two business cycle dating methods". Journal of Economic Dynamics and Control 27 (9), 1691–1694.

Hamilton, J.D., Kim, D.H. (2002). "A re-examination of the predictability of economic activity using the yield spread". Journal of Money, Credit and Banking 34, 340–360.

Hamilton, J.D., Perez-Quiros, G. (1996). "What do the leading indicators lead?" The Journal of Business 69 (1), 27–49.

Hamilton, J.D., Raj, B. (2002). "New directions in business cycle research and financial analysis". Empirical Economics 27 (2), 149–162.

Harding, D., Pagan, A.R. (2002). "Dissecting the cycle: A methodological investigation". Journal of Monetary Economics 49 (2), 365–381.

Harding, D., Pagan, A.R. (2003). "A comparison of two business cycle dating methods". Journal of Economic Dynamics and Control 27 (9), 1681–1690.

Harding, D., Pagan, A.R. (2005). "Synchronisation of cycles". Journal of Econometrics. In press.

Härdle, W., Vieu, P. (1992). "Kernel regression smoothing of time series". Journal of Time Series Analysis 13, 209–232.

Hendry, D.F. (1995). Dynamic Econometrics. Oxford University Press, Oxford.

Hendry, D.F., Krolzig, H.-M. (1999). "Improving on 'data mining reconsidered' by K.D. Hoover and S. Perez". Econometrics Journal 2, 167–191.

Hendry, D.F., Krolzig, H.-M. (2001). "Computer automation of general-to-specific model selection procedures". Journal of Economic Dynamics and Control 25 (6–7), 831–866.

Hodrick, R.J., Prescott, E.C. (1997). "Postwar US business cycles: An empirical investigation". Journal of Money, Credit and Banking 29, 1–16.

Hornick, K., Stinchcombe, M., White, H. (1989). "Multilayed feedforward networks are universal approximators". Neural Networks 2, 359–366.

Johansen, S. (1988). "Statistical analysis of cointegration vectors". Journal of Economic Dynamics and Control 12, 231–254.

Kapetanios, G., Marcellino, M. (2003). "A Comparison of Estimation Methods for Dynamic Factor Models of Large Dimensions". Working Paper No. 489, Queen Mary, University of London, Department of Economics.

Keilis-Borok, V., Stock, J.H., Soloviev, A., Mikhalev, P. (2000). "Pre-recession pattern of six economic indicators in the USA". Journal of Forecasting 19, 65–80.

Kim, C.-J. (1994). "Dynamic linear models with Markov switching". Journal of Econometrics 60, 1–22.

Kim, C.-J., Murray, C. (2002). "Permanent and transitory components of recessions". Empirical Economics 27, 163–183.

Kim, C.-J., Nelson, C.R. (1998). "Business cycle turning points, a new coincident index, and tests of duration dependence based on a dynamic factor model with regime switching". The Review of Economics and Statistics 80, 188–201.

Kim, M.-J., Yoo, J.-S. (1995). "New index of coincident indicators: A multivariate Markov switching factor model approach". Journal of Monetary Economics 36, 607–630.

Kling, J.L. (1987). "Predicting the turning points of business and economic time series". Journal of Business 60 (2), 201–238.

Koch, P.D., Rasche, R.H. (1988). "An examination of the commerce department leading-indicator approach". Journal of Business and Economic Statistics 6 (2), 167–187.

Koopmans, T.C. (1947). "Measurement without theory". Review of Economics and Statistics 29, 161–179.

Kozicki, S. (1997). "Predicting real growth and inflation with the yield spread". Federal Reserve Bank of Kansas City Economic Review, Fourth Quarter.

Krolzig, H.-M. (1997). Markov Switching Vector Autoregressions. Modelling, Statistical Inference and Application to Business Cycle Analysis. Springer, Berlin.

Krolzig, H.-M. (2004). "Predicting Markov-switching vector autoregressive processes". Journal of Forecasting. In press.

Krolzig, H.-M., Marcellino, M., Mizon, G.E. (2002). "A Markov-switching vector equilibrium correction model of the UK labour market". Empirical Economics 27 (2), 233–254.

Lahiri, K., Moore, G.H. (1991). Leading Economic Indicators: New Approaches and Forecasting Records. Cambridge University Press, Cambridge.

Lahiri, K., Wang, J. (1994). "Predicting cyclical turning points with leading index in a Markov switching model". Journal of Forecasting 13, 245–263.

Layton, A.P. (1996). "Dating and predicting phase changes in the US business cycle". International Journal of Forecasting 12, 417–428.

Layton, A.P. (1998). "A further test of the leading indicators on the probability of US business cycle phase shifts". International Journal of Forecasting 14, 63–70.

Layton, A.P., Katsuura, M. (2001). "Comparison of regime switching, probit and logit models in dating and forecasting US business cycles". International Journal of Forecasting 17, 403–417.

Li, D.T., Dorfman, J.H. (1996). "Predicting turning points through the integration of multiple models". Journal of Business and Economic Statistics 14 (4), 421–428.

Lieli, R.P. (2004). "A flexible framework for predicting binary variables". Job Market Paper, UC San Diego.

Lindgren, G. (1978). "Markov regime models for mixed distributions and switching regressions". Scandinavian Journal of Statistics 5, 81–91.

Lubrano, M. (1995). "Bayesian tests for co-integration in the case of structural breaks: An application to the analysis of wages moderation in France". G.R.E.Q.A.M. 95a19, Universite Aix-Marseille III.
Lütkepohl, H. (1987). Forecasting Aggregated Vector ARMA Processes. Springer-Verlag, Berlin.
Lütkepohl, H. (2006). "Forecasting with VARMA models". In: Elliott, G., Granger, C.W.J., Timmermann, A. (Eds.), Handbook of Economic Forecasting. Elsevier, Amsterdam, pp. 287–325. Chapter 6 in this volume.
Marcellino, M. (2003). "Forecasting EMU macroeconomic variables". International Journal of Forecasting 20, 359–372.
Marcellino, M. (2004). "Forecast pooling for short time series of macroeconomic variables". Oxford Bulletin of Economics and Statistics 66, 91–112.
Marcellino, M., Stock, J.H., Watson, M.W. (2003). "Macroeconomic forecasting in the Euro area: Country specific versus Euro wide information". European Economic Review 47, 1–18.
Marcellino, M., Stock, J.H., Watson, M.W. (2005). "A comparison of direct and iterated AR methods for forecasting macroeconomic series h-steps ahead". CEPR WP 4976. Journal of Econometrics. In press.
McCulloch, R., Tsay, R. (1994). "Statistical analysis of economic time series via Markov switching models". Journal of Times Series Analysis 15, 523–539.
McGuckin, R.H., Ozyildirim, A., Zarnowitz, V. (2003). "A more timely and useful index of leading indicators". Working Paper.
McNees, S.K. (1991). "Forecasting cyclical turning points: The record in the past three recessions". In: Lahiri, K., Moore, G.H. (Eds.), Leading Economic Indicators: New Approaches and Forecasting Records. Cambridge University Press, Cambridge.
Mitchell, W., Burns, A.F. (1938). "Statistical indicators of cyclical revivals". NBER, New York. Reprinted in: Moore, G.H. (Ed.), Business Cycle Indicators. Princeton University Press, Princeton, 1961. Chapter 6.
Mizon, G.E., Marcellino, M. (2006). Progressive Modelling: Non-Nested Testing and Encompassing. Oxford University Press, Oxford. In press.
Moneta, F. (2003). "Does the yield spread predict recessions in the Euro area?" ECB Working Paper No. 294.
Moore, G.H. (1983). Business Cycles, Inflation and Forecasting, second ed. Ballinger Publishing, Cambridge, MA.
Moore, G.H., Shiskin, J. (1967). "Indicators of business expansions and contractions". NBER Occasional Paper No. 103.
Moore, G.H., Zarnowitz, V. (1986). "The development and role of NBER's business cycle chronologies". In: Gordon, R.J. (Ed.), The American Business Cycle: Continuity and Change. University of Chicago Press, Chicago, pp. 735–779.
Neftci, S.N. (1982). "Optimal prediction of cyclical downturns". Journal of Economic Dynamics and Control 4, 225–241.
Niemira, M.P., Klein, P.A. (1994). Forecasting Financial and Economic Cycles. Wiley.
Osborn, D., Sensier, M., Simpson, P.W. (2001). "Forecasting UK industrial production over the business cycle". Journal of Forecasting 20 (6), 405–424.
Otrok, C., Whiteman, C.H. (1998). "Bayesian leading indicators: Measuring and predicting economic conditions in Iowa". International Economic Review 39, 997–1014.
Pagan, A. (2005). "Some econometric analysis of constructed binary time series". CAMA WP 7/2005.
Patton, A., Timmermann, A. (2003). "Properties of optimal forecasts". CEPR DP4037.
Phillips, K.R. (1998–1999). "The composite index of leading economic indicators: A comparison of approaches". Journal of Economic and Social Measurement 25 (3–4), 141–162.
Potter, S.M. (1995). "A nonlinear approach to US GNP". Journal of Applied Econometrics 10, 109–125.
Proietti, T., Moauro, F. (2004). "Dynamic factor analysis with nonlinear temporal aggregation constraints". Econometrics 0401003, Economics Working Paper Archive at WUSTL.
Qi, M. (2001). "Predicting US recessions with leading indicators via neural network models". International Journal of Forecasting 17, 383–401.
Raj, B. (2002). "Asymmetries of business cycles: The Markov-switching approach". In: Ullah, A., Wan, A., Chaturvedi, A. (Eds.), Handbook of Applied Econometrics and Statistical Inference. Marcel Dekker, pp. 687–710. Chapter 31.

Ravn, M.O., Sola, M. (1999). "Business cycle dynamics: Predicting transitions with macrovariables". In: Rothman, P. (Ed.), Nonlinear Time Series Analysis of Economic and Financial Data, vol. 1. Kluwer Academic, pp. 231–265. Chapter 12.

Sargent, T.J., Sims, C.A. (1977). "Business cycle modeling without pretending to have too much a priori economic theory". In: Sims, C., et al. (Eds.), New Methods in Business Cycle Research. Federal Reserve Bank of Minneapolis.

Shephard, N. (1994). "Partial non-Gaussian state space". Biometrika 81, 115–131.

Sichel, D.E. (1994). "Inventories and the three phases of the business cycle". Journal of Business and Economic Statistics 12 (July), 269–277.

Sims, C.A. (1989). "Comment on Stock and Watson (1989)". In: Blanchard, O., Fischer, S. (Eds.), NBER Macroeconomics Annual. MIT Press, Cambridge, MA, pp. 395–397.

Sims, C.A., Stock, J.H., Watson, M.W. (1990). "Inference in linear time series models with some unit roots". Econometrica 58, 113–144.

Stock, J.H., Watson, M.W. (1989). "New indexes of coincident and leading economic indicators". In: Blanchard, O., Fischer, S. (Eds.), NBER Macroeconomics Annual. MIT Press, Cambridge, MA, pp. 351–394.

Stock, J.H., Watson, M.W. (1991). "A probability model of the coincident indicators". In: Lahiri, K., Moore, G.H. (Eds.), Leading Economic Indicators: New Approaches and Forecasting Records. Cambridge University Press, Cambridge, UK.

Stock, J.H., Watson, M.W. (1992). "A procedure for predicting recessions with leading indicators: Econometric issues and recent experience". NBER Working Paper Series No. 4014.

Stock, J.H., Watson, M.W. (1993). "A procedure for predicting recessions with leading indicators: Econometric issues and recent experience". In: Stock, J.H., Watson, M.W. (Eds.), Business Cycles, Indicators, and Forecasting. The University of Chicago Press, Chicago, pp. 95–153.

Stock, J.H., Watson, M.W. (1999a). "Business cycle fluctuations in US macroeconomic time series". In: Taylor, J.B., Woodford, M. (Eds.), Handbook of Macroeconomics, vol. IA. North-Holland, Amsterdam.

Stock, J.H., Watson, M.W. (1999b). "A comparison of linear and nonlinear univariate models for forecasting macroeconomic time series". In: Engle, R.F., White, H. (Eds.), Cointegration, Causality, and Forecasting: Festschrift in Honour of Clive W.J. Granger. Oxford University Press.

Stock, J.H., Watson, M.W. (2002a). "Macroeconomic forecasting using diffusion indexes". Journal of Business and Economic Statistics 20, 147–162.

Stock, J.H., Watson, M.W. (2002b). "Forecasting using principal components from a large number of predictors". Journal of the American Statistical Association 97, 1167–1179.

Stock, J.H., Watson, M.W. (2003a). "Forecasting output and inflation: The role of asset prices". Journal of Economic Literature 41 (3), 788–829.

Stock, J.H., Watson, M.W. (2003b). "How did the leading indicator forecasts perform during the 2001 recession". Federal Reserve Bank of Richmond Economic Quarterly 89, 71–90.

Stock, J.H., Watson, M.W. (2006). "Forecasting with many predictors". In: Elliott, G., Granger, C.W.J., Timmermann, A. (Eds.), Handbook of Economic Forecasting. Elsevier, Amsterdam, pp. 515–554. Chapter 10 in this volume.

Swanson, N.R., Ghysels, E., Callan, M. (1998). "A multivariate time series analysis of the data revision process for industrial production and the composite leading indicator". In: Engle, R.F., White, H. (Eds.), Cointegration, Causality, and Forecasting: Festschrift in Honour of Clive W.J. Granger. Oxford University Press, Oxford, pp. 47–75.

Swanson, N.R., White, H. (1997). "A model selection approach to real-time macroeconomic forecasting using linear models and artificial neural networks". The Review of Economics and Statistics 79, 540–550.

Teräsvirta, T. (2006). "Forecasting economic variables with nonlinear models". In: Elliott, G., Granger, C.W.J., Timmermann, A. (Eds.), Handbook of Economic Forecasting. Elsevier, Amsterdam, pp. 413–457. Chapter 8 in this volume.

Timmermann, A.G. (2006). "Forecast combinations". In: Elliott, G., Granger, C.W.J., Timmermann, A. (Eds.), Handbook of Economic Forecasting. Elsevier, Amsterdam, pp. 135–196. Chapter 4 in this volume.

Vaccara, B.N., Zarnowitz, V. (1978). "How good are the leading indicators?" In: Proceedings of the Business and Economic Statistics Section. American Statistical Association, pp. 41–51.

van Dijk, D., Teräsvirta, T., Franses, P.H. (2002). "Smooth transition autoregressive models – A survey of recent developments". Econometric Reviews 21, 1–47.

Walsh, C.E. (2003). Monetary Theory and Policy, second ed. The MIT Press.

Watson, M. (1991). "Using econometric models to predict recessions". Economic Perspectives, Research Periodical of the Chicago Federal Reserve Bank, September/October.

Wecker, W.E. (1979). "Predicting the turning points of a time series". Journal of Business 52 (1), 35–50.

West, K.D. (1996). "Asymptotic inference about predictive ability". Econometrica 64, 1067–1084.

West, K. (2006). "Forecast evaluation". In: Elliott, G., Granger, C.W.J., Timmermann, A. (Eds.), Handbook of Economic Forecasting. Elsevier, Amsterdam, pp. 99–134. Chapter 3 in this volume.

Zarnowitz, V., Boschan, C. (1975a). "Cyclical indicators: An evaluation and new leading indexes". Business Condition Digest May 1975. Reprinted in: US Department of Commerce. (1977). Handbook of Cyclical Indicators, pp. 170–183.

Zarnowitz, V., Boschan, C. (1975b). "New composite indexes of coincident and lagging indicators". Business Condition Digest November 1975. Reprinted in: US Department of Commerce. (1977). Handbook of Cyclical Indicators, pp. 185–198.

Zarnowitz, V., Braun, P. (1990). "Major macroeconomic variables and leading indicators: Some estimates of their interrelations, 1886–1982". In: Klein, P.A. (Ed.), Analyzing Business Cycles: Essays Honoring Geoffrey H. Moore. Armonk, New York, pp. 177–205.

Zellner, A., Hong, C. (1991). "Bayesian methods for forecasting turning points in economic time series: Sensitivity of forecasts to asymmetry of loss structures". In: Lahiri, K., Moore, G.H. (Eds.), Leading Economic Indicators: New Approaches and Forecasting Records. Cambridge University Press, Cambridge, UK, pp. 129–140.

Zellner, A., Hong, C., Gulati, G.M. (1990). "Turning points in economic time series loss structures and Bayesian forecasting". In: Geisser, S., Hodges, J., Press, S.J.A., Zellner, A. (Eds.), Bayesian and Likelihood Methods in Statistics and Econometrics: Essays in Honor of George A. Barnard. North-Holland, Amsterdam, pp. 371–393.

Zellner, A., Hong, C., Min, C. (1991). "Forecasting turning points in international output growth rates using Bayesian exponentially weighted autoregression, time-varying parameter and pooling techniques". Journal of Econometrics 49, 275–304.

Zellner, A., Min, C. (1993). "Bayesian and non-Bayesian methods for combining models and forecasts with applications to forecasting international growth rates". Journal of Econometrics 56, 89–118.

Zellner, A., Rossi, P.E. (1984). "Bayesian analysis of dichotomous quantal response models". Journal of Econometrics 25, 365–394.

Zha, T. (1998). "A dynamic multivariate model for use in formulating policy". Economic Review 83 (First Quarter 1998).

Chapter 17

FORECASTING WITH REAL-TIME MACROECONOMIC DATA

DEAN CROUSHORE*

University of Richmond

Contents

* Thanks to participants at the Handbook of Economic Forecasting Conference in 2004 and the University of Maryland macroeconomics seminar, and to two anonymous referees for their comments. Tom Stark (Philadelphia Fed) deserves credit for helping me think about many of these issues.

Handbook of Economic Forecasting, Volume 1
Edited by Graham Elliott, Clive W.J. Granger and Allan Timmermann

DOI: 10.1016/S1574-0706(05)01017-7

Abstract

Forecasts are only as good as the data behind them. But macroeconomic data are revised, often significantly, as time passes and new source data become available and conceptual changes are made. How is forecasting influenced by the fact that data are revised?

To answer this question, we begin with the example of the index of leading economic indicators to illustrate the real-time data issues. Then we look at the data that have been developed for U.S. data revisions, called the "Real-Time Data Set for Macroeconomists" and show their basic features, illustrating the magnitude of the revisions and thus motivating their potential influence on forecasts and on forecasting models. The data set consists of a set of data vintages, where a data vintage refers to a date at which someone observes a time series of data; so the data vintage September 1974 refers to all the macroeconomic time series available to someone in September 1974.

Next, we examine experiments using that data set by Stark and Croushore (2002), Journal of Macroeconomics 24, 507–531, to illustrate how the data revisions could have affected reasonable univariate forecasts. In doing so, we tackle the issues of what variables are used as "actuals" in evaluating forecasts and we examine the techniques of repeated observation forecasting, illustrate the differences in U.S. data of forecasting with real-time data as opposed to latest-available data, and examine the sensitivity to data revisions of model selection governed by various information criteria.

Third, we look at the economic literature on the extent to which data revisions affect forecasts, including discussions of how forecasts differ when using first-available compared with latest-available data, whether these effects are bigger or smaller depending on whether a variable is being forecast in levels or growth rates, how much influence data revisions have on model selection and specification, and evidence on the predictive content of variables when subject to revision.

Given that data are subject to revision and that data revisions influence forecasts, what should forecasters do? Optimally, forecasters should account for data revisions in developing their forecasting models. We examine various techniques for doing so, including state-space methods.

The focus throughout this chapter is on papers mainly concerned with model development – trying to build a better forecasting model, especially by comparing forecasts from a new model to other models or to forecasts made in real time by private-sector or government forecasters.

Keywords

forecasting, data revisions, real-time data, forecast evaluation

JEL classification: C82, E30

1. An illustrative example: The index of leading indicators

Figure 1 shows a chart of the index of leading indicators from November 1995, which was the last vintage generated by the U.S. Commerce Department before the index was turned over to the private-sector Conference Board, which no longer makes the index freely available. A look at the chart suggests that the index is fairly good at predicting recessions, especially those recessions that began in the 1960s and 1970s. (For more on using leading indicators to forecast, see Chapter 16 by Marcellino on "Leading indicators" in this Handbook.)

But did the index of leading indicators provide such a useful signal about the business cycle in real time? The evidence suggests skepticism, as Diebold and Rudebusch (1991a, 1991b) suggested. They put together a real-time data set on the leading indicators and concluded that the index of leading indicators does not lead and it does not indicate!

To see what the real-time evidence is, examine Figure 2, which shows the values of the index of leading indicators, as reported by the Department of Commerce in its publication *Business Conditions Digest* in September 1974. The index appears to be on a steady rise, with a few fits and starts. But nothing in the index suggests that a recession is likely. And the same is true if you examine any of the data vintages before September

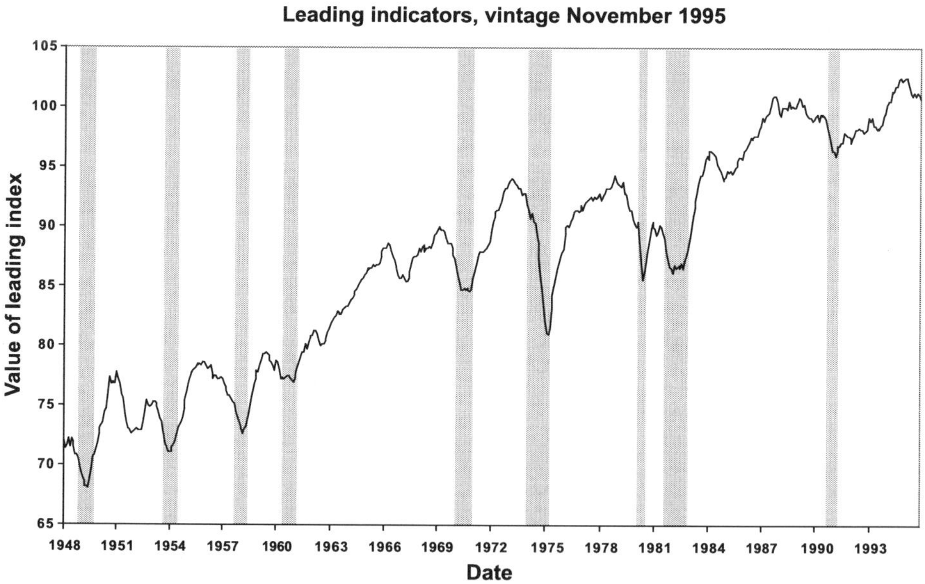

Figure 1. This chart shows the last vintage of the index of leading indicators from the Commerce Department in November 1995 before the U.S. government sold the index to the Conference Board. Note that the index declines before every recession and seems to provide a useful signal for the business cycle. Source: *Survey of Current Business* (November 1995).

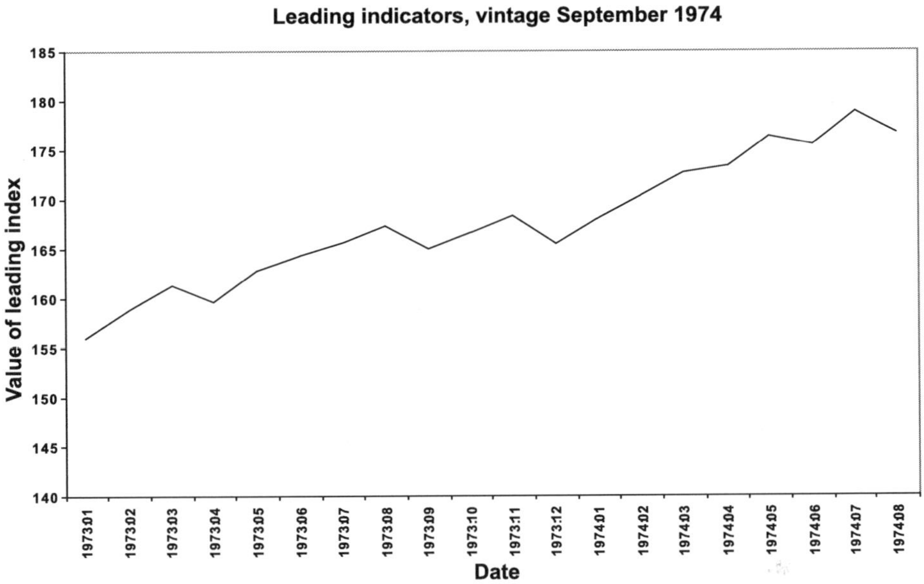

Figure 2. This diagram shows the value of the index of leading indicators from January 1973 to August 1974, based on the data vintage of September 1974. No recession is in sight. But the NBER declared that a recession began in November 1973. Source: *Business Conditions Digest*, September 1974.

1974. Unfortunately, a recession began in November 1973. So, even ten months after the recession began, the index of leading indicators gave no sign of a slowdown in economic activity.

Naturally, the failure to predict the recession led the Commerce Department to revise the construction of the index, which they did after the fact. The data entering the index were revised over time, but more importantly so were the methods used to construct the index. Figure 3 shows the original (September 1974 vintage) index of leading indicators and the revised index, as it stood in December 1989, over the sample period from January 1973 to August 1974. The index of leading indicators looks much better in the later vintage version; but in real time it was of no value. Thus the revised index gives a misleading picture of the forecasting ability of the leading indicators.

2. The real-time data set for macroeconomists

Until recently, every paper in the literature on real-time data analysis was one in which researchers pieced together their own data set to answer the particular question they wanted to address. In the early 1990s, while working on a paper using real-time data, I decided that it would be efficient to create a single, large data set containing real-time data on many different macroeconomic variables. Together with my colleague Tom

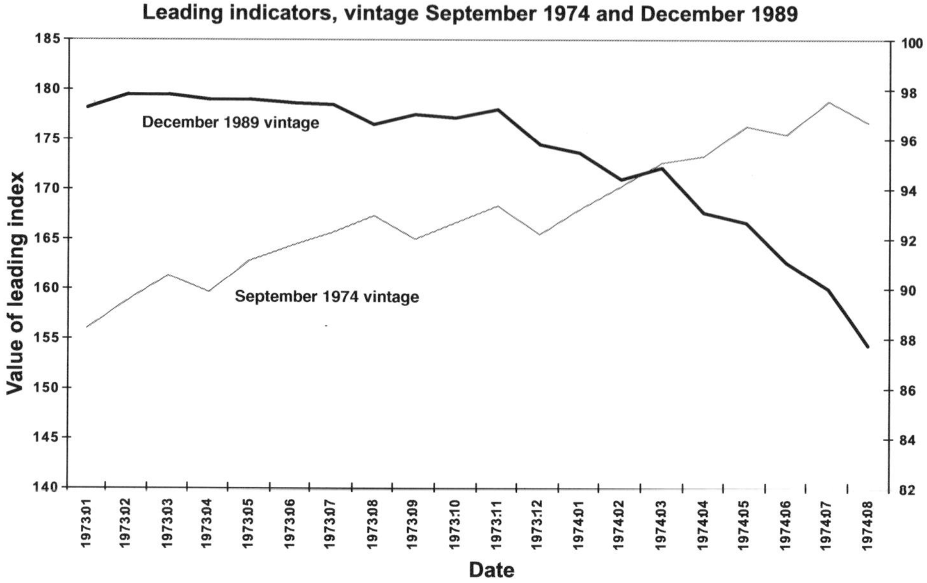

Figure 3. This diagram shows the value of the index of leading indicators from January 1973 to August 1974, based on the data vintages of both September 1974 and December 1989. The revised version of the index predicts the recession nicely. But in real time, the index gave no warning at all. Source: *Business Conditions Digest*, September 1974 and December 1989.

Stark at the Federal Reserve Bank of Philadelphia, we created the Real-Time Data Set for Macroeconomists (RTDSM) containing real-time data for the United States.

The original motivation for the data set came from modelers who developed new forecasting models that they claimed produced better forecasts than the Survey of Professional Forecasters (a survey of forecasters around the country that the Philadelphia Fed conducted). But there was a key difference in the data sets that the researchers used (based on latest available data that had been revised many times) compared with the data set that the forecasters used in real time. Thus we hatched the idea of creating a set of data sets, one for each date in time (a vintage), consisting of data as it existed at that time. This would allow a researcher to test a new forecasting model on data that forecasters had available to them in real time, thus allowing a convincing comparison to determine if a model really was superior.

In addition to comparing forecasting models, the data set can also be used to examine the process of data revisions, test the robustness of empirical results, analyze government policy, and examine whether the vintage of the data matters in a research project. The data set is described and the process of data revisions is explored in Croushore and Stark (2001) and many tests of empirical results in macroeconomics are conducted in Croushore and Stark (2003).

The RTDSM is made available to the public at the Philadelphia Fed's web site: www.phil.frb.org/econ/forecast/reaindex.html. The data set contains vintages from November 1965 to the present, with data in each vintage going back to 1947Q1. Some vintages were collected once each quarter and others were collected monthly. The timing of the quarterly data sets is in the middle of the quarter (the 15th day of the middle month of the quarter), which matches up fairly closely with the deadline date for participants in the Survey of Professional Forecasters. The data set was made possible by numerous interns from Princeton University and the University of Pennsylvania (especially a student at Penn named Bill Wong who contributed tremendously to the data set's development), along with many research assistants from the Federal Reserve Bank of Philadelphia. In addition, some data were collected in real time, beginning in 1991. The data are fairly complete, though there are some holes in a few spots that occurred when the government did not release complete data or when we were unable to find hard copy data files to ensure that we had the correct data for the vintage in question. The data underwent numerous edit checks; errors are possible but are likely to be small.

Variables included in RTDSM to date are: Variables with Quarterly Observations and Quarterly Vintages: Nominal output, real output, real consumption (broken down into durable, nondurable, and services), real investment (broken down into business fixed investment, residential investment, and change in business inventories), real government purchases (more recently, government consumption expenditures and gross investment; broken down between federal and state-and-local governments), real exports, real imports, the chain-weighted GDP price index, the price index for imports, nominal corporate profits after taxes, nominal personal saving, nominal disposable personal income, nominal personal consumption expenditures, and nominal personal income; Variables with Monthly Observations and Quarterly Vintages: Money supply measures M1 & M2, money reserve measures (total adjusted reserves, nonborrowed reserves, and nonborrowed reserves plus extended credit; all based on Board of Governors' definitions), the adjusted monetary base (Board of Governors' definition), civilian unemployment rate, and the consumer price index; Variables with Monthly Observations and Monthly Vintages: payroll employment, industrial production, and capacity utilization. New variables are being added each year.

Studies of the revision process show that a forecaster could predict the revisions to some variables, such as industrial production. Other variables, such as payroll employment, show no signs of predictability at all. Some variables are revised dramatically, such as corporate profits, while others have very small revisions, such as the consumer price index.

The data in RTDSM are organized in two different ways. The data were initially collected in a setup in which one worksheet was created to hold the complete time series of all the variables observed at the vintage date. An alternative structure, showing all the vintage dates for one variable, is shown in Figure 4. In that structure, reading across columns shows you how the value of an observation changes across vintages. Each column represents the time series that a researcher would observe at the date shown in the column header. Dates in the first column are observation dates. For example, the upper left data point of 306.4 is the value of real output for the first quarter of 1947, as recorded in the data vintage of November 1965. The setup makes it easy to see when

Date	Vintage					
	Nov65	Feb66	May66	...	Nov03	Feb04
47Q1	306.4	306.4	306.4	...	1481.7	1570.5
47Q2	309.0	309.0	309.0	...	1489.4	1568.7
47Q3	309.6	309.6	309.6	...	1493.1	1568.0
⋮	⋮	⋮	⋮	⋱	⋮	⋮
65Q3	609.1	613.0	613.0	...	3050.7	3214.1
65Q4	NA	621.7	624.4	...	3123.6	3291.8
66Q1	NA	NA	633.8	...	3201.1	3372.3
⋮	⋮	⋮	⋮	⋱	⋮	⋮
03Q2	NA	NA	NA	...	9629.4	10288.3
03Q3	NA	NA	NA	...	9797.2	10493.1
03Q4	NA	NA	NA	...	NA	10597.1

Figure 4. The data structure of the real-time data set for macroeconomists. Each column of data represents a vintage, so reading the column shows you what a researcher observing the data at the date shown in the column header would observe. Reading across any row of data shows how the data value for the observation date shown in the first column was revised over time.

revisions occur. In Figure 4, note that the large changes in values in the first row are the result of changes in the base year, which is the main reason that real output jumps from 306.4 in vintages November 1965, February 1966, and May 1966, to 1481.7 in vintage November 2003, to 1570.5 in vintage February 2004.

How big are data revisions?

If data revisions were small and random, we would not worry about how they affect forecasts. But work with the RTDSM shows that data revisions are large and systematic, and thus have the potential to affect forecasts dramatically.

For example, suppose we consider the revisions to real output in the short run by looking at the data for a particular quarter. Because of changes in the base year, we generally examine revisions based on growth rates. To see what the revisions look like in the short run, consider Figure 5, which shows the growth rate (seasonally adjusted at an annual rate) of real output in 1977Q1, as recorded in every quarterly vintage of data in RTDSM from May 1977 to May 2005.

Figure 5 suggests that quarterly revisions to real output can be substantial. Growth rates vary over time from 4.9% in recent vintages, to 5.2% in the first available vintage (May 1977), to as high as 9.6% in vintages in 1981 and 1982. Naturally, short-term forecasts for real output for 1977 are likely to be greatly affected by the choice of vintage.

Although Figure 5 shows that some short-run revisions may be extreme, smaller revisions associated with seasonal adjustment occur every year in the data. To some extent,

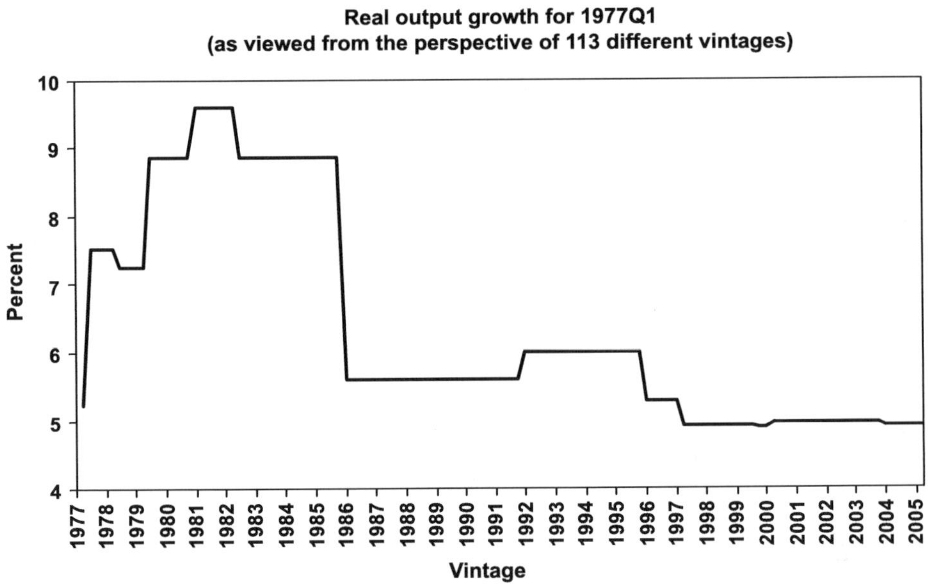

Figure 5. This graph shows how the growth rate (seasonally adjusted at an annual rate) of real output for the observation date 1977Q1 has changed over vintages, from the first release vintage of May 1977 to the vintage of May 2005.

those revisions are predictable because of the government procedures for implementing seasonal adjustment, as described in Chapter 13 by Ghysels, Osborn and Rodrigues "Forecasting seasonal time series" in this Handbook.

Though Figure 5 might be convincing for the short run, many economic issues depend not just on short-run growth rates but on longer-term growth rates. If data revisions are small and average out to zero over time, then data revisions are not important for long-run forecasting. To investigate the issue of how long-term growth rates are influenced by data revisions, Figure 6 illustrates how five-year average growth rates are affected across vintages. In the table, each row shows the average growth rate over the period shown in the first column from the vintage of data shown in the column header. Those vintage dates are the vintage dates just before a benchmark revision to the national income accounts, except for the last column which shows the data as of May 2005.

Figure 6 shows that even average growth rates over five years can be affected significantly by data revisions. For example, note the large differences in the columns labeled '95 and '99. Real output growth over five-year periods was revised by as much as 0.5 percentage point from the 1995 vintage (just before chain weighting) to the '99 vintage.

In summary, in both the short run and the long run, data revisions may affect the values of data significantly. Given that data revisions are large enough to matter, we next examine how those revisions affect forecasts.

Period	Vintage year							
	'75	'80	'85	'91	'95	'99	'03	'05
49Q4 to 54Q4	5.2	5.1	5.1	5.5	5.5	5.3	5.3	5.3
54Q4 to 59Q4	2.9	3.0	3.0	2.7	2.7	3.2	3.2	3.2
59Q4 to 64Q4	4.1	4.0	4.0	3.9	4.0	4.2	4.2	4.3
64Q4 to 69Q4	4.3	4.0	4.1	4.0	4.0	4.4	4.4	4.4
69Q4 to 74Q4	2.1	2.2	2.5	2.1	2.3	2.6	2.6	2.6
74Q4 to 79Q4	NA	3.7	3.9	3.5	3.4	3.9	4.0	3.9
79Q4 to 84Q4	NA	NA	2.2	2.0	1.9	2.2	2.5	2.5
84Q4 to 89Q4	NA	NA	NA	3.2	3.0	3.2	3.5	3.6
89Q4 to 94Q4	NA	NA	NA	NA	2.3	1.9	2.4	2.5
94Q4 to 99Q4	NA	NA	NA	NA	NA	NA	3.9	4.0
99Q4 to 04Q4	NA	NA	NA	NA	NA	NA	NA	2.6

Figure 6. Average growth rates over five years for benchmark vintages (annualized percentage points). This table shows the growth rates over the five year periods shown in the first column of real output for each benchmark vintage shown in the column header.

3. Why are forecasts affected by data revisions?

Forecasts may be affected by data revisions for three reasons:

(1) revisions change the data input into the forecasting model;

(2) revisions change the estimated coefficients; and

(3) revisions lead to a change in the model itself (such as the number of lags).

To see how data revisions might affect forecasts, consider a forecasting model that is an AR(p). The model is:

$$Y_t = \mu + \sum_{i=1}^{p} \phi_i Y_{t-i} + \varepsilon_t. \tag{1}$$

Suppose that the forecasting problem is such that a forecaster estimates this model each period, and generates forecasts of Y_{t+i} for $i = 1, 2, 3 \ldots$. Because the forecasts must be made in real time, the data for the one variable in this univariate forecast are represented by a matrix of data, not just a vector, with a different column of the matrix representing a different vintage of the data. As in Stark and Croushore (2002), denote the data point (reported by a government statistical agency) for observation date t and vintage v as $Y_{t,v}$. The revision to the data for observation date t between vintages $v-1$ and v is $Y_{t,v} - Y_{t,v-1}$.

Now consider a forecast for date t one-period ahead (so that the forecaster's information set includes $Y_{t-1,v}$) when the data vintage is v. Then the forecast is:

$$Y_{t|t-1,v} = \hat{\mu}_v + \sum_{i=1}^{p} \hat{\phi}_{i,v} Y_{t-i,v}, \tag{2}$$

where the circumflex denotes an estimated parameter, which also needs a vintage subscript because the estimated parameter may change with each vintage.

Next consider estimating the same model with a later vintage of the data, w. The forecast is:

$$Y_{t|t-1,w} = \hat{\mu}_w + \sum_{i=1}^{p} \hat{\phi}_{i,w} Y_{t-i,w}. \tag{3}$$

The change to the forecast is:

$$Y_{t|t-1,w} - Y_{t|t-1,v} = (\hat{\mu}_w - \hat{\mu}_v) + \sum_{i=1}^{p} (\hat{\phi}_{i,w} Y_{t-i,w} - \hat{\phi}_{i,v} Y_{t-i,v}). \tag{4}$$

The three ways that forecasts may be revised can be seen in Equation (4). First, revisions change the data input into the forecasting model. In this case, the data change from $\{Y_{t-1,v}, Y_{t-2,v}, \ldots, Y_{t-p,v}\}$ to $\{Y_{t-1,w}, Y_{t-2,w}, \ldots, Y_{t-p,w}\}$. Second, the revisions lead to changes in the estimated values of the coefficients from $\{\hat{\mu}_v, \hat{\phi}_{1,v}, \hat{\phi}_{2,v}, \ldots, \hat{\phi}_{p,v}\}$ to $\{\hat{\mu}_w, \hat{\phi}_{1,w}, \hat{\phi}_{2,w}, \ldots, \hat{\phi}_{p,w}\}$. Third, the revisions could lead to a change in the model itself. For example, if the forecaster were using an information criterion at each date to choose p, then the number of lags in the autoregression could change as the data are revised.

How large an effect on the forecasts are data revisions likely to cause? Clearly, the answer to this question depends on the data in question and the size of the revisions to the data. For some series, revisions may be close to white noise, in which case we would not expect forecasts to change very much. But for other series, the revisions will be very large and idiosyncratic, causing huge changes in the forecasts, as we will see in the literature discussed in Section 4.

Experiments to illustrate how forecasts are affected in these ways by data revisions were conducted by Stark and Croushore (2002), whose results are reported here via a set of three experiments:

(1) repeated observation forecasting;
(2) forecasting with real-time versus latest-available data; and
(3) experiments to test information criteria and forecasts.

Before getting to those experiments, we need to first discuss a key issue in forecasting: What do we use as actuals? Because data may be revised forever, it is not obvious what data vintage a researcher should use as the "actual" value to compare with the forecast. Certainly, the choice of data vintage to use as "actual" depends on the purpose. For example, if Wall Street forecasters are attempting to project the first-release value of GDP, then we would certainly want to use the first-released value as "actual". But if a forecaster is after the true level of GDP, the choice is not so obvious. If we want the best measure of a variable, we probably should consider the latest-available data as the "truth" (though perhaps not in the fixed-weighting era prior to 1996 in the United States because chain-weighted data available beginning in 1996 are superior because growth rates are not distorted by the choice of base year, as was the case with fixed-weighted data). The problem with this choice of latest-available data is that forecasters would not anticipate redefinitions and would generally forecast to be consistent with government data methods. For example, just before the U.S. government's official statistics were changed to chain weighting in late 1995, forecasters were still forecasting the fixed-weight data, because no one in the markets knew how to evaluate chain-weighted data and official chain-weighted data for past years had not yet been released. So forecasters continued to project fixed-weight values, even though there would never be a fixed-weight actual for the period being forecast.

One advantage of the Real-Time Data Set for Macroeconomists is that it gives a researcher many choices about what to use as actual. You can choose the first release (or second, or third), the value four quarters later (or eight or twelve), the last benchmark vintage (the last vintage before a benchmark revision), or the latest-available vintage. And it is relatively easy to choose alternative vintages as actuals and compare the results.

Experiment 1: Repeated observation forecasting

The technique of repeated observation forecasting was developed by Stark and Croushore (2002). They showed how forecasts for a particular date change as vintage changes, using every vintage available. For example: Forecast real output growth one step ahead using an AR(p) model on the first difference of the log level of real output, for each observation date beginning in 1965Q4, using every vintage possible since November 1965, using the AIC to choose p. Then plot all the different forecasts to see how they differ across vintages.

Figure 7 shows a typical example of repeated-observation forecasts from 1971Q3. In this example, forecasts are constructed based on data from vintages August 1971 to May 2005, all using the same sample period of 1947Q1 to 1971Q2. The range of the forecasts is just over 3 percentage points.

The range of the forecasts in Figure 7 across vintages is relatively modest. But in other periods, with larger data revisions, the range of the forecasts in a column may be substantially larger. For example, Figure 8 shows the same type of graph as Figure 7, but for 1975Q4. Note the increased range of forecasts. The increased range occurs because changes in base years across vintages affected the influence of changes in oil prices in 1975Q4, far more than was true for 1971Q3. In Figure 8, we can see that oil price shocks led to big data revisions, which in turn led to a large range of forecasts. The forecasts for 1975Q4 range from 4.69 percent to 10.69 percent.

Based on repeated-observation forecasts, Stark and Croushore suggested that inflation forecasts were more sensitive to data revisions than output forecasts. They found that the average ratio of the range of forecasts for output relative to the range of realizations was about 0.62, whereas the average ratio of the range of forecasts for inflation relative to the range of realizations was about 0.88. Possibly, inflation forecasts are more sensitive than output to data revisions because the inflation process is more persistent.

Another experiment by Stark and Croushore was to compare their results using the AIC to those of the SIC. Use of AIC rather than SIC leads to more variation in the model

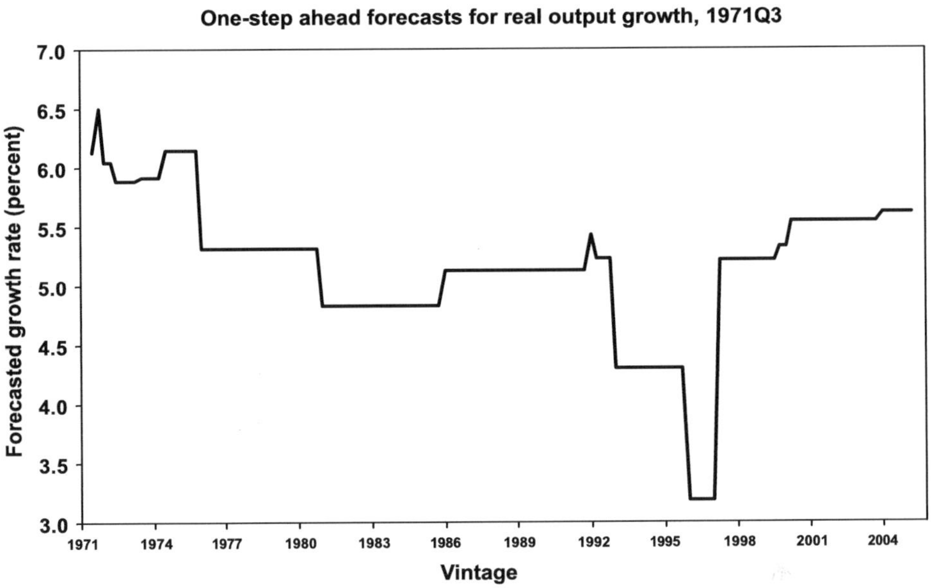

Figure 7. This figure shows the repeated observation forecasts for 1971Q3 made by forecasting with data from vintages August 1971 to May 2005, all using the same sample period of 1947Q1 to 1971Q2. The horizontal axis shows the vintage of data being used and the vertical axis shows the forecasted growth rate of real output for 1971Q3.

chosen and thus more variability in forecasts across vintages. The AIC chooses longer lags, which increases the sensitivity of forecasts to data revisions.

To summarize this section, it is clear that forecasts using simple univariate models depend strongly on the data vintage.

Experiment 2: Forecasting with real-time versus latest-available data samples

Stark and Croushore's second major experiment was to use the RTDSM to compare forecasts made with real-time data to those made with latest-available data. They performed a set of recursive forecasts. The real-time forecasts were made by forecasting across vintages using the full sample available at each date, while the latest-available forecasts were made by performing recursive forecasts across sample periods with just the latest data vintage.

A key issue in this exercise is the decision about what to use as "actual", as we discussed earlier. Stark and Croushore use three alternative actuals:

(1) latest available;
(2) the last before a benchmark revision (called benchmark vintages); and
(3) the vintage one year after the observation date.

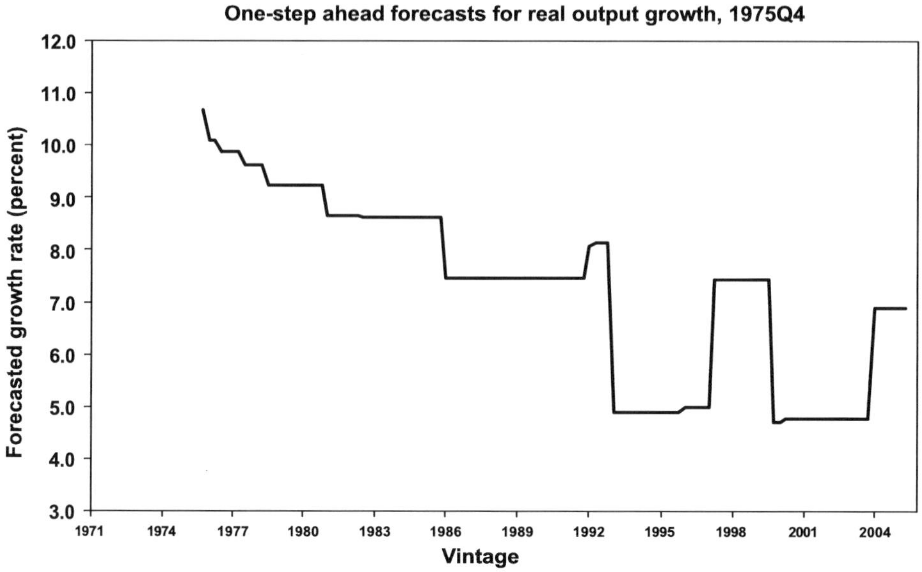

Figure 8. This graph is set up as in Figure 7, but shows forecasts for 1975Q4. The range of the forecasts is much larger than in Figure 7.

A priori, using the latest-available data in forecasting should yield better results, as the data reflect more complete information. So, we might think that forecasts based on such data would be more accurate. This is true for inflation data, but perhaps not for output data, as the Stark and Croushore results show.

One result of these experiments was that forecasts for output growth were not significantly better when based on latest-available data, even when latest-available data were used as actuals. This is a surprise, since such data include redefinitions and rebenchmarks, so you might think that forecasts based on such data would lead to more accurate forecasts.

However, Stark and Croushore showed that in smaller samples, there may be significant differences between forecasts. For example, in the first half of the 1970s, forecasts of output growth based on real-time data were significantly better than forecasts of output growth based on latest-available data, which is very surprising. However, in other short samples, the real-time forecasts are significantly worse than those using latest-available data. So, we can not draw any broad conclusions about forecasting output growth using real-time versus latest-available data.

Forecasts of inflation are a different matter. Clearly, according to the Stark and Croushore results, forecasts based on latest-available data are superior to those using real-time data, as we might expect. This is true in the full sample as well as sub-samples.

Stark and Croushore suggest that forecasts can be quite sensitive to data vintage and that the vintage chosen and the choice of actuals matters significantly for forecasting results. When model developers using latest-available data find lower forecast errors than real-time forecasters did, it may not mean that their forecasting model is superior; it might only mean that their data are superior because of the passage of time.

Experiment 3: Information criteria and forecasts

In one final set of experiments, Stark and Croushore look at the choice of lag length in an ARIMA$(p, 1, 0)$, comparing the use of AIC with the use of SIC. They examine whether the use of real-time versus latest-available data matters for the choice of lag length and hence the forecasts made by each model. Their results suggest that the choice of real-time versus latest-available data matters much more for AIC than for SIC.

Elliott (2002) illustrated and explained some of the Stark and Croushore results. He showed that the lag structures for real-time and revised data are likely to be different, that greater persistence in the latest-available series increases those differences, and that RMSEs for forecasts using revised data may be substantially less than for real-time forecasts. Monte Carlo results showed that the choices of models made using AIC or BIC is much wider using real-time data than using revised data. Finally, Elliott suggested constructing forecasting models with both real-time and revised data at hand, an idea we will revisit in Section 5.

4. The literature on how data revisions affect forecasts

In this section, we examine how data revisions affect forecasts, by reviewing the most important papers in the literature. We begin by discussing how forecasts differ when using first-available compared with latest-available data. We examine whether these effects are bigger or smaller depending on whether a variable is being forecast in levels or growth rates. Then we investigate the influence data revisions have on model selection and specification. Finally, we examine the evidence on the predictive content of variables when subject to revision. The key question in this literature is: Do data revisions affect forecasts significantly enough to make one worry about the quality of the forecasts?

How forecasts differ when using first-available data compared with latest-available data

One way to illustrate how data revisions matter for forecasts is to examine a set of forecasts made in real-time, using data as it first became available, then compare those forecasts to those made using the same forecasting method but using latest-available data.

The first paper to compare forecasts using this method was Denton and Kuiper (1965). They used Canadian national income account data to estimate a six-equation macroeconomic model with two-stage-least-squares methods. They used three different data sets:

(1) preliminary data (1st release);
(2) mixed data (real time); and
(3) latest-available data.

Denton and Kuiper suggest eliminating the use of variables that are revised extensively, as they pollute parameter estimates. But they were dealing with a very small data sample, from 1949 to 1958.

The next paper to examine real-time data issues is Cole (1969). She examined the extent to which data errors contribute to forecast errors, focusing on data errors in variables that are part of an extrapolative component of a forecast (e.g., extrapolating future values of an exogenous variable in a large system). Cole finds that:

(1) data errors reduce forecast efficiency (variance of forecast error is higher);
(2) lead to higher mean squared forecast errors because of changes in coefficient estimates; and
(3) lead to biased estimates if the expected data revision is nonzero.

Cole's results were based on U.S. data from 1953 to 1963. She examined three types of models:

(1) naïve projections, for which the relative root-mean-squared-error averages 1.55, and is over 2 for some variables, for preliminary data compared with latest-available data;
(2) real-time forecasts made by professional forecasters, in which she regressed forecast errors on data revisions, finding significant effects for some variables and finding that data revisions were the primary cause of bias in about half of the forecasts, as well as finding a bigger effect for forecasts in levels than growth rates; and
(3) a forecasting model of consumption (quarterly data, 1947–1960), in which coefficient estimates were polluted by data errors by 7 to 25 percent, depending on the estimation method, in which she found that forecasts were biased because of the data errors and that "the use of preliminary rather than revised data resulted in a *doubling* of the forecast error".

Cole introduced a useful technique, following these three steps:

(1) forecast using preliminary data on model estimated with preliminary data;
(2) forecast using revised data on a model estimated with preliminary data; and
(3) forecast using revised data on a model estimated with revised data.

Then comparing forecasts (1) and (3) shows the total effect of data errors; comparing forecasts (1) and (2) shows the direct effect of data errors for given parameter estimates; and comparing forecasts (2) and (3) shows the indirect effect of data errors through their effect on parameter estimates.

Given that data revisions affect forecasts in single-equation systems, we might wonder if the situation is better or worse in simultaneous-equation systems. To answer that question, Trivellato and Rettore (1986) showed how data errors contribute to forecast errors in a linear dynamic simultaneous-equations model. They found that data errors affect everything: estimated coefficients, lagged variables, and projections of exogenous variables. They examined a small (4 equation) model of the Italian economy for the sample period 1960 to 1980. However, the forecast errors induced by data revisions were not large. They found that for one-year forecasts, data errors led to biased coefficient estimates by less than 1% and contributed at most 4% to the standard error of forecasts. Thus, data errors were not much of a problem in the model.

Another technique used by researchers is that of Granger causality tests. Swanson (1996) investigated the sensitivity of such tests, using the first release of data compared with latest-available data and found that bivariate Granger causality tests are sensitive to the choice of data vintage.

A common method for generating inflation forecasts is to use equations based on a Phillips curve in which a variable such as the output gap is the key measure of economic slack. But a study of historical measures of the output gap by Orphanides (2001) found that such measures vary greatly over vintages – long after the fact, economists are much more confident about the size of the output gap than they are in real time. To see how uncertainty about the output gap affects forecasts of inflation, Orphanides and van Norden (2005) used real-time compared with latest-available data to show that ex-post output gap measures are useful in forecasting inflation. But in real time, out-of-sample forecasts of inflation based on measures of the output gap are not very useful. In fact, although the evidence that supports the use of the output-gap concept for forecasting inflation is very strong when output gaps are constructed on latest-available data, using the output gap is inferior to other methods in real-time, out-of-sample tests. Edge, Laubach and Williams (2004) found similar results for forecasting long-run productivity growth.

One of the most difficult variables to forecast is the exchange rate. Some recent research, however, showed that the yen–dollar and Deutschemark–dollar exchange rates were forecastable, using latest-available data. However, a real-time investigation by Faust, Rogers and Wright (2003) compared the forecastability of exchange rates based on real-time data compared with latest-available data. They found that exchange-rate forecastability was very sensitive to the vintage of data used. Their results cast doubt on research that claims that exchange rates are forecastable.

Overall, the papers in the literature comparing forecasts made in real time to those made with latest-available data imply that using latest-available data sometimes gives quite different forecasts than would have been made in real time.

Levels versus growth rates

A number of papers have examined whether forecasts of variables in levels are more sensitive or less sensitive to data revisions than forecasts of those variables in growth rates. The importance of this issue can be seen by considering what happens to levels and growth rates of a variable when data revisions occur. Using the log of the ratio between two successive observation dates to represent the growth rate for vintage v, it is:

$$g_{t,v} = \ln \frac{Y_{t,v}}{Y_{t-1,v}}.$$

The growth rate for the same observation dates but with a different vintage of data w is:

$$g_{t,w} = \ln \frac{Y_{t,w}}{Y_{t-1,w}}.$$

How would these growth rates be affected by a revision to a previous observation in the data series? Clearly, the answer depends on how the revision occurs. If the revision is a one-time level shift, then the growth rate will be revised, as will the level of the variable. However, suppose the revision occurs such that $Y_{t,w} = (1+a)Y_{t,v}$ and $Y_{t-1,w} = (1+a)Y_{t-1,v}$. Then the level is clearly affected but the growth rate is not. So, how forecasts of levels and growth rates are affected by data revisions is an empirical question concerning the types of data revisions that occurs. (Most papers that study data revisions themselves have not been clear about the relationship between revisions in levels compared with growth rates.)

Howrey (1996) showed that forecasts of levels of real GNP are very sensitive to data revisions while forecasts of growth rates are almost unaffected. He examined the forecasting period 1986 to 1991, looking at quarterly data and using univariate models. He found that the variance of the forecasting error in levels was four times greater using real-time data than if the last vintage prior to a benchmark revision had been used. But he showed that there is little (5%) difference in variance when forecasting growth rates. He used as "actual" values in determining the forecast error the last data vintage prior to a benchmark revision. The policy implications of Howrey's research are clear: policy should feed back on growth rates (output growth) rather than levels (output gap). This is consistent with the research of Orphanides and van Norden described above.

Kozicki (2002) showed that the choice of using latest-available or real-time data is most important for variables subject to large level revisions. She showed that the choice of data vintage is particularly important in performing real out-of-sample forecasting for the purpose of comparing to real-time forecasts from surveys. She ran tests of in-sample forecasts compared with out-of-sample forecasts using latest-available data compared with out-of-sample forecasts using real-time data and found that for some variables over short sample periods, the differences in forecast errors can be huge. Surprisingly, in-sample forecasts were not too much better than out-of-sample forecasts. In proxying expectations (using a model to try to estimate survey expectations), there is no clear advantage to using real-time or latest-available data; results vary by variable. Also, the choice of vintage to use as "actuals" matters, especially for real-time forecasts, where using latest-available data makes them look worse.

In summary, the literature on levels versus growth rates suggests that forecasts of level variables are more subject to data revisions than forecasts of variables in growth rates.

Model selection and specification

We often select models based on in-sample considerations, or simulated out-of-sample experiments using latest-available data. But it is more valid to use real-time out-of-sample experiments, to see what a forecaster would have projected in real time. A number of papers in the literature have discussed this issue. Experiments conducted in this area include those by Swanson and White (1997), who were the first to use real-time data to explore model selection, Harrison, Kapetanios and Yates (2002), who showed that forecasts may be improved by estimating the model on older data that has been revised, ignoring the most recent data (more on this idea later in this chapter), and Robertson and Tallman (1998), who showed how real-time data matter for the choice of model in forecasting industrial production using the leading indicators, but the choice of model for forecasting GDP is not affected much.

Overall, this literature suggests that model choice is sometimes affected significantly by data revisions.

Evidence on the predictive content of variables

Few papers in the forecasting literature have examined the evidence of the predictive content of variables and how that evidence is affected by data revisions. The question is: Does the predictability of one variable for another hold up in real time? Are forecasts based on models that show predictability based on latest available data useful for forecasting in real time?

To address the first question, Amato and Swanson (2001) used the latest-available data to show that M1 and M2 have predictive power for output. But using real-time data, that predictability mostly disappears; many models are improved by *not* including measures of money.

To address the second question, Croushore (2005) investigated whether indexes of consumer sentiment or confidence based on surveys matter for forecasting consumption spending in real time; previous research found them of marginal value for forecasting using latest-available data. His results showed that consumer confidence measures are not useful in forecasting consumption; in fact, in some specifications, forecasting performance is worse when the measures are included.

In summary, the predictive content of variables may change because of data revisions, according to the small amount of research that has been completed in this area.

5. Optimal forecasting when data are subject to revision

Having established that data revisions affect forecasts, in this section we examine the literature that discusses how to account for data revisions when forecasting. The idea is that a forecaster should deal with data revisions in creating a forecasting model. The natural venue for doing so is a model based on the Kalman filter or a state-space model. (This chapter will not discuss the details of this modeling technique, which are covered thoroughly in Chapter 7 by Harvey on "Unobserved components models" in this Handbook.)

The first paper to examine optimal forecasting under data revisions is Howrey (1978). He showed that a forecaster could adjust for different degrees of revision using the Kalman filter. He ran a set of experiments to illustrate.

In Experiment 1, Howrey forecasted disposable income using the optimal predictor plus three methods that ignored the existence of data revisions, over a sample from 1954 to 1974. He found that forecast errors were much larger for nonoptimal methods (those that ignored the revision process). He suggested that new unrevised data should be used (not ignored) in estimating the model, however, but the new data should be adjusted for bias and serial correlation. In Experiment 2, Howrey forecasted disposable income and consumption jointly, finding the same results as in Experiment 1.

Harvey et al. (1983) considered how to optimally account for irregular data revisions. Their solution was to use state-space methods to estimate a multivariate ARMA model with missing observations. They used UK data on industrial production and wholesale prices from 1965 to 1978. Their main finding was that there was a large gain in relative efficiency (MSE) in using the optimal predictor rather than assuming no data revisions, with univariate forecasts. With multivariate forecasts, the efficiency gain was even greater. The method used in this paper assumes that there are no revisions after M periods, where M is not large, so it may not be valid for all variables.

Other papers have found mixed results. Howrey (1984) examined forecasts (using state-space methods) of inventory investment, and found that data errors are not responsible for much forecast error at all, so that using state-space methods to improve the forecasts yields little improvement. Similarly, Dwyer and Hirano (2000) found that state-space methods perform worse than a simple VAR that ignores revisions, for forecasting levels of M1 and nominal output.

One key question in this literature is that of which data set should a forecaster use, given so many vintages and different degrees of revision? Koenig, Dolmas and Piger (2003) attempted to find the optimal method for real-time forecasting of current-quarter output growth. They found that it was best to use first-release data rather than real-time data, which differs from other papers in the literature. This is similar to the result found earlier by Mariano and Tanizaki (1995) that combining preliminary and revised data is sometimes very helpful in forecasting. Patterson (2003) illustrated how combining the data measurement process and the data generation process improved forecasts, using data on U.S. income and consumption.

These papers suggest that there sometimes seems to be gains from accounting for data revisions, though not always. However, some of the results are based on data samples from further in the past, when the data may not have been of as high quality as data today. For example, past revisions to industrial production were clearly predictable in advance, but that predictability has fallen considerably as the Federal Reserve Board has improved its methods. If the predictability of revisions is low relative to the forecast error, then the methods described here may not be very helpful. For example, if the forecastable part of data revisions arises only because seasonal factors are revised just once per year, then the gains from forecasting revisions are quite small. Further, research by Croushore and Stark (2001, 2003) suggests that the process followed by revisions is not easily modeled as any type of AR or MA process, which many models of optimal forecasting with data revisions require. Revisions appear to be nonstationary and not well approximated by any simple time-series process, especially across benchmark vintages. Thus it may be problematic to improve forecasts, as some of the literature suggests. In addition, improvements in the data collection process because of computerized methods may make revisions smaller now than they were in the past, so using methods such as the Kalman filter may not work well.

One possible remedy to avoid issues about revisions altogether is to follow the factor model approach of Stock and Watson (1999), explained in more detail in Chapter 10 by Stock and Watson on "Forecasting with many predictors" in this Handbook. In this method, many data series, whose revisions may be orthogonal, are combined and one or several common factors are extracted. The hope is that the revisions to all the data series are independent or at least not highly correlated, so the estimated factor is independent of data revisions, though Stock and Watson did not test this because they would have needed real-time data on far more variables than are included in the Real-Time Data Set for Macroeconomists. The only test extant of this idea (comparing forecasts from a factor model based on real-time data compared with latest available data) is provided by Bernanke and Boivin (2003). They found that for the subsample of data for which they had both real-time and latest available data, the forecasts made were not significantly different, suggesting that the factor model approach is indeed promising for eliminating the effects of data revisions. However, their results could be special to the situation they examined; additional research will be needed to see how robust their results are.

Another related possibility is for forecasters to recognize the importance of revisions and to develop models that contain both data subject to revision and data that are not subject to revision, such as financial market variables. This idea has not yet been tested in a real-time context to see how well it would perform in practice.[1]

In summary, there are sometimes gains to accounting for data revisions; but predictability of revisions (today for U.S. data) is small relative to forecast error (mainly seasonal adjustment). This is a promising area for future research.

6. Summary and suggestions for further research

This review of the literature on forecasting and data revisions suggests that data revisions may matter for forecasting, though how much they matter depends on the case at hand. We now have better data sets on data vintages than ever before, and researchers in many other countries are attempting to put together real-time data sets for macroeconomists like that in the United States. What is needed now are attempts to systematically categorize and evaluate the underlying determinants of whether data revisions matter for forecasting, and to develop techniques for optimal forecasting that are consistent

[1] Thanks to an anonymous referee for making this suggestion.

with the data process of revisions. This latter task may be most difficult, as characterizing the process followed by data revisions is not trivial. A key unresolved issue in this literature is: What are the costs and benefits of dealing with real-time data issues versus other forecasting issues?

References

Amato, J.D., Swanson, N.R. (2001). "The real time predictive content of money for output". Journal of Monetary Economics 48, 3–24.

Bernanke, B., Boivin, J. (2003). "Monetary policy in a data-rich environment". Journal of Monetary Economics 50, 525–546.

Cole, R. (1969). "Data errors and forecasting accuracy". In: Mincer, J. (Ed.), Economic Forecasts and Expectations: Analyses of Forecasting Behavior and Performance. National Bureau of Economic Research, New York, pp. 47–82.

Croushore, D. (2005). "Do consumer confidence indexes help forecast consumer spending in real time?". Conference volume for conference on "Real-Time Data and Monetary Policy", Eltville, Germany. North American Journal of Economics and Finance 16, 435–450.

Croushore, D., Stark, T. (2001). "A real-time data set for macroeconomists". Journal of Econometrics 105, 111–130.

Croushore, D., Stark, T. (2003). "A real-time data set for macroeconomists: Does the data vintage matter?" Review of Economics and Statistics 85, 605–617.

Denton, F.T., Kuiper, J. (1965). "The effect of measurement errors on parameter estimates and forecasts: A case study based on the Canadian preliminary national accounts". Review of Economics and Statistics 47, 198–206.

Diebold, F.X., Rudebusch, G.D. (1991a). "Turning point prediction with the composite leading index: An ex-ante analysis". In: Lahiri, K., Moore, G.H. (Eds.), Leading Economic Indicators: New Approaches and Forecasting Records. Cambridge University Press, Cambridge, UK, pp. 231–256.

Diebold, F.X., Rudebusch, G.D. (1991b). "Forecasting output with the composite leading index: A real-time analysis". Journal of the American Statistical Association 86, 603–610.

Dwyer, M., Hirano, K. (2000). "Optimal forecasting under data revisions". Unpublished working paper.

Edge, R.M., Laubach, T., Williams, J.C. (2004). "Learning and shifts in long-run productivity growth". Unpublished manuscript.

Elliott, G. (2002). "Comments on 'Forecasting with a real-time data set for macroeconomists'". Journal of Macroeconomics 24, 533–539.

Faust, J., Rogers, J.H., Wright, J.H. (2003). "Exchange rate forecasting: The errors we've really made". Journal of International Economics 60, 35–59.

Harrison, R., Kapetanios, G., Yates, T. (2002). "Forecasting with measurement errors in dynamic models". Unpublished manuscript.

Harvey, A.C., McKenzie, C.R., Blake, D.P.C., Desai, M.J. (1983). "Irregular data revisions". In: Zellner, A. (Ed.), Applied Time Series Analysis of Economic Data. U.S. Department of Commerce, Washington, D.C., pp. 329–347. Economic Research Report ER-5.

Howrey, E.P. (1978). "The use of preliminary data in econometric forecasting". Review of Economics and Statistics 60, 193–200.

Howrey, E.P. (1984). "Data revision, reconstruction, and prediction: An application to inventory investment". Review of Economics and Statistics 66, 386–393.

Howrey, E.P. (1996). "Forecasting GNP with noisy data: A case study". Journal of Economic and Social Measurement 22, 181–200.

Koenig, E., Dolmas, S., Piger, J. (2003). "The use and abuse of 'real-time' data in economic forecasting". Review of Economics and Statistics 85, 618–628.

Kozicki, S. (2002). "Comments on 'Forecasting with a real-time data set for macroeconomists'". Journal of Macroeconomics 24, 541–558.

Mariano, R.S., Tanizaki, H. (1995). "Prediction of final data with use of preliminary and/or revised data". Journal of Forecasting 14, 351–380.

Orphanides, A. (2001). "Monetary policy rules based on real-time data". American Economic Review 91, 964–985.

Orphanides, A., van Norden, S. (2005). "The reliability of inflation forecasts based on output gaps in real time". Journal of Money, Credit, and Banking 37, 583–601.

Patterson, K.D. (2003). "Exploiting information in vintages of time-series data". International Journal of Forecasting 19, 177–197.

Robertson, J.C., Tallman, E.W. (1998). "Data vintages and measuring forecast model performance". Federal Reserve Bank of Atlanta Economic Review, 4–20.

Stark, T., Croushore, D. (2002). "Forecasting with a real-time data set for macroeconomists". Journal of Macroeconomics 24, 507–531.

Stock, J.M., Watson, M.W. (1999). "Forecasting inflation". Journal of Monetary Economics 44, 293–335.

Swanson, N.R. (1996). "Forecasting using first-available versus fully revised economic time-series data". Studies in Nonlinear Dynamics and Econometrics 1, 47–64.

Swanson, N.R., White, H. (1997). "A model selection approach to real-time macroeconomic forecasting using linear models and artificial neural networks". Review of Economics and Statistics 79, 540–550.

Trivellato, U., Rettore, E. (1986). "Preliminary data errors and their impact on the forecast error of simultaneous-equations models". Journal of Business and Economic Statistics 4, 445–453.

Chapter 18

FORECASTING IN MARKETING

PHILIP HANS FRANSES*

Econometric Institute, Department of Business Economics, Erasmus University Rotterdam
e-mail: franses@few.eur.nl

Contents

* I thank participants at the Rady Handbook of Economic Forecasting Conference (San Diego, April 2004), and two anonymous referees, Gerard Tellis, Richard Paap, Dennis Fok, and Csilla Horvath for many helpful suggestions. Lotje Kruithof provided excellent research assistance.

Handbook of Economic Forecasting, Volume 1
Edited by Graham Elliott, Clive W.J. Granger and Allan Timmermann

DOI: 10.1016/S1574-0706(05)01018-9

Abstract

With the advent of advanced data collection techniques, there is an increased interest in using econometric models to support decisions in marketing. Due to the sometimes specific nature of variables in marketing, the discipline uses econometric models that are rarely, if ever, used elsewhere. This chapter deals with techniques to derive forecasts from these models. Due to the intrinsic non-linear nature of these models, these techniques draw heavily on simulation techniques.

Keywords

forecasting, marketing, Koyck model, Bass model, attraction model, unobserved heterogeneity

JEL classification: M30, C22, C23, C53

1. Introduction

In their recent bestseller, Kotler, Jain and Maesincee (2002, p. x) state that "Today's businesses must strive to satisfy customers' needs in the most convenient way, minimizing the time and energy that consumers spend in searching for, ordering, and receiving goods and services". Obviously, these authors see an important role for marketing activities to support that objective.

At the same time this statement indicates that marketing activities can be targeted at the level of an individual consumer's level, and that time is an important factor. Time can consider the speed at which consumers can respond, but it also concerns the ability to evaluate the success or failure of marketing activities. For a quick evaluation, one benefits from detailed data, observed at a high frequency, and preferably including performance data of competitors. With the advent of advanced data collection techniques, optic scanner data and web-based surveys, today's decisions on the relevant marketing activities can be supported by econometric models that carefully summarize the data. These basically concern links between performance measures like sales with marketing input like prices and advertising. Direct mailings, for example, can now be targeted at specific individuals, bonus offers in retail stores can be given to only a selected set of consumers, and the shelf position of certain brands is chosen with meticulous precision.

One of the academic challenges in this area is to design econometric models that adequately summarize the marketing data and that also yield useful forecasts, which in turn can be used to support decision-making.[1] The last few decades have witnessed the development of models that serve particular purposes in this area, and this chapter will describe several of these.[2] The second feature of this chapter is to demonstrate how forecasts from these models can be derived. Interestingly, many of these models specific to marketing are intrinsically non-linear, and as will be seen below, so simulation-based techniques become mandatory, see also Teräsvirta's Chapter 8 in this Handbook on forecasting from non-linear time series models.

The outline of this chapter is as follows. Section 2 briefly reviews the type of measures that are typically used to evaluate the performance of marketing efforts. These performance measures are sales, market shares, purchases, choice and time between events.[3]

[1] This chapter will be dedicated to models and how to derive forecasts from these models. The implementation of these forecasts into decision-making strategies is beyond the scope of this chapter, see Franses (2005a, 2005b) for further discussion. Also, there is no discussion of stability of models, which could affect forecasting performance. Given the possibility that market conditions change over time, this is an important topic for further research.

[2] Many models in marketing research amount to straightforward applications of models in applied econometrics, like univariate time series models, multivariate time series models, dynamic regression models, and so on, and these will not be discussed here.

[3] This chapter abstains for a discussion of how conjoint analysis, where stated preferences for hypothetical products are measured, can help to forecast revealed preferences measuring actual sales or adoption. This is due to the fact that the author simply has not enough experience with the material.

These variables are the outcomes of marketing activities that can concern pricing strategies, promotional activities, advertising, new product introduction, but can also concern the consequences of competitors' actions. Section 3 discusses a few models that are typically used in marketing, and less so, if at all, in other disciplines. Section 4 demonstrates how forecasts from these models can be generated. This section adds to the marketing literature, where one often neglects the non-linear structure of the models. Section 5 concludes this chapter with a few further research topics. The aim of this chapter is to demonstrate that there is an interesting range of econometric models used in marketing, which deserves future attention by applied econometricians and forecasters.

2. Performance measures

One of the challenging aspects of marketing performance data is that they rarely can be treated as continuous and distributed as conditionally (log) normal. Perhaps sales, when measured as quantity purchased times actual price, can be assumed to fit the classical assumptions of the regression model, but sales measured in units might sometimes be better analyzed using a count data model. Other examples of performance measures are market shares, with the property that they sum to 1 and are always in between 0 and 1, and the amount or the percentage of individuals who have adopted a new product. This adoption variable is also bounded from below and from above (assuming a single adoption per consumer). One can also obtain data on whether an individual makes a purchase or not, hence a binomial variable, or on whether s/he makes a choice amongst a range of possible products or brands (multinomial data). Surveys using questionnaires can result in data that are multinomial but ordered, like ranging from "strongly disagree" to "strongly agree" on, for example, a 5-point scale. Finally, there are marketing data available which measure the time between two events, like referrals to advertising cues or, again, purchases.[4]

2.1. *What do typical marketing data sets look like?*

To narrow focus towards the models to be reviewed in the next section, consider a few typical data sets that one can analyze in marketing.

Sales

Sales data can appear as weekly observed sales in a number of stores for one or more chains in a certain region. The sales data can concern any available product category, although usually one keeps track of products that are not perishable, or at least not

[4] Of course, as with any set of data in any discipline, marketing data can contain outliers, influential data, missing data, censored data, and so on. This aspect is not considered any further here.

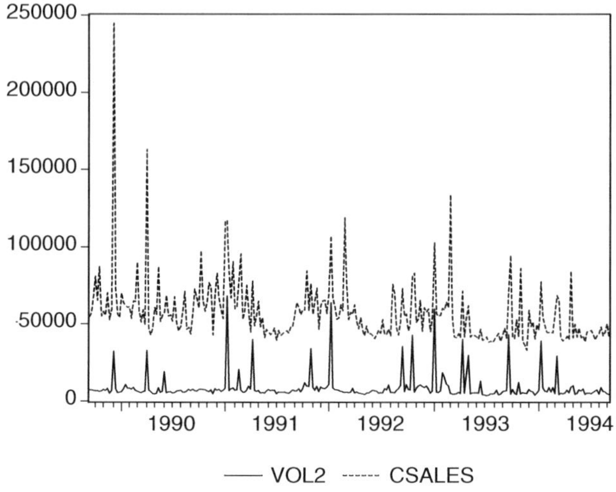

Figure 1. Sales of a brand and category sales, weekly data, 1989–1994, Dominick's Finer Foods.

immediately. Typical sample sizes range from 2 to 8 years. Usually, one also collects information on marketing instruments as "display", "feature", and "price". Preferably, the price variable can be decomposed into the regular price and the actual price. As such, one can analyze the effects of changes in the regular price and in price promotions (the actual price relative to the regular price). When one considers product categories, one collects data on all brands and stock keeping units (SKUs). Subsequently, these data can be aggregated concerning large national brands, private label brands and a rest category including all smaller brands. The data are obtained through optic scanners. With these data one can analyze the short-run and long-run effects of, what is called, the marketing-mix (the interplay of price setting, promotions, advertising and so on), and also the reactions to and from competitors. A typical graph of such weekly sales data is given in Figure 1, where a large amount of substantial spikes can be noticed. Obviously, one might expect that these observations correspond with one-week promotions, and hence one should not delete these data points.

An important area concerns the (dynamic) effects of advertising (or any other instrument) on sales. How long do these effects last? And, what is most interesting to econometricians, what is the appropriate data interval to estimate these effects? This topic has important implications for marketers, policy makers, and legal scholars. For managers, the duration of the advertising effects has implications for planning and cost allocation. If the effects of advertising last beyond the current period, the true cost of that advertising must be allocated over the relevant time period. And, if the effects of advertising decay slowly and last for decades, advertising may have to be treated as an investment rather than as an expense.

The duration of this so-called advertising carryover can have important legal implications. If the effects of advertising last for decades, firms involved in deceptive advertising would have to be responsible for remedies years and even decades after such a deception occurred. Similarly, firms might be responsible for the advertising they carried out several decades earlier.

The available data on sales and advertising often concern annual or at best monthly data. Unfortunately, for the analysis of short-run and carry-over effects, one may want to have data at a higher frequency. An intriguing data set is presented and analyzed in Tellis, Chandy and Thaivanich (2000). The advertiser in their study is a medical referral service. The firm advertises a toll free number which customers can call to get the phone number and address of medical service providers. Consumers know the service by the advertised brand name that reflects the toll free number that is advertised. When a customer calls the number, a representative of the firm answers the call. The representative queries the customer and then recommends a suitable service-provider based on location, preferences, and specific type of service needed. Typically, the representative tries to connect the customer to the service-provider directly by phone, again bearing in mind the quoted statement in Kotler, Jain and Maesincee (2002). Any resulting contact between a customer and the service provider is called a referral. Customers do not pay a fee for the referral, but service providers pay a fixed monthly fee for a specific minimum number of referrals a month. The firm screens service providers before including them as clients. The firm began operations in March 1986 in the Los Angeles market with 18 service providers and a USD 30,000 monthly advertising budget. Around 2000 it advertised in over 62 major markets in the U.S., with a multi-million dollar advertising budget that includes over 3500 TV advertising exposures per month. The primary marketing variable that affects referrals is advertising. A nice aspect of this data set is that it contains observations per hour, and I will return to this particular data set below.[5]

Market shares

Market shares are usually defined by own sales divided by category sales. There are various ways to do calculate market shares, where choices have to be made concerning how to measure sales and prices. Next, one might weight the sales of competitors depending on the availability across outlets.

One reason to analyze shares instead of sales is that their time series properties can be more easy to exploit for forecasting. Outlying observations in category sales and in own sales might cancel out, at least approximately. The same holds for seasonality, and even perhaps for trends of the unit root type. Indeed, various empirical studies suggest that, at least for mature markets, market shares tend to be stationary, while sales data might not be. A second reason to analyze market shares is that it directly shows how well the own brand or product fares as compared with competitors. Indeed, if category sales

[5] It should be mentioned that the nature of this data set precludes any permanent effects of advertising on performance as the firm does not observe repurchases, and hence the firm does not know which customers become regular users of the referred service.

increase rapidly, and own sales only little, then own market share declines, reflecting the descending power of the brand within the category.

An argument against using market shares is that models for sales allow to include and jointly forecast category sales. Also, the introduction of new brands in the observed sample period is more easy to handle than in market share models.[6] Furthermore, another reason for analyzing sales instead of shares is the possible category expansion effects of marketing actions such as advertising and price promotions.

It is important for the material below to reiterate the obvious relation between market shares and sales, as it is a non-linear one. Take S_t as own sales and CS_t as category sales, then market share M_t is defined as

$$M_t = \frac{S_t}{CS_t}. \tag{1}$$

As the right-hand side is a ratio, it holds that

$$\mathrm{E}(M_t) \neq \frac{\mathrm{E}(S_t)}{\mathrm{E}(CS_t)}, \tag{2}$$

where E denotes the expectations operator. Additionally, CS_t contains S_t, and hence the denominator and the numerator are not independent.

Typical graphs of weekly market shares appear in Figure 2. Again one can infer various spikes in one series, and now also similar sized spikes but with different signs for the competitive brands' market shares.

New product diffusion

The data on the adoption of a new product, which usually concerns durable products like computers, refrigerators, and CD-players, typically show a sigmoid shape. Often the data concern only annual data for 10 to 20 years. See, for example, the data depicted in Figure 3, which concern the fraction of music recordings that are sold on compact discs, see Bewley and Griffiths (2003). This sigmoid pattern reflects a typical product life cycle, which starts with early innovators to purchase the product, and which ends with laggards who purchase a new product once almost everyone else already has it.

If the diffusion process is measured in terms of fractions of households owning a product, such data are bounded from below and from above. Hence, the model to be used shall somehow need to impose restrictions also as the data span usually is rather short and as one tends to want to make forecasts closer towards the beginning of the diffusion process than towards the end.

[6] Fok and Franses (2004) provide a solution for the latter situation.

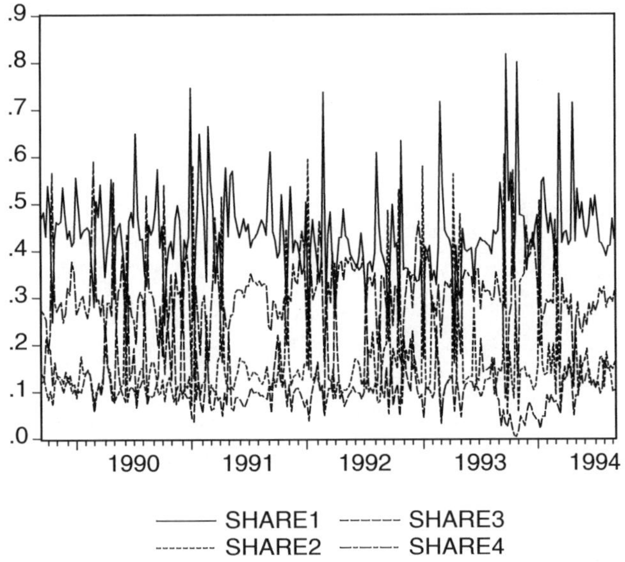

Figure 2. Market shares for four brands of crackers (one is "rest"), weekly data, 1989–1994, Dominick's Finer Foods.

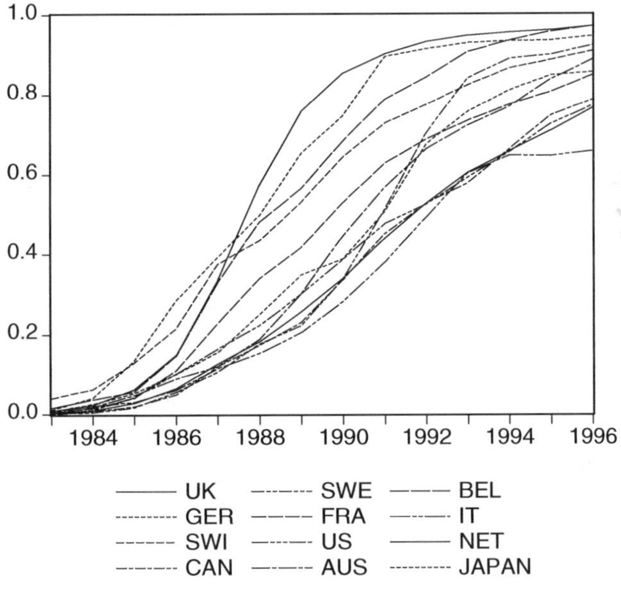

Figure 3. Market penetration of compact discs, 1983–1996.

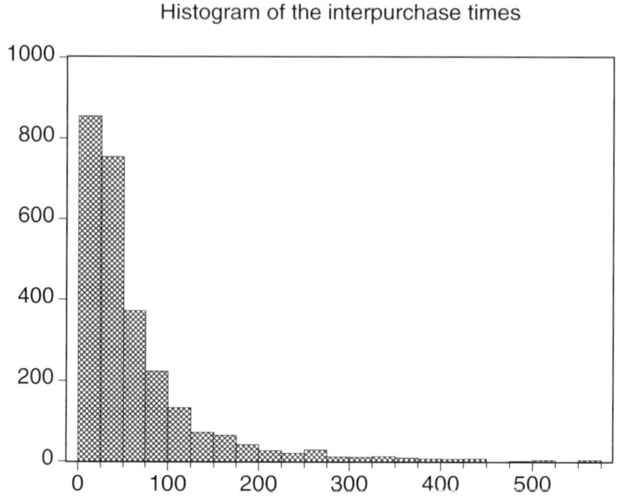

Figure 4. Histogram of the number of days between two liquid detergent purchases.

Panels with N and T both large

Finally, various data in marketing are obtained from observing a sample of N households over T periods. There are household panels with size N around 5000. These keep track of what these households purchase as the households have optic scanners at home, which they use again to document what they had bought on their latest shopping trip. This way one can get information on the choice that individuals make, whether they respond to promotions, and their time between purchases. A typical graph of such interpurchase time appears in Figure 4. In fact, such data allow for a full description of consumption behavior; see, for example, van Oest, Paap and Franses (2002).

Retail stores keep track of the behavior of their loyalty program members and keep track of everything they purchase (and not purchase). Charities store past donation data of millions of their donators, and insurance firms keep track of all contacts they have with their clients. Those contacts can be telephone calls made by the client to ask for information, but can also be direct mailings sent to them. Sometimes these data are censored or truncated, like in the case of a charity's direct mailing where only those who received a mailing can decide to donate a certain amount or not to donate.

2.2. What does one want to forecast?

Usually, these performance measures are of focal interest in a forecasting exercise. Depending on the data and on the question at hand, this can be done either for new cross sections or for future time series data. For example, for new product diffusion it is of interest to forecast whether a product that was recently launched in country A, will also

Table 1
Typical models in marketing

Type of data	Sampling frequency	Model
Sales	Monthly, weekly	Regression Koyck model
Market shares	Weekly	Attraction model
New product diffusion	Annual	Bass model
Consumer panels	Monthly, many households	Multi-level model Hierarchical Bayes Latent class

fly in country B. Another example concerns a new list of addresses of potential donators to charity, which cannot all be mailed and a selection will have to made. One then looks for those individuals who are most likely to donate, where these individuals are somehow matched with similar individuals whose track record is already in the database and who usually donate. Additionally, one wants to forecast the effects of changes in marketing instruments like price and promotion on own future sales and own market shares.

In at least two situations forecasting in marketing concerns a little less straightforward situation. The first concerns sales and market shares. The reason is that one usually not only wants to forecast own sales and category sales, but preferably also the response of all competitors to own marketing efforts. This entails that econometric models will contain multiple equations, even in case the interest only lies in own market shares.

A second typical forecasting situation concerns the adoption process of a new product. Usually one wants to make a forecast of the pattern of new to launch products, based on the patterns of related products that have already been introduced. This should also deliver a first guess value of the total amount of adoptions at the end of the process. For that matter, one needs a certain stylized functional form to describe a typical adoption process, with parameters that can be imposed onto the new situation. Moreover, once the new product is brought to the market, one intends to forecast the "take-off" point (where the increase in sales is fastest) and the inflection point (where the level of the sales is highest). As will be seen in the next section, a commonly used model for this purpose is a model with just three parameters, where these parameters directly determine these important change points in the process.

3. Models typical to marketing

The type of data and the research question guide the choice of the econometric model to be used. In various situations in marketing research, one can use the standard regression model or any of its well-known extensions. For example, in the case of time series data, one often uses vector autoregressive (VAR) time series models and associated impulse response functions, see Dekimpe and Hanssens (2000), Nijs et al. (2001), and Pauwels and Srinivasan (2004), among others. Also, one sees a regular use of the logit or probit model for binomial data, and of the ordered regression model for ordered data, and of the multinomial logit or probit model for unordered multinomial data. Interestingly, the use of the, not that easy to analyze, multinomial probit model is often seen, and this is perhaps due to the assumption of the independence of irrelevant alternatives is difficult to maintain in brand choice analysis. Furthermore, one sees models for censored and truncated data, and models for duration and count data. Franses and Paap (2001) provide a summary of the most often used models in marketing research. However, they do not address in detail the econometric models that are specifically found in marketing, and less so elsewhere. This is what I will do in this chapter. These models are the Koyck model to relate advertising with sales, the attraction model to describe market shares, the Bass model for the adoption of new products, and the multi-level regression model for panels of time series. Each of these four types of models will be discussed in the next four subsections.

3.1. Dynamic effects of advertising

An important measure to understand the dynamic effects of advertising, that is, how long do advertising pulses last, is the so-called p-percent duration interval, see Clarke (1976), Tellis (1988), and Leone (1995), among others. A p-percent duration interval measures the time lag between an advertising impulse and the moment that p percent of its effect on sales has decayed.

Denote S_t as sales and A_t as advertising, and assume for the moment that there are no other marketing activities and no competitors. A reasonable model to start with would be an autoregressive distributed lags model of order (p, m) (ADL(p, m)). This model is written as

$$S_t = \mu + \alpha_1 S_{t-1} + \cdots + \alpha_p S_{t-p} + \beta_0 A_t + \beta_1 A_{t-1} + \cdots + \beta_m A_{t-m} + \varepsilon_t. \quad (3)$$

This model implies that

$$\begin{aligned}
\frac{\partial S_t}{\partial A_t} &= \beta_0, \\
\frac{\partial S_{t+1}}{\partial A_t} &= \beta_1 + \alpha_1 \frac{\partial S_t}{\partial A_t}, \\
\frac{\partial S_{t+2}}{\partial A_t} &= \beta_2 + \alpha_1 \frac{\partial S_{t+1}}{\partial A_t} + \alpha_2 \frac{\partial S_t}{\partial A_t}, \\
&\vdots \\
\frac{\partial S_{t+k}}{\partial A_t} &= \beta_k + \sum_{j=1}^{k} \alpha_j \frac{\partial S_{t+(k-j)}}{\partial A_t},
\end{aligned}$$

where $\alpha_k = 0$ for $k > p$, and $\beta_k = 0$ for $k > m$. These partial derivatives can be used to compute the decay factor

$$p(k) = \frac{\frac{\partial S_t}{\partial A_t} - \frac{\partial S_{t+k}}{\partial A_t}}{\frac{\partial S_t}{\partial A_t}}. \tag{4}$$

Due to the very nature of the data, this decay factor can only be computed for discrete values of k. Obviously, this decay factor is a function of the model parameters. Through interpolation one can decide on the value of k for which the decay factor is equal to some value of p, which is typically set equal to 0.95 or 0.90. This estimated k is then called the p-percent duration interval.

Next to its point estimate, one would also want to estimate the confidence bounds of this duration interval, taking aboard that the decay factors are based on non-linear functions of the parameters. The problem when determining the expected value of $p(k)$ is that the expectation of this non-linear function of parameters is not equal to the function applied to the expectation of the parameters, that is $\mathrm{E}(f(\theta)) \neq f(\mathrm{E}(\theta))$. So, the values of $p(k)$ need to be simulated. With the proper assumptions, for the general ADL model it holds that the OLS estimator is asymptotically normal distributed. Franses and Vroomen (2003) suggest to use a large number of simulated parameter vectors from this multivariate normal distribution, and calculate the values of $p(k)$. This simulation exercise also gives the relevant confidence bounds.

The Koyck model

Although the general ADL model seems to gain popularity in advertising-sales modeling, see Tellis, Chandy and Thaivanich (2000) and Chandy et al. (2001), a commonly used model still is the so-called Koyck model. Indeed, matters become much more easy for the ADL model if it is assumed that m is ∞, all α parameters are zero and additionally that $\beta_j = \beta_0\lambda^{j-1}$, where λ is assumed to be in between 0 and 1. As this model involves an infinite number of lagged variables, one often considers the so-called Koyck transformation [Koyck (1954)]. In many studies the resultant model is called the Koyck model.[7]

The Koyck transformation amounts to multiplying both sides of

$$S_t = \mu + \beta_0 A_t + \beta_0\lambda A_{t-1} + \beta_0\lambda^2 A_{t-2} + \cdots + \beta_0\lambda^\infty A_{t-\infty} + \varepsilon_t \tag{5}$$

with $(1 - \lambda L)$, where L is the familiar lag operator, to get

$$S_t = \mu^* + \lambda S_{t-1} + \beta_0 A_t + \varepsilon_t - \lambda\varepsilon_{t-1}. \tag{6}$$

The short-run effect of advertising is β_0 and the long-run or total effect is $\frac{\beta_0}{1-\lambda}$. As $0 < \lambda < 1$, the Koyck model implies that the long-run effect exceeds the short-run effect.

[7] Leendert Marinus Koyck (1918–1962) was a Dutch economist who studied and worked at the Netherlands School of Economics, which is now called the Erasmus University Rotterdam.

The p-percent duration interval for this model has a convenient explicit expression and it is equal to $\frac{\log(1-p)}{\log\lambda}$.

Even after 50 years, the Koyck model is often used and still stimulates new research, see Franses (2004). For example, the Koyck model involves the familiar Davies (1987) problem. That is, under the null hypothesis that $\beta_0 = 0$, the model

$$S_t = \mu^* + \lambda S_{t-1} + \beta_0 A_t + \varepsilon_t - \lambda\varepsilon_{t-1}, \tag{7}$$

collapses into

$$S_t = \mu^* + \varepsilon_t, \tag{8}$$

where λ has disappeared. Solutions based on the suggestions in Andrews and Ploberger (1994) and Hansen (1996) are proposed in Franses and van Oest (2004), where also the relevant critical values are tabulated.

Temporal aggregation and the Koyck model

Temporal aggregation entails that one has to analyze data at a macro level while the supposedly true link between sales and advertising happens at a higher frequency micro level. This is particularly relevant nowadays, where television commercials last for just 30 seconds, while sales data are available perhaps only at the daily level. There has been substantial interest in handling the consequences of temporal aggregation in the marketing literature, see Bass and Leone (1983), Assmus, Farley and Lehmann (1984), Clarke (1976), Leone (1995), and Russell (1988). These studies all impose strong assumptions about the advertising process. A common property of all studies is that they warn about using the same model for micro data and for macro data, as in that case the duration interval will be overestimated, when relying on macro data only.

Recently, Tellis and Franses (2006) argue that only a single assumption is needed for the Koyck model parameters at the micro frequency to be retrievable from the available macro data. This assumption is that the macro data are K-period sampled micro data and that there is only a single advertising pulse at time i within that K-period. The size of the pulse is not relevant nor is it necessary to know the dynamic properties of the advertising process. This is because this particular assumption for advertising entails that the K-period aggregated pulse data match with the size of the single pulse within that period.

Consider again the K-period data, and assume that the pulse each time happens at time i, where i can be 1, 2, or, K. It depends on the location of i within the K periods whether the pulse will be assigned to A_T or A_{T-1}, where capital T indicates the macro data. Along these lines, Tellis and Franses (2006) show that the Koyck model for the micro data leads to the following extended Koyck model for K-period aggregated data, that is,

$$S_T = \lambda^K S_{T-1} + \beta_1 A_T + \beta_2 A_{T-1} + \varepsilon_T - \lambda^K \varepsilon_{T-1}, \tag{9}$$

with

$$\beta_1 = \beta_0\big(1 + \lambda + \cdots + \lambda^{K-i}\big) \tag{10}$$

and

$$\beta_2 = \beta_0\big(\lambda^{K-i+1} + \cdots + \lambda^{K-1}\big), \tag{11}$$

and where $\beta_2 = 0$ if $i = 1$.

As the parameters for S_{T-1} and ε_{T-1} are the same, Franses and van Oest (2004) recommend to use estimation by maximum likelihood. The total effect of advertising, according to this extended Koyck model for K-period aggregated data, is equal to

$$\begin{aligned}\frac{\beta_1 + \beta_2}{1 - \lambda^K} &= \frac{\beta_0(1 + \lambda + \cdots + \lambda^{K-i}) + \beta_0(\lambda^{K-i+1} + \cdots + \lambda^{K-1})}{1 - \lambda^K} \\ &= \frac{\beta_0}{1 - \lambda}.\end{aligned} \tag{12}$$

Hence, one can use this extended model for the aggregated data to estimate the long-run effects at the micro frequency. Obviously, λ can be estimated from λ^K, and therefore one can also retrieve β_0.

To illustrate, consider the Miami market with 10776 hourly data, as discussed in Tellis, Chandy and Thaivanich (2000). Given the nature of the advertising data, it seems safe to assume that the micro frequency is 30 seconds. Unfortunately, there are no sales or referrals data at this frequency. As the hour is the least integer time between the exposures, K might be equal to 120, as there are 120 times 30 seconds within an hour. As the advertising pulse usually occurs right after the entire hour, it is likely that i is close to or equal to K. The first model I consider is the extended Koyck model as in (9) for the hourly data. I compute the current effect, the carry-over effect and the 95 percent duration interval. Next, I estimate an extended Koyck model for the data when they

Table 2
Estimation results for extended Koyck models for hourly and daily data

Parameter	Hourly frequency[a]	Daily frequency[b]
Current effect (β_0)	0.008648	1.4808
Carry-over effect ($\frac{\beta_0}{1-\lambda}$)	4.0242	5.2455
95 per cent duration interval	1392.8 (30 seconds)	218.77 (days)

[a]The model estimated for the hourly frequency assumes that the micro frequency is 30 seconds, and that the aggregation level is 120, amounting to hours. The λ parameter is estimated to be equal to 0.997851, as $\hat{\lambda}^K$ is 0.772504. There are 10776 hourly observations. The parameter β_2 is not significant, which suggests that i is indeed close to or equal to K.

[b]The model for the 449 daily data is again the extended Koyck model, which includes current and lagged advertising. The model also includes 6 daily dummy variables to capture deterministic seasonality. The λ parameter is estimated to be equal to 0.9864.

are aggregated up to days. In this case daily dummy variables are included to capture seasonality to make sure the model fits adequately to the data. The estimation results are summarized in Table 2.

Table 2 shows that the 95 percent duration interval at the 30 seconds frequency is 1392.8. This is equivalent with about 11.6 hours, which is about half a day. In sharp contrast, if I consider the Koyck model for daily data, I find that this duration interval is about 220 days, or about 7 months. This shows that using the same model for different frequencies can lead to serious overestimation of the duration interval. Of course, the proper model in this case is the extended Koyck model at the hourly frequency, which takes into account that the micro frequency is 30 seconds.

3.2. The attraction model for market shares

A market share attraction model is a useful tool for analyzing competitive structure across, for example, brands within a product category. The model can be used to infer cross-effects of marketing-mix variables, but one can also learn about the effects of own efforts while conditioning on competitive reactions. Various details can be found in Cooper and Nakanishi (1988) and various econometric aspects are given in Fok, Franses and Paap (2002).

Important features of an attraction model are that it incorporates that market shares sum to unity and that the market shares of all individual brands are in between 0 and 1. Hence, also forecasts are restricted to be in between 0 and 1. The model (which bears various resemblances with the multinomial logit model) consists of two components. There is a specification of the attractiveness of a brand and a definition of market shares in terms of this attractiveness.

First, define $A_{i,t}$ as the attraction of brand i, $i = 1, \dots, I$, at time t, $t = 1, \dots, T$. This attraction is assumed to be an unobserved (latent) variable. Commonly, it assumed that this attraction can be described by

$$A_{i,t} = \exp(\mu_i + \varepsilon_{i,t}) \prod_{j=1}^{I} \prod_{k=1}^{K} x_{k,j,t}^{\beta_{k,j,i}}, \tag{13}$$

where $x_{k,j,t}$ denotes the kth explanatory variable (such as price level, distribution, advertising spending) for brand j at time t and where $\beta_{k,j,i}$ is the corresponding coefficient for brand i. The parameter μ_i is a brand-specific constant. Let the error term $(\varepsilon_{1,t}, \dots, \varepsilon_{I,t})'$ be normally distributed with zero mean and Σ can be non-diagonal. Note that data availability determines how many parameters can be estimated in the end, as in this representation (13) there are $I + I + I \times I \times K = I(2 + IK)$ parameters. The $x_{k,j,t}$ is assumed to be non-negative, and hence rates of change are usually not allowed. The variable $x_{k,j,t}$ may be a $0/1$ dummy variable to indicate the occurrence of promotional activities for brand j at time t. Note that in this case one should transform $x_{k,j,t}$ to $\exp(x_{k,j,t})$ to avoid that attraction becomes zero in case of no promotional activity.

The fact that the attractions are not observed makes the inclusion of dynamic structures a bit complicated. For example, for the model

$$A_{i,t} = \exp(\mu_i + \varepsilon_{i,t}) A_{i,t-1}^{\gamma_i} \prod_{j=1}^{I} \prod_{k=1}^{K} x_{k,j,t}^{\beta_{k,j,i}} \tag{14}$$

one can only retrieve γ_i if it is assumed that $\gamma = \gamma_i$ for all i. Fok, Franses and Paap (2002) provide a detailed discussion on how to introduce dynamics into attraction models.

The second component of the model is simply

$$M_{i,t} = \frac{A_{i,t}}{\sum_{j=1}^{I} A_{j,t}}, \tag{15}$$

which states that market share is the own attraction divided by total attraction. These two equations complete the attraction model.

To enable parameter estimation, one simply takes one of the brands as the benchmark, say, brand I. Next, one divides both sides of (15) by $M_{I,t}$, takes natural logarithms of both sides to arrive at a $(I-1)$-dimensional set of equations given by

$$\log M_{i,t} - \log M_{I,t} = (\mu_i - \mu_I) + \sum_{j=1}^{I} \sum_{k=1}^{K} (\beta_{k,j,i} - \beta_{k,j,I}) \log x_{k,j,t} + \eta_{i,t} \tag{16}$$

for $i = 1, \dots, I-1$. Note that the μ_i parameters $(i = 1, \dots, I)$ are not identified. In fact, only the parameters $\tilde{\mu}_i = \mu_i - \mu_I$ and $\tilde{\beta}_{k,j,i} = \beta_{k,j,i} - \beta_{k,j,I}$ are identified. This is not problematic for interpretation as the instantaneous elasticity of the kth marketing instrument of brand j on the market share of brand i is given by

$$\frac{\partial M_{i,t}}{\partial x_{k,j,t}} \frac{x_{k,j,t}}{M_{i,t}} = \beta_{k,i,j} - \sum_{r=1}^{I} M_{r,t} \beta_{k,r,j} \tag{17}$$

$$= (\beta_{k,j,i} - \beta_{k,j,I})(1 - M_{i,t}) - \sum_{r=1 \wedge r \neq i}^{I-1} M_{r,t} (\beta_{k,j,r} - \beta_{k,j,I}). \tag{18}$$

The attraction model has often been applied in marketing, see Leeflang and Reuyl (1984), Naert and Weverbergh (1981), Kumar (1994), Klapper and Herwartz (2000), and several recent studies. Usually, the model is used for out-of-sample forecasting and to evaluate competitive response, see Bronnenberg, Mahajan and Vanhonacker (2000). Fok and Franses (2004) introduce a version of the model that can be used to describe the consequences of a new entrant in the product category.

Despite the fact that the model is often used for forecasting, the proper way to generate forecasts is not trivial, and in fact, rarely considered in detail. The reason for this non-triviality is that the set of seemingly unrelated regression equations is formulated in terms of the logs of ratios of market shares. However, in the end one intends to forecast the market shares themselves. In the next section, I will demonstrate how appropriate forecasts can be generated.

3.3. The Bass model for adoptions of new products

The diffusion pattern of adoptions of new products shows a typical sigmoid shape. There are many functions that can describe such a shape, like the logistic function or the Gompertz function. In marketing research, one tends to focus on one particular function, which is the one proposed in Bass (1969). Important reasons for this are that the model captures a wide range of possible shapes (for example, the logistic function assumes symmetry around the inflection point while the Bass model does not) and that the model parameters can be assigned a workable interpretation.

The Bass (1969) theory starts with a population of m potential adopters. For each of these, the time to adoption is a random variable with a distribution function $F(\tau)$ and density $f(\tau)$, and a hazard rate assumed to be

$$\frac{f(\tau)}{1-F(\tau)} = p + qF(\tau), \tag{19}$$

where τ refers to continuous time. The parameters p and q are associated with innovation and imitation, respectively. In words, this model says that the probability of adoption at time t, given that no adoption has occurred yet, depends on a constant p, which is independent of any factor, hence innovation, and on a fraction of the cumulative density of adoption, hence imitation.

The cumulative number of adopters at time τ, $N(\tau)$, is a random variable with mean $\bar{N}(\tau) = E[N(\tau)] = mF(\tau)$. The function $\bar{N}(\tau)$ satisfies the differential equation

$$\bar{n}(\tau) = \frac{\mathrm{d}\bar{N}(\tau)}{\mathrm{d}\tau} = p\big[m - \bar{N}(\tau)\big] + \frac{q}{m}\bar{N}(\tau)\big[m - \bar{N}(\tau)\big]. \tag{20}$$

The solution of this differential equation for cumulative adoption is

$$\bar{N}(\tau) = mF(\tau) = m\left[\frac{1-e^{-(p+q)\tau}}{1+\frac{q}{p}e^{-(p+q)\tau}}\right], \tag{21}$$

and for adoption itself it is

$$\bar{n}(\tau) = mf(\tau) = m\left[\frac{p(p+q)^2e^{-(p+q)\tau}}{(p+qe^{-(p+q)\tau})^2}\right], \tag{22}$$

see Bass (1969) for details. Analyzing these two functions of τ in more detail reveals that $\bar{N}(\tau)$ indeed has a sigmoid pattern, while $\bar{n}(\tau)$ is hump-shaped. Note that the parameters p and q exercise a non-linear impact on the pattern of $\bar{N}(t)$ and $\bar{n}(t)$. For example, the inflection point T^*, which corresponds with the time of peak adoptions, equals

$$T^* = \frac{1}{p+q}\log\left(\frac{q}{p}\right). \tag{23}$$

Substituting this expression in (21) and in (22), allows a determination of the amount of sales at the peak as well as the amount of the cumulative adoptions at that time.

In practice one of course only has discretely observed data. Denote X_t as the adoptions and N_t as the cumulative adoptions, where t often refers to months or years. There are now various ways to translate the continuous time theory to models for the data on X_t and N_t. Bass (1969) proposes to consider the regression model

$$\begin{aligned} X_t &= p(m - N_{t-1}) + \frac{q}{m} N_{t-1}(m - N_{t-1}) + \varepsilon_t \\ &= \alpha_1 + \alpha_2 N_{t-1} + \alpha_3 N_{t-1}^2 + \varepsilon_t, \end{aligned} \tag{24}$$

where it is assumed that ε_t is an independent and identically distributed error term with mean zero and common variance σ^2. Note that (p, q, m) must be obtained from $(\alpha_1, \alpha_2, \alpha_3)$, but that for out-of-sample forecasting one can use (24), and hence rely on ordinary least squares (OLS).

Recently, Boswijk and Franses (2005) extend this basic Bass regression model by allowing for heteroskedastic errors and by allowing for short-run deviations from the deterministic S-shaped growth path of the diffusion process, as implied by the differential equation in (20). The reason to include heteroskedasticity is that, in the beginning and towards the end of the adoption process, one should be less uncertain about the variance of the forecasts than when the process is closer to the inflection point. Next, the solution to the differential equation is a deterministic path, and there may be various reasons to temporally deviate form this path. Boswijk and Franses (2005) therefore propose to consider

$$\begin{aligned} \mathrm{d}n(\tau) = \alpha\Big[p\big[m - N(\tau)\big] + \frac{q}{m} N(\tau)\big[m - N(\tau)\big] - n(\tau)\Big]\,\mathrm{d}\tau \\ + \sigma n(\tau)^{\gamma}\,\mathrm{d}W(\tau), \end{aligned} \tag{25}$$

where $W(\tau)$ is a standard Wiener process. The parameter α in (25) measures the speed of adjustment towards the deterministic path implied by the standard Bass model. Additionally, by introducing $\sigma n(t)^{\gamma}$, heteroskedasticity is allowed. A possible choice is to set $\gamma = 1$. Boswijk and Franses (2005) further derive that the discretization of this continuous time model is

$$X_t - X_{t-1} = \beta_1 + \beta_2 N_{t-1} + \beta_3 N_{t-1}^2 + \beta_4 X_{t-1} + X_{t-1}\varepsilon_t, \tag{26}$$

where

$$\beta_1 = \alpha p m, \tag{27}$$

$$\beta_2 = \alpha(q - p), \tag{28}$$

$$\beta_3 = -\alpha \frac{q}{m}, \tag{29}$$

$$\beta_4 = -\alpha, \tag{30}$$

which shows that all parameters in (26) depend on α.

Another empirical version of the Bass theory, a version which is often used in practice, is proposed in Srinivasan and Mason (1986). These authors recognize that the Bass (1969) formulation above may introduce aggregation bias, as X_t is simply taken as the discrete representative of $n(\tau)$. Therefore, Srinivasan and Mason (1986) propose to apply non-linear least-squares (NLS) to

$$X_t = m\big[F(t;\theta) - F(t-1;\theta)\big] + \varepsilon_t, \tag{31}$$

where θ collects p and q. van den Bulte and Lilien (1997) show that this method is rather unstable if one has data that do not yet cover the inflection point. How to derive forecasts for the various models will be discussed below.

3.4. Multi-level models for panels of time series

It is not uncommon in marketing to have data on a large number of cases (households, brands, SKUs) for a large number of time intervals (like a couple of years with weekly data). In other words, it is not uncommon that one designs models for a variable to be explained with substantial information over dimension N as well as T. Such data are called a panel of time series. Hence, one wants to exploit the time series dimension, and potentially include seasonality and trends, while preserving the panel structure.

To set notation, consider

$$y_{i,t} = \mu_i + \beta_i x_{i,t} + \varepsilon_{i,t}, \tag{32}$$

where subscript i refers to household i and t to week t. Let y denote sales of a certain product and x be price, as observed by that particular household (where a household can visit a large variety of stores).

Hierarchical Bayes approach

It is not uncommon to allow the N households to have different price elasticities. And, from a statistical perspective, if one were to impose $\beta_i = \beta$, one for sure would reject this hypothesis in most practical situations. On the other hand, the interpretation of N different price elasticities is also not easy either. Typically, one does have a bit more information on the households (family life cycle, size, income, education), and it might be that these variables have some explanatory value for the price elasticities. One way to examine this would be to perform N regressions, to retrieve the $\hat{\beta}_i$, and next, in a second round, to regress these estimated values on household-specific features. Obviously, this two-step approach assumes that the $\hat{\beta}_i$ variables are given instead of estimated, and hence, uncertainty in the second step is underestimated.

A more elegant solution is to add a second level to (32), that is, for example,

$$\beta_i \sim \mathrm{N}\big(\beta_0 + \beta_1 z_i, \sigma^2\big), \tag{33}$$

where z_i is an observed variable for a household, see Blattberg and George (1991). Estimation of the model parameters can require simulation-based techniques. An often used method is termed Hierarchical Bayes (HB), see Allenby and Rossi (1999) among various others.

An exemplary illustration of this method given in van Nierop, Fok and Franses (2002) who consider this model for 2 years of weekly sales on 23 items in the same product category. The effects of promotions and distribution in $x_{i,t}$ are made a function of the size of an item and its location on a shelf.

Latent class modeling

As segmentation is often viewed as an important reason to construct models in marketing, another popular approach is to consider the panel model

$$y_{i,t} = \mu_i + \beta_{i,s} x_{i,t} + \varepsilon_{i,t}, \tag{34}$$

where $\beta_{i,s}$ denotes that, say, household-specific price elasticity, can be classified into J classes, within which the price elasticities obey $\beta_{i,s} = \beta(S_i)$, where S_i is element of $1, 2, \ldots, J$, with probability $\Pr(S_i = j) = p_j$. In words, $\beta_{i,s}$ corresponds with observation i in class j, with $j = 1, 2, \ldots, J$. Each household has a probability p_j, with $p_1+p_2+\cdots+p_J = 1$, to get assigned to a class j, at least according to the values of $\beta_{i,s}$. Such a model can be extended to allow the probabilities to depend on household-specific features. This builds on the latent class methodology, recently summarized in Wedel and Kamakura (1999). As such, the model allows for capturing unobserved heterogeneity.

This approach as well as the previous one involves the application of simulation methods to estimate parameters. As simulations are used, the computation of forecasts is trivial. They immediately come as a by-product of the estimation results. Uncertainty around these forecasts can also easily be simulated.

A multi-level Bass model

This section is concluded with a brief discussion of a Bass type model for a panel of time series. Talukdar, Sudhir and Ainslie (2002) introduce a two-level panel model for a set of diffusion data, where they correlate individual Bass model parameters with explanatory variables in the second stage.

Following the Boswijk and Franses (2005) specification, a panel Bass model would be

$$X_{i,t} - X_{i,t-1} = \beta_{1,i} + \beta_{2,i} N_{i,t-1} + \beta_{3,i} N_{i,t-1}^2 + \beta_{4,i} X_{i,t-1} + X_{i,t-1}\varepsilon_{i,t}. \tag{35}$$

As before, the β parameters are functions of the underlying characteristics of the diffusion process, that is,

$$\beta_{1,i} = \alpha_i p_i m_i, \tag{36}$$

$$\beta_{2,i} = \alpha_i (q_i - p_i), \tag{37}$$

$$\beta_{3,i} = -\alpha_i \frac{q_i}{m_i}, \tag{38}$$

$$\beta_{4,i} = -\alpha_i. \tag{39}$$

As the effects of p and q on the diffusion patterns are highly non-linear, it seems more appropriate to focus on the inflection point, that is, the timing of peak adoptions, T_i^*, and the level of the cumulative adoptions at the peak divided by m_i, denoted as f_i. The link between p_i and q_i and the inflection point parameters is given by

$$p_i = (2f_i - 1)\frac{\log(1 - 2f_i)}{2T_i^*(1 - f_i)}, \tag{40}$$

$$q_i = -\frac{\log(1 - 2f_i)}{2T_i^*(1 - f_i)}, \tag{41}$$

see Franses (2003a).

Fok and Franses (2005) propose to specify $\beta_{1,i}, \ldots, \beta_{4,i}$ as a function of the total number of adoptions (m_i), the fraction of cumulative adoptions at the inflection point (f_i), the time of the inflection point (T_i^*), and the speed of adjustment (α_i) of $X_{i,t}$ to the equilibrium path denoted as $\beta_{k,i} = \beta_k(m_i, f_i, T_i^*, \alpha_i)$. The adoptions that these authors study are the citations to articles published in *Econometrica* and in the *Journal of Econometrics*. They relate m_i, f_i, T_i^*, and α_i to observable features of the articles. In sum, they consider

$$\begin{aligned} X_{i,t} - X_{i,t-1} = {} & \beta_1(m_i, f_i, T_i^*, \alpha_i) + \beta_2(m_i, f_i, T_i^*, \alpha_i)N_{i,t-1} \\ & + \beta_3(m_i, f_i, T_i^*, \alpha_i)N_{i,t-1}^2 + \beta_4(m_i, f_i, T_i^*, \alpha_i)X_{i,t-1} \\ & + X_{i,t-1}\varepsilon_{i,t}, \end{aligned} \tag{42}$$

where $\varepsilon_{i,t} \sim \mathrm{N}(0, \sigma_i^2)$ with

$$\log(m_i) = Z_i'\theta_1 + \eta_{1,i}, \tag{43}$$

$$\log\left(\frac{2f_i}{1 - 2f_i}\right) = Z_i'\theta_2 + \eta_{2,i}, \tag{44}$$

$$\log(T_i^*) = Z_i'\theta_3 + \eta_{3,i}, \tag{45}$$

$$\alpha_i = Z_i'\theta_4 + \eta_{4,i}, \tag{46}$$

$$\log \sigma_i^2 = Z_i'\theta_5 + \eta_{5,i}, \tag{47}$$

where the Z_i vector contains an intercept and explanatory variables.

This section has reviewed various models that are often applied in marketing, and some of which seem to slowly diffuse into other economics disciplines.

4. Deriving forecasts

The previous section indicated that various interesting measures (like duration interval) or models (like the attraction model) in marketing research imply that the variable of interest is a non-linear function of variables and parameters. In many cases there are no closed-form solutions to these expressions, and hence one has to resort to simulation-based techniques. In this section the focus will be on the attraction model and on the Bass model, where the expressions for out-of-sample forecasts will be given. Additionally, there will be a discussion of how one should derive forecasts for market shares when forecasts for sales are available.

4.1. Attraction model forecasts

As discussed earlier, the attraction model ensures logical consistency, that is, market shares lie between 0 and 1 and they sum to 1. These restrictions imply that (functions of) model parameters can be estimated from a multivariate reduced-form model with $I - 1$ equations. The dependent variable in each of the $I - 1$ equations is the natural logarithm of a relative market share, that is, $\log m_{i,t} \equiv \log \frac{M_{i,t}}{M_{I,t}}$, for $i = 1, 2, \ldots, I - 1$, where the base brand I can be chosen arbitrarily, as discussed before.

In practice, one is usually interested in predicting $M_{i,t}$ and not in forecasting the logs of the relative market shares. Again, it is important to recognize that, first of all, $\exp(\mathrm{E}[\log m_{i,t}])$ is not equal to $\mathrm{E}[m_{i,t}]$ and that, secondly, $\mathrm{E}[\frac{M_{i,t}}{M_{I,t}}]$ is not equal to $\frac{\mathrm{E}[M_{i,t}]}{\mathrm{E}[M_{I,t}]}$. Therefore, unbiased market share forecasts cannot be directly obtained by these data transformations.

To forecast the market share of brand i at time t, one needs to consider the relative market shares

$$m_{j,t} = \frac{M_{j,t}}{M_{I,t}} \quad \text{for } j = 1, 2, \ldots, I, \tag{48}$$

as $m_{1,t}, \ldots, m_{I-1,t}$ form the dependent variables (after log transformation) in the reduced-form model. As $M_{I,t} = 1 - \sum_{j=1}^{I-1} M_{j,t}$, it holds that

$$M_{i,t} = \frac{m_{i,t}}{\sum_{j=1}^{I} m_{j,t}} \quad \text{for } i = 1, 2, \ldots, I. \tag{49}$$

Fok, Franses and Paap (2002) propose to simulate the one-step ahead forecasts of the market shares as follows. First draw $\eta_t^{(l)}$ from $\mathrm{N}(0, \tilde{\Sigma})$, then compute

$$m_{i,t}^{(l)} = \exp(\tilde{\mu}_i + \eta_{i,t}^{(l)}) \prod_{j=1}^{I} \left(\prod_{k=1}^{K} x_{k,j,t}^{\tilde{\beta}_{k,j,i}} \right), \tag{50}$$

with $m_{I,t}^{(l)} = 1$ and finally compute

$$M_{i,t}^{(l)} = \frac{m_{i,t}^{(l)}}{\sum_{j=1}^{I} m_{j,t}^{(l)}} \quad \text{for } i = 1, \ldots, I, \tag{51}$$

where $l = 1, \ldots, L$ denotes the simulation iteration. Each vector $(M_{1,t}^{(l)}, \ldots, M_{I,t}^{(l)})'$ generated this way is a draw from the joint distribution of the market shares at time t. Using the average over a sufficiently large number of draws one can calculate the expected value of the market shares. This can be modified to allow for parameter uncertainty, see Fok, Franses and Paap (2002). Multi-step ahead forecasts can be generated along similar lines.

4.2. Forecasting market shares from models for sales

The previous results assume that one is interested in forecasting market shares based on models for market shares. In practice, it might sometimes be more easy to make models for sales. One might then me tempted to divide the own sales forecast by a forecast for category sales, but this procedure leads to biased forecasts for similar reasons as before. A solution is given in Fok and Franses (2001) and will be discussed next.

An often used model (SCAN*PRO) for sales is

$$\log S_{i,t} = \mu_i + \sum_{j=1}^{I} \sum_{k=1}^{K} \beta_{k,j,i} x_{k,j,t} + \sum_{j=1}^{I} \sum_{p=1}^{P} \alpha_{p,j,i} \log S_{j,t-p} + \varepsilon_{i,t}, \tag{52}$$

with $i = 1, \ldots, I$, where $\varepsilon_t \equiv (\varepsilon_{1,t}, \ldots, \varepsilon_{I,t})' \sim \mathrm{N}(0, \Sigma)$ and where $x_{k,j,t}$ denotes the kth explanatory variable (for example, price or advertising) for brand j at time t and where $\beta_{k,j,i}$ is the corresponding coefficient for brand i, see Wittink et al. (1988). The market share of brand i at time t can of course be defined as

$$M_{i,t} = \frac{S_{i,t}}{\sum_{j=1}^{I} S_{j,t}}. \tag{53}$$

Forecasts of market shares at time $t+1$ based on information on all explanatory variables up to time $t+1$, denoted by Π_{t+1}, and information on realizations of the sales up to period t, denoted by $\mathcal{S}_t$, should be equal to the expectation of the market shares given the total amount of information available, denoted by $\mathrm{E}[M_{i,t+1} \mid \Pi_{t+1}, \mathcal{S}_t]$, that is,

$$\mathrm{E}[M_{i,t+1} \mid \Pi_{t+1}, \mathcal{S}_t] = \mathrm{E}\left[\frac{S_{i,t+1}}{\sum_{j=1}^{I} S_{j,t+1}} \,\middle|\, \Pi_{t+1}, \mathcal{S}_t \right]. \tag{54}$$

Due to non-linearity it is therefore not possible to obtain market shares forecasts directly from sales forecasts. A further complication is that it is also not trivial to obtain a forecast of $S_{i,t+1}$, as the sales model concerns log-transformed variables, and it is well known that $\exp(\mathrm{E}[\log X]) \neq \mathrm{E}[X]$. See also Arino and Franses (2000) and Wieringa and Horvath (2005) for the relevance of this notion when examining multivariate time series models. In particular, Wieringa and Horvath (2005) show how to derive impulse response functions from VAR models for marketing variables, and they demonstrate the empirical relevance of a correct treatment of log-transformed data.

Fok and Franses (2001) provide a simulation-based solution, in line with the method outlined in Granger and Teräsvirta (1993). Naturally, unbiased forecasts of the I market shares should be based on the expected value of the market shares, that is,

$$\begin{aligned}\mathrm{E}[M_{i,t+1} \mid \Pi_{t+1}, \mathcal{S}_t] \\ &= \int_0^{+\infty} \cdots \int_0^{+\infty} \frac{s_{i,t+1}}{\sum_{j=1}^{I} s_{j,t+1}} \\ &\quad \times f(s_{1,t+1}, \ldots, s_{I,t+1} \mid \Pi_{t+1}, \mathcal{S}_t)\, \mathrm{d}s_{1,t+1}, \ldots, \mathrm{d}s_{I,t+1},\end{aligned} \tag{55}$$

where $f(s_{1,t+1}, \ldots, s_{I,t+1} \mid \Pi_{t+1}, \mathcal{S}_t)$ is a probability density function of the sales conditional on the available information, and $s_{i,t+1}$ denotes a realization of the stochastic process $S_{i,t+1}$. The model defined in the distribution of S_{t+1}, given Π_{t+1} and $\mathcal{S}_t$, is log-normal, but other functional forms can be considered too. Hence,

$$\big(\exp(S_{1,t+1}), \ldots, \exp(S_{I,t+1})\big)' \sim \mathrm{N}(Z_{t+1}, \Sigma), \tag{56}$$

where $Z_t = (Z_{1,t}, \ldots, Z_{I,t})'$ is the deterministic part of the model, that is,

$$Z_{i,t} = \mu_i + \sum_{j=1}^{I} \sum_{k=1}^{K} \beta_{k,j,i} x_{k,j,t} + \sum_{j=1}^{I} \sum_{p=1}^{P} \alpha_{p,j,i} \log S_{j,t-p}. \tag{57}$$

The I-dimensional integral in (55) is difficult to evaluate analytically. Fok and Franses (2001) therefore outline how to compute the expectations using simulation techniques. In short, using the estimated probability distribution of the sales, realizations of the sales are simulated. Based on each set of these realizations of all brands, the market shares can be calculated. The average over a large number of replications gives the expected value in (55).

Forecasting $h > 1$ steps ahead is slightly more difficult as the values of the lagged sales are no longer known. However, for these lagged sales appropriate simulated values can be used. For example, 2-step ahead forecasts can be calculated by averaging over simulated values $M_{i,t+2}^{(l)}$, based on draws $\varepsilon_{t+2}^{(l)}$ from $\mathrm{N}(0, \hat{\Sigma})$ and on draws $S_{i,t+1}^{(l)}$, which are already used for the 1-step ahead forecasts. Notice that the 2-step ahead forecasts do not need more simulation iterations than the one-step ahead forecasts.

An important by-product of the simulation method is that it is now also easy to calculate confidence bounds for the forecasted market shares. Actually, the entire distribution of the market shares can be estimated based on the simulated values. For example, the lower bound of a 95% confidence interval is that value for which it holds that 2.5% of the simulated market shares are smaller. Finally, the lower bound and the upper bound always lie within the [0, 1] interval, and this should be the case for market shares indeed.

4.3. Bass model forecasts

The Bass model is regularly used for out-of-sample forecasting. One way is to have several years of data on own sales, estimate the model parameters for that particular series, and extrapolate the series into the future. As van den Bulte and Lilien (1997) demonstrate, this approach is most useful in case the inflection point is within the sample. If not, then one might want to consider imposing the parameters obtained for other markets or situations, and then extrapolate.

The way the forecasts are generated depends on the functional form chosen, that is, how one includes the error term in the model. The Srinivasan and Mason (1986) model seems to imply the most easy to construct forecasts. Suppose one aims to predict X_{n+h}, where n is the forecast origin and h is the horizon. Then, given the assumption on the error term, the forecast is

$$\hat{X}_{n+h} = \hat{m}\big[F\big(n+h;\hat{\theta}\big) - F\big(n-1+h;\hat{\theta}\big)\big]. \tag{58}$$

When the error term is AR(1), straightforward modifications of this formula should be made. If the error term has an expected value equal to zero, then these forecasts are unbiased, for any h.

This is in contrast with the Bass regression model, and also its Boswijk and Franses modification, as these models are intrinsically non-linear. For one-step ahead, the true observation at $n+1$ in the Bass scheme is

$$X_{n+1} = \alpha_1 + \alpha_2 N_n + \alpha_3 N_n^2 + \varepsilon_{n+1}. \tag{59}$$

The forecast from origin n equals

$$\hat{X}_{n+1} = \hat{\alpha}_1 + \hat{\alpha}_2 N_n + \hat{\alpha}_3 N_n^2 \tag{60}$$

and the squared forecast error is σ^2. This forecast is unbiased.

For two steps ahead matters become different. The true observation is equal to

$$X_{n+2} = \alpha_1 + \alpha_2 N_{n+1} + \alpha_3 N_{n+1}^2 + \varepsilon_{n+2}, \tag{61}$$

which, as $N_{n+1} = N_n + X_{n+1}$, equals

$$X_{n+2} = \alpha_1 + \alpha_2(X_{n+1} + N_n) + \alpha_3(X_{n+1} + N_n)^2 + \varepsilon_{n+2}. \tag{62}$$

Upon substituting X_{n+1}, this becomes

$$\begin{aligned} X_{n+2} = {} & \alpha_1 + \alpha_2\big(\alpha_1 + \alpha_2 N_n + \alpha_3 N_n^2 + \varepsilon_{n+1} + N_n\big) \\ & + \alpha_3\big(\alpha_1 + \alpha_2 N_n + \alpha_3 N_n^2 + \varepsilon_{n+1} + N_n\big)^2 + \varepsilon_{n+2}. \end{aligned} \tag{63}$$

Hence, the two-step ahead forecast error is based on

$$\begin{aligned} & X_{n+2} - \hat{X}_{n+2} \\ & \quad = \varepsilon_{n+2} + \alpha_2\varepsilon_{n+1} \\ & \qquad + \alpha_3\big(2\alpha_1\varepsilon_{n+1} + 2(\alpha_2+1)N_n\varepsilon_{n+1} + 2\alpha_3 N_n^2\varepsilon_{n+1} + \varepsilon_{n+1}^2\big). \end{aligned} \tag{64}$$

This shows that the expected forecast error is

$$E\big(X_{n+2} - \hat{X}_{n+2}\big) = \alpha_3\sigma^2. \tag{65}$$

It is straightforward to derive that if h is 3 or more, this bias grows exponentially with h. Naturally, the size of the bias depends on α_3 and σ^2, which both can be small. As the sign of α_3 is always negative, the forecast is upward biased.

Franses (2003b) points out that to obtain unbiased forecasts for the Bass-type regression models for $h = 2, 3, \ldots$, one needs to resort to simulation techniques, the same ones as used in Teräsvirta's Chapter 8 in this Handbook. Consider again the Bass regression, now written as

$$X_t = g(Z_{t-1}; \pi) + \varepsilon_t, \tag{66}$$

where Z_{t-1} contains 1, N_{t-1} and N_{t-1}^2, and π includes p, q and m. A simulation-based one-step ahead forecast is now given by

$$X_{n+1,i} = g(Z_n; \hat{\pi}) + e_i, \tag{67}$$

where e_i is a random draw from the $\mathrm{N}(0, \hat{\sigma}^2)$ distribution. Based on I such draws, an unbiased forecast can be constructed as

$$\hat{X}_{n+1} = \frac{1}{I}\sum_{i=1}^{I} X_{n+1,i}. \tag{68}$$

Again, a convenient by-product of this approach is the full distribution of the forecasts. A two-step simulation-based forecast can be based on the average value of

$$X_{n+2,i} = g(Z_n, X_{n+1,i}; \hat{\pi}) + e_i, \tag{69}$$

again for I draws, and so on.

4.4. *Forecasting duration data*

Finally, there are various studies in marketing that rely on duration models to describe interpurchase times. These data are relevant to managers as one can try to speed up the purchase process by implementing marketing efforts, but also one may forecast the amount of sales to be expected in the next period, due to promotion planning. Interestingly, it is known that many marketing efforts have a dynamic effect that stretches beyond the one-step ahead horizon. For example, it has been widely established that there is a so-called post-promotional dip, meaning that sales tend to collapse the week after a promotion was held, but might regain their original level or preferably a higher level after that week. Hence, managers might want to look beyond the one-step ahead horizon.

In sum, one seems to be more interested in the number of purchases in the next week or next month, than that there is an interest in the time till the next purchase. The modelling approach for the analysis of recurrent events in marketing, like the purchase timing of frequently purchased consumer goods, has, however, mainly aimed at explaining the interpurchase times. The main trend is to apply a Cox (mixed) Proportional Hazard model for the interpurchase times, see Seetharaman and Chintagunta (2003) for a recent overview. In this approach after each purchase the duration is reset to zero. This transformation removes much of the typical behavior of the repeat purchase process in a similar way as first-differencing in time series. Therefore, it induces important limitations to the use of time-varying covariates (and also seasonal effects) and duration dependence in the models.

An alternative is to consider the whole path of the repeat purchase history on the time scale starting at the beginning of the observation window. Bijwaard, Franses and Paap (2003) put forward a statistical model for interpurchase times that takes into account all the current and past information available for all purchases as time continues to run along the calendar timescale. It is based on the Andersen and Gill (1982) approach. It delivers forecasts for the number of purchases in the next period *and* for the timing of the first and consecutive purchases. Purchase occasions are modelled in terms of a counting process, which counts the recurrent purchases for each household as they evolve over time. These authors show that formulating the problem as a counting process has many advantages, both theoretically and empirically. Counting processes allow to understand survival and recurrent event models better

(i) as the baseline intensity may vary arbitrary over time,
(ii) as it facilitates the interpretation of the effects of co-variates in the Cox proportional hazard model,
(iii) as Cox's solution via the partial likelihood takes the baseline hazard as a nuisance parameter,
(iv) as the conditions for time-varying covariates can be precisely formulated and finally, and finally
(v) as by expressing the duration distribution as a regression model it simplifies the analysis of the estimators.

5. Conclusion

This chapter has reviewed various aspects of econometric modeling and forecasting in marketing. The focus was on models that have been developed with particular applications in marketing in mind. Indeed, in many cases, marketing studies just use the same types of models that are also common to applied econometrics. In many marketing research studies there are quite a number of observations and typically the data are well measured. Usually there is an interest in modeling and forecasting performance measures such as sales, shares, retention, loyalty, brand choice and the time between events, preferably when these depend partially on marketing-mix instruments like promotions, advertising, and price.

Various marketing models are non-linear models. This is due to specific structures imposed on the models to make them more suitable for their particular purpose, like the Bass model for diffusion and the attraction model for market shares. Other models that are frequently encountered in marketing, and less so in other areas (at least as of yet) concern panels of time series. Interestingly, it seems that new econometric methodology (like the Hierarchical Bayes methods) has been developed and applied in marketing first, and will perhaps be more often used in the future in other areas too.

There are two areas in which more research seems needed. The first is that it is not yet clear how out-of-sample forecasts should be evaluated. Of course, mean squared forecast error type methods are regularly used, but it is doubtful whether these criteria meet the purposes of an econometric model. In fact, if the model concerns the retention of customers, it might be worse to underestimate the probability of leaving than to overestimate that probability. Hence the monetary value, possibly discounted for future events, might be more important. The recent literature on forecasting under asymmetric loss is relevant here; see, for example, Elliott, Komunjer and Timmermann (2005) and Elliott and Timmermann (2004).

Second, the way forecasts are implemented into actual marketing strategies is not trivial, see Franses (2005a, 2005b). In marketing one deals with customers and with competitors, and each can form expectations about what you will do. The successfulness of a marketing strategy depends on the accuracy of stake-holders' expectations and their subsequent behavior. For example, to predict whether a newly launched product will be successful might need more complicated econometric models than we have available today.

References

Allenby, G., Rossi, P. (1999). "Marketing models of consumer heterogeneity". Journal of Econometrics 89, 57–78.

Andersen, P.K., Gill, R.D. (1982). "Cox's regression model for counting processes: A large sample study". Annals of Statistics 10, 1100–1120.

Andrews, D.W.K., Ploberger, W. (1994). "Optimal tests when a nuisance parameter is present only under the alternative". Econometrica 62, 1383–1414.

Arino, M., Franses, P.H. (2000). "Forecasting the levels of vector autoregressive log-transformed time series". International Journal of Forecasting 16, 111–116.

Assmus, G., Farley, J.U., Lehmann, D. (1984). "How advertising affects sales: Meta-analysis of econometric results". Journal of Marketing Research 21, 65–74.

Bass, F.M. (1969). "A new product growth model for consumer durables". Management Science 15, 215–227.

Bass, F.M., Leone, R. (1983). "Temporal aggregation, the data interval bias, and empirical estimation of bimonthly relations from annual data". Management Science 29, 1–11.

Bewley, R., Griffiths, W.E. (2003). "The penetration of CDs in the sound recording market: Issues in specification, model selection and forecasting". International Journal of Forecasting 19, 111–121.

Bijwaard, G.E., Franses, P.H., Paap, R. (2003). "Modeling purchases as repeated events". Econometric Institute Report, 2003-45, Erasmus University Rotterdam. Revision requested by the Journal of Business and Economic Statistics.

Blattberg, R.C., George, E.I. (1991). "Shrinkage estimation of price and promotional elasticities – Seemingly unrelated equations". Journal of the American Statistical Association 86, 304–315.

Boswijk, H.P., Franses, P.H. (2005). "On the econometrics of the Bass diffusion model". Journal of Business and Economic Statistics 23, 255–268.

Bronnenberg, B.J., Mahajan, V., Vanhonacker, W.R. (2000). "The emergence of market structure in new repeat-purchase categories: The interplay of market share and retailer distribution". Journal of Marketing Research 37, 16–31.

Chandy, R.K., Tellis, G.J., MacInnis, D.J., Thaivanich, P. (2001). "What to say when: Advertising appeals in evolving markets". Journal of Marketing Research 38, 399–414.

Clarke, D.G. (1976). "Econometric measurement of the duration of advertising effect on sales". Journal of Marketing Research 8, 345–357.
Cooper, L.G., Nakanishi, M. (1988). Market Share Analysis: Evaluating Competitive Marketing Effectiveness. Kluwer Academic, Boston.
Davies, R.B. (1987). "Hypothesis testing when a nuisance parameter is present only under the alternative". Biometrika 64, 247–254.
Dekimpe, M.G., Hanssens, D.M. (2000). "Time series models in marketing: Past, present and future". International Journal of Research in Marketing 17, 183–193.
Elliott, G., Komunjer, I., Timmermann, A. (2005). "Estimation and testing of forecast rationality under flexible loss". Review of Economic Studies. In press.
Elliott, G., Timmermann, A. (2004). "Optimal forecast combinations under general loss functions and forecast error distributions". Journal of Econometrics 122, 47–79.
Fok, D., Franses, P.H. (2001). "Forecasting market shares from models for sales". International Journal of Forecasting 17, 121–128.
Fok, D., Franses, P.H. (2004). "Analyzing the effects of a brand introduction on competitive structure using a market share attraction model". International Journal of Research in Marketing 21, 159–177.
Fok, D., Franses, P.H. (2005). "Modeling the diffusion of scientific publications". Journal of Econometrics. In press.
Fok, D., Franses, P.H., Paap, R. (2002). "Econometric analysis of the market share attraction model". In: Franses, P.H., Montgomery, A.L. (Eds.), Econometric Models in Marketing. Elsevier, Amsterdam, pp. 223–256. Chapter 10.
Franses, P.H. (2003a). "On the diffusion of scientific publications. The case of Econometrica 1987". Scientometrics 56, 29–42.
Franses, P.H. (2003b). "On the Bass diffusion theory, empirical models and out-of-sample forecasting". ERIM Report Series Research in Management ERS-2003-34-MKT, Erasmus University Rotterdam.
Franses, P.H. (2004). "Fifty years since Koyck (1954)". Statistica Neerlandica 58, 381–387.
Franses, P.H. (2005a). "On the use of econometric models for policy simulation in marketing". Journal of Marketing Research 42, 4–14.
Franses, P.H. (2005b). "Diagnostics, expectation, and endogeneity". Journal of Marketing Research 42, 27–29.
Franses, P.H., Paap, R. (2001). Quantitative Models in Marketing Research. Cambridge University Press, Cambridge.
Franses, P.H., van Oest, R.D. (2004). "On the econometrics of the Koyck model". Econometric Institute Report 2004-07, Erasmus University Rotterdam.
Franses, P.H., Vroomen, B. (2003). "Estimating duration intervals". ERIM Report Series Research in Management, ERS-2003-031-MKT, Erasmus University Rotterdam. Revision requested by the Journal of Advertising.
Granger, C.W.J., Teräsvirta, T. (1993). Modelling Nonlinear Economic Relationships. Oxford University Press, Oxford.
Hansen, B.E. (1996). "Inference when a nuisance parameter is not identified under the null hypothesis". Econometrica 64, 413–430.
Klapper, D., Herwartz, H. (2000). "Forecasting market share using predicted values of competitor behavior: Further empirical results". International Journal of Forecasting 16, 399–421.
Kotler, Ph., Jain, D.C., Maesincee, S. (2002). Marketing Moves. A New Approach to Profits, Growth, and Renewal. Harvard Business School Press, Boston.
Koyck, L.M. (1954). Distributed Lags and Investment Analysis. North-Holland, Amsterdam.
Kumar, V. (1994). "Forecasting performance of market share models: An assessment, additional insights, and guidelines". International Journal of Forecasting 10, 295–312.
Leeflang, P.S.H., Reuyl, J.C. (1984). "On the predictive power of market share attraction model". Journal of Marketing Research 21, 211–215.
Leone, R.P. (1995). "Generalizing what is known about temporal aggregation and advertising carryover". Marketing Science 14, G141–G150.

Naert, P.A., Weverbergh, M. (1981). "On the prediction power of market share attraction models". Journal of Marketing Research 18, 146–153.

Nijs, V.R., Dekimpe, M.G., Steenkamp, J.-B.E.M., Hanssens, D.M. (2001). "The category-demand effects of price promotions". Marketing Science 20, 1–22.

Pauwels, K., Srinivasan, S. (2004). "Who benefits from store brand entry?" Marketing Science 23, 364–390.

Russell, G.J. (1988). "Recovering measures of advertising carryover from aggregate data: The role of the firm's decision behavior". Marketing Science 7, 252–270.

Seetharaman, P.B., Chintagunta, P.K. (2003). "The proportional hazard model for purchase timing: A comparison of alternative specifications". Journal of Business and Economic Statistics 21, 368–382.

Srinivasan, V., Mason, C.H. (1986). "Nonlinear least squares estimation of new product diffusion models". Marketing Science 5, 169–178.

Talukdar, D., Sudhir, K., Ainslie, A. (2002). "Investigating new product diffusion across products and countries". Marketing Science 21, 97–114.

Tellis, G.J. (1988). "Advertising exposure, loyalty and brand purchase: A two stage model of choice". Journal of Marketing Research 25, 134–144.

Tellis, G.J., Chandy, R., Thaivanich, P. (2000). "Which ad works, when, where, and how often? Modeling the effects of direct television advertising". Journal of Marketing Research 37, 32–46.

Tellis, G.J., Franses, P.H. (2006). "The optimal data interval for econometric models of advertising". Marketing Science. In press.

van den Bulte, C., Lilien, G.L. (1997). "Bias and systematic change in the parameter estimates of macro-level diffusion models". Marketing Science 16, 338–353.

van Nierop, E., Fok, D., Franses, P.H. (2002). "Sales models for many items using attribute data". ERIM Report Series Research in Management ERS-2002-65-MKT, Erasmus University Rotterdam.

van Oest, R.D., Paap, R., Franses, P.H. (2002). "A joint framework for category purchase and consumption behavior". Tinbergen Institute report series TI 2002-124/4, Erasmus University Rotterdam.

Wedel, M., Kamakura, W.A. (1999). Market Segmentation: Conceptual and Methodological Foundations. Kluwer Academic, Boston.

Wieringa, J.E., Horvath, C. (2005). "Computing level-impulse responses of log-specified VAR systems". International Journal of Forecasting 21, 279–289.

Wittink, D.R., Addona, M.J., Hawkes, W.J., Porter, J.C. (1988). "SCAN*PRO: The estimation, validation, and use of promotional effects based on scanner data". Working Paper, AC Nielsen, Schaumburg, Illinois.

AUTHOR INDEX

n indicates citation in a footnote.

SUBJECT INDEX

HANDBOOKS IN ECONOMICS

1. HANDBOOK OF MATHEMATICAL ECONOMICS (in 4 volumes)
   Volumes 1, 2 and 3 edited by Kenneth J. Arrow and Michael D. Intriligator
   Volume 4 edited by Werner Hildenbrand and Hugo Sonnenschein

2. HANDBOOK OF ECONOMETRICS (in 6 volumes)
   Volumes 1, 2 and 3 edited by Zvi Griliches and Michael D. Intriligator
   Volume 4 edited by Robert F. Engle and Daniel L. McFadden
   Volume 5 edited by James J. Heckman and Edward Leamer
   Volume 6 is in preparation (editors James J. Heckman and Edward Leamer)

3. HANDBOOK OF INTERNATIONAL ECONOMICS (in 3 volumes)
   Volumes 1 and 2 edited by Ronald W. Jones and Peter B. Kenen
   Volume 3 edited by Gene M. Grossman and Kenneth Rogoff

4. HANDBOOK OF PUBLIC ECONOMICS (in 4 volumes)
   Edited by Alan J. Auerbach and Martin Feldstein

5. HANDBOOK OF LABOR ECONOMICS (in 5 volumes)
   Volumes 1 and 2 edited by Orley C. Ashenfelter and Richard Layard
   Volumes 3A, 3B and 3C edited by Orley C. Ashenfelter and David Card

6. HANDBOOK OF NATURAL RESOURCE AND ENERGY ECONOMICS
   (in 3 volumes). Edited by Allen V. Kneese and James L. Sweeney

7. HANDBOOK OF REGIONAL AND URBAN ECONOMICS (in 4 volumes)
   Volume 1 edited by Peter Nijkamp
   Volume 2 edited by Edwin S. Mills
   Volume 3 edited by Paul C. Cheshire and Edwin S. Mills
   Volume 4 edited by J. Vernon Henderson and Jacques-François Thisse

8. HANDBOOK OF MONETARY ECONOMICS (in 2 volumes)
   Edited by Benjamin Friedman and Frank Hahn

9. HANDBOOK OF DEVELOPMENT ECONOMICS (in 4 volumes)
   Volumes 1 and 2 edited by Hollis B. Chenery and T.N. Srinivasan
   Volumes 3A and 3B edited by Jere Behrman and T.N. Srinivasan

10. HANDBOOK OF INDUSTRIAL ORGANIZATION (in 3 volumes)
    Volumes 1 and 2 edited by Richard Schmalensee and Robert R. Willig
    Volume 3 is in preparation (editors Mark Armstrong and Robert H. Porter)

11. HANDBOOK OF GAME THEORY with Economic Applications (in 3 volumes)
    Edited by Robert J. Aumann and Sergiu Hart

12. HANDBOOK OF DEFENSE ECONOMICS (in 1 volume)
    Edited by Keith Hartley and Todd Sandler
    Volume 2 is in preparation (editors Todd Sandler and Keith Hartley)

13. HANDBOOK OF COMPUTATIONAL ECONOMICS (in 2 volumes)
    Volume 1 edited by Hans M. Amman, David A. Kendrick and John Rust
    Volume 2 edited by Leigh Tesfatsion and Kenneth L. Judd

14. HANDBOOK OF POPULATION AND FAMILY ECONOMICS (in 2 volumes)
    Edited by Mark R. Rosenzweig and Oded Stark

15. HANDBOOK OF MACROECONOMICS (in 3 volumes)
    Edited by John B. Taylor and Michael Woodford

16. HANDBOOK OF INCOME DISTRIBUTION (in 1 volume)
    Edited by Anthony B. Atkinson and François Bourguignon

17. HANDBOOK OF HEALTH ECONOMICS (in 2 volumes)
    Edited by Anthony J. Culyer and Joseph P. Newhouse

18. HANDBOOK OF AGRICULTURAL ECONOMICS (in 4 volumes)
    Edited by Bruce L. Gardner and Gordon C. Rausser
    Volumes 3 and 4 are in preparation (editors Robert Evenson, Prabhu Pingali and T. Paul Schultz)

19. HANDBOOK OF SOCIAL CHOICE AND WELFARE (in 2 volumes)
    Volume 1 edited by Kenneth J. Arrow, Amartya K. Sen and Kotaro Suzumura
    Volume 2 is in preparation (editors Kenneth J. Arrow, Amartya K. Sen and Kotaro Suzumura)

20. HANDBOOK OF ENVIRONMENTAL ECONOMICS (in 3 volumes)
    Edited by Karl-Göran Mäler and Jeffrey R. Vincent

21. HANDBOOK OF THE ECONOMICS OF FINANCE (in 2 volumes)
    Edited by George M. Constantinides, Milton Harris and René M. Stulz

22. HANDBOOK OF ECONOMIC GROWTH (in 2 volumes)
    Edited by Philippe Aghion and Steven N. Durlauf

23. HANDBOOK OF THE ECONOMICS OF GIVING, ALTRUISM AND RECIPROCITY (in 2 volumes)
    Edited by Serge-Christophe Kolm and Jean Mercier Ythier

24. HANDBOOK OF ECONOMIC FORECASTING (in 1 volume)
    Edited by Graham Elliott, Clive W.J. Granger and Allan Timmermann

All published volumes available

FORTHCOMING TITLES

HANDBOOK OF EXPERIMENTAL ECONOMICS RESULTS
Editors Charles Plott and Vernon L. Smith

HANDBOOK ON THE ECONOMICS OF ART AND CULTURE
Editors Victor Ginsburgh and David Throsby

HANDBOOK OF LAW AND ECONOMICS
Editors A. Mitchell Polinsky and Steven Shavell

HANDBOOK OF THE ECONOMICS OF EDUCATION
Editors Eric Hanushek and Finis Welch

HANDBOOK OF ECONOMICS OF TECHNOLOGICAL CHANGE
Editors Bronwyn H. Hall and Nathan Rosenberg

Edwards Brothers Malloy
Ann Arbor MI. USA
November 7, 2013